Advanced Business

SECOND EDITION

Jon Sutherland & Diane Canwell

with Stuart Merrills

Hodder & Stoughton

A MEMBER OF THE HODDER HEADLINE GROUP

For Alun and Stuart Canwell

Orders: please contact Bookpoint Ltd, 39 Milton Park, Abingdon, Oxon OX14 4TD.
Telephone: (44) 01235 400414, Fax: (44) 01235 400454. Lines are open from 9.00 - 6.00,
Monday to Saturday, with a 24 hour message answering service.
Email address: orders@bookpoint.co.uk

British Library Cataloguing in Publication Data
A catalogue record for this title is available from The British Library

ISBN 0 340 65521 6

First published 1994
Second edition 1995
Impression number   10 9 8 7 6 5
Year   2004 2003 2002 2001 2000 1999 1998

Typeset by Greengate Publishing Services, Tonbridge, Kent.
Printed in Great Britain for Hodder & Stoughton Educational,
a division of Hodder Headline Plc, 338 Euston Road, London NW1 3BH
by Scotprint Ltd, Musselburgh, Scotland.

Contents

Introduction   *v*

Acknowledgements   *vi*

An Introduction to the Advanced GNVQ in Business – A Student's Guide   *vii*

GNVQ Core Skills – A note for lecturers   *ix*

A key to the symbols used in this book   *x*

1   *Business in the economy*   *1*

1.1   Analyse the forces of supply and demand on business   1
1.2   Analyse the operation of markets and their effects on business and communities   26
1.3   Examine the effects of government policies on markets   41
Unit 1   Test questions   76

2   *Business organisations and systems*   *79*

2.1   Investigate business organisations   79
2.2   Investigate administration systems   125
2.3   Analyse communication in a business organisation   155
2.4   Analyse information processing in a business organisation   181
Unit 2   Test questions   194

3   *Marketing*   *197*

3.1   Investigate the principles and functions of marketing in organisations   197
3.2   Propose and present production developments based on analysis of marketing research information   219
3.3   Evaluate marketing communications designed to influence a target audience   241
3.4   Evaluate sales methods and customer service to achieve customer satisfaction   284
Unit 3   Test questions   310

4   *Human resources*   *313*

4.1   Investigate human resourcing   313
4.2   Investigate job roles and changing conditions   343
4.3   Evaluate recruitment procedures, job applications and interviews   383
Unit 4   Test questions   409

5   *Production and employment in the economy*   *412*

5.1   Analyse production in business   412
5.2   Investigate and evaluate employment   429
5.3   Examine the competitiveness of UK industry   446
Unit 5   Test questions   469

6	*Financial transations, costing and pricing*	*473*
6.1	Explain added value, distribution of added value and money cycle	473
6.2	Explain financial transactions and complete supporting documents	488
6.3	Calculate the cost of goods or services	517
6.4	Explain basic pricing decisions and break-even point	531
Unit 6	Test questions	543
7	*Financial forecasting and monitoring*	*546*
7.1	Explain sources of finance and financial requirements of business organisations	546
7.2	Produce and explain forecasts and a cash flow for a small business	562
7.3	Produce and explain profit and loss statements and balance sheets	575
7.4	Identify and explain data to monitor a business	586
Unit 7	Test questions	601
8	*Business planning*	*604*
8.1	Prepare work and collect data for a business plan	604
8.2	Produce and present a busines plan	632
8.3	Plan for employment or self-employment	653
	Glossary of business terms	*683*
	Index	*690*

Introduction

Welcome to the second edition of Advanced Business. There have been a great many changes since our preparation for the first edition in September 1994. We have followed a very similar format to the original edition, but hope you will find this new book even more user-friendly and comprehensive than before. The glossary has been considerably enlarged and covers the majority of the key words, jargon and phrases that will become familiar to the students.

We have followed all of the performance criteria, ranges and evidence indicators Element by Element across the eight Mandatory Units of the learning programme. You will find that each of the Units is capable of being tackled independently. However, when we reach Units 7 and 8, there is a presumption that many of the earlier Units have already been tackled. At all times we have used the most up-to-date documentation from NCVQ and the awarding bodies in the preparation of the materials included in this book. This has not been a particularly easy task, since there have been a number of changes in the past year.

Throughout the 28 Elements that form the substance of the eight Units, you will find a common format which attempts to cover not only all of the performance criteria, but also the core skills. Each Student Activity is labelled with the appropriate performance criterion relating to the particular task. (This is abbreviated as PC.) Along with this we list the appropriate core skills that we have identified as being inherent in that activity. (These are abbreviated as COM –

Communication, IT – Information Technology and AON – Application of Number.) There is also, in many cases, an indication of the time that should be allocated to these activities. However, if the activities involve research or the use of information technology, no time has been indicated. The Element Assignments form the major means of gathering evidence and in all cases, cover all of the performance criteria in that particular Element. At the end of each Unit (except Unit 8) there is a 30-question multiple-choice mock test which follows the same format as the real end tests themselves.

The major reason for our choice of format relates to the accessibility of information and immediacy of use to address each performance criterion and range statement. Many of the competitors have opted for a more conventional 'chapter' approach. Personal experience, coupled with feedback from students and institutional purchasers of the first edition, has shown that our approach was both successful and helpful.

We would like to thank Stuart Merrills for his invaluable assistance in the preparation of some of the economics-based Elements. We feel that his contribution has improved upon the economics sections of the previous edition.

We hope that you will find this book an invaluable tool in the successful completion of this award and that GNVQ Advanced Business proves to be a sound foundation for your future career plans.

Jon Sutherland and Diane Canwell
September 1995

Acknowledgements

The authors would like to acknowledge the help and support of the following organisations in the preparation and illustration of this book:

ACCA
Advertising Standards Authority
Alliance and Leicester Building Society
Allied Lyons plc
Anglia Television Group plc
Arbitration & Conciliation Service
Association for Consumer Research
Avon Cosmetics Ltd
Banking Information Service
Barclays Bank plc
Berkeley Scott Associates
British Airports Authority
British Coal Corporation
British Exporters Association
British Franchise Association
British Nuclear Fuels plc
British Petroleum plc
British Union For The Abolition Of Vivisection
British Venture Capital Association
Brook Street Bureau
Commission For Racial Equality
Companies House
Cunard Line plc
Department of Trade and Industry
Equal Opportunities Commission
Federation of Recruitment & Employment Services
Federation of Small Businesses
Fisons plc
Geest plc
Great Yarmouth Business Advisory Service Ltd
ICOM
Inland Revenue Department
Ipswich & Norwich Co-operative Society Ltd
Kingfisher plc
Kwik-Fit Holdings plc
Ladbroke Group plc
Law Society
Livewire
Lloyds Bank plc
Lowestoft Job Centre
Market Research Society
Marks & Spencer plc
Mercury Communications Ltd
Midland Bank plc
Miguel Torres, S.A.
Mobil Oil Company Ltd
National Westminster Bank plc
Norfolk & Waveney Chamber of Commerce & Industry
Norfolk & Waveney Technical Education Council
Norfolk Small Business Initiative
Office of Fair Trading
OFWAT
Peugeot Talbot Motor Company Ltd
Race Relations Employment Advisory Service
Rank Organisation
Rentokil Ltd
Sharp Electronics (UK) Ltd
Small Business Bureau
Smith & Nephew plc
Storehouse plc
Suffolk Technical Education Council
Tesco Stores Ltd
University of Cambridge
Voluntary Service Overseas
Yorkshire-Tyne Tees Television Holdings plc

The authors would also like to thank the following for their valuable assistance in the production of this book:

Stuart Canwell
Maurice Cowley
Alan Hopley
Huw James
Christine Shorten
Delphine and Pat

An Introduction to the Advanced GNVQ in Business – A Students' Guide

What is the Advanced GNVQ in Business? Let's start by explaining what GNVQ stands for: it means General National Vocational Qualification. In other words, this is a course that has been designed so that you can not only gain knowledge of business, but are actually able to use it in the workplace. Depending on the grade you get for this course, it will be the equivalent of two good A level passes. There are two other things about the course that are worth remembering. Firstly, you will gain some useful skills that could get you a job at the end of the course and, secondly you can use the qualification to get on to a University course either at Higher National Diploma or degree level.

The Advanced course asks you to complete the following:

- eight mandatory units – everyone will have to study these
- four option units – you may have a choice of these if your centre offers a wide variety
- three core skill units – you will be marked on these throughout the course

The eight mandatory units cover the business skills and knowledge that will provide you with an understanding of the ways in which businesses work, and what it is like to work in one.

The option units cover some of the other features of business and allow you to concentrate on things that interest you. There are some rules about the options you can choose, but your tutor will be able to tell you about these.

The core skills cover **application of number** (some maths, statistics and graphs etc.), **communication** (written, oral and visual) and **information technology** (the use of computers to present and use information).

A NEW COURSE MEANS NEW THINGS TO REMEMBER

There are plenty of new words and phrases that you will have to learn. There is no need to worry about them too much at the moment, they will become clear as you get into the course. Here are some of the main ones that you will come across:

1 *Unit.* This is part of the course. There are 15 units to complete, eight mandatory, four options and three core skills.
2 *Elements.* These are parts of the units. There are usually three or four in each of the units. These split up the units into easy-to-understand parts.
3 *Performance criteria.* These are probably the most important of all. Each of the elements is split up into three or more performance criteria, which ask you to prove that you can do or understand something. The course work that you will be asked to do will be aimed at helping you with this evidence.
4 *Range statements.* The performance criteria are split up into a number of statements which are all related to one another. The range covers all of the things that make up the wider performance criteria. You will find information on each of the range statements in this book to help you understand what is meant by them. The range statements that are printed in bold on the specification are known as 'range dimensions' and you will cover all of these. The other parts of the range statements are known as 'range categories' and you may not have to cover all of these in the course of your studies.
5 *Evidence indicators.* These are descriptions of what you will have to produce as evidence that you understand each of the performance criteria. The activities throughout the book will help you collect this evidence, but the most important way of doing

this is to undertake the assignment at the end of each of the elements. These assignments give you a series of tasks which exactly match the performance criteria. This is the minimum amount of work you will have to do if you want to claim that you have covered all of the performance criteria.

6 *End tests.* These are one-hour multiple choice tests that you will be asked to sit during the course. They can be attempted several times if you have trouble with them and your tutor will be able to give you the dates of the tests. Once you have passed these and completed all of the assignments covering all of the performance criteria of a unit, you have passed that unit. You will only have to sit an end test for each of the mandatory units, although some of the more practical ones may not have an end test. You do not have to do one for your options or the core skills, so you will only have to do seven different tests.

7 *Portfolios.* This is where you keep the evidence you have collected to show that you have covered all of the performance criteria. You must make sure that your portfolio is up to date and that you have put all your marked work into it. The ways in which these portfolios are put together will depend upon the way your school or college has decided to organise them.

8 *Resubmission.* This is a polite way of saying that there is something wrong with the piece of work you have submitted. You may have missed out some of the tasks or answered them badly. Whatever the reason, you will be asked to do the piece of work again. It may only concern one small area of the work, but you will not have covered all of the performance criteria. You will only be expected to re-do the parts of the work that were not good enough in the first place.

9 *Grading themes.* There are four grading themes for the course. These are important as your grades for these will decide whether you get a pass, merit or distinction for the whole of the course. The grading themes are:

- *Planning* – in which you need to show that you are well organised in getting your work sorted out and that you have made sure all of the tasks have been covered. You will also need to show that when you plan how you are going to do a piece of work you keep an eye on your progress (this is called monitoring)
- *Information seeking and handling* – this shows that you can figure out what information you will need to complete a piece of work and that you have mentioned where you have got the information from
- *Evaluation* – you may find this difficult in the

beginning, but your tutor will be able to give you some more advice about dealing with this. You need to look at your planning and try to say what problems you have in completing the work. The evaluation is your chance to look back at the way you tackled a piece of work and what you think (after having finished it) of your performance.

- *Quality of outcomes* – this means that you can get a grade for the way in which the piece of work has been put together (i.e. have you covered all of the tasks well?) and your use of language and communication skills

10 *Verification.* There are three different people who will look at your work. The first is pretty obvious and this is the person who has set the work and will mark it. The second person is another member of the staff of the college or school who will check the marking of the person who marked it in the first place. This person is known as the Internal Verifier. The third person is the External Verifier who will not be a member of staff of the college or the school. This person is employed by the awarding body (BTEC, City & Guilds or RSA).

GETTING GOOD GRADES

The grade that you get will be based on just one in three of all the grades you get for all of your work. The good news is that this is the best third of the work! You will only pass or be asked to resubmit work that is not worthy of a merit or a distinction. Above all, you should collect and keep all the work you have done. You should also make sure that your tutors have filled in a sheet and signed it to show that you have completed a part of the course every time you get a piece of work back from one of them.

You will be encouraged to take responsibility for what you do throughout the course. This means that when you have been set a piece of work to do, you should get on with it as soon as possible. Letting the work build up just means that you will be putting yourself under pressure later in the course. It will also cause you problems with your tutors – remember that they are only human too and would not want to have to mark everything you should have done weeks ago in the last few days of the course.

We know that this might all sound rather daunting. There are some things about this course that are similar to GCSEs, but the biggest difference is that you will need to keep up-to-date with the course work as there will be quite a lot more to do than on a GCSE course. The other major difference is the fact that you will only have to sit seven one-hour tests spread out over the whole of the two years.

Don't worry too much if this has left you wondering what it's all about. You will begin to understand as you get further into the course. Remember that this is your course and that the tests are pretty straightforward and used only to check that you have understood the unit itself. If nothing else, keep up-to-date with the course work.

We really hope that you will enjoy this course. We have tried to make this book as useful as possible and we are sure that you will find nearly everthing that you need in it. The options are covered in another book and we have followed the same system of covering all of the units, elements, performance criteria and range. By the time that you start your options, we are sure that you will know as much about the course as we do!

Good luck.

Jon Sutherland and Diane Canwell

GNVQ Core skills – A note for lecturers

As we pointed out in the Introduction, we have designed the learning, assessment and evidence gathering activities, bearing in mind the Unit specifications demanded within the programme. It is important to think of the core skills as an integral part of the learning programme. Core skills require continuous assessment and testing throughout the programme. In practice, not only will you assess the core skills on more than one occasion, but you will also find that the particular elements that make up each core skill are similarly tested repeatedly. This process is perfectly acceptable since it reaffirms the candidate's ability to reproduce a particular achievement on a number of occasions.

The new core skills are somewhat more complex and detailed than any previous version. Whilst we have repeatedly used the core skills, they have only been detailed to Element level. In order to address the performance criteria for each Element it would have been necessary for us to have included a complex matrix which cross-checks each of the performance criteria and their related range. Bearing in mind that core skills, performance criteria and range are just as important as the other mandatory performance criteria and range, we would advise you to map them yourselves once you have decided which of the Student Activities and Element Assignments you intend to use.

A key to the symbols used in this book

This indicates a comprehensive series of tasks that are designed to cover all of the performance criteria of a particular element.

This indicates that the activity is intended to be carried out individually.

This indicates that the activity is intended to be carried out by a group.

This indicates the suggested time needed to complete the activity.

This indicates that the activity or assignment has been designed so that evidence can be gathered for stated application of number elements.

This indicates that the activity or assignment has been designed so that evidence can be gathered for stated communication elements.

This indicates that the activity or assignment has been designed so that evidence can be gathered for stated information technology elements.

Analyse the forces of supply and demand on business

PERFORMANCE CRITERIA

A student must:

1 explain **demand** for goods and services

2 explain how businesses decide on goods and services to **supply**

3 **analyse** the demand and supply interaction

4 explain the **effects on business decisions** of changes in the conditions of **demand** and **supply**

5 report research findings about **demand** and **supply** interaction and the price and sales for a particular product

6 suggest future changes in **demand** and **supply** of particular products

RANGE

Demand: *satisfying customer needs and wants, effective demand, spending and income, demand curves, price and income elasticity, causes of change in demand (income, tastes, advertising, prices of other goods)*

Supply: *profit motive, public service motive, opportunity cost, choice of products, availability of finance for business, relationship between price and quantity supplied, elasticity of supply, supply curves, changes in supply, effect of customers, effect of competitors*

Analyse *in terms of: market price for a product, market volume for a product*

Effects on business decisions: *shifts in demand curves, shifts in supply curves, changes in market price and quantity sold, economies of scale, changes to break-even position*

1.1.1 Explain demand for goods and services

DEMAND

No matter whether you are a customer or an organisation, young or old, we all have various wants and needs. The difference between these two desires has a great effect upon how we try to get them and what we will do in the process. You could say that I **want** a new car, but what I **need** is a reliable form of transport. It doesn't have to be a new car.

Goods and services are produced because people, (consumers) want and need them. No matter who you are, everybody has the same basic needs. For example, it does not matter if you are the richest or the poorest person in the world, we all require food, clothing and shelter in order to survive.

Having obtained these basic needs, people acquire (or seek to acquire) their wants, the goods and services that will enable them to improve their basic standard of living.

We all make a series of regular purchases every day, newspapers, cigarettes, canned drinks, chocolates and other food items. The reasoning behind our purchases can be related to our tastes or our opinion of a particular product. Organisations will seek to influence our decision-making when we make a purchase, but we will be looking at this later.

Also, every now and then, we make special purchases. These are things that we really have to think about before we buy them. Perhaps they are expensive, perhaps they are a luxury. Organisations which make these products, like cars, TVs, stereo systems and furniture, have to try to predict what the demand will be like for these products and make sure that they have produced enough of them to satisfy demand. These producers of products will have to be ready to react to sudden changes in demand, and be prepared to gear up their production should demand increase in a short space of time. Above all, the product that they make should aim to satisfy the demands of the buyer. If it doesn't then the buyer will not be satisfied and is unlikely to buy from that organisation again. To be successful, the organisation has to have sufficient products available, at the right price and in the right place. These are the basic business skills required to succeed and survive in a very competitive area of activity. In business jargon, we can use the words **production, pricing** and **distribution.**

SATISFYING CUSTOMER NEEDS AND WANTS

The ultimate success of any company is related to providing for the needs and wants of the customer. Indeed, to be really successful, an organisation must stay ahead of all its competitors. Having a large market share is one thing, but being a market leader is just as important.

Let us return to the question of customers' needs and wants. Just what is the difference between the two? A need is something essential. This, of course, includes the need to eat, drink and keep warm. On the other hand, a want is a specific desire for something you may not necessarily need. If you are hungry, this is a need, but you may want a McDonald's.

Organisations spend huge amounts of money trying to assess and manipulate the wants of customers. If it were not for our wants, then there would be no choice in products at all. Marketing experts know this and attempt, by various means, to influence what customers (consumers) want.

The simple fact that one product has slightly different features, colours, tastes or smells to another means that our essential need is transformed into a want.

The same can be said, to some extent, in the industrial sector of the market. Organisations here will also purchase consumer durables (in their case capital goods like machines), consumables (in industry these will be oil, raw materials and office stationery) and services (perhaps the services of an advertising agency or an accountant). Perhaps the choice is not so great as in the consumer market, but there are definite differences between similar products and services offered by a range of companies.

Technology, design, research and development are continually introducing new products and services on to the market. In many cases, new products or services simple replace older ones, making them obsolete. Occasionally, a new product or services may enter the market that offers possibilities that could not have been dreamt of a few years ago. No one would have believed that there could one day be a machine which would replace the need to hand-write additional copies of a book, but it happened when the first printing press was designed. No one would have believed that the huge pools of copy-typists which most large organisations employed would be replaced by a machine called a photocopier.

These products, whether they are replacing an existing one or not, have to cater for either a need or a want. In the case of replacement, there is an existing need. In the case of a want, this may have to be generated by an expensive advertising campaign which tries to convince the consumers that they really do want one!

student activity

(PC 1.1.1, COM 3.1, 3.2)

In groups of three, try to make a list of the 10 most demanded items that a family would require. Then make a list of the 10 most demanded fashion items.

In your two lists are there a lot of producers of each item or just a few?

Using your conclusions why do you think this is so? Compare your findings with those of the other groups in your class.

EFFECTIVE DEMAND

Needs and wants therefore represent the demand of consumers for goods and services. However, needing or wanting something is not enough to be able to turn that desire into reality. **Effective demand** occurs when consumers not only wish to buy a product but also have the money to be able to pay for it, thus making their demand for goods and services effective.

Therefore the demand for a particular product or service is sometimes reliant on the price the consumer is willing to pay, but this is not the whole story. We need to consider something called 'market demand'. This is the amount of a product of service that will be demanded during a particular period of time. Here are some of the factors that will influence that consumption rate:

1 *Price* – in most cases the higher the price charged for a particular product or service, the lower the demand for it. As the price falls, there should be a corresponding higher demand for that product or service. One thing to note here is that despite the cost, even if it is very low, there is only a comparatively limited demand. Eventually, all those who need it will have it.

2 *Income* – this refers to the income of consumers. They may want the product or service but may not have the income to be able to consume it at the rate that they would really like.

3 *Availability* – the desirability of a good or service and the means to effectively purchase it does not necessarily mean that the good or service is available to be chosen.

SPENDING AND INCOME

Obviously, one of the main determinants of which products are bought and the amount that people are able to pay is the actual income that they have available to spend.

A basic assumption is that consumers with higher incomes have more money available to spend than those with lower incomes and that as income increases, consumers can consume more (as they have more income that they can spend). However, this is not exactly the case. If we split the range of goods and services into two different categories, calling them inferior and superior, then we can begin to see the choices consumers have. The inferior goods and services are comparatively cheap. The superior goods and services are expensive. When consumers have more income, they can spend it on more inferior goods and services, which in effect means that they are consuming more. Consumers could switch over to superior goods and services, which are more expensive, so they would use up the additional income, but not actually consume more. The alternative way of looking at this is to say that they do actually consume more just by buying more superior goods and services.

An example of this occurs when, due to a rise in income, consumers switch from buying a supermarket's own-label product to a product with a more up-market brand name. The consumers aren't in effect consuming any more, they are consuming exactly the same amount, but having switched from an inferior to a superior product they are paying more for the privilege.

DEMAND CURVES

Demand is defined as the quantity of a given good or service that consumers wish to purchase at a particular point in time at a particular price.

Thus a demand curve shows the quantity of a particular good or service that consumers wish to purchase at each conceivable price.

Figure 1.1.1 on p.4 shows the relationships between price and quantity demanded assuming all things remain constant, i.e. if the price of the particular good or service was, for example, £10.00 per unit then 2,000 units would be the quantity demanded and if the price was to fall to £5.00 then 8,000 units would be the quantity demanded.

Thus a demand curve shows the negative relationships between price and quantity demanded, i.e. at the higher prices the quantity demanded falls and at the lower prices the quantity rises. A demand curve is derived quite simply by plotting price (on the vertical axis) against quantity (on the horizontal axis). By plotting all the points and joining them up we obtain the demand curve.

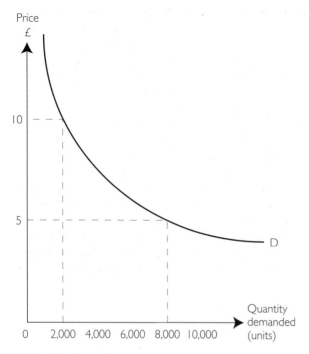

FIG. 1.1.1 *Demand curve.*

ELASTICITY OF DEMAND

The degree of responsiveness of demand to changes in conditions is therefore known as its elasticity. There are three main types:

- elastic demand
- inelastic demand
- unitary elasticity

and three main forms:

- price elasticity
- income elasticity
- cross elasticity

We will go on now to look at each of these in turn.

PRICE AND INCOME ELASTICITY

Elasticity of demand is a term used to describe the quantity of a product or service demanded and how that demand is affected by price and other changes. Merely for the consumer to want a product or service is not sufficient; there are several other factors to be taken into consideration. These are;

- the consumer's ability to pay
- the other demands on the consumer's income
- the desire the consumer has to acquire the product or service
- the benefits and advantages that may be received by acquiring the product or service
- other sacrifices that may have to be made in order to acquire the product or service

Some products or services will be purchased regardless of the price. There has only been a gradual decline in the sales of cigarettes, for example, despite enormous price rises. When we consider the simple relationship between supply and demand, we are not taking sufficient note of price sensitivity. This means that certain products or services may be price sensitive, in other words, the demand may be directly affected by price. Demand tends to be elastic if the product or service has some of the following features:

- if it is a luxury
- if there are cheaper alternatives
- if it is very expensive in relation to total income

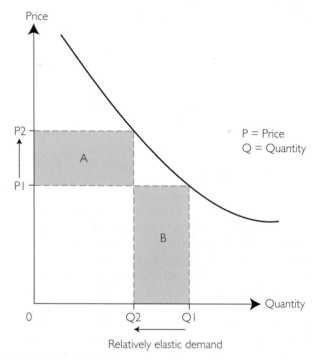

FIG. 1.1.2 *Elastic demand graph.*

Figure 1.1.2 shows a relatively elastic demand curve. A rise in price from P1 to P2 causes the quantity demanded to fall from Q1 to Q2. The proportional fall from Q1 to Q2 is much greater than the proportional rise in price P1 to P2. The product in the demand curve is sensitive to price changes and is termed elastic.

The total revenue that a firm receives can be calculated by:

price × quantity = total revenue

It can be seen therefore that with an elastic demand curve a rise in price from P1 to P2 causes the total revenue to fall. The increase in revenue from the price rise (area A) is offset by the fall in revenue caused by the decrease in quantity demanded (area B). That is, area B > area A. Thus total revenue (TR) falls.

Conversely if there was to be a fall in price this would cause a proportionally larger increase in the quantity demanded and total revenue would rise.

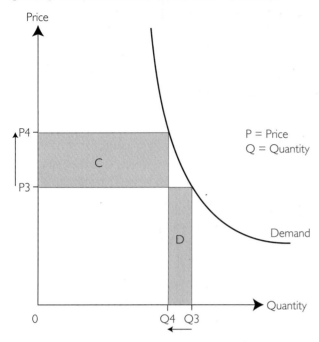

FIG. 1.1.3 *Inelastic demand graph.*

Alternatively, some products or services are inelastic, which means that regardless of the price, we will still be prepared to pay. A good example of this would be the services of a professional such as a photographer or a solicitor. Figure 1.1.3 shows such a demand curve. Despite the rise in price from P3 to P4 the proportional change in quantity from Q3 to Q4 is less than the proportional change in price. Thus the product in Figure 1.1.3 is not as sensitive to price changes as that in Figure 1.1.2 and so it is termed inelastic. With an inelastic demand curve a rise in price from P3 to P4 causes the total revenue to rise as area C > area D. That is, because the product is insensitive to price changes the fall in quantity from Q3 to Q4 is not sufficient to offset the entire revenue gained from the price rise from P3 to P4. Conversely a fall in price causes total revenue to fall as well, as there is not a sufficient increase in quantity demanded.

With **unitary elasticity** the proportional change in price causes the same proportional change in quantity demanded.

Thus, as Figure 1.1.4 shows, total revenue stays exactly the same at all prices as area E = area F.

There is a simple formula which describes the elasticity of demand:

price elasticity of demand
$$= \frac{\text{percentage change in quantity demanded}}{\text{percentage change in price}}$$

Calculating elasticity is quite difficult, but all organisations will consider this when thinking about price changing. In some circumstances, reducing the price will have little effect on the demand, particularly if the demand is insensitive to price. When demand is sensitive to price, the organisation will have to risk losing some of its market share.

Income elasticity of demand describes how responsive demand is to changes in income. Simply, a rise in income should signal a rise in demand. This effect is more likely at the luxury end of the market, and is unlikely to affect products and services at the lower end of the market. In fact, in some cases, a rise in income can signal a negative demand. In this case, consumers shun products or services which they consider inferior or substandard as they can afford more expensive alternatives. The formula for calculating income elasticity is:

income elasticity of demand
$$= \frac{\text{percentage change in quantity demanded}}{\text{percentage change in income}}$$

To complicate matters, there is another formula which describes the effect on demand for one product when the price of another changes. This is called the **cross elasticity of demand**:

cross elasticity of demand
$$= \frac{\text{percentage change in demand for product x}}{\text{percentage change in price of product y}}$$

This formula is only useful when the two products are substitutes for one another. By the term substitute we mean goods that can be readily exchanged for each

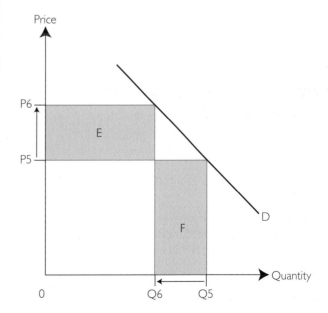

FIG. 1.1.4 *Unitary elasticity graph.*

other e.g. butter and margarine, or Fiestas and Novas, or even telephones and letters.

If the two goods or services being compared give a positive cross elasticity of demand then this indicates that they are substitutes for each other. For example, a rise in the price of butter causes an increase in the quantity of margarine demanded as people switch their consumption to the cheaper alternative.

If, however, the cross elasticity of demand is negative then the goods and services are said to be complementary, that is they are dependent on each other, e.g. petrol and cars, CDs and CD players. So a rise in the price of petrol, for example, would cause a fall in the demand for cars and vice versa and a fall in the price of CDs causes a greater demand for CD players.

The only other situation is that where the cross elasticity of demand is zero and therefore the two products have no effect on each other and are said to be independent. For example, a rise in the price of baked beans would have absolutely no effect on the number of people taking public transport.

student activity

(PC 1.1.1, COM 3.1)
In groups of two or three consider the effect that an advertising campaign for a particular product might have on its various elasticities.

CAUSES OF CHANGE IN DEMAND (INCOME, TASTES, ADVERTISING, PRICES OF OTHER GOODS)

From our simple demand curve (Figure 1.1.1) we have seen that a change in price causes a movement along the demand curve and thus a new level of quantity of goods and services demanded. However, it is not only a change in price that can cause movements and shifts in the level demanded by individuals.

INCOME

The level of goods and services demanded by an individual is largely dependent on his or her level of income, (see spending and income on p.3). It is generally assumed that the greater the income a person possesses the more he or she will spend. The effect upon an individual demand curve is determined by the 'income elasticity of demand' for that particular product and whether that product is regarded as inferior or superior.

TASTES

A major influence on the level of demand for a product is consumer tastes, fashions and trends. For example, consider the demand for flared trousers in the 1990s compared to that in the 1960s and 1970s. Changing consumer tastes can therefore have a large impact on what is demanded and what isn't.

In recent years there has been a growing trend toward environmentally friendly products, thus causing an increase in the quantity demanded of those products perceived as being 'green'. One of the clearest examples of this can be seen in the toiletries market as demonstrated by the success of such companies as The Body Shop and the availability of cruelty-free make-up products.

ADVERTISING

Whether we notice it or not consumers are consistently bombarded by advertising and marketing strategies, (see Unit 3 on marketing), and although as individuals we like to consider in the main that we are immune to such devices the effect of advertising campaigns on the level of demand for goods and services and consumers' perceptions can be exceedingly influential.

Advertising is used by companies to try to raise the demand for their goods and services. They can do this in several ways. The first is to increase consumer awareness to the fact that their products exist and where they can get them from. Obviously nobody is going to go out and buy a product that they don't know about. By making more consumers aware of their products companies hope that more people will buy them and thus increase demand.

Secondly, companies use advertising to try to create the perception that their product is better than that of their competitors in one way or another, e.g. better quality, more functions, better after-sales service etc, in the hope that consumers will switch from buying one brand to another.

And lastly, advertising is used as a means of creating a particular 'image' or brand name for a product.

student activity

(PC 1.1.1, COM 3.1)
In groups of two or three consider the launch of a new product, e.g. a chocolate bar, canned drink or even a type of car. How is advertising used to increase the demand for these products?

PRICES OF OTHER GOODS

As already discussed, if a product is a substitute or a complementary product then a change in its price or that of a related product can have a substantial effect on the level of demand.

In the case of substitute goods, consider the effect of a change in price of butter on the level of margarine demanded. From our simple demand curve we can see that if the price of a good or service (butter) rises, then the quantity demanded falls. However, what has happened in this situation? Does this mean that those people who are no longer buying butter because it is too expensive are now going without? No, in this example, because there is an easy substitute available (margarine), consumers will have switched their demand to the more readily affordable substitute.

Alongside this, the demand for some products is related to the level of demand for others. In this scenario the two products are termed complements e.g. cars and petrol, cigarettes and lighters. Consider the effect of a rise in the price of cigarettes. This has the effect, hopefully, of causing fewer people to smoke as it becomes too expensive. However, as these individuals stop smoking there is no need for them to buy cigarette lighters anymore. Thus a rise in the price of one complementary good causes a fall in the demand of the other.

student activity

(PC 1.1.1)
Find out the number of people who gave up smoking in the last year. Try to estimate the effect this had on the number of cigarette lighters sold.

Another aspect to be taken into consideration when discussing the effect of prices of other goods is the effect of a change in the price of the goods of a direct competitor. (These can be regarded as the same as substitute goods as one make of VCR can readily be substituted for another.)

1.1.2 Explain how businesses decide on goods and services to supply

SUPPLY

PROFIT MOTIVE

Supply obviously refers to the quantity of products or services available. As you may have already realised, demand is not necessarily the quantity actually bought. Equally, supply is not the quantity actually sold. Generally speaking, the higher the price a product or service can command in the market, the greater quantity there is available. High prices will give many new producers the opportunity to enter the market as well as encouraging existing producers to make more. The relationship between price and quantity is reflected in the way the supply curve slopes upwards. This is similar to demand, but assumes that all other factors remain the same. When there is a rise in the costs of producing something, this automatically reduces the profitability of that product or service.

The profit that a company receives is the difference between the price at which the product has been sold and the total cost of providing/producing it. The number of units of any particular product that a company is prepared to supply is therefore dependent upon the price at which the product can be sold compared to the cost of producing it. As previously stated, it generally follows that the higher the price a product can command, the greater the quantity that will be produced. This is because the profits rise on each unit sold (assuming all other things, e.g costs remain constant). This encourages the company to produce and sell more products. Figure 1.1.10 on p.14 shows this relationship in the form of a supply curve.

PUBLIC SERVICE MOTIVE

Not all goods and services are provided by private businesses desirous of making profit. Some goods and services are supplied by the government and local government. In the main these are areas which the private sector would not wish to supply as there is no real profit motive possible, and the government recognises that such services would not be provided by private businesses at all or not sufficiently for all members of the public to benefit from them. Examples of these are education, the police force, national defence (army, navy, air force) and the National Health Service. The government provides such services to all members of the public either free, financed by taxation, or at a price which the vast majority can afford.

The post office is an interesting example. As can be seen by the number of existing private delivery businesses there is a sufficient profit motive for private enterprise to take an active role in this industry. However, it is only the fact that the post office is run by the government for the benefit of all people that guarantees, for example, that remote rural communities have an equivalent postal service to that of other areas. (To supply such communities on a commercial basis would be unprofitable.)

We cover this topic in more detail in a later section of this Unit.

OPPORTUNITY COST

As discussed previously in this chapter there is no limit to what consumers need and want. However, it is impossible for all these demands to be met. Each country has only a limited, finite level of resources. All goods and services, whether supplied by private business or by government, need to make use of these 'scarce resources'. The main problem therefore is how these should be managed. There are many answers to this problem, but they all address the same three questions:

- what should be produced?
- how should it be produced?
- who should produce it?

All goods and services require certain 'Factors of production'. The four main factors of production are:

- land
- labour
- capital
- enterprise

1 *Land* – This includes all of the physical resources like coal, timber, minerals and crops.
2 *Labour* – This includes all the available physical and mental efforts of people.
3 *Capital* – This includes not only money but anything which is used to make other things, e.g. machines.
4 *Enterprise* – These are the skills which people have and the risks they take bringing the other three factors together.

As we have said, not all countries use the same methods to organise their economy. One of the ways of looking at different economies is to measure the amount of influence the government has on decision making.

If these resources are used to provide a particular good or service they are then used up and cannot be used to provide another. Thus one way of describing this situation is to say that the cost of using any resource in production is not the amount you actually paid for it, but the cost of not using it to produce the next best alternative.

Definition: Opportunity cost is the amount lost by not using a resource in its next best alternative use.

For example, if you only have £10.00 and decide to use it to buy a new CD or tape you cannot then use it to go out with your friends.

student activity

(PC 1.1.1 COM 3.1)
Consider the amount of money you had to spend over the last week. What did you spend it on and what alternatives did you have to sacrifice? Compare your list of outgoings with those of the rest of your group.

CHOICE OF PRODUCTS

The choice of products available is dependent therefore on how businesses and government answer the three questions:

- what to produce
- how to produce it
- who should produce it

and thus decide upon how resources should be allocated. One of the major influences upon this is to what extent the government and local authorities take it upon themselves to provide goods and services which may not be provided by the private sector, and thus to what extent they control the allocation of resources. There are three main types of economy:

- free market economy
- planned economy
- mixed economy

In a **free market** the government is not involved in controlling the resources, all decisions are made by buyers or sellers. Buyers will only buy goods that they believe offer value for money. If buyers or consumers think they would get better value from buying something else then they will buy that. Those that make the goods, known as producers, have to constantly adjust their output of goods to match consumer demands. In the real world there is not a single country that can claim to be a truly free market. To a greater or lesser extent, all governments meddle with the economy.

There are some advantages and disadvantages of a free market. These include:

1 *Advantages*

- consumers will buy what they think will give them the most satisfaction and value for money
- the most popular goods are likely to be produced in huge quantities and at low prices
- most resources will be channelled into goods which are popular. It is unlikely that unpopular goods will be widely available
- scarce resources are not wasted on goods which will not sell
- the free market can respond to change very quickly when buying trends make the producing of old-fashioned goods unprofitable

2 *Disadvantages*

- large and powerful companies have much more influence than smaller companies
- although all production is linked to consumers' willingness to buy, those consumers with more money have more influence
- the free market does not guarantee the poorest consumers will have their basic needs provided for
- in a free market it is common for some large companies to be the only producer of particular goods (these are known as monopolies)
- the free market only really works when consumers know exactly where and at what price they can buy goods, in other words the consumers do not always know where the best bargain is
- advertising in a free market is very powerful. The information given to the consumers is often misleading. It is difficult for consumers to know when they are being told the truth

A **planned economy** is on the opposite side of the scale from a free market system. The government, through central planning, needs to know how much each region of the country is able to produce and exactly what its needs will be. From this information it can give out the available resources. This system has not worked very well in the long run, and only China and Cuba still operate this way. A planned economy has advantages and disadvantages.

1 *Advantages*

- the combined effort of the whole country can be used to achieve targets of production

- all parts of the country are dependent upon one another, and this is a powerful way of ensuring all areas of the country remain united in their efforts.
- basic needs of the people can be fulfilled. If there is high unemployment these basic needs can be reduced in price so that they are affordable
- long-term planning can be made for all resources and all industries
- there is no wasteful duplication of production
- all goods and services can be distributed fairly

2 *Disadvantages*

- since there is no competition then the quality of the products suffers. This also removes the rewards that individuals would normally get for their own effort and enterprise
- factory managers and regional planners will always over-estimate what they need to complete a project so that they can obtain more than their fair share of the resources. Resources are therefore wasted because each of the regions of the country like to think that they are more important than others
- because everything is centrally planned a lot of paperwork needs to be completed. This is known as bureaucracy, and means that the cost of running a planned system is high
- because all decisions must go through the bureaucracy decision making is slowed down
- when the planned economy fails to produce enough of particular goods individuals who can obtain these goods sell them at high prices themselves. This is known as the underground economy

Mixed economies have features of both the free market and planned systems. The mixed economy is also the most common type. There is a level of government involvement, but also a large element of private enterprise. Most Western European countries use this system, where three main groups are of equal importance: the producer, the government and the consumer. The producers are private owners who are free to decide how their own resources are used. They decide what to produce, how many to produce (quantity) and the quality of the product.

The government has control over some resources and runs most of the services needed by the country, e.g. health care, welfare services and defence. It has the power to influence producers and consumers. This is usually done by imposing laws or high rates of tax to discourage the over-buying of certain goods, e.g. alcohol and tobacco products.

The consumers are a very powerful but disorganised group. Individuals have their own needs and wants.

They have the choice of buying from a range of goods on offer. Their decisions are heavily influenced by price, availability and advertising.

The advantages and disadvantages of a mixed economy include the following:

1 *Advantages*

- the mixed economy combines the best elements of planned and free markets
- the government should be able to influence how resources are used
- the government also provides a 'safety net' for the weaker members of society who are unable to provide for themselves, e.g. the unemployed, the elderly, the sick
- the government, with the help of the producers, is able to make sure that the market runs smoothly and that there is effective competition within the market to keep prices low

2 *Disadvantages*

- the mixed economy also combines the worst elements of the free market and planned economies
- the government interferes with initiative and enterprise by imposing restrictive laws
- competition will always favour the strong at the expense of the weak. Larger businesses will always be able to offer what appears to be a better deal as they are in a position to buy the resources they need at lower costs

Thus it can be seen that the choice of products available is determined by whether or not the allocation of resources is determined entirely by private enterprise (free market). In a free market the availability and choice of goods and services is focused in the main upon those which are perceived as providing satisfaction to consumers, and resources are not wasted upon goods which will be unpopular. This means, of course, that some goods and services might not be provided at all and that consumers on lower incomes may not have their basic needs provided for at all.

In a planned economy, on the other hand, basic needs will be provided for, although the level of choice of products may be severely restricted, e.g. if consumers are thirsty they are given something to drink but they do not have a choice of beverages or different flavours, such as would be provided by private enterprise as they sought to satisfy the market demands of consumers and to compete against each other.

However, in a mixed economy both the best and worst aspects of each type of economy are achieved, with a wide choice of products being available through free market competition and the provision of goods and services to meet people's basic needs and to cover those areas like national defence. The government is also able to influence how resources are used and the availability of products through legislation. (See section on competition policy.)

AVAILABILITY OF FINANCE FOR BUSINESS

It must be realised that no matter how much a business may wish to supply a particular good or service, because of the degree of profit to be made, it may not always be able to do so.

One of the easiest ways to consider this is if we look at the case of a national monopoly like British Gas. As this company enjoys a monopoly position providing a product that a large proportion of the population uses, it is able to achieve abnormal, (very high), profits (see section on monopoly). This is obviously a situation that many companies would wish to enjoy. However, the existence of barriers to entry, such as the high finance cost of the capital equipment needed to undertake this type of business venture prevents many businesses from doing so. Similarly in less extreme situations, the lack of available finance for businesses can prevent them from achieving lower costs, through bulk buying, for example, or by being able to purchase new machinery and equipment. If they had access to finance they would be able to produce goods and services at a level of efficiency sufficient to enable them to be able to enter a market, and supply a particular product or service and thereby make a profit.

RELATIONSHIP BETWEEN PRICE AND QUANTITY SUPPLIED

The price of a product in relation to the amount that it costs to produce has a very powerful influence on the quantity (number of units) that companies are willing to supply. In conjunction with the profit motive discussed earlier, private companies will only supply a product if there is the possibility of making a profit by

student activity

(PC 1.1.1, COM 3.1)
Research and identify at least five examples of each type of economy. Is one particular type of economy more common than another? Is one type of economy more successful than another? Do certain types of economy tend to be in one area of the world? Research this activity in pairs and feedback your findings to the remainder of the group.

doing so. In this respect it follows that the higher the price a company can charge for a particular good or service the more profit they will make. The higher the price the more units a company will wish to supply, and the more companies will wish to supply that product.

To understand how this system works we need to take a closer look at the relationships between **costs**, **volume** and **profit**. To be able to understand the relationships between costs, volume and profit we have to understand the nature of the variables themselves.

Profit, as previously stated, can be seen as the difference between the revenue received from selling the product and the total cost of providing it. Volume can quite simply be considered as the quantity sold. Costs, on the other hand, need more careful consideration.

Costs can be classified into three main types:

- fixed costs (FC)
- variable costs (VC)
- total costs (TC)

I *Fixed costs* – fixed costs can be considered as those costs which do not vary with the amount being provided in the time period being considered. An example of fixed costs would be rent, costs of machinery, etc. They are costs which do not change whether the company is producing anything or not. It does not matter if a certain company is producing 0, 1,000 or 10,000 units of production, its rent for premises remains fixed at £5,000 per month.

2 *Variable costs* – variable costs can be considered as those costs which are incurred in direct relation to the amount being produced, e.g. labour, raw materials, etc. Thus if the quantity being produced is zero then the variable costs equal zero as well. Consider the following example.

In order to make one unit of production for D. B. Ltd the following variable costs are incurred:

- Labour = £2.00
- Raw materials = £3.00
- Total variable costs per unit = £5.00

Thus if the company were to make 0, 1,000 and 10,000 units of production:

- Total variable costs for 0 units of production = 0 × £5.00 = 0
- Total variable costs for 1,000 units of production = 1,000 × £5.00 = £5,000
- Total variable costs for 10,000 units of production = 10,000 × £5.00 = £50,000

3 *Total cost* – total cost is merely the sum of fixed costs and variable costs at the given level of production. For example, consider the production possibilities of D. B. Ltd for one month. These are presented in Table 1.1.1.

TABLE 1.1.1 *D. B. Ltd*

Output (Quantity of units/products)	Fixed costs (FC) (£)	Variable costs (VC) £5 per unit (£)	Total costs (FC + VC) (£)
0	5,000	0	5,000
1,000	5,000	5,000	10,000
5,000	5,000	25,000	30,000
10,000	5,000	50,000	55,000

0:30

student activity

(PC 1.1.1, COM 3.1, 3.2, AON 3.1)
In groups of three make a list of as many costs incurred by a business as you can think of. Try to classify them into fixed and variable costs. Are there some costs which could fall into either class? Why might this be? Consider the time periods involved.

The exact nature of the relationships between costs, volume and profit can more easily be seen when viewed diagrammatically. Using the figures from Table 1.1.1, Figure 1.1.6 on p.13 represents this. The only additional information required is the price at which each unit of production is to be sold. Assuming a selling price of £6.50 per unit we get:

Output	Total revenue
0	0
1,000	£6,500
5,000	£32,500
10,000	£65,000

As can be seen from Figure 1.1.5 on p.12, fixed costs remain the same over all levels of production and as such are plotted as a horizontal straight line. Total costs (TC), remember, is the sum of fixed costs and variable costs, and start from where the fixed costs line intersects the vertical axis. TC can be plotted by calculating total costs at selected levels of production (as shown in Table 1.1.1). Similarly total revenue (TR) can be plotted by calculating total revenue at selected levels of sales (as shown above).

The diagram in Figure 1.1.5 is known as a break-even chart. It can be seen that when the total revenue line and total cost line intersect:

TR = TC

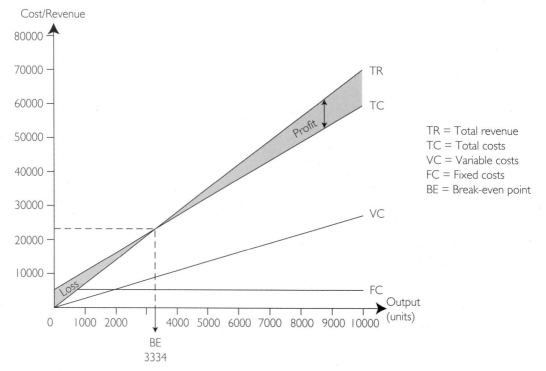

FIG. 1.1.5 *A break-even chart for D.B. Ltd, showing the relationship between costs, volume and profit.*

This is known as the break-even point, i.e. at this level of production and sales the business makes no profit and no loss. To the left of the break-even point total costs incurred are greater than the total revenues received and the difference between the two lines represents losses. To the right of the break-even point total revenue is greater than total costs and the difference between the two lines represents profit. It is evident from our diagram that the more that is produced and sold the greater the difference between the TR and TC lines and hence the greater the amount of profit.

Thus it can be seen that suppliers will expect a higher degree of profit the higher the volume of output and sales, despite the fact that total cost also increases with higher levels of production. If we now assume that the selling price of our product is not £6.50 but £8.00 (Figure 1.1.6), we can see the amount the company needs to produce before it breaks even and starts to make a profit has dropped from 3,334 units to 1,667 units. This means that at a higher price level the company will start to make a profit at lower levels of production. Thus more companies, and especially those who were not efficient enough to enter the market and make a profit before, are now willing and able to do so.

Therefore the higher the price a good or service can command, the more businesses there are who are willing to provide it and the more businesses there are who are able to provide it.

It must be noted, however, that in real situations fixed costs may vary with the volume of production.

For example in order to attain higher levels of productive capacity a company may have to purchase or rent extra machines, so a stepped fixed cost line would probably be more accurate. It is also unlikely that the variable cost and true total cost and total revenue lines will be straight, e.g. as businesses are likely to both give and receive discounts for bulk buying and to incur extra costs such as overtime. It is also assumed that businesses are able to sell all their production at the stated price, but as we shall see this may not always be the case.

We cover, in some detail, the preparation of break-even charts in Unit 6.

ELASTICITY OF SUPPLY

Elasticity of supply is a term used to describe the quantity of a good or service supplied and how that supply is affected by price changes. The price elasticity of supply is dependent upon the following factors:

- whether or not any spare productive capacity exists
- if any barriers to entry exist
- the speed with which producers can increase or decrease the level of supply

As with the price elasticity of demand, there are three possible outcomes:

- elastic
- inelastic
- unitary elasticity

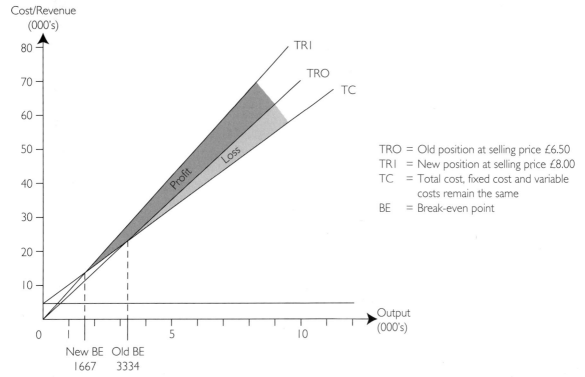

FIG. 1.1.6 *A diagram showing the effect of a rise in selling price on D.B. Ltd's break-even position and level of profit.*

Supply tends to be elastic when producers are able to respond to changes in demand and price quickly. For example businesses may possess spare productive capacity with their existing resources and may therefore be able to expand production quickly in response to increased demand. With elastic supply curves a small change in price causes a proportionally larger change in the quantity supplied. Figure 1.1.7 shows an elastic supply curve. A rise in price from P1 to P2 causes the quantity supplied to increase from Q1 to Q2. The proportional rise in quantity supplied from Q1 to Q2 is much greater than the proportional change in price P1 to P2. Thus the product in Figure 1.1.7 is sensitive to price changes and is termed elastic.

Figure 1.1.8 on p.14, on the other hand, shows an inelastic supply curve. Supply tends to be inelastic when producers are unable to respond to changes in price quickly: for example in agricultural markets it can take several months to plant crops and wait for them to grow. Alongside this, if spare capacity does not exist or the cost of entering the market is prohibitive, producers are unable to respond and so changes in the quantity supplied in a market are restricted. In Figure 1.1.8 we can see that a change in price from P3 to P4 causes proportionally very little effect on the quantity supplied, from Q3 to Q4.

The other scenario which may exist is unitary elasticity (Figure 1.1.9 on p.14). This is where the proportionate change in price is matched by the exact same proportionate change in quantity supplied, that is:

$$\frac{\text{proportionate change P5 to P6}}{\text{proportionate change Q5 to Q6}}$$

There is a simple formula which describes the elasticity of supply:

$$\text{price elasticity of supply} = \frac{\text{percentage change in quantity supplied}}{\text{percentage change in price}}$$

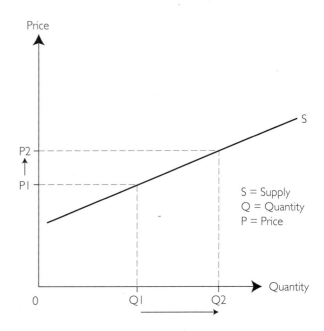

FIG. 1.1.7 *Elastic supply graph.*

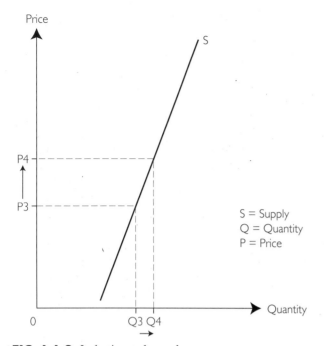

FIG. 1.1.8 *Inelastic supply graph.*

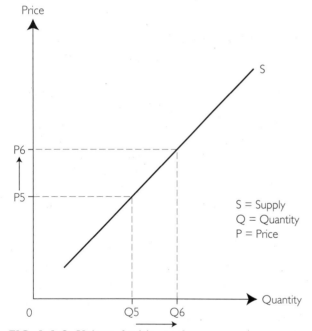

FIG. 1.1.9 *Unitary elasticity graph.*

SUPPLY CURVES

Supply is defined as

The quantity of a given good or service that businesses (sellers) wish to provide at a particular point in time at a particular price.

Thus a supply curve shows the quantity of a particular good or service that businesses wish to sell at each conceivable price.

Figure 1.1.10 shows the relationship between price and quantity supplied assuming all things remain constant, i.e. if the price of the particular good or service was for example £10.00 per unit then 8,000 units would be the quantity businesses would want to supply, and if the price were £5.00 per unit then the quantity supplied would be 2,000 units. This is in total agreement with the relationship between cost, volume and profit discussed previously in this Element.

Thus a supply curve shows the positive relationship between price and quantity supplied. At higher prices the quantity supplied rises and at lower prices the quantity supplied falls. A supply curve is derived quite simply by plotting price (on the vertical axis) against quantity (on the horizontal axis). By plotting all the points and joining them up we obtain a supply curve. Note, however, that the supply curve does not go right to the origin as nobody would be willing to supply a product if they were to receive zero price. Thus prices must reach a certain level before there is enough incentive to supply that product. (This level is dependent on the product, e.g. for a loaf of bread, approximately 45p, for a Ferrari £70,000.)

Another reason for this relationship between price and quantity supplied is that, at lower prices, some businesses are not able to produce the good or service efficiently enough to be able to make a profit. At this particular price level these firms will therefore not supply as they cannot do so profitably. However, as the price for the product rises more and more firms are able to produce and sell the product for a profit and so more businesses enter the market, thus increasing the total quantity of units supplied.

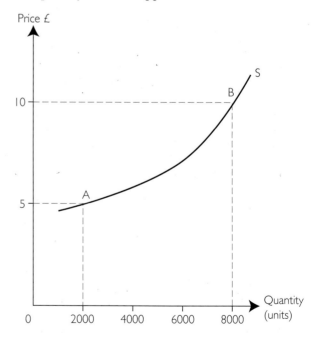

FIG. 1.1.10 *A supply curve.*

Thus the positive relationship between price and quantity supplied is two-fold. First, those organisations already in the market will seek to produce more as price rises, to take advantage of increased profits, and extra supply is generated by those firms which now enter into the market.

CHANGES IN SUPPLY

The most important factor in determining the quantity supplied is, as previously discussed, price. For example, in Figure 1.1.10 a change in price from £5.00 to £10.00 causes a movement along the supply curve from point A to B and thus a change in the quantity supplied from 2,000 to 8,000 units. However, price is not the only factor to be taken into account when considering the determinants of supply. We must also consider:

- *Costs of changes in factor prices* – such as the cost of raw materials or the level of wages. For example, if the cost of raw materials rises without an increase in productivity and sales then the quantity supplied may well be reduced.
- *Changes in technology* – improvements in technology make it possible to produce higher quantities of goods and services with fewer factors of production (raw materials, labour, etc). Therefore supply is likely to increase.
- *The number of firms in an industry* – as we have seen, if more firms enter a market then the level of supply is expected to increase.
- *Exogenous factors* (conditions outside the normal market forces) – government policy, for example: if the government imposes a tax on a particular good or service it has the same effect as an increase in one of the factors of production.

Other influences on quantity supplied include the actual objectives of the firms themselves (and it should be noted that not all businesses are solely project maximisers); the introduction of new legislation such as health and safety measures which may result in higher costs; and even such simple considerations as the weather (especially relevant for agricultural industries).

EFFECT OF CUSTOMERS

Essentially, an organisation can be one of the following:

- *Market orientated* – in which case the organisation responds to perceived market need derived from marketing research. The effect of customers on the organisation in this case would be considerable, since the organisation would only choose to supply products that it expected the customers to purchase. Once an organisation has identified a potential market which has a need that requires to be satisfied, it will attempt to supply that market at a level which offers both good market penetration and reasonable profit return.
- *Product orientated* – in which case the organisation has a fixed range of products to offer the market. It has no real choice about what it supplies but it does have a choice about how much to supply. The level of supply will be affected by the efficiency of the sales force in terms of gaining sales and the willingness of the customer to pay the price which has been set for the product. These organisations are somewhat vulnerable to other organisations stepping into their market and supplying products at a lower price which may not be cost effective to the original organisation.
- *Production orientated* – in which case the organisation is very firmly fixed to finding markets for a set level of supply. The production rate is fairly constant and the organisation is restricted to only making minor changes in its production output. These organisations need either to be extremely cost effective and able to supply products at an acceptably low or competitive price, or to have a very good sales force who can not only flood existing markets, but find alternative markets.

EFFECT OF COMPETITORS

It should not be thought that a market can cope with a finite level of supply. Markets are always developing and growing, if not in the home or traditional market, then elsewhere in the world. Obviously, the impact of competitors on the supply available to a market will have an impact on all organisations' market share. The level of market share held by an organisation will constantly be under threat from its competitors. As we will see in other Units, organisations employ various techniques in order to take market share from one another. The degree to which effort has to be put into this type of operation will be dependent upon the predictions, trends and forecasts made by an organisation. It will be able to ascertain whether it needs to make extra effort to take market share away from a competitor, particularly in the light of the market demand remaining fairly stagnant. Organisations will always be on the lookout to take the opportunity of grabbing market share from a competitor, particularly if that competitor is suffering temporary financial difficulties. Organisations will look at company reports and will act against an organisation which shows poor profits or results.

An alternative to trying to take market share away from a competitor is to seek alternate markets for the product. Organisations which have intensive and non-stop production lines may be unable to make a serious dent on the competitors share of the market. They will seek alternative uses for the product and try to convince customers in other markets to consider their product.

1.1.3 *Analyse the demand and supply interaction*

ANALYSIS:

MARKET PRICE AND MARKET VOLUME FOR A PRODUCT

If we combine supply and demand curves on to the same graph, we can attempt to calculate something known as the **equilibrium price**. The equilibrium price occurs when the quantity bought equals the quantity offered on the market. At all other prices there is what is known as disequilibrium. Competition between purchasers of the products or services will force the price up to the equilibrium (this is when demand exceeds supply). Competition between sellers will force the equilibrium down when supply exceeds demand. The equilibrium price is often referred to as the natural market price as market forces will always have an effect on the equilibrium.

Table 1.1.2 and Figure 1.1.11 show the effect of combining a demand curve (Figure 1.1.1) and a supply curve (Figure 1.1.10).

TABLE 1.1.2 *Supply and demand*

Price per unit (£)	Quantity demanded	Supplied
10.00	2,000	8,000
5.00	8,000	2,000

As can be seen in Figure 1.1.11, market equilibrium and thus the equilibrium or market price occurs at point E where the quantity demanded equals the quantity supplied.

In theory there is an automatic market mechanism in which producers and consumers respond to price signals and co-ordinate their activities accordingly until the market equilibrium price is reached. In simplistic terms the market mechanism works in this way at points to the right of the equilibrium point. Supply is greater than demand and therefore businesses are producing excess stocks of products which they can't sell. Therefore suppliers must drop their prices in order to attract more buyers, thus moving closer towards the equilibrium. To the left demand is greater than supply. There is excess demand in the economy thus prices will be joined up towards the equilibrium. Eventually the market forces tend to bring both consumers and

producers closer and closer to the equilibrium point until the equilibrium market price is reached (EP), as shown in Figure 1.1.11.

Thus at the equilibrium point there exists a national market price and market volume where producers and consumers are able to trade, and there is no incentive for any further change in the price of the product and the quantity demanded and supplied. This is because at this price the quantity demanded (QD) by consumers is exactly equal to the quantity that companies are willing to supply (QS). That is:

QD = QS

This holds true for any market. No matter what the type of good or service on offer there exists a market equilibrium price and market equilibrium volume.

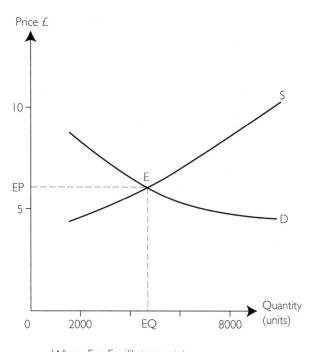

Where E = Equilibrium point
EP = Equilibrium market price
EQ = Equilibrium market quantity (volume)

FIG. 1.1.11 *The interaction of supply and demand.*

1.1.4 Explain the effects on business decisions of changes in the conditions of demand and supply

EFFECTS ON BUSINESS DECISIONS

SHIFTS IN DEMAND CURVES

So far we have primarily concerned ourselves with the effect on demand of price and movements along a particular demand curve. If it is only a price change that takes place then we simply move to a different point along the same demand curve. However if some factor other than price changes, then the effect is a movement (shift) of the entire demand curve either right or left. Demand is therefore also influenced by:

- *Income* – changes in income, changes in the effective spending power of households, e.g. an increase in income is liable to lead to an increase in demand.
- *Consumer tastes or preferences* – for example, changes brought about by fashion may cause demand in a particular market to increase.
- *Price of related goods*
  (a) complementary – as previously mentioned a rise in the price of a complementary good causes a fall in the demand for another, e.g. petrol and cars
  (b) substitute – an increase in the price of the substitute good causes a rise in the demand for another, e.g. margarine and butter.
- *Population* – changes in the size and age of population will affect the quantity and type of products demanded.
- *Expectations of future prices* – if consumers expect future prices to rise then they will buy more now,

causing a shift in the demand curve. Thus news that coffee crops have failed and that coffee prices are due to rise may cause consumers to go out and 'stock up' on coffee before the price rise takes place.

If for any of the above reasons the level of demand for a product is increased this causes a shift to the right, and conversely a shift to the left indicates a decrease in demand at each and every conceivable price. These are demonstrated in Figures 1.1.12 and 1.1.13.

Figure 1.1.12 illustrates the situation when, because of changes in the determinants of demand, market demand is increased. More is now demanded at each and every price. The possible causes of this increase may be:

- increase in level of income
- market product becomes fashionable (could be due to seasonal fluctuations)
- price of substitute rises
- price of complementary good falls
- increase in size of market population
- expected increase in future prices

Figure 1.1.13 illustrates the opposite situation, when, as a result of changes in the determinants of demand, market demand is decreased, and less is now demanded at each and every price. The possible causes of such a decrease may be:

- decrease in level of income
- market product becomes unfashionable
- price of substitute falls

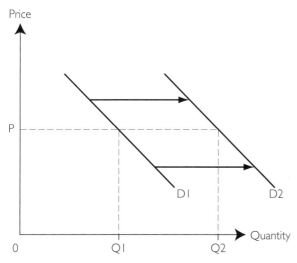

FIG. 1.1.12 *Shifts in demand curves (A).*

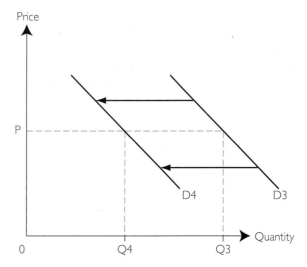

FIG 1.1.13 *Shifts in demand curves (B).*

- price of complementary good rises
- decrease in size of market population
- expected decrease in future prices

SHIFTS IN SUPPLY CURVES

Similarly, with supply we have concerned ourselves only with movements along the supply curve that are caused by responses to changes in price. However, a change in the non-price determinants of supply will result in shifts of the supply curve.

As previously mentioned in '**Changes in supply**'on p.15, the main non-price determinants of supply are:

- changes in factor prices
- changes in technology
- number of firms in the industry/market
- exogenous factors such as government policy
- future price expectations

If for any of the above reasons the level of supply of a product is increased, this again, as with demand, causes a shift to the right. Conversely, a shift to the left indicates a decrease in supply at each and every conceivable price. These are demonstrated in Figures 1.1.14 and 1.1.15.

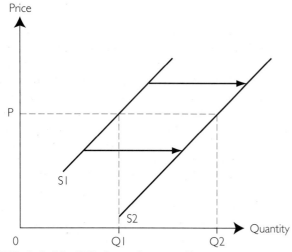

FIG. 1.1.14 *Shifts in supply curves (A).*

Figure 1.1.14 illustrates the situation where, because of changes in the determinants of supply, market supply is increased. More is now supplied at each and every price. The possible causes of this increased supply may be:

- technological advance
- decrease in factor prices, e.g. raw materials
- government policy, e.g. removal or decrease of imposed tax on product
- more firms entering market, total number of firms increasing
- expected increase in future selling price

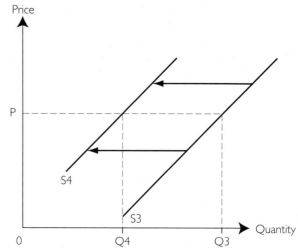

FIG. 1.1.15 *Shifts in supply curves (B).*

Figure 1.1.15 illustrates the situation where, because of changes in the determinants of supply, market supply is decreased. Less is now supplied at each and every price. The possible causes of such a decrease may be:

- increase in factor prices, e.g. wages
- government policy, e.g. increase in or imposition of a tax on product
- firms leaving market, total number of firms decreasing
- expected decrease in future selling price

CHANGES IN MARKET PRICE AND QUANTITY SOLD

The easiest way to demonstrate the effect of shifts in demand and supply curves on the market price and quantity sold is to take each possible instance and represent it diagrammatically.

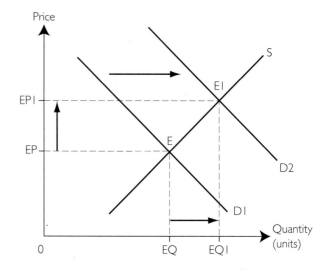

FIG. 1.1.16 *The effect of a rightward shift in demand on market price and quantity sold.*

Figure 1.1.16 shows the effect of a rightward shift in demand with the supply curve remaining static, i.e. more is demanded at each and every price. This has the effect of raising the market equilibrium price from EP to EP1 and the quantity demanded and supplied from EQ to EQ1.

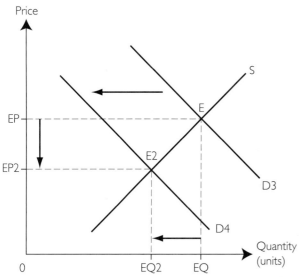

FIG. 1.1.17 *The effect of a leftward shift in demand on market price and quantity sold.*

As can be seen from Figure 1.1.17, with a leftward shift in demand, less is being demanded at each and every price. Therefore this has the effect of decreasing the equilibrium price and quantity from EP and EQ to EP2 and EQ2 respectively.

A rightward shift in supply, as shown in Figure 1.1.18, i.e. more being supplied at each and every price causes a drop in market price from EP to EP1 and a rise in quantity sold from EQ to EQ1.

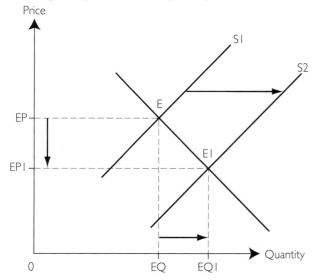

FIG. 1.1.18 *The effect of a rightward shift in supply on market price and quantity sold.*

Conversely a leftward shift in supply, i.e. less being supplied at each and every price, causes a rise in the equilibrium price and a drop in the equilibrium quantity (see Figure 1.1.19).

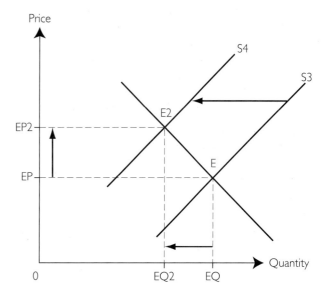

FIG. 1.1.19 *The effect of a leftward shift in supply on market price and quantity sold.*

The effects of changes in demand and supply in specific markets are very much dependent on the type of market and the market conditions which are prevalent at the time. As a general rule, however, if an increase in supply occurs at the same time as a decrease in demand then the market price of the product will fall. Conversely, if there is an increase in the demand for the product alongside a fall in the quantity supplied then the price of the product will rise. However, if there is an increase in demand and supply then the only thing we can be certain of is that output will increase. Similarly, if both supply and demand decrease simultaneously then output will probably fall. In both these cases, however, we cannot make predictions as to what will happen to price, it may either increase or decrease.

As mentioned above, the type of market – whether it is consumer market, industrial market or intermediate market – is also relevant. The current market conditions also play a major factor in determining the effect of changes in supply and demand. In particular the degree of competition within the market is significant. For example, in conditions of monopoly or oligopoly changes in demand may have very little effect on quantity supplied and price, whereas under imperfect conditions (and perfect conditions), where there are large numbers of producers and consumers within the market-place, and there is a large degree of competition, it becomes very difficult for any single entity to influence the market price.

Factors such as government intervention and legislation can prevent the market mechanism from operating freely: for example, the government may put price controls on certain products to keep them available for the majority of the population, whereas if allowed to follow its own course, the market equilibrium price might be much higher, or lower (especially in some agricultural/dairy industries).

Thus there are in reality very few perfectly free markets, and in most cases there are often other influences in addition to those of supply and demand.

ECONOMIES OF SCALE

There is an obvious link between the number of products an organisation sells and its potential to grow. When a company needs to grow more quickly, it may choose to buy or merge with another company. However, most early growth is made by identifying and exploiting a gap in the market. If traditional markets for products are in decline, a company which is well-positioned to sell its excess production elsewhere is less likely to be seriously affected. An alternative way of dealing with this problem is to look for another way for customers to use the product. Whisky distilleries, for example, which have seen a gradual decline in demand, have found it impossible to discover an alternative use for their product. They had, to some extent, coped with earlier declines in demand by exporting the majority of their whisky to the Far East. In Japan, which had been a huge market for Scotch whisky, the tables were turned as enterprising Japanese businessmen started producing their own version of whisky.

As we mentioned earlier, a good way for a company to expand its business is to increase the number of units it produces. As the number of units manufactured gradually increases, so do the profits, as the individual cost for each unit falls. This fact is known as an economy of scale. It basically means that the company can buy greater quantities of raw materials in bulk, it can use its premises and employees more efficiently and all its overheads (fixed costs) are spread more thinly. Overheads refer to such things as heating, lighting, insurance, rent, rates and loans. In addition, with this increased profitability, the company is able to keep pace with technological changes and invest money in research and development and always be in a position to raise additional money for emergencies or the purchase of another company.

When an organisation becomes a large-scale manufacturer, it is able to mass produce goods at relatively low prices, it will always be catering for comparatively stable markets (in other words, the future demands for its products are fairly safe), but it will have had to invest very heavily in machinery.

The ideal situation for a large-scale producer of manufactured goods is to create a global market for its products. It would be even more ideal if this product did not have to be substantially changed before it could be sold in other countries. The fewer the changes, the lower the cost to the manufacturer.

On the other hand, a large-scale manufacturer, involved in various different countries, is likely to suffer quite badly if there is a recession across the world. Some of the largest organisations have had to contend with losses running into billions of pounds as a result of over-extending themselves. The growth process needs to be carefully considered and must not outstrip the real demand for the product.

Companies which have suffered massive losses have blamed various features of their organisation, including:

- The more widespread the company is, the harder it is to manage efficiently.
- Growth beyond their 'optimum' size. In other words, it would have been better to have created another company to handle the production and not to have produced the goods themselves.
- Large organisations with huge numbers of staff tend to suffer from poor communications.
- There is a tendency for considerable numbers of employees to feel that they have no real power in the organisation and therefore they are not well motivated.

These reasons, taken together, are known as diseconomies of scale.

Increasingly, the service sector is dominated by large companies. We have already pointed out that the service sector is, indeed, a large one. Many of the same problems that face a large-scale manufacturing organisation will be faced by service organisations. The major difference is that they do not necessarily produce products, but provide services. In effect, if they suffer problems, they will have to shed staff and dispose of premises.

FIG. 1.1.20 *Carlsberg Tetley, a division of Allied Lyons, shows that large organisations have the ability to not only produce the product but retail it too.*

CHANGES TO BREAK-EVEN POSITION

An in-depth explanation of break-even is given in Unit 6. In this Unit see the section **Relationships between price and quantity supplied**.

In general terms we can assume the following relationships take place. If there is a rise in the market equilibrium price without a corresponding rise in costs companies will stand to make greater profits. In particular, the contribution per unit will rise. Thus the break-even level of production will fall, meaning that companies will break-even at lower levels of output and

therefore stand to make profits earlier. Conversely if the market price were to fall the break-even level of output would rise as each unit of output contributes less towards profits than it previously did. In this instance companies have to reach higher levels of output before they break even and are able to make a profit. If this state of affairs were to continue in the long run it could force the less efficient businesses out of the market especially if it were to cause them to drop below their break-even level of output.

Consider the following situation. Figures 1.1.21 and 1.1.22 on p.22 show the market equilibrium position of a particular product X and the break-even chart for a particular company within that market (IN PRO Ltd) respectively. Table 1.1.3 shows IN PRO Ltd costs and revenue schedules and Table 1.1.4 shows product X demand and supply schedules. It can be seen from Figure 1.1.21 that the equilibrium price for product X is £6 per unit and that equilibrium market demand and supply is 70,000. If we assume that the market is indeed in its equilibrium position and that IN PRO Ltd commands 10 per cent of the market share, combined we get the current position for IN PRO Ltd as shown in Figure 1.1.22 on p.23.

To see the effect on changes to break-even position we might consider the effect of a leftward shift in the demand curve, i.e. less is being demanded at all conceivable price levels, because there has been a decrease in the level of consumers' income caused by the government's raising income tax. Figure 1.1.23 on p.23 shows the effect that this will have on price and quantity demanded and supplied.

As we can see, the equilibrium selling price of product X has dropped to £5.00 and the equilibrium volume has fallen from 70,000 to 60,000 units. Assuming that IN PRO's market share remains at 10 per cent this enables them to make and sell 6,000 units at £5.00 each while their costs of production (fixed, variable and hence total cost) remain the same. This will have the effect of changing the company's break-even position to that shown in Figure 1.1.24. It can be seen that the effect has been to change IN PRO's total revenue schedule from TR to TR1. This is caused by the fall in price and the quantity that IN PRO can supply and sell. This change in the total revenue schedule has the knock-on effect of raising the company's break-even position from BE 5,000 units where TR = TC to BE1 10,000 units where TR1 = TC. However, the company is only able to produce and sell 6,000 units, not 10,000 and so is now in a position of making a loss. If this situation were to persist the company would be forced to switch production to another product and leave this market for product X or to go into liquidation.

TABLE 1.1.3 *Break-down of costs and revenue schedule of IN PRO Ltd*

No of units (£)	Fixed cost (£)	Variable cost (£4 per unit)	Total cost (£) (variable + fixed)	Total revenue* (£)	Profit (£)	Loss (£)
0	10,000	zero	10,000	zero	zero	10,000
1,000	10,000	4,000	14,000	6,000		8,000
2,000	10,000	8,000	18,000	12,000		6,000
3,000	10,000	12,000	22,000	18,000		4,000
4,000	10,000	16,000	26,000	24,000		2,000
5,000	10,000	20,000	30,000	30,000	break-even	
6,000	10,000	24,000	34,000	36,000	2,000	
7,000	10,000	28,000	38,000	42,000	4,000	
8,000	10,000	32,000	42,000	48,000	6,000	
9,000	10,000	36,000	46,000	54,000	8,000	
10,000	10,000	40,000	50,000	60,000	10,000	

*Total revenue: sales = quantity × price.
Selling price is £6 per unit.

TABLE 1.1.4 *Market demand and supply schedule of Product X*

Demand Price (£)	Quantity (units)	Supply Price (£)	Quantity (units)
2	110,000	2	30,000
3	100,000	3	40,000
4	90,000	4	50,000
5	80,000	5	60,000
6	70,000	6	70,000
7	60,000	7	80,000
8	50,000	8	90,000
9	40,000	9	100,000

student activity

(PC 1.1.1, AON 3.1, 3.2)
With the aid of diagrams consider the effect of a left-ward shift in supply in IN PRO's break-even position. N.B. plot the original market equilibrium graph (Figure 1.1.21) on an A4 piece of graph paper, shift your supply curve and then use your graph to estimate the new equilibrium price and volume.

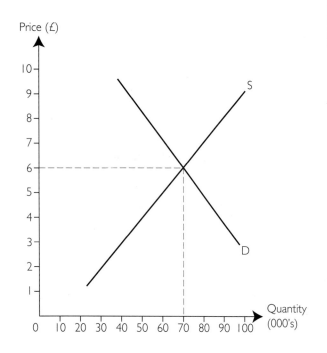

FIG. 1.1.21 *Graph showing market equilibrium price and volume for Product X.*

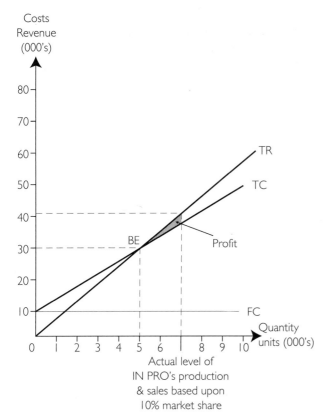

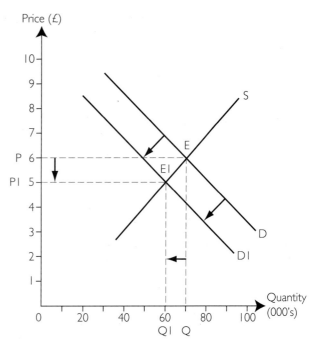

FIG. 1.1.23 *The effect of a leftward shift in demand in the market equilibrium for Product X.*

FIG. 1.1.22 *A break-even chart showing current level of output and break-even position of IN PRO Ltd.*

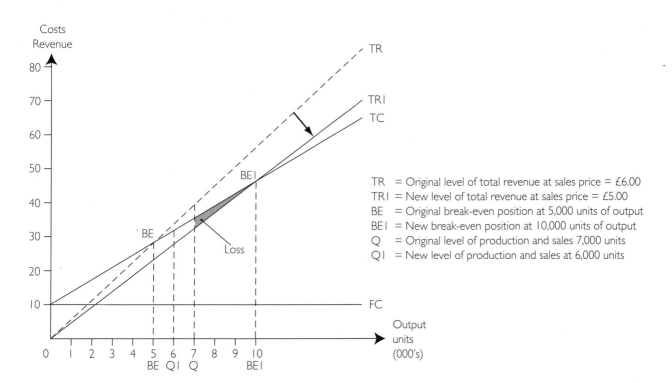

TR = Original level of total revenue at sales price = £6.00
TR1 = New level of total revenue at sales price = £5.00
BE = Original break-even position at 5,000 units of output
BE1 = New break-even position at 10,000 units of output
Q = Original level of production and sales 7,000 units
Q1 = New level of production and sales at 6,000 units

FIG. 1.1.24 *A chart showing IN PRO's new break-even position after a change in market equilibrium from E to E1.*

1.1.5 Report research findings about demand and supply interaction and the price and sales for a particular product

You will be expected to look at this aspect in much greater detail in the assignment at the end of Element 1.1. However, you should look at the following student activity as preparation for the end of Element assignment.

student activity

(PC 1.1.5, COM 3.4, AON 3.1, 3.2, 3.3)
Wilkinson Walkmans produce a basic portable stereo cassette player. They have calculated the following:

Quantity supplied	Price	Quantity demanded	Price
1,100	£25	3,600	£25

Given that a 10% rise in price will have the following effects:

- quantity supplied will rise by 15%
- quantity demanded will fall by 17%

Given that a 10% fall in price will have the following effects:

- quantity supplied will fall by 15%
- quantity demanded will rise by 17%

Construct a graph which shows the interaction of demand and supply with the price and sales.

1.1.6 Suggest future changes in demand and supply of particular products

Again you will be asked to look at this aspect in the assignment at the end of Element 1.1; however, for last-minute practice consider the following student activity:

student activity

(PC 1.1.6, COM 3.4)
Wilkinson Walkmans need to forecast the probable impacts on their sales and demand for the product in light of the following:

- portable CD players are about to drop to around £50 each

- cassette tape prices are about to increase by 20%
- DAT tape portable players are about to hit the market and will sell for around £100

Consider the probable future changes in demand and supply for Wilkinson Walkmans' product.

ELEMENT 1.1

a s s i g n m e n t

(PC 1.1.1–6, COM 3.2, 3.3, 3.4, IT 3.3 (3.1, 3.2*), AON 3.1, 3.2, 3.3)

In order to develop your understanding of the concepts regarding demand and supply, you will need to conduct research on two products. You will be asked to illustrate the concepts with supply and demand curves using data which you have collected. This may be either primary (in other words data you have collected yourself) or secondary data (information which you have obtained from a previously published source). If you find the data collection difficult or impossible, then you will be given simulated data by your tutor which will allow you to construct supply and demand curves.

Remember that demand and supply curves are based on the concept that if the price of a product increases, then the quantity demanded will fall.

TASK 1

(PC 1.1.1–2)

In the form of a report which analyses two products, first identify the causes of change in demand and supply for your two chosen products.

TASK 2

(PC 1.1.3–4)

You should now analyse how the interaction between demand and supply is influenced by decisions made by the business in regard to your two chosen products.

TASK 3

(PC 1.1.5)

You should also consider, within the body of your report, the relationships between the following:

- price
- quantity demanded
- quantity supplied

TASK 4

(PC 1.1.5)

The next part of your report should address the importance of competitors and customers in terms of their effect upon the following:

- demand
- prices
- supply and the consequence of shifts in demand and supply in terms of output or sales

TASK 5

(PC 1.1.6)

Your report should also make it clear that when equilibrium exists between supply and demand, both the price and sales of a particular product will be determined. You should also indicate the effects on price and sales, of changes in demand and supply and also identify two probable changes in demand and supply for your two chosen products.

NOTES

You can use simple graphical models to highlight the demand and supply relationships. Your report should be word processed. It will probably focus upon either local or national examples of business actions.

You may be asked to perform all of these tasks as part of a more comprehensive report which covers the whole Unit.

*may be claimed if you choose to use a software package in the presentation of your graphs

Analyse the operation of markets and their effects on business and communities

PERFORMANCE CRITERIA

A student must:

1 *explain* **types of markets**

2 **compare competition** *within markets*

3 **analyse** *the behaviour of businesses in different markets*

4 **evaluate** *the* **social costs** *of market operations*

5 **evaluate** *the* **social benefits** *of market operations*

RANGE

Types of markets: *competitive, non-competitive; monopoly, oligopoly*

Compare competition: *for customers and sales, for market share, for product superiority, for price, between businesses to shift demand curves, effect on consumers*

Analyse *in terms of: competitive pricing strategies (skimming, expansion pricing, penetration pricing, destruction pricing, price wars); price makers, price takers; non-pricing strategies*

Evaluate social costs *in terms of: effects on the environment (depletion of natural resources, pollution), effects on health, effects on employment*

Evaluate social benefits *in terms of: effects on employment, investment, training*

1.2.1 Explain types of markets

TYPES OF MARKETS

In a mixed economy, such as we have in the UK, the way in which resources are used and allocated is affected largely by the amount of competition between buyers and sellers. As we have seen, the interaction between market supply and demand curves affects the determination of market price and volume. Obviously the amount of competition within a market then is reliant upon the number of buyers and sellers within that market. It can be seen that the greater the number of buyers and sellers the greater the amount of competition. However, the allocation of resources is not always determined by the equilibrium price, markets are not always allowed to operate freely. The conditions within a market can be influenced by a number of factors thus different competitive market situations can be identified. Markets are classified into competitive and non-competitive markets as:

Competitive	Non-competitive
Perfect competition	Oligopoly
Imperfect competition	Monopoly

COMPETITIVE MARKETS

PERFECT COMPETITION

Perfect competition is a market situation where the following seven conditions apply:

1 A large number of buyers operate.
2 A large number of sellers operate.
3 No single buyer or seller is large enough to be able to exert an influence over the market price for the product.
4 The products being offered by all sellers are homogeneous, i.e. they are identical, there is no preference for any particular company due to price, quantity, after-sales service etc.
5 Perfect information is available between buyers and sellers regarding prices throughout the market.
6 Freedom of entry to and exit from the market, i.e. sellers are able to enter the market and compete on the same basis as existing sellers if there is a sufficient profit motive for them to wish to do so.
7 There is perfect mobility of factors of production and consumers, i.e. there is not occupational or geographical restriction to prevent resources and consumers moving freely.

A perfectly competitive market is represented diagrammatically in Figure 1.2.1. From our seven conditions it

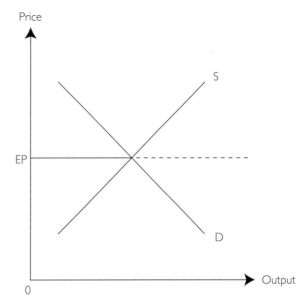

FIG. 1.2.1 *Determination of market price through interaction of supply and demand.*

can be seen that each individual supplier (seller) within the market must have a perfectly elastic demand curve. This is shown in Figure 1.2.2. If the firm were to raise its price above the market price it would sell nothing at all. This is because, as a result of conditions 5 and 7, consumers possess perfect information and know that the product is available cheaper elsewhere and there are no restrictions preventing them from going and buying it from wherever it is cheapest.

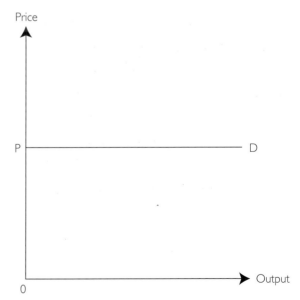

FIG. 1.2.2 *Individual company's demand curve within the market.*

27

Therefore under conditions of perfect competition the seller will only sell at the market price. Under these conditions fierce competition exists between suppliers for potential customers and as a result the market price is as low as possible and only the most efficient companies will survive. The conditions discussed above are, however, slightly unrealistic, and perfect competition does not in practice exist (although some markets like the stock exchange come close). However, it acts as a useful model for comparing real-life market conditions where either one side (e.g. buyers) or the other (e.g. sellers) has an advantage over the other.

IMPERFECT COMPETITION

This is sometimes termed monopolistic competition and is the more common market situation. This is where there is a large number of firms within a market each of which possesses a small percentage market share. They do not all supply exactly the same products as they differentiate them in some way, e.g. different hi-fis have different functions. In addition, consumers do not possess perfect information and freedom of movement. For example, you may learn that the particular hi-fi you want is £30 cheaper in Leeds, but if you live in London or Aberdeen this is of no use to you at all. This has the effect of enabling each firm to act as a very small monopoly as it is able to charge prices that vary a little from those of its competitors. The level of sales an individual company achieves is therefore dependent on price, and demand is not perfectly inelastic but becomes the more normal left-to-right downward-sloping curve. Short-run barriers to entry will exist but any industry continually achieving supernormal and abnormal profits will in the long run attract new entrants into the market causing demand for each individual company to fall until levels of normal profit are reached.

NON-COMPETITIVE MARKETS

MONOPOLY

Monopoly in its pure sense is a market situation in which ALL the production of a good or service is controlled by one firm or individual who dominates the market. This situation again is extreme and rarely exists. Under current UK law a monopoly is defined as a business which possesses 25 per cent or more of total market share.

The monopoly therefore has some control over the price of the product or the output which is sold and is able to influence the market for its own gain. However, if the monopoly wishes to sell more of its product it must reduce the price and if it wishes to increase the price then it must accept that quantity sold will decrease. The monopolist cannot control both these variables at the same time as it cannot determine demand.

Monopolies exist for four main reasons:

1 Companies may possess such a large share of the market that they can influence the market as a whole.
2 They may exist because of natural considerations like geography, i.e. one firm may be the only firm supplying a particular location or region.
3 They may exist through the formation of trading cartels, where several firms are working in conjunction with one another to agree price and output levels.
4 They may exist through the formation of trade associations to represent an industry as a whole.

For monopoly power to exist however, the monopolist must be able to prevent potential competitors from entering the market and must have a product which cannot easily be substituted for another.

Barriers to entering a market can take several forms:

- legal barriers such as patents, licences, etc.
- significant cost advantages in production, e.g. control of a national resource
- large amounts of initial capital investment required, e.g. electricity and national grid
- natural monopoly: sometimes it is not profitable for more than one firm to exist in an industry

EFFECT OF MONOPOLY

The lack of competition in a monopolistic market means that there is no outside incentive for the monopolist to achieve optimum efficiency. Therefore the situation results in a lower quantity being produced at a higher price than would be the case under conditions of competition. This also means that allocative efficiency does not occur either, i.e. resources are not being used efficiently or allocated to their most efficient usage.

However, it must be noted that not all monopoly effects are necessarily bad. As in the cases outlined above monopolies are able to take advantage of economies of scale and can be more efficient than several small firms. However, there is no guarantee that the monopolist will pass this on in the form of lower prices. Also as in the case of natural monopolies such as gas, electricity and water the introduction of competition would involve the wasteful duplication of expensive distribution networks. We discuss this further when we consider monopolies, mergers and restrictive practices.

OLIGOPOLY

Oligopoly market conditions exist in the situation when there are several relatively large firms which dominate

Focus study

MONOPOLY PRICING

The privatisation of water has been a stunning success in financial terms. Dividend payouts have increased by an average of 63 per cent a year. Between 1991 and 1993, turnover per employee increased by 8 per cent a year and profits per employee rose by over 21 per cent a year. If only the rest of the industry had performance as successful as that of the water industry.

However, these figures are a matter of concern because the water industry is displaying all the worst consequences of what happens when monopolies are privatised without effective regulation. In the case of water, both the taxpayer and the consumer have been taken to the cleaners. In the case of the taxpayer this is because the water industry was grossly undersold, even before allowing for the cancellation of debts of almost 5 billion pounds, on which hefty interest charges would have had to be paid. These same companies are now shelling out 1.5 billion pounds in dividends each year and not paying much corporation tax either. The improved financial position is the result not of increased efficiency, but of *monopoly pricing*. If the government had retained the companies but allowed them to do the same thing, it would now be receiving 1.4 billion pounds in dividends – a far better return for the taxpayer than privatisation.

The water industry was given what is now seen to be a ludicrous price increase formula (the annual rise in the retail prices index plus 5 per cent) in order to finance investment in cleaner water. The National Consumer Council (NCC) finds it very difficult to get accurate figures of reinvestment from the water companies' accounts (even though there are no competitors to justify confidentiality) but concludes that the price rises 'were clearly not justified'. Consumers have paid £2 billion in higher prices because of the above inflation. In some cases, prices have doubled. The solution is simple. The water companies must be told the party is over. They must be given a strict pricing regime which forces them to improve efficiency in a way that privatisation alone has proved incapable of.

student activity

(PC 1.2.1, COM 3.2)
Individually, referring to the above Focus Study, explain in your own words how the water industry has been able to make such profits.

Then, in groups, briefly discuss the advantages and disadvantages to consumers of the increase in charges since the privatisation of water.

What measures could be taken to regulate the water industry and rectify this position?

Again individually, try to find out the level of profits made by other utilities since privatisation. Discuss your results in class.

capital inputs and which thus create larger-scale organisations to provide them, creating an effective barrier to entry of smaller-scale operations. Examples of oligopolies operating in the UK are cars, soap powders, petrol, drinks manufacturers and chocolate manufacturers.

student activity

(PC 1.2.1, COM 3.2)
List 15 types of chocolate bar and 15 canned drinks. Conduct research into who manufactures each one. Compare your results with those of other members of your class. What do you find?

a market. This type of market is becoming more prevalent in economically developed countries, e.g. UK and Europe, America, Japan. The reason for this is the increasing number of mergers and take-overs, and the increasing number of products which require intensive

As there are only a few major competitors within the market individual firms are very sensitive to the actions of the others and before any firm makes any changes to its own position, e.g. on price, it has to assess the 'reactions' of its competitors, i.e. it must decide whether it will go along and raise its prices in conjunction with others or hold the price at its existing level and attempt to attract more customers by being cheaper. The fundamental belief of each oligopolist is that its rivals will match any price cuts so as not to lose market share but will not match any price rises in an attempt to gain more market share. Thus highly competitive oligopolistic markets can again be identified by the initiation of price wars or frequent fluctuations in price and highly intensive promotional campaigns.

A high degree of competition can be exceedingly beneficial to the consumer as it leads to lower prices and encourages suppliers towards technical innovation, i.e. the development of new products, flavours, functions etc. A good example of this is the current market for game consoles.

Most oligopolies, however, recognise the danger involved in initiating a price war. First, there is no firm guarantee they will win. Secondly, the effect is to lower prices and hence profits. Therefore oligopolists tend to group their prices within an acceptable margin of each other and tend to keep these prices stable, concentrating on promotion and product differentiation to gain market share.

This movement towards a relatively stable price does not always happen through the independent decisions of the oligopolists. Oligopolists often collude to develop a collective pricing strategy. They may, as

student activity

(PC 1.2.1)
For several days whilst watching television keep a record of the types of products advertised. Which ones occur most frequently? Why do you think this may be?

already mentioned, form a cartel and act as a monopoly, e.g. OPEC, or undertake such strategies as exclusive dealing and full-line pricing. We deal with restrictive practices, monopolies, mergers and fair trading Acts in Unit 1.3.

The recent 1992 opening up of Europe and the increasing ease of international trade have also contributed to the formation of oligopolies as companies merge for protection against foreign importers and become stronger themselves to be able to compete in an open European market.

1.2.2 Compare competition within markets

COMPARE COMPETITION

FOR CUSTOMERS AND SALES

As we have seen, the type of market conditions which prevail influence the degree of competition for customers and sales. Under conditions of pure monopoly for example no such competition exists as by definition there is only one supplier in the market and thus it does not need to compete. However, such companies are still desirous of increasing the number of customers and the level of demand for their product and so will undertake to find new markets for their product. Alongside this it must be recognised that the most obvious form of monopoly in the UK, such as British Gas, must also compete with the electricity industry to determine which will be the major supplier of domestic fuels for example. At the other extreme perfect competition means there must be intensive competition for customers and sales as price and product are identical.

However the ways in which firms compete for customers and sales are more readily to be seen with imperfect

competition and oligopoly and these are discussed later in this Unit with regard to price strategies and non-pricing strategies. Figure 1.2.3 outlines the degree of competition for customers and sales in each type of market.

FOR MARKET SHARE

Although a case could be made that the competition for market share is greater between oligopolists than in imperfect competition, as we have seen that fierce competition within an oligopoly can take place, it must be remembered that oligopolists have a tendency to explicitly or implicitly collude with one another.

Alongside this we have to consider the degree to which any change affects a company in a particular market. In the case of oligopoly a 0.5 per cent rise in market share may mean very little to a company which already possesses perhaps 14–15 per cent of the market. On the other hand a 0.5 per cent rise in market share to a company in an imperfectly competitive market could represent an increase in turnover of one sixth if its original market share were 3 per cent. In this respect

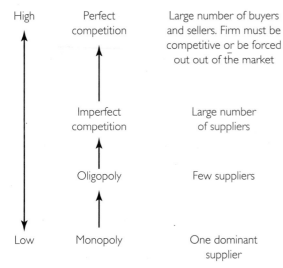

FIG. 1.2.3 *The degree of competition for customers and sales under different market conditions.*

in imperfect competition, the battle for market share and the improvement of it is divided up into much smaller segments than with oligopoly (see Figure 1.2.4).

In the case of monopolies, they possess such a dominant position in the market that there is very little or no competition against them, and there is no incentive for a monopoly which is probably receiving abnormal profits to change its position.

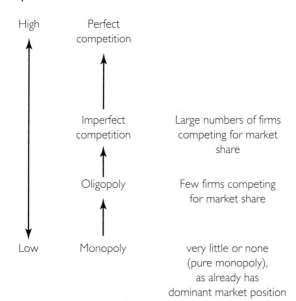

FIG. 1.2.4 *The degree of competition for market share under different market conditions.*

FOR PRODUCT SUPERIORITY

Oligopoly is by far the most competitive in terms of competition for product superiority. As previously noted oligopolists are very wary of using prices as a method of gaining customers, sales and market share for fear of initiating a price war. In this respect they tend to use product differentiation and product superiority as the main means by which they compete (see Figure 1.2.5).

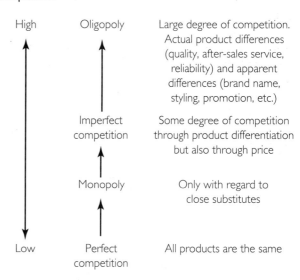

FIG. 1.2.5 *The degree of competition for product superiority under different market conditions.*

Product differentiation and superiority can be achieved in many ways:

- actual differences between competing products in terms of quality, after-sales service, reliability, etc
- apparent differences, brand images, promotion, etc.

If consumers perceive one product to be better than another for any reason, then if those products are within a very close price range, they will usually purchase the one they perceive to be the best, as they attempt to maximise their satisfaction.

Under conditions of imperfect competition companies also use product differentiation and promotional and/or marketing techniques to achieve product superiority, but they are also able to use the price of their product to influence the level of demand.

However, research and development into new products and production techniques is very expensive and due to the size differential is more easily undertaken by oligopolists. Under conditions of monopoly, they would only compete with close substitutes, if necessary.

Under perfect competition all suppliers possess the same product and so no product superiority can exist.

See Unit 3 for a more in-depth study of this subject.

FOR PRICE

In terms of competing for price it must be remembered that in perfect competition all firms are price takers, as any attempt to raise prices above the market equilibrium will result in no demand for that firm at all due to the perfectly elastic demand curve. Under monopoly conditions, the monopolist is totally dominant within the market and has the ability to determine the market price itself, i.e. it acts as a price maker.

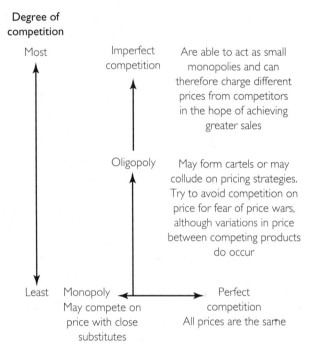

FIG. 1.2.6 *The degree of competition for price under different market conditions.*

Under conditions of oligopoly, competition as to price can take one of several forms. The oligopolies may form a cartel and use their joint power to act as a monopolist and dictate market price or quantity. They may compete with each other in non-price ways: consider the soap powder market. The two main producers of these products, Procter and Gamble and Unilever, would appear to be in fierce competition with each other – judging by the number of television and newspaper advertisements and promotions. However, their competitive practices rarely involve the prices of the products themselves.

When oligopolies do compete on price they may use one of several pricing strategies. (See section on pric-

ing strategies on p.33). For example, when launching a new product they may use the penetration pricing strategy, i.e. the company gives its new product an initially low price in order to gain market share while relying on the rest of its business to support it. However, such competitive pricing measures will usually be restricted to the short term for fear of promoting a price war.

In conditions of imperfect competition, price is one of the major tools for achieving customers, sales and market share. As previously mentioned there are a large number of firms in imperfect competition all competing for a limited market share. Thus rather than a few large companies we have the situation of many small and medium firms. However, the low budgets of these companies prevent them from undertaking expensive R and D projects, thus preventing some forms of technical innovation and product differentiation.

BETWEEN BUSINESSES TO SHIFT DEMAND CURVES

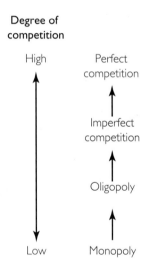

FIG. 1.2.7 *The degree of competition between businesses to shift demand curves under different market conditions.*

Obviously the direction in which companies wish to achieve a shift in demand is to the right, so causing the level of demand to be increased at all prices. Companies can expect a rightward shift in demand to occur for the following reasons:

1 Increase in level of **income** of consumers

- cannot directly be improved by business actions

2 Market product becomes **fashionable**

- can be influenced by advertising, brand imaging, etc.

3 Price of a **substitute good** rises

- individual firms cannot dictate competing firms' prices unless they can force up competitors' costs, e.g. have a dominant position in supply of raw materials

4 Price of **complementary goods** falls

- cannot be influenced by individual firms unless they gain control of supply of complementary goods

5 Increase in size of **market population**

- no direct influence by individual firms

6 Expected increase in **future prices**

- firms may leak information about expected future price rises to encourage a short-run shift in demand. However, unless expected price rise occurs this situation will only be for a short time

We can see therefore that any company which is successful in causing a shift in its individual demand curve to the right will expect to increase the level of sales at the current market price. (See Element 1.1, Shifts in demand curves on p.17 for an illustration of this effect.) Competition to shift demand curves increases in direct relation to the number of companies operating within the market, as the greater the number of companies the greater the number trying to shift their individual market demand curve to the right. Again it must be noted that oligopolies may collude in order to achieve this.

Even monopolies will attempt to shift their demand curve and if they can achieve this they will generate more sales at the market price and then gain more profit.

EFFECT ON CONSUMERS

Obviously the degree of competition in a market has an effect on consumers in such matters as market price, efficiency of production, degree of product differentiation etc.

PERFECT COMPETITION

The effect of perfect competition is to allow only those companies that can produce the product most efficiently to enter the market and survive. Due to the large number of buyers and sellers in the market, fierce competition exists. Therefore, the market price is driven down as low as possible and this is very beneficial to the consumer. However, perfect competition assumes that all suppliers produce and sell a homogeneous product, so the degree of product differentiation and consumer choice is effectively nil.

IMPERFECT COMPETITION

Under imperfect competition market conditions some short-term barriers to entry do exist, so that a firm may be able to make higher than normal profit, and suppliers have some degree of control over the price they can charge for their products. Thus the situation is that firms will not produce and sell at the lowest possible price as they would under perfect competition. But prices are not allowed to run rampant, businesses must still remain fairly efficient to stay in the market as the existence of supernormal or abnormal profits attracts more and more businesses into the market, causing individual firms to receive less demand at each and every price. However, under imperfect competition product differentiation can take place, thus allowing for a greater degree of consumer choice, and encouraging businesses to keep developing their products.

1.2.3 *Analyse the behaviour of businesses in different markets*

ANALYSIS:

COMPETITIVE PRICING STRATEGIES

The different forms of pricing policy are commonly described as follows:

PENETRATION PRICING

This occurs when an organisation sets an initially low price, in order to gain market share. In setting a low price, the organisation relies upon profits from other areas of its business activity to temporarily subsidise a new product or service in its initial launch period.

PRICE SKIMMING

If the organisation is in the fortunate position of being first into the market with a new product or service, it may be able to charge a considerably higher price to people who wish to be the first to take advantage of the new item. This pricing policy is often used when the demand for a product is price inelastic.

TO RECOVER INVESTMENT QUICKLY

This policy is designed to achieve a fast profit and return on the investments made. Prices are set without any specific regard to demand for the product or service.

PSYCHOLOGICAL PRICING

Organisations recognise that there are particular price barriers which should not be breached as they will affect customers' willingness to purchase products. Thus an organisation will price a £10.00 product at £9.99 to artificially stay within the preconceived boundary.

CUSTOMARY PRICING

Organisations may set their prices according to the customers' expectation of how expensive a product should be. If the price is higher than expected, then sales will be affected.

ODD PRICING

This is a form of psychological pricing, in which the price appears to be much more acceptable at a level between two clear and even prices, such as 19p instead of 18p or 20p. To some extent, odd pricing has become a feature of many products with the inclusion of VAT.

PRESTIGE PRICING

Certain products or services may be made to appear exclusive by the setting of an artificial price, which is far in excess of the real value of the item. This form of pricing is particularly true of all luxury goods and is, perhaps, one area of pricing where the comparative competitors' pricing levels are irrelevant.

COST-PLUS PRICING

This is a simple form of calculating the price of a product as it is linked to the total costs incurred in producing, distributing and promoting the product and a specified profit margin.

TARGET PRICING

Target pricing is used to achieve the break-even point and relies on several assumptions being made regarding demand. The target price may relate to the position the product has reached in its life cycle.

LIFE-CYCLE PRICING

This form of pricing relates to the comparative demand for the product at various points during its life cycle. When there is a high demand, the price may be increased, and when demand falls, so too will the price.

DISCRIMINATION PRICING

This pricing policy is one that is used in particular in the service industries when normal demand is low. Certain 'quiet' periods of the day, month or year are identified as times for discrimination price policies to be implemented. In other words, customers find that it is cheaper to make use of the service at these quieter times and this generates additional demand.

COMPETITION PRICING

Many organisations consider their competitors' pricing policies when setting their pricing levels. From a careful consideration of their competitors' price levels, they are able to ascertain what is the accepted price and can set their pricing levels in relation to this 'standard' price. This is a good way of product positioning.

PROMOTION PRICING

This form of pricing is used to attempt to maintain market share by the use of particular promotional devices. These devices include short-term price reductions or the offering of more volume or weight or product for the same price.

TRADE DISCOUNTS

Organisations which purchase products or services from a supplier, and are not at the end of the distribution chain, do not have to pay the full recommended retail price for the item. They pay a price known as the trade price. This trade price is related to either the total value of the order or the number of products ordered.

EARLY PAYMENT DISCOUNTS

To persuade customers to settle their accounts as early as possible, organisations may offer additional discounts. These assist the cash flow of the supplier. At the same time, the discounts allow the purchasers to make a bigger profit when they sell on the product or service. A variation of the early payment discount is the discount available to those who choose to pay in cash immediately. Such payments save the supplier from the delays associated with payment by cheque, such as waiting for a cheque to be cleared, or waiting for it to be sent on in due course.

QUANTITY DISCOUNTS

This is a common form of discount and enables customers to obtain the products or services at a lower unit price by purchasing in bulk.

TENDERS

Tendering has become an increasingly accepted method of pricing. Here it is the supplier of the product or service who sets (in isolation) the price he/she wishes to be paid for that product or service. An organisation wishing to purchase a product or service calls for tenders to supply it and several organisation will simultaneously put in tenders to provide it. The buyer

Focus study

COMPETITIVE PRICING STRATEGIES

Extract taken from Office of Fair Trading's 'Fair Trading: Future challenges' by The Director General of Fair Trading, 1995.

One kind of behaviour which is widely regarded as an offence under competition law concerns predatory pricing. The concern here is that a firm with deep pockets may charge low prices for a time with the intention of driving a rival out of the market and creating a dominant position which enables excess profits to be earned. It can evidently be difficult to distinguish between vigorous marketing, perhaps involving efforts to get a product established, from predation. In order to guide businesses and help our own analysis, we have specified a three-part test to establish whether or not predation is taking place. The first part of the test is that losses are being incurred – though accountants will see immediately that this is not a straightforward matter. Secondly there must be an intention to drive others out of the market. Intention can often not be observed directly, of course, but this really means that there is no other convincing explanation of the pricing strategy. Thirdly, predation must be feasible. If entry to the industry is easy, for example, predation is not likely to work, because as soon as one rival has been eliminated and prices increased, another is likely to enter.

An industry that has seen a good deal of complaint about predatory behaviour is the bus industry. Most of the bus industry has now been opened to competition, either through direct competition on the roads or through competition in a tendering process for local authority subsidies to operate routes which are of social importance but not commercially viable. The privately owned successors to the former government-owned companies, in most cases, commenced with monopolies. There is still, today, relatively little head-to-head competition but such competition as does develop tends to do so as a result of a decision by a small firm to enter the market on a few routes in a local area. Entry is not very difficult because the investment required is low, and in this respect and in other respects, entry barriers are also low. If the initial entry is successful the firm may expand to provide competition in a more broadly based manner. I see it as very important that everything possible should be done to give this emergent competition a reasonable opportunity. A little head-to-head competition plus the threat of new entry is likely to be the best incentive we have in the bus market for some time to come.

However, the structure of the bus industry makes it relatively easy to 'see off' competition through predatory behaviour. If firms are shown that they will not be allowed to get away with this, they will presumably conclude that it is not worth the effort to try. If, on the other hand, they are allowed to get away with it, the expectation of meeting predation will come to be a strong barrier to entry for those contemplating it and competition will not happen. The threat of competition cannot be sustained if it never actually takes place.

My Office has received numerous complaints about predation. In some cases, the complaint concerns a straightforward issue of price-cutting. In others, the predation may take other forms, including uneconomic increases in the number of buses operating on a route, sometimes supported by 'wild-western tactics' such as employing lookouts to spot competitors' buses and arrange for one belonging to the firm concerned to pull out just in front of it. I have investigated a number of cases and, although I have not always been convinced that the complaints are well-founded, I have taken action in some of them.

Unfortunately, action under the competition law can never be fast. No competition offences are subject to prohibition in the general law on anti-competitive practices although there are special laws on restrictive trade agreements and resale price maintenance. In cases of complaints about predation, I must either make a reference to the Monopolies and Mergers Commission under the Fair Trading Act or if I decide to proceed under a related piece of legislation, the Competition Act, I must conduct a preliminary investigation at the end of which I can seek undertakings from firms about their future behaviour: if they are unwilling to give such undertakings, I can again enforce my wishes only after making an MMC reference. Firms – the victims of predation – have collapsed while this has been going on.

Furthermore, there is no penalty for the behaviour, no compensation for the victims, only a constraint for the future. Penalties can be levied only if an Order is broken or breaches occur of undertakings given in accordance with statute. The potential benefits of predatory behaviour might seem likely to outweigh the costs even if – perhaps especially if – a firm intends not to resist any regulatory action which is taken against it.

Some of my functions in securing effective competition come under special Acts of Parliament. Where specialist regulatory bodies exist, as with solicitors and barristers under the Courts and Legal Services Act or the professional accounting bodies under the Companies Act, I have the special function of reviewing their rules and reporting about any matters which seem to me to be significantly anti-competitive. My report goes to the government minister who can order a change in the rules.

Focus study

PREDATORY PRICING

Parfitt's Motor Service (PMS) has been in direct competition with Stagecoach since December 1993, when the country's biggest bus company took over Red and White Services of Merthyr.

The two co-existed peacefully for eight months, until Stagecoach approached PMS in September with an offer to buy the company.

PMS rejected the offer saying, 'It was an insult, way below the price we consider was right. We were also given the impression that if Stagecoach took over, 95 per cent of our employees would be made redundant within a very short time. We were not keen.'

Since PMS rejected Stagecoach's offer, Red and White Services has embarked on a ferocious campaign to increase its market share in the Merthyr Valley. On October 17, it introduced a £2 unlimited travel ticket – a strategy described by PMS as 'suicidal'.

PMS responded by lodging a complaint of predatory pricing with the OFT. One of their concerns centred on a meeting to discuss the bid.

'It was made clear that it would be pointless for us to go back to them after a period of time with a white flag as by then it would be too late,' Mr Parfitt said.

Stagecoach strenuously denied making any reference to a white flag. 'We told them that we would do whatever was necessary for the best interests of our company, as I think any managing director would do for their company.' He welcomed any OFT investigation.

   `0:45`

student activity

(PC 1.2.3, COM 3.1, 3.2)
In pairs, answer the following questions:

- Explain what you understand by the term predatory pricing.
- Why did Stagecoach initiate such a price strategy?

In groups of two or three investigate what has happened to the number of bus companies and prices in your local area since deregulation of the industry.

will then assess these offers and choose the best in terms of price and other criteria.

DISTRIBUTION PRICING

This is a form of pricing policy whereby a supplier undertakes to destroy its competitors' sales either by drastically reducing the price of its product or, when introducing a new product, using an artificially low price in order to switch demand from the competitors' product to its own.

EXPANSION PRICING

This occurs when a company has moved into a situation allowing it to take advantage of economies of scale, thus bringing down its costs and enabling it to lower prices.

PRICE WARS

Price wars occur when one company attempts to grab extra market share by lowering its price as compared with its competitors and undercutting them. The other companies in the market respond by lowering their prices more than the instigator and a price war ensues, in which each supplier attempts to gain sales by undercutting prices.

PRICE MAKERS AND PRICE TAKERS

As previously mentioned under **monopoly** on p.28–9, it is possible for monopolists and, to a much lesser extent, firms with imperfect conditions and oligopolies to have a certain amount of control over either price or quantity. They cannot control both at the same time as they do not control demand. In such a situation the company is either a price maker or a price taker. It can either set the price (price maker) and accept the level of output demanded at that price, or determine the level of output it wishes to achieve and then take the price that is determined by the market for firms selling that level of output (price takers).

NON-PRICING STRATEGIES

As already discussed in the unit, advertising, sales promotions, product differentiation and the marketing efforts of an organisation are all aimed at attempting to compete on a non-price basis. We will see later in Unit 3, how different organisations put these strategies into practice and in Unit 8, you will have opportunities to create your own.

1.2.4 Evaluate the social costs of market operations

EVALUATION OF SOCIAL COSTS

EFFECTS ON THE ENVIRONMENT (DEPLETION OF NATURAL RESOURCES, POLLUTION)

As we have seen in the course of this Unit so far, except under conditions of perfect competition, the market system (laws of supply and demand) does not always work efficiently. There are various reasons for this, and we shall look first at the fact that the price system does not necessarily register all the costs that are associated with production. An obvious example of this is pollution of air and water. This results from production methods but the price system takes no account of the ill effects such pollution may have on others. Social costs (and benefits) are those costs that are borne by society as a whole or incurred by individuals who do not consume the good or service which generated the cost. However it is often very difficult to measure social costs and put a value upon them. Indeed it is often very difficult to notice them in the first place, let alone find the cause.

Social costs can occur as a result of a number of factors:

1 *Production on consumption* – the adverse effects of pollution on recreational areas, e.g. chemical pollution in rivers and lakes causing a danger to water sports.
2 *Production on producers* – the adverse effect of pollution caused by one method of production on another form of production, e.g. chemical pollution in rivers and lakes causing diseases in livestock.
3 *Consumption on production* – e.g. traffic congestion caused by private motorists increases transport and delivery costs for businesses.
4 *Consumption on consumption* – litter caused by some consumers prevents others from using recreational facilities.

Governments, consumers and businesses are becoming more and more aware of what effect their actions have on the environment. As mentioned, an obvious social cost of production is pollution to air and water. Factories churn out by-products into the air, e.g. sulphur dioxide and smoke, and dump chemical waste into rivers etc. However, it is not only private businesses which are to blame, consumers are also at fault. Each time consumers purchase and use products containing CFCs (chloro-fluorocarbons) for example, they contribute towards pollution. Consumers usually consider only the private costs involved and not the social costs their activities place on the environment. In recent years several important environmental considerations have been and are continually being highlighted by the media.

student activity

(PC 1.2.4, COM 3.1, 3.2)
In groups of four, survey 50 to 100 people. How many still drive cars that take leaded petrol and are not filtered with a catalytic converter?

GLOBAL WARMING OR THE GREENHOUSE EFFECT

The more pollutants are released into the atmosphere the thicker the atmosphere becomes, causing heat generated by the sun's rays from escaping.

HOLES IN THE OZONE LAYER

Increasing concern is being expressed at the decrease in the ozone layer surrounding the earth. It is feared that as the ozone layer is eroded, more and more of the harmful UVA and UVB rays from the sun will penetrate the earth's atmosphere causing a widespread increase in the incidence of skin cancer and probably worse for the planet, restricting plant growth. Combined with global warming this could turn large areas into virtual deserts: look at the recent droughts in central and northern Africa.

ACID RAIN

The expulsion of acidic gases, such as sulphur dioxide, into the atmosphere, and the mixture of these with moisture in clouds, causes rain drops to have a slightly acidic content. The results of this 'acid rain' have been the destruction of large areas of Scandinavian woodland and damage to flora and fauna throughout the world.

Other environmental considerations that should be taken into consideration include the destruction of the South American rain forests. In many cases this takes place not for the wood the trees provide, but to make way for mines to extract metals and minerals or to be used as farmland. Lastly we must consider the effect of rubbish generated by humans. Every single business activity and household in the UK generates waste, over 20 per cent of which is dumped into the sea. We are not even going to attempt to discuss here the effects of nuclear by-products and nuclear accidents such as the melt-down at Chernobyl.

Alongside these considerations of pollution we should also look at the effect we are having on the level of natural resources around the world. Take gas, for example. Every time somebody lights up their gas oven they are burning a scarce and finite resource, i.e. once burnt the gas cannot be reclaimed and re-used, it is gone. Also by not taking into account the full cost of such factors as pollution, which are generated by the activities of businesses, the price system will not bring about an efficient allocation of resources (allocative efficiency), thereby perhaps not putting them to their best use.

EFFECTS ON HEALTH

The effects of such activities on the health of the nation and the social costs of this are obviously quite extreme. In some cases air pollution can cause respiratory infections, cancer, burning eyes and skin infections. There are also the effects caused by water pollution to humans, fish and wildlife in general. Such an effect on health carries a cost in itself, as the more people suffer from such infections, the more strain is put upon health-care systems and the more costs are incurred in treating them. Another effect is that as resources become more and more scarce they become more and more expensive. Thus families and individuals on low incomes can no longer afford them, and if we again take our example of gas, we see that this would cause adverse health conditions if people were no longer able to afford to heat their homes.

EFFECTS ON EMPLOYMENT

The effects generated by social costs on employment are twofold in nature. First, if all companies were to take into account the private costs of production plus the social costs, this would necessitate a rise in prices, causing the level of demand within the economy to fall. However, consumers already pay for these social costs by means of rates and taxes. Thus the offset of social costs on employment can be seen as being adverse.

If we assume that this means that people are either underemployed or unemployed then they will suffer because they receive a lower income than if they were in full-time employment. The more disposable income a person has, the more goods and services he/she can afford. People in the lower income brackets conversely can afford less. As we saw in the previous section, not being able to afford goods and services can lead to poor or ill health, e.g. if you cannot afford a balanced diet, suitable clothing and shelter. Similarly, worries about future employment can cause ill health as well, ranging from tension and stress to depression and nervous breakdown. Coupled with ill health from pollution this could be serious problem. The effect upon employment can be imagined if you think about this from the point of view of an employer: which would you rather employ, somebody who suffers from poor/ill health and is liable to take time off or somebody who is fit and healthy? You can see that there is a type of spiral effect. Unemployment can cause lack of income and ill health, ill health reduces the possibility of gaining employment.

Another factor to be considered is that as businesses become more aware of their social responsibilities, and as consumers demand greener and cleaner goods, they may well invest in more modern machinery and production techniques, and these often lead to job losses. New technology and modern production practices are becoming increasingly less and less labour intensive.

However, there is another side to this. The pressure on business and the demands of consumers have created new industries and markets for green, environmentally friendly products and have thus created some new employment opportunities.

1.2.5 Evaluate the social benefits of market operations

EVALUATION OF SOCIAL BENEFITS

It is possible for the activities of consumers and producers to have beneficial effects for one another. Social benefits can occur as a result of:

1 *Production on consumption* – e.g. horticulturists growing fields of flowers which are nice for passers-by to look at.
2 *Production of production* – e.g. the discharge of warm water into lakes and rivers increases fish breeding and leads to increased catches by fishermen.
3 *Consumption on production* – e.g. consumers' waste vegetable products being used as fertiliser to improve farmers' crops.
4 *Consumption on consumption* – e.g. by painting your house to look more attractive you improve the whole street.

EFFECTS ON EMPLOYMENT, INVESTMENT AND TRAINING

Social benefits are such things as health, education etc. and also those products which produce a benefit to others, who may not even directly consume the product. One example of this would be that curing one person of a contagious disease has the extra benefit of preventing anyone else from catching it, even though these others did not receive the treatment themselves.

Education and training possess many social benefits. If education was left entirely to provision by private enterprise, parents would have to pay school fees. Some would be unable to do so or may choose not to do so. The benefits gained from education are enjoyed not by the parent but by the children, and the money saved by the government in not providing education could be put to other uses. However, the government sees education for all as a social benefit, as more highly educated and trained people stand a better chance of employment, earning higher incomes, enjoying a wider range of cultural and leisure activities and bringing benefits to others through social interaction. In this respect, the training of employees after education has finished also provides social benefits. Even though training of the workforce is expensive it provides businesses with more efficient and multi-skilled workers. Even if the employees leave their job, training provides benefits to those who employ them next. The greater the degree of training provided by businesses the greater the benefits for all. Increased levels of training also improve employment prospects and help to remove some of the social costs associated with unemployment and uncertain employment prospects. That is, improved employment prospects and levels of income help to combat some of the social costs which cause ill/poor health.

Another effect on employment has been the creation of new markets and the setting up of new businesses as consumers switch from ordinary products to greener, more environmentally friendly ones. Government legislation has also helped in this regard, e.g. by insisting that all new cars take unleaded petrol and are fitted with catalytic converters.

The amount of investment taking place has an effect on the level of employment as well. If the government considers that particular items bring social benefits the government can encourage consumption of such items by subsidising them and encourage investment in such industries or invest in them directly themselves, hopefully improving employment levels. However, in some cases increased investment may allow a business to invest in new environmentally friendly production techniques which result in job losses.

Many social benefits are financed from government expenditure. As previously discussed in this Unit, many services such as education and health, if left entirely to private enterprise, would not be provided at a level that everyone could afford. Thus as education, health etc. are seen as such major social benefits they are provided by the government. This involves major expenditure on building new hospitals, schools etc. and provides many jobs in the economy, ranging from those employed in actual construction by private industry, to those employed as staff in the new services as teachers, nurses, etc. Another major social benefit provided in the UK by the government is investment in the infrastructure such as road and rail networks. Although there may be some social costs associated with building such communication networks, an economic exercise termed cost-benefit analysis is used to see if the social benefits outweigh the social costs. If they do, the project will be provided. For example, the social costs involved in building a new motorway could be the damage caused to wildlife and the countryside, whereas the benefits may be reduced congestion on existing roads and, therefore, reduced times and costs of delivery. Alongside this the new motorway may well improve communications to an isolated community, and encourage businesses to set up in areas which were suffering from unemployment problems due to bad road and rail connections.

ELEMENT 1.2

a s s i g n m e n t

(PC 1.2.1–5, COM 3.2, 3.3, AON 3.1, 3.2, 3.3, IT 3.2, 3.3)

The purpose of this Element has been to help you develop an understanding of the role of competition in markets and the effect competition has on markets. In this assignment you will be asked to make a study of two different markets and produce evidence which describes and explains the operation and effects of the market. You will also be asked to consider social costs and benefits. It is worth remembering that a social cost to some is a benefit to others.

TASK 1

(PC 1.2.1–3)

Identify two markets, one which is competitive and one non-competitive. In other words, private or public sector monopolies or oligopolies. You should consider the following:

- the size of the suppliers
- the strength of demand in the markets
- comparison between two businesses in one market which show shifts in demand curves, and why these shifts have occurred

TASK 2

(PC 1.2.2)

In the second part of your report you should describe how competition has an effect on the customer's choice and the quality of products available.

TASK 3

(PC 1.2.3)

You should now go on to describe how competition affects the pricing and non-pricing strategies employed to enhance a business's or product's market position.

TASK 4

(PC 1.2.4–5)

Finally you must address the costs and benefits of the operation of markets in relation to the costs and benefits on the wider community.

NOTE

Your report should be word processed.

Examine the effects of government policies on markets

PERFORMANCE CRITERIA

A student must:

*1 explain the **reasons for government intervention** in markets*

*2 explain the **ways** governments can influence markets*

*3 **evaluate** the effects on markets of **government policies***

RANGE

Reasons for government intervention: *to increase competition, to regulate competition, to counteract anti-competitive activities, to ensure fair and honest trading, to protect consumers, to protect environmental and social interests, to stimulate consumer demand, to improve levels of employment, to control inflation, to stimulate growth*

Ways: *regulation, deregulation, control of monopoly, monetary policy, fiscal policy, legislation, public ownership, privatisation*

Evaluate *in terms of: business confidence, changes in employment opportunities, growth, consumers' disposable income, effects on demand, trading conditions*

Government policies: *interest rates, personal income tax, corporate tax, Value Added Tax (VAT), public services wage levels, public spending, investment, regional assistance, single market*

1.3.1 *Explain the reasons for government intervention in markets*

Before we go into some detail regarding the reasons for government intervention, it would be useful at this stage to take a look at the different economies in operation in the UK and in Europe at the moment. One of the ways of looking at the different economies is to measure the amount of influence the government has on decision making. We can do this by first looking at the economic management in general terms.

There are several different types of economy, ranging from a totally free market in which the government concerned has no influence over the allocation or the control of resources, and the decision as to what is produced and consumed is controlled by private individuals and businesseses, to a totally planned or command economy, where all decisions on control and allocation of resources are made by the central government with no involvement from private individuals or businesses. In reality these two extremes of economy do not exist. In current times the closest economy to a free market is Japan, where although the majority of decisions are made by the private sector, there is still some government intervention, especially in terms of taxation and tariffs, and government investment in infrastructure and some public services, for example national defence. Conversely, the closest economies to that of a planned or command type economy are probably those of China and Cuba. In these countries, although the governments attempt to operate an almost totally planned economy, there is still some degree of private enterprise and underground economic operations. The actual type of economy in operation in any particular country is dependent upon the social and political climate at the time. Recent years have seen many Eastern bloc countries, in particular, with the break up of the USSR, move away from planned economies towards a more free type of market economy. The ethos behind a planned economy is that through central decision making the scarce resources of the country can be used to their best advantage as the whole country's efforts are directed towards achieving desired production targets with no wasteful duplication. Alongside this, the country's population should be unified as all parts of a free economy are dependent upon one another. All goods and services are distributed fairly and equally and, therefore, even in areas of high unemployment, the basic needs of the people can be fulfilled. However, in practice there are several drawbacks to operating this type of economy. Firstly, as all decisions for the whole economy are made by the

central government, this involves a lot of bureaucracy (paperwork) and greatly slows down the decision-making process, resulting in the loss of efficiency. This can result in the failure to produce or supply enough of a particular good or service; and create a situation in which those individuals who can obtain these goods will capitalise on their good fortune and sell them on at inflated prices for their own personal gain. Similarly, as theoretically all individuals should receive a fair and equal share, the incentive for increased effort and enterprise is removed. Alongside this there is no effective competition and therefore no incentive to make the products better, leading to a drop in quality. For example, if everybody has the same car and if that car gets you from A to B it does not need leather seats, sports trim and alloy wheels.

This lack of consumer choice and poor standard of production combined with the individual's inability to contribute to the decision-making process is one of the leading factors in the recent move by several countries towards a more free economy. It is believed that in a free economy due to competition, a more diversified and higher quality product will be supplied as consumers will only buy products that will provide them with the greatest satisfaction for their money. Suppliers will, therefore, channel the country's scarce resources into goods and services that are popular with consumers, thus such goods are likely to be produced in high quantities and at lower prices and wastage of resources will be avoided as goods which are unpopular and will not sell will not be produced. Alongside this, as decisions are made by a lot of individuals and businesses, they can respond to changes in trends and fashions very quickly, thus avoiding the bureaucracy inherent in planned economies. However, in free economies the apparent advantages do not always come to fruition. Competition leads to the waste of resources as goods and services are duplicated, large companies and, in particular, monopolies can have an artificial influence on the allocation of resources and the price at which goods and services are offered and the use of advertising provides a very powerful tool for influencing consumers. The main criticism of the free economy is that as all the resources are controlled by the private sector, there is no guarantee that the poorest consumers will have their basic needs provided for, as those consumers who have more money have more influence over producers. In reality the most prevalent type of economy is that of a mixed or social economy and in this type of economy there is both government involvement (public sector) and private enterprise (private sector), which both have a measure of control over the country's resources. The degree of influence of either sector varies from country to country. Most western countries use this type of economy and this is the type of economy that recently planned economies are moving toward. The mixed economy combines the best elements of a planned and free economy. Consumers have the choice to buy from a range of goods and can influence the market with their needs and wants. Private enterprise make decisions on how their resources are used, which means that they decide what and how to produce and the quality of the product, whilst the government has control over some of the productive resources, runs most of the country's services, for example health, welfare and defence and can influence consumers and producers in terms of laws, taxes and tariffs. Thus, the ways in which governments do and can intervene in the workings of an economy and their reasons for doing so, are somewhat dependent upon the type of economy in question.

student activity

(PC 1.3.1, COM 3.1, 3.2, 3.4)
Carry out research and identify at least five examples of countries who, over the last 50 years, have changed from one type of economy to another, for example from a planned economy to a mixed economy. From your research, does it appear that these countries are more or less successful as a result of the change?

Carry out this research in pairs and present your findings to the remainder of your group.

REASONS FOR GOVERNMENT INTERVENTION

One would assume that in a free or mixed market, the individual consumer has the maximum freedom to consume and spend as he/she sees fit. Consumption patterns will determine the supply of all products and services and ensure that any scarce resources are not wasted. Unfortunately, there are several problems with this system and successive governments have inter-

vened to control or manipulate the market. Above all, governments do not want the market to fail. Market failures unfortunately are all too common and may have resulted from the following circumstances:

- the economy is not sufficiently developed to accommodate changes in demand
- products or services are not available in sufficient quantities to match demand, or there has been over-production which has resulted in a glut in the market
- demand in a particular market may have collapsed suddenly
- small or new organisations may be unable to compete due to the dominance of a market by a particular organisation

Before the beginning of this century, the government played only a minor part in the running of the economy. However, various circumstances have determined that the government should play a greater role and involve itself in almost every aspect of business activity. It is important to realise that the government must take a macro view (wide view) of the operations of businesses and how they impact upon the economy. It is for this reason that the government is involved in all of the areas detailed below. You should not consider this to be a comprehensive list as we are sure you can think of other areas of the economy in which the government is involved.

TO INCREASE COMPETITION

As we have seen earlier in this Unit, increased competition tends to lead to a more efficient use of resources, as those firms which are unable to produce efficiently enough are forced out of the market. If there is insufficient competition in a market, such as in conditions of monopoly or oligopoly (where only one or a handful of companies compete for market share), a small number of companies can have a strangle-hold on the market, and therefore can charge excessive prices for their products. Such organisations can charge high prices because the consumers have nowhere else to buy them and, as mentioned above, this can cause inefficient use of resources as there is no need for the company to produce its products as efficiently as possible due to the lack of threat from any competition.

TO REGULATE COMPETITION

Since 1948 successive governments have produced a range of legislation in order to stimulate competition within the economy. Generally referred to as competition policy, these Acts try to ensure free and fair competition in the market-place. There are five principal Acts of Parliament governing UK competition policy; these are:

1 *The 1948 and 1965 Monopolies and Mergers Act*

As previously mentioned, we say there is a monopoly when a single organisation substantially controls a particular market. This is not an acceptable state of affairs, as the organisation may be able to control both price and supply within that market. As far as the government is concerned, a monopoly situation is not in the public interest. In recent years, those responsible for monitoring monopolies have been re-named the Monopolies and Mergers Commission (MMC). With the 1965 Act the government provided itself with the means to automatically refer merger proposals to a Mergers Panel. This panel reports back within six months and simply states whether or not the proposed merger is against the public interest. Serious cases are then referred to the Secretary of State who can make an order to counterbalance the state of affairs.

2 *The Restrictive Trade Practices Act 1956*

Under this Act, a Restrictive Practices Court was established to investigate and rule upon organisations working together to fix market prices. Such an agreement between organisations is known as a cartel. Interestingly, in variance with the basic premise of English law, under which a suspect is presumed innocent until proven guilty, in restrictive practices cases, the organisations must prove that the agreement is not against the public interest in order to avoid action being taken against them.

3 *The Competition Act 1980*

This Act effectively broadened the scope of activities that could be undertaken by the Director General of Fair Trading and the MMC. They could now investigate public sector organisations, which were brought into the range of the legislation. Each case is still investigated to assess its particular benefits and costs to the free running of the market, but it is no longer the view that mergers in themselves are undesirable. Indeed, a monopoly may be acceptable under certain circumstances.

4 *The Fair Trading Act 1973*

This key Act attempts to tackle the problem of competition. Defining a monopoly as an organisation controlling more than 25 per cent of a market, this gave the Director General of Fair Trading considerable powers. Of particular interest to the Director was any organisation attempting to distort the operation of a market by using anti-competitive pricing practices. Should the Director rule that the organisation's activities are unacceptable, the organisation is automatically referred to the MMC. Again, the Secretary of State may rule that the organisation must immediately cease this unacceptable behaviour.

5 *The Resale Prices Act 1976*

This Act seeks to establish the right of retailers to be

student activity

able to charge whatever price they wish for a particular product. In essence, therefore, this Act seeks to prevent dominant suppliers from being able to impose standard prices upon retail outlets, and to discourage suppliers from giving less favourable prices to those retailers who do not follow the suppliers' standard pricing policy. Again, such cases which do occur are dealt with by the Restrictive Practices Court.

FIG. 1.3.1 *The Office of Fair Trading issues many publications, such as this one on cartels.*

Focus study

MERGERS

Extract taken from Office of Fair Trading's 'Fair Trading: Future Challenges' by The Director General of Fair Trading, 1995.

Another well-known area of the work of my Office is the scrutiny of mergers. Here, my role is to advise the Secretary of State whether a merger raises concerns which should be investigated by the MMC to judge whether or not it may operate against the public interest. This is an important area of activity because a merger may create a dominant position in a market and it is better to prevent the establishment of a dominant position in the first place than to face the need to take action subsequently to prevent the abuse of that position.

It is perhaps worth emphasising that competition at the international level may be an important factor in assessments of mergers. If the firms concerned operate in a genuinely international market, then a merger which creates a large share of the UK markets may still be acceptable if the firms will genuinely face effective competition from firms in other countries. Sometimes a merger is advocated on the grounds that it will enable the firm to perform more strongly in international markets and, although I would not argue that a merger was acceptable if it created a strong monopoly position in the UK, this will not be a likely result if the market is genuinely an international one and competitive at that level.

Few cases nowadays do actually create a single firm with an overwhelmingly large share of a market. Some of the most difficult cases concern markets in which a merger will create a duopoly – strong dominance by two firms together. Such a merger may be objectionable on the grounds that it enables the two firms easily to adopt a policy of avoiding vigorous competition and thereby enjoy the fruits of some monopoly power. However, depending on the circumstances, a duopoly may be fiercely competitive. The detergent industry seems to be a good example of this. It is a strong duopoly, in the hands of Unilever and Procter and Gamble, but recent news about the behaviour of the firms suggest that it is vigorously competitive. Sometimes a merger which creates a duopoly can even increase competition, because it creates two more equally matched firms. The final assessment will often depend upon the ease with which other firms can enter the market.

Activity on the merger front has been fairly quiet recently. We had about two hundred cases which qualified for consideration under our size tests in 1993; mergers are running at a slightly higher level in the current year. However, only one industry, involving three cases, has given us serious concern during the current year and these cases have been the mergers of the Channel 3 television companies, beginning with Granada and London Weekend Television. These firms, of course, broadcast in different areas which in some respects are different markets. They participate in national networking arrangements, but these arrangements are subject to scrutiny by my Office under a specific provision of the broadcasting legislation.

Our concerns relate to certain kinds of advertising. The Channel 3 companies co-operate in selling their advertising and the mergers appeared likely to create strong concentrations within that market. This might have been particularly significant for advertisers who wished to achieve extensive coverage without necessarily covering the whole country. For such companies, the merger would have reduced the choices available and therefore altered the balance of the market power. The television companies were willing to offer undertakings that they would arrange their advertising sales in such a way that no one selling organisation held significantly more than twenty-five per cent of the market and the Secretary of State decided, on my advice, to accept these undertakings.

As you may know, government policy has recently emphasised the importance of reducing burdens on business. It has been concerned that regulations are growing rapidly to the point where the resulting cost burden is heavy. Regulations are more easily introduced than abandoned. It is all too tempting for politicians to develop a new regulation to deal with each problem of which they become aware, losing sight of the cumulative effect. Directives of the European Commission are adding to this problem. A bill to facilitate and promote deregulation is now well on the way to the statute book.

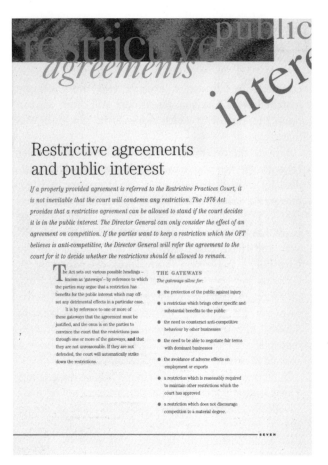

FIG. 1.3.2 *The Office of Fair Trading leaflet on restrictive agreements.*

TO COUNTERACT ANTI-COMPETITIVE ACTIVITIES

The five parliamentary acts we have just looked at are the main means by which the government attempts to counteract the anti-competitive practices undertaken by companies. One of the main forms we have looked at is that of mergers and the formation of cartels, i.e. agreements formed between suppliers to achieve domination of a particular market. These types of agreements can take several forms, which may include:

● agreements to limit the supply of the product to inflate prices
● agreements to fix a standard price
● agreeing to have standard contractual terms (this is not as common as the two other forms)

However, it is not only agreements between suppliers that take place. Suppliers and retailers may well collude in the formation of a reciprocal trading agreement. In this situation each company involved agrees to trade only with the other. This, in essence, effectively eliminates any competition and, additionally, means that a supplier and a retailer may enter into long-term contractual

(PC 1.3.1, COM 3.4)
If you were concerned as to the price charged for a particular product or service, how would you go about complaining? Which agencies would offer you help and advice? You can begin your research by visiting your local Citizens' Advice Bureau.

FIG. 1.3.3 *The Office of Fair Trading booklet on anti-competitive practices.*

agreements. In return for a beneficial price a retailer/distributor agrees to provide only that supplier's products for a long period of time, thus effectively restricting any competitors' products from entering the market.

It should be noted though, that retailers and distributors do not always enter into anti-competitive agreements with suppliers through choice. In some situations dominant suppliers may be able to force distributors and retailers into restrictive trade agreements. For example, as previously discussed in connection with the Resale Prices Act, suppliers may force retailers to accept a minimum resale price or may allow them to stock and sell the supplier's major product only if the retailer agrees to stock the full range of products provided by the supplier. This type of imposed agreement is termed 'full line forcing'. A good example of this may be if a newsagent wished to stock a particular brand and flavour of crisps which he knew to be popular and the supplier only agreed to provide him/her with stock if he/she agreed to purchase some less popular flavours as well. Another version of this type of agreement is referred to as 'tie in sales' when the purchase of one product is related to the purchase of another. A good example of this is when an organisation purchases a new car – part of the warranty agreement may be that all servicing and supply of parts must be carried out by the manufacturer or dealership.

To combat such anti-competitive trading practices the government passed the Acts outlined above, which constitute the government competition policy.

TO ENSURE FAIR AND HONEST TRADING

Despite the government legislation which attempts to counteract anti-competitive agreements and prohibit the formation of mergers and cartels, etc., this by no means ensures that companies will conduct their business transactions in a fair and honest manner.

The job of keeping an eye on organisations and their trading activities is primarily carried out by the government's Department of Trade and Industry and specifically by the Director General of Fair Trading. This post was created under the 1973 Fair Trading Act which led to the formation of the Office of Fair Trading (OFT). It is the role of the Office of Fair Trading and the Director to refer any activities which may be seen to be prejudicial to the economic interests of the consumer to the Consumer Protection Advisory Committee, who, in turn, report to the Secretary of State. The Secretary of State, following their recommendations, may then enact appropriate legislation to make such practices illegal. These practices may include:

- misleading consumers as to the terms and conditions on which goods and services are supplied
- methods of salesmanship employed with consumers, i.e. subjecting consumers to undue pressure
- methods of securing payment causing the terms of the agreement to be deemed so adverse as to be oppressive
- any practice which is considered to be illegal, e.g. false trade descriptions, dealing in stolen property, etc.

student activity

(PC 1.3.1, COM 3.1)
Look at the Focus Study below. Answer the following questions, and discuss your responses with the remainder of your group.

1 Why is the Office of Fair Trading concerned by the Mortgage Corporation's activities?
2 What is the process that must be gone through in order for the OFT to 'revoke the lender's licence'?
3 Under the provision of which Act is the mortgage company acting unfairly?

Focus study

OFFICE OF FAIR TRADING

The Mortgage Corporation was investigated by the Office of Fair Trading after complaints from Surrey Trading Standards Office that it had been harassing borrowers.

Trading Standards is compiling a report on the company for the OFT based on more than 80 complaints from borrowers. They will ask the OFT to consider revoking the lender's licence or disciplining it in another way.

A spokesperson for the OFT said 'We will naturally look at any complaints received centred on 'aggressive tactics'. Borrowers claim they have been repeatedly and needlessly brought before the courts. 'The courts do not grant a repossession order and borrowers sink further into debt as the court's costs are added to their arrears.'

One borrower claimed he was dragged to court nine times without a repossession order being granted, while in another legal proceedings were started against a borrower whose repayment was £1.57 short.

A spokesperson for the organisation in question said that the company would co-operate with any investigation and that they were confident that when the full facts of any case were available, they would be found to have acted in an entirely appropriate way.

Once a matter has been referred to the Secretary of State and has been found to comprise unfair conduct, then the party concerned must not undertake that activity again or he/she may be liable to imprisonment. In addition to the Office of Fair Trading there are many other Acts which help to ensure fair and honest trading takes place. Some of these include:

1 *The Trade Descriptions Acts 1968 and 1972* – these Acts make it a criminal offence to supply false or misleading information about goods, services, accommodation or facilities. However, this only applies to sales conducted as part of a trade or business and not to private sales. The Acts also make it an offence to make misleading claims over sales prices (although this is covered more thoroughly in the 1987 Consumer Protection Act).

2 *The Consumer Credit Act 1974* – this allows only firms which have a licence from the OFT to offer credit (including banks, etc.). It includes numerous offences such as failure to supply copies of consumer credit agreements and trading without an OFT licence. It makes firms which supply the credit jointly responsible for the goods and services rendered, together with the company which sold them.

3 T*he Weights and Measures Act 1985* – this makes it a criminal offence to give a short measure or short weight or even to possess weighing and measuring equipment which does not give accurate quantities. This Act allows trading standards officers to visit garages, public houses, shops, supermarkets, etc. to check such equipment.

4 *The Foods and Drink Acts 1955, 1976, 1982 and the Food Safety Act 1990* – these make it an offence to sell goods which are unfit for human consumption. Food intended for human consumption must meet the 'food safety requirements'. This requires that all reasonable precautions in preparation, storage, transport and sale of goods are carried out. An example of this is ensuring that cooked and uncooked meats are not stored in the same container.

It must be noted, however, that despite all the legislation that may make you think otherwise, the vast majority of businesses do conduct their trading activities in a fair and honest manner, and will do their utmost to ensure that consumers are satisfied with their products.

TO PROTECT CONSUMERS

In addition to the work of the OFT, the Consumer Protection Advisory Committee and the various Acts to help promote competition with honest and fair trading, there is a separate section of government intervention which deals wholly with the protection of consumers. Offences in this area can be roughly divided into two types – those which fall in the sphere of civil law and those which fall into criminal law.

As we have seen, companies involved in the supply,

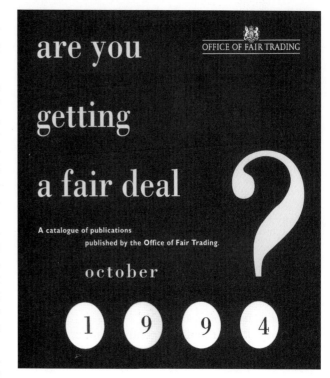

FIG. 1.3.4 *The Office of Fair Trading booklet, 'Are you getting a fair deal?'*

retailing or distribution of goods and services are restricted in these activities by legislation designed to promote competition, efficiency and fairness. Civil law protects consumers mainly in the area of contract law and provides one party with a course of action if the contract is broken by the other party. This covers such areas as false statements and mis-representation of products and enables the innocent party to sue for damages or have the contract rescinded.

The area of criminal law comes into play when one of the statutes covered by one of the numerous Acts is broken. This will usually lead to prosecution by a local authority, the Director General of Fair Trading or by the Secretary of State in the magistrates and Crown courts.

The Consumer Protection Act 1987 is primarily concerned with price and the pricing policy of organisations. No doubt many of us have been caught out when purchasing a product, and finding that the price quoted is not the true price. This may be because the sale period has ended, the price quoted did not include VAT, or the claimed price reduction is untrue. This Act states that the organisation must clearly state the 'real' price of a product, not make unfair or untrue comparisons between products and price, and not make false statements about price reductions.

You will often see, particularly in a sale, one of two statements on a price ticket:

- that the product was available for a period of time at a previously higher price. It may not necessarily have been available in that store, but in another location owned by that organisation, and this fact will be stated on the ticket
- that the product has been specifically bought in and offered at a low price for the sale period only

The Consumer Protection Act further covers the consumer who is offered unsafe goods whatever the circumstances.

Some of the watchdog bodies have been set up by the government in order to monitor organisations' activities, particularly in their dealings with the public. Others have been set up by a particular industry to keep a check on their member organisations. This has been done to ensure that standards are maintained and that any adverse publicity resulting from a disreputable trader does not damage the industry as a whole. Some examples of these watchdog organisations are:

1 *Citizens' Advice Bureaux* – the principal duty of this chain of offices is to act as a mediator in disputes between organisations and consumers. They are also responsible for a variety of other advisory matters, not necessarily relating to consumer rights.
2 *National Consumer Council* – this council is responsible for representing the consumer in disputes and problems with government departments, nationalised industries, local authorities and other businesses.
3 *Environmental Health Department* – this organisation operates a series of local offices which investigate matters relating to food and hygiene. They have the power to enforce legislation relating to food hygiene and may even close businesses which break the regulations.
4 *British Standards Institution* – this organisation, which operates on funds received from the government and voluntary donations, is concerned with setting minimum standards in all aspects of business and industry. It is best known for the BSI Kitemark which it issues. This denotes that a product has been manufactured to and reaches the standards laid down by the British Standards Institution.
5 *Consumer and consultative councils* – these organisations have been set up to monitor the operations of nationalised industries, and to ensure that they do not abuse their monopoly by charging too high a price or providing a poor level of service.
6 *Trade associations* – there are a large number of these associations which deal with specific industries or services. They offer assistance, information and advice to their members. In addition, they may also devise a voluntary code of practice. We deal with them later in this Element. A good example of trade associations

is ABTA (Association of British Travel Agents).
7 *Advertising Standards Authority* – this independent organisation is involved in ensuring that all advertisements are 'legal, decent, honest and truthful'. Its British Code of Advertising Practice gives the advertising industry a clear set of rules to follow.
8 *The Chartered Institute of Marketing* – this is another independent organisation that attempts to ensure that its members have high professional standards, particularly in terms of honesty and integrity.
9 *Independent Broadcasting Authority* – this organisation monitors the activities of television and radio stations and ensures that particular standards are maintained. Recently, it has been concerned about a new marketing technique known as 'placement' which involves popular programmes featuring and recommending particular brand names or products. Although placement is well established in America, the IBA has ruled that it is unacceptable in Great Britain.

student activity

(PC 1.3.1, COM 3.1, 3.2, 3.4, IT 3.1, 3.2, 3.3)
In groups of four, contact and obtain leaflets or brochures from at least six of the above organisations. Having done this, summarise the main areas of activity of each of the organisations and compile your findings in the form of word processed fact sheets which could be made available via the Citizens' Advice Bureaux and local libraries.

TO PROTECT ENVIRONMENTAL AND SOCIAL INTERESTS

Organisations are becoming increasingly aware of the **environmental concerns** of the public. Whether they have adopted this interest in environmental issues as a marketing ploy, as the sceptics would say, or whether they truly believe that they should take a greater interest in this area, is open to debate.

Despite the age of the planet, it has only been in the past few decades that man has managed to destroy and pollute extensively. Environmental awareness has been forced to the top of the agenda by a variety of pressure groups, political organisations and the media.

As far as government is concerned, the only way to ensure that businesses adhere to environmental considerations is by regulation. In the UK the 1990

Environmental Protection Act has begun to regulate industrial pollution. This Act details controls on land, air and water and also covers areas such as noise pollution, public nuisance caused by litter, etc. and the disposal of waste which could be hazardous to health and the environment. The integrated pollution control (IPC) relates to some 5,000 industrial processes and aims to regulate all pollution whether it be on land, air or water. This Act is enforced by the Inspectorate of Pollution. In addition to this comprehensive coverage, local authorities are required by central government to monitor another 27,000 more complex processes. Organisations are required to render all potential pollutants harmless before releasing them.

In 1986 the American government formed the Environmental Protection Agency which publishes a toxics release inventory which obliges organisations to submit an annual list of pollutants released. Meanwhile, in the UK the Environmental Protection Act established the idea of environmental auditing. These 'green' audits are intended to show any weaknesses in environmental management systems and any breaches of standards.

The European Commission in 1990 produced a draft of their own environmental audit which proposed to require companies to submit similar lists, although, at present, this is only a voluntary scheme.

Another reason, in the area of social interests, for government intervention is to eliminate inequalities of opportunity. In a free market it is very difficult for a government to establish conditions under which organisations can compete on an equal basis. Since the key feature of a free market is that market forces determine the success or failure of an organisation, it should not be forgotten that smaller and less efficient organisations tend to fail. As far as government intervention in the operation of organisations is concerned, it is able to keep a close eye on fair trading, monopoly situations and potential mergers. It is at the individual level that the government finds it difficult to provide the ideal circumstances for equality of opportunity. True equality of opportunity may only be established when all individuals in society begin with the same base chance of success or failure. We know that inequalities exist even before an individual is born. His/her parents may be comparatively rich and therefore able to offer their offspring a better start in life. However, the establishment of universal, compulsory education, at least to the age of 16, has gone some way towards levelling the chances and opportunities. In the present political climate it is believed that with intelligence, good ideas and some assistance from government agencies, any individual may be successful. To this end, the government has established a range of advice and information centres, together with incentive programmes to assist new entrepreneurs and enterprises. The Enterprise

Allowance Scheme (which has now reached the end of its life) provided new business people with a safety net of £40 per week during their first year of operation. Despite this, there was still a failure rate of over 90 per cent. New businesses in particular suffer from lack of funding, knowledge and opportunity to succeed.

student activity

(PC 1.3.1, COM 3.1, 3.2)
Most forms of government policy are aimed at ensuring that the average citizen in society is able to provide for him/herself. Try to profile the average citizen. Do you think such a person really exists?

In nearly all countries, governments have involved themselves in providing for **essential needs**. These include health, education, law enforcement, transport and housing. Governments provide these services, funded by taxation, to ensure that the basic infrastructure of the economy is maintained. Without the maintenance of these services, individuals and businesses alike would find it impossible to operate. Although some individuals and businesses may be able to provide for themselves in almost all of these areas, the vast majority of the population find themselves reliant upon the government-subsidised services. There has been a gradual move towards the privatisation of many of these services, but privatisation does not necessarily mean the elimination of the provision of these services by the government. In many cases, the privatisation process merely means that the provider of the service is no longer a government department or agent, but is effectively a subcontractor who provides the service on the government's behalf.

student activity

(PC 1.3.1, COM 3.1)
Try to identify another three examples of essential needs apart from the ones we have already listed. Discuss this in pairs.

THE ENVIRONMENT: A CHALLENGE FOR BUSINESS

The DTI launched its Environmental Programme in May 1989. It did so because the protection and improvement of the environment is a major issue at home and abroad – and not least an issue for business.

Since then the pressures for environmental improvement have grown apace and have a significant impact on business. There have been strengthened controls on substances which deplete the ozone layer; negotiations have started on an international Framework Convention on Climate Change; and consumers have continued to demonstrate a desire for goods which have minimal impact on the environment.

The *White Paper on the Environment, This Common Inheritance*, set out the Government's environmental policies and objectives for the 1990s and stressed the important role business needs to play in achieving a better environment.

All these developments, and others, continue to present both threats and opportunities for your business. It is now more than ever the case that, to remain competitive, and indeed to survive, firms need to develop environmental strategies incorporating better environmental performance and products.

In keeping with this gathering momentum DTI has continued to develop and expand its own activities in the environmental field. DTI's Environment Unit brings together all of the Department's widespread interests in environmental issues.

This brochure sets out what the Environment Unit does and what business can do to meet the environmental challenge. It gives guidance too on the practical ways DTI can help business by offering advice, encouraging best practice and supporting research and development.

Environmental issues impact on all businesses. If you are not already planning your firm's response, the time to do so is now.

FIG. 1.3.5 *The Department of Trade and Industry's environmental programme was launched in May 1989 as a result of the government's white paper on the environment called 'This Common Inheritance'.*

The term **public goods** or **services** refers to provisions provided for the country as a whole. These include the police force, the prison service and the fire service. It is not feasible for each individual in society to pay directly for these services. Although some individuals may be able to afford expensive personal or property protection, the majority of the population require a society-wide protection. Increasingly, some of these public goods or services are being privatised, but this does not mean privatisation in the accepted sense of the word. The privatisation of prisons, for example, merely refers to private organisations subcontracting from the government the responsibility of running the service. There are two further important considerations to look at when we are considering public goods or services, namely:

● *non-rival in consumption* – this refers to the point that if a particular individual benefits from a public good or service this does not prevent other individuals from consuming or benefiting at the same time. The level of service should be sufficient for a number of simultaneous demands on the service to be met fairly easily. The state, in providing the service, will try to ensure that the cost of providing that service does not exceed the overall benefit that society gains

● *non-exclusive* – if individuals refuse to pay their share towards the service provided, it is very difficult to exclude them from the benefits that all individuals receive. If someone has not paid his/her council tax, this does not mean that the police force (which receives some of its funding from this source) will not respond to an emergency call. Individuals who do not pay their contribution towards services are effectively enjoying a free ride at the expense of those who are willing to pay. In the final analysis, this means that all willing payers will end up paying more to subsidise the free-riders

Products or services which fall into the category of merit goods could be provided by the private sector.

Focus study

PRIVATISATION/PUBLIC OWNERSHIP

Government activity costs a lot of money and there has been a great change in the last decade in what governments can spend. Bearing in mind that all spending has to be financed through taxation or borrowing, restrictions have developed in both. If the power of government's spending is curtailed, where can investment for vital UK industry come from?

The UK government decided over 10 years ago that public ownership should be a thing of the past. They pioneered privatisation throughout the 1980s. Perhaps the most revolutionary was the first major privatisation campaign – the selling off of council houses. Telecommunications, airlines, gas, electricity and water soon followed. Instantly these businesses no longer required the government to find money for investment via taxation or borrowing. With the privatisation of coal and the railways in progress there are very few industries or services left in public hands.

The nationalised industries back in 1979 were costing the tax-payer around £50m. a week in losses alone. Today the government receives through taxation £60m. a week from their profits. From 1983–5 the average investment required to be found out of taxation and borrowing for gas, electricity and water averaged out at around £3.6bn. each. In comparison, in 1991–2, these utilities, now in private hands, achieved a £6bn. investment level each.

Examples of merit goods include the National Health Service, museums and education. There are two main reasons why the government chooses to provide these merit goods, these are:

1 *Equity* – in a society which recognises equality of opportunity, it is important to give all individuals a fair chance. In this respect, the provision of free education to all tries to address the fact that the poorer sections of the community could not afford a good education for their offspring. Those with high incomes can always choose to use private education, but the majority of the population have no other choice but to use state education.

2 *Externalities* –the provision of a particular service from which all members of the population can benefit, has positive benefits for society as a whole. If the majority of the population is literate and well educated, then the assumption is that the economy will be more successful. Externalities are also known as the social benefits, but they are hard to quantify. In

0:20

student activity

(PC 1.3.1, COM 3.1)
Present government policy seems to be moving towards reducing the number of publicly owned providers of goods and services. What is your opinion of this privatisation process? Should certain vital goods and services be controlled by the government and not by private enterprise? Discuss this as a group.

some respects the government may choose to ignore the social benefits and concentrate on the social costs of providing the service. This is a rather negative view to adopt, but an increasingly more popular one. The philosophy behind looking at social costs and ignoring social benefits is linked to the desire of many individuals to allow everyone to choose exactly where and how to spend their income. Following on from this, we must assume that if key services are not provided by the state, then we can expect lower taxation – which in turn releases more income to be expended as and where the individual sees fit.

student activity

(PC 1.3.1, COM 3.1)
Merit goods and services include hospitals, which are gradually becoming fund holders in their own right (in other words they are required to manage their own budgets).

Carry out research on your local hospital and try to discover the impact this process may have had. You may also find useful information on this subject in your local press.

Discuss your findings as a group.

TO STIMULATE CONSUMER DEMAND

One of the reasons why a government may intervene in particular markets or in the economy as a whole is to stimulate consumer demand. Governments can do this in several ways. This subject is discussed in more detail elsewhere in this Element, but primarily the government would intervene in the following ways:

- by reducing the level of taxation, either direct or indirect, in order to increase consumers' overall disposable income
- by increasing the amount of transfer payments, such as social security benefits and pensions, etc.

The government can stimulate demand for specific products, therefore, by reducing the level of taxation on that product (if it is already being taxed), or by providing a subsidy. The government may also affect the level of consumer demand by influencing the level of its own expenditure and other economic factors such as interest rates.

By stimulating consumer demand the government may hope to achieve a positive influence on the level of employment. In other words, the greater the demand for goods or service, the more people are needed in employment to provide them or to raise the level of aggregate demand and thus promote growth in the domestic economy.

TO IMPROVE LEVELS OF EMPLOYMENT

To be classified as being unemployed, an individual must be actively seeking work. The way in which the figure of the number of unemployed is calculated has come under severe criticism from a variety of sources. The Department of Employment uses a fairly broad measure to calculate unemployment, this being those who are registered as unemployed and eligible for benefit payments. However, the official figures are said to grossly underestimate the true levels of unemployment. The figures do not include the following:

- those who have not registered as being unemployed as they are too proud to admit to being unemployed
- students and housewives
- those who are on employment training programmes
- those who are working part-time or in seasonal or temporary occupations

The reasons for unemployment are threefold:

- there has been a growth in the number of people seeking work over the last 20 years, in fact it has risen by nearly three million
- with the elimination of many trade barriers, the UK in particular has suffered from high levels of market penetration from foreign competition
- the UK unfairly has a poor industrial relations reputation. It is widely believed that the British worker is not as reliable or stable as some of his/her European counterparts

Unemployment itself may take many forms. Some of the main types of unemployment are as follows:

1 *Structural unemployment* – this is where there is a mismatch of available labour skills to industrial needs. It may be that skilled workers are available in different parts of the country, but they are not necessarily available where they are required.

2 *Cyclical unemployment* – this form of unemployment is caused by periods of downturn in business activity. Typically these cycles are known as 'booms' and 'slumps'. A slump is best defined as a recession, and is a time in which there are higher levels of unemployment.

3 *Frictional unemployment* – this type of unemployment, although temporary, refers to individuals moving from one job to another. The time spent unemployed between these jobs is a permanent feature of the economy. A small percentage of individuals can always be found in this classification.

4 *Seasonal unemployment* – this should not be confused with cyclical unemployment, although the two have many of the same features. Seasonal unemployment is typical of the tourist and leisure industry.

student activity

(PC 1.3.1, COM 3.1)
Identify five major types of seasonal employment in your own area. Discuss as a group the availability of this seasonal employment and identify any individuals in the group who have engaged in seasonal employment.

5 *Regional unemployment* – certain areas within the UK suffer from lower wage levels as they are comparatively at a disadvantage in terms of their location. In such areas, the loss of any industries have a more serious effect as it is less likely that alternative employment may be found.

6 *Technological unemployment* – as industries become automated, information technology equipment in its various forms will replace workers.

7 *Real wage unemployment* – this is caused by wages being too high for all members of the workforce to be in employment. Employers simply cannot afford to take on new staff. These periods are marked by the activities of powerful trade unions and possibly weak governments.

student activity

(PC 1.3.1, COM 3.1)
Can you think of any particular regions which are currently suffering from severe regional unemployment? Why do you think this has occurred? Discuss in pairs.

8 *Residual unemployment* – there is always a small percentage of the population who, for various reasons, are unable to work. While strictly speaking they may not be classed as being unemployed (as technically they are not seeking work), this category will include the physically and mentally disadvantaged.

Unemployment can have severe effects on the economy, these include:

1 *Loss of income to the country* – the unemployed not only pay little or no taxation, but they actually cost the Exchequer funds. It is calculated that the average unemployed person costs the country upwards of £10,000 per year.

2 *Inequality* – unemployed people are, naturally, worse off than their employed peers. The levels of benefit do not adequately compensate them for being unemployed.

3 *Resource wastage* – the mere fact that a number of individuals are unemployed means that the economy is not performing to its maximum potential. If we consider working individuals as a resource, the economy is not using its resource potential to full effect.

In addition to these economic considerations, there are also social effects arising from unemployment. These include:

1 *Increased crime* – as a result of boredom and frustration.

2 *Poorer health* – arising from the inability of unemployed individuals to provide for themselves nutritionally and medically.

3 *Loss of status* – as a net result of being unemployed, particularly in the long term.

4 *Loss of work ethic* – as unemployed people become depressed and demoralised and eventually lose the will to work.

Unemployment itself can have serious implications for businesses, these include:

- a reduction in demand for products and services which, in turn, will affect sales and profits
- reduced wage rates, although beneficial to the employer, mean that some jobs would be considered marginal by employees, as they may pay only slightly more than the available benefits
- reduction in trade union power. Again this may be welcomed by employers, but, as trade unions lose power and members through unemployment, they become easier prey for unscrupulous employers who wish to take advantage of the situation

student activity

(PC 1.3.1, COM 3.2, 3.4, IT 3.1, 3.2, 3.3)
Using local and national newspapers as your research tools, identify any social problems in your own area which have been associated with unemployment. Individually, having identified the social problems in your local area, offer suggestions as to how these social problems could be alleviated. List the social problems and your solutions and present them in the form of a letter addressed to your local Member of Parliament. Your letter should be word processed.

TO CONTROL INFLATION

As we have mentioned earlier in this Unit, one of the main objectives of post-war governments has been to control the rate of inflation and achieve relative price stability within the economy. Inflation causes the general price level of goods and services within the economy to rise, without a corresponding rise in income. This has the effect of lowering the value of consumers' and businesses' money. This, in turn, makes it more expensive for businesses to provide their goods and services.

Inflation also has the effect of lowering the competitiveness of domestic products (exports) in international trade as they become relatively more expensive, and of increasing the competitiveness of imports as they become relatively cheaper. Alongside this, inflation can also cause the level of investment in industry to fall as uncertainty and lack of business confidence sets in. Combined with this is the fact that investors tend to switch their investments into non-productive resources as they seem to hedge against inflation. This occurs as borrowers gain and lenders lose under inflation as the amount of money paid back is worth less.

Government policies to curb inflation could include the following fiscal policies:

- the introduction of higher taxes to reduce demand (this is only applicable if inflation is demand-pull inflation)
- the reduction of the amount of government expenditure. Again this will curb the amount of demand

However, it is important to note that, following on from our earlier comments on employment, both these measures would lead to increased unemployment.

Another way the government could curb inflation (or attempt to do so) would be to introduce some monetary policies, including:

- raising the rate of interest, to reduce the money supply and hence lower demand. Again this can lead to increased unemployment, especially if the higher rate of interest causes exchange rates to rise. This would make exports relatively expensive and imports relatively cheap

- the government can tighten credit facilities and restrict the amount of credit available both to consumers and to businesses. This would also cause the level of demand to fall, but alongside this there would be a corresponding drop in the level of investment funds available to businesses

TO STIMULATE GROWTH

Another objective of government is economic growth. The only way to achieve an increase in the standard of living is to provide a real increase in people's wealth and this can only be achieved by realising economic growth. The government can influence the level of economic growth by using policies which affect the level of private investment or by switching resources from consumption to investment in physical capital and people.

The government can also provide incentives to private investors for investing in research and development. It would do this because technical advances are the most important in terms of productivity gains. In other words, aggregate output can only be increased by using more factor inputs (land, labour, capital and raw materials). Alternatively, technical advances can be made which allow existing levels of input to be used more effectively.

1.3.2 Explain the ways governments can influence markets

INFLUENCING MARKETS

REGULATION

So far in this Element we have concentrated primarily on UK government and EC legislation to control various practices and situations which prevent or restrict the degree of competition taking place within a particular market. However, it is not always necessary for governments to go as far as enforcing parliamentary Acts to regulate or promote competition within a market. Some of the ways a government could influence markets by enforcing regulations are listed below.

COMPETITIVE FRANCHISING AND LICENSING

Under the system of competitive franchising, rather than have companies compete for a share of the market and have one or two achieve a dominant position in which they can exercise undue influence upon that market, companies compete for the entire market under a system of competitive tendering. Those companies who wish to trade within a particular market compete for the franchise or licence to do so. In theory the most efficient firm should be the one willing to pay the most for the franchise. It can afford to pay more for the right to trade in the market as it can supply the product more efficiently and therefore more cheaply. Once the franchise has been awarded all competition for that market ceases. However, the overall effect has been that although a state of monopoly still exists, the government has ensured that the most efficient monopolistic supplier is in place.

The government then usually sets up a form of licensing agreement with the successful organisation whereby the company buys an annual licence from the government in order to retain the franchise. This has two main benefits; first the government receives a share of the abnormal profits made possible by monopoly conditions; secondly it allows the government to regulate the market without excessive legislation and intervention. In essence, if the monopoly does not behave itself, the government will simply revoke its licence.

A recent example of this form of competitive franchising occurred under the 1990 Broadcasting Act where companies were invited to bid for the rights to broadcast in the ITV regions.

VOLUNTARY REGULATION BY INDUSTRY

Government legislation is often very bureaucratic and full of red tape. As such, it can be very costly and time consuming. There is also the added problem that making new legislation and statutes takes time and often Parliament has more pressing business to undertake. For this reason the government encourages trade associations to some degree to regulate themselves. They do this by what are known as voluntary codes of practice which are a statement made by the trade association with the aim of achieving a common acceptable standard of trading and behaviour which it expects from its members. These are used instead of legislation and therefore, if broken, are not legally enforceable. However, they do provide a basis for dealing with customer complaints rather than going through lengthy legal proceedings in court. In recent years governments, through the Office of Fair Trading, have tried to encourage more and more trade associations and other organisations to adopt such codes because:

- less legislation and government intervention allows businesses to operate more freely and thus allows the natural laws of supply and demand to do so as well
- if the government passes legislation it then has to appoint someone to see that such legislation is carried out and to deal with any breaches of it. The less legislation, therefore, the cheaper it is liable to be for the government

PRICE CAPPING

Another way in which the government may seek to regulate businesses is by using a strategy known as price capping. This prevents businesses (usually monopolies) from charging exorbitant prices for goods and services. The way in which price capping works is quite straightforward:

- the government or regulating body (such as OFWAT – the regulating body of water companies) sets an upper limit on the price that the industry can charge
- the limit is then regularly reviewed to take into account inflation, changes in costs of production, etc.

LICENSING

Although licensing is used in competitive franchising and as such is already partially covered earlier in this Element in the discussion of that topic, it is also a tool used by governments and, in particular, local authorities, as a means of regulating businesses in particular industries. The main examples of such industries are casinos and related gambling activities, public houses and off-licences and restaurants. Restaurants also come under the Health and Safety and Hygiene Certificate regulations. In this way any business which is seen to be conducting its trading activities improperly simply has its licence revoked and is not granted a new one.

DEREGULATION

In order to promote competition and fair trade it is not always necessary to have more legislation and regulation in an industry. In some cases, deregulation is used. This involves the opening up of a market to more businesses and competition. Deregulation has taken place amongst many of the previously state-owned monopolies such as National Express Coaches (1980), local bus services (1985) and British Telecom. This has been a popular policy with the Conservative Government since 1979. The reasoning behind this policy is that by opening the markets up to increased competition, consumers should be able to enjoy lower prices, higher quality of goods and services and, hopefully, increased innovation, as companies try to get an edge on each other.

However, deregulation does have its critics. One of the main concerns is whether or not deregulation will offer all that is promised. For example, consider the coach and bus industries. Although it is true that prices have generally fallen and there are now many more routes and companies choose from (in many cases), companies concentrate on the more profitable routes to town and city centres and between cities themselves. This inevitably leaves outlying districts and, in particular, rural areas to suffer. Is this the improvement in quality of service expected?

In recent years, due to the 1990 Broadcasting Act, we have seen the deregulation of the broadcasting industry. We have already mentioned this under the competitive franchising section of this Element. While, no doubt, this deregulation has increased consumer choice, with the introduction of satellite systems, there have been widespread fears of a drop in quality and service.

Focus study

PRICE CAPPING

Extract taken from the Office of Fair Trading's 'Fair Trading: Future Challenges' by The Director General of Fair Trading, 1995.

The government's concerns seems to me to be well-founded. Regulation evidently has a cost and that cost can exceed the benefits. The costs, after all, have to be borne by consumers in one way or another. We must be ready, in appropriate cases, to acknowledge a problem but conclude that consumers should be left to take care of themselves and the government should not intervene.

This line of thought has implications for competition policy too. A policy of deregulation does not mean that a business should be free in general to pursue anti-competitive practices or create and abuse dominant positions. However, action under competition law does involve a cost and it is possible for the costs to exceed the benefits. Because of this, we are now adopting the routine of considering the costs and benefits of action under our powers for each case and the policy for deregulation has encouraged us to do this rather more systematically and thoroughly than we might otherwise have done.

However, I would not want this to be interpreted as implying a significant softening of competition policy. One has to remember that a decision on one small market may influence behaviour in other small markets. For example, as I have already mentioned, competition in the bus industry often takes place at a local level. If anti-competitive behaviour were allowed in one bus market, others might conclude that action would not be taken against their adopting similar practices. The benefits of action under the competition law may go beyond the particular market concerned and this may justify action under a cost-benefit test.

I may have given the impression, in what I said earlier, that I regard UK competition law as capable of improvement. That is indeed the case. I believe that vigorous competition is a most effective weapon for securing consumers' well-being. The almost complete absence in British competition law of clear-cut offenses which can be penalised by fines is an indisputable weakness. The deterrent effect of fines is likely to be substantial. Our present system – 'every dog is allowed one bite' – may have been appropriate twenty years ago when people were much less familiar with the concepts of competition policy; but today it appears increasingly to be an out-of-date model.

CONTROL OF MONOPOLY

Although we have alrready looked at monopolies and the specific legislation regarding them several times, it is worth taking a more in-depth look at monopolies here as they are such an extreme case.

The legal definition of a monopoly is a company which possesses 25 per cent or more of the market share and exists because of barriers of entry of some sort. These can be:

- natural
- legal
- strategic
- absolute cost advantages
- economies of scale

It is important to note here once again that monopolies can occur at local, national and international levels.

Monopoly is an area of concern to the government for various reasons, the prime ones being:

- due to lack of competition, if there is sufficient demand, the monopolist may well be able to charge excessive prices
- as there is little or no competition there is no incentive for the monopolist to look for more efficient ways of production
- monopoly has a tendency to redistribute wealth from the consumer to the monopolist

All of these reasons have the common theme of being detrimental to the consumer in some way. For this reason the government takes a particular interest in the activities of monopolies and the potential formation of monopolies (mergers).

The main vehicles for monitoring the activities of monopolies and potential monopolies are the Director General of Fair Trading (DGFT), the Monopoly and Mergers Commission and ultimately the Secretary of State. We have also given details about these posts and their functions above under the 1948 and 1965 Monopolies and Mergers Acts and the 1973 Fair Trading Act.

It is the role of the DGFT to keep a watchful eye on British industry and to deal with allegations and complaints about anti-competitive practices and abuses of monopoly power. If he/she feels that grounds for a further enquiry are justified, the case is then reported to the Monopolies and Mergers Commission. It is up to the commission to decide whether or not the organisation involved has been acting 'against the public interest'. The commission will then make a report to the Secretary of State either stating 'no further action necessary' or suggesting possible action to be taken. The Secretary of State will then take appropriate action, either seeking undertakings from the company that such practices will cease (with the DGFT closely monitoring them) or, in severe cases, seeking to obtain legal orders to prevent such practices by the organisation in the future.

In the case of mergers, again the Director General will undertake a preliminary investigation and decide whether or not to forward the details to the commission. There are, however, two instances in which a potential merger is automatically investigated:

- if the total gross assets of the organisation exceed £30m.
- if either organisation has 25 per cent of the market share or if, as a result of the merger, a market share of 25 per cent or over would be achieved

Again, if a merger is reported to the Monopolies and Mergers Commission, it is up to it to decide whether or not such a merger is for or against the public interest. Despite the arguments against monopolies, it is not always the case that 'adequate' competition will not exist or that the situation involved would actually be to the benefit of the public. For example, in industries which require a great deal of capital equipment, larger and more monopolistic organisations are often able to take advantage of economies of scale and, by doing so, produce the product more cheaply than would otherwise be the case. In some cases, governments have even promoted the formation of such monopolies.

However, it must be noted that as business activities become more and more widespread in terms of global and inter-company connections and the formation of implicit and explicit cartels, it is becoming increasingly difficult for the anti-competitive practices of monopolies, mergers and cartels to be dealt with.

MONETARY POLICY

Monetary policy by the government deals with the following:

- supply of money circulating in the economy
- interest rates
- exchange rates

The government uses the above to influence the level of demand, investment, inflation, employment and growth (again, we discuss the effects in more detail later in this Element). In simplistic terms, the government can use the above to encourage or discourage the amount of money which consumers and organisations spend. This includes not only their personal income, but also the level and ease of obtaining credit. By influencing the way in which spending takes place, and the amount of that spending, the government can, in turn, expect all of the above to take place.

Focus study

CONTROL OF MONOPOLY

Extract taken from the Office of Fair Trading 'Fair Trading: Future Challenges' by The Director General of Fair Trading, 1995.

Refusal to supply, of course, is far from being the only basis for investigations under the monopoly provisions of the Fair Trading Act. Other cases have concerned excess profits, price recommendations by trade or professional associations and preference by firms with strong positions upstream in the supply chain of its own downstream operation over those of competitors. The actual cases are too numerous for me to give a comprehensive picture of them here. However, the case of compact disc supplies is worthy of comment, partly because it was the subject of a lot of publicity following a controversial clearance by the MMC.

I first became concerned about compact discs because of complaints about price differences between Britain and the USA. International price comparisons are often triggers for investigations as to how well a particular market may be working. The mechanics of the price comparisons can be controversial but, in the case of compact discs, prices were said to be much cheaper in the United States than in Britain. A price difference alone is not sufficient for me to take action. One needs to find evidence of anti-competitive behaviour or abuse of a dominant position before action can be justified. However, that justification seemed to be provided by so-called parallel import restrictions. This means, essentially, that the record companies have segregated the US and UK markets; discs supplied for sale in the United States could not be exported to the UK. My concern about this restriction was that discs could perhaps be sold more cheaply in Britain if they were exported from the United States so that the restriction was a material impairment of competition. The issue was examined by a Select Committee of Parliament and they expressed concern. I therefore decided on a reference to the MMC.

The MMC took the view that, although price differences existed, they were not as great as had been claimed. Furthermore, the MMC did not believe that profits in the industry were excessive. Neither of these findings is conclusive because the restriction might still be having a detrimental effect on consumers, for example by limiting incentives to improve efficiency. However, the MMC took the view that parallel import restrictions were justified because they made it easier to control piracy. The intellectual property aspect of this case was decisive.

Monetary policy is concerned with the control of the quantity and price of money in the economy. As long as individuals are spending money at a rate faster than the supply of products or services, then prices will inevitably rise. There is a strong link between the quantity of money available and the level of inflation.

FIG. 1.3.6 *Interest rates naturally affect all bank borrowing and influence deposits in banks, loans and overdrafts.*

Money cannot simply be described as coins and notes. There are many other forms of money. These include credit cards, cheques and credit payments. In order to control the amount of money available, the government will set the interest rate at a level to deter people from borrowing, or encourage them to do so. As well as attempting to control the quantity of money the government will also try to set the price of money. Such activity relates also to the interest rate. In addition, the government will keep a close eye on the retail price index (RPI) which serves as an indicator of inflation. By keeping pay settlements below the increase in the RPI, the government will be effectively reducing the amount of money available in the economy. On the other hand, if the government allows pay settlements to exceed the change in the RPI then it will be allowing the injection of more money into the economy. In the first instance, the RPI will drop, in the latter it will increase. Both of these circumstances may give the government cause for concern.

FISCAL POLICY

Fiscal policy refers to the government's policy on the following:

- public spending
- various taxes
- public borrowing

The government uses the above to influence the level of demand, inflation, employment and economic

Student banking

Starting student life means all sorts of changes. As well as studying hard and having a good time, you'll need to pay for all types of living expenses such as rent, food, household bills, books and so on. You may find your grant just won't stretch to cover all of this. Barclays have produced a package to help you manage your money more effectively.

THE BARCLAYS STUDENT BANK ACCOUNT PACKAGE

WHAT DOES IT GIVE ME?

The choice is yours. You may just want a cheque book and a Barclaybank card, which is a cash dispenser card only. Or maybe you'd prefer the versatility of the Barclays Connect card – a debit card, cash dispenser and cheque guarantee card all in one – so you have less to carry around. You may also need a credit card – Barclaycard Visa. You can apply for whatever card best suits your needs.

FIG. 1.3.7 *Banks have recognised the importance of providing services for individuals even before they actually reach the job market.*

growth (the effects of these are discussed elsewhere in this Element). In simplistic terms we can say that these criteria are achieved by the government changing the amount of money it spends in relation to the amount of money it collects and the different tax methods by which it collects it.

The government also uses fiscal policy for a number of other reasons, which include:

- to finance its own expenditure on health, education, armed forces, etc.
- to help people on lower incomes in the form of transfer payments, such as pensions, social security, etc.
- to give incentives to industry, e.g. grants, loans, subsidies, etc. (see regional policy on p.72–3)
- to discourage consumers from buying products which may be considered detrimental, e.g. very high taxes on tobacco
- to protect domestic industries by controlling imports (this can also help with the balance of payments)

At nearly every point in recent history, the government has been operating a deficit budget, i.e. spending more than they receive in taxes. In order to make up the shortfall, they must acquire money from other sources. This is known as the public sector borrowing requirement (PSBR). A balanced budget occurs when government spending is matched by tax income. Recent governments have attempted to reach this balance by spending as little as possible and relying on private individuals to provide for themselves. Rarely does a government have a surplus budget, as this would mean that the government had taken more in taxes than it was spending.

There are additional advantages and disadvantages of these various forms of 'balancing the books'. If the government is operating a deficit budget, there is a danger of inflation growing, as it becomes increasingly more expensive to borrow money. A surplus budget, on the other hand, can help reduce inflation by cutting down the amount of disposable income each individual has, in other words, reducing demand.

The main sources of tax income are:

- income tax taken from each individual from money earned
- corporation tax paid by businesses on their profits
- value added tax paid on the value of products or services at each stage of their production (this VAT proportion increases as products move from raw materials to finished goods)
- national insurance paid by both employees and employers to provide benefits
- inheritance tax paid on property and money left in wills
- stamp duty paid on financial transactions which involve large sums of money

student activity

(PC 1.3.2, COM 3.2, 3.4)
Find out the latest figures on government expenditure plans. Try to find out how these figures differ from those of last year. What have been the most significant changes in expenditure? Have some particular departments gained or suffered as a result of expenditure realignment? Present your findings in the form of a table.

Focus study

FISCAL POLICY AND MONETARY POLICY

Not merely has VAT been introduced on fuel, but there are serious increases in national insurance contributions and important cuts in personal allowances and tax reliefs. The present government's policies on income tax have meant that they have not confronted their fiscal difficulties with the traditional tax distribution logic of increases in direct taxation, especially at the top rate. The direct consequence of this has been to load the burden onto the middle and low income earners. But in so doing, they have reversed the earlier mission 'to take people out of tax'. We now have the highest proportion of taxpayers in the working population that there has ever been. Whilst interest rates have fallen, millions of households have had the benefit of this taken away from them by higher deductions from their wages or salaries.

student activity

(PC 1.3.2, COM 3.1)
Individually, consider the following with regard to the above Focus Study:

- what is the difference between indirect and direct taxation?
- what is meant by the last sentence of the Focus Study?

Now, in groups, discuss why the government has followed this course of action rather than actually raising income tax itself.

LEGISLATION

So far in this Element we have discussed a number of different parliamentary Acts which affect the way in which organisations can and cannot operate:

- Trade Descriptions Acts 1968, 1972
- Consumer Credit Act 1974
- Fair Trading Act 1973
- Weights and Measures Act 1985
- Food and Drink Acts 1955, 1976, 1982
- Food Safety Act 1990
- Consumer Protection Act 1987
- Environmental Protection Act 1980
- Monopoly and Mergers Act 1965

There are other ways in which government can affect the trading activities of organisations. One example of this would be the recent changes in Sunday trading laws which now allow certain types of businesses to open and trade on Sundays. Another change along similar lines to this occurred in 1988 when licensing hours for selling wines, beers and spirits were extended from 11 am to 11 pm.

Focus study

SUNDAY TRADING

Until now shops have been allowed to stay open until 9 pm one day between Monday and Saturday and until 8 pm on other days between Monday and Saturday.

The age of open-all-hours shopping has dawned – but consumers may not notice. Shops can trade at any time of the day or night under Home Office regulations which came into force recently. A Home Office spokesperson was quoted to have said that it may well be that nothing will change and that there will not be much demand for shopping at two or three in the morning.

The new regulations, part of a government drive to cut bureaucracy which hinders business, were included in the Deregulation and Contracting Out Act, which received Royal Assent in November 1994.

A Home Office Minister said that the change would be of particular benefit to customers of local convenience stores. 'Shopkeepers will be able to decide which hours they wish to open from Monday to Saturday to maximise their business opportunities and profitability. Shoppers will have greater choice over the times they can shop.'

Retailers said the new rules would not lead to a revolution. 'We are not going to see drastic changes in retail opening hours, but it will allow people more flexibility,' said a spokesperson for the retail industry. 'It will particularly give smaller shops the chance to open for longer if there is enough customer demand,' Retailers feel that general late night opening is a very retrograde step and exposes women shop workers travelling home to very real dangers, particularly where stores are in lonely out-of-town locations.

`0:40`

student activity

(PC 1.3.2, COM 3.1, 3.2)

In pairs, consider the following questions related to the Focus Study on p.61 and attempt to answer them to the best of your ability:

1 What do you think the major impacts on retail businesses will be due to these changes?

2 Why does the government wish to cut down on the amount of bureaucracy?

3 What effect will Sunday opening and later opening hours have on employment and employment conditions?

Other considerations may be, for example, the need to obtain planning permission before new premises can be built. This has recently been brought more to the forefront as increasingly large out-of-town supermarket complexes are being developed. Various other types of legislation including employment law and health and safety at work regulations affect organisations, but these are discussed in great detail elsewhere in the book.

PUBLIC OWNERSHIP

There is a vast range of public sector organisations, with an equally vast range of objectives. Three main areas are:

- the government
- people who operate and work in the public sector
- how they relate to the public

The government is very deeply involved in the business life of this country, as indeed are governments throughout the world.

Depending upon the kind of policies that governments adopt, the prosperity of the country, which is measured by the success of the businesses in that country, can be either helped or hindered. The influence of the government is far-reaching. Increases in government expenditure or the creation of controls over businesses, or, indeed, support for business in a particular area, can have a marked effect.

The government has the means to create wide-scale changes in business activity. The following are good examples:

- if the government increased interest rates this would reduce the general level of spending in the economy, and at the same time it would make it difficult for businesses which have borrowed money to finance projects
- when the government gives a contract to one firm rather than another, it can make the future of the business very secure, or conversely destroy its possibility of surviving
- if the government reduces personal taxes, this may, in fact, prove to be beneficial. The more money a person takes home, the more inclined that person is to work harder. This is known as increasing productivity
- if the government reduces taxes on a particular product, for example lead-free petrol, this could affect demand for that product. This in turn could lead to changes in how the product is supplied since the supply would need to be increased to match the increased demand

The government plays a massive role in the economy in general. Here are some examples:

- some particular goods and services are actually provided by the government because it is felt that every single person is entitled to that product or that service. A good example is health or education
- some goods or services from which everyone benefits can only be provided by the government if they are actually going to be provided properly. A good example is the police
- the government is interested in reducing inequality. This could mean that people who are relatively well off pay a higher tax. This in turn generates money to give to those who are less well off. Many people, however, think inequality is a good thing as it is an incentive for people to help themselves. Any increases in taxation, of course, will mean that those earning higher salaries are taxed at a higher rate, and in turn may be less motivated
- the government needs to make sure that the economic system as a whole is running well. It will pass laws to protect consumers or to prevent companies from controlling particular goods or services. It will take measures against polluters or those involved in anti-social behaviour

In other words, the government really sets the rules by which all businesses must comply.

Over time, as situations change, the government finds itself required to make amendments to the rules. How do they change? Who loses and who benefits when they change? This will be dealt with later.

student activity

(PC 1.3.2, COM 3.1)
In pairs, consider the following problems:

1 What would the government do if a company produced a product which was harmful to the public?
2 What would the government do if a company was found to be deliberately polluting a river?
3 What would the government do if a particular area of the country was suffering from a very high level of unemployment?

When we think about the government, the places Downing Street, the Houses of Parliament and Whitehall come to mind. Although these are important and are examples of the government in action, the government consists of many other parts. There are many organisations which are controlled by the government in some way. Some of these are what are known as public enterprises or public corporations. Here are some examples:

- British Coal
- The Bank of England
- The Post Office

Since 1979, however, many public corporations have been privatised. Examples of these are:

- British Telecom
- British Gas
- Electricity generation

But why did the government get involved in running these organisations in the first place? Here are some examples of reasons:

- one of the main reasons is to avoid waste and duplication. In the past many services have been offered by different companies. Essentially they were offering the same thing
- many of these organisations offer services which could not be run profitably. The big debate here is whether a private company would invest in supplying gas or electricity to a remote village when even in the long term it would not be able to make a profit
- the larger the organisation the more benefits there are in terms of production. Organisations which produce lots of output are able to buy their raw

materials more cheaply, their labour can be more concentrated and consequently their prices can be lower

- the government is always interested in the level of employment. In setting up public corporations the government might be taking this into consideration. A good example of such thinking is the relocation of tax offices and social security offices, whereby vast headquarters have been set up in relatively remote areas of the country that are suffering high unemployment
- one of the biggest arguments in favour of public corporations is that the government needs to control the vital basic goods and services that everybody needs. This is known as the infrastructure. This includes the transport network, water and energy. It is argued that the government has a responsibility to make sure that this is supervised and maintained well

PRIVATISATION

The process of privatisation which turns public corporations into companies owned by shareholders has been continuing since 1979 and is sure to step up in the 1990s. There are two reasons for this privatisation process:

- many people argue that state-run businesses are not very efficient, perhaps because they have no competition, and they never suffer the threat of going bankrupt because the government will always bail them out
- it is believed that as many people as possible should have shares in businesses. The idea is that everyone, no matter how rich or poor, should be encouraged to buy a few hundred pounds worth of shares in major enterprises like British Telecom. And, indeed, they have done so

As privatisation rolls into areas which have not been affected so far, such as the National Health Service, where trust status is almost another word for privatisation, there have been considerable worries. Competition in areas such as health can often lead to cost-cutting policies which will only mean the deterioration of standards.

One of the major arguments against privatisation is the debate about whether it is right to sell people shares in industries which in effect they already own. The theory behind this is that if the government is representative of the people of the country and runs services for the people then those services are owned by the people, since they are state owned.

One of the ways of safeguarding the running of a public corporation is to set up an independent body which keeps an eye on it. This organisation copes with complaints made against the enterprise and tackles the enterprise should it wish to put up prices or cut services.

Although these public corporations operate independently, they are controlled to some extent by the government at all times. It is the government's responsibility to make decisions about closing down parts of the business or investing large sums of money to improve it. On a day-to-day basis the chairperson of the enterprise and the other managers make decisions about wages, prices and industrial relations, but the government does still interfere when these areas affect the public.

Just as a limited company needs to make an annual report to its shareholders, so too does a public corporation. It presents its annual report to the government minister responsible for taking care of it. This government minister makes a report in Parliament to the Members, who will then make criticisms or support the corporation and how it is being run. At the same time a committee made up of Members of Parliament meets on a regular basis to keep an eye on the day-to-day running of the corporation and reports back to Parliament on how it is being operated. This is known as a Select Committee.

In addition to public corporations, there are two other areas in which the government gets involved in the business world:

- when an activity is actually run by a government department. A typical example of this is Customs and Excise, which deals with the supervision of and collection of taxes due on products entering and leaving the country
- where the government has a shareholding in a public company

Perhaps the most common form of government organisation is one which touches our lives the most, and this is local government. In the UK certain services are run by locally elected councillors. These councils usually run business organisations such as swimming pools, sports centres, bus services, car parks, shopping centres and public conveniences.

Just like public corporations, local council activities have also been affected by privatisation. The particular process that is used in this respect is that of tendering. The local council details the service which it wishes to offer for tender. Companies interested in running the service put sealed bids into the council explaining what it would cost to run the service and what they would be providing. The company that offers the lowest tender is given the job. It is then the council's responsibility to monitor how effective the company is in providing the service. If a company fails to reach certain standards then the contract is taken away from it. Local government pays for this by receiving a grant direct from central government and by collecting local taxes. These have been known as rates and community charge (poll tax) and is now called council tax.

The local council also subsidises loss-making activities such as parks and leisure centres which obviously provide benefits to the community.

student activity

(PC 1.3.2, COM 3.1)
In pairs, try to answer the following questions:

1 What is meant by nationalisation?
2 What is meant by privatisation?

Identify four public corporations and four recently privatised corporations.

In the role of a group of people who use a local swimming pool on a regular basis, try to decide whether it would be good or bad for you, as users, if the swimming pool were to be privatised.

1.3.3 *Evaluate the effects on markets of government policies*

EVALUATION

IN TERMS OF BUSINESS CONFIDENCE

Government intervention and specific government policies can have a very high impact on business confidence. Whether businesses feel confident or not about current and future market and economic conditions, plays a large part in how they behave.

For example, if current government policy is to control inflation and to keep prices stable, and the government intends to maintain this stance, businesses can then make forecasts with a greater degree of accuracy and certainty. Businesses use these forecasts to estimate future demand for their products and in turn, therefore, future expected profits. The more accurate their predictions are, or can be, the better able they are to make correct decisions as to what path their business should take. However, if there were no such policy to control inflation, unexpected or incorrectly predicted levels of inflation could cause costs to increase unexpectedly and thus expected revenue to fall. If organisations are confident about future market conditions then they are much more liable to undertake new investments and hence create growth and employment. A similar argument can be used for interest rates, taxation and to some degree exchange rates.

student activity

(PC 1.3.3, COM 3.1)
In groups of two or three, discuss the effects on organisational confidence of a government policy to increase interest rates and a policy to decrease corporation tax. Consider one impact on consumer spending and employment in each case.

CHANGES IN EMPLOYMENT OPPORTUNITIES

At various times, governments have employed both fiscal and monetary policy to control unemployment. Fiscal policies used by governments include:

- increasing public spending which, in turn, generates economic activity and helps to expand employment
- reducing taxation, which gives individuals more disposable income and helps to generate additional demand
- providing general support for businesses by offering incentives to investment and assisting and reducing the complexities of exporting

Since 1979 the government has been preoccupied with the use of monetary policy to manage the economy. The manipulation of interest rates has been used to control the money supply. Lower interest rates are more attractive to borrowers than savers, as they encourage people to take on credit or loans in order to spend. With the availability of cheaper money, businesses are likewise more inclined to invest. It is believed that this policy will help reduce unemployment. In reality, it is only just beginning to have an effect after nearly 16 years.

Specific policies, or direct measures, taken by the government to tackle unemployment include:

1 *Investment in education and training* – funded through the Technical Enterprise Councils, a number of schemes, such as YT and Target Training are run which are specifically aimed at the long-term unemployed and at employers.
2 *Enterprise schemes* – which offer various financial and tax incentives to help, in particular, small or new businesses.
3 *Reducing the value of social security* – to act as a disincentive to individuals and force them back into work. Present government philosophy is moving towards the introduction of a 'Workfare' along American lines, where individuals who receive benefits are required to involve themselves either in training or in community programmes. If they do not, then the benefit will be suspended.
4 *Reduction in trade union power* – as we see elsewhere in the book, the government has introduced a wide range of legislation aimed at reducing trade union power. The policy has been targeted at removing the 'closed shop', and reducing the power of picketing and the effectiveness of strikes. In addition, as we have already mentioned, weaker trade unions mean lower pay settlements.
5 *Advice and information* – the government has sought to create a comprehensive range of advice centres throughout the country to aid the unemployed.

These include Job Clubs, Restart and enhanced Job Centres.

6 *Regional assistance programmes* – depressed areas may benefit from a variety of grants and tax relief schemes to businesses. These policies are specifically aimed at areas with high unemployment in the hope that they will alleviate pressure on local businesses.

GROWTH

As previously stated in this Element, the only way to achieve a rise in the standard of living is by achieving economic growth. Governments obviously have this as one of their main objectives for the following reasons:

- if people perceive their standard of living to be increasing they will probably re-elect the government responsible
- steady and consistent economic growth is a good indication of a healthy and buoyant economy

Government policies can be used to stimulate more demand in the economy, however, the only true way to achieve real and effective growth is by increasing real investment in the economy. By real investment we mean investment other than that to replace worn-out capital equipment. One of the main ways in which governments can do this is by a lowering of the rate of interest. Since each investment is only profitable if it pays back more than it costs, it follows that the lower the rate of interest, the less organisations have to pay back on money they have borrowed for investment purposes. Therefore, the lower the rate of interest, the more profitable investment projects become and so the amount of investment spending will increase.

Expectations and organisational confidence also play a large role in the amount of investment undertaken. For example, organisations which are confident that future profits will increase will undertake more investment than if they consider that future profits may fall.

CONSUMERS' DISPOSABLE INCOME

We have already mentioned effective demand and income elasticity in this Unit, and you may wish to refer back to this discussion before continuing.

Different government policies will obviously have different effects on consumer income. However, it is important to note here that governments do not only affect the amount of income that people have to spend; through taxation, for example, by lowering the rate of income tax, but actually manipulate the amount of money an individual receives. Individuals then have more money to spend, and increase the level of demand in the economy. Conversely by raising income tax the government lowers the level of spending and demand. The government can also affect the way in which people use their money. By raising interest rates the government does not affect the level of income that any individual receives, but it does encourage people to save more and spend less, and vice versa if it lowers the rate of interest.

student activity

Increasingly consumers are buying more and more goods and services on credit and again the government can use interest rates to encourage greater or lesser amounts of spending in this way. In pairs, discuss how they do this.

Under recent Conservative governments a consistent policy of reducing direct taxation such as income tax has been followed. Why might the government do this and what would be the effect on the economy? Discuss this in pairs.

Another consideration to be taken into account are payments made by the government to individuals such as transfer payments, for example social security benefits, pensions, child allowance and income support. Alongside these considerations are those people employed by the government itself, civil servants, armed forces personnel, police, etc. The government can easily and very quickly affect a large portion of the nation's consumers' disposable income by simply increasing the level of their payments, thus increasing the amount they have to spend, or conversely decreasing such payments.

EFFECTS ON DEMAND

Obviously the way in which the government intervenes in the economy and the activities of organisations can have a huge effect on the level of demand.

By using direct tools such as legislation the government can affect changes in the type of goods and services consumers demand and their overall spending. A prime example is government legislation concerning particular products. Obviously this will have a drastic effect on the amount consumers spend on it, although there may be some residual demand serviced by the underground economy. Consider illegal drugs as an example. However the main way in which government affects demand within the economy is by its current fiscal and monetary policies.

TRADING CONDITIONS

Obviously the trading position of an organisation is quite clearly linked to the level of demand in an economy. The higher the level of demand, the more sales an organisation can expect to make. Alternatively, the lower the level of demand, the less likely it is to have high sales. However, government policies have an effect on more than just the level of demand in the economy.

Governments can directly affect an organisation's trading position by altering the amount of direct tax it has to pay on profits (corporation tax) and by using legislation to increase or decrease competition within a particular market. One of the major influences on an organisation's trading position, however, is the availability of finance for investment. An increase in the amount of corporation tax, for example, means that companies have less retained profit to plough back into the organisation itself. Alongside this, a rise in the rate of interest will reduce the amount of investment as the cost of borrowing money increases. In other words, the higher the rate of interest, the more one has to pay back. As we have seen, real investment is the only true way organisations can become more efficient and achieve growth.

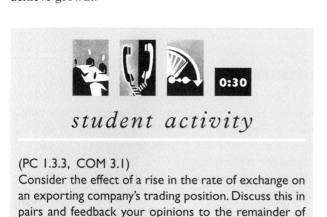

student activity

(PC 1.3.3, COM 3.1)
Consider the effect of a rise in the rate of exchange on an exporting company's trading position. Discuss this in pairs and feedback your opinions to the remainder of your group.

Of course, we must also consider the areas of availability of employees and the level of inflation on an organisation's trading positions. However, these are discussed in more depth in other sections of this Element.

GOVERNMENT POLICIES

FISCAL POLICY

As previous discussed, fiscal policy concerns the government's level of taxation and expenditure. Figure 1.3.8 presents this information simply.

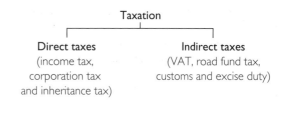

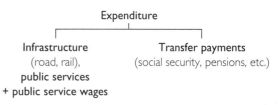

FIG. 1.3.8 *Fiscal policy.*

Obviously, there are two main ways in which the government can effect fiscal policy: it can either raise or lower the level of taxation or raise or lower the level of its own expenditure. The effect of the change in these variables on demand is outlined in Figure 1.3.9.

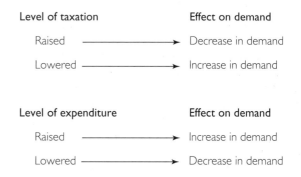

FIG. 1.3.9 *Effects of changes in fiscal policy.*

It must be noted that some policies have a much greater and quicker impact on the level of demand than others. The effect of an increase in direct taxation such as a rise in income tax has a direct and immediate impact on the level of consumers' disposable income. This thus reduces the level of demand. If the government were to increase the level of indirect taxation (say VAT) the overall effect would again be to decrease the level of demand. However, as indirect taxation is effective on consumer spending only on those items affected by the tax, the decrease in the level of demand obviously takes longer to have an impact.

MONETARY POLICY

Again, as we have previously mentioned, monetary policy is concerned with the supply of money circulating in the UK (Figure 1.3.10).

student activity

(PC 1.3.3, COM 3.1, 3.2)
In groups of two or three, consider the different forms of government expenditure. Which do you think would have the most immediate effect on demand? List your considerations in ranking order of importance. Compare your list to those of the remainder of the group.

FIG. 1.3.10 *Monetary policy.*

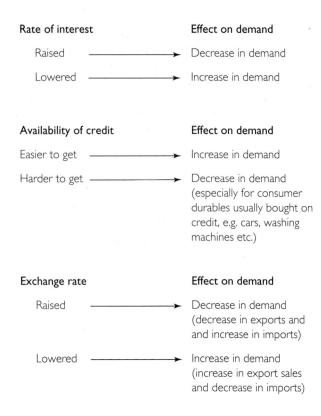

FIG. 1.3.11 *Effect of changes in monetary policy.*

In a similar way to fiscal policy, by means of monetary policy measures the government (through the Bank of England) can raise or lower the rate of interest. It can also make credit facilities easier or harder to obtain and it can vary the rate of interest. Once again, changes in these variables will have an effect on the level of demand. These are outlined in Figure 1.3.11 on p.68.

Again, we can see that different policy instruments will have a varying degree of effect on demand. A rise in interest rates (especially if coupled with a decrease in the availability of credit) causes purchases made on credit to become relatively more expensive and consumers will put off such purchases. This is especially the case if they think that interest rates in the future will fall. Additionally, a higher rate of interest encourages people to save more money and receive returns on it rather than spend it.

However, if we consider exchange rates, these fluctuations in the value of the pound primarily have the effect of altering the relative price of exports and imports. In other words, if the exchange rate goes up it becomes more expensive for other economies to buy our exports and cheaper for UK organisations to buy imports. This brings about a drop in the level of demand for domestic goods and services.

INTEREST RATES

The simplest way to think about interest rates is to assume that these control the price of borrowing money. The Bank of England, in consultation with the government, sets the general level of interest rates in particular economic situations. By changing the interest rate government policy has the following impact on businesses:

- high interest rates will reduce the money tied up in stock and release capital as organisations seek to avoid overdrafts. The net effect of this is that organisations produce less and employ fewer people
- higher interest rates will also affect suppliers who face similar problems and may be required to increase prices to the consumer. This, in turn, may have a detrimental affect on an organisation's ability to compete in the international market
- as interest rates increase, demand will fall, since consumers will have to pay more for their credit facilities. Some goods, as we have already seen, are price-sensitive and this increase in credit costs may deter consumers from purchasing products
- rises in interest rates will, however, strengthen the pound, thus encouraging foreign investors to put money into the UK economy. In order to invest in the UK foreign organisations must buy sterling and

their buying activities will increase the demand on that currency. As we know, greater demand may increase price. This is also true for currencies

- a rise in interest rates does, as we have already said, make UK firms less competitive, but on the other side of the coin, it does mean that the prices of imports into the UK will also fall. This may lead to a further problem as imports outpace exports

student activity

(PC 1.3.3, COM 3.1, 3.2)
How will interest rates affect an organisation's ability to manage its debts? Write down your considerations and then compare them to those of a partner.

The effects of changes in the interest rate depend on the size of the change. If higher interest rates are coupled with a high inflation rate then organisations and consumers alike are not overly concerned. But when inflation is low and interest rates are high we are less likely to borrow.

Increasingly, the UK government has been interested in the interest rates of other European countries. This new level of interdependence has been promoted by the EU, which is keen to see interest rates in harmony throughout Europe. Nevertheless, certain EU member states are suffering from more serious economic problems than others and are forced to increase their interest rates correspondingly. The effects of these increases may be seen as either advantages or disadvantages, dependent upon whether one is importing from or exporting to those countries.

PERSONAL INCOME TAX AND CORPORATION TAX

Personal income tax and corporation tax are both forms of taxation which are termed 'direct taxation'. These are taxes which are targeted at individual entities and are based upon level of earnings. In other words, income tax is paid upon an individual's income and the more you earn, the more you pay. Corporation tax is paid upon company net profit, the higher the amount of net profit earned, the more tax is payable. There are both advantages and disadvantages:

student activity

(PC 1.3.3, COM 3.1, 3.4)
Find out the interest rates in the following countries:

- UK
- Germany
- USA
- Japan

As a group discuss the reasons for the differences in interest rates in these countries.

Focus study

INTEREST RATES

The Chancellor of the Exchequer's firm action to keep control of inflation by raising interest rates won the approval of the financial markets, but was greeted with dismay by business leaders, industrialists and mortgage lenders.

The second increase in borrowing costs has provoked cries of betrayal and warnings that consumers, already hit by higher taxes and mortgage rates, would be reluctant to spend.

The Halifax Building Society, Britain's largest society, expressed disappointment over the move, saying it would further damage the fragile recovery in the housing market.

The Federation of Small Businesses said that the rate rise would bring more business failures, and the British Chambers of Commerce said that consumer spending could come to a stop.

Tim Melville-Ross, Director General of the Institute of Directors said the decision would make investment, crucial to the recovery, more expensive.

Howard Davies, Director General of the CBI, urged the Chancellor to act decisively to restore confidence in the government's fiscal strategy, arguing that continued uncertainty would be damaging and could lead to even higher interest rates.

▌ *Advantages*
- this is usually progressive in the sense that, taken with benefits, it is effectively redistributing income in favour of low income groups

student activity

(PC 1.3.3, COM 3.1)

Referring to the previous Focus Study, answer the following questions and discuss your opinions with the remainder of the group:

1 Name three types of organisation which are unhappy with a rise in interest rates.
2 Why might consumer spending come to a stop?
3 How will a rise in interest rates adversely affect the UK economic recovery?
4 Explain the role of expectations with regard to the Director General of the CBI's comment.

- the amount raised by direct taxation increases as income rises
- it is anti-inflationary
- the exact cost to each individual in society is easily measured and calculated

2 *Disadvantages*
- there is a disincentive effect, in that the more you earn, the more you pay
- it is said that direct taxation stifles initiative and enterprise by overtaxing
- it is comparatively easy to evade or avoid payment of taxation
- direct taxation may act as a disincentive to foreign investors as well as those at home.
- it is comparatively expensive to collect
- by taxing savings, the value of these savings is substantially reduced

Direct taxation has a higher impact than indirect taxation in terms of a policy instrument as it immediately affects the disposable income of individuals and the level of profits returned by companies. Indirect taxation, on the other hand, takes time to filter through. As a means of reducing demand in the economy an increase in a direct tax such as income tax would have a far more immediate effect than the introduction of an individual tax on a particular or type of product.

VALUE ADDED TAX (VAT)

VAT (value added tax) was introduced on 1 April 1973 and is known as an indirect tax. In other words, it is a tax imposed upon people's spending. VAT is collected by the government at each stage of production and dis-

tribution. Each organisation pays VAT on the value of goods it purchases, and then charges VAT on the value of the goods and services it supplies. The business effectively pays no tax as any VAT incurred in purchasing is passed on in sales to the consumer. As indirect taxes are based upon spending they are often seen as hitting people on lower-incomes harder than the more well off. Consider the following situation:

- Bob, aged 47, earns £75,000 p.a. as a professional journalist. He drives a 2.9 injection Scorpio, M reg.
- Mavis, aged 64, receives £7,200 p.a. in pensions. She drives an 850cc Mini, Y reg.

Yet they both pay the same amount of road fund tax. Essentially, this means that richer people have a proportionally lower tax bill than the poor.

VAT has both advantages and disadvantages:

1 *Advantages*
- payment is often convenient as indirect taxation may be paid in instalments or at source
- to some extent indirect taxation can be considered to be voluntary since its payment is linked to consumption
- unlike direct taxation, it does not adversely affect incentive or enterprise
- since it is often paid at source, it is harder to evade payment
- indirect taxation is considered to be a fairly flexible form of taxation
- the funds received from indirect taxation can be used to fund specific purposes

2 *Disadvantages*
- indirect taxation can be considered to be a regressive form of taxation in that, although it takes a lower percentage of an individual's income, it may not necessarily take a lower amount as income rises
- indirect taxation tends to penalise certain types of consumption. If the taxation policy is not sufficiently thought through, then it may adversely affect the ability of a particular industry to operate
- unlike direct taxation, the burden of indirect taxation is hard to calculate since it is only when specific purchases are made that the indirect taxation comes into operation

As a policy instrument indirect taxes are still effective in raising revenue for the government, and are also reasonably effective in achieving government objectives. However, as indirect taxation only comes into effect as and when consumers spend money on a particular item, then the implementation of the derived effect takes time to filter through.

student activity

Find out the government's total income last year, and the sources of taxation income that contributed to it. How much difference is there between this income and the expenditure of the government? Present the findings of your group in the form of a graph.

PUBLIC SERVICES WAGE LEVELS

It is important to remember when discussing government involvement and the public sector that we are not only concerned with national government (and areas such as nationalised industries and the civil service) and related services (such as police, armed forces, etc.) but that we are also concerned with all those employed by local government as well. Although in recent years there has been a trend towards local government services being offered to private companies on a competitive tendering basis, for example refuse collection, there are still large numbers of people employed by local government, or who are paid by local authorities. A prime example of this is the payment of salaries to teachers.

student activity

Try to find out what percentage of people in employment in the UK are employed by the public sector.

One of the easiest instruments that government can use to implement its fiscal policies is the level of expenditure on public service wage levels and the number of people it employs. Obviously, by raising or lowering the number of employees and level of income of people employed in the public sector, the government can have a large influence over the level of disposable income its employees receive. This directly influences levels of spending and demand within the economy.

PUBLIC SPENDING

The government finances its public expenditure (on roads, health, education, etc.) by the collection of taxes such as income tax, VAT, corporation tax and many others, e.g. import tariffs.

The government can control its expenditure in three main ways:

- *budget deficit* – where expenditure is greater than the revenue collected
- *budget surplus* – where expenditure is less than the revenue collected
- *balanced budget* – where the government spends the same amount as it collects in tax revenue. This is a very difficult position to achieve as for example it is virtually impossible to predict with total accuracy the amount of revenue that will be received from indirect taxes such as VAT

The reasons for government expenditure can be classified into four main categories:

1 *The provision of public goods* – those goods and services that government supplies because private enterprise may be unwilling or unable to do so, e.g. National Defence.
2 *The provision of social services* – health care, education, housing and transfer payments.
3 *To increase industrial efficiency* – first the government believes that certain industries will be more efficient if run by the government (see **public ownership** on p.62–3) and secondly the government can use grants and subsidies to improve the performance of the private sector.
4 *To influence the level of economic activity* – thus an increase in public spending can increase demand and reduce unemployment, whereas a reduction in public spending can reduce the level of demand in an economy, raise unemployment and lower inflation.

If the level of demand and other economic objectives is judged to be at the right level the government will introduce a balanced budget where the reduction in demand caused by taxation is counterbalanced by government spending. If the government considers the level of demand in the economy to be too low then it will initiate a budget deficit, i.e. government spending to increase demand outweighs the reduction in demand caused by taxation. The government finances this deficit by borrowing. Lastly if the government thinks that demand in the economy is too high then it will introduce a surplus budget, in which revenue from taxation exceeds government expenditure and the demand caused by government spending is less than the fall in demand due to taxation. The government can therefore achieve budget deficits and surpluses by raising and lowering taxation and raising and lowering its own expenditure.

INVESTMENT

We discuss the question of investment in some detail in the section of this Unit on **regional policy** (below).

Investment by the government itself is an important area of investment in the UK economy because the government undertakes investment not only for commercial gains but also for social considerations and it allows the government a good means by which to influence economic activity.

In the past most investment projects were undertaken by the government within its own nationalised industries and as such were undertaken in much the same way as a private company would undertake such projects. However, in certain situations the government may well undertake investment projects which are not necessarily profitable. For example, the government may well undertake to open new rail networks to ease the congestion and pollution caused by an overcrowded road network. Throughout this Unit we have seen various ways in which the government can influence investment levels in the private sector.

REGIONAL ASSISTANCE
REGIONAL POLICY

Regional policy seeks to address the inequalities between particular regions. Some economists feel that regions should be left to their own devices and that market forces should determine whether a region succeeds or fails. If a region is suffering from high unemployment, then it is inevitable that organisations which establish themselves there can impose lower pay rates on their workers. The theory is that the comparative advantage that results from high unemployment will mean that the region will benefit in the medium to long term. Unfortunately, the market is not as discriminating as these economists feel it should be. The UK, in particular, has a national wage bargaining system, which means that in certain occupations, the wage rates are exactly the same despite regional variations in employment levels. There are many other factors that may determine the location of an industry in a particular region, such as the availability of raw materials or communication links. It is too simplistic to cite labour skills as the sole reason for the location of an industry in a particular region. The theory of market forces also presupposes that labour is comparatively mobile and is able to move from region to region in search of employment. The fact of the matter is that the majority of individuals are immobile. This is for two main reasons:

1 *Occupational immobility* – this form of immobility is related to the fact that many people have only some skills and are untrained in other skills. They are thus unsuitable for employment in alternative occupational areas. The government provides a range of retraining programmes to help ease this form of immobility.

2 *Geographical immobility* – individuals are reluctant to move to new areas of the country, or to Europe for that matter, for a variety of reasons. These include:

- family ties, including children
- social ties
- housing difficulties
- comparative additional expenses of moving into more expensive areas

The young are more likely to be willing and able to move, but it is they who contribute significantly to local economies. If we assume that most younger people are in employment, then they are already contributing a large proportion of their income to local businesses and this, in turn, generates more employment. Emigration of these people from an area has a multiple effect on that area, since demand for local goods and services will be reduced, thus increasing unemployment. Gradually, the area will suffer a decline as organisations close or move from that area.

Government policy on regional development can take a number of different forms. These include:

1 The siting of central government departments in regional areas. The government operates a policy of positive discrimination in choosing a depressed area to site its services. The Vehicle Licensing Agency, which is responsible for the monitoring and licensing of all motor vehicles within the UK, has been sited in Swansea. This area has been suffering from high levels of unemployment and the move has resulted in many positive effects on the local economy.

2 The government offers a range of incentives to industry to help reduce costs in moving to or setting up in a depressed area. The government has built a number of purpose-made factories and lowered the cost of rent and rates to encourage organisations to resettle in depressed areas.

3 Labour costs can also be reduced by offering a subsidy to industries to attract them to select a depressed area when considering a move.

4 Certain regions can be designated as special areas which will, in turn, receive additional help and assistance from the government. Development areas can be split into three distinct types:

- *special development areas* – those in need of the maximum help

- *intermediate areas* – those with particularly high levels of unemployment
- *development areas*

The EU also assists these regions through its regional development fund and encourages its money to be spent on building up infrastructure and encouraging organisations to establish their businesses in the EU.

student activity

(PC 1.3.3, COM 3.1)
Try to identify the nearest area which benefits from some form of assistance from the government. Assess the impact of this enhanced status. How has it affected the unemployment figures? As a group, try to identify any aspects of your own local area which have similar problems to that of the area closest to you which is receiving assistance. Why do you think that your local area has not received assistance or the level of assistance the other region has obtained? Discuss these factors at first in pairs, and then feedback your comments to the remainder of your group.

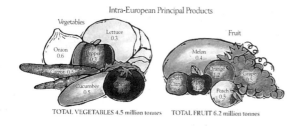

FIG. 1.3.12 *This illustration shows the internal trade within Europe of fruit and vegetables as calculated by Geest plc.*

SINGLE MARKET

The European Union (EU) Commission, based in Brussels, prepares and proposes a range of laws based on the agreed treaties signed by member states. Once these are passed, the implementation of the policies is monitored by the Commission.

The Council of Ministers decides whether policies should become law. These ministers (one from each member state) consider the proposals and must all agree before a policy can become law. Increasingly, the European Parliament is becoming involved in decision making. The impact of EU law has had wide-ranging effects at all levels and to all activities of businesses.

FIG. 1.3.13 *It is likely that the 15-member EU will be enlarged with the inclusion of 12 further nations. This process may be slowed down by the creation of the European Economic Area and Association Agreements with East European countries. This intermediate step is intended to give the current member states time to complete the programmes of economic and monetary union.*

THE MAASTRICHT TREATY

Many people will have heard of this treaty, but despite a considerable amount of press coverage, there is still confusion as to the point and nature of the legislation. Its main points are that:

- individuals whose country is part of the EU have the right to live or work anywhere within the community
- there is some level of co-operation and agreement with regard to transport networks, energy policies and communications throughout the EU
- the EU funds many research and development projects
- the EU monitors environmental issues
- throughout the EU there is some common recognition of academic and vocational qualifications
- the EU strictly monitors and controls the entry of new countries into the EU
- member states co-operate on educational issues
- member states co-operate on public health issues
- member states develop a range of consumer laws
- particular attention is paid to the protection of regional culture and language
- the EU states move towards a single market (which allows the free movement of goods and services throughout the EU)

Another aspect of the Maastricht Treaty is the Social Chapter. Although this has not been adopted by the UK, it has been accepted by all other EU members (1989). The proposals of the Social Chapter include the following:

- a maximum 48-hour working week
- the improvement of working conditions of employees
- an EU-wide attempt to reduce high levels of unemployment
- the formalisation of the negotiation process between employees and employers

- the goal of preventing 'social dumping' whereby organisations move to EU member states which have lower pay rates and less protection for employees.

student activity

(PC 1.3.3, COM 3.1)
Try to assess the reasons why the UK is refusing to adopt the Social Chapter of the Maastrich Treaty. Discuss the probable reasons as a group.

student activity

(PC 1.3.3, COM 3.1, 3.4)
Can you find any evidence of social dumping in the UK? Use newspapers as your main source of information and discuss your findings as a group.

The **exchange rate mechanism** was created to control the rate of exchange of currencies between members of the EU. The purpose is to give organisations and individuals the opportunity to purchase products and services in any EU currency and be well aware of the exact exchange rate (within some limits). Many EU members consider that the adoption of a standard currency throughout Europe is essential to ensure that Europe operates effectively as a single, strong market. To this end, they have created the ECU (European Currency Unit) which, although it has been minted in many countries, has not been generally accepted as a viable exchange currency.

The UK, in particular, sees the Maastricht Treaty as being the first stage in a process leading to the eventual loss of sovereign power and ability to make its own decisions. By giving up its sovereignty, a country is passing on decision making to the EU, the European Parliament, the European Central Bank, and this could lead to joint decision making by Europe as a whole. If countries were to accept a single currency, many people feel that the government would lose its ability to use monetary policy to control the supply of money and the level of interest rates.

THE UK AND EU COMPETITION POLICY

The European Commission is the executive arm of the European Union. Its main function is to propose EU policy and legislation which is then deliberated on by the council of ministers. If the council of ministers agrees to the proposals then it is the European Commission's role to ensure that EU member states comply with such legislation. There are various commissioners, e.g. those for agriculture, finance, education and competition.

It is also the European Commission's role to see that trade agreements, which might result in restrictive practices, causing restrictive, or distorted or limited competition between member states, do not occur. Articles 85 and 86 of the Treaty of Rome lay out the main provisions on competition of European law which are applicable to the UK. Article 85 is primarily concerned with the prohibiting of practices between member states and Article 86 seeks to prevent large dominant companies (those with a 25 per cent or greater market share) abusing their position within the EU. The intention is to bring the UK and other EU member states into line with each other on competition legislation, although this obviously would lead to less control by national governments. With the relaxing of trade barriers, e.g. import quotas and tariffs, within the EU, the business environment between member states is becoming increasingly integrated. It is therefore important to have a common regulatory body rather than independent national ones, as national regulatory bodies might well tend to be 'biased' towards their domestic companies if the result were a net overall gain to their nation's economy. Alongside this, as firms become increasingly involved in other member states' markets, it becomes increasingly difficult for national regulators to control foreign companies operating in their domestic economy and also increasingly difficult for national regulators to control domestic companies in other member states.

ELEMENT 1.3

a s s i g n m e n t

(PC 1.3.1–3, COM 3.1, 3.2, 3.3, 3.4, AON 3.3)
In this Element it is hoped that you have appreciated the impact of government intervention on markets and the subsequent effects on businesses. This assignment is a series of research tasks which culminate in an oral presentation which should last 15–20 mins.

TASK 1

(PC 1.3.1)
Prepare notes which explain the reasons why governments intervene in markets.

TASK 2

(PC 1.3.2–3)
Looking at two particular government policies which affect either local or national markets, assess how the markets have been influenced by this legislation.

TASK 3

(PC 1.3.1–3)
Using the title 'Why governments try to intervene in markets' prepare a 15–20 minute oral presentation which focuses on arguments for and against government intervention. You should support your oral presentation with any visual aids you feel are relevant.

UNIT I

t e s t   q u e s t i o n s

Focus 1

SUPPLY AND DEMAND

I   Which of the following persons has a need?

(a) somebody who would like a new leather jacket
(b) somebody who is hungry
(c) somebody who has not got a personal stereo
(d) somebody who requires a new car

2   Decide whether each of the following statements is true or false:

(i)   the normal demand curve slopes downwards from left to right
(ii) if the price of a product or service increases then demand will rise as well

(a) True/True
(b) True/False
(c) False/False
(d) False/True

3   Which of the following best describes price elasticity of demand?

(a) the percentage change in demand when quantity supplied rises
(b) the rate of change in demand in response to a change in price
(c) the level of demand at each and every conceivable price
(d) the effective change in demand when consumer disposable income increases

4   Inferior goods are characterised by which of the following statements?

(a) as price rises demand also rises
(b) they usually possess unitary demand curves
(c) as consumer disposable incomes rises demand falls
(d) they usually have no close substitute

5   Decide whether each of the following statements is true or false:

(i)   the demand for bread is usually highly elastic
(ii) a rise in the price of bread causes a fall in the demand for cakes

(a) True/True

(b) True/False
(c) False/True
(d) False/False

6–8 All of the following statements are related to demand and supply:

(a) a drop in income causing less to be demanded and supplied at each and every conceivable price
(b) more is demanded at each and every conceivable price
(c) a rise in the price of one product causes a rise in demand for another
(d) the percentage change in quantity supplied is proportionately less than the percentage change in price

Which of the above relate to the following?

6   Cross elasticity

7   A rightward shift in the demand curve

8   An inelastic supply curve

9   Look at Fig. 1.3.14. The typical shift in the supply curve for chocolate bars may have been caused by:

(a) a fall in the price of chocolate bars
(b) an increase in consumer income
(c) an increase in the cost of cocoa powder
(d) a rise in the price of chocolate bars

10   Look at Fig. 1.3.15. Which of the following would cause a fall in the market equilibrium price and a rise in the equilibrium volume?

(a) a rightward shift in demand
(b) a leftward shift in supply
(c) a leftward shift in demand
(d) a rightward shift in supply

Focus 2

COMPETITIVE AND NON-COMPETITIVE MARKETS

11–13 The following statements all apply to different types of competitive market:

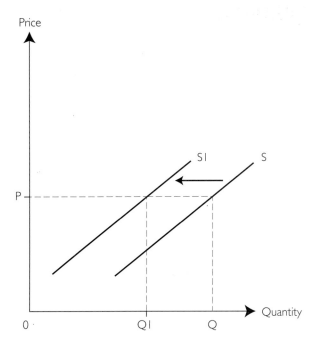

FIG. 1.3.14 *A supply curve.*

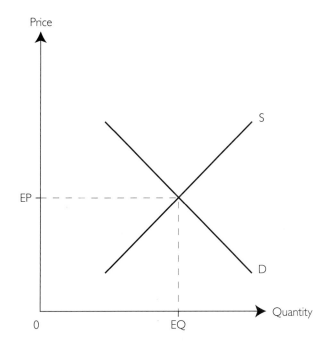

FIG. 1.3.15 *Equilibrium price.*

(a) a large number of sellers with product differentiation
(b) a company which has 25 per cent or more of the market share
(c) a company which is the only supplier in a market
(d) all suppliers in the market have a homogeneous product

Which of these best describes the following?

11 A pure monopoly

12 Imperfect competition

13 Perfect competition

14 Decide whether each of the following statements is true or false:

(i) a monopolist is able to influence both price and quantity
(ii) a monopolist cannot control both price and quantity at the same time

(a) True/True
(b) True/False
(c) False/True
(d) False/False

15 A price taker is:

(a) a company which responds to a drop in price of a competitor by dropping its price even lower
(b) a company which decides the price of its product and accepts the quantity demanded at that price
(c) a company which sets its level of output and accepts the market price
(d) a company which is imperfectly competitive in market conditions

16 Decide whether each of the following statements is true or false:

(i) oligopoly refers to markets which are dominated by several large businesses
(ii) oligopolistic markets are decreasing as international businesses become more competitive

(a) True/True
(b) True/False
(c) False/True
(d) False/False

17-19 Which of the following pricing strategies best fits the descriptions in 17–19?

(a) target pricing
(b) penetration pricing
(c) discrimination pricing
(d) promotion pricing

17 A strategy to encourage customers to use a service during off-peak times

18 A pricing strategy used to achieve the break-even point for a product

19 A strategy of setting an initially low price in order to gain market share

20 Decide whether each of the following statements is true or false:

(i) social costs are those non-private costs of production which are borne by people directly consuming the product itself

(ii) if an investment project generates any social costs the government will not undertake it

(a) True/True
(b) True/False
(c) False/True
(d) False/False

Focus 3

LEGISLATION AND GOVERNMENT POLICY

21 Which of the following is a current government objective?

(a) to increase the level of social services
(b) to restrict trade from European competitors
(c) to increase the population of the UK
(d) to maintain a stable balance of payments

22 Decide whether each of the following statements is true or false:

(i) in order to increase demand the government may use fiscal policies such as lowering interest rates

(ii) if interest rates go down investment will increase as consumers save more

(a) True/True
(b) True/False
(c) False/True
(d) False/False

23 Full line forcing is:

(a) a restrictive trade practice
(b) a government policy to increase employment
(c) a strategy to force retailers into a minimum resale price
(d) a measure of consumer protection

24–26 The following are all types of fiscal policies:

(a) decrease direct taxation
(b) increase government expenditure
(c) decrease government expenditure
(d) increase indirect taxation

Which would the government use to achieve the following?

24 Improve the level of education in the UK

25 Increase the level of consumer disposable income

26 Reduce the level of demand for cigarettes

27 Decide whether each of the following statements is true or false:

(i) inflation reduces the level of real income of consumers

(ii) inflation is calculated by measuring the changes in value of stocks and shares

(a) True/True
(b) True/False
(c) False/True
(d) False/False

28 Regional policy and assisted area status in particular is useful to a region that has:

(a) a high level of under-exploited natural resources
(b) an area that suffers from high rates of inflation
(c) a bad road and rail network
(d) an ageing population

29 Which of the following organisations oversees dealings between suppliers and consumers?

(a) the Home Office
(b) the Monopolies and Mergers Commission
(c) the Equal Opportunities Commission
(d) the Office of Fair Trading

30 To raise the rate of exchange:

(a) governments would increase the rate of interest
(b) governments would raise levels of taxation
(c) the Bank of England would print more bank notes
(d) the government would loosen trade barriers between the EU member states

ELEMENT 2.1

Investigate business organisations

PERFORMANCE CRITERIA

A student must:

1 explain the **objectives** of **business organisations**

2 explain the **differences** between **types of ownership**

3 **compare organisational structures**

RANGE

Objectives: *manufacturing, providing services, financial (profit, profit improvement, not for profit); market share, public service*

Business organisations: *private sector, public sector; charities*

Differences: *type of liability (limited, unlimited), use of profit (owners, shareholders, government), sources of finance, control of organisation, legal obligations*

Types of ownership: *sole trader, partnership, private limited company (Ltd), public limited company (plc), franchise, co-operative, public (state, local authority)*

Compare in terms of: *size, location, type of product, functions, meeting business objectives, changes (to organisational structures, to location, to functions)*

Organisational structures: *simple, divisional (by function, by product, divisions of multinationals), matrix, centralised, decentralised, flat, hierarchical*

2.1.1 *Explain the objectives of business organisations*

OBJECTIVES OF BUSINESS ORGANISATIONS

Throughout this Element you should be aware that regardless of whether an organisation is industrial, commercial or service orientated, it may have a variety of different objectives. Sometimes these objectives (often specifically stated in writing) may not be borne out by the organisations' actions. As we will see, organisations often find themselves in situations which require them to radically reconsider not only their objectives, but their entire purpose. Some of these influences, as we will see, are out of the hands of the organisation. Legal changes, for example, may require an organisation to re-evaluate (overnight) the way in which it either produces or markets a product. Equally, internal pressures such as financial problems can cause an organisation to abandon its most important objectives. Also, changes in ownership can radically affect the way in which the organisation pursues its published objectives.

In most respects, the purpose of any organisation is to be successful. This success is, however, measured in many different ways, which are dependent upon the type of organisation concerned. A good starting point for any organisation is to set down guidelines for activity that act as a standard from which it can measure itself. There is always likely to be a major difference between the organisation itself and how it operates, and the ideal types of organisation to achieve success. It is only when the organisation has clearly set out its goals and objectives that it can identify shortcomings or problems and seek solutions to them.

Many businesses begin with setting out their aims, purposes and objectives in a **business plan**. This is a formal statement of their goals. However, in reality, the day-to-day achievement of these goals may differ from the business plan. Organisations do not exist in isolation. The environment in which they operate is constantly changing. Therefore the organisation must be flexible. Any change may require organisational change when old ways of operating are no longer efficient or advisable in the new circumstances.

A **mission statement** differs from a business plan as it looks at what the organisation actually stands for. Generally, this is an agreement between both managers and employees. These agreed goals are often more valuable as they have the common consent of all those involved in the organisation. The individuals involved have a shared point of view and perhaps some common ideas of how to achieve them.

student activity

(PC 2.1.1, COM 3.1)
What would you expect to find in a business plan? How would a business plan be organised? Who would be responsible for putting the business plan together? Who would want to see a business plan? How closely do businesses stick to their business plans? Discuss this in pairs and orally report your findings to the rest of your group.

student activity

(PC 2.1.1, COM 3.1, 3.4)
The institution in which you are studying this programme will probably have a mission statement. Try to discover what it is and put it into your own words.

Once an organisation has established its goals, it must then find methods of achieving them. These are known as the **strategy** and **tactics.**

Strategies are the major ways to achieve the objectives and tend to be fairly long term in their approach, e.g. increase turnover by 50 per cent in 10 years.

Tactics, on the other hand, are more short term and flexible. These are the individual parts of the main strategy, e.g. in order to increase turnover by 50 per cent in 10 years we need to increase our product range and find cheaper suppliers.

So, strategy answers the question of how the organisation intends to get where it wants to go, and tactics are the means by which it achieves the strategy.

As we will see, businesses exist for many different reasons, and perhaps the most common is profit, but it is certainly not the only one. Being happy and satisfied is as strong a reason for running an organisation, and this is why many people like to work for themselves. Also the freedom to make your own choices can be good compensation for having to work for an organisation that is interested only in profit.

MANUFACTURING

An industrial or manufacturing organisation primarily exists to construct, assemble or otherwise make a product. It is during this process (known as the production process) that an organisation 'adds value' to the raw materials or components they began the process with, and will eventually produce some form of finished goods. This production process can take many forms, including:

- a car tyre manufacturer uses rubber during the production process to produce car tyres, however, the final selling price of the car tyres is far in excess of the original cost of the rubber. In other words, during the production process the added value aspect makes the rubber (in its new form as car tyres) more valuable
- a furniture manufacturer constructing various items from wood (or lumber) will similarly put the raw materials through a series of production processes to make tables, chairs, desks, etc. Again, the value of the wood after it has gone through the production process is significantly more than that of the tree from which it came

student activity

(PC 2.1.1, COM 3.2)
Make a list of at least 10 manufacturing organisations that you can think of. What raw materials would they use?

As we will be analysing the effectiveness and efficiency of various organisations in a multitude of different aspects later on, at this point we can identify some of the key manufacturing objectives.

1 *Method of production* – In any industry, there are universally accepted methods of production. However, there are many other factors which determine the organisation's choice of production method. These determinants include:

- available investment
- target customer (perhaps the organisation is producing hand-made products for the more wealthy customer)
- availability of skilled labour
- availability of affordable and applicable machinery
- availability of raw materials (these raw materials may be completely 'raw' or part processed already)
- location (this is particularly true of organisations manufacturing goods in the third world).

2 *Scale of production* – as you will see elsewhere, the scale of production (in other words, how many products the organisation produces), is an important determinant in the way the organisation operates. Larger-scale production can mean cheaper raw materials and more efficient methods of production. Obviously, the greater the production the more the organisation desires better productivity levels from its employees (this means that the organisation requires them to be more efficient).

3 *Location* – any organisation that wishes to do more than survive in a competitive market must take great care in choosing the sites of its factories. Great economies can be made by being close either to the source of raw materials (where the raw materials are grown or mined, for example) or to where the raw materials can be easily accessed (via good transportation links). Equally, the organisation should be aware that there are avoidable costs which it can save by being close to the market in which it wishes to sell its finished goods.

PROVIDING SERVICES

The commercial or service organisation does not, by definition, actually manufacture goods. Increasingly, however, the boundaries between manufacturing and services are blurred. An organisation which produces computer software will now be involved (either directly or indirectly) with the manufacture of the finished product and be in a position to market the product itself.

Manufacturing organisations have, in the past, been reliant upon the commercial or service sector to act as a point of contact between the end-user (customer) and themselves. As competition has grown manufacturers have sought to reduce the distribution chain and try to deal directly with the customer. This is not always possible and certainly the commercial or service sector of the economy is without doubt the largest employer in Europe. Many of the objectives which we will look at shortly are common to many organisations whether they are manufacturers or service providers. There are, however, some features of a service provider which are not common to a manufacturer. These include:

- more direct contact with the customer
- comprehensive after-sales service
- ability to provide information to customers on demand
- possibly a greater understanding of the market (since the organisation will stock or deal with a variety of different manufacturers' products)
- in understanding customers' requirements, it is able to identify the correct products to stock

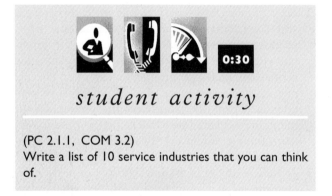

student activity

(PC 2.1.1, COM 3.2)
Write a list of 10 service industries that you can think of.

FINANCIAL (PROFIT, PROFIT IMPROVEMENT, NOT FOR PROFIT)

This rather broad objective encompasses, for many organisations, their principal objective. The exact set and mix of financial objectives will be dependent upon a wide variety of circumstances. Essentially, these may include:

- the nature of the market in which the organisation operates
- the period of time during which the organisation has been operating
- the requirements of the investors
- the availability and awareness of customers
- the level of competition
- the market share held by the organisation (see pp.84–5)
- the size of the organisation
- the range of products being produced by the organisation
- the type of organisation (see pp.85–7)
- the management style employed by the organisation (see pp.116–20)
- the stated objectives of the organisation

Some of the major financial objectives include:

1 *Breaking even* – this objective can often be used to describe the attitude of a charity or a non-profit-making organisation (e.g. a local authority or a government department). Any profits that are made are simply ploughed back into the organisation to cover running costs and purchase more products in order to continue the cycle. This can be termed 'ticking over' and is another objective often adopted by organisations in times of recession.

2 *Expanding the range of products or services* – the more products or services an organisation offers, the more likely that organisation is to survive and succeed. Organisations which only offer a single product or service can often find themselves in great difficulty if demand for what they offer reduces or disappears.

There are, however, dangers of offering too wide a range of products or services as an organisation may not be considered to be the expert or a market leader in any of them. In addition, the organisation is also exposing itself to the risks of several markets failing.

3 *Maximising profits* – this is when there is the largest possible difference between how much something has cost to produce and how much you can sell it for. In order to achieve this the organisation needs to know as much about the customer and the market as possible. It needs to know where to get its supplies at the cheapest possible rate, the most economical way of getting the product to the customer and the maximum price the customer would be prepared to pay for the product.

4 *Maximising sales* – on the face of it, this would appear to be similar to maximising profits, but this is not the case. It does not necessarily follow that by achieving high sales you are achieving high profits. There may be only a small profit to be made from each product. It is only when you sell many thousands of a product that you make a reasonable profit. This particular objective is most common in the retail trade, when different branches of the same organisation compete with one another to achieve high sales figures. The employees of the branches may even be given considerable cash bonuses to encourage them to sell more.

5 *Providing a return for shareholders and owners* – this objective aims to provide a steady and acceptable level of profit to the owners of the organisation. You should understand that here we have made a distinction between owners and shareholders. This will be covered in greater detail later.

Shareholders are owners of the business, but may only have a small stake in it and look for profits in the form of dividends from the shares they own.

Owners, on the other hand, may be sole traders, partners or major shareholders, who again are looking for income from the organisation related to how much of that organisation they own.

6 *Providing a steady income* – in some ways, this is the opposite to sales and profit maximisation. An organisation which states that providing a steady income is its principal objective is saying that it would rather attain realistic goals than overstretch itself. This is perhaps a cautious approach to business, but it is one that is often the most workable. Being able easily to meet sales targets, deliver goods on time and maintain high standards of quality may mean the difference between survival and failure in an uncertain business world. Many of the organisations which grew very quickly in the 1980s overextended themselves in pursuit of short-term profits. We can now see that companies which plodded along through the 1980s are still trading successfully, having provided themselves with a steady income in good times and bad.

CHARITABLE (NOT FOR PROFIT) BODIES

There is a bewildering range of different charities which cater for all segments of society and involve themselves in fundraising and the distribution of resources and information. This information increases the public's awareness of an issue or a problem.

Objectives of charities include:

1 *Raising awareness of an issue* – either through conventional advertising and marketing, or by word of mouth or reputation, various organisations strive to make us aware of the issues which they represent. In this respect, they must compete against all of the other organisations attempting to do the same.
2 *Stimulating action* – this can be measured in two major ways. The more obvious one is financial, to encourage the public to send donations or sign covenants to make regular contributions to the organisation. As important as this is the goal of convincing the public to make some other kind of response to an issue. This may be in the form of signing a petition or perhaps writing to a minister or government official in support of a particular issue. The call for the banning of live animal exports has spawned a series of responses from the RSPCA, Compassion In World Farming and other animal-orientated organisations. Each has its own preference in attempting to encourage us to support the issue by direct action in some way.
3 *Providing advice and support* – many charities provide vital support and advice to the public in areas that are neglected by the government. This is particularly true of health concerns (such as AIDS) and childrens' issues (such as Childline – an organisation set up to help combat abuse and bullying). This support is vital since there are no 'official' or government sponsored alternatives.
4 *Distributing resources* – whether this is in the form of cash (such as grants and pensions given to war veterans by the British Legion) or physical resources (such as recreational facilities donated by charities for the old) or the organisation of holiday trips for the under-privileged or orphans (such as the Variety Club of Great Britain), this is the main way that most of us recognise the activities of a charity.

MARKET SHARE

Market share is the percentage of sales held by a particular organisation. There are two basic ways in which this market share can be measured:

- the value or revenue generated by the sales
- the volume or units sold

It is important for an organisation to keep abreast of its market share in relation to its major competitors in order to assess its position in that market. It should be noted that even though an organisation may increase its sales, this may not necessarily mean that it has increased its market share. If the market is growing faster than the organisation's market share is growing, then it is losing pace with its competitors. Short-term increases in sales (and profits) may hide the true situation from the organisation.

Amongst the variety of market share-related aspects or objectives, the following are perhaps the most important:

1 *Being the market leader* – a market leader is an organisation that tries to sell more products than all of its rivals, or perhaps all of its rivals combined. There are considerable advantages to being a market leader, since every other organisation's products are compared to yours. Once this status has been achieved profit maximisation may also follow as you can produce products more cheaply than your rivals because you are producing so many more than they are. A part-way stage of achieving market leadership is to set an achievable level of market share. In other words, the organisation may not directly seek to be the market leader straight away, but will move towards this in stages.
2 *Beating the competition* – this objective is similar in a sense to being a market leader, however, beating the competition may just relate to achieving higher sales. Measuring this objective in terms of success is difficult, but can usually be assessed by the level of profit or reputation.
3 *Organisational growth* – the larger an organisation is, the more likely it is to attract investors and be able to produce products on a vast scale. Being big brings its own particular problems. Keeping track of business activity such as sales, stock and profit requires many extra employees. Should a company grow too

quickly and outstrip its ability to keep track of things, it runs the risk of overtrading. It is, therefore, very important for an organisation to be able to monitor all activities when it is growing fast.

4 *Customer service* – most organisations now appreciate the importance of an efficient and effective customer service programme. In the past, organisations only paid lip-service to this crucial aspect of their operations. It should not be forgotten that customer service is as vital to an organisation which does not have direct contact with its customers as it is to those that deal with customers on a day-to-day basis. In this respect, when we consider customer service we should not simply focus upon the commercial or service sector of the economy. It should also be remembered that both public and private sector organisations are under increasing pressure to provide comprehensive customer service programmes.

Some of the main customer service considerations are:

- *efficiency and responsiveness* – organisations now value the need to be immediately responsive to customers' requirements. This may be achieved in many ways, such as answering the telephone quickly, having sufficient products always in stock and being able to repair products at relatively short notice.
- *sales service* – throughout the organisation's contact with customers, it is vital for the business to do all it can to ensure total satisfaction. Well-trained staff and efficient and effective systems are important to make sure that all has been done to achieve this goal.
- *after sales service* – the organisation's responsibility, as far as the customer is concerned, does not cease when the product or service has been sold. It is an increasingly important feature of organisations that they have enhanced and developed their after-sales service. This may mean having sophisticated systems in place to cope with complaints, queries and returns of damaged or faulty goods.

PUBLIC SERVICE

Despite large-scale privatisation, there still exist numerous organisations which provide a public service in some form. Primarily, these include:

- central government departments
- local authorities
- QUANGOs (organisations appointed by the government to provide certain services)
- directly or indirectly funded organisations (such as hospitals and colleges)

3:00

student activity

(PC 2.1.1, COM 3.2, 3.3, AON 3.1, 3.3, IT 3.1, 3.2, 3.3)
An organisation monitoring the quantity of products returned for replacement due to fault would need to keep computerised records of these exchanges or refunds.

How would it estimate the amount of money to be set aside for this purpose?

Using a graph or pie chart produced by means of computer software, prepare an estimate assuming that 5 per cent of your chosen product will be returned as faulty.

If this was the case in your organisation, what steps would need to be taken to improve this situation? Present your findings in the form of a word processed report.

- specialist organisations (such as those set up to advise businesses and direct certain government initiatives)

In the past many public services were that in name only, they did provide a service, but they were not necessarily accountable or responsive to public needs. Recent government legislation now requires them to be accessible, responsive and efficient.

Some of the key public service considerations include:

1 *Providing benefits and grants* – organisations such as the DSS or councils are responsible for providing a range of benefits and grants, either to the unemployed or students. In this respect, the public service aspect of the organisation is obvious, but there are less obvious ways in which some public sector organisations can also provide vital services.

2 *Providing advice and guidance* – councils and central government, through a range of different sub-organisations, provide a vast range of support services to industries and individuals. These services include business advice and guidance through the Department of Trade and Industry, and more local support for business via Chambers of Commerce. Individuals can obtain useful advice on demand through the Citizens' Advice Bureaux that are common in nearly all towns and cities.

3 *Collection and monitoring* – the Inland Revenue not only collects income tax and other forms of taxation

based on profits from business, but also provides useful business advice on matters such as financial control and monitoring.

Customs and Excise, which is responsible for the collection and monitoring of VAT (Value Added Tax), provides useful guidelines for the collection, payment and monitoring of this 'sales tax'.

4 *Data collection* – many central government departments routinely collect data which will be of great use to businesses. Data are readily available on employment trends, family expenditure, growth or decline of markets and export information.

5 *Other objectives* – there are other purposes of organisations that do not neatly fit into the categories identified above, since they are not necessarily profit related, or anything to do with market share.

- *freedom* – as we have already mentioned, many people set up a business in order to work for themselves. They prefer the opportunity to make their own decisions and be their own boss, and, of course, take all the profits and risk all the losses.
- *survival* – when times are bad and the economy is in recession, a company may simply seek survival. This may be measured by the company's ability to maintain existing staff levels, keeping customers and not having to close branches or retail outlets.

student activity

(PC 2.1.1, COM 3.1, 3.4)
We have tried to identify the major objectives of most organisations. Which do you think are the most important? Put the objectives into ranking order of importance. Once you have done this, look at your top five and try to come up with reasons why you have chosen these as being the most important.

Compare your decisions with those of the rest of the group.

BUSINESS ORGANISATIONS

It is probably easier to think of an example of a business organisation than try to define what a business organisation actually is. Although, as we will see, business organisations can differ enormously, they do have some common features. These are:

- they often use resources that are in limited supply (such as human resources, money and materials)
- they provide something (either a product or a service)
- they normally compete with other organisations

As we will see later, each organisation must undertake a wide variety of different tasks or functions to ensure that it operates well within the area in which it is involved. Some of the functions include:

- *managing employees* – usually through a personnel (or human resources) department
- *selling products or services* – providing customers with the product or service which they require
- *distributing the product or service* – ensuring that customers have access to what they need
- *purchasing products or services* – ordering stock for either short-term use or long-term needs
- *marketing a product or service* – researching the customers' needs and then promoting the product or service
- *keeping financial records* – to monitor the success of the organisation

Also, an organisation must ensure that when it needs to make a choice it makes the correct decision. This may involve a wide variety of considerations which will have an impact on the decision. It usually involves the use of resources, which may be limited, so the organisation must ensure that it makes the right decision as often as possible.

Business organisations do not always have the same purpose. Perhaps the most common, as we will see later, is the profit motive, but not all organisations are driven by this goal.

PRIVATE SECTOR

Generally, the private sector is made up of organisations that are independent of the government. A little later on in this Element we will investigate the specific nature of each of the main private sector organisations, but for now we need to make some simple distinctions between them:

1 *Sole traders* are organisations usually run or operated by one person.
2 *Partnerships* are organisations of groups of people.
3 *Limited companies* are organisations that are owned by shareholders.
4 *Franchises* are organisations that have been set up by buying the name of an established organisation.
5 *Co-operatives* are organisations of groups of people who have joined together to be more efficient and effective.

PUBLIC SECTOR

The public sector consists of organisations that are either owned or controlled by the government. The most common forms of public sector organisation are:

1 *Government departments* or the civil service, who are responsible for running government activities in a specific area (such as the Department of Trade and Industry which assists other businesses).
2 *Local government,* such as county, metropolitan, district or borough councils whose task it is to provide services, assist business and promote the area.
3 *Public corporations* or enterprises, such as the Bank of England or British Rail (although many parts of this may have been privatised by the time you read this), whose task it is to provide services in a particular part of the economy. These are also known as nationalised industries.
4 *QUANGOs* (Quasi-Autonomous Non-Governmental Organisations) which are funded by the government to provide services. Examples of Quangos include OFTEL (which monitors the communications industry) and the Arts Council (which provide grants to artists, theatres and film makers).
5 Many organisations were once public enterprises or Quangos, but have been *privatised.* These include British Telecom, British Gas, British Airways and the various water boards.

CHARITIES

As we have already mentioned, charities have a different perspective on business activity than that of many other organisations. Charities have been described as the following:

1 *Non-profit making* – charities are not necessarily in operation to provide a profit, although a modest profit that could be ploughed back into the operation could be useful. After all, the profit motive is not there as technically charities are not owned by anyone, nor do they have shareholders who require dividend payments.
2 *Non-loss making* – perhaps this is a slightly better description, but still not quite true. It is obviously advisable for the organisation not to have to dip into its reserves to support its activities. Some organisations, throughout the recession, found their income diminishing and had no other choice. Even the Church of England has had to dispose of assets.
3 *Profit-making* – this can be said to be true of many charities these days. They do produce a profit from their merchandising and other fundraising activities, but the money is not distributed to shareholders or owners. In most cases, the funds are either used to support new activities, purchase equipment, expand into new countries, or are simply transferred into a reserve fund for contingencies.

An organisation with a 'charitable status' is exempt from many of the legal obligations of a normal organisation. This is not to say that it must not comply with such things as health and safety requirements, or contracts of employment, but that any profits it makes are not taxable.

In recent times, in addition to the well-known and long-established charities like Dr Barnardo's, Oxfam, Help the Aged, etc. many schools have adopted this form of organisation.

LOCAL BUSINESS ORGANISATIONS

Whether you live in a city or town or in the countryside, there is a network of business organisations to cater for nearly all of your immediate needs and wants. Some may be part of the public sector (such as refuse collection or health care), others will be provided by the private sector (such as supermarkets, newsagents and chemists). Other organisations may not necessarily provide products or services for the local community, but may provide these for the national or international market (such as a mine, or a food processing operation, or a government department).

student activity

(PC 2.1.1, COM 3.2, 3.3, AON 3.1, IT 3.1, 3.3)
Undertake a brief audit of your most immediate retail shops. How many of them are independent and local? How many of them are part of nationally owned chains? Are there any internationally owned outlets? Present your findings in the form of a table, by means of a computer software package.

NATIONAL BUSINESS ORGANISATIONS

There are a wide variety of organisations that operate on a national basis in this country. In all sectors of the economy, we can find examples of businesses that have established themselves in nearly all the major population centres of the UK. In manufacturing terms, food processing tends to be based around the areas which produce the required raw materials. Birds Eye Wall's, for example, are positioned to exploit the availability of fish and vegetables. They are careful to choose their location since the processing of the freshest possible produce is essential in maintaining their image.

In the service area of the economy, we will find banks, building societies, travel agents, betting shops and newsagents creating national networks to cover the spread of the population over the country.

INTERNATIONAL BUSINESS ORGANISATIONS

Many organisations have become multinationals or conglomerates, by acquiring or building up their businesses all over the world. For some organisations this is a result of the type of business that they are involved in:

1 *Oil companies* discover oil in many parts of the world, refine the crude oil, ship it to storage areas and then distribute it via petrol stations (e.g. BP and Shell).
2 *Computer manufacturers* market and sell their products world-wide. Although they may research and manufacture in only one or two countries, they must have support, sales and marketing operations world-wide (e.g. IBM and Apple).
3 *Retail organisations* have sought alternative markets throughout the world; this is particularly important if their major market is in recession or decline (e.g. Marks & Spencer).
4 *Franchise organisations*, like retail businesses, see expansion abroad to be the best course for the future and have encouraged people to set up franchises in areas of which the original organisation has little or no knowledge (e.g. The Body Shop).

5 *Manufacturing organisations* need to be able to produce products in the market in which they compete. This may be to overcome import duties or quotas set by the host country or simply to take advantage of lower wage rates and set-up costs (e.g. General Motors, Nissan and Ford).

The term **conglomerate** best describes an organisation that has interests in a variety of different business ventures. An organisation in this position can avoid sudden or gradual downturns in profits for a particular product or in a particular market by distributing its operations and investments around the world.

International organisations can also take advantage of the differences in the value of currencies, as well as the economic growth or recession in different countries. They have enormous buying power and it is thought by many people that they can exert too strong an influence on countries desperate to retain their investments.

These international organisations do suffer from some problems that can be encountered as a result of their size. It is often difficult to maintain any sense of international corporate identity. Modern technology, such as video-conferencing, e-mail and faxes have gone some way to solving this problem.

Just as it is comparatively easy to 'buy into' a market if an organisation has the financial strength, so it is also easy to dispose of companies that form part of the organisation if they fail to live up to their promise of profits.

2.1.2 *Explain the differences between types of ownership*

DIFFERENCES

We must now turn our attention to the exact nature of difference in terms of the following criteria:

- liability
- use of profit
- sources of finance
- control of the organisation
- legal obligations

In many cases, we identified the key aspects when we looked at the different types of business ownership. It is perhaps more valuable to consider the nature of these differences in a comparative manner. We have attempted to put all of the main differences into a single table (Table 2.1.1 on p.89). For more detail either refer to the previous descriptions or the short notes which help explain the table itself.

TYPE OF LIABILITY (LIMITED/UNLIMITED)

As we will see in later Units, the term **liability** applies to debts which may be incurred by a business. Liabilities (in terms of a balance sheet for example) are the sources of finance.

Limited liability means that the owners or shareholders are financially responsible for only the amount that they have invested in the business. In this sense, their personal belongings, property and cash are protected from claims by creditors.

In limited liability cases, the creditors can only claim (and share) cash up to the value of the shareholders' original investment in the organisation. Any potential creditor would know whether or not an organisation has limited liability by noting the addition of Ltd. (private limited company) or plc (public limited company) after the name of the organisation in question. A creditor would not often see this as a potential risk, but it can mean that in the early stages of a creditor's relationship with a new organisation, it may insist on full or part payment for goods and services before delivery.

The obvious advantage in limited liability firms is the fact that potential shareholders know that they only risk their investment and not their whole lifestyle and wealth when buying shares in a limited company.

USE OF PROFIT (OWNERS, SHAREHOLDERS, GOVERNMENT)

Profit itself is what is left from revenue after the costs have been deducted. Therefore:

revenue − costs = profit

There are, of course, several types of profit, and it is advisable to understand these in basic terms first (although we will look at this in greater detail in a later Unit). A profit and loss account is the best place to begin. This is simply a statement which records all of the organisation's revenue and costs over a period of time. The statement begins with the total revenue (sales total), from which is deducted the cost of sales (cost of purchasing the goods and services subsequently sold and any other directly attributable costs). This gives us the **gross profit** (not the final profit as more costs must still be deducted).

From the gross profit we must now deduct the organisation's overheads (indirect and fixed costs such as salaries, rent, lighting and heating). This leaves us with the trading or operating profit. From this the cost of or revenue from 'one-off items' is either added or deducted. This may be revenue from the sale of property, or deductions from the payment of redundancy packages or payments into a pension scheme. After this calculation, we are left with the **pre-tax profit**.

Not surprisingly, we now take the tax away from this total (corporation tax in most cases, but in smaller businesses, this may be Schedule D – self-employment tax).

The next total, after the tax deduction, is **profit after tax.** In the cases of limited companies, they must now pay a dividend to their shareholders. A dividend is a share of the profits. The total left, is known as the **retained profit.**

So what happens to this retained profit? In most cases, the main use of this cash is reinvestment. This may take a variety of forms:

- purchase of new materials
- payment of long-term liabilities (such as loans)
- purchase of premises
- acquisition of another organisation
- acquisition of another organisation's product or service (for the purpose of owning and producing it in the future)

Smaller organisations may use profit to expand their operations. A sole trader, for example, may choose to create a partnership with others and relocate to larger premises. Perhaps the sole trader needs to upgrade or replace machinery or vehicles?

Larger organisations may choose to use their profits to acquire smaller or related organisations. This is known as a merger (when two organisations mutually agree to join together) or a take-over (when one organisation buys another one).

As we have seen from the explanation of the distribution and gradual reduction of profits, the cash needs to go to a number of different individuals, groups and organisations. Tax is the unavoidable consequence of profit. The government insists on clear and honest accounting of the transactions carried out by all organisations, regardless of size or structure.

Any owner or shareholder of an organisation also insists on a slice of the profits. After all, the original investments were made to reap the financial benefits of the organisation's activities. As we will see later, larger organisations which have shareholders have a complex job in deciding the level of dividend or profit share.

More simple, in one respect, is the distribution of retained profit to partners. This distribution is usually made on the basis of seniority or the level of the original investment in the partnership.

For a sole trader, the distribution could not be easier. If the organisation is wholly owned and run by a single individual, then he/she will retain all of the profit. Many sole traders will have 'sleeping partners' who do not take an active role in the business. However, they will expect a share in the profits at the appropriate time.

TABLE 2.1.1 *Differences between various types of business organisation*

Type of business organisation	Criteria				
	Liability	*Use of profit*	*Source of finance*	*Control of organisation*	*Legal obligation*
Sole trader	Unlimited	Reinvest self	Own assets Loans, grants	Direct	All ★
Partnership	Unlimited †	Reinvest partners	Own assets Loans, grants	Direct	All ★
Private limited	Limited	Reinvest shares	Shares, loans Grants	Directors Managers owners	All ★
Public limited	Limited	Reinvest shares	Shares, Loans Grants	Directors Managers owners	All ★
Franchise	Limited/ Unlimited ‡	Reinvest Franchisor Franchisee	Own assets Franchisor Loans, grants	Managers Franchisor	All ★
Co-operative	Usually limited	Reinvest Members	Members Loans, grants	Members Managers	All ★
Central government	n/a	Re-used Treasury	Treasury	PM Cabinet Ministers Civil Servants	Most ¶
Local government	n/a	Re-used	Council tax Rates/rent Central government	Councillors Officials	Most ¶
Quangos	n/a	Re-used Treasury	Central government	Appointees Central government	Nil★★
Charity	Limited/ Unlimited	Reinvest in cause in question	Donations Covenants, grants	Trustees	Most §

★ Including employment, civil, trade union, health and safety etc.
† Except in limited partnerships
‡ Dependent upon the organisation of the franchise
§ Dependent upon the structure and charitable status
¶ Except for some laws depending on nature of authorities
★★ Only those imposed by central government

Multinationals or international organisations have complex arrangements in dealing with profits. They are in an excellent position to 'move' profits from one part of the organisation to another to avoid paying tax. In some cases, profit-making parts of the organisation will be deemed to 'owe' another less profitable part of the organisation and thus the profit will have been 'removed' before the stage when tax is payable. This is not illegal, but a much-used benefit of operating in a variety of countries. Profits in this case can often be used to bolster or support struggling parts of the organisation. This can cause animosity between the different parts of the organisation as the successful parts feel that they are subsidising the inefficiencies of another part.

SOURCES OF FINANCE

We will be considering the sources of finance available to different businesses in Unit 7, however, at this point it is worth identifying not only some of the major sources of finance, but also their conditions and terms.

We can identify the principal sources of finance first in terms of the length of time that they are available. In this respect, we will make the distinction between short-, medium- and long-term and permanent availability.

We will look at each type of organisation in turn, examining briefly the finance available, length of availability and its probable use.

SOLE TRADER

- *permanent sources of finance* – owner's capital, profit reinvestment. Usually used for the purchase of fixed assets and organisational growth
- *short-term sources of finance (up to three years)* – credit, overdrafts, factoring, short-term personal or bank loans, hire purchase. Credit would be used for the purchase of stock. Overdrafts and factoring would be used for the purchase of stock, paying wages and to provide working capital. Short-term loans and hire purchase would be used for the purchase of relatively cheap assets
- *medium-term sources of finance (3–10 years)* – medium-term bank or personal loans, hire purchase, credit, leasing. Loans would be used for the purchase of fixed assets. Other sources would be used for buying assets in order to maintain sufficient working capital
- *long-term sources of finance (over 10 years)* – loans or grants from government agencies, mortgages, long-term bank or personal loans. These sources of finance would be used for either the purchase of fixed assets or as an alternative to using working capital

PARTNERSHIP

- *permanent sources of finance* – partners' capital, profit reinvestment. Again, these would be used for the purchase of fixed assets and general organisational growth
- *short-, medium- or long-term sources of finance* – as sole trader

LIMITED COMPANIES

- *permanent sources of finance* – issue of new shares, building up reserves. Again, these would be used for the purchase of fixed assets and general organisational growth
- *short- or medium-term sources of finance* – as sole trader
- *long-term sources of finance (over 10 years)* – as sole trader, but in addition debentures and redeemable preference shares. These two new sources of finance would be used for an immediate increase in available working capital

In the summary above, we have used a number of business terms which you have not yet encountered. It is perhaps a good idea to try to give a basic definition of these, although, again, you will find far more information in Unit 7.

1 *Asset* – basically, we can subdivide this term into fixed or current assets. The former would include premises, equipment, shop fittings and vehicles. The latter refers to the items needed by a business on a day-to-day basis. This will include stock and any cash either in the bank or in the business's safe.

2 *Working capital* – this is the day-to-day finance required for running a business. It is used to pay for the raw materials and running costs and also importantly, funds the credit which may have to be given to customers. As we will see later, it is important for the business to have sufficient working capital as this may affect its ability to pay immediate debts and other costs.

3 *Factoring* – this is a service provided by banks and other financial institutions which advance 80 per cent of the value of invoiced sales and organise the collection of that debt. This service can be used by a business to ensure that its cash is not tied up in unpaid bills.

4 *Debentures* – this is a fixed-interest long-term security which is secured against an asset. Debentures are used as an alternative to share issues as a means of raising long-term capital. For example, a 10 per cent debenture would pay 10 per cent of the loan each year until the end of the loan period.

5 *Preference shares* – these are a way of paying a fixed dividend and offer far greater security than an ordinary share. They are not linked to the profitability of the business, as the dividend is fixed, but, in the event of the business failing, preference shareholders will be paid back their investment as a priority.

CONTROL OF ORGANISATION

One of the clearer definitions of management, since it is this that actually controls the organisation, is a much used phrase:

a manager helps the organisation to achieve its goals by helping others to achieve their objectives

We will be looking at some of the functions and duties of managers and other individuals in an organisation later in the book. At this point, we will look at the general co-ordination and control of organisations.

If the individuals within an organisation are to achieve their goals then it is the job of the management to create a means for them to do so with the minimum of disruption and confusion.

There needs to be a coherent pattern of co-ordination and control, not only for the employees' sake, but also for the management to be assured that their directions are clearly understood and followed. To be truly effective, they must encourage motivation, commitment, common values and a clear and agreed corporate mission or strategy.

The impact of this control will differ from organisation to organisation as, after all, the exercise of power will depend on the nature of the individual manager. Many of the controlling features within an organisation are actually unwritten and unspoken, and employees will learn to understand the rules and expectations of the business and the ways in which things are done.

VERTICAL CONTROL

In hierarchical (or formal) organisations, the business will maintain control through the following:

- policy statements (written or oral)
- statements of responsibility
- organisational charts
- written procedures

All work is controlled vertically; this means that an individual receives instructions from his/her immediate superior, who in turn is instructed by his/her superior, and so on. As the instructions are passed down the lines of authority, it is important to ensure that the corporate objectives and goals are maintained.

Having clear lines of authority makes it easier for decisions to be made and to ensure that they are implemented. The more junior individuals in the organisation are protected from potentially conflicting instructions as they know to whom they are answerable. The major problem with this form of control is that some of the subtleties of the instructions are lost as the message passes through the levels of management. At the bottom of the organisation it can often appear that some of the rules and procedures are petty and unhelpful, despite the fact that these instructions began further up the lines of authority with the very best of intentions.

LATERAL CONTROL

When an organisation grows larger and its activities more varied, it becomes increasingly difficult to maintain control. There are various remedies to this problem, but one of the most effective is 'networking'. This informal means of communication and interchange of ideas is crucial to an effective manager trying to keep abreast of the ever-changing policies and procedures of the organisation. In this connection, managers value their relationships with other managers. It is crucial that they understand what is going on elsewhere and how decisions made at higher levels are impacting upon the business.

More complex structures are looked at on pp.110–116 such as the matrix and the decentralised structure.

CONTROL SYSTEMS

Within the same industry, using the same technology and catering for the same markets, you will often find organisations that approach this problem quite differently. Typically, we may find any of the following:

- orderliness and preparedness
- detailed planning procedures
- scheduling
- annual operating plans
- individuals' performance plans

At the other extreme, and equally as common, we will find:

- 'muddling through'
- 'adapting as and when'
- 'taking things as they come'

Smaller and newer organisations have a tendency to follow the latter range of control systems, after all, they need to adapt to problems and opportunities as they arise. Unfortunately, control systems at this stage, however chaotic, take root in the organisation and are difficult to change. Controls do become tighter as the need to respond to external considerations (such as banks, interest rates and complaints) become more important. These tighter controls need to be carefully managed, since adaptability may still be of importance. It is a careful balancing of needs that has to be achieved if the organisation is to maintain adaptability as well as more formal controls.

The degree of employee participation in the control and co-ordination of the organisation can also differ. Some organisations favour an autocratic method of control (tightly controlled and not involving the employees in decision making), or a more democratic method (where employees take an active role in the decision making and control). As we will see later, there are many methods and theories of management, but many organisations do not have a great degree of internal control at all. Some organisations are controlled externally by legislation, as we will soon discover, a good example being a nuclear power station. Such an organisation is bound (quite rightly) by a huge range of laws to prevent accidents and disasters.

LEGAL OBLIGATIONS

The implications of the legal obligations will be looked at in the specific Units relating to them later on in the book.

UK AND EC EMPLOYMENT LAW

Employment legislation is considered by many people to be a minefield of legal requirements and restrictions. Many of the laws have been designed to protect the individual employee in situations where he/she may be unfairly treated by a powerful employer. Some may say

Focus study

CONTROL OF ORGANISATION

Electrolux expanded very quickly in the 1980s, buying, amongst others, a rival company called Zanussi. It now consists of some 35 national marketing companies, supporting 29 international product development and production organisations.

Each of the development and production organisations provides goods for the 35 national marketing companies to sell to that country.

Each country is co-ordinated by a manager who is accountable to the parent company. There are a handful of managers who co-ordinate the activities of all production and development organisations and the marketing companies. Over the years, they have tried to create structures and systems to maintain control and direction, but they still believe that these cope with only 80 per cent of the problems and workloads. In this sense, Electrolux is not uncommon in having fairly rigid rules and procedures in place for certain controlling functions, but having to 'take things as they come' in many instances.

that the laws have only served to reduce the number of full-time employees, as employers move towards part-time and short-contract labour, which is not so comprehensively protected by law. All of the following laws are currently in force in the UK, although another whole batch of laws and regulations are contained within the EU's proposed Social Charter (which at the time of writing the UK government has opted not to accept).

1   *Disabled Persons (Employment) Act 1958*
    An employer with 20 or more employees must employ a minimum of three registered disabled persons. Certain organisations can obtain an exemption certificate due to the hazardous nature of their work. On the other hand, certain organisations are required to give disabled persons priority in selection and recruitment to particular positions, e.g. electronic switchboard operators.

2   *The Factories Act 1961*
    This Act covers a wide range of different organisations, focusing on the use of machinery. The key features of this piece of legislation are:

    - the employer must provide toilet and washing facilities
    - premises should be adequately heated and ventilated
    - the employer must make sure that floors, stairs

and passageways are not obstructed in any way
    - all floors should have a non-slippery surface
    - potentially dangerous machinery should be fenced off to protect employees
    - there must be are adequate fire escapes, well sign posted and regularly maintained
    - fire doors themselves should never be locked or obstructed

3   *The Offices, Shops and Railways Premises Act 1963*
    This Act concentrates on conditions within shops and offices and provides a number of clear guidelines to the employer, including:

    - in work areas, the temperature must never drop below 16°C
    - the employer must ensure that there is an adequate supply of fresh air
    - following on from the Factories Act 1961, this legislation states that the employer must provide enough toilet and washing facilities in relation to the number of staff. He/she must also make sure that there is hot and cold running water as well as soap and clean towels
    - again, following on from the Factories Act 1961, this legislation states that an employer has to provide suitable lighting wherever employees are expected to work or move around
    - the employer must ensure that there is at least 12 square metres of working space per employee

4   *Equal Pay Act 1970*
    This important Act stated that women, performing a similar job to men, should be treated in every way equally. This includes not only pay and conditions, but opportunity for promotion and recognition.

5   *Race Relations Act 1970*
    This very complicated piece of legislation aims to protect individuals against discrimination on the ground of race, colour, nationality, national origin or ethnicity.

6   *The Rehabilitation of Offenders Act 1974*
    Individuals who have criminal convictions need not necessarily mention these on their job application forms or during interviews. Some convictions, after a certain period of time, are considered to be 'spent' (no longer applicable). If an employer subsequently discovers that an employee has 'spent' convictions and decides to dismiss him/her because of them, then this is illegal.

7   *Health and Safety at Work Act 1974 (HASAW) and EU Directives on Health and Safety*
    Before this Act, employees were protected against hazardous working conditions under a number of different pieces of legislation. HASAW aimed to bring all of these together and extend the protection

of employees under a single Act. The main points of the Act are:

- it stated general duties of an employer across all types of industry and commerce
- it created a system by which HASAW could be enforced (by the Health and Safety Executive and local authorities)
- it created the Health and Safety Commission which aimed to help employers understand the regulations and develop codes of practice
- it was backed up by the imposition of a series of legal obligations on the employer who risked facing criminal proceedings for failure to follow them
- it imposed minimum safety regulations and introduced improvements to the working environment

The work of HASAW has been followed up by a number of EU Directives covering such areas as safety signs at work, employees handling hazardous materials and guidance regarding avoidance of major hazards.

New regulations and codes of practice are being designed continually and now cover nearly all work activities, both in the private and the public sector. Steps are now being taken to cover any gaps in the legislation, or to make it easier to understand and implement.

8 *Sex Discrimination Acts 1975 and 1986*
The original Act covers discrimination on the grounds of gender. It is equally applicable to both males and females. The Act also covers discrimination relating to marital status.

The amended Act of 1986 extended protection against discrimination to employers employing five or fewer people. It also included for the first time employees working in a domestic capacity for private employers and employees working for professional associations.

9 *Employment Protection (Consolidation) Act 1975 and 1978*
The original Act, substantially amended in 1978, covers the main features of a contract of employment. In addition, it requires employers to provide a contract of employment within 13 weeks of commencement of employment. We will be looking at contracts of employment in much more detail later in the book.

10 *Employment Acts 1980–1990*
Since 1979 successive governments have taken steps to limit trade union power. The main points of each of the laws are as follows:

- *1980:* picketing (attempting to prevent other employees, customers, deliveries, etc. from entering or leaving the premises during industrial action) was restricted to the premises involved in the dispute and was not permitted at any of the organisation's other premises. The Act also restricted 'blacking' (employees refusing to handle goods from an organisation whose employees are in dispute). It also became illegal to sack an employee who refused to join a trade union, whereas before this certain occupations required compulsory membership of a trade union (known as a 'closed shop'). These 'closed shops' were further restricted by the law requiring 80 per cent of employees to agree that there should be one in existence
- *1982:* this law restricted the reasons for calling an industrial dispute in the first place. The reasons had to be related directly to employment matters and could in no way be political. A more damaging part of the Act, as far as trade unions were concerned, was that they could now be sued by employers for any loss of business to other organisations as a result of industrial action. A trade union's funds could now be seized by the courts to pay for damages. Following on from the restrictions made on 'closed shops' in 1980, the law stated that trade union members must vote on whether 'closed shops' should continue
- *1988:* for the first time, individual members of trades unions were given the right to take their union to court to prevent industrial action. This right only applied when the union itself declared there should be industrial action, and a ballot had not been taken. Union members were also protected under this law against disciplinary procedures for not having taken part in industrial action. Employees could now work for organisations which had 'closed shops' and not join the union, in the knowledge that they would keep their jobs
- *1989:* this amended Act required employers to provide some form of document which stated the terms and conditions under which an individual is employed. This is not a contract of employment, and does not have all the details of one
- *1990:* this Act outlawed the dismissal of an individual who refused to join a trade union. Secondary action (union members taking industrial action in support of other union members) was made illegal. Unions became responsible, legally and financially, for any unofficial industrial action taken by members. All industrial action had to be approved by a majority of members in a secret ballot. Any union members

involved in unofficial industrial action could be singled out by the employer and dismissed

11 *Trade Union Act 1988*

This Act clearly stated that all industrial action must be agreed in advance by a majority of union members in a secret ballot.

12 *EU Directive, 'An Employer's Obligation to Inform Employees of the Conditions of Employment Relationships' 1991*

The most important feature of this EU Directive is a change to the nature of the contract of employment. Employers are now required to provide the following information, within two months and not the original 13 weeks:

- the location of the work
- the job title
- the type of job (by categories)
- a job description
- paid leave entitlements
- hours of work
- collective agreements made organisationally/nationally

This is the first stage of a comprehensive range of legislation designed to ensure that employees throughout the EU have an employment contract, and know exactly what is required of them. The intention is also to treat employees working on a part-time basis as equals to full-time employees in most respects.

13 *Trade Union Reform and Employment Rights Act 1992*

This law was designed to assist the rapid creation of jobs by clearly stating exactly what an employer has to provide for the benefit of the employees. This includes a written statement which covers the main conditions of employment (pay, holiday entitlement and hours worked).

Female employees are entitled to take 14 weeks maternity leave in the knowledge that their job is secure for them to return to should they desire to do so after the pregnancy.

Employees who have responsibility for ensuring that Health and Safety Regulations are adhered to, and whose employers have broken those regulations, are protected under this law from having the employer take action against them.

14 *Management of Health and Safety at Work Regulations 1992*

This major piece of legislation aims to provide a systematic and well-organised set of guidelines in relation to health and safety. They include the following:

- employers are required to assess any potential risks employees may have to face and take preventive measures to cope with them
- this risk assessment must be continually monitored by a group of employers working closely with at least five employees
- employers are required to employ specialists whose sole responsibility it is to implement the preventive measures, as well as to provide information for all other employees within the organisation
- employers are further required to carry out regular screenings of their employees to make sure that they have not suffered any ill-effects as a result of carrying out their duties. If appropriate, any health hazards which have been identified should be addressed immediately
- employees who have been given the duties of Safety Representatives should be regularly consulted, provided with time and space to carry out their investigations and given the authority to act on them

15 *Health and Safety (Display Screen Equipment) Regulations 1992*

This Act is designed to protect employees who spend considerable amounts of their working hours in front of a computer screen. The main points of the legislation are:

- employees must receive sufficient breaks from the screen
- work should not be repetitive and the employee should be given a variety of tasks
- basic safety requirements must be satisfied as regards the screen itself, the design of the keyboard, as well as the shape and height of the desk and chair being used
- regular eye tests must be provided by the employer and if the employee needs special spectacles in order to carry out his/her tasks, they should be provided by the employer
- sufficient lighting should be provided in the room where the employee is using the computer, as should proper ventilation

16 *Provision and Use of Work Equipment Regulations 1992*

This Act covers all equipment from major production line machinery to hand-held tools. The legislation requires employers to:

- take into consideration how and where equipment will be used, and choose the least hazardous methods of production
- purchase only equipment that conforms with any applicable EU safety directive

- ensure that employees are given sufficient information to enable them to use any equipment safely. Where appropriate, training and retraining should be offered
- ensure that all equipment is regularly serviced
- ensure that potentially dangerous machinery has appropriate guards to prevent injury
- provide protection for those using hazardous materials
- ensure that work is carried out in an environment which has sufficient light
- display any relevant warnings regarding potential dangers

17 *Manual Handling Operations Regulations 1992*

These regulations were implemented to assist in the avoidance of unnecessary injury at work. This Directive covers lifting, pushing, pulling, carrying and moving objects at work, and offers advice as to the correct manner by which these should be carried out.

18 *Personal Protective Equipment at Work Regulations 1992*

The term 'personal protective equipment' includes life jackets, harnesses, head, hand and foot protection, glasses and goggles and clothing designed to be visible at all times and in all conditions. The Directive states that the protective equipment must be fit for the purpose for which it is intended, as well as actually fitting the employee. The equipment must conform with EU regulations and it must be suitably stored, cleaned regularly and replaced if defective. In addition, employees must be trained in the correct use of the equipment.

student activity

(PC 2.1.2, IT 3.1, 3.3)
Assess these pieces of legislation in terms of the relative protection they offer employees and employers. On balance, who do you think is the better protected? Consider each Act separately and present your findings in the form of a word processed document.

CONTRACTS OF EMPLOYMENT

As we have seen so far, the employer has a number of duties towards the employee. This can be seen very clearly in the contract of employment. This really for-

malises the relationship and is seen as a legally binding document on both the employer and the employee.

A contract of employment should lay down all of the following points:

- job role – the precise nature of the job
- job title
- pay details – how it is paid, frequency of payment
- additional payment details – such as which salary/wage scale the individual will be placed on, when overtime can be undertaken, how bonuses and commission may be earned
- start times and finishing times of work
- total number of hours worked per week, before overtime
- number of paid days off for holidays, etc. and any restrictions on when these may be taken
- sick leave and maternity leave details, duration and entitlement to such leave
- pension schemes, with details of contributions made by employer and employee
- grievance procedures – stating who the Grievance Officer is and the process of the grievance procedure itself
- period of notice to be worked/given
- number of weeks or months notice required (by either side) in the event of resignation or termination of employment

In addition to these legally required details, the employer may wish to inform the employee of the following:

- rules and regulations to be followed by employees
- codes of behaviour expected of the employees
- the nature and availability of sports and social activities and welfare facilities offered
- a full organisational chart so that the employee identifies where he/she fits into the overall scheme of things

CIVIL LAW

Civil law covers disputes between individuals and suppliers. When a transaction is made this is, in effect, a contract. If one side suffers a loss in any way from the contract, then the injured party may sue.

CRIMINAL LAW

Criminal law tends to deal with more widespread abuses related to sales transactions. If an organisation sells a product that is harmful or dangerous to the community in general, then it will be the government (through the law courts) that will take action against the organisation. Under criminal law, an organisation or individual found guilty is liable to fines, imprisonment, or both.

CONTRACT OF SALE

As we have already said, when goods or services are provided, the consumer should expect that they are fit for the purpose for which they were intended. If a product does not meet the consumer's requirements, then he/she may expect a replacement. If the product is wholly unfit then the consumer may expect his/her money back. These basic rights form part of the Sale of Goods Act. The companion law is the Trade Descriptions Act. This makes it a criminal offence to wrongly describe a product. In other words, any description of the product must be accurate.

The Weights and Measures Act attempts to ensure that the quantity stated on the box, container or bag matches the weight of the contents inside. It is an offence under this Act to claim a particular weight and supply a lighter one.

The Food and Drugs Act deals with food and medicines specifically. Under this Act an organisation cannot supply a harmful product and must always make sure that any instructions as to the use or preparation of the product are clear. For example, uncooked red kidney beans contain a toxic substance which is eliminated by cooking them for the correct period. Suppliers of this product must ensure that any packaging states very clearly the potential hazards. Also under this Act, there are rules that apply to certain foodstuffs such as sausages. Sausages must contain a defined amount of meat to be called a sausage. If they do not, then they must be alternatively labelled.

THE CITIZENS' CHARTER

The Citizens' Charter sets out consumer rights which indicate that, particularly as far as public services are concerned, the consumer should expect a certain level of service. It states that if the service does not meet this standard, the consumer should expect compensation. This system is regulated by a number of separate organisations (some of which we will look at later). It is further suggested that once an organisation's services reach a particular standard, then it will be able to claim a 'chartermark'. This chartermark is intended to give a consumer a clear indication that he/she will receive a high-quality service.

In the first phase of the Citizens' Charter an organisation releases a list of 'promises', which clearly states exactly what consumers should expect from that organisation. From this set of promises consumers should now know what their rights are as regards service.

The main reason for the development of the Citizens' Charter is to control publicly run organisations, such as local authorities and to maintain some level of control over 'opted-out' organisations, such as hospitals or schools and colleges.

student activity

(PC 2.1.2, COM 3.1, 3.2, IT 3.1, 3.3)
In groups of three, in the role of the manager of a local authority's refuse collection service, produce a Citizens' Charter covering your promises of service.

Discuss and compare your charter with those of the remainder of the group. Your charter should be word processed.

GUARANTEES AND OTHER LEGAL PROTECTION

A guarantee or a warranty is basically an undertaking by the manufacturer to replace or repair a product, or parts of a product, should they prove to be defective, and to do this free of charge, and as quickly as possible. A typical guarantee would include the following:

- the product will be repaired free of charge if faulty because of defective materials used in its manufacture
- the product will be repaired free of charge if faulty because of defective workmanship
- the product will be repaired free of charge if found faulty within the first 12 months
- the manufacturer will require a proof of purchase such as a receipt or credit card voucher
- the product must be repaired or replaced only at the manufacturer's service centre or approved service centre
- if it is discovered that the fault is not the result of defective parts or workmanship, but due to negligence by the consumer or retailer, then the manufacturer is not obliged to repair or replace free of charge
- optionally, the consumer may choose to extend the guarantee or warranty period by paying an additional charge. In this case, the manufacturer extends its

student activity

(PC 2.1.2, COM 3.1)
In pairs, discuss the warranties you would expect to find when purchasing a pocket calculator.

offer of replacement or repair for the period purchased

We will be looking at the Sale of Goods Act and the Trades Descriptions Act later on in this Unit, but there are some other laws which similarly protect consumer rights:

THE CONSUMER PROTECTION ACT

This Act is primarily concerned with price and the pricing policy of organisations. No doubt many of us have been caught out when purchasing a product, to find that the price quoted is not the price in reality. This may be because the sale period has ended, the price quoted did not include VAT, or the claimed price reduction is untrue. This Act states that the organisation must clearly state the 'real' price of a product, not make unfair or untrue comparisons between products and price, and not make false statements about price reductions.

You will often see, particularly in a sale, one of two statements on a price ticket:

- that the product was available for a period of time at a previously higher price. It may not necessarily have been available in that store, but in an alternative location owned by that organisation, and this fact will be stated on the ticket
- that the product has been specifically bought in and offered at a low price for the sale period only

The Consumer Protection Act further covers the consumer who is offered unsafe goods, whatever the circumstances.

THE SUPPLY OF GOODS AND SERVICES ACT

This Act was created to cover loopholes in the Sale of Goods Act. The older Act did not include services, hired goods or part exchanges. All goods or services 'purchased' under these conditions are now covered. In respect of services this Act protects the consumer against poor workmanship, long delays and hidden costs.

FISCAL – VAT, PAYE AND PENSIONS

Organisations must keep accurate financial records to meet their obligations regarding their tax liability. All organisations have direct taxes to pay which are related to their profits (known as Corporation Tax), and they may also be responsible as a tax collector with regard to the PAYE (Pay As You Earn) of their employees.

The employer also has the additional responsibility of the calculation and collection of National Insurance and will have an individual responsible for the monitoring of this function. The calculations need to be correct and paid on time.

An individual may receive a pension from two different sources, both of which involve the employing organisation in some respect. These are:

❙ *State pensions* – the organisation has an administrative responsible for the collection of contributions from the individual until he/she retires. From then on the state takes over responsibility for the payment and administration of the pension. In addition, an individual may choose to pay SERPS (State Earnings Related Pension Scheme) contributions in order to 'top up' his/her pension.

A BRIEF WORD ON SALARIES

When are salaries paid?

- salaries for monthly paid staff are generally paid on the 14th of each month. Paid two weeks in advance and two weeks in arrears, they can be paid into a bank account or a Society account.

How do I change the details of where my salary is paid?

- simply notify the Payroll Department in writing, preferably giving a month's notice.

How is my National Insurance contribution worked out?

National Insurance contributions are paid to finance State benefits such as unemployment pay, State sickness benefits and State pensions and are calculated as a percentage of gross earnings.

- Your N.I. letter as shown on your payslip will most probably be a 'D' or an 'A'.

- if you pay 'D' rate National Insurance it means you are a member of the Society's pension scheme.

- if you pay 'A' rate National Insurance it signifies that you are not.

- you contribute less on 'D' rate than on 'A' rate because in return for lower N.I. contributions, the Pension Scheme gives the D.H.S.S. certain guarantees about the benefits payable at retirement.

What about my income tax?

Income tax is paid on taxable income and is determined by your tax code and the rate of income tax currently in force. It is a complex area where a variety of factors govern the amount you will pay.

- if, for example, your code is 260L this will mean you are able to earn up to £2,600 p.a. before paying tax. Any money earned after that will be subject to Income Tax.

- for more information about **calculating your Income Tax**, contact the Payroll Department.

- if you have a query about your **code**, contact: H M Inspector of Taxes, 44 Abbey Street, Leicester. Tel: Leicester (0533) 510041. Tax reference number: L6273. Always quote your personal tax reference number.

FIG. 2.1.1 *The Alliance and Leicester Building Society provides all employees with a very user-friendly booklet called 'Your Pay'. The section on salaries explains very clearly an employee's obligations in terms of PAYE and national insurance.*

2 *Occupational pension schemes* – the other form of pension is known as an occupational pension scheme, by which the individual pays the employer separate contributions which may be topped up by the employer. Although the employing organisation is responsible for carrying out all the administrative tasks related to this pension scheme, it does receive the benefit of all its contributions being tax-deductible.

Pensions

We have two first class contracted-out Company pension schemes which will help you to protect your dependants and provide for your retirement.

If you are aged 20 or over you can apply to join the relevant scheme immediately. If you are 25 or over with 1 year's service you are automatically included in the appropriate scheme, unless you have completed the form available from the Pensions Department to say you do not wish to join. (Our pension schemes are for permanent employees only).

+ You can obtain a pensions guide and question and answer booklet along with further details from your Staff Manager.

Additional Voluntary Contributions (AVCs)

Members of both pension schemes have the opportunity to improve their pension benefits by making Additional Voluntary Contributions (AVCs). AVCs are worth considering if you think your pension may be too small when you retire.

However, AVCs should only be considered as a long term investment because you cannot gain access to the funds until you retire. Whether AVCs are for you depends on various factors such as age, length of service, etc.

+ Pension arrangements are very important. Your Staff Manager will be able to give you more details before you make a decision.

FIG. 2.1.2 *Tesco PLC, the national food retailing giant, offers an attractive company pension to its employees, who are given additional opportunities to make voluntary contributions to enhance their pension benefits.*

TYPES OF OWNERSHIP

There are many ways in which a business can be organised, from a small one-man business to a multinational organisation. You will find that the majority of the business organisations covered earlier in this section are representative of the private sector, but we have also covered the public sector in some detail in our consideration of public corporations.

THE SOLE TRADER

The sole trader is perhaps the most common type of business organisation although in recent years the numbers of such businesses have been declining, for a number of reasons, which we will look at later on.

The sole trader is responsible for all actions that the operation undertakes. This individual will be responsible for borrowing all the money required and actually running the business on a day-to-day basis. Perhaps the most common sorts of sole traders are craftsmen and women – plumbers, decorators, electricians, mobile hairdressers, window cleaners and chiropodists.

Sole trader businesses cover a very wide range of activities, but they all have some features in common, including the way they got started, and the fact that the business can always normally be run by one person, although that person has to be very flexible and needs to be willing to work very long hours.

There are quite a number of advantages to setting up as a sole trader:

● there are no real legal formalities to complete before commencing to trade
● there are no real legal requirements governing the layout of accounts
● the annual accounts do not have to be audited
● decisions can be made quickly since only one individual is involved
● the owner has the freedom to run the business his/her own way

There are also a number of disadvantages:

● capital is limited to the owner's savings or profits or any other money he/she can borrow
● the owner has sole responsibility for debts – if the owner does fall into financial difficulties he/she may have to sell personal possessions to meet the business debts
● responsibility for a range of activities falls upon the shoulders of the one person who runs the business. So, in other words, the owner is responsible for running the business – dealing with paperwork and customers, filling in tax returns and dealing with day-to-day contact with any employees or subcontractors he/she might use
● the success of the business is always dependent on how hard the sole trader wishes to work
● any unforeseen accident or illness could seriously affect the business since all responsibilities rest on the shoulders of that one person

student activity

(PC 2.1.2)
Consult your Yellow Pages Directory and try to identify at least 10 local sole traders.

THE PARTNERSHIP

A partnership may be formed as a way to overcome the problems a sole trader may have in raising capital. A partnership consists of between 2 and 20 people who set up in business together and share the responsibility for that business. Each partner is required to contribute some capital and the profits and the losses are shared between all of the partners. The control of the business is the responsibility of all of the partners and decisions made by one partner are always binding on the others.

In partnerships, all partners have what is known as unlimited liability. This means that any debts incurred by the partnership have to be met by all the partners.

Individuals may enter into a partnership with one another without any real formal written agreement, but in practice they usually draw up a partnership agreement. This is a set of rules which will hopefully help avoid disagreements between the partners.

The agreement usually includes the following:

- the amount of capital to be contributed by each partner
- the ratio in which the profits and losses are to be shared. Usually this is worked out in relation to the amount of capital each of the partners has put in. So, in other words, the more capital each partner has put in, the more profits he/she will be entitled to
- the salaries, if there are any, that are going to be paid to specific partners
- the rules for admitting and expelling partners
- the voting rights of partners – they may have an equal or an unequal share of the decision making
- the rules for ending the partnership

On the question of limited liability, there is an option which allows a partnership to have limited liability for some members of the partnership – this is known as a limited partnership. In such partnerships, certain partners are known as sleeping partners. They take no part whatsoever in the decision-making process of the business, and should the business fall they stand to lose no more than their original investment in the business. Therefore, they have limited liability. In contrast, the other partners, known as the general partners, still face unlimited liability. In law, there must always be at least one partner with unlimited liability.

The most common form of partnership though, is the ordinary partnership where all partners play an active role in the running of the business. In the event of losses being incurred, each partner has unlimited liability.

It is very important for people setting up a partnership with unlimited liability that all the partners are trustworthy, honest and hard-working. Otherwise, the mistakes of one may affect all the others financially.

Partnerships are commonly found in the accounting and legal professions, where specialists will join together in a partnership to make the business more attractive to prospective clients.

There are a number of advantages and disadvantages in setting up a partnership. The advantages are:

- as we have said earlier, it is easier for partners than sole traders to raise capital because all of the partners can pool their resources and have access to more capital
- partners can share their expertise and their efforts
- partners can arrange to cover one another at times of illness or holidays, or even lunch breaks
- a partnership, like a sole trader, has the advantage of not having to publish its accounts or have them audited
- additional capital can be raised by introducing more partners into the partnership

There are a number of disadvantages too:

- a partner is personally liable for all of the firm's debts
- disagreements can arise between partners about the amount of effort that each of them puts in
- partnerships can only raise limited amounts of capital as compared with businesses like limited companies (which we will talk about later on)
- decision making can be slow since all partners have to be consulted
- the death or retirement of a member can bring a partnership to an end if such a rule is written into the deed of partnership
- all profits must be shared

student activity

(PC 2.1.2, COM 3.1)
Investigate at least five local accountancy firms and try to discover the number of partners in each of these businesses. Discuss your findings in small groups.

PRIVATE LIMITED (LTD) AND PUBLIC LIMITED COMPANIES (PLC)

The limited company is fast becoming one of the most common forms of business organisation. A limited company is a separate organisation in law from its shareholders and directors.

As with a partnership, individuals put capital into the business – these are known as shareholders – and they own part of the business and will share any profits that are earned. They elect a number of directors who will actually run the business on their behalf.

The law requires a meeting of shareholders to be held once a year, and minuting of matters that may be discussed is required. Shareholders really have little part in the day-to-day running of the business, although they may also be directors.

A number of Companies Acts have been passed over the years which protect the interests of shareholders, as well as those of creditors who are owed money by limited companies.

It is relatively simple and reasonably cheap to set up a company. In order to set up a limited company, two documents must be drawn up:

1 The first is known as a **memorandum of association**. This is really the company's rule book. The kinds of thing that you would find in a memorandum of association are:

- the name of the company
- the address of the registered office
- the company's activities
- the type and amount of capital which has been invested to set the company up

2 The second is what is known as the **articles of association**. These deal with the inside working of the company. They detail the following:

- the procedures that have to be followed at an Annual General Meeting, known as an AGM
- the duties of the directors of the company
- the voting rights of the shareholders
- how profits and losses are distributed among shareholders
- details of how company officers will be appointed
- details of how accounts will be kept and recorded
- the rules and procedures of issuing shares and transferring shares to other people

Once these two documents have been drawn up, the next step is to send them to Companies House. If everything is in order, the Registrar of Companies will issue a certificate of operation, which in effect is like a birth certificate.

There are essentially two different types of limited company. Both of them have a minimum of two shareholders.

1 The first is known as a **private limited company**. You can always tell that a company is a private limited company when the word Limited or Ltd is written after the company name. The shares in a private limited company are not freely available to the general public and the transfer of shares is agreed only by the directors. Private limited companies are usually family concerns, or were originally family concerns. This is the form of organisation often chosen when a sole trader wants to expand or wishes to retain control of the company.

2 The second type of limited company is a **public limited company**. These tend to be larger concerns. They are allowed to raise capital through selling their shares on the Stock Exchange. This gives them greater flexibility in raising capital. They still only need two people to form a public company, and there is no stated maximum number of shareholders.

The process of creating a public company is very similar to that of creating a private company. Once a public company has received a certificate of operation it will prepare a prospectus, which is basically an invitation to the public to buy shares. The people forming the company must decide how those shares are to be sold, and how many shares will be allocated to each prospective buyer. The Registrar of Companies will then issue a trading certificate. This means that the business is now up and running.

One feature common to both types of limited company is that they must file a set of audited accounts with the Registrar of Companies. This set of accounts must include:

- a directors' report
- an auditors' report
- a balance sheet
- the source of application of funds
- an explanation of the accounts

We will deal with all these items later on in the book.

It is also necessary for public limited companies to file an annual return. This gives the details of the directors, shareholders and any other information that is actually required by law. All this information is kept on file at Companies House, and is always open to inspection by members of the public for a small fee.

There are a number of advantages in setting up a limited company as compared with being a sole trader or partner:

- shareholders have limited liability
- it is easier to raise capital through shares
- it is often easier to raise finance through banks
- it becomes possible to operate on a larger scale since, when additional capital is required, additional shares are offered to the public
- it is possible to employ specialists
- suppliers tend to feel a bit more comfortable in trading with legally established organisations

- directors are not liable, provided they follow the rules
- it is easy to pass shares down from one generation to another and in this way control may be kept by the same families
- the company name is protected by law
- there are tax advantages attached to giving shares to employees
- a company pension scheme can give better benefits than those that are available for the self-employed
- the ill-health of shareholders does not affect the running of the business

There are a number of disadvantages associated with becoming a limited company:

- the formation and running costs of a limited company can be expensive
- decisions tend to be slow since there are a number of people involved
- employees and the shareholders are actually distanced from one another
- all the affairs of the company are public, with the audited accounts and annual returns that the company makes being produced
- legal restrictions, under the various Companies Acts, are fairly tight and there are very heavy penalties for companies which break the rules
- large companies are often accused of being impersonal to work for and to deal with
- rates of tax on profits are often higher than those that sole traders and partnerships have to pay

student activity

(PC 2.1.2, COM 3.2, 3.3, IT 3.1, 3.3)
Study a local private company. Who actually owns it and who controls it? Is this the same person or group of people?

Having completed your research, present your findings in the form of a word processed report, attaching any diagrams, photographs, etc. that you feel would enhance your work.

FRANCHISE

The franchise is a form of organisation which has been imported into the UK and the rest of the world from America, where over a third of all retail businesses are operating on what is known as a franchise basis. Again,

this is becoming a very popular form of business organisation in the UK. The main features of franchising are as follows:

1. Franchising really amounts to hiring out or licensing the use of product lines to other companies. A franchise agreement allows another company to trade under a particular name in a particular area. The firm which sells the franchise is known as the franchisor.
2. The person who takes out the franchise needs a sum of money for capital and is issued with a certificate from the franchising company. This person is known as the franchisee. The franchisee usually has the sole right of operating in a particular area. Some examples of franchises can be seen in many of our High Streets – Pizza Hut, Prontaprint, The Body Shop and Spud U Like.
3. Another important feature of the franchise agreement is that the franchisee agrees to buy all of its supplies from the franchisor and the latter makes a profit on these supplies.
4. The franchisor also takes a share of the profits made by the franchisee's business, without having to risk any capital or be involved in the day-to-day management of the business.
5. The franchisee, on the other hand, benefits from trading under a well-known name and enjoys a local monopoly. In other words, each franchisee is the only business to operate under that name in a particular area.
6. The franchise agreement allows people to become their own boss without the normal kinds of risks of setting up a business from scratch.

student activity

(PC 2.1.2, COM 3.1)
In the role of a potential franchisee, investigate the franchise opportunities open to you. Which information sources would you use in order to find this information? Discuss this in pairs.

CO-OPERATIVES

Co-operatives are an increasingly popular type of business organisation. In the past co-operatives were found only in agriculture or retailing. More recently there has been a growth in the number of co-operatives in services and in small-scale manufacturing.

In a co-operative all the people who form part of that organisation join together to make decisions, share the work and also share the profits.

The first successful co-operative was a retail co-operative. It was set up at the end of the last century in Rochdale when weavers joined together to start their own shop selling basic grocery items. Their profits were shared, as was the amount of money they spent, and everyone had an equal say in how the shop was run.

The basic idea behind the Rochdale Co-op (see the Focus Study on p.103) still stands and Co-ops may be seen in High Streets throughout the country. Nowadays, Co-ops are registered as limited liability companies.

FIG. 2.1.3 *The Ipswich and Norwich Co-operative Society Limited is one of many co-operative businesses in the UK.*

Another major area in which co-operatives are found is in production, both in manufacturing and food production. In this type of organisation all the members share the responsibility for the success or failure of the business and work together, making decisions together and taking a share of the profits.

These co-operatives suffer from a number of problems:

1 They often find it difficult to raise capital from banks and other bodies because the co-operatives are not in business just to make a profit.
2 The larger co-operatives have discovered that they must set up a solid management structure in order that decisions can be made.
3 In food production, several farmers will set up what is known as a marketing co-operative, in which each farmer takes responsibility for a particular part of the production of a food, whether it is packaging, distribution or advertising.

Focus study

FRANCHISES

By the turn of the century McDonald's aim to have 1,000 outlets in the UK, and of that total it is expected some 300 will be franchised restaurants.

McDonald's joined the franchising business relatively late (1986), and favour granting additional franchises to existing franchise holders. The franchise deal, in the first instance, runs for some 20 years. McDonald's are very careful in choosing their potential franchise holders, they can pick and choose as the enquiry numbers are large. They look for outgoing people, with a good financial mind, enthusiastic and quite aggressive in business terms. They also favour individuals setting up franchises in their own town or area.

Training lasts for some nine months. There is a 'Hamburger University' in north London and the total cost of the training is around £40,000 per franchisee.

A typical franchisee would need to find some £125,000 (around 40 per cent of the cost of setting up the restaurant).

If an individual wanted to franchise an existing McDonald's restaurant then the cost would be between £100,000 and £1m.! If a potential franchisee is particularly good, but does not have the full 40 per cent investment capital, then with £40,000 a deal could be struck. The balance is paid over a three-year period by putting the restaurant's profits back into the business.

The McDonald's franchise operation has been extremely successful, with only one franchisee having dropped out so far, although some have not made it through the training period. Even with the McDonald's name and reputation, there is no guarantee of success – as with all business ventures it will only be successful if you work extremely hard.

student activity

(PC 2.1.2, COM 3.1)
Again, consulting your local Yellow Pages, try to identify any co-operative organisations in your local area. In which business sectors are they operating? Discuss this with the remainder of your group.

Most of this section, as we will see, is concerned with the more conventional form of co-operative. Increasingly, an ideal way for smaller retailers (in particular) to compete with larger organisations is to join a co-operative alliance. These alliances, also known as 'buying groups', offer many of the advantages that larger organisations enjoy, particularly in relation to purchasing stock. Independent small businesses through their membership of a co-operative alliance or buying group, can obtain many of the following:

● higher levels of discount
● lower initial basic prices
● cheaper or enhanced delivery services

- greater access to a wider variety of products
- enhanced credit terms
- benefits from co-operative marketing and advertising

Prime examples of these types of co-operative alliance or buying groups are:

- *Toymaster* – an independent buying group for toy and hobby shops
- *Spar* – an alliance of independent grocers and off-licences

An additional benefit is passed on to the customer (in most cases) by lower prices or at least prices competitive with those of the major chains.

PUBLIC (STATE, LOCAL AUTHORITY)

There is a vast range of public sector organisations with an equally vast range of objectives. We are going to look at three main areas:

- the government itself
- the people who operate and work in the public sector
- how they relate to the public

STATE

It depends on your point of view whether you approve or not, but the fact remains that the government is involved very deeply in the business life of this country, as indeed are governments throughout the world.

The prosperity of a country, which is measured by the success of the businesses in that country, can be either helped or hindered by the kind of policies which its government adopts. The influence of the government is far-reaching. Increases in government expenditure or the creation of controls over businesses, or indeed support for businesses in a particular area, can have a marked effect.

The government has the means to create wide-scale changes in business activity. Here are some examples:

1. If the government were to increase interest rates this would reduce the general level of spending in the economy, and at the same time it would make it difficult for businesses which have borrowed money to finance projects.
2. When the government gives a contract to one firm rather than another firm it can make the future of the business very secure, or indeed destroy its possibility of survival.
3. If the government reduces the personal taxes that people pay then this may, in fact, prove to be beneficial. The more money a person takes home, the more inclined that person is to work harder. This is known as increasing productivity.
4. If the government were to reduce taxes on a particular product, for example, lead-free petrol, then this

Focus study

CO-OPERATIVES

1994 saw the 150th anniversary of the founding of the first co-operative in Rochdale, Lancashire. Twenty-eight working men formed the Rochdale Equitable Pioneers Society with just £28. They opened a shop where they sold good, wholesome food at reasonable prices. Nowadays, the co-operative movement has never been bigger, the experiment has been copied in over a hundred countries world-wide.

The Co-op is the UK's biggest farmer, with over 45,000 acres of land. They are foremost in the move to stop the testing of products on animals and have not done so since 1984. They were the first supermarket chain to ban CFCs, they have also banned ivory and fur products in their stores and do not allow fox hunting to take place on their land.

Japan has one of the biggest ranges of co-op stores, with a replica of the original Toad Lane shop in their training centre, and even the Imperial Palace in Tokyo has a co-op store for employees.

Co-ops have not just restricted their involvement to farming and the sale of products through their supermarket chains. The Co-op Bank was the first to offer free banking (1973), they support the film industry, brass bands, and make donations to the arts. They financially support Members of Parliament, Members of the House of Lords, EuroMPs, and hundreds of Labour councillors. They are active in the insurance industry, undertaking 170,000 funerals per year, and own the largest hypermarket in the UK in Stockton-on-Tees (covering an area the size of five football pitches).

Internationally, there are 700m. co-op members, one in three Americans are members of co-ops and in Moscow there is a road called Rochdale Street in memory of the pioneers.

Commercially, the movement has been a great success, 99 Tea is the biggest selling 'own brand' in the world, a staggering 5m. cups of tea are drunk every day!

could affect the demand for that product. This in turn can lead to changes in how the product is supplied since the supply would need to be increased to match the increased demand.

The government plays a massive role in the economy in general. Here are some examples:

1. Some goods and services are actually provided by the government because it is felt that every single person is entitled to that product or that service. Good examples of this are health or education.

2 Some goods or services from which everyone benefits can only be provided by the government if they are actually going to be provided properly. A good example of this is the police force.

3 The government is very interested in trying to reduce inequality. This could mean that people who are relatively well off pay a higher tax. This in turn generates money to give to those who are less well off. Some people, however, think that inequality is a good thing because it gives people an incentive to help themselves. Any increases in taxation, of course, will mean that those who are earning higher salaries are taxed more, and in turn they could be less motivated.

4 The government needs to make sure that the economic system as a whole is running well. It passes laws to protect consumers or to prevent companies from controlling particular goods or services. It will take measures against polluters or those involved in anti-social behaviour. In other words the government really sets the rules by which all businesses must comply.

Over time, as the situation changes, the government finds itself required to make amendments to the rules. How do they change? Who loses and who benefits when they change? We will look at these questions later on.

PUBLIC ENTERPRISES

When we think about governments we automatically tend to think about Downing Street, the Houses of Parliament and Whitehall. Although these are important and they are places where the government can be seen in action, the government has many other parts, including organisations which are controlled by the government in some way. These are known as public enterprises, or public corporations. Here are some examples of these:

- British Rail
- British Coal
- the Bank of England
- the Post Office

Since 1979, however, many public corporations have been returned to private hands. Examples of these are:

- British Telecom
- British Gas
- electricity generation

But why did the government get itself involved in running these organisations in the first place? Here are some of the reasons:

1 One of the main reasons is to avoid waste and duplication. In the past many services were offered by different companies. Essentially they were offering

FIG. 2.1.4 *BP, now a successful multinational, was once publicly owned.*

the same thing. For example, in the past private railways ran similar services from the same towns, often having lines running parallel to one another.

2 Many of these organisations offer services which could not be run profitably. The big debate here is on whether a private company would invest in supplying gas or electricity or water to a remote village when even in the long term it would not be able to make a profit.

3 The larger the organisation the more benefits there are in terms of production. Organisations which produce lots of output are able to buy their raw materials more cheaply, their labour can be more concentrated and consequently their prices can be lower.

4 The government is always interested in the level of employment. A good example of this thinking is the relocation of tax offices and social security offices, whose vast headquarters have been set up in relatively remote areas of the country suffering high unemployment. In setting up a public corporation the government might be taking this into consideration.

5 One of the biggest arguments in favour of public corporations is that the government itself needs to control vital basic goods and services which everybody needs. These are known as the infrastructure. This includes the transport network, water and energy. It is argued that the government has a responsibility to make sure that this is supervised and maintained well.

The process of privatisation which turns public corporations into companies owned by shareholders is proceeding rapidly and is sure to step up in the 1990s.

One of the ways of safeguarding the running of a public corporation is to set up an independent body which keeps an eye on it. This organisation copes with complaints that are made against the enterprise and tackles the enterprise should it wish to put up prices or cut services.

Although these public corporations operate independently, they are controlled to some extent by government at all times. It is the government's responsibility to make decisions about closing down parts of the business or investing large sums of money to improve it. On a day-to-day basis the chairperson of the enterprise and the other managers will make decisions about wages, prices, industrial relations, but the government does still interfere when these decisions affect the public.

We have seen that a limited company needs to make an annual report to its shareholders. So, too, does a public corporation, but it presents its annual report to the government minister who is responsible for taking care of it. This government minister makes a report in Parliament to the Members, who will then make criticisms or support the corporation and how it is being run. At the same time a committee made up of Members of Parliament meets on a regular basis to keep an eye on the day-to-day running of the corporation and reports back to Parliament on how it is being operated. This is known as a Select Committee.

In addition to public corporations, there are two other areas where the government gets involved in the business world.

1. The first is when an activity is actually run by a government department. A typical example of this is **Customs and Excise**. They deal with the supervision and collection of taxes due on products entering and leaving the country.
2. The second is when the government has a **shareholding** in a **public company**.

Perhaps the most common form of government organisation is one which touches our lives the most, and this is local government. In the UK certain services are run by locally elected councillors. These councils usually run business organisations such as swimming pools, sports centres, bus services, car parks, shopping centres and public conveniences.

Just like public corporations, local council activities have been affected by privatisation. The particular process used by councils is that of tendering.

The local council details the service it wishes to offer for tender. Companies which are interested in running the service put sealed bids in to the council explaining what it would cost to run the service and what they would be providing. The company that offers the lowest tender is given the job. It is then the council's responsibility to monitor how effective the company is in providing the service. If a company fails to reach

certain standards then the contract is taken away from it. Local government pays for these services by receiving a grant direct from central government and by collecting local taxes. These have been known as rates and community charge and is now called council tax.

Local councils also subsidise loss-making activities such as parks which obviously provide benefits to the community.

Perhaps the strangest form of business organisation is known as a QUANGO. This stands for 'Quasi Autonomous Non-Governmental Organisation'. These are organisations that have been set up by the government to carry out a specific task. In other words, they have been set up to take responsibility for a certain area of the government's business. A good example of this is the Equal Opportunities Commission.

student activity

(PC 2.1.2)
Identify five other QUANGOs apart from the Equal Opportunities Commission.

Focus study

QUANGOS

There is one QUANGO for every 10,000 people in the UK. Nearly 75,000 people are QUANGO members and at a local level, this means that there are twice as many QUANGO members as elected councillors.

Some 99 per cent of QUANGOs are not subject to investigation and monitoring by an ombudsman. Only a third are audited by either the National Audit Office or the Audit Commission, and over 90 per cent do not have to invite the public to their meetings or an annual general meeting.

It is claimed that QUANGOs have taken over the responsibility of decision making and public spending that should be the role of elected individuals. A labour government would abolish these QUANGOs and restore the power to local or nationally elected authorities. At the very least, they would make them subject to supervision by an ombudsman.

2.1.3 *Compare organisational structures*

COMPARISONS

There are many factors which may determine the nature of the organisational structure. We will identify some of them later, but now let us consider them in a slightly different way. Essentially, all the factors fall into two categories:

1 *Internal* – caused by factors within the organisation itself.
2 *External* – caused by factors which may not be in the control of the organisation.

Having made this distinction, we cannot really say that the internal factors are 'self inflicted' as the organisation may need to restructure to gain greater efficiencies or 'iron out' certain problems. The external factors may have been brought about by actions initiated by the organisation in the past. An example of this may be the development of a new product or service that radically changes (over a period of time) the requirements of the customer, the source of raw materials or the need to obtain alternative sources of finance.

Having established that there are numerous forms of business structure, we can now confuse the issue by saying that organisations are never static and are always evolving and changing. First, in this section, we will look at the various criteria which determine the changes themselves.

SIZE

Changes in the size and scope of an organisation's objectives can often mean a radical rethink in the structure of the business. Some organisations may opt for a new and more flexible structure as they diversify and expand. Simply 'tacking on' new parts to an existing structure does not always work. The chain of command and the exercise of authority can become difficult if the organisation experiences 'organic growth'. This growth and consequent structure 'add ons' do not really address the need to restructure. Perhaps the organisation is growing too fast to contemplate a radical change and needs to wait until the 'growth spurt' has slowed down. The danger with this philosophy is that the organisation may have outgrown the structure and be experiencing severe difficulties as a result.

In terms of size itself, the organisation does need to adopt a structure which not only best suits the nature of its operations, but takes into account the fact that not all operations will be carried out at a single site. Equally, the organisation needs to consider whether it is advisable to maintain a hierarchical structure or a more formal structure if the organisation has diversified into a number of different product areas or markets. It is often the case that the senior management, whilst striving to control the organisation as it has always done, does not even understand what some parts of the organisation are doing. If they lack understanding, how can they impose any kind of structure or method of decision making upon them? As we will see later on pp.116–20, this can very much depend upon the management style preferred or adopted by the management of the organisation.

This is perhaps the most obvious reason for changes in the organisational structure. Simpler forms of organisational structure are more relevant in smaller businesses, but as the organisation grows it needs to adapt to even more complex requirements.

Most organisational structures are based on the assumption that the business will expand. This is not the only form of growth. Diversification and changes in the structure are often advisable in preference to simply growing bigger and maintaining the existing general nature of the structure.

LOCATION

As businesses grow, they may need to consider relocation in order to achieve sustained and permanent growth. Moving closer to the source of raw materials, skilled labour or better distribution points may be key considerations in this move. More obvious is the move brought on by growth itself. Perhaps the organisation simply needs larger premises in order to continue its operations successfully.

As previously mentioned, an organisation which has a variety of sites needs to adopt a slightly different structure to accommodate the problems of communication and overall control. Within a single site operation, the organisation must also consider the most appropriate structure for their business. Again, this may depend upon the nature of the business. In service industries, for example, the organisation would be structured towards providing customer service as a priority. For manufacturing organisations, the bulk of the structure considerations would be related to the production process itself, with other departments supporting and servicing the production unit.

Organisational structure may, of course, be related to the premises in which the organisation is located. An inappropriate building may preclude the restructuring of the business since the physical location of each part of the organisation remains fixed. This state of affairs is particularly true of organisations which add on new extensions and buildings to their site without really considering the implications of their placement or location. In these cases, the organisation may not have had the time to spend considering the future when immediate demands for expansion and new accommodation were pressing.

TYPE OF PRODUCT

The changes in structure may be brought about by the nature of the business itself. If the organisation has a variety of diversified products or services, it may be logical to organise in such a way as to separate the management and production in order to establish specific profit centres. Equally, this organisation (often product-based) revolves around the need to attract expertise in a particular area in such a way that the individuals can identify with a particular product or service rather than a whole organisation.

FUNCTIONS AND MEETING BUSINESS OBJECTIVES

As with the type of product the organisation produces, the specific function of the organisation may bring about changes in structure. As we have already said, businesses have a wide variety of different goals. These differing goals and objectives will determine the historical structure of the organisation, as well as the structure best suited to taking that organisation into future successful years. In general terms, an organisation can fall into any of the following categories:

1 *Formal organisations* – these can be defined as those that have established the express purpose of achieving a particular goal or aims or objectives. These sorts of organisations have clearly defined rules and instructions as well as quite highly developed communication between different parts of the organisation. Good examples of these sorts of operations include most businesses, governments and international institutions.

   Because there are so many different forms of formal organisation, we need to clarify this large group a little more carefully. One of the easiest ways is to separate them into productive and non-productive categories, i.e. those that manufacture and those that provide a service.

2 *Informal organisations* – these are also known as social organisations. These tend not to have clearly defined goals; examples of these include families or communities.

The function of the organisation (the reason why it is in operation and the objectives set at the beginning) will strongly determine the type of organisational structure in place. Should these objectives not be met, or should they have to be amended during the course of time, then radical changes to the organisational structure may have to be made.

CHANGES (TO ORGANISATIONAL STRUCTURES, TO LOCATION, TO FUNCTIONS)

As we have mentioned earlier, organisations tend to change their type as they mature or grow. A sole trader may begin a business career with no intention of changing the type of business at all. Growth, changes in legislation or tax incentives may encourage the sole trader to become a limited company. With this change, the organisation will probably need to take on a different structure in order to cope with the new demands placed upon it. Individuals who were employed on a casual and 'when needed' basis may become permanent members of the workforce. Specialists, such as accountants, who had been paid and retained when required may have to be permanently incorporated into the structure.

   With this change in structure and type of business may come a change in ownership itself. If a sole trader enters into a partnership, the ownership will now be split between the original owner and the new partner(s). Equally, a sole trader or partnership that becomes a limited company (particularly a plc) will have to cope with structural and control changes demanded by the shareholders.

   Another form of ownership change is the disposal of an organisation to another party. If this is the case, inevitably, the new owners will institute changes merely because they wish to stamp their own authority and presence on the organisation. Many of these changes will be seen, by the employees in particular, as being changes only for the sake of change and they will have little faith in or degree of support for them.

CHANGES IN WORKING ARRANGEMENTS

As we will see later, technology has a part to play in the changing structure relating to working arrangements. Generally, new demands on the organisation can force change in the working arrangement. These may include:

- change in hours worked (shifts, etc.)
- level of manning (due to technology)
- greater supervision (quality control)
- total hours worked
- relocation to new premises
- multi-skilling (undertaking new and varied tasks)
- re-designing of job tasks

student activity

(PC 2.1.3, COM 3.2, IT 3.1, 3.3)
In the role of a small garage owner, consider the impact on working arrangements in the following circumstances:

- you have just acquired a new dealership with a car manufacturer
- you have just been appointed as an AA/RAC breakdown service
- you have just bought an adjoining building to carry out MOTs

Consider each point separately and present your findings in the form of a word processed report.

CUSTOMERS' REQUIREMENTS

There is, quite rightly, a greater emphasis on the customer and meeting the customers' needs. The traditional concerns with the internal problems and running of the organisation, and, indeed, 'office politics' have slowly given way to other concerns.

Customers require and demand greater levels of service, advice and after-sales service. To this end, the restructuring of the organisation will be needed to provide support for these services, not to mention the training of all staff to cover these considerations.

COMPETITION

As we have discovered already, competition can have a direct impact on the organisational structure.

Any organisation which ignores what the competition is doing may be doomed to failure. Structural changes are often copied within a business sector, particularly if the first organisation to restructure is obviously more competitive and successful. We will return to this aspect shortly.

Apart from the obvious effects on the internal functions and activities of the organisation, competition may force the organisation to consider restructuring in order to stay competitive. A competitive edge, or the ability to 'stay ahead' of the competition can mean the difference between success or failure. All aspects and parts of an organisation can have a role to play in maintaining this advantage over the opposition. Here are some examples of how the structure and the consistent parts of the organisation can contribute:

- *Administration* – by streamlining procedures and cutting down on wastage
- *Sales* – by following up sales leads, customer service and ensuring that key customers are especially well provided for in all aspects
- *Marketing* – by ensuring that products and services are fully researched and supported with appropriate advertising and promotion
- *Distribution* – by maintaining swift, efficient and reliable delivery at all times to all customers
- *Accounts* – by ensuring that all invoicing, statements and other financial documents are correct at all times

student activity

(PC 2.1.3, COM 3.1)
Can you think of other ways that an organisation could remain competitive? Make a list in pairs and compare your list with those of the remainder of your group.

CHANGING MARKETS

The organisation must always be aware that a currently stable situation will not always remain stable. The organisational structure may need to change radically if there is a sudden or unexpected market change. We will see in the Marketing Unit (Unit 3) and the Business Planning Unit (Unit 8) how changes can be dealt with in specific terms, but we need to address how the structure of an organisation may be affected by change. Principally, the organisation may:

- ensure that employee numbers are sufficient to take up extra work, or be capable of redeployment
- ensure that employees are multi-skilled and require minimum retraining to undertake new duties
- ensure that production facilities are flexible enough to respond to changes in production at short notice

- ensure that the management is aware of the necessity to 'keep an eye' on the market, including making regular checks on the competition and market trends
- ensure that the product or service is not wholly reliant on a single market

As we will see later, the nature of a market can depend upon your interpretation. Market can mean:

- the **volume of sales** in total for a product or service
- the **demand** within a specific region for a product or service

student activity

(PC 2.1.3, COM 3.1)
Can you think of any other definitions of the work 'market'? Discuss this in pairs.

Focus study

MARKET CHANGES

Since 1980 trends in drinking habits have changed enormously. There are a number of ways to measure the drinking habits of the population, but consumption is perhaps one of the clearer indicators.

Beer drinking has declined from an average of 147 litres per head per year (counting drinkers over 15 and including off-licence and supermarket sales) to a low of 123 litres in 1993. Consumption of spirits has also fallen since 1980, from 2.2 litres per head per year to 1.9 litres. Cider drinking is becoming more popular now: in 1980 only 5 litres were drunk on average per head per year; this has risen to 9.5 litres.

Wine drinking has shown a marked increase over the same period. In 1980, some 10 litres were drunk per head per year on average, whereas the total now is nearly 17.5 litres.

Among non-alcoholic drinks, by comparison, there has been a significant rise in the consumption of mineral water. There were no figures for 1980, but in 1985 the average consumption was 0.5 litres per head, but by 1993 the figure was nearly 8 litres.

DEMOGRAPHICS

The availability of suitable employees and the proximity to a large market (in population terms) can have an influence on the structure of an organisation.

student activity

(PC 2.1.3, COM 3.1)
In the role of a manager of a public house, say how you would respond to changes in the market's demand. Could you predict the changes before they happened? Discuss your proposed changes with the remainder of your group.

With regard to the availability of employees, the structure may have to be adaptable and include more part-time or casual employees than the organisation would like. Such employees cannot be fully integrated into the organisational structure since they are not full-time or permanent. We will investigate this aspect in a later Unit.

Closeness to markets (in demographic terms) may be a problem for some organisations. If an organisation produces goods which either are inappropriate for the immediate market, or the population density is not great, then it may need to consider having more employees located in various places around the country and closer to the market concentrations. In this sense, conventional organisational structures may not be appropriate since the level of autonomy at these remote sites will need to be developed and accepted. In this respect, the organisation must be willing to allow local decision making to happen (within set guidelines).

Focus study

DEMOGRAPHICS

Tele-working, or working from home via a computer link (modem, etc.), is becoming a useful solution to the availability of labour and the high costs of business premises. The Telecottage Association has just launched the first formal qualification for tele-workers. The 20-week course has been approved by City and Guilds and contains aspects of self-management and communications.

TECHNOLOGY

Gradually, computerised management information systems are making it possible to streamline management and structures. On a higher level, the use of computers allows much greater flexibility in structural terms. It is no longer necessary to locate all of the employees in one large building or a connected series of premises. Outlying units can be directly 'plugged into' the organisation, regardless of their location.

Technology also changes the nature of the structure in relation to production itself. Automation means fewer employees on the shop floor and more in management and supervisory positions. Again, we shall return to this aspect later.

Technology, particularly in the field of information and telecommunications, has radically changed the structure of organisations. The impact on the structure of organisations can best be seen by following the historical development of information systems:

- the invention of the typewriter, in the eighteenth century led to the reduction in the need for all documents to be handwritten
- the invention of morse code at the beginning of the nineteenth century meant that you could communicate (almost instantly) with anywhere in the world
- the invention of the telephone at the end of the nineteenth century meant that organisations could communicate readily and directly orally
- the invention of the cellode ray tube began the gradual invention of screens
- in 1920 electronic typewriters were produced, which reduced the need for so many typists
- after the Second World War, the calculator was developed, leading to structural changes in accounting and finance
- by 1950 a business could long-distance direct dial using the telephone, reducing the number of people in the older forms of communication (such as letter delivery)
- in 1956 IBM produced the disk drive, leading to restructuring of office equipment needs and staffing
- in 1964 IBM released a basic form of word processor, leading eventually to a reduction in administration and secretarial employees
- in 1971 Intel produced computer chips, greatly reducing the cost of computers and speeding up structural change
- now we have mobile phones, lap-top computers, video phones and total and wide area networked computers, all of which have had marked effects on the structure of organisations

Provided an organisation has a reliable form of technology, then it can concentrate on other issues.

student activity

Can you identify any other inventions which have radically affected employee numbers or the structure of an organisation?

Discuss your thoughts with the remainder of your group.

ORGANISATIONAL STRUCTURES

Many organisations have traditionally been organised in a form of pyramid structure. Individuals at each level of the pyramid (or hierarchy) are fully aware of their rank and their position in the organisation. Each individual should also know his or her particular role within the organisation. As we will see, this formalised 'chain of command' is well suited to allow orders and instructions to be passed down the pyramid and for information to be readily transmitted up the pyramid. The structure depends on many factors. These include:

1. *The number of employees* – in effect the actual size of the organisation.
2. *Type of premises used* – a multi- or split-site organisation with a number of different branches would need to be organised in a radically different manner from an organisation which is based in a single building.
3. *Type of business*

  - If the organisation is in the **primary** sector, it is likely to be organised in such a way as to allow as efficient processing of the raw materials as possible, and may be based around a single mine, forest or quarry.
  - A **manufacturing** organisation may either carry out all of its processing procedures on a single site, or need to transport partly finished goods to other specialist sites. Organisation in this case may be based on the single factory unit, or a cluster of factories which contribute towards the finished product. Distribution organisations tend to be organised in a regional, national or international framework. Depending on the bulk of goods being distributed, the organisational structure will be complex in certain geographical areas and simpler in others. In other words, if the

organisation is busy in one area, the size and complexity will reflect this. As with many organisations, good communications between the regions are vital and a separate part of the organisational structure may concentrate on dealing with communications.

- In the **retailing** sector the obvious organisational structure is that of the branch. However, many functions of the business are carried out centrally. These services tend to be of a managerial, financial or buying nature, and this allows the individual branches to concentrate on the selling process.
- **Professional** services tend to operate on the basis of a number of specialist individuals who are assisted by a variety of support staff. Often these support staff are drawn from a 'pool' of clerical and secretarial employees.

4 *The number, type and size of the clients* – if the organisation deals with only a handful of clients, then the structure need not be overly complex. On the other hand, if it is dealing with literally millions of retail customers, then the demands on the structure may be much greater.

5 *The past structure and history of the organisation* – an old-fashioned organisation which has successfully managed to survive for many years may not see the need to change its structure. It may not appreciate the benefits of reorganisation and may be structured in such a way as to prevent the possibility of growth or adaptation to new demands.

6 *The current structure* – this can again be a positive or negative influence on the day-to-day running of the business. If the organisation has recently undergone changes, it will be unlikely to adapt to further changes without encountering considerable problems.

7 *The future needs* – the need to constantly react to changing demands, diversify into new areas and respond to changes in legislation are all strong reasons to consider how the organisation is structured.

As we have seen, the structure of an organisation will vary depending on the nature of a number of factors:

- the size and nature of the market in which it operates
- the type of business it is involved in
- the maintenance of good communications
- the size of the organisation
- the number of branches, outlets and sites
- the type and number of clients
- how much it is affected by government legislation
- impact of new technologies

- nature and extent of responsibilities and obligations
- past and current structure
- future plans
- complexity of business activity

At this point we shall look at all the different varieties of organisational structure and later try to assess their appropriateness in different situations.

SIMPLE ORGANISATIONAL STRUCTURES

The simplest organisational structure is that of the person who work on his/her own. This person would obviously be responsible for everything that the organisation does. Someone, for example, who set up a Mail Order business would be responsible for buying in products, designing the catalogue, getting it printed, carrying out market research to find the kind of person who would buy the products, researching a mailing list, sending out catalogues, taking orders, despatching goods, dealing with any correspondence, paying bills, banking cheques, doing the accounts and a hundred other things. In this situation the individual who is running the business is at the centre of everything.

The larger the organisation, the more need there is for people who specialise in a particular area. Good examples of these are bank managers, solicitors, accountants. All of these people have specialist skills and can take some of the responsibility off an individual business person's shoulders.

As a business expands it needs to employ people, some part-time, some full-time. As the business expands the person who set up the company needs to think about what has to be done. The business needs to be organised in the best possible way to meet the objectives that have been set for it. The owner of the business needs to define exactly what individuals do, precisely what the various departments are responsible for. Who will supervise the employees? Who should tell them what to do? Where does everyone fit into the organisation? And who is ultimately responsible? This is known as the division of labour and specialisation.

The division of labour involves breaking down the process of producing things or providing services into clearly defined specialist tasks. The fact is that if the process is broken down into these separate tasks then production can actually be increased. Instead of one person trying to do everything, everybody who works as part of the production process of goods or services specialises. Specialisation means being more efficient. What kind of advantages are there in specialisation?

1 Resources can actually be concentrated where they are needed the most.

2 If the worker becomes more efficient at doing a particular job he/she becomes more skilled.

3 Specialisation allows greater output. This means that each item produced is made more cheaply because the labour involved in producing it is less for each unit.

4 If people specialise then they can pass on their skills and experience to others and help them become more efficient.

5 If people specialise then hopefully they can get a better standard of living. By specialising people can develop their own talents and are able to trade what they can do with other people.

6 By specialising in one job a person can do that job well rather than doing lots of jobs badly.

There are some disadvantages of specialisation:

1 Specialisation can often lead to jobs becoming very boring. Simple repetition of the same task day in day out demoralises people and they can become less efficient.

2 Specialisation is always dependent on how good or efficient the specialists in the previous task were. If workers are not as efficient or as fast at every stage of production this can cause bottlenecks.

3 There is a tendency in specialisation for workers to become little more than machines. This, in turn, could lead to loss of skill.

4 Specialising actually reduces a worker's ability to adapt to change.

5 Those who specialise have only a narrow view of the product or service which they are actually producing. Someone who makes an article from start to finish has a better overview and can help to make things more efficient in the long run.

DIVISIONAL ORGANISATIONAL STRUCTURES (BY FUNCTION, BY PRODUCT, DIVISIONS OF MULTINATIONALS)

Larger organisations often need to take a radically different approach to their structure. In particular, organisations whose operations are complex and span several different countries find it impossible to adopt more traditional forms of organisational structure. As we will see, there are three major methods (which are all essentially divisional in nature) that can be used to facilitate control, efficiency and communications, these are:

1 *Division by function* – in this form of structure the organisation has identified its key functions and has either an individual (or in the case of larger organisations, a department) which oversees this function throughout all subdivisions of the organisation.

2 *Division by product* – as we will shortly see (Figure 2.1.5), Philip Morris, a multinational organisation, has identified not only trade name subdivisions, but below this, product subdivisions. Each subdivision is semi-autonomous (partly independent) but has clearly stated goals, objectives and profits to achieve.

3 *Divisions of multinationals* – again, using the Philip Morris example, and bearing in mind that the organisation operates in a variety of different countries throughout the world, it is logical that the organisational structure reflects this diversity and potential control headache. In this way, as we will see, an organisation such as this can choose to invest, examine or sell off a subdivision as it sees fit.

Departmentalisation is the process by which an organisation has certain functions which it carries out, grouped logically under a particular manager. There are usually five ways of grouping employees or the things an organisation does. These are:

1 by what they **produce** – known as the product
2 by their **function** – in other words what they do for the organisation
3 by **process** – which means how they do it
4 by **geographical area** – which may be various regional offices or separate companies
5 by **type of customer** – for example they may deal with other business organisations, or they may deal with retail

FUNCTIONAL ORGANISATIONAL STRUCTURES

A functionally based organisational structure is usually designed around the specific parts of the organisation that produce, market and sell the product or service. The actual substructure of the organisation may take a variety of forms, either hierarchical or flat, for example.

Typically, a structure adopting the functional system will be controlled by a managing director who is supported by a range of senior managers. Each of the managers has responsibility for the direction of a specific function of the organisation. These functions could include:

● advertising
● finance and accounting
● personnel
● production
● purchasing
● sales

PRODUCT DIVISIONS

An alternative to basing the organisational structure on function is to base it around product(s) or ranges of

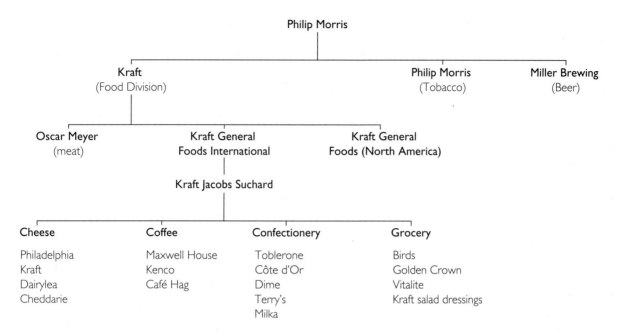

Note: At the product end of the operation, the majority of the brands are available in at least four European countries. In terms of the confectionery, for example, they are market leaders in Austria, Belgium, Denmark, France, Norway and Sweden. In ground coffee, they are Europe's leading brand.

FIG. 2.1.5 *Philip Morris — a multinational organisation.*

products. As we will see when we consider the divisions of multinationals, it is easy to identify how an organisation has grown (organically by acquiring other organisations and incorporating them into the larger organisation, but maintaining their individual identity). Such a structure might also show that the organisation values its individual brand names or product names (particularly in cases where the same product is known under various different names across the world). An example of this is the Snickers bar which was known by this name in all countries except the UK. In order to establish its name world-wide, Nestlé decided to give up the name Marathon for ease of marketing, distribution and promotion.

Another reason for dividing an organisation by product is to establish a series of cost or profit centres. Essentially, this means that specific spending related to a particular product can be identified, as can any profits generated by that product.

If a multinational organisation acquires another organisation in a different country, it is probably not a good idea immediately to change the name of a 'household name' which may have been trading very well for a number of years. Again, for this reason, we will find divisions by product where, in some cases, the situation was beneficial to the purchaser, and in others, the name will be changed to that of a more internationally known trade or brand name.

DIVISIONS OF MULTINATIONALS

Large multinationals may have literally dozens of separate companies or divisions being directed, to some extent, by a head office or 'holding company'. Typically, in real terms, the head office is comparatively small. This is always dependent upon the degree to which the head office is involved in the day-to-day running of the subsidiaries.

Each of the individual companies or divisions is relatively autonomous (or free) to make its own decisions on general matters. It is only at corporate level that the head office exerts its influence upon them. General guidelines would, of course, have been created by the head office to ensure that there is guidance on most decisions that have to be made.

Unilever, the multinational chemicals giant, is divided up into some 500 separate companies, 50 of which operate in the UK alone! All of the 500 operate under guidelines issues by the parent company. In each country there is a national manager who has responsibility for all facets of the organisation's activities. The role of co-ordinating the efforts of the different national managers is undertaken by a director in the parent company. It is this individual who assists in setting the policies for each country grouping. In this way, the organisation as a whole and in any one country, can respond to developments whether related to the competition, consumers or government.

MATRIX ORGANISATIONAL STRUCTURES

This form of organisational structure provides the opportunity to dispose of the more normal departmental boundaries. Typically used in Japan, this system allows for teams to be created that consist of a number of individuals from various different parts of the organisation but brought together to undertake a particular task. This can mean that individuals may have their regular manager to answer to, as well as the project leader.

The system appears to work quite well, and has the advantage that team members are able to meet without direct reference to their departments. Also, it allows more individuals to be brought in to use their expertise when needed. Unfortunately, it is often the case that both managers (departmental and project) make too great a demand on the time and effort of the individuals. There is also a blurring of the lines of accountability, particularly if the project flounders or fails.

CENTRALISED ORGANISATIONAL STRUCTURES

There are two different ways of looking at centralised structures, both of which contain features of many of the other types of organisational structures. Indeed, they may actually be organised in another way, but they have centralised features.

1 *Centralised services* – this version of a centralised structure involves the reorganisation of key services to provide for the organisation as a whole. In this structure, it would be common to find the reprographics (printing functions) centralised and controlled in such a manner as to provide cross-organisational services. Central control means that the service should be more efficient in terms of work through-put and output, and it also attempts to keep costs down (by the non-duplication of staff roles, etc.).
2 *Centralised decision making* – in larger organisations that do not favour a decentralised approach to decision making, it may be preferred to concentrate command and decision functions in a few individuals. They will be supported by a variety of employees and will be responsible for cross-organisational decision making. Organisations favouring such a structure are often more traditional, or they rely on the expert knowledge of a handful of specialist individuals.

The main advantages of a centralised organisational structure are:

● decisions can be made quickly
● specialist staff can be used
● larger discounts can be obtained by centralising purchasing

The main disadvantages are:

● there is little opportunity for total decision making
● individuals lack the opportunity to learn about the decision-making process
● centralised power can be misused

DECENTRALISED ORGANISATIONAL STRUCTURES

In recent years, some major organisations have recognised that relying on a pyramid structure has prevented quick and necessary decisions and change from taking place and have adopted a new form of structure, which is commonly known as decentralisation. This is the exact opposite to having centralised services which assist individual branches or sites. Each part of the organisation that carries out a distinctly different function in the organisation is given a level of autonomy. This means that they are allowed, up to a point, to make decisions for themselves without the permission or consent of the directors or the central office. This allows each sub-organisation to be more flexible and responsive to its own needs and customers without having to wait for a central office to consider any points of concern that have been passed on to them. Most typically the structure consists of a central 'holding' company (these are the owners of several companies who, while they are interested in the profits and decisions made by their companies, do not meddle in the day-to-day business) which has devolved (passed down power and authority) responsibility to each company forming part of the group.

The main advantages are:

● local decisions can be made by local managers
● individuals can learn about the management process
● head office managers can concentrate on the strategic decisions
● there is a greater overall freedom of decision making

The main disadvantages are:

● the organisation can be difficult to supervise and control
● conflict often occurs between different parts of the organisation
● unless the policies are clear, then the decisions made can be in conflict with corporate strategy

FLAT ORGANISATIONAL STRUCTURES

This is essentially a version of the hierarchical structure, but it has a number of different features. It should be remembered, however, that this is still a pyramid-style structure, but one with few layers.

The theory behind having fewer layers in the pyramid is that decisions can be made quickly and efficiently. Each layer is able to communicate easily with other layers and the organisation avoids the danger of becoming 'bureaucratic'. This simpler structure is generally found in organisations operating from a single site where directors and other decision makers are readily available for consultation and guidance. Employees find it easier to understand the reasoning behind the directors' decisions and therefore feel more a part of the organisation and less isolated.

Equally, junior managers and other employees are more motivated as they are often given more responsibility through delegation.

HIERARCHICAL ORGANISATIONAL STRUCTURES

The best way to understand what a hierarchical structure looks like is to imagine a pyramid. At the top of the pyramid are the owners or major decision makers of the organisation. As we look further down the pyramid the shape of the organisation broadens as more employees are involved at each level. At the base of the pyramid are the majority of the employees and below them are the customers. Responsibility, power and authority are all much greater at the top of the pyramid than at the bottom. Decisions flow down the pyramid affecting successive layers of employees.

This form of structure is said to have a 'pecking order' as the higher up the pyramid you are as an employee, the more power and authority you have. Equally, we can see that the lower down the pyramid you are, the less influence you have on the organisation as a whole.

The reason for this hierarchical structure is that important decisions need to be made by those who have expertise and experience along with enough authority to make sure that the decision is implemented. Those at the top of the pyramid take all the credit for success, but also bear the consequences of failure.

Typically, we would see a structure that would begin with directors at the top of the pyramid making decisions for heads of department below to pass on to middle managers who would then tell the junior members of staff to implement them. The higher an individual is in the pyramid, the less likely he/she is to understand precisely how decisions are implemented at the lower levels. These individuals may just have an idea of overall strategy and base their decisions on information received via the various layers below them. Each time information passes from layer to layer, the relative importance of what has been said may change. It is therefore likely that those at the top of the pyramid will have a distorted view of the organisation and how it really works.

For those at the bottom of the pyramid, the directors will seem remote, unable to understand the organisation's needs and unwilling to change decisions which may adversely affect the day-to-day running of the business.

The main advantage of this structure is that each layer sees the organisation in its own peculiar way. Each layer will have different opinions, priorities and interpretation of the overall organisational policy.

The main version of the hierarchical structure is the steep pyramid. In this version of the hierarchical structure there are many layers of management. The reason for the number of layers may be that the organisation operates in several different locations and needs to duplicate the administration in order to function efficiently. Alternatively, the nature of the business may be very complex, requiring the processing of many orders, messages, pieces of information or complaints.

Because the structure is multi-layered and complicated, those further down the pyramid find it difficult to understand how and why decisions are made and the organisation may find it impossible to make sure that the employees follow through 'corporate decisions' (general statements of policy and procedures). The organisation may also suffer from being 'bureaucratic'. This means that decisions must pass through so many layers that they take a very long time to put into operation, and the systems designed to help implement them become more complicated than they need to be.

CO-OPERATIVE ALLIANCE ORGANISATIONAL STRUCTURE

As we have mentioned earlier when looking at co-operatives as a form of business organisation, these are organisations run by a group of individuals with a financial interest in their success and a say in how their own organisation is managed.

The more straightforward co-operative has already been described in full, however, but there is another type of organisation, a co-operative alliance, the nature of which may be somewhat different. This form of organisation, is rather like the divisions of a multinational. In other words, each member (or independent business) is free to make its own day-to-day business decisions. The members, unlike the divisions of a multinational, are not accountable to a head office in respect of their profits or decisions. It is only when we consider the purchasing function of the organisation that we can more readily draw parallels with a multinational. In this respect, we should consider the purchasing function as being centralised. Each independent business does not order directly from the supplier, rather, they order via a central office or buying group.

The costs of the central office or buying group employees are offset by an extra few per cent of discount offered by the suppliers but not passed on to the independent businesses. In other words, the viability of this central purchasing unit is reliant upon the business fortunes of the members of the alliance. In times when the independent businesses are purchasing relatively large quantities (collectively), the purchasing unit can make a reasonable profit. In difficult times, when the purchase levels are lower, they may find it difficult to cover costs.

Normally, the independent businesses will be visited by the suppliers direct in order to inform them of new product availability or ideas. However, the independent businesses will not (necessarily) buy direct from that supplier. Suppliers are well aware of this situation and although they would prefer the independent business to buy direct (since they would not have to offer such large discounts), the buying group alliance is honoured.

The central purchasing unit, in whichever form it takes, will probably have regional representatives who can inform the independent businesses of special offers, trends and promotions. They will also co-ordinate marketing and advertising which is usually paid for by means of a subscription by the independent businesses. By pooling the advertising and marketing budgets, the members of the organisation can acquire far better deals from the media and printers.

OTHER ORGANISATIONAL STRUCTURES

1 *Geographically based structures* – Retail businesses generally use this form of structure as it best fits with the demands that will be made of regional and local managers. Using a traditional hierarchical structure, in the main, the organisation will take the form of a relatively small head office, which supports a number of regional offices. These regional offices have various support functions to assist the outlets within that area. In other cases, manufacturing organisations may have a similar structure, particularly when they have widely dispersed factories throughout the country.

student activity

(PC 2.1.3, COM 3.1)
What organisations can you think of that may use the geographical method of structuring? Discuss this in pairs.

2 *Market-based structures* – Some organisations are structured to cater for each of their major markets. If an organisation produces a wide range of different products, it may well be advised to have separate

companies or subsidiaries to exploit each market (see also divisions of multinationals on p.113).

3 *Product-based structures* – In many respects this is a similar structure to that of the market-based organisation. Each company/division or unit will be responsible for all of the activities related to a particular product. The product divisions will also have their own manufacturing, accounting, sales and purchasing departments.

student activity

(PC 2.1.3, COM 3.1)
What organisations can you think of that may use the product-based method of structuring? Discuss this in pairs.

4 *Mechanistic* – These are functionally divided with clearly identifiable chains of command. Each task carried out by the individuals making up the organisation is clearly defined. In this way orders filtering through from the top of the organisation are carried out to the letter. Because of this accountability and rigid structure organisations like this seem to take on the qualities of a machine, hence the name.

5 *Organic* – In these organisations, many of the job roles have been somewhat blurred, as the definition of tasks and duties change according to the needs of the organisation. Individuals work as part of a network, where communication is easy and the authority to make decisions is readily available. Although there are roles within the organisation that relate to the direction of the work, the actual carrying out of the tasks can differ according to the nature of the work in hand.

6 *Bureaucratic* – These are largely hierarchical in structure, but with a high reliance on adhering to the rules of the organisation and following accepted procedures.

7 *Autocratic* – Again, these usually have a hierarchical structure, in which the decisions are made by a single individual who requires unquestioning support and reaction to his/her directives.

MANAGEMENT STYLES

Each management role involves the use of authority and some degree of leadership. Organisations can be described as 'power systems'. Individuals who become employees have to give up some of their independence in order to function within the organisation.

Just how the authority is used in the organisation can determine how the organisation actually functions and also affects all of its internal relationships. In the army, for example, a clear line of responsibility, authority and power has been established and is clearly understood. The new recruit knows he/she is dependent upon the sergeant, and the sergeant knows to salute and take orders from the officer. In a business organisation, these clear distinctions may not be so obvious. What is clear is that any leader or manager does require a degree of obedience from the subordinates. The notion of leadership implies that the individuals in a management position have the 'right' combination of skills and abilities. The manager needs to be able to obtain effective performance from the employees. The manager does not just need these personal skills and abilities, but also needs to be aware of the employees' needs. As we shall see, some leadership styles ignore the needs of the employee entirely.

Leadership style refers to the way in which the individual manages the employees. The leader's style may result in the following:

- respect
- affection
- trust
- loyalty

The two key aspects of leadership hinge upon the manager's attitudes and abilities to delegate and consult. This is a recurring theme in the leadership styles we will now consider.

POWER AND AUTHORITY THEORY

The German social scientist, Max Weber, was very interested in management style and organisational structure. He identified three different types of organisations and used these to illustrate his theory:

1 *Charismatic leadership* – where the employees were devoted to their leader and worked hard as a result (e.g. a political party).
2 *Rational-legal leadership* – due to the skills and expertise of the leaders, they are respected and accepted by the employees.
3 *Traditional leadership* – when the authority is derived from custom and practice.

MANAGEMENT PROFILE THEORY

Henry Fayol, a French social scientist, developed a list of key management qualities and functions:

1 *Division of work* – all employees know what their duties are.
2 *Authority* – clear, unambiguous and complete.
3 *Discipline* – rigid and firm if required, but in any case clearly understood.
4 *Unity of command* – all aspects of the organisation are managed in the same manner.
5 *Unity of direction* – the organisation has a clear corporate strategy.
6 *Subordination* – individuals within the organisation put the business first and their personal interests and needs second.
7 *Remuneration* – a fair wage for a fair day's work.
8 *Centralisation* – essentially a cost-effective measure, but ensures that like tasks are concentrated and not duplicated.
9 *Scalar chain* – all individuals within the organisation know their own position within it. This is easily achieved by the production of an organisational chart.
10 *Order* – the organisation does its best to avoid conflict within the organisation.
11 *Equality* – basically, equal opportunities, regardless of age, sex, sexual orientation, handicap or creed.
12 *Stability of tenure* – making sure that the employees are not concerned and worried about their job security.
13 *Initiative* – the organisation encourages the creation of ideas and readily accepts them if they will work. Also, this means that certain decisions can be made without reference to senior managers.
14 *Esprit de corps* – a French saying, derived from the military, which means that there is a 'company spirit'. In other words, individuals are proud to support the aims and objectives of the organisation.

SOLIDARITY THEORY

The Australian, Elton Mayo, investigated factories to discover why individuals feel more or less content with their job and role. Mayo found three quite interesting things:

- that output and motivation (interest in the job) improved when employees were being observed by him
- that peer pressure (from work mates) contributed to the level of support by the individuals within that group
- that the group had strong feelings about what was possible and reasonable and that this was as important as their reaction to demands from the management

SELF-ACTUALISATION THEORY

The American sociologist, Abram Maslow, produced a theory that motivation and leadership style should be based upon the employees' needs. Although this may sound one-sided, it showed that it was in the organisation's best interests to consider the fact that a well-motivated employee needs to acquire or be given certain support and incentives.

The 'hierarchy of needs', as it became known, is a well-researched and applied leadership style of management. What it says is that every individual needs a series of ever-more complex achievements and goals in order to be truly motivated. The first needs are 'physiological needs'. These are the most basic 'life-supporting' needs, such as food, housing, warmth and clothing, and individuals' first motivation in working is to satisfy these needs.

The second level, known as 'safety', refers to the employees' belief that they are secure in their job and do not face the sack for a trivial or unimportant reason.

Building on to this is the third need, 'social belonging'. This means that the individual is socially acceptable. This may be seen in the nature of the job, the job description, job title or the way in which society in general views the job he/she does.

The fourth level of need is known as 'esteem'. This is the way in which the individual is viewed as a person and as an employee. An individual who has achieved respect from his/her colleagues and has good solid standing in the country in respect of the job he/she undertakes is likely to be more motivated than others who have not.

The final level of the needs of the employee is called 'self-actualisation'. This refers to the individual's belief that he/she has achieved (career-wise) what he/she set out to achieve. The individual is content that he/she can do the job well and has received recognition for doing so. It should be noted that an individual cannot be expected to achieve those higher states of motivation until the basic ones have been gained first.

MOTIVATION AND HYGIENE THEORY

Frederick Herzberg's investigation of accountants and engineers in the USA brought forward another angle to the theory of leadership, motivation and management. He identified five major motivations, and we will look at these first.

1 *Achievement* – that the individual feels that something has been accomplished by his/her labours.
2 *Recognition* – that others (and management) realise that the role the individual is playing in the organisation is important and is appreciated.
3 *The work itself* – that the job provides variety and interest and is not crushingly boring.
4 *Responsibility* – that the employee has enough freedom to make his/her own decisions and that the individual is given a job role that meets or reaches his/her potentials.
5 *Advancement* – that the employee perceives that

he/she can be promoted if his/her skills and performance warrant it.

The *hygiene factors* that Herzberg identified are features of the work or organisation that help to maintain an individual's 'good feelings' about the job, but do not necessarily motivate in themselves. Typical hygiene factors include:

- wages/salaries
- bonuses/commission
- working conditions
- supervision (quality of)
- working environment
- job security

X AND Y THEORY

McGregor, an American management consultant identified two radically different leadership and management styles:

1 *Theory X* – where organisations and their management believe that the employees are lazy and do not work hard unless they are very closely supervised. In these organisations tough and unrelenting managers would be common.
2 *Theory Y* – where organisations and their management believe that their employees do want to work hard. They can be relied upon and will perform well if the organisation provides a reasonable and supportive working climate.

SUPPORTIVE RELATIONSHIPS THEORY

Likert, another American theorist, put forward the notion that if the management created an environment where individuals were encouraged to 'network' and support one another, then the employees would be able to work well together. Specifically, he cited that a good and effective leadership style would:

- be helpful and friendly
- be concerned with employees welfare
- be supportive
- be fair, but firm
- encourage employees' development
- support staff with problems
- protect weaker employees
- be expert and well organised
- be good at planning
- live up to employees' expectations of them

TRAIT THEORY

In this theory, a number of key qualities were identified which helped map out the ideal management and leadership style. These were:

- articulateness (good speaking skills)

- convincingness
- co-operativeness
- decisiveness
- determination
- drive
- initiative
- ability to get things done
- insight (forward-looking)
- perception (can see future pitfalls)
- self-assuredness (confident)

It is probable that there are many other ideal traits.

student activity

(PC 2.1.3)
Can you think of at least another five ideal traits?

STYLE THEORY

The style theory maintains that the leadership style of the management is first dependent on the following:

- the nature of the organisation's business
- the historical management
- the structure of the organisation

These theorists then propose that leaders will be in one of the following categories:

- *dictatorial* – where the leadership style is harsh and unremitting. Employees are expected to do as they are told at all times
- *benevolent autocratic* – where the leadership is less strict, but adheres to very clear (and historical) sets of rules and procedures
- *consultative* – where the organisation encourages employees to take a role in the decision making
- *democratic* – where the organisation positively encourages participation from all employees at all stages of the decision-making process

LEADERSHIP GRID THEORY

Several management consultants have supported this theory of leadership and management style. Essentially, it is a follow-up of Style Theory. This theory contends that leaders believe either that:

- employees need support in achieving a goal or completing a task, or
- the task and job in hand are more important than

the needs of the employees

Obviously, the ideal leadership style lies somewhere between the two.

CONTINGENCY THEORY

Fielder, yet another American theorist, put forward the theory that leaders switch from being task orientated to employee orientated, depending upon how the leader was getting on with his/her employees at the time.

Many theorists do not accept this view as research has shown both of the following:

- a task-centred approach was always successful regardless of the leader's relationship with his/her employees
- an employee-centred approach was always most successful, regardless of the relationship status

'BEST FIT' THEORY

In this theory, the balancing of three elements makes up the leadership style. The three elements are:

- *the task* – the job in hand
- *the employees or team* – those who will undertake the task
- *the leader* – the individual responsible for directing the team and allocating the tasks

If you imagine a triangle, with a short base and longer verticals, you will begin to understand the nature of this theory. The two most important elements are represented by the long verticals, and the subordinate third element occupies the base. In a situation where a quick decision and action needs to be undertaken, then the leader and the task occupy the verticals, with the employee on the base (subordinate).

PAY-BACK THEORY

This theory is typified by the phrases 'nothing for nothing' or 'what's in it for me?' Career-orientated employees would drive hard bargains and always negotiate with their managers on the questions of role, tasks and duties.

MANAGEMENT BY OBJECTIVES THEORY

Using this theory, the organisation establishes and supports a range of meetings to discuss the following:

- objectives and targets to be achieved by the employees
- setting a timescale for the above
- negotiation of the objectives
- agreeing the objectives with the employees
- setting the deadlines
- quantifying the objectives (i.e. how they will be measured)

The outcome of this theory is a more task-based leadership style. It is a feature of the implementation of this theory that employees are often ignored during the process and they then have to suffer the consequences of ill-considered demands and deadlines.

One outcome of the management by objectives theory was the development of staff appraisal, performance measuring and more reasonable pay scales.

EXPECTANCY THEORY

Vroom, Lawler and Porter put forward this theory to suggest that the relationship between people's behaviour at work and their goals was not as simple as was first imagined. The theory proposed that:

- each individual has different goals
- individuals will only try to achieve their goals if they think that they have a reasonable chance of achieving them

One way of classifying goals is the following:

- a direct goal is achieving better performance
- an indirect goal results from achieving the direct goal

The value of the goal, in personal terms, affects motivation and behaviour.

Focus study

PRIVATE V. PUBLIC

New Force Co. Ltd.

1 *Purpose of organisation*

New Force is a franchised distributor of electrical components. Distributors act as the 'middlemen' between the customer and the producer of a product or service. The producers tend to want to sell their products in reasonable quantities and to achieve this they appoint distributors, who act rather like regional warehouses for them. The distributor deals directly with the customer (or end-users) who do not, necessarily, want to buy in bulk. The distribution industry is known for its fierce competition and often small profit margins. Therefore, in order to survive, a company has to be extremely efficient.

2 *Type of ownership*

New Force is a small to medium-sized distribution company servicing the electronics industry. New Force is a private limited company, whose major shareholder is Phil Cunningham. It operates from an industrial unit on a trading estate in Kent. Many of New Force's competitors are of a similar size and ownership type. It is only when such organisations reach a point at which they diversify into the distribution of different electrical components that they tend to become public limited companies.

3 *Organisational structure*

New Force's organisational structure reflects the fact that it is mainly a sales-orientated organisation. It does not manufacture products, but concentrates on the sale and distribution aspects. New Force's organisational structure is quite simple, as Figure 2.1.6 illustrates.

New Force's organisational structure may appear to be quite hierarchical in nature, but Phil Cunningham is keen to allow his employees freedom and the ability to make decisions without always clearing them with him first.

4 *Job roles*

(a) Phil Cunningham – Managing Director

Phil's main daily task is the management of the organisation. However, he has several other roles to undertake:

- he is the main point of contact with his suppliers
- he negotiates and places orders with suppliers
- he accompanies members of the sales team on visits to important clients when needed
- he liaises with, and offers suggestions to his suppliers regarding new product ideas
- he is responsible for placing and writing advertisements (mainly in the trade press)

Phil relies on his key employees, Donald Sullivan (to ensure stock levels are correct and that orders are despatched), Jasuinda Patel (to ensure the financial condition of the company is readily accessible), Jenny Anderson (to ensure that the sales team are working well and are supported) and Toni James (to ensure that Phil's activities and duties are organised and well structured).

(b) Jenny Anderson – Tele-sales/Field Sales Manager

Jenny's job is extremely hectic, she directs the work of five people, two based in the office and three who are 'out on the road'. Jenny directs the telephone sales efforts of Patricia Johnston and Richard Lewis, who systematically 'cold-call' potential customers and telephone existing contacts set up by the Field Sales team. The three Field Sales employees, John Dixon, Arthur Hemmings and Chris Herold are all given sales targets and expected to visit a number of customers each day.

(c) Jasuinda Patel – Accounts Manager

Jasuinda's job is to ensure that the financial information relating to New Force is as up to date and accessible as possible. She directs Shirley Price in carrying out the routine book-keeping operations. Jasuinda is also responsible for credit control, debt collection and the mailing of statements of accounts to the customers.

(d) Donald Sullivan – Stores Manager

Donald's main job is to ensure that the stock levels are maintained at the agreed level and to make sure that Frank Righton and John Horne despatch the orders within 24 hours of receiving the order. He informs Phil when stock levels are approaching re-order level so that Phil can contact the suppliers.

(e) Toni James – PA (Personal Assistant) and Secretary

Toni's job involves ensuring that Phil does everything that he needs to do in a particular day. Phil admits that without Toni he could not possibly cope with the demands of the company. Toni prioritises the tasks Phil needs to complete and carries out many of the duties Phil delegates to her. Her role is so key to the running of the organisation that Phil fully accepts (as do the rest of the company) that Toni deputises for him in his absence.

(f) John Dixon, Arthur Hemmings, Chris Herold – Field Sales Team

These three employees are very experienced and know the market very well. They each have responsibility for a part of the country (see the organisational chart). They are answerable directly to Jenny Anderson and Phil Cunningham. They act as the liaison and main sales contact with all customers and potential customers.

Clerical support is provided by Patricia Johnston and Richard Lewis. If John, Arthur or Chris need additional help to impress or convince a new customer to do business with New Force, then they will call on Phil Cunningham.

The three territories are roughly equal (perhaps the Midlands is slightly better in terms of existing customers) and the three Field Sales Team members receive commission for their efforts on top of a relatively small basic salary.

(g) Frank Righton and John Horne – Despatch

Frank and John are responsible to Donald Sullivan and work in the warehouse/despatch area of the unit. They check stock when it arrives against delivery notes and then make sure that it is placed in the correct storage bay in the warehouse. They use a computerised stock control system which allocates each electrical component a particular number and code.

When orders come via Jenny Anderson or the Tele-sales Team (in the form of a computer printout or 'picking list') they collect together the order and pack it carefully into polystyrene boxes for despatch. Because of the relatively high value of the electrical components, New Force uses Securicor for deliveries. In some cases, particularly if Phil Cunningham or one of the Field Sales Team is going to visit the customer, they will take the order with them.

Frank and John are answerable to Donald Sullivan, although he knows that they are capable of sorting the work-load out between them.

(h) Patricia Johnston and Richard Lewis – Tele-sales/Sales Support

Patricia and Richard, both relatively new to the company, are tele-sales specialists. Patricia's former

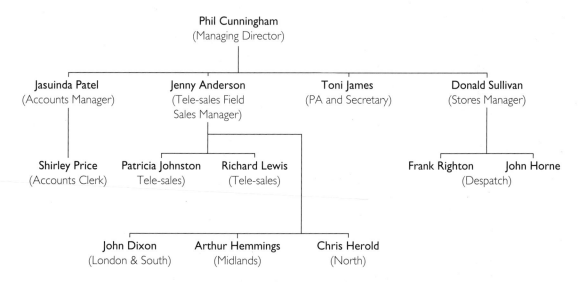

FIG. 2.1.6 *Organisational structure of New Force.*

employer, a local newspaper, was also quite heavily involved in tele-sales. Richard, on the other hand, is completely new to the job, having just finished studies at college. In addition to their tele-sales activities, they also provide clerical support for Jenny Anderson and the Field Sales Team.

(i) Shirley Price – Accounts Clerk

Shirley is the youngest member of the company, she works directly for Jasuinda Patel. Shirley's day is mainly taken up with checking invoices, filing, basic book-keeping and generally helping Jasuinda with the financial work. She is learning quickly and has been given additional responsibilities such as liaising with the Field Sales Team with regard to their expenses claims and commission payments.

5 *Functions of the organisation*

When Matsushia, a very large Japanese manufacturer of electrical components acquired SDS Ltd., New Force had to radically change its whole operation. SDS Ltd. had been New Force's main supplier. With the change of ownership, New Force had to forge new links with the Japanese owner and hope to continue the business relationship that had been working well.

The existing track record that New Force had with SDS Ltd. had a great influence in persuading Matsushia that New Force would be able to achieve the sales figure it promised. Phil Cunningham had several meetings with Masushia's new UK Director, and one of the main agreements was that New Force should increase its commitment to Matsushia as its main UK distributor. To this end, New Force had to increase their marketing and advertising effort. Phil Cunningham knew that this would take up an increasing amount of his time, and therefore had to take on new employees. Phil had been part of the Field Sales Team, but took on John Dixon to replace himself.

New Force uses two main media for its advertising. The first is *Electronic Components*, a magazine serving the electronic industry. Its circulation is small, but the readership is very highly representative of New Force's potential customers. Specific targeting of customers is important with specialised products such as electronic components. The second major medium is New Force's catalogue. This is now produced every six months and is available to all customers. An important function of the Sales Team is to distribute and mail out the catalogue twice a year.

All of the other functions of the organisation are designed to back up the sales effort. Rapid despatch is vital in a market where such a response is imperative. Efficiency in all areas is equally vital to keep New Force's market advantage. New Force is a very professional organisation. Matsushia holds briefing programmes to inform distributors about the uses of new products, and all of New Force's 'front-line' Sales Team and Phil Cunningham always attend these seminars. Being able to provide this 'know-how' is a very valuable marketing tool for the distributor and one that should not be underestimated. New Force had ridden out the recession and is set to expand in the next decade.

Gorlesworth District Council

1 *Purpose of organisation*

GDC has been involved in improving the environment for many years. Activities such as providing parks and open spaces, controlling pollution and regulating development are part of its everyday work. Although GDC is involved in many other activities not related to the environment, we will focus on the environmental considerations for the purposes of this Focus Study.

The future health and well-being of the area is dependent upon a healthy environment, and to this end, the council promotes a set of environmental policies or an environmental charter. The following objectives, which essentially determine the purposes of the council are:

- to protect the habitat of all wild animals, birds, fish and insects
- to promote the concept of tidiness and freedom from pollution
- to encourage the conservation and management of trees and vegetation
- to promote an interest in natural history, the countryside and the architectural environment
- to reduce the impact of roads and buildings on the environment
- to encourage the laying of underground power lines and other lines related to communications

2 *Type of ownership*

GDC is responsible for an area in a fast-growing region of the UK. Its role, as required by central government, is to encourage a partnership between community, commercial, voluntary and environmental agencies. Funded by central government funds, the council must also raise money from rates, rents, fees for services provided and other grants. The council is led by a Chief Executive called Matthew Ellough, although Matthew is an employee in the strictest sense of the term. The council's policies and decision making are carried out by the elected councillors. Matthew's function is to ensure that these policies and decisions are carried out in the most efficient and cost-effective manner. In addition to this, there are innumerable pieces of legislation which must be monitored, recorded and implemented by the council on behalf of central government.

3 Organisational structure

The organisational structure of the council is very complex. For this reason, we have concentrated on a single area of the council's activities. The Health and Housing Department is situated in Clapham Road, Gorlesworth and the work is carried out by two separate divisions – the Housing Division and the Environmental Health Division. Again, for reasons of clarity and space, we will focus upon the Environmental Health Division which is also divided into two separate sections. Since Gorlesworth is on the coast, the council has a Food and Port Health Section, as well as an Environmental Control Section.

The former section is responsible for the following:

- the quality of food processed and sold within the Gorlesworth area
- health education – the Community Physician gives regular talks to schools and organisations on health-related topics such as healthy eating, exercise, smoking and alcohol abuse
- infectious disease control – the Environmental Health Officer works with the Community Physician to assist in the investigation of infectious diseases and the prevention of them spreading
- associated port activities

The latter section is responsible for the following:

- the monitoring of pollution – clear air is essential and accidents which cause air pollution are investigated
- noise control – noise can emanate from factories, discos, sporting events, road works or even neighbours. A monitoring and a means of dealing with noise nuisance is an integral part of the duties
- occupational health and safety – too often individuals are injured in accidents at work, as well as at home. If premises do not conform with health and safety requirements then a report will be passed on to the appropriate enforcing authority
- public health nuisance
- recycling – a recycling officer is based within the environmental health division and deals with the provision of facilities to recycle glass, paper, cans, old clothing and waste oil
- canine control – a dog warden service is provided to enforce local by-laws, deal with strays and give advice to pet owners
- drainage
- private sector housing
- improvement grants
- pest control – a comprehensive pest control service is provided free to all domestic users (with the exception of wasps' nests). Commercial premises are charged according to the treatment required

4 Job roles

Help, advice and information on the above topics is provided by a number of different officers. The specific roles are as follows:

- John Durrant – Health and Housing Management
- Jim Bracey – Marine Pollution and Environmental Health
- Gail Bowcock – Housing and Environmental Pollution
- Jim Johnson – Food and Port Health
- Lawrence Dybal – Grants
- Penny Goldspink – Recycling
- David O'Leary – Pest Control
- Peter Thomas – Dog Warden
- Maurice Cowley – Community Physician

5 Functions of the organisation

With the department having an involvement in matters as far ranging as litter control and the design of public buildings, it is clear that work can only be carried out by dealing with matters in a sympathetic and professional manner.

The department is the agent for the County Council Highways Department, and it is therefore involved in dealing with congestion in the town. The provision of pedestrianisation and traffic calming has been successful, as, too, have new provisions for cyclists.

The local water authority, in conjunction with GDC, is responsible for the sewerage system. This includes the maintenance and repair of sewers, pumping stations and sewerage outfalls into the sea.

The design of public buildings is also fundamental in order to maintain an area's character. New council buildings are constructed using current energy conservation techniques and materials. Efforts are made to ensure that quality landscaping and tree replanting are an integral part of any new development.

The Environmental Protection Act commits GDC to new levels of responsibility in keeping public areas clean and free from litter. Domestic and trade waste disposal requires significant staff resources for inspecting areas and supervising contractors.

Another issue involving the department is the environmental improvement of the beaches: recently Gorlesworth achieved two blue flag beach awards.

GDC sponsors competitions such as 'the best kept village' to engender conservation within the

area. This is coupled with the improvement of parks with a view to improving the environment for wildlife.

The department is also actively involved in endeavouring to increase areas covered by local by-laws for the control of dogs. The eventual aim is to free the district of dog fouling in all public areas, roads and footpaths.

ELEMENT 2.1

a s s i g n m e n t

INVESTIGATING ORGANISATIONS

(PC 2.1.1, 2.1.2, 2.1.3, COM 3.2, IT 3.1, 3.2, 3.3)
In order to provide evidence for this Element, you are required to produce a report. You must ensure that you cover all of the tasks in order to cover the three performance criteria of this Element. If you are unable to source information about either a private or a public sector organisation, you will be able to use New Force as an example of a private sector organisation, or Gorlesworth District Council as an example of a public sector organisation. This means that you will have to find a third organisation which is in the private sector to complete the necessary explanations and comparisons.

TASK 1

(PC 2.1.1, 2.1.2)
In the form of a word processed report you must compare and analyse three business organisations, one from the public and two from the private sector. In your comparison and analysis, you should include the following:

- main objectives of the organisation
- broad financial objectives (profit or not-for-profit motives)
- any objectives which conflict with one another
- how the financial differences between the organisations influence the objectives
- how the legal differences between the organisations influence the objectives

- how the organisation is owned and controlled

Show your comparisons by means of graphical materials produced using a computer software package.

TASK 2

(PC 2.1.3)
You should also include in your report the following aspects of the organisational structure:

- an organisational chart for each business
- a comparison of the organisational structures in terms of how they help the business achieve its objectives
- a comparison of the organisational structures in terms of how they hinder the business in achieving its objectives

TASK 3

(PC 2.1.3)
Having illustrated and described the organisational structures, you must now consider the following:

- suggest two changes that can be made to the structures
- what are the reasons behind these suggested changes?
- what will be the effect of these changes?
- how will the organisations' effectiveness in meeting their objectives be influenced by these changes?

Investigate administration systems

PERFORMANCE CRITERIA

A student must:

1 identify the **administration systems** which support **functions** of business organisations

2 explain the **suitability** of one **administration system** in an identified business organisation

3 identify how **information technology** developments can change **administration systems**

4 suggest **improvements** to an **administration system**

RANGE

Administration systems: *purpose, processes, procedures, equipment (hardware, software)*

Suitability *in terms of: fitness for purpose, value for money, security, health and safety*

Information technology: *hardware, software, networks, commercial administration packages*

Improvements *in service, in procedure, in equipment, in training*

2.2.1 Identify the administration systems which support functions of business organisations

ADMINISTRATION SYSTEMS

The operation of administration systems is vital since the activities of the organisation must be co-ordinated and planned. If inadequate administration systems are in operation, then the organisation may suffer from a lack of efficiency and effectiveness since it does not have access to all relevant information. Administration systems inevitably involve some form of filing, whether it is a paper-based filing system or one based on a computer system. We must look at the various areas of business activity and identify the main types of system and the reasoning behind the adoption of these systems.

The systems which an organisation has in place should aim to establish a means by which the efficiency and effectiveness of all operations are assessed. All systems rely on the way in which the organisation is structured and the comparative importance with which individuals within the organisation view the system.

Any system is only a series of sub-systems which themselves may be split into additional sub-systems. It is, therefore, important that the organisation monitors all parts of the system. The systems should be designed in such a way that they can be amended or can evolve to meet the requirements of the organisation. In order to understand the ways in which organisations work, we need to understand how they can assess the efficiency and effectiveness of all their operations.

EFFICIENCY OF OPERATION

The simple way of describing the efficiency of operations is to consider how the organisation uses its available resources to produce specific outputs.

student activity

(PC 2.2.1, COM 3.1)
Identify some criteria to measure efficiency and effectiveness that could be used for a variety of different organisations. Compare your criteria with those of the remainder of your group.

Efficiency requires the organisation to make this process as smooth as possible.

EFFECTIVE CONTROL OF BUSINESS FUNCTIONS

Effectiveness is concerned with how the organisation achieves its objectives and goals. At its simplest, if an organisation meets its declared objectives and goals, then it is being effective. However, the amount of resources deployed to achieve these objectives or goals should also be measured in order to assess effectiveness.

In other words, we cannot assess how successful an organisation is simply by considering efficiency or effectiveness separately. We need to consider both, since an organisation needs to operate efficiently and effectively and its operations need to be co-ordinated. Even if only one part of the organisation fails in its task then we cannot state that the organisation is truly efficient or effective. One or more features in the organisation's systems must be deficient if one part of the organisation is underachieving.

Systems obviously play a vital role here. They are the means by which the organisation is able to operate as a whole entity. Any organisation can have good ideas and well-motivated personnel, but without systems to ensure that vital functions are carried out, then these may be doomed to failure. Organisations need not necessarily rely on their own personnel to provide the design and running of systems. They may employ outside specialists or consultants who are conversant with Organisation and Methods (O & M) Analysis. In recent years many organisations have employed this vital tool to improve efficiency and effectiveness. They have often done this by engaging outside agencies to study and analyse their existing systems.

Whether the systems of an organisation evolve from existing systems, or are radically redesigned, O & M specialists base their assessment on scientific analysis of the organisation's systems. As we have seen, systems are vital to measure the performance of an organisation and to assess whether it is reaching its declared objectives. However the systems have originated, they will always be open to criticism and to the charge that it is the systems themselves that are responsible for inefficiencies or their lack of effectiveness.

PURPOSES, PROCESSES AND PROCEDURES

However we define administration systems, we can identify a common thread within them. Each of the procedures we will look at later consists of a relatively simple process:

Inputs	Process	Output
(Information, via faxes, telephone, quotation, monies, etc.)	(The system by which this information is handled, e.g. input into computer, analysis, costings, etc.)	(Supply of a response, e.g. letter, memo, report, telephone call, fax, etc.)

In effect we can split the 'process' part of the diagram into two parts to make it clearer:

- storage of information (either manually or by computer)
- analysis of information

This may appear to be too simple a definition of the process, but as we will see, the complexities of the operation very much depend upon the context in which the process takes place.

The term administration systems needs to be defined before we can accurately determine the purpose of these systems or the procedures carried out. These are the generally accepted descriptions of administration systems:

activities carried out by managers to determine the aims and policies of the organisation

control of the day-to-day running of the business

As we have said, the running of an organisation requires an organised approach if it is to be efficient and effective. Administrative tasks will be carried out at all levels of the organisation. In a larger organisation, administration will be carried out by the Administration Department, but in smaller businesses the administration may be carried out by a single individual who will be responsible for all forms of administration. Whoever is responsible for carrying out these administrative tasks, the basic purposes for these procedures remain the same. These are:

- providing support systems for all resources used by the organisation
- the keeping of records relating to the activities of the organisation
- monitoring the performance of the business's activities

The activities of an organisation may be classified as routine or non-routine. We need, at this stage, to look at these in a little more detail:

1 *Routine*
Routine activities mean those carried out on a regular basis. Some individuals will be responsible for administration functions which will not differ regardless of any other activities carried out by the organisation. Examples of such functions may include:

- the processing of invoices
- the filing of business documents and information

student activity

(PC 2.2.1)
Identify another five routine activities which would be carried out on a regular basis by an organisation.

2 *Non-routine*
Other individuals will carry out a series of non-routine activities. They will have to be more adaptable as the demands of each day will differ greatly. These individuals will not be able to predict the demands upon them with any great accuracy. On a single day they may have a series of meetings or tasks to perform without prior notice or instruction.

The routine functions of an office can be easily organised through the establishment of systems to handle them. An office organised in this way will base its procedures upon previous experience and will know with great accuracy the demands that will be placed upon it. In situations when an individual or department must carry out a non-routine function, they must be able to rely upon a separate series of procedures to support them. A support system may have to be created for that specific purpose.

SUPPORTING RESOURCES

Many organisations have found the need to provide administrative systems or procedures in order to support the resources used by the organisation. These resources can fall into three main categories:

1 *Human resources* – many organisations have recognised that human resources are the most important resource they have. The deployment of these human resources, as much as any other factor, will determine the successfulness of the organisation.
2 *Financial resources* – this is the capital (or money) that the organisation has received from its trading activities.

student activity

1:30

(PC 2.2.1, COM 3.1, IT 3.1, 3.3)
Assess the comparative amounts of time spent by the following individuals on routine and non-routine tasks:

- an accounts clerk
- a receptionist
- a shop manager
- a tele-sales assistant

Present your findings in the form of a pie chart for each individual, using computer software to produce this information.

3 *Physical resources* – these are slightly more complicated, and administrative systems need to be in place to fully support the following:

- land
- premises
- equipment
- plant and machinery
- copyrights
- patents
- trade marks

In the managing of any of these resources, it is a priority that the organisation establishes a series of systems (which often take the form of a departmentalised structure) to assist in the efficient running of the administration function.

RECORDING AND MONITORING BUSINESS PERFORMANCE

Maintaining an efficient and accurate recording system of business activity is essential to all forms of businesses. Records are kept for the following four main reasons:

1 *To fulfil statutory obligations*
Various legislation requires organisations to keep detailed records of business activity. In the main, these tend to focus on financial and staff considerations. A record of business activity should be kept for VAT and tax inspections and with regard to staff, both tax and national insurance deductions and contributions should be recorded. Company legislation requires organisations to provide information for investors, customers and company employees.

IR 53

THINKING OF TAKING SOMEONE ON?

PAYE for Employers

FIG. 2.2.1 *The Inland Revenue provides comprehensive guidance to employers on such matters as the calculation of PAYE for their employees. This booklet, IR 53, is particularly useful and extremely informative.*

2 *To assist future planning*
Comprehensive data on the following may be vital to assist managers in future decision making:

- costs
- product details
- market research
- customer complaints
- profit margins
- supplier details

These records are maintained in order to allow managers to make decisions on the basis of past experience.

3 *Evidence of transactions*
The following records will provide a system for tracking all income and expenditure relating to the organisations business activity:

- purchases made
- sales made
- dates of transactions

- organisations and individuals with whom transactions have been made
- payments received and pending
- personnel records
- stock levels
- staff training and development
- accurate minutes of meetings

student activity

0:30

(PC 2.2.1, COM 3.1)
Identify the location of these forms of information within an organisation. Who would have access to them and what purposes would they have in using them? Discuss this in pairs.

4 *Monitoring performance*

An organisation must attempt to identify any problems arising from its business activities and have in place a system which can quickly highlight these. Finance is the key area to monitor, as financial information may be sourced from various parts of the organisation. Each individual manager is responsible for controlling and monitoring the expenditure of his/her department and will need to analyse this expenditure to assist in future planning. Expenditure may be compared from two different viewpoints:

- *intra-firm comparisons* – where expenditure is compared with that of last year
- *inter-firm comparisons* – where comparisons are made in relation to the expenditure of competitors

Many organisations have adopted management information systems provided by computer software packages to organise, store and monitor their financial data. The information stored is accessible to all interested parties within the organisation and can be used to provide necessary information on an immediate basis. We will be looking at this aspect of information technology systems later in this Unit.

EQUIPMENT (HARDWARE, SOFTWARE)

In this section it is necessary to look at the equipment used within the administrative section of an organisa-

0:45

student activity

(PC 2.2.1, COM 3.1, IT 3.4)
For what reasons would an organisation make intra-firm comparisons and inter-firm comparisons? What would be the outcome of these comparisons? What computer software would make the accessing of such information immediate?

tion, and the varying ways that equipment is put to use. Certainly, for administration purposes, the computer has made radical changes to the day-to-day running of a business. It has also changed the daily duties or tasks of the personnel working on the administration side of an organisation. Information technology, essentially, does very much what the manual systems do, but as we can easily imagine, it does this work far faster and (hopefully), more efficiently and accurately. We look in more detail at the job roles of different individuals in a later Unit within the book. In addition, in a later section of this Unit, we look at developments in information technology in some detail. For the purpose of this performance criterion, we need to look more closely at the hardware and software which make up computer systems.

HARDWARE

Whenever a business considers a new computer system, two basic points must be established:

- what is the computer itself capable of?
- what can the software do and what are its limitations?

Hardware, or the computer itself, is the physical components of the system. As we will see, the computer is only as good as the software it is capable of running. The actual versatility of the computer is related to the flexibility of the software and its ability to process data (or manipulate it).

For those of you who have a good working knowledge of computers and their applications, our apologies, but the requirements of this performance criterion and the related range require us to have a look at the basics.

As you might remember, we defined administration systems as being the process through which information is handled in some way. In many respects, this is exactly how a computer works.

Essentially, we can define the operations of a computer using the following chart:

INPUT DEVICES	CENTRAL PROCESSING UNIT (CPU)	OUTPUT DEVICES
	MEMORY/DISK	

Regardless of how sophisticated the computer may be, the heart of the machine is the CPU (Central Processing Unit). The CPU is a complex construction of micro-electronic circuitry and components mounted on 'boards'. These boards simply act as a means of connecting all the parts of the CPU.

The input devices, as featured in the diagram, include the keyboard or a bar-code scanner. These are the means by which information is put into the computer (hence input).

Output devices, or how the information is displayed or 'got out of' the computer, include the monitor (screen) or printer. Alternatively, the memory or disk may be the place that you choose to keep the information for further use.

We shall look at some of these in a little more detail:

DISPLAYS

Commonly a display is the viewing screen. Normally, the viewing screen or VDU will show a combination of text and graphics. Depending on the screen resolution (in other words, the sharpness or clarity of the monitor), the viewer will be able to see various images made up of pixels (picture elements). The more pixels there are on the screen, the better the quality of picture.

KEYBOARDS AND ALTERNATIVES

The keyboard is perhaps the most common, but not necessarily the most convenient, method of inputting information into the system. A keyboard will be touch sensitive and arranged in a standard QWERTY format. There are a number of alternatives to the keyboard however. These include:

1 *Mouse* – a hand-held device which is used to move the cursor around the screen. Clicks on the mouse allow the user to perform various functions from on-screen icons or text.
2 *Joystick* – commonly used in computer games, these operate in a similar manner to a mouse. However, they are slightly more sophisticated in the sense that they allow greater flexibility in terms of angles of movement.
3 *Light pen* – this is a photo-electric or light-sensitive device which interacts with the screen once touched.

A light pen is particularly useful in computer aided design (CAD).

4 *Touch screen* – this is a logical extension of the light pen but allows the user to interact with the screen by the use of his/her finger.

PRINTERS

There is a wide diversity of printer types available. They are usually identified by use of the following criteria:

- speed
- quality of print
- impact
- non-impact

Specifically, printers may be identified as being one of the following:

- impact dot-matrix printers
- line printers
- thermal printers
- electro-sensitive printers
- laser printers
- ink-jet printers

FIG. 2.2.2 *The Alliance and Leicester's use of advanced information technology has helped the company to offer a high quality service and competitive rates.*

DATA CAPTURE EQUIPMENT

As we have already mentioned, most information is normally originally formatted in a manner in which humans can read it. Computers need to be able to 'read' this information and to transform it into their own binary language. The principal devices that have been designed to capture information, in other words, to allow the computer access to this information, include the following:

- *optical character readers* – which are able to read stylised characters also readable by humans

- *optical mark readers* – which enable the computer to read marks in pre-set positions, such as multiple choice papers or market research questionnaires
- *bar code readers* – commonly found in many shops, which enable the computer to read via a light pen or laser scanner
- *magnetic ink character readers* – commonly used for sorting and processing cheques. These are very stylised characters, printed in ink containing iron
- *digitisers* – which automatically transform graphics in particular into a binary format on the screen
- *voice recognition devices* – this relatively new system allows the computer to understand simple words and phrases and interpret them as commands

FIG. 2.2.3 *Barclays Bank's Computer Operations division was formed to provide services to the commercial market and boasts some of the most sophisticated computer technology in the UK. Its operations are extremely highly thought of by customers and its customer service teams have recently gained BS 5750.*

SOFTWARE

The processes by which computer systems handle information can be categorised under the following headings:

- word processing
- spreadsheets
- data bases
- graphics packages
- accounts packages
- sales packages
- invoicing packages
- stock control packages
- desktop publishing
- computer aided design and manufacture
- management information systems

We shall now look at each of these in a little more detail:

WORD PROCESSING

Essentially, a word processor is a computer with a keyboard used for entering text. Word processors may thus be used for all forms of business documentation. They have a number of advantages over the manual system (typewriters).

- it is comparatively easy to identify and correct typing errors (there is usually a spell-checking facility available)
- page numbering may be available automatically
- an instant word count may be available
- the document may be edited and re-edited, particularly useful when sending a similar letter to various addresses
- multiple copies may be made
- all printed copies are of the same quality
- documents may be saved for future reference or use
- a line-draw facility may be available to aid the ruling of tabulated work
- a wide variety of print styles and character fonts is available

SPREADSHEETS

Spreadsheets are designed to manipulate numerical data. Spreadsheet programs consist of the following:

- a number of cells – each of these cells may be labelled to perform a particular function
- the cell may be a number or text or a formula
- calculations may be made, provided the spreadsheet has been pre-designed to perform a particular function

Spreadsheets are particularly useful in the displaying of numerical data. A good example of the use of a spreadsheet would be in the updating of a football league table, when the spreadsheet has been organised in such a manner that:

- results of football matches are inputted
- the spreadsheet updates the league table by allocating the appropriate number of points to each team
- the spreadsheet then re-sorts the league after each football result has been entered

Spreadsheets offer a number of advantages over their manual counterparts:

- they are designed to be easy to learn and use
- they have a wide variety of uses
- they are comparatively cheap
- they can be personalised for each organisation
- they have been 'debugged' and tested

However, spreadsheets need to be carefully designed prior to use and may suffer from incorrect design features which fail to show the correct information in an appropriate format.

being designed. Computer aided design requires complex calculations to be made and may only be satisfactorily used on powerful computers.

Computer aided manufacture (CAM), as the title suggests, is involved in the actual manufacturing process. It can control the following:

- automated production lines
- robots
- manufacturing systems
- process control

Organisations often use an integrated CAD/CAM system which allows the CAD-produced design to be relayed straight to the production line where the process is monitored by the CAM system.

MANAGEMENT INFORMATION SYSTEMS

Management information systems offer a number of features to the organisation:

- they can produce information of a sophisticated nature
- they can provide information at a crucial period of decision making
- they can aid the decision-making process
- they can process information stored in databases

Essentially, an MIS should assist managers in making decisions by allowing them access to hitherto unobtainable forms of data.

student activity

(PC 2.2.1, COM 3.1, IT 3.4)
What would you expect to find in a management information system? How would you make the best use of its abilities and functions? In pairs, list the facilities you think would be available and their uses. Compare your list with those of the remainder of your group.

FUNCTIONS OF BUSINESS ORGANISATIONS

We have already considered some of these functions in general terms, but now we need to look at them (and other functions) in more detail.

Every organisation has its own way of structuring the functions that it carries out. Here are some of the more common ones. Not all the positions described below exist in every organisation. Factors such as the nature of the operations of the organisation and its size and complexity affect the need for functions such as these and for separate departments and staff to carry them out.

RESEARCH AND DEVELOPMENT (R & D) AND DESIGN

By working closely with the marketing department, who keep a constant check on competitors' products and services, the R & D department may be informed of the need for a new product. Equally, the R & D staff may be developing new products or ranges in their own right.

The main function of the R & D department is not only to design new products, but to work out the most efficient and logical method of producing them. The R & D staff will, after a number of exhaustive tests, pass on their designs and proposed methods of production to the production department. This department will then be responsible for putting the product into production.

Routinely the R & D department will test random samples of products being manufactured to ensure that they comply with the quality standards set by the organisation, as well as by government legislation. In some organisations, this function is separated from the R & D department and is supervised by a quality assurance/control department.

The R & D department will also test competitors' products to see how they have been manufactured and whether the organisation's products compare favourably to them. Additionally, they will keep a close eye on the technological advances made within their area to see if the design and production processes can be improved.

student activity

(PC 2.2.1, COM 3.1, 3.2, AON 3.1)
Using the information given above, design a form (in pairs) which an R & D department could use to assist them in the development of a new product. What information would they need on the form to record the process from the initial idea or request to the presentation of the product to the production department and sales department?

MARKETING

The main function of the marketing department is to try to identify customer requirements. There is also an element of trying to predict customer needs into the future. The marketing department works very closely with the sales department, and it is important that the two communicate well.

The starting point for most marketing functions is to carry out extensive research on a particular market to try to discover exactly what customers want, where they want it, how much they want to pay for it and the most effective way of getting the message across. This is known as the marketing mix. We will be dealing with this in more detail later in the book.

student activity

(PC 2.2.1, COM 3.2, AON 3.1, IT 3.1)
If you were a member of the marketing department, responsible for carrying out market research for the product in the previous activity, what information would you need? Design a market research questionnaire which would successfully provide you with the necessary information. Word process your document.

The marketing department will need to work closely with the R & D department and the production department in developing attractive and sellable products. This work will also include the constant updating of existing products to cater for changes in taste and demand.

One of the more obvious responsibilities of the marketing department is the design and development of advertising ideas and marketing campaigns. This design and development process will take account of the needs of the sales department and any other interested area of the organisation.

As a part of its regular market research procedures, the marketing department will monitor changes in trends and fashions that affect their customers. Some information is readily available as statistical tables published by the government, but much information must be researched as required by the organisation itself.

COMMUNICATIONS

Effective communication is the responsibility of all parts of the organisation. Each function, department or division has some degree of responsibility for communicating decisions and policies as well as general information.

Most organisations have a central administration. The main function of the administration department is to control paperwork and to support all the other departments by servicing their needs for secretarial work – filing, mailing, handling data, etc..

As offices have becomes more accustomed to using computers, administration departments have shrunk in size because many of the tasks carried out by such departments can now be carried out simply at the desktop with a networked computer. We will look at this aspect in more detail later.

One of the functions most commonly still carried out by an administration departments is that of organising office services. The manager in charge of office services is responsible for training, advising departments about how their space should be organised, supplying equipment, stationery and setting up an effective communication system within the organisation, which obviously includes the telephone and the mailing of documents.

The administration department will also provide a centralised purchasing service for office supplies and storage. It also operates as a 'pool' of business stationery and corporate materials, e.g. memorandum and letterhead paper, and will co-ordinate the mass printing of the stationary. Allied to this it will control the large central photocopying facilities, providing a fast and efficient reprographic facility, which may include photocopying, collating and binding of documents.

Traditionally, administration departments have been responsible for arranging insurance for the organisation and the monitoring of leasing agreements (cars, equipment and premises).

FINANCE (ACCOUNTS, FINANCIAL CONTROL)

The main function of accounting systems is to provide managers with the means to exercise financial control over their departments so that they may implement budgetary control. A budget relies on a plan, which is made on the basis of estimates of future spending and income. The budget will also try to allocate any expenses in relation to particular objectives set by the organisation. Depending upon the size of the organisation, this may be across the whole of the organisation, or on a departmental basis. Budgetary control is established by careful consideration of the following:

1 The organisation will define its objectives and try to allocate the expenditure related to each of them.
2 The organisation will establish standard operating procedures which relate to specific strategies and tactics in meeting the objectives.

Profit & Loss Account
FOR THE 26 WEEKS ENDED 3RD JULY 1993

Geest PLC Interim Report 1993

53 weeks ended 2nd January 1993 £000		Notes	26 weeks ended 3rd July 1993 £000	26 weeks ended 27th June 1992 £000
	Turnover			
605,826	Continuing	2	332,687	325,478
53,101	Discontinued	2	-	33,284
658,927			332,687	358,762
(586,278)	Cost of sales	2	(302,243)	(318,983)
72,649	**Gross profit**		30,444	39,779
(55,943)	Administrative expenses	2	(26,369)	(27,371)
2,412	Less 1991 provision	2	-	1,584
(1,839)	Operating exceptional items	3	(734)	-
17,279	**Operating profit**	2	3,341	13,992
174	Income from investments in associated undertakings		(35)	143
(1,176)	Provision for loss on operations to be discontinued		-	-
(20,860)	Loss on disposal of discontinued operations		-	-
4,788	Less 1991 provision		-	-
205	**Profit on ordinary activities before interest**		3,306	14,135
2,922	Interest receivable		255	1,288
3,127	**Profit on ordinary activities before taxation**	1	3,561	15,423
(5,966)	Taxation on profit on ordinary activities		(1,139)	(4,473)
(2,839)	**Profit on ordinary activities after taxation**		2,422	10,950
117	Minority interest		124	(42)
(2,722)	**Profit/(loss) for the financial period**		2,546	10,908
(5,793)	Dividends		(2,655)	(2,645)
(8,515)	**Retained (loss)/profit**		(109)	8,263
(3.8p)	**Earnings per ordinary share**	4	3.6p	15.3p
8.1p	**Dividend per ordinary share**		3.7p	3.7p

FIG. 2.2.6 *The Profit and Loss Account of Geest plc, covering the first half of 1993. Also contained in the Interim Report are the balance sheet, cash-flow statement and interim financial statements.*

student activity

(PC 2.2.1, COM 3.1, 3.2)
Define the following with reference to Figure 2.2.6, by writing a paragraph on each item. Discuss your written work with the remainder of your group, comparing your statements with theirs.

- profit and loss account
- balance sheet
- cash flow statement
- interim financial statements

3 The organisation will establish systems to monitor the actual spending on each objective, as opposed to the estimated expenditure.

4 The above monitoring of the objectives in relation to the standards set will be made at various times and may take the form of interim reports.

5 The organisation must have in place a series of procedures in order to react to any differences between the estimated and the actual spending. This is particularly important if there is an overspend and may result in the re-examination of the organisation's operating systems. Most organisations expect to have to constantly redefine their operating standards and monitoring systems in order to maintain efficiency.

The accurate monitoring of budgets is essential to all businesses for the following reasons:

1 It allows the organisation to clearly define its aims and policies.

2 It allows the organisation to develop an overall corporate strategy.

3 It allows the key decision makers of the organisation to keep a careful eye on all budgets.

4 It allows the organisation to monitor actual performance against estimated activity.

5 It should improve the organisation's efficiency and the deployment of resources towards the meeting of specific objectives.

student activity

(PC 2.2.1, COM 3.2, AON 3.2, IT 3.1, 3.3)
Assess how the production of financial data may assist in the monitoring of business performance and the meeting of targets. How can budgets be amended if they appear to be heading for an overspend? Prepare a memorandum to your superior, informing him/her of an anticipated overspend on your departmental budget, and suggesting ways of avoiding an overspend before the end of the financial year. Your memorandum should be word processed, showing your calculations in full.

In relation to the creditworthiness of a customer, most organisations will have set a particular policy at high management level. In large organisations, there may be an individual with specific responsibility for credit control and the setting of customers' credit levels. In smaller organisations, as we have mentioned, an individual may have to take on this responsibility in addition to other tasks. Regardless of the particular situation in the organisation, an efficient credit system should include the following features:

- credit checks – which include the taking up of bank and trade references and reference to credit agencies
- establishment of credit levels and what terms apply to these limits
- action to be taken in the case of credit breaches – this will involve a system being created to determine at what particular stage action will be taken. It will include a series of letters requesting payment. The style and tone of these letters is important in order to avoid unnecessary complications, both legally and personally, with the customer

Credit ratings are often based on sales experience with a particular customer. Credit ratings given to customers should reflect their ability to pay at some point in the future.

student activity

(PC 2.2.1, COM 3.2, IT 3.1)
Design and write a letter aimed at obtaining an outstanding debt from a customer. Bear in mind that you should always be clear and courteous. Word process your letter and print two copies.

Specifically then, the major requirements of the administrative system within a finance or accounts department are:

- to record information
- to store records either manually or using a data base or specific accounts software
- to have these records available for inspection by the Inland Revenue (for tax purposes)
- to have these records available for inspection by Customs and Excise (for VAT purposes)
- to have these records available for inspection by the company's auditors
- to report on the financial health of the organisation at the end of the year

It is vital that these systems work, as the organisation will need them for the following:

- planning
- decision making
- financial control

It is usual, particularly in larger organisations, for the Chief Accountant (or equivalent) to be a member of the Board of Directors.

PRODUCING GOODS

The production department is involved in all functions which revolve around producing goods or services for the customer.

This department monitors levels of wastage to ensure the most efficient use of resources and checks the cost of raw materials and parts purchased to make sure that profit margins are maintained.

As new products are developed, and technology changes, the production department will be responsible for purchasing all the necessary plant and equipment required, as well as organising the production process.

In consultation with the sales department, the production department must make sure that it can manufacture or supply customers with the quantity of goods required at the time they have been requested. The tight monitoring of production levels means that the production department should know how long it would take to produce sufficient products to fill a particular order. Advance planning and close liaison with the sales department are vital to ensure that deadlines can be met.

Regardless of how many units of products are being produced, the production department is also responsible for the maintenance of quality. Each product must meet a number of strict quality standards and must, to all intents and purposes, be exactly the same every time. Periodically products will be randomly selected from the production line and tested by either the R & D department or the quality assurance/control department.

A good production department will monitor methods of production used by all major competitors and allied industries and will take steps to implement any useful methods of production used elsewhere.

Increasingly, as production becomes steadily more automated, the production department will also have to design computer programs which can handle the new processes.

Focus study

QUALITY ASSURANCE

When an old lady was awarded £1.9m. in damages after being burned by a cup of McDonald's coffee, it only goes to prove that even the most stringent quality assurance can go wrong.

McDonald's serve some 28m. people in their restaurants world-wide each day, the business is worth $25bn. per year, with 14,000 restaurants in 70 countries. They actually have a staggering 225m. customers each year and the majority were satisfied with the quality of service.

In 1994 McDonald's were awarded the highest level of safety by the Royal Society for the Prevention of Accidents (RoSPA). Every single restaurant has a safety co-ordinator, everybody is trained in health and safety and every restaurant has at least one qualified first aider.

Quality standards have always been important to McDonald's – they have quality, service, cleanliness and good value as their catch words.

McDonald's continually audit and inspect their restaurants – both arranged inspections and unannounced visits – to ensure that quality standards are maintained at all times.

PROVIDING SERVICES

Whether an organisation is producing goods or providing a service, there are still certain criteria which it would have to meet on a regular basis. For organisations providing services only (not manufacturing goods), the following criteria would be equally important and would be carried out on a regular basis by the administration systems in place within that organisation. These criteria include:

1 They must be ready, willing and able to provide a wide variety of information instantly and on demand. Their meetings (particularly if they are in the public sector) may be open to the public and information packs should be available on request.

2 They must be fully aware of how much a customer would be willing to pay for their service.

3 They must be fully aware of how much it is costing to provide the service. Costs could include the following:

- premises
- workforce
- development costs
- training costs
- cleaning costs
- administration costs

Costs can be either short term or long term. Short-term costs tend to be fairly fixed in the sense that it is difficult to change the level of expenditure in a short period of time. If an organisation providing a service needs to respond financially to sudden changes in the market, then it may be unable to find the additional funding required. Long-term costs, on the other hand, tend to be more variable. These costs will be incurred whether the organisation is producing goods or not. Therefore, administration systems need to be in place to monitor these costs.

4 They must be aware of the competition within the market in which they are dealing and the price these competitors are charging.

5 They must be aware of the quality of service their competitors are providing.

6 They must ensure that the service they are providing is constantly monitored with regard to efficiency, effectiveness and quality.

HUMAN RESOURCING

The main features of the personnel department will be looked at in other Units of this book, but the key consideration is the management of the human resources of the organisation. In addition, the department is responsible for the well-being of the workforce so that they can contribute fully to the organisation itself. Specifically, a personnel department will deal with the following areas related to employees:

- hiring and firing
- education and training
- staff welfare
- industrial relations

In order to carry out these functions, the staff must deal with a range of administration work, which mainly relates to the maintenance of personnel records. The personnel department will maintain records on all members of the workforce, both full and part time. The organisation will require the personnel department to store information regarding the following:

- name, address and date of birth of employee
- sex, marital status, number of dependants and next of kin of employee
- nationality and place of birth of employee
- national insurance number and tax details of employee
- education and qualifications of employee
- past and present employment record of employee
- present job role(s) and responsibilities of employee
- salary details of employee
- appraisal interview(s) and outcome(s)
- any disciplinary action taken against the employee
- an assessment of the potential of the employee
- any staff development undertaken or required by the employee

The system by which this information is collected and stored must be flexible enough to be updated on a regular basis. The information relating to particular employees should be available to relevant members of staff upon request (but only those with authority to access such records).

student activity

(PC 2.2.1, COM 3.2, AON 3.1, IT 3.3)
Design a personnel record which would allow for the successful storing of all of the above details of an employee. This record would need to be flexible in its use. You may use computer software to produce this record.

Specifically, the human resourcing department or personnel department is responsible for providing the administrative systems which relate to:

- statutory and legal requirements
- confidential personnel records
- organisation and provision of support for employee activities and relations

The information which must be recorded to comply with statutory and legal requirements falls into the following main categories:

1 Records of Statutory Sick Pay (SSP) which the employer has to pay to any employee who is absent from work through illness for more than four days. These records must be kept for inspection by the Department of Social Security. SSP is payable for up to 28 weeks.
2 Records of Statutory Maternity Pay (SMP) which the employer has to pay employees who are absent from work to have a baby. This SMP is payable to women who have been working for the organisation for at least 26 weeks.
3 Taxation records – the employer is required to deduct income tax on behalf of the Inland Revenue. This system is known as Pay As You Earn (PAYE).

To comply with the rules, the employer has to set up administrative systems to record the following:

- total tax paid by employee
- employee's national insurance contributions
- employer's national insurance contributions
- total amount of SSP paid to employee
- total amount of SMP paid to employee

Normally, these figures are kept on a form P11 provided by the Inland Revenue. Many organisations now use a computerised system to keep track of these payments and collections.

DISTRIBUTION

Since distribution deals with the transferring of products from the supplier to the customer, there needs to be an accurate and efficient system in place to monitor the location and status of all dealings. The distribution function may fall under the control of the marketing department, just like sales. It is the aim of the distribution department to seek to fulfil the following requirements:

- keep distribution costs competitive
- evaluate alternative distribution methods
- decide whether to deal directly with retailers
- decide whether to rely on wholesalers
- reduce administrative costs by dealing directly only with larger customers
- analyse and evaluate seasonal fluctuations in distribution
- accurately identify the location of all products at all stages of the distribution process (from a centrally

FIG. 2.2.7 *As part of their service to customers, Geest Wholesale Services have a network of nine distribution points throughout the UK, making them the only national operator in their market sector.*

located warehouse within the organisation, through transportation to arrival and storage at the customers' premises)

Specifically, administration systems must be in place to handle the following functions:

- checking goods into the warehouse
- checking goods out of the warehouse
- a selection system for choosing products to be distributed. This is particularly important in the case of perishable goods where a stock rotation system is essential in order to ensure that products do not deteriorate as a result of being stored when they should have been earmarked for distribution. There are two versions of this system, known as:
  - FiFo – the first in first out system. This bases distribution on the premise that goods stored for the longest period of time should be distributed first
  - LiFo – the last in first our system, particularly important for organisations which distribute seasonal or fashionable products which require immediate distribution as opposed to their standard items, which are held in bulk storage
- moving products around within the warehouse, whether this is done by a manual or automated system
- establishing a system which identifies specific loca-

tions within the warehouse for particular products
- keeping stock control levels in order to assist the re-ordering function of the organisation

student activity

(PC 2.2.1, COM 3.1)
How would you identify the differences between the distribution and warehousing facilities of an organisation? Discuss your views first with a partner and then with the remainder of your group.

The principal concerns of the transportation aspects of the organisation are:

- to ensure that products are delivered to the right person/organisation
- to ensure that products are delivered at the right time
- to ensure that the products are delivered in a perfect and undamaged condition
- to ensure that transportation costs are kept to a minimum

The choices relating to the above considerations may depend on the following:

- weight of products to be delivered
- value of products to be delivered
- volume of products to be delivered
- speed of delivery required
- insurance implications
- whether the transportation is carried out by the organisation or a contractor

Administration systems will have to be in place to cope with a variety of different transportation methods, but, preferred methods will already have been established and be clear.

MAINTENANCE (BUILDING, EQUIPMENT, SITES)

It is essential for an organisation to establish administration systems to cope with the various service functions. A maintenance system will be required to fulfil the following requirements:

- regularly inspect all plant and machinery
- record any actions taken as a result of inspections
- instruct maintenance staff to deal with any problems identified by the inspection

FIG. 2.2.8 *The Office Machine Maintenance Division of Rentokil PLC provides a service for leasing, rental, sales and maintenance of photocopiers and fax machines. Rentokil brings its experience and reputation for high quality service to an industry sector in which service is vital. Major brands are sold with service and maintenance provided under contract with the aim of reducing down-time from breakdowns and maximising the reliability and performance of equipment.*

- create a full inventory of all plant and machinery
- maintain records of action taken by maintenance staff
- identify particular plant and machinery which may be prone to deterioration or breakdown
- establish an additional maintenance schedule for vulnerable plant and machinery
- regularly inspect the buildings/premises to ensure that they do not require repair
- monitor an ongoing system of repairing, redecorating, re-roofing, repairing guttering etc.
- ensure that all legal obligations are carried out (e.g. fire exits or alarms, etc.)

PROVIDING CUSTOMER SERVICE

This function includes the parts of the organisation which have direct contact with the customer. We also include marketing here, since they may have a responsibility for customer service in terms of advertising, promotion and quality assurance. The exact relationship between sales and marketing will very much depend upon the organisation itself.

The key functions of sales staff are to control and organise the selling and distribution of the organisa-

tion's products and services. The sales function may often be found within the marketing department of an organisation, but the sales operation will always be supported by administrative personnel and various sales representatives. As with any other managerial function, the sales manager will be responsible for the establishment and revision of systems which will ensure the smooth running of the sales operation. In addition, he/she may have specific targets to meet and must maintain budgetary control over these. Communication is a key feature of a good sales department, as the staff must be able to handle all communications with customers. They will also be responsible for the maintenance of any relevant records and exercise some control (via a credit controller) over the availability of credit to customers.

Dealing with customers requires the establishment of systems to handle enquiries and problems efficiently. These systems will also require the sales department to keep records of any enquiries made, orders received and other documentation which maintains an up-to-date record of customer transactions.

PRIDE

YOUR PERSONAL COMMITMENT

It cannot be stressed enough that the considerable benefits available to your staff and your company from the Customer Awareness Training programme will depend more upon you and your manager's commitment and involvement than upon any other factor.

This detailed guide outlines the scope of the programme and has been produced to help with the task ahead.

However, should you have any queries regarding aspects of the C.A.T. Programme, please contact the Sales and Marketing Institute on 0203 884400.

FIG. 2.2.9 *Peugeot Talbot's Pride programme for its dealers, which concentrates on customer awareness training.*

When sales staff have contact with customers, whether this is by telephone or personal visit, administration systems must be in place to ensure that the details of any conversation, negotiation or problems have been recorded accurately. This information will be held by the sales department and will include many of the following:

- name and phone number of customer's chief buyer
- discounts agreed
- creditworthiness
- specific customer requirements

- delivery arrangements
- size of customer order
- frequency of customer order

student activity

(PC 2.2.1, COM 3.2, AON 3.1)
Design a form which would be appropriate for the recording of the above data. Compare your form to those of your peers.

The documentation and administration systems used by the customer service wing of an organisation will very much depend upon the nature of the organisation itself. However, some generalisations can be made about the types of information that should be recorded:

- processing of sales information (through invoices/ order forms and letters, etc.)
- marketing research (including data collection and analysis)
- customer care details (guarantees or warranties, etc.)
- customer service (dealing with complaints, etc.)
- sales promotions (all non-advertising marketing such as special offers, etc.)
- advertising (planning, monitoring, etc.)
- support services (via personnel for training and development etc.)
- general sales administration

PROVIDING INFORMATION TECHNOLOGY SERVICE

The information technology or computer services department's responsibility includes computing (hardware and software), maintenance of data bases, telecommunications, and other technological office developments. As most organisations are now incorporating computers into almost everything they do, the number of truly separate information technology or computer services departments is diminishing.

The information technology or computer services manager must not only be aware of new developments in technology, but also know how to use them. These managers will also supply all support and guidance to help others accomplish this too.

As we intend to identify information technology (IT) developments which can change administration

---

Focus study

CUSTOMER SERVICE

Many retailers, hoteliers and restaurant chains have used 'under-cover' customers to assess how their outlets and staff perform. The concept of the 'mystery shopper' has now moved to the financial institutions of banks and building societies.

The high street banks and building societies are very worried about their image. They have a low standing in public opinion and want to turn this around. In the year 1994–5 they will spend some £2m. on 'mystery shopper' surveys to assess their staffs' abilities to respond to customers' needs and problems.

The TSB itself is expected to spend some £200,000, but do not want the operation to be seen as a method of weeding out staff who do not come up to scratch. LAUTRO,* the regulator of life and unit trust companies, also uses 'mystery shoppers' to test members' levels of training, competence and ability to cope with customer demands.

* Now replaced by the Personal Investment Authority (PIA)

---

systems in a subsequent section of this Element (on pp.146–50), suffice to say here that new technology has made devastating changes to administration systems and their procedures over recent years. These changes are not restricted to the acquisition of computers, but extend also to facsimile machines, advanced and sophisticated telecommunication systems and robotics for production departments. We look at these in much more detail in the following section of the book.

Focus study

INFORMATION TECHNOLOGY

UK companies increased the amount they spent on computer systems last year. This increase in spending was attributed to a growth in corporate confidence. Research carried out found that expenditure on new technology rose by an average of 15 per cent compared with a 0.2 per cent prediction at the start of the year. Local and central government organisations led the boost in spending, adding 20 per cent to their information technology budgets.

2.2.2 *Explain the suitability of one administration system in an identified business organisation*

SUITABILITY

Suitability refers to the quality of the administrative system in terms of its ability to support the function for which it was designed. Obviously, if the system is not suitable, then the quality of the service provided by the organisation will be affected in a detrimental manner. If, for example, the organisation has in place a system for dealing with customer complaints, but nothing is done about the monitoring or conclusion of such problems, then this system is not suitable for the purpose. Equally, if the organisation has developed a new product and the advertising or promotion of that product has not reached the intended market, then this system is inadequate and not suitable. In other words, if the administration system does not support the function of the organisation, then it is not successfully assisting the organisation to meet its objectives. If the administration system in place is found to be unsuitable, then amendments or improvements will have to be put into place to rectify the faults and improve the service.

Obviously, in order for an administrative system to be deemed suitable, the following criteria have to be met:

1 The administrative system should be **fit for the purpose** for which it was intended.
2 It should be cost-effective – the system should provide **value for money** with regard to the end product achieved.
3 The system should be **secure**, in terms of both cost-effectiveness and accessibility of information.
4 The system should meet health and safety requirements – it should not cause any safety problems either to the members of staff in the carrying out of their duties, or to customers or clients involved in the supply of the service.

Many organisations do not take full advantage of their computer technology. Projects are often fragmented across several different departments.

Whilst reading this, you should begin to consider an organisation and its use of information technology and try to make some initial assessments using the above list of criteria.

FITNESS FOR PURPOSE

Suffice to say here that any administrative system must be seen to work successfully. If the process is too long-winded or complicated this could detract from the speed of operation. In addition, a system which is not fit could result in the lack of motivation of the individual(s) involved in the administration of the system itself.

Equally, an unfit administration system could result in:

- *the loss of prospective and actual sales* – if the sales and marketing systems are not adequate
- *the loss of goodwill from customers* – if the customer service systems are not adequate
- *the loss of money for the organisation* – if the credit control system is not adequate to monitor the credit worthiness of other organisations. In addition, if the administrative system in place to chase up bad or aged debts is inadequate, then the organisation could face delay in customers' payment of outstanding and long-term bills
- *loss of reputation* – if the quality of the products is not monitored and amended accordingly, or if the distribution system is not efficient enough
- *suitable personnel being hired* – if the human resources section of the organisation has a poor administrative system, then the recruitment and selection process will be affected
- *unmotivated personnel* – if staff training, appraisal and development are not administered correctly, then staff will see no prospect of promotion or career development
- *expensive raw materials* – if the purchasing department is not working with a suitable administration system, then it will not be finding out current prices and delivery times from alternative suppliers of raw materials. This, obviously, would add to the cost of the finished product

Some 80 per cent of business organisations, regardless of their size, use some form of sales and marketing software. Studies have shown that some 65 per cent of these organisations claim that the software has exceeded their objectives and expectations. Many admit that they could achieve much greater benefits by fully understanding the complexities of their systems. This means that general knowledge of computer technology even in the largest of businesses is still inadequate. In this respect alone, we can make some judgement about a system's fitness for purpose. If it is not fully accessible and understandable to even the computer literate, then there must be some shortfalls in the explanation, manuals and ease of use of the system.

When technology has been introduced it is usually to gain a competitive advantage. As we will see, investment in software tends to be directly aimed at boosting sales productivity rather than any other business objective.

Many organisations, as we have already said, fail to fully integrate their installation of computer technology. Different projects take place within the organisation in isolation. Equally, these different parts of the organisation are more or less ahead of the norm in terms of application, development and training. In many cases, there is not even a direct link between the computer systems used by the sales and marketing departments. If such a link were in place then they would be able to refine their marketing campaigns and focus their joint energies on achieving greater market penetration.

In many cases, the lack of application of information technology and enhanced administration systems is the failure of the IT people within the organisation.

VALUE FOR MONEY

The administration system an organisation adopts must also be cost effective. This is whether the system itself is value for money to the organisation as a whole.

It could be that all of an organisation's administration systems are of equal cost. This, though, is very unlikely. In practice, the cost of the system will be determined by the following:

- the number of employees involved in administering the system
- the position of those employees within the organisation
- the resources required by the organisation to carry out this system
- the income generated as a result of the provision of the system

Obviously, if it is costing the organisation a great deal of money to carry out the administration of the system in order to support just one particular function, then this system could not be considered to be cost effective.

If a new organisational structure is introduced, this may possibly result in a change to the administration system, and the value for money of the systems must be compared. It is necessary to make comparisons from several different angles, not necessarily from the point of view of those who carry out the tasks every day. The organisation will need to measure the benefit to the organisation as a whole.

Whether the system is value for money will also be dependent upon the benefits gained by the organisation as a result of the amendments. One of the benefits, in addition to the cost effectiveness, is the efficiency of the new system.

Obviously, the initial outlay on a new system will be large, but organisations tend to take a longer view and look to the future cost effectiveness that the system will bring. If the system can ensure that the right information reaches the right person at the right time, then unnecessary wastage can be avoided, thus contributing to the cost effectiveness of the organisation as a whole.

As we mentioned earlier, the initial investment in a new information technology or administration system should be linked to a perceived positive future benefit which the organisation will enjoy. In many cases, an organisation will make some kind of attempt to measure the impact of the introduction of new systems and set a date or a specified period of time by which the positive benefits will be expected to make an impact on the day-to-day running of the business. In this respect, in the 'bidding process' for selection of any new system, any individual or group of individuals who identify a new system that they consider to be desirable, will need to fully justify the investment.

The concept of value for money may not be immediately apparent, since the organisation may have to take a longer view, in terms of possible pay-backs the system may give them. This longer-term view, which may not be seen clearly by budget holders or the accounts section of the organisation, has to be explained in the simplest possible terms. We must not assume that budget holders or the accounts section will fully understand the implications and probable benefits of the system.

Usually, a substantial memorandum or report will have to be written which outlines the uses and benefits of the system, and provides some projected future cost savings. It is only when this task has been carried out that any budget holder can objectively assess whether the system offers true value for money.

SECURITY

Regardless of the nature of the organisation's business activities, there is always a need for certain security measures. This may simply mean that the organisation does not wish its competitors to find out any information about its operations. Other organisations, on the other hand, may have more sensitive data which need to travel throughout the organisation by means of its administrative systems. This is particularly true of organisations involved in financial and credit facilities. Perhaps even more sensitive from this point of view are organisations which are involved in the production of military equipment.

Obviously, any changes to the organisational structure of the organisation would need to take security into account. The existing administration systems, even if they have been amended, would need to pay special attention to the likelihood of loss of information because of poor security arrangements.

As you will find elsewhere in this Unit, security of data and systems may be paramount to avoid unauthorised access. Whilst this unauthorised access may not be for criminal purposes, the organisation may not wish to allow more junior members of their workforce access to sensitive data such as financial information.

Systems can be introduced to all computer networks to bar non-password holders from access, tampering or extraction of data. If we extend our considerations to other forms of administration systems, the organisation will need to have a series of security checks in place to ensure that manual systems are not compromised or tampered with.

Simple systems like 'call barring' can effectively restrict the use of telecommunication systems to authorised users only. Only certain extensions will be granted the function of external calls, national calls or international calls. This simple system can effectively reduce an organisation's telephone bills.

One of the most frequently reported forms of security breach is that of hacking. Indeed, any organisation which has external computer links with remote sites may fall prey to unauthorised access into its computer system. Although hackers may have a rather unfavourable public image, they are, in fact, extremely adept computer users.

An organisation should take every precaution to ensure that its connecting lines are as secure as possible and, if they have been breached, then sophisticated password security devices should be installed.

A vital form of communication for businesses, although not strictly speaking an administration system, is the mobile telephone. This form of communication device is not only essential to the sales force but also often used by delivery drivers to update their warehouse as to their estimated times of arrival and length of time taken at each destination. There is a new form of hacker who, using fairly sophisticated scanning devices, can read the mobile phone's number and code. Having gained these two codes, the hacker can then re-programme the chip on another mobile phone and make unauthorised calls using the original mobile phone's number and code. This form of theft is becoming more and more prevalent in the UK and estimates have been made that it costs the telecommunications industry upwards of £1.5m. per day in unauthorised calls.

HEALTH AND SAFETY

As all business organisations have to be aware of and adhere to the regulations laid down in the Health and Safety at Work Act (1974), it is imperative that any administrative systems in place within the organisation do not place any employees in an unsafe or unhealthy environment. If you need to, refer to the section on the Health and Safety at Work Act, Unit 1, before commencing your next piece of work.

The health and safety implications of using computer technology have been outlined in the previous Element. When we extend our consideration of the health and safety concerns to administration systems in general, we should consider the following:

- does the system entail any significant threat to the health or well-being of the user?
- has the user been sufficiently trained and educated in the correct use of the system?
- does the system offer significant benefits which offset any particular threat to the user?
- does the user require any particular protective equipment or clothing?
- are there any implications relating to the use of the equipment which involve additional ventilation or lighting?

Obviously, many administration systems and, indeed, computer systems are often no significant threat to the user. They will, of course, have been thoroughly tested by the manufacturer and will have to conform with a number of health and safety laws.

student activity

(PC 2.2.2, COM 3.2, 3.4, IT 3.3, 3.4, AON 3.1)
To fulfil the requirements of this performance criterion you must now investigate the suitability of an administration system in an organisation. You could undertake this activity during work placement, whilst undertaking part-time work or within your school or college.

You must assess the suitability of the system in terms of its fitness for purpose, its value for money, its security aspects and any health and safety considerations.

You should present your research findings in the form of a word-processed report.

2.2.3 *Identify how information technology developments can change administration systems*

INFORMATION TECHNOLOGY

We have already mentioned in the previous section that information technology has made radical changes to the duties and tasks and the speed of output of personnel carrying out administrative jobs. We intend in this section to look at specific developments in hardware, software, networks, and commercial administration packages.

Administrators are now expected to work with computers and a wide range of electronic equipment used for processing and communicating various types of information. Because of this, they can be described as office technologists, rather than clerical assistants. We look in more detail at the way these changes in technology have affected, or will affect, an individual's work load and productivity in the next section.

Information technology has brought with it a brand new language. Knowing and understanding computer terminology is now essential, as it is used so frequently within business today. Obviously, the extent of benefits from computerisation will vary from organisation to organisation, depending on the complexity of their administration systems. The ability to extract information quickly and distribute it immediately, is of no use if that information is inaccurate or out of date. For these reasons, the selection of hardware and relevant software packages is essential, as is the need for staff training and re-training.

Before we look at developments in some detail, it may be useful at this stage to list some of the computer language in common use, with a brief explanation of each term:

- *buffer* – a part of memory used as a temporary store for the holding of data. Many printers have this buffer facility
- *byte* – a measure of computer memory
- *cursor* – a small flashing block or dash on the screen which indicates where the data will be input
- *disk drive* – a device for storing and retrieving data (these can be hard disks or floppy disks)
- *operating system* (OS or sometimes DOS, for disk operating system) – part of the software that is contained on disk which, when loaded into the memory of the computer, allows the system to be used
- *hard copy* – the printed copy of the information
- *interface* – a term used to describe the processing of data between two systems or sub-systems

- *local area network* (LAN) – a system that connects a number of microcomputers in order that they can share common resources. Even though they are sharing these resources, each microcomputer can act independently of the rest
- *mainframes* – normally these are large computers which may support hundreds of computer terminals, microcomputers, printers, and storage units. Mainframe computers are often used as centres for supporting remote systems. These remote systems can communicate data through links covering long distances
- *stand alone system* – most microcomputers are stand alones. They are capable of working independently of any other system

Let us now look at some of the developments in information technology, with regard to administration systems:

HARDWARE

Anyone who has any knowledge of computers will be aware that their appearance and performance have changed dramatically over recent years. Most significant for individuals working on machines on a regular basis are the following:

- the ability to upgrade machines either by means of an interface, or more recently, with a mini tower case
- advanced sound cards and CD-ROMs have enabled a new wave of software for this new technology
- multimedia applications on CD-ROM can allow you to use an interactive encyclopaedia or proofread a spreadsheet
- portable computer systems offer a solution to those individuals who need to work 'on the move'. These systems now offer:
  - CD-ROM facilities
  - internal speakers
  - internal microphones and amplifiers
  - audio system cards
  - floppy disk drives
  - removable hard disks
  - mains battery chargers
  - carry cases

  thus making them excellent pieces of equipment for those who travel in their job, but still need to maintain links with the organisation itself

- many computer systems are now supplied with built-in applications as standard, e.g. MS-DOS 6.22, Windows for Workgroups 3.11, plus a pre-installed anti-virus

Naturally, with so many new developments, it is, for some, becoming increasingly difficult to keep up to date with what is new and what has been around for some time. Many computer suppliers are aware of this and publish the warning that due to the complexities of particular technologies, some upgrades require a certain level of technical experience. In such cases, they would advise that the installation be carried out on-site (at the premises of the purchaser or upgrader). This, obviously, will add to the expense of upgrading or installing the machine.

In addition to the changes in the complexity of the hard drives of the computer, there are some developments which are of benefit to the user on a more personal and comfort-related basis. These include:

- adjustable brightness and contrast of the screen
- the choice of mix of colours on the screen
- adjustable position of the screen
- adjustable position of the keyboard
- more compact machines – in general, they are less bulky nowadays and take up less space on a desktop

Printers, like the computer, have also advanced dramatically in recent years. The amazing array of printers available has bewildered many would-be purchasers. Increasingly, laser and ink-jet printers have gained a reputation for being the quickest and most efficient printers available on the market at present. Certainly, those that have the following features are regarded as being the 'best buys', although price is obviously a determining factor:

- 360 dpi resolution (this is for sharper print and superior colour – in the case of colour printers)
- quiet printing – very important when more than one printer is housed in one office
- a variety of fonts
- a variety of typefaces
- a good paper capacity, to avoid the constant refilling of the paper feeder
- compatibility with a variety of software packages
- a memory of its own, to allow for several printing jobs to be requested consecutively. If the printer itself has a good memory (approx 4 Mb), then it stores the information sent from the computer until a suitable printing slot is open

Desktop scanners have also made what used to be repetitive and time-consuming work much easier and quicker, with the added benefit of improving the presentation of the work. It is possible, using a desktop scanner, to carry out the following tasks:

Focus study

MOBILE USERS

IBM has launched a new version of its voice recognition system. This new system allows users to dictate notes and figures to their lap-top computers.

The development of a card, replacing the adaptor boards used on desktop computers, has made this innovation possible. At present a similar version installed on a PC desktop would cost £755. It is anticipated that the new lap-top (or notebook) version will cost £855.

- the 'scanning' of pages of existing text using optical character recognition equipment, thus doing away with the need to key large chunks of text into the computer
- the editing and manipulation of text, as well as the editing of photographs and captions
- the changing of shapes, colours and details, which can be merged with other shapes and backgrounds
- the storing of letters, clippings, memos, articles, pages from books and diagrams in a computer, rather than filing them away

Obviously, if an organisation had the use of a desktop scanner, this would radically change the day-to-day duties of the administrator. Tasks like filing and photocopying, which had previously been regularly carried out would no longer be needed. The whole emphasis of the job role would be changed.

SOFTWARE

It would be impossible for us to give you a comprehensive list of the available software at the present time. The availability of new (and improved) software changes weekly, if not daily. As we mentioned earlier, the choice of software will depend very much on the functions carried out by the organisation and the use to which the information generated is put.

We intend in this section to discuss software in terms of the integrated packages which are used most commonly in industry today, or are at least available on the market should organisations or individuals wish to purchase them. Most of these packages include a built-in tutorial which takes the user through the facilities offered on a step-by-step basis. Also available is a 'help' facility which the user can refer to should he/she need assistance. Readily available are the following:

- Borland Office 2.0
- CA Simply Business
- Lotus SmartSuite 2.1
- Microsoft Office 4.2
- Microsoft Office Professional v4.3
- Microsoft Works 3 for DOS
- Microsoft Works for Windows v3

It should be borne in mind that these are integrated packages. That means that they combine the software we discussed earlier, i.e. word processing, spreadsheet, data base, communications and graphics, into one program. The software can be installed onto the hard drive of the computer, and floppy disks can be used to save work. Specifically, a program like Microsoft Works could carry out the following functions:

1 *Word processing*

- creating a document
- correcting a document
- formatting a document (i.e. changing paragraphs, margins, fonts and font sizes)
- placing borders around a paragraph
- creating columns and tables
- linking information from another Works document, e.g. spreadsheet
- copying and moving text, charts, objects, formats and styles – this avoids repetitive typing and helps ensure the accuracy of the document
- creating headers and footers (lines of text which you require to appear at the head (top) and the foot (bottom) of each page of the document)
- creating page numbering
- checking spelling and counting the number of words contained within the document
- including drawings or illustrations from a bank of pictures stored in Microsoft (clipart)
- allowing the drawing of diagrams or illustrations within the word processed document

2 *Spreadsheet*

The Microsoft Works for Windows Spreadsheet can be used for basic or complicated calculations. A simple home budget can be created, as can a full business book-keeping system with automatically updated sales and income categories. The following processes are possible using this package:

- creating a basic spreadsheet
- changing the spreadsheet by changing text, values, formulae, number formats
- changing the spreadsheet by copying and moving cell contents, changing the column width and row height, or shading cells for emphasis
- entering formulae
- viewing the spreadsheet on the screen

- inserting and deleting rows and columns
- changing fonts, font sizes, font styles and colours
- automatically formatting tables
- linking information from a word processed document or from a data base
- organising cell entries in alphabetical or numerical order
- naming groups of cells for references and calculations
- creating, modifying and printing charts (bar charts, pie charts, scatter charts, radar charts, 3-D area charts, 3-D line charts and graphs). This facility includes the option to 'explode' a pie slice on a pie chart

3 *Data base*

With the Microsoft Works for Windows Data base, it is possible to create a filing system to organise, for example, customer records, mailing lists, inventories. Up to 32,000 records can be created. The following can be carried out using this program:

- creating a form for entering information
- inputting information onto the form
- making changes to or amending the information
- adding and deleting fields and changing field names
- changing fonts, font sizes, font styles and colours
- changing number formats
- adding borders, colours and shading to a form
- adding drawings and other objects to a form and changing their size and position (and also layering the objects which have been incorporated)
- linking information from a word processed document or a spreadsheet document
- incorporating clipart into the data base
- using mathematical formulae and functions to create calculating fields
- organising records in alphabetical or numerical order
- selecting specific records for printing purposes

4 *Communications*

With Microsoft Works for Windows and a modem, it is possible to communicate with one another, from computer to computer. We cover the facilities available from this particular section of the program in the next Element of the book. This Unit specifically covers communication, e.g. electronic mail. For the moment, we will look at the facilities available using Microsoft Works for Windows communication package:

- connect with and communicate to another computer
- send and receive information

- connect with a 'bulletin board' to view up-to-the-minute news and sports, plus technical, legal, medical, political, business and other specialised information
- participate in forums for discussing current issues
- make travel arrangements and book hotel accommodation, buy and sell stock and even shop

NETWORKS

Networking allows microcomputers to be linked together in such a way as to enable them to share information and to centralise the distribution of data. The microcomputers will also share the control of the program. In other words, a member of staff who is working on some software relevant to accounts information can input the latest data on a customer. Once that information has been inputted, then all the other linked microcomputers will receive the same information. This is particularly useful when an organisation requires software or applications to be used by more than one person at the same time, or have several people inputting different aspects of the same information at the same time. By using this computerised method, it is possible for one person to extract information for his/her own purpose without having to disturb another member of staff in their duties.

The number of machines that can be linked by networking is very flexible and can be upgraded to suit a particular organisation's needs. Obviously, this is an expensive and complicated area. Most organisations seek advice from specialists before embarking on the installation of a network.

Users of a network system would need to be familiar with the following procedures:

- how to log into the system – it would be advisable for an organisation to have a series of either user names or passwords to allow access into the system. We deal with this is more detail when we cover the security aspect of this Element on pp.144–5
- how to choose the application they need
- how to log out

Many organisations have a number of computers connected to one another so that data may be transferred between terminals. These take the form of either a LAN system or a WAN system. We shall look at these in some detail:

LAN SYSTEM (LOCAL AREA NETWORK)

A LAN system consists of a number of terminals connected together so information and functions can be shared. Each terminal can be considered to be a workstation.

Information should be considered as a resou the sharing of this information provides benef who are involved. Users do not have to rely on disk-based updates of information, as the simple inputting of information at one terminal instantly fulfils the task.

WAN SYSTEM (WIDE AREA NETWORK)

This slightly more sophisticated variety of networking enables terminals to be linked in various remote locations in much the same way as a LAN system. In the UK British Telecom provides the majority of land lines connecting terminals in a WAN system. The use of satellites extends WAN systems world-wide. This enables individuals to engage in tele-working as well as providing offices abroad with instant access to the information stored by the parent company.

Major corporations will employ a LAN and a WAN system working together in order to provide a full range of network facilities. Each office will have its own LAN system but be connected with all other offices by a WAN system. They will all have access to the head office's mainframe via the WAN system.

COMMERCIAL ADMINISTRATION PACKAGES

The term multi-tasking (or multi-user) means very much the same as networking. The difference is that rather than having several microcomputers linked together, one computer has a number of terminals attached to it. This means that each of the terminal keyboards is not actually attached to its own computer, so cannot be termed a computer itself.

Any member of staff, even if at a remote terminal (one that could be miles away from the computer itself), would need to know how to log in, access information and log out. User names or passwords would also be a security consideration for organisations adopting the multi-tasking form of computerisation.

Any organisation considering the choice of either a networking or a multi-tasking form of computerisation would need to take account of a number of factors, including:

- will the system be sufficient on a long-term basis? – it would be ineffective to install a system which could become overloaded too quickly
- is the system upgradable? – can more microcomputers or additional terminals be added in the future?
- does the master processor have sufficient memory to enable it to function effectively?
- will the system be quick enough? – this is important if bottlenecks are to be avoided

- is staff training or retraining necessary? – if so, (and it most likely will be), then is this a viable proposition, in terms of cost and possible disruption?

The choice between a networking and a multi-tasking system is never a clear-cut one and organisations need to consider the following (plus many other factors)

before making a final decision:

- the type of work to be carried out
- the 'loading' of the system
- the response times required
- the support available

2.2.4 *Suggest improvements to an administration system*

IMPROVEMENTS

We have talked in some detail about the different ways an organisation may find it necessary to bring about change elsewhere in this Unit. We need to look here at the ways the administration department can support such changes within the organisation. The installation of a networking system or a multi-user (terminals-based) computer system can help support such a change. Hopefully the organisation would have made very extensive enquiries and sought advice regarding the correct hardware and software for its own purposes. Certainly, if an organisation has successfully 'computerised' then this will mean a very drastic change for some members of staff with regard to their job roles, work load and job satisfaction.

If the changes the organisation has undertaken (or is undertaking) are related to the amount of information technology it has in place, then it can be expected that the following aspects of its operations would be affected:

- the **work load** (including the job role) of individuals within the organisation
- the **service** the organisation is able to provide to its customers
- the rate at which an organisation is able to **produce goods** ready to sell to its customers

Obviously, if an organisation makes a great change, then the administration systems in force within that organisation will also have to change. These changes will, automatically, change the roles of the individuals within the organisation to a greater or lesser degree.

The term work load refers to the duties and responsibilities that an individual undertakes on a regular basis. These may include:

- having the responsibility for one particular department or section
- having the responsibility for one particular administrative system

- having the responsibility for one particular section of an administrative system
- the carrying out of specific tasks on a daily, weekly or monthly basis (e.g. the checking of invoices or the preparation of a monthly departmental budget)

Many of these duties can either be carried out manually by the individual, or can be completed by the use of computer software.

IN SERVICE

We have looked in some detail at customer service on pp.141–2 of this Element. We need to look now at the ways the administration systems can support a change within the organisation with regard to the service that organisation provides for its customers and clients.

Naturally, the success of the service the customers receive is vital to the success of the organisation, as well as the image and perception of the organisation as viewed by competitors.

The ways in which customer service provisions can be affected by organisational change include the following:

- *advertising* and *promotion* – a poor administrative system will not assist the organisation in the promotion of any new or existing products or services
- *quality assurance* – obviously, if the careful monitoring and testing of products and services is not carried out successfully, then the organisation may be considered to have failed
- *selling* and *distribution of products and services* – this is vital to the success of the organisation. If a suitable administrative system is not in place to constantly contact existing and new customers in order to sell goods, then the organisation is making no money. Equally, if products or services have been promised to a customer, then it must be ensured that they arrive at the specified time and in prime condition

- *communication* with new and existing customers – if the organisational structure changes so drastically that poor communication channels are the result, then the service provided to the customer could deteriorate. This deterioration would result in the customer seeking products or services elsewhere
- *credit control* – if administrative systems are not in place to monitor the credit of customers, then the following could be the result:
  - the organisation could lose money
  - the organisation could lose goodwill from the customer
- the handling of *enquiries* – it is important that a quick and efficient telephone system is in operation. In addition, it is equally important that enquiries are handled quickly and efficiently. A first-time customer would not consider approaching the organisation again if his/her first impression was one of sloppiness and inefficiency

Provided the service supplied to customers is improved as a result of any organisational change, then the organisation should grow and flourish.

IN PROCEDURE

If the administrative systems within the organisation are to support the change that has taken place, then the work loads of the members of staff will also have to change in order to support the organisation as a whole. This change will mean that the individual may be:

- *busier* – this will add pressure to complete work on time and accurately. An individual who is too busy will make mistakes
- *less busy* – it may be that hours have been cut for part-time members of staff, or that 'job sharing' has been introduced
- *supervising* more individuals – or alternatively, supervising fewer individuals than he/she had previously been responsible for
- *more efficient* – if the changes have been successful, then the members of staff carrying out their duties will be able to do so in a more effective manner
- *less efficient* – if the changes have been unsuccessful, then obviously the standard of work produced or levels of communication links will hinder the individual

Focus study

IT IMPACT

There are psychological approaches to keeping staff motivated in times of organisational restructuring or upheaval.

British companies no longer have employees who stay in the same place for years. Change has become a way of life, particularly to IT specialists. These specialists are very often at the heart of many corporate restructuring programmes.

Some companies are now looking at new ways to keep staff motivated during periods of upheaval. One approach applies some psychology to efforts to help individuals, groups or even entire organisations to accept the new demands of change.

Companies are looking at new ways, such as teleworking, to reduce costs. This move does mean transferring individuals, groups or teams into new structures. Some concern has been voiced at such a move and it is said that the consequences have not been explored thoroughly. 'When you take an organisation through change you have to raise the tolerance threshold of individuals. If people are asked to start working from home, you create problems if you lack the mechanisms to raise their thresholds' says Vyla Lejeune Rollins, an organisational psychologist with KPMG. She claims that provided an organisation works creatively and constructively with its employees, then

they can be helped into new roles. People involved in IT, in particular, tend to find their motivation in the tasks they perform.

Among the techniques advocated are workshop sessions and exercises for groups and individuals, in order to allow individuals to explore their own feelings about the changes they are involved in – what they find enjoyable, exciting and motivating.

This process can reveal that organisational change or restructuring is not for everyone.

Alternatively, it can be rewarding. Hoskyns, a service supplier organisation used to be organised in divisions determined by the type of service provided. After realising that their clients often had overlapping requirements, Hoskyns decided to implement a three-tier structure – division by industry sector, then five service lines. Hoskyns claim that their staff want to feel they belong to an office and to be locally managed with continuity of their careers and management. They also claim that their staff want technology to be introduced on an ongoing basis.

When the needs of the staff are satisfied, then they feel they are being invested in and can see a number of career options and opportunities. When they are not, there are barriers, either real or imagined, in the way of the progress of the individual and the organisation.

student activity

(PC 2.2.3, COM 3.3, IT 3.1)
Thinking about one administrative system in particular, write a list of the ways you think that the duties, tasks and responsibilities of one individual could be changed as a result of organisational restructuring. What duties would they no longer have to fulfil? What additional responsibilities might they have to undertake?

Compare your list to those of the remainder of your group. Once this comparison has been made, word process a short report which outlines your findings.

Essentially, the way in which procedural change(s) are adopted will make a radical difference to the way in which the administration systems are able to support that change. Hopefully, if administrative duties are carried out more efficiently and effectively, then the result will be an improved service to the customers and it should be possible to improve productivity.

IN EQUIPMENT

Over the past 200 years highly complex equipment and technology have been developed. In terms of the administration systems, we should look at the accessibility and availability of information which can assist people in their work duties. Although this rapid development in technology has signalled the emergence of a number of specialists who need to be consulted in regard to the installation and use of the equipment, many people are now capable of using this equipment.

The Information Society as it is often called, began in the 1950s. The silicon chip made many of the computer advances possible. For organisations the identification of suitable administrative and information systems is an ongoing concern. They need to ensure that they are constantly up to date and have in place reliable systems and procedures to guarantee the smooth running and profitability of the business. It is all a question of information flowing in and out of the organisation in the most efficient manner. As we have mentioned elsewhere in this Unit, each organisation must make its own decision with regard to the applicability of administration systems. There can be no over-arching criteria which can be imposed on any business. It very much depends on the type of information handled, sources used and, indeed, the destination of that information.

Even within one organisation, the needs of different departments for administration systems will differ. The different types of information handled by different departments includes the following:

1 *Administration* – whilst dealing with most office equipment, they will also be concerned with printing and colour copying. Many individuals will work at a computer.
2 *Accounts* – data about purchases, sales, expenses and running costs. Most employees work from computer systems.
3 *Sales* – handling information regarding sales, marketing, products and complaints. A computerised system would be desirable in the management of these complex issues.
4 *Marketing* – market information, product testing and details of competitors. Software applications could assist in the analysis of such information.
5 *Personnel* – information relating to employees, pay rates, employment law and manpower audits. Such information which must, by law, be kept, is often stored on computer data bases.
6 *Production* – information regarding cost effectiveness, production costs and information on raw materials and parts, etc. The production department would require an efficient computer system for up-to-date figures and stock levels.
7 *Research and development* – analysing reports on new processes and developments, carrying out product tests and gauging competitors' activities all benefit from the use of efficient computer administration systems.
8 *Computer services* – naturally, this part of the organisation would be at the forefront of computer and administrative developments, as well as having to test new software programs and handle any faults on other departments' systems or networks.

IN TRAINING

If an organisation instals some form of new technology which will carry out these duties more quickly, then obviously the work load of the individual will be affected to some degree. Let's look at some of the ways work load can be changed:

● the *individual's job title* may be changed – a different title can make the individual feel and seem to others to be more or less important within the organisation
● the *individual's position within the structure of the organisation* may be changed – the position in the structure could have been changed in the following ways:
  – the individual may previously have reported to one line manager only. The change may now require

that person to report to a series of people with authority

– alternatively, the individual may previously have reported to several other people. The change may now mean that he/she has only one line manager

- the *responsibilities of the individual* may have changed – perhaps only with regard to specific job tasks and duties, but in the case of supervisory or managerial positions, perhaps with regard to these supervisory or managerial functions

- the *individual's level of competence to do the job* may have changed – particularly if the individual has been with the organisation for a long time in the same job. If the job has changed to such an extent that that person is no longer deemed to be competent, then this can have major effects on the individual

- the *individual may no longer be considered to hold the personal attributes required* – if this were felt to be the case, then the individual might be asked to engage in some training with regard to personal development

- the *qualifications held by the individual may no longer be relevant* – certain occupations require particular levels of competence related to qualifications as a base. If the change in the organisation has affected the individual's job role, title, tasks and duties, his or her current qualifications may not be sufficient for the new role

- the *individual's experience may not be sufficient* – this is particularly difficult for young employees. The concept of transferrable skills is important here. This term relates to the identification of skills performed in a different situation which may show that the individual should be able to acquire the new skills required

IN PRODUCTIVITY

In much the same way that the service offered to customers could be improved, so too could the level of productivity. Obviously, any organisation developing a new product will encounter some problems. Often, these problems do not manifest themselves until a product is actually in production.

For the purpose of identifying any likely problems, the R & D department will test products during early production runs. Similarly, the production line supervisors or foremen (and sometimes the operatives) may suggest ways in which production costs can be cut and the rate of production increased.

The administrative systems in operation during the production process need to be adequate to ensure that the following criteria are met:

1 *The design of the product is correct* – with regard to the amount of raw materials, manpower and time that may be wasted.

2 *The quality of the finished products is acceptable* – stringent quality standards (e.g. BS 5750) have been in place in the UK for several years. These standards cover production itself, warehouses, shops and offices and are a means of ensuring that the quality of products and services in the UK meet those of other countries. In order to comply with these standards, many organisations have appointed Quality Assurance Officers.

3 *The product is cost effective* – production runs or batches must be planned and executed to ensure that the best resources are being used. Much time is spent on the future planning of production runs. These runs need, when they do take place, to be smooth, uninterrupted and cost effective. Obviously, overheads like lighting, heating and manpower also have to be taken into account. At times when an organisation is particularly busy, or when a job has to be completed by a certain time, then overtime may have to be worked. This additional cost must also be taken into account when the question of cost effectiveness is being addressed.

4 *Communication links between the sales team and the production line are essential.*

If an organisational restructure or change has been carried out successfully, then it is very likely that the above points will be adhered to. If, on the other hand, the change has been implemented poorly, and the organisation is not meeting its customers' demands for products, then the future for the organisation is in danger.

ELEMENT 2.2

a s s i g n m e n t

(PC 2.2.1–4, COM 3.1, 3.2, 3.3, 3.4, AON 3.1, 3.3, IT 3.1, 3.2, 3.3, 3.4)

In order to show that you have covered the necessary performance criteria for this element, you must:

● identify the **procedures** which contribute to an administration system in an organisation
● identify the **processes** which contribute to an administration system in an organisation
● identify the **equipment** which contributes to an administration system in an organisation

If you do not have access to an external organisation, then you should consider studying the systems used in your own school, college or work place.

TASK 1

(PC 2.2.1, 2.2.2)

In report format, explain the suitability of a system used in one business organisation for the purpose of supporting one or more functions of the organisation. You should use the aspects covered in the range statement at the beginning of Element 2.2 as your headings.

TASK 2

(PC 2.2.3, 2.2.4)

In your report, you should explain how information technology is changing or has changed the administration system. You should also suggest ways in which the administration system could be improved.

TASK 3

In addition to your written report you should prepare a 15-minute presentation supported by notes explaining your investigation and findings.

Remember that your report should be word processed and that you should include, if possible, any supporting material such as print-outs, screen dumps or copies of operating manuals.

Analyse communication in a business organisation

PERFORMANCE CRITERIA

A student must:

1 identify **communication** in and between business organisations

2 identify and explain the **objectives of** internal and external **communication**

3 **analyse** the effectiveness of **communication** in a business organisation

4 explain possible **positive** and **negative effects** of changes to communications

5 suggest changes to improve **communications** in a business organisation

RANGE

Communication: *internal, external; communication channels (restricted, open), using electronic technology; to meet special needs*

Objectives of communication: *provide information, give instructions, keep people up to date, make checks, receive feedback, negotiation, confirmation*

Analyse *in terms of: ease of use, ease of access, efficiency of user (health, stress), interaction between people, interaction between organisations, confidentiality, security*

Positive effects: *improved speed of communication, improved access to communication, potential for communication to wider audience*

Negative effects: *incompatible equipment, cost, exclusion from communication, threat to security*

2.3.1 *Identify communication in and between business organisations*

COMMUNICATION

Central to the efficient running of any organisation is the clear and effective channelling of all communications. It is a fundamental requirement of all those in a position of authority, and some who are not, to be able to communicate in a clear and effective manner. To be a good manager or administrator, an individual will need to spend a great deal of time communicating with others, as communication is, of course, a two-way process.

To be a good communicator takes practice and experience. Here are some of the key things to remember when you are communicating. It does not matter who you communicate with – it could be friends, parents, teachers or potential employers – they will all gain an insight into you, and how you conduct yourself, by what you say and how you say it:

- you should always **speak clearly**
- **try not to speak too quickly or too slowly**
- you should **use the right words** for the situation; do not be too complicated or simplistic
- you should be able to **listen** to what the other person is saying so that you can respond properly
- you should **show confidence**; both in yourself and in what you say
- you should try to **put the other person at ease**
- you should **think** about what you say and try to make your responses logical and easy to follow
- you should try to **use the right tone** for the situation; do not be too aggressive or passive or allow your feelings to confuse what it is you have to say
- if you have a regional accent, while this is fine in most situations, if it is too strong or broad, you should **talk slightly more slowly** than normal
- if you think that your voice is not pleasant to listen to, perhaps too high, try to **lower the pitch** of your voice a little. You can help counter this problem by controlling your excitement or speed of talking
- you should **never interrupt** someone who is speaking, wait until he/she has finished
- take care to **use the right tone of voice**, as this can affect how the other person receives what you say. The same statement may be either acceptable or unacceptable, depending on your tone

It is important to identify the main sorts of communication and look at their purposes within the organisation.

INTERNAL COMMUNICATION

The way in which an organisation is structured will determine the channels through which communication is made. There is a definite relationship which needs to be identified – in terms of an individual's position, authority and status within an organisation. Depending on these factors, an individual will be more receptive and accessible through the establishment of an effective communications system. Information needs to flow freely around an organisation. In a small business, it is easy for everyone to know exactly what is going on, but in larger organisations, the flow of information may be awkward and disrupted at various points. Indeed, certain individuals within the organisation will impose barriers to communication to avoid information overload. They will not be interested in or able to handle the sheer volume of information and will have nominated other individuals to perform monitoring tasks on their behalf.

In order to determine how effective the channels of communication are within an organisation, we must look at whether the right information has reached the right person at the right time. If there are any barriers that prevent this from happening, then they must be overcome in order to increase the effectiveness of that individual. The way in which an organisation is structured will often determine how hard or easy it is to get the information through to the right person. Organisations may consider fundamental changes in their structure if these barriers appear to be insurmountable.

Once the information has reached the correct person, it must be in such a format as to allow that individual immediate understanding. If the information is unclear, misleading or ambiguous in any way, then the channels of communication, however good they are, have been wasted.

Many basic forms of communication are applicable to both internal and external situations. The skills of communication are similar whether one is dealing with colleagues or customers. The different needs of these two groups may determine the exact style of the communication. Internal communications can very often be dealt with in an informal manner. We shall look at the various forms of internal communication in turn a little later in this section, but first let us look at communication in general in more detail.

student activity

(PC 2.3.1, COM 3.2, IT 3.1)
List ways in which the lack of good communication within an organisation could affect the performance of that business. What implications do poor internal communications have on the business image and efficiency of a business?

Work in pairs on this activity. After your discussions have taken place, your findings should be presented in the form of an informal word processed report.

The five main types of communication skills are:

- listening
- speaking
- reading
- writing
- information technology

In addition, we must also consider communication that is carried out using none of the above. This is known as non-verbal communication or body language. Let us look at these skills in a little more detail:

1 *Listening* – during the course of a day, we may listen to a number of different people. It is a rare person who will remember everything that has been said to him/her. This is particularly the case if the way in which conversation is listened to is unstructured and confused. In order to use listening as effectively as possible, the individual must:

- actually hear the message itself
- interpret the message
- evaluate the message
- act upon the message and make use of the information it contains

It is a good idea to take notes during a conversation. Some people find it helpful to use a tape recorder.

2 *Speaking* – speaking need not necessarily take place face to face. It may also take the form of a telephone conversation. The use of questioning techniques is important in clarifying the exact nature of the message. To be an effective communicator the individual should have the following qualities:

- clearly know his/her own role in the conversation
- be aware of the receptiveness and interest of those listening

- in some cases, be aware of the listener's own knowledge of the subject of the conversation

Being an effective communicator means making sure that the listener is always attentive and that any points raised within the conversation are not ambiguous.

3 *Reading and writing* – we have chosen to take these two skills together since the writer of the message must be acutely aware of how the message will be received by the reader. To be an effective writer an individual must take the following facts into account when presenting the information:

- that the information might be read by a variety of people in different situations
- that complex information needs to have sufficient background description in order to make it clear
- that the information should be capable of having a long life, in the sense that it may be referred to many times in the future

As with many other forms of communication, the written word may suffer from being ambiguous. Even the most informal of messages needs to be clear. Organisations use standard formats for a variety of written communication. These systems have been designed to avoid ambiguity. Certain forms of written communication can be easier to understand than others, but the writer should ensure that the reader always has sufficient information in order to form an opinion if required. The presentation of data, for example, should be carefully considered since financial information, in particular, can often be misleading or unclear.

4 *Information technology* – information technology has transformed the way in which much information is processed, handled and distributed. The availability of computer facilities throughout organisations has meant that information can be relayed quickly and effectively. This is, of course, vital to the success of a business, but does require that individuals within the organisation be sufficiently trained on many different computer software packages

5 *Non-verbal communication or body language* – as we will see, not all messages rely on the spoken or written word. We can 'read' a great deal into the way in which someone uses his/her body to convey information. Each gesture or facial expression has its own particular meaning. Being able to read these gestures and expressions is a skill in itself, not to mention being able to use these gestures and expressions yourself. An individual will use non-verbal communication in order to support the message he/she is giving or receiving. This form of communication is intended to make the message clearer.

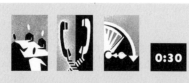

(PC 2.3.1, COM 3.1)

In pairs, alternately taking the role of listener and speaker, carry out the following exercise to evaluate your own skills. First, recount a recent event in your life to your partner, then ask him/her to paraphrase this conversation back to you. Now it is your turn. See how well you listen to your partner's conversation by paraphrasing to him/her what you have heard.

Although you may not have heard of the term, we all use non-verbal communication (NVC). It is important to know how to use it, what it means and how you can read other people's NVC. Let's start with the face and what that can give away about what you are really saying:

- raising the eyebrows could show surprise or disbelief
- if your pupils dilate, this could mean either anger or love
- opening your eyes wide might show hostility
- grinning would show that you accept what is being said or are simply friendly

We are sure that you can think of many more of these facial expressions.

Gestures, on the other hand (no pun intended), can also give interesting clues as to what the speaker really means.

- pointing, to identify someone or something directly when referring to it
- giving a thumbs-up sign, to signify agreement or acceptance
- shaking your head, to show disagreement
- fiddling with something, such as jewellery, a tie or the strap of a bag may infer nervousness
- pacing up and down may show impatience or boredom
- looking at your hands, or fiddling with something may show disinterest

Posture shows some interesting things too:

- standing upright shows alertness
- sitting in a hunched position shows nervousness
- lounging in a chair, on the other hand, shows ease
- standing with your shoulders hunched, shows that you are miserable or depressed

Where you stand or sit, in relation to the person you are talking to, can show some important things:

- you are likely to stand closer to a person whom you know well
- where you stand, and how close to a person, may depend upon your nationality or upbringing
- the nature of the circumstances in which you met the person to whom you are talking will have an effect on how close you stand to that person

(PC 2.3.1, COM 3.1)

In pairs, discuss a topic of your choice, preferably one which interests you. While communicating note the different NVCs used by your partner. What do they indicate to you? After five minutes compare your lists with one another.

Internal communication in organisations will include the following methods:

MEMORANDA

Internal memoranda are used for communication between different departments within the same organisation. These are often called memos. An example of a memo is given in Figure 2.3.1. You will see that it is normally shorter than a business letter and usually deals with one particular subject. When more than one point is being made it is normal to number them.

Memos are not signed in the same way as a business letter, but the person issuing the memo would normally initial it at the end.

REPORTS

Although reports issued or received by an organisation can be either informal or very formal, both types contain certain common elements, although not necessarily in the same format.

A report may contain research which has been carried out for a specific purpose. It may be the findings and recommendations of work that has been carried out for a specific purpose. Or it may be an account of something which has taken place and been reported on. A report will contain the following headings:

- *terms of reference* – this will state what you have been asked to do. It may be that you have been asked to conduct research on a particular topic

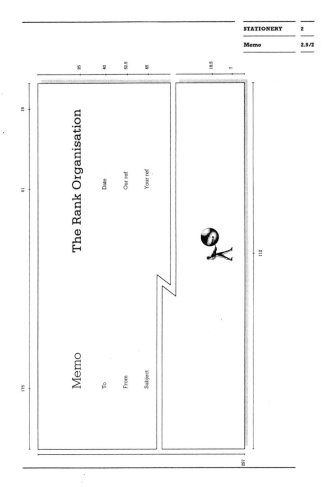

STATIONERY	2
Memo	2.9/2

FIG. 2.3.1 *This illustration shows an example of Rank Organisation's standard stationery requirements. Note the structure of the memorandum document.*

- *procedure* – this will say how you have gone about gathering the information you are stating
- *findings* – in this section you would state what facts you have found out. You would not make statements about your recommendations at this stage, but simply state facts
- *conclusion* – this would be a general statement about your findings. Again this is not the place you would make recommendations, but it is where you would conclude and sum up your findings
- *recommendations* – on the basis of your findings and conclusions you would make recommendations for future research or projects

It is usual to sign and date a report. Sometimes it is helpful to break down the headings used in a report. This could be done by using a series of numbers, for example:

   1 Establishment of company catering facilities
      (a) Lunch period arrangements
      (i) Arrangements of seating

student activity

(PC 2.3.1, COM 3.2, IT 3.1, 3.2)
Compile a report on the effectiveness of different forms of communication. In this report you should include all the advantages and disadvantages as well as the features of each type of communication. You should use the correct report format, which should be word processed.

PREPARING A SUMMARY

It may be that during the course of your work you will be asked to use the written form of communication called summarising. This means that you are given a long article or report and have to read it and present the information more briefly. The original document may be long and complicated, so it is necessary that you understand the information you read before you start. You would then take out the unnecessary facts and write a shorter information pack. The following are guidelines for carrying out this task:

1 Read through the whole document first, rather than trying to understand everything as you go through.
2 Re-read the document more thoroughly. You could highlight the areas of importance at this stage, or cross out the unnecessary information.
3 Make a list of the items you have to use and that it is important to include.
4 Compare your list with the main document to make sure you have not forgotten anything important.
5 Write a draft summary. It may be that a superior should check this for you at this stage. Once you are happy with this draft, you may want to write a final draft.
6 Once the final draft has been agreed, you can write the final summary.

WRITING A PROJECT

Just as you write projects for your college work, so you may be asked by your employer to write a project for him/her. If this task is new to you, it may be useful to look at some of the guidelines for completing projects:

1 *Preparation* – the first thing you need to find out is the date for completion of the project. Allow yourself plenty of time to research and write up the information.

2 Secondly, find out exactly what is required of you. How long does the project have to be? How many pages of typing or writing is expected? Is there a limit to the number of words submitted?

3 Do you have to submit the project in a certain format? Are there set headings you are expected to use?

4 Where will you find the information you need? Make a list of the sources of information you will need to use. These may include:

- your local library
- local and national newspapers
- local and national radio and television
- banks
- building societies
- post offices
- citizens' advice bureaux
- chambers of commerce

Many other organisations offer assistance in project work. It will obviously depend on the type of research you are carrying out.

PAPERS AND BRIEFS

These documents take the form of additional information provided by individuals to assist decision makers. In other words, their key function is to enable others to make the right decision. These documents will include essential background information on a particular subject, usually written by an individual with a particular interest or experience in this area. A discussion document also gives essential background material, but in addition offers advice as to the decision which should be made. These documents will usually include a series of arguments for and against a particular course of action and these must be considered in the process of arriving at a preferred conclusion.

NOTES

These short, often informal, forms of communication take the form of handwritten pieces of information. Under this heading, we may include telephone messages, informal arrangements and details of informal short meetings.

NOTICEBOARDS

If an organisation wishes to pass a message on to a number of employees, it may place information on its staff noticeboards. These messages may be formal or informal. Perhaps there is a change to normal organisational procedures, or maybe a social event is being planned by the organisation's personnel department.

Notices allow the quick and easy sending of information to a large number of people. Noticeboards can also be used by individuals wishing to inform employees of items for sale or of events planned.

NEWSLETTERS

Another way that an organisation can inform all of its employees of matters of interest is by issuing a newsletter. Several larger organisations use newsletters to contact all members of staff, particularly where they have different branches around the UK. These newsletters can include both formal and informal information. They may state the fact that a director is retiring, or, even, that one of the sales assistants has recently given birth to a baby.

AGENDAS

The success of a meeting will be largely determined by the way in which it has been organised in advance. The document that is used to inform those who are to attend a meeting about the nature of that meeting is known as an agenda.

Essentially, an agenda has the following format:

- apologies for absence
- minutes of the last meeting
- matters arising from the minutes
- reports
- motions
- any other business
- date of next meeting

```
                    A G E N D A

for the Annual General Meeting of the Gt Yarmouth Camera Club

1    Apologies for absence

2    Minutes of the last meeting

3    Matters arising

         3.1  Subscription fees

         4.2  Planned exhibition

4    Final plan for next exhibition

5    Purchase of new equipment

6    Any other business

7    Date of next meeting
```

FIG. 2.3.2 *This shows the normal layout of a typical agenda. The format is standard for most organisations.*

MINUTES OF MEETINGS

Minutes are the record of meetings and include the following:

- a list of those present at the meeting
- decisions made
- discussions which have taken place
- tasks allocated to individuals

- reports received from individuals
- actions to be taken in the future
- details of individuals to whom decisions made refer

It is the responsibility of an appointed individual (usually a secretary capable of taking shorthand) to record and prepare formal minutes. These are then typed and distributed to members present at the meeting, together

```
          MINUTES OF THE ANNUAL GENERAL MEETING
             OF THE GT YARMOUTH CAMERA CLUB
   Held at the Bendix Hotel, at 7.30 on Friday 7th January 199-.

Present:        Mr J Clyde (in the Chair)
                Mr B Butler
                Miss S Smith
                Mr J Thompson
                Mrs B Brett
                Mr A Sharman
                Mrs P Hunt

1    Apologies for absence

     Apologies for absence were received from Mrs Bryant and
     Miss Leech.

2    Minutes of the last meeting

     The Minutes were read and signed as being a true and
     accurate record.

3    Matters arising

     3.1  Subscription fees

          It was agreed that the fees would be increased to £15
          with effect from 6 April.

     4.2  Planned exhibition

          A sub-committee was formed in order that plans for
          next year's exhibition could begin to be under way.
          Mr Sharman would chair the sub-committee and
          volunteers would be sought to assist in some fund-
          raising activities.

4    Final plan for next exhibition

     As the exhibition is only now 3 weeks away, it was decided
     to hold an Extraordinary Meeting to discuss the final
     arrangements in more detail.  It was felt that more could
     be achieved by doing this than trying to cover all items on
     this Agenda.

5    Purchase of new equipment

     The Treasurer reported that funds are very low at the
     moment, and although members had been requesting some new
     dark-room equipment, he felt it would be unwise to spend
     any money until after the exhibition had been held.

6    Any other business

     There being no further business, the meeting closed at
     9.15.

7    Date of next meeting

     The date of the Extraordinary Meeting was arranged for
     Friday 14th January at 7.30.

     The date for next year's Annual General Meeting would be
     arranged at a later date.




     .................................
          Chairman
```

FIG. 2.3.3 *The minutes shown here relate to the agenda in Figure 2.3.2. You will see that all items appearing on the agenda have been covered in the minutes, showing the outcomes of discussions.*

with the agenda of the next meeting. This is to ensure that a correct and true account has been made of the previous meeting and that it may be agreed in the next meeting that the minutes present an accurate account of what happened.

Although minutes should be concise and precise, they should not lose any accuracy in this process. The writing style required may seem short and abrupt and often a form of numerical recording is used against each minuted item. The subsequent distribution of the minutes further assists members present by reminding them of decisions made and any actions which they personally have to take.

Certain organisations, in particular local authorities, must have their minutes available for public inspection. The details of any motions voted upon or amendments made to these motions must be clearly detailed in the minutes for public perusal.

EXTERNAL COMMUNICATION

Most business organisations spend a considerable amount of their time communicating with their customers. Some of this communication, as we have already seen, will take the form of face-to-face or verbal communication. However, it is essential that some of these communications are supported by written evidence of agreements made.

In our day-to-day life, we use written communications, and it is just as important when writing a personal letter to a friend or a note to one of the family as in business correspondence, that we ensure our spelling and grammar are correct. In all organisations, neat, accurate and reliable written communication is vitally important.

Organisations are often very concerned about how external organisations view them. The view of external organisations is often affected by the way in which they receive information from that organisation. While the organisation will try to respond in an appropriate manner, it must take care to ensure that its reputation is maintained at a high level in all the communication methods it uses.

External communications include the following:

COMPLETION OF FORMS

In everyday life, as well as in the business world, there are a large variety of forms to complete. When carrying out this task, there are some useful guidelines you should follow to ensure that you make a neat and accurate job of completing forms:

1 If possible take a photocopy of the form so that you can practise first. If this is not possible, complete in

pencil first to avoid messy crossings out.

2 Read the form thoroughly before you even consider starting to complete it.

3 Make sure you know how to complete the form before you start, and that you have all the information required readily to hand.

4 Check to see if there is any instruction regarding the colour of pen to use. Some forms stipulate 'use black pen'.

5 Check to see if there is any instruction regarding the style in which you have to complete the form. Some forms stipulate 'use block capitals only'.

6 Use your neatest handwriting.

7 Try to complete all parts of the form. If there is some information you do not have readily to hand, then do not send the form off until it is fully completed.

student activity

(PC 2.3.1)

What would your impression be of an organisation which failed to return a telephone call or to reply to some form of correspondence you had sent? With this in mind, identify areas where you consider it important for an organisation to have good communication with customers and suppliers.

Form initiation

The initiation and design of forms is a specialised activity and the following guidelines are, of necessity, technical in nature. Basically, one can distinguish between forms that are wholly, or in part, subject to data processing constraints and those free from such constraints.

Form design

There are two important aspects of form design. Firstly, there is the efficiency of the form which, because of its appearance and layout, aids use. Secondly, there is the Rank corporate style which by its consistent application creates a positive impression.

The visual arrangement and appearance of any form should aid clarity of information content as well as legibility and ease of use, both by the person entering information on the form and by the person who needs to retrieve selected information from the form.

Where there is a hierarchy of importance, a distinction must be made between hierarchy in terms of form content and structure, and hierarchy in terms of actual reading. When forms are regularly used by staff, most wording is no longer actually read and the typography must aid recognition and location; but considerations of familiarity do not as a rule apply to forms or those portions of forms used by members of the public, and the typography must aid legibility.

It should be borne in mind that type size is not an indicator of importance and that simultaneous emphasis on many items is counter productive.

Design guidelines for forms

Plan the basic layout giving consideration to the contents, order and general position of the information to be included. Take any constraints into account at the planning stage. Position the name of the company, title of the form and symbol. Divide the form into horizontal positions and vertical columns, based on the likely amount of information each entry will require. Use the entire printable area of the paper and try to achieve a balanced appearance.

Plan and lay out the form roughly first, using the grid printed at the end of this section.

When the basic layout has been finalised, fine detailing can begin. Each caption should be positioned exactly on a grid co-ordinate, therefore conforming to 12pt vertical divisions and 5 or 6 character horizontal divisions. This will enable the typist to position all entries automatically without constant re-alignment and adjustment.

Align all information horizontally and vertically into columns wherever possible.

When all wording required has been positioned use vertical and/or horizontal rules to create boxes and separate the areas of information. Distances between words and rules should be consistent both vertically and horizontally. One weight of rule is generally sufficient, but a thicker weight can be used for emphasis or the division of information into areas.

Check that the layout is appropriate, clear and the positioning of all information is correct before involving a printer.

STATIONERY	2
Forms	2.10
Introduction	2.10/1

FIG. 2.3.4 *Within Rank Organisation's corporate identity manual, they clearly detail exactly how forms should be created and designed. This attention to detail ensures that the corporate image is consistent throughout the organisation.*

8 Check thoroughly everything you have completed before you send it off. If possible ask someone else to look at it – sometimes you do not see your own mistakes.

INVITATIONS

Informal and formal invitations may be sent or received by organisations. When these are being issued in bulk, they are normally printed by a specialist company and simply prepared for postage within the organisation. An invitation will usually contain the following information:

- the address of the person sending out the invitation
- the date the invitation is sent out
- the names of the people acting as host/hostess at the event
- the date of the event
- the venue of the event
- the time of the event
- the reason for the event (e.g. 18th birthday party)
- RSVP – this is a request for a reply and is taken from the French phrase 'répondez s'il vous plaît'. Sometimes a deadline for replies is also given

student activity

(PC 2.3.1, COM 3.2, IT 3.1, 3.2)
Design an invitation card using a word processor for an organisation of your choice. This should relate to a public open day. Only specific individuals will be invited. Word process your invitation.

BUSINESS LETTERS

A business letter, unlike a memorandum, is one that would be sent outside the organisation. It is important that such letters are neat, accurate and well presented.

The headed paper used by an organisation for its business letters forms part of its corporate image. The examples shown in the following figures give the information an organisation would wish each of its customers or clients to see regularly:

- the name and address of the organisation
- the telephone number, fax number and/or telex number of the organisation
- the registered address of the organisation, as this may be different from the postal address
- the company registration number
- the names of the directors of the organisation

FIG. 2.3.5 *Cunard Line Ltd.'s rather impressive letterhead.*

- any other companies the organisation may represent or be affiliated to

The layout or format of the business letter will usually also be part of the organisation's corporate image, and different organisations have their own rules about the way in which a letter should be displayed. It is common to use the fully blocked method of display which means that each part of the letter commences at the left hand margin.

student activity

(PC 2.3.1, COM 3.2)
In your own student role, write a letter in correct business format requesting information from an organisation of your choice. You should ask specifically for their company report.

COMPANY TRAINING

Peugeot Talbot Motor Company PLC
Registered Office: Aldermoor House, P.O. Box 227, Aldermoor Lane, Coventry CV3 1LT
Telephone: 0203 884000 Fax: 0203 884001 Telex: 311914
Registered in England No. 148545

FIG. 2.3.6 *Peugeot Talbot's Company Training Division's let-terhead. Note the inclusion of the crest following the gaining of the Queen's Award for Export Achievement in 1992.*

LETTERS OF COMPLAINT

Organisations will, in their business activities receive a number of complaints from their customers, or indeed suppliers. Many will express strong emotions, particularly if money is involved. It is important for the organisation to respond in a helpful and constructive manner. A good letter of complaint from the complainant's point of view should follow these guidelines:

- set out the facts clearly
- be relevant
- be polite
- state that the complainant requires a favourable response

The organisation, in response to the letter of complaint, may have to write a letter of apology. This may involve the following, in addition to the apology:

- financial compensation
- an offer to replace the goods
- an undertaking that the situation will not arise again
- an undertaking that an individual within the organisation has been disciplined

student activity

(PC 2.3.1, COM 3.2)
In the role of an irate customer, write a letter of complaint concerning the poor service you have received when requesting information from a sales assistant in a retail outlet.

If the organisation discovers that the complaint is without justification then, in order to maintain goodwill, a token offer may be made.

Whatever the circumstances, justified or unjustified, letters relating to customer complaints should be carefully put together. They should always use restrained language, such as 'Please be assured that this situation will not arise again'. With the best will in the world an organisation is prone to errors and cannot really guarantee that something similar will not happen at some point in the future.

All letters of complaint should be dealt with promptly but some may need enquiries to be undertaken before the complaint can be addressed.

student activity

(PC 2.3.1, COM 3.2)
In the role of the manager of the retail outlet concerned in the previous activity, write a letter of apology in response to the complaint.

CIRCULARS, STANDARD LETTERS AND DIRECT MAIL

These forms of letters are often used for advertising purposes. Standard letters, in the main, can also be used for inviting individuals to attend job interviews.

These sorts of letters take the form of a basic word processed letter which is merged using computer software with a datafile containing names and addresses.

Such letters are not always personally addressed and they may simply refer to the 'occupier'. This is particularly true of circulars as many thousands of these may be distributed in a particular mail shot. Circulars have three main goals:

- to create an impact by using a striking headline or picture
- to encourage the reading of the letter by using the appropriate language or stating boldly that the individual will receive a free gift for example
- to be memorable by using appropriate slogans in large type

REFERENCES AND TESTIMONIALS

Many organisations are required at various times to provide references or testimonials for individuals. References are much more common and testimonials need not necessarily relate to an employee of an organisation.

I *References* – often references are written on a standard form provided by a potential employer. In other cases, a letter can be written in relation to a number of guidelines laid down by the potential employer. These references are always written by an individual who has some knowledge of the applicant and will contain statements regarding that individual's abilities, character, quality of work and performance.

student activity

(PC 2.3.1, COM 3.2)
In the role of a manager, write a reference for one of the members of your group.

2 *Testimonials* – a testimonial is essentially a letter of commendation. It has not been written with a particular job in mind, but contains general information regarding the individual. Organisations may be asked to write testimonials for other individuals who are not necessarily employees.

The writing of references and testimonials provides the organisation with some moral problems. A reference should be truthful as far as the organisation is aware. The organisation must be careful not to make defamatory statements which could harm the reputation of an individual. The writer needs to strike a balance between the truth and tact. In other words, when reading a reference, one should often look for what is not said. There is no legal obligation to provide a reference or a

testimonial and much can be inferred from an employer choosing not to give a reference to an individual. It should be noted that employers must give permission before their name and address is given to a potential employer. In some cases, a potential employer will contact a previous employer by telephone if a quick decision is needed.

COMMUNICATION CHANNELS (RESTRICTED, OPEN)

Obviously, whatever the type or size of an organisation, there will be confidential material which should not be for the use or inspection of everyone in general.

In order to restrict the amount of communication which goes on within the organisation, it is usual for some of the channels to be restricted. Let us look at the two types of channels of communication separately:

I *Restricted* – restricted channels of communication allow the organisation to keep the information in question available to only a few selected individuals in the organisation. This information may include:

- *confidential material* regarding a new product or range of products – only those involved in the development of this product(s) will be entitled to view, for example, the list of materials involved in the production process
- *employee files* – only the personnel department and possibly the line manager of the employee concerned will be allowed access to this information
- *application forms* – only the personnel department and possibly the line manager of the post involved will be allowed access to this information
- *management information systems*, for example, can ensure that information goes to specified individuals only. This can contribute to the control, confidentiality and security of the information

2 *Open* – open communication channels tend to be those types of communication where everyone within the organisation is at liberty to see and be aware of the information involved. Examples of open communication channels are:

- *noticeboards*
- *newsletters*
- *minutes* of meetings which are circulated to all staff
- non-confidential *internal mail* which is distributed openly
- *multi-user systems*, which offer significant advantages to an organisation in the case of non-

restricted information. Access to this information via a multi-user computer system will involve the availability of numerous terminals throughout the organisation

In order to ensure that all employees are aware of the limitations of access to restricted information, confidential labels or sealed internal post envelopes will be used.

Obviously, if an organisation uses electronic mail systems for the communication of internal and external correspondence, then systems will be in place to ensure that monitors are not left switched on or displaying information whilst the employee is out of the office. Similarly, passwords and user codes will be used to restrict the access to information contained on disk within the computer system.

USING ELECTRONIC TECHNOLOGY

The installation of information technology was initially met with a great deal of scepticism. Many organisations adopted information technology without any serious regard to the uses to which it would be put. However, more recently, organisations have recognised the need to use information technology and to develop employee skills to handle its functions.

The skills required fall into two main categories – general and specialist skills. We shall look at these in detail first before considering the nature of the electronic technology itself.

1 *General skills* – nearly all jobs have been affected in some way by the adoption of electronic technology. As a result, most employees must know in general terms how this technology works. Increasingly, technological systems have been integrated via a networking system and are no longer the relatively simple stand alone desktop PC.
2 *Specialist skills* – nearly 1 per cent of the working population can now be considered to have specialist technology skills in relation to the use of computers. Specialists will have particular skills in one or more computer functions, and they may include the following:

- word processing
- desktop publishing
- data base
- spreadsheet
- graphics

As we have said, technology has transformed businesses and as a result many benefits have been enjoyed. These benefits include the following:

student activity

(PC 2.3.1, COM 3.1)
As a group, audit the specialist technology skills available between you. How were these skills acquired and are there areas concerning electronic technology that all of you lack?

- cost reductions
- simplified and efficient workflows
- increased responsiveness to customer needs
- additional job satisfaction
- ability for employees to learn new skills

While the adoption of technology can be seen as a positive step, it is essential that all computers be user-friendly. The recent introduction of the Graphical User Interface has allowed technology to be more easily understood by the use of icons. All an operator needs to do is to use a mouse to click onto an icon which, in turn, redraws the screen and offers a new set of options.

The 'windows' systems allows the operator to undertake a series of simultaneous tasks by over-writing new screens onto the existing screen. In this way, other files may be perused and referred to and the user may then return to the original document. This system is fast becoming the industry standard.

As we have already mentioned, computer systems enable an individual to carry out the following main tasks, which include:

- the **recording** of information
- the **checking** of information
- the **sorting** and **classification** of information
- the **summarising** of data
- the **calculation** of financial data
- the **storage** and **retrieval** of information
- the **reproduction** of information
- the **communication** of information to remote terminals

Specifically, these processes are covered by the following:

1 *Word processing* – the main function of a word processing package is the manipulation, storage and retrieval of text. In addition, a modern word processing system will allow graphics to be inserted into the text and via a data base will provide names and addresses for mail shots.

2 *Desktop publishing* – DTP systems have been developed by merging the functions of word processing and graphics packages. On a DTP system the operator has the facility to use a variety of different typefaces, fonts and styles in conjunction with various illustrations. It is possible to produce a very professional document using a DTP package.

3 *Data bases* – the storage of information is important to most business organisations. The construction of a data base that will provide the information you require needs careful consideration. When constructing a data base the designer must know what information will be required from the data base and what information needs to be input into the data base in order to fulfil these demands. The data base is capable of producing information in various forms such as bar charts or line graphs. To get the full benefit from a data base it is essential to ensure that the information recorded is constantly updated.

4 *Spreadsheets* – the task of a spreadsheet package is to manipulate and organise numbers. Spreadsheets are used when making calculations and forecasts. Provided the correct information has been entered into the spreadsheet package, then the computer can calculate a number of useful totals.

Through networking and the creation of integrated software packages, an operator is able to access all of these key technological functions simultaneously and gain access to information from the individual terminal and the mainframe computer system.

TELECOMMUNICATIONS

Telecommunications have had a drastic impact on the communications systems of organisations. At a stroke, many new forms of telecommunication have replaced traditional forms of communication. We shall begin by looking at the three forms of telecommunication:

1 *Enhanced telephone systems* – in recent years modern telephone systems have been developed to provide many new features, including:

- visual display of number dialled
- a redial button
- a secrecy button
- a timer so that the call cost may be estimated
- a memory facility for all regularly dialled numbers
- the day, date and time
- conferencing

Switchboards, too, are much more sophisticated and allow the telephone operator to assess the status of

---

SOFTWARE USED WITHIN PEUGEOT

WINDOWS - Word :- A word processing package used primarily for typed documents.

       - Lotus :- A package used for spreadsheets.

       - Freelance :- Used primarily to produce OHP's and slides.

The Company is moving steadily towards a total windows environment. Windows and the packages that go with it require modern hardware. Those people who have slightly older machinery use some of the older packages, primarily Displaywrite which is a word processing package and DOS Lotus which is a spreadsheet package. These are increasingly being phased out as the company continues to expand its modern hardware.

Another form of software used by the company are databases. These are used to set up large databanks of information. An example is the Assisted Development Programme (ADP) in which a record is kept of all employees partaking on some sort of course within the scheme. The records holds their names, address, course, cost, date of course and tax paid.

Other than the software used above the company is linked up through a mainframe network. A couple of examples of the uses of this are included, these being MEMO an electronic Mail System and Cyborg a Computerised Personnel Information System.

FIG. 2.3.7 *A brief summary of software employed by Peugeot Talbot – from their detailed information package on information technology.*

each individual line on the system. Switchboards can also identify which extension should be dialled in response to a particular call. They also have the facility to log calls and record them, thus assisting in the monitoring of unauthorised personal calls made by employees and enabling the cost of the calls to be attributed to particular departments and their budgets.

Cellular phones enable individuals to be contacted in remote locations and important information to be transmitted wherever that individual may be. A hands-free system has been developed for car phones in order to avoid the perils of telephone use and driving.

An alternative to cellular phones, and in many respects cheaper, is the radio-pager. These enable the individual carrying the radio-pager to be contacted and given a short message or telephone number. Additional facilities available on a radio-pager are:

● using the PABX system (private automatic branch exchange) an individual may be 'bleeped' to inform him/her that there is a message
● multiple radio-pagers may be 'bleeped' simultaneously
● there is a short visual display consisting of either the telephone number to be contacted or brief details of the message

Answering machines have become a vital part of business communications, despite the fact that people are not keen on talking into machines. When the individual called is not available, or when there is no-one to take the message on an extension, then the answering machine can receive the message.

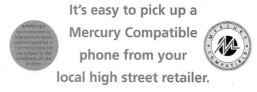

It's easy to pick up a Mercury Compatible phone from your local high street retailer.

To help you choose the one which best meets your needs, start by consulting this leaflet.

All the phones featured in this leaflet are Mercury Compatible, which means they have a dedicated Mercury button and display the "Mercury Compatible" symbol.

Mercury Compatible phones enable you to make fast, trouble-free connection to Mercury's network at the convenient touch of a button.

There is a wide range of styles of Mercury Compatible phones available with up-to-the-minute features to choose from at affordable prices. You can buy them from high street retailers – stockists for each phone are listed in this leaflet. Alternatively, you can buy any of them from the Mercury Customer Centre at 67 Theobalds Road, London WC1 (near Holborn Tube). Telephone 071 971 8500 for details of their mail order service.

So... the choice is yours.

FIG. 2.3.8 *A page from Mercury Communications' 'Mercury Compatible Phones' booklet, which lists some 30 different enhanced telephone systems.*

student activity

(PC 2.3.1, COM 3.1)
In the role of a sole trader operating a washing machine repair service, devise a suitable message which could be left on an answering machine.

2 *Facsimile machines* – another way an organisation may choose to communicate with its customers or clients is by the use of the facsimile machine, colloquially known as the 'fax' machine. The word facsimile means 'an exact and faithful reproduction of' and applies to text, photographs and graphic images. An added benefit of a fax machine is that an organisation is not limited to what it can send. It is also useful for organisations which need to contact companies overseas. Fax machines are left on for 24 hours a day, and do not have to be continually monitored through the night. This means that the time differences between countries are not a problem.

3 *Electronic mail* – this offers all of the facilities provided by fax and telex, but is paperless. Electronic mail offers the additional advantage of being able to store messages when the destination terminal is busy. Electronic mail systems offer a variety of common features, including:

● terminals to prepare and store messages
● a communication link with other workstations within the network
● a central controlling computer

- a directory of addresses
- a central mailbox
- a system which dates the message
- a function that notes that the message has been received by the addressee
- a facility to multiple-address so that all members of a particular working group are sent the message simultaneously
- a prioritising system so that messages can be identified as important or routine
- a storage facility in order to keep in the memory those messages that have not yet been received
- compatibility with existing equipment and computer systems

Electronic mail offers a number of advantages in relation to other forms of communication, including:

- savings on stationery and paper costs
- savings on telephone costs
- rapid transmission
- integration with other systems
- recording of all transmissions so that accurate costings may be obtained
- allowing employees to tele-work
- allowing the addressees to peruse their electronic mail at their leisure

Another version of the electronic mail system may be found in the electronic data interchange which enables individuals to exchange business documents using the same communication system.

Electronic diaries and calendars are becoming increasingly common and allow individuals to make diary entries and searches on particular days or events, thus avoiding the need to enter information manually in a personal handwritten business diary.

Electronic noticeboards and viewdata now allow a mass of information to be accessed via workstation screens. This is provided in the UK by Prestel and is essentially an interactive system which allows viewing and transmission of information.

student activity

(PC 2.3.1, COM 3.1)
In the role of office services manager, what positive steps could you take to ensure that information within the organisation reached its destination quickly and efficiently? Discuss this in pairs.

Videotex is the general name for all computer based information systems which provide information and make information available to a wide variety of users. Videotex is divided into two main areas – viewdata and teletext. Viewdata uses the telephone system to make contact, but teletext is broadcast via the television signal.

TO MEET SPECIAL NEEDS

Obviously, another vital function of communication systems is to ensure that the maximum number of individuals are able to take part in that communication process. In any organisation, there may well be individuals who have special needs. Alternatively, the customers of that organisation may also have special needs. We will identify and address the main remedies required to cater for those with special needs.

SIGN LANGUAGE

People with a hearing impairment may require sign language to aid communications. Although many deaf people can lip read, a business should not rely on this as being their only means of communication with deaf people.

Focus study

SIGN LANGUAGE

Two young unemployed deaf men have recently developed a pocket-sized guide to sign language. The guide that they produced received a runners-up award in the 1993 BT Young Deaf Achievers Scheme.

The Thornaby Young Deaf Enterprise Project won the 1994 Touche Ross Award for Ideas for Youth, jointly sponsored by *The Times* and Touche Ross, with their new CD-Rom version. This dictionary will prove to be invaluable not only to the deaf, but also as a useful resource for businesses.

BRAILLE

Braille is an alphabet that was designed to be read by the blind. Each letter of the alphabet consists of a pattern of raised dots on a 3×2 grid. A braille printer (or embosser) can now be connected to a personal computer which has translation software to convert normal word processed text into braille characters. There is also a speech synthesiser to tell the operator what buttons have been pressed. The obvious applications for businesses include the ability to respond in braille to enquiries, and to produce sales literature and other materials in braille.

AUDIO VISUAL AND ELECTRONIC VOICE

Speech is the fastest and easiest way to communicate. Despite the wide availability of the fax machine and electronic mail, most of us still reach for the telephone when we need to give or receive information quickly. In addition to this, there are still many people who have little or no keyboard skill, thus making it almost impossible for them to use electronic mail.

Much research has been carried out over recent years on computer systems which can translate speech into typed text. Recent developments in the amount of power and memory available mean that systems are beginning to become available.

All speech recognition systems work in a similar way. After recording and digitising the speech signal, they compare it to a lexicon of possible words to find the best fit. This works in much the same way as a spell-checker works on a word processing package.

When speech recognition technology becomes more mainstream, new applications will emerge. One possibility is to put the software onto a credit-card sized device, so that smaller, lighter devices can accept speech input. Slightly further ahead is the possibility of 'smart' mobile phones. It is not possible at the moment to telephone your office PC or switchboard and dictate to it. If, however, smart phones can be incorporated, then this would be a possibility.

2.3.2 Identify and explain the objectives of internal and external communication

OBJECTIVES OF COMMUNICATION

One of the key objectives of all organisations is successful communication both within the business and with customers and clients.

Although all people consider themselves to be good communicators, this is not always the case. In any organisation with a large number of employees, it is obvious that communication problems will be encountered if the correct systems are not in place to monitor the information provided to those individuals. Should these systems prove to be inefficient, then gaps occur between the intended instruction and the action taken by the individual. These breakdowns in communication can be costly to an organisation, both in terms of efficiency, and financially. With this in mind, much research has been carried out to try to analyse what problems can be encountered if poor communication systems are in place, and to identify how they can be improved.

We look at the **objectives** of communication, both internal and external, in more detail now, but later in this Unit we look at how effective communication can be, and some ways it could possibly be improved.

In order to evaluate the impact that communication systems have on specific businesses, it is essential that we consider a number of common measures:

- accuracy of the system
- whether the system creates efficiency
- whether in relation to alternative methods of communication, the system used is cost effective
- whether the system is secure against unauthorised access

We shall look at each of these in a little more detail later in this section.

PROVIDE INFORMATION

The role of any manager within an organisation will inevitably involve many communication responsibilities. These often take the form of more personal qualities, as communicating well is one quality that can make or break a manager. A manager who is a good communicator will be far more likely to achieve set objectives than one who does not communicate so well.

Providing information, either to his/her line manager, or, on the other hand, to his/her subordinates will be a key function of a manager within any organisation, regardless of its size or function.

A manager may need to provide information for the following reasons:

- in order to help his/her team to make a decision
- in order to help his/her team solve a problem
- in order to delegate some responsibility to another member of his/her team
- in order to motivate his/her team
- in order to inform his/her line manager of developments

- in order to supply feedback to a group of managers at their regular meeting

Obviously, some of the above situations will not cause a manager any communication problems. Alternatively, some of the ways in which the manager provides information can cause a degree of stress or tension.

With regard to the provision of information in external communications, then naturally, the content of the communication will differ, but hopefully, the standard of the communication will remain the same.

Whether a communication is internal or external to the organisation, there are some factors to consider in judging whether the communication is successful, including:

- what is the best means of getting the message across?
- is this the best time to put this information over?
- think about the way the information is going to be provided – it may be that verbal communication would be the best channel, but with this method there is no record of what has been said. Alternatively, lots of graphs and numbers can be boring and the impact can be lost
- will I need to use information technology to provide the information? Before the information is passed on it should be remembered that electronic technology is very quick. Once the message has been sent, then it is irretrievable
- will I require any feedback from the provision of this information? If so, how and what is the best way of requesting this?

student activity

(PC 2.3.2, COM 3.1)
We have said that a manager would need to provide information either to subordinates or to team members. What form do you think this information is likely to take? What information would a manager need to pass on and why? Discuss this in small groups.

GIVE INSTRUCTIONS

Another objective of communication is to give instructions to subordinates or fellow team members. This objective could use several of the methods of communication that we have mentioned, but we will specifically deal here with the verbal method of communication.

When talking to another member of staff in order to give him/her instructions relating to a specific project or task, it is important to remember the following:

- ensure that you are clear with your instructions
- take each stage step by step
- make sure you have any relevant written documentation relating to the instruction to hand. This will be useful to clarify a point which might be complex
- ensure that you give clear instructions regarding the deadlines involved
- give the recipient the opportunity to ask questions about the instruction
- ensure that the recipient knows that he/she can come back to you for further information if necessary
- ensure that the recipient of the instruction knows who else to contact should he/she require additional help or information
- try to make the recipient of the instruction aware of the reason for the task or project so that he/she knows why he/she has been asked to do something
- allow the recipient of the instruction to provide you with some form of feedback about the carrying out of the instruction

student activity

(PC 2.3.2, COM 3.1)
In pairs, alternating your roles, give instructions to your partner for a specific job or task he/she is to carry out. Make sure you explain yourself clearly and allow your partner to ask any relevant questions. Mark each other out of 10 on your performance at giving instructions.

KEEP PEOPLE UP TO DATE

This objective of communication is often a combination of the last two points, i.e. to keep people up to date you need to provide them with information and to give them instructions for their future tasks.

Keeping people up to date on the objectives and activities of the business organisation is vital if the employees are to remain well motivated and informed about the business. Without this relevant information, employees themselves become poor communicators. In addition, it has been proved that if people lack knowledge about the organisation as a whole they may lack effective social skills.

Over a period of fifty years, all types of organisations have grown enormously. This, in part, has been due to the technological developments that have taken place simultaneously. There are some organisations that have up to 10,000 employees working on one site. In such a situation, unless there are good communications that allow people to feel they are being kept fully up to date about the objectives and aims of the organisation, the individuals will feel unfulfilled. Such an outcome would not only be unfair, as those individuals spend a great deal of their working lives being committed to the organisation, but also counter-productive for the organisation itself.

MAKE CHECKS

Making regular checks on the standard and quality of the communication channels open to the organisation should be of prime importance. In addition to checking the success or otherwise of the communication processes themselves, the organisation would use communication methods to ensure the following:

- that employees are receiving correct information and instructions
- that employees are being kept up to date
- that employees are being given the opportunity to make feedback
- that the administrative systems in place within the organisation are working successfully
- that any possible changes to the administrative systems are carried out quickly and efficiently to the best effect
- that customers are happy with the quality, standard, delivery and transportation of the goods or services
- that the after-sales service is being provided to its best effect

Such checks on communication processes and administrative systems would not be carried out on a one-off basis, but would be systematically approached on a regular basis.

RECEIVE FEEDBACK

We have mentioned feedback several times already in this section. Organisations would consider that one of the main objectives of communication systems is the opportunity to allow feedback from their employees and from their customers.

Feedback comes in several forms:

- from a message which could be sent using any of the communication channels
- from instructions given or information provided
- from customers as to the service being provided or the goods being produced

Unless feedback is provided promptly and unambiguously, then the communication process is likely to be frustrated and inefficient. When a message is sent the recipient, however busy he/she may be at the time, should take steps to provide feedback to the sender of the message. This feedback may simply be a reply to say that the message has been received and is being dealt with. Alternatively, when written communication is involved, this may take the form of a written acknowledgement to say that their letter, memorandum or letter of complaint is being dealt with.

With oral communication, in, say, the giving of instructions or the provision of information, some kind of feedback is necessary to ensure that the recipient has understood what is being said or asked of him/her. This feedback can sometimes be just a 'yes' or a nod of the head. For the speaker, this feedback is important, to ensure that he/she does not feel they are talking to an empty room.

Feedback from any form of communication helps to cement the understanding of the recipient and to allow the sender of the message to feel secure that he/she has provided the correct information and that it will be dealt with.

NEGOTIATION

We talk in some detail about the negotiation processes of trade unions and the conditions of work and pay scales in Unit 4. Negotiation, whatever the topic of conversation, is a very important element of the communication system for all organisations and is a crucial management skill. Good skills in negotiation require the manager to secure the desired outcomes for the organisation by ensuring that the others within the organisation accept what is being said.

If negotiations have been successful, then both parties in the process will feel they have achieved what they set out to do. It is fair to say that negotiation processes tend to work through the same stages, regardless of the topic of negotiation. These stages are:

- *Stage 1* – when both parties in the negotiation process prepare themselves for what they consider to be the ideal outcome
- *Stage 2* – both parties tend to 'test one another' with their proposed outcomes
- *Stage 3* – when the non-contentious parts of the negotiation are decided. This is done to provide goodwill. Both parties agree to the sections which neither party has a problem with

- *Stage 4* – some trading off takes place. By this we mean that either party will give in to sections that are not really important to them in order to gain a small advantage over the other party
- *Stage 5* – when, due to the comments and decisions made by the other party, the good negotiator will spot a favourable balance

Good negotiation skills include the following:

- the ability to decide in advance what is the worst acceptance point and when negotiations should be called off
- knowing what parts of their package they are prepared to give up
- having good knowledge of the views of the other party
- knowing when they have asked for enough and should stop
- ensuring that all agreed conditions, concessions and undertakings have been taken note of and recorded (this may be in the form of minutes of the meeting)
- trying to ensure that the other party does not feel they have lost face

CONFIRMATION

This objective of communication is something we are all likely to have used in the past. Confirmation, in verbal communication, can literally mean the nod of the head or the word 'yes'. Alternatively, it can mean a telephone call to confirm receipt of a message or goods.

In written communication, this can mean a letter sent to an organisation to confirm an order or the receipt of goods. It can also mean a letter to a hotel to confirm accommodation arrangements made over the telephone, or to a travel agent confirming flight bookings made over the telephone.

Whatever method of communication is used to confirm arrangements, it should be remembered that it is polite to respond to any communication. It makes the recipient more determined to deal with the communication and, similarly, it gives the sender peace of mind that the communication is being dealt with. It would be pertinent to remember here what we have said earlier about the non-confirmation of receipt of letters of application and application forms for positions advertised by an organisation. It is safe to say that everyone would feel happier to receive a letter of confirmation that says 'we have received your letter and your application is being dealt with' rather than to hear nothing for weeks and then find out the post has been filled!

student activity

(PC 2.3.2, COM 3.2, IT 3.1)
Word process a letter of confirmation to a hotel of your choice. You should confirm that you have booked two single rooms for the nights of Friday and Saturday, 28 and 29 April 19… Your requirements are on a bed and breakfast basis, with accommodation including bath or shower.

2.3.3 *Analyse the effectiveness of communication in a business organisation*

ANALYSIS

For this performance criterion, you will need to analyse the effectiveness of communication in a business organisation from the point of view of interpreting and drawing conclusions from selected information which you should judge for its subjectivity or objectivity. In order to do this you may wish to use the institution in which you are studying this programme, or take the business organisation which you used in Element 2.1. In analysing the effectiveness of the communication used within this organisation, you will need to address the following:

- the **ease of use** of the communication
- the **ease of access** to the information
- the efficiency of use in terms of the user, with regard to **health** and the **stress** experienced by that individual
- the effectiveness of the communication system with regard to the **interaction between people**
- the effectiveness of the communication system with regard to the **interaction between organisations**
- the effectiveness of the communication system with regard to **confidentiality of information**
- the effectiveness of the communication system with regard to **security**

Before you look at the student activity at the end of this section, you may find it useful to look at the brief notes we give on each of the above.

EASE OF USE AND EASE OF ACCESS

In order to evaluate the ease of use and the ease of access of a communication system, we need also to think about the person who is using the system. Obviously, the system itself is only as effective as the person using the system. It is imperative that all business documentation is produced in an error-free way.

Communication systems specialists take the view that the reduction in human involvement with the processing of information and communication takes many of the errors out of the processes. If a business can rely on a foolproof communications system, then the accuracy factor is taken for granted. Others may take a more sceptical view and state that reliance on electronic technology means that humans are less aware of the process, therefore they find it more difficult to identify errors and inaccuracies. The sophistication of systems should mean that to a large extent the systems are totally reliable.

A sophisticated communications system should offer a business flexibility and the ability to respond to change and market requirements. With improved communications between remote parts of an organisation a greater interchange of information should occur. The sharing of ideas can be problematic at a more traditional level based on paper. Paper-based filing systems, for example, lack the immediacy of access that can be enjoyed from on-screen systems. A good communication system should also help efficiency in terms of work flow and operations by ensuring that congestion and delays in the interchange of information can be identified and information re-routed by an alternative channel.

With increased efficiency the organisation will receive a useful additional benefit in that it will appear to external organisations to be more responsive and professional.

If the communications system is sufficiently user-friendly then employees will enjoy a more stimulating and satisfying work experience. If employees can be freed from boring and routine tasks, then there is more opportunity for them to stretch their talents to the benefit of the organisation. This will, in itself, increase efficiency since fewer employees are involved in mundane duties.

student activity

(PC 2.3.3, COM 3.1, 3.2)
In the role of the business administration manager of an organisation, list the criteria that you would use in order to assess the ease of use and ease of access of communications systems. Discuss your list with those of the remainder of your group.

EFFICIENCY OF USER (HEALTH, STRESS)

Working with a computer can be a very demanding job. Someone who is skilled in the techniques of word processing can spend a lot of time looking at the screen. This is not just for the inputting of the information, but also for the proof-reading of the text which has been entered. This requires a great deal of concentration if it is to be carried out efficiently and accurately. Similarly, the entering of accounting or other numerical data requires a level of concentration which can be very demanding. Most people using computers find they get very tired very quickly, particularly if they have been looking at a computer screen for more than an hour.

Obviously, being over-tired will affect the effectiveness, efficiency and accuracy or the computer user. In order to ensure that it adheres to government legislation regarding breaks to be given to computer users, an organisation must make sure that someone in authority has the responsibility for checking that regular breaks are taken and that the correct lighting and screen arrangements are made.

Naturally, if an organisation wants an efficient and happy workforce, then it will do all it can to ensure that they are working under good conditions. This is particularly important when considering health and the stress experienced by a user of a computerised system. The following should be addressed and constantly monitored:

- the temperature in the room – this can affect the performance of the computer as well as the user
- no food and drink should be allowed in the computing room
- regular breaks from the machine should be allowed
- if possible, a variety of tasks should be undertaken during the course of the working day

- the posture of the user should be monitored – a user who is in an uncomfortable position for any length of time will inevitably suffer long-term health problems. Adjustable chairs should be provided which incorporated footrests and correct back support
- the angle and the height of the screen should be monitored. If these are not positioned correctly, then the user becomes more quickly tired and errors can result
- avoid the likelihood of having operators suffer from RSI (repetitive strain injury). This is an increasingly common problem for individuals who regularly carry out repetitive jobs such as typing or word processing. If the individual does not vary the tasks, then RSI can occur in the wrists or lower arms

Focus study

REPETITIVE STRAIN INJURY

An industrial radiographer, whose job entailed checking parts for Trident submarines, has been awarded compensation of £72,000. His job involved making repeated adjustments to a turntable carrying metal castings whilst they were being x-rayed. It was proved that his injuries had been caused by the excessive, repeated force of movements he had to make in the course of his work.

Additionally, if a user is not sure precisely what is required of him or her with regard to the work he or she is carrying out, then this leads to lack of motivation and frustration.

INTERACTION BETWEEN PEOPLE AND INTERACTION BETWEEN ORGANISATIONS

When you are analysing the communication system which you are going to evaluate in terms of its efficiency, you will also need to address the question of whether it is adequate in terms of its ability to allow members of the organisation to interact. In addition, you will also need to look at the system with regard to the way it interacts with other organisations.

Interaction between people within the organisation could include different communication systems which may take the following forms:

- internal telephone systems
- documentation used within the organisation only

- electronic mail
- a mail distribution system
- a filing system
- a computerised system which is used for internal use only

student activity

(PC 2.3.3, COM 3.1, 3.2)
List any other communication systems you can remember which may be used to allow people within organisations to interact. Compare your list with those of the remainder of the group.

To fulfil this performance criterion, you also need to analyse communication systems which allow organisations to interact with other organisations.

student activity

(PC 2.3.3, COM 3.1, 3.2)
What interaction between organisations can you remember? List the ones you can think of and then join with a partner to merge your individual lists. Now feedback your findings to the remainder of your group.

CONFIDENTIALITY AND SECURITY

Whatever the nature of the organisation's business activities, there is always a need for certain security measures to be in place. This may simply mean that the organisation does not wish its competitors to know some of the following confidential information:

- any information regarding its customers
- any information regarding the rates of discount offered
- any information regarding the credit limits offered to the organisation
- any information relating to the production costs and targets of the organisation

- any information relating to the distribution arrangements of the organisation
- the current financial status of the organisation

Perhaps even more sensitive in terms of security and confidentiality are organisations involved in the production of military equipment, for example. We have mentioned hackers elsewhere in the book when discussing security measures, particularly in terms of information technology users.

The communication systems of an organisation are particularly vulnerable in terms of security to unauthorised users. Communication systems rely on shared channels to transfer information from machine to machine. The use of security codes has gone some way to address this problem. Other confidentiality and security devices in common use are those which allow limited levels of access into the system. By means of a security code numbering system, individuals can only gain access to limited numbers of levels of the system. In this way more junior members of staff are limited in the amount of information they can access, whilst, at the same time, the procedure serves as a back-up security system. Because access is limited, a hacker would need to know the correct procedure before gaining access to information. In addition, if there is information that is not necessarily security sensitive, but which is confidential and to which limited access is required, it would be less likely for this to be accessed by the wrong individuals within the organisation.

2.3.4 Explain possible positive and negative effects of changes to communications

POSITIVE EFFECTS

When an organisation makes the decision to change all or part of its communication system, it can have very positive effects on the performance of that organisation. Alternatively, the effects could have negative results. We look at the negative results in detail a little later in this section, but for now we concentrate on the positive effects a change in communication may have.

IMPROVED SPEED OF COMMUNICATION

Whenever an organisation considers the installation of a new communication system, it must approach this from the point of view of the benefits that will be accrued. Given the fact that the acquisition, financing and implementation of a new communication system will be a long and laborious task, the benefits need to be significant.

A modern computerised communication system should improve the following:

- storage of data
- retrieval of data
- processing of data
- saving of time

A computerised system can undertake a number of tasks simultaneously and does not necessarily require an individual to be present. The printing of standard letters, statements, price lists, balance sheets, trading and profit and loss accounts can be done by simply accessing the correct file, pressing a series of buttons and switching on the printer. Among other positive benefits in terms of the speed of use is the fact that a computerised system can generate order lists when stock levels are reaching re-order level.

IMPROVED ACCESS TO COMMUNICATION

An organisation which makes the investment in improved communication systems will be able to ensure that the majority of employees have improved access. If an individual can work from his/her terminal or enhanced telephone system and acquire the necessary information to undertake a task, then there must be positive benefits over the more manual and time-consuming traditional systems. An organisation which has terminals on the majority of employees' desks will be able to send messages and instructions to specific or all individuals. Likewise, these individuals can gain immediate contact with work colleagues even in remote locations in a matter of seconds. With this immediacy of contact, individuals will not have to spend valuable time seeking out particular people or calling informal meetings with them.

POTENTIAL FOR COMMUNICATION TO WIDER AUDIENCE

Many of the comments that we have made in relation to the improved access to communication within the organisation are equally applicable to communication with a wider audience. In this respect, we would include the following:

- remote locations which are part of the same organisation
- associated organisations such as suppliers and distributors
- agents, licensees and representatives overseas
- professionals associated with the organisation such as accountants and solicitors
- requests from and responses to customers or clients

NEGATIVE EFFECTS

Many of the negative effects which we will consider in this section of the Element in relation to communication systems can often be thought of as temporary or short term. Many of the negative aspects involved in the installation of new communication systems only occur in the 'teething stage' when the system has been installed for the first time. Not only has the organisation had to cope with the expense and upheaval of the installation, but also faces a period of transition when it has to incorporate the new communication system into its normal daily activities.

INCOMPATIBLE EQUIPMENT

If the organisation is considering radically overhauling its communication systems, then one of the basic problems it may find is that the present system is not capable of being integrated into the new system, or vice versa. Although many modern communication systems are compatible, there are always changes in specification which render the previous version unable to handle the demands that the new installation needs.

Most organisations will consider replacing equipment when they appreciate that their present systems are obsolete. Given that rapid changes are being made in technology, an organisation has to be absolutely sure that it is making the right decision to install new equipment at any particular time. The replacement of some of the peripheral equipment such as telephones or printers may not cause any serious problem of incompatibility. However, there is no point in installing new telephones which can offer such services as memory store and automatic redial, if the switchboard is unable to cope with these functions. There will come a point when incompatibility is a concern and this is when the whole system is overhauled and scrapped.

COST

The costs of installing new communication systems, and in particular computerised communication systems, include the following:

1 *Direct costs* – which include all costs incurred from the time the computer system is proposed to the time when it is installed and running for the first time. These also include the running costs of the system throughout its lifetime.

2 *Direct immediate costs* – this is, of course, the actual costs of buying and implementing the system. Normally this would have to be financed immediately or at least within normal terms of credit. There is a danger here that the costs will escalate beyond that which has been budgeted.

3 *Hardware costs* – these are the most obvious short-term direct costs, but remember that all equipment depreciates and this is particularly true of communication systems. There will always be a temptation to upgrade and replace hardware as new developments are made.

4 *Software costs* – these are similar in many respects to hardware costs and there is the temptation to upgrade software as new versions enter the market. The cost of software may be particularly high if it has been especially written for the organisation.

5 *Installation and cabling costs* – these can vary according to either the system used or the nature of the premises and may escalate even further if the locations needing to be linked to one another are remote.

6 *Direct long-term costs* – these, of course, include maintenance and repair. Many organisations take out a maintenance contract and it is possible that, in the lifetime of the system, an organisation may pay more for the maintenance contract than it paid for the communications system in the first place. Organisations need to ensure that the maintenance contract covers all parts and equipment. If the organisation employs someone with considerable technical experience then that person may be able to undertake the majority of the maintenance work and any damage or breakdown of the system will be covered by the normal insurance policy.

EXCLUSION FROM COMMUNICATION

With the installation of new communication systems there is an ever present danger of excluding certain individuals from using the equipment to its best effect. If the equipment which has been chosen has been selected to carry out functions which were hitherto undertaken manually, then it is in the organisation's interests, particularly in terms of efficiency, to ensure that all employees understand the benefits of the system. Staff training and development should be an ongoing process, beginning with the prime users of the equipment who can then cascade their understanding to colleagues or subordinates. As new staff join the organisation, they should receive a short induction programme and be encouraged to attend training courses to assist them with the use of the equipment if they are not familiar with it.

THREAT TO SECURITY

Any data that are on a computer system are valuable simply because they are there. Someone, at some time, had to input the data onto the system, so at the least the organisation has had to pay for that person's time. Obviously, such items as lists of customers and discounts and production levels could be directly useful to a competitor. Given that the computer is a tangible asset, how can we determine the tangibility of the data on a computer system? Whatever your answer to this question, the data are still an asset. Accidental or malicious erasure could seriously affect the organisation.

Failures and corruptions can be minimised by taking daily back-ups.

Passwords are another method of ensuring that access is limited to those who have a legitimate right to use the system and any good encryption codeword will be a considerable barrier to unauthorised entry. If individuals can get access to your computer system, they can literally take a copy of all of your records in a matter of minutes. The combination of a competitor who does not really care where the information has come from, and an employee willing to undertake the task can spell disaster.

2.3.5 *Suggest changes to improve communications in a business organisation*

In order to fulfil the requirements of this performance criterion, you need to suggest changes in order to improve communications in a particular business organisation. Working on the assumption that it may be difficult to investigate an organisation and make an assessment of its current communication systems, we have provided a short Focus Study on a fictitious organisation which does require some major reappraisal of its present communication systems.

Focus study

'THE AD SHOP'

The Ad Shop was founded by Derek Worthing four years ago and has grown considerably despite the fact that it is based in a small town. The Ad Shop has three main categories of sales. These are:

- sales through its single retail outlet
- sales to other organisations in bulk via the warehouse
- sales to individuals and organisations via a mail order catalogue

The Ad Shop has a limited supplier base consisting of:

- four large UK-based organisations
- six small UK-based organisations
- around ten overseas organisations handled through a single import agent

The structure of the organisation is as follows:

- retail staff: 3
- drivers and packers: 3
- stores keeper: 1
- administration: 3
- managerial (Derek): 1
- total number of staff: 11

The Ad Shop has a turnover of £2.9m. per year and handles an average of 280 orders per month.

There are some 32 regular bulk purchasers and around 900 mail order customers. The Ad Shop stocks around £200,000 worth of items in the warehouse and the retail outlet, made up of around 1,500 different products.

Derek was very keen to develop the mail order side of his business and realised that he needed to computerise the system in order to cope with the additional administration. The initial steps Derek decided on were:

- placing advertisements in the local and national press for his catalogue
- ordering a new print run of his catalogues
- purchasing a stand alone computer with a printer
- purchasing an accounts package which included:
  - sales and purchase ledger
  - nominal ledger
  - sales invoicing

Focus study (continued)

He arranged for one of the administration staff to go on a four-day course in order to understand the operations of the computer and the software package. Whilst both Derek and one of the administration staff were involved in these activities they neglected other activities. Orders were sitting in the in-tray and invoices were not being sent out. After the training the Ad Shop staff valiantly attempted to catch up, however, this was to be the calm before the storm. When people started to reply to the advertisements, and when the catalogues had been sent out, orders started coming in at around 120 a day. He simply could not cope.

student activity

(PC 2.3.5, COM 3.1, 3.2, 3.3, 3.4, IT 3.1, 3.2, 3.3, 3.2) Referring to the previous Focus Study, Derek obviously needs help. In the role of consultants who have been called in by Derek, prepare a short and accessible report which addresses his current problems and offers practical solutions to immediately advise him. Bearing in mind that Derek is not a multinational and does not have unlimited funds, your suggestions should be appropriate for his financial situation.

You should present your short word processed report in the form of short points and include any facts, figures or suggestions of sourcing equipment.

ELEMENT 2.3

a s s i g n m e n t

(PC 2.3.1–5, COM 3.1, 3.2, 3.3, 3.4, IT 3.1, 3.2, 3.3)
You may find the investigative aspects of this assignment somewhat difficult. Perhaps you should take advantage of the opportunities offered to you by other means to obtain the information you will require. These other methods of information gathering include:

- work experience
- visiting organisations
- visits from individuals in industry
- case studies provided by your tutor

You will also need to have some practical knowledge of some of the communication systems.

TASK 1

(PC 2.3.1–2)
Compile a report which looks at two examples of internal and two examples of external communication systems within business organisations. You should also consider how the business organisation uses its communication systems to help it achieve its objectives.

TASK 2

(PC 2.3.3)
You should also analyse one internal and one external electronic communication system and consider their effectiveness in:

- enabling access to information
- improving interaction between individuals
- establishing and maintaining confidentiality and security

TASK 3

(PC 2.3.4–5)
In the final part of your report you should outline two proposals for changes to communication systems within a business organisation. Your proposal should be justified in terms of:

- beneficial effects to the organisation
- positive and negative effects of change

Your report should be word processed.

Analyse information processing in a business organisation

PERFORMANCE CRITERIA

A student must:

1 explain the **purposes** *of* **information processing**

2 describe **information processing** *in one business organisation*

*3 **analyse** the effectiveness of* **information processing** *in one business organisation*

4 explain the **effects of the Data Protection Act** *on* **information processing**

RANGE

Purposes: *receiving information, storing information, using information, communicating information*

Information processing: *manual systems; single-purpose systems (word processing, number processing, spreadsheets, data bases, graphics processing); multi-purpose systems*

Analyse *in terms of: fitness for purpose, cost and value for money, efficiency, information retention, security*

Effects of the Data Protection Act: *on individuals: access to information, security, ownership, accuracy, on business: ability to sell information to others, cost of meeting the Act*

2.4.1 Explain the purposes of information processing

PURPOSES

Information processing systems may be either manual or electronic. They both handle data, processing them in some specific way in order to produce an end goal.

The processing systems of electronic systems comprise of both hardware and software. The information processing system itself is carried out by a program. It is useful to define these three key terms at this point, although we have already covered them in some detail in Element 2.2.

1 *Hardware* – this describes the physical, mechanical components of the computer system, such as the keyboard, monitor, disk drive(s) and printer(s).
2 *Software* – software is the pre-designed computer package which provides the information and processes by which the hardware can handle particular forms of information. These are also known as programs.
3 *Programs* – as you may have realised, programs are software, but are written in a complex computer language aimed at providing a flexible and foolproof system by which information may be processed.

Let us now look at the particular forms of hardware and how each part of that hardware interrelates with the whole system:

1 *Memory* – often known as RAM (random access memory) has five specific purposes:

- to store programs being utilised in the processing of data
- to temporarily store the data itself
- to store information awaiting processing
- to store information being processed
- to store information generated as a result of the processing function

2 *The CPU* (central processing unit) can be considered to be the real brain of the computer. It performs the following functions:

- monitors current operations
- ensures that all components within the system meet the requirements of the software in use
- carries out arithmetic processing of data
- carries out logical processing of data

3 *Input and output* – in order for the machine to process data the information must be in a form which the machine understands. Computers cannot understand the same language that we speak or write. The computer has to convert all information into a binary language. This information, once it has been translated into the binary language, is known as input. Output essentially translates binary language back into a format which is understandable to us. The computer converts the binary language and displays it, either on the screen or on to paper via a printer.

4 *Backing store* – in order to fulfil many of the functions that are required, the computer must be able to file information. This information may be found in two places:

- *memory* – it is not practical or desirable to store much information here since it may be destroyed or over-written. Certain computers do not have an inbuilt resident memory and all files stored in memory are destroyed if the computer is turned off
- *magnetic disks* – an alternative location for the storage of information is on either magnetic tape or disk. Data files can be stored in these locations for retrieval in the future.

Before we look at the purposes of information processing in more detail, we should look at the basic uses of information processing systems. The main considerations are:

- the storing of information
- the distribution of information
- the use of information
- the communication of information

We shall look at these individually.

RECEIVING AND STORING INFORMATION

A useful comparison to make here is the difference between a filing cabinet and a computer storage system. Both have the following features:

- information is stored in a logical manner
- the information is readily retrievable, provided the user is aware of where that information is stored
- a system has been created in order to ensure that the right information goes to the correct place 'in the files'
- it is possible to update and amend information as required

- there is the opportunity to access and duplicate the information when required
- there should be a system by which irrelevant or out-of-date information is 'weeded out' periodically to ensure that the system is not overloaded with irrelevant details

Obviously, the manual version of information storing will require greater physical space. There is also the danger that important documents may be misfiled or lost. This is also true of computer systems. At a key stroke, a file may be accidentally erased or routed to a location not intended.

student activity

(PC 2.4.1, COM 3.1, IT 3.4)
In groups of three, consider all the ways in which a computer could be beneficial in the storage of information. How would an organisation ensure that there is easy access to this information at all times?

USING INFORMATION

A manual system can suffer from the restrictions of there being only one file in existence. This means that only one individual may have access to this file at a time. A way around this problem is to duplicate the file so that all interested parties may gain access to a copy simultaneously. However, this simply adds to the paper mountain and adds considerably to the overall storage problems. Certain computer systems can suffer from the same problems. Unsophisticated computer systems may only allow a single user access to a file at a particular time. Equally, if the system is disk based, then access to the relevant files relies on a number of disk copies being made. With this system, there is always the danger of a file being updated by a particular user, while all other users are dealing with out-of-date information.

COMMUNICATING INFORMATION

As we have already mentioned earlier in this Unit, there is a wide variety of communication systems. Some of the manual systems do have their advantages in as much as they are, to a large extent, personal communication processes. Computer communication systems can suffer from being impersonal and give a sense of isolation to the user. Whether the information being communicated to a particular individual is routed via a manual or an electronic system, there is still no guarantee that the individual will read or take note of the information. To date, there has been no system designed to ensure that the recipient does respond to information given. Certain computer systems will, however, require the recipient to acknowledge receipt of the information, but this is really no more sophisticated than ticking a circulation list.

INFORMATION PROCESSING

We covered the different systems available for the carrying out of information processing in some detail in Element 2.3 when we discussed the effects of information technology on the administrative and communication systems of an organisation. You may find it useful to refresh your memory before continuing.

MANUAL SYSTEMS, SINGLE-PURPOSE SYSTEMS (WORD PROCESSING, NUMBER PROCESSING, SPREADSHEETS, DATA BASES, GRAPHICS PROCESSING) AND MULTI-PURPOSE SYSTEMS

Single-purpose systems, or the software used, tend to relate to independent functions such as word processing, data bases, spreadsheets and graphics processing. Whatever application is used, whether it be a single-purpose system or a multi-purpose system, it is vital that the application actually does what you want it to. The following questions should be asked:

- does it do the job you want it to do?
- will it serve its purpose for a reasonable amount of time?
- is it compatible with the current system?

We should now consider some of the applications available using information processing systems:

WORD PROCESSING

This is quite a straightforward computer application. It can do what most organisations need for their business or administrative functions, e.g. write letters, reports and documents.

Many organisations now produce their printed documents by means of a word processing package instead of using typewriters. Such a package has several advantages over a typewriter:

- the text can be read through easily
- mistakes can be easily corrected
- changes can be made without the need to retype the whole document
- work can be stored for future reference
- work can be altered for a different occasion

These benefits are particularly useful in the case of very long and complicated documents.

Most word processing packages will have the following valuable features:

- the ability to edit text
- help screens which show you how to carry out certain functions which are available within the package
- a spell-checking facility. This is ideal for someone who is not good at spelling. It scans the text and compares your spelling with a built-in dictionary. If an error is discovered the correct spelling can be entered. Additions can be made to the dictionary if required
- a thesaurus – this allows you to choose alternative words to the ones you have used
- a word count to count the number of words in the document
- a print preview or the facility to view the document before it is printed
- mail merge or mail shot facilities – these allow a standard letter to be merged with several names and addresses. This is very useful and time saving for an organisation which wishes to distribute the same letter to several different organisations or customers

NUMBER PROCESSING

Another application area that has developed rapidly over the last few years is the computerised number processing facility. In this instance the computer's role is that of a calculating machine. It is possible, using this method of application, to process information of a numerical nature for the following tasks:

- accounts packages normally offer sales, purchase and nominal ledgers, either as individual modules or completely integrated packages
- payroll packages
- order processing packages
- invoicing packages
- a fixed asset register
- stock control packages
- job costing and bill of materials packages

Naturally, before an organisation decides to embark on a computerisation of the above functions, it must clearly identify the areas that it needs to integrate. In addition, it would also need to identify the amount of activity within each of these areas.

SPREADSHEETS

A spreadsheet package is the computerised equivalent of an accounts department's ledger. The name spreadsheet is derived from the 'spreading of the business's accounts on a piece of paper'. The computer user can enter number, formulae or text into each of the columns. Columns are the vertical sections of the spreadsheet and rows are the horizontal ones. A cell is one section of the spreadsheet.

This screen-based calculating machine allows information to be input in the form of text, numbers or formulae and the subsequent printing of the information. This information can be printed in the form of an exact replica of the screen itself, or in the form of a graph, a line graph, bar chart, pie chart or more complicated forms of graphics.

It is possible to change any number within the spreadsheet at any time and the new results will automatically be shown. The ability of the package to carry out this function makes it a very powerful, useful and popular system.

Spreadsheets can be used by an organisation in order to:

- hold records
- depict sales and costs
- determine what prices will maximise profits
- detail the costs accumulated for a specific job
- carry out financial planning and budgets
- undertake tax, investment and loan calculations
- produce statistics
- merge spreadsheet information in order to show accounts from more than one department or branch
- convert currency
- organise the timetabling and planning of staff

DATA BASES

The term 'data base' relates to what can be called an electronic filing system. In fact, most accounting software and spreadsheets are specialised data bases. Most organisations would use and maintain a data base in one form or another in order to:

- collect and store information regarding customers or clients
- to profile products sold or purchased
- to collect and store personnel records

A data base is a collection of records. Each record is structured into fields and each field contains specific information. The desired structure and range of records can be flexible and can be compiled by the operator. It is a formal way of storing information. The record might be a collection of facts about a specific product, client or supplier. It could also hold a list of records regarding stock, prices and number of units sold.

Before embarking on the installation of a data base system, an organisation would need to ensure that the package would be suitable. In addition, it would need to decide whether a general package would suffice or whether one that is more closely related to the activities of the business were required.

GRAPHICS PROCESSING

The capabilities of a computer with regard to graphics processing will very much depend on the hardware involved and the software available. It is therefore important that an organisation considers carefully the requirements of the application, so that the correct hardware is acquired. This will avoid the necessity to upgrade the machine, which is an expensive option.

The resolution of the screen limits the ability to display graphics of a suitable quality. Desktop publishing can make extensive use of graphics for digitising photographic images and for displaying a range of type fonts in different pitches.

Obviously, one major area of use of graphics processing is the design side of an organisation. Technical and engineering drawing can be carried out with precision and accuracy. In addition to the excellence of the standard of work produced, the ability to store and subsequently retrieve and amend work can be of enormous value. Although graphics design and graphics processing packages can be very expensive, the business activities of the organisation will determine whether it is cost effective to install such a system. The following can be carried out using a graphics processing package:

- computer aided design
- the design of stationery
- the production of simple pictures

student activity

(PC 2.4.1, COM 3.1, IT 3.4)
Apart from the short list given above, to what other uses might an organisation put a graphics package? Why would such packages be useful for this task? Discuss this in pairs and then compare your lists with those of the remainder of your group.

MULTI-PURPOSE SYSTEMS

We have already mentioned integrated packages in our discussion of accounts and business applications. Integrated accounts is an obvious example of the integration of applications. To some extent, integrated applications can be seen as a single application, as opposed to a collection of different applications. There are several applications available that integrate the individual applications we have already mentioned, i.e. word processing, spreadsheet, data base and graphics.

We have listed some of these packages and their capabilities in Element 2.3 of this Unit.

Many benefits can be derived from purchasing an integrated package as opposed to a single package, including:

- all the computer requirement problems could be solved at one time
- it should prove cheaper than buying each application separately
- only one package has to be learnt, as opposed to several
- there is only one set of documentation to consider
- the key strokes or function keys tend to be similar throughout the different applications

When using a multi-purpose system, it is possible to transfer information from one application to another, e.g. to transfer information from a spreadsheet or data base file into a word processing document.

Alternatively, a multi-purpose system can have some disadvantages over the use of a single-purpose system:

- it is not a specialist package, so no one application is the most sophisticated available
- for a person who is using the system for the first time, the integrated package may appear overwhelming
- the training time and the cost involved in learning all the applications can be expensive for the organisation

Of course, when we consider information processing, we cannot ignore the fact that communication both within the organisation and from organisation to organisation has also been affected by the new technology available via the computer. The Internet and e-mail cannot be ignored here. The Focus Study given below should help to inform you of the dynamic influence these two inventions are having on the business activities of some of the more sophisticated and advanced organisations.

student activity

(PC 2.4.1, COM 3.2, 3.4, IT 3.1, 3.2, 3.3, 3.4)
Using the Focus Study on page 186 as your basis, compile a word processed report which considers the implications of services like e-mail and the Internet to organisations. In addition, consider the implications of the spread of such services through the general public. What existing systems and services could be affected?

Focus study

INFORMATION PROCESSING

The Internet may not prove to be such a threat to traditional letter-sending as people seem to think. Technology means new opportunities for the Royal Mail, but also new challenges too. E-mail is quickly becoming adopted by organisations and is also spreading into the consumer world. For a few pounds a month, anybody who owns a personal computer and a modem can hook into the Internet and exchange unlimited electronic mail with more than 20 million other people around the world.

Conventional postal services are now beginning to consider the long-term implications of a world in which e-mail will be cheaper and quicker than posting a letter. They have already lost business since the invention of the fax machine.

Conversely, some have their doubts, as they feel that too little information or statistics are yet available which state the true effect of e-mail on industry. E-mail forms the bulk of traffic on the Internet and related electronic networks but much of it consists of short and rapidly written notes which are passed from one colleague to another.

The Internet's quoted 20m. addresses include university students whose mailboxes often remain technically active after they leave their course.

People also have different attitudes towards e-mail, particularly when companies try to use it as a direct-marketing medium. Dataquest has used focus groups to ask computer users how they feel about receiving mail through an electronic network, and have found that they are hostile to the idea, particular in certain areas of Europe.

Marketing through networks is more likely to take place through advertising in electronic newsletters and virtual shopping stores than through direct approaches to individuals. It is expected that the next technological breakthrough for Europe is that post offices will move away from simple delivery services towards offering a complete service to commercial customers. A direct mail company would create its entire direct-marketing campaign on desktop computers, compile its list of mail targets and then transmit the information electronically to the post office. The mail agency would then control the printing and assembly of the mail shot and, finally, deliver it.

2.4.2 Describe information processing in one business organisation

In order to meet the performance criterion of this Section, it is necessary for you to investigate and describe the information processing activities of one particular business organisation. The business organisation can be one of your own choice. If this proves to be difficult, you may decide to use the institution in which you are studying this course as your example. You should identify the organisation you wish to use for your study and then carry out the following student activity. The information you gain in the completion of this activity will be useful to you in the completion of the assignment at the end of Element 2.4.

student activity

(PC 2.4.2, COM 3.2, 3.3, IT 3.1, 3.2, 3.3, 3.4)
Once you have identified the organisation whose information processing systems you wish to study, you should consider its systems with regard to the following:

- the type of systems used
- how the systems increase or decrease the work opportunities for the staff
- any training implications involved

Your word processed report should fully describe the information processing carried out by your organisation.

2.4.3 *Analyse the effectiveness of information processing in one business organisation*

ANALYSIS

Just how effective an information processing system is in relation to an organisation's business activities can be measured in terms of the following:

- whether the system is **secure** both as far as the business is concerned, and in terms of its compliance with the requirements of the Data Protection Act
- whether the system is **efficient** in terms of its collection, processing and storage of information
- whether the system is **cost effective** in the sense of suitability for its purpose and whether all the features of the package have been fully implemented

FITNESS FOR PURPOSE, EFFICIENCY, COST AND VALUE FOR MONEY

Just how efficient an information processing system is may be dependent upon the way in which the system was originally designed. This can be a slightly more complex consideration, and includes the following:

- how the components of the information processing system were selected
- whether they fit the purpose of the information processing system itself
- how the information processing system interrelates with the administrative procedures required to operate the system
- whether the information processing system is backed up by a sufficiently powerful computer to run it. If the computer is not sufficiently powerful, users may experience reduced response times as the computer desperately tries to handle the complex system
- whether the system fits the purpose for which it was purchased. If the system was designed to handle a lower level of business activity than the organisation is now experiencing, then it may find difficulties in handling all the information it is required to process
- the implementation of the system itself may be acceptable on a mechanical level, but the users of the system may not be trained sufficiently and would thus be unable to operate it efficiently

In terms of cost effectiveness, the basic equation is that the cost of the system should be less than the value of the information it produces. When one considers the costs of adopting an information processing system, one must include the following:

- hardware costs
- software costs
- maintenance costs
- specialist staff costs
- training costs
- insurance costs
- security system installation costs
- the costs of providing the necessary legal working environments for such equipment

student activity

(PC 2.4.3, COM 3.1, IT 3.4)
In pairs, consider the circumstances in which an organisation may find that manual systems of communication and information storage are preferable to electronic methods.

INFORMATION RETENTION AND SECURITY

A good information processing system should provide a range of controls in order to enable it to carry out its functions efficiently and in a secure manner:

- prevent loss of information through software error
- prevent loss of information through procedural errors such as incorrect key strokes
- prevent loss of information as a result of accidental hazards such as loss of power
- protection of all information from being disclosed to unauthorised individuals
- protection of all information from accidental modification
- protection of all information from deliberate corruption
- restriction of access to this information

In certain circumstances, which are often beyond the control of the organisation itself, files may suffer permanent or temporary damage. These hazards are:

- fire
- flood
- mechanical malfunction
- programming errors
- human error
- malicious damage

Most organisations will ensure that they have back-up files housed in secure locations which can be loaded back into the system should the master files be damaged.

We shall deal in Element 2.4.4 with the provisions of the Data Protection Act 1984 as these provisions relate to information processing systems.

student activity

(PC 2.4.3, COM 3.2, 3.4, IT 3.1, 3.2, 3.3, 3.4)
In order to meet the performance criterion of this section, it is necessary for you to consider further the information processing systems in the organisation you investigated in the previous performance criterion. You now need to consider the information processing systems in terms of their effectiveness. In order to do this, you should consider the following:

- the efficiency of their use
- the time taken to produce information
- the speed at which information can be processed
- the volume of work involved
- the ease of use for the operator of the system

The collection of this information will assist you in the assignment at the end of Element 2.4 and should now be stored on a computer for future retrieval.

student activity

(PC 2.4.3, COM 3.1, IT 3.4)
If the institution in which you are undertaking this programme of study has a network computer system, investigate in general terms the security measures which have been implemented. Are they sufficient to ensure that all information is retained and secure, or can you think of any alternative measures that could be taken to improve the measures? Discuss this first in pairs, and then in larger groups.

2.4.4 Explain the effects of the Data Protection Act on information processing

EFFECTS OF THE DATA PROTECTION ACT

ON INDIVIDUALS

As you will see from the list below, an individual about whom an organisation has information stored, does have specific rights, including:

- **access** to that information
- **the right to challenge** inaccurate information

If an organisation fails to comply with the Data Protection Act in this respect, then the individual affected has a right to be compensated.

There are some exceptions to this, however, and these are:

- where the individual has supplied the information him/herself
- where the organisation has taken 'all reasonable care' to acquire the information
- where the information relates to payroll matters
- where the information relates to pension details
- where the information is used only for statistical purposes and, in addition, does not specifically identify individuals

student activity

(PC 2.4.4, COM 3.1)
How would you go about discovering whether the information stored about you as an individual is correct? Discuss this as a group.

ACCESS TO INFORMATION

The Data Protection Act attempts to ensure that stored information is only put to specific lawful purposes. While it is difficult to maintain this degree of certainty about the use of the information, most organisations tend to use stored information for its specifically stated purpose only. Problems will inevitably arise when there is an interchange of this information between different organisations. The organisation which initially collected the data may have had a specific purpose in mind. However, the organisation which has acquired the information may have different motives altogether. The transmission of sensitive information from one organisation to another can pose considerable problems both to the individual and to the Data Protection Registrar. In particular, information stored regarding an individual's creditworthiness may include a number of inaccuracies which have not been identified. If the individual subsequently discovers that inaccuracies have been made then it is a difficult task to trace the transmission and use of the original inaccurate information in order to ensure that all information stored at whatever location is, indeed, accurate.

student activity

(PC 2.4.4, COM 3.1)
Information regarding customers is regularly traded between organisations. How would an organisation ensure that the information being passed on does not adversely affect the individual or the organisation itself? Discuss this in pairs.

SECURITY

As with any data storage facility, an organisation will take steps to ensure that unauthorised access is avoided. The Data Protection Act, however, makes this a legal requirement and, therefore, unauthorised access can mean fines for the organisation which has suffered the breach of security. The sensitivity of some of the material stored is such that it could be used for criminal or other unlawful purposes by an unauthorised entrant. The sensitivity of the information is further heightened by the fact that the individual whose information is stored in the system may be unaware that it is actually there. If unauthorised entry is gained and this information is used by others, then the individual may suffer as a result.

OWNERSHIP

Most organisations keep detailed records which may include the following:

- customers' names and addresses
- customer transactions
- customer credit information
- specific information regarding customers, such as their political affiliations (in recent years certain high street banks have admitted that they keep details of customers' political allegiances)
- staff records
- personal information regarding employees' domestic situations
- disciplinary action taken against employees

Organisations obviously store a great deal more information than this, but the Data Protection Act relates specifically to the way in which this information is used. The Act attempts to prevent this information being used to harm an individual. The Act requires all organisations or individuals who hold personal details regarding other individuals on computer to register with the Data Protection Registrar. If an organisation or individual fails to do this, then they may be fined up to £2,000. The Registrar needs to know the following:

- what sort of information is held
- what use is made of the information
- who else has access to this information
- what methods were used to collect the information

The Registrar must ensure that the data conforms with the Act. Specifically, this means that the Registrar must ensure that the information complies with the codes given below:

- that the information has been collected in an open and fair manner
- that the information is only held for lawful purposes
- that the uses to which the information is put are disclosed to the Registrar
- that the information held is relevant to the purpose for which it is held
- that the information is accurate
- that the information is up to date
- that any irrelevant or inaccurate information is destroyed
- that individuals can be told about the existence of the information
- that individuals can challenge inaccurate information
- that the information is kept confidential
- that the organisation takes steps to ensure that unauthorised access is avoided

student activity

(PC 2.4.4, COM 3.1, 3.2)
Consider, from a personal point of view, the Data Protection Act and try to assess the range and amount of information which may be stored by organisations concerning you. Write a list of any considerations you can think of and then compare your list to those of the remainder of your group. How much do they vary?

ACCURACY

The fifth principle of the Data Protection Act states that:

personal data shall be accurate and, where necessary, kept up to date

The Act gives further guidance on interpreting this principle. 'Accurate' means correct and not misleading as to any matter of fact. A mere opinion, which does not purport to be a statement of fact, cannot be challenged on the grounds of inaccuracy.

The Act contains special provisions which apply to information obtained from the data subject or from third parties. These are dealt with fully within the Act. Stated briefly, a data user who wishes to rely on these provisions must ensure that both the fact that the information has come from such a source and any challenge by the data subject to the accuracy of the information are recorded.

If these requirements are complied with, the fact that the personal data are inaccurate does not result in a breach of this principle.

The Registrar will seek to establish that there is a factual inaccuracy and will also wish to see whether the data user has taken all responsible steps to prevent the inaccuracy. The matters which he may wish to consider will include:

- the significance of the inaccuracy
- the source from which the inaccurate information was obtained
- any steps taken to verify the information
- the procedures for data entry and for ensuring that the system itself does not introduce inaccuracies into the data
- the procedures followed by the data user when the inaccuracy came to light

If an individual suffers damage because of inaccurate personal data held about him/her by a user, he/she is entitled to claim compensation from the data user. An application for compensation must be made by the individual to the court. The Registrar cannot award compensation.

ON BUSINESS

In order to decide whether or not the Data Protection Act affects the activities of an organisation, it will be necessary to ascertain whether the organisation uses any of the following equipment:

- word processors
- microcomputers
- minicomputers
- mainframe computers

The organisation should remember that it makes no difference whether the equipment is owned or leased. It is not the equipment itself that is important, but the use of that equipment for the storage and processing of data. The control of the data is in the hands of the organisation.

If the organisation does use any of the above equipment, then the following questions need to be addressed:

- is the equipment used for the processing of accounts payable and accounts received?
- is the equipment used for the checking of credit ratings?
- is the equipment used for the payroll and storage of personnel data?

- is the equipment used for marketing and sales information?
- is the equipment used for the storage of general management information?
- is the equipment used for the production and manipulation of letters and text?
- is the equipment used for the transmission of electronic mail?

If the organisation does use its equipment for any of the above purposes, then these activities are not subject to the restrictions imposed by the legislation.

On the other hand, if the organisation does store and use personal data and has to ensure that these are properly secured, then they do require special attention. The data protection laws frequently refer to specific types of personal data which are either prohibited or which must have special safeguards, as detailed earlier. These data relate to:

- racial origin
- political opinions
- religious beliefs
- health

If an organisation uses a computer service bureau to process personal data, it is not the responsibility of the organisation to ensure that they are securely processed. The computer service bureau has to register that it provides processing services to other organisations and must conform to the requirements laid down in the Act for security and confidentiality.

If an organisation's computer system holds any data regarding the following, then it must ensure that it conforms to specific domestic legislation:

- the sexual life of employees
- any criminal convictions of employees
- the colour of skin of employees
- the use of intoxicants by employees
- the intimacy of the private life of its employees
- the trade union membership or otherwise of its employees

ABILITY TO SELL INFORMATION TO OTHERS

The personal data held by the data user may include information which identifies another individual as well as the data subject, e.g. a relative or associate of the data subject or a person who has given information to the data user about the data subject. In replying to a data subject's request, the data user need not disclose the information unless the other individual has consented to the disclosure. The data user, however, must still give

as much information as possible to the data subject without revealing the other individual's identity. This may involve editing the information to remove names or other identifying details. Information should not be withheld under this provision merely because the data user suspects that the data subject may be able to guess the other individual's identity. The provision applies only where anyone lacking the data subject's special knowledge could reasonably be expected to identify the other individual from the information.

The fact that another individual's consent may be required should never prevent the data user from replying at least partially to the request. When he/she has received the request, together with enough information about identity and location, the data user should therefore always reply within 40 days. The reply should consist of:

- confirmation that personal data about that individual are held
- a copy of as much of the information as can be given without disclosing the identity of the other individual who has not consented

student activity

(PC 2.4.4, COM 3.2, 3.4, IT 3.1, 3.2, 3.3, 3.4)
There are several exemptions and restrictions set down in the guidelines relating to the Data Protection Act. Obtain a copy of these leaflets and research the following:

- what data are exempt from the regulations?
- what disclosures are prohibited by law?
- how likely is it that data relating to one individual could be accessed and purchased by another individual or organisation?

Present your findings in the form of a word processed report.

COST OF MEETING THE ACT

Obviously, one of the negative effects of the implementation of the Data Protection Act for an organisation could be the costs involved.

If the organisation is large and the amount of information stored is of a nature to require registration with the Registrar, then some expense will be involved in overseeing the input of such data. It may be necessary for the organisation to employ an individual to control and monitor this process. Such a Data Protection Officer would have the responsibility of monitoring the additions, deletions and use of information. This could involve a great deal of time in man hours and expense in terms of salary for the organisation.

student activity

(PC 2.4.4, COM 3.1, 3.4)
Again, as in the previous activity, obtain copies of the guidelines regarding the implementation of the Data Protection Act. You will find that your college or local library will have copies. Try to estimate the cost to an organisation of complying with the legislation. Does it cost more for an organisation than it does for an individual? Discuss your findings with the remainder of your group.

ELEMENT 2.4

a s s i g n m e n t

(PC2.4.1–4, COM 3.2, 3.3, 3.4, IT 3.1, 3.2, 3.3, 3.4)
You have already identified a business organisation whose information processing systems you wish to investigate. For the purpose of this assignment, and in order to fulfil the performance criterion of this Element, you should carry out the following tasks. Your tasks should take the form of a word processed report.

TASK 1

(PC 2.4.1)
The first part of your report should explain the purposes of the information processing applications that are carried out within your organisation. You should ensure that you address the following:

- the way the information is **received**
- the way the information is **stored**
- the way the information is **used**
- the way information is **communicated** both within and outside the organisation

TASK 2

(PC 2.4.2)
The second part of your report should describe the information processing systems used in your business organisation. You should consider the following:

- is the system a **single-purpose system?**
- or is the system capable of operating **several tasks** at the same time?

In addition, you should address the question of the impact these systems have on the following:

- the increased or decreased **work load** of the staff

- the increased or decreased **work opportunities** of the staff
- the **training** which was required or will be required

TASK 3

(PC 2.4.3)
In Part 3 of your report you should analyse the effectiveness of the information processing system in your organisation. Specifically, you should consider the following:

- the time taken
- the speed
- the volume of work
- the ease of use

The work you carried out in a previous Student Activity should be useful to assist you in the completion of this section.

TASK 4

(PC 2.4.4)
In the final part of your report you should illustrate the effects of the Data Protection Act on the organisation with regard to the following:

- the rights of individual employees to personal access to information
- the security of the information
- the ownership and accuracy of the information held by the organisation

UNIT 2

test questions

Focus 1

OBJECTIVES OF BUSINESS ORGANISATIONS

1–3 There are a number of ways in which an organisation sets out its aims, purposes and objectives, including:

(a) a business plan
(b) a mission statement
(c) organisational strategy
(d) organisational tactics

Which of these are described by the following?

1 Agreed goals which have common consent or shared point of view

2 The formal statement of the organisation's goals

3 Short-term and flexible ways of achieving objectives

4 The following statements have been made about business organisations:

(i) a conglomerate is an organisation that has interests in a variety of different business ventures
(ii) an organisation which has charitable status is not exempt from the legal obligations of a normal organisation

Are these statements?

(a) True/True
(b) True/False
(c) False/True
(d) False/False

5 Which of the following organisations does not enjoy a degree of protection in terms of limited liability?

(a) Ltd.
(b) plc
(c) QUANGO
(d) Franchise

Focus 2

OWNERSHIP AND ORGANISATIONAL STRUCTURE

6 A Memorandum of Association outlines which of the following?

(a) the duties of the directors
(b) a brief statement including an organisation's activities and investments made
(c) the general procedures to be followed at an AGM
(d) details of how the accounts will be kept and recorded

7 What does CCT stand for?

(a) Charitable Co-operative Trust
(b) Compulsory Company Tender
(c) Company Contract Trustees
(d) Compulsory Competitive Tender

8 In terms of organisational structure, which of the following areas of business activity would use the concept of branches?

(a) manufacturing
(b) primary sector
(c) retail sector
(d) professional services

9 The following statements have been made about specialisation:

(i) by specialising in one job a person can do that job well rather than doing lots of jobs badly
(ii) specialisation can often lead to jobs being boring

Are these statements?

(a) True/True
(b) True/False
(c) False/True
(d) False/False

10–12 The following are different types of organisational structure:

(a) decentralised
(b) flat
(c) product divisions
(d) matrix

Which organisational structure is described as?

10 A Japanese form of structure created to allow different individuals to be brought together to form a task

11 An organisation with a high level of autonomy

12 An organisational structure which encourages employees to take on greater responsibility

Focus 3
ADMINISTRATION SYSTEMS

13 The following statements have been made about the monitoring of business performance:

(i) intra-firm comparisons are where comparisons are made in relation to the expenditure of competitors
(ii) inter-firm comparisons are where expenditure is compared to that of last year

Are these statements?

(a) True/True
(b) True/False
(c) False/True
(d) False/False

14 An organisation uses MIS for which of the following purposes?

(a) to assist the running of automated production lines
(b) to help design complex items
(c) to provide information for managers
(d) to assign codes to each product

15 The administration department provides a centralised purchasing service. Which of the following would not fall within their regular functions?

(a) memoranda and letterheads
(b) the issuing of sales invoices
(c) purchase of photocopiers
(d) purchase of insurance and leasing agreements

16 UK companies have increased the amount they have spent on computer systems year by year. The average increase in this expenditure has risen by which of the following percentages?

(a) 0.2%
(b) 20%
(c) 15%
(d) 6%

Focus 4
COMMUNICATION SYSTEMS

17 What are NVCs?

(a) non-vocational communication
(b) normal visual communication
(c) non-verbal communication
(d) non-visual codes

18 Which of the following is not used for internal communication?

(a) telephone
(b) letter
(c) memo
(d) report

19 The correct sequence for a report is:

(a) Terms of reference, procedure, findings, conclusions, recommendations
(b) findings, conclusions, procedure, terms of reference, recommendations
(c) procedures, terms of reference, findings, conclusions, recommendations
(d) terms of reference, findings, conclusions, procedure, recommendations

20 The following statements have been made about forms of external communications:

(i) an invitation will include répondez s'il vous plaît
(ii) a business letter should ensure that the registered address is the same as the postal address

Are these statements?

(a) True/True
(b) True/False
(c) False/True
(d) False/False

Focus 5
INFORMATION PROCESSING

21 There have been a number of harmful effects on the users of computers. Which two of the following are more likely to have harmful effects?

(i) computer noise
(ii) radiation
(iii) screen flicker
(iv) repetitive keyboard actions

(a) (i) and (ii)
(b) (i) and (iv)
(c) (ii) and (iii)
(d) (iii) and (iv)

22–24 The following are types of computer applications:

(a) windows
(b) spreadsheets
(c) data bases
(d) desktop publishing

Identify which application is being described by the following statements:

22 Tables of numbers which can be altered and organised

23 A graphical interface allowing several tasks to be carried out at the same time

24 A system capable of manipulating text and importing graphics

25 The following statements have been made about computers:

(i) computers rely on the operator to tell them what to do
(ii) it does not matter what information is input into a computer, it will always sort it out for you

Are these statements?

(a) True/True
(b) True/False
(c) False/True
(d) False/False

26 What is user-definable software?

(a) software purchased as part of the deal when acquiring a computer
(b) easily adaptable software
(c) easy-to-use software
(d) software with good graphics packages

Focus 6
DATA PROTECTION ACT

27 What is the role of the Data Protection Registrar?

(a) to ensure that complaints are swiftly dealt with
(b) to make sure that individuals who request it are removed from computerised data
(c) to ensure that organisations using and storing data have made themselves known
(d) to personally vet the type and purpose of data stored

28 The following statements have been made about the Data Protection Act:

(i) the Data Protection Registrar awards compensation to individuals who have claimed misuse of data by a data user
(ii) an individual who suffers damage due to inaccurate personal data being held about him/her is entitled to claim compensation

Are these statements?

(a) True/True
(b) True/False
(c) False/True
(d) False/False

29 The following two statements have been made about the Data Protection Act:

(i) an organisation is exempt from the Data Protection Act if the equipment is leased
(ii) it is the use of the equipment for the storage and processing of data that is covered by the Data Protection Act

Are these statements?

(a) True/True
(b) True/False
(c) False/True
(d) False/False

30 The Data Protection Act states that 'personal data shall be accurate and where necessary kept up to date'. What is meant by the word accurate in this context?

(a) it should not be misleading
(b) it should be correct
(c) it should be both correct and not misleading
(d) it should be in a format which cannot be challenged

Investigate the principles and functions of marketing in organisations

PERFORMANCE CRITERIA

A student must:

1 discuss **marketing principles** and **marketing functions**

2 explain how the **marketing principles** underpin the **marketing functions**

3 explain an organisation's need to have a **customer focus** while meeting its **own needs**

4 **analyse marketing activities** in **business organisations**

5 explain the **growth of organisations** which relates to marketing

RANGE

Marketing principles: *anticipate market needs and opportunities, satisfy customer expectations, generate income and/or profit, maximise benefit to the organisation, manage effects of change and competition, co-ordinate activities to achieve marketing aims, utilise technological developments, enhance customers' perception (of the organisation, of the product)*

Marketing functions: *manage change, co-ordinate marketing planning and control, implement marketing mix (product, place, promotion, price), ensure survival of business, branding*

Customer focus/organisations' own needs: *market orientation versus product orientation, cost of customer service versus productivity, cost of customer service versus profitability, cost of customer service versus accountability*

Analyse marketing activities *in terms of assessing market needs (marketing research), satisfying customer requirements, managing effects of change, managing effects of competition, co-ordinating role (marketing, planning, control), generating maximum income and/or profit (sales and sales channels), optimising customer perception (customer service, marketing communications)*

Growth of organisations *through product development, markets (market development, market share, new market, new customers, retained customers)*

3.1.1 Discuss marketing principles and marketing functions

MARKETING PRINCIPLES

Before we investigate the main principles and functions of marketing, it would probably be a good idea to try to define exactly what **marketing** is.

If we begin by stating that marketing puts customers first and foremost in terms of the organisation's activities, we are beginning to get somewhere. The principal role of a business, as we have seen, is to meet the customer's needs. If an organisation can successfully use its premises, machinery, employees and materials, it can go some way to being successful. However, it is only when it can successfully market its products or services that it can be truly profitable and successful in the long run.

The Chartered Institute of Marketing provides a fairly good start at a definition:

> 'Marketing is the management process responsible for identifying, anticipating and satisfying customer requirements profitably.'

We shall return to these specific aspects later, but we should not forget that the implementation and use of marketing will differ from organisation to organisation.

The implementation techniques may include the following:

- market research
- sales forecasting
- product research
- advertising
- public relations
- sales promotions
- sales skills

It is also important to consider marketing as a concept which is one part of all the aspects of an organisation. It is not enough for a business to have a marketing department and believe that all of its marketing activities are dealt with by that department. From the top of the organisation down to the most lowly of employees, marketing should be a daily part of the activities of all members of the organisation. In other words, marketing is directly involved in:

- research (of competitors, of customer demand, etc.)
- development of products and services
- production processes
- finance
- distribution
- after-sales service
- all other activities of the organisation

Let us now turn our attention to the specifics and consider the fundamental nature of the principles of marketing and how they are applied in reality. One other point that should be borne in mind is that not all organisations necessarily have all of these principles uppermost in their list of priorities. Indeed, the importance placed on the marketing functions and the approach to these functions may be very different in profit-making and non-profit-making organisations. Equally, some charities or other organisations that fall into the non-profit-making field may be just as concerned with marketing as businesses whose sole aim is to make profits and be as efficient in this respect as possible. There is some debate about the 'professional' nature of some charities and other organisations, but in fairness, this should really be seen in context. Some of these organisations began in rather humble circumstances and were created to provide a service where there had been no traditional or governmental support. These organisations, because of the economic climate, have found that they were under increasing pressure to adopt many of the marketing tactics used by other more conventional business organisations. These non-profit-making organisations have had to adapt very quickly to the need to survive in an increasingly competitive market. The idea of a 'market', in the charity scene, has been a notion that, in the past, many of these organisations closed their eyes to. The impact of the National Lottery, for example, is such that some charities have reported a reduction in donations of as much as 70 per cent. This factor alone has made many charities begin to re-evaluate their marketing efforts. Increasingly, as we will see, these organisations recognise that they must adapt to survive.

ANTICIPATE MARKET NEEDS AND OPPORTUNITIES

Customers' needs, wants, desires and requirements change all the time. Anticipating what will be needed in the future is quite an art. The preliminary task of an organisation is to try to identify what the customers want and not what the organisation thinks that they want.

Overall market demand and customer demand are often beyond the direct control of an individual organisation. Whilst the demand and the patterns of need generated by the public in any region or market are unique to that market, the underlying factors are the same. These factors are relatively easy to measure, as we will see shortly.

It is possible to categorise the main determinants of demand, or needs, under the following headings:

● economic
● demographic
● geographical
● socio-cultural
● comparative price
● mobility
● government or legislative
● media communications

Demand also responds to changes in the supply of products and services. Supply is an important determinant of demand and demand is an important determinant of supply. Let us return to the eight points that we have mentioned already and analyse their influence on the demand for products:

1 *Economic* – the influence of economic variables can be seen in countries that have enjoyed a growth in the average disposable income per capita over the past few decades. The majority of the population have experienced a steady rise in the real value of their incomes. As a result, their disposable income has increased. The relationship between income and expenditure is known as the **income elasticity of demand**. If the population has a 10 per cent increase in their disposable income and this is matched by a similar increase in demand for a product, then the market is known as **income elastic**. If, on the other hand, the change in demand is less than the rise in disposable income, then the market is called **inelastic**. A typical example of an elastic market is the travel business. If people have more disposable income, then the number of people travelling abroad or going on holiday increases in proportion. It is a little more complex than this, as the travel business broadly splits into two parts. The elastic part is the vacation side of the business, whilst the inelastic side of the market is the holidays that people take to visit relatives abroad. If we stay with this example, then the increases in travel abroad are one thing, but the customer requires greater levels of quality and other improvements.

2 *Demographic* – this criterion is far slower to have an influence on the demand and needs of the market than economic factors, but it is not a factor that should be ignored. This factor includes the following:

● the age distribution of the market
● the average household size of the market

● the composition of the household (i.e. the number of adults and children)
● the education level of the market

3 *Geographical* – for populations living in the northern hemisphere, the weather has a great influence on the products and services demanded. This is particularly true of leisure activities and related products. Next to the weather is the size of the community in which individuals live. Large urban areas and suburban areas tend to generate more demand than the less populated and wealthy rural areas.

TABLE 3.1.1 *Households by size, Great Britain (per cent)*

Household size (persons)	1961	1971	1981	1991	1993
1	14	18	22	27	27
2	30	32	32	34	35
3	23	19	17	16	16
4	18	17	18	16	15
5	9	8	7	5	5
6 or more	7	6	4	2	2
No. of households (millions) (=-100%)	16.2	18.2	19.5	21.9	22.9
Average household size (no. of people)	3.1	2.9	2.7	2.5	2.4

Source: Office of Population Censuses and Surveys; Department of the Environment; The Scottish Office Environment Department; General Register Office.

4 *Socio-cultural* – this term is used to describe the broad trends in attitudes which influence the motivation of the customer. These also have a wider implication if we consider that many of the core attitudes of individuals are held by the majority of the population. Luxury goods are a measure of an individual's status in society. An individual who consumes relatively expensive products may perceive this consumption as a measure of his or her worth in society. The full marketing implications of this factor have been exploited very well by businesses. The trend towards exclusive or comparatively expensive products is ongoing.

Another factor to consider here is that some

TABLE 3.1.2 *Households: by type of household and family, Great Britain (per cent)*

	1961	1971	1981	1991	1993
One-person households					
Under pensionable age	4	6	8	11	11
Over pensionable age	7	12	14	16	16
Two or more unrelated adults	5	4	5	3	3
One-family households					
Married couple★ with:					
No children	26	27	26	28	28
1–2 dependent children★★	30	26	25	20	20
3 or more dependent children	8	9	6	5	5
Non-dependent children	10	8	8	8	7
Lone parent★ with:					
Dependent children★★	2	3	5	6	7
Non-dependent children	4	4	4	4	3
Two or more families	3	1	1	1	1
Number of households (millions) (=100%)	16.2	18.2	19.5	21.9	22.9

★ Other individuals who were not family members may also have been included.
★★ May also include non-dependent children.
Source: Office of Population Censuses and Surveys; Department of the Environment; The Scottish Office Environment Department.

student activity

(PC 3.1.1, COM 3.4, AON 3.3)
Referring to Table 3.1.1, draw a bar graph, or other graph of your choice, that illustrates this information. You should then try to consider the implications of the spread of household size in relation to the following products:

- washing powder
- children's nappies
- bread

Compare your conclusions about the probable demand with those of the rest of your group.

student activity

(PC 3.1.1, COM 3.4, AON 3.3)
Table 3.1.2 gives more detail than Table 3.1.1. Create a series of graphs for the following:

- one-person households
- two or more unrelated adults
- one-family households
- lone-parent households
- two or more families

Once you have done this, try to discern any particular trends in the figures over the period 1961 to 1993. What implications may there be for the products that you looked at in the previous Student Activity?

products tend to be more expensive at some times of the year and cheaper at others. A good example of this is the general availability of fresh fruits and vegetables at times of the year when, technically, they are 'out of season'. Individuals will still buy these products at a premium or higher price as part of their belief that this consumption reflects their lifestyle and socio-cultural position in society.

5 *Comparative price* – this reflects the value to the consumer in relation to their spending power. The concept of comparative prices is very complex and quite hard to predict with any hope of accuracy. Price is, without doubt, one of the principal determining factors of demand. Effective marketing can seek to exploit the comparative price factor. This is particularly true when we consider products that are competing with one another across international boundaries. Within each country a different set of economic factors may determine the price that needs to be charged for a product or service. This is amplified by the fact that if the product is to be distributed outside the country, then it comes into contact with products that have been produced under very different economic conditions. Such economic influences will include the following:

- inflation
- wage levels
- cost of raw materials

student activity

(PC 3.1.1, COM 3.1)
In pairs, try to come up with some other economic factors that would influence the price of a product. In the role of an organisation that produces products with high costs as a result of the economic factors, how would you compete against an organisation that operates in a cheaper environment?

The other aspect of this is the fact that some organisations have completely different attitudes to the price that they will charge for their product, regardless of the fact that they are operating in the same environment. This is when the aspects of quality, craftsmanship, method of production and distribution come into the equation.

6 *Mobility* – the use of public means of transport inevitably declines as car ownership increases. Apart from non-leisure travel, such as much of inter-city travel by road, rail and air, there are some important parts of the travel infrastructure that are determinants in the demand for a product or service. The general willingness of the individual customer to travel considerable distances to visit a particular outlet or location cannot be underestimated. The demand for factory shopping is so great that one company, based in Somerset, has reported that customers will travel from as far away as South Wales. Coach and bus companies have found many niches to exploit. Witness the number of day excursions to popular shopping centres and other attractions.

7 *Government or legislative* – Although government and other regulatory factors will determine the legality of and may exercise control over the production of certain products and services, organisations do attempt to lobby decision makers, particularly if they believe that legislation will adversely affect demand and therefore profits. Deregulation, on the other hand, very much affects the level of competition in a market and may well increase the overall demand since the customer is able to make use of the service or purchase the product for the first time. Liberalisation of rules and regulations has to be tempered with the continuing need to protect the customer from anti-competitive activities by organisations, particularly in the first few months of deregulation. Only by keeping a close eye on the developments of the market after deregulation, can the government ensure that the customer gets a good deal. The simple replacement of a public monopoly with a private one does nothing to increase the demand. The reverse might well mean that the demand would decrease if the new private monopoly chose to push up the price of the product or service. For this reason, the government will often appoint a watchdog or ombudsman, whose task it is to make sure that anti-competitive practices are stamped out or not allowed to develop.

8 *Media communications* – this is the final consideration, and has a powerful influence over the demand for products or services. Television watching is far and away the most popular form of leisure activity. The average person in the UK watches some 19 hours of television per week. The cumulative impact of so many hours of watching has to have an influence on the demands of a customer. The massive and continuous exposure to this medium alone will impact upon the consumption patterns and hence the demand for products and services.

At lower levels, the radio and the print media will have an impact on the demand too. Drawing attention to a particular product or service may be one thing, achieved by advertisements, but anticipating customer needs is another. Keeping a close eye on the activities of the organisations which supply goods and services (in terms of advertising and other promotions) is one useful way of anticipating customer needs. A truly successful organisation will take a rather more pro-active approach in this respect and will carry out market research on the impact of and awareness stimulated by advertising in the media. We will return to this topic in later parts of this Unit.

SATISFY CUSTOMER EXPECTATIONS

Customers, obviously, demand that their requirements are met. They are always looking for benefits that a product or service can offer them. As we will see later, the subtle use of the marketing mix may have a vital role to play here. After all, the key elements are always:

- having the right product available
- having the product available at the right price
- having the product available in as many places (outlets) as possible
- having the product in stock at all times, both in the warehouse and the outlets

Customer expectations are a notoriously difficult thing to measure. It is only through continuous market research and the monitoring of customers' reactions to its products and services that an organisation can begin to build up a profile of customers' expectations.

Today, an increasing number of businesses are recognising the commercial advantages to be gained from the high quality of service, state of-the-art technology, competitive pricing, and comprehensive management reporting provided by Mercury Communications.

In addition, Mercury users benefit from an innovative product line and the highest standards of customer care.

FIG. 3.1.1 *Mercury Communications is a prime example of an organisation which markets its sevices to businesses. This illustration is an extract from its brochure on the Mercury 2200 service which is specifically designed for business users.*

Some of the more obvious expectations of customers can be addressed as a matter of course. Indeed all organisations can identify the key expectations that relate to their particular area of business. Some of the expectations may include the following:

- accurate and reliable information about the product or service
- prompt and courteous advice and feedback regarding questions about the product or service
- wide availability of the product or service
- consistency in the quality, style, colour or other standardised features of the product or service
- reliable and responsive after-sales service, maintenance or technical back-up after the purchase of the product or service
- good, competitive pricing structures that encourage the customer to return to the same organisation time and time again for the purchase of the product or service
- a consistent public image of the organisation that neither undermines nor embarrasses the customer

student activity

(PC 3.1.1, COM 3.1)
In pairs, try to think of some other basic customer expectations. Are these expectations fair? Does the customer expect too much from the supplying organisation? How much real effort should be expended by an organisation in the pursuit of ensuring that customers' expectations are met and often exceeded? Once you have drawn up a list of expectations, discuss the other questions arising from this with the rest of the group.

GENERATE INCOME AND/OR PROFIT

Generating income from sales or producing a profit for the organisation are always essential for any business. Clearly, organisations cannot survive without ensuring that sales income exceeds the costs incurred. We have looked at this concept in other parts of the book. At this stage, we will restrict our comments to the more general aspects. Generating extra income does not necessarily mean that the organisation will achieve greater profits. Also, the profit motive is not always the driving force behind the move to increase sales income. In the short term, the organisation may wish to try to increase its market share, and this may be at the expense of lower profits for a short while. By making extra investments and, perhaps by reducing the price of a product, the organisation may gain extra market share, but it may not gain extra profits. There is also a balance to be considered. If the organisation tries to expand its operations too quickly, then it may face the problem of over-trading. In this instance, the organisation cannot find enough working capital to ensure that the immediate debts of the organisation can be paid when they fall due.

Marketing provides a useful series of tools to the organisation that can have an impact on the level of sales. We will be looking at many of them in the remainder of this Element and the rest of the Unit in general. Whether it is marketing's responsibility simply to inform the potential customer about the product or service, or whether the role is deeper than that, the sales increase motive will usually remain paramount.

MAXIMISE BENEFIT TO THE ORGANISATION

As we will see in Element 3.4, the measurement of the effectiveness of marketing communications methods can be quite complex, but at the same time, rather revealing. Essentially, regardless of the methods employed to measure the effectiveness of the marketing, the organisation may derive some main positive benefits. These are:

- greater knowledge of the customer and the market
- a greater knowledge on the part of customers about the product or the organisation
- a greater, or retained market share
- an increase in sales
- establishing the product or service as the market leader, or protecting its position
- a high level of quality assurance

The other major benefits that may come to the organisation are more functional or control benefits. These include:

- co-ordination of the marketing effort
- matching the marketing effort with the corporate image or mission statement of the organisation
- monitoring and fulfilment of customers' expectations
- the ability to manage and respond to change
- the ability to take advantage of, use and understand breakthroughs in technology

As we have mentioned, the measurement of marketing communications is covered in the last Element of this Unit, while the other aspects such as co-ordination can be found elsewhere in this Element.

MANAGE EFFECTS OF CHANGE AND COMPETITION

In business, as with almost any other area of life, the only really constant and dependable piece of information to work on is that things are always changing.

An increasingly important function of the marketing efforts of an organisation is to attempt to manage this change. This statement alone appears to be impossible. How can an organisation 'manage change'? Surely, the nature of change itself means that much of it is unpredictable? Perhaps, but at the very least, the organisation needs to identify the sources of the potential change and to have in place a series of measures or proposed policies to combat them.

This begins with an appraisal of the external factors that may influence the organisation. In other words, we are considering the changing environment in which the organisation operates, which includes the activities of the competition. It is vital that the organisation does this since it needs to be sure that it can react more effectively and efficiently than its competitors, no matter what the changes may involve.

A solid formation of the strategies to be employed often begins with a PEST analysis. This form of analysis addresses the four major external influences on the organisation. These are:

1 *Political and legal* – where the organisation is affected by changes in legislation or government decision making. Equally, any form of political instability may affect the smooth running of the organisation and its ability to respond in a meaningful way.

2 *Economic* – where the organisation is affected by the economic policies of the government of the country in which it is based, or the more indefinable changes in the world's economic situation. A world recession, such as the ones that occurred in the 1980s and early 1990s determined how successful an organisation could be in the world markets. Other such factors which fall into this category are:

- inflation
- economic growth or contraction of country
- consumer consumption patterns
- the distribution of income within a country
- the protectionist policies adopted by countries

3 *Social* – where the organisation is affected by the nature of the society within which it operates. Typically, these factors will include:

- demographic changes
- migration of people
- age of the population
- the population's culture
- social trends
- family size

4 *Technological* – where the organisation is affected by developments in the manufacturing process. The net effect of these changes may influence such things as the cost effectiveness of the current methods of production, particularly when comparing the processes with those of the competitors.

Focus study

MANAGING THE EFFECTS OF CHANGE AND COMPETITION

The fierce competition between washing powder manufacturers took an unexpected turn in the middle of 1994. Unilever distributed 11m. free samples of their new Persil Power to almost every home in the UK. This was in reaction to claims by their main market rival Procter and Gamble about the effect of Persil Power on clothes. The enormous Unilever campaign was one of the biggest direct marketing exercises ever undertaken and was part of Unilever's £25m. support campaign for Persil Power.

Unilever hoped that it would end reports about the destructive power of their new brand. Procter and Gamble had undertaken a series of tests on Persil Power and claimed that the product rendered cotton cloth ragged after fewer than 30 washes.

Procter and Gamble have claimed that they did not invent this story about Unilever's product, neither did they encourage individual customers to make complaints. Unilever, on the other hand, claim that Procter and Gamble had descended to the depths of competitive activity in trying to 'rubbish' their new product. At the end of the day the consumers, having received free samples of Persil Power, will be the judge.

CO-ORDINATE ACTIVITIES TO ACHIEVE MARKETING AIMS

In order to implement the marketing aims of the organisation in a co-ordinated manner some planning is required. We will be looking at this aspect a little later in this Element (see PC 3.1.4). At this point, it would be valuable to examine the overall marketing process in terms of the activities normally undertaken by an organisation and see how these can be co-ordinated in an efficient manner.

Implementing marketing policy or aims can be seen as a cyclical process. Certain activities should be undertaken before it is appropriate or wise to venture further through the marketing process. In this respect, we can identify four main stages of the marketing

student activity

process. These are:

1 *The initial phase* – which involves carrying out marketing research to discover want the customer needs are; this will also include an analysis of the competition (their strengths and weaknesses) and an investigation of the types, nature and performance of products already available.

2 *The strategy phase* – this involves the setting of objectives and the clear setting out of the marketing activities required in order to achieve these objectives.

3 *The operational phase* – this phase actually puts all of the planning into action. All of the marketing activities mentioned in Element 3.4 are included in this phase, such as television advertising and sales promotions.

4 *The control phase* – this, as we have mentioned earlier, is the stage in which the organisation attempts to assess the effectiveness of the marketing activities.

The organisation may face the prospect of having gone through all of these phases and then discover that the marketing activities have either been ineffective or do not accord with the marketing aims as set out at the beginning of the exercise.

The organisation will, in such cases, revert back to the first phase of the operation and begin again, trying to identify any mistakes or misinterpretations that may have been made. In any event, the organisation will continually feed new research findings into the process to hone and improve the marketing activities and their effectiveness.

UTILISE TECHNOLOGICAL DEVELOPMENTS

If there is one factor that can seriously impact upon the marketing activities, or for that matter the activities of the organisation as a whole, it is the advent of new technology. Many of us forget that technology that we depend upon on a day-to-day basis was not available in the recent past. Technological innovations may impact upon the marketing activities in the following ways:

1 *The unstoppable pace of technology* – opportunities in new fields of technology which open up new markets are much greater than in the past. The organisation, rather than working from a set of marketing possibilities, is faced with the prospect of having to handle radically different situations day by day. Some marketing consultants have likened this aspect of marketing to playing a game of cards, when the hand you have is changing every three or four seconds. In other words, how do you plan for the unexpected?

2 *Impact on all industries* – innovations tend to feed upon one another. A breakthrough by one organisation will lead to another trying to outdo it. A breakthrough in one field, such as the chemicals industry, will release new products onto the market that can revolutionise other industries. It is rather like a chain reaction of changes, with each new discovery fuelling the next. The distance between the retail outlet and the scientific lab is shortening day by day. A good example of this is the development of the meat substitute called Quorn. Based on a fungus, this new product has allowed manufacturers to produce new foodstuffs that mimic meat. Because of improvements in food flavourings, it is now impossible to tell the difference between a Quorn 'steak pie' and a real one. In terms of marketing activities, new techniques and ideas had to be developed to sell this innovative product to the public.

3 *Research and development* – marketing personnel are closely linked to the research and development efforts of the organisation. An organisation cannot afford to stand still while the competition spends money on developing new products. The marketing personnel need to keep abreast of new developments and appreciate, at the earliest opportunity, the marketing opportunities.

ENHANCE CUSTOMERS' PERCEPTION OF THE ORGANISATION, PRODUCT OR SERVICE

Marketing plays an important role in enhancing the corporate or organisational image. An effective and well-managed company should be market sensitive and aim to create greater customer satisfaction. Public relations efforts cannot possibly succeed in their goals if the company is unable to show itself capable of performing well and demonstrating reasonable efficiency. Good trading performance, coupled with strong customer loyalty, goes a long way in maintaining a sound and positive corporate image.

Marketing can help the corporate or general image of the organisation in the following ways:

1 *Product publicity* – getting the products onto TV or featured in newspapers and magazines.

2 *Informing* – continually feeding information to the public and other interest groups.

3 *Media relations* – co-ordinating advertising, sales promotions, press releases, etc. It is in the organisation's interest to release as much information as possible to counteract any chance that the public misunderstands or has a negative impression of the organisation.

4 *Creating awareness* – by fostering strong and positive attitudes to the organisation this will help add to the reputation of the organisation's products and services. If the brand name is well established and respected, then any problems associated with the organisation itself can be kept at a distance.

5 *Developing the corporate image* – marketing can be involved throughout the whole process, starting with marketing research that attempts to find out what customers' expectations of the organisation are, to the analysis of customer behaviour. Targeting policies, advertising and selling and any attempt to readjust the perceptions of the organisation that may be necessary are also integral roles. Optimising the marketing opportunities and constantly pushing news of the organisation's successes should be tempered with the need to be honest if the organisation has made a mistake.

The enhancement of product image encompasses many of the activities an organisation will employ to protect its market share or standing in the market. Promotions and sponsorships have become particularly popular in recent years. A number of organisations sponsors television programmes (for more details see Element 3.4). The image of the television programme helps to enhance the customers' perceptions of the product.

National Power were unfortunate in their sponsorship of the 1990 World Cup. The unexpected defeat of the English team, which meant that they did not qualify for the finals, not only curtailed the television coverage, but also damaged National Power's credibility. Martell Cognac, which sponsored the disastrous 1993 Grand National horse race, similarly suffered a loss of face as a result of the fiasco.

GUIDELINES FOR USE AND REPRODUCTION
OF THE LOGOTYPE

The logotype shown below is the copyright of Anglia Television Limited, and
may not be reproduced or transmitted in any form or by any means without
the prior permission of Anglia Television Limited. The logotype consists of
both the symbol and the words 'Anglia Television Limited' and must be used in
its entirety.

Applications of the logotype must conform to one of the standard designs
shown on the artwork supplied. No other arrangement of the symbol and
wording, or typestyle, or colour is permissible; nor may the logotype be linked
to any other typography or graphic device.

For any circumstances where the specifications given are not suitable, please
contact the Public Relations Manager for further instructions.

COATED STOCK
60% Cyan
UNCOATED STOCK
60% Cyan

COATED STOCK
100% Cyan
40% Black
65% Magenta
UNCOATED STOCK
100% Cyan
24% Black
60% Magenta

COATED STOCK
100% Yellow
15% Magenta
UNCOATED STOCK
100% Yellow
15% Magenta

COATED STOCK
100% Black
UNCOATED STOCK
100% Black

Colour on Black

White out of Black
or Colour

Colour on White

Black on White

FIG. 3.1.2 *Anglia Television is
another prime example of an organisation which has produced clear
guidelines for its logo to enhance its corporate image. You will notice the Anglia
logo on many programmes such as 'The
Chief', 'Survival' and 'Knightmare'.*

student activity

(PC 3.1.1, COM 3.1)
As a group assess whether you think that it is more
important to enhance customer perception of the
organisation itself or of its product? Try to reach some
kind of consensus.

FIG. 3.1.3 *Allied Lyons' Tetley Tea sponsors the British TV
series 'The Darling Buds of May'. This has an audience of 13 million in the USA and the organisation considers this an ideal way
of enhancing its product image.*

3.1.2 Explain how the marketing principles underpin the marketing functions

MARKETING FUNCTIONS

One of the most common forms of marketing organisation is the division of the marketing department into specific functions. As we explained in Unit 2 when we considered the job roles of various individuals that you might find in the marketing department, each of their central job roles or tasks performs a vital function within the marketing process.

The principal rationale behind separating responsibilities or functions is to enable each individual to carry out both operational and planning activities. By reporting to a senior manager, perhaps a marketing director, people can be entrusted to carry out tasks within their own specialism. Again, if we refer back to another section in Unit 2 in which we considered a function-orientated organisation, you can recognise that each of the specialists effectively manages different products, territories or customers. Obviously, in the case of an organisation whose markets or products are similar to one another, a functionally-based organisational structure is perhaps inappropriate. We will now consider the principal marketing functions and explain how they relate to the marketing principles which we have already outlined at the beginning of this Element.

MANAGE CHANGE

Even the best laid plans are subject to interference by any number of external or internal variables. It is not sufficient to develop just one plan. Provisions need to be made not only to adjust plans when necessary, but also to consider the alternatives which may send the planning process into new areas. It is important to have control over the marketing process, and there are a number of ways in which the organisation can attempt to maintain control, either by means of a top-down system (in which senior management closely monitor or review the situation), or by developing marketing sub-systems which attempt to monitor themselves.

CO-ORDINATE MARKETING PLANNING AND CONTROL

We can best explain the control systems appropriate to marketing by looking at them in turn:

1 *Top management control* – one of the best ways to control the functions and activities of the marketing department is to treat them as a profit centre. This means, in effect, that the marketing department acts as an independent middle man that purchases products and services from the manufacturing side of the organisation and then sells them into the market. In this way, the profit made will be the difference between the company's sales and the marketing department's costs. It will then be relatively easy to look at ratios of profit in relation to investment in the department.

2 *Marketing's control over company sub-systems* – there is a constant battle in many organisations for ultimate control over the key activities. Using this control model, the marketing director would attempt to incorporate related activities such as production, stock control, distribution and purchasing. In seeking increased authority and power, the marketing director is attempting to gain greater control over internal variables that may affect his/her department's efficiency.

3 *Marketing's control over outside agents* – in the previous control model, we considered the marketing department's attempt to gain authority over internal factors. In this model the marketing department turns its attention to external agents, such as wholesalers and advertising agencies. In many cases, the performance, cost effectiveness and efficiency of these external agencies are out of the control of the organisation, let alone the marketing department. In extreme circumstances, the organisation may be convinced by the marketing department to acquire shares in the outside agencies in order to achieve adequate controls. In any case, the marketing department will seek to put very tight restrictions on the outside agency and clearly state its responsibilities.

4 *Marketing's control over personnel* – one of the age-old problems which a marketing department may face is the inability to make meaningful and productive business relationships with other employees. If the marketing director or his/her department has some say in the recruitment and selection of employees with whom he/she will have regular dealings, then a degree of additional control may be achieved.

5 *Marketing's control over external influences* – as we mentioned earlier, any marketing plan can be seriously undermined by a factor which either has not been considered or is beyond their control. Flexibility is the key word in this respect. The marketing management needs to be able to make the right changes and put them into immediate effect.

This will involve having a good information system and having a range of contingency plans ready.

6 *Marketing's control over special projects* – special projects, such as the development of a new product, a major advertising campaign, or the organisation's move into a new market-place may be considered at board level without the involvement of the marketing department. The first problem is keeping the projects on schedule as well as within budget. It is obviously essential for the marketing department to be involved at the earliest possible stage in the conception of a new project so that it is aware of the additional pressures and duties which it will be expected to perform.

One feature that we have not addressed so far is that of efficiency. Many organisations may employ efficiency engineers who are skilled in helping people perform their jobs better. In terms of the marketing function, we can identify three main areas where specific efficiencies may be achieved:

I *Sales force efficiency* – is the sales force larger than it needs to be to do the job? How can tasks which are currently be handled by sales people be transferred or eliminated? Are individual sales personnel using their time to the best effect?

2 *Advertising efficiency* – it is widely accepted that many organisations spend too much on advertising. Is the organisation's advertising agency charging a proportionate amount compared to the organisation's expenditure? Do product managers have reasonable budgets? Is the sales revenue derived from advertising in proportion to the advertising spending?

3 *Distribution efficiency* – in distribution, there are always areas where economies can be made. The physical distribution process which includes stock levels, warehousing and transportation should be consistently under review. Improvements in delivery, especially in high volume operations such as food deliveries, can identify massive savings with simple re-routing exercises.

IMPLEMENT MARKETING MIX (PRODUCT, PLACE, PROMOTION, PRICE)

The marketing mix is the combination of strategies and tactics, company policy, techniques and activities to which resources can be allocated in such a way that the organisation's objectives can be achieved. The marketing mix itself is concerned with the practicalities of achieving the marketing objectives. How can the organisation translate its marketing objectives into viable and working marketing activities? The marketing mix assists in the following way:

student activity

(PC 3.1.2, COM 3.1)
In the role of an organisation which has a comprehensive delivery and distribution system, where would you begin in your assessment of the service? What factors would you have to consider before radically changing the distribution network? Discuss this as a group.

I *Strategic considerations* – what products or services should the organisation produce, and how will it achieve satisfaction of the market needs? These choices will be limited by the level of the organisation's resources, thus the organisation should limit its activities to what it deems to be potentially fruitful for markets or products.

2 *Tactical considerations* – what sales tactics or promotional tools will the organisation employ in its attempts to achieve the sales objectives?

3 *Planning considerations* – what is the organisation's long-term commitment to the product or service?

4 *Resource considerations* – how much of the resources of the organisation can be channelled into advertising and sales promotions and when can the organisation expect a return on the research and development of the product?

5 *Operational considerations* – to what extent does the organisation expect its marketing department to generate the necessary marketing and advertising ideas and materials?

The marketing mix aims to ensure that:

● the right product is available
● the price is right
● the product is available in the necessary outlets
● the product is available when the customer needs it

In conjunction with these four main points, the marketing mix should also be responsible for making sure that the appropriate tool is employed to help persuade the customers that they should consider the organisation's product and make the purchase.

The marketing mix can be more clearly defined as relating to the following, also known as the Four Ps:

● product
● price

student activity

(PC 3.1.2, COM 3.1)
How does an organisation determine what is the correct promotional tool for their product or service? Discuss this in pairs.

student activity

(PC 3.1.2, COM 3.1)
How would the marketing mix in a retail outlet and a wholesale organisation differ? Discuss this in pairs.

- place
- promotion

The four parts of the marketing mix are extremely interdependent and cannot really be considered separately. Here are some examples of the interdependence:

1 The brand image of the product or service should be reinforced by the pricing policy; in other words, a customer will be prepared to spend more on what he/she considers to be a reputable brand. The price charged is relative to the customer's perception of the product and not necessarily its quality.
2 The level of advertising and sales promotion can strongly influence the customer's perception of the product.
3 If an organisation intends to distribute a product intensively, there will be a large sales force promoting the product in every market, and making sure that it is available where and when demand requires it.

If the organisation makes alterations to one aspect of the marketing mix, this will mean that there will be a knock-on effect to the other parts of the marketing mix. If the price is reduced significantly, then this may alter the product's standing in the market. This is not to say that a slight adjustment to one of the aspects of the marketing mix will not pay dividends. Slight alterations may be seen in a positive light by the customer, and it is therefore the skill of the marketing manager and his/her understanding of how the four elements interrelate that determine the success or failure of the organisation's objectives.

ENSURE SURVIVAL OF BUSINESS

At the heart of this consideration is performance measurement. There are many sophisticated ways of performance measurement which aim to alert the management to possible problems. Some of the ways in which problems can be identified at the earliest point include:

1 *Expense and revenue deviation charts* – these show the sales quotas required and the expense budgets for particular sales regions. Periodically updated, these will show quota attainment, expense attainment and poor or good performance.
2 *Ratio analysis* – you could use the expense and revenue deviation charts to calculate ratios. However, there are several other methods which involve ratios and percentages, including:

- expense to sale ratios
- gross profit to sales ratios
- percentage of goods sold at discount
- percentage of returned goods
- ratio of back orders to current stocks
- salesperson turnover, i.e. number of salespersons joining and leaving the organisation
- bad debtors' ratios

Cross-ratio analysis will also reveal a number of interesting and significant factors. These are essentially, as we have said, alerting devices to possible problems in marketing performance.

BRANDING

Every organisation faces a number of decisions in relation to the branding of its products. A brand is a name, term, sign or design that differentiates the product from the competition. A brand name is the name by which the product is most generally known, such as Coke, Hoover and Ford. Some brand names have become generic, in the sense that the name Ford covers a number of different products. In other cases, such as Filofax, the name refers to one particular type of product. The trade mark is part of all of this since this is a brand given legal protection because it is capable of being identified as a separate item. Branding is the term usually used in establishing the brand name, trade marks or trade names of a product, organisation or range of products.

Why should an organisation rush into branding its products? Surely this means extra expense? The costs of legal protection and packaging alone can run into hundreds of thousands of pounds. Here are some of the reasons why:

- the brand name may be needed so that the organisation can simplify the handling of the product
- the brand name may be important for legal reasons, and if there are patents for the protection of some of the product's unique features, it may prevent copying
- the brand name may infer some level of quality or quality assurance, and the customer will be able to identify the product and be assured of its quality
- the brand name may be part of the overall marketing strategy. The product, through the brand name, will have a history or a tradition. A good example of this is the Levi branding
- the branding idea and requirements may not come from the manufacturer at all. It may be that the distributors see that the product would be easier to market and handle with a unique identity

The **brand wars**, as they are known, are raging in supermarkets and other retail outlets across the world. In this battle, the two sides are:

- the **manufacturers' brands**, which tend to be more expensive and are supported by advertising and promotions
- the **distributors' brands**, or **own-label brands**, which are offered at lower prices, but do not have the advantage of as much media exposure as the manufacturers' brands

The bottom line is that there is only a limited amount of space on any of the shelves in the outlets. Supermarkets give more prominent display to their own-brand products than to the manufacturers' brands.

There are at least three main brand strategies to consider:

1 *Family brands against individual brands* – some manufacturers choose to put all of their products under the organisation's name, however, there are some sub-variations of this:

- *individual brand names* – followed by many organisations; these mean that the product has a completely distinctive identity. Good examples include: Radion, Surf, Persil and Bold
- *blanket family names* – in this version, the organisation uses the same name for all products, such as Heinz
- *separate family names for all products* – where the organisation has a number of separate 'divisions' or parts which have a range of products each. Kingfisher, the owners of Woolworths, also own other retail chains, but each has its own identity

- *trade name plus individual product name* – this policy is used by organisations such as Kelloggs. They describe their products as Kelloggs Corn Flakes, Kelloggs Rice Crispies etc.

2 *Brand extension* is a method of using a successful product's name to launch new products onto the market. The washing powder manufacturers use this technique all the time with words like 'improved' or 'better than ever'. Alternatively, the brand extension policy may involve the production of variants of the main product all of which are offered at the same time. Cars are good examples of this – you can purchase a standard model, a diesel version, a turbo version, an estate version or a 'limited edition'.

3 *Multi-brand strategy*, on the other hand, is the development of two or more brands which compete with one another. Procter and Gamble pioneered this strategy, having introduced one washing powder as early as the 1950s and then, subsequently, producing other brands with different powers and ingredients.

student activity

(PC 3.1.2, COM 3.1)
Why would an organisation bother to start a multi-brand competition within its own operations? Surely, there are enough competitors out there anyway? Discuss your possible reasons in pairs and then feedback your findings to the remainder of the group.

If you have been wracking your brains about why organisations would actively compete with themselves, then this may be the answer. If your organisation manufacturers or supplies a number of products that roughly perform the same function, and you support them with advertising and get them into the retail outlets, then where are the other competing organisations' products going to go if you have taken up all of the shelf space?

Focus study

BRANDING

In April 1993 Philip Morris, the world's largest consumer products group, took one of the biggest gambles of its business life. It slashed the price of its top-selling cigarette brand Marlboro by 20 per cent. This was an attempt to counteract the brand's collapsing sales in the face of massive competition from low-priced generic cigarettes.

Price cuts have also been embraced by other leading cigarette manufacturers such as Benson and Hedges and Virginia Slims. JRJ Nabisco, manufacturers of Camel and Winston reported a $900m. dip in sales from 1993 to 1994.

Brands are no longer a licence to print money. Own-label products will flourish when brands are over-priced. The price of Marlboro, for example, was as much as double the price of discounted cigarettes and as a consequence its market share dropped from 24.5 per cent to 21.5 per cent in the space of a month.

student activity

(PC 3.1.2, COM 3.1)
In the middle of 1995 the Co-Op announced that it would be revealing the sources of all of its own-label products. Perhaps this is the beginning of a trend which will enable customers to make more objective decisions about their perception of own-label products.

As a group, discuss whether you would be more or less likely to consider buying own-label products if you knew, for example, that the biscuits were made by McVities, or the baked beans by Heinz.

3.1.3 Explain an organisation's need to have a customer focus while meeting its own needs

CUSTOMER FOCUS/ ORGANISATION'S OWN NEEDS

Juggling the two considerations of customer focus and organisational needs may prove to be a constant problem for an organisation. In this section we will be considering the various ways of measuring the cost, effectiveness and impact of customer service against the sometimes conflicting requirements of the organisation itself.

MARKET ORIENTATION VERSUS PRODUCT ORIENTATION

There are, in effect, two very different approaches to business: one is known as the market-orientated approach and the other is known as the product-orientated approach. Now attempt the Student Activity on the right.

A market-orientated organisation has, in essence, embraced the concepts of marketing. To these organi-

student activity

(PC 3.1.3, COM 3.1)
Before you read on, what do you think these two different approaches actually mean? Which do you think is the better approach? Discuss your ideas with the rest of the group.

sations, the customers are the most important aspect of the business. They will make strenuous efforts to ensure that the customers get what they need. The entire organisation is geared up to provide for the needs, wants and aspirations of the customers.

A product-orientated organisation, on the other hand, begins (not surprisingly) with the product. The whole effort of such an organisation revolves around finding out the best ways to sell its products or services.

Let us restate these two opposing viewpoints and follow the logic behind each of the approaches. This is the approach of a market-orientated organisation:

- what do people want?
- how many do they want?
- how much will they pay?
- can we make a profit by providing for their wants?
- if we can; we we'll make the product/provide the service

The organisation is geared to the needs of the customer. It notes and acts on quality, reliability and price. In other words, the organisation is wholly market orientated and looks to that market to provide vital information about what it should produce.

The alternative view, and sadly a very common one, is the complete opposite, as we have seen. A product-orientated organisation would change the sequence of questions to the following:

- these are the products that we can make, aren't they?
- yes, we're good at that. Let's make more of them
- hang on, who are we going to sell them to?
- never mind that, that's the sales people's job, isn't it?
- great! That's true. Let's make some more, eh?

This approach does not take into account what the customer needs. The organisation only thinks in terms of what it makes and what it wants to do. If the organisation has produced something and it does not have a buyer, then the whole effort of the organisation switches to supporting the sales team. However, and this might sound negative, but some organisations are really very good operating in this way, they gear the whole organisation to selling and may even produce goods or services that the sales force feel 'comfortable' selling.

COST OF CUSTOMER SERVICE VERSUS PRODUCTIVITY, PROFITABILITY AND ACCOUNTABILITY

When we consider the organisation's need to achieve and sustain productivity in relation to the level of customer service it offers, we are, perhaps, focusing on time. If we assume that the organisation is committed to customer service, then we must also assume that it is prepared to invest employees' time in seeking this satisfaction. It should be remembered that whilst an employee, particularly a retail assistant, is dealing with a customer service-related issue, then he or she is not available to close other sales of a more straightforward nature with other customers. Equally, a salesperson who is dealing with a complex customer service enquiry is unavailable to take calls or enquiries that may result in a more profitable sale. For these sorts of reasons, it has become apparent to

Focus study

CUSTOMER ORIENTATION

The process of checking service excellence is becoming an increasingly important responsibility for management. British Airways, whose reputation and profitability was at rock bottom in the early 1980s, initiated their 'putting people first' campaign and has reaped considerable benefits.

IBM, for example, has suffered from telling its customers what they need rather than asking them what they want. Their pre-eminence in the market has probably suffered irreparable damage. Dell Computer Corporation, a $2bn. American computer manufacturer has seen sales grow by up to 100 per cent per year. By offering the twin benefits of sales direct from the manufacturer and unlimited telephone problem solving support, they have become extremely customer orientated. They have identified 16 major requests that customers make of them and have taken steps to make their response as efficient as possible.

many organisations that there is a need for a discrete customer service section. The staff of such a section will field the bulk of complex enquiries or complaints, only referring them to the 'front-line staff' when they cannot handle the situation themselves. In a manufacturing environment, employees may be constantly interrupted by visitors who require customer service on an immediate basis. Again, whilst handling these enquiries, the employee cannot proceed with his/her own tasks and duties. In all of these cases, assuming that the organisation does not have a discrete customer service section, productivity will be lost. There needs to be some kind of balance established between the need to provide customer service and the productivity requirements of the organisation. The other aspect which is involved here is that in smaller firms, where individuals undertake a wide range of different duties, they cannot be expected to perform routine tasks if they are constantly bombarded with customer service problems.

Turning to **profitability** in relation to customer service, it has been established that if an organisation manages to retain a customer for a considerable period of time, then that customer's business with the organisation becomes increasingly more profitable. Loyal customers who make repeat sales offer the following benefits:

- their spending will increase over a period of time
- they may purchase other products offered by the organisation

- they are likely to recommend or refer friends or acquaintances to the organisation
- they are less price-sensitive than new customers

Against this is the fact that loyal customers may cost more to acquire in the early stages of the organisation's relationship with them. This cost, though, is more than outweighed by the additional benefits mentioned above, as well as the probable savings in terms of reduced day-to-day customer service costs relating to that customer and the inevitable loss of sales, and therefore profit, if that customer should be lost.

On the subject of **accountability**, we return to the thorny problem of actually assessing the potential income derived from customer service activities. It is very difficult to identify sales achieved from existing customers which were either the result of their normal spending intentions or sales achieved as a result of customer service. Obviously it very much depends on who you are or where you are in the organisation. Those involved in customer service would claim that these increased sales were as a result of their efforts, whilst the sales department would claim that they can take credit for the sales.

student activity

(PC 3.1.3, COM 3.1, 3.2)
At first in pairs, and then as a group, try to identify methods that you could employ to regain the defecting customers mentioned in the Focus Study below.

Focus study

COST OF CUSTOMER SERVICE VERSUS ACCOUNTABILITY

As we have mentioned above, in connection with accountability and customer service, it is often difficult to try to set some kind of value to the process of customer service. However, Coopers and Lybrand, a management consultancy firm, have suggested that around 60 per cent of all complaints by business customers are nothing to do with the product itself. The way in which customers are handled is the most common cause of customer complaints.

Rather than being irritated by complaints, organisations need to learn that complaints can give them important feedback. Research has shown that out of any 100 complaints from dissatisfied customers only 4 are seasoned complainers, who will complain about anything regardless of the level of service. Twenty-five of the 100 will defect to the competition and 75 per cent of these will never return. Perhaps the worst aspect is the 10 lost customers who will tell up to 20 other people about their dissatisfaction.

3.1.4 Analyse marketing activities in business organisations

ANALYSE MARKETING ACTIVITIES

ASSESSING MARKET NEEDS (MARKETING RESEARCH)

Although we will be considering market needs and in particular marketing research in Element 3.2, we must stress here that an organisation needs to evaluate its marketing opportunities. **Market need** can be seen as the demand for a product and the volume that will be bought by defined customer groups within defined geographical areas, over a defined time period, within a defined marketing environment, as a result of a defined marketing campaign. Yes, that does sound very complicated, but we are only stating the obvious. The important point is for the organisation to establish what these needs and demands may be. It can do this by looking at the potential need for a product or by looking at the total volume required by the market. This can be achieved by marketing research. The other criteria can also be addressed by the marketing research process.

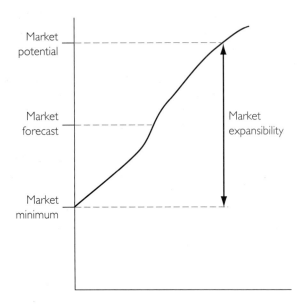

FIG. 3.1.4 *Market needs in a specified time period.*

Figure 3.1.4 illustrates something known as market expansibility. We will explain the meaning of each of the terms used on the graph:

- *market minimum* – this is the level of need or demand within the market without high marketing expenditure. In other words, this is the base level of need, regardless of promotion
- *market forecast* – this is the probable level of need as expressed in sales which will occur if a marketing campaign is undertaken
- *market potential* – this is the probable real level of need which could only be achieved if the organisation invests considerable sums of money over an extended period of time. You should remember that the market potential is almost infinite, since the organisation would be constantly expanding into new markets allied to the main market, either geographically or by some other linkage
- *market expansibility* – this is therefore the probable difference between the conversion of base needs and the actual market potential. The further the market minimum and the market potential are apart from one another, the greater the market expansibility

SATISFYING CUSTOMER REQUIREMENTS

Obviously, once an organisation has established that there are market needs, it must turn its attention to satisfying the specific customer requirements. We can regard an organisation which produces a product range as being fully aware that its products may fulfil customer requirements. It is only by extending or expanding its range that it can adequately ensure that all customer requirements are satisfied. In other words,

it is not sufficient to produce a single product and hope that it will be suitable for all customers. Variations need to be developed which can address specific customer requirements within what may seem a narrow band of requirements. Car manufacturers have realised that simply bringing out a single model will not satisfy all customer requirements. Through marketing research they will have identified discrete market segments within their probable target market. Some may want performance cars, some may want personalised cars, others may want limited editions, estates, or hatchbacks. This essential product differentiation addresses the need to cover all the variations of customer requirements, regardless of the fact that they may only be subtle or cosmetic differences.

MANAGING EFFECTS OF CHANGE AND COMPETITION

As we mentioned earlier, managing the effects of change is a vital function of the marketing department, and in many cases, it may be undertaken as a result of actions taken by competitors. With very few exceptions, most organisations are continually locked in battle with their competitors, many of whom will offer very similar products. Indeed, their prices may be the same and their distribution channels similar. Both short-term and long-term strategies need to be developed in this battle of wits. Principal among the weapons used are the four Ps. To the victor will come greater market share, additional sales revenue and ultimately higher profits.

Competition is just one of the change-making considerations that the organisation may have to face. Again, as we mentioned earlier, planning and control of the marketing process will prove to be the major way of overcoming the challenges presented. The next section of this performance criterion will mention some techniques used by marketing departments to combat the potentially damaging effects of unpredictable change.

CO-ORDINATING ROLE (MARKETING, PLANNING, CONTROL)

Managers, in particular marketing managers, are responsible for the planning, organising, directing and controlling within their area of influence. All these controlling and co-ordination activities are fundamental in assisting the manager to make the right decisions. The formulation of the marketing plans, and any strategy strongly allied to them, is linked to the manager's ability to control the resources at his or her disposal. As with most tasks in business, success depends on getting things done by individuals within the organisation. The management of human assets needs very careful handling as motivation, training and selection are the key features of leadership.

We all have ideas about what a manager does, indeed we discussed this topic at length in Unit 2. As you will remember, there are dozens of theories of management. Most managers learn how to manage the hard way through a process of trial and error. This is not a satisfactory situation, as organisations need a manager to be effective from day one. Out of this need has arisen some concept of a scientific approach to managerial skills. This process of professionalisation requires the manager to establish the fundamentals of management and then transfer them to the situations in which he/she may find him/herself.

Planning is an essential feature of all of this: it requires that the manager sets a series of objectives from which he/she begins to formulate a strategy. Within this strategy there is some notion of a time-scale which considers the implementation and achievements of these plans. Just how these objectives are set may depend upon the nature of the business. There are a number of key steps that hold true regardless of the circumstances:

1 An **analysis** of the performance, both current and past, of all products.
2 A **review** of the marketing opportunities and possible threats.
3 **Relating** these plans to the overall corporate strategy.

Once the marketing objectives have been set, the manager must determine which route to take to achieve these objectives. Many of the key phrases and tactics are taken from military terminology, such as flanking or encirclement. Broadly speaking, a marketing strategy is the way in which the organisation proposes to achieve its marketing objectives. It should always include consideration of the following:

- the **selection** of marketing targets
- market **positioning**
- an appropriate **marketing mix**

GENERATING MAXIMUM INCOME AND/OR PROFIT (SALES AND SALES CHANNELS)

Many believe that organisations will always seek, or should seek, to maximise their profits above any other objective. This is a common statement because:

- for most organisations profit maximisation is the formal purpose
- the competitive pursuit of maximum profits will create greater economic welfare for the organisation
- profit maximisation provides the management of the organisation with an extremely unambiguous criterion for decision making

Against this are other statements which can be held to be equally as true for most organisations, these are:

- that the management of large organisations, particularly those with a large number of shareholders, are no longer closely controlled by a small ownership group. In the light of this they are able to pursue alternative objectives other than profit maximisation
- that profit maximisation is not as unambiguous in terms of decision making as one would expect, as it does not feature in short-term risk taking and the probable long-term benefits
- in setting a price for products or services, the management often seeks to identify an acceptable price which will lead to regular sales against a higher price that will maximise profits in the short term

Having established these contradictory statements, we are now in a position to identify the trade-offs that an organisation must make:

- obtaining short-term profits against long-term growth
- having a good profit margin in the face of competition
- assessing the direct sales effort against market developments
- further penetration of existing markets against developing new ones
- identifying related (as opposed to unrelated) market opportunities
- balancing profits against social responsibility
- going for growth rather than stability
- being careful or taking fewer risks as against entering a potentially high-risk market

Each organisation will have to define a profitable balance using each set of conflicting objectives. Organisations which are attempting to meet their profit objective may be tempted to make immediate savings, particularly in research and development, which are the very areas on which the organisation will depend for its long-term growth.

OPTIMISING CUSTOMER PERCEPTION (CUSTOMER SERVICE, MARKETING COMMUNICATIONS)

The organisation's long-term viability may very well depend upon the customers' perception of the organisation. In this connection we need to identify two key areas upon which the organisation depends:

- customer service
- marketing communications

Figure 3.1.5 attempts to provide a cross-referencing mechanism which measures the relative strength of orientation – organisational versus customer orientation. At point A the actions taken by the organisation are detrimental to both the organisation and its customers.

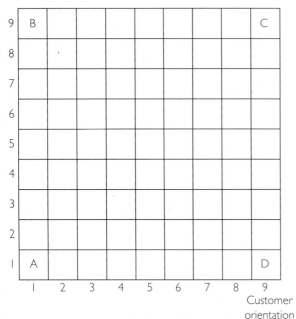

Organisational orientation

Customer orientation

FIG. 3.1.5 *The marketing matrix.*

(PC 3.1.4, COM 3.1, 3.3, AON 3.1, 3.3)
As a group, agree on 10 organisations with which you are all familiar. Having drawn up this list, then construct a marketing matrix and individually position the 10 organisations on the grid. Try to do this in secret and once you have completed the task compare your results with those of the rest of the group.

Typically, the employees may be openly hostile to customers and have little motivation. This state of affairs may exist for organisations which do not have any direct competition. At location B we have the ideal situation. The organisation has matched its objectives with the requirements of the customer. Point C is the epitome of a product-orientated organisation (see next performance criterion for more detail). At point D the organisation's employees are rather too helpful and accommodating to customers. This is to the detriment of, and involves avoidance of, the organisation's objectives.

As we will see later on in this Unit, marketing communications methods operate as the first point of contact between an organisation and its potential customers. The nature, style, effectiveness and quality of the marketing communication methods employed will have a direct impact on the customers' perceptions of the organisation. If the marketing communications techniques used are deemed inappropriate or unappealing, the customers may well be deterred before the organisation has had a chance to convert any interest into sales. Conversely, if the organisation gets its marketing communications techniques right, then even the most sceptical or cynical customer may be encouraged to enter into a relationship with the organisation.

3.1.5 *Explain the growth of organisations which relates to marketing*

GROWTH OF ORGANISATIONS

Marketing should be seen as one of the principal methods of obtaining and sustaining **market growth**. Making constant contacts with the potential target customer group, the organisation can attempt to ensure that it sustains growth. Whether the organisation seeks development of products and markets, or takes a more revolutionary view that the changes need to be rapid and all-encompassing, the organisation must not stand still and ignore what is going on around it. To this end the organisation must address both product development and market development in a systematic and pragmatic manner. Key decisions will have to be made before it embarks on the development of a new product or expands into a new market. As we have seen above, there is a balance between many of the competing objectives of marketing.

PRODUCT DEVELOPMENT (INNOVATION, MODIFICATION, TECHNOLOGICAL BREAKTHROUGH)

As we already know, a product is something that satisfies a customer's need. We should broaden this somewhat and include services as well as products. Of course, even though a need might exist, there may not be a product to satisfy that need.

The **product mix** is the range of products offered by a particular organisation. Each of these products is linked to a particular need within a particular market. Product mix should not be confused with the product line, which usually refers to the range of products that are aimed at one particular market.

A collection of product lines makes up the product mix and the extent of this product mix is known as the **product mix width**. The final definition to remember is the product mix consistency. This relates to how the individual product lines fit into the product mix. A number of questions amply explain what this means:

- are the products complimentary?
- are they different, requiring different approaches in terms of sales and marketing techniques?
- do they demand different approaches in terms of technology or production process?

We have seen that marketing strategy basically comprises of three main areas:

1 The setting of the means by which the organisation intends to achieve its objectives.
2 The period of time over which these objectives are proposed to be met.
3 The resources that are available to be deployed to achieve these objectives.

	Current products	New products
Current markets	Market penetration	Product development
New market potential	Market development	Diversification

FIG. 3.1.6 *Growth and development matrix.*

MARKETS (MARKET DEVELOPMENT, MARKET SHARE, NEW MARKET, NEW CUSTOMERS, RETAINED CUSTOMERS)

The fundamental goal is **profitability**, but this can only be achieved by gradual growth. This, of course, can be achieved by a number of different methods. They include the following:

- the research and development of **new ideas** which can become profitable products and services
- the **purchase** of other organisations that relate in some way to the original organisation
- **mergers** with other organisations that relate in some way, or are complementary to, the original organisation
- **subcontracting** or licensing the production of other products from other organisations to increase the product range with the minimum of investment and delay

Profits are the key to the continued, or for that matter any, growth. The organisation needs to take a serious look at its resources which will, in turn, generate the profits it desires. These resources, of course, include the following:

- finance
- plant
- manpower
- organisational ability
- recognition of the organisation's marketing possibilities

A satisfactory marketing mix is dependent upon the recognition of the market's needs, the recognition of the organisation's objectives and the planning of a strategic marketing philosophy which incorporates the various methods of obtaining these objectives. Consideration of the needs of the market must look at how to serve all of the different segments of the market. Any decision that arises out of this should ensure co-ordination in the application of the organisation's efforts to reach each of the market segments. The development of the marketing plan should involve a clear definition of the problems, which include:

- the **collection** of the facts
- the **analysis** of the data
- the **selection** of the appropriate marketing mix
- choosing the appropriate **solutions**

The elements that make up the marketing mix are very diverse and may include both external and internal considerations. Among the external factors that may affect the marketing plan are the following:

- socio-economic influences that can affect the users of the organisation's products
- government regulations, including restrictions on business, that can also have an impact on the long-term plans of the organisation
- seasonal changes
- changes in market demand
- technological developments
- product obsolescence
- competition

Here are some of the internal factors that should be considered as a part of the marketing mix:

- market research
- product quality
- pricing
- product development
- product range
- sales force, aids and promotion
- after-sales service
- advertising
- stock levels
- credit
- public relations
- packaging
- sampling

ELEMENT 3.1

assignment

(PC 3.1.1–5, COM 3.1, 3.2, 3.3, 3.4, AON 3.1, 3.2, 3.3, IT 3.1, 3.2, 3.3)

In order to claim understanding of the range and show competence in the performance criteria, it is necessary for you to look at the marketing principles detailed in this Element. In addition, you will be expected to analyse the marketing activities of two different organisations and explain how they have achieved growth through product and marketing development.

TASK 1

(PC 3.1.1–3)

Prepare a 20-minute oral presentation which focuses on the following:

- the key marketing principles discussed in this Element
- how these marketing principles are used to manage the marketing functions of the organisation
- how organisations can balance their own requirements and objectives with the needs of the customer

TASK 2

(PC 3.1.4)

This task, together with the last task, requires you to analyse two different organisations. One should be a profit-making organisation and the other should be a non-profit-making organisation. The focus of the report, in relation to the marketing activities mentioned in this Element, should be centred on how the two organisations achieve growth by using product development and market development.

TASK 3

(PC 3.1.5)

In this last part of the assignment and the second part of the report, you are required to:

- assess how the businesses (organisations) evaluate market needs by using marketing research
- in order to do this, you will need to look at how the marketing personnel use the information that is gleaned from the marketing research
- you should also analyse the marketing and selling activities of the organisations and see how they use them to generate maximum income and, in the case of the profit-making organisation, to maximise profit

NOTES

You may wish to read the next Element to give you a fuller understanding of the marketing research techniques involved. Also, if you look at Unit 6, in particular Element 6.4, you will be able to appreciate the pricing considerations. The last thing to note is that the practices of organisations involved in producing, marketing and selling fmcgs (fast-moving consumer goods) have had a massive impact on the marketing efforts of all other types of organisations, even charities.

Your report should be word processed.

Propose and present production developments based on analysis of marketing research information

PERFORMANCE CRITERIA

A student must:

1 *identify* **marketing research methods** *and explain their* **suitability** *for selected products*

2 *analyse* **marketing research information** *from different* **sources** *for its contribution to* **marketing decisions** *for selected products*

3 *propose and justify* **product development** *with reference to* **marketing research** *information*

4 *present proposals for* **product development** *to an audience*

RANGE

Marketing research methods: *interview, observation, questionnaire, survey, panel discussion, telecommunications, focus groups, field trials, piloting; qualitative research methods, quantitative research methods*

Suitability: *accessibility, fitness for purpose, validity, cost, time, reliability*

Marketing research information: *sales trends, changes in sales of new products, changes in sales of existing products, changes in market share, changes in profitability of businesses in the market, product substitution, customer behaviour, buying patterns, customer preferences, competitor activities*

Sources: *government statistics, other published statistics, primary market data, secondary market data*

Marketing decisions: *product (type, features, packaging), place, promotion, price, timing, sales methods*

Product development: *innovation, modification, technological breakthrough*

3.2.1 Identify marketing research methods and explain their suitability for selected products

MARKETING RESEARCH METHODS

Millions of pounds are spent on marketing research in the UK alone each year. Nearly 10 per cent of what you spend in the shops ends up being spent on marketing research in one guise or another. Before we go any further let us try to define exactly what marketing research is:

> marketing research is the systematic collection and analysis of data which looks specifically at the customers' attitudes, needs, opinions and motivations within the context of political, economic, social and technological influences

Simply put, marketing research is using scientific methods to collect information that is relevant to the product or service in question.

In order to reduce risk an organisation needs to know about the intended market for the product that it is going to launch. Marketing research refers to the research into markets specifically, but strictly speaking, marketing research refers to any aspect of the marketing process that requires investigation. Throughout this Unit we will look at the different types of marketing research, their context and their probable use. Regardless of the type of market research or marketing research to be undertaken, a number of broad criteria hold true:

- what is your budget?
- what is your time-scale?
- how accurate does it need to be?
- who exactly do you want to survey?
- where are the people you want to survey?

INTERVIEW

This is a very common method of gathering research information. The interviewer can select the 'victim' and question him/her face to face. The most frequently used method is to ask questions from a formally structured questionnaire – often with a pre-determined range of answers. Here are the advantages:

- high response rate because each respondent is selected
- a fairly low rate of refusal to answer
- if structured well the questionnaire is easy to analyse
- misunderstood questions can be explained

- deliberate 'wrong' answers can be eliminated easily
- additional information can be noted without asking the respondent (e.g. age or sex)
- answers are not considered, they are immediate and probably more truthful
- you can ask reasonably personal questions
- because the respondent does not have to read the questionnaire it can be longer and more involved than one which the respondent is required to read and complete

There are, however, several disadvantages, including the following:

- the cost is high as you have to pay for the interviewer's time
- there may be interviewer bias in noting down the answers, after all some answers may have to be interpreted by the interviewer
- there may be some inaccuracies if the respondent is in a hurry to leave and just says something to get it over with
- interviewers need to be selected and trained before they can begin the task
- speed of collection is related directly to length of the questionnaire and the availability of appropriate respondents

OBSERVATION

It is often claimed that observation is a much more objective method of obtaining data than questioning. Primarily, observation is undertaken in the following ways:

- by individuals
- by the use of diaries
- by the use of instruments

Within the marketing research area, observation is generally used in the following circumstances:

- *retail studies* – when auditing is undertaken by monitoring the data captured by EPOS
- *distribution checks* – which are observations centring on brands offered in different retail outlets
- *comparison shopping* – when organisations look at the prices of products in competitors' stores
- *observing people* – particularly used when a new technological development has been introduced. This method includes analysis of the behaviour of individuals. Usually this method is undertaken

covertly, or, in other words, without the person under observation being aware of it. Awareness might lead to modification of behaviour

QUESTIONNAIRE

The key point to remember is that a well-constructed questionnaire will give far better results than an ill-considered one. If things are unclear you run the risk of annoying the respondent and losing his or her co-operation. Questionnaires contain different types of questions, which fall into four main categories. We shall look at these in a little more detail:

1 *Closed questions* – the respondent is asked to answer the questions from a range of set answers. Usually the answers are simply yes or no, but in other cases may include 'don't know'. The questions could offer a wider range of answers but the more answers the more likely that the respondent will get confused.

2 *Open questions* – the respondent is given the opportunity to answer the question however he/she sees fit. There is no multiple choice of preferred answers and the questionnaire has to be structured in such a way as to allow plenty of space for the response.

3 *Direct questions* – these are very similar in some respects to a closed question style. They require an exact or specific answer, sometimes a simple yes or no and at other times a more detailed but specific answer. An example would be 'Do you own a Sega Mega Drive?'

4 *Indirect questions* – these are very general and attempt to discover the respondent's attitudes about certain issues. A series of questions will be asked that will build up a detailed picture of attitudes or behaviour. As the interviewer has to interpret much of what is being said and will identify what he/she sees as the more important parts of the response you do need to have well-trained interviewers.

Additionally, the time spent with each respondent is longer than for any other method, hence it is expensive. What this type of questioning does reveal can be very interesting and it is unlikely that the other forms of questions will get as much in-depth material.

Having looked at the different types of question we can break down the actual types of questionnaire into two basic categories, the **structured questionnaire** which relies mainly on closed questions with the occasional open question and the **unstructured questionnaire** which mainly makes use of direct and indirect questions. Structured questionnaires are simple to fill in, as respondents are just required to tick the appropriate box, whereas the unstructured questionnaire must rely on the skills of the interviewer as the questions themselves are merely a guide to the direction in which the interviewer should go.

As a guide for the interviewer using unstructured questionnaires, there are two main ways of measuring and recording the respondent's attitudes. The techniques are known as the Likert Scale and the Semantic Differential Scale.

Figure 3.2.1 shows a Likert Scale question. The Semantic Differential Scale asks respondents to mark their opinion on a sliding scale of seven (which is the usual). Figure 3.2.2 shows an example of this.

In both cases the researcher would compile the results and reach an 'aggregate' total for each of the questions. In other words the researcher would both look at the range of answers to the questions and also discover which answer was the most common.

What do you think are the advantages and disadvantages of fresh vegetables against frozen ones? Tick the appropriate box.

	Strongly Agree	*Tend to Agree*	*Don't agree or disagree*	*Tend to disagree*	*Strongly disagree*
Fresh vegetables are healthier	☐	☐	☐	☐	☐
Fresh vegetables are less convenient	☐	☐	☐	☐	☐
Frozen vegetables are better quality	☐	☐	☐	☐	☐
Frozen vegetables are more expensive	☐	☐	☐	☐	☐

FIG. 3.2.1 *A Likert Scale question.*

Please rate your day out at the Theme Park. Circle the number you have chosen:

very good value for money	7	6	5	4	3	2	1	poor value for money
very good range of rides	7	6	5	4	3	2	1	poor range of rides
food stalls very good	7	6	5	4	3	2	1	bad food, poor service
staff helpful & courteous	7	6	5	4	3	2	1	staff bad mannered
great family day out	7	6	5	4	3	2	1	not good for families
strongly recommended	7	6	5	4	3	2	1	will not recommend

FIG. 3.2.2 *The Semantic Differential Scale.*

SURVEY

Survey research is one of the most common methods of collecting primary data and can provide information on the following:

- attitudes
- beliefs
- feelings
- behaviour
- knowledge
- personal characteristics
- ownership

Survey research itself is concerned with the administration of questionnaires, which we have already looked at in the previous section of this performance criterion. The interpretation of the word survey that we will address in this section is that of the conventional form of personal interviews using questionnaires or some other form of structured questioning.

The survey researcher will be concerned with the following:

- sampling
- questionnaire design
- questionnaire administration
- data analysis

We will return to these aspects when we consider the suitability of each marketing research method.

Essentially, there are two different sorts of interview type. These are:

1 *Direct surveys* – which involve personally asking the respondent to fill in or answer questions from a questionnaire.
2 *Indirect surveys* – the alternative method, of mailing the questionnaire to the respondent.

There are alternative views of the merits, use and interpretations of direct and indirect surveys and these are:

- *direct* – best used when the respondent knows the general area of interest and concern of the questionnaire

- *indirect* – used when the questions are such that it is difficult for the respondent to appreciate the purpose of the questionnaire

As we mentioned, the survey method need not necessarily be questionnaire-driven. There are, in fact, four main ways of structuring the survey technique:

1 *Structured direct* – when the respondent is asked to answer a series of pre-specified and relatively simple questions. This method is used particularly in the case of postal or telephone surveys.
2 *Unstructured direct* – used particularly for preliminary or exploratory surveys and may simply focus upon general issues regarding the topic of research.
3 *Structured indirect* – particularly used for gauging responses to words, phrases or pictures.
4 *Unstructured indirect* – a technique not often used in marketing research but a system that is useful for encouraging the respondent to talk about the subject freely with only the occasional prompt from the interviewer.

PANEL DISCUSSION

This information-gathering technique relies on asking the same people a range of questions over a period of time. This method is often used to check on changing attitudes. There are three main types of panel:

1 *Consumer purchasing panels* – where data are collected by a number of methods and which looks at a customer's purchases of and attitudes to particular products or types of product.
2 *Test panel* – where a group of people are asked to field-test new products before their launch. This is particularly useful in the household product field or in the case of specialist equipment such as hospital items.
3 *Audience panel* – this is where audience figures for TV and radio come from. Here the viewing or listening patterns are recorded using a computerised system and all the members of a family are involved.

If you are using the last method, then the respondents can be anywhere and you can ask very detailed questions and expect intelligent and useful responses. The two forms of panel discussion usually involve inviting a selected group to a mutually acceptable location and in both cases you will be able to collect in-depth and intelligent responses. There are a number of advantages associated with panel discussions, including:

- they are a good trend indicator
- you can analyse changes and assess them in relation to external factors that may have influenced them
- you can collect very detailed information about the habits and attitudes of the individuals, thus providing very valuable background information

There are, however, a number of disadvantages, including:

- a regular panel can be upset by deaths or panelists moving away from the area
- panels tend to attract more intelligent people and there is a tendency that the less articulate will be excluded
- panelists may adopt uncharacteristic behaviour as they know they are being watched
- it is expensive to recruit panelists
- there will be a need to replace any panelists who leave
- the panelists will expect some kind of reward

TELECOMMUNICATIONS

This method is very popular in the USA but very prone to a low response rate due to people's reluctance to be canvassed for information on the telephone. It is, after all, an invasion of privacy, although, of course, the person can always hang up rather than respond. Otherwise the technique is almost identical to face-to-face interviewing. One of the other advantages of telecommunication interviews is that the interviewer can instantly input the response onto a computer and then the management system can begin analysis.

There are a number of advantages associated with telephone interviewing. These are:

- it is a very quick way of getting through a lot of interviews
- interviewers only need to be in one place and can be easily supervised
- the costs are significantly lower than personal interviews
- a sample can be taken from across the country without incurring high travel costs
- this is one of the only ways of accessing certain individuals who are hard to canvas by any other method

Naturally there are also some disadvantages:

- the system is useless in contacting those who are not on the telephone
- it is difficult to establish the age or social class of the respondent without asking him or her
- you will inevitably annoy people by phoning at the wrong time of day
- it is harder to get and retain the attention of the respondent
- it is difficult for the interviewer to prove his or her identity and the aim of the enquiry
- unless you are using a bought-in data base of names and phone numbers you will not be able to access ex-directory subscribers

POSTAL

Accompanied by a letter, postal surveys are sent out to a sample of the population in the hope that they may be returned. Often a second letter is necessary to remind the chosen sample to fill in the questionnaire. Most of these surveys will also offer a small gift or entry into a prize draw to encourage a higher response rate. Another technique is to enclose questionnaires in magazines. Again, respondents will be enticed by promises of gifts or prizes. Using this technique it is important to make sure that the questionnaire is straightforward and easy to fill in, otherwise you run the risk of the potential respondent not bothering to answer the questions. There are a number of advantages to this system of data collection:

- it is relatively easy to access a wide sample of the population
- this method is much cheaper than the personal interview
- there are no field expenses
- as there is no interviewer, no training is required
- the interviewer cannot influence the response in any way
- it is a good way to reach target groups that are difficult to access in any other way
- within certain limitations, the respondent has as much time as he or she likes to fill in the questionnaire

There are a number of identifiable disadvantages, however:

- it is unlikely that the sample will be representative as you will only get responses back from those who can be bothered to fill them in
- unless the questionnaire is easy to complete and any incentives offered are attractive, then the refusal rate will be high
- there is a strong possibility that questions may be misunderstood
- questions need to be highly structured, giving less

scope for additional information

- mailing lists are expensive to keep up to date, they are very labour intensive
- plenty of time should be put aside for a slow trickle of replies over the weeks
- personal questions should be avoided as these may deter respondents from filling in the questionnaire
- the answers may not come from the person that the questionnaire was intended for. The respondent may be a different person or he/she may have asked the opinion of someone else

FOCUS GROUPS

The standard focus group is usually between 8 and 12 individuals. The respondents are selected according to a pre-determined sampling plan and meet at a central location that has a facility for filming and taping. The discussion is led by a moderator. Usually the focus group will talk for up to three hours. The moderator's role is to:

- establish rapport with the group
- structure the rules of the group interaction
- set the objectives
- provoke discussion
- summarise the group's responses

Focus groups are used by many organisations and are particularly valuable in establishing probable responses and reactions to new product ideas. A focus group will often be presented with a prototype of the intended product and be asked to comment on aspects of it including its shape, size, colour and texture. There are a number of advantages associated with focus groups, including:

- each individual member of the focus group can expand on his or her opinions
- it is possible to acquire detailed and accurate information
- since this is a more stimulating environment than in some of the other methods of obtaining opinions, respondents are likely to be more forthcoming
- as this is a discussion, spontaneous responses can be very valuable
- focus groups involving young children often work well
- the respondents do not have to be literate
- the focus group may be either observed 'live' or filmed for future reference

Focus groups also have a number of disadvantages, including:

- since there is a considerable investment in time and effort involved, it is sometimes difficult to get a truly random sample

- there is sometimes a tendency for respondents to give deliberately false impressions
- a single very vocal individual may skew the responses of the rest of the focus group
- the role of the moderator is a key determinant and in many cases moderators are unable to provoke discussion or steer the conversation in the correct direction
- the members of the group often exhibit abnormal behaviour

FIELD TRIALS

Field trials offer the possibility of obtaining a degree of realism absent in many other forms of survey. Unfortunately field trials also are largely out of the control of the researchers, as there are simply too many variables. Typically, there are four main types of field trial:

- test marketing
- controlled store and mini-market tests
- simulated tests
- standard market tests

We shall briefly address each one in turn:

1 *Test marketing* – this form of field trial often involves the development of a new product or service. In other words, the organisation attempts to create all of the conditions and techniques that would be employed in the national or international marketing of a new product or service. Test marketing is not necessarily restricted purely to new products or services, but may also be used for the following:

- evaluating price changes
- evaluating new packaging
- varying the distribution channel
- assessing the impact of new advertising
- assessing individuals' reactions to new initiatives or ideas

2 *Controlled store and mini-market tests* – in controlled store testing a few outlets in a specified area are used to assess the sales and reaction of customers. In mini-market tests a larger number of outlets are chosen and an attempt is made literally to flood a limited market with the product or service. The researchers will be able to assess the impact only through sales data as they will be unable to observe the reactions of customers since there are too many different locations. These tests are also considerably less visible to competitors than are other forms of field trials. Since the product or service is distributed directly to the field trial sites then distribution costs are low. Unfortunately there are three major disadvantages, which are:

- the difficulty in making precise projections if there are only a limited number of outlets used or the community chosen is too small
- these field trials do not offer any indication of how well the product or service will sell without the retailers' input
- it is seldom possible to duplicate advertising campaigns used in these tests on a national or international basis

3 *Simulated tests* – these are mathematical estimates of potential market share based on initial customer reactions to the product. As with any mathematically based prediction, there are innumerable variables which may introduce error. The accuracy of these simulated tests is somewhat debatable and these tests are often used only as a means of deciding whether the product will go on to a controlled or standard market test.

4 *Standard market tests* – selecting an area suitable for a standard test marketing programme is perhaps the most important decision. The choice is based on the following criteria:

- the sample area must be large enough to produce meaningful data
- the sample area must not be so big as to incur high expenses
- the sample area must be one that can be targeted in isolation using advertising and promotional techniques
- the demographic features of the area must be fairly similar to those of the larger market area
- the sample area must be self-contained in terms of outlet spread and product availability
- the sample area must be reasonably representative in terms of its penetration by competitors
- the area must not have any peculiarities which may introduce error during analysis

PILOTING

Piloting is the testing of the proposed marketing research. It is not to be confused with exploratory research which seeks to determine the research design. Piloting itself tests the design and helps to determine costs. In many respects the phrase 'better safe than sorry' is the whole philosophy behind piloting. There are definite advantages in trying to establish how the intended sample of the main marketing research programme will respond. Extensive piloting work will ensure that the full marketing research programme actually addresses the subject matter in hand and that it does not go off at a tangent. If nothing else, the piloting work will identify who is really required as respondents for the main survey itself. It will also be able to identify important sub-groups that will have to be represented in the main sample. In other words, piloting allows the organisation to consider the size of the sample, and the proportions of various groups within it, for the main marketing research programme.

student activity

(PC 3.2.1, COM 3.1)
Which of the techniques described above would you use for the following research programme and why?

- an investigation of young women's attitudes to the type of advertising directed at them

Note the advantages and disadvantages of the choice that you have made and compare these with the advantages and disadvantages of other techniques. Discuss your findings with the remainder of your group.

QUALITATIVE AND QUANTITATIVE RESEARCH METHODS

Qualitative research methods often provide the context in which you will find quantitative facts. Essentially, qualitative information refers to opinions, beliefs and impressions held by individuals. You will also be able to identify from this information such things as motivation and other such influencing factors. Any form of focus group or panel will give you a qualitative set of data.

Quantitative research, on the other hand, focuses more closely on strict numerical data in various forms. Typically, the use of observation, and in particular research which does not require the respondent to give a subjective response, can be considered quantitative in nature.

SUITABILITY

ACCESSIBILITY, FITNESS FOR PURPOSE, VALIDITY, COST, TIME AND RELIABILITY

What then of the argument about using insiders or outsiders? There are six main areas of consideration, not all of them necessarily relevant to each case but several will be important each time. The first area of consideration is that of **cost**. An obvious thought really, as it is clearly more expensive to 'buy in' help from outside than to use your own staff. But what about the cost of using people from within your organisation? If they carry out the research they can not do their normal work. Is there a cost to the organisation if they fail to do this work?

Secondly there is the question of **expertise**. Do your own people have the skills needed? Some research techniques are fairly basic and do not require a great deal of skill or experience but some are quite sophisticated. Similarly, the analysis of the data needs to be carried out by the right person. Perhaps the analysis is beyond your immediately available skills.

On the other hand, knowledge of the product or service is much more likely to be the domain of your insiders. You would have to teach the outside organisation about you, your company and your products or services. This is both time-consuming and expensive.

It follows from what we have said above about 'in-house' people and their knowledge of the company and what it is about, that they may be too close. The question of **objectivity** is important. Conclusions drawn from the research may be unconsciously biased and tainted by their own preconceived ideas and prejudices.

The question of equipment, more commonly called **resources**, is another key factor. Specialist computer programs or particular testing equipment may be needed as may the ability to sample people in different parts of the country. It may not prove possible or economically viable to train your own people to use specialist equipment or indeed to buy what you need just for this one exercise.

Finally, and by no means less importantly, there is the question of **confidentiality**. No matter who you use, once information about a new product or process leaves the confines of your own company and direct control there will be a nagging feeling about its safety. In most cases the fear is irrational and unfounded and the information is probably more safe than when it was with you. But people do worry and not without reason, since millions can be made through industrial espionage. Many companies, for a variety of reasons, never use outside marketing agencies. These include household names such as Marks & Spencer and Sainsbury's. In their highly competitive market secrecy is vital and disclosure disastrous.

It is fairly obvious to most people that marketing research is carried out for a specific reason. That reason should invariably be that you will gain more in the long term from what you have learnt than it cost you in the short term to find out. Easier said than done. Calculating the costs of research is fairly easy; you will know how many people are involved, what equipment you will need, any specialists you will have to pay and what it will cost to process the information to get it into a presentable and usable form. The problem is, how do you work out just what the value of the information is?

How can you compare the straightforward costs of collecting and processing data with the benefits derived from your knowledge of it?

student activity

Do you think that knowledge gained through market research is vital to making the right decision? How would you weigh up the delay in making the decision whilst market research is going on against making the decision that you think is right now? Discuss this in pairs.

Two key thoughts are relevant here. The first is: what is the relative profitability of the alternative decisions open to you before you undertake the marketing research? After all, you might be trying to choose one or another, and the benefit of each should be measurable. The other point is: how will the information directly affect your decision making? Will it make a positive contribution or will it just be another factor to worry about?

Perhaps, if you are still concerned (for financial reasons or otherwise) about whether you need marketing research or not, when you see the phases that the research process needs to go through you will find that simply considering the process directs the mind. In some cases that may be enough for you to get what you want out of the exercise before you have gone through all the stages of the research process.

The first step in the research process has to be to **define the problem**. It is here that you, as the client or director of the research, specify exactly what you hope to achieve from the research. What are the major objectives? If these cannot be achieved then the research is worse than useless.

Next you need to decide what **methods** are to be employed in the **collection of the data**. As we have already discussed there are effectively three main sources of information. The primary sources of information are usually the ones that cost you money to collect because they are often specific to your needs and involve the more common forms of data collection such as surveys, interviews and observations. The secondary sources tend to be cheaper as they are often already collected but are usually less useful and only helpful as background information.

student activity

(PC 3.2.1)
How many people do you think would be a minimum representative sample? Could you sample, say, 10 people and present them as representative? If you interviewed everyone in your group as representatives of their age groups would the sample be accurate?

The third stage is to decide on the **scale** of the information gathering. This is known as sampling. Basically you need to ask just how many people you are going to include in your research. You could probably interview all Conservative Members of Parliament or the residents of one small area of the country, but you could not possibly interview everyone who owns a Ford car or all of Britain's smokers. Sampling decisions are crucial because you will need to make up your mind about how many people would be a representative sample, balancing this against the cost of sampling a larger number.

The fourth stage is making your mind up about how the data that have been collected are to be **analysed**. Which statistical procedures are going to be employed to look at the information? You should consider this question in relation to what you wanted in the first place. What are you looking for? The analysis should give you the answers to the questions you have posed.

The fifth consideration relates to **time and resources**. You may well have considered these already before you undertook to start the research but it could be here that you decide not to pursue the research any further. This is where you will have to put a price on the research so that you can finally decide whether the research is worth whatever it is going to cost you. Also you may not have considered just how long it is going to take to collect the data to answer the questions that you want answered. Will the process take too long? Can you afford to wait?

The sixth stage is the point of no return. Having outlined the parameters of the research and looked at how much information you are going to collect and how to analyse it to get the answers that you want, and of course put a monetary figure on the whole exercise,

it is here that you get the **go-ahead** or not. Agreement here on the five preceding stages is vital otherwise the research process terminates straightaway.

student activity

(PC 3.2.1, COM 3.2, AON 3.1, 3.2, 3.3)
How would you decide on the cost effectiveness of research? Work out a simple research process and try to cost it. The results may surprise you!

The final three stages, seven, eight and nine, are the putting into practice what you have already agreed in the first five stages. Namely they are: **collecting** the data, **analysing** it and then **reporting** back on the findings to the person or persons that the research is for.

student activity

(PC 3.2.1, COM 3.2, AON 3.1, 3.2, 3.3, IT 3.1, 3.2, 3.3)
Individually, using a software package, create a matrix which cross references the marketing research methods discussed in the Focus Study on page 228 and the following criteria:

- accessibility
- fitness for purpose
- validity
- cost
- time
- reliability

Head each cross-referencing matrix with one of the following research problems and fill in the matrix as you feel appropriate:

- washing powder
- hand-held televisions
- decaffeinated tea bags

Focus study

MARKETING RESEARCH METHODS

As the advertisement says, 8 out of 10 owners who expressed a preference said their cats preferred it. Many people now believe that if you want accurate information for marketing research, you are better off asking the cat. Marketing research organisations set themselves up as being expert and scientific. However, test results in many recent polls have proved to be either inconclusive or even false. Another good example of this is in relation to television programmes. If you believe market research it will tell you that programmes such as *Spitting Image* and *Blind Date* are in the 'preference to view' category. The fact of the matter is that audience figures for both programmes have dropped considerably. So what is the truth and where can you find it?

Organisations invest huge amounts of money in order to obtain the most accurate and up-to-date market information. So are they just throwing their money away? The large research organisations obviously disagree. They claim that they find questions and not answers. Research can be ideal in discovering the kind of questions that you need to ask about your product or service and not necessarily what people think of it. Critics of market research point to the predictions they made about the result of the 1992 General Election. With the exception of one market research organisation, they all predicted a hung Parliament. They were wrong. Some cite this as a prime example of the end of quantitative research. On the qualitative research end, group discussions and focus groups have become all the rage, but the problem with qualitative research is that it only gives information from another individual's perspective.

The critics of qualitative research claim that you will only get obvious and simplistic results from this sort of research. The other major problem which has been unmasked is that large numbers of the participants in these focus groups and discussion groups are in fact fakes. They are paid between £20 and £30 for a 90-minute session. Surely this is simply fraud?

The Japanese, on the other hand, launch a product first then research it. Admittedly they have had some failures, but largely they are successful. Whether this is testimony to their business sense or the depths of their pockets in terms of advertising spending is another question.

3.2.2 Analyse marketing research information from different sources for its contribution to marketing decisions for selected products

MARKETING RESEARCH INFORMATION

In order to analyse the marketing research information you will be required to look at averages, tables and graphs which display market trends. We have constructed two fictitious organisations and created data to help you carry out this analysis.

FIG. 3.2.3 *Through consistent market research Tesco PLC has managed to focus closely on satisfying the needs of customers. The company has developed stores, introduced new products, new pricing policies, customer service standards and technical innovations, all driven by the aim to satisfy customers.*

Focus study

ALLSTAR SPORTS

Founded in 1975, Allstar Sports is run by Alun and Stuart Johns. They began trading as a conventional sports outfitter in the east end of London. Having established the company they saw good growth throughout the remainder of the 1970s and the early 1980s. When their cousin, Christine Shorten, left university after obtaining a business studies degree, she was invited by the brothers to join the company as their marketing and sales director. Fairly swiftly

Christine began to revolutionise the business. By the mid-1980s they had acquired a small industrial unit and were importing trainers from the Far East. Having set up a regional distribution network to other retail outlets, Allstar Sports began to look nationally for markets and business opportunities. Having weathered the recession of the late 1980s and early 1990s, Allstar Sports began to cast its eye again on the lucrative import and distribution market.

Focus study

CAINES CANNED DRINKS

The ancestors of Michael Caine were fortunate enough to have built a farm in an area which boasted a natural spring. For several generations the Caine family simply used the spring as their primary source of water. It was not until the 1930s that Joshua Caine, Michael's great grandfather, began to look at the commercial possibilities of this pure water source. After he launched Caine Pure Table Water in 1933, it quickly became a rather popular product in middle and upper class homes. The sales were not spectacular, but Joshua Caine was always grateful and rather amused that anyone would consider purchasing bottled water. After the Second World War his eldest son, Peter, inherited the farm and the spring. Peter had more of a commercial eye and engaged an advertising agency to reposition the product in an attempt to gain greater popularity. Caine Pure Spring Water, as it was now known, was relaunched in 1952 with the not-too promising slogan of 'Caine canes your thirst'. The product launch, although successful in part, was not destined to make Peter a rich man. By the 1960s, with Peter fast

losing his interest in the spring water, the rights were sold to Richardson Glass who had been the bottlers. Jim Bonner, the sales director of Richardsons made the decision to retain the Caine family name in order to use their reputation to form the base of a relaunch. He also hit upon the idea of carbonating the water. By the early 1980s Caine Pure Carbonated Spring Water had achieved a 6 per cent market share, much to the annoyance of the Caine family, who only retained a 1 per cent share of profits.

In 1994 Michael Caine, now the owner of the land upon which the spring is located, sold the farming concern and bought a major shareholding in Richardson Glass. Events had gone full circle and the Caine spring was now back in the hands of the Caine family. Michael had been impressed with Jim Bonner's relaunch and decided to retain him as marketing director.

Both Michael and Jim decided that diversification was the key to success. If they could sell bottled water then why could they not sell canned drinks using the pure water source?

SALES TRENDS

student activity

(PC 3.2.2, AON 3.1, 3.2, 3.3)
Allstar Sports – Sales trends

The following data relate to the main product ranges offered by Allstar Sports. The yearly sales figures for trade sales are given in Table 3.2.1.

Using appropriate graphs, plot these figures and try to predict what the sales trends will be for the next five years.

TABLE 3.2.1 *Allstar Sports annual sales*

Product name	1988	1989	1990	1991	1992	1993	1994	1995
Flash	6,990	6,216	5,478	4,871	4,011	3,383	2,518	1,665
Sprinter	9,978	9,872	9,340	9,616	9,488	8,821	8,473	8,216
Pro	–	–	–	102	541	687	794	638

CHANGES IN SALES OF NEW PRODUCTS

student activity

(PC 3.2.2, AON 3.1, 3.2, 3.3, IT 3.1, 3.2, 3.3)
Caines Canned Drinks – Sales of new products

Caines launched six canned drinks in the early summer of 1995. The sales figures for the first six months are shown in Table 3.2.2.

TABLE 3.2.2 *Caines Canned Drinks sales*

Sales per month ('000)

Name of product	May	June	July	Aug.	Sept.	Oct.
Apple	52	84	87	93	86	81
Pear	35	32	32	36	23	17
Peach	38	40	39	42	41	42
Lemon	63	92	98	104	95	92
Lime	35	37	39	40	35	32
Strawberry	27	25	26	25	17	14

Analyse the changes in the sales of these products, paying particular attention to the seasonal nature of demand. In the role of Michael/Jim, decide whether any of the range should be dropped or relaunched. What is the reasoning behind your decisions? Present a word processed report to summarise your reasons.

CHANGES IN PROFITABILITY OF BUSINESSES IN THE MARKET

student activity

(PC 3.2.2, AON 3.1, 3.2, 3.3)
Allstar Sports – Profitability

The figures given in Table 3.2.3 relate to the production costs and list prices of Allstar Sports' three main product lines.

TABLE 3.2.3 *Allstar Sports: profitability*

Product	Production cost (£)	Selling price (£)	Discount (%)
Flash	16.98	45.00	40
Sprinter	29.94	62.00	40
Pro	28.63	74.00	40

Using the last two years' sales figures and assuming that the price remained the same for the two years, what was the comparative profitability between the three products? Does this information shed any additional light on the viability of Allstar's product range?

CHANGES IN SALES OF EXISTING PRODUCTS

 1:30

student activity

(PC 3.2.2, COM 3.1, 3.2, AON 3.1, 3.2, 3.3)
Allstar Sports – Sales of existing products

Alun, Stuart and Christine knew that they had to do something as their sales figures were not exactly promising. They engaged the services of a marketing research company and asked them to carry out a survey regarding the reasons for customers purchasing a particular brand of trainer. The results are in Table 3.2.4.

The respondents were able to tick as many reasons for purchasing as they felt necessary, hence the high percentages. The bad news was that out of the sample of 258 individuals aged 16–35, only 11 actually mentioned any of Allstar Sports brands.

How many of these reasons for the choices in buying the brands can Allstar Sports seriously expect to influence? What further research should they undertake in order to ascertain their next course of action? Discuss this as a group.

TABLE 3.2.4 *Purchases of trainers*

Reason for buying the brand	No. of responses (%)
It is my favourite make	91
I had a pair of these last time	89
They are the ones in fashion	63
I wanted to try something new or different	37
I saw them advertised on TV	31
Someone recommended them	29
They were cheaper than other brands	25
The shop had a money-off offer	25
I saw them advertised on a poster	14
I saw them advertised in a magazine	12

CHANGES IN MARKET SHARE

 2:00

student activity

(PC 3.2.2, AON 3.1, 3.2, 3.3)
Caines Canned Drinks – Market share

Whilst accurate sales figures of competitors were hard to come by, Caines managed to calculate their ranking in the canned drink market. They were not surprised to find that they were not even in the top 20. As a comparative exercise, Caines decided to look at the movement in market share of the major competitors over the same period of months that their product had been on the market.

Plot graphs for each of the products featured in the table and also calculate the average ranking market share position for each product over the six-month period.

TABLE 3.2.5 *Market share of canned drink market*

Name of product	Ranking order by market share					
	May	June	July	Aug.	Sept.	Oct.
Coca-Cola	1	1	1	1	1	1
Pepsi Cola	2	2	2	2	2	2
Diet Coke	3	3	4	4	4	3
Pepsi Max	7	6	7	7	8	7
Tango	4	4	3	3	3	4
Lilt	5	5	5	6	5	5
IrnBru	6	7	6	5	6	6
Sunkist	8	8	9	9	7	8
Tizer	9	9	8	8	9	9
Lucozade	10	10	10	10	10	10

PRODUCT SUBSTITUTION

student activity

(PC 3.2.2, COM 3.1, 3.2, IT 3.1, 3.2)
Caines Canned Drinks – Product Substitution

Referring back to the student activity which looked at changes in sales of new products, you will remember that you have already identified the products which have not really taken off. Suggest viable alternatives to replace the dropped product(s) as Caines are keen on maintaining a six product range. Justify your decisions and attempt to identify which of the remaining products your new product(s) are likely to perform as well as. You should present your decisions in the form of a word processed report.

CUSTOMER BEHAVIOUR, BUYING PATTERNS AND CUSTOMER PREFERENCES

student activity

(PC 3.2.2, COM 3.2, 3.4, AON 3.1, IT 3.1, 3.2)
Allstar Sports – Customer behaviour buying patterns and customer preferences

There did not seem to be any particular reason, apart from the massive advertising spending of the major competitors, for Allstar's products to be performing so badly. In the role of a marketing consultancy produce a questionnaire which addresses the nature of customer behaviour, buying patterns and customer preferences in relation to the purchase of trainers. You should construct your questionnaire in such a way as to facilitate the easy analysis of the data. Remember that you should pay particular attention to the need to be objective and to provide the respondent with the maximum opportunity of responding in a natural and unprompted manner. Your questionnaire should be word processed.

Avon's Environmental Mission is to:

- Conserve usage of energy and raw materials.
- Reduce waste to a minimum.
- Recycle materials as much as is possible.
- Avoid pollution of air, land and water.
- Improve the working environment.
- Meet – and exceed where possible – environmental regulatory standards.
- Support local community environmental initiatives.
- Train employees in good, environmental practices.

FIG. 3.2.4 *Many orgainisations have recognised the consumer's interest in environmental issues. Avon UK state that both their management and their employees are highly committed – in every aspect of their business – to finding ways to demonstrate this. They have taken special steps to care for the environment.*

COMPETITOR ACTIVITIES

2:00

student activity

(PC 3.2.2, COM 3.2, 3.3, 3.4, AON 3.1, 3.2, 3.3, IT 3.1, 3.2, 3.3)

Caines Canned Drinks – Competitor activities

Caines realised that they were not in the premier division as far as canned drinks were concerned. In fact, they were probably somewhere in the middle of the third division. Nothing brought this home more clearly to them than their discovery of the advertising expenditure of the major competitors. They were staggered to discover that in a single month many of the major competitors had spent Caine's yearly marketing budget.

TABLE 3.2.6 *Advertising expenditure (£'000s)*

Brand	July 1995	Annual spend
Coca-Cola	1,025	5,518
Tango	349	4,727
Lucozade	656	4,652
Pepsi Max	000	4,474
Pepsi Cola	98	3,493
Sunkist	365	3,266
Lilt	711	2,195
IrnBru	458	1,844
Tizer	518	1,439

Jim and Michael realised that this probably did not give the whole picture, then they stumbled upon some data which showed whether viewers or readers remembered the advertisement.

TABLE 3.2.7 *Recall of advertisements*

Brand	Recall (%)
Coca-Cola	57
Tango	41
Pepsi Cola	27
Pepsi Max	18
IrnBru	16
Lilt	16
Tizer	11
Lucozade	9
Sunkist	9

Michael and Jim realised that these two different measurements of competitor activity needed to be cross referenced.

Undertaking this job for Caines, formulate your own graphical representation of these two sets of figures which illustrate the relationship between advertising spending and the recall of the advertisement. Produce your graphical representation by use of computer software.

SOURCES OF MARKETING RESEARCH INFORMATION

Marketing research covers the obvious markets, but also what we noted in our first definition. Broadly speaking there are three main sources of information that the marketing researcher is interested in:

- information within the company which already exists but which may be in a form that is not particularly usable
- information external to the company which already exists and is much more expensive to track down than internal data
- information which may or may not be within the company, and is usually external to the company, but which does not exist in a usable form at all. Commonly this information is customer opinion, attitude or buying traits

We can further identify these types of information and categorise them more simply:

- information within the company, such as sales figures, is known as internal information
- information external to the company, such as government reports or published marketing reports, is known as secondary information
- the third information source, often characterised by market research opinion polls, is known as primary information

Marketing research makes a positive contribution to a business by helping in the decision-making process. There are many different types of marketing research, the main ones being:

1 *Market and sales research*
- estimating market size of new markets
- estimating potential growth of an existing market
- identifying market characteristics and segments
- identifying market trends
- sales forecasting
- collecting data on existing customers
- collecting data on potential customers
- collecting data on competitors

2 *Product research*
- customers' attitude to new products
- comparing competition with own products
- finding alternative uses for existing products
- market testing proposed products
- investigating customer complaints
- packaging research
- generating new ideas for new products

3 *Research on promotion and advertising*
- choosing the right advertising medium
- analysing effectiveness of advertising
- establishing sales areas
- evaluating present sales techniques
- analysing sales force effectiveness
- establishing sales quotas

4 *Distribution research*
- location of distribution centres
- handling products (efficiency)
- transport costs and comparisons
- storage efficiency and needs
- retail outlet locations

5 *Pricing policy*
- demand
- perceived price
- costs
- margins

The scope of marketing and market research is very broad. In fact almost every aspect of the production, promotion, sales and after-sales life of a product is scrutinised at some point for one particular purpose or another.

GOVERNMENT STATISTICS

Throughout the book we have used a number of tables prepared by the government or government agencies. Perhaps one of the more useful and often-used aspects of government statistics is the standard industrial classification. It essentially breaks down the different markets and organisations which make up the economy into ten distinct divisions, these are:

student activity

(PC 3.2.2, COM 3.1)
Before you read any further and find out how things are usually done, decide how you would research the following if you were being asked to launch a new product:

- is the product needed?
- how would you set the price?
- how would you decide on the packaging?

Try to identify the research methods and just how reliable you think they are. Discuss this in pairs.

- division 0 – agriculture, forestry and fishing
- division 1 – energy and water supply industries
- division 2 – extraction of minerals and ores, manufacture of metals, mineral products and chemicals
- division 3 – metal goods, engineering and vehicle industries
- division 4 – other manufacturing industries
- division 5 – construction
- division 6 – distribution, hotels and catering, repairs
- division 7 – transport and communication
- division 8 – banking, finance, insurance, business services and leasing
- division 9 – other services

student activity

(PC 3.2.2, COM 3.1, 3.2)
In pairs, locate the full listing of the standard industrial classification and identify at least three industries per division.

It is not just the UK government that produces useful statistical information; other government-related organisations and bodies also produce a wide variety of data, these include:

- the European Union which publishes such data as the *General Statistical Bulletin*

- the United Nations which produces a *Demographic Yearbook*
- the OECD which⁻ publishes *Main Economic Indicators*
- the IMF which releases a *Balance of Payments Yearbook*

OTHER PUBLISHED STATISTICS

There are a number of different agencies or commercial research organisations which produce a variety of statistical information relating to a huge variety of different topics. These agencies and research organisations collect or buy information which they then compile in report form and sell on to other organisations. Typical examples of agencies or commercial research organisations include:

1 *Mintel* – which produces short reports on a single specific consumer market and includes details on the following:

- market size
- projected growth
- market share of main competitors
- advertising spending
- market trends

2 *Euromonitor* – which produces keynote reports which at around 75 pages give a broad outline of the nature and specific characteristics of a particular market.

3 *Retail Audits* – collect data from supermarkets and other large retail chains on sales figures of particular products. This audit service is very useful for suppliers in assessing how effective their marketing has been and its impact upon other organisations' sales and market share

In addition to these commercial organisations, various trade associations produce some very useful data. These bodies include:

- the Market Research Society
- the Advertising Association
- the Chartered Institute of Marketing

PRIMARY MARKET DATA

Information systems, if set up correctly, should channel useful information to the marketing department of a company. A marketing information system worth anything should pass on only the useful information and should sift out the irrelevant. There are four facets of information that are useful and should make up the elements of a marketing information system. These are:

1 *Internal accounting* – which reports orders, sales, stock, incoming cash and outgoing cash.

Market Research

Abstracts

- available on IBM compatible disk
- abstracted from over 40 publications
- leading UK, European and US sources
- indexed by author and subject
- coverage from 1963
- available in 3 formats

MRS

Setting the professional standard

FIG. 3.2.5 *Market Research Abstracts – a service offered by The Market Research Society.*

student activity

(PC 3.2.2)
Using your college library or the local library, try to find the Directory of British Associations. In it you will find specific trade associations relating to various industries. Bear this book in mind when you consider the Element 3.2 Assignment, which follows shortly. You would be wise to contact any trade association that you feel is relevant to the product that you choose to feature in your presentation.

2 *Marketing intelligence* – a firm set of procedures that ensures the information on new developments that may affect the business is collected and calculated.

3 *Marketing research* – systematic collection and analysis of information useful to the decision makers of the company.

4 *Analytical marketing* – a system which analyses relevant marketing data in a scientific manner.

SECONDARY MARKET DATA

Before an organisation goes to the expense of paying for primary research it is prudent for it to look at what information is already available. Surprisingly, whatever the subject, there will be something. Secondary data, which are either already in existence under your noses but not in the right format, or readily available from somewhere else, are a great deal cheaper than starting from scratch.

Published data, which are available in most good commercial reference libraries, and often in the main libraries of larger towns, include some of the more obvious (and weighty) tomes as well as some seemingly rather boring and starchy items. In the book line there are titles like *Regional Trends* or the *General Household Survey*. Datastream is a computer data base facility and Prestel can be accessed via a TV with an adaptor. Other sources are local chambers of commerce, which have good libraries and links, and leads to other sources of information.

student activity

(PC 3.2.2)
Visit your local public library or the library in your institution and have a look in the reference section at what is available in the way of resources. Try to identify the following:

- where you would find details on the more successful and well-known organisations in the UK. This should include their turnover and profitability
- the name of your local councillor
- details of the local unemployment figures

MARKETING DECISIONS

The ideal mix of price, place, product and promotion will obviously differ from product to product. In some cases, price is more important. This is particularly true in the case of own label products versus branded products. At other times the promotion method chosen and its effectiveness is more important than the price itself. In this section we will look at the various marketing decisions required as a result of receiving marketing research information.

PRODUCT (TYPE, FEATURES, PACKAGING)

There are innumerable methods of determining the exact nature of a product in terms of its type, features and packaging. Without going into too much detail, we can identify the following methods:

- *consumption system analysis* – which looks at how the product is actually used by customers in normal conditions
- *benefit/needs analysis* – which addresses the needs or desires of customers and attempts to provide a product which will address these needs or desires
- *brainstorming* – when a group of individuals is selected to give immediate feedback on the product
- *synectics* – a more structured version of brainstorming which tries to encourage heavy users of a similar product to discuss and come up with ideas
- *problem inventory analysis* – a way of discovering what problems customers have with existing products and as a result discovering how new products or variations can make positive improvements
- *attribute listing* – which attempts systematically to list all the attributes of a product and see whether the modification of any of these attributes will improve it
- *morphological* – which is generally used to generate new product ideas and includes a listing of all of the attributes of the product, listing alternative uses of the product

Obviously, market testing or field trials, which we have discussed earlier in this Element, play a part in establishing the type, features and packaging of any product. Just how much heed an organisation pays to the results of a field trial may very well determine the ultimate success or failure of the product.

PLACE

Determining the spread or availability of a product is obviously another key determining factor which can be influenced by marketing research information. Choosing the appropriate distribution channel is just as important since this will determine how production relates to the demand (in terms of orders) for the product. As we have mentioned elsewhere in the book, if demand has been generated then the last thing the organisation wants is for its customers to have difficulty in obtaining the product.

Don't settle for an ordinary credit card

What would you expect a credit card to give you? Convenience? An extra financial resource for unexpected expenses? Flexibility?

Of course, these things are very important, and you'll get them all with a Barclaycard.

But today, you really should be looking for much more. And with Barclaycard you'll find it. Because by possessing a Barclaycard you'll have access to a whole range of complimentary benefits and services:

International Rescue – helps solve problems when you're abroad.
Purchase Cover – insurance for most Barclaycard purchases.
Travel Accident Insurance – for travel paid for with your card.
Barclaycard MasterCard – a second, totally separate account.
Free Additional cards – for your partner.

You don't have to bank with Barclays to apply for a Barclaycard. So if you're looking for your first credit card, or to improve on your existing card, look no further. Barclaycard gives you so much more.

FIG. 3.2.6 *Even the well-established Barclaycard is continually re-packaged and re-launched, as can be seen from this recent leaflet, 'Barclaycard – so much more than a convenient way to pay', August 1993.*

PROMOTION

Again, choosing the appropriate promotional or advertising method is essential to ensure that the product receives the attention and interest which the organisation hopes for. In the next Element we identify and discuss the relative effectiveness of each form of media communication. Obviously some of the media communication systems are inappropriate for certain types of product. It is rare, for example, to find advertisements for tractors on television.

PRICE

Setting a product's price is very much a question of where the product is in terms of its positioning in the market. In any market there is a broad range of different price structures. From the cheapest product to the most expensive branded version, depending upon the nature of the market and the product in question, the differences may run into several hundreds of pounds. Particularly in high-cost products, it is essential that the

FIG. 3.2.7 *Geest plc import bananas from the Windward Islands and since these are a comparatively fragile fruit, they require careful handling and packaging at all stages of their distribution.*

FIG. 3.2.8 *Tesco's own-label products, coupled with their highly succesful multi-saver price promotions, offered discounts or free products on 400 items in their largest stores. The campaign was promoted on television, in the press and in the stores themselves with the quotation, 'Tesco has never given away so much free!'*

organisation identifies the right price band in which to place the product.

TIMING

Scheduling, in the form of a timetable, is another essential component of the marketing process. From information derived from marketing research, an organisation will be able to establish the approximate time-scales involved in the development, testing, launch and promotion of a specific product. In many cases an organisation will follow the example set by an existing product offered by a competitor. However, in the case of a new product this can be somewhat more problematic since there is no bench-mark to compare it with.

SALES METHODS

Again, choosing the appropriate distribution channel – which may involve consideration of direct or indirect sales methods – is a key component in achieving fast results in terms of sales. Maximising the opportunity for the customer not only to view the product in a retail outlet but also to have the opportunity to purchase the product must be one of the organisation's ultimate goals. As we discuss in Element 3.4, the sales techniques involved in selling different products differ widely. Although there are no prescribed ways of selling anything, there are, however, some tried and tested methods. An organisation could do far worse than look at previous experience or competitors' sales methods to see which would be the most appropriate for its new product or service.

3.2.3 Propose and justify product development with reference to marketing research information

PRODUCT DEVELOPMENT

New product development is the process through which new product ideas are screened, analysed, developed, tested and finally launched as a new product on the market. This final stage can be described as 'the culmination of a rigorous process of elimination'. Two statements really highlight the need for and risks of new product development by business firms:

- the development and successful marketing of new products is perhaps the single most important factor in long-term growth and profitability for a company
- this proverb flashes through his head – the many fail, the one succeeds

These two statements really outline the need for new product development by companies, and the risk involved in developing a successful new product.

There are several stages involved in new product development:

1 *Generation of ideas* – every new product starts off as an idea. Ideas come from within the organisation itself, e.g. from research and development, the marketing department, executives and workers. Alternatively they come from outside the firm, from customers, technology, inventions and competition.

2 *Screening of ideas* – the main purpose of the first stage in the product development process is to increase the number of good ideas. The main purpose

of all the succeeding stages is to reduce the number of ideas. The main purpose of screening is to eliminate ideas which are out of line with company objectives or resources, or which carry high-risk cost and little profit opportunity.

3 *Testing the product concept* – given the revised short list, product concept testing is then carried out. This is where market research can begin to play an important role. This is where you present the consumer with the idea of the product, using written descriptions, photographs or films to convey the idea. It is important to look for an interested reaction to the product. The firm that has a relatively vigorous screening of ideas should be left with a few well screened products. It then examines the technical feasibility of the products and looks at such questions as production costs and the investment needed in research and development.

4 *Development* – this is the product testing stage. Once some prototypes of the product have been made, the product is tested in controlled conditions (laboratory) to gain consumer reaction to the product, pack, name, etc., so that the firm can compare it with established products. Ratings are also needed so that adjustments can be made, e.g. is it too sweet, too dark, etc.? This development stage can be very long and it could be a number of years before the company puts the product into commercial production.

5 *Test marketing* – up to this stage the reaction of potential customers has not been tested under normal

marketing conditions. The idea here is to launch a product in a restricted area in order to make generalisations about the country as a whole and also as a defensive measure if it is found that the product does not sell, in order to avoid further losses. There are three main functions of test marketing:

- to make predictions about the national launch
- to find out what went wrong during the test marketing stage
- to experiment with different tactics

Research plays a vital role in this stage and it is important that as much data as possible are collected in order to give an indication of how the product will sell nationally. However, it must be emphasised that all products passing this stage are not necessarily successful nationally.

6 *National launch or commercialisation stage* – described as the 'culmination of rigorous process of elimination'. By this time the marketing plan should have been worked out, salesmen, dealers, etc. should be equipped for the launch and public relations geared for the product's introduction. Management responsibility within the firm should be established for the launching and continued progress of the product. However, even after the launch of the product the organisation may have failed to anticipate reactions and problems and here again research can be important in gauging full-scale consumer reaction to the product.

The whole process of new product development is one of continued elimination of ideas at successive stages of new product development. Each stage becomes increasingly costly to an organisation.

The commercialisation stage is the introductory stage of the product's life cycle. Lead times from product ideas to the commercialisation stage can often take two to three years or longer.

INNOVATION

Continuous innovation is essential for the long-term survival of companies. Because it is its purpose to create a customer, any business enterprise has two basic functions – marketing and innovation. A failure by companies to innovate has been termed 'marketing myopia'. This term was used in relation to the railroads

in the 1930s – 1960s in the USA when the argument was voiced that they had lost freight trade because they were product orientated whereas other commercial carriers were marketing orientated and provided better transportation services for customers.

Failure to innovate has hit many companies in the past and they have subsequently paid the price. Other, more visionary companies are increasingly trying to insure themselves against the inevitable obsolescence of their existing products; the increasing expenditure on research and development by companies is a reflection of this trend.

MODIFICATION

The release of the product onto the market should never be seen as the end of the marketing research involvement in the operation. It is only through continual monitoring and surveying techniques that an organisation will establish whether the product fully addresses the needs of the customer. Constant attention must be given to the modification of products in order to ensure that they do address customer needs. Innovation or modification in this sense needs to be tempered with a certain degree of caution. An organisation would be ill advised to replace or significantly modify a product before it has had a chance to establish itself on the market. All too often a product will be replaced by a modified version which, in effect, renders the original product obsolete. Subtle and gradual changes are the best ways of ensuring that the product meets the ever-changing demands and requirements of the customer.

TECHNOLOGICAL BREAKTHROUGH

Whether the technological breakthrough refers directly to the nature or features of the product or whether it refers to a technological breakthrough in terms of the production process, again product substitution needs to be tempered by the need to avoid undermining current products or services. Again, a gradual introduction of the technologically superior product or service is probably the best way of handling the situation. You only need to look at the prices currently being charged for seemingly obsolete computers to appreciate the fact that each technological breakthrough renders previous generations of products obsolete, or, at least, comparatively undesirable.

3.2.4 *Present proposals for product development to an audience*

This performance criterion forms an integral part of the Element 3.2 Assignment. However, before you begin to prepare the presentation it would be wise to look at Unit 2 again for hints and tips on presentation technique.

ELEMENT 3.2

a s s i g n m e n t

(PC 3.2.1–4, COM 3.1, 3.2, 3.4, AON 3.1, 3.2, 3.3)
This Element assignment asks you to make a presentation to an audience of fellow students, assessors or visitors. You will have to outline your proposals for the development of a product. You should base your proposal on an analysis of marketing research information from two different sources.

TASK 1

(PC 3.2.3)
Propose a product and justify your choice by selecting appropriate marketing research methods.

TASK 2

(PC 3.2.1)
Having identified your selected marketing research methods, undertake this research and collate your findings, which will be included in your presentation.

TASK 3

(PC 3.2.2)
Analyse competitor activities and suggest probable changes that you could make to the product in the light of your investigation.

TASK 4

(PC 3.2.3)
As evidence that you have made an appropriate marketing decision in relation to the marketing research information collected, now outline the following:

- features of the product
- packaging of the product
- identification of sales outlets
- product promotion
- selling price
- the timing of marketing, communication and sales

TASK 5

(PC 3.2.1)
Having undertaken your research and selected your product, now assess the relative value of qualitative and quantitative research. You must do this regardless of the fact that you may not have used one of these types of research.

TASK 6

(PC 3.2.4)
Now present your proposals to an audience. Your presentation should be supported by appropriate numerical information and any illustrative material you feel appropriate.

NOTES

You are not necessarily expected to carry out any primary research of your own. However, if your product choice is obscure enough you may not be able to find any published data. In any case, as you will discover, many of the published data are neither accessible nor directly appropriate for your needs. Certain information should also be approached with some scepticism, particularly if it has been prepared by a trade association or an individual organisation. They may have a hidden agenda in making their market appear to be more successful than it actually is.

Evaluate marketing communications designed to influence a target audience

PERFORMANCE CRITERIA

A student must:

1 *explain the suitability of* **advertising** *and* **publicity** *for promoting products and the image of an organisation*

2 *identify and give examples of* **public relations** *to promote products and organisations*

3 *evaluate* **sales promotion methods** *for their effectiveness in reaching a* **target audience**

4 *evaluate the effect of marketing communications on product performance*

5 *explain the growth in* **direct marketing methods** *in terms of customer need and new technology*

6 *explain the effects on marketing communications of* **guidelines and controls**

RANGE

Advertising: *newspaper, magazine, TV, poster, radio, cinema*

Publicity: *sales literature, signage, vehicle livery, stationery, point-of-sale (POS)*

Public relations: *press releases, sponsorship, lobbying, community relations*

Sales promotion methods: *competitions, coupons, special offers, free mail-ins, loyalty incentives*

Target audience: *socio-economic group, age, lifestyle, gender*

Product performance: *sales levels (volume, value, growth), repeat sales, brand loyalty, customer loyalty, product life cycles, product awareness*

Direct marketing methods: *direct mail, tele-marketing, selling off-screen, selling off-page*

Guidelines and controls: *Advertising Standards Authority, Code of Advertising Practice (CAP), codes of practice*

3.3.1 Explain the suitability of advertising and publicity for promoting products and the image of an organisation

In this Element we will be investigating the various marketing communication methods and means, such as advertising, public relations, sales promotion and direct marketing which are designed effectively to communicate to, and influence the decision making of, the target audience.

ADVERTISING

Advertising provides information for the customer and has been around for centuries. Essentially, it aims to provide the customer with the following:

- information about the product
- what the product does
- how the product works
- how much the product costs
- where the product can be obtained

In addition to these basic messages, the advertisement should also be persuasive and attempt to convince the customer to buy this product as opposed to another similar product.

Organisations choose to advertise for the following reasons:

- they want to increase demand for their products
- they want to establish a particular price for the product
- they want to create an image for their new product
- they want to change or enhance the current image of the product
- they want to create brand loyalty for their product
- they want to raise awareness, emotion or concern for an issue (particularly in the case of charities)
- they want to protect, maintain or increase their market share
- they want to tell the customers about their product, particularly if it is new and innovative. In other words, they want to educate the customer

All of the different advertising media maintain audience figures and profiles. The media planner can attempt to match the organisation's product and message with the appropriate medium. It is unlikely that any one medium will get the message across to all of the proposed target audience. The concept of 'opportunity to see' (OTS) refers to the penetration of the

student activity

medium into the whole of the adult population of the UK. In other words, the bigger the OTS, the better the advertising medium. But, as we will see later, the bigger OTSs which can be considered mass media methods, do not necessarily target the audience very well. Some of the smaller OTSs are targeted more at specific segments of the market and the population. The OTS figures of the major media are given in Table 3.3.1.

TABLE 3.3.1 *OTS figures*

Type	Per cent
Outdoor advertisements (posters, buses, etc.)	nearly 100
Television advertisements	over 90
Sunday newspapers	around 75
Daily newspapers	nearly 70
Commercial radio	nearly 40
Weekly magazines	around 40
Monthly magazines	nearly 40
Cinema	around 5

Unfortunately, the choice of medium is not quite as simple as the figures in Table 3.3.1 might suggest. From these figures it would seem logical to use only outdoor advertising. But if the planner considers the question of cost effectiveness, it obviously costs more to advertise in certain media than others. The new formula that we can use is called cost per thousand

Focus study

ADVERTISING

Tinned and packet soups are fairly regularly advertised on TV. The top brands such as Batchelors and Campbells have boosted their advertising spend to take advantage of Heinz's decision to stop their TV advertising.

Despite the decision made by Heinz, the present division in market share is as shown in Table 3.3.2.

TABLE 3.3.2 *Market share for soups*

Brand	Share (%)
Heinz	69
Own label	28
Batchelors	21
Sainsbury's	16
Campbells	13
Batchelors Cup-A-Soup	13
Knorr	8
Baxters	5

The reasons for customers choosing to purchase a particular brand of soup are rather interesting. The reasons given are stated in Table 3.3.3

Given that 90 per cent of the advertising spending for all brands goes into TV advertising, and magazines take a mere 8 per cent, the extra expenditure on TV advertising does not seem justified in terms of its influence in encouraging customers to buy a particular brand.

Soup is one of the 'low-risk' purchases, i.e. customers are willing to try different brands because the unit price is low.

In 1993, Heinz spent over £1m. in 'above the line' advertising. In other words, this was their spending on consumer media such as TV, magazines and newspapers. The fall to just £30,000 in 1994 should have enabled other manufacturers to take some of Heinz's market. Other brands did increase their advertising spend at the same time. Campbell's increased spending by 33 per cent and Batchelors by 35 per cent.

TABLE 3.3.3 *Reasons for purchase of soups*

Stated reason	
The customer always bought a particular brand	86
The customer was tempted by the packaging	25
The customer wanted to try a new brand	23
The customer wanted to buy a cheaper brand	20
The customer saw the brand advertised on TV	13
The customer bought as a result of recommendation	11
The customer had a money-off coupon	10
The customer was sent a money-off coupon in the mail	9
The customer saw the brand advertised in a magazine	7

student activity

(PC 3.3.1, COM 3.1)
What is unfair about the percentage shown for cinema audiences in Table 3.3.1? In terms of the OTS criteria, is this a fair comparison? Discuss this in pairs.

(CPT). This is a far fairer way of making comparisons but, as we will see, it still has some problems. The CPT is based on the numbers of the target audience who view, listen to or read that media. We then divide this figure by the cost of the advertisement. This will give us the CPT. Roughly speaking, the CPTs for the various media are as shown in Table 3.3.4.

The price comparisons in Table 3.3.4 are not really particularly fair, as you cannot compare unlike media

TABLE 3.3.4 *CPT of various media*

Type	Cost
Outdoor	around 30p
Television	around £3.25 (regions vary)
Newspapers	nearly £3
Magazines/supplements	around £1.40
Commercial radio	around 80p
Cinema	around £18

student activity

(PC 3.3.1 COM 3.1)
Why bother to advertise in any medium other than TV or outdoors? After all, aren't they more likely to help you reach the maximum number of potential customers? Discuss this as a group.

in such a crude manner. The size of the advertisement, its length or the colour used have to be factored in to the equation.

One of the key considerations to look at is the **frequency** of the advertising the business is considering. This is known as the **threshold**: by this it is meant that a business has to advertise beyond a certain level to get any sort of response or impact. The threshold is worked out on the OTS basis, and this means that you would have to show the advertisement a number of time to ensure that a sufficient number of people have seen it.

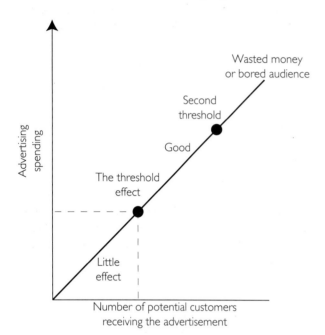

FIG. 3.3.1 *The threshold concept.*

There is another point on the graph plotting spending against audience size (Figure 3.3.1). This is the point when the advertiser has 'over spent' and the advertisement starts to lose its impact and effectiveness. There can be a negative impact here, the audience can get bored or irritated that the same advertisement or range of advertisements are being used so often. At this point it is wise for the advertiser either to terminate the campaign or switch to different advertisements. The trick is knowing when this will happen.

Working out the right medium for a product is hard enough, so here are some ideas about how to go about this:

- your budget may limit your options
- finding an affordable medium may not mean that you have chosen the right one
- all of the potential audience need to be contacted, if possible
- you need to show/publish the advertisement as often as is possible to maximise the OTS

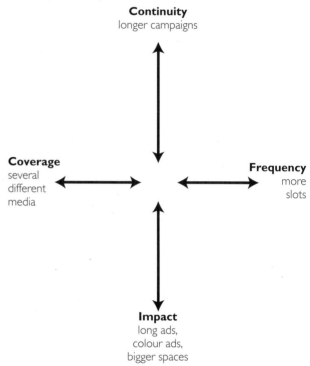

FIG. 3.3.2 *A diagram which illustrates the media planner's dilemma.*

- cost effectiveness is important, choose a cheaper medium if this means that you can run more advertisements for a longer period of time
- the medium itself should actually help enhance the image of your business or product

This balancing act can be summed up in what is known as the 'media planner's dilemma'. See Figure 3.3.2 to consider the elements of this problem.

Taking account of all of these considerations means that the media planner has to compromise. The key thoughts are:

- the **continuity** of the campaign
- the overall **coverage** of the campaign
- the **impact** of the campaign
- the **frequency** of the advertisements

It is a rare individual who can juggle all of these competing requirements. Those that are able to do so are paid an enormous amount of money!

Let us now turn our attention to the different media and try to assess the effectiveness of each type, their value for money and other advantages and disadvantages.

NEWSPAPER

There is a considerable choice of national newspapers available for the potential advertiser. Sales figures (or circulation figures) differ widely. For accurate circulation figures, it is always advisable to look at the ABC of the newspaper. This means that the sales figures have been audited by an independent organisation and have been certified as being true. There are some inherent advantages and disadvantages of newspaper advertising, and we will begin our investigation of this medium by looking at these. The advantages are:

- over 85 per cent of the adult population can be reached by the combined sales of national and local newspapers. A great many individual advertisements would have to be placed in order to achieve this level of coverage
- each newspaper has a distinctly different readership which allows for more accurate targeting and segmentation
- the flexibility of giving short or long notice in booking advertisements is a key feature of daily newspapers
- many people believe the printed word more than any other form of advertising
- many national newspapers offer the facility of 'split runs', in other words, you may advertise in a specific area of the country within a national newspaper if you wish
- the message that you are trying to get across may be long and complex, such as in financial advertising, making it more suitable for this medium
- many newspapers offer special features, sections or special days to help you target your message
- an increasing number of newspapers have colour sections which offer better opportunities. The problems that formerly existed with colour print on newspaper-quality paper have been addressed

The disadvantages are:

- many people think that newspaper advertising is boring. It is thought that many of the advertisements lack impact, although the introduction of colour has helped this
- most newspapers are read on the day that they are printed, therefore the advertisement has a very short life
- the growth of the 'free' newspaper market has diluted available income. Further, it has meant that many newspapers simply consist of advertisements with very little editorial content. Advertisements tend to 'get lost' in the mass of advertising

MAGAZINE

With well over a thousand magazines available in the UK alone, the advertiser has the choice of specialist or general interest magazines that are published with frequencies ranging from weekly to quarterly. The range of magazines is really quite bewildering and is constantly

student activity

(PC 3.3.1, COM 3.1)
Is there any point in advertising in free local weekly newspapers? Are they just full of advertisements and not really 'newspapers' at all? How would you objectively assess their value? Discuss this in groups of three.

Focus study

NEWSPAPERS

Daily newspapers' sales may have dipped over the last 10 years, but Sunday newspapers have fared even worse. From a high of 114.4m. sales per week, national newspaper sales have fallen to 102.6m. This is a decline of some 10.3 per cent. Sunday newspapers, over the same 10-year period have fallen by 16 per cent. Adult readership has dropped by 13.5 per cent for dailies and by 12.6 per cent for the Sunday papers.

student activity

(PC 3.3.1, COM 3.1)
Considering the information in the above Focus Study, how do you think this will influence media buyers in their choice of newspapers as an advertising medium? Discuss this as a group.

changing, but many have done a lot of work that helps the advertiser by specifically catering for a particular audience.

There are a number of advantages and disadvantages that we can associate with magazine advertising. We will address the advantages first:

- segmentation and targeting can be precise as the magazine may have done this for its own purposes and, by providing a full reader breakdown, can save the advertisers from having to undertake this themselves

- special interest magazines have a considerably longer life than most other magazines. The editorial content is well read and the advertisements are given much more attention than those in general interest magazines
- magazines tend to have a longer life than newspapers in any case.
- magazines tend to have a greater 'pass-on' rate, in other words more people read each copy of the magazine
- advertisements that appear in well-known and respected magazines may well have increased impact and credibility
- the better quality paper and more sophisticated printing techniques used by magazines allow the advertisers to use up-market advertisements (extra colours, etc.)

There are some disadvantages to consider:

- there is quite keen competition for the attention of customers with many high-quality advertisements and interesting editorial material
- the readership figure breakdown is usually less complete for magazines than for newspapers; indeed the smaller circulation magazines may have no independent audits of their true circulation figures
- an advertiser should not expect an instant response from an advertisement as the 'shelf-life' of a magazine is comparatively longer than that of a newspaper, as is the 'digesting' period of the reader to consider the content of the advertisement
- magazine production schedules have long lead and cancellation times for advertisements and these make 'spur of the moment' decisions very difficult
- high-quality advertisements inevitably mean high production costs to create the original for the advertisement

In many respects, the world of magazine advertising is not unlike that of newspapers. Magazines tend to vie for advertising in a much more aggressive manner than newspapers. It is often possible to get special deals for new advertisers and regular advertisers who make a long-term commitment. The main thing to remember about the magazine advertising possibilities is that there are magazines and advertising rates to suit any pocket.

TV

Up until quite recently viewing was almost equally split between the BBC and the ITV networks. The commercial stations now have a slight advantage. Another factor to be taken into account is satellite television, which is beginning to have a marked impact on the viewing figures of both of the terrestrial broadcasting

student activity

(PC 3.3.1, AON 3.1, 3.2, 3.3)
Using the source *British Rate and Data* (BRAD), which you should find in the reference section of any reasonable library, compare the advertising costs of newspaper and magazine advertising. What are the relevant advantages and disadvantages that you discover?

Focus study

MAGAZINES

The top 5 magazine publishers account for some 60 per cent of the circulation revenue. The next 10 per cent is split between ten companies. The percentages of circulation control are as shown in Table 3.3.5:

TABLE 3.3.5 Circulation control of magazines

Publisher	Per cent
IPC	25
EMAP	15.2
BBC Magazines	8.7
Bauer	7.9
National Magazine Co.	4.2
Others	39

student activity

(PC 3.3.1, AON 3.1, 3.2, 3.3)
Using BRAD again, try to identify at least five magazines owned by the main companies mentioned above. Try to find similar magazines that cater for the same kind of market. Make some comparisons between the prices charged for advertising and their relative circulation figures. Which magazines offer the best value for money in advertising terms?

groups. The ITV network consists of around 14 regional stations, plus GMTV and Channel 4. Each station's share of the audience depends upon the population density of the region. London and the Thames area (covered by London Weekend Television and Carlton) have some 22 per cent of the population, the Channel Islands only 1 per cent. These figures will have an impact on the pricing structure for advertisements in the regions, based on the population density.

There are a number of advantages and disadvantages associated with television advertising. The advantages are:

- TV is extremely useful in getting simple and uncomplicated messages to the vast majority of the population. Most homes have a TV set and therefore, on a purely statistical basis, everyone has an opportunity to see the advertisement
- generally speaking, the impact should be good. Creativity is high and is assisted by the use of colour and sound
- it is widely agreed that people are more receptive to advertisements in a relaxed atmosphere (homes are usually relaxed, but not necessarily so!)

- in a highly competitive market such as this, attractive discounts are offered to new and regular advertisers
- the sophisticated collection and analysis of viewing data helps the media planner target the audience more accurately
- the regional nature of the independent television network offers the planner the opportunity to segment the country into manageable advertising areas
- the regional nature of the network also offers the possibilities of test marketing an area with an advertisement, or in some cases a product, before 'rolling out' into the UK as a whole

There are a number of disadvantages, however:

- production costs, except for the most basic of advertisements, are high
- air time can be extremely expensive, particularly at peak times. For example, in the Thames region, a 30-second slot would cost in excess of £40,000. The same slot would cost as little as £2,000 for the Border region (with a 1 per cent share of the population)

FIG. 3.3.3 *This map illustrates not only the organisation of Anglia Television, but also the infrastructure of the area.*

— County Boundaries
Airports
Cargo Ports
Ferry Ports
Main Studios
News Centres

- high income and well-educated groups tend not to view as often as the rest of the population. Therefore, TV may not be the right medium for them
- tests have proved that viewers' attention wanders during advertising breaks
- the population's wide use of the video recorder may mean that your expensive and clever advertisements are never watched (except at fast forward)

The available advertising time is at present limited, only seven minutes per hour being allowed for advertising purposes. Charge rates are calculated according to the particular time of the day, assumed audience sizes and demand from other advertisers.

student activity

(PC 3.3.1, COM 3.1)
Do you think that the BBC should offer advertising possibilities? Research the cost of TV advertising, using BRAD, and try to work out the peak viewing hours. Discuss this as a group.

Sports, particularly those appealing to men, are very well supported in audience figure terms. Film premieres, soap operas and classy dramas are also watched by millions. But it is the major sports events which excite the advertisers as they vie for the limited slots available. A really popular sports event can attract figures in excess of 25m. Here are some of the most popular sports events of 1993/4:

The FA Cup Final (BBC1, May 1994)	30m.
The European Cup Final (ITV, May 1993)	24m.
The Coca-Cola Cup Final (ITV, May 1994)	28m.
The Cup Winners Cup Final (ITV, May 1994)	29m.

These figures can account for 66 per cent of the total viewers at a particular time. You will note that the majority of the big audience pullers were on ITV. It was interesting to note that the BBC screened female-orientated programmes to compete with these sporting events. In homes with only one TV set, there would have been quite a fight for the remote control!

POSTER

We should really broaden this category and call it outdoor advertising. It covers advertising carried on buses, taxis and trains. Other, more static sites include sports

Focus study

TELEVISION

There have been depressing viewing figures for television over the last few years, but this does not tell the whole story. Television advertising is still extremely effective. The other major feature is the strong emergence of satellite and cable advertising potential. Whilst the average adult watches 14 hours of 'terrestrial' television per week (that is BBC1, BBC2, ITV and C4), the average satellite television watcher sits in front of the TV for 18.5 hours per week. This may be as a result of the 25 or more channels available, but it means that satellite subscribers can watch up to 32 per cent more commercial television than terrestrial viewers. Some 12 channels dominate the satellite viewing figures.

student activity

(PC 3.3.1, COM 3.1)
What do you consider to be the relative advantages and disadvantages of advertising on terrestrial and satellite television? Discuss as a group.

student activity

PC 3.3.1, COM 3.1, 3.2)
These male-orientated sports events are the advertisers' dream. What sort of products would be advertised during these programmes? Can you identify at least five different types of product that would achieve a good OTS in the commercial breaks? Compare your written list with those of the remainder of your group.

stadia, balloons (the really big ones!), milk bottles and even parking meters.

The most obvious form of outdoor advertising is the poster and you will find these literally everywhere. They do lack the impact (quite often) of TV and other more intimate advertising methods, but do seem to remind people about the advertising message.

There are a number of advantages and disadvantages of outdoor advertising that are worth noting, and we shall look at the advantages first:

- outdoor advertising has very high OTSs
- comparatively, outdoor advertising has a very low CPT
- outdoor advertising offers a wide range of colours and sizes
- there is a wide choice of sites
- in many cases, the advertisement may be the only one on view
- sites tend to be sold on a monthly or quarterly basis
- there is a gradual effect with these advertisements as the audience will see them a number of times and then subconsciously remember the advertisement without actually studying it
- there are great opportunities to be innovative, such as the use of three-dimensional advertisements with cars, giant microwaves or similar items 'stuck' to the poster

As with all forms of advertising, there are a number of disadvantages:

- printing costs can be high for the short runs needed for the posters
- there is a long booking and cancellation period required
- there is some very debatable and spurious research regarding the number of people who will view a particular site
- poster sites can be 'missed' or ignored by the public
- only short and snappy messages tend to work
- graffiti tends to be a problem
- prime sites are often booked for considerable periods by the big advertisers and so are not available
- sites are usually not available on an individual basis, normally a package of sites is sold to the advertiser offering a mix of site locations

student activity

(PC 3.3.1, COM 3.2)
Do you notice poster or bus advertising? How would you assess the effectiveness of such advertisements? Try to list at least ten advertisers that use poster or bus panels in your area.

Most outdoor advertising is handled by a small number of agencies or contractors. They sell a mixed package of sites which are intended to get the message across to a wide section of the population. Popular sites are tied up for years under the concept of TC (Till Countermanded) which means that advertisers can keep sites until they say that they do not want them any more.

Costs can vary enormously – you can buy a package of some 400 sites for around £700,000 per month. Bus rears can cost about £50 each, but they are bought in multiples (often around 30–50):

Focus study

TRANSPORT ADVERTISING

The Original Passenger Picture Show (TOPPS) launched an on-bus television service for some 800 vehicles in the Midlands and north-west of England in November 1994. The recall of travellers on the buses showed that around 50 per cent of them remembered a particular advertisement shown on the bus. The other major finding of the research done to support the campaign was that 38 per cent of the travellers were 14–24 year olds, while only 13 per cent were over 65. Interestingly, the travellers, when asked about their reason for using the bus replied that it was either for shopping (65 per cent) or for going to work (20 per cent).

student activity

(PC 3.3.1, COM 3.1)
What lessons can be learned about this form of outdoor advertising? Do the figures, in terms of age groups and reasons for travelling, give some additional indication as to the type of advertisement that would work on such a site? Discuss this in groups of four.

RADIO

The 1990s have seen an explosion in radio. Networking, such as that used by the television stations, is becoming more common, particularly in the case of music stations. Not surprisingly, the medium is

Focus study

POSTER SITES

Poster contractors have been suggesting that the results of a recent test may herald a dramatic increase in outdoor advertising. A £250,000 initiative spearheaded by Maiden Outdoor boosted a new bubble-bath product called Scallywags to a 26 per cent market share in just six weeks. The key to success was the identification of sites that would be seen by housewives and children.

At the same time, other research has shown the following:

- that the campaign was remembered by 36 per cent of housewives and children
- that the campaign was remembered by some 36 per cent of tube travellers
- that these totals meant that 40 per cent of those who remembered the advertisement intended to buy the product

student activity

(PC 3.3.1, COM 3.1, 3.2)
Using the figures above, how do you now rate outdoor advertising as a potential method of getting a message across to the public? Try to identify at least 10 sites in your local area that would have matched the criteria of the Scallywags campaign. Compare your list to those of the remainder of the group.

dominated by the larger stations, usually based in London, Manchester, Birmingham or Liverpool. The emergence of Virgin Radio, Talk Radio UK and Classic FM has signalled a major change in the balance of power in radio. Their long-term impact on the medium and their overall profitability has yet to be really tested.

There are a number of advantages and disadvantages that should be looked at. These are the advantages:

- the medium is ideal for urgent and immediate advertising announcements
- with widespread stereo use, sound effects and gimmicks are far more effective than on TV
- a business can advertise precisely to a set area

- production costs for radio are comparatively low
- good discounts are available
- short notice may be given to the stations in terms of bookings and cancellations, so the flexibility is high

The disadvantages are:

- national campaigns are still hard to co-ordinate
- radio has the reputation of being a low-impact medium, used as a background or as 'aural wall-paper'
- as with TV, national advertising can be expensive if you add up all the costs of advertising with each of the small stations

Listeners are fed up with the BBC stations and are turning to commercial radio in a big way. Despite the fact that the recession severely dented the advertising income of many of the commercial stations, they are now beginning to show very healthy profits again. Radio accounts for some 2.5–3 per cent of all advertising spending. On the basis of US experience, it is thought that radio could take up to 10 per cent of all advertising spending. More sober voices claim that the figure is more likely to be around 4–5 per cent.

TABLE 3.3.6 *Fall in listeners for BBC radio stations, 1993–4*

Radio One	−21 per cent
Radio Two	−7 per cent
Radio Four	−3 per cent

There are two main routes through which radio air time can be booked. First, there are brokers who handle the sales for each of the stations. Secondly, the stations themselves sell air time through their own offices and sales force. Discounts can be attractive, as it is rare to buy a single advertisement. The concept of Total Audience Package (TAP) is used to give the advertisers a chance to target the maximum number of listeners in a whole advertising package. In this way, the radio station sells a package which adds up to a number of listeners over a number of advertisements. The advertisers state the number of people to whom they wish to expose their advertisement and the station offers a series of advertisements to suit.

CINEMA

Cinema advertising has spent some time as the poor relation, but it is making a big comeback. Attendance figures are up and so is the advertising spend. This is an ideal medium for the younger customer and businesses have not been slow in recognising this aspect.

The advantages of cinema advertising are:

- local advertising is cheap and relatively simple
- the medium has great visual impact and sound effects

student activity

(PC 3.3.1, COM 3.1)
Radio advertising is a relatively young medium. Do you think that you can accurately target the segment to which you wish to pass on your message? How well do the radio stations detail their audience figures? Discuss in pairs.

Focus study

COMMERCIAL RADIO

Commercial radio has been recognised as the fastest growing advertising medium in the UK. According to the Radio Advertising Bureau, there is a 25 per cent year on year growth in sales revenue from advertising. However, since 1992, there has been a 2 per cent drop in the number of listeners. The biggest fall-off is in the 15–24 and 55+ age groups. Virgin, the station that has had the most impact, attracts some 3.25m. listeners, accounting for around 2.8 per cent of all the listeners.

Classic FM is up too, with weekly listeners of some 4.8m. This represents a 6 per cent increase from the previous year. Atlantic 252 is up to 4.93m. (3.1 per cent of all listeners).

The BBC is the main loser, with listeners to Radio 1 dropping to 14.7 per cent of the listening public. It is still, however, the market leader in this growing and competitive market.

- this medium is ideal for the under 25 market
- the medium is ideal for testing the effectiveness of advertisements that will later appear on TV
- the medium allows spirits to be advertised

There are, however, some disadvantages:

- there is a relatively small audience
- production costs are high as separate copies of the advertisement have to be provided for each screen
- buying advertising space can be more difficult than for some of the other media

student activity

(PC 3.3.1)
Research the viewing figures of your local radio station(s). What is its market share and how do its advertising prices relate to its listening audience?

Focus study

CINEMA

The Cinema Advertising Association is a trade organisation of cinema advertising contractors. Its purpose is to monitor, promote and maintain standards of cinema advertising. It also conducts research into cinema and cinema advertising.

CAA research has shown that the emergence of the multi-plex (at an investment of £600m.) has had a marked effect on the fortunes of cinema in the UK. In 1993, the number of multi-plex screens had increased to 625, from the 1985 level of just 10.

Advertising revenue has increased on a year by year basis over the past 10 years, and now accounts for nearly 1 per cent of all advertising spending. The national average for a 30-second commercial is around £73.00. The total number of screens available in the UK has risen to 1,862, predominantly in the higher population density areas.

The CAA offer an Audience Discount Package which guarantees the price on a CPT basis. The average cost is around £28.00.

student activity

(PC 3.3.1, AON·3.1)
Obviously, the number of cinemas is growing in the UK. Cinema going suffered a severe slump in the 1970s, but is now steadily growing again. Try to find out how many cinema screens were in your local area 20 years ago, 10 years ago and now. What has been the growth rate?

PUBLICITY

The publicity side of the marketing effort can often be considered as an internally generated method, with advertising materials such as the following being used:

- sales literature
- signs and other messages on the premises, etc.
- vehicle livery, including the organisation's name and product names
- stationery and other items such as compliment slips
- point-of-sale (POS) materials to assist the marketing of a product within retail outlets

We shall look at each of these forms of publicity and try to consider their relative use and effectiveness. Public relations, as we will see later, ties in very well with the publicity efforts of organisations. These are often used jointly to obtain vital customer awareness and to heighten the image of the organisation in general.

SALES LITERATURE

Sales literature plays a vital role in the ongoing marketing effort of any organisation. It aims to convey to the customers the vital information about the product, service or selling organisation that will aid them in making a purchasing decision. To this end, the sales literature needs to be as professional as possible, with a strong company image and some degree of clarity and standardisation. As we mentioned earlier in this Unit, there is often a communications problem that inhibits some parts of an organisation from understanding what other parts are doing. In the sales literature area, it is vital that all parts of the organisation know the content of the material and what claims are being made. In some cases, prices and availability have been mentioned in sales literature and the sales department has not been informed of this. They have been faced with the embarrassment of callers quoting from the sales literature and not being able to respond. The importance of communication of the content can, therefore, not be underestimated.

Sales literature includes the following:

- brochures
- leaflets
- information booklets
- sales letters
- compliment slips

Brochures and leaflets can be used to send out responses to sales enquiries or for direct mail campaigns. They can also be given out to salespersons to help to reinforce the sales message. Many potential customers expect sales literature, since it adds credibility to the business. Brochures and leaflets can be relatively cheap although, as we have already mentioned, the style and

FIG. 3.3.4 *This example of sales literature, produced by Witley Press for Norton, is aimed at the profession. It is clear and straightforward and contains all necessary information. Note that it does not include prices; this extends the life of the leaflet.*

student activity

(PC 3.3.1, COM 3.1)
Can you think of some more examples of the use of sales literature and types of material that would contain sales information? Firstly in pairs, and then in groups, consider your ideas.

tone needs to be consistent. They should not look cheap and nasty, but should be of reasonable quality and follow any conventions that the business has established in terms of logos and slogans, etc. Brochures should not be packed with lots of technical details, unless of course, the business is selling technical or specialist equipment. Leaflets are perhaps more flexible,

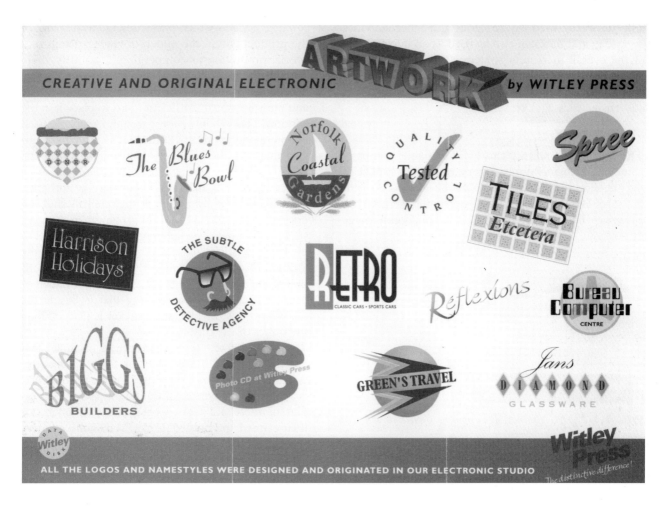

FIG. 3.3.5 *This company offers a comprehensive service to businesses and can design these logos and type styles for as little as £100.*

since they are cheaper to produce and can be used for a variety of different purposes.

SIGNAGE

The company name or logo can be very important for any organisation attempting to get its name into the minds of potential customers. The design work should not really be done by an amateur, it is far better to pay a relatively small fee to a professional organisation that can really make the most of the business name and any other features of the organisation.

The correct use of signage and all its implications in terms of the image that it helps to build, is yet another part of the overall marketing strategy that so many organisations ignore. Without a clear and professional-looking logo and type style, the organisation runs the risk of appearing to be rather unprofessional and amateur.

VEHICLE LIVERY

Any organisation that uses vehicles would be foolish not to use these mobile marketing devices as a means of publicising its products and services. No doubt, there are hundreds of thousands of vans, trucks, lorries

FIG. 3.3.6 *Rentokil, the market leader in pest control and environmental health, uses the company name on all vehicles. Note particularly the use of the 'By Appointment' on the side of the van.*

and cars being used for deliveries and other activities every day and they can also be used as an integral part of the overall marketing strategy. Publicity can range from the simple use of the business name, nature of business, address and telephone number to the use of advertising messages on vehicles.

STATIONERY

The use of logos and clearly identifiable company names and slogans on stationery is another aspect of the marketing effort that should not be ignored. As with the sales literature, particular care should be given to ensuring that the stationery has a consistent image throughout.

With compliments

FIG. 3.3.7 *TEC Business Development Centre compliment slip.*

POINT-OF-SALE (POS)

These are materials that are used to display and promote products within a retail outlet. The most common examples of this form of marketing are:

1 *The dump bin* – which is a container or box in which the product is displayed in the retail outlet. Typically, these dump bins will have the name of the product clearly visible and will have a back card giving the dump bin greater prominence in the shop. The size of these dump bins varies according to the size of the product or the level of stock held by the outlet. You will find dump bins in many different outlets containing items as diverse as video tapes and confectionery, pharmaceuticals and books. Free-standing dump bins would normally be placed near doors, near the till or at the end of an aisle. The smaller, less conspicuous form of dump bin would normally be placed beside the till.

2 *Window poster* – which publicises the availability of the product within the outlet, or carries details of a special promotion or competition. Obviously, there is a limit to the available space for these posters and the retailer would have to feel that the content, size and message was of sufficient merit to place it in the window. The window poster would, ideally, be used in conjunction with the dump bin as a further reinforcement of the product's availability within the shop.

3 *The shelf-sticker* – in cases when there is not sufficient space for a dump bin, or the retailer's shelving does not allow the use of a dump bin, then the shelf sticker is the next best alternative. Typically, the use of the shelf sticker would permanently signify the location of a product within the shop. Good examples of the use of the shelf sticker include the shelf or counter-level confectionery tray that is beside the till. Within this tray, the shelf sticker is placed along the ridges of the tray.

4 *The compartment* – typically a freezer or chiller that has the name of the product or the manufacturer upon it. This acts as a dispenser for the product and is a permanent fixture within the shop. Good examples of these are Coca-Cola's chiller cabinets for their canned and bottled drinks, Mars confectionery freezers for their range of iced products or a Slush Puppy frozen drinks dispenser. The retailer has to pay for the cabinet or dispenser, at a subsidised price, on the understanding that only that product or product line is sold from that container. There have been some problems with these dispensers, when retailers have sold other products from the dispensers. The suppliers have contended that this is in breach of the agreement. Many retailers either have refused to conform with the agreement (leading to the supplier taking back the dispenser) or have asked the supplier to take the dispenser back.

Obviously, the retailer has the final say about using any of this POS material or equipment. Suppliers are keen to offer incentives or discounts if the retailer is prepared to have the POS items in the shop. Often, the stock carried in the POS dispenser will be on special offer (to the retailer) or will be on a sale or return basis for a defined period.

3.3.2 *Identify and give examples of public relations to promote products and organisations*

PUBLIC RELATIONS

There has always been a certain degree of scepticism surrounding the measurability of this area of activity. A common way of measuring the effectiveness of public relations exercises was to look at the number and length of the articles and news stories written about the organisation in question. The number of times the organisation's name or products were mentioned in the media served as the only method of measurement.

It is true to say that public relations is one of the more intangible aspects of marketing, but after all, what is the difference between trying to measure the effectiveness of advertising and trying to measure the effectiveness of public relations? The biggest difference, without doubt, is the amount of money that organisations are prepared to spend on either activity. Public relations is the poor relative in this respect.

Focus study

PUBLIC RELATIONS

Tracking the effectiveness of a public relations exercise can be somewhat easier if you investigate a single issue event. National 'No Smoking Day' relies entirely on public relations and has consistently achieved success. It has achieved awareness levels of around 80 per cent of the adult population, without any advertising back-up. The real value of the public relations exercise has to be measured in terms of how many people give up smoking as a direct result of the public relations campaign. In 1993, some 2m. people took part in No Smoking Day and around 50,000 are still not smoking.

The main targets of public relations efforts, generally, are:

- the general public, often targeted by community relations exercises such as sponsorship events
- the company's employees, being seen as increasingly important now that the workforce is perceived as an asset rather than a necessary evil or a potential source of confrontation
- the banks and the stock exchange to whom the organisation must look for confirmation of its financial soundness and its prospects
- the customers of the organisation, for whom PR must run alongside the advertising and general marketing policy. It is vital to educate customers as to the superiority of a product or service as well as to maintain general interest and awareness in the target group
- the media, an integral part of a well-organised PR campaign, as any organisation is keen to strike up a good relationship with the press, television or radio

Some typical forms of PR are detailed later, but let us look at the more general tasks that PR aims to perform:

1 *Identifying specific interest groups* which will be able to influence the public towards the organisation. The organisation will have to identify the objectives of these interest groups and assess the resources that are available to them. Examples of interest groups are pressure groups and investors. Once the interest group has been identified, the group's attitude to the organisation must be ascertained. How does the interest group operate? What are its strengths? The PR operation must form part of a plan to influence the interest group and project a favourable image to them. The organisation must also be able to deflect any criticism levelled at it by the interest group.

2 PR should also offer *counselling and advice* to the management of the organisation and keep it updated on the attitudes and opinions of the organisation as perceived by the general public and interest groups. The creation of forecasts of what might happen in the future should be a vital part of this, so as to enable the organisation to respond positively to off-set potential problems and criticisms.

3 *Publicising* the organisation's products and activities is an integral part of the overall marketing policy and duties. PR plays an important role in the launch of a new product and can be a key factor in the development of new ideas. PR aims to keep interested parties informed of trends, developments and launches on a continual and rolling basis.

4 In the area of *media relations*, the PR element of the organisation needs to try to get press, radio or TV coverage. The media can be used to educate or inform the public about a certain product, service or activity with which the organisation is involved. Good examples of these are the use of Richard Branson's media grabbing skills by Virgin and Anita Roddick's adeptness in pushing The Body Shop message home to the general public. As we will see

shortly, the use of press releases is ideal in this respect.

5 *Creating awareness* and a positive attitude towards the organisation on a corporate level is extremely useful. This activity seeks to increase overall interest and awareness but is not specifically related to a particular product or service. The use of sponsorship, as we will see, can help this cause immensely.

6 PR also aims to *lobby the decision makers* in both government and professional organisations, to persuade them to promote legislation, regulations, codes of practice or attitudes that are favourable to the organisation.

student activity

(PC 3.3.2, COM 3.1)
Organisations which have a large and active PR department have a disproportionate share of the coverage in the media as compared with smaller and less active organisations. Is this fair, and how could this be offset by smaller organisations? Discuss as a group.

PRESS RELEASES

This is a public relations statement issued to the media by an organisation in order to gain some editorial coverage favourable to the organisation.

When an organisation has a news item, either a staff member of the organisation will write the press release, or a professional marketing agency will be engaged to write it on behalf of the organisation. The main aspects of writing a successful press release are:

- it should stick to the facts
- it should be brief
- the contents of the press release should be summarised in the first paragraph
- it should contain the organisation's name and telephone number and must also give a contact name
- it should contain a quotation from the person responsible for the item. This gives it a human angle
- a photograph should be attached, if relevant, to increase the chances of the press release being used

It is also a good idea for anyone who has to write press releases to try to get to know the editor or some journalists at a newspaper or magazine that might possibly feature your organisation. If the organisation has a news story, then an initial phone call should be made to offer an 'exclusive' to the newspaper. This might be an even better way than sending out a number of press releases to several different newspapers.

An organisation should also try to send articles and press releases to the trade press in the hope that they might feature the organisation's news or developments.

It is always worth remembering that the better the press release, the better the chances of the newspaper using it. Also, if the press release is written like a news story, then there is every chance that the story will be printed in full. Journalists are busy people and if you make their jobs easier for them, then you have a great advantage.

SPONSORSHIP

UK businesses spend around £250m. sponsoring sport each year. This figure is growing by about 10 per cent per year. According to the organisation Sports Marketing Strategy, sponsorship accounts for some 5 per cent of all advertising spending world-wide. Although sports advertising is aimed at reaching a mass audience, it is argued that since so many sponsorship deals are being struck this dilutes the effect. When was the last time that you bought something after seeing the name of a business or a product on the chest of your favourite sports personality?

Sports sponsorship is more than just image building. It is about selling products too, but the former aspect is the more dominant. When a client has been sold on the concept of sponsorship, media monitoring exercises are carried out to indicate the exposure levels which measure the success or failure of the venture. Sponsorship supporters do admit that not enough research is being carried out to measure the real objectives of the sponsorship or, for that matter, the possible up-turn in sales that may result.

Normally, a business, product or brand is tracked against the trends in the market to try to show what effect the sponsorship has had. Sponsorship is very strong on brand-building. Once the target market has been identified, the business will know a lot about the target group, their lifestyles, income and age, etc. If the target group is young and active, then the business would be wise to associate itself with an active and exciting sport.

For some businesses, sponsorship deals that run to £750,000 or so are really just 'petty cash' in comparison with the massive advertising spending that may be going on at the same time. TV sponsorship has really come of age in the last few years. Just over half of advertisers and agencies are more likely to consider the possibilities of sponsoring TV programmes than a year ago. They now view sponsorship as being extremely useful for brand enhancement and for targeting specific markets and audiences.

Although around 80 per cent of advertisers state that they do not have a specific sponsorship budget, they also state that if they do use sponsorship then the costs are not taken out of the advertising budget. The main reasons for advertisers not to consider sponsorship are:

- poor targeting possibilities (i.e. of the audience type)
- budgetary restrictions of the business
- over-pricing of the sponsorship deal
- lack of control over how their name/brand will be used

Some 42 per cent of advertisers claim that TV sponsorship helped to build brand awareness, and 56 per cent said that it improved the image of the business. Some of the more prominent TV sponsorship deals in 1994 were:

Passengers (C4)	Pepsi
Don't Forget Your Toothbrush (C4)	Polaroid
Italian Football (C4)	Carlsberg Export
NFL (C4)	Budweiser
The Word (C4)	Swatch
Gamesmaster (C4)	McDonald's
World Cup (ITV)	Panasonic
Play Your Cards Right (ITV)	The Sun
You Bet (ITV)	Daily Mirror

student activity

LOBBYING

The term 'lobbying' takes its name from a political activity which involves trying to influence members of parliament in the lobby (entrance hall) of the Houses of Parliament. In business terms, lobbying takes on a wider role and involves the practice of attempting to influence any decision maker for the benefit of the organisation or the industry in general.

It is at this, the industry or trade, level that the majority of lobbying is undertaken. Federations or associations that represent a particular trade or industry will act on

Focus study

SPONSORSHIP

Sponsors paid more than £152m. to be associated with the World Cup Finals in 1994. That figure appears to be very small when we consider the amount that the top 19 World Cup sponsors invested in advertising over the same period. This support advertising ran to a staggering £6.6bn. world-wide!

The returns were great too, as some 31bn. people watched the World Cup Finals world-wide. However, the fact that England failed to make the finals cost an estimated £30m. in lost advertising. The USA was the big market in which the sponsors wished to make an impact. The organisers of the World Cup, aware that football was a rather unknown and unloved sport compared to baseball, American football, ice hockey and basket ball spent an estimated £20m. on promoting the event to the Americans.

The two-tier sponsorship deals managed to attract some household names such as Coca-Cola, McDonald's and General Motors (each paying between £10m. and £13m.). The second tier, or 'marketing partners' paid around £4.6m. each.

McDonald's final bill, in sponsorship-related costs, ran to £46m. They were more than pleased with their investment: they believed that it would have been impossible to have gained the exposure that the World Cup gave them with that level of spending.

their members' behalf to try to obtain a higher profile and become part of the decision-making process. They will attempt to become advisers to government or other bodies, being consulted when there is an issue that affects the industry.

COMMUNITY RELATIONS

Large organisations may well have a dedicated community relations department. The main feature of this form of marketing is to heighten awareness of the organisation within the local community, as well as to support local charities and issues.

This relatively cheap form of marketing or public relations can bring very positive benefits to an organisation in helping to mobilise support for the organisation. The feeling that the organisation is an integral part of the local community needs to extend beyond the obvious job-providing role. Many smaller communities may be economically reliant upon one or two businesses and the organisation needs to be seen as a positive aspect of the local community and not just as a job provider.

Focus study

LOBBYING

The British Exporters Association is a lobbying organisation for UK exporters. It is particularly active in lobbying for export credit insurance. This is a government service which guarantees payment for UK exporters in the event that the foreign importer fails to pay the invoice for an order. This is, of course, of vital importance to the exporter since potential bad debts that are difficult to retrieve can mean severe cash-flow problems or worse. One of the major lobbying goals is to try to convince the Export Credit Guarantee Department to charge lower premiums to UK exporters. The premiums are significantly higher than in other European countries such as France and Germany. In 1991, the export credit insurance business was privatised.

The lobbying effort of BExA has included deputations to:

- the Department of Trade and Industry
- the Industrial Finance Division of the Bank of England
- the Export Credit Guarantee Department
- the Director-General of Export Promotion

Community relations exercises can go badly wrong (see the Focus Study on the right), but charitable donations and other community relations exercises are very good for the organisation's general image. If the organisation chooses the right kind of cause or event, then it can expect great dividends from this relatively cheap method of marketing.

Visits and open days are very useful methods too: by inviting the public to view its operations, an organisation can help improve the public's understanding of what it is about. The Body Shop, for example, encourages the public to have a look at its operations and arranges regular guided tours of the premises in Littlehampton. There are exhibits, original packaging and a mock-up of the first Body Shop to interest the visitors. The tour begins and ends at the Body Shop retail outlet on the factory site where the public can buy products and merchandise that are not available anywhere else.

Focus study

COMMUNITY RELATIONS (CHARITY FUND-RAISING)

The Flora Aerobathon 94, held in April, was a disastrous flop. In 1993, some 26,000 people were attracted to the London venue alone without the benefit of a significant advertising spend. In 1994, despite a £1.2m. advertising budget, only 17,000 people turned up to the five venues.

Flora had expected around 140,000 people to attend and had projected that the event would raise some £3m. for six national charities.

Publicity was carried on 55m. Flora margarine tubs, with TV advertising in most areas and additional radio advertising in others. The event turned out to be the biggest flop in living memory. The Aerobathon collapsed with debts of over £1.2m. The income raised from the nationwide event amounted to only £340,000.

The charities had agreed to 'write off' the first £150,000 per venue to cover the costs of the event. Initially, there were to have been six venues, so the total write-off would have amounted to £900,000. This would have contributed greatly to subsidising the estimated £1.5m. costs of the whole event. The Royal Marsden Hospital was to have received the first £500,000. This meant that the event would have had to total some £1.25m. before any of the other charities got a penny.

Flora itself is one of the creditors, being owed some £300,000. At least it received the publicity and the increase in brand awareness. Other creditors were not so lucky: they face financial disaster.

student activity

(PC 3.3.2, COM 3.1)
Do you think that even Flora can claim that it has achieved additional publicity and brand awareness? Do you feel that it should have covered the costs of the other companies involved? Is any publicity good publicity? Discuss in pairs.

3.3.3 Evaluate sales promotion methods for their effectiveness in reaching a target audience

SALES PROMOTION METHODS

Sales promotion, known as 'below-the-line' expenditure, can account for up to half of all marketing spending. Trade sales promotions are very common, such as bulk-order discounts, or rebates based on the amount spent over a year with a supplier. The main aim of any sales promotion is to increase sales. This may sound fairly obvious, but the tactics used can be somewhat more complex than in advertising. Sales promotions, in order to be classified as successful, should generate short-term increases in the sales volume and value. During the period of the sales promotion, the customer should also be encouraged to purchase more regularly or in greater quantities per purchase than he/she would normally do.

Most sales promotions are short term. Certainly in the case of fmcgs (fast-moving consumer goods), such as baked beans, confectionery and coffee, the sales promotions may be continuous. Organisations that produce these products will roll one sales promotion straight into the next, without a break.

Offering plastic dinosaurs or merchandise associated with the latest film release can give a brand a temporary edge over competitors who are only offering breakfast bowls to customers who collect ten tokens. For many products, such as cereals or petrol, the sales promotion replaces the price cut. Price wars do nothing for any of the organisations involved other than to affect their profit margins and divert attention away from the quality of the product or service. Having said this, temporary price cuts or special offers can be seen as an alternative method of sales promotion, but not one that is favoured by suppliers. Short-term special offers are

fine if the product is a new one that needs to be established in the market-place, but otherwise they are avoided if possible.

Sales promotions are very much tied in with the concepts of customer loyalty, brand loyalty and the general rewards given to customers who stick with a particular brand name.

student activity

(PC 3.3.3)
We will be identifying some of the major variants of sales promotions in this Element, but some of them require investigation and research. In pairs, research the meaning of the techniques listed in the Focus Study on page 260 and report your findings and examples back to the rest of the group.

COMPETITIONS

This form of sales promotion has a twofold objective. First, it seeks to maintain brand loyalty. Secondly, it hopes to increase the frequency of use and purchase by existing customers. It is unlikely that new customers will be attracted to the product just because of the competition. The competition must offer attractive and desirable prizes or a good cash win. Each and every entrant in the competition must have a fair chance of winning. Competitions are subject to tight controls and must conform to legislation. This is related to the element of skill involved. Usually the entrant has to put a number of points or features of the product in order and then complete a 'tie breaker'. The tie breaker is usually a slogan or similar that begins with: 'Yum Yum breakfast cereal is a great start to the today because...'. Competitions are very good tools in convincing retailers to give the product extra shelf space.

There is one good story related to competitions that is worth retelling. A certain individual purchased a vast quantity of a particular cat food in order to win a new car. The rules of the competition stated that the entrant had to put the five main features of this car into a

student activity

(PC 3.3.3, COM 3.1)
Why bother with sales promotions at all? Surely, running a sales promotion only shows that the organisation's advertising and other marketing activities are not working? Discuss as a group.

Focus study

SALES PROMOTION METHODS

The Institute of Sales Promotion is fighting against the EU's plans to harmonise the rules and regulations that govern the use of sales promotions throughout Europe. The Institute fears that common rules and regulations will prevent the use of 'country specific' sales promotions methods that definitely work in a particular country. The laws in the UK are some of the most liberal in the EU. In comparison, the Germans have rules and regulations covering nearly every type of sales promotion method.

Table 3.3.7 attempts to identify the significant differences between the major European countries with regard to sales promotion techniques.

TABLE 3.3.7 *Sales promotion techniques in major European countries*

Technique	UK	IRL	SP	GER	F	BEL	NL	IT
On pack price cuts	y	y	y	y	y	y	y	y
Branded offers	y	y	y	m	y	n	y	y
In-pack premiums	y	y	y	m	m	y	m	y
Multi-buys	y	y	y	m	y	m	y	y
Extra product	y	y	y	m	y	m	m	y
Free product	y	y	y	y	y	m	y	y
Re-usable pack	y	y	y	y	y	y	y	y
Free mail-ins	y	y	y	n	y	y	y	y
Collecting tokens	y	y	y	m	m	m	m	y
Competitions	y	y	y	m	m	m	m	y
Self-liquidating	y	y	y	y	y	y	m	y
Free draws	y	y	y	n	y	n	n	y
Lotteries	m	m	m	m	m	m	m	m
Cash-off vouchers	y	y	y	n	y	y	y	m
Cash-off purchase	y	y	y	n	y	y	y	m
Cash back	y	y	y	m	y	y	y	m
In-store demonstrations	y	y	y	y	y	y	y	y

KEY: y = allowed by law; n = not allowed by law; m = maybe, dependent upon certain conditions

particular order. The individual worked out all of the permutations of the five features and bought the necessary number of cat food tins to make a multiple entry. The individual then filled in the tie breaker with the same slogan for each of the entries, then sat back to wait for the car to be delivered. The individual did not win because the tie breaker was not very good. The car was not won. The punchline to the story is that the individual did not own a cat! The moral of this tale is that although the majority of competitions have a 'skill' or 'judgement' element to them, either they are just like a lottery (in the sense that anyone with a brain can get the answer right), or the main point of the competition is to get some decent tie breakers from the entrants.

COUPONS

The collection of coupons is a time-honoured method of short-term sales increases. Normally, the customer will be required to collect a number of coupons and fill in an address slip to send off for the featured item.

Focus study

COUPONS

Hoover's Free Flights scheme, in which customers could apply for two free flight tickets to the USA or Europe after purchasing a £100 Hoover product, turned into a fiasco. Something was deeply wrong with the whole idea. An estimated 300,000 people applied for tickets. Around 15,000 people were being booked onto flights per month. The hold-ups were unacceptable and in both the UK and the USA, Hoover had to answer for their poor preparation of the sales promotion. Disgruntled customers had to deal with applications that had 'gone missing' and other unexplained delays. The Hoover Holiday Pressure Group sought to take High Court action against the company in their attempt to get their promised tickets.

student activity

(PC 3.3.3)

This prime example of how a sales promotion should not work, seriously back-fired on Hoover. They could not cope with the demand or the administration of the sales promotion. This is perhaps a lesson in the fact that sales promotions need to be very well organised.

Research the background and outcome of the Hoover promotion. What do you think they should have done to ensure that the promotion worked?

SPECIAL OFFERS

Sales promotion battles are fought every day in the supermarkets and other retailers. Special offers abound, the results are good, some 20 per cent of the value of an average shopper's basket is related to special offers.

Focus study

SPECIAL OFFERS

Duracell and their rival Energizer face the same dilemma every Christmas. The run-up to the season of goodwill is a great time to sell batteries. With Duracell offering 12 batteries for £6.49, Energizer's offer of 'buy two, get one free' gave you 12 for £6.38, a difference of just 9p. So what were the advantages to either organisation? Did the special offer really increase their battery sales in the run-up to Christmas or not? How was their market share affected?

The offers were great for the customer, the price levels acceptable and in keeping with the major supermarkets' philosophy of reducing brand name products in price.

The dilemma for Duracell and Energizer is not whether to reduce prices and offer special deals, but the price they would have to pay if they didn't. With one brand doing it, the other just HAD to follow. Simple market realities. The special offers were not really for the benefit of the customer, although they did benefit in terms of cost, but were simply to maintain and protect market share and sales.

student activity

(PC 3.3.3, COM 3.1)

If you go to a supermarket and look at two similar competing brands, what is the real price difference between the two? Are they both offering special deals at the moment? Taking these into account, what is the real difference between the two promotions? Are they really very similar? Discuss this in pairs.

In-store, price-based promotions are extremely common: the main versions include the following:

- 10 per cent extra free
- buy two, get one free
- 10 per cent off

Such promotions can account for up to 75 per cent of the promotional budgets of the major companies. Organisations and analysts consider them to be a plague, infectious and dangerous, that should be avoided if possible. If this is the case, then why is everyone using them? Some critics state that the costs outweigh the benefits, pointing out that the use of these promotions can cause the following:

- massive demand is generated in a short period of time
- the organisation has to ensure that sufficient supplies are available to cope with the demand generated by the promotion
- as a consequence of this, the organisation suffers supply inefficiencies
- the organisation also has to change, temporarily, the packaging of the product (i.e. to state the nature of the offer)
- the organisation has to have additional employees on hand to deal with the extra production, distribution and other supply-related concerns

The other interesting aspect of special offers is that customers often perceive that the discounting is offered by the retailer and not the supplier. This may be good for the retailer, but offers no potential benefit to the supplier.

Marketing directors and consultants often compare special offers to an arms race. They know that it is not a sensible thing to be doing, but no one will do the sensible thing. That is, to stop doing it. If a single organisation declares unilaterally that it will stop, then it is the one that will suffer because it can be sure of one thing – the others won't stop.

FREE MAIL-INS

This form of promotion, which often offers a seemingly attractive gift or reward to the customer, is another variant on keeping loyal customers.

In many cases, the free mail-in service simply allows the organisation to send out product or service information to the interested party. This is nearly always given some form of 'added value' by the inclusion of recipes, hints, tips, health-care ideas or some other similar gimmick.

The main point of the exercise is to get the existing or potential customer to make the first contact with the organisation. In this way, the organisation can 'capture' a great deal of information about the customer. The free mail-ins are often accompanied by a fairly comprehensive form or coupon that requires the respondent to give some details about him or herself. This can prove to be invaluable to the organisation in terms of market research, etc. Upon receipt of the free mail-in request, the organisation will promptly send out the required information. This opens a dialogue between the organisation and customer. In turn, the organisation can send other materials to the customer in the hope that this will generate a sale.

A more common alternative to the postal version of the free mail-in is the use of a freephone, or local call system. In a similar way, the customer's details can be logged and used for the organisations benefit at a later date.

LOYALTY INCENTIVES

The Promotion Handling Association contends that the way that loyalty incentives are handled can mean the difference between gaining the customer for life or turning him or her off the product for life. When a customer gets involved in a loyalty incentive sales promotion, it is often the start of an on-going relationship with the organisation or the end of a long-term history of purchases.

There is no fool-proof method of making sure that the loyalty incentive scheme will work. If the customer does not receive the gifts or rewards when he or she expects them, then complaints and bad feelings are inevitable. A hot-line is one way of handling this aspect of the operation. When things do go wrong, the organisation needs to have a plan to save the situation and retain that loyalty despite the difficulties.

The Persil Fun-Fit scheme aimed to promote the concept of fun and fitness for children. It began with the collection of on-pack points that could be redeemed for sports equipment. Some 33,000 registered organisations could also buy certificates and badges to reward children's efforts. When things did go wrong, the organisation wrote and apologised to those who complained. Often as not, the complainant wrote back and thanked the organisation for the prompt reply and apology.

The Casa Buitoni Club has 70,000 members. Each receives a monthly newsletter and can call a freephone number for advice and information on pasta cooking. The newsletter not only gets a good response from the members in terms of calls, but also ensures that the customers keep buying the products.

Getting things in the post is exciting. If a loyalty scheme only offers poor quality rewards and gifts, then the gift is undervalued. It is important to make sure that the gifts are worth having.

Many loyalty schemes are run by specialist fulfilment houses on behalf of the promoting organisation. They have sophisticated data bases and are well versed in the needs of customers. Computer technology is at the heart of all good loyalty schemes. In situations when there are large volumes of goods that need to be in the right place at the right time, computer technology is the only real way of ensuring that this happens.

Shell Smart cards, another loyalty programme, reward customers for buying forecourt products with a range of gifts. This provides Shell with very detailed data on the purchasing habits of the customers at each of the Shell outlets. The benefits, therefore, are two-fold. First, the customer is made to feel valued and is rewarded for his or her loyalty. Secondly, the organisation has the advantage of a 'captured' section of the buying group and can collect vital marketing information.

TARGET AUDIENCE

SOCIO-ECONOMIC GROUP, AGE, LIFESTYLE, AND GENDER

As we have seen in the previous Element, there are a number of ways of identifying the target audience for a particular product or service. Just how successful the techniques we have mentioned above are, in terms of accurately identifying and influencing the target market, can be somewhat debatable.

Any organisation that claims to be market orientated will have a clear idea of what their principal targets may be. The trick is to make sure that any promotional activity addresses the needs of the customer type and fits in with the customer profile.

In considering the question of **socio-economic groups**, we need to understand the differing attitudes of the various segments of society. As we have seen earlier in this Unit, we can make some sweeping judgements about what will, and what will not appeal to

Focus study

TARGET AUDIENCE

American jeans manufacturers used to sell their products by trading in the concept of the 'American Dream'. They have radically changed their approach to try to cash in on the new images of life and society in general. One series of advertisement for Pepe Jeans, costing some £10m. Europe-wide, features very negative and depressing views on life. Centring on such concepts as teenage suicide and hanging parents' cars from a crane over a dock and with absolutely no use of chart-potential music, the aim is to shock. The designers of the advertisements claim that if the parents of the target market (teenagers) knew what their children really thought then they would realise that the advertisements reflect reality.

Before the age of 12, most children wear own-label jeans. The same is true for the over 35s. Pepe contend that their targeting is based more on attitude than on age. The core market, for them, is 12 to 25.

Levi's aim at a slightly older market, between 20 and 35, although the core is 12 to 25.

Wrangler identifies its core market as the 20s to 30s. Their 'City Slickers' campaign, with the actress putting out a flaming hay bale with her jeans, focused on the practical nature of the clothing and not the fashion aspect. In this respect, the advertisements have done well. The use of a woman as the principal in the advertisement has led to a 140 per cent increase in the sales of Wrangler jeans to women.

The UK denim market is worth over £900m. per year. Levi has a 22.6 per cent share, Wrangler a 6.4 per cent share and Pepe a 6 per cent share.

different people. Perhaps in no other major method of segmentation can we see the divide in society, both in real terms and in the ways in which advertisers perceive the differences.

Remember that this classification does not only refer to the existence or lack of money. Socio-economic factors are far more deep rooted than that. Your background, education and other factors can have a great impact on your outlook on life and your buying behaviour too. Advertisers have not been slow to recognise this, and they will attempt to use different techniques to try to attract the various groups in a multitude of different ways. Indeed, versions of the same product are produced for the consumption of individuals in different socio-economic groups. The placement, approach and style of advertisements are tailor-made to suit the particular (supposed) differences between the classes. After all, class is still the criterion we are talking about when we consider socio-economic classifications.

student activity

(PC 3.3.3)

Try to identify at least three products that appeal to different socio-economic groups. You may have to refer back to the section on socio-economic classifications to remind yourself of them. Once you have identified these products, think about how the promotional and advertising techniques differ to cater for each of the socio-economic groups. How appropriate are they for these groups?

student activity

(PC 3.3.3)

Consider the denim advertisements on TV, in magazines and on poster sites. Do you think that they are aimed at your particular age group? What are the features of the advertisements that either appeal to you, or do not appeal at all?

Age, as we have seen earlier in this Unit and in the last Focus Study, can clearly determine the nature of an organisation's promotional activities. The organisation running the promotion makes certain assumptions. Obviously, it seeks to attempt to appeal to the different age groups in different ways. Whilst free gifts, personalities and film tie-ins may appeal to the younger age groups, price and special offers may be appropriate for the older target groups.

Lifestyle may be linked to the socio-economic grouping of the target audience. Again, some assumptions are made. Families will be targeted with special offers, convenience and health. The young, with a lifestyle of their own, may be attracted by exciting advertisements and special promotions linked to their leisure interests. There is the presumption that the older and more steady your lifestyle the more comfortable and 'safe' you want your products to be.

With regard to **gender**, there is a whole industry building up to market products and services to women. It has now been recognised, and none too early, that women are not just interested in how their washing powder performs when faced with 'those hard to remove stains'.

Focus study

TARGET AUDIENCES: WOMEN

The infamous advertisement that features a woman eating a Cadbury's Flake may not, on first impressions, appeal to women. It does. Not for the rather sexist reasons it may appeal to men, but because women perceive the advertisement in a different way to men. They see the woman as being the focus of the advertisement. They see a woman who is indulging herself and relaxing.

The Gossard Wonderbra advertisement carries the line 'say goodbye to your feet'. This advertisement, with few complaints and lots of awards, is very successful.

On the other hand, this move towards female-orientated advertisements can go wrong. An advertisement which carried the line 'at last a turbo for women drivers' did not refer to a car, but to a vacuum cleaner. Someone, somewhere, had not got the right idea at all.

3.3.4 Evaluate the effect of marketing communications on product performance

In assessing product performance in relation to the chosen marketing communication method, there are a number of factors to consider. The first of these is that of product performance itself. As we will soon see, successful product performance is the principal measure of effectiveness since it involves the following:

- sales level
- repeat sales
- customer loyalty
- brand loyalty
- product awareness

Whilst many of these factors can be considered in their own right, they are part of the overall product life cycle. As we will see at the end of this performance criterion, there are significant reasons for the product to show specific characteristics at various stages of its existence.

PRODUCT PERFORMANCE

An organisation needs to see an appreciable change during and after a particular advertising or promotional campaign. Without some measurement of success or failure, the organisation will not know whether the campaign has worked or not.

One of the most popular and workable ways of measuring product performance is to adopt the Boston Consultancy Group's model of product definitions. In essence, the categories attempt to measure the market share against the growth of the market.

As you can see from Figure 3.3.8, four categories of product have been identified. These are:

1 *Stars* – these are products that have cost considerable amounts of money to launch successfully into the market-place. Once they are there, the performance of the product is good, with good cash returns. In reality, although they provide good returns, they only cover expenditure on the product in terms of marketing budgets. Note that these products perform well in a growing market.

2 *Cash cows* – these products have a high market share, despite the fact that the market is no longer growing at a good rate. Although the product may need advertising and promotional support, the product delivers a good level of return. The balance is definitely positive and the product is putting cash back into the organisation. This type of product provides most of an organisation's profit. The product may have been a Star in the past and has successfully made the transition into a Cash cow.

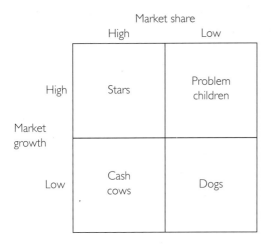

FIG. 3.3.8 *The Boston Consultancy Group product evaluation matrix.*

3 *Problem children* – despite the fact that the market is growing well, these products are not performing well. Regardless of the investments made in terms of advertising and promotion, these products are marginal and a constant drain on the resources of the organisation.

4 *Dogs* – against a back-drop of a poor market, these products are performing spectacularly badly. These, too, are a drain on the resources of the organisation. These products have probably never performed well and are unlikely ever be viable.

Another way of looking at the performance of a product is to consider the nature of the expected sales and market share against the reality of the situation. We will look at this aspect after we have investigated the following Focus Study.

student activity

(PC 3.3.4, COM 3.2, 3.3, AON 3.1, IT 3.1, 3.2)
Using the data in the Focus Study, try to assess the effectiveness of the advertising budget against the advertisement recall (the ability of the viewer to remember the advertisement) and the market share.

To aid you in your assessment of the figures, draw a bar chart that superimposes the three sets of figures. Once you have done this, word process a memorandum for the attention of a marketing director of a new brand of washing powder. Your memorandum should outline the lessons that can be learned from the data.

Focus study

PRODUCT PERFORMANCE

The success of the low-spending Daz washing powder brand shows that some high-profile advertising can radically change the fortunes of a product. Even in this very competitive market, where brand loyalty is high and purchasers invariably are immune to advertising, there is some hope, as Table 3.3.8 illustrates.

TABLE 3.3.8 *The washing powder market*

Product name	Market share (%)	Advertisement recall (%)	Annual expenditure (£)
Persil	28	48	23,187,000
Ariel	26	43	23,601,000
Daz	20	54	12,610,000
Bold	14	25	7,311,000
Sainsbury	9	–	–
Radion	5	26	4,892,000
Fairy	5	8	6,922,000
Other own label	5	–	–
Surf	4	16	4,457,000
None	–	9	–

The Danny Baker campaign, run by Daz, is top of the league as far as recall is concerned. Daz, however, spend less than half the money that Persil and Ariel invest. Daz has benefited more than any other brand from the desire to be different. A third of all purchasers stated that this was the reason for buying the product.

SALES LEVELS (VOLUME, VALUE, GROWTH)

As we mentioned in the last section, there are a number of different ways of assessing the performance of a product. Remember that we are assessing this performance against the impact of the marketing communication methods that have been employed by the organisation. We can best begin by simply listing the most common evaluation methods:

● what were the expected sales and profit figures?
● what is the relative market share and how was this affected by the campaign?
● what are the current and supposed threats in the future to the long-term prospects of the product?

Let us briefly analyse these concerns and try to address the question of product performance in terms of the more measurable data such as sales figure and market share.

When we consider the **expected sales and profits**, we need to look at the prior performance as well as the projected. In this respect, the organisation needs to know the performance levels of the product before, during and after the campaign. By keeping a close eye on these, the organisation will be able to assess whether the product has been significantly affected by the campaign itself. Against this, there are the movements in the size and needs of the market. The wise analyst will be able to filter these out and give a clearer idea of the actual impact.

The **market share** question is always an important one. Without an advertising or promotional campaign, the product may begin to lose its share of the market. The question is, will the product actually gain any market share by the use of a campaign? It is certain that the product will begin to disappear from the minds of the customers if the product is not marketed.

The **potential threats** to the product are a very real and constant danger. New technology, as well as new competitors, may affect the standing of the product. Equally, if customer spending patterns change, then the volume of sales and overall profitability may be affected.

student activity

(PC 3.3.4, COM 3.1)
Looking at the market share in the Focus Study, do you think that Sainsbury will automatically bounce into second place? How do you think that the acquisition of the Texas chain will affect the profitability of the Homebase operation? Do you also think that the imminent arrival of a major new competitor will drastically affect the balance of power in the market? Discuss these questions in pairs.

REPEAT SALES

Typically, we can identify the repeat sales potential of the products offered by an organisation in terms of the nature of the buying habits of its customers. There are three main categories of customer in this respect. These are the primaries, the secondaries and the tertiaries. The classifications should not be confused with the industrial sectors of the economy; they have a very different meaning. Let's have a look at the nature of these three different customer groupings:

Focus study

SALES LEVELS

The DIY retailing business can be a very risky one. Many of the organisations involved have seriously misjudged the market. With Sainsbury's move to buy Texas, there may be a new casualty. Sainsbury's own some 82 stores; to consider buying the 200 Texas stores is perhaps one step too many.

Table 3.3.9 shows the current market share (before Sainsbury's purchase of Texas) in 1994:

TABLE 3.3.9 *Current market share of DIY stores (per cent)*

B&Q	15.0
Texas	9.0
Do It All	5.1
Homebase (Sainsbury's)	3.6
Great Mills	2.7
Wickes	2.7
Fads	1.5
Focus	0.8
Other DIY retailers	59.6

In 1993, Texas only managed to produce £7.8m. profit on £690m. turnover. The expected price for the takeover is around £150m. The owners of Texas, Ladbrooke, may be rather canny individuals. The expected arrival on the DIY scene of the American giant, Home Depot, may radically change the face of DIY retailing in the UK. It is suggested that many of the operators of stores could not survive in a new, revitalised, competitive market-place.

1 *The primaries* – these customers form the hard core of the repeat sales. After going to some expense to actually get these customers in the first place, organisations can rely on the primaries as their main source of regular income. These customers may be few in number, but they are very valuable to the organisation. These individuals invariably make repeat purchases, and it is mainly to keep them that the organisation offers customer incentives and loyalty rewards.

2 *The secondaries* – although there are more of these, the secondaries tend to be irregular purchasers and, as such, occasionally make repeat purchases. Again, this group is valuable and is usually the target of the organisation's advertising campaigns.

3 *The tertiaries* – these are the majority of potential customers that do not purchase from the organisation very regularly at all. These individuals, often difficult

to target in advertising terms, and not really interested in targeted sales promotions, seem immune to many of the marketing techniques of the organisation. The best that the organisation can hope for is to convert these into secondaries.

As you can see from Figure 3.3.9, the primaries tend to be mostly in the loyal and habituals categories. For a full description of the categories mentioned in the figure, see the section on customer loyalty on p.268. The majority of secondaries tend to be either habituals or variety seekers. The tertiaries, on the other hand, are more likely to be variety seekers or switchers. If we consider this figure in terms of repeat sales, we can see that the primaries and the secondaries offer the best opportunities to gain repeat sales. The tertiaries are a dead loss, there is little chance of convincing them to become more loyal.

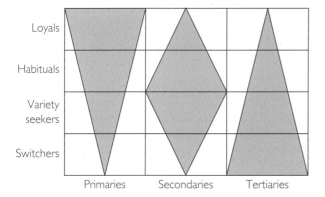

FIG. 3.3.9 *Repeat sales cross referencing loyalty and customer type.*

student activity

(PC 3.3.4, COM 3.2, AON 3.3)
As you will see from Figure 3.3.9, there are some lessons to be learnt in terms of the targeting of marketing techniques towards the different categories.
  Draw up a chart which identifies the type of marketing communication that would be most appropriate for each of the categories cross referenced in the figure.

BRAND LOYALTY

If you want loyalty, buy a dog! This is the practical philosophy adopted by marketing experts. There are some

TABLE 3.3.10 *Aspects of brand loyalty*

Measure/indicator	Loyalty level		
	High	Average	Low
Full-time workers	yes		
Part-time workers			yes
Unemployed		yes	
No children	yes		
Has children			yes
Male		yes	
Female			yes
Unmarried	yes		
Married		yes	
Hectic lifestyle			yes
Steady lifestyle	yes		
Late afternoon shopper	yes		
Evening shopper		yes	
Morning shopper			yes
Saturday shopper	yes		
Weekday shopper		yes	
As & Bs★			yes
Cs★	yes		
Ds & Es★		yes	

★ socio-economic groupings

student activity

(PC 3.3.4, COM 3.2)
What can the information in Table 3.3.10 tell us about the nature of the brand-loyal customer? What are the major measures and indicators? Write a profile of the typical loyal, fairly loyal and disloyal customer using this table.

very interesting aspects to the nature of brand loyalty, and we have attempted to distil these into Table 3.3.10.
  The brand label wars have over-spilled into new areas of conflict. In past years, the various brand names fought it out in the supermarket and other retail outlets across the world. Now there is a new threat to the long-term viability of the brand name, that even threatens their existence. The emergence of the 'own label' or product ranges carrying the name of a supermarket chain, are cutting very deeply into the market share of the branded products.

Focus study

BRAND LOYALTY

The 1994 the fourth quarter profits of Coca-Cola showed an operating profit of £530m. This was on an annual sales income of £2.4bn. Consumption of the products made by Coca-Cola have risen by some 750m. units in the same period. Against this rather good set of figures is a cloud building above the Coca-Cola giant.

During 1994, own-label products have taken 6.7 per cent of Coke's market share. At the same time, Pepsi has lost 1.6 per cent. Coke took immediate action with a £4m. advertising campaign in the run-up to the 1994 Christmas period. It was aimed at Sainsbury's Classic Cola and Virgin Cola, amongst many other contenders.

student activity

(PC 3.3.4)
If you were in charge of Coke's massive advertising budget, what would you do to try and arrest the gains of the own-label brands?

CUSTOMER LOYALTY

In order to retain the customers that it may have acquired, it is essential that an organisation creates a sustainable improvement programme. The key factors of this retention are:

● to have the **right kind of customer** – who is responsive and feels valued at all times
● to have the **right products** – that are appropriate for the customer and match the strengths and weaknesses of the organisation itself
● to have the **right distribution channels** – that are appropriate to the needs of the customers and are responsive to any changes that they may require
● to have the **right customer service** – that is responsive, clear and courteous
● to have **loyal employees** – who wholeheartedly endorse and carry out the organisation's policies and procedures, and at times work on their own initiative
● to carry out **'defector' analysis** – that aims to identify the reasons behind a customer switching from the organisation to another supplier

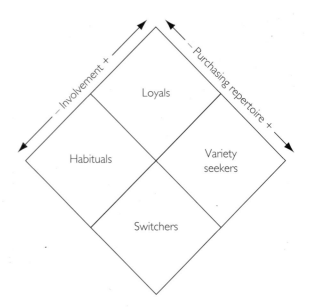

FIG. 3.3.10 *Customer purchasing styles.*

The classifications or categories featured in Figure 3.3.10 need some explanation. The definitions of the terms used are:

1 *Loyals* – these are customers who are the hard core of the organisation's customer base. These individuals remain loyal to the product or product range and need to be occasionally rewarded for their loyalty. They tend to feel involved in the product as they recognise it as reflecting their needs, lifestyle and way of life. The purchasing repertoire, or the number of different products that they buy within a certain category of products, is low. In other words, they tend to stick with the same product and rarely experiment with alternatives.

2 *Habituals* – these are customers who invariably purchase a particular brand or product. They feel that the product broadly addresses their needs and do not tend to experiment very often with alternative products.

3 *Variety seekers* – these customers tend not to be very loyal. In fact they have many of the characteristics of switchers, but are not so unpredictable. They feel that they need to 'ring the changes' from time to time. In this respect, they are reasonably good customers who could be tempted to try another brand if there was a special promotion or some other incentive.

4 *Switchers* – these customers are only occasional purchasers of the brand or product. They experiment with a variety of different brands and display little sign of loyalty to any of them. They are unpredictable and may be influenced by the most mundane and seemingly unimportant reasons.

We will be addressing some specific methods of ensuring customer satisfaction in Element 4 of this Unit.

PRODUCT LIFE CYCLES

As we saw in the first Element of this Unit, considerable thought needs to be given to the introduction of a new product into the market-place. The product life cycle itself is an excellent way of trying to make plans. It should be recognised that, except in some circumstances, a product has a limited life span. In other words, there is going to be a point in the future when the product is no longer in demand by the customer.

This life span has very definite phases; from a beginning of zero sales, the product will pass through a period when the sales are increasing, then a 'plateau' will be reached. Finally, the product's popularity will fade away into nothingness. The typical life cycle of a product is illustrated in Figure 3.3.11.

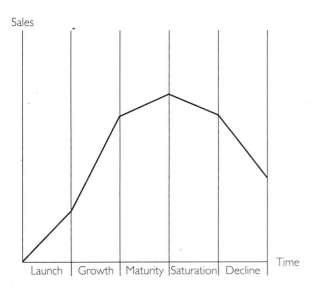

FIG. 3.3.11 *Standard product life cycle.*

The stages or phases of the product life cycle can be defined in the following manner:

1 *Launch* – in this first phase the marketing activity needs to be intense. A great deal of the organisation's time and resources needs to be invested during this period to ensure that the product gains acceptance in the market-place. The growth in sales is slow, but gradually gains pace as customers become aware of the product.

2 *Growth* – the sales are rising more quickly now. The product is heading to the point where profits are reaching a maximum. The marketing activity still needs to be high as this is the point when new competitors may enter the market and abruptly end the growth period of the product.

3 *Maturity* – by this phase the majority of the customers have embraced the product and are steadily making repeat purchases. More new competitors are entering the market-place and the organisation needs to continue to support the product to ensure that this maturity period does not come to a premature end.

4 *Saturation* – at this phase of the life cycle, the product has normally reached its full potential and the maturity period is now over. The impact of the competitors is beginning to bite into sales and the organisation will notice a dip in sales and volume. The organisation will have a choice here. If it chooses to allow the cycle to continue on its 'natural' course, then the product will move into the decline phase. On the other hand, the organisation may choose to give extra support to the product, which may mean that it has every chance of returning to maturity, or indeed, of entering a new growth period. We will look at this aspect after we have considered some of the life-cycle variants.

5 *Decline* – the product has now become rather staid or old-fashioned. The customers have moved over to other, newer, products and are steadily abandoning the original. By this stage, if the organisation has had its wits about it, it will have introduced a new or improved version of the product and this would have begun its own new life cycle. Again, we will return to this aspect shortly

As you can imagine, a number of variations can occur in a product life cycle. Not everything goes to plan, and some products have a very short or long life cycle. We will now look at the variations. These are very roughly based on the work carried out by Cordon and Raybaud:

1 *Slow-take-off life cycles* – this type of product takes an extremely long time to have any significant impact on the market or the potential customer. A good example of this would be the CD, which took a long time to overtake the LP or the cassette. It has now, effectively, taken over the market – until the next item of technology gains acceptance.

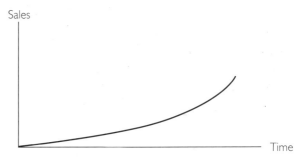

FIG. 3.3.12 *A slow-take-off life cycle.*

2 *Immediate success life cycles* – these are usually very innovative and exciting new products. They immediately capture the imagination of customers and achieve 'overnight' success. A very good example of this would be the National Lottery or a new drug that tackles a previously 'untreatable' illness.

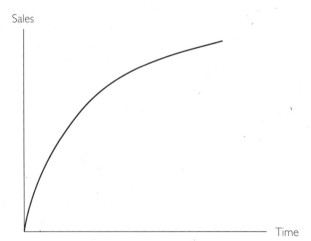

FIG. 3.3.13 *Immediate success life cycle.*

3 *Burn-out life cycles* – these products, although gaining significant market penetration in the beginning, fall off in popularity very quickly. Typically, these would include gimmicky products or products that only are applicable to particular occasions. Good examples of these would be World Cup merchandise or (if you can remember them) deeli-boppers. These were head bands with balls or shapes on the end of long springs!

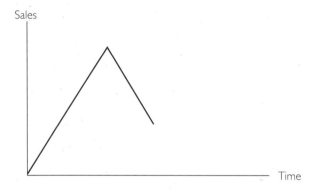

FIG. 3.3.14 *A burn-out life cycle.*

4 *Devotee life cycles* – these products gain considerable popularity for a time and then fade off to a residual level of popularity. The classic example of these is skateboards, which have had great success in the past, but now only a few people are still buying them. There were a number of skateboard shops around the country, but now only a handful still survive. Another good example was the metal detector.

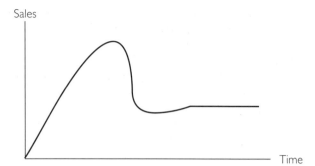

FIG. 3.3.15 *A devotee life cycle.*

5 *Failed life cycles* – these products are basically flops. They may have gained momentary interest and sales, but quickly fell away into obscurity. The classic example of these would be the Sinclair C5, or perhaps more controversially, the black Action Man doll.

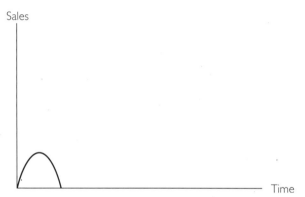

FIG. 3.3.16 *A failed life cycle.*

6 *Long life cycles* – these are the products that every organisation dreams about. They just go on and on. Sales continue to be strong over a considerable period of time and only seem to waver when a new competitor comes on to the market. The organisation responds with more advertising or a sales promotion and the product quickly responds in turn. Products such as the Mars Bar or certain car models are good examples.

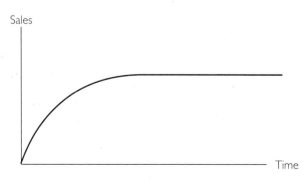

FIG. 3.3.17 *A long life cycle.*

7 *Relaunch life cycles* – these products gain the necessary support from the organisation in times of need. When the product begins to look as if it is heading into saturation or decline, the organisation promptly relaunches it. Perhaps this involves a new campaign or new packaging, but the underlying popularity is maintained. Good examples of these types of product include Cider brands and Ribena.

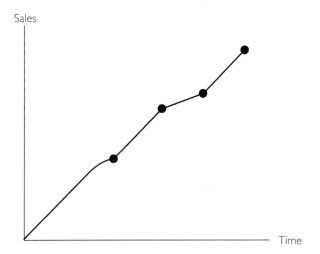

FIG. 3.3.18 *A relaunch life cycle.*

8 *Hiccup life cycles* – with these products there are two main reasons for the apparent initial failure of the product. There may have been an ill-considered or poor marketing campaign that failed to capture the imagination of the public. Alternatively, the product may have been introduced at a time when there was significant marketing activity by the existing brands in the market place. Examples of these include Pepsi Max and Seven Up. Each had a rather shaky start and needed to be relaunched a number of times.

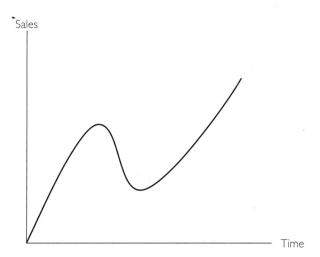

FIG. 3.3.19 *A hiccup life cycle.*

9 *Seasonal life cycles* – obviously, there are some products that only sell at particular times of the year. The organisations that produce them are geared up to bring their marketing campaigns into action in the lead-up to each of the applicable periods in the year. Fireworks manufacturers advertise and expect sales in October and November, Christmas cards only sell (in great numbers, unless you buy surplus stock in January!) during November and December. Sun-tan lotion (normally) only sells in the run-up to the summer holiday period.

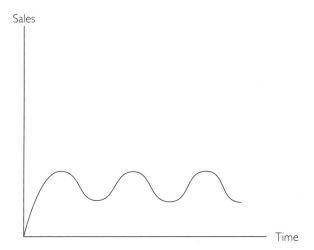

FIG. 3.3.20 *A seasonal life cycle.*

Obviously, most organisations are not stupid enough to let their products reach a terminal stage of their life cycle without making plans. This means that the organisation needs to have a series of products ready to 'phase in' at particular times so that the life expectancies of the products overlap. In Figure 3.3.21, we have tried to illustrate this point.

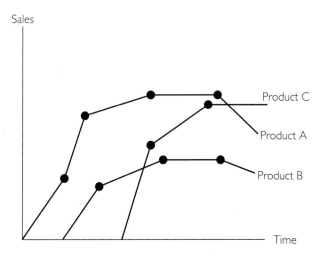

FIG. 3.3.21 *Multiple life cycles.*

student activity

(PC 3.3.4, COM 3.1)

As a group, discuss the following statement after having identified at least one more example of a product that would fit each of the above variations of life cycles:

'an organisation that is faced with the prospect of a failure in sales terms has neither carried out enough market research, nor has sufficiently supported the product with a marketing budget'

Using the technique of multiple life cycles, an organisation can ensure that at least one of its products is enjoying popularity, and consequently high sales, at a time when another product is in decline. The organisation can then 'switch' its support to the successful or 'newer' product. It should also be remembered that some of the products may carry out the same function. With regard to the products illustrated in Figure 3.3.21, Product A may be the same as Product C while Product B may be a failed replacement for Product A.

student activity

1:00

(PC 3.3.4, AON 3.1, 3.2, 3.3)

Draw a similar graph to that in Figure 3.3.21 using the same kind of ideas for the following products:

- Product A – achieves high sales very quickly, then reaches a plateau and stays there
- Product B – has a slow sales growth, reaches a short plateau, then fades off
- Product C – has a slow sales growth, reaches a low plateau, then is relaunched and exceeds Product A before reaching a new plateau

Stagger the release of each of the products by six months.

PRODUCT AWARENESS

Product awareness, at least in terms of the customer, can be looked at in a variety of different ways. Perhaps the best way to start looking at this aspect of product performance is to consider the model called the innovation adoption model (see Figure 3.3.22). This is a method of measuring the way in which customers are willing to accept and try out a new product.

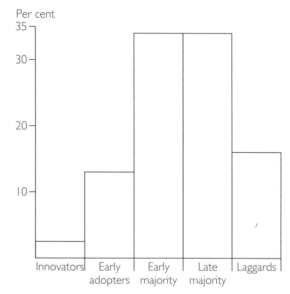

FIG. 3.3.22 *Everest Roger's innovation adoption model for new products.*

Let's have a look at the classifications in Figure 3.3.22 in a little more detail:

1 *Innovators* – these are the people who are the first to purchase a new product, particularly in the case of new technology such as CDs, DAT and satellite dishes. In many respects these are techno-freaks or 'trendies' who really must be the first to buy or try a product. They will often buy a product even before it is advertised as they may be keen on keeping an eye open for new innovations and ideas.

2 *Early adopters* – this larger group of customers is still ahead of the majority of the population. They tend to buy very early, but only after the product has been on the market for a few weeks. They usually buy after the product has received initial reviews or has been featured in the media as a new innovation. Typically, their purchases would be made in the first few days of the advertising campaign for the product.

3 *Early/late majority* – these are the bulk of the purchasers of the product. The early majority are just ahead of the rest in becoming owners or users of the product. The bulk of purchases would be made in the first few weeks of the product's availability. For the late majority, this would mean purchasing the product after the launch and into the main (continuing) advertising campaign for the product. They would normally only buy when the product has 'proved' itself in the market-place.

4 *Laggards* – this group, significantly large, embraces the product after the rest of the customers have either tired of it, or have been using it for some time. These people would be purchasing technology and other durables well into the product's life cycle. In this respect, the laggards may be just the people who will ensure that the product has a continued life expectancy.

Product awareness, in itself, is the key purpose of the marketing communications process. As we saw in the previous section of this Element, the product life cycle amply explains the nature of product awareness. Above all, it also shows clearly the acceptability of the product in terms of whether the customer is willing to purchase it.

3.3.5 *Explain the growth in direct marketing methods in terms of customer need and new technology*

DIRECT MARKETING METHODS

Many businesses have recognised the importance of talking to their customers directly. The recent growth of retail store cards and affiliated credit cards (like GM's credit cards) have helped direct marketing to grow by 70 per cent in the past five years.

One of the more interesting angles in the growth of direct marketing is the emergence of relationship marketing. This means that a business attempts to sell a range of other products to a customer with whom it has already formed a link. This can mean a life-long partnership between the business and the customer, obviously a desirable thing.

The key to success is the identification of the customer's buying behaviour and a knowledge of his or her aspirations. Smart cards, for example, give instant information about the buying habits of the customer and directly reward him or her for staying loyal to the business.

The growth of 0800 and 0345 numbers shows that advertisers are beginning to become aware of the possibilities in this area. This is a vital, and efficient, method of attaining a direct response from the customer.

The growth of direct mail, for example, amply shows the emergence of this form of marketing as a force to be reckoned with:

1988	£550m.
1989	£780m.
1990	£980m.
1991	£900m.
1992	£950m.
1993	£910m.

DIRECT MAIL

Direct mail only becomes junk mail when it is badly targeted. Direct mailings have a rather mixed reputation in the minds of most people. Statistics from the Direct Mail Information Service reported that in 1985 some 83 per cent of consumers who opened a direct mail package did not read it. Ten years later, the figure is almost exactly the same. This should be considered in the light of the fact that targeting is supposed to be more accurate and other aspects of direct mailings have been improved. Something is going wrong.

Business-to-business direct mailing has an even worse record. In 1991, around 88 per cent of the mail was opened and not read, and in 1993 the figure had only dropped to 84 per cent. In 1991, direct mail to other businesses achieved a pitiful 2 per cent response rate. This figure fell to a low of 1 per cent in 1994.

Direct mail, it is argued, is not often seen as an integral part of the marketing mix. Direct mail departments are often operating in isolation. This is borne out by the fact that many businesses which have trading relations with another business receive direct mail urging them to become a customer. The destination of this mail is always the bin.

Direct mail is considered to be a tactical medium. It is aimed at responding to competitors in ways that advertising cannot. Most direct mail campaigns are measured only in terms of how many responses they generate, but a longer-term view needs to be taken.

Rather than being a 'cold mailing' device, in the sense that the business is mailing out to non-customers, direct mail should be used to reinforce existing relationships. When this is the philosophy, then the letter-opening percentage is far higher.

Focus study

DIRECT MAIL

The businesses that are more successful in direct mailings tend to be those that send out increasingly smaller volumes, rather than try to blanket the whole population. The latter is expensive and brings a low percentage of responses.

The Royal Mail, for example, has managed response rates of around 10–20 per cent. This is based on mailings of under a thousand each time, rather than 50,000 plus. They claim that good response rates are reliant on making sure that the mailing talks to the customer directly and addresses his/her concerns and needs. Good direct mail needs to be creative and not the tired old thick package of pre-printed sales letters.

TELE-MARKETING

Tele-marketing is the systematic use of the telephone to achieve business objectives in sales, customer care, market growth, promotions, market research and database building. Quite a complex concept? Many businesses are taking the plunge and developing tele-marketing operations, but the set-up costs are very high. There are two basic choices: should the business attempt to do it in-house or should it use one of the growing number of agencies that offer the service?

Setting up a tele-marketing operation involves recruitment, training, equipment and software. In addition the structure of the organisation needs to be reconsidered as many businesses are unsure of where the tele-marketing effort fits into traditional structures.

Agencies can earn quite a lot of money by running a pilot tele-marketing exercise for their clients, and they then follow this up with consultancy work advising them on how to set up and run the operations in-house. Starting small has definite advantages: the key is gradually to build up the data base and the relationship with the customers.

The Automobile Association (AA) runs one of the biggest tele-marketing operations in the UK, but was very cautious when it started. It began by using the tele-marketing method to gain membership renewals and recognised the advantages of having started the operations in-house. The AA recognised that if it used an agency, there was a time lag between the agency and the Association, and this could cause problems.

The greatest uses of tele-marketing are in:

- direct response television advertising
- product recall lines
- membership renewals

The extremely sophisticated software available allows the caller to be able to cope with the most difficult calls.

Personalised telephone marketing can make a customer feel cared for and can help the business retain that person's loyalty. Just as badly targeted direct mail can become regarded as junk mail, telephone marketing is only intrusive when the person picking up the phone does not understand the reason for the call.

Research has shown that 68 per cent of customers do not make repeat purchases after the initial purchase. Tele-marketing aims to address this and tries to make the customer pleased that the business has taken the time and effort to make the follow-up call. Less than half a per cent of tele-marketing calls, on the follow-up basis, are refused by the customer. The positive benefits can mean as much as a 40 per cent increase in repeat business from tele-marketing. In this respect, tele-marketing is well worth considering.

Focus study

The Bank of Scotland use a 'predictive dialler' for making tele-marketing calls. This computerised system automatically works its way through a list of contact numbers. It screens out engaged numbers and unanswered calls. This cuts out any frustration for diallers, as well as putting up on the screen the customers' account details for reference. The system is very sophisticated: it can even avoid ringing women when a soap opera is being shown on TV! It also blocks out calls to men when there are sports programmes on TV. The predictive dialler system has increased the number of contacts per operator per hour from eight to 40.

It has been recognised that the integration of mailings and tele-marketing is essential. A follow-up call after a mailing has been sent, or a call then the mail-out, further increases the probability of creating business. An outbound call costs around £6, compared to £1 for a mailing, so the strategy of using tele-marketing has to be worked out thoroughly to cover the high expenses.

SELLING OFF-SCREEN

The tele-marketing industry that relates to television advertising is another growing marketing area. Some 15 per cent of all advertisements on TV carry a telephone number. The UK is still well behind some other countries in the development of this field of sales. In the USA, for example, tele-marketing has penetrated some 54 per cent of all TV advertisements. Indeed, if you include all of the shopping channels in the USA, it has been estimated that some 28 per cent of all air-time (i.e. total of all advertisements and programmes screened) is related to DRTV (Direct Response Television). The response to advertisements tends to happen in the first 12 minutes after the advertisement has been screened; after this period the response dies away. It is, therefore, very important that the technology used to 'capture' the enquiries or orders is up to the job. Talking computers are fine, but the majority of callers would prefer to speak to a 'real' person. The response levels run to 100 calls per split second and technology is not yet up to that level of activity.

SELLING OFF-PAGE

The big five home shopping, catalogue-based businesses account for some 86 per cent of all sales of this type. These businesses recruit agents who show the catalogue to customers and take orders on the business's behalf. They take delivery from local warehouses, distribute the goods and collect payments. In return, they receive commission and, more importantly, the purchasers get free credit.

This agency cost structure adds about 20 per cent to the price of the goods. This gives them a potential sales disadvantage over other methods of purchasing the same products.

Direct mail-order companies, such as Next Directory, Racing Green, Cotton Traders, Extend, Damart and Kaleidoscope do not pay commission as they have no agents. These are enjoying growth at the moment, at the expense of the bigger operators who still use the agent system.

The 10 largest businesses in this field showed a profit margin of around 17 per cent of turnover (which was £2.81bn.). The more traditional organisations cater to the 25–45 age group, leaving the other, direct-sale, businesses to handle the younger age groups.

3.3.6 Explain the effects on marketing communications of guidelines and controls

GUIDELINES AND CONTROLS

All forms of business activity need to have some guidelines and some degree of control to ensure that customers are protected from unscrupulous organisations. There is nowhere that this is more true than in the field of marketing and advertising. Within this field the following organisations are in the forefront of maintaining guidelines and controls:

- the Advertising Association
- the Incorporated Society of British Advertisers
- the Advertising Standards Authority
- the Market Research Society
- the Chartered Institute of Marketing
- the Office of Fair Trading
- the Association of Household Distributors
- the Association of Media Independents
- the Broadcast Advertising Clearance Centre
- the Cinema Advertising Association
- the Council of Outdoor Specialists
- the Direct Mail Services Standards Board

- the Direct Marketing Association
- the Institute of Practitioners in Advertising
- the Institute of Sales Promotion
- the Mailing Preference Service
- the Mail Order Traders Association
- the Newspaper Publishers Association
- the Newspaper Society
- the Outdoor Advertising Association
- the Periodical Publishers Association
- the Proprietary Association of Great Britain
- Royal Mail Letters
- Scottish Daily Newspaper Society
- the Scottish Newspaper Publishers Association

Whilst some of these organisations are not member-based and may not have an overt written code of practice, they all support the Code of Advertising Practice.

The general subject of consumer protection is worth mentioning here in that many of the concepts and basic rights apply to customers before, during and after a sale has been made. The Office of Fair Trading plays a part in this, promoting the following:

- that any information, or statements about a product or service should not affect the customer adversely
- that in cases when the customer's rights have been infringed the matter should be investigated by the Consumer Protection Advisory Committee
- that all industries should be encouraged to develop a code of practice that all members will adhere to
- that organisations which break any statutory regulations or codes of practice are dealt with
- that the OFT will produce consumer protection literature to ensure that all customers know their rights

We will return to the subject of more general codes of practice at the end of this Element.

ADVERTISING STANDARDS AUTHORITY

The Advertising Standards Authority is the independent self-regulatory body responsible for supervising the content of non-broadcast advertisements in the UK.

Focus study

ADVERTORIALS

The Advertising Standards Authority (ASA) has recently published new guidelines to control the confusion readers may have about these features. The appeal of this form of advertising is that it adds credibility to the business or product being advertised. The market is growing fast, the 1993 figures were up 22.3 per cent.

The ASA has called for greater care to be taken in protecting customers. The term advertorial should not be used when, patently, a feature is an advertisement. It should be labelled as such. The responsibility of assessing the feature is the joint role of the advertiser, the advertising agency and the publisher of the newspaper or magazine.

The ASA goes on to say that such features should be subject to the British Code of Advertising Practice since money has changed hands for the editorial space.

January 1994

CODE
of Conduct

MRS

The Market Research Society

FIG. 3.3.23 *The Market Research Society's Code of Conduct which outlines the rules and responsibilities of those carrying out marketing research.*

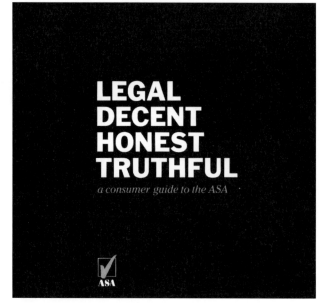

**LEGAL
DECENT
HONEST
TRUTHFUL**

a consumer guide to the ASA

✓
ASA

FIG. 3.3.24 *The Advertising Standards Authority's complaints procedure.*

It is estimated that there are some 25m. advertisements published annually in the UK. The ASA spot-checks thousands of them (and indeed sales promotions) as part of its rigorous monitoring programme.

The ASA also advises thousands of advertisers, agencies and publishers on how to avoid using misleading or offensive advertisements that may lead to complaints being made. The aim is avoidance, since not only are complaints costly but they may involve adverse publicity and criticism of the industry.

The ASA operates on a levy charged on all advertisements. This levy, only 0.1 per cent of the advertisement's cost, is collected on the ASA's behalf by the Advertising Standards Board of Finance. This separation of functions helps to ensure that the ASA maintains its independence.

The ASA has the power to investigate any complaint and to assess the advertisement's compliance with the Code of Advertising Practice (see the next section of this Element). The ASA rarely tells the advertiser to stop the advertisement immediately, as the advertiser is given time to give his or her side of the story.

If the advertisement is found to be unacceptable under the rules of the Code, then the advertiser will be told to withdraw the advertisement or to amend it. Failure to do so will lead to the suspension of the advertiser, or possibly to the withdrawal of privileges and to the publishers of magazines and newspapers being advised not to accept this organisation's advertising.

Further refusal may lead to the advertiser being referred to the OFT for refusing to abide by the Code. Under the Control of Misleading Advertisements Regulations (1988) the organisation can be restrained from using the advertisement ever again.

The ASA covers all advertisements in the following areas of the media and marketing activities:

- newspapers
- magazines
- posters
- direct marketing
- sales promotions
- cinema
- video cassettes
- teletext (not ITV)

Advertisements on TV and cable are covered by the Independent Television Commission. Radio is regulated by the Radio Authority.

Claims made on packets and labels are the preserve of the Trading Standards or Environmental Health Officers.

In conclusion, the ASA deals only with what is written or shown in an advertisement or a promotion. Complaints must be made in writing to the ASA with as much detail about the advertisement as possible (and preferably a copy of the advertisement should be enclosed).

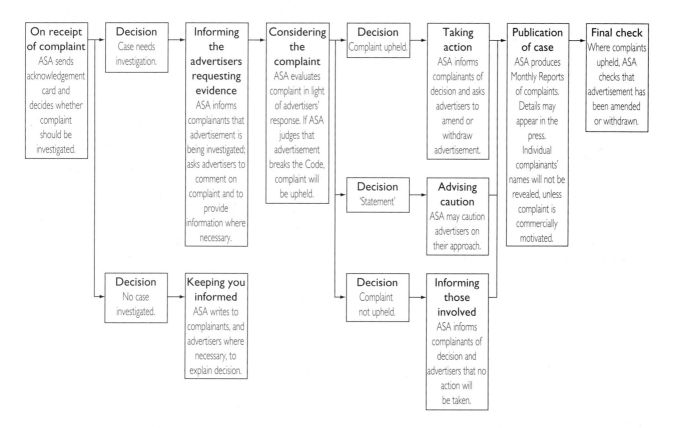

FIG. 3.3.25 *The British Code of Advertising Practice which lays down what is and what is not acceptable in advertisements – from the Advertising Standards Authority's booklet 'Advertising Under Control'.*

Focus study

ADVERTISING STANDARDS AUTHORITY

In March 1995, a much reported case was covered in the marketing press. It involved the advertising strategy of Colgate (run by Colgate Oral Care). It was an example of 'knocking copy', which means that the advertisement openly criticised a competitor. There is nothing particularly odd to that, but it used an advertising slogan used by one of its competitors as part of its advertisement. It stated that Colgate's Plax mouthwash was approved by the British Dental Association and that Listerine (owned by Warner Wellcome Consumer Healthcare) was approved 'by a dragon called Clifford'. Quite amusing in its own right, but it was suggested that the advertisement had broken the British Code of Advertising Practice. Specifically, it states that: 'advertising should not make unfair use of the goodwill attached to the ... advertising campaign of any other business'.

Colgate also faces another problem with the ASA, in that the endorsement by the BDA incurs an annual fee. The ASA states that all financial relationships for product endorsements must be mentioned in the advertisement. It did not. Colgate, meanwhile, was confident that the advertisement was within the spirit and codes of the law.

CODE OF ADVERTISING PRACTICE (CAP)

The full version of the Code of Advertising Practice is included here, but the main points of the Code are:

- that the advertisement should be legal
- that the advertisement should be decent
- that the advertisement should be honest
- that the advertisement should be truthful

When a complaint is received by the ASA, the first thing that it does is to decide whether the complaint needs to be pursued. The ASA will pursue any complaint of an advertisement that breaches any part of the Code. The ASA will not entertain complaints made by competitors unless there is a major breach of the Code. In cases when a member of the public makes a complaint, his or her identity is never revealed.

The advertiser is asked to make comments about the complaint, and at the same time the publishers of the advertisement will be informed that a complaint is being investigated. If the case appears to be particularly serious, then the advertiser will be told to stop the advertisements immediately.

The advertiser must now reply to the accusations. If relevant, he/she must supply proof of any claim made in the advertisement. Once the response from the advertiser has been received, then the next stage is to evaluate his/her comments in the light of the complaint. In some cases, additional evidence may be sought from the complainant or the advertisers, or perhaps the testimony of an expert adviser. At the end of the investigation, the Secretariat submits a recommendation to the ASA Council. A copy of this will be sent to the complainant, the advertiser or the agency.

If the Council's decision is in support of the complaint, then the advertiser will be instructed to withdraw the advertisement in its present form. It should be remembered that all members of the advertising industry have agreed to adhere to the Code. Persistent breaches of the Code will mean referral to the OFT.

CODES OF PRACTICE

As a response to government pressure and indeed pressure from customers, many industries have developed their own codes of practice. These often go beyond the legal requirements and aim to provide a comprehensive set of preventative codes to protect the customer. Many of these codes have been developed in consultation with the OFT and are designed not only for the protection of the customer, but also for the maintenance of the greatest levels of customer satisfaction and peace of mind as possible. A good example of such a code is that of ABTA (Association of British Travel Agents) who offer financial protection to customers who have booked holidays with their members.

The Chartered Institute of Marketing has produced a code of practice which its members are obliged to follow. Indeed, it is a prerequisite of membership that the organisations or individuals must accept this code of practice. The CIM demands the highest levels of professional behaviour of its members, particularly in relation to honesty and integrity at all times.

THE BRITISH CODE OF ADVERTISING PRACTICE

This summary of the Code contains much of its thinking and many of its major rules. Those involved in the preparation of advertisements should refer to the Code in full.

The Code is published by the Committee of Advertising Practice (CAP) for the advertising industry and is supervised by the Advertising Standards Authority.

THE ESSENCE OF GOOD ADVERTISING

All advertisements should be

- legal, decent, honest and truthful
- prepared with a sense of responsibility both to the consumer and to society
- in line with the principles of fair competition generally accepted in business.

INTRODUCTION

The Code is the body of rules by which, the British advertising business has agreed, the overwhelming majority of the advertisements it produces should be regulated. The only substantial group of advertisements not covered by the Code are television, cable and radio commercials, and these are subject to very similar codes operated by the Independent Television Commission and the Radio Authority.

The Code establishes a standard against which any advertisement may be assessed. It is a guide both to those concerned with commissioning, creating and publishing advertisements and to those who believe they may have reason to question what an advertisement says or shows.

The Code is applied in the spirit as well as the letter.

The first edition of the Code was published in 1961. This is the 8th edition.

SCOPE

The Code's rules apply to:

- advertisements in newspapers, magazines and other printed publications
- indoor and outdoor posters and other outdoor advertisements, including aerial advertisements
- cinema and video-cassette commercials
- advertisements on viewdata services, excluding those on ITV
- advertising material such as brochures and leaflets or newspaper/magazine inserts.

- list and database management in direct marketing.

*The Code's rules do **not** apply to:*

- broadcast commercials on TV, radio and cable
- advertisements in media principally intended for circulation outside the UK
- advertisements addressed to members of the medical and allied professions in their professional capacities.

Communications and material of the following kinds are not regarded as advertisements for the purposes of this Code:

- statutory, public, police and other official notices
- material published as a matter of record only
- non-advertising matter (eg works of art) exhibited on billboards or other advertising sites used primarily for advertisements
- private correspondence, as distinguished from personalised or individually addressed circulars
- oral communications, including telephone calls
- press releases and other public relations material

- the contents of books and of press editorial columns, even if either has the outward semblance of advertising material
- packages, wrappers, labels, tickets and the like, except to the extent that either:

a) they advertise a sales promotion, or a product other than the one they contain, or are attached to, or

b) they are depicted in an advertisement, in which case any words, pictures etc which are reproduced in a legible or otherwise comprehensible manner are subject to the Code.

Material which is not shown (eg because it is on the opposite side of a pack to that depicted) is not subject to this Code, though it may entail obligations under the British Code of Sales Promotion Practice.

DEFINITIONS

For the purposes of the Code

- A *product* is anything that is capable of forming the subject matter of an advertisement. It is most often a tangible object of trade, but may also be, for example, a service or facility, an idea, a cause or an opportunity
- A *consumer* means any person likely to be reached by a given advertisement (and not only a member of the general public, or one of those directly addressed)

- A *claim* is to be understood as applying to both express and implied claims.

INTERPRETATION

The opinion of the ASA on any matter concerning the interpretation of the Code is final.

Conformity with the Code is assessed in the light of an advertisement's probable effect when taken as a whole, and in context. In applying these criteria, particular attention is paid to:

- the characteristics of the likely audience for the advertisement
- the medium by means of which the advertisement is communicated
- the nature of the advertised product
- the nature and content of any associated material made available contemporaneously to consumers by the advertiser.

GENERAL RULES

Primary responsibility for observance of this Code falls upon advertisers, and remains with them even when delegated, for practical purposes, to an advertising agency or other intermediary.

This provision in no way affects the responsibility of advertising agencies, which contract as principals, in their relations with publishers.

Substantiation

Before offering an advertisement for publication, the advertiser should have in his hands all documentary and other evidence necessary to demonstrate the advertisement's conformity to the Code. This material, together, as necessary, with a statement outlining its relevance, should be made available without delay if requested by the ASA.

Legality

Advertisements should contain nothing which is in breach of the law, nor omit anything which the law requires.

Advertisements should contain nothing which is likely to bring the law into disrepute.

Decency

No advertisement should contain any matter that is likely to cause grave or widespread offence. Whether offence is likely to be caused and, if so, of what gravity, will be assessed in each case in the light of the standards of decency and propriety that are generally accepted at present in the United Kingdom.

Some advertisements, which do not conflict with the preceding paragraph, may nonetheless be found distasteful because they reflect or give expression to attitudes or opinions about which society is divided. Where this is the case, advertisers should carefully consider the

FIG. 3.3.26 *'The Code of Advertising Practice' (continued on Pages 280–281)*

effect that any apparent disregard of the sensitivities involved may have upon their reputation and that of their product, and upon the acceptability, and hence usefulness, of advertising generally.

The fact that a product may be found offensive by some people is not, in itself, a sufficient basis under the Code for objecting to an advertisement for it. Advertisers are urged, however, to avoid unnecessary offence when they advertise any product which may reasonably be expected to be found objectionable by a significant number of those who are likely to see their advertisement.

Honesty

No advertiser should seek to take improper advantage of any characteristic or circumstance which may make consumers vulnerable; as, for example, by exploiting their credulity or their lack of experience or knowledge in any manner detrimental to their interests.

The design and presentation of advertisements should be such as to allow each part of the advertiser's case to be easily grasped and clearly understood.

Truthful presentation

No advertisement, whether by inaccuracy, ambiguity, exaggeration, omission or otherwise, should mislead consumers about any matter likely to influence their attitude to the advertised product.

Whenever an advertisement is likely to be understood as dealing with matters capable of objective assessment upon a generally agreed basis, it should be backed by substantiation. The adequacy of such substantiation will be gauged by the extent to which it provides satisfactory evidence that the advertisement is both accurate in its material details and truthful in the general impression it creates.

Advertisements which contain material of the kinds described below are not to be regarded, for that reason alone, as in conflict with the Code's rules on truthful presentation:

a) Obvious untruths, exaggerations and the like, the evident purpose of which is to attract attention or to cause amusement and which there is no likelihood of consumers misunderstanding

b) Incidental minor inaccuracies, unorthodox spellings and the like which do not affect the accuracy or truthfulness of the advertisement in any material respect.

Matters of opinion

Substantiation is required for all advertisements with the following exceptions:

• Any subjective opinion expressed by an advertiser on the qualities or desirability of his own products, so long as it is clear that what is being expressed is an opinion and that the Code's rules on matters of fact and fair competition are observed.

• Any advertisement, from whatever source, whose principal function is to influence opinion in favour of or against any political party or electoral candidate, or on any matter before the electorate for a referendum.

Advertisements by central or local government or those concerning government policy, as distinct from party policy, are subject to all the Code's requirements on substantiation without exception.

Quotation of prices

The Code makes no general requirement that the cost to the consumer of an advertised product should be stated in an advertisement (but see page 11: Children).

Use of the word 'free'

When a product is advertised as being 'free', incidental costs which will necessarily be incurred in acquiring it, and which are known to (or can be accurately assessed by) the advertiser, should be clearly indicated; and when such incidental costs exceed those that

would typically arise if a comparable product was bought from a comparable source, the product advertised should not be described as free.

Advertisers should not seek to recover the cost to them of a product which they describe as free

• by imposing additional charges they would not normally make

• by inflating any incidental expenses they may legitimately recover (eg cost of postage), or

• by altering the composition or quality, or by increasing the price, of any other product which they require to be bought as a precondition of the consumer obtaining the 'free' product.

Except in the context of a free trial, the word 'free' should not be used if payment for an advertised product is only deferred.

Testimonials

Except when the opinion quoted is available in a published source, in which case a full reference should be made available on request, the advertiser should be able to provide substantiation for a testimonial in the form of a signed and dated statement, containing any words which appear in the advertisement in the form of a direct quotation, and with an address at which the author of the statement may be contacted.

Recognisability

An advertisement should always be so designed and presented that anyone who looks at it can see, without having to study it closely, that it is an advertisement.

Guarantees

Words such as 'guarantee' should not be used in an advertisement if, in consequence, there is any likelihood of consumers mistakenly believing, when such is not the case, that it is the advertiser's intention to confer on them, or procure for them, a legal right to recompense or reimbursement.

Where it is intended that such a legal right be created, it should be made clear to consumers, before they are committed to purchase, whether their right lies against the advertiser or against a third party (as it may do, for example, where insurance schemes are used to prolong warranties).

Subject to the provisions of the two preceding paragraphs, there is no objection to the use of 'guarantee' in a colloquial sense ('Guaranteed to cheer you up' of a film, for example).

Availability

Except in circumstances

a) in which the advertisement makes clear that any advertised product is subject to a limitation on availability, or

b) in which such a limitation is inherent in the nature of the product (eg theatre tickets),

advertisers should be able to show that they have reasonable grounds for supposing that they can supply any demand likely to be created by their advertisement.

Products which cannot be supplied should not be advertised as a way of assessing potential demand.

Fear and distress

Without good reason, no advertisement should play on fear or excite distress.

Violence and anti-social behaviour

Advertisements should neither condone nor incite to violence or anti-social behaviour.

Advertisements for weapons and for items such as knives, which offer the possibility of violent misuse, should avoid anything, in copy or in illustration, that may encourage such misuse.

Protection of privacy and exploitation of the individual

Except in the circumstances noted below advertisements should not portray or refer to any living persons, in whatever form or by whatever means, unless their express prior permission has been obtained.

FIG. 3.3.26 *'The Code of Advertising Practice' (continued)*

The circumstances in which a reference or portrayal may be acceptable in the absence of prior permission, are the following:

- generally, when the advertisement contains nothing which is inconsistent, or likely to be seen as inconsistent, with the position of the person to whom reference is made, and when it does not abrogate their right to enjoy a reasonable degree of privacy

- in the special case of advertisements the purpose of which is to promote a product such as a book or film, when the person concerned is the subject of that book, film etc.

Unsolicited home visits

When advertisers intend to call on those who respond to their advertisement, with a view to making a sale, they should either make this clear in the advertisement or should explain their intention in a follow-up letter. In both cases, respondents should be given an adequate opportunity to refuse the salesman's call and the advertiser should help respondents to communicate their decision by providing either a reply-paid postcard or instructions as to how to make telephone contact.

Safety

As a general rule, advertisements should not show or advocate dangerous behaviour or unsafe practices except in the context of the promotion of safety.

Exceptions may be permissible, in circumstances in which emulation is unlikely. Special care should be taken with advertisements directed towards or depicting children or young people.

There should be no suggestion in any advertisement that there is a 'safe' level for the consumption of alcohol, or that a product can mask the effects of alcohol in tests on drivers. All advertisements for breath test products should include a prominent warning on the dangers of driving after drinking.

The alcohol content of some 'low alcohol' drinks is none the less such as to make it unwise to consume them in quantity before driving or engaging in any other activity for which complete sobriety and command are needed. Advertisers should take care that such drinks are not advertised in any way which may lead to such inappropriate consumption.

Denigration

Advertisers should not seek to discredit the products of their competitors by any unfair means.

Imitation

No advertisement should so closely resemble another advertisement as to be likely to mislead or confuse.

PARTICULAR CATEGORIES OF ADVERTISEMENTS

The Code contains rules covering specific categories of advertisements.

Categories covered are health claims; hair and scalp products; vitamins and minerals; slimming; cosmetics; direct response advertising, marketing and mail order; financial services and products; employment and business opportunities; limited editions; children; media requirements; alcoholic drinks; and cigarettes and tobacco.

The Code is very detailed in each of these areas, and the examples below give an indication of the types of rules included.

Health claims

No advertisement should employ words, phrases or illustrations which claim or imply the cure of any ailment, illness or disease, as distinct from the relief of its symptoms.

No advertisement should cause those who see it unwarranted anxiety lest they are suffering (or may, without responding to the advertiser's offer, suffer) from any disease or condition of ill health, or suggest that consumption or use of the advertised product is necessary for the maintenance of physical or mental capacities, whether by people in general or by any particular group.

Slimming

The only way for a person in otherwise normal health to lose weight, other than temporarily, is by taking in less energy (calories) than the body is using ie burning up excess fat the body has stored. A diet is the main self-treatment for achieving a reduction in this excess fat.

FIG. 3.3.26 *'The Code of Advertising Practice' (continued)*

Diet plans and certain aids to dieting are the only products which may be offered in advertisements as capable of effecting any loss in weight. Claims that weight loss or slimming can be achieved wholly by other means are not acceptable in advertisements addressed to the general public.

Direct response advertising, marketing and mail order

All mail order and direct response advertisements should indicate the period within which the advertiser undertakes to fulfil orders, or, when appropriate, provide services. Except in certain circumstances, the period should not be greater than 28 days from receipt of order.

All reasonable steps should be taken to ensure that lists and databases used to market consumer products and service are accurate and up-to-date, that they avoid duplication of mailings to the same name and address and that prompt action is taken, upon request, to correct personal information.

Financial services and products

All advertisements within the scope of this section should be prepared with care and with the conscious aim of ensuring that members of the public fully grasp the nature of any commitment into which they may enter as a result of responding to an advertisement.

Advertisers should take into account that the complexities of finance may well be beyond many of those to whom the opportunity they offer will appeal and that therefore they bear a direct responsibility to ensure that in no sense do their advertisements take advantage of inexperience or credulity.

Employment and business opportunities

Advertisements for schemes in which a person is invited to make articles at home should

- contain an adequate description of the work to be done

- make clear whether the home-worker is to be employed by the advertiser or will be self-employed, and

- whenever possible, indicate what level of earnings may realistically be expected. If, as when a scheme is in its infancy, no reliable forecast of earnings can be made, no claim as to earnings attainable should be attempted.

Children

Advertisements should contain nothing which is likely to result in physical, mental or moral harm to children, or to exploit their credulity, lack of experience or sense of loyalty.

Direct appeals or exhortations to buy should not be made to children unless the product advertised is one likely to be of

interest to them and one which they could reasonably be expected to afford for themselves.

No advertisement should cause children to believe that they will be inferior to other children, or unpopular with them, if they do not buy a particular product, or have it bought for them.

Alcoholic drinks

Advertisements should be socially responsible and should not encourage excessive drinking. In particular, they should not exploit the young, the immature, or those with mental or social incapacities.

Advertisements should not be directed at people under eighteen whether by selection of the medium or context in which they appear, or by reason of their content or style of presentation. People shown drinking in advertisements should always clearly be adults.

Advertisements should not depict activities or locations in connection with which the consumption of any drink whatever would be unsafe or unwise. Particular care requires to be taken with advertisements which depict powered vehicles of any kind and especially motor cars.

Cigarettes and hand rolling tobacco

The Cigarette Code is the outcome of discussions between the Department of Health (on behalf of the UK Health Departments), the manufacturers and importers of cigarettes (as represented by the Tobacco Advisory Council and the Imported Tobacco Products Advisory Council) and the ASA.

The essence of the Code is that advertisements should not seek to encourage people, particularly the young, to start smoking or, if they are already smokers, to increase their level of smoking, or to smoke to excess, and should not exploit those who are especially vulnerable, in particular young people and those who suffer from any physical, mental or social handicap.

student activity

(PC 3.3.6)
The case study featured in the illustration in Figure 3.3.27 shows the clear instructions given to the media as a result of the ASA's findings. Can you identify any advertisements in recent newspapers or magazines that make wild claims about the product or service? Do you think that the ASA should be investigating them?

Annual Report 1993   11

Case study: not on my patch

ASA has become all too familiar with the sharp end of mail order advertising over the years. No case in 1993 more typified the reasons why than that of unauthorised transdermal nicotine and slimming patches.

"Giving up is easy – I've done it lots of times", runs the hardened career smoker's favourite gag. At the end of 1992, though, would-be kickers of the habit had cause to believe there was new hope – with the help of the nicotine patch.

Previously only available on prescription, their status had been recently reconsidered by the medical authorities. A number of potent licensed patches had become freely obtainable over the local chemist's counter. Manufactured by major pharmaceutical companies, these patches were licensed in November 1992 after thorough testing for safety and to make sure they dispensed nicotine through the skin into the bloodstream as they claimed. All advertisements for the patches were sent for checking by the ASA before they were published.

But in early 1993, the opportunists struck. The Authority began receiving enquiries from national newspapers about off-the-page advertisements for new patches which were untested and unlicensed. Similar in appearance to a sticky plaster, they were easy to produce and quick to sell. Advertisements placed by a number of mail order companies made unacceptable claims that their product was all that was needed to give up ("or your money back"). Untested, these 'alternative' patches never were shown to work.

Our advice to media was unequivocal: the advertisements should not be run until the legality and safety of the patches had been established by the Department of Health. After a short time, the advertisements stopped appearing.

Within weeks, however, the first derivative of the patch fad surfaced: the slimming patch. This product contained seaweed extracts which, when taken by mouth, were licensed as an "aid to weight loss". But there was nothing to show that the patch could deliver these extracts through the skin. Again, we issued strong advice against these advertisements, and media responded quickly and positively.

An evening primrose oil patch made a brief appearance, as did a vitamin C patch. In both these cases, the advertisers were happy to take advice to ensure that untoward claims were avoided.

FIG. 3.3.27 *'Case study: not on my patch', taken from the Advertising Standards Authority Annual Report 1993.*

ELEMENT 3.3

a s s i g n m e n t

(PC 3.3.1–6, COM 3.1, 3.2, 3.3, 3.4, AON 3.1, 3.2, 3.3, IT 3.1, 3.2, 3.3)
In order to achieve and display understanding of the performance criteria of this Element, you will have to produce a word processed report which evaluates the following:

- advertising
- publicity
- public relations
- sales promotion

This will have to be a comparative investigation into two different organisations. You do not have to look at any of the marketing communications methods in great detail, but you should appreciate that they are a key component of the total marketing process.

TASK 1

(PC 3.3.1–3)
The first part of your report should explain why the two organisations use particular types of marketing communications to promote their products and image.

TASK 2

(PC 3.3.1–3)
You should now evaluate how the marketing communications these organisations have adopted assist them in reaching their specified target audience.

TASK 3

(PC 3.3.4)
This section of the report should evaluate the effect of marketing communications on the two organisations in terms of the following:

- product sales
- product awareness

- customer loyalty
- brand loyalty
- length and nature of the product life cycle

TASK 4

(PC 3.3.5)
Taking one of the organisations, you should investigate the use of direct marketing techniques and explain the following:

- how customer needs have changed
- how technology has changed in marketing terms
- the reasons behind the growing use of direct marketing

TASK 5

(PC 3.3.6)
In this last part of the report, you need to identify marketing communications which may contravene the British Advertising Code of Practice. This does not have to be in relation to the two organisations and can be a general investigation. You should also explain why particular forms of marketing communication need controls.

NOTES

You do not necessarily need to investigate two particular organisations if this proves impossible. You can draw on your own observations of marketing communications and examples included in this Element and other Units. Your institution may provide you with case study materials. Alternative sources of information include the following:

- Marketing Week magazine
- Campaign magazine
- CD ROM newspaper data bases
- ASA Monthly Report

Evaluate sales methods and customer service to achieve customer satisfaction

PERFORMANCE CRITERIA

A student must:

1 compare **direct** and **indirect sales methods** for their suitability to meet the **needs of customers** and **organisations**

2 describe **sales campaign methods**

3 explain and give examples of **responsibilities of salespersons**

4 explain the importance of effective **sales administration** to an organisation and its customers

5 evaluate **customer service** in terms of the **needs of customers** and **organisations**

RANGE

Direct sales methods: *TV, radio, factory, tele-sales, door-to-door, pyramid, catalogues*

Indirect sales methods: *distribution channels (national, international), direct factory, retail, wholesale, distributor, agents*

Needs of customers: *quick and easy purchasing, clear and accurate information, clear refund procedure, easy exchange of goods, complaints procedure, special service to meet special needs*

Needs of organisations: *to make a profit, to retain market share, to secure customer satisfaction*

Sales campaigns methods: *sales letters, sales memos, sales conferences, sales meetings*

Responsibilities of salespersons: *presenting appropriate image, customer care, point-of-sale service, product knowledge, after-sales service, sales administration, knowledge of Sale of Goods Act, knowledge of Trades Description Act, communicating effectively*

Sales administration: *order processing, credit clearance, credit control, customer accounts, delivery schedules, security, prospecting*

Customer service: *to meet the needs of external customers (sales, complaints, information, problems); to meet the needs of internal customers (help, information)*

284

3.4.1 Compare direct and indirect sales methods for their suitability to meet the needs of customers and organisations

DIRECT SALES METHODS

Generally speaking, the shortest channels are often the most costly. If an organisation wishes to sell direct then it needs to achieve a good market coverage. In addition to this, it also needs to ensure that the sales force, transportation and warehousing are organised in an efficient manner. Balanced against these considerations will be a greater profit margin. By not using middlemen or intermediaries, the manufacturer or supplier does not have to take a cut in their profit margins. By being closer to the end-users of the product or service, the organisation is in a much better position to anticipate and meet its customers' needs. There has been a trend for manufacturers to shorten their distribution and sales channels as much as possible and to employ comparatively expensive marketing and advertising campaigns to 'pre-sell' their products to the customer.

TV

Taking their lead from American practice, many UK suppliers of consumer products have begun to use television as their principal means of sales distribution. Indeed, many of the earlier users of this form of sales method were UK subsidiaries of US firms, such as Time-Life Warner, which produces CDs, tapes and books. Charities have not been slow in recognising that this medium also offers them advantages in terms of quick customer response. Many advertisements have been screened which depict harrowing scenes aimed at manipulating the emotions of the viewer. With the advent of the wide use of credit cards and switchcards, the facility to make an immediate purchase or donation has been significantly enhanced.

In choosing to use this form of sales or distribution channel, organisations have obviously considered its advantages over other more conventional means of distribution. These organisations have certainly invested considerable sums of money in telecommunications systems as well as ensuring that their distribution and despatch methods are efficient.

As we will see shortly, there is a similarity between this form of distribution channel and tele-sales. They are both pro-active in the sense that they are actively directed towards the customers themselves rather than relying on middlemen or more conventional forms of distribution. Perhaps the major difference is that direct sales derived from television advertising is not as intrusive as tele-sales may be. The sales climate in the UK is still relatively conservative. The more pushy techniques employed by the Americans would not really work very well in this country.

Having said this, we have ignored the impact of American-style home shopping via satellite and cable. It seems incredible that viewers will watch what really amounts to an extended advertisement demonstrating the various uses of product and then be offered the opportunity to buy it. In many respects this form of advertising leading to a direct sale is very similar to the more traditional in-store demonstrations of products. Anyone who has been to the Ideal Home Exhibition, for example, will have been exposed to multi-purpose vegetable choppers, all-purpose cleaners and unbluntable knives. Most of these advertisements are direct imports from the USA. Interestingly, they are also repeated with over-dubbed European languages so you can be convinced in French and German as well as English.

RADIO

As we have seen earlier in this Unit, radio is still a comparatively new medium in terms of advertising and marketing. Radio does have the advantage of being significantly cheaper than television, whilst the major disadvantage is that it cannot allow demonstration or viewing of the product before purchase. In this respect, direct sales via radio seem to be restricted to audio-based products, such as recordings and music. The advent of national commercial radio has made this medium much more adaptable and usable. The potential market penetration of commercial radio has led organisations which have been using television for similar purposes to switch some of their advertising and marketing activities over to radio.

FACTORY

It is not unusual for customers to travel considerable distances in order to save at least 30 per cent on their purchases. Whilst it may be questionable whether the customers actually save any money when they add in the cost of the travel, there is always the added anticipation and excitement of not knowing what may be on offer once they get there. There are around 550 of these factory shops operating at present in the UK. The direct factory versions which stock a variety of different products from a range of manufacturers are discussed later in this performance criterion. This American-style alternative to conventional means of distribution allows manufacturers to sell the following kinds of goods:

- slightly damaged stock
- returns
- cancelled orders
- last season's products
- samples
- discontinued lines

student activity

(PC 3.4.1)
Using your local yellow pages, try to identify any factory sale outlets in your immediate area.

TELE-SALES

Research has shown that in the USA an average telephone user would be on the phone for 18 minutes per day. Six minutes per week of this would be spent buying over the phone. In comparison, the UK user only uses the phone for four minutes per day, spending only 30 seconds a week purchasing over the phone.

There is something of an emerging 'tele-culture' in the UK and recent research has shown that the 'tele-philes', or ardent supporters of the telephone, now account for 47 per cent of the population. The 'tele-phobes', on the other hand, now account for only 16 per cent. It would now appear that the UK is ready for the extensive use of tele-sales techniques to develop new channels of sales and distribution. As we have seen in previous Elements of this Unit, tele-marketing or tele-sales is definitely on the increase. Again, recent research has shown that organisations are shifting across to more pro-active tele-marketing and tele-sales techniques. It is now estimated that some 13 per cent of organisations have active tele-sales teams.

Traditionally, the telephone sales technique was confined to non-consumer products. We should make the distinction here between tele-marketing, which is, in effect, ordering by phone, and tele-sales which is a form of direct marketing. Prospective customers are contacted via the telephone with the salesperson working from a pre-prepared script either on paper or on screen. This initial contact is made to smooth the way for a follow-up call from another salesperson, or, indeed a visit from a sales representative. This form of cold calling is considerably less expensive than cold canvassing, the latter being the door-to-door cold sales technique.

Obviously the number of calls per year that an organisation wishes its salespersons to make is dependent upon the product, its service and the nature of the customer. However, W. Tally, some 30 years ago, devised a way in which you could calculate the effectiveness of the salesperson. This technique can be as valid for door-to-door sales as for tele-sales. The technique involves:

- grouping customers into categories according to the value of the products bought and their potential in the future
- assessing the call frequency or number of calls on a particular customer per year for each category of customer
- totalling the required work load per year by multiplying the call frequency and number of each customer in each category
- making an estimate of the average number of calls made by each sales representative per week
- calculating the number of working weeks per year
- calculating the average number of calls a sales representative can make each year
- calculating the number of sales representatives needed by dividing the total number of annual calls by the average number of calls made by each sales representative per year

This may sound incredibly complicated, but it is essential if the organisation is to ensure that the tele-sales effort is cost effective.

This is a form of prospecting or, in other words, actively seeking 'hot leads' to ensure that sales representatives only visit or contact customers who have a potential in terms of interest to convert to a sale.

DOOR-TO-DOOR

There was a time when few homes were safe from the inevitable knock on the door from a sales representative. Clutching a large suitcase, this individual would then launch into a pre-prepared sales patter in a vain attempt to convince the householder to buy items from his or her exciting range of household cleaning products, or similar. Whilst there has been a marked downturn in this type of activity, we should not forget some of the more traditional forms of door-to-door sales which still go on to this day. As we will see in the Focus study, perhaps one of the most enduring forms of door-to-door sales involves the milkman.

Focus study

DOOR-TO-DOOR SALES

In the past the Milk Marketing Board was the monopolistic buyer of all milk and dairy farmers were required to sell their milk to the Board at a guaranteed price. Now that the MMB has been replaced by Milk Marque it must buy its milk on a competitive basis. This had led to a rise in milk prices triggering a rise in the price of each pint of milk sold in the shops. With doorstep milk delivery dropping by around 12 per cent per year, some milk delivery operations are down to 45 per cent of their previous milk rounds. Perhaps there is some light at the end of the tunnel, since the price increases have meant that supermarket milk is now more expensive than it was. The principal cause in the previous drop in door-to-door milk deliveries was the lower price at supermarkets. However, the convenience and reliability of milk deliveries continues to be an enduring feature of many people's purchasing habits. There is a feeling that eventually milk deliveries will be a thing of the past. In order to try to combat this, milkmen are offering an ever wider range of related and unrelated products to supplement the dropping demand for home delivered milk. The milk processors, who, in effect, pasteurise or skim the milk before bottling, are faced with a difficult situation. They supply the supermarkets in bulk as well as running their own home delivery services. It may only be a matter of time before they consider the complications and extra expense involved in home deliveries to be uneconomic.

`0:20`

student activity

(PC 3.4.1, COM 3.1)

As a group consider the Focus Study above, and try to identify an effective course of action which could be implemented by a milk delivery operation to address the problems mentioned.

PYRAMID

Pyramid selling has become something of a religion or as others would claim, a disease caught from America. Using its supporters' terminology, this form of sales channel is known as network marketing. Pyramid sales organisations sell products ranging from soap powder to water filters. Essentially, the system works by asking people to recruit friends or relatives to become representatives or salespersons in their own right. These individuals, in turn, recruit even more people. One of the areas which blurs legality with illegality is that some organisations do not actually have anything to sell. The organisation asks you to recruit other people and pays you for doing so. These recruits in turn recruit other individuals and are paid for doing that, and so on, and so on. The DTI is keeping a very close watch on this.

Over the past 5–10 years pyramid selling or network marketing or multi-level marketing, whichever you choose to call it, has become increasingly popular. Many people have turned to this form of selling as a means of supplementing their income.

Focus study

PYRAMID SELLING

In the middle of 1994 the DTI called in liquidators to deal with three pyramid sales operations. These were 3T Publications, Alchemy Marketing and Quillpunch. All were considered to have been acting against the public interest. Individuals who got involved with these three organisations were required to make an initial investment but their profitability and returns were very much dependent upon the number of recruits they brought in. As long as there was a steady stream of new recruits, the recruiters would be enjoying a good income. 3T, for example, a Yorkshire-based firm, promised around £460 profit within eight months of investing £160. The problem was that the investments made by those who had been recruited were not invested but were simply redistributed to those higher up the levels. It was inevitable that as recruitment tailed off, the organisation was bound to fail. The 8,000 members of 3T who paid on average £1,500 each are very unlikely to see any of it back. One individual paid in more than £19,000 and claimed to have received £18,000 of it back as well as £1,600 per month. This was very much the exception to the rule.

The kind of money-making or chain-letter scheme featured in our Focus Study is a great cause of embarrassment to the more genuine network marketing organisations. Many adopt slightly different techniques, which include door-to-door sales, catalogues or party plans. It was predicted some years ago that in time, 75 per cent of all products and services would be sold via pyramid selling operations, but this might be slightly optimistic. However, the industry has achieved nearly £1bn. in sales revenue in the last year.

The majority of products sold by such methods are cosmetics, clothing, housewares, electrical goods, diet plans, books and toys. It is estimated that something in the region of 460,000 people are involved in marketing these products direct.

There are some success stories. A couple in Kent, after losing their previous business, got involved with a book distribution network and are now earning around £3,000 per month. This is from an initial investment of just £500. Since many less ethical pyramid selling operations claim that they are 'get rich quick' schemes, the DTI, in particular, continues to keep a very close eye on them.

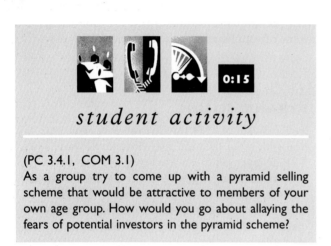

student activity

(PC 3.4.1, COM 3.1)
As a group try to come up with a pyramid selling scheme that would be attractive to members of your own age group. How would you go about allaying the fears of potential investors in the pyramid scheme?

CATALOGUES

One of the principal advantages of running a catalogue-based operation is that the business does not have to spend large sums of money on city-centre locations, or, indeed, relatively expensive customer facilities such as parking or restaurants. Often you will find the headquarters or fulfilment centre of a catalogue operation located on a rather unattractive industrial estate. The most popular form of mail order is via enormous catalogues produced by such companies as Kays, Littlewoods, Great Universal Stores and Grattans. These operations are under considerable pressure from other operations such as Avon Cosmetics, Betterware and Oriflame which have catalogues which are 'presented' to potential customers by individuals who receive a commission from sales. Other companies are also exerting pressure on the more conventional catalogue market and have begun to bridge the gap between strict mail order service and direct customer retailing. In fact these organisations, such as Argos and Pastimes, have retail outlets. The former has a catalogue but you cannot buy its products by mail order. The catalogue, in effect, replaces the need for Argos to have extensive showrooms displaying the vast range of stock on offer. The latter, although still achieving a large proportion of its sales via the conventional mail order market, uses its retail outlets in two ways. First, they give the customer the opportunity to actually view and handle the product and then, perhaps, to purchase via mail order. Secondly they obviously enable the customer to purchase immediately just as he or she would in a normal retail outlet.

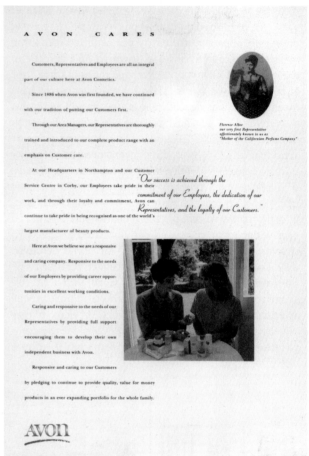

FIG. 3.4.1 *Avon Cosmetics is a widespread and respected company that uses both catalogues and door-to-door methods of selling its products.*

INDIRECT SALES METHODS

Direct sales methods are not suitable for every organisation. Indirect sales methods may be more appropriate. Deciding on the correct sales or distribution channel is crucial as this is one of the more stable aspects of an organisation's operations. Changing a channel can be expensive. Basically, a manufacturer has four different types of distribution to choose from, namely:

● *direct* – as we have seen, there is a variety of different techniques, but principally they involve the exclusion of a middleman

- *selective* – this is when the manufacturer decides to sell only through a limited number of middlemen
- *intensive* – this is when the manufacturer attempts to achieve the maximum number of outlets selling its products
- *exclusive* – this is when the manufacturer decides to artificially restrict the number of stockists of its product in order to ensure that only the most reliable outlets are used

DISTRIBUTION CHANNELS (NATIONAL, INTERNATIONAL)

The distribution or sales channel chosen by the manufacturer or supplier will depend very much upon the nature of the product or service, and, indeed, on the nature and location of the customer. Essentially, we can identify five distinct ways of distributing products or services within a national market. Many of these will involve the services of a wholesaler or a middleman. In each of the distribution methods we will look at we will try to identify examples of products which would be distributed in this manner. The five channels of distribution are:

1 *Manufacturer → wholesaler → retailer* – this is perhaps the most common method of distribution. This allows the manufacturer or supplier to produce products in bulk and distribute large quantities to the wholesaler. The wholesaler will house or store sufficient quantities of the products (or services) in order to supply a number of retailers over a particular time period. The retailers, in turn, will then be able to order smaller quantities in order to supply their customers directly.

2 *Manufacturer → customer* – increasingly manufacturers have recognised that there are greater profits to be made by supplying to the customer directly. As this system cuts out the middlemen, such as the wholesaler and retailer, it does mean greater profits to the manufacturer or supplier. As we will see later in this performance criterion, the growth of the factory shop method of distribution is seen as a very good way of disposing of over-stocked items at reduced prices. Both manufacturer and customer benefit from this form of distribution, the former being able to dispose of excess stock and realise the value of the stock immediately, and the latter being able to obtain products and services at reduced prices.

3 *Manufacturer → retailer* – this system effectively cuts out the need to use wholesalers. Some large retail chains are, in effect, wholesalers and distributors in their own right. If a chain has hundreds of shops across the country, it can buy products and services direct from the manufacturer at sufficiently low prices to preclude the need for using wholesalers. Manufacturers have recognised that, particularly in the case of supermarkets, they have no option but to deal with them direct.

4 *Manufacturer → wholesaler* – this is another popular way of buying products which is very common in the USA. In the UK this is typified by the cash and carry operation. In effect, the cash and carry outlets operate rather like wholesalers, in that they do sell directly to retailers who will then sell the goods on, but they also supply customers directly, provided they buy in bulk. There are some restrictions on this type of operation: some cash and carry outlets may require their customers to pay a small membership fee, or at the very least, to be issued with an identity card. The term cash and carry is perhaps rather confusing, since it is not purely a cash facility. There may be lines of credit available to regular customers, and, at the very least, customers will be able to pay by credit card or charge card. These establishments have recognised that there is a large demand even from individual customers to buy in comparative bulk. Customers will recognise the advantages of buying in bulk, particularly for special occasions, such as weddings or parties, etc. Before the limitations on the personal importation of alcohol and tobacco from the Continent, cash and carry outlets were the traditional place to buy stocks of alcohol for parties and celebrations.

5 *Manufacturer → specialist* – this distribution system refers to manufacturers who supply specialist merchants catering for tradesmen. A builders merchant, for example, would supply a wide variety of materials to carpenters, electricians, plumbers and bricklayers. Such businesses operate to some extent rather like a cash and carry, and may limit access to bona fide tradespersons. In most cases the tradesperson will have an account or line of credit with the specialist merchant and be billed monthly. This is obviously beneficial to the tradespeople since they will not have to pay cash if they return to the builders merchant a number of times in a day to complete a job.

The UK is in most respects geographically small. Given that the prime motivation behind selling into markets is the desire to sell more, sooner or later the UK market will be saturated. Therefore, organisations need to consider entering the international arena and competing with other organisations selling internationally already. International selling is as old as trade itself and stems from, as we have said, the inability of the home market to satisfy the long-term profit objectives of the organisation.

student activity

(PC 3.4.1, COM 3.1, 3.3, 3.4, AON 3.3)
Referring to the map of Geest Wholesale Services illustrated in Figure 3.4.2, suggest the location of three further distribution centres which would significantly improve the delivery time to customers. You should consider, before deciding on the location, whether the immediate catchment area has sufficiently high levels of population.

Any look at international selling needs to begin with an investigation of the structure of selling, or, in other words, the distribution or sales channels. There are, of course, a number of ways of achieving an efficient international sales or distribution channel or network, and these are:

I *Direct representation* – in this version, sales representatives travel from the base of the organisation to various locations overseas. Distribution is achieved by direct export. Obviously, to achieve this, the sales representatives need to be well versed in the languages, customs and geography of the overseas market. Another key skill required is that of time management, as this is crucial in ensuring that the sales representative invests sufficient time commensurate with the expected returns from the overseas customer.

BOURNEMOUTH	HEREFORD	LIVERPOOL
Geest Wholesale Services 0202 393333	Geest Wholesale Services 0432 273094	Dan Wuille 051 220 9341/4
		LIVERPOOL
BRISTOL	**LONDON**	Francis Nicholls 051 228 6301
Burgess Webb & Squire 0272 773631	Geest Wholesale Services 071 720 8355/6	**MANCHESTER**
		Houghton
CARDIFF	**SOUTHAMPTON**	Millington 061 223 3132
Dan Wuille 0222 399877	Burgess Webb & Squire 0703 221212	**PRESTON**
		Geest Wholesale
CARDIFF	**SOUTHAMPTON**	Services 0772 50643
William Bradnum 0222 341412	Helliwell 0703 226400	**WOLVERHAMPTON**
		Francis Nicholls 0902 452145
	SOUTHALL	**BRADFORD**
	Geest Wholesale Services 081 848 4561/2	Trueloves 0274 725244/5
	BIRMINGHAM	**GATESHEAD**
	Francis Nicholls 021 622 4603	William Hardy 0914 879441
	BIRMINGHAM	**LEEDS**
	Newnes 021 622 3060	Francis Nicholls 0532 494950/3
	COVENTRY	**LEICESTER**
	Francis Nicholls 0203 456232	Francis Nicholls 0533 549660
	DERBY	**MIDDLESBROUGH**
	Geest Wholesale Services 0332 32131	William Hardy 0642 246522
	GLASGOW	**NOTTINGHAM**
	Francis Nicholls 041 552 8857	Francis Nicholls 0602 503222/6
		SPALDING
		Greens 0775 760061

GEEST

Geest Wholesale Services

WHITE HOUSE CHAMBERS SPALDING LINCS PE11 2AL TEL: 0775 761111 FAX: 0775 710766

FIG. 3.4.2 *Geest Wholesale Services: this illustration shows the location of wholesale operations throughout the UK mainland. Note the concentration of distribution centres in the Midlands.*

2 *Local representation* – using locally recruited sales representatives, who are either trained in the overseas country or, in many cases, undertake training at the organisation's base, to represent the organisation in the host market. A certain level of independence and decision-making ability is necessary since the local representative will only make periodic visits to the organisation's base but will probably receive regular updates or occasional visits from headquarters personnel. In some cases, the relationship is taken one stage further in that the local representative and the supplying organisation enter into a joint selling venture or marketing campaign. In essence then, local representation is very similar to the relationship a sales agent may have with a supplier.

3 *Structured representation* – an organisation involved in international selling will create an overseas version of its home operation. This ensures both direct management reporting and immediate accountability. The Japanese follow this system, by establishing a range of representatives for each major market who report directly to their superior in Japan. The natural progression from this distribution and sales channel is to set up assembly or manufacturing plants in countries which prove to be particularly profitable.

4 *Export commission houses* – these are based in the supplier's country and act as an agent through which purchases of products or services are made. The ECHs do not actually buy the products or services themselves and then resell them, they merely act as a middleman, earning a commission on the value of the deal. Obviously one of the problems with this kind of relationship is that if the supplier and the ultimate buyer get to know one another's identity, then there is a danger that they will by-pass the ECH, thus being able to come to some amicable deal between them.

5 *Export merchant* – this is a trader who buys and sells for the purposes of export. These export shippers tend to specialise in a particular field and have considerable knowledge both about products and the potential market. The EMs have their own distinct distribution and sales channels and tend to use a network of contacts across the world. Again, the EMs run the risk of being by-passed, but they do tend to demand fairly good prices from suppliers so that the price to the end-user would be difficult to beat if the supplier chose to supply direct.

6 *Export agent* – again, working in the supplier's market, they have created a network of sales representatives and contacts. The supplier may not necessarily know that he or she is dealing with an export agent. A supplier may believe that he or she is dealing directly with the buyer.

The manufacturer or supplier has to decide upon the distribution and sales channel that will best suit their own product or service. It should be borne in mind that in many overseas markets organisations tend not to have sales representatives on their payroll. Salespeople tend to be self-employed and, as such, will often be representatives for a variety of companies. Trying to control these agents is very difficult for a supplier or manufacturer. They invariably cover enormous distances and may be selling competing products from different suppliers. Indeed, in terms of their circulation around the possible buyers of the product, they may only visit a customer once every three or four months. This poses something of a problem, since the supplier's products are under-represented for long periods of time.

The other major concern with international sales is the handling of complaints or returns, particularly if the distribution or sales channel is tortuously long. The supplier or manufacturer may find themselves in a position where there are literally hundreds of thousands of pounds of faulty or damaged stock lying in warehouses around the world. At some point all of these will return in some state or other to the supplier.

Realistically then, in terms of breaking into an overseas market and having sufficient and accountable representatives in that market, the supplier is reduced to just three choices:

1 *The overseas commission agent* – who takes a commission on the sales gained plus a modest operating charge. It would also be advisable to establish a *del credere* relationship with an agent since this means that the agent takes responsibility for the bad debts of customers whom he/she has supplied.

2 *Distributor* – essentially this relationship is that of a buyer and re-seller. The distributor will have a number of sales representatives, showrooms and warehouses in the overseas market. Obviously a good relationship must be maintained with this distributor since there is a level of detachment in that the sales and marketing function is no longer in the hands of the supplier. In this respect, the relationship with the distributor may be difficult since he/she will only re-order when stock levels have been reduced to the re-order level. This is obviously satisfactory as far as the distributor is concerned but it may mean that the supplier is not alerted early enough to ensure that re-orders are despatched quickly enough.

3 *Licensee* – this relationship usually involves the right actually to manufacture the product or service in the overseas market. Again there are some questions of control, particularly with regard to accurate auditing of the production and sales figures. The licensing agreement may prohibit the supplier from supplying directly into that market. This could cause problems, particularly if the licensee is not doing a very good job. The supplier will be tied to the licence holder for a set period of time, although the supplier may be able to circumvent this restriction by requiring the licence holder to either produce and sell a specified number of units or achieve a particular sales volume.

student activity

(PC 3.4.1, COM 3.1)
In pairs, consider the most appropriate distribution channels for the following products in an overseas market:

- a range of posters featuring top UK chart personalities
- a range of garden gnomes with the faces of football personalities
- a range of new sports hats with integral sunglasses

DIRECT FACTORY

This term may prove to be somewhat confusing but actually refers to factory outlets which are shopping centre-style developments in which leading manufacturers sell their products at knock-down prices. These enormous warehouses, often in excess of 200,000 sq. ft., are another import from the USA. Concentrating on the sale of seconds, end-of-line or clearance goods, these factory warehouse operations are usually in out-of-town locations. Preliminary predictions estimate that town or city centre retail outlets will be affected by as much as a 5–10 per cent drop in their sales. The catchment area involved is enormous. One such scheme based in Somerset has been attracting customers from as far away as South Wales.

RETAIL

Retail outlets vary considerably. Some aspects that differentiate them include the following:

- size
- type of outlet
- location of outlet
- range of products stocked

When we consider the various sorts of retail outlet, without going into enormous detail, we can identify three major types:

1 *Personal service retail outlets* – this is perhaps the more traditional form of retail outlet. The sales assistants will be readily available to give you advice or information and pass on their knowledge of the product(s) available. In other words, the employee serves you personally, will carry through the transaction and will be a point of contact should you return to the outlet for any reason.
2 *Self-selection* – in this form of outlet you use a basket or trolley and select the products you require. These are, in effect, very similar to supermarkets, except that in self-selection stores there are often a number of different service points or cashiers. Good examples of these include Boots the Chemist, British Home Stores and Marks & Spencer.

FIG. 3.4.3 *A British Home Stores retail outlet in a shopping arcade. Note that the outlet is on two levels. It would have cashier or customer service points at each exit.*

3 *Self-service* – this type of retail outlet can differ enormously in size. From the smallest corner shop to the largest hypermarket, they all employ the same format in terms of layout. Typically they would have a single entrance point and a single exit point. Customers enter the store and collect either a basket or a trolley and then proceed up and down the aisles selecting the products they wish to purchase. Once the customer arrives at the check-out desk the products are unloaded onto a conveyor belt or table top beside the till and the check-out operator or cashier processes the goods and these are then packed. Depending upon the technology used by the outlet,

the processing may take the form of ringing the price up on the cash register, or, as is becoming more common, there will be a barcode reader which will register the price automatically.

student activity

(PC 3.4.1)
In pairs, carry out an audit of your local shops and categorise them into the types identified above. Which type of operation is the most common and why?

WHOLESALE

Wholesalers purchase products from the manufacturer and distribute them to retailers. By virtue of the fact that the wholesaler is able to buy significantly greater quantities of products in one order, they are able to obtain them for lower unit costs than the retailer may hope to achieve. It should be borne in mind that this 'discount' or 'trade price' obtained from the manufacturer is only a fraction of both the original cost of the product and the final selling price. Once the retailer has purchased the products from the wholesaler he/she will then either mark the price up to the recommended retail price or fix the price on their own. There are a number of advantages in purchasing products from a wholesaler, including:

- since the wholesaler buys in bulk this means that the manufacturer does not have to store vast quantities of products
- wholesalers tend to buy from more than one manufacturer and can therefore offer a wider range of products to the retailer
- the retailer will be able to view the 'next season's products' before they officially enter the retail outlets
- wholesalers will be willing to sell smaller quantities of products to the retailer than the latter could obtain by means of a direct deal with the manufacturer
- many wholesalers also offer the retailer the opportunity to pay for his/her purchases at the end of each month by invoice

There is another form of wholesaler that we have not considered so far and this is known as a voluntary group wholesaler. A group of small retailers will join together in order to approach a wholesaler and arrange for their orders to be considered as a single order. Alternatively, a group of retailers may join together and open their own warehouse, which then gives them the opportunity of being able to buy branded products, in particular, at lower unit costs and thus acquire higher levels of discount than they would normally be able to do if they were purchasing individually.

DISTRIBUTOR

A frequent complaint about using distributors is that because they are independent businesses they can set the final selling price to the end-user. In many cases the price is a significant factor which may determine the product's success or failure. If the market is particularly price sensitive then the manufacturer may be well advised to avoid using distributors unless they are willing to agree a reasonable level of mark-up and a correspondingly fair selling price.

It is essential that the manufacturer develops a good relationship with its distributors since to all intents and purposes the distributor is the manufacturer in that market place. Also, the manufacturer will have to decide whether to use a large number of small distributors who are capable of covering relatively limited areas of the country or to use a smaller number of regional distributors. There are, of course, regional differences in culture or business practice and it may be advantageous for a manufacturer to take advantage of a distributor's undoubtedly superior knowledge of the locality.

AGENTS

Again, a certain degree of care should be taken in choosing agents, particularly agents in overseas markets. It is usual for agents to have other interests and the manufacturer or supplier should ensure that these other interests do not conflict. The agent needs to have a good reputation as well as a sound financial basis. Agents can be fairly key figures in the success or failure of a product and once a suitable agent has been found the manufacturer needs to monitor his/her performance and progress. It is usual practice for an agent to be taken on for a trial period and then the contract may be extended if the relationship proves to be successful. The agent needs to gain a good knowledge and appreciation of the product or product range as soon as possible and this is usually facilitated by in-house training programmes set up by the manufacturer. Obviously if the product is of a complex or technical nature this training should be compulsory and part of the agreement. The degree of autonomy given to an agent will obviously vary from agreement to agreement, but in order for the agent to make a valuable contribution to the development of a market, he/she does need some autonomy.

NEEDS OF CUSTOMERS

The needs of customers have been discussed at various points elsewhere in the book. However, we can summarise the factors involved by looking at the following considerations:

- the organisation must be able to establish what the customer's needs are
- the organisation needs to interpret them into clear needs
- the organisation needs to mirror these needs in the production and distribution of products and services
- the organisation also needs to ensure that any products or services provided meet exacting quality standards in order to achieve long-term customer satisfaction and probable repeat sales

QUICK AND EASY PURCHASING

If there is one thing that will ensure that a potential customer becomes a non-customer, this is the non-availability of the product. If the customer experiences difficulties in finding a stockist of a product, or, once having found this outlet, discovers that the purchasing process is complex, then he/she is likely to turn to an alternative product and supplier. Obviously, to alleviate this potential problem and facilitate an immediate and simple purchasing process, the organisation must have chosen its distribution or sales channels wisely. As we have discussed earlier, different products have different levels of availability, often related to some form of perceived exclusivity. This is also the case for products of a technical or complex nature, since only competent stockists with expert staff on hand can accurately match the product with the customer's needs.

The concept of the 'one-stop shop' has definitely arrived, particularly when we consider hypermarkets or supermarkets, which offer not only a wide range of consumable products, but also dry cleaning, post office services, restaurants, petrol and even banking. The proximity of all of these services is aimed at providing the customer with the easiest possible means of taking advantage of the variety available. Whilst this may have led to a downturn in the fortunes of city centre and town centre shops, it has meant that there have been extensive developments in out-of-town or suburban sites. The alternative to the street of single shops in town centres is the conglomeration of do-it-yourself, home furnishing, gardening, car parts and maintenance and electrical goods stores on out-of-town sites. With the ease of parking and the short walk from store to store, these have proved to be an attractive alternative to the shopping mall or shopping centre. All of these retail developments have been inherited from the American experience. Some have taken several years to take off and be embraced by the British public.

student activity

(PC 3.4.1, COM 3.1)
As a group, attempt to assess the impact of large supermarkets on the more traditional forms of retailing in your area. How, if at all, have the smaller retail outlets responded to the challenge of one-stop shopping? If they have not, what would be your suggestions?

When we consider that the customer now has the choice of shopping locally, or in a shopping centre, or in an out-of-town site, by phone or from a catalogue, there appears to be no area that has not been exploited by manufacturers, suppliers and retailers. Shopping has never been easier or simpler. It is without doubt that shopping will become even easier in the future, particularly with the development of new telecommunication systems which enable the consumer to purchase a variety of goods from home.

CLEAR AND ACCURATE INFORMATION

There is a statutory or legal obligation for organisations to provide clear and accurate information about their products or services. It is, however, beneficial to an organisation to make sure that its customers receive the highest level of information and accuracy before, during and after the sales process. Depending upon the distribution or sales channel chosen by the organisation, this will be more or less in the control of the manufacturer or the original supplier. Obviously, the more distance there is between the manufacturer or supplier and the end-user, the less control the former has on the information transmission system. In such situations, the manufacturer would be at pains to ensure that at every point or stage in the distribution process sufficient information, either in terms of sales literature or training, is passed down from level to level. Some organisations value the use of mass product briefing sessions to stockists or distributors of the product, or will support the sales force at the point-of-sale with regular visits by experienced sales representatives. The dissemination of printed material is essential and is often undertaken with the assistance of the retail outlets. Joint publication of sales literature or mini-catalogues is fairly routine in this area.

CLEAR REFUND PROCEDURE

If a customer requests a refund or replacement the employee dealing with the request should be aware of the organisation's policy in such matters. If the employee does not have the authority to refund or replace then he/she should always refer the matter to a senior member of staff who should be aware of the policy.

Some retail outlets, such as Marks & Spencer, who have a no quibble refund policy, will have special cash registers which are only used when money needs to be refunded to a customer.

Research has shown that customers are more inclined to purchase from a retail outlet which provides a clear receipt as this is not only proof of purchase but also a guarantee that a refund will be given if the product proves to be unsuitable in some way. It should be noted that refunds are generally given in the same manner as the payment was made, in other words, a cash sale is refunded in cash, but a credit card sale is refunded by the use of a credit card refund voucher.

EASY EXCHANGE OF GOODS

As with refunds, there are occasions when a customer may request that a product be exchanged for another item of stock. Again, the employee dealing with such a request needs to know the exchange policy of the organisation and should always check the item for signs of use, damage or missing parts. Provided the product appears to be in good order, then an exchange may be undertaken. This is, of course, assuming that the customer has some form of proof that he/she purchased the product from that retail outlet, or at least from part of that particular chain of retail outlets. It is unfortunately all too common for certain individuals to attempt to exchange goods purchased elsewhere, or perhaps obtained in a less legal manner, for other goods.

COMPLAINTS PROCEDURES

A customer may be dissatisfied for a number of reasons, including the following:

- the product he or she purchased is faulty
- he/she requires a product which the store does not stock or which is out of stock
- he/she has received poor service
- he/she has a problem which nobody seems to be able to help with

In many cases organisations will have a formal complaints procedure for customers who are dissatisfied. It is usual practice for complaints to be referred to the manager who is empowered by the organisation to act on behalf of them and make any on-the-spot decisions to help rectify these types of situations. There are some

student activity

(PC 3.4.1, COM 3.1)

In pairs, simulate your responses to the following refund or replacement queries:

1 A customer enters a record shop and produces a CD. The customer explains that this CD was purchased on his/her behalf by a friend as a birthday present. Unfortunately the customer already has this CD but has no means of proving that the CD was purchased in this shop.

2 An elderly gentleman returns to a large do-it-yourself superstore. He is dragging behind him a petrol mower. Walking up to the customer service desk he explains that the mower refuses to start. Upon being questioned about the procedures he took in starting the lawn mower he confesses that he has filled the fuel tank with diesel.

3 A customer returns to a car spares outlet having purchased only a matter of hours before a can of undercoat spray. Having prepared the surface of his car and masked off the areas he did not wish to spray, he followed the instructions on the can and proceeded spraying onto the body work. He now has a red car with a large patch of bright green paint. The label stated that the can contained white primer. Since the car is not very old he is very annoyed.

4 A young woman returns to a clothes shop clasping a carrier bag containing a dress. She has proof of purchase and the garment was definitely purchased from this outlet. She purchased the garment very late on Saturday afternoon. It is now lunch time on Monday. She claims that she has changed her mind and does not like the garment any more. Upon close inspection the garment is seen to have a stain and shows signs of having been worn.

key stages here which, regardless of the formal complaints procedure, should be followed:

- when listening to the complaint do not interrupt, and give the customer the opportunity to explain the situation
- always appear to be sympathetic to the customer
- in particularly complicated cases make sure that you write down all the details

- when you have done this, check the main points of the complaint with the customer
- even if the customer is abusive, always try to remain calm and polite
- if you feel you cannot solve the situation yourself, keep calm and refer the matter to a senior member of staff
- never give the customer a vague response or an unbelievable excuse
- never blame anyone else directly
- even if provoked, do not lose your temper
- never try to infer that the complaint is not really a problem, it is in the eyes of the customer
- always tell the customer exactly what you are going to do, particularly if this involves having to refer to another person or company
- above all, never make any promises which you cannot personally fulfil or ensure will be fulfilled

SPECIAL SERVICE TO MEET SPECIAL NEEDS

As each customer is an individual in his or her own right, it is not surprising that they may have a range of special needs which will require a different level of service. We can identify the following types of customer who may have special needs, and we attempt to look at any special services they may require:

1 *Children* – unless you are involved in a retail outlet, it is highly unlikely that day-to-day contact with children as customers will be normal. Children are not always accompanied by adults and it is in this respect that children may require special levels of service. The child may not be able to communicate on an adult level and may need additional assistance when either choosing or paying for a product. It is always advisable to treat a child just as you would treat an adult: you should not assume that because of a child's relatively tender age he/she is incapable.
2 *Special needs* – this rather broad category includes customers with hearing difficulties, the blind or partially sighted and the physically and mentally handicapped. Each will have their own particular requirements and many retail outlets have taken steps to ensure that both access and layout of their outlet facilitates ease of use by such customers.
3 *Foreign customers* – although the majority of overseas visitors may have some ability to speak and understand English, this may not be the case with overseas customers who are attempting to purchase products via the telephone. In larger organisations, attempts will have been made to identify employees who are able to speak foreign languages and these individuals may be contacted in the event of any communication problems.

NEEDS OF ORGANISATIONS

Each organisation will have a different set of objectives, as we have discussed in other Units of the book. The exact nature of these objectives, particularly in relation to sales, tend to focus upon three major concerns:

- to make a **profit**
- to retain or improve **market share**
- to secure **customer satisfaction**

We will address these three considerations in the remainder of this section of the Element.

TO MAKE A PROFIT

It is often said that the organisation's success is measured by its ability to make a profit and also that as the organisation grows, so too does its profits. Equally, as the profits increase the organisation is better placed to expand so really we must consider whether profits come before growth or growth comes before profits. There is no absolute answer to this, but for an organisation to realise any form of profit it must make a sale. Before it can do this it must identify a customer, and before this, it must ensure the customer is satisfied.

Profit as a term has different meanings in different contexts. Here we are particularly concerned with two meanings:

- profit is the **increase in overall profit** over a particular period of time
- profit is the **amount earned** by a particular product or product range

In terms of the first definition, the organisation is endeavouring to sell more, probably by expanding its range of customers. In the second definition, the organisation is more concerned with increasing the amount of profit generated by each sale.

As we have seen, there are other considerations, such as volume versus profit. It might be thought that as sales increase so do profits by the same factor. In the real world this does not really happen. Whilst an organisation may be able to take advantage of economies of scale in relation to increases in sales volume, it may be faced with having to reduce the product's selling price to ensure increased sales volume.

So how does this relate to the sales methods employed by the organisation? The sales management needs to make sure that a higher proportion of sales is achieved for every contact with a potential customer. This means effective selling techniques and therefore the management needs to think about the following:

- they need to have a **clear strategy**
- they need to look at **alternative plans**
- they need to consider **possible solutions**

- they need to make sure that **policies** are put into **practice**
- they need to **monitor results**

To sell more often requires putting much more effort into the following:

- paying more attention to the **customers** and in particular to their **needs**
- a re-examination of the **sales process** and selling **techniques**
- considering spending **longer with each customer** in order to ensure that the sale is closed
- considering expanding the **range of products and services** on offer
- making sure that all of the above are monitored
- making sure that additional costs are not incurred and that they do not exceed the additional sales achieved, otherwise the additional profit will be wiped out

TO RETAIN OR IMPROVE MARKET SHARE

As we have said elsewhere in the book, the question of market share can be an all-consuming passion for particular organisations. In order to achieve any measure of market share sales targets must be set and year-on-year exceeded. This is not the whole picture, as we need to consider what the competition may be doing at the same time. The other external factor which may or may not be within the sphere of influence of the organisation is the market growth, or the increase in the number of customers wishing to buy a product. Close monitoring of the external factors may have one part to play in this equation, but many of the sales techniques and innovations used within the organisation will contribute to a large degree to the success or failure in retaining or improving market share.

Whilst a sales assistant in a retail outlet may not have a clear view as to the nature or status of the organisation's market share such employees should be considered an integral part of the overall effort. Once again, we return to the concept of establishing the needs of the customer and matching the products or services provided by the organisation to that need. Without establishing this close and vital relationship it is impossible for the organisation to make any impact upon the distribution of market share.

TO SECURE CUSTOMER SATISFACTION

The retention of customers and the consequent likelihood of repeat sales are largely influenced by the level of customer satisfaction that an organisation can achieve. Customers are considerably more discerning and demanding these days than they were in the past. Whilst they do not necessarily expect something for nothing, there are minimum levels of customer service,

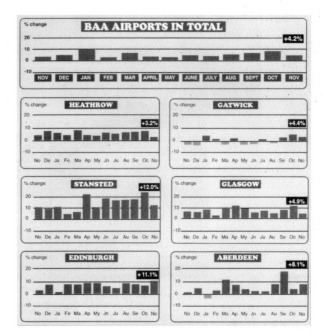

FIG. 3.4.4 *BAA's interest in their market share and in particular the level of passenger handling throughout their seven airports illustrates their interest in retaining and improving their market share (the figures are for 1993).*

student activity

(PC 3.4.1, COM 3.3, 3.4, AON 3.3, IT 3.1, 3.2, 3.3)
Referring to Figure 3.4.4 which details the passenger throughput of BAA's airports, convert the graphs into table form, including all of the six featured airports. You should use a suitable software package for the presentation of your table.

and in particular after-sales service, which are demanded as a matter of course.

Naturally, sales representatives or sales assistants who are in the front line in terms of contact with customers, must bear the brunt of any potential customer complaints or problems. Despite the fact that customers who are satisfied rarely come back to an organisation and praise its staff for their efforts and help, a measure of this satisfaction can be seen by comparing the level of customer complaints with the total number of customers dealt with. Again, many organisations have instituted extensive and complex customer satisfaction policies. Some organisations are considerably further ahead in this field than others. Again, despite the fact that legislation is pushing the maintenance of customer satisfaction to its absolute limits, many organisations have chosen to exceed customers' expectations.

WOOLWORTHS AND CUSTOMER CARE

Woolworths is committed to ensuring that staff offer the highest standards of customer care. Woolworths people are trained to be proficient and confident when dealing with customers, and to have extensive product knowledge.

This is summed-up in Woolworths Customer First Policy, "We serve ourselves best by serving our customers first" and implemented through the Customer First Skills Training Programme, which is the standard induction course for all sales staff.

The vast majority of customer enquiries are successfully resolved at store level, but to support the work of stores Woolworths operates a central Customer Relations Department from its Head Office.

By letter or phone, this department handles over 10,000 customer enquiries every year.

FIG. 3.4.5 *A section from literature issued by Woolworths, focusing on their customer care commitment.*

3.4.2 Describe sales campaign methods

SALES CAMPAIGN METHODS

Sales campaign methods employed by organisations seek to address both the internal and external communication functions. In this section of the Element we will be looking at internal communication systems which can assist the sales force to keep aware of products, organisational objectives and promotional campaigns. These include internal or sales memos, sales conferences and sales meetings. We will also be looking at sales letters which, of course, can be used for a variety of purposes, such as establishing first contact with a potential customer or following up a previous contact that may have been made.

SALES LETTERS

Sales letters are still one of the most valuable means of communicating with customers. The success of such a letter obviously depends upon its nature, particularly in terms of its personalisation. Essentially, sales letters fall into one of three categories:

- part of a direct mail shot which may be personalised although it may not be specifically targeted. This is known as prospecting
- a follow-up sales letter in response to a specific enquiry regarding a product or service.
- a follow-up sales letter in response to a more general enquiry, perhaps for a catalogue or a price list

Obviously, there is no particular use in sending out hundreds of sales letters without having some mechanism to follow them up. In the case of prospecting, as we will see later, the response rate is unlikely to be very high. It is, therefore, important to inform the recipient of the letter that some kind of additional contact will be made in writing, in person or by telephone. This problem of lack of response is even more acute when the potential customer has made the initial contact with the organisation. The customer, having expressed some interest in the organisation's products or services, should be more receptive to a follow-up contact. Typically, the following procedure will be set in motion in response to a request for information:

1 The requested information is collected or prepared and a sales letter is produced to be included in the package.
2 The sales letter informs the potential customer of the next action that the organisation will undertake.
3 Once the package has been sent, a sales representative responsible for the area in which the potential customer lives is informed of the customer's name, address and telephone number and nature of enquiry.
4 Organisations that do not have a national sales force may inform the local stockist of the product or service and leave them to do the follow-up work.
5 An organisation that does not have a national sales force or a network of stockists, but relies on fulfilment from a central location, will follow up the enquiry by telephone or by an additional sales letter.
6 The organisation will allow a reasonable period of time for the customer to assimilate the information included in the package.
7 The organisation will then contact the customer, and through whichever means the organisation has chosen there will be an attempt to close the sale.

It should be noted that there is a distinct difference in procedure when an organisation is prospecting for potential customers and when there are potential customers who have made an initial contact with the organisation themselves. The latter are known as 'hot' customers, in the sense that they have already partially expressed a desire to purchase the product or service. Organisations would be foolish to ignore them since the conversion of a 'hot' customer is considerably easier than 'cold' contact under other circumstances.

Sales letters, or for that matter any form of communication with existing customers, need not necessarily be for a specific purpose. By having an on-going dialogue with customers organisations seek to continually re-establish a good working relationship, as well as to instil a degree of trust and a sense of reliance.

SALES MEMOS

It may be logistically difficult to require a sales force to meet on a regular basis. This is particularly true of organisations which have a network of salespersons covering national or international markets. The sales force will need to be informed of any decision or situation which may affect their sales effort. Typically, the

student activity

(PC 3.4.2, COM 3.2, IT 3.3)
In the role of a sales representative, working for a photocopy paper supplier, write a sales letter which would be appropriate as a means of introducing yourself to potential customers.

information they need would include the following:

- changes to products
- bonuses available
- targets for a set period
- requests for paperwork or administration to be completed

A sales memo is usually used as a back-up to verbal contact with the sales force. It is, in effect, a tangible record of the conversation.

Alternatively, if the information is sufficiently complex, the organisation may choose to use a sales bulletin.

Sales memos and sales bulletins are also useful for periodic contact with existing customers, as an alternative to a sales letter. Once a working relationship has been established with a customer or stockist, then they may be considered, to some extent, an integral part of the communication network. To this end, items such as memos or bulletins, which could be considered to be purely internal in nature, may be employed as an external communication.

SALES CONFERENCES

One of the major concerns of any sales department is to increase sales. Good methods to enthuse the sales force are therefore vital. The major benefits of a sales conference are:

- all of the sales representatives are there and they are a captive audience
- if the conference is large, then it may appear special and can engender enthusiasm
- it allows sales representatives from all over the country or the world to get together and share their experiences
- it serves as a reminder to the sales representatives that they are a part of an organisation and not simply out on their own

A successful conference will have the following characteristics:

- realistic **objectives**
- a firm **agenda**
- a **co-ordinator** to organise the event
- an appropriate **venue** which:
  – is easy to get to
  – has suitable rooms
  – is comfortable
  – is unlikely to have interruptions
  – has adequate parking facilities
  – has useful facilities to hand, such as overhead projectors, large video screens, etc.
- an inspirational **speaker**
- provision for special diets and catering needs
- a credible and valuable conference **appraisal questionnaire**

SALES MEETINGS

Sales meetings can be some of the most boring events inflicted on employees. There are, however, a number of variations which would help make them more interesting and informative. These include:

- *inspirational meetings* – where a noted external speaker is engaged to enthuse the audience
- *topical meetings* – which concentrate on a single up-to-the-minute subject
- *question and answer meetings* – where sales representatives are assessed as to their ability to handle new procedures or policies
- *discussion meetings* – following a speech the sales representatives are given the opportunity to discuss the subject
- *quiz meetings* – which are rather more up-beat versions of the question and answer meetings. Every individual will be given a chance to answer a question and prizes will be awarded
- *problem-solving meetings* – where a specific problem needs to be addressed and all those present have an opportunity to contribute to the discussion
- *advertising meetings* – which consider new campaigns and may involve a representative from the advertising agency. The sales representatives will be encouraged to comment on the proposed advertising campaign
- *factory meetings* – where production representatives explain and discuss products with the sales force
- *sales training meetings* – which focus on a single or a series of related aspects giving practical help and advice on their implementation
- *merchandising meetings* – which present the sales force with proposed new point-of-sale and display materials

3.4.3 Explain and give examples of responsibilities of salespersons

RESPONSIBILITIES OF SALESPERSONS

Personal selling is an important element of the promotional variable in the marketing mix. For many companies the salesperson is the key intermediary, the presenter of offerings and the interpreter of consumer needs. The salesperson's job is shot through with technical skills, leadership and trusteeship – he/she goes into the environment and, so to speak, takes the skin of the organisation with them when they go – he/she is the organisation so far as his/her prospects and clients experience it. Selling and sales management are sophisticated and highly developed business functions with influential positions in the corporate plan. The main functions of a salesperson are set out in Table 3.4.1.

Another responsibility of a salesperson is to organise the sales force. This is usually organised on the basis of:

- geographical area
- product types
- customer types
- customer size
- a combination of the above

There are other important decisions concerning the sales force apart from its organisation, including the following:

- the size of the sales force
- importance of various sales force activities
- type of person required
- levels of management required
- systems of payment to be adopted

Organisations use various methods to motivate salespeople, including:

- *remuneration* – various methods may be used:
  – salary only – this provides security for the sales-

TABLE 3.4.1 *Functions of salespeople*

Non-call functions	Call functions	Encounter functions
To locate potential buyers	To obtain interviews	To present oneself
To estimate sales potential	To deliver goods	To supply product information
To gather information	To check stock	To diagnose customer situation
To select calls	To display stock	To reassure
To sequence calls	To demonstrate	To put a proposition
To plan customer approach	To instruct	To select and sequence information
To report:	To provide service	
● own activities	To negotiate terms	
● competitor activities	To take an order	
● customer activities	To collect cash	
To maintain records		

person, but also means there is no incentive for extra effort
- commission only – this maximises effort, but may deter some applicants, and may cause stress when low sales are achieved
- salary and commission – achieves a balance between incentives and security, but incentives for effort are still limited

- a **company car**
- payment of **insurance** by the organisation
- attractive **pension funds**
- payment of the salesperson's **expenses**
- effective **training**
- **prizes** for the highest sales in a set period

As well as the remuneration and other benefits outlined above, there are other factors that have to be taken into account. Salespeople have irregular hours, they usually work alone and when sales are going badly there is a danger that a salesperson may lose confidence. In order to overcome some of these problems a number of methods can be used, including:

- regular sales meetings
- providing help in the field
- encouragement of suggestions for improved company operations
- reducing unnecessary administrative procedures
- arranging sales contests

Training is essential in selling. New salespeople should always be provided with a period of induction and organised training. Continuous sales training is necessary to ensure good consumer relations, good selling, planning and morale. Different methods of training will usually include some of the following:

- knowledge of the product range
- company policies
- sales techniques
- complaints procedures
- competitors' products, sales, services, etc.

- report writing procedures
- the use of samples, literature, etc.
- the psychology used in buying and selling
- job satisfaction and motivation
- establishing goodwill with customers

The size of the sales force, and how an organisation chooses to deploy it depend on a number of factors, including:

- the product and customer range
- the geographical dispersion of the customers
- the number of actual or potential customers
- the size of potential orders
- the frequency of call rate by the salespeople
- the company resources available

In designing sales territories, organisations must consider the need to reduce travel and expense as much as possible, to divide work loads equally, to provide adequate sales potential for motivation purposes, and to provide for simple administration and control.

The sales force often works without direct supervision and, therefore, control standards are needed to ensure that the salesperson's performance is up to standard. Methods used may include an analysis of total volume, revenue, comparison with past performance, progress towards targets, etc. All these measures relate to the products sold. However, other factors that may be considered here include the number of sales made by the salesperson, new accounts opened, the accuracy of paperwork, and feedback from customers. The general appearance of the salesperson, his/her product knowledge and relations with customers may also be taken into account.

PRESENTING APPROPRIATE IMAGE

Establishing a clear corporate image is one thing, but it is often said that first impressions are everything. It is, therefore, essential that all employees involved in sales-related activities adopt the organisation's stance on image projection.

Many organisations will adopt the more obvious methods of projecting this image. Examples will include the wearing of uniforms, badges or name tags or the requirement to be smart and presentable. This image projection cuts across many sales activities, and in particular customer service. An organisation which has spent a considerable amount of time and effort on establishing a corporate image will be at pains to ensure that its employees assist in this communication channel.

CUSTOMER CARE

There are a wide range of characteristics which could be associated with customer care, including:

- interpersonal relationships between the employees and the customer
- activities involved in the placing and receiving of orders as a response to customer requirements
- activities related to how the product is delivered and when
- availability of after-sales service for maintenance, repair and advice
- customer complaints procedure

Obviously, if a customer is satisfied with the service he/she receives from an organisation, this will lead to the following:

- repeat sales
- the customer recommending the organisation to a third party
- compliments and testimonials

Conversely, dissatisfaction may result in the following:

- loss of the customer with consequent loss of repeat sales
- numerous customer complaints
- unfavourable feedback from the customer to friends and associates

In order to institute an effective customer care programme, an organisation must:

- be responsive to customer needs
- have a quality approach to distribution
- instil and maintain the right attitude among employees
- encourage employees to establish a rapport with customers
- continually upgrade and improve the product or service
- ensure that the organisation is customer-driven
- have clear market-orientated objectives
- provide an effective after-sales service

POINT-OF-SALE SERVICE

With many products, there is no point of contact between the end-user and the sales force. The organisation has, therefore, no control over how the product is displayed or, indeed, what a salesperson may say to the customer. Undoubtedly many potential sales are lost because a salesperson in a retail outlet lacks knowledge or understanding of a product. In order to combat this, many organisations employ comprehensive point-of-sale materials. As we have mentioned elsewhere in this Unit, these include dump bins, posters and sales literature.

The responsibilities of the salesperson for point-of-sale material differ, according to which type of salesperson he or she is:

1 The salesperson employed by the supplying organisation, whose duty it is to 'install' or provide point-of-sale material in any outlet which requests it, or to convince outlets to devote space to it, needs to ensure that the sales-people in the outlet understand what should be done with the point-of-sale material and are appraised of the content of any sales literature.

2 The salesperson employed by a retail outlet, must make him/herself aware of the nature and uses of the point-of-sale material provided by the supplier. Normally this point-of-sale material will be an integral part of an on-going marketing or sales promotion campaign and the salesperson will be expected to embrace this. Any stock taken from the warehouse or deliveries will be placed within the point-of-sale display area. It may be necessary also to put 'special offer' stickers or other promotional attractors on the products to signify the special promotion.

PRODUCT KNOWLEDGE

It is obviously essential that a salesperson has good product knowledge. Essentially, this involves the following:

- knowledge of the organisation's own products
- an understanding of the benefits of the products
- an understanding of how the product works
- similar understanding of the competitors' products
- an appreciation of the relative strengths and weaknesses of the organisation's own products and those of competitors

AFTER-SALES SERVICE

As we have said elsewhere in the book, an effective after-sales service attempts to address the probable reasons for a customer returning to an organisation after making a purchase. Essentially we can classify the reasons as follows:

- the customer may require information
- the customer may require a related service
- the customer may need a complimentary product or service

- the customer may need to be reassured about a particular situation
- the customer may need assurance of quality
- the customer may have a problem which needs to be addressed

student activity

(PC 3.4.3, COM 3.2, 3.4)
Using the above list of product knowledge requirements, try to identify product knowledge needed for the following:

- toothpaste
- a vacuum cleaner

Discuss this as a group and attempt to make a comprehensive list of product knowledge requirements.

student activity

(PC 3.4.3, COM 3.1)
As a group, can you think of other reasons why a customer may return to an organisation after having purchased a product or service?

Businesses spend millions of pounds per year in after-sales service. British Airways, for example, receive around 100,000 complaints about the service they have provided from their millions of customers. They ensure that every single complaint or after-sales enquiry is investigated to the customer's satisfaction.

British Gas actually go one stage further and advertise in the hope that they can induce customers to complain if they are not satisfied with the services provided.

The following should be an integral part of the service provided by a salesperson in dealing with customer service enquiries:

- always put the customer service requirement first, before other operations
- resist the temptation to create a service which has an end in itself and loses the point of the original need

- always ensure that the customer gets what he/she wants when he/she wants it
- always treat the customer with respect and follow the concept that the customer is always right
- always remember that without customers there is no business

SALES ADMINISTRATION

Record keeping is obviously important in any aspect of business. We cover in great detail in Unit 2 various administrative systems which organisations could have in place. A sales representative would normally keep the following information:

- the names and addresses of organisations with whom he/she has contact
- the name, telephone extension and position of the contact at each of these organisations
- dates of meetings which have already taken place
- dates of meetings scheduled for the future
- an assessment of each organisation's potential
- an identification of each organisation's buying needs and habits
- a record of past sales
- a record of complaints and problems
- a record of the organisation's credit limits
- feedback from the customer on various aspects of the supplying organisation's activities

We will be looking at some of the aspects of sales administration in the next performance criterion of this Element.

student activity

(PC 3.4.3, COM 3.2, IT 3.1, 3.2, 3.3)
Using the above list of customer information which should be held by a sales representative, design a suitable record sheet covering each of the items, using computer software.

KNOWLEDGE OF SALE OF GOODS ACT AND TRADES DESCRIPTION ACT

Naturally, a sales representative will need to know the main points in the following Acts which are relevant to his/her function:

- Sale of Goods Act 1979 and 1994
- Sale of Goods (Amendment Act) 1994
- Trades Descriptions Act, 1968 and 1972

According to the Sale of Goods Act, goods must be of merchantable quality. In other words, they must be fit for the normal purpose for which they were purchased. This Act comes into force as soon as the seller has offered the product for sale and the buyer has accepted it. The contract need not have been written and if the seller breaks the contract, then the buyer is entitled to have his/her money back or the goods replaced. Buyers do not have to accept a credit note, despite what sales assistants may say.

The terms of the Trades Descriptions Act (1968 and 1972), particularly in respect of the following, are also relevant:

- that false descriptions of the product or service are not made
- that no misleading statements or claims are made in respect of the product or service

It should be remembered that this law applies not only to the packaging of the product itself, but also to any advertisements, posters, labelling or point-of-sale material. The Trade Descriptions Act comes into force when a customer complains that he/she has been misled or the product has been sold with an incorrect description.

COMMUNICATING EFFECTIVELY

Being in close day-to-day contact with customers, the sales representative will need to have at least average communication skills. The inability to communicate effectively with a customer can not only cost the organisation sales, but also may result in unnecessary misunderstandings. Most organisations have established clear procedures which they expect their salespeople to follow. However, the day-to-day implementation of this policy may not be under the direct control of those who constructed the procedures. It is, therefore, essential for organisations to ensure that salespeople are given regular refresher courses on dealing with and communicating with customers effectively. In Unit 2.3 we identified and investigated the key methods of communication and interaction with others, both within and outside the organisation.

Obviously, as well as having basic communication skills, the sales representative will also have to prove that he/she is reliable in all the methods of communication he/she uses. In other words, if a salesperson says he/she will telephone the customer, then he/she must do so. If he/she promises to send some further information, then he/she must do so.

3.4.4 Explain the importance of effective sales administration to an organisation and its customers

SALES ADMINISTRATION

We have talked earlier about the responsibilities of sales representatives for administration as it affects customers. Now we intend to look at the way the organisation itself should control the administration systems which support sales to customers.

ORDER PROCESSING

Obviously, when a sales representative visits an organisation or customer, it is hoped that he/she will receive an order for goods or services. Alternatively, an independent customer may simply telephone to place a repeat order for goods. Whatever the case, it is imperative that the processing of these orders is carried out in an efficient and effective way.

The sales team, either by means of direct contact with customers, or by telesales, will have in place a series of steps which they will have to take when receiving an order. These may include:

1 With telephone orders, they should ensure that they obtain an order number from the customer. This order should then be confirmed in writing.
2 In the case of telephone orders, in particular all the details of the order, including the quantity, unit price, any reference numbers, etc. must be repeated to the customer, to ensure that they have been correctly understood.
3 When the written confirmation of the order is received, or when a written order arrives at the sales office, the details should all be checked to ensure that the customer has not made any errors.
4 When a sales representative takes an order directly from a customer, he/she should also ensure that all details on the order form have been correctly completed.
5 Before any confirmation of order is sent to the customer, the sales department needs to contact the warehouse to ensure that the goods are available for despatch. If there is any problem with availability, the customer should be informed immediately.
6 Before goods are despatched to the customer the warehouse must make sure that the goods being sent tally with those ordered. Any discrepancies could cause drastic problems to the customer and bad repercussions for the organisation.
7 The accounts department needs to be aware of all the details on the order form so that they can issue an invoice to the customer. In addition, the details of the total amount of the order would be sent to the customer by means of a Statement of Account, which is a request for payment for the goods.

CREDIT CLEARANCE AND CREDIT CONTROL

There is an inevitable amount of risk associated with sales if business objectives are to be met. The riskiness or otherwise of a particular customer needs to be assessed. To do this, information, control and monitoring are needed. Normally there are standard steps to be taken in ensuring that a customer is not too significant a risk. These include:

1 Asking the prospective customer for bank references.
2 Asking the prospective customer for at least two trade references. Information obtained from them should include:

- trade credit that they give to that customer
- their opinion of whether the customer represents a good or bad risk

3 Asking a credit reporting agency for a report on the customer.
4 Asking the prospective customer for a copy of his/her company's report, accounts, balance sheet or profit and loss account, which you can then pass on to your own accounts department.
5 Visiting the business and meeting the owners and making sure that they answer any queries you may have.

There is a variety of different methods of making sure that you offer the correct credit terms to customers. Typically, credit terms include:

- cash with order
- cash on delivery
- payment within seven days
- payment on a weekly basis for goods received the previous week (this is known as weekly credit)
- payment on a monthly basis for goods received the previous month (this is known as monthly credit)
- payment within 30 days after delivery (30 days credit)

Offering a discount for early payment can serve as a useful incentive to ensure that payments are made on time if not before. For example, you could offer a 1 per cent discount for payments made within seven days of issuing the invoice. It is important if this kind of system is introduced that customers are made aware that they are only entitled to the discount if they meet the conditions. Late payers, may be required to make an additional payment for administrative or interest purposes.

CUSTOMER ACCOUNTS

In order to ensure that an organisation meets its objectives and makes a profit, the administration systems which are in place have to carefully monitor how customers pay for their goods or services.

Obviously, one factor that has to be taken into account is the credit the customer is allowed. Monitoring how the customer pays and the regularity of payments is essential if the organisation is not to find itself with a series of aged debtors (people who owe them money).

The accounts department and/or the credit control department of the organisation will monitor each customer individually to ensure that he/she pays for the goods or services purchased on a regular and acceptable basis. In order to make sure that the customer is fully aware of the balance owing to the organisation, the accounts department will issue a Statement of Account which will itemise the transactions which have taken place during the financial period in question. A reliable customer should then pay this balance in full.

If a customer is not quite so reliable with his/her payments, then the sales team need to be informed of this. The last thing the organisation will want to do is to sell more products or services to a customer who already owes it money. A series of letters (becoming increasingly demanding) will be sent to the customer advising him/her that they have reached their credit limit and that payment of the account is now required in full. The sales team would be informed that the customer is in debt to the organisation and that no further goods or services should be provided until the account has been cleared.

DELIVERY SCHEDULES

Distribution or delivery is one of the four Ps in the marketing mix. It obviously involves not only the physical distribution of the products to the locations where they are required, but also choosing the right channel of distribution.

The concept of physical distribution management (PDM) addresses the need for managers to consider the following:

- developing administrative systems to control the movement of products
- managing the administrative systems
- monitoring the administrative systems

If a distribution system is in place then the organisation will be able to inform its customers of the probable delivery time for the product or service ordered. Obviously some products may need more lead time than others, if they are manufactured on an individual basis.

SECURITY

You can refer back to Unit 2 for further details about security, however, there are a number of security issues involved in this performance criterion.

We can split the security issue into the following sub-divisions:

- confidentiality
- customer record security

In terms of **confidentiality,** we must consider such aspects as ensuring that the sales representatives are aware that certain information is on a privileged basis and that they should not divulge such information to customers. This will be particularly true when an organisation is planning something or when it is in financial difficulty. In the first instance competitors may glean information from shared customers and may be able to undermine the marketing or sales promotion campaign before it has begun. In the second instance, if a customer has knowledge that a supplier is having financial difficulty, then he/she may be tempted to seek alternative suppliers on the assumption that present arrangements may not last for very much longer. Whether the financial difficulties being experienced actually become serious or not, the mere act of looking for an alternative source may lead to a customer defecting to a new supplier.

Since **customer records** may contain confidential information about payments, credit levels and discounts, it is advisable that these records are not available to individuals who may unwittingly disclose information to a third party. There are two concerns here if this should happen:

- not only would the customer be immensely annoyed, if not embarrassed, by the disclosure of the information
- but also the customer's competitors may gain an unfair advantage if they know the terms and conditions as well as the trading history of the organisation

With the advent of networked computer systems which allow hitherto unparalleled levels of information to be available, there is a need to limit access. If an organisation allows relatively junior employees to access confidential or sensitive information regarding customers there is always a risk of disclosure to a third party. Although this may not happen as a result of malicious intent or for monetary gain, the employee may, inadvertently, mention something which he/she should not really have known about. The solution is obvious and many organisations have openly embraced the concept of locking out unauthorised personnel by the use of codes or key words.

PROSPECTING

As we mentioned earlier, prospecting is the search for customers and subsequent contact with them in order to secure a sale. It is probably more common in the field of industry than in retail operations, as the majority of customers in retail make the initial contact with the organisation.

One of the major problems with salespeople who have been working for an organisation for a number of years is that they have a tendency to rely upon established customers to provide them with repeat orders. If this level of sales activity is sufficient, then the sales representative is not encouraged personally to seek new business. Human nature being what it is, even the more

brash and confident sales representative would prefer to visit established contacts, than to try and sell to strangers.

student activity

(PC 3.4.4, COM 3.1)
As a group assess the principal sources of information required for prospecting in relation to the following products or services. In other words, where would you find appropriate names and addresses to begin a prospecting exercise?

- a chilled bottled water dispenser
- a printing service which offers the printing of logos and slogans on tee-shirts and sweatshirts
- a service which offers the collection of recyclable materials such as old bottles, used batteries and drinks cans

3.4.5 Evaluate customer service in terms of the needs of customers and organisations

CUSTOMER SERVICE

We have covered many of the customer service requirements in relation to sales, complaints, information and problems as they relate to **external** customers. In order to put your knowledge of these services into practice, you should read the Focus Study on p.308 (which is fictitious) and attempt the Student Activity which follows it.

Before you do this, we should mention the needs of **internal** customers, particularly in terms of help they may need and information they may be seeking.

TO MEET THE NEEDS OF EXTERNAL CUSTOMERS (SALES, COMPLAINTS, INFORMATION, PROBLEMS) AND TO MEET THE NEEDS OF INTERNAL CUSTOMERS (HELP, INFORMATION)

In any organisation, regardless of its size, certain departments or divisions will have to service other

parts of the organisation. This is particularly true of the following departments:

- accounts
- administration
- personnel
- sales

Whether they require assistance in the form of a specific project or whether they require information, they should be treated in exactly the same way as you would treat an external customer. Whilst no money will actually change hands, although in some cases departments will 'charge' other departments for services provided (such as a reprographics unit charging the various departments for photocopies), a professional and courteous service should always be provided.

Focus study

MEETING THE NEEDS OF EXTERNAL CUSTOMERS

The small supermarket chain Baileys has seven stores in central Norfolk. It is a family-run concern and despite having been established over 30 years ago, it is now facing problems. The shops do not have the advantage of being small local stores (the average store size is 4,000 sq. ft.) or of being large supermarkets. When the stores were established (the last one was opened in 1981), they were in small towns and reasonable sized villages, and it was considered by the company that they were good locations with reasonable catchment areas. Baileys could not have predicted the opening of large out-of-town supermarkets which have had a drastic effect on their business. In the early stages the chains' prices compared well with those of corner shops, but now, with the supermarket price-cutting war, Baileys has been left way behind.

The Board met recently and working from reports provided by store managers and head office personnel, they ascertained the following:

- they cannot possibly compete in price terms with supermarkets
- the quality and range in these supermarkets is much better than in Baileys
- the large supermarkets are at least five or six times bigger than Baileys' average store
- being located in the centre of a market town is no longer an advantage as car parking is difficult
- by comparing the average customer's spending in Baileys and in the supermarkets, they discovered that customers on average spend around £7 in Baileys against over £40 in supermarkets
- traditional customers of Baileys are now happy to travel considerable distances to visit the supermarkets. Even those without a car can take advantage of the free buses provided by the supermarkets

Baileys were very interested in customer attitudes about the probable disadvantages of supermarkets and they identified the following:

- there seemed not to be sufficient staff in the supermarkets
- the quality of fresh produce was criticised
- in most supermarkets there were no price tickets
- there were often long queues at the check-outs

This all sounded promising until the results of an exit questionnaire was analysed. Baileys had commissioned a local marketing consultancy to interview 500 customers leaving their stores. It was bad news:

- Baileys' own-label products were considered extremely poor quality
- the customers did not think much of the employees' appearance or helpfulness
- the stores appeared tatty and underfunded
- it was difficult to move trolleys or prams around the stores
- Baileys did not have a good range of convenience items, such as pre-packed salads or ready to cook meals

There were a few positive points:

- the quality of Baileys' fresh produce was considered to be good
- customers appreciated Baileys' local delivery service
- Baileys '8 til 8' opening times were very much appreciated

The Board of Baileys obviously need to reappraise the whole of their business strategy. They have to re-examine the needs of their customers or face eventual closure.

student activity

(PC 3.4.5, COM 3.2, 3.4, AON 3.3, IT 3.1, 3.2, 3.3)
In the role of Baileys sales director, respond to the instruction from the Board to create a new strategy which addresses the needs of the customers. The Bailey family are perfectly prepared to invest considerable sums of money in a total overhaul of their operations if you think this is necessary. You should present your key findings and recommendations in the form of a confidential internal memorandum to the Board. Your memorandum should be word processed and you should submit any tables, charts or diagrams that you think would be of use to them in making their decision.

ELEMENT 1.3

assignment

(PC 3.4.1–5, COM 3.2, 3.3, 3.4, AON 3.1, 3.2, 3.3, IT 3.1, 3.2, 3.3)
This Element is designed to help you understand the final objective of marketing, which is making the sale. If possible, in the preparation of the report which forms the centre of this Assignment, you should try to study the sales operations of an existing business. If this proves to be impossible, your tutor should be able to provide you with a simulated business.

TASK 1

(PC 3.4.1–2)
In the first part of your report you should compare the sales methods used by two different sales organisations. You should also, now focusing on just one organisation, look at a specific sales campaign.

TASK 2

(PC 3.4.3–4)
In this part of your report you should explain the responsibilities of salespeople in providing customer service. As a back-up to this you should also investi-gate the importance of sales administration within your two chosen organisations and how this addresses the needs of the customer, as well as the needs of the organisation.

TASK 3

(PC 3.4.5)
Your report should conclude with a summary evaluating the customer service provided in a particular organisation which meets the needs of both internal and external customers.

NOTES

Your report should be word processed. You could consider looking at one organisation which has been successful and one which has been unsuccessful in its sales operations, although this may be difficult. In relation to Task 1 it would be advisable to look at two organisations which employ different sales methods, in other words direct and indirect.

UNIT 3

test questions

Focus 1

MARKETING PRINCIPLES AND FUNCTIONS

I   What would be the most likely reaction of an organisation already dominant in the market to a new product entering that market?

(a) carry out market research on the new product
(b) sponsor a promotional event
(c) drastically reduce price
(d) step up the advertising campaign

2   The principal function of branding is to:

(a) ensure that the product is not copied
(b) be able to charge a higher price
(c) differentiate the product from other products
(d) ensure that all supermarkets stock the product

Focus 2

CUSTOMER FOCUS/ORGANISATION'S OWN NEEDS

3   The following two statements have been made about the focus of organisations:

(i)   a market-orientated organisation analyses the market's needs first and then produces products
(ii) a product-orientated organisation is geared up to produce a new range of products should it discover there is a need

Are these statements?

(a) True/True
(b) True/False
(c) False/True
(d) False/False

4   Customer retention is:

(a) ensuring that the organisation does its best to encourage repeat sales
(b) ensuring that the organisation does not keep the customer waiting for too long to fulfil an order
(c) ensuring that the customer's interest is kept during the sales pitch

(d) ensuring that the organisation always has the minimum number of customers required to remain profitable

Focus 3

MARKETING RESEARCH METHODS AND SOURCES

5–7   There are a number of methods for collecting primary data. These include:

(a) interviews
(b) telecommunications
(c) post
(d) observation
Which of the above would:

5   Give a low response rate

6   Be regarded as unnecessarily intrusive by the respondent

7   Look at how customers behave in certain situations

8   Data on a company obtained through Companies House are an example of which form of data?

(a) government statistics
(b) other published statistics
(c) primary market data
(d) secondary market data

Focus 4

PRODUCT DEVELOPMENT

9   At the initial stages of product development, which of the following is not necessarily a concern?

(a) pricing
(b) competition
(c) profit
(d) packaging

Focus 5

ADVERTISING AND PUBLICITY

10–12 The following figures represent the OTSs of some major forms of media:

(a) 90%
(b) 70%
(c) 40%
(d) 3%

Which of the above percentages relate to the following marketing media?

10 Television

11 Cinema

12 Radio

13 The following two statements have been made:

(i) magazines tend to have a longer life than newspapers and have a higher pass-on rate
(ii) magazines have longer lead and cancellation times for advertisements

How are these statements best described?

(a) True/True
(b) True/False
(c) False/True
(d) False/False

14 In planning an advertising campaign an organisation would normally consult:

(a) a television company
(b) a public relations agency
(c) an advertising agency
(d) the board of directors

Focus 6

PUBLIC RELATIONS AND SALES PROMOTION

15–17 There are a variety of different sales promotions techniques, including the following:

(a) self liquidating premiums
(b) money-off
(c) user competitions
(d) free premium offers

Which of the above is best described by the following?

15 A sales promotion technique which seeks to maintain brand loyalty by increasing the frequency of use

16 A sales promotion technique which offers the customer a reduced price on repeat purchases in exchange for several proofs of purchases

17 A sales promotion technique which offers the advantage of an additional sample

18 The following two statements have been made:

(i) public relations encompasses all of the actions of and communications from an organisation
(ii) public relations is commonly concerned with setting the record straight if the organisation has been criticised

Are these statements?

(a) True/True
(b) True/False
(c) False/True
(d) False/False

19 A loyalty incentive is best described as:

(a) rewarding sales people for exceptional levels of activity
(b) encouraging potential customers to become customers
(c) rewarding existing customers for their repeat purchases
(d) offering marketing managers a prize for successful campaigns

Focus 7

GUIDELINES AND CONTROLS

20 What is the ultimate sanction that the Advertising Standards Authority can use in the event of an organisation breaking the Code of Advertising Practice?

(a) to demand the withdrawal of the advertisement
(b) to request the withdrawal of the advertisement
(c) to ask for the advertisement to be amended
(d) to pass the matter on to the Office of Fair Trading

21 The Advertising Standards Authority makes a levy on all advertisements and it is collected on its behalf by:

(a) the Advertising Standards Board of Finance
(b) the Code of Advertising Practice
(c) Newspaper Publishers Association
(d) Association of Media Independents

22 The following statements have been made:

(i) Advertisements on radio are regulated by the ITC
(ii) Written or visual print advertisements are regulated by the ASA

Are these statements?

(a) True/True
(b) True/False
(c) False/True
(d) False/False

Focus 8

DIRECT AND INDIRECT SALES METHODS

23–25 There are a number of different direct sales methods which include:

(a) pyramid selling
(b) tele-sales
(c) factory sales
(d) direct response

Which of the above is best described by the following?

23 A direct sales channel which allows the organisation to dispose of excess stock

24 A pro-active sales technique now adopted by around 30 per cent of organisations

25 A direct sales technique now commonly known as network marketing

26 The following statements have been made:

(i) a licensee is an individual or organisation that has the right to manufacture a product in an overseas market
(ii) a distributor is a buyer and re-seller of products

Are these statements?

(a) True/True
(b) True/False
(c) False/True
(d) False/False

Focus 9

SALES ADMINISTRATION AND CUSTOMER SERVICE

27 Prospecting is an essential activity of the sales force. A good definition of this is:

(a) visiting existing customers and attempting to increase sales via internal contacts
(b) visiting existing customers and attempting to increase sales by trying to convince them to buy other products from your range
(c) making initial contact with a potential customer
(d) responding to initial contact made by a potential customer

28–30 There are a number of different ways of dealing with credit terms for customers. The following are variations of these terms:

(a) cash with order
(b) weekly credit
(c) monthly credit
(d) 30 days credit

Which of the above is best described by the following?

28 A statement would be sent out to inform the purchaser of the amount owing

29 No credit

30 No credit would be given if payment for goods was made 10 days after the invoice was received

Investigate human resourcing

PERFORMANCE CRITERIA

A student must:

1 analyse *the rights of employers and employees*

2 *explain* **employer** *and* **employee responsibilities** *in human resourcing*

3 *describe* **procedures** *available to* **employers** *and* **employees** *when rights are not upheld*

4 *explain the* **roles of trades unions** *and* **staff associations**

5 *explain employers'* **methods for gaining employee co-operation**

RANGE

Analyse *in terms of: contracts (pay, holiday pay, sick pay, procedures for disciplinary action), health and safety regulations, non-discriminatory legislation*

Employer responsibilities: *clarify business objectives, offer and facilitate training and professional development, manage change; recruitment, negotiation of pay and conditions, handle disciplinary procedures, handle grievance procedures, implement non-discriminatory legislation (Sex Discrimination Act, Race Relations Act, Equal Pay Act), implement health and safety regulations, meet quality standards*

Employee responsibilities: *compliance with terms of contract, compliance with health and safety at work, non-discriminatory behaviour, work towards organisational objectives, meet customer needs, to other employees, meet quality standards*

Procedures for employers: *negotiations (with individuals, with trades unions, with staff associations); negotiations through Advisory Conciliation and Arbitration Services (ACAS), industrial tribunals, court action*

Procedures for employees: *negotiations (with employer, through trades unions, staff associations) negotiations through Advisory Conciliation and Arbitration Services (ACAS), industrial tribunals, court action, industrial action*

Role of trades unions and staff associations: *negotiating pay and conditions, giving advice and information, defending employees' rights, resolving conflict*

Methods for gaining employee co-operation: *representation, consultation, team working, employee share ownership, quality circles, job security*

4.1.1 *Analyse the rights of employers and employees*

ANALYSIS

Employers are under a common law duty to ensure that reasonable care is taken to provide their employees with:

- a safe place of work
- safe working methods
- appropriate training
- safe equipment

Obviously, it is hard to establish the nature of reasonable care. It is not usually sufficient that the employer simply provides a safe system of work. He/she must ensure that these systems have been put fully into effect. If, for example, legislation requires that all employees use safety equipment whilst using machines, it is the employer's responsibility to make sure that the safety equipment is actually used. The employer cannot use the defence that the employees were told to use the safety equipment, or that a subordinate was delegated to make sure this happened. As we will see, the Health and Safety at Work Act and other regulations carry a criminal sanction if breached. With regard to some of these regulations, the employer will know absolutely what has to be done, but in others, the instructions are more vague.

student activity

(PC 4.1.1, COM 3.1)
Individually, try to define the term 'reasonable care'. What do you think should be implied in your definition? Compare your definition with those of the remainder of your group.

Certain legislation merely establishes a minimum standard, or prohibits certain actions. In the case of industrial accidents, damages or injunctions may be placed upon the employer for breaches of the legislation.

We will now turn out attention to the specific rights which bind both employers and employees.

COMPLIANCE WITH TERMS OF CONTRACT (PAY, HOLIDAY PAY, SICK PAY, PROCEDURES FOR DISCIPLINARY ACTION)

As we have already seen in Unit 2, the employer has a number of duties towards the employee. This can be seen very clearly in a contract of employment. This document really formalises the relationship and is seen as a legally binding document on both the employer and employee. A contract of employment should lay down all of the following points:

1 Job role; what is the precise nature of the job?
2 Job title.
3 Pay details; how it is paid, frequency of payment.
4 Additional payment details, such as which salary/wage scale the individual will be placed on.
5 When overtime can be undertaken.
6 How bonuses can be earned.
7 How commission can be earned.
8 Start times and finishing times of work.
9 Total number of hours to be worked per week.
10 Number of paid days off for holidays, etc. (and any restrictions).
11 Sick leave details, duration and entitlement.
12 Maternity leave details, duration and entitlement.
13 Pension schemes, including contributions made by employer and employee.
14 Grievance procedure details.
15 Period of notice to be worked or given.
16 Resignation or termination details.

The employer may also wish to inform the employees of the following:

- company rules and regulations
- codes of behaviour (including dress code, etc.)
- organisational chart
- availability of social activities

Just as the employer will be expected to fulfil his/her obligations as set out in the contract of employment, so, too will the employee. The employee will be expected to comply with all aspects of the contract of employment, and furthermore, will be required to accept responsibility for his/her actions at work.

Confidentiality is important; the employee should also take care not to release any information of a sensitive or secret nature to the media or competitors.

student activity

0:20

(PC 4.1.1, COM 3.1)
In the role of an employer, draw up a list of sensitive information and sources which you would expect to remain confidential. How would you clearly state to your employees the fact that this information should remain secret? What steps would you take to ensure limited access? What steps would you take against employees breaching the confidentiality of such documents?

COMPLIANCE WITH HEALTH AND SAFETY REGULATIONS

If legal requirements are broken by either employers or employees, in effect, one side or other has been negligent. The aggrieved party may then begin legal proceedings. The health and safety requirements with which any employer must comply are:

- to provide **a safe working environment**
- to provide **adequate welfare facilities**
- to ensure **entrances** and **exits** are **safe**
- to ensure **equipment** and **systems** used are **safe** and regularly **serviced**
- to make sure that items needed for use in **handling** or **storage** are **safe**
- to make sure that **dangerous** or **toxic materials** are housed in **safe** containers
- to provide **instruction,** training or supervision regarding working practices and materials used
- to ensure that all **accidents** are rigorously **investigated** and the causes promptly dealt with

English law requires not only a **standard** of care, but also a duty of care. Other European countries have created clearer definitions. The German law (Article 823(1) of their civil code) states:

a person who, wilfully or negligently, unlawfully injures the life, body, health, freedom, property or other rights of another is bound to compensate him for any damage arising therefrom.

Specifically relating to health and safety at work, the German civil code (Article 831(1)) states:

a person who employs another to do any work, is bound to compensate for any damage which the other

unlawfully causes to a third party in the performance of his work. The duty to compensate does not arise if the employer has exercised necessary care in the selection of the employee; and, where he has to supply apparatus or equipment or to supervise the work, has also exercised ordinary care as regards such supply or supervision, or if the damage would have arisen notwithstanding the exercise of such care.

student activity

1:00

(PC 4.1.1, IT 3.1, 3.3, COM 3.3)
Identify a particular health and safety concern of your own choice. Create a simple flowchart which describes the actions to be taken in the event of a breach of this health and safety matter. Produce your flowchart by means of a computer software package.

COMPLIANCE WITH NON-DISCRIMINATORY LEGISLATION

Even today, many individuals suffer discrimination on various grounds. Within employment, employees are protected to some extent by a series of laws and regulations. The main groups who suffer from discrimination are:

- women
- ethnic minorities
- the disabled
- the young
- the old
- those with an alternative sexual orientation
- certain religious groups

Many organisations have adopted equal opportunities policies, although they are not yet required to do this by law. The Equal Opportunities Commission has designed a standard policy which employers can use. This covers a wide variety of different situations, and includes the following:

- that to have an equal opportunities policy is a desirable thing
- that it should be strictly adhered to
- that all forms of direct and indirect discrimination are clearly defined

TABLE 4.1.1 *European Law – A comparison of rights and responsibilities*

	CONTRACT OF EMPLOYMENT	DISMISSAL	GRIEVANCE	REDUNDANCY
AUSTRIA	Salaries paid in 14 instalments. After 5 years contracts may be terminated with 6 months notice.	Reasons include: disloyalty disobedience, competing (privately) with employer.	If unfairly dismissed up to 3 months' wages to be paid.	Details must be given to Labour Authority, including age, sex, responsibilities and qualifications for appraisal.
BELGIUM	Includes a probationary period (1–12 months). No written contract is required by law.	Provided notice is given either party may terminate the contract.	Under the Belgian Law on employment contracts no reason is required for dismissal.	Formula includes: length of service, difficulties in finding a new job, age, job role and salary.
FRANCE	Can be written or oral. If these contradict one another, then the situation most favourable to the employee is taken. Also may include a trial period.	Reasons include: incompetence, longterm illness, age, retirement, gross misconduct, economic problems.	Whether personal or economic reasons for dismissal, employee may ask for an industrial tribunal to hear the case.	Certain protection for older employees with families or for single parents and disabled. Also redundant employees have priority if employer recruits within a year.
GERMANY	Usually written, normal contractual obligations. 18 days minimum holiday entitlement. Payment is made in 13, 14 or 15 instalments.	Long notice periods, specified usually in contract of employment. Normal dismissal reasons.	Heard in the employment court. Total compensation does not usually exceed Dm 36,000.	
GREECE	Includes a 2-month trial period. Normal contractual obligations. Salaries paid in 14 instalments.	Phased dismissal procedures. Also includes temporary dismissal.	Employee can challenge validity of dismissal, etc. If not legal then employee can demand reinstatement and back pay.	Provided legal compensation is paid, although employer must taker into account seniority and family commitments.
EIRE	Very comprehensive legislation covering contracts. Reasonably long notice periods.	Wrongful dismissal outlawed. Statutory compensation of up to 104 weeks pay.	Claims made through either Rights Commissioners or Employment Appeals Tribunal. Complex Legislation.	If employee has worked for at least 104 weeks, then compensation is due. No rules regarding choice of redundant employees.
ITALY	Oral or in writing. Fixed-term contracts last a minimum of 5 years. Also includes trial period.	Normal reasons, but does not protect the over-60s, those in trial period, house-keepers and executives.	Claims through arbitration bands if up to 22 months to pay.	Complex, but may entitle employee to up to 80% of salary or be considered 'early retired'.
LUXEMBOURG	In writing and in duplicate. All other normal contractual obligations. Long notice periods.	Employee must be interviewed before dismissal by law. Otherwise reasons apply.	Court of appeal hears complaints and imposes judgements.	Usually for economic reasons.
NETHERLANDS	Maximum 2-month trial period, fairly simple contract of employment.	Employment controls cannot be terminated without a permit from the district labour office.	The National Court will settle blame and require compensation to be paid. This is called a 'golden handshake'.	Employment contracts can be terminated by mutual consent and agreement of the Judge of the Court.
PORTUGAL	Normal contractual obligations. Written contract required for temporary work, or for permanent. 15–30 day probation period.	Notification within 30 days of reasons. Trade Union must be informed.	If deemed unfair, employer pays salary from dismissal date to date of court hearing.	Normally 1 month's salary for each year or part year worked.
SPAIN	Written or oral. All main contractual obligations. Variable trial periods.	'Serious and blameworthy non-fulfilment by employee'. Normal reasons apply.	If dismissal is unlawful, then the employer makes a payment of 45 days pay per year employed, or may have to re-employ.	Normally 20 days' salary per year worked.
UK	Usually written, particularly in the case of redundant employment 13 weeks max. (and in writing).	Many legitimate reasons, including misconduct, capability or any other 'substantial' reason.	Employee may use an industrial tribunal. Maximum rewards vary, but between £6–10,000 or up to 52 weeks pay.	Complex calculation. Dependent upon years worked and rate.

WORKING HOURS	EQUALITY	TRADE UNIONS
Working Time Act states hours not to exceed 8 per day or 40 per week. Even with overtime, hours must not exceed 50 per week.	Equal Treatment Act covers sexual discrimination, and covers all areas of work. Employer must prove discrimination did not occur.	Only 1 Trade Union body is recognised — Austrian Federation of TUs. This organisation is responsible for collective agreements.
Normal working week is 39 hours, although employees can work for up to 46 hours per week for a 12 week period.	In 1983 new laws covered sexual discrimination and restrictions relating to family status in all aspects of work.	5 main nationally recognised bodies to undertake collective bargaining. Employer must supply meeting rooms if over 200 employees are union members. Shop stewards allocated paid time.
Mainly 35 hours per week Also working day must have regular breaks. Prohibits work on Sundays or public holidays.	Federal law forbids discrimination. Violation means automatic fines and compensation.	When collective agreements made the Federal Minister of Labour delivers them 'binding'. All employees (regardless of TU membership) are bound by them.
Usually 40 hours per week. Employer may require employees to 'overwork' an extra 8 hours with higher rate of pay.	No discrimination allowed on the grounds of sex, race or religion, etc.	Collective agreements made locally or nationally. Trade union officials legally protected. Court or Arbitration called in if dispute is unproven then judgement is legally binding on both parties
Covered under Conditions of Employment Act and Protection of Young Persons (Employment) Act.	Many laws, including Anti-discrimination (pay) Act, and Promotion of Equality Employment.	Industrial Relations Act (1990) requires pre-strike ballots, Establishment of Labour Relations Commission (covering conciliation and advice).
Normally no more than 8 hours per day, 48 hours per week.	Comprehensive, particularly in relation to sex, equality and the disabled.	Not normally recognised, but nearly always consulted.
Standard 40 hours over 5 days. Overtime must be agreed by the Minister of Labour.	Law considers that equality is expected. Minimum salaries apply regardless of sex.	Collective agreements run for 6 months or more. Trade Unions recognised and must be part of negotiations to make a collective agreement.
Dutch Act on employment states maximum 15 hours to be worked		Quite powerful. Collective bargaining agreements are made legally by the Dutch Ministry of Social Affairs and Employment
Normally 8 hours per day, 48 hours per week or for clerical staff, 7 hours and 42.	Legislation covers sex discrimination, the disabled and students.	Both worker committees and trade unions, latter involved in industrial actions etc. Strike notice required.
Normally 40 hours per week. No more than 80 hours overtime per year paid at 17.5% of usual pay.	Statute of Workers covers sex, race, marital status, religion, politics and trade union membership.	Key role in collective bargaining. Trade unions seen as vital to economic prosperity. Collective agreement legally binding.
No limitations except for those under 18 or in specific occupations.	Unlawful to discriminate in terms of gender, marital status, race, membership of trade union.	Collective agreements not necessarily legally binding. Individuals particularly, not bound by collective agreements.

- that the organisation states its commitment to equal opportunities and further states that it is in the best interests of the organisation and employees to do so
- that all employees are made aware of the policy
- that any preconceived ideas which the employees may have regarding those who are subject to discrimination are addressed
- that staff are trained to maintain the policy
- that recruitment and promotion are equal for all
- that training is offered on an equal basis to all
- that the employment contract does not inadvertently discriminate against anyone
- that the organisation's facilities are open to all
- that an individual is nominated to monitor the policy
- that the policy is regularly reviewed and updated according to need
- that any grievances related to discrimination are dealt with in a prompt and fair manner
- that no individual suffers victimisation in the course of his/her duties within the organisation

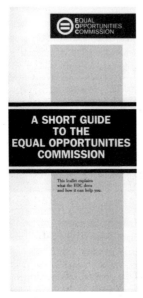

FIG. 4.1.1 *This short guide to the Equal Opportunities Commission explains the role and functions of the EOC.*

The concept of equal pay for an equal day's work is the foundation of the Equal Pay Act. The Equal Pay Act came into force in 1975. Its purpose was to eliminate discrimination between men and women in terms of the following:

- basic rates of pay
- payments for overtime
- payments for bonuses
- payments for piece-work
- working hours
- holidays
- sick leave entitlement

Focus study

EQUAL OPPORTUNITIES COMMISSION

The Equal Opportunities Commission was created to ensure the effective enforcement of the Sex Discrimination Act and the Equal Pay Act and also to promote equal opportunities between the sexes.

The EOC has the power to carry out investigations and if it is satisfied that the practices are unlawful, it can then issue non-discrimination notices requiring the practice to cease.

The EOC has the power to require any individual to provide information or attend hearings to give evidence.

The EOC has the power to help individuals prepare and conduct complaints in either courts or tribunals. In some cases, where issues raise important aspects of principle, the EOC will clarify the legal position.

As well as carrying out investigations, the EOC makes recommendations to the government regarding the operation of existing law.

The EOC takes legal proceedings in its own right against individuals or organisations.

The EOC is also involved in research and educational work relating to equal opportunities.

student activity

(PC 4.1.1, COM 3.1, 3.2)
What is sex discrimination? There are two kinds of discrimination:

- direct discrimination – which involves treating a woman less favourably than a man because she is a woman
- indirect discrimination – which favours one sex more than another for unjustifiable reasons

Try to think of examples of direct and indirect discrimination. If you were the EOC, how would you identify them? Think of examples in pairs, write them down and swap your examples with another pair. Look at the examples of discrimination and work out the best way which you could use to identify and rectify the situation.

The right to equal pay for work of equal value, which was given in effect by the 1983 amended regulations, now forms a part of the Equal Pay Act.

The Act may be used by workers of all ages, including:

- apprentices
- part-time workers
- temporary workers
- home workers
- the self employed
- contract workers
- employees over normal retirement age

The term 'like work' can actually be defined as 'of a broadly similar nature'. In other words, if an individual can show that the work carried out is the same or broadly similar, then in legal terms, the case has been proven. We shall look at some specific examples when we consider the employer's implementation of non-discriminatory legislation and an employee's responsibility to behave in a non-discriminatory manner.

Focus study

EQUAL PAY

Some 20 years have passed since the Equal Pay Act came into operation. Women still earn only 79 per cent of men's full-time hourly earnings. They tend to cluster in 'women's jobs', often under-valued and under-paid. Women provide the bulk of part-time workers, with low pay and fewer opportunities for overtime or bonus earnings. The abolition of the Wages Councils has further widened the gap. Performance-related pay systems have been identified as having bias that affects not only pay, but also training and promotion opportunities.

Britain introduced regulations in 1984 to provide for equal pay for work of equal value. Unfortunately, due to the complexity and limitations of the legal system, they have had little impact on the 'inequality gap'. The laws and related administrative provisions have failed to provide justice to women and ensure equal pay.

The Race Relations Act 1976 makes racial discrimination unlawful in the following areas:

- employment
- training
- education
- the provision of goods, facilities and services
- the disposal and management of premises

0:20

student activity

(PC4.1.1, COM 3.1)
As a group, discuss what you think is meant by 'women's work'. How would you research the actual adoption and implementation of equal pay and conditions to dispel this myth?

The Act gives an individual the right of direct access to the courts or industrial tribunals to gain a legal remedy for unlawful discrimination.

The Act established a Commission for Racial Equality. The Commission's remit includes:

- enforcement of the legislation
- promotion of equality of opportunity
- the fostering of good relations between different racial groups
- advisory responsibilities to the government on the working of the Act
- the Act as a principal source of information
- discretion to assist individuals who feel they have been discriminated against
- assisting organisations to implement equal opportunities

1:05

student activity

(PC 4.1.1, COM 3.1, 3.2, IT 3.1)
In pairs, and using CD-ROM data bases of newspaper articles (if available), try to find an example of racial discrimination within the workplace. Having printed out the article, give a brief explanation of it, in the form of a presentation to the rest of the group. Your presentation should focus on the specific breaches of this legislation. If the case has not been judged by a court as yet, try to make a judgement of your own on whether there is a case to answer.

Focus study

RACIAL EQUALITY

The Race Relations Act came into force in 1977 and applies to discrimination before or after that date. The Act repealed the former Race Relation Acts of 1965 and 1968. It also abolished the Race Relations Board and the Community Relations Commission.

The Act defines two specific kinds of racial discrimination, again we can classify these as direct or indirect. Direct racial discrimination occurs when an individual treats another individual less favourably on racial grounds. The term racial grounds covers the following:

- colour
- race
- nationality
- ethnicity
- national origins

Indirect racial discrimination can be best described as that which occurs when an individual requires specific conditions to be satisfied as a result of being a member of a particular racial group. In other words, the individual discriminating is requiring the victim of the discrimination to comply with additional conditions that he or she would not necessarily have to meet if he or she were not a member of that racial group.

It is unlawful for an employer to discriminate on any of these grounds in relation to employment.

4.1.2 Explain employer and employee responsibilities in human resourcing

EMPLOYER RESPONSIBILITIES

COMPLIANCE WITH TERMS OF CONTRACT

The employer must take care when advertising a job, as the advertisement is considered to be the beginning of the formation of the contract of employment. Once a candidate for a particular job accepts employment on the basis of the advertisement details, then to some extent, much of the contract of employment has already been decided. Before an employer finally accepts a candidate as an employee, he/she will usually take up references. If a prospective employer receives unfavourable references about the candidate, then he/she is quite within his/her rights to withdraw the job offer. In reality, just how the employer interprets the content of a reference is open to question.

A contract of employment is really like any other contract. It gives both parties rights as well as obligations. The contract, as we mentioned earlier, identifies formally what was really agreed during the interview or selection process. Normally, a contract of employment will contain the following commitments, either directly or by inference:

1 The employer will pay wages/salaries.
2 The employer will provide work.
3 The employer will pay any reasonable losses or expenses incurred by the employee in the course of his/her work.
4 The employer will provide a reference if required by the employee.
5 The employer will provide safe working conditions and practices.
6 The employer will not act in such a way as to breach the trust and confidence given by the employee.
7 The employer will provide necessary information relating to the employee's work, pay, conditions and opportunities.
8 The employer will always act in good faith towards the employee.

student activity

(PC 4.1.2, COM 3.1)
What do you understand by the phrase 'breach of trust and confidence'? Discuss this as a group.

CLARIFY BUSINESS OBJECTIVES

Obviously, it is in everyone's interests to identify the exact business objectives as laid down in either a company's mission statement or other company documentation. As we have already mentioned in Unit 2, the specific business objectives can be wide and somewhat imprecise. In addition, business objectives may differ from time to time. Objectives are the medium to long-term targets which help the business to achieve its mission statement. The strategies and tactics involved in achieving the objectives are usually those which will have a direct impact upon the employees.

There are numerous methods of ensuring that employees are conversant with a company's current business objectives. Rather than rely on rumour and misinformation (which is usually rife in many organisations), it is advisable that the organisation ensures that a true picture and statement of objectives is given. Organisations employ some of the following means of ensuring that this vital information (particularly important if there are changes in business objectives), is passed on to employees:

- staff meetings
- newsletters
- company newspapers
- bulletin boards
- noticeboards
- e-mail
- press statements
- corporate videos
- letters sent direct to all employees

An organisation which fails to ensure that its employees are appraised of any key changes in company policy or objectives may find itself working 'against' the employees. This may not be a wilful act, but may result from actions born out of lack of information. To suddenly impose radically different working practices or procedures without consultation (as we will see later) can lead to unrest and diminished motivation among the employees.

It is also advisable for an organisation to clarify the business objectives in order to prepare employees for possible training and development. An organisation which is able to look ahead and, to some extent, predict its future business objectives, is an organisation which will find that employees are not only conversant with, but in step with, the new business objectives.

As we will see, many features of human resourcing that forward planning. In many respects, these relate to the management of change and predictions of future requirements of the organisation.

   `0:20`

student activity

(PC 4.1.2, COM 3.1)
Individually, try to identify the business objectives of

- an organisation for which you may have worked in the past
- an organisation for which you currently work on a part-time basis (including weekends)
- the organisation in which you are studying this programme

Discuss the business objectives you have identified with the rest of the group.

OFFER AND FACILITATE TRAINING AND PROFESSIONAL DEVELOPMENT

Training basically falls into four separate categories, which are:

1 *On-the-job training* – which refers to training carried out whilst at work. It may be delivered by in-house training personnel, or by 'bought-in' specialists.
2 *Off-the-job training* – which refers to training carried out at a location other than the workplace. It may require access to specialists or specialist equipment, not necessarily currently available in the workplace.
3 *Part-time training* – which refers to the 'mode' of training itself. This category includes day-release, evening classes and short courses. This type of training is usually paid for, at least in part, by the employer and relates directly to required job skills.
4 *Full-time training* – which refers to short- or even long-term training courses which take the employee out of the work situation for an extended period. Such training may be necessary because the employee needs to be trained in a complex area which could not be taught on a part-time basis.

Most organisations run special courses, either at the workplace or in an alternative location. The nature of the training may involve specialist management skills, health and safety or supervisory skills. It is usually key personnel who are chosen to attend these courses and they are then expected to pass on the knowledge they have acquired to the rest of the members of their work teams (this is known as **cascading**).

The types of skill required for a business can range from knowledge of new software packages to more

TRAINING DEPARTMENT INDUCTION COURSE

The programme will include:-

- the functions of building societies

- Alliance & Leicester's main products

- business objectives and your role in helping to meet them

- Alliance & Leicester customer service

- communication and teamwork

- telephone techniques

- education and training opportunities

Attendance confirmed by: _____
                                        (Training Officer)

Date: _____

FIG. 4.1.2 *The Alliance and Leicester Building Society is one of many major organisations to consider the importance of training from the very beginning of an individual's working life with the organisation.*

general managerial skills. The area of work which the individual is involved with, will dictate the type of training he/she needs. Personal skills development has become a very popular area of training in recent years and will attempt to offer guidance in the following areas:

- time management
- stress management
- supervisory skills
- leadership skills
- management skills
- communication skills
- counselling skills
- negotiation skills
- assertiveness skills
- coping with meetings

Most people will start their careers with few or no qualifications. Most individuals will have at least some basic understanding of English, or Mathematics, but it is only when they begin to consider what their career goal may be, that they should start to gain qualifications which will help them achieve their goal. Depending on the time and effort put in, individuals can slowly progress in their collection of qualifications. At the same time, particularly if the individual is in work,

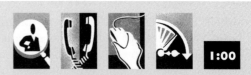

student activity

(PC 4.1.2, COM 3.1, IT 3.1)
In relation to the course which you are now attending, try to identify a particular skill for which you would like to receive training. How would you like this training to be delivered and do you think that it would be better to undertake this training within the institution, or at another location? Try to draw up a short list of topics within the skill area you have identified, which could form the foundation of the training programme. You should present this list in a word processed format.

he/she will be gaining additional responsibilities as a result of the qualifications he/she has achieved.

Whether we are considering training or qualifications, we must make two more important distinctions which relate to the nature of the course of study, and concern whether it is vocational or non-vocational.

Vocational training or qualifications are those which relate directly to the job or job area. It does not necessarily matter whether the individual is in work or not, since the programme should be designed to offer the learner the opportunity to practise the type of skills required for a particular job. This has become a very popular area, much supported by employers, who see this as the only useful and relevant way of preparing individuals for work within industry, commercial services or technology.

In some respects, you would think that the **non-vocational** course is the complete opposite to a vocational course. This may not necessarily be the case. Typically, a course which falls into this category will not have a direct relevance to a particular job and may be more general in nature. Alternatively, non-vocational courses may be academic and provide a wide range of knowledge which is not necessarily applied. Individuals who have followed such courses will need to undertake further training to learn how to put into practice the extensive knowledge they have gained on their academic course.

MANAGE CHANGE

As we mentioned in Unit 2, one of the key skills required of a successful manager is the ability to manage change. Change can be a painful experience to both employer and employee. Considerable research has been undertaken to establish how people cope with

student activity

(PC 4.1.2, COM 3.1, 3.2)
In pairs, using the following sources of information, prepare a short list which should include at least five vocational and non-vocational courses:

- your college library
- your local library
- your careers office
- your careers officer (if you have one)

change and what their reactions are likely to be in different circumstances. Research by Elizabeth Kubler Ross, a psychologist, identified seven stages in an individual's reaction to change:

1 *Shock* – when the change is first discovered. A typical response would be 'I don't believe it!'

2 *Denial* – where the individual will assert that 'it won't affect me'.

3 *Frustration and anger* – where the individual considers him/herself to be the victim, a typical response being 'why me?'

4 *Depression and apathy* – where the individual asserts that he/she cannot cope and is fed up.

5 *Experimentation* – where as a result of the first four stages, the individual now undertakes to 'give it a go'.

6 *Accepting the reality of change* – when the individual realises that the new situation is 'not as bad as I thought it was'.

7 *Integrating the change* – where the individual gradually develops new codes of behaviour and attitudes which incorporate the change. Typical responses at this stage are 'I never thought it would work, but I am coming to terms with it'.

Another feature of change within the work situation concerns the exact nature of the change and how it comes about. In other words, we can identify two distinct forms of change:

- changes over which employees have no control
- changes in which the employees had some part

A simple way of ensuring that changes are implemented in a logical and fair manner is to adopt the SMART approach. The letters of this acronym spell out the following:

- *Specific* – making sure that the changes proposed are clearly stated
- *Measurable* – ensuring that the changes can be monitored and calibrated easily
- *Achievable* – ensuring that the changes are not too all-encompassing and complex and are reasonable
- *Realistic* – following on from the achievable nature of the change, the organisation should not expect too many changes too quickly
- *Timed* – ensuring that the changes are paced and do not swiftly follow other changes. Also, if possible, the change has been implemented at an appropriate point in the development or activities of the organisation

RECRUITMENT

The recruitment and selection process, as we will see in Element 4.3, can be a complex and time-consuming matter. The purpose of recruitment is to attract a sufficient number of well-qualified or appropriate candidates to fill the requirements of the job(s). The purpose of selection is to first define exactly what the requirements are and then adopt an effective 'filtering system' to ensure that the candidates fit those job requirements. Organisations may have radically different approaches to the way in which they recruit or select individuals. Clearly, depending upon a number of criteria, the organisation will choose to adopt one of the following methodologies:

1 *Casual recruitment and selection* – where an individual is recommended by a current employee, or an individual has been working on a part-time basis for the organisation and is well known there. In this instance, the individual may not necessarily go through the standard recruitment and selection process, but may simply be appointed to the job.

2 *Formal* (objective and scientific) – other organisations have developed complex recruitment and selection procedures. They may use expensive selection techniques, such as bio-data (a diagnosis questionnaire which identifies psychological traits), handwriting analysis or referral to assessment centres. Formal procedures are usually found in larger organisations, or when unemployment is high and it is relatively easy to attract a large number of potentially appropriate candidates.

Whichever recruitment and selection process is employed, organisations frequently find themselves in the position of failing to select the correct candidate. The main reasons behind this include:

- the organisation's failure to define clearly the exact nature of the job
- the organisation's failure to brief interviewers correctly – to ensure they are all looking for the same thing

- a failure to realise what the selection process has been designed to achieve
- a failure to use the correct selection procedures for a particular job

There are many reasons why an organisation may find itself in a position to have to recruit or select new employees. As we have mentioned in Unit 2, expansion or diversification may involve the employment of new members of staff. Equally, changes in technology or working practices may involve the gradual replacement of employees. If an organisation has a disproportionate number of employees in the older age bracket, it may find itself with a constant need to replace retiring members of staff. Termination of employment or resignation, as a result of an employee's decision, may make recruitment and selection an immediate priority. This is particularly true if the employee leaving the organisation held a key post at a particularly crucial time in the development of the organisation. This form of termination of employment cannot be easily predicted by the organisation, but the organisation should be prepared (at fairly short notice) to advertise, recruit and select a replacement. As we will see in Element 4.2, job roles can be complex, as can the reasons that determine changes in these job roles. Changes in working conditions, such as the establishment of short-term contracts or flexi-hours, may have an impact on employees' willingness to remain with an organisation. Equally, the comparative expense involved in replacing an individual, particularly if this is not a key role, may be outweighed by the benefits of simply appointing a known individual.

In all cases, the organisation is faced with a potentially expensive and time-consuming activity which does not stop when the individual signs his/her contract of employment. The gradual integration or induction of the new employee may not happen over a period of days. It may take the new employee a matter of weeks or months to be a fully functioning and effective member of staff. The organisation needs to realise this and to take all possible steps to ensure that employees, particularly key members of staff, are retained and highly motivated.

NEGOTIATION OF PAY AND CONDITIONS

Negotiation is a vital communication skill which any credible or effective manager should be able to cope with. Possibly the key to all negotiations is the balance of relative power between the negotiators. In the field of sociology, many researchers have been preoccupied with notions of power and authority. If you refer back to Element 2.1, you will see that some of the leadership theories are derived from sociological research. In the 1950s, the sociologists French and Raven identified eight different sorts of power and it is in relation to

these that we can begin our investigation into the nature of negotiations. We will be considering specific negotiations in relation to trades unions, courts, industrial tribunals and ACAS later in this element.

The types of power identified by French and Raven were:

1 *Positional power* – which derives from an individual's position within the organisation relative to other individuals. This form of power is particularly in evidence when negotiations occur between managers and their direct employees.
2 *Information power* – which derives from differences between people in terms of their access to important information. An individual who lacks access to information can be controlled by another individual who has that information. In other words, some individuals find themselves dependent upon those who have acquired the information already (possibly by virtue of their position within the organisation).
3 *Control of rewards* – individuals in managerial or supervisory positions within an organisation have the ability to dispense rewards to less senior members of staff. Again, these members of staff are dependent upon their supervisor or manager.
4 *Coercive power* – this power is related to the ability of a manager or supervisor to punish less senior members of staff. Once again, the less senior employees are dependent upon their supervisor or manager.
5 *Alliances and networks* – this type of power is derived from both an individual's access to information and his/her relative position within the organisation. More senior individuals are members of stronger alliances and networks and can use this to exercise power and authority.
6 *Access to and control of agendas* – setting the ground rules or topics to be discussed within a negotiation process is obviously a determining factor to the outcome of the negotiations. If an individual can set the agenda or, in other words, determine what will be discussed, then the negotiation process has already been somewhat undermined before it even begins.
7 *Control of meaning and symbols* – particularly in jargon-ridden organisations, the use of language or other strange symbols to explain situations can radically affect the negotiation process. Access to these symbols and their meaning can strongly determine the effectiveness of negotiators who are not conversant with the jargon.
8 *Personal power* – the adoption of characteristics similar to those of an individual that you feel is a good role model may have a determining effect on the negotiation process. It may, indeed, determine your stance and effectiveness as a negotiator, particularly if you cannot easily replicate the desirable qualities.

Having established the determinants of the basis of power in negotiations, we shall now turn our attention to the specific points which relate to pay and conditions. Obviously, many aspects of pay and conditions are covered under government legislation, but, there is considerable latitude available to employers in establishing pay and conditions for their employees.

In any competitive negotiation, such as those concerning pay and conditions, individuals should give consideration to the question of where the negotiation begins. A key to the success of the negotiations is to manage the context of the relationship in which the negotiation takes place. As we have seen, the balance of power between the negotiators is crucial, as is the need to establish good communication links.

One of the first rules of negotiation is that you should always avoid making the 'opening bid' as, when you do this, you are giving away a considerable amount of information before the other negotiating party has established his/her position. In situations when the employer is forced to make the opening bid, it is essential that he/she does not make an offer which is insulting. If the opening offer does insult the other party, then it is possible that he/she may withdraw from the negotiations and consider more drastic forms of action (as we will see later in the Element).

A competitive negotiator, particularly on the employer's side, should be well versed in the tactics of offering concessions. It is often thought that in competitive negotiation situations, the offering of concessions is seen as a sign of weakness. To this end, particularly on the employer's side, concessions should be kept to a minimum. Both sides will have already established, before the negotiation process begins, an ideal solution to the situation. This is known as 'BATNA' (Best Alternative To A Negotiated Agreement). Whether you are an employer or an employee, your BATNA should always be kept secret.

HANDLE DISCIPLINARY PROCEDURES

It is inevitable that disputes will often arise between the employer and the employees. As we will see later in this Element, the procedures employed by organisations and the role of trades unions or external organisations can be crucial to the settlement of such disputes.

ACAS (Advisory Conciliation and Arbitration Services) have approved the disciplinary procedure illustrated in Figures 4.1.3, opposite, and 4.1.4 on p.326, the key aspects of which are:

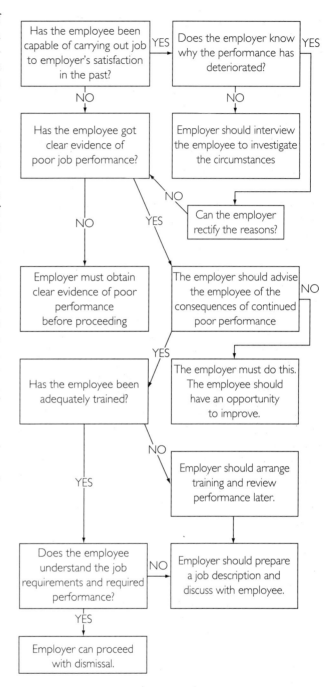

FIG. 4.1.3 *This flowchart illustrates the procedure to be followed when an individual demonstrates lack of capability or poor performance.*

- that the disciplinary procedure is written down
- that all employees have access to the disciplinary procedure
- that employees are aware who operates the disciplinary procedure

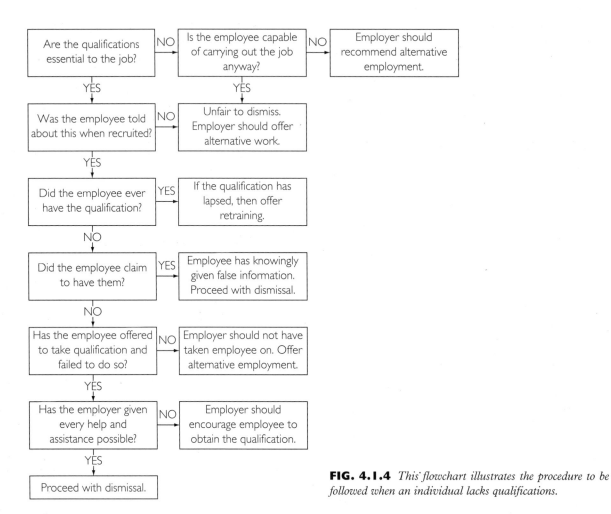

FIG. 4.1.4 *This flowchart illustrates the procedure to be followed when an individual lacks qualifications.*

HANDLE GRIEVANCE PROCEDURES

Most organisations of any size have accepted grievance procedures to deal with problems arising from their employees.

The ACAS Employment Handbook offers the following advice:

> grievance procedures should aim to settle a grievance fairly, quickly and as closely as possible to the point of origin, and help to prevent minor disagreements developing into more serious disputes. For this reason, it is usually advisable for the first stage to be between the employee and his/her immediate supervisor or line manager. This can also help to maintain the authority of the supervisor and can often lead to the issue being resolved directly between the parties without the involvement of a representative.

It is in neither the organisation's nor the employee's interests to allow the grievance procedure to carry on for any length of time. To this end, many organisations have stipulated the following:

- that the first stage of the procedure must be completed in 24 hours
- that the second stage is completed within 3 days

All organisations would obviously prefer to resolve their own internal disputes. In some cases, this is not possible and an external organisation may have to be involved or invited to help settle the issue. We will be looking at the role of ACAS in the next section of this Element. If you wish to refer to the recommended grievance procedures as laid down by ACAS, you should turn to Unit 2.

IMPLEMENT NON-DISCRIMINATORY LEGISLATION

In order to establish the fact that inequality exists within the working environment, it is probably a good idea to try to define what equality actually means. Perhaps an easy definition would be whether all individuals or groups of individuals are treated as favourably as one another, regardless of the situation. It is essential that equality of treatment and opportunity is encouraged, so as to foster good working relationships within the

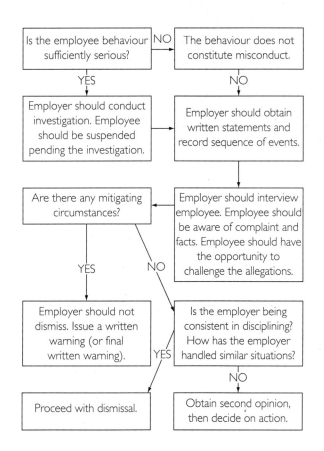

FIG. 4.1.5 *This flowchart illustrates the procedure to be followed when an individual commits an act of gross misconduct.*

working environment and to make the best use of all employees' abilities.

The word **unjustifiably** is a key one when we consider discrimination, for it is **unjustifiable discrimination** that overwhelmingly is the root cause of problems.

Other significant considerations include the following:

- does any individual receive different treatment?
- is any individual suffering a disadvantage?
- is there any legal or other justification for such inequality?

In all cases, it is essential that the organisation establish the facts behind any alleged discrimination. To this end, the employer may be legally obliged to make such an investigation.

Clearly, as we mentioned in the previous part of this Element, certain groups suffer from higher levels of potential discrimination. Let us look at some of the facts behind the discrimination aimed at these groups:

1 *Women* – the following facts regarding women are pertinent here:

- women make up in excess of 40 per cent of the working population
- canteen assistants or workers in similar occupations are predominantly female (over 97 per cent)
- cleaners are predominantly women (some 92 per cent)
- nurses are predominantly women (some 92 per cent)
- only 12 per cent of the members of the 'professions' are women

2 *Ethnic minorities* – the term racial minority refers to those who share some of the following characteristics: race, colour, nationality, ethnic origin. The key features to remember about ethnic minorities are the following:

- West Indians and Asians account for only 5 per cent of the UK population
- many live in areas with acute housing problems
- many live in areas where there are acute educational problems
- many live in areas with high unemployment
- a member of an ethnic minority is more likely to fail to be selected for a job than a white person
- work offered tends to be poorly paid and of low status

3 *Disabled* – this generic term covers a multitude of different individuals. Some views about disabled people should be borne in mind:

- many employers believe that they will be inefficient
- many employers believe that they will be unreliable
- many employers will not be prepared to pay for special facilities

Some of the more obvious forms of discrimination include the following:

- *victimisation* – where an individual has been treated unfairly
- *pressure to discriminate* – where individuals within the organisation are encouraged by others to discriminate
- *instruction to discriminate* – when an individual uses his/her power and authority within an organisation to apply pressure on others to discriminate
- *segregation* – where, on racial grounds, an individual is forced to work alone or in a different location from the rest of the employees

A solution to the possibility of discrimination is for an organisation to institute a policy of positive action or positive discrimination in an attempt to put right inequalities or poor treatment in the past. In such a situation an organisation positively encourages groups previously discriminated against to apply for jobs and, indeed, gives them preference. Within the working environment these groups are given every opportunity to 'catch up' in terms of experience and qualifications. It should be noted, however, that overt positive action, particularly in the recruitment process, may inadvertently discriminate against others.

Achieving equality within the working environment is essential to the organisation both morally and legally. In terms of the latter consideration, the employer may be required to pay compensation for any unlawful discrimination. In order to ensure that equality is paramount an organisation should ensure the following:

- that procedures are in place which take account of objectivity and equality
- that training and guidance are given to all employees
- that regular checks are made regarding procedures, practice and policy
- that it takes immediate action when necessary
- that it keeps records to show that reasonable steps have been taken in the pursuance of equality

Commitment to equality is also essential, not only in relation to those to whom legislation is applicable, but to all employees and groups of employees.

IMPLEMENT HEALTH AND SAFETY REGULATIONS

As we have mentioned earlier, an employer must provide a reasonable standard of health and safety. This responsibility extends to cover the following different groups of individuals:

- employees
- visiting workers (such as individuals servicing machinery or production line equipment)
- customers
- visitors and representatives from other organisations
- the general public

It is also worth remembering that this responsibility extends beyond the premises themselves, to any health and safety problems which may arise from the work undertaken within those premises.

Bearing in mind that the local authority has the right to enter an employer's premises at any time, the management of health and safety regulations should be an ongoing process. An inspector may insist on examining equipment and legally enforcing the requirements of the health and safety legislation.

Ideally, the employer should follow a set of procedures which include the following:

- notify the local authority responsible for health and safety of the business name and address

- contact either the Environmental Health Department (in the case of offices, shops, restaurants and warehouses) or for other businesses the Health and Safety Executive area office
- obtain employers' liability insurance
- display the insurance certificate in the workplace
- prepare a written statement of health and safety policy (this applies if the employer has more than five employees)
- display the health and safety law poster, or distribute a leaflet which contains this information
- make an assessment of the potential risks within the workplace
- maintain a written record of this risk assessment (if the employer has more than five employees)

student activity

(PC 4.1.2, COM 3.1, 3.2, IT 3.1)
In pairs, using the sources of information listed in the activity on p.1106 and CD ROM databases, obtain at least two of the following booklets:

- HSE, The Law on Health and Safety at Work
- HSE, Report that Accident (HSE 21)
- HSE, Five Steps to Risk Assessment
- HSC, Writing your Health and Safety Policy Statement (HSC 6)
- HSC, Health and Safety at Work: the Act Outlined (HSC 2)
- HSC, Health and Safety at Work – Advice to Employers (HSC 3)
- ACAS, Health and Employment

Having obtained these, write a short (no more than one side of A4) general health and safety policy statement applicable for an office environment. Your report should be word processed.

MEET QUALITY STANDARDS

Quality can be rather subjective. It is only in cases where you can measure exactly the quality of the product (such as an item of clothing, for example) that any form of objective assessment can be made. One way around this is to gradually build up the image or reputation of the product to suggest quality.

Quality is dependent upon the following aspects:

- appearance of the product

- the packaging
- the reliability
- the performance
- the service offered (before, during and after the sale has been made)

Many organisations institute quality audits or other mechanisms aimed at maintaining high quality standards. Obviously, the nature of this monitoring process is largely dependent upon the type of business involved. As we have intimated, organisations which do not actually produce products as such may find it difficult to make any objective quality assessment. Some other ways of measuring quality are:

- measuring the speed and reliability of response to customers' enquiries
- maintaining a strict rule on the number of 'rings' before the telephone is answered
- ensuring that administrative procedures are in place to record any customer complaints and to monitor these regularly

EMPLOYEE RESPONSIBILITIES

COMPLIANCE WITH TERMS OF CONTRACT

The employee has a responsibility to the employer to work in a loyal, conscientious and honest manner. He/she is also expected to accept any reasonable and legal directions from his/her superiors. In essence, this means adhering to the terms of the contract of employment. As we have seen, the contract of employment can be a very detailed document and is considered to be legally binding once both parties have signed. By law, all employees must have received a contract of employment within 13 weeks of commencing employment. As we mentioned earlier, the employer is required to exercise a duty of care towards his/her employees, provide sufficient work to do, pay the employee at due times and complete a number of records on behalf of the employee. These will include details of:

- PAYE deductions
- national insurance contributions
- pension scheme contributions

In addition to the obvious obligations the employee may have, he/she will be expected to:

- act in good faith towards the employer
- keep trade secrets confidential
- obey any reasonable orders
- give faithful service to the employer
- account for any cash received from other sources (this is to make sure that the employee does not accept bribes or fees from external organisations in the pursuit of his/her normal activities)

student activity

COMPLIANCE WITH HEALTH AND SAFETY AT WORK

Just as the employer must take heed of the requirements of the legislation, so must the employee. Employees may, however, suffer harm or injuries which are not necessarily the fault of the employer.

If an employee is negligent and causes injury to him/herself or another person, then the employer can find him/herself in a difficult position. The employee may claim that it was not really his/her fault. As long as the employer provides safe working conditions, then apart from accidents caused by negligence, there should be no real concerns here.

Another possible area of concern is when an employee deliberately puts someone else's life in danger. Depending on the circumstances, he/she could not only be dismissed, but be the subject of criminal and civil proceedings.

NON-DISCRIMINATORY BEHAVIOUR

Employees should obviously be made aware of the employer's policies regarding correct behaviour as regards discrimination. The employer, as we have mentioned earlier, is responsible for ensuring that the various pieces of non-discriminatory legislation are adhered to within the workplace.

It is worth remembering that the anti-discrimination policies of an employer are based upon the legislation itself. This covers both indirect and direct discrimination.

WORK TOWARDS ORGANISATIONAL OBJECTIVES

As we mentioned earlier in this Element, the exact nature of the employer's business objectives may be somewhat difficult to grasp. This is particularly true if the employer frequently changes the focus and direction in which the organisation is moving. To this end, it is obviously the employer's responsibility to attempt to inform the employees at each stage when the business objectives are altered. Specifically, this will be done by employing forms of internal communications such as newsletters, posters and notices.

As an employee, it is difficult to respond to the needs of the organisation without prior knowledge of its organisational objectives. Broadly speaking, the employee should be aware of the basic organisational objectives as it is probable that these under-pinning aims will not change even if there are short-term alterations to some objectives.

MEET CUSTOMER NEEDS

In order to help employees understand customer needs, the organisation needs to inform employees about the following:

● why will they buy?
● what does the customer want?
● what are the benefits and features of the organisation's service?

In relation to the product itself, the employee must know the following:

● the appearance of the product
● what is the product made of?
● what colours are available?
● how is it packaged?
● what is the speed and reliability of delivery?
● how does the organisation deal with faults?
● how frequent are maintenance visits (if applicable)?
● what quality levels are desired?
● how does the price compare to that of competitors?

The last obvious consideration is how much will the customers buy. Not only is this information useful in ensuring that employees are sufficiently briefed on the customer, but it is also useful for sales and cash forecasts.

Regular training and staff development is obviously required in order to ensure that the organisation's employees are not only up to date with product availability, but intimately know the characteristics of products currently available.

student activity

(PC 4.1.2, COM 3.1, 3.2, IT 3.1)
In pairs, try to obtain some of the following booklets relating to anti-discrimination legislation:

● EOC, A Guide for Employers to the Sex Discrimination Acts 1975 and 1986
● EOC, Code of Practice
● CRE, Racial Discrimination and Grievance Procedures
● CRE, Indirect Discrimination in Employment
● CRE, Code of Practice
● DE, Union Membership Rights and Non-Membership Rights, (PL 871)
● DE, Employment Rights for the Expectant Mother (PL 710)
Note: EOC stands for Equal Opportunities Commission
CRE stands for Commission for Racial Equality
DE stands for Department of Employment

Having obtained these valuable sources of information, choose one of the following topics:

● racial discrimination
● sex discrimination
● trade union discrimination

Prepare a short briefing paper which addresses the employee's responsibilities in relation to combatting these forms of discrimination. Your briefing paper should be word processed.

4.1.3 Describe procedures available to employers and employees when rights are not upheld

PROCEDURES FOR EMPLOYERS

Procedures are necessary for the many cases that inevitably arise in relation to the following:

- breaches of an organisation's regulation or codes of practice
- breaches of the state's regulations or codes of practice
- times when an employee perceives that he/she has been wronged or ill-treated

In many cases, potential disputes may be negotiated without having to resort to the involvement of:

- trades unions
- staff associations
- ACAS
- industrial tribunals
- court action

Many other negotiations seek to save the employee from having to resort to industrial action.

NEGOTIATIONS (WITH INDIVIDUALS, WITH TRADES UNIONS, WITH STAFF ASSOCIATIONS)

As we have already mentioned, the need to negotiate on a variety of different topics or problems may arise on a regular basis. Depending upon the scale or importance of the potential problem, the employer may have to proceed first with negotiations. These negotiations may proceed at an individual level, involving the employee in question and his or her immediate line manager. However, as is the right of an employee, a trade union may be involved at this early stage. Employees have the right to ask for a trade union representative to be present during all negotiations.

In later stages of negotiation, perhaps when the situation cannot be solved at the individual level, a trade union may be called in to assist in the negotiation process.

We have already looked at the negotiation of pay and conditions, disciplinary procedures, grievance procedures and the implementation of non-discriminatory legislation earlier in this Element.

Trades unions and staff associations become involved (generally) in such areas as:

- annual pay rounds
- consultation on new developments within the organisation
- disciplinary and grievance procedures

It should be realised that although organisations like trades unions and staff associations do become involved in negotiations, these should still be considered 'internal' negotiations. It is only when the trade union feels it is necessary to ask for assistance from their regional office or headquarters that negotiations take on a more difficult and complex nature.

Beyond the involvement of a trade union, at any level, the inclusion of external organisations give further weight and gravity to the situation.

The basic role of trades unions and, indeed, staff associations is to negotiate on a collective basis. The potential conflicts between managers and shop stewards or staff representatives rest largely upon the following:

- their dependency upon one another
- their co-operation
- their mutually beneficial approach
- their relative bargaining power
- their respect of each other's rights

There must be mutually accepted procedures which will outline the framework within which negotiations take place. This is essential since it establishes a level of stability. The balance of power within these negotiations will inevitably lead to one side or the other wishing to alter the rules and procedures. In order to avoid conflict in relation to the procedures, it is essential that both sides are flexible.

Throughout the 1970s and early 1980s, changes in legislation relating to industrial relations significantly changed the balance of power between trades unions and employers. Indeed, the concept of 'the right to manage' is enshrined in many of these laws. In other words, government legislation has determined that the balance of power lies with the employer.

Negotiations effectively, and regardless of the exact subject matter of the negotiations, involve the following:

- the distribution of money
- the distribution of status
- the distribution of power
- the ability to achieve objectives
- the willingness to collaborate
- the desire to compete

NEGOTIATION THROUGH ADVISORY, CONCILIATION AND ARBITRATION SERVICES (ACAS)

ACAS is an independent organisation that offers employers, trade unions and individuals the opportunity to obtain unbiased assistance in relation to disputes. ACAS enjoys a reputation for impartiality and is recognised by employers and employees alike as being a valuable and reliable source of assistance.

As well as its primary objective to resolve disputes, it also offers a wide range of employee-related advice.

In an arbitration situation, the two sides will turn to ACAS when they feel that they have exhausted the procedures open to them to resolve the problem internally. ACAS will listen to the two parties involved and consider their arguments and will then provide a solution which both parties must accept. It is a prerequisite for ACAS that both sides agree, before they begin the arbitration process, that they will abide by the decision made.

On the conciliation side, again, ACAS will listen to both sides of the argument and attempt to resolve the situation by encouraging those in dispute to move closer to one another's point of view.

ACAS also publishes useful statistical information on employee relations. It looks at disputes which have gone as far as industrial tribunals and recommends good practice in employee relations.

INDUSTRIAL TRIBUNALS

Industrial tribunals are made up of individuals who have specific knowledge of employment law. The chairperson of a tribunal is either a barrister or a solicitor with at least seven years experience. The other members of the industrial tribunal include two lay people (individuals who do not have a specific allegiance to either employers or employees). These lay people are either nominated by either the CBI (Confederation of British Industry) or the TUC (Trades Union Congress). The members of the tribunal all have an equal say and decisions are made by majority verdict. Industrial tribunals are somewhat more accessible than other courts. An individual may simply fill in a form. He/she need not resort to the professional assistance of a solicitor, or, indeed, have any representation at the hearing. The tribunal does not take place in a court room and all of the usual complications that are associated with courts are avoided.

As there are no court fees, it is inexpensive to take a case to an industrial tribunal.

Normally, an industrial tribunal is involved in complaints regarding unfair dismissal. The ex-employee must first ask ACAS to decide whether the case needs to be taken to an industrial tribunal.

TABLE 4.1.2 *Applications to industrial tribunals in Great Britain*

	Percentage
Unfair dismissal	57
Wages Act	15
Redundancy payment	12
Equal pay, sex and race discrimination	8
Other	7

Source: Employment Department.

student activity

(PC 4.1.3, COM 3.1)
Referring back to Unit 2, where we discussed the various reasons for unfair dismissal, discuss as a group why cases of unfair dismissal are significantly more common at industrial tribunal level.

In excess of 25,000 complaints of unfair dismissal are lodged yearly, but only a quarter of these are actually heard by an industrial tribunal. In this respect, the role of ACAS in dealing with complaints means that three-quarters of all potential industrial tribunal hearings are not necessary.

Once a complaint reaches an industrial tribunal around one-third of complaints are upheld. Although this may seem that employers tend to 'win' more often than not, lessons still need to be learned by employers who have allowed the complaint to go as far as an industrial tribunal.

Individuals who have had their complaints upheld by an industrial tribunal are entitled to compensation, reinstatement or re-engagement.

COURT ACTION

If an employer or employee makes an appeal on a point of law made by an industrial tribunal, then they can refer to the Employment Appeals Tribunal. The EAT consists of a High Court Judge and two lay people. It is the role of the EAT to uphold or reverse the findings of an industrial tribunal. In some cases, admittedly rare, appeals may be made to the Court of Appeal or to the House of Lords (the House of Lords being the highest court in the country).

PROCEDURES FOR EMPLOYEES

Situations occasionally arise when an employee finds him/herself in a position that leads to a potential dispute with his or her employer. For the various reasons detailed in the previous section on procedures for employers, we can recognise that some of the causes of disputes originate with the employer, whilst others are the result of an employee's perception of an unfair situation.

The possible responses are fairly clear when the situation relates to breaches of regulations or codes of practice. However, when an employee perceives that he/she has been wronged or ill-treated, the exact course the dispute may take will differ from situation to situation.

Again, as with the procedures for employers dealt with above, the negotiations may involve internal or external bodies. In many cases, the primary concern is not only to solve the dispute, but also to manage the negotiation at as low a level as possible. It is often not in the interests of either the employer or the employee to involve external bodies or organisations, since this heightens the tension between the two parties and may well lead to the situation getting out of hand.

NEGOTIATIONS (WITH EMPLOYER, THROUGH TRADES UNIONS, THROUGH STAFF ASSOCIATIONS)

Many different topics, problems or disputes may arise on a regular basis, and there will usually be specified methods of conducting negotiations on these matters. With regard to breaches of regulations, legislation and codes of practice, set procedures have been outlined by government legislation or ACAS. It is worth remembering that even at the lowest levels of negotiation, an individual employee has the automatic right of representation if he/she so wishes.

In consultations and negotiations which involve pay and working conditions, the procedures begin at a significantly higher level than in situations when a simple dispute needs to be resolved. In the case of annual pay rounds or the negotiations relating to new terms and conditions of work, a trade union will almost certainly be involved at the earliest possible opportunity.

Annual pay rounds which, in effect, attempt to set the pay rises for the majority of the workforce for the next year, tend to take the form of a series of consultation meetings at which differing views are exchanged. It is often important for the employees, in particular, to have expertise on hand in the form of a trade union official, who has knowledge of good practice and of other pay negotiations. These consultations and negotiations are often fraught and, as we point out later in this Unit, the negotiation process is a complex one. Each side will begin the negotiations demanding more than it actually expects or hopes to achieve. Since the management of the organisation will probably have a personnel expert who will lead the negotiations on behalf of the business, the employees need to have a similarly qualified individual who can represent them.

Staff associations and, in particular, their officials play a similar role to that of a trade union representative, but their role and power is often somewhat different from that of a trade union official. As we will see later, many staff organisations have negotiated away the right to take industrial action. There is a tendency, therefore, for employers to consider negotiations undertaken by staff associations as less important and potentially contentious. In both trade union and staff association cases the progress of the negotiation will certainly depend upon the status of the relationships between management and the workforce. Indeed, many negotiations are influenced by the course of previous negotiations and the general inter-personal relationships between the individuals involved in the negotiations.

Again, as we mentioned in the previous section with regard to employers, many negotiations, particularly those concerning pay and conditions, revolve around the distribution of scarce resources. The willingness of the organisation to give an additional share of profits or resources accrued as a result of the labours of the workforce is a key feature in the success or failure of the negotiation process. Both sides need to show, regardless of previous negotiation history, a certain willingness to collaborate with one another and, above all, to show a degree of respect for one another's position and desires.

NEGOTIATION THROUGH ADVISORY, CONCILIATION AND ARBITRATION SERVICES (ACAS)

In the previous section relating to employers, we explained how ACAS fits into the negotiation process. ACAS should not be seen simply as a means by which the opposing party, whether it be employer or employees, is forced to accept a particular proposal. ACAS is equally valuable to both sides, regardless of the distance between the initial, or negotiated, positions.

On an individual basis, ACAS may be the only channel through which to resolve a particular dispute relating to either grievance or disciplinary procedures. However, provided ACAS guidelines have been followed, then there may be a tendency for the ACAS judgement to simply 'rubber stamp' the decision that has already been made. In this event, as we will see in the next sections, the individual has the right of appeal.

Perhaps the most valuable service that ACAS can offer an individual is impartial and objective advice. There are many situations where either employers or employees resolve to take their problems to an industrial tribunal, but find that ACAS can, at least, mediate or supply information and advice to diffuse the situation.

The outcome of a referral to ACAS should not be seen simply as either winning or losing an argument. There are lessons to be learnt regardless of the nature of the ACAS judgement.

INDUSTRIAL TRIBUNALS

Industrial tribunals have been set up in such a way as to be as little threatening as possible. They do not in many ways resemble the commonly held perception of a court. Despite the possible involvement of a barrister or solicitor, they do not carry with them the expense one would normally associate with court action. In many respects, industrial tribunals represent the last opportunity to resolve a dispute before considerable time and expense needs to be invested in solving the dispute.

The majority of cases heard by industrial tribunals involve unfair dismissal. If you refer back to the table which detailed applications to industrial tribunals (Table 4.1.1), you will see that the significant majority of cases obviously arise from an employee feeling that he/she has been unfairly dealt with. Significantly, the lower percentages relating to wage payments, redundancy payments, equal pay, sexual and racial discrimination can be seen as a result of the extensive legislation relating to these areas. Unfair dismissal still remains a rather grey area since, in the majority of cases, there is no clear right or wrong. Indeed, the employer's and the employee's perception of fairness can be so widely different that it would be difficult to realise that they are considering the same set of circumstances.

Compensation, reinstatement or re-engagement are the usual remedies if a case is upheld. An individual will have to decide whether he/she wishes to resume employment with an employer who has treated him/her, both in his/her eyes and the court's, in an unfair way. Equally, employers, having proceeded through a complex and probably expensive legal argument with the employee, may not be all that keen to re-employ that individual. In these cases, compensation is usually the solution.

COURT ACTION

Just as the employer has the right to refer an unacceptable judgement made by ACAS or an industrial tribunal to a higher court, so too does the employee. Court action can, of course, be extremely expensive. If the employee is a member of a trade union, the organisation will step in and provide legal assistance and pay for the court action to proceed. Obviously, there is some degree of 'trade-off' if the dispute has reached this level of seriousness. The employee and the trade union need to be assured that not only do they have a reasonable chance of winning the case, but also that the compensation payable will include the payment of their legal fees by the employer. In many cases, disputes which have reached this stage are resolved 'out of court'. This means that the two parties involved have realised that the complexities of the dispute will mean that a protracted court case will serve no useful purpose to either side. The employer, if he/she feels that the adverse publicity involved in the court case will seriously affect their standing in the market-place, may be prepared to offer compensation in return for the case being dropped by the employee. Equally, the employee or his/her representatives may feel that nothing more can be gained by pursuing the case any further. They may offer the employer a settlement in order to terminate the proceedings.

The Employment Appeals Tribunal, as we have mentioned earlier, offers the first stage in the appeals procedure. The High Court judge, who chairs this tribunal, has the power to overturn decisions made by the industrial tribunal. If either party decides to proceed beyond the EAT, then the case can be referred to either the Court of Appeal or even the House of Lords. It is rare for cases to reach this level of seriousness; however, some cases are considered to be 'cases of principle' and will be vigorously pursued to the very end by either the employer or the employee. Indeed, judgements made at this high level may have implications for other cases in later years. The foundation of UK law is often based upon precedents. This means that judges will refer back to similar cases and judgements made in the past and make their decisions based upon their outcomes.

INDUSTRIAL ACTION

In the event that a trade union believes that management decisions are detrimental to its members, it may consider taking industrial action. Such action may take several forms and some may be more damaging to the organisation than others.

The main types of action fall into the following categories:

1 *Withdrawal of goodwill* – this includes employees refusing to work overtime, refusing to cover for absent colleagues, refusing to attend meetings out of their normal working hours.

2 *Go slow* – this is a form of industrial action where the employees continue to work, but only at the slowest

possible pace. This will mean that they will lose any productivity bonuses, but will receive their basic pay. This is a particularly good form of action when the employer needs production to be at the optimum.

3 *Working to rule* – this is similar to the withdrawal of goodwill, but also includes following every single rule and regulation as required by the organisation, regardless of the fact that some of these may be out of date and not yet replaced.

4 *Days of action* – these involve the withdrawal of labour for single or groups of specified days. The employer will be informed in advance that labour will be withdrawn. The employer will, of course, lose vital production during these days and the employees will lose pay. In the event that single days of action do not bring about a change of heart from the employer, then more regular days of action may be planned. This may culminate in a full strike.

5 *Strikes* – again these involve the withdrawal of labour, usually when the situation has deteriorated sufficiently to make this action necessary. As we saw in Unit 2, there are many pieces of legislation which relate to the taking of strike action. In particular, the trade union must undertake a secret ballot in order to ascertain whether the majority of its members support this form of action. It is usual for these striking employees to 'picket' the premises of the organisation.

6 *Blacking* – this form of dispute often relates to action taken against an organisation other than the one in which the trade union members work. This is usually as a result of a dispute which has occurred at this other organisation, and the blacking is undertaken to support this dispute. Blacking involves refusing to handle any goods, enquiries or other business activities relating to this other organisation. Before South Africa achieved democracy, certain unions blacked

TABLE 4.1.2 *Labour disputes: working days lost in the United Kingdom, 1971–1993*

	Millions
1971	13.6
1972	23.9
1973	7.2
1974	14.8
1975	6.0
1976	3.3
1977	10.1
1978	9.4
1979	29.5
1980	12.0
1981	4.3
1982	5.3
1983	3.8
1984	27.1
1985	6.4
1986	1.9
1987	3.5
1988	3.7
1989	4.1
1990	1.9
1991	0.8
1992	0.5
1993	0.6

South African produce such as Cape fruits and vegetables. It was felt that in refusing to handle these goods, they would be supporting the cause for majority rule in that country. In the event, despite the claims of producers, wholesalers and distributors that this action only served to harm South African workers, the new leaders of that country have wholeheartedly praised the actions of workers across the world for their support during the struggle for democracy.

4.1.4 Explain the roles of trades unions and staff associations

ROLES OF TRADE UNIONS AND STAFF ASSOCIATIONS

An employer does not have to recognise a trade union unless he/she feels that it would be beneficial to the organisation. Therefore, organisations may adopt any of the following policies in relation to the recognition of unions:

- full recognition of a variety of different unions relating to different sections of the workforce within the organisation
- full recognition of a single union representing all or the majority of the workforce
- refusal to recognise any trade union
- the establishment of a staff association as an alternative to trades unions

As we will see, trade unions are fairly widely recognised across the country as the primary route for negotiations. In cases where there are a variety of different trade unions operating in a single organisation, there will be a joint union committee to facilitate the negotiation process. Nearly all unions are affiliated to the TUC (Trades Union Congress). This organisation aims to speak for the entire trade union movement, particularly in its negotiations with the government.

TABLE 4.1.3 *Trade union membership as a percentage of the workforce in the United Kingdom, 1971–1992*

	Per cent
1971	45.8
1972	46.8
1973	46.1
1974	47.3
1975	49.1
1976	50.3
1977	52.1
1978	52.2
1979	52.4
1980	52.6
1981	50.6
1982	49.4
1983	47.0
1984	45.1
1985	44.2
1986	42.7
1987	41.0
1988	39.4
1989	37.8
1990	37.3
1991	37.3
1992	36.1

`0:20`

student activity

(PC 4.1.4, COM 3.1)

The percentage of employees in the workforce who are members of trade unions has fallen significantly since 1971. Over the 21-year period to 1992, trade unions have lost approaching 20 per cent of their membership. As a group, try to assess why there has been this significant fall in membership. Can unemployment be the main reason for the fall? Are there any other major reasons that you can think of?

Although legislation has been passed restricting the activities of trade unions (see Unit 2), the primary need for their existence still remains.

In effect, there are four different types of union, but the distinction between them is becoming increasingly less obvious. The four types of unions are:

1 *Craft unions* – these are the earliest type of trade union and were formed to cater for crafts persons who had received an apprenticeship. The membership of a craft union consists of individuals all of whom work with the same basic range of skills. These unions are still relatively powerful, since they control the number of skilled crafts persons entering the workforce. Craft unions restrict their membership by having very strict entrance qualifications and charging high membership rates. There are still some fields in which a person cannot work in that occupation unless he/she is a member of a specified union.

2 *Industrial unions* – traditionally, these unions were formed to cater for all employees (regardless of grade and job) within a particular industry. Good examples of this type of union are the National Union of Mineworkers and the National Union of Railwaymen.

3 *Occupational unions* – unlike the industrial unions, the occupational unions recruit from a wide range of different industries, but always from the same occupational group. A good example of this type of union would be the National Union of Public Employees, which recruits manual workers from hospitals, councils, schools and colleges.

4 *General unions* – initially, these unions catered for individuals not covered in the three categories above. The first general unions concentrated on unskilled workers, offering a wide range of benefits for a relatively low subscription rate. General unions have thrived in recent times as new industries have emerged and older, more traditional ones have declined. Often, these general unions are the result of several smaller, more specialist unions merging with one another.

Whatever type of union exists in a workplace, the basic functions of unions remain the same. A union exists to protect and promote the interests of its members. It essentially does the following:

- acts as a pressure group which promotes the interest of its members
- acts as a pressure group which protects the position of its members
- acts as the main instrument for bargaining with the employer
- at national level, acts as the main instrument of bargaining with the government

TABLE 4.1.4 *Trade union membership by gender and occupation, Autumn 1993, Great Britain*

	Percentages		
	Males	Females	Total
Managers and administrators	19.5	19.4	19.5
Professional	38.4	56.4	45.5
Associate professional and technical	33.6	52.9	43.1
Clerical and secretarial	35.9	24.7	27.4
Craft and related	28.7	27.8	28.6
Personal and protective service	39.6	22.2	27.9
Sales	11.9	11.2	11.5
Plant and machine operatives	42.5	33.1	40.6
Other	32.4	24.2	28.1
All in employment	30.7	28.0	29.5

0:40

student activity

(PC 4.1.4, COM 3.1, 3.2, 3.3, AON 3.3, IT 3.1, 3.3)
Using the data contained in Table 4.1.3 plot a graph using computer software which contains the breakdown of gender and occupation in relation to trade union membership. Using the graph, can you identify particular occupations which are more or less likely to attract males or females to join unions related to that trade or job?

All unions are formed and financed by their members. They are run by full-time officials, voted or appointed into place by the members. Unions are independent of employers; they do not rely on them for funding. The union must also organise its own facilities and not necessarily rely on the employer to offer space within the organisation's own premises.

Trade unions carry out a multitude of different tasks in pursuit of looking after their members' interests. We will look at many of these in more detail later, but here are some of their major functions:

- protecting the wages of the members, particularly in times of recession
- negotiating the working hours required by the employer
- negotiating the working conditions
- monitoring health and safety
- providing a range of benefits including pensions, sick pay, unemployment pay, injury benefits and strike pay

- representing the interests of the members in times of dispute with the employer

In addition to these tasks, unions undertake a number of political duties relating to employment. They will actively negotiate with the government and opposition parties to further the cause of their members.

With a few notable exceptions, all employees are entitled to join a trade union and take advantage of the benefits offered, both protection and facilities.

0:20

student activity

(PC 4.1.4, COM 3.1)
To what extent do you think that trade unions, despite their relative lack of power, can have a positive impact upon employers' decision making? Discuss this as a group.

Staff associations in many organisations have either replaced trade unions or have been the only option, as far as employees are concerned. Staff organisations tend to have the following features:

- they have been designed by the employer
- they are run by the employer on behalf of the employees
- they are subsidised or fully funded by the employer
- they do not have the same roles or objectives as trade unions
- they are generally 'no strike' organisations
- they are the main route by which the organisation consults its workforce
- they tend to offer a similar range of welfare facilities as trade unions
- they are invariably separate organisations and not linked nationally
- membership is usually compulsory
- they are viewed with suspicion by trade unionists since they lack the power associated with independence

Trade Union Membership

We recognise the Union of Shop, Distributive and Allied Workers (USDAW) as the sole representative and negotiating union for all grades excluding senior store management.

Senior store management are represented by the Supervisory, Administrative and Technical Association (SATA) which is a separate division of USDAW.

Our relationship with USDAW has developed over many years and we encourage you to join.

FIG. 4.1.6 *Tesco Retail's staff handbook makes it clear that company policy is to recognise the Shopworkers' Union, USDAW.*

NEGOTIATING PAY AND CONDITIONS

National pay policies, which are often created by the government or by employers' organisations, have an inherent notion of 'pay restraint'. This means that to all intents and purposes, an absolute limit has already been set on the probable pay rise for the next year. In the light of this, trade union officials must negotiate the best possible deal that they can obtain for their members. Against a backdrop of the government's assertion that large pay increases will simply fuel inflation, employees are blamed for undermining the economy of the country if their pay claims are too great.

At a local level, issues which relate to pay and conditions will normally be undertaken either at regional or organisational level. Trade union officials will meet representatives of the employer and new deals will be struck.

Issues which affect a specific organisation, such as the introduction of new working conditions, will involve the union branch officials and senior management. In some cases, a negotiation process will precede the publication of the proposed changes to working conditions. The new working conditions may thus be seen as a collaborative effort between the employees and the employers.

GIVING ADVICE AND INFORMATION

Given the increasingly complex nature of employment and the need to adhere to a bewildering variety of legislation, it is essential that employees are given accurate and reliable advice and information. Trade unions provide their members with information on the implementation, practice and reality of legislation.

In giving advice and information to its members, the trade union is able for the most part to put employees on an even level with their managers. It is often said that information is power and the absence of knowledge of the relevant legislation can be seen as a definite disadvantage in many cases.

The branch officials within an organisation will, of course, keep their members appraised of developments within the organisation itself. Equally, it is their role to pass on relevant information which comes to them via the trade union headquarters or regional representatives. This constant interchange of information is vital to their members since seemingly distant decisions may have drastic impacts upon their members' pay and working conditions.

DEFENDING EMPLOYEES' RIGHTS

Despite the fact that many rights are protected by legislation, there are always situations where unscrupulous employers will seek to take advantage of their employees. Without branch officials or representatives from

student activity

(PC 4.1.4, COM 3.1, 3.2, 3.3, IT 3.1, 3.3)
Using the yellow pages or your local telephone directory, obtain the address of a trade union which operates in your area. Write a word processed letter to the union requesting information booklets regarding their range of advice available to members. Explain that you are a student and that you require the information to fulfil a particular aspect of your course.

Once you have obtained this information, read the booklets and prepare a short (10 minute) presentation on the advice offered by the union and contained in the booklets which you have collected. Make your presentation to the rest of the group.

You should ensure that if possible each member of the group contacts a different union. In the event that there are insufficient unions in your local area, you should each choose to concentrate on a particular aspect of the advice given by the union.

the staff association keeping an eye on the activities of management, members may find themselves in situations that are unacceptable but which are too late to reverse.

A well-informed branch official or staff association representative will be able to inform management if a decision may breach a particular piece of legislation. In addition employers have an ethical duty to behave in a reasonable manner towards their employees. Any breaches of reasonable behaviour are a little more difficult to monitor, and, indeed, they are more difficult to react against. Nearly all organisations have unwritten customs and practices whereby certain activities and circumstances are covered by traditional ways of doing things. Employees' representatives will be keen to maintain these customs and practices since they may not appear in contracts of employment, rules and regulations or policies and procedures of the organisation.

In the case of a dispute or, indeed, a disciplinary or grievance procedure, a trade union representative may be called in by the employee to act as a source of information or, simply, as a 'witness' to the events that take place. This function is fully supported by legislation and may enable the dispute or grievance to be dealt with at a relatively low level.

RESOLVING CONFLICT

The traditional view of trades unions is that their primary involvement in an organisation or industry is in the handling of conflicts and complex disputes. The term conflict can, of course, be used for a variety of seemingly uncontentious issues. Conflict itself occurs quite naturally whenever two parties disagree over a certain issue or the implementation of a policy. The trade union representative within the organisation will, of course, be involved if the conflict merits his/her input. Equally, if the employee requires or asks for trade union involvement, then it is the union's responsibility to offer assistance.

A trade union representative will only involve him/herself in conflicts which relate to that union's members. It should be remembered that an employee who does not keep up his/her membership and pay of membership or subscription fees may find him/herself technically disqualified from representation.

Within the structure of the trade union movement and trade unions themselves, certain individuals become involved in the handling of conflict at different levels, as follows:

- *shop stewards/branch officials* – will negotiate with management about issues within the working environment concerning their members
- *regional official* – who will be called in by the branch for additional information, guidance and authority
- *national executive* – which represents the union at national level and is involved in collective bargaining

It is this final role of collective bargaining that signifies the importance of the trade union movement as far as employees are concerned. The ability to negotiate at a national level often involving hundreds of thousands of members is a widely accepted and workable method of achieving results. Over the years many potential problems and disputes have been resolved by negotiations being carried out at national level with employers' federations, the government or other organisations.

   `0:30`

student activity

(PC 4.1.4, COM 3.1)
As a group, in the role of the executive committee of BIFU, consider what action you could take to protect your members. Given that the banks and building societies are reporting record profits, how can you attempt to ensure that your members are given the opportunity to prove their worth before more waves of redundancy hit them?

4.1.5 *Explain employers' methods for gaining employee co-operation*

Many organisations, while recognising that employees are a valuable resource in terms of their work output, have largely ignored their ability to offer specialist knowledge which could aid the operations of the organisation. Ssome employers, however, have installed schemes aimed at tapping this hitherto unused resource. Sceptics often claim that many of these schemes are simply paper or PR exercises aimed at trying to give the appearance of being more enlightened. Many progressive organisations have installed very effective forms of employee representation and consultation. As regards representation, the traditional forms obviously included trade union organisations. As we have seen in recent years many trade unions have decreased in size and power, while at the same time staff associations have become more common.

Employee relations become increasingly important as job tasks become more complex. Individuals who have a responsibility for key organisational activities need to feel that the organisation offers them rather more than monetary rewards. As we will see, complex infrastructures have gradually evolved to support key employees. We will also find that this development may be largely related to the need for the organisation to retain these key employees and offer them some level of ownership.

METHODS OF GAINING EMPLOYEES' CO-OPERATION

REPRESENTATION AND CONSULTATION

There are various forms of employee representation and consultation. Some organisations have formed **joint consultative committees** in which employees are given the opportunity to involve themselves in decision making. These committees hold regular meetings at which decisions made by the management are relayed to the workforce and a forum for discussion is provided. Such committees also meet to discuss and negotiate matters relating to industrial relations, such as working conditions, disciplinary procedures and pay.

These committees will take the form of:

- an advisory body
- a consultative body
- a negotiating body

Another form of employee consultation is known as employee participation. This has come about because organisations have recognised that the workforce has considerable skills and good ideas which could be used for the mutual benefit of employer and employees. There are various versions of employee participation and they include the following (although we will be looking at some of these specifically later in this Element):

- *employee briefing sessions* – where the employees are given useful and relevant information regarding the objectives of the organisation
- *quality circles* – where the employees meet on a voluntary basis to discuss their work and how systems and procedures may be improved
- *transfer of responsibility* – when employees take on some of the decision making previously undertaken by management
- *worker directors* – where employees attend meetings of the board of directors. In Europe this idea has proved to be very successful in improving the quality of decision making at board level. It also gives the board the opportunity to hear the views of the workforce at first hand rather than relying on the various layers of management to relay the employees' wishes and ideas. Further, this system tends to mean that the employees are more committed to decisions made by the board. Finally, it helps reduce employer/employee conflict as the employees have a greater idea of the overall problems faced by the organisation

student activity

(PC 4.1.5, COM 3.1)
Assess the impact of the above forms of employee consultation in the light of reduced labour disputes in the UK. Discuss this as a group.

TEAM WORKING

Employees rarely work in an organisation alone. Often teams are created, either formally or informally, in order to bring together the skills of individuals. Organisations will spend considerable time and effort in order to make sure that the teams created are able to function with much greater efficiency than groups of individuals undertaking the tasks alone.

In the interests of employee co-operation, team working is seen as a valuable means of ensuring that employees gain a greater understanding of the job task as a whole, as well as being given the opportunity to work with other individuals outside their normal working situations.

Teams are able to generate a high degree of loyalty, not only to themselves but to the organisation. One of the particular problems with regard to team work is that the teams often resent being split up after the task has been completed.

If you refer back to Unit 2, where we discussed the theories of Fayol, you will see that his fourteen-point management theory included 'Esprit de Corps'. This is, in effect, team work. The common purpose and co-operation involved in team work offers considerable benefits to both the individuals involved and the organisation in general.

EMPLOYEE SHARE OWNERSHIP

In recent years, employers have recognised that a degree of personal ownership on the part of the employee engenders much greater dedication, productivity and motivation. Organisations which use this form of participation include Marks and Spencer plc and the John Lewis Partnership.

The availability and issue of shares is usually dependent upon the number of years of service an employee has accumulated. Normally, shares will be made available to employees at a particular time of the year. A share offer may take place either when usual Christmas bonuses are paid, or, at the end of the financial year once the organisation's performance and profits have been calculated. Employees are not forced to take these shares instead of their bonus and they are often given the opportunity to take a cash payment instead. However, this cash payment is not as financially attractive as the shares which have been offered. Usually the shares come with some limitations, particularly in regard to the period for which the employee has to keep the shares before selling them.

These shares are just like any other ordinary share and the owners will receive any dividends payable and will be able to assess their worth by consulting published stocks and shares figures.

QUALITY CIRCLES

A quality circle is a discussion group which meets on a regular basis to:

- identify quality problems
- investigate solutions
- recommend suitable solutions

The members of the quality circles are ordinary members of the workforce and may include a individual with specific skills such as:

- an **engineer** in the case of complex products
- a **quality inspector** (if the organisation has a quality control department)
- a **salesperson** to give information on customer perspectives

Quality circles were first created in the 1950s in the Toyota motor company. In the 1980s this Japanese form of employee participation and consultation was adopted on a large scale in both Europe and the USA. Quality circles aim to use untapped knowledge from the factory floor, as well as giving employees the opportunity to show their knowledge and talents in terms of problem solving.

JOB SECURITY

Job security, in essence, is the knowledge that the job is guaranteed for the foreseeable future. Employers have recognised that a lack of job security can engender poor motivation and morale. Although it is difficult to guarantee that a job will last for the foreseeable future, employers are keen to stress that as long as the organisation continues along its projected course, then the job will be secure.

For the employee, a gradual process of multi-skilling and job enlargement is essential to ensure that job security is maintained. By broadening the range of activities and tasks undertaken, the employee can, to a large extent, make him/herself 'indispensable'. This should, however, be taken in the context of the organisation being much greater than the sum of all its parts. In this respect, no individual, regardless of rank, role or job title, is indispensable.

student activity

(PC 4.1.5, COM 3.2, IT 3.1)
Referring back to the previous Focus Study, in the role of a banking employer, prepare a short statement which addresses the fears of your employees concerning job security. This short statement should be word processed.

ELEMENT 4.1

a s s i g n m e n t

(PC 4.1.1–5, COM 3.1, 3.2, IT 3.1, AON 3.1)
In order to fulfil the performance criteria of this Element, it is essential that you analyse the rights and responsibilities of employers and employees. In addition, you should look at the procedures available to employees and employers in upholding these rights. Finally, you should also consider the role of trade unions and staff associations and how they provide advice, information, legal representation and negotiation skills.

TASK 1

(PC 4.1.1)
In the form of a report, detail the main features of the contract of employment which relate to pay and disciplinary procedures.

TASK 2

(PC 4.1.2)
Comparing two different working environments, assess their compliance with the following:

- health and safety regulations
- non-discriminatory legislation

TASK 3

(PC 4.1.3)
Also in your report you should describe the procedures available to employees and employers for upholding rights relating to the following:

- health and safety regulations
- non-discriminatory legislation

TASK 4

(PC 4.1.4)
Also in your report you should explain the role of trades unions and staff associations and how they play a part in the negotiation process, particularly relating to pay and conditions. You should also detail their provision of advice, information and legal representation.

TASK 5

(PC 4.1.5)
In the final section of your report you should explain how an employer's responsibilities are met in relation to two of the following:

- negotiating pay and conditions
- handling disciplinary procedures
- handling grievance procedures
- obtaining employee co-operation

Your report should be word processed and contain any relevant statistical data which may relate to your findings.

Investigate job roles and changing conditions

PERFORMANCE CRITERIA

A student must:

1 identify **job roles** in business organisations

2 describe **responsibilities** for human resources in job roles

3 explain reasons for change in working conditions

4 **evaluate** change in **working conditions**

5 propose a **plan** for a business **implementing change** to **working conditions**

RANGE

Job roles: director, manager, supervisor, operative, assistant

Responsibilities: to identify business objectives, to work with others, to meet targets, to monitor performance, to implement change in working conditions, to provide training, to give advice, to discipline, to handle grievances

Reasons for change: labour mobility, improving productivity, improving employee motivation, adapting to technological changes, employing new skills

Working conditions: fixed short-term contracts, long-term contracts; pay, benefits; flexible (hours, location, work space, multi-skilling, job sharing)

Evaluate in terms of: costs to business, benefits for business, costs to individuals, benefits for individuals

Plan to implement change through: planning, training, monitoring progress

4.2.1 Identity job roles in business organisations

This Element deals with the complex nature of job roles within organisations. Each individual, no matter how senior, carries a broad range of responsibilities. To a greater or lesser extent, legislation has a bearing on the activities of all individuals. Some things to bear in mind throughout any investigation of job roles are:

- the **employer** should clearly identify what the employee is expected to do
- the **employee** should be well aware of what the employer expects of him/her
- **both** the **employer** and **employee** should be content that the employee is capable of doing the job. If not, then steps should be taken to ensure that the employee can perform to the best of his/her abilities

We will be using a number of key terms in describing exactly what individual job roles are. These are:

- *authority* – can the individual command others to carry out tasks? In other words, does the individual have any real power?
- *accountability* – who is the individual responsible to? How many superiors have responsibility for the individual?
- *responsibility* – what exactly are the tasks or duties related to the job and what level of independence does the individual have?
- *rights* – what should the individual reasonably expect from the employer? What should the employer reasonably expect from the employee?

ROLES

DIRECTOR

Directors are essentially members of the **board** which controls an organisation. The most senior member of the board is known as a **managing director**. Before looking at directors in general, we shall consider this key role first.

It is the responsibility of the managing director to preside over board meetings. A managing director's main responsibilities are:

- to exercise all powers and duties of a director
- to exercise power and responsibility in the name of the board on a day-to-day basis

The managing director is chosen by other members of the board. In making their choice they will be looking for an individual with a number of important qualities, amongst which are the following:

- wide business experience
- a proven track record of success
- the ability to make decisions under pressure
- to be prepared to answer for any decision made and to stand by those decisions
- to be accountable to the board and ultimately the shareholders
- to be a driving force behind the policies and objectives of the organisation and the fulfilment of the same
- to have excellent communication skills
- to act as a representative and ambassador for the organisation in a variety of situations

It is the managing director who is actually responsible for the implementation of policy formulated by the board, and who represents the board itself at all times. To some extent, the managing director has to interpret the wishes of the board, and develop a clear programme of organisational objectives. Further, he/she must know which key members of staff can be relied upon to follow through his/her policy decisions to successful completion. At all times, the managing director must keep the board informed of any problems, decisions or crises that may occur and of which they should be made aware.

The minimum number of directors depends on the type of organisation. In private companies, there need only be one. In a public company two is the minimum. A directorship has a dual function:

- direction of activities
- management of staff and their activities

FIG. 4.2.1 *Deputy Chairman and Managing Director Clinton Silver (left) has special responsibility for merchandise. Managing Director Keith Oates is responsible for finance. These are two key Marks & Spencer PLC executives.*

The main difference between these two functions is that direction tends to be longer term whilst management involves day-to-day decision making.

Direction is essentially the implementation of the board's policies. If a director is an **executive director,** this means that he/she works full time for the organisation and has responsibility for a particular part of the organisation. A **non-executive director** may be part time and may concentrate on a particular aspect of policy with which he/she has experience.

Management as carried out by executive directors can be complex as many find it difficult to separate the direction and management roles. They may have a good idea of the nature of the organisation's policies and have a reasonably clear impression as to how this policy may be implemented. Unfortunately, day-to-day decision making may mean that the executive director has to make decisions which are sometimes at odds with the organisation's policy. One way around this problem is to organise the board of directors into two separate units. Board members will serve on one or other of the units (with the exception of the managing director who will serve on both). One unit of directors will deal with overall policy, and the other unit will concentrate on day-to-day implementation of policy. In this way, any conflict between policy and management of decision making is avoided.

The main responsibilities of the directors, therefore, are:

- to exercise their power and authority in good faith and for the benefit of the organisation
- to put aside their personal interests and always put the organisation first
- to endeavour to be professional when managing the affairs of the organisation

A director should, therefore, display care and skill at all times. Obviously, non-executive directors, who have been included on the board for their experience and expertise in a particular area, are expected to be even more professional in their conduct on behalf of the organisation. At the same time, these non-executive directors may not have the skill or expertise of a normal board member. Such directors are often helped by an employee who will assist them in procedural matters.

Both public and private limited companies are required by law to have a **company secretary**. Essentially, this is an administrative post and may be at director level. Certainly the company secretary will be expected to either sit on the board or regularly attend meetings. A company secretary has a variety of tasks and duties, the most common of which are:

- to keep all **records** as required by law which include a register of members of the organisation

- to keep **minutes** of the board and other director's meetings
- to keep the organisation's **legal documents** secure
- to keep the organisation's **seal** secure – the seal is the organisation's name and registration number
- to arrange the directors' **meetings**
- to ensure that any information required by the **Registrar of Companies** is completed
- to act as the representative of the organisation when the organisation enters into a **binding contract**

student activity

(PC 4.2.1, COM 3.1, 3.2)
In pairs, make a list of legal documents which you think a company secretary would be responsible for.

There is a legal requirement to look into the financial affairs of organisations on an annual basis. This examination, known as **auditing,** is undertaken to ensure that any facts or figures relating to finance given by the organisation are true and accurate. Under normal circumstances, auditing is done mainly for the benefit of the shareholders.

It is usual for the auditors to be a professional business, not connected in any way to the organisation being audited. Only registered auditors may carry out auditing work. There are a number of limitations as to who may act as an auditor for an organisation. These are:

- the auditor must not be an officer or servant of the organisation being audited
- the auditor may not be the partner of, or employed by, an officer or servant of the organisation
- the exclusion extends to any subsidiaries of the organisation and their employees and partners
- the auditor must not have any relationship with the organisation being audited
  The auditor looks at two main areas:
- the organisation's accounts
- what the organisation has said in relation to these accounts to members of the company

MANAGER

Below the level of director, there are a number of layers of managers. It is the duty of a manager to undertake tasks and duties as delegated to him or her by a director. In effect, it is the manager who takes responsibility for the day-to-day decision making and implementation of organisational policy. A manager will be accountable to the director and ultimately the board and shareholders via any other managers senior to him/her.

A manager would usually have a far better working knowledge of the organisation than even an executive director. Directors, therefore, tend not to interfere with basic decision making, and providing they consider the managers competent and reliable, are happy to delegate their authority to the various levels of management.

The exact duties of managers very much depend on the following:

- the level of responsibility
- the department or function of the organisation for which they are responsible
- the nature of the organisation to which they belong

Shortly we will be looking at some specific managerial roles and identifying the key tasks, duties and responsibilities of managers.

FIG. 4.2.3 *Managers at various levels play key roles in the decision-making process of an organisation.*

---

student activity

0:20

PC 4.2.1, COM 3.2
In the role of an auditor, draw up a list of documents which you would expect to be given access to by an organisation during an audit.

AUDITORS' REPORT

Kwik-Fit Holdings plc and its Subsidiary Companies

ARTHUR
ANDERSEN

ARTHUR ANDERSEN & CO SC

18 Charlotte Square
Edinburgh EH2 4DF

To the Members of KWIK-FIT HOLDINGS PLC

We have audited the accounts on pages 16 to 32 in accordance with Auditing Standards.

In our opinion the accounts give a true and fair view of the state of affairs of the Company and of the Group at 28 February 1993 and of the Group profit, total recognised gains and losses and cash flows for the year then ended and have been properly prepared in accordance with the Companies Act 1985.

Arthur Andersen.

Chartered Accountants and Registered Auditor
18 March 1993

FIG. 4.2.2 *Statement by Kwik-Fit Holdings PLC auditors, Arthur Andersen, that the accounts have been audited in accordance with auditing standards.*

student activity

0:20

(PC 4.2.1, COM 3.1)
Discuss the following:

Managers are the ones who do all the work. Directors just grab the glory and blame managers if things go wrong.

SUPERVISOR

Supervisors tend to be the next tier down in the organisational structure below managers. Essentially they are team leaders or organisers of specific projects or functions of the organisation. It is relatively difficult, in some cases, to recognise the exact difference between a manager and a supervisor. Perhaps it is easier to think in terms of the actual managerial responsibilities involved. Supervisors tend to deal only with day-to-day tasks and to direct individuals under their control in the pursuit of efficiency. Supervisors do not necessarily have wider scale managerial responsibilities. They will usually answer to a manager who takes on these functions.

There is an interesting point to be made regarding the status of supervisors, particularly in regard to employers' use of the word supervisor itself. One way around having to offer a higher level of salary is simply to call an individual's job role 'supervisory', rather than 'managerial'. There is a perception that managers should receive higher rates of pay. In order to avoid this, an organisation may choose to call its managers supervisors. Women, in particular, often find themselves offered supervisory posts when, in fact, their job role is clearly a management one.

In industrial organisations, there are quite large numbers of supervisors. They have responsibility for specific functions of the production process and have relative independence in their choice of the deployment of employees to achieve success.

In an office environment, a supervisor will tend to have responsibility for ensuring that all individuals have been allocated sufficient work, that the work produced is of an acceptable standard and that the secretarial duties fully support the other operations of the organisation.

student activity

(PC 4.2.1, COM 3.1)
As a group, try to identify the principal differences between a supervisor and a manager. = In the role of an employer, try to decide whether you think it would be preferable to give an individual the job title of 'manager' instead of 'supervisor'. What possible benefits do you think the organisation would obtain by doing this?

OPERATIVE

The term operative is a relatively new term which is applied to a wide variety of different job roles. Perhaps the main feature of the term operative is that it infers some form of manual labour. Strictly speaking, the term operative refers to the operation of machinery or equipment. More recently, this term has been adopted to encompass many non-manual activities. Indeed, in a fast food outlet such as McDonalds, the counter staff are referred to as operatives.

One aspect of the working environment that we should not ignore is employees working in an organisation rarely work on their own. More often teams are created, either formally or informally, to carry out specific tasks. A team is basically a group of individuals or operatives working together towards a single common objective. When working as a member of a team, people need to know which members of the team have the power and authority, in other words, who is actually directing the efforts of the team. It is common to find a supervisor fulfilling this role. To be a successful team member, a number of skills are required. These include:

● the ability to communicate
● an understanding of the objective of the task
● the ability (gained through training) to carry out a variety of roles within the team

Employers have recognised the advantages of team building and many have been prepared to pay for residential training programmes aimed at enhancing team building.

FIG. 4.2.4 *Team work at all levels and in all work situations is a vital component of work activity, as can be seen in the work of these Costa Rican pineapple growers, picking fruit for Geest plc.*

ASSISTANT

This job title infers a subsidiary role in the organisation. Derived from the term 'to assist', an assistant, by definition, helps a more senior member of staff. Typically, we would find the word assistant attached to job titles such as 'shop assistant', 'catering assistant', 'administrative assistant', 'clerical assistant', 'editorial assistant' and 'personal assistant'.

Despite the fact that these job roles may not appear to be particularly key in an organisation, the mere fact that the more senior member of staff needs an assistant means that the individual fulfilling this role is also a vital member of staff. Many managers who have personal assistants working for them would find it impossible to do their jobs without the able support of a well-motivated colleague. Again, the exact nature of the assistant's role within the organisation is very much dependent upon the nature of the job and the organisation itself.

The term assistant is again used in some cases to downgrade the perception of the job. Again, this may be used as a means of offering a lower salary. A shop assistant, for example, may have enormous responsibility in not only the day-to-day shop work activities, but also cashier responsibilities, stock-taking and ordering, customer service and security of premises. It should not be assumed that if the job title includes the word assistant this is a junior post.

JOB FUNCTIONS

As we have already inferred, the jobs people actually do within an organisation are clearly dependent upon three major criteria. These are:

- the size of the organisation
- the type of organisation
- the function of the organisation

Perhaps a good starting point in trying to assess exactly what a job entails is to discover what an organisation needs. Once this has been done, jobs can then be designed to fulfil the various functions required by the organisation. However, things are not always this simple. The majority of organisations have evolved over a number of years and the jobs undertaken by individuals working for them have changed gradually. In fact, many jobs have expanded to incorporate duties somewhat different from those they were originally intended to perform. In many cases, if an individual looks at his/her original contract of employment, it is not unusual to find that the current tasks and duties undertaken are radically different from those specified in the contract.

The result of this change is that some employees find themselves extremely over-worked, while others cope well with the tasks required of them, yet others still are under-worked. An organisation which allows such an imbalance of work to persist will find that it will adversely affect the smooth running of the organisation.

The solution appears to be simple, but is not often used. Each time an individual leaves an organisation there is an opportunity to evaluate exactly what his/her job entailed and assess whether certain duties can be re-allocated. The more progressive thinking organisations regularly conduct a process of job review and evaluation. This process aims to look in detail at each job role and see if any features of the job need to be changed to take into account the following:

- development of different working practices
- new demands
- different demands
- technological developments

The smaller the organisation, the more complex each individual employee's job may be. Employees may have to be capable of carrying out a wide variety of duties, often unrelated to one another. Not only would the owner of a small business be a managing director, but he/she may also be responsible for the following:

- recruitment, training and promotion of employees
- supervising employees
- dealing with wages and salaries
- other financial considerations
- purchasing and ordering
- actively seeking contracts

student activity

(PC4.2.1, COM 3.2)
In the role of a small business owner, complete the list above assuming that you are unable to delegate anything to assistants or employees.

The small business owner will have to rely on his/her small number of employees to carry out their duties largely unaided, and will have to turn to a number of professionals to deal with more complex situations, such as accountants, bank managers or solicitors. Their services will have to be 'bought in' either on an as-and-when basis, or on a retainer basis.

In larger organisations, different functions tend to be split into distinct areas, as we have seen. These areas may include many of the departmental divisions which we have looked at in Unit 2. Before we consider the responsibilities that relate to job roles, it may be useful to reconsider some of the key features. We will begin by looking at the various levels of management and authority and then try to identify the five main types of job.

The layers of authority and power in an organisation tend to follow a similar format, regardless of size, type and function of organisation. These are:

1 *Director level* – who set broad organisational policies and objectives.
2 *Senior management level* – who set the policies and procedures which will ensure the implementation of the organisation's objectives; some executive directors may be included at this level.
3 *Middle management level* – whose task it is to actually ensure that the objectives are implemented on a day-to-day basis and to direct managers and supervisors in the course of their duties.
4 *Junior management level* – whose task it is on a day-to-day basis to liaise with middle managers with regard to policy and supervisors in the direction of employees.
5 *Supervisors* – whose responsibility it is to ensure that tasks as directed by the levels of management are carried out promptly and efficiently.
6 *Operatives, assistants, workers, staff* – who make up the bulk of the organisation and whose role it is to actually deal with the job in hand.

We will now try to identify the five different types of job. This will help us in assessing the exact nature of job roles and attempt to put them into the context of the organisation. These are:

1 *Professional* – this category includes solicitors, accountants, dentists, doctors and architects, all of whom display a certain degree of specialist knowledge in a particular area. In recent years, although many professionals would strenuously disagree, new professionals have joined this group. They are mainly related to new areas of work outside the traditional professional fields. Examples of these would include computer analysts, personnel managers, marketing executives and the bewildering variety of management and business consultants.
2 *Managerial* – this category is a very wide one, but essentially it includes managerial and supervisory posts. Some occupations which we have already mentioned as being professional, can also be referred to as being managerial, such as personnel managers and marketing managers.
3 *Technical* – this relatively recent occupational category type (although this occupational group has existed ever since there have been machines), essentially refers to those individuals who are responsible for the setting up and maintenance of machinery and technological equipment. Within this category

we will find computer programmers, television camera operators, sound recordists and production line technicians.
4 *Administrative* – this category is also fairly wide and includes any job which could be considered to have clerical or administrative responsibilities. Typical examples are secretaries, receptionists, word processor operators and switchboard operators.
5 *Manual* – essentially this category covers all manual workers who operate various different types of equipment or machinery. It is necessary to make three sub-divisions in order to more clearly define this category, these are:
   ● skilled – in this sub-section we would find tradespersons, such as carpenters, plumbers, bricklayers, roofers and tilers. Members of this sub-section usually belong to a guild or association related to their trade
   ● semi-skilled – in this sub-section we would find partially trained individuals, or those who have been trained to use a particular piece of equipment or
   ● machinery. They would usually assist a skilled person and be an assistant or 'mate'
   ● unskilled – in this sub-section we would find workers who are not trained for a specific role, but may, nevertheless, have a specialist ability in some respect. These include labourers, factory operatives, warehouse packers and cleaners.

student activity

(PC 4.2.1, COM 3.1, 3.2)
Individually, list and categorise the occupations undertaken by all members of your immediate family. Into which of the categories listed above do those occupations fit? Compare your list with that of the rest of the group.

Every organisation has its own way of structuring the functions that it carries out. Here are some of the more common ones. Not all the positions described below exist in every organisation. Factors such as the nature of the operation and its size and complexity affect the need for functions such as these and for separate departments and staff to carry them out.

THE ADMINISTRATION DEPARTMENT

Most organisations have a central administration. The main function of the administration department is to control paperwork and to support all the other departments by servicing their needs for secretarial work – filing, mailing, handling data, etc.

The main staff of any administration department are:

1 *Chief administration officer or office services manager* – oversees all major functions of the department, allocates work received from other departments (and routine administrative duties) and carries responsibility for the smooth running of the department.

2 *Secretariat supervisor* – allocates and monitors all work carried out by the secretaries, audio typists, shorthand typists, word processor operators and typists.

3 *Word processor operator* – under the guidance of the secretariat supervisor, the word processor operator undertakes work from a variety of different sources and is responsible for the presentation and safe storage (on disk or hard copy) of this work and for ensuring that any deadlines related to the work are met.

4 *Secretary* – usually works directly for one or more managers. It is the secretary's responsibility to ensure that any information in the form of messages, memos, letters, reports, etc, is brought to the attention of the manager. In addition, a secretary is responsible for routine letter and note-taking, on behalf of the manager, as well as keeping track of all his/her diary commitments (sometimes his/her personal diary too). The secretary may also arrange meetings for which his/her manager may be responsible. At all times the secretary must ensure that only relevant information and individuals which really need the time of the manager are brought to his/her attention. A secretary's skills may include the ability to work with audio tapes, word processors and to take shorthand.

5 *Audio typist* – works for several people in the organisation, possibly based in a 'pool'. His/her duties include typing from audio tapes which have been prepared by various individuals and he/she will need to ensure that this work is completed to the given deadline, in a neat and accurate way.

6 *Shorthand typist* – works for several individuals within the organisation. He/she takes dictation from the manager and is responsible for transcribing this and typing up the document in a neat and accurate way. A shorthand typist is usually present to note the decisions taken at any company meetings.

7 *Typist* – types routine documents within the organisation. To a great extent this role is gradually being taken over by word processor operators, as increasingly organisations are tending to buy word processors rather than typewriters.

8 *Messenger* – distributes of both internal and external documents. The role is particularly useful in organisations which have a number of sites close to one another, or in situations when the organisation's customers are located in the immediate vicinity. Messengers are still used in the City of London. However, many functions traditionally carried out by messengers have been replaced with the availability of facsimile machines, modems and electronic mail.

9 *Records supervisor* – responsible for ensuring that all necessary documents are safely, securely and accessibly stored. Despite the fact that technology has substantially reduced the need to store vast amounts of paper documents, there are many reasons why organisations still prefer to have hard copies of documents available for inspection. Upon receiving a request for information the records supervisor instructs a records clerk to retrieve and deliver the required documentation.

10 *Records clerk* – allocated work by the records supervisor. Responsible for retrieving the required information and ensuring its safe delivery by internal mail, personal delivery or by messenger. The records clerk also takes note of who has requested the information, the date of the request and the date of return. This 'Out' card is completed in order to keep track of the documents and ensure their safe return.

11 *Librarian* – responsible for acquiring and maintaining resources relevant to the organisation's activities. These may take the form of books, reports, periodicals and newspaper cuttings. This resource is then available to all members of the organisation who may need to conduct research into a specific area related to their work. It is the librarian's task to ensure that the information is as up to date as possible and that all staff are aware of its availability.

12 *Mail room supervisor* – responsible for the handling of all internal and external mail. The office is commonly known as the post room. This location acts as a central collection point of letters, packages and parcels. Some may be bound for literally any part of the world while others may be internal mail or bulletins. The various pieces of mail are either collected by a mail room assistant, or delivered by various individuals within the organisation. It is the mail room supervisor's responsibility to make sure that all outgoing mail is weighed, franked and made ready for collection by the Post Office. The mail

room supervisor also notes (for internal cost allocation) the postage totals for each department within the organisation.

13 *Mail room assistant* – working under the direction and instruction of the mail room supervisor, the mail room assistant may carry out a variety of different tasks:

- collect mail from the various departments
- deliver mail received each morning to the relevant person(s). Before this can be done, the mail needs to be sorted and perhaps re-routed to another site
- weigh, frank and put outgoing mail into the correct Post Office bag ready for collection or delivery to the Post Office
- note postage costs of each department and ensure that the mail room supervisor has up-to-date figures for these
- ensure that the Post Office leaflets kept in the mail room are current

14 *Telephone/switchboard supervisor* – since many organisations rely heavily on the internal and external telephone system, this key post is vital to the smooth running of most operations. This supervisor ensures that all telecommunication needs are met and that the switchboard system is capable of fulfilling the demands of the organisation. In addition, the supervisor makes sure that the switchboard is constantly staffed and that, at times when the organisation is closed for business, an answerphone can record incoming calls, or can give useful information to callers.

15 *Switchboard operator* – in many cases, a customer's first contact with an organisation is via the telephone. It is therefore most important that the switchboard operator answers the calls swiftly and is helpful and responsive to the caller. A good switchboard operator knows exactly who the caller needs to speak to about a particular matter (despite the fact that the caller may not ask for a named individual) and knows from memory the extension number of most members of staff.

16 *Cleaning supervisor* – all organisations, whether or not they have a constant flow of visitors, need to ensure that the premises are kept as clean and tidy as possible. Organisations which have sensitive technological equipment may even need to ensure that the work areas are as dust-free as possible. The cleaning supervisor allocates his/her cleaning staff according to the demands of each particular work area. Periodically, floors and windows may need to be given special attention and may require specialist equipment/subcontractors to carry out the necessary work.

17 *Cleaners* – usually given a particular area of the premises for which he/she is responsible. The main cleaning duties include emptying of bins, clearing away of empty boxes and packing materials, hoovering and dusting and routine general cleaning duties. Specialist cleaners may be employed to sanitise telephones, clean word processors with anti-static sprays and clean carpets or polish floors.

student activity

(PC4.2.1, COM 3.2)
Draw up an organisation chart which shows the operations of an administration department. You should include all of the above posts. Indicate with arrows the lines of responsibility and decision making.

THE ACCOUNTS OR FINANCE DEPARTMENT

The accounts department supervises all matters involving finance. Computers and calculators are used extensively. An accounts department is split up into two further sections:

- the day-to-day accounting procedures are handled by the **financial accounting** section. Essentially they keep track of all incoming and outgoing cash or credits
- the **management accounting** section concentrates on analysing the figures and trying to predict possible income and outgoings into the future

The accounts or finance department records and monitors sales, purchasing, manufacturing costs, running costs (lighting, heating, etc.), dividends to shareholders, payment of salaries and wages and departmental and organisational budgets.

At all times, the accounts department must know whether the organisation is operating at a profit. They do this by checking that revenue from sales is greater than costs. The directors, shareholders and senior managers need to have access to this information instantly. This is presented in various forms, such as balance sheets and profit and loss accounts. We will look at these in much more detail in a later Unit of the book.

This department is also responsible for maintaining records of financial transactions required by law, e.g. the payment of tax and national insurance and pension fund arrangements.

The officers of this department are:

1 *Company accountant* – it is the company accountant's responsibility to maintain an up-to-date record and analysis of income and expenditure. The company accountant has a number of accounts specialists who monitor, on his/her behalf, various financial aspects of the organisation. At any time, the company accountant may be asked for detailed information about the financial status of the organisation, and must be able to respond immediately. There are a number of legal and statutory requirements that an organisation must fulfil and it is the responsibility of the company accountant to ensure that all of these obligations are met. The company accountant is directly accountable to the board of directors for his/her actions and decisions.

2 *Accountants* – various accounts specialists are employed to carry out specific monitoring and analysis of financial data. These accountants oversee the flow of data received regarding sales, purchases, running costs and other expenses. In addition, they provide essential accounting information such as gross profit, net profit, turnover and relative profitability of different areas of the organisation. In larger organisations they may keep track of the performance of investments in other organisations and regularly monitor the financial strengths and weaknesses of subsidiary companies.

3 *Credit controller* – monitor the orders placed and the payment history of customers in order to establish their reliability as payers. Each customer has a set credit limit (rather like an agreed overdraft) and the credit controller must endeavour to make sure that customers do not exceed this limit. In cases of late or non-payment of invoices, it is the credit controller who contacts the customer in question in an attempt to secure payment. The credit controller takes into account how long the customer has been purchasing from the organisation and may well look back into the past to see if there have been any previous problems with regard to payment.

4 *Accounts clerk* – carries out routine day-to-day accounting duties, as directed by either the chief accountant or senior accountants. This may involve either manual figure work, or the use of the increasingly popular range of accounting software. It is usually the accounts clerk's role to prepare figures for analysis by the more senior accountants. In some organisations, one duty of an accounts clerk is to maintain and issue petty cash to those who request it by the presentation of a validly signed voucher.

5 *Payroll clerks* – working closely with the personnel department, the payroll clerk is responsible for ensuring that the correct wages or salaries are paid to every member of staff. The payroll clerk must be familiar with income tax and national insurance and pension scheme contributions. Depending on the size of the organisation, the payroll clerk may have to undertake these tasks manually, or in a larger organisation, he/she may be assisted by a software package. In some organisations where the wages structure is complex, or is related to performance and output, this job may not be as straightforward as one might imagine.

student activity

(PC 4.2.1, COM 3.1, 3.2)
In the role of an accounts clerk, decide what action would you need to take should the following arise:

- you are processing a cheque which has not been signed
- you receive petty cash vouchers which do not correspond with the attached receipts

Having completed your list of actions to take, compare and discuss with the remainder of your group.

THE SALES DEPARTMENT

The sales department's main responsibility is to create orders for goods and services. Many organisations enjoy a large sales force which operates either, in the case of retail stores, on a local level, or, in the case of organisations which supply to other organisations, on a regional basis.

The greater the emphasis on selling to individual customers, the larger the sales force, and those organisations which rely on heavy advertising to stimulate interest in their goods or services can have a relatively small sales team.

In terms of organising the efforts of the sales employees, the sales department draws up a detailed sales plan which includes targets to be met by each area or region of the sales force. Also included in this will be the level of profit which can be expected from each and every product.

Working closely with the marketing department, the sales department regularly supplies sales information regarding sales levels, activities of competitors and requests from customers for new or improved products. The sales force compile the raw data about their sales figures on a weekly basis for interpretation by the sales manager, who will then pass this information on for analysis by the marketing department.

In order to stimulate sales, the sales department may develop a range of point-of-sale material (including posters, leaflets and boxes with the company logo) and other promotional materials.

The officers of this department are:

1 *Sales manager* – his job entails the co-ordination of the organisation's sales efforts. The sales manager is usually located at the head office with an administration staff who monitor the performance of the various national, regional and area sales managers and teams. In positions such as this, a considerable amount of the salary is related to sales performance. Periodically the sales manager visits his/her sales team in the field to assess their effectiveness and to keep in touch with current customer demands.

2 *Assistant sales manager* – deputising for the sales manager, this individual takes on a range of sales-related responsibilities and may often be the first point of contact for the various members of the sales force. It is the assistant sales manager's role to help the sales manager formulate the sales policy of the organisation.

3 *National sales manager* – in larger organisations, there is a need to co-ordinate the sales efforts on a country-by-country basis. National sales managers are usually given considerable freedom to formulate a sales policy which is the most effective for the country in which they operate. Normally, a national sales manager will have a wide knowledge of the country in which he/she works and may even be a national of that country. Other organisations may not have national sales managers, as they may have entered into an agreement with a foreign company which will represent the interests of the organisation in the field.

4 *Regional sales manager* – just as different countries have their own peculiarities, regions within a country also have theirs. Different sorts of industry and commerce tend to cluster around particular towns or cities. The regional sales manager will have an intimate knowledge of the needs of these businesses, which may be different from the national needs. The regional sales manager will be located within the region for which he/she has responsibility and will be required to regularly analyse any changes in the local economy which may affect sales.

5 *Area sales manager* – working under the direction of the regional sales manager, an area sales manager is responsible for a part of the region. In some cases, this may mean a single city or county. Again, a good working knowledge of the needs of the area is essential in co-ordinating the sales effort. The area sales manager regularly accompanies sales representatives when they visit customers and is able to offer on-the-spot advice and guidance.

6 *Sales representatives* – these individuals form the backbone of the sales team. Constantly on the road, visiting both existing and potential customers, they will be in direct contact with their area sales manager via mobile or car phones. Since the bulk of their salary is directly related to the sales they generate, they are always under pressure to meet their targets in order to achieve their bonuses. The image of the sales representative in his company car, is well known. In reality, they may be very well trained sales people, with an expert knowledge of their field and extremely useful to their customers. They are, after all, the first point of contact and may well become a useful 'partner' in building up a business.

7 *Tele-sales assistant* – working from central, national, regional or area offices, these individuals not only take direct orders for goods and services from the customer, but also receive regular orders from the sales representatives. Operating with up-to-date lists of customer contacts from the sales representatives, they attempt to gain new sales or arrange for one of the sales representatives to visit the business. They are particularly well trained in telephone skills and normally have useful information to hand via a desktop computer.

8 *Invoice clerk* – processes all orders generated by either the sales representatives or the tele-sales team. Essentially, the documents produced form both a list of required products for the warehouse to despatch and a record for the accounts department of products sold. The invoice clerk is in regular contact with the warehouse to ensure that the sales team is aware of the stock levels of each product.

student activity

In the role of the sales director, prepare a memo which answers a note from the personnel department. The note states that at the end of the month you will lose the services of your invoice clerk. Your memo should state your reasons for wanting to keep this individual and should be word processed.

THE MARKETING DEPARTMENT

The main function of the marketing department is to try to identify customer requirements. There is also an element of trying to predict customer needs into the future. The marketing department works very closely with the sales department, and it is important that the two communicate well.

The starting point for most marketing functions is to carry out extensive research on a particular market to try to discover exactly what customers want, where they want it, how much they want to pay for it, and the most effective way of getting the message across.

The staff in this department are:

1 *Marketing manager* – responsible for planning, organising, directing and controlling the marketing efforts of the organisation. Increasingly, they are professional individuals who are well versed in formulating a marketing plan which is workable within the limitations of the organisation. In effect, they are responsible for establishing the organisation's marketing objectives (known as the strategy) and deciding how the overall objectives may be achieved (known as the tactics). All organisations have a 'corporate image', which means that everything the organisation produces, from letterheads to finished products, has the same overall look. The marketing manager will decide exactly how the corporate image relates to each and every aspect of the company.

2 *Assistant marketing manager* – deputising for the marketing manager, and co-ordinating the efforts of each of the product/brand managers are the main responsibilities of the assistant marketing manager. It is this individual's role to implement the marketing strategy across all aspects of the organisation and to ensure that the corporate image is consistent.

3 *Product/brand manager* – responsible for co-ordinating the marketing plan relating to a single product. A brand manager, on the other hand, may be responsible for a range of products which have the same brand name. In both cases, the individuals will have to organise all activities relating to their product(s), including advertising, sales promotions, launches, re-launches and packaging.

4 *Marketing research analyst* – millions of pounds are spent each year on marketing research. Nearly 10 per cent of the retail price of every item is spent on marketing research alone. Marketing research is the systematic collection and analysis of data which looks specifically at the customers' attitudes, needs, opinions and motivation and anything which influences these. In order to minimise the risks involved in launching a new product, the organisation needs to know as much as possible about the potential customer, competition and any other factors which may affect sales. This specialist uses existing statistical data, as well as commissioning new market research as may be required.

5 *Advertising manager* – responsible for co-ordinating the advertising budget of the organisation. Working in close co-operation with various other members of the organisation, the advertising manager should be able to identify the best media for the advertising of the product. Additionally, the advertising manager negotiates with magazines, newspapers, radio and television companies to achieve the best possible price. In many organisations, the advertising manager's function is taken over by an outside advertising agency which places and co-ordinates all advertisements.

6 *Promotions manager* – there is a narrow line between the responsibilities of a promotions manager and those of an advertising manager. Essentially, the promotions manager co-ordinates all marketing strategies apart from advertisements. These include special offers, competitions, trial offers, money-off vouchers, point-of-sale material and exhibitions.

student activity

(PC 4.2.1, COM 3.1)
In the role of marketing manager where would you look for information on changes in customer trends and fashions? Discuss this in groups of three.

THE INFORMATION TECHNOLOGY OR COMPUTER SERVICES DEPARTMENT

The information technology or computer services department's responsibilities includes computing (hardware and software), maintenance of data bases, telecommunications, and other technological office developments.

The staff of this department are:

1 *Departmental manager* – it is the responsibility of the departmental manager to provide a round-the-clock and comprehensive service back-up for the organisation's computing and data processing requirements. Within his/her area of influence, the manager co ordinates the design of computer programs to manipulate data for the various departments.

2 *Assistant departmental manager* – under the direction of the departmental manager, responsible for acquiring and maintaining all computer software and hardware. In order to carry out this task, he/she delegates various aspects to specialist managers. In co-ordination with the departmental manager, they will ensure that sufficient support is given to all computer-based communication systems within the organisation.

3 *Data processing manager* – maintains a detailed record of the organisation's stored information, which must be constantly updated and always accessible. The manager also ensures that sensitive information is protected from access by unauthorised persons. On a regular basis, the data processing manager also makes sure that back-up copies of all data stored have been made and kept in secure and fireproof locations.

4 *Computer services manager* – keeps a constant overview of new developments in order to inform the departmental manager of more efficient ways of storing and manipulating data. It is also this individual's responsibility to install and maintain new or updated versions of software as they become available. Further, his/her team of servicing engineers regularly checks all of the organisation's computer equipment. In some organisations, this service function has been bought in from computing service specialists.

5 *Computer programmers* – these specialist individuals create computer software needed by the various departments, so that information may be processed and analysed according to changing needs.

6 *Computer operators* – responsible for the inputting of data and the manipulation of existing information at the request of various departments within the organisation. Routinely, they update information from a variety of sources, deleting or modifying as required. Organisations have become increasingly reliant on computer-based information and need constant access to reliable and contemporary data.

THE RESEARCH AND DEVELOPMENT DEPARTMENT

Key research and development personnel are:

1 *Research and development co-ordination manager* - it is the responsibility of this manager to coordinate the development of products and services to prototype level. All products and services must be rigorously tested before they are put into production and offered to the customer. The individual who fills this post is likely to be a technical expert within a specific field. He/she must be aware of the technological requirements and any production problems related to these. Normally, this manager is given clear instructions as to the organisation's requirements for a new product or service, but will have to work very closely with the production manager in order to develop a product which the organisation is capable of producing.

2 *Researchers* – once the departmental manager has been given a brief to develop and test a new product or service, researchers investigate all aspects of this product or service. They refer to any scientific reports which relate to the area of interest, as well as investigating competitors' products. In effect, they produce a report which offers a series of alternatives from which the developers can work. This report is also circulated to any other interested party in the organisation.

3 *Product/service developers* – these individuals are specialists in their own field. They will have been chosen for their knowledge and ability to apply their skills. It is their responsibility to work from the information given to them by the researchers and to develop a working version or versions of the product. This product is then subjected to exhaustive testing to ensure that it meets the requirements of the organisation, safety tests and the needs of the customer. At all stages of the development, the production department will advise the developers of any production considerations.

student activity

(PC 4.2.1, COM 3.1)
Discuss the following statement:

Computers have taken the human factor out of too many business decisions.

student activity

(PC 4.2.1, COM 3.1)
What kind of R & D would be carried out by a manufacturer of frozen foods? Discuss this as a group.

THE PRODUCTION DEPARTMENT

The production department is involved in all functions which revolve around producing goods or services for the customer.

The staff of this department are:

1 *Production manager* – responsible for manufacturing products to the correct specification, quality, price and safety levels. Production managers tend to have considerable technical knowledge, and to understand the production process intimately. He/she works closely with the R & D manager, as well as the sales manager. It is the production manager's role to turn new product ideas into finished products and supply the regular needs of the sales department.

2 *Assistant production managers* – given the responsibility by the production manager of overseeing the smooth running of the various production lines. They work in close co-operation with the production line managers to ensure that production levels and product quality are maintained in relation to demand. The assistant production managers are technically competent and may have a good working knowledge of the machinery.

3 *The buyer* – must ensure that he/she has purchased sufficient stocks of raw materials and components to enable the production lines to run efficiently. The buyer must be able to predict demands for all raw materials, components and machinery by close examination of sales figures, past, present and projected. An essential duty of the buyer is to obtain all items at the best possible prices. The buyer may be able to negotiate favourable extended credit terms from regular suppliers. He/she is also responsible for making sure that all items ordered are received in good time.

4 *Production line manager* – responsible for the smooth running of a part of the production department which produces a single product or product range. The production line manager is given quotas to achieve by the production manager or assistant production manager and has to organise his/her staff to meet the deadlines.

5 *Production line supervisor* – it is this individual's responsibility to deploy the members of his/her work team to the maximum possible effect. The supervisor monitors the performance of both the work team and the machinery and regularly reports to the production line manager regarding any potential problems. This supervisor is the main point of contact between the employees and the management structure of the organisation. In the event of potential problems with the machinery, he/she will liaise with the service engineers.

6 *Service engineers* – it is the service engineer's role to ensure that any defects or breakdowns in machinery within the production department are swiftly and efficiently dealt with. He/she must inform the production manager and the relevant production line manager of any need to close down a production line for the purposes of maintenance, service and cleaning. The service engineers need to keep a stock of basic components in order to be able to repair machinery on the spot.

7 *Production line operatives* – depending on the type of production in which the organisation is engaged, the production line operatives are responsible for either a repetitive task or a series of related tasks. Many production lines have been developed so that only routine duties need to be carried out by humans. In these cases, production line operatives tend merely to feed the machines with raw materials

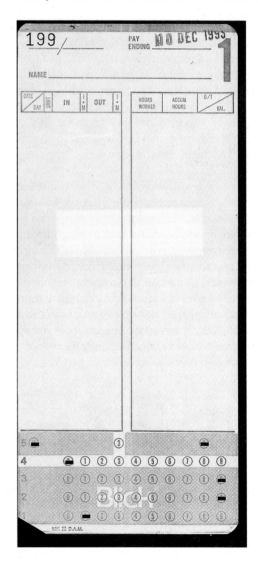

FIG. 4.2.5 *This is a clocking-in card used by employees at Sharp Electronics (UK) Ltd.*

and components and do not actually take part in the production process itself. In situations when the production is less automated, production line operatives are involved in the production of goods to completion. Many organisations run their production lines continuously and therefore require their production line operatives to work shifts.

student activity

(PC 4.2.1, COM 3.1, 3.3 AON 3.3, IT 3.1)
In the role of a production manager, design a time sheet for completion by employees, to replace a system similar to that used by Sharp. Your time sheet should be produced using computer software.

THE STORES/WAREHOUSE

This service department should keep a careful check on the stock levels of all items for which it has overall responsibility and should inform the relevant department should stocks begin to approach their minimum stock level.

The staff are:

1 *The warehouse manager* – is responsible for the smooth running of the warehousing facilities of the organisation. He/she co-ordinates all warehouse staff in an effort to ensure that goods both inwards and outwards are dealt with quickly and efficiently. The warehouse manager designs the storage facilities in such a way as to enable easy access to the most used items. He/she must also keep a close eye on the stock levels of all stored equipment, products, components and raw materials.

2 *Operatives* – take their instructions from the warehouse manager. They are responsible for reporting any problems to their immediate manager, and for ensuring that they carry out their tasks quickly and efficiently. Upon receiving an order via the sales department, warehouse operatives 'pick' the order and pack it ready for distribution. Others may be concerned with the goods inwards part of the warehouse operation, and check goods received against orders made by the organisation. Should there be any discrepancies, the warehouse manager should be informed and he/she will contact the relevant person. Some warehouse operatives operate machinery such as fork-lift trucks.

student activity

(PC 4.2.1, COM 3.1)
There are many rules and regulations which control the working conditions of a driver. Research the laws and restrictions which relate to this occupation. Choose one law in particular and when you have carried out your research, present your findings to the remainder of your group.

THE DISTRIBUTION/TRANSPORT DEPARTMENT

The staff of this department are:

1 *The distribution manager* – designs, runs and maintains a cost-effective way of ensuring that products reach their correct destination, in a suitable state, at the right time. The distribution manager works in close co-operation with the sales department whose staff inform him/her of orders placed by customers, as well as expected delivery dates. The distribution manager tends to control the operations of the warehouse and all storage facilities. He/she informs the production department when stock levels reach the re-order level. This information is received from the warehouse manager.

2 *Transport manager* – responsible for maintaining and running the fleet of delivery vehicles which service the distribution requirements of the organisation. He/she liaises closely with the distribution manager, the warehouse manager and the sales department. The transport manager is also responsible for keeping service records and vehicle registrations, as well as any related insurance for the fleet. He/she also negotiates any leasing or purchasing agreements relating to vehicles. He/she directly co-ordinates the work of the drivers, vehicle service engineers and the administration staff within his/her department.

3 *Drivers* – directly answerable to the transport manager, who issues them with delivery rounds. In certain cases, particularly in larger organisations, there may well be a need to have regional distribution points with small warehousing facilities and attached drivers/delivery men or women.

THE PERSONNEL DEPARTMENT

The main function of the personnel department is the recruitment and organisation of individuals required for the various functions needed to run the organisation.

The staff of this department are:

1. *The personnel manager* – ultimately responsible for the recruitment, retention and welfare of all staff. In this role the personnel manager is involved in the designing of job descriptions and job specifications, the interview process, any training required by employees, staff problems and handling any necessary documentation relating to termination of employment for whatever reason. The personnel manager is also involved in the co-ordination of staff facilities such as catering, sport, leisure and social activities. He/she monitors and fulfils any staff development requirements. The personnel manager is the first and main point of contact with the management structure in trade union negotiations.

2. *The assistant personnel manager* – deputises for the personnel manager in various situations, and has regular duties delegated to him/her. The assistant personnel manager is usually the first point of contact for employee problems and individuals enquiring about possible vacancies within the organisation. The personnel manager and the assistant personnel manager between them offer a confidential counselling service to all employees. The assistant personnel manager is also responsible for the maintenance of comprehensive staff records.

3. *Clerical assistants* – routine personnel duties, such as the maintenance of staff records and work logs. Various duties are delegated to them by either the personnel manager or the assistant personnel manager and it is essential that these are carried out with confidentiality always in mind.

student activity

(PC 4.2.1, COM 3.2, IT 3.1)
In the role of personnel manager, draft an advertisement for the following position:

JOB TITLE	CLEANER
HOURS	07.00-09.30 DAILY
PAYMENT	£2.73 PER HOUR
PREVIOUS EXPERIENCE PREFERRED	

Once you have decided on the content of your advertisement, produce two copies from computer software.

THE CUSTOMER RELATIONS OR PUBLIC RELATIONS DEPARTMENT

The customer relations department is the main point of contact for customers who have complaints about products or services supplied by an organisation. A smooth, efficient and courteous response to customer complaints is a key feature in ensuring that the organisation's reputation is maintained. Many products now have on their labels a short sentence stating that if a customer has any problems with the product, he/she should simply return it to the manufacturer for a refund or replacement. This is an offer in addition to the legal requirement that a product must be fit for the use for which it was intended and has gone a long way to enhance organisations' reputations for being fair.

Traditionally a public relations department was the main channel by which an organisation passed on news and information about its activities and products to the media and other interested parties. In recent years, organisations have realised the need to project a strong, positive image to the public. This role has expanded to include close contact with the public. Requests for information about an organisation and its operations are dealt with by the public relations department, which may well have developed a range of booklets and other materials for this purpose.

The staff of a public relations department are:

1. *The public relations officer* – responsible for fostering a good relationship with the media, in the hope that they will consider giving the organisation both editorial space and favourable news reporting. He/she maintains a comprehensive data base of media contacts, to whom extensive mail shots will be sent. The public relations officer is also responsible for the writing of press releases. He/she also produces a range of booklets and leaflets concerning the operations of the organisation.

2. *The customer relations officer* – while the public relations officer is concerned with media and news coverage, the customer relations officer concentrates on existing and potential customers. He/she responds to customer enquiries, providing a range of information packs on request. In addition, the customer relations officer also co-ordinates activities within the community projects department. If a customer has a serious complaint about the products or services of the organisation, the customer relations officer will be available to assist in the solving of any problem.

THE COMMUNITY PROJECTS DEPARTMENT

In many of the larger organisations throughout the UK a community projects department has been set up with a responsibility to make sure that the local community is made aware of exactly what the organisation is doing. In some organisations this work is carried out by a public relations officer. Other areas in which this department is involved are liaison with other local businesses, close contact with the local education service and the maintenance of an effective environmental policy.

Such departments are not usually large, and may consist only of:

FIG. 4.2.6 *BP believe that the best way of contributing to the community is to create wealth by carrying on their business in an ethical, safe and profitable manner. BP's world-wide expenditure on community support is over £20 million per year.*

The community projects officer – any organisations, having recognised the need to form a closer relationship with the local community, have appointed a community projects officer. In several respects, the duties of this individual are somewhat similar to those of the customer relations officer. However, the community projects officer tends to concentrate on the immediate locality. He/she organises, with the assistance of other local organisations, a range of activities in order to heighten the public's awareness and appreciation of the organisation. This may take the form of sponsoring local events, financing community projects, or offering the organisation's facilities to local groups.

Working with schools close to BP operating centres is just one of the many ways BP people contribute to the community they are part of.

4.2.2 *Describe responsibilities for human resources in job roles*

Every organisation has its own way of structuring the functions that it carries out. In this element we will look at some of the key responsibilities and try to identify the majority of job roles within organisations. You should bear in mind, however, that not all organisations need to address these considerations or responsibilities, or that they have all of these job roles in place. Factors such as the nature of the operations of the organisation and its size and complexity affect the need for functions and for separate departments.

RESPONSIBILITIES

We will first look at the specific responsibilities and try to identify individuals or groups of individuals within the organisation to whom these responsibilities fall. Once we have done this, we will attempt to take each department in turn and identify key job roles and responsibilities. It should always be borne in mind that organisations, even in the same field of business endeavour, will have radically different approaches and priorities.

TO IDENTIFY BUSINESS OBJECTIVES

Clearly, this is the responsibility of the board, the owners or the directors of the organisation. As we have seen, broad business objectives usually are identified via a Mission Statement. The extent to which the more senior individuals involved in an organisation play a part or are interested in the actual technicalities of implementing business objectives varies. One thing is certain: in larger organisations, implementation is devolved down the organisational structure and it is the responsibility of managers and supervisors to ensure on a day-to-day basis that business objectives are addressed. The directors, on the other hand, are more concerned with consistency and with over-arching policy statements and objectives.

TO WORK WITH OTHERS

As we mentioned when considering the nature of teams, it is rare to find individuals within organisations who work on a solitary basis. Regardless of the position of an individual within an organisation, he/she will, at some time or another, on a day-to-day basis, have to involve, rely on or delegate to another person.

Teams work in a variety of different ways. Every individual has a number of traits or characteristics which determine the way in which he/she will be prepared to be involved in and to contribute to the team's activities.

Meredith Belbin identified a number of traits which are relevant to how people work with others. These include the following:

- high or low intelligence
- high or low dominance
- extroversion or introversion
- stability or anxiety

student activity

(PC 4.2.2, COM 3.1)
Consider your group and try to identify which traits individuals hold. Do you think there are any particular types of behaviour which help you to identify traits?

Belbin went on to look at eight different roles within a team. These are:

1 *The chairperson* – who focuses on the objectives of the team and tries to establish work roles for other team members. This person tries to set the agenda and make summaries and is usually a good listener and communicator.

2 *The shaper* – this highly active individual is always involved in the activities of the group. Enthusiastic and energetic, this person is an ideal individual to set achievements for and to motivate.

3 *The plant* – a creative individual who often offers good ideas, but lacks the ability to realise how they can be implemented or developed.

4 *The monitor or evaluator* – this serious individual is quite skilled in analysing and decision making. Not a particularly good 'ideas' person, but will work quite well with 'the plant'.

5 *The company worker* – a good practical organiser, who is methodical and systematic. This individual will find it difficult to cope with ideas that cannot be easily implemented. This individual operates well when directed

6 *The resource investigator* – enthusiastic and sociable, who is prepared to consider almost any new idea. Responds well to encouragement and is usually fairly positive

7 *The team worker* – works well in a team and is popular and supportive. This individual is not competitive and will try to defuse any potential problems in the group. A good listener and communicator.

8 *The completer or finisher* – something of a worrier and with a tendency to get bogged down in detail, this individual likes order and structure. Always concerned with getting the task completed and may sometimes be overly worried about potential mistakes.

A good team will include members who display all of the above traits. Roles and traits will, of course, change and an individual cannot be expected to be one of the above for any considerable length of time. Indeed, individuals may be plants at the beginning of the exercise, and completer/finishers towards the end.

student activity

(PC 4.2.2, COM 3.1)
What is your role in a group? What roles do the other individuals fulfil? Does your role differ according to either the task in hand or the length of time taken up by the task?

TO MEET TARGETS

Targets can be imposed on individuals within an organisation regardless of the nature of the job involved. We should not assume that targets merely refer to financial concerns. Indeed, efficiency-based targets are equally valid. Just how these targets are established is often a considerable cause of concern both for the target setter and for those who have to meet the targets. Equally, a target may simply be a deadline by which a particular task or series of tasks must be completed.

If we begin by establishing the fact that a target is, in fact, a need, then we can begin to investigate how targets may be set and achieved. There are two interesting theories concerning needs-driven targets:

1 *Expectancy theory* – this theory establishes a link between the achievement of a goal or target and the performance of the individuals involved in it. It further goes on to say that provided the individual has the means to achieve the target, then he/she will do his or her best to ensure that the target is met. Individuals make judgements as to whether they will succeed or fail, probably even before they begin the task. Their perception at this stage will have a drastic impact on their ability to complete the task successfully. If individuals perceive their chance of achieving the target as zero, then they are doomed to failure. If individuals feel that they are in a hopeless situation, then they may become apathetic. It is the role of the manager or supervisor to establish a means by which the individual can not only achieve the target, but perceive from the outset that it is achievable. Those involved in performing a task need to have a realistic chance of success.

2 *Gestalt theory* – this theory attempts to interpret motivation and is based on experiments carried out over 70 years ago. The theory states that individuals are interested in order, simplicity and stability. Volvo have embraced Gestalt theory in their reorganisation of their car production processes. Rather than requiring their vehicles are produced on a production line basis, they have split their factories into discrete work areas. A work team is responsible for the entire production of a single vehicle. In this way, they address order, simplicity and stability, and the individual members of the work team are given responsibility and possibility of personally achieving targets without having to rely upon any other external factors.

As we will see later in this Element, there are a number of other methods or procedures which can assist an individual in achieving targets and remaining motivated at all times. It is motivation after all, that will finally determine whether a target is reached or whether the individual can confidently approach a task with some prospect of success.

TO MONITOR PERFORMANCE

Assessing the work performance of individuals within an organisation is the role of the personnel department. But, on a day-to-day basis, performance appraisal may be the concern of line managers and supervisors. They may be required to fill in fairly extensive documentation which charts either individual or team-based performance. There are a number of different ways in which an organisation can appraise performance. These are:

- performance evaluation
- performance review
- personnel rating
- merit rating
- staff assessment
- staff appraisal

We shall focus on the measurement of the individual's performance in terms of his/her personal **attributes** and **motivation.** In the recruitment process an organisation takes care to ensure that any individuals chosen as potential employees match a certain standard in terms of qualities or abilities. They may be formally tested. However, it is only when an individual is actually at work that the organisation can monitor and assess these qualities and abilities. Another factor relating to personal attributes is an individual's preferences regarding **involvement** in various forms of work. Individuals approach different tasks in a variety of different ways, depending upon their interest in undertaking them. Equally, we may use the term preference in relation to an individual's **willingness** to undertake different types of job role and working hours. A good organisation will not impose new working conditions without prior consultation. Within the range of personal attributes, we should also consider **attitude.** An employee should always have a positive attitude towards the organisation and the work. Unfortunately, many jobs do not always live up to the **expectations** of the employee. In other cases, an individual's attitude to work may be related to perceived **job security**. The final consideration when we look at personal attributes is the question of the individual's **motivation.** This will affect his/her efficiency and willingness to undertake a variety of tasks. The morale of the staff is paramount and should be closely monitored by managers. Morale can be easily measured by comparing the output of workers or, in certain cases, by asking the staff to complete anonymous questionnaires.

There are two distinct types of appraisal system which we can call formal and informal systems.

1 *Formal systems of appraisal* – the key considerations of these are:

- they tend to be expensive
- the administration costs are high
- managers may feel embarrassed
- there is a sense of confrontation
- employees may view them with distrust
- the system may not be objective
- the processes are clear
- employees are told how they will be judged
- employees are usually given the opportunity to rectify any negative assessments

2 *Informal appraisal systems* – these may have the following features:

- they may be rather haphazard

- there may be no formal feedback procedures
- managers may find it difficult to make constructive criticisms
- criticisms may be misunderstood
- there are opportunities to exchange views
- as there is no formal feedback procedure, managers will find it difficult to report back to his/her superior

The main purposes of appraisal are:

- to identify employee weaknesses
- to identify employee strengths
- to determine salary increases
- to determine who deserves promotion
- to aid internal communication processes within the organisation
- to determine staff development needs

FIG. 4.2.7 *This assessment sheet, used by Kwik-Fit, aims to consider the personal characteristics and attitude of the individual. Our example comes from their apprenticeship programme.*

ASSESSMENT SHEET

CENTRE | DIVISION

✔ box appropriate for each assessment area

VISIT DATE	Above Standard	Acceptable	Below Standard	Unacceptable	REPORT FOR THE MONTH OF (✔)
TIME-	Always on time	Seldom late	Frequently late	Persistently late	JAN
APPEARANCE	Always clean, tidy and well presented	Generally well turned out	Often untidy	Persistently unkempt	FEB / MAR
ATTITUDE AT WORK	Exceptional attitude and co-operative at all times	Good attitude usually co-operative and helpful	Poor attitude can be unco-operative and unhelpful	Bad attitude Hostile and Aggressive	APR / MAY
INITIATIVE	Takes correct action without supervision	Usually acts on own	Requires frequent supervision	Requires constant detailed direction	JUN / JUL
KEENNESS	Very interested and very keen to learn	Reasonably interested and keen	Slight interest not very keen	No interest in learning new skills	AUG / SEPT
QUALITY OF WORK	Consistently high quality	Good	Fair, room for improvement	Continually makes errors	OCT / NOV
PROGRESS	Has made exceptional progress	Has made progress	Has made poor progress	Little or no progress	DEC

Apprentice _____

Manager _____

Partner _____

R.M. _____

COMMENTS ON ANY ACTION TAKEN:

Signed _ _ _ _ _ _ _ _ _ _ (Apprentice)

Signed _ _ _ _ _ _ _ _ _ _ (Manager)

Date _ _ _ _ _ _ _ _ _ _

SEND TO THE PERSONNEL MANAGER BY THE END OF EACH MONTH

Kwik-Fit

20

CEN 78A

PERFORMANCE APPRAISAL

GUIDELINES AND PREPARATION DOCUMENT FOR EMPLOYEES

INTRODUCTION

These guidelines have been developed to help you prepare for the Performance Appraisal process and should be used in conjunction with the Appraisal and Training/Development Planning record sheet.

In this document the appraisal process is explained under three main headings:

1. PREPARATION AND TIMING
2. COMPLETION OF RECORD SHEET
3. POST APPRAISAL ACTION.

These issues are discussed more fully below.

1. PREPARATION AND TIMING

Successful performance appraisal preparation is best achieved by:

- reading the guidelines and completing the forms well in advance of the appraisal meeting – the appraisal documentation should be issued to you 7 to 10 days prior to your meeting
- agreeing a date/time with your Manager/Supervisor for the appraisal interview
- contributing to the meeting which should be viewed as a two way exchange of information and ideas.

All appraisals should be completed by the end of January.

2. COMPLETION OF THE APPRAISAL TRAINING/DEVELOPMENT PLANNING RECORD SHEET

The format of this preparation document is very similar to that of the record sheet which covers four major sections:

- achievement of objectives/targets for previous year
- methods of working
- dealing with people
- objectives/targets for next year.

Each of these is explained in more detail overleaf.

FIG. 4.2.8 *This Peugeot Talbot performance appraisal form, 'Guidelines and Preparation Document for Employees', shows the criteria upon which employees are being appraised.*

As we have mentioned, there are a variety of different staff appraisal systems. Regardless of the system adopted, the organisation needs to ensure the following:

- that the management is fully committed to the appraisal system
- that there is time to carry out the appraisal process
- that the system is not overly complex
- that there is an agreed timetable for the overall implementation of the appraisal system
- that the managers receive training in order to carry out the appraisor's role
- that employees, as appraisees, receive guidance and information to assist them

In designing the appraisal system, the organisation has a number of alternative techniques to choose from.

These are:

1 *Merit rating* – in this system each employee's characteristics are graded on a scale which ranges from unacceptable to outstanding. Each particular characteristic has been identified and may include some rather subjective characteristics such as attitude or aptitude.

2 *Comparison with objectives* – having set a series of objectives for the employee, the manager then compares performance with these identified targets. Obviously, some objectives are fairly easy to measure but many are open to interpretation.

3 *Behaviourally anchored rating scales* – this technique is basically a complex version of the merit rating system. A manager carrying out the appraisal in consultation with the personnel department considers the job description of each employee and then creates a list of duties and tasks and agrees levels of performance required.

4 *Narrative reports* – this system requires the manager to summarise features of the employee's work. In many respects this is rather like a school report. It is open to bias and does not take into account the fact that the manager may not necessarily remember all of the incidents that occurred over the appraisal period.

5 *Critical incident report* – this is an ongoing system in which the appraisor is expected to record examples of good or bad work performed by the employee. He/she will then pass on the information to the employee in the course of an appraisal meeting. In order for this system to work, not only does the appraisor need to have sufficient time but he/she should also call the meeting as quickly after the incident as possible.

It should be noted that information gathered in the course of an appraisal comes under the Data Inspection Act 1984. The individual being appraised has the right to inspect any information gathered.

Following the appraisal, the employee and appraisor draw up an action plan which includes all matters covered in the appraisal interview. This will form the basis of the next appraisal interview. There will be an opportunity at this meeting for the employee to respond and offer evidence that matters identified in the previous appraisal interview as being unsatisfactory have been rectified.

TO IMPLEMENT CHANGE IN WORKING CONDITIONS

Perhaps the best way for an organisation to ensure that employees derive the most tangible benefits and enhanced conditions of work is for it to consider the various methods of managing the work process itself. A number of attempts have been made to design systems which allow an individual within the work situation to enjoy better conditions of employment. We shall now look at these in some detail:

1 *Job rotation* – many individuals suffer from boredom as a result of having to do repetitive and simple tasks. Under this system, individuals are trained to obtain the skills required in order to carry out many different tasks. This will give them a vital variety of different work experiences. Two points of caution should be mentioned here:

- ´an organisation must care take not to rotate staff too often as inefficiency will result
- an individual who moves from one similarly boring job to another will, in no way, be more motivated

student activity

(PC 4.2.2, COM 3.2, IT 3.1)
In pairs, consider an accounts department and draw up a job rotation system which would give employees the maximum opportunity to experience a wide variety of tasks. Present your considerations in the form of a chart produced using a software package, against which you can mark the order in which the job rotations should occur, the period in which each individual will experience that job role and the main differences between each of the job roles.

2 *Job enlargement* – particularly on a production line, an employee will have to undertake a series of highly repetitive tasks. Not only will they be repetitive, but individually, they will take a short period of time each. An assembly line worker who is simply riveting a front door panel on a car every four minutes will not be achieving a great deal of job satisfaction. Job enlargement means that this individual will be given a greater variety of tasks to perform in the production process. In our example, the riveter would enjoy the prospect of riveting the rear door panels too! Other organisations have taken the job enlargement system to its logical conclusion. They have replaced individual employees carrying out repetitive tasks on the production line by robots and now the employees maintain the robotics as their main activity. Alternatively, as we mentioned earlier, some car manufacturers have dispensed with the production line altogether.

student activity

(PC 4.2.2, COM 3.1)
How would you enlarge the job of an invoice clerk? Discuss this as a group.

3 *Job enrichment* – following the theories of Hertzberg (which you will find in Unit 2), a job enrichment programme aims to provide for the employee's full psychological development. There is a notion here of stretching the employee and making him or her develop skills in a variety of different areas. This challenge is intended to increase the motivation of the individual.

4 *Group work* – extending the job enlargement programme even further, as we intimated, some organisations have created groups of workers or teams to complete whole tasks. The group will be responsible for all aspects of the production process and will, in effect, turn raw materials into finished goods.

A further variation of this technique is to allow groups of workers to operate autonomously. They agree between themselves how, when and by whom certain tasks within the production process are to be carried out. There is a supervisor involved in this process, but this individual is really considered to be a problem-solver and the means of communicating on behalf of the group with the rest of the organisation.

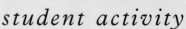

student activity

(PC 4.2.2, COM 3.1)
How would group work help in the running of an administration department? Discuss this as a group.

TO PROVIDE TRAINING

Workforce performance should not be considered to be the sole responsibility of the employee. The employer may have a positive impact upon workforce performance in other ways than simply offering financial incentives. By implementing a comprehensive and well-structured training programme, the employer will be able to identify and rectify shortcomings in the skills and qualifications of the workforce. Although this may be an expensive method of increasing work force performance, an organisation which takes a longer view will be able to count on increased productivity and greater staff loyalty, as well as motivation in the future.

student activity

(PC 4.2.2, COM 3.1)
Should training really be used as an incentive for workers? How might the training programme reflect the corporate policy of the organisation? Discuss in pairs.

TO GIVE ADVICE

Failing to address the needs of individuals within the organisation can give rise to potentially difficult and possibly insurmountable situations.

Managers and supervisors should be aware that individual employees need to be developed and offered training on a reasonably regular basis. The main steps in developing staff are:

- to appreciate that development is important
- to identify personal attitudes towards development
- to identify developmental objectives
- to link developmental objectives with organisational objectives
- to decide methods of development
- to measure the effectiveness of the development

If we broaden the subject of advice to its more general use, then we must consider the importance of access to information and understanding of that information. Simply to circulate material in whichever form does not ensure that each individual within the organisation will either read it or understand it. If the organisation has not taken steps to formally pass on information and ensure its understanding, then it cannot realistically expect employees to be able to pass this information on to either customers or suppliers. As we will see later in this Element, training is essential, and above all, relevant and accessible training programmes are the key to the management of change and good employee relations.

TO DISCIPLINE

The approved disciplinary procedure, as recommended by ACAS, should be both fair and impartial. It includes the following features:

- all stages of the procedure should be **written down** as a record of events
- copies of the **procedures** should be **available** to all employees
- the employer should clearly state **who operates** the procedure
- the employer should clearly state **who was involved** in any particular disciplinary action
- the employer should clearly state what kind of **disciplinary action** would be taken against particular types of infringements disciplinary guidelines
- the employee has the right to have a friend, colleague or trade union **representative present** during all disciplinary interviews
- in most cases, the employee will not be dismissed for a **first offence**
- the employee has the right to **appeal** against the decision made by the employer
- all proceedings should be administered in a **fair manner**
- the employee should not be **unfairly discriminated** against

Normally, the actual disciplinary procedure would work along the following lines:

1 *Verbal warning* – if the employee's conduct, behaviour or performance does not reach suitable and acceptable standards, then he/she will be given a formal verbal warning. This is the first official stage of the proceedings. Usually a time limit is set, and provided the employee reaches the acceptable standard within this time the matter will be dropped.

2 *Written warning* – if the employee persists with the same behaviour that resulted in the verbal warning, or if the offence was sufficiently serious, then a written warning will be issued. This is usually given by the employee's immediate superior.

The written warning details the complaint and clearly states exactly what must be done to rectify the situation. The warning will also state how long the employee has to respond to the warning. If the employee persists then the next stage of the procedure will follow. Again, if the employee complies with the requirements then the matter will be dropped. There is, at this stage, an opportunity for the employee to appeal.

3 *Final written warning* – if the employee continues to fail to improve conduct or behaviour, then a formal written warning will be given. In some cases, employees may find themselves at this point in the disciplinary procedure as a result of a serious disciplinary offence. The employee should be under no illusions that dismissal is imminent.

4 *Suspension* – as an alternative to, or in addition to, a final written warning, an employer may suspend an individual for up to five working days without pay. This is known as disciplinary suspension.

5 *Dismissal* – the final stage of the disciplinary procedure is dismissal itself. To reach this point, an employee must have failed all the requirements laid down in the early stages of the procedure. The employee's most senior, but related, line manager will take the decision to dismiss the employee, usually in consultation with the personnel department. The employee will be given a written statement which includes the reasons for dismissal and the date of termination. It will also include guidance for the employee in case of appeal.

student activity

(PC 4.2.2, COM 3.2)
Write your own version of a formal written warning. What needs to be said and how should the statement be worded?

The termination of the contract of employment is the final act in dismissal. There are a number of legal and ethical obligations which the employer must address to ensure that fairness and objectivity are maintained.

If the employer puts the employee in a position that makes it impossible for him/her to stay in the organisation, this is known as **constructive dismissal**. Courts have found in favour of employees who have been put in this position as a result of actions by their employer. Examples include:

- changes in **wages** without informing the employee
- changes in **location** of the job without consultation
- changes in **duties** without negotiation
- changes in the **job description** without negotiation

In all of these examples, the employer has decided to change certain conditions of work. In some cases, this action will inevitably break the original contract of employment signed by both parties. An industrial tribunal will look carefully at the stages of events and decide whether the actions constitute constructive dismissal. Some breaches of the contract of employment may relate to sexual harassment or discrimination on the grounds of race or colour.

student activity

(PC 4.2.2, COM 3.1)
In pairs, try to identify at least three different situations that an employee may find him/herself in which could be construed as constructive dismissal.

UNFAIR DISMISSAL

The employee's right not to be unfairly dismissed from a job is a fairly important one. The laws relating to this prevent employers from having the right to hire and fire as they see fit. It is, however, a complex issue and whether an individual employee is entitled to claim unfair dismissal is a much argued subject.

Generally speaking, to qualify for a claim of unfair dismissal, the employee must:

- have worked for the employer as a full-time member of staff for two years
- have worked for the employer as a part-timer for at least eight hours a week for five years
- not be over pensionable age

There are certain exemptions and groups of individuals who can never claim to have been unfairly dismissed. These include:

- police officers
- employees who work for an organisation outside the UK
- employees on fixed-term contracts
- members of the armed forces

In cases of dispute between the employer and the employee, ACAS will assist and attempt to resolve the conflict. An official working for ACAS will try to get the two parties to agree rather than having to resort to courts for settlement.

CAUSES OF DISMISSAL

An employer will nearly always have a reason for dismissing an employee, whether the reason is right or wrong. There are, however, four main reasons for dismissal:

1 and 2 *Capability and qualifications* – these two reasons relate to the employee's fitness or competence to do the job. In this sense capability means skill, health, physical or mental ability. In terms of capability, if an employee is shown to be incompetent or

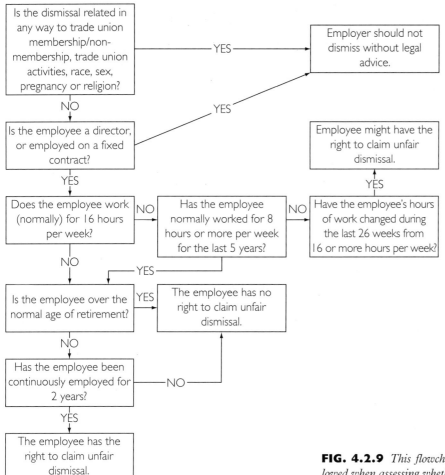

FIG. 4.2.9 *This flowchart illustrates the procedure to be followed when assessing whether there is a claim of unfair dismissal.*

shows serious errors of judgement then the employer may have grounds for dismissal. Qualifications refers to academic, technical or professional qualifications relevant to the job. An example of dismissal in relation to qualifications could occur if an employer required that an employee achieve a certain level of qualification but the employee has subsequently failed to do so.

3 *Redundancy* – if the employer closes down the business, or part of the business, he/she may no longer need the services of some or all of the employees. In such cases, the employer must consult the employees, having fairly selected those to be made redundant, and if possible, offer them alternative employment. There is always a way around the problem of redundancy, particularly if the employer could freeze recruitment and redeploy existing employees, or, indeed, reduce the number of working hours of all employees.

4 *Gross misconduct* – misconduct is a very wide area and includes the following:

- absenteeism – where an employee is away from work too often

student activity

(PC 4.2.2, COM 3.1)
Identify the necessary capabilities and qualifications of individuals employed in the following occupations:

- accounts clerk
- bus driver
- hairdresser

Discuss with the remainder of your group.

- lateness – where an employee constantly turns up late for work
- insubordination – where an employee refuses to carry out instructions from a superior
- incompetence – where the employee shows on several occasions an inability to do the job

- immorality – where the employee behaves in an unacceptable manner, perhaps sexually or morally
- breaking safety rules – where an employee endangers his/her life or the life of others by not taking heed of safety rules, perhaps deliberately
- theft – where the employee has stolen the property of the employer

In reality then, the employer can identify a number of reasons for dismissal due to misconduct. This may mean that the employee could be dismissed under the misconduct guidelines for any of the following:

- wearing offensive badges or tee-shirts
- being involved in questionable activities outside the work place
- consistently making dangerous mistakes

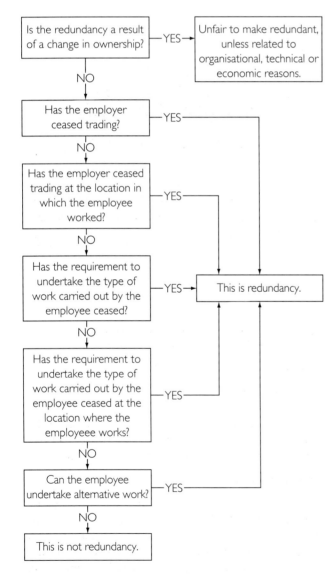

FIG. 4.2.10 *This flowchart illustrates the procedure to be followed when assessing redundancy.*

- an inability to get to work on time
- prolonged and unexplained absences
- inability to take orders or instructions
- the theft of even low value items

Essentially then, the misconduct category fall into two basic areas:

- *statutory contraventions* – in which the employee breaks a legal requirement, e.g., a lorry driver who is banned from driving due to drinking, or an employee who works for a butcher and then grows a beard, thus contravening hygiene and food regulations
- *other reasons* – this broad area is fairly difficult to summarise, but, for example, would include the gradual deterioration in performance of an employee

FAIRNESS AND DISMISSAL

The employer really needs a valid reason for dismissing an employee. At all times the employer's conduct towards the employee, regardless of the situation, must be fair and objective. The employer must not single out an individual because of his/her gender. Women, for example, have a right to be pregnant and should not be discriminated against as a result. If the employer chooses to dismiss an employee on the grounds of his/her gender, then there would have to be very strong reasons to link gender with the requirement and nature of the job.

TO HANDLE GRIEVANCES

If an employer dismisses an employee for any form of misconduct or other reason, he/she must be able to prove the employee's guilt. In one particular case, all the employees of a shop were dismissed after stock had disappeared. This had occurred over a matter of months. An industrial tribunal held that the employer could not dismiss all of them as he/she did not have sufficient grounds to dismiss when perhaps only one of them was the culprit. The employer had, therefore, not proven the guilt of the employees.

There are a number of types of behaviour or practices which would constitute reasons for dismissal, and any individual dismissed for any of these reasons would be fairly dismissed:

- sexual harassment
- racial harassment
- wilful destruction of property
- negligence
- long-term bad time-keeping
- sleeping at work
- gross insubordination
- inability to do the job the employee was appointed to do
- fraud, including the falsification of records

- inability to do the job as a result of being under the influence of alcohol
- inability to do the job as a result of being under the influence of illegal drugs
- fighting resulting in assault
- unauthorised entry into confidential computer records

In all these cases, an individual will be able to make an appeal against decisions made by the organisation to take some form of disciplinary action. Before we consider grievance procedures in general, we should consider some of the reasons for dismissal which are unfair and which are usually the cause of court action and appeals. These are:

- dismissal on the grounds of race
- dismissal on the grounds of religious belief
- dismissal on the grounds of sexual preference/orientation
- dismissal on the grounds of pregnancy
- dismissal on the grounds of irrelevant or spent criminal records
- dismissal on the grounds of trade union membership

Resolving grievances, whether as a result of proposed disciplinary proceedings, or events which take place in the working environment, should really follow a set pattern. The steps are:

1 The employee takes the grievance to his/her immediate superior.
2 If the problem is not solved at this stage, then the employee can ask for intervention by a more senior manager.

3 The senior manager institutes an investigation and hears evidence from both parties.
4 The senior manager now arbitrates informally.
5 If the problem is still not solved, then the senior manager and employee agree to refer the problem to a grievance officer.
6 The grievance officer, usually a member of staff who is not directly involved in the line management chain, looks at the information and evidence from both parties.
7 The grievance officer now calls a meeting and the employee can be accompanied by a friend, colleague or trade union official whilst the case is being reviewed.
8 If the problem is not solved by this stage, then the employee may ask for an industrial or appeals tribunal to hear the case.

student activity

(PC 4.2.2, COM 3.1)
Why do you think it is necessary for many of the above forms of discrimination to be classed as illegal? Discuss this question in pairs.

4.2.3 Explain reasons for changes in working conditions

In this part of the Element, we will investigate the various reasons why job roles and responsibilities evolve or change over a period of time. Indeed, some changes may occur literally overnight, as a result of changes in legislation or organisational restructuring.

REASONS FOR CHANGE

Amongst the reasons which bring about changes to job roles and responsibilities, and indeed, working conditions, we can identify some which are internally driven

(in other words, instituted by the organisation itself), and others which are as a result of external pressures or changes beyond the control of the organisation.

LABOUR MOBILITY

An individual's ability to switch from one job to another is largely dependent upon his or her experience, skills and training. Clerical workers, for example, have highly transferable skills. In many respects, administrative work, is essentially the same even in organisations with different functions. Equally, a builder is not restricted to the construction of homes. To a large degree the skills employed in all types of construction work are the same, regardless of the size of the building.

Individuals who have particularly specialist or unique skills may find it significantly more difficult to obtain alternative employment. They may need expensive retraining before they can be considered for alternative employment.

If individuals consider that they are neither qualified nor experienced to undertake alternative employment, or if the incentive to move is not sufficient, then certain organisations or industries may experience labour shortages. In such situations, organisations must turn to existing employees and encourage them to consider retraining programmes. If you refer back to the description of such motivational techniques as job rotation, enlargement and enrichment, earlier in this Element, you will see that these can be viable alternatives in solving labour and skills shortages.

Particularly in economic situations when individuals are unwilling or unable to consider being 'mobile', as they fear the risk of making an expensive move which may not actually work, the organisation may have to resort to more drastic methods of attracting employees. One would think that when there is high unemployment certain employees would be very easy to recruit. This may be true of semi- or unskilled workers. However, in the case of skilled employees, an attractive pay and 'perks' package may have to be offered to encourage them.

In times of low unemployment, an organisation is faced with having to compete with other organisations for a relatively small number of available potential employees. Again, as is the case with the more skilled workers in terms of high unemployment, the employer must offer significantly better pay and conditions in order to attract new staff.

IMPROVING PRODUCTIVITY

Any business must operate in a manner in which it addresses the needs of the customer. To this end, the organisation must ensure that it has deployed its **resources** in the right proportions. Further, the organisation needs to ensure that it has a sufficient number of **employees** who are experienced, qualified and well trained. The **production process** itself should be as streamlined as possible, as should be the **layout** of the premises in order to facilitate efficiency of operations. Productivity is measured by considering the total output of the organisation and the number of employees involved. The employer will constantly expect this ratio to improve in his/her favour. The main methods of doing this include the following:

- encouraging the employees

- motivating the employees
- analysing output levels
- analysing the number of employees needed to work machinery
- monitoring quality
- continually analysing production processes and methods

Perhaps the first place to start, particularly if the organisation is looking to increase productivity, is the employee. Most employees will respond favourably to the following:

- a good match between the employee and the job
- a clear statement of the employee's responsibilities
- a clear statement of required standards of performance
- encouraging and enabling employees to participate in decision making
- paying a salary or wage commensurate with the tasks performed
- offering incentives or performance-related pay
- offering regular refresher courses for retraining
- supervising effectively
- ensuring that the employee is working in a healthy and non-hazardous environment
- adhering to or abiding by employment legislation and, in fact, exceeding minimum requirements

Machinery, equipment and other forms of technology must also be considered as key factors in assuring that productivity levels are maintained and increased. The organisation should always:

- ensure that old or worn-out machines are replaced
- purchase additional machinery in order to facilitate increased output
- train employees and/or make them aware of how machines may be used to their best effect

In some cases, employers may discover that their employees are working harder, or seem to be doing so, but production and productivity have not increased. In this case, the employer should examine the machinery provided to see whether this may be a possible cause of the lack of productivity increase. Alternatively, employers may notice a productivity increase and at the same time realise that their employees are not putting any more effort into their jobs. If the employer has chosen to offer productivity or performance-related pay, then really the employees are earning this extra money without having to work any harder.

Different organisations, depending on their size or function, use machinery to a greater or lesser extent. It is notoriously difficult to judge productivity levels in occupations where machinery plays small part. The use of machines such as computers, which are widely available in a variety of different organisations, can have drastic effects on productivity. This does not necessarily mean that the employees are more productive in themselves.

The other side of the argument is **productivity,** or more clearly, **profits** accrued from productivity. In this respect we should turn our attention to such matters as the level and use of waste and other by-products as a result of industrial processes. An organisation which minimises these factors will inevitably benefit from increased profits and productivity.

IMPROVING EMPLOYEE MOTIVATION

We have covered many of the leadership and motivational theories in Unit 2, as well as some of the more direct forms of motivation methods, such as job enlargement, enrichment and rotation in this Element. At this stage, we shall look at some of the more fundamental features of developing employees for their own benefit and that of the organisation. We can break down performance and, indeed, the underlying reasons for motivation or lack of motivation, into three main headings:

- knowledge
- attitudes
- skills

We shall look at these in some more detail and consider their application in terms of motivating employees.

1 *Knowledge* – should not simply be seen as the job of schools, colleges or other forms of education. Specific knowledge needs to be acquired throughout the working life of an individual. For the organisation's sake, it should include the following:

- *knowledge of the organisation* – including where the individual fits into the organisation and how he/she may develop
- *knowledge of customers* – including specific details about products and services and how these may or may not meet the expectations of the customer
- *knowledge of the standards required* – including product quality and personal effectiveness within the organisation
- *awareness of professionalism* – including how the organisation views professional behaviour, what are accepted practices and how communication should be undertaken with a variety of different parties
- *knowledge of job* – including the requirements of the job with the resources available and what is expected of the individual

2 *Attitudes* – within any relationship and particularly those in a working environment it is essential that a number of attitudes are clearly defined and appreciated by all employees. These include:

- *fairness* – how people should be treated and the assurance that all people are treated equally
- *openness* – that all dealings should be honest to ensure that both parties have the opportunity to complete the task with full amounts of information
- *respect* – that every individual, regardless of who/she is or the situation, deserves respect and consideration
- *support* – that at times an individual will need support and other times must be prepared to offer support to colleagues
- *responsiveness* – that at all times the individual is prompt and gives feedback when necessary

3 *Skills* – vocational training can do much to ensure that an individual is in a position to respond to change and is able to demonstrate effectiveness. The key components of preparation for change are:

- *knowing the procedures* – how a job should be done and how the organisation expects it to be done
- *following models* – the recognition and adoption of good practice as demonstrated either within or outside the organisation
- *setting criteria* – knowing the standards in terms of quality or output required and what identifies acceptable work output
- *good communications* being able to communicate effectively and having access to information in an understandable format

In short, motivation may be achieved through the following main methods:

- **pay** or rewards
- the **job** itself
- the ability to **participate** in decision making
- the satisfaction of **completing a task**
- the feeling of being fully **informed** of actions taken and to be undertaken

ADAPTING TO TECHNOLOGICAL CHANGES

Organisations which fail to appreciate the need constantly to reappraise their use of technology risk failure. Equally, if employees are unwilling or unable to adopt new working practices, the same net result may occur.

Many organisations have embraced the use of computers and information technology, regardless of the type or function of the organisation. In retailing, for example, the availability of electronic point-of-sale equipment has revolutionised retail selling and stock control. It was viewed with considerable suspicion by employees and organisations themselves before they realised the benefits it offered. Its effect has not been to reduce the number of employees (as had been feared – because there is no longer the need for items to be individually priced), but to free employees to undertake a wider variety of tasks and more interesting activities.

It is perhaps in the field of communications that technology has had the greatest impact. The flexibility and swiftness of telecommunications in particular has enabled organisations to collect, store and evaluate information effectively and efficiently.

Technology has enabled manufacturing organisations to reduce their costs of production and institute Just-in-Time methods of stock control (which means that they do not have to hold large quantities of stock as they are able to produce finished goods very quickly). This change has been coupled with the introduction of robotics on the production line which further reduces the need to disrupt employee working patterns in order to fulfil rush jobs.

EMPLOYING NEW SKILLS

The introduction of new technology does present some short-term problems for organisations. They may find themselves in a position where they are unable to find or attract enough experienced staff. Indeed, if the technology is sufficiently new, these new staff may not exist. In such a situation, a forward-looking organisation will have appreciated this concern already and will have taken steps to institute retraining programmes.

New skills can also be identified as being opportunities for individuals to embrace a new occupation, provided they are aware of the technological advances. In some respects, this pro-active approach can ensure that the individual is well placed to take advantage of short-term skill shortages. An organisation will be only

too happy to acquire the services of such individuals, albeit for a relatively short time.

Even in the most mundane forms of occupation, technological advances may not be the only reason for new skills development. Simple changes in **procedure** may not require significant re-skilling of an organisation's employees. However, in practice, the implementation of any new procedure will involve a certain level of retraining. In such cases, both the organisation and the employee need to be flexible. The organisation should be patient and allow the employee to 'catch up with' new developments and the employee should be prepared to spend time and effort in acquiring these new skills and knowledge of procedures.

Increasingly, as we have mentioned earlier, the multi-skilling of employees can be a solution to short-term potential skill shortages. These adaptable and flexible employees should be able and willing to adopt new procedures and learn to use new technology.

student activity

(PC 4.2.3, COM 3.1)
As a group, try to assess the importance of the reasons for change in working conditions, as detailed above. Which of the reasons do you consider to be of the greatest importance? Try to reach some consensus within the group.

4.2.4 *Evaluate change in working conditions*

WORKING CONDITIONS

Working conditions within an organisation can differ depending on an employee's department, site or rank. Factors which may differ include the technology used, the physical surroundings or the number of people one works with. Furthermore, individuals' qualifications differ, as do the ways in which these are used in the context of a specific job. Obviously, the way in which individuals are paid and how much the pay is controlled by the organisation's policy or government

legislation may also have an impact on conditions. Individuals' training requirements and needs may be different, as may be the opportunities an individual has to gain new qualifications and training.

The basic physical working conditions are governed by health and safety rules. It has long been accepted that employees work much better if the employer takes note of the following:

- that the workplace is well **lit**
- that the workplace is kept at a constant **temperature** regardless of the weather

- that the workplace is **pleasant** and well decorated
- that efforts are made to encourage **health and fitness** to reduce sickness
- that the **hours** worked can be **flexible** to take account of employee's external commitments
- that the workforce receives regular **training** and the opportunity to gain **qualifications**
- that the acquisition or use of skills is **rewarded** either financially or in terms of improved promotion prospects
- that with age, **additional payments** are made to encourage experienced workers to stay with the organisation
- that **trade unions** are recognised and there is a regular dialogue with them
- that, above all, **pay and conditions** should be attractive and competitive

Having said all of this, there is a vast difference in how the points are adopted by individual employers. The physical working conditions of an individual in an administrative job are very different from those of an individual working in industry. The former will enjoy relatively luxurious conditions, with carpets, curtains and blinds, comfortable seating and a clean environment. In a factory, you may find a completely different set of conditions. The environment may be dirty and noisy, the employee may be on his/her feet all day and the job may be physically demanding and the hours long.

Examination of the nature of jobs in the different sectors of industry will show a wide variety of working conditions. Industrial working conditions may present the following questions:

- **where** is the work?
- is the work **outside** or **inside**?
- is the environment **hot** or **cold**?
- does the employee work on **his/her own**?
- is there much opportunity for **contact** throughout the day?
- do the **hours** differ?
- is there a requirement to work **shifts**?
- is the environment **clean**?
- should the employee have regular **health checks**?
- how **safe** is the job?
- how physically **demanding** is the job?
- is there a risk of **injury**?
- does the employee have to wear **protective clothing**?

We will now investigate the key criteria which determine working conditions and attempt to address the reasons behind the changes in these conditions.

student activity

(PC 4.2.4, COM 3.2, IT 3.1)
Assess the working conditions in the following occupations:

- a butcher
- a sales representative
- a sales assistant in a shop
- a nurse

When you have considered all of the above occupations, choose one in particular and word process a report on your findings and opinions.

FIXED SHORT-TERM CONTRACTS

The use of non-standard contracts has come about as a result of the economic recession experienced in recent years. In addition to this, organisations have had to cope with an increasingly competitive international market, and as a result, a level of uncertainty regarding the demand for their products and services. To this end, fixed short-term contracts have become quite common in order to allow the employer to make only a short-term commitment to the employee. In this way, the employer is able to increase or decrease employee numbers as a quick response to changes in demand.

Termination of a fixed short-term contract is normally regarded as dismissal in legal terms. However, provided both parties agree to exclude the employee's right to redundancy payment (assuming that the fixed-term contract is for two years or more), and also to waive the right to compensation for unfair dismissal (provided the contract was for over one year), this means that fixed short-term contracts are flexible and attractive to both employer and employee.

In essence, fixed short-term contracts not only provide the employer with the opportunity to respond to short-term fluctuations in demand, but also enable the employer to deal with projects or tasks on a one-off basis, or to bring in specialists to carry out a particular function. Areas of employment which have significantly increased their use of fixed short-term contracts are:

- health
- education
- distribution

In fact, most public sector organisations find that the fixed short-term contract allows them to reduce their long-term commitments in the knowledge that their potential future budgets may not be wholly predictable.

LONG-TERM CONTRACTS

Although fixed short-term contracts are finding considerable favour with some employers and employees, long-term contracts are still the norm. These open-ended contractual agreements form the most common basis of the relationship established between the employer and the employee.

Some changes and clarifications have been made which act as a guide to employers in the formulation of contracts of employment. As we have already seen in Unit 2 and Element 4.1, there are a variety of under-pinning rights and responsibilities for both parties.

PAY

The changing nature of contracts obviously has an impact upon the pay received by the employee. One of the more obvious impacts is that the employee is only paid for hours worked. Whilst this arrangement may be beneficial to the employer, it does mean that the employee cannot predict his/her income beyond the short term. The nature of these new contracts may mean that the employee has guaranteed work only for limited periods of time. These work periods may be punctuated with considerable amounts of unemployment. Whilst flexible working conditions and their relationship to pay may allow the organisation more accurately to budget for particular contracts or projects, the employee is faced with the prospect of having to seek work elsewhere. This makes it very difficult for the employee to make any long-term financial commitments, such as a mortgage or a loan. Without guaranteed work and the pay associated with it, financial institutions would be unwilling to risk significant loans.

BENEFITS

Whilst the majority of benefits are protected by government legislation, there is something of a grey area relating to part-time or casual workers. Broadly speaking, they are disadvantaged in the sense that they may not be entitled to sick pay or holiday pay. Also, short periods of work may not be sufficient to qualify for statutory benefit payments by the DSS, or, indeed the Unemployment Benefit Office. The details of these benefits are as follows:

I *Holiday pay* – in comparison with all other major European countries, the UK has possibly the most meagre level of both public holidays and annual statutory leave entitlement. In fact, under current legislation, there is no statutory annual leave entitlement in the UK. The only other European country which does not have statutory annual leave entitlement is Italy.

In the European league table of holiday entitlement plus public holidays, the UK is firmly bottom. Spain leads the table with a total of 38 days (25 days minimum annual leave plus 13 public holidays). The vast majority, if we include both annual leave and public holidays, have in excess of 25 days. In the UK, by contrast, there are 8 public holidays plus a rather low annual leave entitlement (on a sliding scale depending upon the number of years worked).

Organisations have taken advantage of the high rates of unemployment to institute relatively low holiday pay entitlements. Indeed, part-time workers, temporary workers and those on fixed short-term contracts may find that they have no paid holiday entitlement at all.

Employees, particularly those working on an hourly-rate basis, have to decide between the cost of working and the consequent loss of leisure time against the payment received from that work. This is an example of **opportunity cost,** as, if the employee works extra hours he/she loses leisure time and, conversely, by taking leisure time he/she loses wages.

The Social Charter, as proposed by the EU, was intended not only to improve but to attempt to harmonise working conditions throughout Europe. The UK not only requires its employees to work longer hours (an average of 43.6 per week) than employees elsewhere in Europe but, as we have said, offers far less paid holiday entitlement.

2 *Sick pay and maternity pay* – as we have already discovered in Unit 2, employers have to pay a minimum amount of sick pay to employees aged 16 or above, if they have been off sick for more than four consecutive days. Statutory sick pay (SSP) is paid by the employer just like normal pay. The employer is required by law to keep records of absences due to sickness and the payment of SSP for inspection by inspectors from the Department of Social Security.

In 1993 an investigation was undertaken by a House of Commons Watchdog Committee, under the supervision of the then Social Security Secretary, Peter Lilley. The investigation discovered that there were some 70,000 errors in the payment of Statutory Sick Pay and Statutory Maternity Pay. The total cost of this was in excess of £250m. This amounted to nearly 30 per cent of all payments. The payment of SSP and SMP costs the UK something in excess of £1bn per year.

Statutory Maternity Pay, although not strictly speaking sick pay, should be included here. As we have seen in Unit 2, there are fairly strict rules governing the payment of this benefit. Maternity pay and leave vary between the different countries of the EU. Perhaps the most generous country is Denmark, which allows leave for both parents of six months. In the UK there is no entitlement for the father to claim paternity leave unless the employer is sufficiently enlightened and prepared to allow this vital benefit.

Obviously, considering the enormous pressure on the UK's budget, steps have been taken not only to attempt to reduce sick and maternity payments, but also to ensure that payments are not made in error or fraudulent claims made.

3 *Redundancy terms* – the vast number of redundancies in the second half of the 1980s and early 1990s brought many problems to the UK. Long-term unemployed middle-aged former employees swamped the job market just as employers froze recruitment and employment prospects. The consequent effects on health, law and order, not to mention marriages, proved to be an increased cost which the UK had to fund. This form of unemployment is disastrous both to the individual and to the economy in general. As we saw in Unit 2, there are strict rules and regulations governing termination of employment and whether such termination constitutes redundancy, as well as redundancy payments themselves.

Many organisations employed the last-in, first-out system to identify potential redundancy candidates. This is a reasonable way of approaching the problem, but employers should also be aware of the employees' skills, length of employment service, performance and many other factors.

Personnel units within organisations were inundated with requests for counselling by individuals selected for redundancy. Working closely with both local and central government agencies, they attempted to find alternative employment for the redundant individuals. Retraining was essential as most individuals affected needed to acquire or improve their skills in order to match the local job market.

Redundancy packages which, in effect, encouraged individuals to accept either voluntary redundancy or early retirement, were fairly attractive. The lump sums involved often ran into tens of thousands of pounds, with the prospect of also receiving pension enhancements which would further buffer the drastic effect of unemployment. Many individuals reinvested, in some cases somewhat unwisely, in businesses of their own, only to discover that due to the recession, their new business was not able to survive. Organisations which make redundancy payments are entitled to rebates which may encourage them to offer more generous lump-sum and enhanced pension benefits.

FLEXIBLE

One of the implications of changing working conditions is that employees are expected to be far more flexible in their approach to and availability for work. The principal areas included here are hours worked, location of the work, work space available, multi-skilling needs and job-sharing opportunities. We will address these concerns in the following section:

▌ *Hours* – there are innumerable variations in the hours worked by employees, as a result of changes in working conditions and patterns. The main variations are:

(a) Shifts: shift working, or the working of non-standard hours, has long been an accepted method of ensuring either that the production process is 'manned' at all times, or that individuals are available to provide essential services on a 24-hour basis. Shift working is absolutely essential in such occupations as the emergency services. It is obvious that the fire brigade, police force or ambulance service, for example, could not operate on a 9–5 basis.

In manufacturing, where shift work is also an accepted norm, the requirements of the production process necessitate such working hours. If the manufacturer employs flow production for example, then it is essential that the production line is manned at all times. Whilst additional payments may be made to employees working unsociable hours, this cost is insignificant compared to that of constantly stopping and starting the flow production process.

In some cases, employees may be required to work for a period during the day then, after a short break, for a period of nights. Alternatively, the contract may require the employee to work a mixture of days and nights.

(b) Flexi-hours: flexible working arrangements, such as flexi-time, allow some 2.5 million people to take advantage of the opportunity to arrange the hours to suit both themselves and their employers. Normally, employees will be expected to work during the core time – usually 10 am–4 pm – but they can then choose to make up the balance of the hours at some point between 8 am and 6 pm. Alternatively, employees may choose to work longer hours for short periods of time and thus 'build up' days off.

(c) Compressed working weeks: certain organisations choose to close early on Fridays, or perhaps close on Fridays altogether. This means that employees work longer hours between Monday and Thursday. This can prove to be a suitable arrangement since the organisation can concentrate its business activities on four full working days which are fully manned by all employees who have the advantage of enjoying an extended weekend.

(d) Compressed annual hours: certain employees will find that their contracts simply stipulate the number of hours they will be expected to work throughout the year. With such arrangements, they may be able to work extremely long hours for short periods of time (provided this does not breach legislation) and then be able to benefit from long breaks at the end of these work periods.

2 *Location*

(a) Home working: it is now possible, due to technological advances, for an individual to undertake job tasks at home, via a computer linked to his/her employer's premises. There are, however, more traditional forms of home working, largely in the clothing industry. A form of piece-work which allows an individual to work at his/her own rate, provided that certain quotas are

reached, has been common for decades. Employers using this form of production or processing of garments, or a similar skilled or semi-skilled function, will be able, very quickly, to respond to changes in demand. They will have a 'pool' of 'out-workers' to whom they will deliver part-finished products and simply inform the employee of the piece-rate and the date by which the finished goods should be ready.

Within certain limitations, an individual may be able to undertake other employment in addition to the home working commitment. There is nothing to stop an individual from engaging in home working during the evenings or weekends. Indeed, in terms of computer access and the cost of enhanced telephone lines, employers may positively encourage home workers to do this.

Many organisations have tried to use home working, but have discovered that it is unsuitable for some individuals who feel isolated through lack of social contact throughout the day, and thus become unmotivated.

FIG. 4.2.11 *This is a time sheet as used by employees of the Department of Trade and Industry. Note that it includes a full breakdown of all work, activities and tasks undertaken.*

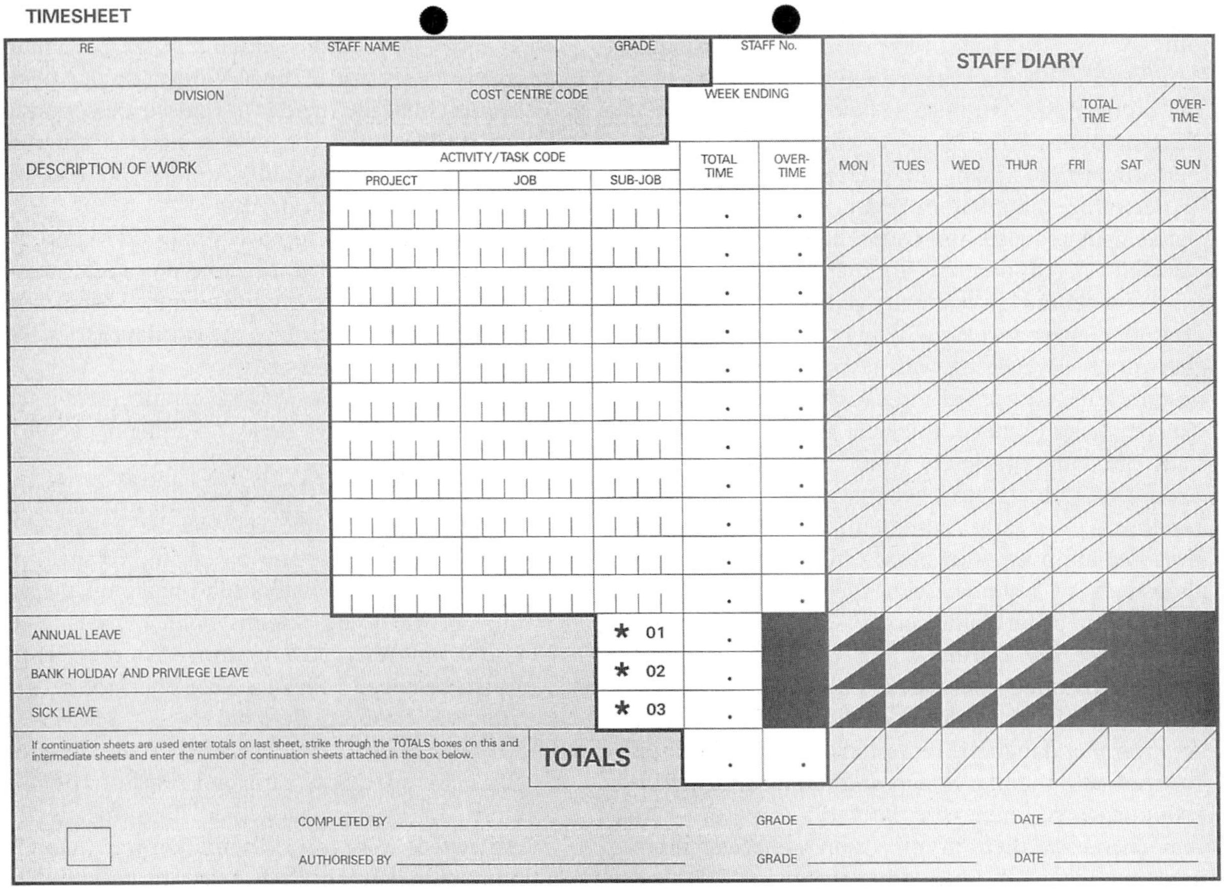

student activity

(PC 4.2.4, COM 3.1)
Identify three occupations where home working would be appropriate. Discuss your list with a partner.

(b) Mobility: an employee may be expected to be geographically mobile as an essential part of his/her job. Individuals, particularly those who are involved in maintenance, will be expected to carry out their duties in a variety of different locations. This may mean that the working location may differ every day, or at the very least, the individual may have to work for short periods of time in a variety of different locations. In some cases, this may even mean working in different countries at various times during the year. This flexibility requires not only the willingness of the employee (and, of course, an ability to handle any domestic problems which may arise from this mode of work), but also that the employer rewards the employee for the disturbances to his/her life.

student activity

(PC 4.2.4, COM 3.1,3.2)
In pairs, draw up a list of at least 10 different occupations that would require a high degree of geographical mobility. You should think of occupations where the employee is in full-time employment and not simply moving around the country in search of work.

3 *Work space* – increasingly, organisations have recognised the positive benefits which may be accrued from making their working environments open plan. A series of workstations are established within a fairly 'free form' environment, where the exact delineation between different sections or departments of the organisation are quite blurred.

Some organisations have taken the work space revolution to its most logical conclusion. In such organisations, admittedly rather 'arty' establishments, the desk has been abolished. Communal working areas are available and all individuals are issued with a portable computer which may be plugged into the main network at a variety of points in the building(s). These organisations have also addressed the problem of filing and storage, and positively discourage their employees from collecting paperwork and attempting to store it anywhere. In the electronic office of the next century it is envisaged that paper will become redundant and all transactions, documents and information will be available via a computer screen.

There is a statutory minimum requirement in terms of work space per employee. However, this is openly ignored by the majority of employers. Indeed, it is rare to find anyone who actually knows what the statutory minimum is.

student activity

(PC 4.2.4, COM 3.1)
Using your college or local library, try to find out what the statutory minimum work space should be for each employee. Report your findings back to the rest of the group and discuss whether you feel this is sufficient.

Many organisations also have a 'clear desk policy'. Essentially, this means that at the end of each working day the employees must remove all paperwork from their desks. There are two main reasons for this:

- much of the information may be of a sensitive or confidential nature and it would be unwise to allow unauthorised individuals to have access to it
- the organisation values the appearance of a clean and tidy office environment and indeed, the clear desk policy assists operatives to carry out thorough cleaning duties

4 *Multi-skilling* – since the introduction of trade union legislation aimed at reducing the power of employees in relation to employers, the subject of demarcation has all but disappeared. In the past, demarcation was a common reason for industrial disputes.

Demarcation is essentially to do with the clear definition of job descriptions, tasks and roles. Trades unions fought against the blurring of these definitions. Multi-skilling requires individuals to perform a broader range of activities within the workplace. It is now commonplace for a machine operative to undertake most basic forms of machine maintenance. Previously, demarcation demanded that any maintenance work should be carried out by an individual employed specifically for that task. While multi-skilling offers greater job satisfaction in terms of giving greater job variety, it has meant the loss of many jobs. A fringe benefit of multi-skilling has been, in some cases, higher rates of pay. Multi-skilling has also given organisations the following benefits:

- since machine operatives carry out most maintenance, there is less 'down time'
- machinery, as a result of this, is more productive
- following on from these two points, the organisation should be more competitive
- a natural result of all of the above is that the organisation should be able to offer better pay and conditions to its workforce

5 *Job sharing* – has become increasingly popular in recent years. Employers have discovered that job sharers are very beneficial to the organisation since these employees approach the job in a fresh and positive manner, as they have only had to work for part of the week. Employers also benefit from the fact that there are two individuals with different ideas to solve particular problems. Individuals involved in job sharing will normally be able to choose their working hours, but most commonly, they will either work for two and a half days per week each, or mornings only, or one week on, one week off. This type of arrangement ideally suits individuals with commitments outside the workplace, such as child care.

student activity

(PC 4.2.4, COM 3.1)
Identify at least three occupations in which job sharing might be appropriate. Having chosen your three occupations, compare them with those chosen by a partner from within the group.

EVALUATE CHANGES TO WORKING CONDITIONS IN TERMS OF COSTS AND BENEFITS

Needless to say, changes in working conditions can prove to be either beneficial or costly to the business organisation or individual employees. In this performance criterion we shall briefly investigate the probable costs and benefits involved. It should be noted that without specific reference to particular organisations or individuals, only general statements can be made.

COSTS TO BUSINESS

We can identify changes in working conditions as being either internally driven or the result of external change or pressure. It would be rare to find an example of an organisation which institutes working conditions of a radically different nature which would involve unnecessary additional costs. However, it should be pointed out that costs must be regarded as being short, medium and long term. An organisation would be perfectly prepared to accept the burden of additional costs for the short term in the knowledge that benefits would accrue in the longer term.

Thus, an organisation may consider radically changing its manufacturing or production process, for example, knowing that the costs of instituting the changes may be high, but that in the long term productivity and profitability would improve. Returning to the example of Volvo cars, they inevitably incurred huge costs in restructuring their work teams and factories. The mere act of removing the assembly line machinery and constructing discrete work areas was not achieved without significant cost. However, in the longer term, not only did employee motivation increase, but quality was improved and consequent productivity increases led to higher profitability.

The other side of the coin are changes which are wrought by external organisation such as central government in the form of new legislation. The government is well aware that making drastic changes to working conditions imposes intolerable strain on both the employer and employee. Therefore, in consultation with employers or at the very least with employers associations, such as the CBI, the government would choose to phase-in changes in working conditions over a period of time.

More radical changes may be instituted if the government recognises, or is made to recognise, a particular abuse of power or an unacceptable level of discrimination. Such overnight changes would only affect organisations which were 'guilty' of abuse or discrimination and would not really affect more progressive organisations.

BENEFITS FOR BUSINESS

Many changes to working conditions may, as we have seen, cost the organisation in the short term but will have long term benefits. Legislation which either harmonises or formalises working conditions must be seen as a benefit to both employer and employee. Organisations can avoid unnecessary employee problems and other matters which have to be dealt with as a result of poor working conditions if they rectify the conditions themselves. Generally speaking, most organisations not only adhere to legislated standards of working conditions, but actually exceed them.

As we have mentioned, employers are very keen, particularly in relation to changes in contracts and modes of working, to ensure that the new levels of flexibility offered by these contracts are matched with a flexibility of their own. Despite the fact that the UK still suffers from high unemployment, working conditions have not significantly been reduced as a result. It is the presence of employment legislation which has to a large part ensured that unscrupulous employers have not taken advantage of their employee's lack of power.

COSTS TO INDIVIDUALS

With changing patterns of work requiring greater flexibility from employees, it would be foolish to say that all of these changes have been accepted and integrated without a problem. Individuals within certain organisations have discovered, at least in part, that their working conditions have deteriorated to some degree. If, for example, an individual found that he/she was now required to work longer hours for the same rate of pay, or that holiday leave entitlement had been reduced, or that he/she was expected to be more productive without a subsequent increase in pay, we could expect some form of industrial dispute. However, the fact of the matter is that the number of days lost as a result of industrial action has reduced in a time when working conditions have been significantly altered. This is largely due to the fact that employment legislation brought into effect during the 1970s has seriously reduced the power and effectiveness of trade unions and other employee organisations. The reasoning behind this, as we swa in Element 4.1, was to give employers a greater degree of power and authority in relation to the trade unions and employee organisations.

BENEFITS FOR INDIVIDUALS

As with any change, there are always winners and losers. Perhaps one of the most publicised changes in working conditions was that of trainee doctors in the National Health Service. They had been expected to work in excess of 100 hours per week, often on 24-hour call. As the health authorities were able to choose these partially qualified doctors from a significantly larger pool than there were posts available, they could insist upon working conditions that would be unacceptable in almost any other area of employment. The media often quoted examples of mistakes or errors made by these housemen, as they were called, as a result of their fatigue and lack of rest. The government was eventually forced to recognise that these individuals were being required to undertake work far in excess of the norm. There is now legislation which significantly reduces the demands upon these individuals.

More generally, the introduction of new legislation governing working conditions can only be to the benefit of the employee. If nothing else, the legislation formalises or recognises good practice in terms of instituting basic levels of working conditions which must be met. Employers cannot afford to ignore legislation in this area. Employees are fully within their rights under law to seek redress, compensation or immediate action if the employer breaches the legislation.

4.2.5 Propose a plan for a business implementing change to working conditions

PLANNING TO IMPLEMENT CHANGE

In any proposed change in either job role or working conditions, we must begin by establishing the fact that the whole process is very much reliant upon the ability of the management.

Assuming that the manager has the following characteristics, we can expect a fairly smooth implementation of change:

- an effective manager manages relationships with employees rather than managing the employees themselves
- management skills, particularly in terms of negotiation, communication, learning ability and the setting of goals, are essential management techniques
- an effective manager learns from the experience of management rather than having a theoretical knowledge
- an effective manager recognises that no two individuals are the same and people cope with stress or change in many different ways

We shall now address the stages in which the implementation of change takes place.

IDENTIFYING GOALS

As we have mentioned, the difference between an effective manager and a poor one is in their ability to recognise goals and identify methods by which these goals may be attained. The first stage in implementing change is to actually identify the goal itself. The following questions need to be asked at this stage:

- what is it we are trying to do?
- what is the point of the change?
- who will it affect?
- what is in it for the organisation?
- what are the short-, medium- and long-term prospects?
- what are the constraints involved?
- what is the time-scale?
- do we have the technology, equipment or machinery?
- how will the employees respond?
- who has overall responsibility for the change?

student activity

(PC 4.2.5, COM 3.1)
Can you think of any other criteria which may be relevant in establishing goals? Discuss this in pairs.

THE PLANNING PROCESS

Individuals set about the process of planning in many different ways. In general, however, we can recognise the following features of the planning process:

- in relation to the objectives a plan should include what needs to achieved and by whom
- the plan should also identify the key factors involved
- above all, the plan should include a list of actions and timings

Having determined what is to be achieved, the plan should address the following:

- what will be the changes in **working conditions**?
  - will managers have to **delegate** more?
  - will there be a change in the **location** of the work?
- will there be a change in the way in which **teams** work?
  - are new **procedures** necessary?
  - does the organisation have to be **restructured**?
- what are the **training** requirements?
  - what new **skills** will need to be learnt?
  - how will they be **acquired**?
  - what will be the **format** of the training?
- will there be changes in the **communications** procedures?
  - will it make communication more **difficult**?
- does the organisational **structure** support the new conditions?
  - does someone need to be appointed to **oversee** the new changes?
- how will **individual** employees be affected?
- how will **groups** in general be affected?
  - who will be **affected**?
  - who will **not** be **affected**?
  - who, therefore, needs to be **informed**?

- what **information** has to be relayed?
  - **who** needs to be **consulted**?
  - **when** should they be **consulted**?
  - **how** will the changes be **presented**?
- what are the **likely reactions** or resistance to the change?
  - **what** are the anticipated reactions?
  - **who** will present the greatest resistance?
- what is the estimated **cost** of the change?
- what is the **timetable** for introducing the change?
  - should **milestones** be identified?
  - what **steps** need to be achieved?
- how will the changes be **measured** and monitored?
  - by **whom**?
  - **how**?
  - **when**?

Once the effects of the changes have been thought through in detail, the following issues need to be addressed:

- the more **complicated** the change, the more need there is for schedules to be drawn up
- assuming there are **limited resources**, how realistic is the timetable?
- what will be the **net effect** on the day-to-day running of the organisation whilst the changes are being undertaken?

SETTING TARGETS

As we have mentioned in the previous sections, the establishment of milestones, or means by which the progress of the change can be planned and monitored, is essential. Certain targets or objectives must be readily identifiable in order to assess not only the progress of the change but its current impact on the organisation. If we are looking at significant structural or physical changes relating to the premises of an organisation, it is fairly easy to recognise and establish these targets. However, when we are considering less tangible changes in working conditions, we must, perhaps, examine the reactions of the employees or their gradual acceptance of the changes. It may be quite difficult to use these as means of measuring or recognising that the target has been reache. Regular meetings and subsequent feedback from employees is essential in ensuring that changes are being made in the smoothest and most beneficial manner.

Normally, when changes are implemented, a specific individual will be responsible for the monitoring and evaluation process. Indeed, this individual's time and effort may be solely directed at the implementation of the change. Unfortunately it is not always possible to spare a person to concentrate only on the monitoring and evaluation process and an employee may have to undertake this work in addition to his/her normal day to day duties. In this case, the individual may find it difficult to address both job roles.

TRAINING

With any change in working conditions there may be a need to train, retrain or refresh individuals' understanding and knowledge. Factored into the overall implementation plan should be a rolling programme of training. Obviously, the amount of training depends upon the nature of the change in working conditions. In the field of health and safety, particularly when new legislation has been introduced, significant amounts of training may be required. If, for example, individuals are required to wear new protective clothing or to maintain equipment for the first time, then these changes may have a significant impact upon their productivity for a short period of time.

If new equipment or machinery has been installed to be used in the manufacturing process, again significant retraining may have to be undertaken. The suppliers of new equipment often include in their quotation to the purchasing organisation a basic training programme for all operators or users of the machinery.

MONITORING PROGRESS

Again, as we have mentioned earlier, there may be one individual who can be identified as the 'driving force' behind the change. This individual will have been prepared in advance and should know about the nature of the changes and any significant impact that may occur. Ideally, this individual should not only be conversant with the change but also be a good communicator. In monitoring the implementation of the change it may be necessary for this individual to come into conflict with those who are involved in actually instituting the change or those who are affected by the change. Resistance to change can often identified as the change is near completion. Although resistance may be greater in the earlier stages of the implementation of the change, the individual responsible for monitoring the change, by means of careful communication, may be able to allay fears and dispel myths.

In most cases, however, insufficient attention is given to the monitoring of the change or its progress. If the organisation has not clearly thought through how it will ensure that the change keeps to its timetable, then delays may be inevitable. In more formal situations, the organisation may require that certain documentation is completed and feedback given at the identified milestones.

MONITORING PROGRESS

If, as is generally the case, things do not go according to plan, the organisation and the individual responsible for the implementation may find themselves in a difficult situation. If the production process has been drastically affected by the change(s), but the change is not significantly completed as yet, then there may be drastic effects upon the viability and profitability of the organisation.

The organisation needs to take a pragmatic view in setting the targets and establishing the timetable. It would be foolish to assume that the changes would be completed according to the pre-planned timetable. In this respect the organisation must have a contingency plan ready in order to address the problems that may occur if the change is behind schedule.

A rigorous review of progress is essential as the organisation needs to have the opportunity to re-set targets and timetables, as well as investigating the ramifications of the time delay.

The relaying of information is essential throughout the whole process of change. Organisations should call regular meetings, particularly with those most affected by the change. These feedback opportunities should not be ignored as employees may have good ideas or suggestions to overcome problems and aid development and implementation.

ELEMENT 4.2

assignment

(PC 4.2.1–5, COM 3.2, IT 3.1)
In order to fulfil the requirements of the performance criteria of this Element, it is necessary not only to investigate job roles and responsibilities but also to consider working conditions and potential changes.

In a report format, which should be word processed, address the following tasks. You may need to investigate a particular business organisation and follow the progress of a change in working conditions. You should not be overly concerned with the nature of the change in working conditions, since any of the following will be acceptable:

- changes in the contract of employment
- changes in hours worked
- changes in pay
- changes in redundancy terms
- any other relevant change in working conditions

TASK 1

(PC 4.2.1)
Identify five individuals within a business organisation who hold a range of job roles.

TASK 2

(PC 4.2.2)
Describe their responsibilities in terms of the following:

- identifying targets

- meeting targets
- working with others
- training needs
- disciplinary considerations
- impact of changes in working conditions

TASK 3

(PC 4.2.3)
You should explain why working conditions are always subject to change and describe in depth one reason for a change in working conditions.

TASK 4

(PC 4.2.5)
In this part of the report, you are expected to create a plan to implement change. Begin by identifying one area of change from the list given above.

TASK 5

(PC 4.2.4)
You must now justify and evaluate the possible costs and benefits to the business organisation and its employees.

TASK 6

(PC 4.2.2)
Finally, in your plan, you should identify those job roles which would have a responsibility for implementing the change.

Evaluate recruitment procedures, job applications and interviews

PERFORMANCE CRITERIA

A student must:

1 Assess the effectiveness of **recruitment procedures** in attracting and recruiting applicants

2 Explain how **job descriptions** and **person specifications** match applicants with vacancies

3 Produce and evaluate **letters of application** for clarity and quality of presentation

4 Produce and evaluate **curricula vitae** for clarity and quality of presentation

5 Practise and appraise **interviewer techniques**

6 Practise and appraise **interviewee techniques**

7 Explain and give examples of **legal obligations** and **ethical responsibilities** in **recruitment procedures** and interviews

RANGE

Recruitment procedures: advertising vacancies, short-listing, dealing with references, assessing candidates, confirming employment, dealing with unsuccessful candidates

Job descriptions: job title, position within organisational structure, duties and responsibilities

Person specifications: personal attributes and achievements, qualifications, experience, competence

Curricula vitae: name, date of birth, address, telephone number, education and training, qualifications, other relevant achievements, interests, references

Interviewer techniques: opening the interview, asking questions, asking follow-on questions, using body language, closing the interview, giving feedback

Interviewee techniques: preparing, showing confidence, using body language, listening to questions, responding to questions, asking questions, being clear and concise

Appraise in terms of: *own performance in demonstrating interviewer and interviewee techniques, interaction between participants, success of interview (meeting its intended purpose, meeting legal obligations, meeting ethical responsibilities)*

Legal obligations: *equal opportunities, contract of employment*

Ethical responsibilities: *honesty, objectivity, fairness, confidentiality*

4.3.1. Assess the effectiveness of recruitment procedures in attracting and recruiting applicants

RECRUITMENT PROCEDURES

The main purpose of offering a new post to prospective candidates is to meet an identified organisational need. As we have mentioned, the creation of a new post will involve the definition of the following:

- a job description
- a job specification
- a person specification

Before we look at the methods of external recruitment, we will first consider the question of **internal recruitment**. It is often possible for an employee currently engaged by the organisation to fill a job vacancy. There are advantages and disadvantages for both the individual and the organisation in considering internal recruitment. The **advantages** are:

- the individual knows a great deal about the organisation
- the organisation can save considerable sums of money on recruitment costs
- the organisation can save considerable sums of money on induction costs
- promotion within the organisation is seen as an incentive to other employees

  The disadvantages are:

- since the individual already knows the policies and procedures of the organisation, he/she may be unable to offer any new ideas or innovations
- an external candidate usually works very hard in the initial period of employment
- the individual who has filled the vacant job position will have to be replaced in his/her previous position
- by choosing one individual the organisation has had to ignore or overlook other individuals within the organisation

student activity

(PC 4.3.1, COM 3.1)
As an applicant for a job within the organisation in which you are presently working, what real advantages do you think you would have to offer, which could enable you to succeed in your bid to gain a new post? Discuss this in groups.

ADVERTISING VACANCIES

In order to seek external candidates, the organisation must begin its recruitment campaign by advertising the vacant post. An advertisement should include the following:

1 the job title
2 a brief job description
3 the nature of the organisation's business
4 the market sector in which the business is active
5 the geographical location of the vacancy
6 the salary range
7 the organisation's address
8 a specific person to whom all applications must be made
9 a telephone number for candidates to contact
10 qualifications required
11 experience required
12 any limitations the organisations may wish to place upon the post (age or additional skills required)

Another method is to use a commercial employment agency which will attempt to recruit on the organisation's behalf for a commission or a fee. Alternatively, the organisation may decide to employ a temporary person. In this case, the organisation pays the employment agency and the employment agency then pays the individual after having taken its commission.

The final alternative is to use a government-run employment agency which will fulfil a very similar role to that of a commercial employment agency. The major difference is that such agencies do not, at present, require commission or a fee to fill a post. Local job centres, career services or employment services are the main agencies involved.

student activity

(PC 4.3.1, COM 3.1)
What facilities and services do government-run agencies offer? Investigate your local office in the course of your research. Present your findings to the remainder of the group.

FIG. 4.3.1 *This is an example of an advertisement placed by Berkeley Scott Selection, a private recruitment agency.*

Exactly where the employer chooses to place the advertisement, if this is the route preferred, will very much depend on the job itself. There are countless magazines and newspapers that offer the chance of finding the right person for the job. A useful start is a regularly updated guide called *British Rate and Data* This lists most of the magazines and newspapers published in the UK. It includes the cost of advertising, the circulations and a brief profile of the type of readership. It is also wise to contact the advertising manager for additional information and a 'rate card', which details all of the available discounts, introductory offers and special issues. This may be of enormous help in determining when to place the advertisement.

Generally speaking, the higher the circulation, the higher the cost of advertising. The employer will have to balance the cost of the advertisement against the level of response likely from a larger circulation publication.

As we mentioned earlier, recruitment agencies and consultants will take on the task of actually sifting through the candidates and fielding enquiries from applicants, but the employer still needs to do the basic work of drawing up the job description, job specification and details relating to job title and pay and conditions.

The private recruitment agencies, such as Berkeley Scott Selection (see Figure 4.3.1), employ some thirty full-time consultants who deal with management recruitment in a number of fields. We will be looking at

Queens Moat Houses

INTERNATIONAL HOTELIERS

HOTEL MARKETING
ROMFORD BASED

CORPORATE MARKETING MANAGER

LEISURE MARKETING EXECUTIVE

COMPETITIVE SALARY AND BENEFITS PACKAGES

Queens Moat Houses, a leading UK hotel company with a superb portfolio of hotels, are moving forward aggressively in the marketplace, having recently completed a major organisational restructure and recruited a number of high profile professionals at senior management level. The sales and marketing strategy which is currently being implemented will establish a strong brand awareness and a coherent offer to the marketplace, and the team are dynamic, positive and highly motivated to achieve the company's goals and objectives.

Two new opportunities have been created within the marketing department to assist in the production of a diverse and creative range of programmes and initiatives during 1995. Experienced and ambitious, with a fresh, enthusiastic approach, the successful candidates will enjoy recognition, career development and an open, cheerful management style.

You will take responsibility for all aspects of corporate marketing, providing support to the sales teams, developing a number of loyalty programmes and new products for the corporate market. You will also be responsible for joint marketing ventures with Queens Moat Houses' partners in associated industries, and for liaison with representation companies. This position requires a broad range of applied marketing skills and a practical and "hands-on" approach to the marketing function within the Hospitality industry.

Reporting to the Marketing Manager you will assist in the production of a diverse range of offers to this market. Projects include new branded leisure products, reader and on-pack offers, weekend and leisure break programmes and a wide range of promotions. This is a super opportunity to further develop your marketing skills and experience in an environment where you will be involved in all aspects of marketing services.

Please send your CV in the first instance quoting ref:DW6199 to Dee Wilson, Sales & Marketing Division, Berkeley Scott Selection, Berkeley House, 11-13 Ockford Road, Godalming, Surrey, GU7 1QU. Tel: (0483) 414141. Fax (0483) 414457.

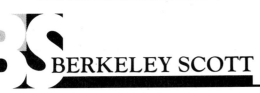

BERKELEY SCOTT

the role of specialist recruitment agencies in Unit 8.

A private recruitment agency will place the advertisement in relevant magazines, newspapers and journals for the employer. It will also have a data base of potential employees who have already registered with it. In return for assistance in obtaining the right person for the job, the agency charges the employer anything from 6–20 per cent of the employee's first year's earnings.

Table 4.3.1 sets out the most suitable, and usual, places for advertising particular jobs.

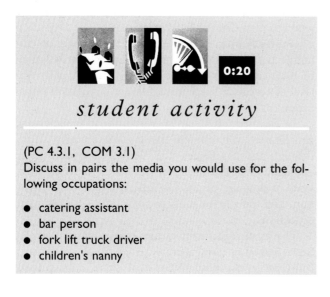

student activity

(PC 4.3.1, COM 3.1)
Discuss in pairs the media you would use for the following occupations:

- catering assistant
- bar person
- fork lift truck driver
- children's nanny

Research has shown that potential employees are attracted to job advertisements which infer the following (bearing in mind that this must be supported by reality!):

- good prospects
- interesting work
- creative possibilities
- quality and reputation of the organisation
- an opportunity to use intelligence
- job security
- good working environment

The wording of an advertisement is also very important. It is a good idea to use the word 'you' when referring to the individual needed and using the word 'we' in the case of the organisation.

Employers devote considerable amounts of time to recruiting employees. It is perhaps at this stage of the recruitment process that many mistakes may be made. An employer might do one or more of the following:

- be over-critical – when the employer fails to recognise a good potential applicant by too rigidly adhering to preconceived ideas about what he/she is looking for

TABLE 4.3.1 *Advertising jobs*

Type of job	Usual advertising chosen
Clerical workers	Local advertisements (press) Job centres Letters of enquiry from potential candidates
Shop assistants	Local advertisements (press) Notices in shop window Job centres Word of mouth
Unskilled manual workers	Notice outside factory Job centres Word of mouth Occasional local advertisements (press)
Semi-skilled manual	Notice outside factory Job centres Word of mouth Occasional local advertisements (press) Occasional local radio
Skilled manual workers	Local advertisements (press/radio) Notice outside factory Job centres Word of mouth
Trainees	Job centre Colleges/schools Local advertisements (press/radio) Letter of enquiry from potential candidate
Salesperson	Local/national advertisements (press/radio) Enquiry from potential candidates
Professional (and technical)	National advertisements (specialist magazines/journals) Recruitment centres Letters of enquiry from potential candidates
Management trainees	Recruitment consultants/agencies Colleges/universities National advertisements (press)
Senior management	National and professional magazines and journals Recruitment consultants/agencies Letters of enquiry from potential candidates
Secretaries	Employment agencies Local advertisements (press) Specialist magazines (such as free papers/journals, etc.)

- be under-critical – when the employer finds it hard to sift out the good candidates from the less suitable ones. The employer may end up needing to interview all of the applicants
- not setting criteria – when the employer has all of the applications in and finds it difficult, due to lack of preparation, to sift through the applicants and make any form of decision about them
- making snap decisions – when the employer looks at the applications and decides that one of the candidates is ideal. Having formed this impression, the employer cannot really make an objective judgement about the other applicants
- taking too much time – when the employer either finds it difficult to conduct the sifting process, or is unable to devote enough time to the task

There will always be some people who do not exactly tell the whole truth on their application forms. This may be because the application form is not very well designed. The gathering of information about an individual needs to be as accurate as possible. Before the employer goes to the expense of interviewing the individual, there are some checks that can be made, as we will see in the next section of the Element.

If we assume that the advertisement for the available position was appropriate and successful in attracting the right candidates, then the sifting-out process should not just mean sorting out the unsuitable candidates from those that the employer thinks are worth actually seeing. The short-list process should be a question of ranking the candidates against the criteria that have already been identified. Even if there are candidates who look interesting 'on paper' but do not match the criteria, then the employer would be advised not to bother seeing them. If the employer is tempted, there is a risk that time may be wasted in the long run.

Once the candidates have been ranked, those that most closely match the criteria are the ones to call for interview. If, and sometimes this is the case, even the short-listed candidates do not 'fit in' after the employer has seen them, then the whole process may have to be repeated. It is for this reason, in the main, that the short-list process is so important.

DEALING WITH REFERENCES

Taking up references should, in most cases, merely confirm the employer's impression of the candidate. The references should also confirm that the candidate has had particular work experience and has achieved certain qualifications.

When taking up references, it is advisable to provide a straightforward form for the referee to fill in. It is also a matter of courtesy for the employer requesting the reference to provide a self-addressed, stamped envelope.

Also, in most cases, the employer should also include a brief description of the job involved. At this stage it may also be a good idea to confirm that the potential employee has to work a particular length of notice or has to complete studies until a specified date.

Some employers include on their application forms a box to tick in relation to the taking up of references. Usually, this refers to the timing of the taking up of references. In some cases, employees would prefer that their current employer does not know about their applications until the last possible time. The prospective employer should note this request, not for reasons of secrecy but more to comply with the candidate's wishes. In most cases, references will not be taken up until the candidate is short-listed with the probability of being asked for interview. It is perfectly acceptable both for the employee to make this request and for the employer to respect it.

The interpretation of references is something of a fine art, as is the writing of one. The reader must read between the lines to interpret what is said and what is not said. A fair-minded employer, giving a reference, will even give a suspect employee a reasonable reference under most circumstances. In some cases, the current employer may actually want to 'off-load' the useless employee on an unsuspecting new employer! When writing references, particularly in cases when the potential employer who has made the request does not give guidelines, an employer would normally cover the following:

- duties/responsibilities
- current salary (including bonuses, etc.)
- job role and title
- service record
- absences (sickness, etc.)
- honesty and integrity, etc.

Some employers state that references are not really worthwhile. Particularly in larger organisations, it is unlikely that the referee would know the employee very well. Another problem may arise because the potential employer, having only a brief period with the candidate, may form a different judgement about him/her from that stated by the referee, who may know the candidate well.

There is no legal obligation to provide a reference and, in any case, judgements made in a reference are often subjective or qualitative. Comments about a candidate's ability are only really reliable when they are measurable. References tend also to be written in such a way as to avoid offending the candidate. It is often a good idea for the potential employer to follow up a written reference with a phone call to the referee. It may be that, in conversation, some more pertinent or relevant facts and comments may be forthcoming.

student activity

(PC 4.3.1, COM 3.2, IT 3.1)
In pairs, compose a reference for your partner. He/she has applied for a position as a clerical assistant in a large engineering organisation. Word process your reference and compile a covering letter to accompany it.

ASSESSING CANDIDATES

We will be looking at the assessment of candidates later in this Element. However, it is a good time to look at some of the basic criteria that relate to the assessment process. If a candidate has reached the stage of being assessed for a job, then the employer needs to be absolutely certain that the individual on paper (the details on the application form) match the individual attending the interview. This might sound rather strange and it is not meant to suggest that the interviewee may be an imposter! In many cases, a good candidate 'on paper' is a poor one in the flesh. The employer's expectations may not be satisfied by the individual when he/she meets him/her.

There are some key points that will help the employer in his/her assessment of the candidates. These are:

- try to observe the candidate at all times. How does he/she react to situations and different circumstances?
- make sure that any checks that need to be made have been made (such as references and certificates, etc.)
- if applicable, test the candidate. There are various ways of doing this, such as multiple-choice tests, aptitude tests, bio-data, psychometric tests, scenarios and role plays, etc.
- if there is a query or question about the background, experience or qualifications of the candidate make sure that these are addressed

The selection interview is a notoriously unreliable method of choosing a potential employee, but a good interviewer will be able to pick up on many unspoken and unguarded features about the candidate. As we will see later, body language or non-verbal communication can give very interesting clues about an individual. A good interviewer, as we will see later, should:

- ask probing questions
- always be polite
- listen well

- observe the candidate's behaviour
- check that the candidate is attentive at all times

CONFIRMING EMPLOYMENT

The successful candidate should be notified at the earliest opportunity. It is also wise not to contact the unsuccessful candidates until the successful one has confirmed in writing that he/she will be taking up the post. In some cases, the successful candidate may change his/her mind about accepting the position and an employer who has already told the unsuccessful candidates about the outcome of the recruitment procedure will have burned all his/her bridges. The only course open is then to re-advertise and bear all the expenses and go through the process once again. In some cases, it has been known for successful candidates to accept the offer, then after a few days (and after the employer has rejected all of the other candidates) contact the employer and say that he/she has changed his/her mind. This may be a genuine change of mind, but in some instances the existing employer (remember that the employee is probably still working out his/her notice) has offered the employee a better deal so not to lose his/her experience or skills.

The offer of a position, which should be confirmed by the employer in writing, is normally subject to certain conditions. These tend to be:

- satisfactory references (if not already taken up)
- a medical examination (if appropriate)

Provided these are acceptable, then a date will be set for the new employee to join the organisation.

student activity

(PC 4.3.1, COM 3.2, IT 3.1)
Following on from the previous Student Activity, and assuming that your partner has been successful in his/her application for the job, now word process an acceptance letter which confirms the appointment.

DEALING WITH UNSUCCESSFUL CANDIDATES

Everyone, at one stage or another, will receive a rather dismissive photocopied rejection letter following an interview or you may not hear anything at all. Others will simply receive a rather terse and brief phone call telling them that they have been unsuccessful.

Good practice in dealing with unsuccessful candidates is as important as dealing with those who have been chosen for employment. Employees may promise to keep the details of the unsuccessful candidate on file. They may also promise to let the unsuccessful candidate know if a position arises in the future. It is always a good idea not to make promises that the employer is not able to deliver. It is important to remember that an unsuccessful candidate may be a customer too. In this respect, careful treatment of unsuccessful candidates is as important as any other marketing technique.

The employer should always be aware that an individual who does not match the requirements of the job may, if appointed, be a source of problems in the future. It is far better not to appoint and to re-advertise than to take the risk of employing someone who is merely the best of a relatively poor group of candidates.

Some employers are perfectly willing to give unsuccessful candidates some feedback on how they performed at the interview stage of the selection process. The employer, although this may cause some anxiety in the unsuccessful candidate, should be frank and offer straightforward criticism. It is far better to tell the unsuccessful candidate about his/her shortcomings than to leave him/her wondering what went wrong. After all, the unsuccessful candidate may have felt that his/her performance at interview was very good, whereas the employer/interviewer saw serious problems and had misgivings about the candidate.

In all cases, letters, telephone calls and other communications to the unsuccessful candidates should be made promptly and be courteous. The candidate invested time and effort in the application and recruitment process and should be given the respect that this deserves. Equally, if the employer promised to pay expenses for travel/subsistence, etc. to all candidates, this should be done promptly upon receipt of expenses claims forms.

student activity

(PC 4.3.1, COM 3.2, IT 3.1)
Still imagining the same situation as in the last two Student activities, now word process a letter to your partner informing him/her that he/she has been unsuccessful on this occasion in obtaining a position with your organisation.

PLANNING INDUCTION PROGRAMME

Any new employee, regardless of the rank or job title, will (hopefully) feel very positive when beginning the job. This is particularly true if the organisation has planned a comprehensive **induction** or training **programme.** The employer is well advised to have organised this in advance and not simply to offer induction or training on an *ad hoc* basis.

The main aims of the induction process are:

- to ensure that the new employee attains **effectiveness** and **efficiency** at the earliest opportunity
- to ensure that the new employee gains **commitment** to the organisation as soon as possible
- to ensure that the new employee is **familiarised** with the organisation, job role and procedures
- to ensure that the new employee adopts the organisation's **attitudes and philosophy** as quickly as possible

The new employee would have had some impressions of the organisation before the interview. A good candidate would have researched the organisation and found out as much as possible. During the interview process, these impressions would have either been confirmed or undermined. In general terms, the employer wants the new employee to be committed and efficient; the employee wants many things too. Amongst these are:

- acceptance by colleagues
- information to help settle in
- accurate job description and role
- an individual to turn to if confused or unhappy
- to have all the 'tools' available to do the job
- clear understanding about the rules, regulations and procedures

Many of these are provided by a good induction programme. Ideally, the induction package should include the following information:

- a brief description of the organisation
- number of employees
- location(s) of the organisation
- products or services offered by the organisation
- pay scales
- holiday entitlements
- pension arrangements
- hours of work
- other conditions of work
- sickness arrangements
- disciplinary and grievance procedures
- trade union membership
- staff perks (including subsidised facilities)
- travel and subsistence rules and arrangements
- medical facilities
- welfare facilities

- canteen facilities
- health and safety regulations and procedures
- education and training programmes available

Normally, these matters should all be covered in a staff handbook. The handbook should be clear and concise and be a ready reference volume for daily use.

Organisations have recognised that the majority of employees who leave in, say, the first six months do so as a result of poor induction programmes. In such cases, no real induction takes place. Employers then run the risk of having individuals working for them with no real idea of the organisational structure, roles or philosophy. From the first day, they feel left out and isolated. It is no wonder that employees in such a position choose to 'vote with their feet' and seek alternative employment.

It is worth remembering that a good employer will invest as much time, money and effort on its employees as it does on its machinery.

4.3.2 Explain how job descriptions and person specifications match applicants with vacancies

JOB DESCRIPTIONS

Obviously, the main purpose of job descriptions and person specifications is to ensure that the individual matches a series of desired criteria. Clearly it is necessary, when actually employing someone, to match particular needs of the organisation. These fall into three main categories:

- accurately matching potential employees with existing vacancies
- making sure that the job design relates to the overall business objectives of the organisation
- being prepared to provide additional training and development if required

JOB TITLE

The job title assigned to a particular collection of tasks, duties and responsibilities should be as appropriate as possible. If the job involves some form of supervisory or managerial responsibility, then it is normal for the job title to be suffixed by the word 'supervisor' or 'manager'.

POSITION WITHIN ORGANISATIONAL STRUCTURE

The job description, as we have said, should clearly state at what level this job will be in the overall structure of the organisation. It is normal for the job holder to know precisely to whom he/she is accountable and for whom he/she is responsible. In addition, the position in the organisational structure will determine the post-holder's inclusion on circulation lists and attendance at meetings.

DUTIES AND RESPONSIBILITIES

The job description must also clearly state the responsibilities of the postholder. These may simply relate to specific job tasks and duties, but in the case of supervisory or managerial positions, they may also relate to these supervisory or managerial functions. The specifics of responsibility should be made very clear to the postholder, although they may be couched in rather general terms. It is only when the individual postholder has acquired some experience of the job itself that he/she will know precisely what is being demanded of him/her.

student activity

(PC 4.3.2, COM 3.2, IT 3.1)
Individually, compose a job description for an advertisement of your choice from a local newspaper. You should be careful to choose an advertisement which contains the maximum amount of information. If the advertisement does not contain the necessary information to complete the job description, then you should make reasonable assumptions of the hidden requirements of the job.

PERSON SPECIFICATIONS

A person specification covers the main characteristics which will be required to undertake the job. These will include:

- the physical make-up of the individual – how he/she looks and whether he/she can speak clearly
- the current attainments of the individual – qualifications, driving licence, if applicable, and previous experience
- the intelligence of the individual
- the aptitudes of the individual – depending upon the job, these may include social skills, listening and communication skills or legible handwriting
- the interests of the individual – any relevant sports or leisure activities, particularly any positions of responsibility held in relation to these
- the disposition of the individual – whether, for example, the individual is capable of coping with a variety of problematic situations such as dealing with customers, for which tact and diplomacy may be required
- the circumstances of the individual – these will include domestic situation and personal relationships and, the availability and willingness of the individual to work overtime or at weekends

This person specification is used in relation to the job specification from which the job description has been written. A typical job specification will include the following:

- physical attributes required
- proficiencies required
- manual skills required
- knowledge skills required
- personality traits preferred
- social skills preferred

The specification itself is usually expressed in the following manner:

- what particular work will need to be carried out
- what knowledge that person will need in order to carry out the tasks
- what judgements will need to be made by that person
- what factors the individual will have to take into account in the course of his/her duties

Employers may find it useful to try to 'weight' the qualities required of the potential employee. Some use a system designed by Alec Rodgers called a Seven Point Plan. In essence, this covers the following:

1 physical make-up
2 attainments
3 general intelligence
4 special aptitude
5 interests
6 disposition
7 circumstances

Let us look at those in a little more detail:

1 *Physical make-up* – this would include some of the following:

- height
- weight
- hearing
- eyesight
- looks
- grooming
- dress
- voice

2 *Attainments* – these generally relate to the education of the individual:

- general education
- work experience
- on or off-the-job training

3 *General intelligence* – this may relate either to tests conducted by the employer or on the employer's behalf or to a more general induction of the candidate's reasoning and intellectual ability.

4 *Special aptitudes* – these are largely based on the exact nature of the job, but may include the following criteria (if appropriate):

- mechanical skills
- dexterity
- word skill (written/oral)
- figure skills (numbers, etc.)
- artistic ability

5 *Interests* – this is another broad category, but it often gives the employer an insight into the candidate's intelligence and use of leisure time. It would include some of the following:

- intellectual interests
- practical interests
- physical/sport interests
- social interests

6 *Disposition* – this is a tricky category, since it can be very subjective. The qualities looked for may include the following:

- acceptability (how easy is the individual to 'get on with'?)
- leadership (any signs of experience?)
- stability (mentally and domestically)
- self-starter skills (will the candidate need to be self-motivated?)

7 *Circumstances* – straightforward category, simply includes the following:

- age
- marital status
- dependents (children)
- geographical mobility/willingness to move location
- home/domicile arrangements (where the candidate lives and financial ties)

After these criteria have been identified, the next job is to categorise them in terms of the following:

- are they essential?
- are they desirable?
- are they not required?
- are they negative?

student activity

(PC 4.3.2, COM 3.2, IT 3.1)
In pairs, using a clerical assistant's job as your example, prepare a list of criteria which you consider to be essential, desirable or required. This list should be word processed.

PERSONAL ATTRIBUTES AND ACHIEVEMENTS

As we have already mentioned, the personal attributes required will be clearly defined within either the job specification or the person specification. However, not all potential employees will be expected to have all of the skills already. An employer should be able to identify an individual who has the potential to fulfil all of the requirements of the job. To this end, it may be a condition upon which the individual is taken into employment, that he/she engages in staff development. The personal attributes already present in the individual should form a useful basis upon which to develop the individual as an ideal employee. Development will normally take the form of on-the-job (learn as you work) or off-the-job (studies undertaken outside the work environment) training. We have already dealt with the nature of staff development earlier in this Unit.

QUALIFICATIONS

Qualifications may play an important part in determining whether a particular individual obtains a position.

Certain occupations require particular levels of competence related to qualifications as a base. The acquisition of qualifications by the individual may be vital in certain career paths. An applicant for a more junior post may not be expected to have proceeded along a specific qualifications path to its logical conclusion. Most employers will encourage individuals to undertake additional studies either within or outside work time. Some employers will be prepared to at least partially finance such additional studies.

In certain career paths, particularly in the professions, the minimum entry requirements in terms of qualifications may be high. An employer in these fields will expect the individual to have pursued several years of personal study.

Most occupations, to a greater or lesser extent, will offer some kind of opportunity to attain additional qualifications. As we have mentioned, individuals will be encouraged to pursue these at the earliest possible opportunity.

EXPERIENCE

Many people will attest that there is no substitute for real experience. It is obviously very difficult for younger employees to obtain experience. To this end, many courses (like GNVQ) attempt to replicate real work situations. Many people entering the job market in their mid to late teens have already had some minimal level of work experience. Perhaps this may have been carried out while at school or college. Employers are keen to see that potential employees have had some such experience as otherwise they have no real indication of whether the individual can cope in a working environment.

Recently employers have begun to recognise the concept of transferable skills. This rather tricky area attempts to identify skills performed in alternative situations which may not necessarily be relevant to the intended work duties but for which the individual should be given some credit. With this in mind, two systems have been developed to cope with transferable skills and all the problems relating to them. These are:

- APL (accreditation of prior learning) – this relates particularly to the level of entry on to a vocational course. Previous studies may have been at a comparable level to those being considered and therefore the individual may be credited with the knowledge he/she has gained. With this credit the individual may become exempt from certain studies on the programme
- APEL (accreditation of prior experiential learning) – this rather broader method of gaining credit can allow an individual to be exempt from certain studies without having previously attended a formal

programme of study. Provided evidence can be produced that the individual has experience in the area, then credit will be given. This is particularly useful for individuals returning to study after having spent a period of time in the working environment

COMPETENCE

As we saw in the previous section, a job specification will clearly state the exact nature of the competences required for the particular post. In general terms, the job description will presuppose certain levels of competence. These may relate to experience, conventional qualifications or general skills.

student activity

(PC 4.3.2, COM 3.1)
In the role of an assessor of transferable skills, consider the credits that may be given to an individual in the following circumstances:

- a female candidate who has recently returned to study after having brought up two children
- a male candidate who has spent the last five years as

- a clerical assistant in an accounts department
- a candidate who has recently left the armed forces. The candidate's previous job was as an aircraft fitter and the chosen course of study is business and finance

Initially consider this in pairs, and then feedback your thoughts to the remainder of your group.

4.3.3 *Produce and evaluate letters of application for clarity and quality of presentation*

Potential applicants will use a variety of sources in their attempt to discover a job which suits their skills, experience and aspirations. Essentially, they may use the following:

- the national daily press
- Sunday newspapers
- professional journals
- trade journals
- television
- radio
- local daily newspapers
- local weekly newspapers
- free newspapers
- career centres
- job centres
- private employment agencies
- word of mouth
- self advertisement

In responding to an advertisement, an applicant needs to consider the following questions:

student activity

(PC 4.3.3, COM 3.2)
Write your own self advertisement offering your services as a potential employee. Where would you place this advertisement?

- am I in a position to apply for this post? (This may include the preparation of a curriculum vitae and a cross-checking of present skills with skills required.)
- what do I already know or what can I find out about the organisation offering the post?
- does the organisation have a good reputation?
- how does it treat its staff?

- are there any possibilities for personal development?
- are there good promotion prospects?
- is it clear to whom I will have to apply?
- do I need to send a letter of application to obtain additional information about the post?
- is the job really for me?
- will I discover that the job is really unsuitable?
- how will they react if I turn down the job after having gone through all the processes of recruitment?

Applying for a position may involve the following:

- obtaining, then filling in an application form
- writing a letter of application
- researching the organisation
- preparing a curriculum vitae

student activity

(PC 4.3.3, COM 3.2, IT 3.1)
If you have not already done so, design your own cv, and print a hard copy using computer software, taking care to include all of your qualifications and experience.

APPLICATION FOR EMPLOYMENT

Name	Address
	Phone No.

Date of birth	Age	Position applied for
Marital status		Names and ages of children

Health give details	Driving licence YES/NO Endorsements YES/NO (give full details)
Are you a registered disabled person YES/NO If yes give registration no.	

Education History: Schools Colleges/Further Education Other	Qualifications obtained:

Previous employment begin with present or last employer and work backwards.

Name of Employer	Position held	From – To	Give full details of job	Rate of Pay

P.T.O.

FIG 4.3.2(A) *This is a typical application form.*

The advertising organisation may require applicants to write a letter of application. The basic rules about writing a letter of application are:

- clearly state in the first paragraph that you are applying for a particular post
- state in this first paragraph where you saw the advertisement for the vacancy
- indicate any enclosures such as an application form or cv
- use the letter of application to summarise your major strengths as detailed in your application form
- stress your suitability for the post
- be enthusiastic

- keep the letter of application short, no more than one side of A4
- many recruitment advisers recommend that this letter of application is handwritten
- use the correct tone
- use the correct layout for a business letter
- make sure that the letter is formal and uses the correct salutations and complimentary close
- state that you are available for interview
- state that you are able to start the job
- make sure that you take a photocopy
- make sure that any examination certificates required have been photocopied; do not risk sending the originals

---

Please give any other information which you feel to be relevant to your application for employment
i.e. Sports, hobbies, ambitions, interests etc.

References please give details of two referees one of whom should be your last or current employer. These references will not be taken up without your permission.

Name	Name
Address	Address

For office use only

Applicant engaged Starting date	YES/NO	Rejection letter sent Date	YES/NO
Engagement letter sent Date	YES/NO	General comments on Candidate	
Personnel File opened	YES/NO		
References applied for (Date)	YES/NO		

FIG 4.3.2(B) *The reverse of the application form*

Alternatives to sending a letter of application are filling in a standard application form or sending your curriculum vitae. We shall consider these two items separately.

An application form may appear to be somewhat daunting in the first instance, but, having reached this stage in your application for the post, it is worthwhile attempting to fill in the details. There are a number of guidelines to consider when filling in an application form, these are:

- photocopy the original and always fill in a rough copy first
- spend some time considering the trickier questions
- make sure that you have spelt everything correctly and used the right grammar
- when filling in personal details, although this is relatively straightforward, make sure that your answers are legible. It is, after all, this first part of the application form that will give a valuable first impression to the reader
- if asked whether you have any specific skills, emphasise the ones which you think are particularly useful for the post
- in mentioning your achievements, try to identify something you have done which can show personal development or initiative on your part

- make sure that you know the examining board and date of all examinations and qualifications taken or in the process of being taken
- carefully consider the inevitable open-ended questions, such as 'why have you applied for this post?' In order to answer these questions you will need to have carefully read the details about the post including any skills or competences required
- choose your referees with care and make sure that they are well-respected members of the community
- before entering anything on the original application form, make sure that you have answered all of the following questions:
  - have I answered everything?
  - are there any time periods in my life unaccounted for?
  - have I actually answered the questions, or have I simply stated something?
  - is my approach positive?
  - do I think that the reader will gain a favourable impression of me?
  - do I need to attach any proof of qualifications or perhaps a photograph?
  - have I been honest and can I substantiate anything I have claimed?

4.3.4 *Produce and evaluate curricula vitae for clarity and quality of presentation*

CURRICULUM VITAE

A curriculum vitae is normally sent when an organisation asks a candidate to 'send full details'. The purpose of a cv, which means 'course of life' is to summarise all personal details and past experience. The way in which cvs are produced is very much down to the individual. Indeed, cvs should be designed to match the specifications of the job applied for.

The style of the cv should be concise and clear. It should include only the relevant facts and figures and should be in note format.

The content of the cv will obviously depend upon the post you are applying for. You should ensure that it fulfils the following criteria:

- it should be no longer than two sides of A4
- it is a summary
- it is well presented
- the tone is positive and optimistic throughout

Additionally, your cv must be typed and you should keep a copy of it and read it before the interview.

With covering letters which often accompany application forms or cvs, use the following guidelines:

- produce a rough draft
- state the post for which you are applying
- quote any reference numbers
- say where you saw the advertisement
- identify any points made in the cv or application for which relate directly to the post
- give reasons for applying for the post
- state convenient interview dates

NAME

This should normally take the format of the surname in capitals first, with the forenames (Christian names) afterwards. The full name should be included (even if middle names are embarrassing!). The name should also indicate the title desired, such as Mr, Mrs, Ms, Dr and Rev.

DATE OF BIRTH

This can be presented as either a simple numerical date of birth (e.g. 24.4.78) or in full (24th April 1978). The day should always be first, followed by the month and the year.

ADDRESS

This should be in full, with the home number, street, town, county and full postcode. It should be presented in the following way:

House number/street
TOWN
County
POSTCODE

TELEPHONE NUMBER

Again, this should be in full, with the STD first (in brackets), followed by a space, then the rest of the number. Alternative telephone numbers where the applicant may be reached should also be included. If such numbers are given, the applicant should make it clear when he/she may be reached on that number. For example, the applicant may state:

01941–662243   (9–5)
01941–644320   (evenings)

EMPLOYMENT HISTORY

The employment history, particularly if you have been working for some time, can be quite difficult to compile. Some basic rules apply, however:

- always work backwards in time (unless directed otherwise on the application form). In other words, give the latest (last) employer first and then the previous one, and so on
- give employer's name in full, along with address
- if required to state tasks, job role and duties, be brief (you may not have much space). Always mention the most relevant details to the job you are applying for
- give dates (as appropriate), try to be accurate
- if there is a gap in the employment record (in terms of the chronological order) make sure that the potential employer realises that you were doing something else (e.g. education, training or unemployed, etc.)

- be truthful, as the potential employer may check your statements. He/she may actually know someone in the organisation you claimed to work for and may phone them. A lie at this stage will terminate your chance of being considered. Also remember that you are obliged to be truthful and will sign the application stating that you have been truthful and honest
- you may be asked for your salary details here, also be truthful
- you may also be required to give reasons for leaving. This may need to be handled with care if you left in unfortunate circumstances

EDUCATION AND TRAINING

Again, the reverse chronological order system applies here. Start with the last education and training undertaken and work backwards in time. Give accurate dates and clearly and fully state the institution(s) that you attended. If the institution has changed its name or status, try to make sure that you give the new name/address and state what it was formerly called. Do not put your qualifications here in detail as this is covered (normally) under the next section of the application form.

QUALIFICATIONS

There is never enough space to put all of the qualifications in here. If necessary use a separate sheet and mark it 'qualifications'. Put the qualifications in reverse chronological order, along with:

- grades obtained (including special grades)
- examining board

Also detail your 'pending' results and the date by which you expect to have attained them.

OTHER RELEVANT ACHIEVEMENTS

Be brief in this section, do not put in irrelevant or inappropriate achievements. The employer may not be interested if you have a 25-metre swimming certificate (unless you have applied for a job in a swimming pool!). Useful achievements include:

- duties/responsibilities at school or college
- special awards (such as Duke of Edinburgh Award Scheme)
- any press coverage

INTERESTS

An employer does not want to be told that you enjoy 'drinking with your mates' or other such interests. Again, be brief, try to come up with interests (truthfully) that may be of interest to the employer and relevant to the job. Be careful not to say things like 'I enjoy reading eighteenth-century literature' (unless you do) as the employer may ask you about it!

REFERENCES

These should always include your present (or last) employer, or your school or college principal or head teacher as appropriate. Do not use direct family members for your referees. If you can find a person of status or responsibility willing to be your referee, then take up

his/her offer. In most cases, two referees will be sufficient, but occasionally three are asked for. This is comparatively rare, but you should always establish beforehand that all referees are willing to act for you.

student activity

(PC 4.3.4, COM 3.2)
Thinking about your own curriculum vitae and the need to obtain referees, write a list of people you feel you could approach to provide a reference for you.

4.3.5 *Practise and appraise interviewer techniques*

INTERVIEWER TECHNIQUES

The interview has two basic purposes:

- to help in choosing the employee
- to help the employee choose the organisation

It is important to structure the interview in such a way as to enable the organisation to find out as much as possible about the applicant and similarly for the applicant to find out as much as possible about the organisation. All essential information should be on hand and the interviewer should pre-prepare questions and answers to potential questions from the interviewee. Let us look at the good practice recommended for interviewers:

OPENING THE INTERVIEW

A few minutes should be spent in putting the applicant at ease. It may be a good idea to open the interview with some questions about his/her interests.

Normally, it is advisable to help set the scene by addressing the following:

- *perceptions* – making sure that the physical surroundings are private. There should be no interruptions or phone calls, etc. Think about the siting of the chairs and tables too
- *social* – make sure that the candidate is greeted

properly and is offered tea/coffee, etc.
- *facts* – help the candidate understand the purpose and content of the interview, tell him or her what to expect

ASKING QUESTIONS

There are many techniques that can be adopted in the asking of questions to interviewees. Some of the more successful are:

1 Ask **open questions** that require the candidate to give more than a simple yes or no response. Remember that you want to know what the candidate is really like.
2 Use **silence** as a way of getting more out of the interviewee.
3 Do **not talk** for more than 30 per cent of the interview time.
4 Try to be **flexible.** If you have a pre-prepared list of questions, do not stick slavishly to them.
5 Take **notes,** but do not be too interested in getting things down on paper at the expense of listening to what the candidate is saying.
6 Make sure that the candidate is willing to accept the job, if offered.
7 If the candidate is suitable, give details about the job and request some feedback on 'how they feel about that'. If not, do not bother with this line of questioning.

ASKING FOLLOW-ON QUESTIONS

Follow-on questions can often reveal more than the initial enquiry. It is not advisable, if you want to get the most out of the interviewee to leap into asking another question before the interviewee has had a chance to finish what he/she was saying.

Always try to use follow-on questions to help the interviewee develop what he/she has said.

It is always a good idea to ask the candidate whether he/she wants to ask anything. You can use this also to get the candidate to tell you about his/her qualities that match the job that may not already have been addressed or included on the application form.

Follow-on questions should be formed in such a way as to clarify, amplify or expand on matters that have been touched upon in initial questioning.

The questions should be fair and not designed to make the candidate feel ill at ease. The level of complexity is obviously important here. The key is, perhaps, not to get too bogged down in the nitty-gritty of detail. An interview is over so quickly that it may be difficult for both parties to gain a fair impression of one another.

USING BODY LANGUAGE

The spoken language is not the only useful form of communication. Body language (or non-verbal communication) is a powerful tool. It can either support what you are saying or undermine it, particularly if the body language is inappropriate.

The following list is an attempt to identify good practice in relation to body language on the part of an interviewer (although many of these features would be useful to the interviewee also):

1 Always face the interviewee.
2 Do not sit directly opposite (this is too aggressive).
3 Try to be natural.
4 Try to have a receptive (relaxed) posture.
5 Try to lean slightly towards the interviewee (this shows an interest in him/her and what he/she is saying).
6 Try to match the body language of the interviewee (but be careful not to look as if you are imitating him/her).
7 Do not dress differently from how you would normally dress for work.
8 Do not behave any differently from your normal behaviour.
9 Try not to be threatening.
10 Use direct eye contact when appropriate.

student activity

(PC 4.3.5, COM 3.1, 3.2)

Here are some good questions for an interviewer to ask at the interview stage. They are designed to get the candidate to reveal a little more about him/herself and are all examples of open questions. These types of questions are often best since there is no pre-determined response. The questions are:

1 What is your current boss like, how would you rate him/her?
2 What aspects of your work do you find the easiest and the most difficult?
3 What has been your greatest success to date?
4 What are your strengths and weaknesses?
5 Why did you apply for this job?
6 What worries you about this job you are applying for, and what excites you about it?
7 Can you describe your ideal boss?
8 What has been your greatest failure to date?
9 How will your friends and family react if you need to move because of this job?
10 What is the most attractive feature of this job which encouraged you to apply?

In pairs, try these questions out on one another. How clear and believable are the answers? Do you think that you are prepared for questions such as these? Keep a written record of your responses.

If you need a job to focus on, then use the support materials (SM 3) that follow the assignment at the end of this Element.

We will see later, from the other side of the interview table, what the interviewer should be doing in terms of body language.

CLOSING THE INTERVIEW

The candidate should feel, by this stage, that he/she has had ample opportunity to respond to all of the questions and to leave the interviewer in no doubt about any of the details or meanings. The interviewer will normally say 'we will need to finish shortly' and then begin to summarise what has been said. The interviewee also needs a last chance to add or clarify.

The full close should include a handshake and thanks from the interviewer. The interviewee should also know when to expect a decision or what is the next stage of the selection process (e.g. a test or second interview).

It is important to leave the candidate at ease and ensure that an ongoing relationship has been established.

GIVING FEEDBACK

As we mentioned in the section on dealing with unsuccessful candidates, giving feedback is vital, both for the employer (to justify his/her decision) and for the employee (to understand his/her shortcomings).

For the successful candidate, this feedback process is equally important, if not more so. The successful candidate should be made aware of any potential failings that he/she has displayed. It is important also for the employer to identify these as they may be the basis upon which decisions are made in regard to training and development of the employee.

A formal appraisal at this stage is relatively rare, but an interviewer should be in a position to offer some

information to the successful candidate and perhaps suggest that certain employee training take place.

It should not be assumed that the successful candidate exactly fits all of the criteria required by the employer. Both parties need to be aware of this and should also be in agreement with the assessment and tone of the feedback information.

student activity

(PC 4.3.5, COM 3.1)
As a group, consider the following two situations:

- feedback that it would be necessary to give to a very poor interviewee
- feedback that it would be necessary to give to a very good interviewee

4.3.6 *Practise and appraise interviewee techniques*

Having reached the interview stage in the recruitment process, the candidate will have received a letter which tells him/her the date and time of the interview. It is now time for the candidate to begin preparations for the interview phase itself. This section will consider the nature of these preparations and aspects of interview technique, including:

- assertiveness
- body language
- framing questions
- listening skills

PREPARING

The potential interviewee will reply to the organisation with a letter or telephone call accepting the interview date. As we advised earlier in this Unit, the candidate will have kept photocopies of the application documents. Now is the time for him/her to re-read all of this documentation and begin to draft a list of possible

questions which might be asked. As we mentioned earlier, it would be wise for him/her to find out as much as possible about the organisation. Specifically, this information should include:

- the nature of the organisation
- the products and services of the organisation
- the markets in which the organisation is involved
- the typical customer of the organisation
- the obvious competitors of the organisation

This information may be obtained from company reports, articles in the press, libraries or, if the candidate is particularly keen, by trying to obtain a tour of the organisation.

The final phases of preparation for the interview should include the following:

- knowing the most reliable and direct route to the organisation
- testing this route beforehand, if possible
- listening to the radio on the day of the interview to find out if there are any traffic hold-ups

- choosing suitable clothes to wear at the interview
- ensuring one is well groomed
- males should have shaved or ensured that their beard is neatly trimmed
- females should not wear too much make-up
- ensuring sufficient travelling time to allow for any possible delays
- in the event of arriving early, the candidate should not enter the premises more than 10–15 minutes before the expected arrival time

SHOWING CONFIDENCE

The question of assertiveness needs to be carefully considered. The interviewee must attempt to get his/her point of view across at all costs, but should not be too aggressive. With regard to speech itself, he/she should take heed of the following points:

- while replying to a question, he/she must look at the person asking the question
- be positive and optimistic in his/her response
- he/she must not lie
- he/she must always answer the question that has been asked; if he/she does not understand, then he/she should ask for the question to be repeated

USING BODY LANGUAGE

The effective use of non-verbal communication is essential in making full use of one's communication skills. In essence, the interviewee should attempt:

- not to fidget
- to take care not to use distracting mannerisms
- to use appropriate facial expressions to express oneself
- to use the hands for appropriate gestures

Typically, non-verbal communication relates to the following parts of the body:

- head
- hands
- fingers
- legs
- feet

Interviewers will be looking at how the interviewee sits and whether he/she displays signs of nervousness and discomfort.

The 'reading' of body language requires a great deal of experience. It is not expected that the interviewee (unless he/she has attended many interviews) will be able to 'read' the messages being given by the interviewer.

As an interviewee you can train yourself both in the use and the reading of body language by applying these basic principles:

- always try to read the body language in the light of what the speaker is saying
- style of dress can give clues about the meaning of body language
- an individual who avoids eye contact may not actually mean what he/she is saying or does not mean it with conviction
- look out for complex multiple or groups of body language signs. A single body language action may not give sufficient clues as to what is actually meant

student activity

(PC 4.3.6, COM 3.1)
Try out body language techniques with a partner. In turns try to convey the following messages without saying anything:

- surprise
- pleasure
- frustration
- boredom
- anger
- nervousness
- alertness
- interest
- attention
- friendship

How do your interpretations differ from those of your partner?

LISTENING TO QUESTIONS

Just as it is important for the interviewee to develop speaking skills in the interview situation, it is also most important to make full use of all listening skills. For a good communicator, listening is as essential as speaking. Particular listening skills include the following:

- concentration on what is being said
- avoiding distractions
- preventing the mind from wandering
- repeating key words or phrases to oneself
- paying particular attention to the gesture and posture of the speaker

- looking at the speaker's non-verbal communication
- being alert for pauses in the speaker's speech
- being ready to respond when required
- giving the speaker feedback, perhaps by nodding
- being alert for opportunities to give personal responses

student activity

(PC 4.3.6, COM 3.1)
Can you think of six questions that you would wish to ask at an interview? Why would they be necessary? Discuss this in pairs.

RESPONDING TO QUESTIONS

Remember that an interview is an information gathering exercise for both you and the interviewer. To give short or non-committal answers to questions will not leave a good impression. Above all, you should not be frightened to say what you believe. The only thing to remember is that you should only really comment on things that you know about. It serves no useful purpose to show understanding when you patently do not understand. This only makes the speaker appear foolish.

The interviewer will, usually, attempt to frame questions in such a way as to get particular responses from you. These question types include the following:

1 *Trust questions* – where the interviewer will ask something that indicates that he/she has faith in your judgement. A typical question would be: 'There is a big problem with sickness at the moment and it causes difficulties in getting orders out to customers in time. What do you think we should do about it?' Be careful here not to make any assumptions; you may not know the organisation well enough to be able to give any detailed advice. Try to be general, but never say 'I don't know'.

2 *Clarifying questions* – in this type of question the interviewer will ask whether you actually understand something fully. An example of this would be: 'You know that we use a computerised stock control system: do you think that you could operate it?' Be truthful again, if you have experience in computers, then this is fine, but do not say you know how to use a system that you do not really understand.

3 *Empathising questions* – these deal with the problems and concerns that the candidate may have. A typical question would be: 'How do you feel about taking a rather junior position in the organisation?'

4 *Open questions* – although we have addressed these already, we should emphasise that these do not really have a right or wrong answer. It is rather the case that the candidate is given the fullest opportunity to reflect and give depth to an answer. These should be used as often as possible.

There is another set of questions that may be asked and these require a slightly different approach. These are:

5 *Criticisms* – where the interviewer may make a statement which expresses some doubt about your experience or ability to do the job. In these cases, a simple response which illustrates that you are capable will suffice. If you do not have the qualities, then do not attempt to bluff the situation out. Honesty is, as they say, the best policy.

6 *Testing* – these questions attempt to determine whether the candidate is capable of making a right or wrong decision regarding a certain question. The interviewer may have preconceived ideas about the correct answer. It is difficult to double-guess what will be required of you. Some clues may be given, by accident, in the body language of the interviewer. If you are certain that you know the right answer, then stick to your guns and say it. A clear response is a good one, regardless of whether the interviewer thinks your answer is correct.

7 *Leading* – these questions attempt to get the candidate to respond in the manner that the interviewer expects. In most cases, it may be a good idea to go along with the interviewer's intentions. If the candidate does respond in the way expected, this may stop any further questions along this line of enquiry.

8 *Closed* – again, as we have mentioned earlier, the interviewer may use this type of question when he/she requires a quick or simple response. Normally, the expected response is either 'yes' or 'no'. In other cases, the candidate may be required to give a date, time, or other straightforward response. These questions do not give the candidate the opportunity to talk about the subject or expand on his/her simple response.

ASKING QUESTIONS

We have already mentioned the nature of questions which may be asked by the interviewer or interview panel. The nature of any question asked by the interviewee should take the following into account:

- he/she should ensure that his/her questions are clear and understood

- he/she should ensure that his/her questions are not covering matters already dealt with
- the questions should not be of the sort that could be considered to be sarcastic or cynical
- the interviewee should not try to be funny
- questions should be asked at the appropriate time
- the interviewee should never butt in or interrupt one of the interviewing panel

Generally speaking, skills include:

- careful control of accent
- clear pronunciation
- good articulation, with particular attention to fully rounded endings to words
- emphasis on the key part of answer or question
- projection of the voice so that all of the panel can hear

BEING CLEAR AND CONCISE

The situation may not offer much opportunity for the candidate to be clear and concise. After all, the candidate can only respond (as well as he/she can) to the questions posed by the interviewer or panel.

The general rule is to make statements that are easy to understand and clear of ambiguities. In this respect, regardless of the nature of the question, take your time and consider what you are saying. Try to say what you want to say and do not leave statements 'up in the air' or unsubstantiated. Always remember that the interview time is restricted. The interviewer has a list of questions and areas of enquiry and he/she may wish to move along fairly rapidly. It is the candidate's responsibility, and in his/her own best interests, to make sure that there is no room for misunderstanding. The interviewer should always be left with the impression that the candidate has fully addressed the questions and given a satisfactory response. It is always better to give a clear and concise response than to waffle about a subject that you are unsure about. A good interviewer will notice this and try to cut the candidate short if he/she thinks that the candidate is wasting or 'playing for' time.

The appraisal of your performance as both interviewer and interviewee will be contained in the Assignment at the end of this Element. This will include an appraisal of the interaction between yourself and the interviewer or interviewee and the success or failure of the meeting. In addition to this, you will also be appraised of your performance in terms of meeting legal and ethical obligations and responsibilities.

4.3.7 Explain and give examples of legal obligations and ethical responsibilities in recruitment procedures and interviews

LEGAL OBLIGATIONS AND ETHICAL RESPONSIBILITIES

Laws relating to the recruitment of staff have already been considered in Unit 2 and elsewhere in this Unit. However, there are a number of specific legal obligations about interviewing of prospective employees.

If an organisation fails to comply with legal requirements then an individual may have recourse to law via a court or industrial tribunal. To avoid possible legal action an organisation would ensure that the recruitment criteria are clear and that any terms of employment are made obvious to the candidate. We need to consider both equal opportunities and obligations regarding the contract of employment in this section.

The main point to remember is that both parties are bound by legal obligations and there is an implicit acceptance of ethical issues such as honesty and integrity. At all stages, both for the interviewer and the candidates, there may be confidential matters that need to be handled with tact, diplomacy and, above all, secrecy.

EQUAL OPPORTUNITIES

We would not be incorrect in stating that it is an organisation's right to choose an individual for a particular post. However, there are a number of pieces of legislation which limit this freedom of choice.

Under the Disabled Persons (Employment) Act 1958, an employer with more than a certain number of employees is required to employ a minimum of 3 per cent of the workforce as registered disabled persons. The only exception to this is if the organisation has an exemption certificate.

Similarly, the Rehabilitation of Offenders Act 1974 protects ex-offenders from discrimination on the grounds of their past life. The Act states that an individual who has a past conviction need not mention 'spent' convictions on his/her job application forms or at interview. He/she must, however, mention any convictions that are not 'spent'. (The length of time that must pass before a conviction is 'spent' depends on the gravity of the offence.)

Under the Employment Protection (Consolidation) Act 1978 an individual cannot be discriminated against on the basis of union membership.

In certain cases, prospective employees are discriminated against on the ground of:

- racial origin
- gender
- sexual orientation
- religion
- age
- disabilities

Legislation now exists to protect prospective employees in all of these circumstances. The legislation covering most of the above reasons for discrimination is contained in the Race Relations Act 1976 and the Sex Discrimination Act 1975.

CONTRACT OF EMPLOYMENT

The tricky problem regarding employment contracts concerns when the contract of employment actually begins. A job advertisement is not an offer of a contract. However, if a candidate is offered the job, then the contract of employment has, in effect, begun. An additional problem here is that an employer may choose to place conditions upon the acceptance of the individual for the post. Particularly, these may relate to the following:

- the taking up of satisfactory references
- the perusal of an educational qualifications certificate
- a medical examination

If the prospective employee fails to fulfil any of the above, then the offer of the post is invalid.

ETHICAL RESPONSIBILITIES

It is in the best interests of both the interviewee and the organisation to ensure that honesty and objectivity prevail throughout the recruitment process. We shall look at these two fundamental ethical obligations in more detail:

HONESTY

It is prudent for the organisation to act in an honest and upright fashion throughout the recruitment process since it does not wish to mislead prospective employees. Great resentment will occur if an employee subsequently discovers that claims and promises made by an organisation during the recruitment process are not capable of being fulfilled. The organisation does not wish to gain a reputation for untruthfulness as this may deter prospective applicants for other posts from applying.

OBJECTIVITY

Objectivity is a key element at every stage of the recruitment process. All those involved in the recruitment process should ensure that they consider only the facts in assessing applicants. An application form often asks whether the applicant knows any individual working for the organisation. If he/she does know someone else, then it is in the best interests of both the individual and the organisation to ensure that this person does not have any input into the recruitment process.

Objectivity should ensure that the organisation chooses the best candidate for the available post and that no other criteria such as prejudices or preferences have had an influence upon the selection.

Although the issues of honesty and objectivity are not necessarily covered in employment law, an organisation wishing to abide by the spirit of these pieces of legislation, as well as prevailing acceptable behaviour, should attempt to take note of both of these considerations.

FAIRNESS

In addition to the considerations in regard to the different forms of discrimination, there is an ethical issue involved in the question of fairness.

Fairness, at all stages of the recruitment process, is essential for the employer. The notion of fairness itself is a difficult one, as how can you actually measure or monitor this subjective judgement of behaviour? The employer needs to leave the candidate in no doubt that he/she has been dealt with fairly. It is quite easy to do this if the employer keeps the candidate informed at all times and to explain (if possible and relevant) why his/her application has not been successful. As the selection process continues the number of candidates will obviously shrink. The employer should continue this policy of giving information and be prepared to debrief as required and at the correct points of the process.

It is also a good idea, and a policy which should ideally be adopted in all cases, for an employer to tell unsuccessful candidates (in particular) why the successful candidate had been chosen. The employer should state what it was about this individual that caused him/her to be chosen, what qualities he/she had, what aspects of the procedure brought these qualities out.

Occasionally the recruitment procedure may be reduced to the level of a farce. This may happen if the employer has already decided on the candidate before the interviews even take place. These cases tend to involve an 'internal' candidate. This means that one of the candidates either works (or worked) for the employer, or is well known to the employer already. For an employer to claim that the recruitment process was fair in these circumstances may be very difficult. However, even when there is a 'preferred' candidate, all steps should be taken not to allow bias to enter into the process. There may be, after all, a better candidate on the short list and the employer may be making the wrong decision in appointing the known individual.

CONFIDENTIALITY

There are legal obligations regarding the confidentiality of information about the candidates (who may later be employees). These obligations refer particularly to personal details. Many of these considerations are included in the employment legislation of the Data Protection Act.

On the other side of the coin, the candidate should respect the wishes of the potential employer to keep certain matters secret. Obviously, the employer would be foolish to reveal too much information at the interview stage. When the candidate has been appointed very different criteria and circumstances apply.

During the recruitment process, it should be remembered that the candidates owe no allegiance to the employer and cannot be expected to understand what is confidential and what is not.

In some situations, a potential employer may require a candidate to sign a non-disclosure statement which legally obliges him/her not to divulge any information about the organisation that he/she may have gained during the recruitment procedures. It may be difficult to police this non-disclosure agreement once the candidate has proved unsuccessful and a certain amount of time has passed.

A candidate applying for a government post may be required to sign the Official Secrets Act. This is a long-term, legally binding agreement that states that no information may be released to others who have not signed the agreement. Any individual who subsequently does divulge information regarding the government organisation concerned may face criminal proceedings as a matter of course.

Normally, however, candidates are not exposed to situations or opportunities that could compromise the secrecy of an organisation. Employers should take steps to ensure that candidates are not put into awkward positions as a result of what they have been told or have witnessed.

ELEMENT 4.3

assignment

(PC 4.3.1–7, COM 3.2, 3.2, 3.3, 3.4, IT 3.1, 3.2, 3.3)
This Assignment, designed to fulfil all of the performance criteria of this Element, is a practical one. It requires you to look at the recruitment procedures in some detail. It is wise to tackle the tasks in the correct order, since there is a level of evaluation required. It will be impossible to evaluate certain procedures.

TASK I

(PC 4.3.1)
Write a report based on the recruitment procedures used by organisations. You may choose the procedures adopted by either:

● a business itself
● a recruitment agency

Your report should focus on the problems that may arise in attracting suitable employees as well as recruiting employees for specific job roles.

TASK 2

(PC 4.3.2)

You must now write two job descriptions with matching person specifications. Also comment on how successful these job descriptions and person specifications have been in matching the applicants contained in the source material that follows this assignment (SM 1)

TASK 3

(PC 4.3.3, 4.3.4)

Write two letters of applications and two curriculum vitae. One should be your own and the other should use the source material that follows this assignment (SM 2). Your cv should have the following qualities:

- clear language
- good appearance
- relevant to job applied for (see (SM3)

TASK 4

(PC 4.3.5)

Prepare two different interview appraisal forms relating to the following:

- one should be a record of self-appraisal
- one should be for appraisal by others (such as staff, peers or visitors)

You will need these for the next task, so prepare these in advance.

TASK 5

(PC 4.3.5)

Having applied for either a real job or the job detailed in SM 3, you must now undertake an interview. You will be observed during the interview.

TASK 6

(PC 4.3.6)

In the role of the interviewer, interview another student for the job detailed in SM 3.

TASK 7

(PC 4.3.5–6)

Having now undertaken the roles of interviewer and interviewee in two different interview situations, you should appraise the following:

- your own performance in demonstrating the various interviewer and interviewee techniques
- provide a commentary on the interaction between the interviewer and interviewee in both situations
- prepare a statement which assesses whether the interview was a success in terms of meeting:
    – its intended purpose
    – legal obligations
    – ethical responsibilities

This statement should be presented in the form of a word processed memorandum to your tutor

TASK 8

(PC 4.3.7)

Using the interview appraisal forms as a basis, write notes which explain the following and say how they relate to the recruitment process:

- racial discrimination
- sexual discrimination
- unethical behaviour

Source material

SM 1: Details of ten candidates

Name: **Ben Hornsby**
Age: 18
Gender: Male
Qualifications: 5 GCSE at C
　　　　　　　GNVQ Advanced Business
Experience: Holiday work in small hotel
　Saturday job in retail outlet

Name: **Richard Ford**
Age: 19
Gender: Male
Qualifications: GNVQ Intermediate Business
　　　　　　　GNVQ Advanced Business
　　　　　　　RSA 1 Word processing
Experience: Evening bar work

Name: **Penny Oliver**
Age: 18
Gender: 　　　Female
Qualifications: 8 GCSE at grade C
Experience: Full-time clerical post (one year) in engineering company

Name: **Brian O'Connell**
Age: 20
Gender: Male
Qualifications 3 GCSE at grade C
Experience 4 years as accounts clerk in a Chartered Accountant's office

Name: **Holly Bryant**
Age: 24
Gender Female
Qualifications RSA 1, 2 and 3 typewriting
　　　　　　　Teeline shorthand 80 wpm
Experience: Secretarial work in various organisations through a temporary agency

Name: **Stuart Davis**
Age: 18
Gender: Male
Qualifications 7 GCSE at level C
　　　　　　　GNVQ Advanced Business
　　　　　　　A level Economics
Experience: 4 weeks work experience only

Name: **Andrew Jones**
Age: 17
Gender: Male
Qualifications: 2 GCSE at level C
　　　　　　　GNVQ Intermediate Business
　　　　　　　RSA Core Text Processing
Experience: Saturday job in a DIY superstore

Name: **Emma Wilkins**
Age: 18
Gender Female
Qualifications: 7 GCSE at level C
　　　　　　　A level Business Studies
　　　　　　　A level Economics
　　　　　　　A level Accounts
Experience: Saturday job as waitress in a hotel

Name: **Fiona Sherman**
Age: 19
Gender: Female
Qualifications: 5 GCSE level C
　　　　　　　BTEC National Diploma in Business
　　　　　　　and Finance
Experience: Shop assistant in Marks and Spencer plc

Name: **Bradley Landale**
Age: 19
Gender: Male
Qualifications: 3 GCSE level C
Experience: 1 year accounts clerk in an oil company
　　　　　　　1 year trainee manager in Sainsburys
　　　　　　　6 months building site work

SM 2: Other candidate with experience

Sally James is 22 years old and left college three years ago after successfully completing a BTEC National Diploma in Business and Finance. Her results were very good and she managed to achieve merits across all of her subject areas. Whilst at school Sally achieved B grades at GCSE in Maths and English, with C grades in Human Biology, Geography, French and Double Science.

Since leaving college Sally has been working for a local firm of surveyors, where she began as an administrative assistant. Having held this post for six months, she was promoted to Office Manager, after the previous postholder retired. Sally is now shadowing one of the surveyors with a view to taking professional qualifications in surveying. She has proved to be a valuable member of staff and her employers think very highly of her. She has significantly improved the efficiency of the office and has shown great initiative.

Whilst at college Sally worked three evenings a week as a waitress in a restaurant and also worked as a shop assistant in Woolworths on Saturdays.

Sally is a keen swimmer and has achieved her Bronze medal for life saving. Her other leisure interests include horse riding, walking and going to nightclubs.

Her referees are her current employer (Karen Irving) and her course tutor (David Walker).

SM 3: Job advertisements and details

WANTED

IMMEDIATE STARTER

Exciting new job opportunity
with

HUGHES AND HENDERSON LTD.

Can you head up and develop a new department for this respected company? A recent joint venture has been established with a French company to market a range of decorative ceramics and terracota tiles in the UK and Ireland. This will mean starting a business from scratch. Are you up to the challenge? You will need to have business qualifications and the ability to communicate.

If you are a HIGHLY MOTIVATED and AMBITIOUS 18–25 year old, and possess SELLING SKILLS, then send your cv to:

Harold Henderson (Director)
Hughes and Henderson Ltd.
6 Kings Road
Wells
Somerset
BA4 5LU

UNIT 4

test questions

Focus 1

EMPLOYER/EMPLOYEE RIGHTS AND RESPONSIBILITIES

I The following two statements have been made:

(i) direct discrimination involves treating a woman less favourably than a man because she is a woman
(ii) indirect discrimination involves favouring one sex more than another for justifiable reasons
How are these statements best described?
(a) True/True
(b) True/False
(c) False/True
(d) False.False

2 Which of the following methods would not normally be employed by an organisation to clarify its business objectives to its employees?

(a) press statements
(b) staff meetings
(c) company newspapers
(d) television advertising

3 Approximately what percentage of individuals in professional occupations are women?

(a) 12%
(b) 22%
(c) 32%
(d) 42%

4 With regard to the implementation and monitoring of health and safety legislation, whose responsibility is it?

(a) the employer
(b) the employees
(c) both employer and employees
(d) the Health and Safety Executive

Focus 2

PROCEDURES FOR EMPLOYERS/EMPLOYEES

5 In cases of dispute between the employer and the employee, which is the correct sequence of appeals?

(a) ACAS, court action, industrial tribunal, House of Lords
(b) ACAS, industrial tribunal, court action, Employment Appeals Tribunal
(c) industrial tribunal, Employment Appeals Tribunal, ACAS, court action
(d) court action, industrial tribunal, ACAS, House of Lords

6–8 The following are different forms of action which can be taken by employees and trades unions:

(a) work to rule
(b) withdrawal of goodwill
(c) blacking
(d) days of action

Which of the above are described in the following questions:

6 Temporary withdrawal of labour

(a) (b) (c) (d)

7 Following only the procedures and regulations as laid down by the employer

(a) (b) (c) (d)

8 Refusing to handle the products of certain organisations or countries

(a) (b) (c) (d)

9 Which of the following types of union cater for workers who are employed in one particular industry?

(a) craft unions
(b) industrial unions
(c) occupational unions
(d) general unions

10 Which of the following statements is true or false?

(i) quality circles must have at least 10 members
(ii) quality circles aim to use untapped knowledge from the factory floor

(a) True/True
(b) True/False
(c) False/True
(d) False/False

Focus 3

JOB ROLES AND RESPONSIBILITIES

11 In which category of job type would you put a carpenter's mate?

(a) skilled
(b) semi-skilled
(c) unskilled
(d) professional

12 Which of the following is NOT a team role as described by Belbin?

(a) the shaper
(b) the plant
(c) the extrovert
(d) the team worker

13 Two of the following techniques are used in appraisal systems. Identify the correct two techniques:

(i) checks on time keeping
(ii) behaviourally anchored rating scales
(iii) critical incidents reports
(iv) accident reports

(a) (i) and (ii)
(b) (i) and (iv)
(c) (ii) and (iii)
(d) (iii) and (iv)

14 The following two statements have been made in relation to job rotation:

(i) an organisation must take care not to rotate staff too often
(ii) an individual who moves from one boring job to another will gain no benefit

How are the statements best described?

(a) True/True
(b) True/False
(c) False/True
(d) False/False

15 Gross misconduct is a legitimate reason for dismissing an employee. Which of the following does not fall into this category?

(a) theft
(b) insubordination
(c) breaking safety rules
(d) sickness

16 Unfair dismissal can occur as a result of action taken by the employer in breach of government legislation. Which of the following would be considered to be an unfair dismissal situation?

(a) fighting at work
(b) computer hacking
(c) pregnancy
(d) sleeping at work

Focus 4

WORKING CONDITIONS

17 Decide whether the following two statements are true with regard to fixed short-term contracts:

(i) they are non-standard contracts that have come about as a result of organisations needing to be more competitive
(ii) they have come about so that employers can change their work force regularly

How are these statements best described?

(a) True/True
(b) True/False
(c) False/True
(d) False/False

18 Which European country offers the most attractive number of annual leave and public holidays:

(a) UK
(b) Greece
(c) France
(d) Spain

19–21 Employees often work under very different sets of working conditions, particularly in relation to the hours worked. These include:

(a) compressed annual hours
(b) compressed working weeks
(c) flexi-hours
(d) shifts

Which of the above are best described by the following statements?

19 Working non-standard hours so that the production line is manned at all times

(a) (b) (c) (d)

20 Working core hours plus making up the balance of the working week to suit the individual

(a) (b) (c) (d)

21 Working a four-day week

(a) (b) (c) (d)

Focus 5
RECRUITMENT AND SELECTION

22 Job centres are a useful place to advertise and recruit for a number of different jobs. Which of the following types of occupation would NOT be suitable for advertising at a job centre?

(a) unskilled manual workers
(b) senior managers
(c) trainees
(d) skilled manual workers

23 Once a candidate accepts a job offer what final checks should be made by the employer?

(a) check references and carry out a medical examination
(b) check references and previous pay slips
(c) carry out a medical examination and check previous pay slips
(d) check references and obtain bank details

24 A staff handbook can be a very valuable source of information for the employee. Which of the following would not normally be contained within a staff handbook?

(a) medical facilities available
(b) canteen facilities available
(c) a statement of the company's financial position
(d) disciplinary and grievance procedures

25 A person specification covers the main characteristics which will be required to undertake the job. Aptitudes of the individual refer to which of the following:

(a) current attainments
(b) physical appearance
(c) leisure interests
(d) listening and communication skills

26 Detailing your employment history is an important feature both for a cv and for the completion of an application form. Which of the following is a basic requirement in providing this information?

(a) giving the history in reverse chronological order
(b) only mentioning the most senior posts held
(c) providing references from each post held
(d) ensuring that a full address is given for each ex-employer, including the post code

Focus 6
INTERVIEWER/INTERVIEWEE TECHNIQUES

27 Non-verbal communication can be best described as:

(a) not saying anything
(b) using body language
(c) making an application for a job in writing
(d) not talking too much

28 When closing an interview, the interviewer should do the following:

(a) say that the interview is over and show the candidate out of the room
(b) tell the candidate immediately whether he/she has been successful or unsuccessful
(c) shake the candidate's hand and thank him/her for coming
(d) write some comments immediately before telling the candidate that the interview is over

29 Closed questions may be used during an interview. However, open questions are a better method of getting the most out of the candidate. Which of the following is NOT an example of a closed question?

(a) what is your age?
(b) what do you think of your current boss?
(c) how long have you been working for your current employer?
(d) what is your current salary?

30 What is a non-disclosure agreement?

(a) an undertaking by the employer not to terminate employment
(b) an undertaking by the employer not to close the factory
(c) an undertaking by the employee not to divulge information about the organisation
(d) an undertaking by the employee not to work for another organisation during his/her period of employment

Analyse production in businesses

PERFORMANCE CRITERIA

A student must:

*1 identify added value in production and ways to **achieve added value***

*2 explain **why businesses aim to add value***

*3 identify and give examples of **factors** which can contribute to **change in production***

*4 **analyse improvements in production***

RANGE

Ways to achieve added value: *quality assurance, productivity, just-in-time (JIT) production, using human resources effectively*

Why businesses aim to add value: *to meet international competition, to meet customer requirements, to improve profit, to survive and grow*

Factors: *price, technology (management information systems (MIS)), robotics, automation, computer-aided design (CAD), computer-aided manufacturing (CAM), contracting out, single sourcing, labour flexibility, legislation, competition, quality standards*

Analyse *in terms of cause of change: impact on production, research and development needed; human resourcing changes; changing customer and supplier relations*

Improvements in production: *better productivity, quality assurance, investing in (research and development, training, technology), reducing pollution, changing working methods*

5.1.1 *Analyse production and ways to achieve added value*

WAYS TO ACHIEVE ADDED VALUE

It may be valuable to look at the more technical side of the added value issue in Unit 6 after having read this Element. It should give you a more complete understanding of the concept as well as a realisation of the economic implications. In this Element, we will be looking at the concept of added value throughout the production process and looking at ways in which the production process can be amended to accommodate the need for added value.

When we consider the concept of production, in its most practical and relevant definition, we can identify it as meaning all the processes which add value to a product or service. We should consider that added value is as applicable to the public sector as it is to the private sector.

VALUE ANALYSIS AND VALUE ENGINEERING

In many respects the concepts of value analysis and value engineering amount to the same thing. Both are organised approaches which aim to achieve high performance at a low cost without affecting the quality. Some people use the term **value engineering** to describe the design of **new products** and **value analysis** in relation to **existing products**.

Value analysis is a common-sense approach to the design or redesign of products, addressing the following matters:

- the determination of the functions of the product
- the development of alternative designs
- the ascertaining of the costs involved
- the evaluation of the alternatives

The needs of the customer would also be factored into the analysis:

- what functions does the customer require of the product?
- what is the appearance of the product, is it acceptable and what the customer is expecting?
- what is the esteem (or snob value) of the product?
- what is the apparent value of the product as far as the customer is concerned in terms of his/her appreciation of the materials used and the labour content?
- what will be the replacement, exchange or disposal value of the product once the customer has finished with it?

Thoughts will then turn to the question of value improvement:

- which areas appear to offer the greatest potential for savings?
- what percentage of the total cost of the product is made up of the costs of items bought in (from other suppliers)?
- what is the percentage of the total costs that can be attributed to labour?
- what is the percentage of the total costs that can be related to materials used?

The total cost of the product is often largely made up of the costs of the bought-in elements of the product. The organisation undertaking the analysis will look at the following in relation to these costs:

- how much do these items contribute to the total value of the product?
- how much do these items contribute to the total cost of the product?
- are all of the features and specifications used at present necessary to maintain the product's quality?
- can any of the components used be substituted for other, less costly, components?
- is there a standard part that can be used for a variety of different products?
- will the adoption of an alternative design mean that the new version of the product can fulfil the same functions?

The first step in the value analysis investigation should include the collection of information:

- about the costs
- about the function of the product
- about the customers' requirements
- from archives about the history of the product
- about the future development of the product design
- from archives and from research about future intentions with regard to the manufacturing process

At this stage, in the attempt to find ways to cut costs and to look for alternative designs and production processes, no reasonable suggestions or alternatives should be ruled out. In this respect, the organisation needs to consider the following in setting the objectives of the value analysis:

- elimination of parts and operations that may not be necessary
- simplification of parts and operations that could be replaced or amended
- the substitution of alternative materials should these prove to be as reliable as those used at present
- the adoption of standard parts that could be used across a range of different products and operations
- the relaxation of manufacturing tolerances (the requirements of the production process that may involve the setting of particular standards and stringent quality checks)
- the utilisation of standard manufacturing techniques
- the elimination of certain unnecessary design features
- the adoption of certain design features that may facilitate manufacture
- the purchase of certain parts and components from suppliers if this should prove to be less expensive than producing them within the organisation itself
- the use of pre-finished materials (again obtained in a part-processed form from a supplier)
- the use of pre-fabricated parts from suppliers
- the rationalisation of the product range
- the substitution of a lower cost manufacturing process
- the rationalisation of the purchase of components, parts and materials from suppliers
- the elimination of waste

QUALITY ASSURANCE

Quality Assurance (QA) is an attempt to ensure that the organisation adopts a series of quality **standards** that have been agreed as part of a system to achieve **customer satisfaction**. In essence, QA tries to address the following concerns:

- the **time and effort** put into product design
- the **technology** used in product design
- the **quality** of the components, materials and parts used
- the **commitment** and efforts of the employees
- the setting up of a **system** that **monitors** and records the quality issues associated with product design and production
- the assurance that the organisation can and, will **deliver on time** with the correct orders of a suitability **high** level of **quality**
- that the organisation is geared up to be able to offer good **advice** before, during and after the sale has been made

An American writer, L P Sullivan, identified seven stages to achieve organisation-wide quality control. He uses two shorthand terms throughout his appraisal of the quality control process, these are:

1. TQC – Total Quality Control, which means that there is a system in place that integrates all the different departments of an organisation in such a way as to ensure that the quality concept is standard and adopted by all parts of the organisation. The main aim, of course, is to achieve complete customer satisfaction with the product and with all of the allied and support systems offered by the organisation. The central issue for this concept is the management of quality control systems which address the following:

   - the specification of the product
   - the customer's expectations of the product
   - the balance between cost and quality

2. CWQC – Company-wide Quality Control, which aims to provide a good quality, low-cost product to the customer. It goes further and states that the organisation should endeavour to offer benefits to the customers, employees and owners of the organisation by addressing their specific needs. CWQC refers to the following concerns:

   - the quality of the management
   - the quality of the human behaviour within the organisation in terms of how the individuals interact and co-operate with one another
   - the quality of the working conditions and general environment
   - the quality of the product itself
   - the quality of the service

student activity

(PC 5.1.1, COM 3.1)
What do you see as the main differences between TQC and CWQC? Discuss this as a group.

The seven stages that we mentioned earlier relate to the concepts of TQC and CWQC. The first three stages relate to TQC and the fourth, fifth, sixth and seventh, to CWQC. The seven stages are:

1. *Stage one* – inspection of the product after production, with audits of the finished products. There will be problem-solving activities which address any variations in quality at this stage and seek ways to rectify them. This is known as being **product orientated**.

2 *Stage two* – the quality assurance checking during the production process. This will include looking at the monitoring of statistical information that can help to identify slight variations in the quality of the product during the production process. This is a **process-orientated** approach to quality assurance.

3 *Stage three* – checking the systems used to monitor and maintain quality assurance in all departments within the organisation. This involves a **systems-orientated** approach to the maintenance of quality assurance.

4 *Stage four* – formulating and instituting a system which aims to make all employees of the organisation think about quality issues and be aware of the concept of quality assurance. This is known as a **humanistic** approach.

5 *Stage five* – looking at the production process and at the product design itself in order to discover a cheaper way of producing the product for the benefit of the organisation and the customers. This is called a **society-orientated** approach.

6 *Stage six* – this stage addresses the need to be cost conscious in the light of any fall in the quality of the product if the costs (or inputs) of the product are reduced. This is called a **cost-orientated** approach.

7 *Stage seven* – this is the attempt to adapt the production process and the nature of the product itself to the needs of the customers and respond to their desires or instructions relating to that product. This is known as a **consumer-orientated** approach

student activity

(PC 5.1.1, COM 3.1)
As a group, try to define exactly what would be done in each of the seven stages. Attempt to identify an example of the kinds of actions that the organisation would take in relation to each of the different stages.

We will be returning to the subject of quality later on in this Element when we consider the factors that can contribute to a change in production.

PRODUCTIVITY

Basically, under the heading of productivity we are considering the best way to maximise the **benefits** between the **cost of inputs** and the **value** of the final product.

student activity

(PC 5.1.1, COM 3.1)
Investigate the following:

● British Standard 5750
● International Standards Organisation 9000

Feedback your findings to the rest of the group.

Although the human factor is a very important consideration in the measurement of productivity, we will only be mentioning this in passing in this section of the performance criteria. There is a specific section devoted to this at the end of this performance criterion.

There are a variety of different ratios that can be used to assess the productivity of the organisation. These are:

● profit/capital employed
● profit/sales
● sales/capital employed
● sales/fixed assets
● sales/stocks
● sales/employee
● profits/employee

In all such ratios, the emphasis is placed upon the sales revenue and profits, however it is possible that both will be affected by market supply and demand factors as well as being influenced by the efficiency of the organisation's operations.

Perhaps a more valuable approach would be to use the integrated **productivity measurement technique**. Various models have been developed, but they all have the following in common: that they look at the whole of the operation of the organisation in a totally dependent and integrated manner. The series of calculations look like this:

1 The added value is compared with employee costs. This is calculated by dividing net earnings by labour costs. This will give us the **net added value labour productivity**.

2 To calculate the **added value productivity**, we divide the added value or net output by the internal expenses of the organisation.

3 We can calculate the **total earnings productivity** by dividing the total earnings by the operational costs.

4 We can calculate the **gross efficiency** of the organisation by dividing the sales revenue (or gross output) by the total inputs.

To sum up, there are three major components of the organisation and its operations that can be looked at in order to get some indication of the productivity of the organisation. These are:

1 *The machinery* – which includes the tools used, buildings, and space, that is, all physical items that have a direct impact on the production or are involved with it in some way. The items measured are:

- the through-put per machine per hour
- the proportion of total available time used
- the total capacity used at any time
- the utilisation of the space available
- the reduction of down-time or under-utilisation
- the original cost of any of the items within this category

2 *The labour* – which includes all of the individuals who are directly involved, or contribute to, the production process (both manual labour and any supervision). Items measured are:

- the output per man hour
- the proportion of total available hours used
- the idle and ineffective time
- the labour cost component

3 *The materials* – which include all items that are consumed directly or indirectly as a result of the production process. The elements measured are:

- the yield (in other words what is created as a result of consuming x tons or volume)
- the wastage level and the use (and value) of the scrap
- the material costs

JUST-IN-TIME (JIT) PRODUCTION

JIT is a Japanese technique which involves the ordering of raw materials and other stock only when they are actually needed. Obviously, the point of the exercise is to reduce the amount of stock held so that costs can be cut to the minimum and as little as possible of the working capital of the organisation is tied up. Production needs to be able to respond quickly and efficiently to the demands of customers. One way of doing this is to have vast stock levels of all of the products that might be needed. Whilst this is possible for some forms of business, particularly in the retail trade, it is not really a viable proposition for an organisation involved in production or manufacturing.

The cost of holding stock on the premises or at a warehouse can be a considerable drain on the resources of an organisation, as it is not only the value of the stock that has to be taken into account, but also the cost of actually looking after it. It has been estimated that around 25 per cent of the value of the stock should be added to the costs to cover warehousing and other associated costs per year.

The key factor to the solution of this problem is for the production organisation to know how long it would take to get the materials needed for the product and to manufacture the finished item. This is known as the 'lead time'. This is the key to JIT: it identifies the lead time and can ensure that the customers receive their orders when they need them. Considerable investment is required for the purchase of state of the art production machinery that can turn orders around in the quickest possible time, but the savings from the reduction in stock levels more than compensate over a period of time.

This technique is not suitable for all forms of production, since the technology is not available for instant or rapid production in all areas of manufacturing.

student activity

(PC 5.1.1, AON 3.3)
As a group, considering the previous section of this performance criterion, try to identify what is being measured by the following calculations or formulae:

- occupancy/space utilisation
- percentage of down-time
- percentage of scrap

student activity

(PC 5.1.1, COM 3.1)
Identify at least four different types of production that could be achieved with the implementation of JIT. Are there any features of these types of production that are common to all four? Discuss your thoughts as a group.

USING HUMAN RESOURCES EFFECTIVELY

This concept implies that the organisation needs to utilise the effectiveness and efficiency of the workforce to reduce costs. Within this is the notion that it is advisable to ensure that working conditions are such that the workforce positively responds to the environment and remains highly motivated.

The Department of Trade and Industry have developed the idea of net output per employee as a productivity measurement. Their formula looks like this:

$$\text{Net output per employee} = \frac{\text{added value per annum}}{\text{total number of employees}}$$

As we have seen above, we can use a more integrated approach in our assessment of the productivity of an organisation. The human resources of an organisation can have a considerable input and thereby can affect productivity.

5.1.2 Explain why businesses aim to add value

WHY BUSINESSES AIM TO ADD VALUE

This performance criterion addresses the more obvious reasons why an organisation would wish to add value to its products or components. As we have seen, the concept of productivity and the measurement of this consideration will largely determine just how successful an organisation can be in its avowed objectives. You must remember that, just as organisations have different organisational objectives, they will also seek to put the following goals in a different order depending upon their own set of circumstances.

TO MEET INTERNATIONAL COMPETITION

As we will see in Element 5.3, there is considerable competition from overseas markets, particularly from Europe. Since the relaxation of trade barriers, there has been increasing pressure on organisations to maintain and improve their profitability. With domestic markets open to all comers, there is a natural concern to reduce production costs and other expenditure whilst maintaining a high level of added value. As we have seen, there are a number of different ways in which an organisation may seek to achieve this, but the bottom line is that it has to respond to this external pressure. If an organisation is unable to maximise its profitability, productivity and added value levels, then there is little hope that it can survive in the world market.

Above all, an organisation must be competitive, in terms of not only of the price of its products, but also the quality and standards that it offers. In other words, the customer, regardless of where he/she is in the world, must believe that the product cannot be bettered. The organisation must work to foster this confidence, despite the fact that some organisation somewhere will be able to undercut it in price terms. It may be the role of the marketing and sales department of the organisation to promote this image, but their efforts can only be successful if the product truly has marketable and saleable qualities that hold up well against all of the competition.

TO MEET CUSTOMER REQUIREMENTS

The meeting of customer requirements is an ever present concern. If an organisation is to be successful in anything other than the short term, then it will have to maintain and improve its ability to achieve customer satisfaction. First it must address the needs or requirements of the customer. As we have seen, this is not the end of the story. The organisation needs to follow through any of the quality-related advantages that it may have achieved in its production processes to provide a fully comprehensive sales and after-sales service.

Many of the comments that we made about international competitiveness hold true for meeting customers' requirements. It is the objective of the organisation to make sure that its products not only are of a high quality and very reliable, but also are marketable to a broad spectrum of customers.

An organisation can usually find a competitor that can match it in terms of quality, but perhaps not also in the range of services and other related aspects offered. These may be the deciding factors that persuade a customer to purchase from the organisation. If an organisation can also offer some other advantage, such as durability? compatibility, resale value or a host of other special characteristics, it can stay ahead of the competition. Obviously, the nature of these additional advantages will depend upon the nature of the product itself.

Meeting customer requirements or achieving their satisfaction will involve the following concerns, many of which have been discussed elsewhere in this book:

- the reliability of the product
- the fitness of the product for the purpose it was intended
- the value for money

- the after-sales service and support
- the packaging
- the customer information available
- the training of the customer to use the product (if appropriate)
- the maintainability of the product in terms of its quality and reliability
- the variety of products offered
- the speed of service
- the civility of the employees dealing with the customers

student activity

(PC 5.1.2, COM 3.1, 3.4)
In pairs, try to rank the points made above in the following cases. Which would be most important for these different types of organisation?

- a retail outlet selling electrical goods
- British Telecom
- a hairdresser's or barber's shop
- a record shop

Once you have done this, compare your ideas with those of the rest of the group.

- the image of the organisation
- the confidence that the customer has in the product and the organisation

TO IMPROVE PROFIT

As we have seen, the measurement of the added value component will have a large part to play in the **profitability** of the organisation. By maximising the added value component, the organisation can make a reasonable profit per unit of production. Alternatively, by reducing the unit added value, the organisation can seek to increase the total sales revenue by being more price sensitive to the market-place. If the organisation can achieve a high level of sales, even with only modest margins and mark-ups, then profitability levels can be maintained or increased.

TO SURVIVE AND GROW

Simply to survive has been an all too common goal of organisations throughout the recession. Despite the fact that the worst of the recession is over, organisations now face a different set of problems, which we have already addressed above, in the section relating to international competition.

Having cut back all costs to a minimum just to survive the lean times of the late 1980s and early 1990s, organisations should be in a better position to grow now that the worst is over. Provided organisations have learnt the painful lessons that resulted in mass lay-offs of employees, the closure of factories and the wholesale abandonment of certain types of production, they will be able to compete in a positive way in the international market.

5.1.3 Identify and give examples of factors which can contribute to change in production

FACTORS

Many factors that contribute to changes in production and this performance criterion addresses those that have the greatest influence. We must remember that organisations often do not have much choice with regard to the adoption of different production methods. Indeed they may be forced to adopt new methods in order to keep up with the competition. New methods particularly in relation to labour flexibility and competition, may also be introduced as a result of external factors such as legislation, either national or European, e.g. EU.

PRICE

Naturally, a price change and the associated pressures can force an organisation to consider a different form of production. This is, perhaps, particularly true of falls in the price of a product which may mean that the organisation has to question its whole process and approach to production.

Changes in technology or in the needs of a market undoubtedly influence an organisation's pricing decisions. Techological change, as we have seen, requires a period of reinvestment and high costs, followed by a gradual pay-back period. An organisation needs to take the longer view here. It cannot radically increase prices in order to get back its investment as soon as possible. The market may not be capable of accepting higher prices, nor will customers accept that the higher and more sustainable quality levels are worth the extra costs. In relation to the market itself, organisations must be constantly aware of the actions of their competitors and their pricing structures. We have looked at pricing policy from different viewpoints elsewhere. In this performance criterion we will look at pricing from the point of view of the production process and the related costs:

1 *Standard material pricing* – whether materials are obtained from the same supplier over a period of time or from different suppliers, there may be differences in the prices paid for the materials at different times of the year, unless a single price is agreed in advance. The organisation may have to factor these differences into the selling price, particularly if the materials cost more in, say, August than they did in March.

2 *Weighted average price* – in this case, an average is struck by adding together the values of the stock already in the warehouse and the stock that is added to it. The value of the materials is then divided by the total quantity of stock.

If the value of the stock in the warehouse is $20 \times 10p = 200p$, and the added stock of 100 is made at a cost of 15p per unit, then we have $100 \times 15 = 1,500p$. The total stock is $(200 + 1,500) = 1,700p$. The weighted average unit price is $1,700/120 = 14.17p$.

3 *LIFO (last-in-first-out) pricing* – here, the price charged is the last price paid. In other words, if an organisation needs to supply 50 units from a stock of 60 units, the price being 15p per unit, then the price is simple, $50 \times 15p = 750p$. If it then takes a delivery of more units at 10p each, then receives another order for more units, the price structure will be different. In this case, it will supply 10 units at 15p and the remaining 40 at 10p.

4 *FIFO (first-in-first-out) pricing* – here the price charged is the price of the earliest received stock from which the order could be supplied. If the order is supplied from stock worth 10p per unit, but the order exceeds the quantity of that stock in the warehouse, then it is 'topped up' with stock received, at a different price, from a later re-supply.

5 *Standard pricing* – here a price is created and all orders are fulfilled at this price. Where the actual price varies from the standard, a variance is declared. A positive variance indicates that the purchase price is greater than the standard and a negative price indicating that is it less. Standard pricing is usually only used as a part of a fully integrated standard costing system.

6 *Replacement pricing* – here a price is set, this being the price which it is anticipated will be paid when the stock is replaced.

TECHNOLOGY

Within this category we are restricting ourselves to ways in which the organisation can achieve a greater level of productivity and add more value to the product without necessarily incurring more costs.

1 *Management Information Systems (MIS)* – you will recall from Unit 2 that the use of MIS has become widespread in many organisations. This intelligent linked system, which enables the user to obtain information instantly often operates as part of the network established in the organisation. The user is able to access financial and other types of information to assist in decision making and problem solving. Ideally, the system should streamline the availability of or access to information to assist in the smooth organisation and running of the production process. With useful information at his/her fingertips, the manager should be able to make informed decisions and not interrupt the operations of the production process whilst he/she flounders around trying to source particular information.

2 *Robotics and automation* – many organisations, particularly in the field of car manufacture or the production of consumer durables, have been using robotics and automated production techniques for many years. With all of the advantages of not being unduly affected by labour considerations, the automated systems can literally work 24 hours per day and 365 days of the year. The only problems that are likely to arise relate to servicing and possible breakdowns. With systems and machinery becoming increasingly more efficient and reliable, these robotic or automated systems do not suffer from the same problems as their predecessors?

Robots have the following main characteristics:

- they are reprogrammable
- they are multi-functional manipulators (i.e. they are capable of carrying out a variety of different tasks that are essentially manual or precise)
- they have a frame that is the main substitute for a human's arm
- they can be programmed to carry out a number of different tasks
- they can carry out very repetitive tasks without tiring or complaining
- they will not be concerned about the working conditions of the organisation
- the pay-back for an investment in a robot is usually around two to three years

- the prices have been dropping over the past few years, and robots now cost between $20,000 and $100,000 each
- they are capable of undertaking tasks at at least five times the speed of a human
- that they can undertake dangerous work that it would be impossible for a human to attempt
- they can manage very skilful and precise tasks, such as brain surgery

3 *Computer-aided design (CAD) and computer-aided manufacturing (CAM)* – the advent of new computerised systems which can assist in the design of new products, or variants of a product, have radically affected the design industry. Traditionally professionals were employed to make physical 'mock-ups' of the product or component for testing purposes, prior to manufacture. It is now possible to use a software package to design the product and to produce a read-out of the full specifications required. This has significantly streamlined the design process and indeed the production process.

Computer-aided manufacture is the next stage, after CAD systems. It is possible to 'import' the specifications and designs from CAD straight into the CAM software and then sit back and wait for the production process to begin. This has, in effect, taken the human element out of the whole equation. With the possible exception of human checking and monitoring of the system, the design and production can be fully computerised and automated.

CONTRACTING OUT

Contracting out, in the present context, should not be confused with the concept of compulsory competitive tendering, or contracting out of local services and amenities which we discussed in an earlier Unit. It is, however, very much part of the same concept. In contracting out in a conventional business, certain tasks, assembly or production are sub-contracted to a third party. In this way, an organisation can employ another business to undertake a specific aspect of its production, leaving it free to concentrate on the tasks that it is good at. Alternatively it may sub-contract additional production requirements at times of high activity.

SINGLE SOURCING

A great deal of criticism has been levelled at UK suppliers, with regards to their flexibility, reliability and quality assurance. It is alleged that there is poor performance in price, quality and delivery.

Since the presence of a large manufacturing organisation can have a major impact in a local economy, in terms of job creation, it is not surprising that, in the interests of stability in that economy, the company would seek to minimise the chances of disruptions to its operation. As a result many large manufacturing organisations which need to be assured of continuity and reliability of supply prefer to establish formal relationships with a certain number of suppliers on whom they can then rely for the majority of their materials and components. They can go a stage further and adopt the concept of single sourcing. This means that a recommended and monitored specific supplier is tied into the manufacturing organisation. To all intents and purposes, the supplier is almost like a subsidiary (except that it is not owned by the manufacturer). This supplier will take on the quality standards of the manufacturer and will adopt the manufacturer's methods of production and flexibility. This means that the manufacturer can rely on the supplier as the latter is wholly dependent upon the former. It can also mean that the manufacturer can demand high levels of service at a reasonable cost. The cost angle is important: the manufacturer must not have too stringent control of this otherwise the supplier may question the viability of the relationship with the manufacturer.

LABOUR FLEXIBILITY

As more and more organisations switch to part-time work, with the approval of the government, many employees risk increased insecurity as a result.

The government's Labour Force Study shows how fast part-time employment has been growing as compared with full-time opportunities. The unquestionable flexibility of part-time work is at the leading edge of human resource management. Although this trend may have been driven by economic circumstances, this part-time surge is definitely a tentative step by organisations out of the recession.

Part-time and flexible working hours and conditions are still very much a feature of women's occupations. For men, part-time work is largely confined to teenagers and those who are close to (or beyond) retirement age. There has been a 50 per cent rise in the numbers of part-time workers among males in their late 40s. There has also been a rise of 17 per cent among women over 60. Despite this apparent flexibility, organisations should not forget the administrative costs and management time involved in employing so many part-time workers.

LEGISLATION

Aside from the more obvious legislation that has been discussed elsewhere, particularly that relating to such issues as consumer protection and employment law, there are a number of other pieces of legislation that can have a direct impact on the nature of the production processes and any changes that might be under consideration. These other pieces of legislation, in relation to the UK, include the following:

- Pollution of Rivers Act
- Deposit of Poisonous Wastes Act
- Clean Air Act
- Health & Safety At Work Act
- local by-laws

Focus study

LABOUR FLEXIBILITY

Marks & Spencer, with over 40 years of experience of employing part-time staff, have something like 70 per cent of their staff on part-time contracts. They do so mainly in order to meet the demand for staff at high peak times during the day or the week. They have identified the following times as the key points when they need part-timers:

- lunch times
- selected evenings
- Saturdays

With their stores open for an average of 70 hours per week, they tend to staff their stores by the hour. They use a complex version of job-sharing and have a discrete part-time management system. This has been computerised and allows each store to schedule its staffing in relation to the flow of the business in that store.

Pay and conditions are on a strictly pro-rata basis. M&S do not use the zero-hours mode of working that is used by some other organisations. Under this system there are no guaranteed hours of work and the part-timer may be telephoned at short notice and told that he/she is not needed for the next shift. M&S give their part-timers a full week's notice if they want them to work extra hours. The basic hours are guaranteed.

 `0:20`

student activity

(PC 5.1.3, COM 3.1)
Try to identify examples of local organisations that use a large proportion of part-time staff. Can you also identify any that operate a zero-hours system? What are the similarities between organisations that use this system? Discuss in pairs.

student activity

(PC 5.1.3, COM 3.1)
As a group, split into threes or more and investigate the legislation mentioned above. Try to identify how these pieces of legislation will affect the production process. Feedback your results and findings to the rest of the group.

COMPETITION

We looked at the various implications of competition in terms of an organisation's need to maintain and improve the added value component of its operations earlier in this Element.

There are a number of other factors that could affect the choice of production process by a UK organisation:

- the United States has made considerable investments in the UK economy. Indeed, American investments have created some 850,000 jobs in this country. This is around 40 per cent of all United States investment in Europe
- conversely, the UK invests heavily in the United States. With investments topping £104bn., UK organisations in the United States employ more than 1m. Americans
- with the UK offering the lowest unit of production labour costs in Europe, this inward investment not only from the United States but from many other countries too is set to increase
- the UK is also a very low-tax country. The rate of corporation tax in France is 34 per cent, in Italy it is 36 per cent and in Germany it is 50 per cent, so the rate of 33 per cent in the UK is very attractive to overseas investors
- the UK is also well ahead of other countries in Europe in terms of productivity, union co-operation and overall stability

However, the advantages are somewhat reduced by the following disadvantages, some of which are common across the rest of the EU:

- energy costs across Europe are some 30 per cent higher than the United States
- telecommunications costs are a staggering 22 times more expensive than in the United States

- air and rail travel is considerably more expensive in Europe than anywhere else in the world
- the EU is set to add to the energy costs by introducing a carbon tax
- the cost of capital is far higher in Europe too, taxation in Europe averages 46 per cent of GDP, against 31 per cent in the United States and 34 per cent in Japan
- despite the recovery in Europe, the spending on education and training is far lower than in the United States, Japan and other major competitors beyond Europe

student activity

(PC 5.1.3, COM 3.1, 3.4)
In the light of what we have just said about competitive differences, how would these affect the production methods employed by European countries? Given that investment is more costly (if the funds are generated from loans within Europe) and that many of the distribution and communication processes are more expensive too, what could be done to help balance the situation?

With regard to the investment of the United States in the UK and vice versa, what do you think are the implications for production processes? Do you think that the production processes used are US in origin and design or British?

Discuss these points as a group.

QUALITY STANDARDS

The implementation of a strong quality standard can involve the following:

- the notion that quality is not just related to the physical production of the product. The institution of a quality standard must be embraced throughout the organisation
- the need for people working for the organisation to understand that the quality standards refer to them and everything that they do
- any system which supports the quality standards also supports the individuals in their attempts to produce quality work
- there must be a commitment to continual quality improvement in all areas of the organisation, not just among production workers

- quality should be measured in terms of what customers want, their needs and requirements, but at the same time it must be able to satisfy the organisation's requirements in terms of production efficiency
- new technology should be incorporated into the organisation as quickly as possible, in particular in areas such as:
  - quality design
  - computer-aided quality management measurement and control
- the goal of continuous improvement should be sought, not only by the management, but also by the rest of the employees, who may have a variety of good ideas that could be easily and efficiently put into practice
- the organisation should have a clear and customer-orientated quality management system that is:
  - easy to understand
  - worth believing in
  - one that individuals want to be part of

Focus study

FACTORS WHICH CONTRIBUTE TO THE CHANGE IN PRODUCTION

Recent surveys have identified some of the major problems which face an organisation seeking to improve its productivity. These can also be seen as a barrier to change itself.
The following are the main **internal** difficulties:

- the lack of employees with the right skills or the desire to adopt more flexible techniques – 35 per cent
- the reluctance of individuals within the organisation to consider or adopt new production methods and plans – 22 per cent
- the high level of absenteeism and labour turnover – 10 per cent
- the lack of management expertise, or inadequate management systems – 10 per cent
- the quality and reliability of incoming parts and raw materials – 5 per cent
- difficulties in establishing quality assurance standards within the organisation – 5 per cent
- reluctance and opposition to the adoption of Japanese-style manufacturing techniques – 2 per cent
- lack of co-operation by the dominant trade union within the organisation – 2 per cent
- problems of being able to recruit or attract the right type of employee within the local area – 2 per cent
- other reasons – 2 per cent

student activity

(PC 5.1.3 COM 3.1, 3.2, 3.4)
In groups, consider the above Focus Study and suggest solutions to the problems faced by organisations in their desire to improve the productivity and competitiveness of their business. Try to identify the reasons which are inherent in the organisation and may be attributed to the lack of managerial expertise. Write down your considerations and then compare them to those of the remainder of the group.

CAUSES OF CHANGE AND IMPACT ON PRODUCTION

Now that we have looked at all of the major factors that could contribute to changes in the production process, we should turn our attention to the analysis of these changes. Given that we are operating from a very broad base and not looking at the production process of any particular organisation, our comments must be of a general nature.

RESEARCH AND DEVELOPMENT NEEDED

As you are no doubt already aware, research and development involves the investigation and invention of new products and methods of producing them. If an organisation invests time and resources in the development of a new production method, it can never be assured that it will ever get a reasonable return on their investments. One of the other key considerations is that an organisation that has invested resources in this development may well be simply opening the door to other organisations which take advantage of the technological innovations without having made any investment themselves.

There are a number of government incentives to encourage organisations to adopt an R&D programme. The government has been actively involved in the allocation of funds to projects that can be seen as being in the public interest. They have been involved in the development of technology such as the micro-chip, offering tax concessions to organisations undertaking research and straightforward sponsorship of R&D. The DTI provides something in excess of £400m per year for these activities.

The UK has a reputation for innovation and changes in technology. Our one main weakness is that we are often the last to actually implement change.

There has to be a co-ordination of the conduct of R&D and the implementation of this as a practical measure. In France, for example, there is a national policy of indicative planning which involves the co-ordination of the economy over a number of years. This means that the advantages of R&D can be readily implemented.

The research and development that relates to the production process in particular includes work on the following:

- computers for production control
- computer-aided design (CAD)
- computer-aided manufacture (CAM)
- robots
- process measurement and control devices

As part of the integration of these systems, we can also identify the following:

- computer-integrated manufacturing (CIM)
- computer-aided engineering (CAE)
- flexible manufacturing systems (FMS)

student activity

(PC 5.1.3, COM 3.1, 3.2, 3.4, IT 3.1, 3.2)
With the exception of CAM and CAD, research the other aids to production as mentioned above. Present your findings in the form of a memorandum to the Managing Director of a manufacturing organisation that is considering investing in new technology. You should explain the nature of each of the above and give a brief assessment of their potential uses. Your memorandum should be word processed.

In economic terms, the impact of new technology on the manufacturing process is likely to produce as many threats as opportunities. The likely problems include:

1 the emergent economies of Eastern Europe are likely to make the jump from their outdated forms of production straight into the micro-electronic field. They may outstrip, in the move to new technology, the United States, Japan and Western Europe.

2 These Eastern European states have far lower labour costs and will be able to produce products at much more competitive prices than the countries of Western Europe.

3 With employment levels in manufacturing already falling in the present advanced countries, the

employment situation will be further affected by the development of the new technologies.

4 Any country or industry that fails to embrace the possibilities of new technology will be left behind. There is no real choice of whether to use the technology or not.

5 The biggest likely gains from new technology are likely to be in terms of productivity and improved product quality.

The decline of the more traditional forms of business which rely on the employment of large numbers of individuals can also be seen as an indicator of the implementation of new technology. The following trends have been recognised:

- it has been commonly recognised that since the beginning of this century, there have been three distinct phases,:
  - the agricultural economy (up to the 1920s)
  - the industrial economy (up to the mid-1950s)
  - the information economy (the remainder of this century)
- agriculture has been in decline in terms of employment, since the start of the century
- industry has been in decline, in terms of employment, since the 1960s
- the service sectors have seen a marked increase in employment since the 1960s
- the rise of information-related employment has shown a marked gradual increase throughout the whole of the century

student activity

(PC 5.1.3, COM 3.1)
As a group, discuss the trends that have occurred throughout this century in relation to the four main types of employment. What is your assessment of what will happen in the new millennium?

HUMAN RESOURCING CHANGES

Human resources considerations have received a great deal of attention over the past few years. There have been some crude attempts to link such concepts as quality circles, participation in the decision-making process and other participative methods with the new production practices and the concept of job security. It is true that in order to adapt the production process and, more fundamentally, to establish and maintain the right attitudes and environment for change, it is necessary to have a co-operative workforce. An organisation, at the same time, needs to have the right employees with the right skills and to have an understanding of the local environment, in terms of regional culture and values.

In terms of human resources as they relate to the production process, there are some six different practices:

1 *Single-status facilities* – in such operations, organisations have eliminated all barriers between the different grades of employee. All employees wear the same work clothes, use the same facilities and participate in morning activities together, such as exercises before starting work.

2 *Systems of communication and involvement* – the most prevalent forms include regular team briefings and other forums for discussion. Performance appraisal would be an integral part of this process and would be used for positive means. It would not be seen as a potential disciplinary procedure.

3 *The provision of staff benefits to all grades of employee* – here, regardless of the rank of the employee, all have equal access to all forms of benefits including medical treatment and social facilities.

4 *High job security* – as a matter of general policy, the key workers in the organisation have considerable job security in return for very clear contractual commitments to the organisation and vice versa.

5 *The use of company-based representative bodies* – together with the establishment of briefing sessions, the organisation would encourage the setting up of company councils and perhaps promote the concept of worker directors.

6 *Temporary workers* – there has been an enormous rise the number of temporary workers employed by manufacturing organisations over the past few years. The number of organisations employing temporary workers rose from 33 per cent in 1987 to 57 per cent in 1992. This practice allows for greater flexibility and enables more workers to be brought in if the production line needs to be manned on a more intensive or long-term basis. It also enables the organisation to cover for sicknesses and absences from a pool of workers who have already had experience of the organisation's working practices and demands.

CHANGING CUSTOMER AND SUPPLIER RELATIONS

Making changes to the production of a product will mean that there will be, inevitably, changes in quality standards. Equally, customers and suppliers may demand changes in the quality of a product. If an organisation fails to respond to these demands then this may cause severe difficulties with customers. The producing organisation needs to keep a close eye on the quality of materials received from its suppliers. If it does not, an inferior batch of materials may slip through the checking procedures and cause problems when the product reaches the end-user. The producer will be held responsible and it may be too late to demand any action from the supplier. If the supplier is not informed instantly that an inferior batch of materi-als has been delivered, then it may either ignore the fact or contend that the batch was delivered and accepted, hence there was no problem at that stage. If the supplier continues to deliver inferior materials then the producer has no other choice but to seek alternative suppliers and terminate its relationship with the existing supplier.

The main problem is that it is the producer or manufacturer (rather than the supplier) that will get the reputation for inferior or below-quality products and this may lead to problems in the market-place.

5.1.4 *Analyse improvements in production*

IMPROVEMENTS IN PRODUCTION

The management methods employed by Japanese manufacturers have had a significant influence on UK and other Western businesses in the last few years. Now that there are a number of Japanese organisations operating their own particular styles of production and management in the UK and the rest of Europe, this has meant that the following has happened:

1 The Europeans have had the opportunity to observe the Japanese techniques first hand. Before this, there had been few opportunities to visit Japan and see these techniques in action.
2 The effectiveness and impact of local demonstrations and open days organised by Japanese manufacturers have speeded this information gathering.
3 The viewing of a Japanese-style manufacturing plant has allowed European organisations to appreciate the transferability of the techniques to their own particular production needs.
4 There has been a realisation that the introduction of these techniques is not linked to the peculiarities of the Japanese culture. The setting up of the Nissan plant in Sunderland has proved that UK employees are capable of adapting and embracing the techniques wholeheartedly.
5 Since the Japanese have led the way in the introduction of these techniques in Europe, the European organisations can learn about the pitfalls and problems that may face them in adopting these procedures.

Japanese-style manufacturing has been the centre of much management literature in recent years, although it has been (quite rightly) pointed out that the practices are not distinctly Japanese in their origins. What the Japanese have managed to do is to incorporate a number of individual methods into a coherent package of improvements that seem to work. This is something that the UK, the United States and the rest of the Western world have so far failed to achieve.

BETTER PRODUCTIVITY

One of the key aspects of the adoption of new production methods has been the elimination of waste and a reduction in the stock levels held by organisations. This factor alone has contributed to higher levels of productivity as it means that there is not so much capital tied up in stock and not contributing to the profitability of the organisation.

Another direct measure of the profitability of an organisation is sales per employee, and there are several different ways of assessing it:

- annual sales per employee, the traditional approach, made purely in monetary terms
- units of output per unit of direct labour input, in which performance is expressed in productivity terms

Operating profits are further confused by the fact that an organisation may not have addressed the need to cut its overheads and streamline its administration costs. Any failure in this respect would affect profitability, but not productivity. This point has to be borne in mind when considering the relative merits of sales per employee and output as methods of assessing performance.

QUALITY ASSURANCE

With the implementation of quality standards and other forms of checking its processes and outputs, an organisation can go a long way to ensuring that the quality threshold is maintained. Equally, it may be necessary for an organisation to consider changes in its management style in order to embrace full quality assurance in every activity and task. The other way of assuring that quality standards are maintained is to attempt to eliminate errors and problems that may arise as a result of lack of training and understanding of the processes. Any such attempt needs to be regularly reviewed and assessed in terms of the impact it may have on the workforce and the overall efficiency of the organisation.

INVESTING IN (RESEARCH AND DEVELOPMENT, TRAINING, TECHNOLOGY)

We have already addressed the question of investment in research and development, but it is worth repeating the fact that there is a constant and ongoing need to make this investment if the organisation hopes to be able to remain competitive. There has to be a balance struck, in the sense that an organisation cannot hope to be wholly innovative at all times, particularly as there will be times when its principal activities should relate to profitability and production levels rather than any attempt to introduce ever more innovative methods of production. At some point, the organisation needs to pause and look for some positive benefits from its investments in the past.

Training is probably the most effective method an organisation can employ in order to achieve its goals in relation to productivity and the maintenance of quality standards.

There has been a tendency in the UK to concentrate on the production of products employing lower levels of technology. As a result the UK's record in education and training is poor. In recent research, the UK was placed 22nd out of 23 industrialised countries in the overall quality of its workforce. The UK produces fewer graduates, engineers and technology specialists than any other country in Western Europe. In a recent EU study, the UK was shown to have only 38 per cent of its workforce engaged in some form of training. This compares rather unfavourably to countries such as Portugal (50 per cent) and France (80 per cent). In the UK, employers devote a pitiful 0.15 per cent of their turnover to training. Against this poor level of investment, the Germans, Japanese and French invest between 1 and 2 per cent.

REDUCING POLLUTION

Environmental policy has received a great deal of attention from the EU over the last decade. There are two main reasons for this:

- the increasing levels of pollution do not stop at the borders of the EU, this has been an increasing cause for concern

student activity

(PC 5.1.4. COM 3.1)
As a group discuss whether you think that the UK's relatively poor position in the world economy is a result of the low levels of investment in training and education. In the role of the government what would you suggest to be the solution? Assess the direct impact that the government could have, as well as the incentives that it could offer industry to encourage them to invest more themselves?

- different standards relating to pollution can seriously affect the competitive edge of industries in countries that have stringent pollution controls. Not only will the countries with poor pollution records be able to produce more and keep up their levels of employment (by using old-fashioned production methods), but they will also be polluting their neighbours

The EU environmental policy was launched (by the EC) in 1972, with all of the legislation created since then coming under the Single European Act in 1987. One of the key considerations, enshrined in policy, is the 'polluter pays principle'.

student activity

(PC 5.1.4, COM 3.1)
What do you think is meant by the 'polluter pays principle' (PPP)? Can you discover any examples of how this principle has been used in practice?
Feedback your findings to the rest of the group and then discuss what you think would be the implications of PPP for an organisation considering the choice of production process.

CHANGING WORKING METHODS

Changing the working methods need not be drastic, but there are always ways in which an organisation can address the nature of the activities, duties and tasks that it expects of its workforce. There are a number of alternatives that we can consider at this point. Included amongst these are:

1 *The establishment of distance working* – this is achieved by the installation of computer terminals either at employees' homes or at remote stations around the country (or the world for that matter). These computer terminals can be linked via networking facilities and can allow instantaneous contact regardless of the time, complexity of message and distance from terminal to terminal.
2 *The establishment of problem-solving work teams* – this can allow the organisation to identify individuals with the complementary skills and experience to tackle problems arising out of the production process. In this way, utilising the dynamics of a hand-picked team, the organisation can obtain quick results that may be able to improve the production process. Above all, with their own experience very much in mind, these individuals should be able to come up with practical and implementable suggestions that can be used whereas external consultants might take a theoretical approach. These 'in-house' experts are readily available and, if a problem arises out of the solution that they have suggested they will (hopefully) be able to rectify it instantly. Typically, to solve a production problem, individuals would be assembled from the design team, the production team and the marketing team. In this way, the overall demands and perceptions of the organisation can be addressed within the single forum of the work team.
3 *Flexibility in working methods* – perhaps the concept of multi-skilling is the greatest example of this type of flexibility.

ADOPTION OF JAPANESE MANUFACTURING TECHNIQUES

We have alluded to these techniques throughout this Element, but we thought that it would be valuable to add another section here which specifically addresses the key Japanese manufacturing techniques and assesses their use in the production process. We will focus on the following:

1 *Cellular manufacture* – the resources in the factory are organised around 'flow-lines' or 'product families' in order to simplify the work flow and increase the accountability. The cellular manufacturing process is quite straightforward. By establishing the nature of the product and its integral parts, the organisation can attempt to work out the most advantageous method of laying out the factory so that the part-finished products can be passed on easily to the next stage of the production process. Similar activities or parts of the production process can be grouped so that they can be carried out in one specific location.
2 *Continuous improvement* – see Kaizen below.
3 *Design for manufacture* – this is a process by which the products are designed so that they can be easily manufactured. This concept is fine if the product is new, but it could be difficult to adopt in the case of existing products.
4 *Just-in-time production* – this is a manufacturing process which is managed in a very tightly co-ordinated way, when minimal stocks are held and production is undertaken on an order-by-order basis. This has been adopted by a large number of organisation who can benefit from the reduced level of investment needed to hold large amounts of buffer stock.
5 *Kanban materials control* – this is a card signalling system that is used to synchronise the outputs of the stages of the manufacturing process. This is particularly useful when the production process involves a number of discrete stages that may be undertaken separately.
6 *Kaizen (continuous improvement)* – this process permits the organisation to learn from problems and constantly improve its manufacturing process. It is manifested by its widespread use of elementary data analysis and problem solving on the factory floor. This is a very useful technique for an organisation to employ in the early stages of its development, when it is not certain of the correct methods to employ when considering the production process. This method is also very valuable to long-established organisations which know that alternative methods are available but are finding it difficult to identify them.
7 *Quality circles* – we have looked at this concept elsewhere, but essentially this involves the establishment of problem-solving or process-improvement groups. Again, a number of organisations have adopted these but their success relies on the participants being assured that their suggestions are taken on board and treated with respect.
8 *Operator responsibility for quality* – this focuses the responsibility for the levels of quality on the production workers themselves. This is very much in contrast to normal Western practice where the responsibility for quality is in the hands the manager, supervisor or specialist.
9 *Set-up time reductions* – these are programmes that are designed to reduce the time needed to prepare the production line for the processing of a particular product. This means that batch sizes can be reduced and the lead time to production can be reduced to a minimum. This requires forward

planning and considerable thought, to make sure that the types of product produced on the production line are similar in some respects. In other words, the order in which the products are made can help to ensure that the product line need not be completely organised before the process can begin.

10 *SPC* – this is a method of monitoring product process performance which uses elementary statistical theory to guide the decisions about adjustments to the process, reducing the variations of technique. Again, this requires some degree of retraining and set-up costs, but has been introduced successfully in a number of organisations.

11 *Total quality control* – this is a production philosophy with an emphasis on:

- error prevention
- continuous improvement
- concept quality in terms of its fitness for use

This is an integral part of Total quality management, which we have looked at elsewhere and which is a key component of quality and production efficiency.

ELEMENT 5.1

a s s i g n m e n t

(PC 5.1.1–4 COM 3.2, 3.3, 3.4, AON 3.1, 3.2, 3.3, IT 3.1, 3.2, 3.3)

The concept of added value is central to this Element. The focus is on production techniques and methodology, but we have also addressed the role of marketing and the use of human resources to achieve added value. You should now have an understanding of the relationships between the different aspects of production.

TASK 1

(PC 5.1.1–2)

In a report format describe the ways in which businesses add value through their production processes. You should also explain why it is necessary to add value.

TASK 2

(PC 5.1.3–4)

Also in your report, you should identify and give examples of the factors which can contribute to changes in the production process. Additionally, you should analyse at least two improvements in production explaining the causes of change and their consequences for businesses, their employees, customers and suppliers.

NOTES

The changing patterns of production should be seen in the context of the development of world markets. Competition and co-operation between different cultures can lead to the adoption of new approaches to production. You may find some useful data if you refer to OECD Reports or World Development Reports. Other useful information can be obtained via the CD ROM in relation to newspaper articles, etc.

This Element links in with Element 6.1 (which looks at the financial aspects of the added value process) and Element 5.3 (which considers the ways in which UK industries can respond to overseas competition). An assignment could therefore be undertaken that encompasses all of these aspects. Your report should be word processed.

Investigate and evaluate employment

PERFORMANCE CRITERIA

A student must:

*1 identify and explain **types of employment***

*2 **evaluate** the effects of changes in types of employment*

*3 identify **implications** of **employment trends** in the local economy*

*4 **evaluate** the **implications of employment trends** in the local and national economy*

RANGE

Types of employment: *self-employed, full-time, part-time, permanent, temporary, contract, non-contract, skilled, unskilled, home-working*

Evaluate *in terms of employee needs (pay, benefits, career progression opportunities, job security, working conditions); business needs (to control costs, to maintain profits, to maintain levels of production, to maintain customer satisfaction)*

Implications for: *employment, unemployment; de-skilling, retraining; male employment, female employment*

Employment trends: *national levels of employment; shift from manufacturing to service industries; full-time and part-time; permanent and temporary; skilled and unskilled; male and female; growth of the 'underground' economy, regional levels of employment; differences in pay*

Evaluate *in terms of: effects on individuals in employment; effects on the unemployed, effects on communities; effects on government revenue and expenditure*

5.2.1 *Identify and explain types of employment*

TYPES OF EMPLOYMENT

You will discover full descriptions of types of employment elsewhere in this book. Indeed other Units focus on the specific nature of these occupational categories. In this Element we will be focusing on the size and probable trends in types of employment, rather than simply describing them.

It may be a good idea to try to assess the comparative size of businesses in terms of the number of employees involved. This investigation of employment share by size of firm is a regular measure undertaken by National Westminster Bank. In their 1994 study they compared the size of the firms, discovering that the percentages of small firms (those with 1–10 employees and large firms (those with more than 500) were similar – around 32 per cent. The categories in between these two widely different sizes held no more than 10 per cent each. This gives some credence to the belief that some of the principal casualties of the recession were small to middle-sized businesses. The very small businesses and very large businesses seemed not to suffer as greatly as the others.

SELF-EMPLOYED

Self-employment showed very strong growth throughout the 1980s. However, this growth trend was severely interrupted by the recession. It is now widely believed that the growth has recommenced. By the year 2000 it is projected that a further 0.5m. people will be self-employed.

Small businesses themselves also account for a growing proportion of employment. During the 1980s there was a growth in the number of small businesses from 1.9m. to 3.1m. They were, however, the main casualties of the recession and in 1992 only 2.8m. survived. Again, this short-term 'blip' has come to an end and there appear to be underlying trends which suggest that small firms and self-employment have recovered and are growing.

FULL-TIME

There has been a trend away from full time employment. It now accounts for around 62 per cent of employment. This is projected to decrease by a further 0.3m. by the year 2001, giving a percentage of just 57 per cent. Many other forms of employment offer considerably more flexibility to both businesses and individuals, as we will see in the next section of this Element.

TABLE 5.2.1 *Self-employed as a percentage of all ethnic groups, Spring 1994, Great Britain*

	Per cent
Pakistani/Bangladeshi	22.4
Indian	18.0
White	12.8
Black ★	6.7
Mixed/Other †	14.4
All ethnic groups ‡	12.9

★ Includes Caribbean, African and others of non-mixed origin.
† Includes Chinese, other ethnic minority origin and people of mixed origin.
‡ Includes: ethnic groups not stated.

Source: Employment Department.

student activity

(PC 5.2.1, COM 3.1)
In pairs, and referring to the Table 5.2.1, try to assess what these figures actually tell you. Why is it that certain ethnic groups are more likely to be self-employed than others?

PART-TIME

Part-time jobs currently account for around 24 per cent of employment. It is projected that by the year 2001 the figure will have increased to 28 per cent, which means an increase of 1.3m. jobs. Since women are the major part-time workforce, this will mean that by the year 2001 they will make up 52 per cent of all part-time workers. This is an increase of over 1.2m. Men will still be the majority of the employed as considerably more men than women are self-employed.

PERMANENT AND TEMPORARY

In the temporary category of employment, nearly half of all jobs are in the secretarial field. Well behind secretarial are publishing, industrial and technical areas of employment. Just ahead of computing and accounting comes catering. Normally the definition of a temporary full-time post is one in which an individual works on a short fixed-term contract, as we have discussed elsewhere. As we will see a little later, when we consider the

TABLE 5.2.2 *Employees and self-employed: by gender and occupation, United Kingdom*

| | Per cent | |
	Males	Females
Craft and related	21.4	2.9
Managers and administrators	19.6	11.3
Plant and machine operatives	13.5	4.3
Professional	11.1	9.2
Associate professional and technical	8.7	10.5
Clerical and secretarial	6.7	25.3
Personal and protective services	6.2	14.8
Sales	5.2	11.2
Other	7.4	10.3

student activity

(PC 5.2.1, COM 3.3, AON 3.3, IT 3.1, 3.2, 3.3)
Using Table 5.2.2, create or design an appropriate graphical representation of these data and then analyse and present in point form the major features or issues of this information. You may use a computer software package to create your graphical representation.

evaluation of types of employment in relation to business needs, employers have increasingly found the use of temporary workers a more attractive prospect.

CONTRACT AND NON-CONTRACT

As we will see later when we consider the 'underground economy', there are still numerous employees who work without the benefit of a contract. These individuals, although they may not be strictly breaking the law, include casual workers and hourly paid employees. Some employers prefer to pay a slightly higher gross pay than they would pay to staff on contracts, and rely on the employee (who may be technically classed as self-employed) to take care of his/her own tax, national insurance and pension schemes. Whilst this may be considered to be the ultimate form of labour flexibility, it does little to justify the supposition that the majority of UK employers are ethical in all their business dealings. Again, if you refer back to other sections of this book you will discover that employers are legally obliged to provide contracts to their employees. Many organisations, as we have said, prefer a more casual approach to the employment of workers. It is strongly suggested that work without a contract is rather like jumping out of an aeroplane without a parachute – there is no protection.

SKILLED AND UNSKILLED

We will be investigating some of the key trends in skills and de-skilling later on in this Element. However, at this point we shall have a look at the skilled and unskilled workforce in more general terms. There are a number of current skill supply issues and, as we have said, the future skill needs of the country will be addressed later. There are three ways of assessing skills. These are:

1 *Core skills* – which are very general skills applicable to almost every kind of job. They, of course, include basic literacy and numeracy, the ability to work with others and some understanding of information technology.
2 *Vocational skills* – these are skills which are needed for a particular occupation but are often less useful outside of these occupations. There is some transferability in these skills. A typical example would be knowing how to operate a specific computer package. A person with this skill would be more likely to be able to use another one than a person without it.
3 *Specific job skills* – the usefulness of this type of skill is often limited to a fairly narrow range of occupations. It would perhaps be more appropriate to call these specific job skills knowledge.

As we will see, the availability of jobs in particular regions of the country is often related to the present skills mix within that region. Certain areas will have a predominance of particular types of occupation and consequently will require significantly more individuals skilled in that sort of work. If we return to the differences between skilled and unskilled work, we will discover that the boundaries between them are becoming increasingly blurred. It is obvious that even some of the more routine unskilled occupations require a little more than basic core skills. Increasingly the need to communicate at a number of different levels coupled with the flexibility of multi-skilling is becoming as relevant for those involved in quite straightforward occupations as for those who are involved in complex operations.

HOME-WORKING

Again, as we have pointed out elsewhere in the book, home-working is a growing trend. The traditional forms of home-working were often restricted to the clothing and textile industries and simple assembly occupations. Increasingly, however, very complex and technologically-based tasks are being undertaken on a routine basis within the home environment. Not only does this new form of occupation offer greater flexibility to the employee, but it also offers significant cost savings for the employer. As there are some 640,000 people currently engaged in some form of home-working, they represent a major minority which cannot be ignored. There is every indication that the trend towards home-working, which also includes tele-working, will continue.

5.2.2 Evaluate the effects of changes in types of employment

EVALUATION CRITERIA

In order to make an evaluation of the effects of changes in types of employment, we obviously need to address the two often opposing viewpoints, those of the employer and the employee. In this performance criterion, you will be required to evaluate how types of employment have changed in at least four different types of employment. This will form an integral part of the Element Assignment. Here, we will only make general comments as the specifics will differ in different types of organisation and will be related to your choice of employment types.

EMPLOYEE NEEDS (PAY, BENEFITS, CAREER PROGRESSION OPPORTUNITIES, JOB SECURITY, WORKING CONDITIONS)

If you refer back to Unit 2 where we looked at the reasons for employees to be motivated or otherwise, you might remember that we mentioned Maslow's hierarchy of needs. Changes in types of employment will obviously have an impact on the basic requirements and expectations that an employee may have in relation to his/her job.

If we begin with **pay**, there has been a tendency, which we mentioned in Element 5.1, for some employers to be keen to move over to part-time modes of employment. These employers will only keep a core of staff on full-time contracts to provide some degree of stability and continuity within the workplace. With such a change in his/her mode of employment an individual may not necessarily suffer any difference in job security but will experience a considerable drop in weekly or monthly income.

Similarly, if an individual moves on to a temporary contract, he/she may experience lulls or periods of inactivity between contracts. These will obviously have a detrimental effect upon his/her ability to make long-term plans and commitments.

Pay, the essential reward for labour provided, gives the individual the first basic requirement of his/her motivational needs. Pay, in most cases, is essential to ensure that the individual remains committed and motivated to the organisation.

Turning to **benefits**, we can readily appreciate that in many cases an individual will not enjoy the same level of non-monetary reward if he/she enters an alternative mode of work other than permanent full-time. In many organisations benefits such as pensions, sick pay, maternity pay and profit sharing are given on a pro-rata basis. Whilst the alternative mode of employment may be convenient for the employee and employer, the relative loss of benefits to the individual may serve as a disincentive in his/her decision to accept a different mode of employment.

A great many employees would not regard **career progression opportunities** as being readily available to them. This lack is perhaps compounded for individuals who do not work on a full-time basis. Not only are the job roles and duties limited and somewhat curtailed compared to their full-time counterparts, but the career progression options are severely limited. although such individuals may be experienced and have more than adequate educational attainments, they are often overlooked by the organisation as merely part-time workers who can address the short-term demands made by the organisation and its customers.

For individuals who are not on a permanent contract, **job security** is the paramount concern. At the end of their contract they will not know whether they will have a job or not. This uncertainty not only undermines their motivation, but also puts into question their loyalty to the organisation. If the organisation has not given them sufficient job security and a commitment to long-term employment, then the employer cannot realistically expect these employees to give loyal and dedicated service. This is not to say that those on temporary contracts do not provide a valuable and essential service to the organisation. On the contrary, they are often the most motivated members of staff, albeit for a short period of time. If they are only engaged on a short-term basis, then many of the long-term complications and falls in levels of motivation will not occur.

Again if we refer back to the discussion of motivational theory in Unit 2, you may remember that Hertzberg identified the physical surroundings and atmosphere of a workplace (i.e. the **working conditions**) as being an important factor in the motivation of employees. Poor working conditions lead to demotivation, whereas there is a tendency for good working conditions to be taken for granted, so that employees receive no positive satisfaction from them. For an individual working on a part-time basis, the availability and use of the physical benefits of a good working environment may tend to be only incidental. The worker may not be in the working environment long enough to appreciate or take advantage of the working conditions. Another aspect is that any additional features which make the working conditions more amenable may not be available during their working hours. This is particularly true of individuals who work in an different hours from the standard 9–5.

TABLE 5.2.3 *People usually* engaged in weekend working, shift work and night work†, spring 1994, United Kingdom*

	Total ('000)	As % of all in employment
Saturday working	6,289	24.6
Shift work‡	4,138	16.2
Sunday working	3,110	12.2
Night work	1,577	6.2

* Respondents were asked if they worked unsocial hours: usually, sometimes or never.

† It is possible for respondents to appear in more than one category.

‡ Includes both weekend and night shifts.

Source: Employment Department.

BUSINESS NEEDS (TO CONTROL COSTS, TO MAINTAIN PROFITS, TO MAINTAIN LEVELS OF PRODUCTIVITY, TO MAINTAIN CUSTOMER SATISFACTION)

The drive towards greater flexibility in working conditions has made businesses look towards alternatives to full-time employment. As we will discuss later, these trends have numerous implications. The main reasons for these changes are:

1 *Varying the number of employed to match demands* – it has been shown that amongst the largest organisations over 80 per cent use temporary workers (temps). Temps account for around 5 per cent of the total number of employees in all sectors.

2 *Sub- contracting* – in 1990 the Workplace Industrial Relations Survey established the fact that 72 per cent of organisations sub-contracted services to

student activity

(PC 5.2.2, COM 3.1, 3.4)

As you can see from the Table 5.2.3, nearly 25 per cent or over 6m. individuals, are required to work on Saturdays as a matter of course. A further 4m. are required to work on a shift basis. The increasing trend towards Sunday working has brought in a further 3m. individuals who work non-standard hours. These unsocial hours are much more the norm than in the past.

As a group, discuss the advantages and disadvantages of working unsocial hours and try to identify the benefits which you would expect in return for working these unsociable hours.

another business. A slightly later study showed that 70 per cent of 'non core operations' are contracted out. This flexibility offers considerable benefits to businesses.

3 *Temporal flexibility* – this consideration involves the varying of hours worked by employees. There is a strong growth in part-time work and indeed new working conditions such as annualised hours contracts and flexi-time have increased to 9 per cent and 12 per cent respectively in all occupations (1993 figures).

4 *Tele-working/home-working* – as we have already seen, this type of work is steadily increasing. In 1992 it was estimated that some 10 per cent of employers use home-based workers and 5 per cent use tele-workers. Some large firms may have as much as 20 per cent of their workforce employed in tele-working or home-working employment systems. In 1994 the Labour Force Survey calculated that there were around 640,000 home-workers.

5 *Functional flexibility* – this enables the organisations to switch staff from one task to another; in other words, it involves multi-skilling. In 1990 some 68 per cent of businesses said that they were actively using this form of flexible working practice. In the same survey 72 per cent of businesses reported that their productivity had increased. By comparison, organisations that did not use this system only claimed a 56 per cent productivity increase.

6 *Restructuring* – in surveys carried out during 1993–4 around half of all major organisations reported considerable structural changes. Unfortunately 80 per cent of these organisations also reported job losses at all levels. Significantly, 70 per cent reported a loss of at least one layer of management.

TABLE 5.2.4 *Employees with flexible working patterns: by gender, United Kingdom*

	Male	Per cent Female	All
Full-time			
Flexible working hours	9.7	15.4	11.7
Annualised working hours	5.6	6.4	5.8
Term-time working	1.1	4.7	2.4
Job sharing	–	0.2	0.1
Nine day fortnight	0.7	0.4	0.6
Four and a half day week	3.2	3.1	3.1
All full-time employees			
(=100%) ('000)	10,573	5,681	16,254
Part-time			
Flexible working hours	7.3	9.1	8.8
Annualised working hours	3.1	5.3	5.0
Term-time sharing	4.9	10.3	9.6
Job sharing	1.8	2.5	2.4
Nine day fortnight	–	–	–
Four and a half day week	–	0.3	0.3
All part-time employees			
(=100%) ('000)	745	4,760	5,506

Source: Employment Department.

7 *Flexible pay bargaining* – during 1990 surveys showed that collective bargaining at organisation level had increased significantly. Local pay bargaining now applies to 48 per cent of manual workers and 43 per cent of non-manual workers.

TABLE 5.2.5 *Average hours usually worked* per week†: by gender, EU comparison, 1992*

	Male	Hours Female	All
Portugal	42.6	38.2	40.6
Greece	41.0	38.1	40.0
Spain	40.7	37.0	39.5
Luxembourg	40.3	35.0	38.4
Irish Republic	41.1	34.4	38.2
Italy	39.4	35.0	37.8
France	39.8	34.6	37.4
United Kingdom	43.3	30.2	37.1
Germany‡	39.6	33.6	37.1
Belgium	38.3	31.8	35.7
Denmark	36.7	31.3	34.1
Netherlands	36.3	25.8	32.1
EC average	40.2	33.1	37.2

* Employees only.
† Excludes meal breaks, but includes paid and unpaid overtime.
‡ As constituted since 3 October 1990.

Source: EUROSTAT.

5.2.3 *Identify implications of employment trends in the local economy*

IMPLICATION CRITERIA

As a part of the Assignment for this Element, you will be expected to identify at least four types of employment that have changed. The implications of these changes are covered in this performance criterion. Since the implications will be different for every locality, we have simply covered some of the aspects which you may need to look at. In order to address the impli-

cations for your local area, you will need to consider the following Student Activity, on p.435:

Having collected these data, you should consider the implications for the local community and the prospect of government expenditure in your local area. You should present your findings as a word processed preliminary report which can be used for inclusion in your Element Assignment.

student activity

(PC 5.2.3, COM 3.1, 3.2, 3.3, 3.4, AON 3.1, 3.3, IT 3.1, 3.2, 3.3)

By contacting your local council or Training and Enterprise Council, you will be able to discover some very valuable sources of local data. As a back-up to these sources, you will also be able to access computer-based data compiled by central government and the EU. As this information is an integral part of the evidence required for this Element, then by undertaking this activity you will have prepared much of the necessary groundwork. In terms of the implications for the local economy, you should focus on the following areas:

- *employment* – levels of employment, principal types of employment, modes of employment (part-time, full-time, etc.)
- *unemployment* – causes of unemployment, average length of unemployment, patterns of unemployment
- *de-skilling* – loss of industrial base, reduced need for skilled employees, alternatives to skilled employees
- *retraining* – available retraining programmes (government, TECs, council), on-the-job training, off-the-job training
- *male and female employment breakdown*

5.2.4 *Evaluate the implications of employment trends in the local and national economy*

EMPLOYMENT TRENDS

It is widely recognised that there has been a recovery in the labour market. Unemployment itself has been steadily reducing since early 1993. From the summer of 1993 to the summer of 1994 employment actually increased by 230,000. It is expected that the longer-term unemployment growth will continue, but at a slower rate. Projections carried out by the Institute of Employment Research suggest the following:

- 1995–1997 – employment growth of 0.6 per cent per year
- 1997–2001 – employment growth of 0.9 per cent per year

If these figures are correct, then by 2001 1.6m. new jobs will have been created.

NATIONAL LEVELS OF EMPLOYMENT

The census of employment which measured the workforce in employment in June 1994 identified the following figures:

- male full-time employment – 96m.
- male self-employment – 2.5m.

- male part-time employment – 1.1m.
- female full-time employment – 5.7m.
- female self-employment – 0.8m.
- female part-time employment – 4.9m.

TABLE 5.2.6 *Civilian labour force: by age, Great Britain ('000s)*

	16–24	25–44	45+	All
Estimates				
1971	5,082	9,725	10,096	24,903
1976	5,095	10,824	9,782	25,700
1981	5,832	11,358	9,052	26,242
1986	6,173	12,455	8,310	26,938
1991	5,536	13,879	8,714	28,129
1993	4,932	13,863	9,094	27,890
Projections				
1996	4,339	14,346	9,477	28,162
2001	4,206	14,678	9,951	28,835
2006	4,434	14,389	10,587	29,409

Source: Employment Department.

TABLE 5.2.7 *Unemployment rates adjusted to OECD concept: international comparison*

	1976	1981	1986	1991	1993
Spain	4.6	13.9	21.0	16.0	22.4
Finland	3.8	4.8	5.3	7.5	11.7
France	4.4	7.4	10.4	9.4	11.7
Canada	7.1	7.5	9.5	10.2	11.1
Australia	4.7	5.7	8.0	9.5	10.8
United Kingdom	5.6	9.8	11.2	8.8	10.3
Italy	6.6	7.8	10.5	9.9	10.2
Belgium	6.4	10.8	11.2	7.2	9.6
Netherlands	5.5	8.5	9.9	7.0	8.3
Sweden	1.6	2.5	2.7	2.7	8.2
United States	7.6	7.5	6.9	6.6	6.7
Germany	3.7	4.4	6.4	4.2	5.8
Portugal	..	..	8.4	4.1	5.5
Japan	2.0	2.2	2.8	2.1	2.5

Source: OECD.

SHIFT FROM MANUFACTURING TO SERVICE INDUSTRIES

There are now around 3m. more jobs in service industries and 1.4m. fewer in manufacturing than there were in 1981. By 1993 almost 45 per cent of all jobs were in the service industries (this includes both private and public sectors). With another 25 per cent of all jobs in the distribution industries, this left less than 30 per cent in manufacturing, the primary sector and the construction industry.

It is expected that this trend will continue until 2001 when it is assumed that around 1.5m. extra jobs will be created in the service industries. At the same time, 0.5m. more jobs will be available in distribution and construction. Over the same period 0.5m. jobs will be lost from the primary sector and manufacturing combined.

The Institute for Employment Research looked at the overall projected employment changes between 1993 and 2001 and discovered the following:

- *primary and utilities sector* – will lose 12 per cent of the workforce
- *manufacturing* – will lose 8 per cent of the workforce
- *construction* – will gain 7 per cent of the workforce
- *distribution and transport* – will gain 6 per cent of the workforce
- *business services and other related services* – will gain 23 per cent of the workforce
- *public services* – will gain 8 per cent of the workforce

This means that the whole economy benefit from an increase of about 6% increase in the total workforce.

FIG. 5.2.1 *Where the jobs are – employees by industry, 1993, United Kingdom.*
Source: Institute for Employment Research 1994.

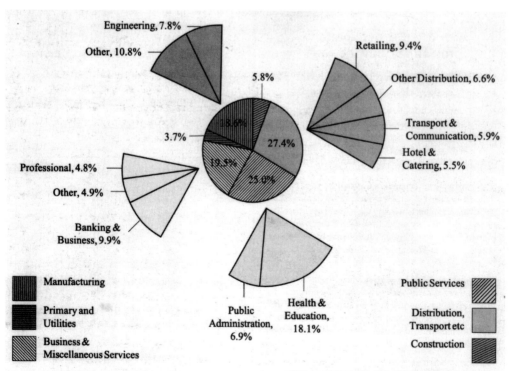

Source: Institute for Employment Research 1994

FULL-TIME AND PART-TIME EMPLOYMENT TRENDS

Technically, part-time workers are those individuals who are working for less than 30 hours per week. There has been considerable growth in this type of employment. Indeed, some 1.4m. extra jobs have been created between 1981 and 1993. During the same period the number of full-time employees fell by 2m. As a direct result of this, the overall percentage of employees engaged in part-time work rose from 21 per cent to 28 per cent.

As we have mentioned previously, part-time employment is still the domain of women. In 1993 women accounted for 80 per cent of part-time workers. In terms of the total number of women working, it was projected in 1981 that 4 per cent would now be in part-time employment as compared with 6 per cent for men. There have been significant changes since then, and the actual figures now are 46 per cent and 11 per cent respectively.

The Institute for Employment Research expects part-time employee positions to rise by a further 1.3m. Coupled with this is a comparative fall in full-time

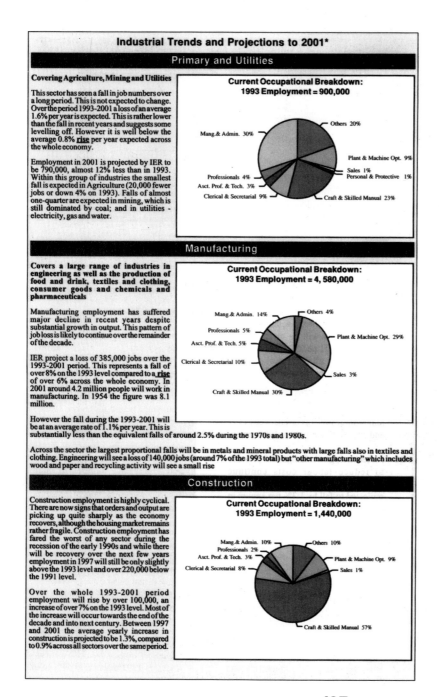

FIG. 5.2.2 PART I *Industrial trends and projections to 2001.*

employment of 0.3m. This will mean that as the number of part-time employees increases it will outstrip the total increase in employees. In other words, by 2001 part-time employment will account for some 32 per cent of all work.

In some specific sectors part-time working is expected to fall slightly. These drops in employment are more than offset by probable increases in the following areas:

- *distribution* – up 23 per cent
- *business and miscellaneous services* – up 38 per cent
- *public services* – up 18 per cent

PERMANENT AND TEMPORARY EMPLOYMENT TRENDS

By referring to Figure 5.2.4, on p.439 which details the workforce in employment, you will see that the majori-

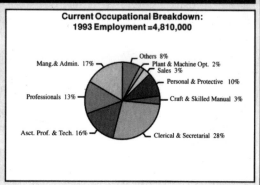

Distribution, Transport and Communications

Covering Retailing and Other Distribution, Hotels and Catering, Transport and Communication

Retailing and other distribution has been the source of major employment growth. Hotels and Catering has recently been affected by depressed demand from customers. Transport and Communication has been hard hit by the recession but is expected to benefit as the economy picks up.

Over the whole sector there are expected to be an extra 370,000 jobs in 2001 compared to 1993. This represents a rise of 5.5% over the same period. Hotels and Catering is expected to benefit most to the tune of 280,000 extra jobs (up almost 21%), there will also be a rise in retailing employment (up 120,000 or 5%).

To partly offset this Transport and Communication employment is expected to fall by 80,000 or 6% largely as a result of technological change, restructuring and reorganisation leading to improvements in productivity.

Current Occupational Breakdown: 1993 Employment = 6,730,000

Mang.& Admin. 24%, Professionals 1%, Asct. Prof. & Tech. 2%, Clerical & Secretarial 12%, Craft & Skilled Manual 10%, Personal & Protective 8%, Sales 21%, Plant & Machine Opt. 12%, Others 10%

Business and Other Services

Covering Banking and Finance, Insurance, Computing and Other Professional Services such as legal services, leisure, recreation and tourism.

The sector as a whole has enjoyed high levels of growth over the past few decades, although there was a net fall in jobs during the recession of the early 1990s.

Over the 1993-2001 period as a whole employment in this area is projected to rise by an average of 2.6% per annum, compared to 0.8% across the whole economy. This rate of increase is significantly less than that during the 1980s.

This rise will mean 1.1 million new jobs or 23% of the 1993 level. By 2001 there will be 5.9 million of these Service jobs. They will represent 23% of all employment compared to only 10% in 1971.

There will be large rises throughout the sector, although Banking and Business Services will see a slightly smaller proportionate rise than professional services (legal services, architects, surveyors etc.) and, particularly, Other Services (leisure activities and media).

Current Occupational Breakdown: 1993 Employment = 4,810,000

Mang.& Admin. 17%, Professionals 13%, Asct. Prof. & Tech. 16%, Others 8%, Plant & Machine Opt. 2%, Sales 3%, Personal & Protective 10%, Craft & Skilled Manual 3%, Clerical & Secretarial 28%

Public Services

Covering health, education and public administration. Not all of these jobs are in, what is traditionally called, the public sector.

Prospects for this sector depend primarily on government policy. During the 1980s employment grew by an average of 1.3% per annum compared to a rise of 0.5% across the whole economy. Between 1993 and 2001 IER expect average rises of 1.0% compared to economy-wide rise of 0.8%.

It is therefore possible to conclude that, while growth will exceed that across the whole economy, the rise will not be quite as great in relation to the rest of the economy as it was during the 1980s.

Over the 1993-2001 period some 500,000 extra jobs will be created. IER expect these to be all in the health and education area with no increase at all in public administration and defence. Almost 6.7m will be employed in the complete Public Services sector by 2001.

Current Occupational Breakdown: 1993 Employment = 5,900,000*

Mang.& Admin. 9%, Professionals 21%, Asct. Prof. & Tech. 18%, Others 9%, Plant & Machine Opt. 1%, Personal & Protective 21%, Craft & Skilled Manual 2%, Clerical & Secretarial 19%

* (excluding HM Forces)

FIG. 5.2.2 PART 2 *Industrial trends and projections to 2001.*

Source: Institute for Employment Research (IER), 1994.

ty of individuals, both male and female, are engaged in full-time employment. However, a significant minority, amounting to some 6m., are involved in part-time work of some description. This growing trend. which we addressed earlier in this Element, has had a significant impact on both regional and national employment figures.

SKILLED AND UNSKILLED EMPLOYMENT TRENDS

Again, as we discussed at the beginning of this Element, there has been considerable change in the balance between skilled and unskilled employment. If you refer back to Element 5.1, you will remember that as new technology is introduced, there is a decreasing

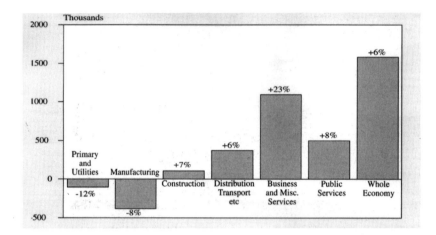

FIG. 5.2.3 *Overall employment change 1993–2001 by broad industrial.*

TABLE 5.2.8 *Employees by gender and industry, Great Britain, illustrating the shift from manufacturing to service industry*

	Males				Females			
	1971	*1981*	*1991*	*1994*	*1971*	*1981*	*1991*	*1994*
Agriculture	2	2	2	2	1	1	1	1
Energy and water supply	5	5	3	2	1	1	1	1
Manufacturing	41	35	29	28	29	19	13	12
Construction	8	8	7	6	1	1	1	1
Distribution, hotels, catering and repairs	13	15	19	20	23	24	25	24
Transport and communications	10	9	9	9	3	3	3	3
Financial and business services	5	7	11	13	7	9	13	13
Other services	15	18	20	21	35	41	44	45
Total ('000s) (= 100%)	13,425	12,277	11,254	10,539	8,224	9,107	10,467	10,363

Source: Employment Department.

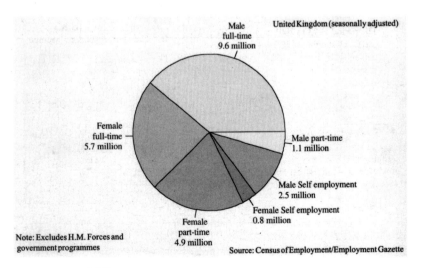

FIG. 5.2.4 *Workforce in employment, June 1994, United Kingdom. Source: Institute for Employment Research 1994. From: Census of Employment/Employment Gazette.*

need for skilled employees. Indeed, many of the skills which were used in the past have been replaced by machinery, automation and robotics.

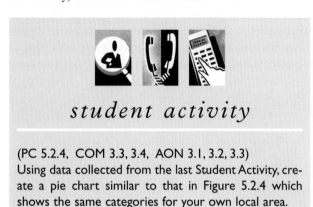

student activity

(PC 5.2.4, COM 3.3, 3.4, AON 3.1, 3.2, 3.3)
Using data collected from the last Student Activity, create a pie chart similar to that in Figure 5.2.4 which shows the same categories for your own local area.

MALE AND FEMALE EMPLOYMENT TRENDS

As we have seen since the 1960s women's employment has risen whilst at the same time men's employment has fallen. The predictions of changes throughout the period 1993–2001 infer that whilst female employment will increase by 1.2m., male employment will fall by 0.2m. The consequence of this is that whilst in 1981 women accounted for only 42 per cent of employees, they comprised 49 per cent of employees by 1993 and they are expected to outstrip their male counterparts for the first time in 2001, with a percentage of 52 per cent.

Since women will outnumber men in all areas except self-employment, this will not mean that they necessarily will make up the lion's share of the workforce in employment. Predictions do vary, but it is expected that the majority of males in employment will fall from its current figure of 54 per cent to at least 52 per cent by the year 2001.

Women's employment is still concentrated in certain sectors of the economy and they outnumber men in the following areas:

● health
● education
● other services
● textiles
● clothing

By contrast, in the construction and mining sectors of the economy, women still represent a mere 10 per cent of the workforce.

Men in the 35–44 age group still have the highest rate of participation in work. By the year 2000 this figure is likely to be 94 per cent. At the same time men over the age of 55 show a considerable decrease.

TABLE 5.2.9 *Full and part-time* employment† by gender, United Kingdom ('000s)*

| | Males | | Females | |
	Full-time	Part-time	Full-time	Part-time
1984	13,240	570	5,422	4,343
1985	13,336	575	5,503	4,457
1986	13,430	647	5,622	4,566
1987	13,472	750	5,795	4,696
1988	13,881	801	6,069	4,808
1989	14,071	734	6,336	4,907
1990	14,109	789	6,479	4,928
1991	13,686	799	6,350	4,933
1992	13,141	885	6,244	5,081
1993	12,769	886	6,165	5,045
1994	12,875	998	6,131	5,257

* Full/part-time is based on respondent's self-assessment. who did not state whether they were full or part-time
† At spring each year. Includes employees, self-employed, government training schemes and unpaid family work.

Source: Employment Department.

Women will play a much greater role in employment than they have ever done in the past. In fact their participation rates are rising whilst men's are falling. The growth rates of women aged 25–34 will reach 77 per cent by the year 2000. This is in comparison to 61 per cent in 1984 and 72 per cent in 1994. In the next age group of women, those aged 35–44 some 81 per cent will be in work by 2000 compared to just 71 per cent in 1984 and 78 per cent in 1994.

During the period 1983–1990 almost two-thirds of all new jobs went to women. From the 1960s there has been a continual rise in women's employment.

GROWTH OF THE 'UNDERGROUND' ECONOMY

The UK's underground economy is said to be worth around £50bn. per year. Research is showing that the underground economy is growing at a faster rate than that of the recorded and official economy.

Typical forms of activity in the underground economy include:

● drug dealing
● sale of stolen goods
● undeclared income from the self-employed
● re-sale of alcohol and tobacco brought into the country duty-free
● professional traders at car boot sales

The underground economy is thought to account for around 6–8 per cent of the GDP. This means that it is worth between £41bn. and £54bn. for the year 1994–95. If this income was identified and taxed, then the income to the government would be around £14.5bn. to £19bn.

The self-employed, it is believed, actually earn around 1.5 times the amount that they declare. With an increase since the late 1970s of nearly 1m. in the number of people who are self-employed, this is a potentially large source of untapped income for the government.

Higher taxes and VAT continue to spur individuals to join the underground economy. With unemployment having fallen by 200,000 in the year 1993–94 and no real increase in the number of jobs in that time, this could signal a vast move into the underground economy. The upturn in business activity is not bringing in the funds that the government was expecting, and this could be a pointer to the size of the underground economy in the UK.

REGIONAL LEVELS OF EMPLOYMENT

The 13 pie charts of Figure 5.2.5 show the industrial structure of employment in the whole of the UK and of each region separately. You can compare the UK structure with that of each region.

The changing occupational structure of employment at regional level is shown in the pie charts. However, we need now to have a look at the projected changes between 1993 and 2001. The categories of occupation as identified by the government are:

- managers and administrators (M and A)
- professionals (Pro)

FIG. 5.2.5 PART 1 *Industrial structure of employment, 1993, United Kingdom and by region.*
Source: Institute for Employment Research 1994.

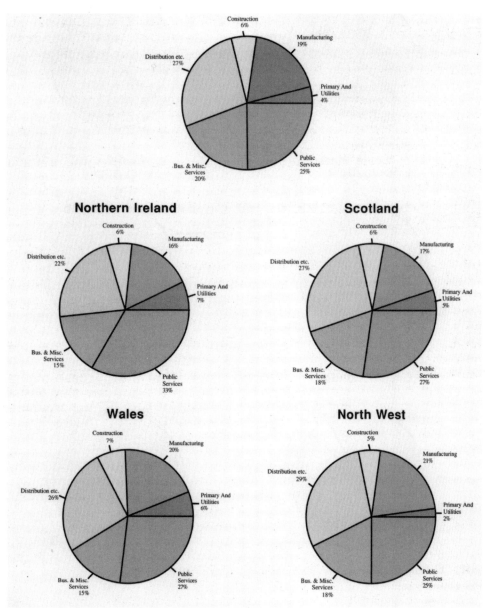

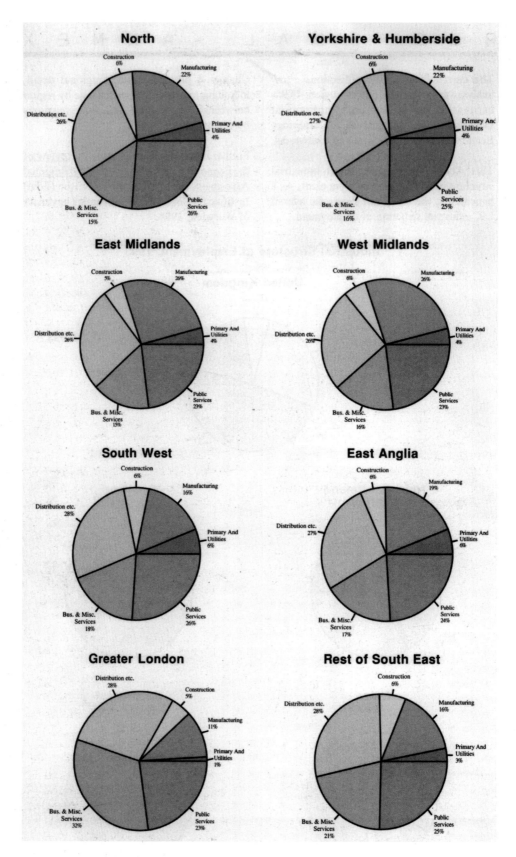

FIG. 5.2.5 PART 2 *Industrial structure of employment,*
1993, United Kingdom and by region.
Source: Institute for Employment Research 1994.

- associate professionals (APro)
- clerical and secretarial (Cler)
- craft and skilled manual (C and SM)
- personal and protective services (P and P)
- sales (S)
- plant and machinery operators (PMO)
- other elementary occupations (OEO)

In order to do this, we will follow the same order of regions and address each one in turn:

1 *UK* – the largest employment group in the UK is the **M and A** category. This accounts for around 4.03m., and is follow closely by the **C** category at 3.95m. It is expected that between 1993 and 2001 **M and A** will increase by 770,000 whilst **C** will fall by 120,000.

2 *Northern Ireland* – there are a total of 620,000 jobs in Northern Ireland, predominantly skewed towards the **C and SM** and **P and P** categories. In the run-up to 2001 it is expected that an extra 30,000 jobs will be created. This is a 5.3 per cent increase and compares rather unfavourably to the projected 6.9 per cent increase across the UK as a whole.

3 *Scotland* – of the 2.2m. jobs in Scotland, **M and A** and **C** categories have significantly lower proportions than the UK average. The **OEO** category is significantly larger. The expectation of a 4.8 per cent growth (or 110,000 extra jobs) by 2001 is the second lowest rate of growth.

4 *Wales* – Wales has some 1.1m. jobs. There is a significant bias towards manual jobs, in other words the **C and S M, PMO** and **P and P** categories are much higher than the UK average. All other categories are significantly smaller in percentage terms. With an expected growth of 7.8 per cent before 2001, this will mean that 90,000 jobs will be created. This is a higher percentage growth than the UK as a whole can expect; the biggest gains are likely to be in the **P and P** category.

5 *North* – there is also a considerable bias towards manual jobs in the 1.2m. workforce here. With the exception of **M and A, Pro, APro** and **C** categories, all other occupational groups are significantly higher in percentage terms. Unfortunately the North will have a 4.8 per cent growth in the run-up to 2001. Although this will mean 60,000 extra jobs, this is the second slowest growth rate in the UK.

6 *North West* – with a significant majority of the 2.6m. jobs in the PMO category, the North West is looking forward to a rather low 4.6 per cent increase before 2001. These extra 100,000 jobs will signal a trend towards the **P and P** category.

7 *Yorkshire and Humberside* – with 2m. jobs in this region there is bias towards the **C and SM, OE**O and **PMO** categories. All other occupational groups are considerably lower in percentage terms than the UK average. Some 120,000 new jobs (5.9 per cent) will come into existence between 1993 and 2001. The **P and P** and **M and A** categories will be the main beneficiaries.

8 *East Midlands* – the East Midlands has considerably more **C, SM** and **PMO** workers in its 1.7m. total. There are lower percentages for all other categories. With a massive increase of 9.1 per cent, 160,000 new jobs will be created between 1993 and 2001. The **P and P** category will increase by at least 33 per cent.

9 *West Midlands* – the 2.15m. jobs in this area are mainly in the **C, SM** and **PMO** categories. With an increase of 120,000 jobs before 2001 this represents a 5.7 per cent growth rate. As in many other regions the **P and P** category will increase the most.

10 *South West* – with just under 2m. people employed, this region has interesting imbalances which favour the **M and A** and **Pro** categories. As a result of de-industrialisation in the area the **PMO** category is significantly lower than the average. Some 200,000 new jobs will be created between 1993 and 2001. This is the largest growth rate, at 10 per cent. Principal beneficiaries will be the **M and A** and **P and P** categories.

11 *East Anglia* – with just 900,000 jobs in this region, there is an imbalance towards the **OEO** and **PMO** categories. All other occupational groups are under-represented. Despite this, East Anglia hopes to enjoy the second fastest growth in the UK between 1993 and 2001, at 9.7 per cent which will mean 90,000 new jobs. It is expected that the **P and P** category will be the main growth area.

12 *Greater London* – with 3.4m. jobs there is an imbalance towards the **M and A, Pro, APro** and **C** categories. Other more manual occupations are under-represented. With an expected growth rate, of just 6 per cent, this will still mean 210,000 more jobs. It is in the categories that are already more dominant that additional growth will occur.

13 *Rest of the South East* – this area, which includes the whole of the South East except Greater London, has a workforce of 4.5m. As it is greatly influenced by London, **M and A** and **C** categories are still dominant. This region is expected to have a growth rate of 8.6 per cent, amounting to 390,000 new jobs, but again the largest beneficiary will be the **M and A** category; however, the biggest proportionate growth will be in the **P and P** occupational areas.

TABLE 5.2.10 *Economic activity rates: by region, showing percentages of those in employment, Great Britain*

Per cent		Per cent		Per cent	
Shetland Islands	76.6	Cheshire	64.6	Lancashire	60.5
Powys	69.8	Central	64.3	Nottinghamshire	60.0
Buckinghamshire	69.4	Fife	64.0	Lincolnshire	60.0
Northamptonshire	69.2	Avon	64.0	Somerset	59.8
Wiltshire	69.1	West Yorkshire	64.0	Borders	59.8
Cambridgeshire	68.8	Tayside	63.9	Northumberland	59.5
Grampian	68.4	Warwickshire	63.8	Dorset	59.2
Highlands	68.3	Derbyshire	63.7	Cornwall and Scilly	59.0
Hertfordshire	68.2	London	63.1	Devon	58.8
Orkney Islands	67.7	Essex	63.1	Strathclyde	58.8
Berkshire	67.5	Staffordshire	63.0	Durham	58.8
Bedfordshire	67.2	North Yorkshire	62.9	Isle of Wight	58.3
Hereford and Worcestershire	67.2	Leicestershire	62.7	Gwent	58.2
Shropshire	66.8	Humberside	62.2	Dyfed	57.5
Surrey	66.5	Greater Manchester	61.5	Tyne and Wear	57.3
Hampshire	66.0	West Sussex	61.2	Clwyd	56.6
Oxfordshire	65.9	Western Isles	61.0	South Yorkshire	55.7
Gloucestershire	65.9	Dumfries and Galloway	60.9	Cleveland	55.7
Suffolk	65.6	West Midlands	60.9	Gwynedd	55.2
Cumbria	65.4	East Sussex	60.6	Mid Glamorgan	54.4
Lothian	65.2	Norfolk	60.6	Merseyside	54.0
Kent	65.0	South Glamorgan	60.6	West Glamorgan	51.7

* The percentage of people either in employment or ILO   *Source:* Employment Department.

DIFFERENCES IN PAY

Whenever you visit a different part of the UK you will discover that there is something of a disparity between the costs of certain basic commodities. Although this disparity may not be significantly great, it does reflect either the local market price sensitivity or the immediate availability of that product. In relation to these regional differences in price, it is often common to find regional differences in pay. These regional differences in pay are often related to the perceived 'cost of living'.

student activity

(PC 5.2.4, COM 3.1)
Using your combined knowledge as a group, try to identify items which are considerably cheaper or more easily available in your own locality than in the rest of the UK. What common features do these products have?

EVALUATION CRITERIA

The more general evaluation criteria which relate to the national economy concern the various effects that employment trends will have on the employed, unemployed, communities and government. In this section of the Element, we have briefly addressed each of the issues involved, although the detail will again be specific to your own chosen local economy and your focus upon the national economy.

EFFECTS ON INDIVIDUALS IN EMPLOYMENT

This criterion concerns the effects on individuals in terms of their personal relationships, attitudes, health, income and spending power.

EFFECTS ON THE UNEMPLOYED

The longer an individual is unemployed, the more chance there is that his/her skills and knowledge will be dissipated. In order to retrain these individuals, a new employer, or, more likely, a government agency will have to incur considerable costs. Obviously the longer a person is unemployed, the greater the loss of his/her potential income and related tax will be to the economy. Indeed, any output which could have been created by these individuals is also lost.

EFFECTS ON COMMUNITIES

The effects on communities can be both tangible (e.g. including wealth, health and security) and intangible (e.g. a rather less definable notion of well-being). Effects on government revenue and expenditure

As employment increases, the amount of tax collected will increase, whilst the costs relating to benefits payments will fall. Obviously, if the reverse is true, then tax income will be reduced whilst the demands for more money to make large-scale benefits payments will increase.

ELEMENT 5.2

a s s i g n m e n t

(PC 5.2.1–4, COM 3.1, 3.2, 3.3, 3.4, AON 3.1, 3.2, 3.3, IT 3.1, 3.2, 3.3)
In order to fulfil the performance criteria of this Element, you are required to identify and explain the different types of employment and evaluate how at least four types of employment have changed. Your evaluation should consider the changes in terms of employee and business needs.

TASK 1

(PC 5.2.1)
Identify national and regional trends in employment in at least one manufacturing and one service industry.

TASK 2

(PC 5.2.2)
Identify national and regional trends in full-time and part-time employment.

TASK 3

(PC 5.2.3)
Identify national and regional trends in male and female employment.

TASK 4

(PC 5.2.3)
Identify the trends in differences in pay nationally and regionally.

TASK 5

(PC 5.2.4)
Explain the implications arising from these trends for the following:

- employed or unemployed people
- local communities
- government revenue and expenditure

NOTES

Following on from Element 5.1, which addressed changes in production, you will now be required to evaluate the ways in which employment is also changing. You will be able to obtain information from the following sources:

- personal knowledge and experience
- local councils and training enterprise councils
- national and EU information sources

This Element also provides you with an opportunity to investigate employment trends which may have a bearing upon your work in Element 8.3.

Your findings should be presented in the form of a word processed report.

Examine the competitiveness of UK industry

PERFORMANCE CRITERIA

A student must:

1 **compare performance** *of the UK economy with its* **major competitors**

2 *describe* **business strategies** *intended to improve competitiveness*

3 *describe* **government strategies** *intended to improve the competitiveness of UK industry*

4 **evaluate business and government strategies** *intended to improve competitiveness*

RANGE

Comparing performance *in terms of: economic growth, investment, inflation, exchange rate; share of world trade, research and development, technological development, productivity*

Major competitors: *European, non-European*

Business strategies *relating to: organisational structure, human resourcing, marketing, scale of production, finance, new technology*

Government strategies: *exchange rate policy, control of inflation, privatisation, deregulation, reducing the role of the government, investment in new technology; improving training and education; taxation to affect aggregate demand, government expenditure, European market integration, participating in the World Trade Organisation (WTO)*

Evaluate *in terms of: market share, sales, revenue, efficiency, productivity, product quality, service, trading conditions, standard of living, levels of employment*

5.3.1 *Compare performance of the UK economy with its major competitors*

COMPARING PERFORMANCE

In this performance criterion, we will be attempting to consider the main measures used in comparing the UK economy with that of its major competitors. Many of the basic comments are not specific to a particular country, but we will be considering the main competitors at the end of this performance criterion. The main measures of comparison are:

- economic growth
- investment
- inflation
- exchange rate
- share of world trade
- research and development
- technological development
- productivity

ECONOMIC GROWTH

This is a measure of the real growth of the **Gross Domestic Product** of a country during a year or over a period of years. Generally, this is taken to show the health of the economy and is a valuable measure for comparative purposes.

INVESTMENT

The levels of **investment** within a country signify the degree of internal and external confidence in that country's economy. A low investment rate, either from internal or external sources, will mean that the country is not really getting the vital injections of capital to ensure that the industrial base is kept modernised or that new industries are supported.

INFLATION

The inflation rate is a measure of the steps taken by a country's government to **control prices** and **price rises**. In countries that suffer from a high inflation rate, businesses experience difficulties in maintaining their competitive edge. The major impacts on business activity as a result of inflation are:

- businesses with high levels of borrowings find that the real value of their outstanding loans has been reduced by inflation
- businesses can benefit from the fact that customers become more price sensitive; this is particularly true of products that are price elastic

- producers of branded products suffer from the fact that customers begin to look for value-for-money products. This price sensitivity leads to greater levels of brand switching and the more competitively priced products do better. Branded products can either be reduced in price to compensate for the loss of demand or increase their advertising expenditure to attract more customers
- employees are customers too – they are aware of price increases and consequently will be more likely to demand wage rises. They will expect wage increases to at least cover the inflationary effects on their incomes

EXCHANGE RATE

Exchange rates are, again, a measure of the **confidence** in a particular country and its currency. Fluctuations in the exchange rate are expected and are a daily state of affairs, it is only when the exchange rate gets out of control and the currency becomes seriously eroded in real value against its major rivals that it will begin to seriously affect businesses. However, even slight fluctuations can mean the difference between profit and loss when dealing with an overseas organisation. If, for example, an organisation agrees to provide an order and sets a price in the purchasing organisation's currency and subsequently the value of that currency drops, then the actual cash received is not worth as much as it had been. If the deal is based on an exchange rate of £1 is equal to 8FF, and the total bill for the order is 8,000FF, a reduction in the value of the French franc to, say, 7.5FF per £1 will mean that the supplier will receive £1,066 instead of £1,000. Conversely, if the French franc increases in value to, say, 8.5FF, then the supplier will only receive £941 instead of £1,000. It can also be seen that changes in the exchange rate will make the prices charged by overseas competitors more or less attractive to customers.

SHARE OF WORLD TRADE

Just as organisations assess of their market share, different countries have a share of **world markets**. As we will see when we investigate some of the key UK competitors, they are more or less active in various markets that make up the total world trade. The trade involved in the European Union is worth some 416bn. ECU in exports and some 487bn. ECU in imports alone. The share of this total business is very much dependent upon many of the factors that we will be looking at later.

student activity

Individually, try to find out what share of the world markets is commanded by the following countries:

- UK
- Japan
- Germany
- France
- Greece

RESEARCH AND DEVELOPMENT

The degree to which the industries, or for that matter the government of a particular country, value investments in **research and development** differs very widely. It is certain that the more industrialised and 'advanced' nations tend to make much investment in this area. The recognise that in order to keep ahead of their competitors, it is essential that a rolling programme of research and development is undertaken. The poorer nations do not have the resources to invest in high-tech research and may restrict their programmes to more appropriate areas such as the improvement of crops and other agriculturally based research.

TECHNOLOGICAL DEVELOPMENT

Again, **technological development** is essential for the organisation and the economy as a whole. There are constant changes in the high-tech field and countries not only need to keep abreast of developments but should also be at the cutting edge of them. Certain countries excel in the area of technological development and lead the way in research, implementation and exploitation of new methods of production and product use.

PRODUCTIVITY

Productivity is a measure of relationship between **inputs** and **outputs**. The greater the difference between the two, the more productive the organisation or country is seen to be. One of the more common forms of measuring productivity is to consider the relationship between the costs of labour and the quantity of goods and services that this labour produces. If the country has a low labour cost but high productivity, then the country can be seen to be more efficient than others. There is a sting in the tail, however: if productivity increases faster than demand then there may be job losses as a smaller workforce is needed to produce the quantity of goods demanded. Productivity itself is seen as one of the major measures of industrial performance and of the level of national wealth.

MAJOR COMPETITORS

The identification of a competitor can be quite crude, as all we are looking for is any country that directly competes in a market-place with the UK. No doubt, there may be some dispute about the actual viability of the competitor, but, in at least one area of business activity competitors do have an impact on the successfulness of the UK industrial and service base.

EUROPEAN

This section seeks to cover the main European competitors as well as the minor ones. Although our classification of major and minor might be questioned, we cover all of countries in the same level of detail. In this section we will look at the countries that made up the EU in 1993, the latest date for which comparative statistics are available:

- Germany
- France
- Italy
- Spain
- Netherlands
- Belgium
- Denmark
- Portugal
- Greece
- Eire
- Luxembourg

We consider the first four to be the UK's major competitors. We have not included any of the former Eastern bloc countries in our comparison, since their economies are largely in chaos and are not, as yet, very credible competitors. Under each country, we list the main areas of specialisation. The letter in brackets after the type of producr or service indicates the economic sector to which it belongs, as follows:

- (a) = agriculture
- (m) = manufacturing
- (s) = services
- (e) = energy

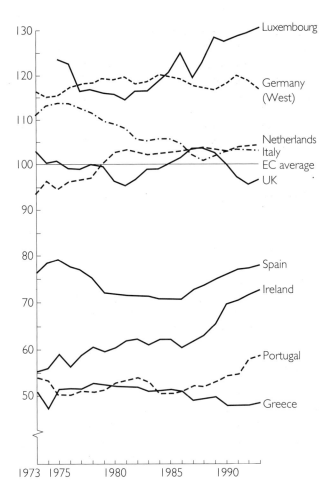

FIG. 5.3.1 *Gross domestic product at current prices per head of population, selected countries, 1973-1993*
Note: PPS; EU average (former East Germany excluded) = 100.
Source: Table E20/Eurostat.

0:30

student activity

(PC 5.3.1, COM 3.4, AON 3.3)
Referring to Figure 5.3.1, identify the following:

- the country which has sustained the most stable level of gross domestic product over the 20-year period
- the country that has had the most unpredictable level of gross domestic product over the 20-year period
- the country that has seen the greatest increase in gross domestic product from 1973 to 1993

GERMANY

Growth in Germany has been rather moderate. The growth rate, in GDP terms, averaged around 2.9 per cent over the period 1984–90. The overall growth rate from 1963 puts Germany behind France, Spain and Italy. Inflation rates and budget deficits have been acceptable, with unemployment comparatively low. For Germany, however, the unemployment rate is still unacceptably high. Three major points can be identified in relation to the health of the German economy:

1 There is a high level of **costs**, particularly in relation to labour costs. This state of affairs is only sustainable if levels of productivity continue to rise. Germany's main trade rivals are the USA and Japan. Germany is good at producing high quality high-tech products, but it needs to continue to devote a large amount of its GDP to research and development to keep ahead of its rivals. Germany has quite stringent environmental legislation and this has not helped to keep costs down.

2 There is something of a problem with the establishment of **new businesses** in Germany. There is a tendency to allow larger businesses to collaborate and this, in turn means that the domestic market is less competitive, but at the same time it does not help new businesses break into the market.

3 The third and, perhaps, most important impact on Germany was the **reunification** with the former East Germany. This has put a tremendous strain on the economy. With massive closures and unemployment spinning out of control in the former GDR, the government has had to put billions into restructuring the economy and supporting the unemployed. As a result of this massive reinvestment, the climb out of the recession was slower than it would otherwise have been. Interest rates stayed abnormally high, despite the recession. Successful reunification depended upon there not being, in effect, two different economies operating in Germany. The slower growth rate of the former GDR has stalled growth, but it is thought that growth in the eastern portion of Germany could in time outstrip the western growth and thus contribute to a much greater combined growth figure.

The main areas of specialism are:

- construction (s)
- electrical engineering (m)
- mechanical engineering (m)
- car manufacture (m)
- metal goods (m)
- chemicals (m)

FRANCE

France's GDP has grown, on average, at a rate of 3.4 per cent since 1960. During the 1980s, this was strengthened by a rise in investment and exports. French policy has achieved:

- relatively low inflation rates
- low budget deficits
- balanced current accounts
- moderate wage increases
- a stable currency

This has meant that French industries have become more competitive and much more active in the export field. Although the recession did affect the French economy, the effect was not as deep as in other countries and it is expected that France will be in a better position once the long-term effects of the recession wear off.

Unemployment has always been quite high, on average around 10 per cent, at worst 12 per cent. Despite the fact that output has increased, the unemployment figures remain stubbornly high. The labour market is quite rigid. In addition, the education system leaves something to be desired. There is particularly high unemployment among the many unskilled workers.

The value of the franc has caused some problems, principally in the area of competitiveness. Although the franc is fairly stable in relation to other currencies, there is little scope for interest rate reductions, a measure that it used by other countries to get themselves out of recession.

The French economy is relatively sound, and it is one of the best placed to take advantage of the lessening of the recession.

The main areas of specialism are:

- tourism (s)
- engineering (s)
- data processing and office machinery (m)
- car manufacture and parts (m)
- aerospace (m)
- nuclear and hydroelectric power (m)
- electrical equipment (m)
- food (m)
- wine, brewing, soft drinks and water (m)
- pharmaceutical (m)
- wool (m)
- dairy products (a)
- livestock (a)
- fruit and vegetables (a)

ITALY

The average growth rate for Italy over the past 33 years has been of the order of 3.6 per cent per year. There are, however, some inherent problems in the Italian economy. These are:

- there is a marked difference between the **north** (industrial based) and the **south** (mainly agriculture)
- the government's support for **local industries** and for tackling **unemployment** has put considerable strain on the economy
- the **national debt** is high and servicing this had meant that money cannot be channelled into the infrastructure which needs vast improvement
- **public services**, such as education, need high levels of investment, there is a distinct lack of suitably qualified management
- **inflation** and **wage levels** are too high, resulting in a fall in competitiveness and the widening of the trade deficit

There have been constant allegations of mismanagement and worse at the highest levels of the government in Italy. Political reforms are under way to try to combat this problem.

The private sector is very capable and versatile, with innovative plans and good managerial skills.

The main areas of specialism are:

- tourism (s)
- design and fashion (s)
- cars and motorcycle manufacture (m)
- textiles, leather, footwear and clothing (m)
- furnishings (m)
- jewellery (m)
- machinery and machine tools (m)
- electrical goods (m)
- wire and cables (m)
- food (m)
- wine (a)

SPAIN

Spain has suffered from high inflation and high unemployment problems. Spain also suffers from very large trade deficits and wide differences in the fortunes of the various regions, with the result that there are very many more problems than solutions. Per capita income is very low, the infrastructure is underdeveloped and the social security system is inadequate.

Despite all of this, Spain has had a higher level of growth over the past 33 years than any of the other major competitors, at 4.3 per cent on average. There is great hope, therefore, that the Spanish economy will pick up in all sectors. The key to success must lie in control of labour costs, otherwise Spain will be unable to withstand the competition of the single market.

The main areas of specialism are:

- tourism (s)

- car manufacturing (m)
- oil refineries (m)
- electrical goods (m)
- wire and cables (m)
- food and drink (m)
- footwear and clothing (m)
- textiles (m)
- rubber products (m)
- wine (a)
- olive oil (a)
- fruit and vegetables (a)

NETHERLANDS

The Netherlands was hit the hardest of all of the EU countries during the recession. Its high social security expenditure has led to:

- high levels of labour cost
- high taxation

These two major costs seriously affected profits during the 1970s and 1980s. Nevertheless, the inflation rate in the Netherlands is one of the lowest in the world. Other advantages are:

- a strong currency
- current account surpluses
- very low budget deficits
- good geographical location
- strong involvement in the export market
- very competitive world-wide

In short, the Netherlands is one of the best placed of the minor competitors to take advantage of its position and relative strengths as the recession comes to an end.
The main areas of specialism are:

- transport (s)
- communications (s)
- trading services (s)
- business services (s)
- chemicals (m)
- telecommunications (m)
- electrical goods (m)
- food processing (m)
- ship building (m)
- dairy products (a)
- horticulture (a)

BELGIUM

Belgium's growth rate and output are fairly average in European terms. It has a manageable level of inflation, currency and competitiveness. It does, however, have some problems, including:

- high national debt
- high public deficits

- high labour costs
- high taxation
- regional differences in terms of priorities and wealth

Although Belgium is having to deal with a crushing level of debt, it too has the advantage of its geographical position in Europe. The longer-term problems of coping with the high debt level are:

- more pressure to increase taxation
- lack of investment in the infrastructure

The main areas of specialism are:

- administration (s)
- transport (s)
- distribution (s)
- banking and insurance (s)
- chemicals (m)
- food and drink (m)
- car assembly (m)
- wool and cotton (m)
- carpets and textiles (m)
- glass (m)

DENMARK

Weak growth in the first 20 years since 1960 makes Denmark appear to be a poor performer. Productivity levels are low as the public expenditure is high. The private sector is a poor cousin to the huge public sector which is the largest in terms of revenue and expenditure in the EU. The main problems are:

- steps to make government less involved have largely failed
- Denmark has a rigid labour market
- wage rates are very low at the bottom end of the scale
- social security costs are very high
- unemployment is unacceptably high

Denmark does have the advantage of:

- good cost competitiveness
- a current account surplus
- an internationally orientated industrial base

The main areas of specialism are:

- transport (s)
- distribution (s)
- trading services (s)
- pharmaceuticals (m)
- machinery (m)
- medical equipment (m)
- ship building (m)
- plastics (m)
- fishing (a)

PORTUGAL

Portugal shares with Spain the highest growth rate of 4.3 per cent, a reflection of the rather poor quality of the Portuguese economy in the past. Having joined the then EC in 1986, Portugal has had to make some changes, including:

- reducing the role of government in the economy
- moving from a protected economy to a more market orientated one

As a major recipient of EU development money, Portugal has been able to consider the following:

- industrial restructuring
- liberalised financial reform
- administrative reform

The main areas of specialism are:

- tourism (s)
- textiles, clothing and footwear (m)
- food processing (m)
- ceramics (m)
- wire and cables (m)
- paper (m)
- wine (a)

GREECE

Since the late 1970s Greece's growth rate has been comparatively poor. As a result of the poor growth and the general low quality of the economic base, Greece has been a major recipient of EU funding. The particular problems which face Greece are:

- serious fiscal imbalances
- an extremely inefficient public sector
- a high inflation rate with little chance of getting it under control
- a poor and uncompetitive range of industries
- an infrastructure that needs a great deal of investment

Unless these fundamental problems are addressed, real GDP growth seems unlikely.

The main areas of specialism are:

- shipping services (distribution and transport) (s)
- tourism (s)
- cement (m)
- clothing and footwear (m)
- textiles (m)
- wool (a)

EIRE

Eire has always been somewhat prone to high inflation rates and current account deficits. This has largely been due to the fact that there was no solid industrial base.

Since the 1980s, this lack has been addressed and much work has been undertaken to attract inward investment. The economy has shifted significantly away from being agriculturally dominated to a mixture of services and manufacture.

Eire has one of the worst records for unemployment in the EU, and in addition has a high population growth, which is not helping this problem. The major structural reforms and policies aimed at the supply side of the economy that have been undertaken in recent years include:

- tax reforms
- reduction of state intervention
- the creation of a more competitive environment

The main areas of specialism are:

- office and data processing equipment (m)
- telecommunications (m)
- medical equipment (m)
- pharmaceuticals (m)
- wire and cables (m)
- dairy products (a)

LUXEMBOURG

With no average growth since the 1960s, Luxembourg is something of a disappointment in growth terms. The country has suffered from deindustrialisation and a loss of its former core industries. Since the late 1980s, things have begun to pick up somewhat, and there has been a growth rate of 4.1 per cent. The country has developed into a major centre for financial services. It has a very high per capita income and is the leader in this respect within the EU. It is forecast that Luxembourg will continue to grow in this area and its economic projections are encouraging.

The main areas of specialism are:

- banking (s)
- insurance (s)
- trading services (s)
- business services (s)

Finally, we examine the UK in the same manner as we considered the other countries.

UK

The growth rate of the UK is the lowest of the 12 states of the EU considered. At only 2.2 per cent over the 30-year period, this low rate is largely the result of the poor performance prior to the 1980s. The service sector has expanded well, at the expense of manufacturing and primary sector activity. The recession hit the UK very hard and high unemployment, coupled with a huge budget deficit, followed. The UK economy still has very serious structural problems.

The main reasons for these weaknesses are:

- the UK economy is very prone to inflation
- investment in research and development has not been very high
- savings are low
- considerable regional differences in unemployment, investment and quality of infrastructure
- the UK industrial base produces largely low-value products that are prone to competition from overseas
- investment in the public sector has been low, patchy and unsustained
- without a flourishing public sector, there is little support for the private sector

On a positive note, there has more recently been considerable external investment in the UK from Japan and other countries such as Germany (e.g. BMW's purchase of Rover). This has substantially modernised certain areas of the industrial base. One of the difficulties is that the recoveries seen in recent years are not based on really firm improvements, and things could go badly wrong once again.

The main areas of specialism are:

- banking, insurance and financial (s)
- business services (s)
- trading services (s)
- chemicals (m)
- pharmaceuticals (m)
- aircraft (m)
- office machinery and computers (m)
- telecommunications (m)
- publishing (m)
- electrical plant and machinery (m)
- brewing and soft drinks (m)
- oil products (e)

NON-EUROPEAN

The UK is still the fifth largest trading nation in the world. The league table looks like this:

1 United States
2 Germany
3 Japan
4 France
5 UK

We have, therefore, restricted our study of the UK's major non-European competitors to the United States and Japan.

UNITED STATES OF AMERICA

As the largest country, after China, in terms of population, it is not surprising that the United States figures fairly heavily in the world trade scene. With a mixture of manufactured goods and other products, the USA is active in nearly every market in the world. The sheer size of the industrial base and the product quality ensures that the USA is reasonably competitive, despite the fact that its products are not always the cheapest alternative.

Focus study

NON EUROPEAN COMPETITORS – UNITED STATES I

The American economy showed a 7.5 per cent increase in its Gross Domestic Product in the last quarter of 1993, but at a cost of increasing inflation and a probable 'overheating' of the economy. Real net exports of goods and services in the last quarter of 1993 were around $2.2bn., against a negative return of $11.1bn. in the previous quarter.

student activity

(PC 5.3.1, COM 3.1)
What do you understand by the term 'overheating'? What could cause this? Discuss this first in pairs then feedback your considerations to the remainder of the group.

JAPAN

Japan's government policy relies on high savings, huge exports and a large external surplus. This means that the yen is nearly always highly valued. Japan uses its high exchange rate to invest its savings in the relatively low-cost countries in the rest of Asia. Labour costs compare favourably, with a Chinese car worker being paid around $35 per month against a German car worker commanding $30 per hour.

Japan dominates the world's capital markets. Although the United States has the largest economy in the world, it consumes 45 per cent of all of the world's capital exports. Japan provides some 80 per cent of the world's capital exports. The United States is highly reliant on Japanese-produced goods to satisfy its enormous consumption levels.

student activity

(PC 5.3.1, COM 3.1)
Japanese investments in the United States have produced a negative return of some 5–10 per cent. At the same time, investments in Malaysia, China and Indonesia have produced a positive return of some 10–20 per cent. The Japanese plan to increase investment in these countries by at least 25 per cent in the next few years.

In the role of Japanese multi-national, how could you justify any investment in countries other than eastern Asia. What is the benefit for the Japanese in investing in the United States? Consider the problem in pairs.

Focus study

NON-EUROPEAN COMPETITORS – JAPAN 1

Japan has been suffering from a severe and long-term recession. The Japanese banks are burdened with bad debts. Japan is facing the possibilities of deflation, deindustrialisation and above all, unemployment.

Inflation is a thing of the past, in fact the prices in the shops are falling. Despite Japan's recession, imports are still rising. Back in 1990, Japan exported some 3.7m. colour televisions and imported around 1.1m. In the first seven months of 1994, Japan exported only 2.1m. and imported a colossal 3.3m. The problem is that the imported televisions are cheaper than their Japanese equivalents and, as a result, Japan is the biggest importer of televisions in the world.

student activity

(PC 5.3.1, COM 3.1)
Visit your local electrical retailer. Where do the majority of the television sets come from? Is the market dominated by a single country or is there a wide spread of different countries of origin? Having carried out your research, present your findings to the remainder of your group.

Focus study

NON-EUROPEAN COMPETITORS – JAPAN 2

The Japanese car industry plays a dominant role in the economy of its country. Japanese vehicles account for the following levels of market share:

- in Japan   93%
- in eastern Asia   86%
- in North America   30%
- in Europe   15%

Although the weak dollar has allowed the United States to overtake the Japanese in terms of world-wide sales for the first time since 1979, Japan completely dominates the east Asian market.

Toyota has just opened a factory to produce one-million cars (intended total sales penetration for the region) in China and Honda is converting its motorcycle production plants in China to operate on a similar scale.

student activity

(PC 5.3.1)
Identify at least three other markets within the UK that Japan has been able to penetrate to obtain, at least, a 15 per cent market share.

student activity

(PC 5.3.1, COM 3.2, 3.3, 3.4, AON 3.3)

Consider the information in Table 5.3.1 and carry out the following tasks:

- plot a graph similar to that used to illustrate the gross domestic product earlier in this section (Figure 5.3.1). Include all of the countries contained in Table 5.3.1, using the EU figure as the base line average

- identify the top five countries in terms of greatest average growth over the 33-year period
- in relation to the data included in this section, try to identify why the UK experienced a negative growth in the period 1991–93, and which countries experienced:
  - a similar drop in growth over the same period
  - a substantial growth over the same period

TABLE 5.3.1 *Real growth rates, 1960–93*

(a) The five major EU countries, USA and Japan

	Germany†	France	Italy	UK	Spain	EC	USA	Japan
1961–79	3.7	4.6	4.8	2.6	5.6	4.0	3.5	7.7
1980–83	0.5	1.4	1.5	0.5	1.0	0.9	0.7	3.3
1984–90	2.9	2.5	2.9	3.1	3.7	2.9	3.1	4.6
1991–93*	1.6	1.3	0.8	−0.6	1.5	1.1	1.0	2.5
1961–93*	2.9	3.4	3.6	2.2	4.3	3.2	2.9	6.0

b) The smaller EU countries

	Netherlands	Belgium	Denmark	Portugal	Greece	Ireland	Luxembourg
1961–79	4.2	4.0	3.5	5.6	6.4	4.5	3.2
1980–83	0.1	1.3	1.0	2.0	0.7	1.4	1.1
1984–90	2.8	2.7	2.4	3.4	2.0	4.5	4.6
1991–93*	1.4	1.1	1.3	1.6	1.6	2.5	1.8
1961–93*	3.1	3.2	2.8	4.3	4.3	4.0	3.2

* 1993: estimates

† Excluding Eastern Germany

Source: Table E19/EUROSTAT.

5.3.2 *Describe business strategies intended to improve competitiveness*

BUSINESS STRATEGIES RELATING TO: ORGANISATIONAL STRUCTURE, HUMAN RESOURCING, MARKETING, SCALE OF PRODUCTION, FINANCE, NEW TECHNOLOGY

Business strategies to improve competitiveness are as diverse as the nature of the business activities themselves. In this section you do not have to be able to identify specific strategies, but you should begin to realise that there are a great many options available. As you will be returning to this method of improving competitiveness in the Element Assignment, it would be a good idea to try to identify an organisation that has made one, some or all of these improvements in recent years. Perhaps you will be able to find an organisation that has a policy of continued change aimed at improving competitiveness.

ORGANISATIONAL STRUCTURE

In earlier sections of this book we addressed the different types of business organisation and their major advantages and disadvantages. Certainly, if an organisation expects to be competitive in the world market, then it may have to consider restructuring the business.

Restructuring can be achieved in a number of ways. An organisation can follow the example of its major competitors and try to impose the same kind of structure. Alternatively, the organisation may discover that it only needs to make minor adjustments to make itself more streamlined and responsive. It is the last two points that are mainly responsible for ensuring that an organisation is capable of coping with external competition. Different organisational structures around the world have evolved to try to take advantage of the nature of markets and to play to the strengths of industry in general.

HUMAN RESOURCING

As we mentioned earlier in this Element and in other sections of this book, the relationship between the labour force and output is one of the principal methods of measuring efficiency and high productivity levels. If you refer back to Element 5.1, you will see that labour

flexibility is one of the key determinants behind an organisation's ability to adapt and respond to changes and levels of competition.

The degree to which the power of the trade unions has been reduced is a measure of the UK government's determination to make UK industry more competitive and responsive. The other major change, this time from the point of view of businesses themselves, is the inclusion of employees in the decision-making process of organisations. Democratisation, if we can call it that, involves consultation with the workforce in order not only to achieve a greater level of consensus within organisations but also to elicit useful and implementable ideas from them. This process has not been fully embraced by all organisations, but a significant number have included this in their appraisal, training and development techniques.

MARKETING

It is of no use to an organisation to continue to produce products that do not enjoy any level of demand in overseas markets. Equally, organisations should be aware of the changing needs of the domestic market. To this end, the continued use of marketing research will uncover a wide variety of useful data sources which will give pointers to potentially beneficial adaptations of products and production processes. Each individual country does have its own peculiarities and organisations cannot expect to sell exactly the same product throughout the world. Products with the same brand name or image have been adapted to suit other markets. Nestlé, for example, have innumerable versions of Nescafé available around the world. Some are very like the British version, but others are stronger or slightly different in colour, or indeed in taste.

The continued development of products and services must also be undertaken if the organisation hopes to remain in a strong competitive position. The monitoring of the competition in the domestic market may be hard enough but if an organisation is active in a number of markets and also has to monitor them, then it is not surprising that the organisation may miss some developments. For this reason, the organisation needs to be assured that it has access to the latest data and developments relating to the products and markets in which it is active. This can be achieved by having a network of representatives available throughout the world, or by engaging the services of marketing research agencies in a particular country.

On the subject of advertising and sales promotions, it should be recognised that the same campaign may not work in different countries. Overcoming the confusion that may be engendered by literal translations of slogans and phrases is hard enough, but the nature of customers within the overseas market may differ enormously from those of the domestic market. Obviously, it is a good idea for an organisation to engage the services of an agency in the overseas market to plan and execute the marketing or sales promotion campaign on the its behalf. The organisation would need to impose very strict controls and conditions to ensure that the agency's ideas and execution of the campaign are not in variance with the overall corporate strategies or objectives.

SCALE OF PRODUCTION

Optimising the scale of production in relation to the needs of the organisation is another consideration that must be approached with caution. Among the other organisations competing in the same market as the UK business, there may be large organisations which have achieved production levels and efficiencies it is impossible to duplicate in the short term. On the other hand, increasing the scale of production can lead to greater productivity. New technology can enable small-scale production to be as competitive.

student activity

(PC 5.3.2, COM 3.1)
Individually, try to discover an example of new technology which has enabled smaller organisations to be competitive. Feedback the results of your investigation to the rest of your group.

FINANCE

In order to remain competitive within the domestic market, let alone a world market, the organisation needs to have systems in place to address the following:

● controls over the cost of labour
● controls over the cost of production
● controls over the cost of marketing in comparison with its effectiveness

As we have seen in Unit 1, and as we will see in Units 6 and 7, financial control is be a primary concern of an organisation which intends to achieve and maintain its competitive edge. If it allows costs to spiral out of control the organisation reduces its ability to inwardly invest and to present a strong and credible option for potential providers of finance. This may lead the organisation to become starved of cash, further compounding its inability to compete.

NEW TECHNOLOGY

New technology itself acts not only as an agent of change but also as a means by which an organisation can gain and maintain a competitive edge. Certainly there have been considerable advances in technology, such as:

● fibre optics
● robotics
● computer-aided design and manufacture
● automation

Organisations which are concerned with remaining competitive in the world market must always adapt, implement or fail. Since new technology is developing at a rate which most organisations find it hard to keep up with, there will always be an organisation somewhere which has decided to embrace the new technology at a time when other organisations are unable to do so. Temporarily this organisation will be at the cutting edge of the industry, provided it understands and can use the new technology, but, inevitably, as technology advances again, a different organisation will take up the ball and run with it.

5.3.3 Describe government strategies intended to improve the competitiveness of UK industry

GOVERNMENT STRATEGIES

In Unit 1 we addressed the two essential types of government policy, namely monetary and fiscal policy. However, there are a number of individual actions (which are not necessarily part of these two key policy directions) that need to be taken in order to ensure that the UK industry remains competitive on the world stage. We deal with these below.

EXCHANGE RATE POLICY

If there is an increase in the money supply this will lead to a depreciation in the pound and a consequent increase in net exports. An increase in the money supply normally reduces interest rates, so if the interest rate falls in the UK but does not fall in one of the UK's competitors, then investors will move their money out of the UK and into the more profitable overseas markets. Unfortunately there is another side-effect. When organisations take their investments out of the UK the demand for the pound decreases (since they are selling their investments in sterling) and, at the same time, the demand for the currency of their new destination of investment will increase. Naturally this means that there is a lower foreign exchange value of the pound relative to these other currencies.

The pound is now worth less and, as a result, customers from overseas markets can purchase UK products at lower prices. At the same time, products from overseas markets cost UK customers more. In the short term this means there will be an increase in demand for UK products, as customers switch from the more expensive imports to the comparatively less expensive domestic product. There is another benefit to this too. Customers in the overseas markets who had been purchasing their own domestic products because they were cheaper than UK imports are now able to buy UK products at lower prices than their own country's goods.

If the government then reduces the money supply and increases interest rates all of the effects detailed above are reversed. However, many of these changes are only temporary since in our description above we have not factored in the actions of other overseas governments who may be undertaking a similar exercise simultaneously.

CONTROL OF INFLATION

Monetary policy is usually the best course of action to control inflation. Unfortunately, whenever there is an attempt to control inflation this often leads to a freezing of wage increases, higher interest rates and higher levels of unemployment. The relationships between these features are complex, but the main point of trying to control inflation is to attempt to prevent costs to UK industry spiralling out of control. One way in which the inflation rate is fuelled is for there to be a cycle of wage rises followed by increased prices, followed by more calls for wage increases. By rigidly controlling prices or wage rates the government can go some way to controlling inflation. Equally, it can control the availability of money in the form of credit, in an attempt to prevent inflation from creeping up. If through high interest rates the government controls and reduces the number of individuals seeking credit, then they simply will not have the money to push prices up. Perhaps more than any other single example of inflation, the housing boom of the early to mid-1980s was fuelled by two main things. The first was the easy availability of cheap mortgages and the second was the over-valuation of houses by surveyors and estate agents. These two factors were inextricably linked. Estate agents and surveyors knew that houses could command far higher prices than they had done previously, as demand was high and money was easy to borrow. It was only when inflation had become a more widespread problem that banks and building societies were forced to be rather more stringent in their assessment of individuals asking for mortgages. As interest rates had risen, the demand for mortgages had decreased. With many borrowers unable to keep up payments, due to the higher interest rates, there were widespread repossessions. When prices fell, many individuals found themselves trapped in properties which they had purchased at far higher prices than the now current market value.

PRIVATISATION

Most of the countries of Western Europe have a mixed economy, in other words, there is a portion of the economy in public hands and the remainder is in private hands. The scale of government intervention in these countries is, of course, far higher in relation to the percentage of the economy which is in public hands. Nationalised industries are owned and operated by authorities which are directly responsible to the government. In recent years, successive governments have been selling off state-owned enterprises. This is, perhaps, in response to the fact that countries such as Japan and the USA, which are very active and successful in the world markets, rely very heavily on private industry. In an attempt to emulate these two successful countries, many nationalised industries have been privatised and these sales have reduced the role of the government in the economy.

DEREGULATION

Regulation in this context refers to a set of rules for the winning of an operation that provides a major public service. They are administered by an agency or authority under the guidance of the government, or perhaps the EU. In the UK regulation really began in the late nineteenth century with the control of railways and canals. As industries were nationalised or the government recognised that a particular organisation had a monopoly, new regulations were brought into force. Although some of the nationalised industries have been privatised, there are still regulators such as OFGAS, OFWAT and OFTEL to keep a watch on their operations. These regulate the gas industry, the water industry and telecommunications industry respectively. A good example of the power of regulation is when British Telecom was told that they could not increase their prices by any more than 6.2 per cent less than the increase in other retail prices.

Deregulation involves the removal of restrictions on the following:

- prices
- product standards and types
- entry conditions (improving an organisation's chances of entering the market)

There is a very strong tendency in the UK now to deregulate; recent examples include the deregulation of the buses and the entry of Mercury Communications into the telecommunications field as a direct competitor to British Telecom.

REDUCING THE ROLE OF THE GOVERNMENT

The economic crises in the 1970s and 1980s brought something of a turning-point in the role of the government and its involvement in the economy. The concept of state intervention began to be abandoned forever. There had been until the 1970s a partnership of sorts, with businesses, labour and the government acting in concert for the greater good of the economy. There was a degree of regulation which provided a framework for the mixed economy. Some of the key industries were nationalised, social security was widespread and fairly comprehensive and the size of the public sector was quite large. So why has there been a breakdown in this consensus and why has the government, particularly since 1979, chosen to dismantle the welfare state and return the key industries to private hands? We can identify the following main causes:

- oil prices were substantially increased in 1973 and 1979
- as a result of the oil price rises, the growth of the western economies slowed down
- this led to a period of 'stagflation', characterised by inflation and a stagnant (not growing) economy
- as a result of this, the government had to find extra money to pay for the enormous numbers of unemployed
- this led to the widening of the welfare safety net, and a considerable increase in expenditure on this
- as the government was receiving less income, the balance between income and expenditure took a negative turn
- because of the deficit, the tax burden on individuals and business increased
- this meant lower profits for businesses, lower investment, lower employment and closures
- this, in turn, meant that there was even greater strain on government expenditure

The Keynesian policies employed by the government (i.e. adjusting demand by controlling credit and currency) could not cope with the new demands on the economy. As a result of the rising costs of inputs, such as energy and labour which are on the supply side of the considerations, the demand-orientated policies of the time could not provide a solution.

Meanwhile, on the international scene, there was an intensification of competition. As individual domestic economies became more and more exposed to international competition, businesses were forced to lower their costs, be more efficient and apply pressure to wages and employment levels.

The government had only one option, to decrease the burdens on businesses and individuals in the hope that this might prove to be the solution. Tax and social security payments were reduced, but at the same time the level of labour protection was reduced.

As a result of all of this, there was a new era of economic theory, and the blame for the problems have been laid at the door of the government. They were too involved in the economy and did not give it sufficient freedom. We need first to look at what the mistakes were, before we look at the measures taken to solve them.

- the welfare state was too big and too expensive
- prices were too heavily influenced by subsidies (e.g.

nationalised industries) and high taxes

- the taxation policy, both direct and indirect taxes, squeezed profits
- the government was too inclined to use monetary policy to cover any deficits

The solution, as we well know, is the free market, or perhaps more accurately a **more free market**. As if to prove the point, the command or planned economies of Eastern Europe collapsed in the late 1980s like a house made of playing cards.

Although not all the principles of the free market have been fully embraced, the free market is still dominant. The call for 'more market and less state' has been the cry of successive governments in the UK and throughout the rest of Europe and beyond. The European Union bases its philosophy on the free market, but there are still very substantial differences between the member states as to the involvement of the government in the economy. We will see this when we look at the question of economic and monetary union.

INVESTMENT IN NEW TECHNOLOGY

Organisations are constantly on the search for new technology which can help reduce the costs of production. They appreciate that they cannot achieve these savings without considerable investment. One of the key considerations they have to address is where they can obtain the investment that they need in order to develop new technology. Formerly many of the nationalised industries took a lead in the development of new technology and methods of production, working on the assumption that their costs would be subsidised or underwritten by the government. With the removal, to a large extent, of these industries from the public sector, the government has had to enter into more direct partnerships with private industry. Obviously investing in or underwriting the development of new technology is an important and key role for the government to undertake. If it is not willing to make investments how can it possibly expect private industry to fund developments?

IMPROVING TRAINING AND EDUCATION

The government has recognised that there is a severe skills gap in the UK. In other words this means, although there may be hundreds of thousands of unemployed, they do not have the necessary transferable skills to make them employable. The government has begun with a package of measures aimed at addressing the level of education and competence of individuals passing through educational and training establishments. The government has instituted a policy which supports a core curriculum which is followed through from primary school until the individual leaves

school. It is assumed that these core skills, knowledge and abilities will provide individuals with a better preparation for the world of work than previously available courses. The government has supported the development of vocational or semi-vocational courses, very much like the one which you are studying in the last few years of schooling and in further and higher education. It is presumed that the development of these courses and other allied training programmes will make the workforce a highly educated and flexible one.

TAXATION TO AFFECT AGGREGATE DEMAND

Aggregate demand is the total level of demand in the economy. Basically it consists of the following:

- the total spending by customers on products and services
- investments made by organisations
- government expenditure
- net revenue from business dealings abroad

Obviously a change in taxation would have an impact on the aggregate demand within the economy. In other words, a taxation increase would mean that customers would have less money to spend in the shops, and the demand for products or services would reduce. Equally, if taxation of organisations was increased they would have less retained profits from which to make investments. A taxation increase would, however, allow the government to spend more and would enable the government to redirect some of the income generated within the economy into projects and developments which it feels are of national importance. Obviously, a taxation increase will affect not only the fortunes of UK goods and services in retail outlets, but also the demand for overseas products and services. There is a more drastic effect which relates to the lowering of investment by UK industry. If industry is unable to sustain levels of investment comparable to those of its overseas competitors, there may be a danger that it will fall behind in technological development and other investment.

GOVERNMENT EXPENDITURE

Government expenditure is the public spending undertaken using the revenue obtained from taxes or other sources. Usually, government expenditure is directed towards improving the infrastructure or towards encouraging organisations to locate in particular areas of the country. Unfortunately, in recent years, a large percentage of government expenditure has had to be invested in the welfare state and, in particular, in supporting the unemployed. The government is faced with a two-fold problem here:

TABLE 5.3.2 *Government expenditure (in £ millions at current prices)*

	1980	1985	1986	1987	1988	1989	1990	1991
Current expenditure								
Military defence	11,327	17,857	18,608	18,669	19,288	20,446	22,178	24,410
National Health Service	11,280	17,212	18,446	20,300	22,362	24,250	26,610	29,812
Education spending								
by local authorities	9864	13,314	14,944	16,235	17,714	18,578	19,849	21,835
Other final consumption	16,469	25,422	27,383	30,145	32,365	35,755	41,241	45,842
Total	48,940	73,805	79,381	85,349	91,729	99,029	109,878	121,899
Gross domestic fixed capital								
formation	5499	6872	7509	7577	6506	9582	12,659	12,173
Value of physical increase in stocks	43	450	−237	−498	−322	−163	156	151
Transfer payments								
Subsidies	5719	7225	6187	6173	5918	5782	6069	5878
Current grants to personal sector	25,524	46,813	50,984	52,494	54,087	56,793	62,002	71,767
Current grants abroad	1780	3427	2233	3277	3248	4278	4597	1049
Capital grants	2193	3319	3002	3216	3806	4233	9273	6769
Total net lending	3551	−1733	−3979	−6375	−5051	−1382	−8589	−9254
Debt interest	10,873	17,715	17,257	18,003	18,255	18,943	18,793	17,097
Total, all expenditure items								
Total as % of GDP(E)								

Source: Central Statstical Office, UK National Accounts, as presented in the Econmics Review, Data supplement, September 1993, p. 22.

- the money spent on unemployment cannot be redirected into developments which would create jobs
- because the government cannot create jobs by investing in the infrastructure, the unemployment level is bound to remain high

As we mentioned earlier, the government is keen to return many nationalised industries into private hands, believing that this not only reduces government expenditure in the form of subsidies, but also actually contributes money to central government in the form of the income from the shares. Again, as we mentioned earlier, the government is particularly active in training

and education, and also makes considerable investments in the development of new technology.

EUROPEAN MARKET INTEGRATION

When the UK joined the European Union, or the European Economic Community as it was known in 1973, it became part of a political and economic union. There has been considerable debate regarding UK's membership of the EU and the advantages and

TABLE 5.3.3 *Government expenditure as a percentage of GDP*

	1960–7	1968–73	1974–79	1980–8
Sweden	34.8	44.3	54.4	62.8
France	37.4	38.9	43.3	50.4
Average EC	33.9	37.1	43.2	48.4
Italy	31.9	36.0	42.9	48.4
Germany	35.7	39.8	47.5	47.9
UK	34.7	39.5	44.6	45.7
Canada	29.3	34.7	39.2	45.1
US	28.3	31.0	32.6	36.0
Japan	18.7	20.5	28.4	33.2

Source: OECD, *Historical Statistics*, 1990.

student activity

(PC 5.3.3, COM 3.2, 3.4)
Referring to Table 5.3.2, explain the following headings:

- capital grants
- gross domestic fixed capital formation

Which of the spending categories has seen the greatest increase over the period 1980 to 1991? Which of the spending categories has seen the lowest average increase over the period 1980 to 1991?

disadvantages can best be summed up by the following:

1 *Advantages*
- the EU offers UK industry the prospect of easy access to some 340m. customers
- the sheer size of the EU offers groups of industries amazing economies of scale
- disposing of trade barriers, and subsequently increasing competition, creates an opportunity to reduce costs, increase efficiency and encourage innovation
- investments from non-EU countries are positively encouraged and no curbs are placed upon such investments
- there is the possibility of much greater redistribution of wealth within the EU as the poorer countries are given the opportunity to catch up with their more successful neighbours
- on an individual level, the EU offers tremendous career opportunities

2 *Disadvantages*
- there have been constant criticisms of the way in which EU funds are spent. The Common Agricultural Policy, in particular is cited as a distorted and unfair way of spending these EU funds
- the EU has been roundly criticised for its bureaucratic nature
- the EU is regarded with a degree of suspicion by non-EU countries and some have gone as far as to suggest that it is a conspiracy to exclude them from the lucrative European markets
- despite the fact that the EU means full European market integration, many member states still put their own national interests before those of the rest of the community

PARTICIPATING IN THE WORLD TRADE ORGANISATION (WTO)

The World Trade Organisation replaces and develops further the principles of of the General Agreement on Tariffs and Trade (GATT). Around 120 countries are involved in negotiations to cut tariff barriers by around 37 per cent, thus opening up global markets in agriculture and services. Unfortunately, many countries, such as the USA, view the talks with considerable amounts of scepticism. Under pressure from the American labour movement, the American government has voiced its concerns about unfair competition from poor countries whose costs of production are significantly lower than those of the more advanced western countries. It is certainly true that these poorer countries do have a competitive advantage, but it lies in lower wages and the USA in particular wants such countries to introduce laws to raise labour costs. There is also a fear that if present trade barriers are eliminated, some countries (or regional groupings of countries) will create new and discriminatory ones.

The WTO is also seen as a means by which the world can be rid of starvation, but the human rights issue is tempered by the fact that many countries will not engage in trade with other countries which have poor human rights records, even though the populations of these countries are starving.

The WTO embraces the concept of free trade. It is difficult to see how government subsidies and investments in their own domestic economies will fit into this concept. The main aim, however, is to reduce protectionism and come up with an international policy that is consistent. It is only when this has been achieved that a truly free and competitive world market will be in existence.

5.3.4 *Evaluate business and government strategies intended to improve competitiveness*

In this performance criterion, we address the impact of business and government policies and strategies on the competitiveness of UK industry and the economy as a whole. Since this is part of the Element Assignment, we will only give you some pointers to lines of enquiry and investigation. For deeper analysis, you will have to do some research yourself and consult the various sources of statistical information available and the media.

MARKET SHARE

As we mentioned earlier, the key to business success is the constant search for new markets, or ways to exploit existing ones. Organisations need to be aware of the possibilities and alert to the threats of the competition. As the EU market develops, taking in more countries and opening new possibilities, there is a danger that UK businesses will come under threat from overseas competitors. Just as the UK can exploit the changing face of Europe, so too can the other member states.

TABLE 5.3.4 *Main economic indicators, 1992*

(a) The five major EU countries

	Germany	France	Italy	UK	Spain
Population (millions)	80.7	57.4	57.9	57.7	39.1
Gross domestic product (GDP)					
Current market prices (billion ECU)	1487	1036	951	804	444
Average real growth in % 1983–92	2.7★	2.1	2.4	2.2	3.2
GDP per head, PPS, EC = 100%	118.7★	111.5	103.5	95.3	76.7
Unemployment rate					
average 1983–92	6.0★	10.1	10.2	10.8	18.0
Inflation (GDP deflator)					
average 1983–92	2.9★	5.7	8.1	5.5	8.0
Gross fixed capital formation					
average 1983–92	20.2★	20.1	20.2	17.5	21.7
(% of GDP at market prices)					
Private consumption					
average 1983–92	61.9★	60.4	61.7	63.0	63.4
(% of GDP at market prices)					
Real unit labour costs					
(1980 = 100)	92.4★	89.8	96.3	101.2	84.5
Exports of goods and services					
(% of GDP at market prices)	33.6★	22.6	19.5	23.7	17.5
Imports of goods and services					
(% of GDP at market prices)	26.5★	21.3	19.3	25.3	20.5
Current balance					
(% of GDP at market prices)	0.9★	0.1	−2.4	−2.7	−3.7

b) The smaller EU countries

	Netherlands	Belgium	Denmark	Portugal	Greece	Ireland	Luxembourg
Population (millions)	15.2	10.0	5.2	9.4	10.4	3.6	0.4
Gross domestic product (GDP)							
Current market prices (billion ECU)	248	169	110	65	61	38	8
Average real growth in % 1983–92	2.4	2.2	2.1	2.7	1.8	3.7	4.1
GDP per head, PPS, EC = 100%	102.9	106.1	106.0	57.5	47.4	70.7	129.1
Unemployment rate							
average 1983–92	6.7	8.2	9.5	4.8	7.7	17.8	1.9
Inflation (GDP deflator)							
average 1983–92	1.6	4.1	4.2	16.8	17.2	4.0	3.5
Gross fixed capital formation							
average 1983–92	20.4	17.6	17.9	25.1	18.5	18.4	24.6
(% of GDP at market prices)							
Private consumption							
average 1983–92	59.3	63.8	53.6	65.5	68.5	58.1	57.6
(% of GDP at market prices)							
Real unit labour costs							
(1980 = 100)	89.0	91.6	89.2	84.5	93.9	64.6	98.3
Exports of goods and services							
(% of GDP at market prices)	53.0	69.5	36.6	28.9	23.7	63.0	90.8
Imports of goods and services							
(% of GDP at market prices)	47.7	66.4	29.1	37.9	32.5	51.5	98.7
Current balance							
(% of GDP at market prices)	3.6	1.8	3.0	−2.1	−3.3	0.1	19.9

★ *Excluding East Germany.*

Source: European Economy, 1993, No. 54.

student activity

(PC 5.3.4, COM 3.2, 3.3, 3.4, AON 3.1, 3.2,3.3)
Individually, assess the data in Table 5.3.4 and pre-pare a short report that looks at three of the countries in the table, including the UK. You should explain what the classifications mean as well as addressing the key comparative data. Your aim should be to compare the three countries and make an assessment of their relative strengths and weak-nesses.

Focus study

MARKET SHARE

Japanese companies are clearly using their UK produc-tion facilities as a springboard into the European markets. As the 1990s dawned, the Japanese stopped trying to increase their market share in this country. They are now targeting the rest of the EU. In 1987, some 36 per cent of all Japanese manufacturers cited the UK as their main target for market penetration, but four years later, this figure had fallen to only 25 per cent. At the same time, the percentage of Japanese manufacturers who gave their target as achieving mar-ket penetration in the rest of Europe rose from 43 per cent to 59 per cent.

SALES AND REVENUE

Sales level or volume of sales is seen as one of the prin-cipal ways of measuring the effectiveness and potential profitability of a business. Without doubt, there have been some success stories among UK companies. Obtaining sales in the face of severe European compe-tition in the EU market still remains one of the major goals of many medium to large UK businesses. Unfortunately, the continuing trade deficit remains stubbornly high. Although improvements have been made since the low of 1989, the trade balance is at least £15bn. in deficit. We will return to this subject of the trading position of the UK later in this performance criterion.

student activity

(PC 5.3.4, COM 3.1)
Can you identify any other European or non-European country that has begun to make inroads into the UK market? What is the nature of their business and why has the UK industry not really responded? Discuss in small groups.

EFFICIENCY AND PRODUCTIVITY

National competitiveness and, consequently, efficiency and productivity are very much determined by the inflation rate. Considerable progress has been made since the poor performance experienced in the late 1980s. The modest wage increases have helped to bring about a sharp rise in productivity. Labour productivity has risen because of the laying off of workers in busi-ness rationalisation programmes. As a result, the real unit labour costs of the total European economy have fallen by 7 per cent over the period 1980–92. At the same time, the Japanese managed to match the decrease, whilst the United States only managed a 1.8 per cent drop.

Using a rather complicated formula, it has been cal-culated that over the 1980–92 period, the following has happened:

- the EU industries have become 12 per cent more competitive
- the United States has become 1.1 per cent more competitive
- the Japanese have become 27.8 per cent less com-petitive

student activity

(PC 5.3.4, COM 3.1)
What do these figures relating to competitiveness tell you? What does the fall in the competitiveness of the Japanese mean to the UK and the rest of Europe? Discuss this as a group.

PRODUCT QUALITY AND SERVICE

As we have mentioned earlier, one of the many reasons for the dramatic fall in the UK's overseas trading in the past few years was the nature and quality of the products it offered. Basically, low–quality manufactured products are often the most prone to fluctuations in the overseas markets. There is no doubt that UK companies produce some world-beating products and services, but they also compete in areas that are flooded with the products of other countries. If we take the products offered by Third World countries, it is impossible for a highly expensive production process in the UK to compete at all. Indeed, there are examples of whole industries being undercut to the extent that they are faced with the prospect of closure. The shipbuilding industry, for example, under pressure from significantly cheaper markets, has all but been closed down as a result.

TRADING CONDITIONS

The trading conditions that apply to the UK in relation to their EU partners are fairly straightforward: there is virtually free access to the market-place for all industries and business ventures. The trading conditions that apply to overseas (non-European) trading nations are rather more complex.

Focus study

PRODUCT QUALITY AND SERVICE

Diplomats are often seen as one of the key markets to tempt when trying to establish visible and prestige products abroad. Some nine UK ambassadors have recently been issued with new Rolls Royce limousines. It was stated by a spokesperson that 'they offered a good deal...the cars are also a shop window for Britain'.

Meanwhile, other European countries also encourage their ambassadors to use their own home-grown products. The Italians are unlucky enough to have to use the Lancia Thema in the UK, a car that was withdrawn from sale over here because of poor sales figures.

The Jaguar, preferred by John Major, has also found favour with the South Africans, Nigerians and Russians. The Germans use the Mercedes. At a cost of up to £96,000 each and with a fleet of over 300 in the UK alone, this is no mean investment.

The Japanese, the home of car manufacturing, rather embarrassingly for them, saw their Emperor use a Rolls Royce for his coronation. It is reported that his preferred vehicle is the Bentley Brooklands, another UK-manufactured prestige car.

student activity

(PC 5.3.4, COM 3.1)
What does this Focus Study tell us about the nature of the quality of UK products? Can you think of any other examples of UK products that are renowned for their quality around the world? Discuss this as a group.

student activity

(PC 5.3.4, COM 3.4)
Individually, investigate the trading conditions of a country outside the EU. What are the restrictions and opportunities in that country for a UK-based organisation? If there are barriers to trade, what is the agreement with the UK regarding the importation of that country's products and services into the UK?

STANDARD OF LIVING

Since the term 'standard of living' is rather a woolly and difficult thing to define, we confine ourselves to saying that it is the ability of individuals to buy products and services that they desire. Alternatively, it could be measured in terms of individuals' real incomes, in other words, their income in relation to pricing levels.

student activity

(PC 5.3.4, COM 3.3, 3.4, AON 3.2, 3.3)
Individually, prepare a series of graphs that can better illustrate the data in Table 5.3.5. Also, try to define the following:

- lowest decile point
- highest decile point

LEVELS OF EMPLOYMENT

The success or failure of UK businesses and the economy as a whole can be directly measured by unemployment rates. Given that there will, inevitably, be regional differences, the unemployment figures as a total are in reverse proportion to the level of activity of the economy and business.

There is record unemployment in the EU, but it is said that the UK has a better chance than some other countries to beat this blight on the economy. With unemployment across the EU expected to hit 11.25 per cent in 1996, this flies in the face of some rather optimistic predictions of growth.

Growth, expected to rise by some 3 per cent in 1996, against a rise of only 1.25 per cent in 1995, is definitely on the positive side. The recovery is rather slow all the same. Inflation is expected to fall to only 3.2 per cent. It is the export market and the increased levels of investment that offer the best hope for the UK in the next few years.

student activity

(PC 5.3.4, COM 3.1)
What does the graph in Figure 5.3.2 tell you about the following:

- the relative provision of welfare and social security in the different countries featured?
- the probable reasons behind the very low figure for Japan and the very high figure of Sweden
- the average level of direct taxes and other contributions across the range of featured countries

Discuss this as a group.

TABLE 5.3.5 *Real* weekly earnings† after income tax, national insurance contributions, child benefit and family credit: by selected family type, Great Britain (£ per week)*

	1971	1981	1991	1992
Single man, no children				
Lowest decile point	98.9	108.0	130.9	134.6
Median	146.3	160.3	211.3	217.6
Highest decile point	231.4	261.0	380.9	390.6
Single woman, no children				
Lowest decile point	63.4	80.6	103.5	107.5
Median	153.5	168.6	219.9	225.8
Highest decile point	238.6	269.4	389.5	402.2
Married man‡, no children				
Lowest decile point	106.1	116.3	139.5	142.9
Median	153.5	168.6	219.9	225.8
Highest decile point	238.6	269.4	389.5	402.2
Married man‡, two children§				
Lowest decile point¶				
Family credit claimed	124.3	134.8	164.3	168.7
Family credit not claimed**	124.3	134.8	156.4	160.3
Median	171.6	187.1	236.8	243.3
Highest decile point	256.7	287.8	406.3	419.6

* At April 1992 prices.

† Figures relate to April each year and to full-time employees on adult rates whose pay for the survey pay-period was not affected by absence.

‡ Assuming no wife's earnings.

§ Aged under 11.

¶ In years up to 1987, there was no entitlement to Family Income Supplement for this category

** Families with capital of more than £3000 would only be eligible to receive reduced amounts of family credit, or may not be eligible at all.

Source: Inland Revenue; Department of Social Security; *Social Trends 1994,* Table 5.13.

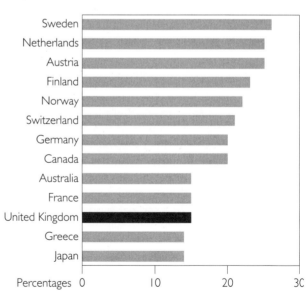

1 Excluding employers' contributions
Source: Central Statistical Office *Social Trends 1994,* Chart 5.14

FIG. 5.3.2 *Percentage of personal income taken by direct taxes and social security contributions[1]: international comparison, 1990.*
Source: Central Statistical Office, *Social Trends, 1994,* Chart 5.14.

student activity

(PC 5.3.4, COM 3.1)
As a group, study Figure 5.3.3 on regional unemployment rates. Discuss why you think that certain regions
of the UK are more or less likely to suffer from consistently high unemployment.

FIG. 5.3.3 *Regional unemployment rates, 1989-1994, United Kingdom.*
Source: Central Statistical Office, Economic Trends, May 1994, Chart 4.3.

student activity

(PC 5.3.4, COM 3.1)
As a group, look at the graph in Figure 5.3.4, which plots the unemployment figures from 1950 to the 1990s. Discuss why the unemployment trends have increased almost consistently over the period. What do you think, caused the downward turn in 1990?

FIG. 5.3.4 *United Kingdom unemployment, 1950-1990.*
Source: Central Statistical Office, Economic Trends.

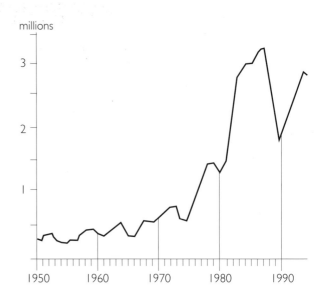

ELEMENT 5.3

assignment

(PC 5.3.1–4, COM 3.2, 3.3, 3.4, AON 3.1, 3.2, 3.3, IT 3.1, 3.2, 3.3)
Having looked at types of production in Element 5.1, you must now extend your investigations to foreign competitors. It may be useful, particularly when the Assignment focuses on a single business and how it faces overseas competition, to consider doing a SWOT analysis first.

TASK 1

(PC 5.3.1)
Produce a series of tables which investigate at least three major competitors of the UK. These tables should include the following as a part of the analysis:

- economic growth
- investment
- inflation
- exchange rate
- share of the world trade
- productivity

TASK 2

(PC 5.3.2, 5.3.4)
Word process a report which describes how one business faces competition. It should describe the strategy used by the business to improve its performance in a competitive world market, and also evaluate the strategy in terms of its effects on employees and the business itself.

TASK 3

(PC 5.3.3, 5.3.4)
Also included in your report should be an evaluation of government strategies which affect business. You should also show how these might help or hinder the business's ability to compete.

NOTES

You should attempt to look at current media dealing with business and government activity. Your library may have a file of articles and newspaper stories that can prove to be a useful source. Alternatively, you may wish to look at the CD ROM Disks available for all of the quality newspapers.

test questions

Focus 1

ADDED VALUE

1-3 The following are different forms of quality assurance:

(a) CWQC
(b) TQC
(c) QA
(d) TQM

Which of the above is best described by the following?

1 a system which integrates all of the departments of an organisation

(a) (b) (c) (d)

2 a top-down adoption of a quality approach to all activities

(a) (b) (c) (d)

3 a method which aims to provide a good quality low-cost product to the customer

(a (b) (c) (d)

4 The Department of Trade and Industry developed a formula to measure productivity. The correct formula is:

(a) added value per unit/total number of employees
(b) added value per annum/total number of employees
(c) added value per unit/total labour costs
(d) added value per annum/total labour costs

Focus 2

FACTORS CONTRIBUTING TO CHANGE IN PRODUCTION

5 The following statements have been made:
(i) robots are multi-functional manipulators
(ii) robots have a frame which mimics the human brain

How are these statements best described?

(a) True/True
(b) True/False
(c) False/True
(d) False/False

6 Compulsory competitive tendering is a version of which of the following?

(a) single sourcing
(b) labour flexibility
(c) contracting out
(d) double sourcing

7 Which of the following pieces of legislation would normally be created and administered by local government?

(a) Pollution of Rivers Act
(b) by-laws
(c) Clean Air Act
(d) Deposit of Poisonous Wastes Act

Focus 3

IMPROVEMENTS IN PRODUCTION

8 The following statements have been made:

(i) UK corporation tax is lower than that in France, Italy and Germany
(ii) the USA has created more jobs in the UK than the UK has created in the USA
(iii) UK investment in the USA exceeds £100bn.
(iv) US investment in the UK accounts for 20 per cent of its total European investments

Which of the two above statements are correct?

(a) (i) and (ii)
(b) (i) and (iii)
(c) (ii) and (iii)
(d) (ii) and (iv)

9 In surveys which have investigated the barriers to change, which of the following was cited as the most common barrier?

(a) lack of management expertise
(b) quality and reliability of incoming parts
(c) high level of absenteeism and labour turnover
(d) lack of employees with the right skills

10 What is a single status facility?

(a) an organisation which produces a single product
(b) an organisation in which all employees wear the same clothes

(c) an organisation which only operates in one market

(d) an organisation which can be clearly identified as a particular form of industrial concern

Focus 4

TYPES AND CHANGES IN TYPES OF EMPLOYMENT

11 By 1992 the number of individuals running their own businesses accounted for which of the following totals?

(a) 2.8m.

(b) 3.1m.

(c) 1.9m.

(d) 2.2m.

12 The following statements have been made:

(i) By the year 2001 full-time employment will have seen a decrease of 0.3m.

(ii) By the year 2001 full-time employment will account for some 61 per cent of all employment

How are these statements best described?

  (a) True/True

  (b) True/False

  (c) False/True

  (d) False/False

13 Which of the following statements is untrue regarding part-time employment?

(a) part-time employment accounts for around 24 per cent of all employment

(b) by the year 2001 this will have increased to 28 per cent

(c) by the year 2001 women will account for 52 per cent of part-time workers

(d) this will mean an increase of 2.2m.

14 The following statements have been made:

(i) employers are not required to pay home-workers statutory sick pay

(ii) home-working accounts for some 640,000 jobs

How are these statements best described?

(a) True/True

(b) True/False

(c) False/True

(d) False/False

15 With regard to a business's need to make changes in types of employment, which of the following has not been identified as a factor?

(a) 72 per cent of organisations sub-contract services

(b) 70 per cent of non-core operations are contracted out

(c) temporal flexibility involves temporary measures to cope with changes in demand

(d) 80 per cent of organisations which have restructured incurred job losses

Focus 5

EMPLOYMENT TRENDS

16 In terms of national employment trends, the following statements have been made:

(i) during the period 1995 to 1997 employment growth is expected to be 0.8 per cent

(ii) during the period 1993 to 1994 employment decreased by 230,000

How are these statements best described?

(a) True/True

(b) True/False

(c) False/True

(d) False/False

17 Which of the following facts regarding national levels of employment is incorrect?

(a) female part–time employment exceeds male part–time employment

(b) male full–time employment exceeds female full–time employment

(c) female self-employment exceeds male self-employment

(d) male self-employment exceeds female self-employment

18–20 The following are percentages of jobs in the various sectors of the economy:

(a) 20%

(b) 25%

(c) 30%

(d) 45%

Which of the above percentages relate to the following sectors?

18 Manufacturing, primary and construction

(a) (b) (c) (d)

19 Service

(a) (b) (c) (d)

20 Distribution

(a) (b) (c) (d)

21 The following statements have been made:

(i) despite the fact that 1.4m. jobs were created between 1981 and 1993, the number of full-time employees fell by 2m.
(ii) during the same period the number of employees engaged in part-time work rose from 21 per cent to 28 per cent

How are these statements best described?

(a) True/True
(b) True/False
(c) False/True
(d) False/False

22 The underground economy has a number of important features. Which of the following is untrue?

(a) if the earnings were taxed, then the income would be around £25bn.
(b) it is estimated that the underground economy is worth upwards of £54bn.
(c) the underground economy accounts for 6–8 per cent of GDP
(d) the self-employed earn in reality 1.5 times what they actually declare

Focus 6
UK ECONOMY AND MAJOR COMPETITORS

23 The following statements have been made:

(i) in terms of GDP growth, Germany lags behind France, Spain and Italy
(ii) the slower growth rate of the former GDR has stalled German growth

How are these statements best described?

(a) True/True
(b) True/False
(c) False/True
(d) False/False

24 With regard to the UK's major European competitors, which of the following statements is incorrect?

(a) Portugal has enjoyed one of the highest GDP growth rates in Europe at 4.3 per cent
(b) One of the main reasons why the Italian economy has failed to improve is government mismanagement

(c) Spanish per capita income is very low
(d) Luxembourg has experienced a growth rate of 4.1 per cent since 1960, largely as a result of its industrialisation programme

25 The UK is the fifth largest trading nation in the world. The correct sequence of the top four is:

(a) Japan, USA, Germany, France
(b) USA, Germany, Japan, France
(c) USA, Japan, Germany, France
(d) USA, Japan, France, Germany

26 The following statements have been made:

(i) Japanese investments in the USA have produced a negative return of some 5–10 per cent
(ii) Japanese investments in Malaysia, China and Indonesia have produced a positive return of some 10–20 per cent

How are these statements best described?

(a) True/True
(b) True/False
(c) False/True
(d) False/False

Focus 7
BUSINESS AND GOVERNMENT STRATEGIES

27 Stagflation is:

(a) when the government has to find extra money for large numbers of unemployed
(b) when the welfare state safety net has been widened
(c) when there is less income coming into the government forcing a higher public sector borrowing rate
(d) when inflation is coupled with an economy that is standing still

28 In terms of European market integration, the following statements have been made:

(i) the EU offers UK industry a prospect of easy access to some 250m. customers
(ii) the Common Agricultural Policy is a fair way of distributing EU funds to under-developed countries

How are these statements best described?

(a) True/True
(b) True/False
(c) False/True
(d) False/False

29 GATT can be seen as an integral part of which of the following?

(a) EU
(b) UN
(c) IMF
(d) WTO

30 Which two of the following statements are correct?

(i) during the period 1980 to 1992 EU industries have become 1.1 per cent more competitive

(ii) during the period 1980 to 1992 the Japanese have become 27.8 per cent less competitive

(iii) EU unemployment in 1996 is expected to reach 11.25 per cent

(iv) EU growth by 1996 is expected to rise by some 6 per cent

(a) (i) and (ii)
(b) (ii) and (iii)
(c) (iii) and (iv)
(d) (i) and (iv)

Explain added value, distribution of added value and money cycle

PERFORMANCE CRITERIA

A student must:

1 explain the **trading cycle** *of goods or services in a business and their added value*

2 explain the **distribution of added value**

3 explain the **money cycle**

4 explain **factors** *for consideration* **when selling**

5 explain **factors** *for consideration* **when buying**

RANGE

Trading cycle: *order, supply, payment; process raw materials or components for a service to meet customer requirements, charge for goods or services; make a return on investment, make a trading profit or loss*

Added value: *value of goods or services supplied; cost of goods or services bought from others; added value created*

Distribution of added value: *wages and salaries, taxes, interest paid to lenders, money required to pay off debts, dividends paid to shareholders, profit retained in the business*

Money cycle: *initial cash, purchase materials, produce goods, sell goods on credit, goods are paid for, residual cash*

Factors when selling: *cash, credit, creditworthiness, payment terms, credit control, bad debt*

Factors when buying: *assessing suppliers, specification, quantity, price, delivery date*

6.1.1 *Explain the trading cycle of goods or services in a business and their added value*

TRADING CYCLE

When an organisation has the necessary labour, capital, raw materials and other resources, this does not necessarily mean that it is in a position to make profits. In this Element we will be considering two separate but inextricably linked aspects of business operations relating to:

- *the trading cycle* – which considers the initial order, processing, fulfilment and eventual profit
- *the money cycle* – which addresses the needs of the organisation to generate cash in order to pay various costs

The key to all of this is the concept of **added value**, in other words, the generation of **profit** over and above the amount of time, effort and resources put into the task or stage of production. It would seem obvious that as a raw material is gradually transformed through various production processes, changing hands and moving from business to business, the price attached to it increases in each consecutive stage of its development.

When we consider the concept of a trading cycle, we are not simply restricting ourselves to looking at the processing of an order and any complexities that may arise during the fulfilment of that order. The trading cycle extends beyond the fulfilment phase and into the area which identifies the reasoning behind the setting of the price charged to the end-user and the probable use of the profit obtained. In some cases we may be able to recognise that the fulfilment and price of an order do not necessarily cover all of the costs which have been incurred during its processing. Whilst an organisation would not consciously process a product from which it could not confidently expect to make a profit, there may be costs incurred during the processing which cause the product to make a loss, or a very low profit.

ORDER

When an organisation receives an order for a product or service, the customer does not necessarily already know the final price for that product or service. This may seem strange, but we can identify particular circumstances where this would be so. Perhaps the product in the form in which it is required has never been produced before. Perhaps the product involves complex processing procedures which have not been tried before. Alternatively, the customer may be seeking the specialist knowledge of the organisation and will be expecting the supplier to quote a price for the product once the supplier has made all the necessary calculations. This is known as tendering for a job and requires the organisation to assess the probable costs of processing the products or services needed to fulfil the order and then to add on a profit margin, thus added value. As we will see, there are a number of criteria involved in making this assessment of the costs, and of establishing the level of profit acceptable or desirable for that particular product. Typically, as we will see later, an organisation will establish a preferred profit margin in relation to such criteria as overhead costs which need to be included, variations in costs which may occur, particularly if the order may need to be fulfilled in the future and the competitors' pricing levels.

When an organisation receives an order, regardless of whether the product has been pre-priced or requires quotation, a number of steps are taken:

1 The organisation makes an assessment of whether it is viable commercially to attempt to accept the order.
2 The organisation may have the products in stock, or may be expecting them to be available shortly.
3 The organisation may have already identified the likely customers for the available products and may have already established an outline deal with the original organisation. In this case:

- the organisation would have to consider producing more of the product (perhaps under different cost implications)
- the organisation may have a full order book which means that in the foreseeable future any products which have been processed already have a definite buyer

4 The organisation may, after having undertaken credit checks or other enquiries, consider that the potential customer is too great a risk, in which case the order will be immediately declined.

Once the order has been accepted, either by direct acceptance of the price quoted in sales literature, or, by the acceptance of a quoted price that has been specially calculated, the organisation is now **contractually obliged** to provide the product. An organisation, having reached this stage, would have to be absolutely sure that it had already covered all the possible eventualities which might result in additional costs being added to the processing operations. Miscalculation at this stage will inevitably mean the difference between profit and loss. The problem also runs deeper. If the organisation supplying the product subsequently realises that the processing of the product will not be profitable, it could decide to decline the fulfilment of the order. This may have either legal or financial implications. Not only this, if the supplier does decide to decline the order after having accepted it, it would be showing signs of inexperience and an unprofessional approach to business dealings. In the business world bad news like this travels very fast. The organisation could now face the prospect of being labelled unreliable or amateurish. It is for this reason that the organisation needs to address the concept of added value throughout each of the key stages of the production process. Clear identification of the probable costs, including a forecast of external influences, will help the organisation to reach its final end-user price. This price-setting task is not the sole responsibility of those involved in the production process. Organisations which employ complex production processes not only seek the advice of production operatives and managers, but also may be influenced by corporate policy in the shape of specified profit margins or mark-ups.

SUPPLY

As we have already identified in Unit 1, there are considerable implications for supply in the issues of the **demand** and the current **market price** for a product or service. Consequently, particularly in respect of the costs which have to be passed onto the customer, the supply aspect of the trading cycle may not necessarily be in the supplying organisation's hands. Unless the supplier has built up a sufficient stock of raw materials or components in order to see itself through a supply shortage, or a period in which prices have been increased as a result of demand, the current market price will have to be paid. This is yet another factor that we will return to when we consider the price charged for the goods or services.

The current state of the supplier's **order book** will also have an influence upon the immediacy of supply. A successful organisation which has built up forward orders which will be fulfilled in a strict and orderly fashion, may have to inform new customers that it is unable to supply until a specified date has been reached. Unfortunately, this potential sale may well be lost because, in the business world, there will always be some other organisation which is able to supply immediately. One of the key requirements in establishing a reputation in any market is to be able to fulfil an order within the shortest possible time. Competitors will always seek to gain advantage in many areas. Delivery times and the availability of supply is yet another key area.

The concept of **just-in-time** (JIT) production, which we discussed in Unit 5, does seek to address the problem of not having huge levels of stock within the organisation. It does not necessarily accommodate the immediacy of supplying needs, however. Consequently, an organisation which has adopted JIT may suffer from external cost implications at a much higher level than an organisation which maintains a buffer stock of raw materials or components to process. These JIT organisations will have to consider their pricing structure and consequent added value potential much more rigorously before arriving at an end-user price. The end-user price of their products is therefore much more likely to fluctuate in line with the different prices charged by their suppliers. They may, however, be able to accommodate a degree of cost increase with the savings that they have made by not having to finance high stock levels and warehousing costs.

Supply, then, relates to the willingness of an organisation to produce, process and deliver products or services demanded by its customers. A constantly varying factor will be the **market price** of the product or service. Simply, the price can rise if the demand is higher than the available supply.

If the demand is high, then the supplier's suppliers will be looking for additional added value which, in turn, will have to be passed on by the supplier to the end-user. If an organisation wishes to offer a stable pricing structure it may, as we have mentioned already, seek to hold considerable buffer stocks to see it over a high demand period. Alternatively, it may have established a pricing structure which incorporates a higher degree of added value than is actually needed in order to maintain sufficient profit. Equally, a wary organisation will have tied its suppliers into a rigid supply agreement which guarantees a fixed price over the period in which the supply will continue. All of this naturally assumes that demand is continuing to rise throughout the period. An organisation may find itself in difficulties if it has agreed fixed prices over a set period only to discover that it could obtain alternative supplies from other suppliers at cheaper rates. A pricing structure that is higher than required does allow a degree of flexibility in the sense that the organisation can reduce prices without drastically affecting profit.

PAYMENT

As we have seen elsewhere in this book, the **terms of payment** which include both credit and discounts, have considerable implications for smooth cash flow of the organisation. Whilst it is obviously beneficial and desirable to obtain as much payment as possible before, during or immediately after the order has been fulfilled, this may not, necessarily, be possible. The key point is that the organisation needs to convert its assets, or in other words, the products or services supplied, into cash as fast as possible. If the payment for the products or services provided is withheld for any reason, then it is not the supplier who is receiving the benefit of that outstanding debt. A balance needs to be established between the supplier and the customer. In many cases, particularly in the case of direct sales to the general public, this consideration may not be relevant. Strict cash sales obviously enable the supplier to bank that cash immediately and use it for other purposes. Cheques and debit card payments mean a delay before the supplier receives the full benefit of the transaction. The delay is longer if payments are made by credit cards or on credit. Both of these, through the different periods of delay, require the supplier, in effect, to finance the borrowing of the customer.

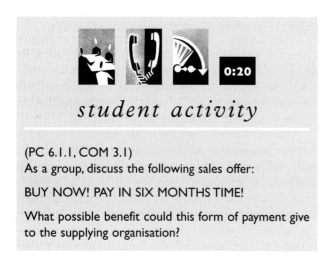

student activity

(PC 6.1.1, COM 3.1)

As a group, discuss the following sales offer:

BUY NOW! PAY IN SIX MONTHS TIME!

What possible benefit could this form of payment give to the supplying organisation?

Normally, in business-to-business deals, payment is always made with agreed **credit terms**. Whilst we may not necessarily consider that having 30, 60 or 90 days to pay the invoice is credit, it is so and needs to be factored into the supplier's calculations in terms of the net effect on its margins or mark-up. In other words, its added value calculations may be affected by the provision of credit terms.

PROCESS RAW MATERIALS OR COMPONENTS FOR A SERVICE TO MEET CUSTOMER REQUIREMENTS

It is probably in the **processing** phase that the supplier will incur the highest level of costs. Not only the raw material and component costs, but also many of the overheads, such as wages, heating, lighting and machinery costs, have to be factored in. Many organisations seek to obtain a contribution from each unit produced which is added to the direct costs of the

processing operation. These contribution payments transacted on paper, identify a portion of the overheads which can be attributed to each unit of production. This process does not add value *per se* to the product, it merely adds extra cost. The added value component emerges when the organisation considers the mark-up or profit margin beyond costs.

An alternative way of looking at this is to say that the added value is the surplus used to pay wages, overheads and other costs. Consequently, products which involve a high degree of personal expertise tend to have a higher added value component.

An organisation's cost curves will show the most **efficient** way of producing each product. The minimum cost is very much dependent upon the production function or production techniques and the prices at which different methods of production can be employed. The organisation will substitute one production method for another if it cannot achieve cost efficiency at lower or, indeed, higher levels of production. One of the other factors which may be a part of this equation is whether the organisation is capital or labour intensive. In the processing of products, external factors may influence either the cost of borrowing funds to purchase or lease equipment (which will affect capital-intensive organisations) or changes in the wage rates and legislation regarding employees (which will affect labour-intensive organisations).

Nevertheless, the input required to process the product will add value to the eventual costs of the product. This is, of course, before any mark-ups or profit margins have been included.

CHARGE FOR GOODS OR SERVICES

Strictly speaking, as we have mentioned earlier, the value added concept involves the cost of bought-in goods and services, plus the desired mark-up or profit margin. When we use the phrase **bought in**, we do not necessarily refer to services purchased from an external organisation. Bought in, in this sense, simply refers to the costs incurred which are external to the product itself. In other words, we mean labour costs, overheads and finance.

Let us assume that a product sells for £5.99. The cost of the bought-in materials (which may be components or raw materials) amounts to £2.00. This means that the added value component is £3.99. However, this is not profit. From this £3.99 we have to deduct wages and salaries, overheads, administration and profit. By taking away the first three components we are actually left with the real profit margin or mark-up.

Another way of calculating the added value component of a product is to express it in percentage terms. In this case, the equation would look like this:

$$\% \text{ added value} = \frac{\text{value added}}{\text{materials}} \times 100$$

Using the same example, we can express the added value component in percentage terms:

$$\% \text{ value added} = \frac{£5.99 - £2.00}{£2.00} \times 100 = 199.5\%$$

We addressed the concepts relating to pricing policy in Unit 1 when we looked at the various alternatives available to organisations in the construction of their pricing strategy. Constructing a pricing strategy around added value is just one way of setting pricing levels. It does not account for many of the external factors, particularly in relation to the competitors. Alternatively, the organisation may begin with an identified percentage of value added and work its calculations back to the component costs. This would, in effect, overlay a desired mark-up or profit margin, regardless of any external influences.

MAKE A RETURN ON INVESTMENT

Not many organisations are in the fortunate position of fully owning, in the strictest sense, all of their assets. **Investment** may refer to the time, effort and resources put into fulfilling a specific order. Obviously, here we are referring to wages, salaries, overheads and other incidental costs. As we mentioned earlier in this Element, an organisation needs to be sure that the added value component involved in processing an order is commercially viable. Commercial viability, as you have probably already appreciated, is measured in many different ways by different organisations. Commercial viability may simply mean the continual use of existing machinery and production processes, or, it may refer more strictly to the acquisition of profit.

Perhaps one of the more accessible methods of identifying the percentage return that an organisation is able to generate as a result of investments made is the formula called **return on capital employed** (ROCE). The formula looks like this:

$$\text{return on capital employed} = \frac{\text{operating profit}}{\text{capital employed}} \times 100$$

This measure of **profitability** enables the organisation to judge the financial benefits of its operations. If the organisation cannot achieve a higher return on capital employed than the current interest rate, then it is not going to be able to make sure that its long-term loan commitments are covered. This may mean that it will have to sell off assets in order to provide cash to cover the shortfall. An average organisation is able to achieve a 20 per cent return on capital employed. In the early stages of an organisation's growth, it may be able to

achieve far higher percentages. If this is the case, then the organisation is able to make even greater investments and, perhaps, consider expansion and the acquisition of larger loans.

student activity

(PC 6.1.1, AON 3.2, 3.3)
If an organisation has an operating profit of £350,000 and the capital employed is £2.5m., what is its ROCE?

MAKING A TRADING PROFIT OR LOSS

Elsewhere in this book we have considered the concept of **breaking even** which is, indeed, one of the most important aspects of business activity. Added value contributes to the probability of an organisation adds breaking even, but only to a point. By adding value in terms of additional costs, it does not address the issue of breaking even. It needs to add additional value in terms of its profit margin or mark-up to do so. It is only when the organisation has added these in that it will make a trading profit. If it has not calculated the incidental added value components correctly, then it will make a trading loss.

It may be valuable to think again about break even before we continue. We will use a worked example first and then ask you to follow a similar procedure in a Student Activity (see p. 478).

ADDED VALUE

As we have mentioned earlier, and obviously alluded to indirectly when we considered the trading cycle, added value is an increase in the market value of a product or component which excludes the cost of materials and services used. In other words, this is **cost plus profit**. Added value is a key concept in both the internal and the external accounting systems of an organisation. Added value is also a useful means of identifying the relative efficiency of a business. It should be noted that the added value concept looks at the internal input costs in such a way that they are not confused with the external input costs, which may be beyond the control of the organisation.

Focus study

MAKING A TRADING PROFIT OR LOSS

Dick Carver is a professional musician. He is a busy man and recently has found that he needs a secretary/bookkeeper. Dick needs to work out his break-even point before taking on the commitment of an employee. His calculations are quite simple:

- prospective assistant's salary: £12,000
- national insurance contributions: £588
- other costs: £350
- total: £12,938

Dick manages to earn from his various concerts, recitals and performances some £40,000 per year. However, he has direct costs of £20,000. He needs to work out his gross profit:

£40,000 – £20,000 = £20,000

His gross profit margin, therefore, is:

$$\frac{£20,000}{£40,000} \times 100 \quad = 50\%$$

Dick's overheads, before taking on an assistant, are around £5,000. If he took on an assistant, his overheads would be £17,938, in other words, the £12,938 for the salary, national insurance and other costs of the assistant, plus his £5,000 overheads.

Dick now needs to find out what his break even point is before he takes on the prospective assistant. He can use the following formula:

$$\frac{overheads}{gross\ profit\ margin} \times 100$$

So Dick's calculation is:

$$\frac{£5,000}{50} \times 100 \quad = £10,000$$

If he does take on an assistant, then obviously his break-even point will change:

$$\frac{£17,938}{50} \times 100 \quad = £35,876$$

He has estimated that he will earn £40,000 so he can afford an assistant. In fact, he only needs to achieve £25,876 worth of business to cover the assistant's cost, but he must also factor in his own personal break-even point, which is £10,000, and this means that he then needs to achieve £35,876. With an estimated income of £40,000 this will still leave him with a margin for error of over £4,000.

student activity

(PC 6.1.1, COM 3.2, 3.3)
Apply the techniques employed in the Focus Study above, in the following series of calculations:
  The following data have been obtained from the records of an organisation:

- production and sales level   20,000 units
- selling price per unit   £13.00
- direct materials   £3 per unit
- direct labour   £4 per unit
- variable overheads   £2 per unit
- total fixed costs   £40,000

Calculate the break-even point in units, and calculate the break-even point in sales.

VALUE OF GOODS OR SERVICES SUPPLIED

The value of the goods or services supplied may depend on a number of different variables. Obviously, if the organisation is processing raw materials into finished products and is responsible for all stages of the production process, then it has a relatively high degree of control over the level of added value involved. Organisations which buy in components or part-finished products do not have this depth and length of control. They purchase products which have had value added to them already. The supplier will have gone through a similar set of calculations prior to selling the components or part-finished products on to the organisation which in turn will continue their processing. In the final analysis, the level of added value of the goods or services supplied is directly related to the price that the customer is willing to pay. An organisation may decide to add value which would raise the price beyond that which the average customer is willing to accept. In such a case, the supplier would have either to accept that it can receive the price which it expected, or to drastically reduce its costs which have contributed to the end-user price.

  In highly competitive markets, the added value concept does, of course, take on a significantly different aspect. Organisations will have to be careful in their overlaying of added value to the product, as they may find themselves unable to compete in a price-sensitive market. Since the majority of customers are now, at least, price aware, if not price-sensitive, the organisation needs to cut back its costs at every stage of the process. The controlling mechanism does not stop here. Once the products have left the supplier, new sets of phases of added value come into operation. Obviously, any organisation which has a part in the distribution of the product will seek a profit margin of its own. Only by imposing a recommended retail price, or some similar price-fixing mechanism, can the supplying organisation be sure that the product will be price competitive once it hits the shelves.

In order to keep costs down and thus reduce the compound effect of added value the organisation needs to apply pressure to each aspect which could add costs. This means that there will be a downward pressure on wages and salaries, the costs of raw materials and components. Similarly, other overheads which must be covered by the organisation will be reduced to their absolute minimum. It is only when an organisation reaches a stage at which economies of scale are possible that it can apportion items such as overhead costs in a less dramatic manner. Obviously, the more units an organisation processes or handles, the fewer costs are imposed upon the individual units. Similarly, wages and administration costs can be apportioned in smaller amounts to each of the units. This may leave room for a greater level of added value to be imposed at the profit margin or mark-up end of the calculation. It also leaves the organisation with considerably more room for manoeuvre when considering price reductions in response to competitor activity.

COST OF GOODS OR SERVICES BOUGHT FROM OTHERS

Any organisation which buys in goods and services from other organisations would be well advised to shop around before entering into any long-term agreements. As we mentioned earlier, there are not only other organisations always willing to offer a similar product at a lower price, but also innumerable suppliers willing to provide raw materials and components or part-finished goods at a lower rate.

In many respects, an organisation buying in goods or services adopts the reverse procedure to that which it imposes on its debtors. The credit available from suppliers is a significant source of finance. However, some suppliers may be short of funds and will chase debts with considerable vigour.

Organisations need to adopt a rather pragmatic view when considering their suppliers. Whilst it may be desirable to enter into an agreement with a supplier who can provide goods and services at relatively low prices, the eagerness of the organisation to accept this deal needs to be tempered with an investigation of the supplier's reliability and reputation. Trying to cut corners and costs in relation to suppliers may bring short-term benefits but may lead to considerable difficulties in the future. To choose as a supplier an organisation that does not have a policy of making a large profit from each sale, may not, in the end, be a wise move. The organisation, as a customer, needs to ask itself why a particular supplier may be able to provide goods and services at a far lower price than the majority of its competitors. Could this supplier know something that the other suppliers do not, is it able to process products at a lower cost (in other words it has achieved economies of scale), or, is it simply under-charging? Some organisations would take advantage of the latter situation and allow the supplier to provide them with goods and services in the certain knowledge that the supplier cannot sustain this level of pricing. It could be argued, after all, that it is not the organisation's worry whether the supplier succeeds or fails. However, long-term relationships with suppliers can prove to be extremely beneficial, since they will be more willing to enter into collaborative partnerships, either in a formal or informal sense. An organisation which continually casts around for the cheapest possible deal may find itself frozen out in times of short supply. It is probably wiser to walk the middle ground, discarding those who are at the top end of the price scale and avoiding those who may be offering the 'deal of a lifetime'.

ADDED VALUE CREATED

As we have already indicated, the most common definition of added value is profit. Before the profit is realised, however, it is necessary to be able to cover the directly applied or overhead costs of the organisation. If the organisation is able to cover the various costs, then it has gone a considerable distance to being able to break even. It is only when added value exceeds the break-even point that the organisation moves into real profit. It is perhaps this part of the added value concept that is most important. Profits mean a number of things, as we will see in the next section of this Element. They enable the organisation to make additional investments, to pay dividends and to retain a certain amount (called retained profit) for contingency purposes. A certain percentage of the profit may also be earmarked for expansion, reorganisation, rationalisation, or acquisition. A profitable organisation should mean continued success, but the organisation should not rest on its laurels once it has achieved a profitable situation. The business world is liable to drastic change overnight. By retaining some of its profit the organisation can offset any short-term fluctuations in demand or supply. Whilst the organisation may be willing, for a limited period, to purchase raw materials, components or part-finished goods at a higher price than it would normally expect, it cannot sustain such a policy indefinitely. The nature of added value has a tendency to push up the end-user price from the moment the raw materials are extracted. In stages, some more dramatic than others, added value will be heaped upon the product. Each layer of supply or distribution will demand its rightful profit in handling the product or service. Consequently, as we have said before, if an organisation is not involved in the total extraction, processing and sale of a product or service, then it may not be able to curb unnecessary levels of added value elsewhere in the trading cycle.

6.1.2 *Explain the distribution of added value*

DISTRIBUTION OF ADDED VALUE

The final destination of the added value component of a product will very much depend upon the nature of the business and the organisation's commitments. Indeed, the distribution also depends on the nature of the organisational structure and its legal form. Equally, added value may be put aside for future use or contingency purposes.

WAGES AND SALARIES

A significant proportion of the added value element of a product is made up of **wages and salaries**. We should begin by making a distinction between these two types of payment to employees. As we have said elsewhere in this book, wages tend to be paid to employees who are directly involved in the production process. These can be considered, therefore, as direct costs in relation to the product and should be calculated and apportioned on a unit-by-unit basis. Salaries tend to be paid to individuals who are involved in non-production activities. In other words, salaries are a component part of the overheads of the organisation, but again, need to be apportioned on a unit-by-unit basis. In other words, the product, by virtue of the fact that it has had added value imposed upon it, makes a unit-by-unit contribution to both salaries and overheads.

TAXES

As an organisation adds value to a product, the tax liability on that product will increase. This is illustrated very clearly in the case of VAT. As an example let us consider raw materials valued at £50 per tonne: they attract VAT on this value, but once they have been processed into finished goods valued at £500 per tonne, they will attract VAT on this much higher value. By adding value to the product the organisation is incurring higher levels of tax liability. Whilst this tax liability forms a part of the added value, it also increases the added value in its own right.

An organisation must ensure that it has made sufficient provision for the payment of taxes in its added value calculations. In the case of VAT, the organisation is able to claim back any VAT it pays to its suppliers, so that it does, in fact, create a VAT bill of its own by adding value to the product itself. In this sense VAT is not an absolute tax, as it can be offset by VAT payments made lower down in the production process.

With regard to other forms of taxation, the added value contributes to a large degree to the organisation's profitability. In turn, the organisation is expected to pay tax on its profits. Therefore the level of added value will determine, indirectly, the amount of tax the organisation has to pay.

INTEREST PAID TO LENDERS AND MONEY REQUIRED TO PAY OFF DEBTS

In establishing the added value component of a product, an organisation needs to pay attention to its outstanding debts and loans. The organisation will has to factor in a adequate margin or added value calculation which can ensure that sufficient funds are made available to pay interest or the capital of a debt. The organisation will begin by calculating its liabilities in terms of interest payments and debts. It will have to establish when these payments have to be made and ensure that added value derived from the production of units is sufficient to cover these liabilities. It would not be enough for an organisation simply to artificially increase the price of units immediately before the time when these liabilities have to be paid. Such an action would have a serious impact on the viability of the product in the market-place. The organisation has to take a longer view and look for a gradual contribution from each unit over a period of time. Certainly, the contribution made by particular units can be earmarked for the payment of regular interest. However, once an organisation reaches the point when a loan must be paid back, it will be necessary for it to have accumulated contributions from added value over a period of months or years.

DIVIDENDS PAID TO SHAREHOLDERS

A vital consideration, in the case of public limited companies, is the requirement to pay their shareholders a reasonable and attractive dividend. Without this provision, organisations cannot reasonably expect individuals to make any kind of investment or commitment to the business. Added value is the main source of finance for dividends. Although there are other sources of finance which may contribute in some way to the payment of dividends, it is the day-to-day process of adding value to products or services that allows the organisation to divert these funds back to the shareholders.

Generally, dividends are paid in relation to the level of profit obtained by the organisation in a given financial year. As we have said earlier, this profit is derived from adding value to the products and services processed by the business. As you may have realised, this profit and the consequent dividend payment do not miraculously appear at the end of the financial year. They have to be planned for and, in this respect,

a small portion or level of added value needs to be factored into each and every unit of production.

PROFIT RETAINED IN THE BUSINESS

An organisation which allows itself to be satisfied with a reasonable return on investments made may not be able to cope with unexpected situations. A prudent organisation will factor in a level of added value to each of the units produced, in order to provide a contingency fund which is capable of dealing with unforeseen financial crises. An organisation cannot guarantee that its machinery, workforce or premises will remain in their current state indefinitely. External factors may also disturb the organisation's forecasts of business performance. In both cases, at fairly short notice, the organisation may have to find new funds to cover unexpected costs.

Retained profit may be earmarked for a specific purpose or may merely held in an interest account, to be deployed should unforeseen events occur.

6.1.3 *Explain the money cycle*

MONEY CYCLE

In Unit 7 we will be addressing the sources of finance available to organisations. In this performance criterion we will be examining the flow of money from an original investment through the purchase of materials, the production and sale of goods, the payment for goods and the use of residual cash. This flow of cash will take place regardless of the nature of the organisation involved. In essence, we consider cash inputs into the organisation, the use of the cash within the organisation and the processes through which cash passes.

INITIAL CASH

An organisation obviously needs cash to purchase essential equipment, raw materials and components in order to fulfil an order and may even need to make a considerable investment to do so. In such a case, it is very important for the organisation to ensure that payment will be made by the customer in full. Actions to ensure this are covered in the next performance criterion. This initial cash may take the form of the following:

- new cash obtained by a loan
- the use of retained profit or residual cash
- credit from suppliers

student activity

(PC 6.1.3, COM 3.1)
In pairs, identify the probable sources of initial cash for an existing organisation wishing to extend its operations, particularly one needing to fulfil a large order.

PURCHASE MATERIALS

The purchasing function is usually carried out by the purchasing and stock section of an organisation. It needs to ensure that it has bought materials at the right time, at the right price, of the right quality and of the right amount. In many organisations, a centralised purchasing unit would have knowledge of a range of suppliers with whom it could negotiate acceptable terms.

Every organisation needs to ensure that it achieves good value for money. This is often achieved by having an accurate data base of suppliers, perhaps graded, using a technique known as 'vendor rating'. This classification of suppliers will involve a value judgement of the suppliers' reliability, quality, service and price. Obviously, the procurement of materials from new suppliers needs to be rather more carefully monitored. It would be advisable for the purchasing organisation to make a number of checks before committing itself to an order. The new supplier's capacity to provide the necessary materials needs to be ascertained as the purchasing organisation has already made a commitment to its customer to supply the finished product and would not want to be let down by a supplier.

The initial cash identified in the first section of this performance criterion will, of course, be used to pay for the essential **materials** required to fulfil the order. Alternatively, it might be necessary for the manufacturing organisation to purchase new or updated **machinery** in order to fulfil the order. Again, similar concerns are involved, including a systematic investigation of the available machines in order to choose the most appropriate.

student activity

(PC 6.1.3)
Using the Yellow Pages directory, identify probable suppliers of the following:

- cement
- electrical cable
- flour
- ceramic tiles

PRODUCE GOODS

Referring back to the added value concept central to this Element, this is the point where the majority of additional costs are calculated. Obviously the organisation will be looking to find the most cost-effective method of producing the products, so giving it more leeway to value for itself. Keeping costs down through efficiency and good productivity may mean the difference between profit or loss on a particular production run. Again, as we have mentioned in other sections of this book, a variety of different methods of production can be adopted and these are more or less appropriate to different forms of product or production level. In small-scale production, it is probably not cost effective

to spend considerable time and resources in setting up a complex production process. It is only when economies of scale may be achieved by the use of complex manufacturing processes that it is worth pre-planning the production process in any great detail. Whatever is decided about the production process, as we have said, an organisation looks for the greatest possible returns in added value terms against the lowest possible real costs incurred.

SELL GOODS ON CREDIT

Having now invested considerable time, effort and cash in obtaining the materials and processing them, not to mention having acquired of the initial cash, the organisation is now faced with the prospect of not being paid immediately for the fulfilment of the order. As we will investigate in the next section of the Element, payment terms and credit control are key aspects in ensuring that payment is made eventually. The organisation has to weigh up the relative advantages and disadvantages of any credit deal it may strike with a customer. Obviously, the longer the period between the investment made in the purchasing and production of the product and the final payment, the longer the supplier has to finance the delay in acquiring the payment.

GOODS ARE PAID FOR

Once the goods are paid for in full, the organisation now has a different set of priorities, in terms of its use of the cash received. It may have been operating on a credit system with its own suppliers and, having received the cash, it can now pay invoices which were presented on longer credit terms. Alternatively, the organisation may have to pay off a loan or divert the funds into other areas of activity. Typically, the payment of an invoice will go some way to financing the purchasing of raw materials and the manufacture of the next order. It is not as simple as this, of course, as the majority of organisations do not work on the basis of a single order at a time. Rather they have a series of orders at various stages of completion. The gradual trickling in of cash from paid invoices is essential to ensure that the production process is not affected by short-term cash-flow difficulties. An organisation would always attempt to have some form of buffer in cash terms to ensure that late payments do not adversely affect its ability to continue operations. Alternatively, it may have turned to providers of finance, such as a bank, for an overdraft facility. In any case, once the goods are paid for, the organisation will have a series of priorities to address.

RESIDUAL CASH

The residual cash, which is, in effect, the profit margin or mark-up after all other financial commitments have been taken into consideration, may now be employed for a variety of specific projects. Equally, this residual cash may be necessary to clear a backlog of debts or loans, or, indeed, may be put aside to ensure that interest payments are made. Many organisations will attempt to siphon off some residual cash as a contingency fund or for a specific development project. If an organisation can identify some residual cash, this means that new projects or developments do not have to be fully financed by borrowing. An organisation would obviously prefer not to have to borrow money every time it needs to either expand or develop in some way. At least a portion of the costs of these activities should come from residual cash. The lender would not expect to have to finance the full cost of these activities and would expect a reasonable contribution from the organisation itself.

6.1.4 Explain factors for consideration when selling

FACTORS WHEN SELLING

Achieving sales is one thing, but the actual collection and frequency of payments from customers is another. An organisation would be well advised to investigate a potential customer before fulfilling the first order. In this way, the supplier can avoid unnecessary hassle or complications at a later date with an unresponsive and potentially insolvent customer. There are a number of factors for a supplier to consider before getting carried away with the prospect of having made a sale. There is no real point in a supplier making a sale to a customer who does not appear to have the wherewithal to honour the debt he/she may have thereby incurred. Credit-worthiness, payment terms and credit control and the rigid enforcement of bad debt collection need to be an integral part of the organisation's monitoring and selling process.

CASH

If an organisation's cash runs out then the business will fail. Cash shortfalls may result from of the following:

- insufficient sales
- costs too high for the sales that were achieved
- insufficient cash to fund the increased number of debtors and stocks

It is, therefore, essential that the organisation knows how much cash it has and how much cash it will need. In other words, the organisation must make an attempt to ensure that its customers pay up quickly, but that its suppliers are prepared to wait.

In this Element, we are considering cash or payments other than credit in terms of their beneficial effects on the operations of the organisation. Clearly, a business makes forecasts about its operations. It is only by the strict control of cash going into and coming out that an organisation can ensure that it has sufficient available cash or working capital to cover immediate debts.

Making cash work for the organisation should involve not allowing large amounts of money to sit in a current account. Some form of account which earns interest is highly recommended. As we will investigate in the remainder of this Element, there are many other factors to consider before entering into a business relationship with another organisation. Taking notes of these can save an organisation from forming disastrous trading relationships with unreliable and potentially insolvent customers.

CREDIT

We need to consider credit from two different points of view. These are:

1 The credit **available to the organisation** from its suppliers in respect of the credit control exercised by suppliers and the payment terms obtained from suppliers. An overdraft is, in effect, a form of credit. It may be an expensive one, but, nevertheless, it is a facility which is used by many organisations. In addition the standard forms of credit such as the use of Access or Barclaycards will provide short-term credit facilities for the organisation.

2 The credit which is **offered by the organisation** to its customers. As we will look at creditworthiness, payment terms and credit control in more detail later, we will restrict ourselves here to more general comments. Obviously it is desirable for an organisation to obtain a degree of credit in any transactions it may undertake. But this desire to obtain credit must be tempered with the understanding that any credit must eventually be paid for. The 'buy now, pay later' concept, which is the key to credit, has the same implications for an organisation as it has for an

individual purchasing electrical equipment or household furnishings on credit terms. Credit is not necessarily free as credit cards in particular, attract a rate of interest based on the amount outstanding. An organisation needs to weigh up whether the interest paid on credit is counteracted by the freeing up of available cash for other means which will provide a greater return.

CREDITWORTHINESS

Taking credit from suppliers is a significant form of finance. Suppliers may be short of funds themselves and need to restrict credit terms as much as possible. When an organisation is short of cash, one of its first steps will be to negotiate improved credit terms with suppliers. Negotiation is always the best course since unauthorised credit may cause considerable bad feeling.

When checking a customer who has requested credit, it is advisable to do the following:

- approach his/her bank for references
- take up two trade references
- ask to see a copy of his/her latest accounts

Alternatively, you could engage a credit reporting agency in order to ascertain what the customer's credit rating actually is. It is the normal practice for organisations to require their customers to pay in full initially. It takes time for an organisation to establish whether a customer is creditworthy.

PAYMENT TERMS

The payment terms negotiated with a supplier or, indeed, with a customer may involve a degree of credit. As we have mentioned elsewhere in this book, there are some common forms of payment terms, including:

- cash with order
- cash on delivery
- payment 7 days after delivery
- weekly credit
- monthly credit
- 30 days credit

For larger organisations with more established trading relations, as much as 120 days credit may be granted. Whilst this may put a considerable burden on the supplying organisation, it does ensure that the relationship between the organisation and the customer remains amicable. Obviously, neither party would be interested in agreeing terms which are not personally beneficial. The key to the negotiation is establishing payment terms which are **mutually beneficial**. Extended payment terms can, in fact, negate any profit that may have been made on a deal, as the supplier will have had to finance the gap between the fulfilment of the order and the payment.

CREDIT CONTROL

In order to control the credit which an organisation offers customers, it needs to keep the following records:

- how much it is owed in total at any given time
- how long it has been owed this money
- who owes this money
- records of sales and payments, including the date for each customer

This information will help the organisation ascertain the creditworthiness of a customer.

Having established a level of credit which may be made available to each customer, it is the job of a credit controller to ensure that customers stay within these limits. Equally, payment schedules which have been agreed between the supplier and the customer should be checked to see if they are being honoured. Action would have to be taken against customers who have failed to make payments on specified dates or those who have failed to respond to payment reminders. As we will see at the end of this performance criterion, action can and will be taken against customers who consistently fail to meet their obligations.

BAD DEBT

Chasing the money that may be owed to the organisation can be a frustrating and time-consuming activity. Certain steps should be taken by all organisations to ensure, as far as possible, that debts do not become bad debts. Strictly speaking, a bad debt is one which the organisation does not have a reasonable chance of recovering. The key steps which all organisations should take to avoid bad debts are:

1 Make sure that all customers know the credit terms. This can be achieved by printing the credit terms on the invoice.
2 If a customer has exceeded the credit limit or has not paid an invoice then the supplier should immediately ask for the money to be paid.
3 A follow-up request should be made in writing or by fax.
4 If there has been no response within 7 days the invoice details should be checked to ensure that the problem is not the result of an error within the organisation.
5 After this check, another letter or fax should be sent. A letter should be sent by registered delivery.
6 If the customer is still unresponsive, the organisation should again telephone. There may be a perfectly valid reason for non-payment which has not yet been communicated to the supplier. If possible, the supplier should ascertain whether the customer has a weekly or monthly cheque run. This

may have been the reason behind the late payment. The supplier's invoice may have arrived a day or two after the monthly cheque run and due to the customer's administrative procedures, may have been ignored until the next cheque run. The supplier then needs to ascertain when the cheque run will be.

7 Assuming there is still no payment after the cheque run date, the supplier should keep the pressure up with continual telephone calls. If the supplier knows the frequency of the cheque runs then he/she should telephone two or three days before each date.

8 If the customer is never available when the supplier phones, then a little subterfuge may be in order. The individual making the phone call should pretend to be someone to whom the customer would wish to speak. Alternatively, the supplier could speak to another individual within the organisation to try and get him/her to apply pressure on the person who will have to authorise and sign the cheque.

9 It is always a good idea to be somewhat unpredictable in debt chasing. Phone calls should be made at different times of the day and different days of the week. Research has shown that Monday mornings are a particularly good time to try.

10 If the supplier manages to make contact with an individual at the customer's organisation and this person has promised to go and find out what is happening, the supplier should not hang up, but should say that he/she will wait for the result of this investigation.

11 If the customer claims that the cheque has already been sent, the supplier should ask the following:

- what was the cheque number?
- how much was the cheque for?
- when was the cheque dated?
- how much was the postage on the letter?

12 If the cheque still does not arrive, the supplier should consider going to collect the cheque him/herself. If he/she manages to get a cheque out of the customer then he/she should bank it immediately and if appropriate use the express cheque clearance procedure. This will counteract any attempt on the part of customer to stop the cheque.

13 Assuming that all of this has failed the supplier must now resort to legal measures. Essentially, there are the following options:

- a formal letter sent by the firm's solicitor, threatening to take legal action such as instigating bankruptcy or winding-up procedures
- threaten to use a debt collection agency

14 These actions may result in payment. If they do not, the supplier may have to engage the services of a debt collection agency. If the supplier has threatened to do so in the past, he/she must follow this through.

15 The last course of action is to issue a writ for the debt and start bankruptcy proceedings, in the case of an individual, or winding-up proceedings in the case of a company. This may necessitate a visit to the Small Claims Court, but a supplier should not take this action without consulting a solicitor.

6.1.5 Explain factors for consideration when buying

FACTORS WHEN BUYING

Many of the factors to be considered when buying a product are similar to those considered when selling a product. An assessment needs to be made of the supplier as well as the quality, specification, price and expected delivery dates. This assessment is as important as ascertaining whether a potential customer is capable of fulfilling his/her financial obligations. Given the fact that an organisation will be reliant on its supplier to provide a comprehensive and responsive service, it is essential that all possible problems relating to that supplier are identified and minimised.

ASSESSING SUPPLIERS

Assessing suppliers requires an **audit** to be undertaken. The elements of this audit obviously differ according to the nature of the business and the reliance that the organisation will have on that supplier. Generally, the following considerations will play a part in the auditing process:

- are there any alternative suppliers who are cheaper but can still maintain the same quality and delivery standards?
- if the organisation is already in a trading relationship with a supplier, can better terms be obtained?

- does the supplier always have sufficient stocks?
- does the supplier fully appreciate the organisation's demands?
- how responsive is the supplier to the organisation's needs?
- is the supplier willing to strike up a relationship with the organisation that goes beyond the normal business relationship, in other words, is the supplier willing to become part of the organisation's decision-making process and will the supplier act as an advisor in certain matters?
- what are the credit terms and terms of payment?

SPECIFICATION

In many cases, an organisation seeking suitable suppliers will present them with a detailed specification giving the exact requirements of the product or component. This will contain a systematic listing of all of the quality aspects of the product, as well as its preferred performance levels. This is a **discriminator** by which the purchasing organisation can establish, or at least narrow down, the list of potential suppliers. Any organisation wishing to supply the product will have to assure the purchasing organisation that it meets a certain quality threshold. The exact measurement of this quality threshold will, of course, depend on the nature of the product. In some cases, the quality aspect will relate to a service. In others, it will relate to the intrinsic nature of a product. Detailing a specification before agreeing on a supplier is an essential tool, not only to ensure that quality standards are maintained, but also to enable the purchasing organisation to identify, for itself, what it really wants from that product. Many of the organisation's decisions will have been influenced by the specifications outlined by their own customers. In other words, the specification clearly states exactly what the purchasing organisation wants.

QUANTITY AND PRICE

Having established a supplier, and given it a clear specification of what is required, the next decision to be made relates to the quantity required. When seeking a supplier, the purchasing organisation may have alluded to particular order levels and probable turnover with that supplier. Indeed, as we will see, the supplier may well have agreed to meet certain specifications on the basis of a presumed long-term commitment by the purchasing organisation.

This naturally leads on to the relationship between the specification, the quantity required and the price charged for the product or service. If a supplier is aware that the purchasing organisation intends to use it as a principal source of raw materials or components, then it may be more willing to be considerably more flexible in terms of quantity and price. In many cases, this relationship is based upon the total level of business over a given period. In other words, there will be a sliding scale of costs related to the actual quantities ordered by the purchasing organisation.

The question or ordering relates directly to the purchasing organisation's capacity to store and process the materials purchased from the supplier. Obviously, the purchasing organisation would prefer to have in stock (and, therefore, liable for payment) sufficient raw materials and components. It could safely operate this way if it were assured that the supplier held a buffer stock for immediate availability. Using the supplier in this way means that the organisation need not tie up cash or space unnecessarily. Suppliers have recognised that flexibility is essential in establishing a long-term relationship with their customers. Whether the organisation purchasing the raw materials or components decides to opt for bulk buying or staggered delivery, the supplier should be more than willing to oblige.

DELIVERY DATE

Again, the question of delivery dates derives from the quantities ordered. The purchasing organisation needs to be assured that promises made in relation to quantities delivered and, indeed, the delivery date, will be fulfilled. An audit of the potential supplier will highlight that organisation's ability to fulfil promises. Obviously, the purchasing organisation, having established that the supplier is capable of meeting its quantity and delivery date promises, will seek even further flexibility. The supplier needs to address the needs of customers and fit in with their required delivery times. Whilst this may simply be a question of not delivering at specific times of the day, more importantly, it means delivering the goods to the purchaser at the time it actually needs them. The purchaser will not want to have deliveries made too far in advance of its need to use them. This will entail warehousing and employee costs which could be avoided if the supplier exercises a greater degree of flexibility. Being able to order and have that order fulfilled at fairly short notice is a key concept of the production method known as **just-in-time**. The whole concept relies on the flexibility of the supplier. The success or failure of JIT is dependent upon the supplier's willingness to become, essentially, part of the production process itself.

ELEMENT 6.1

a s s i g n m e n t

(PC 6.1.1–5, COM 3.1, 3.2, 3.4, AON 3.1, 3.2, 3.3, IT 3.1, 3.2, 3.3)

This Element is concerned with establishing the link between the trading cycle and the money cycle. You should now appreciate that money is essential to the smooth running of a business and that high sales and good profits are not enough to ensure that a business will survive. An organisation needs sufficient working capital to pay creditors, otherwise it may experience delays in receiving orders. The knock-on effect can be drastic and will affect the production and distribution aspects of the organisation. If this happens then the organisation's ability to supply its own customers' orders is restricted and consequently this will lead to an even lower supply of money. In other words, we are addressing the typical cash-flow problems experienced by many businesses.

In order to display an understanding of the performance criteria it is essential that you examine the trading and money cycle of a particular organisation. You will be asked to manipulate these figures and provide an explanation of how the trading cycle matches the money cycle and what other factors are involved.

You must therefore choose an organisation willing to allow you to examine its trading and money cycle. This may prove to be rather difficult since much of the data you will require is of a sensitive and confidential nature. After all, it would be of great use to their competitors. As an alternative, your tutor will provide you with an adequate set of data in order to carry out the various tasks outlined below.

TASK 1

(PC 6.1.1–2)

Produce a diagram which illustrates the trading cycle of one business. You should support your diagram with approximate annual figures. These figures should focus upon the following:

- the accumulated costs of goods or services bought from another business
- the final value of the goods or services when sold to the customer
- the resulting added value or profit

You should also support your findings with suggestions regarding the following:

- how the added value could be distributed
- why profits need to be retained within the business
- how profits are used to pay off debts
- how profits are used to provide dividends to shareholders

TASK 2

(PC 6.1.3)

Using a spreadsheet package, show how the money cycle for goods and services produced by the organisation mirrors the trading cycle for the same goods and services. You should pay particular attention to the fact that the process begins with cash and ends with cash.

TASK 3

(PC 6.1.4–5)

Provide a brief document which explains:

- how a finance or accounts department would consider the following:

  - the creditworthiness of customers
  - the payment terms offered to customers

- why are particular quantities ordered?
- how is the price arrived at and payment terms agreed?
- what is the significance of the delivery date?

You should consider all of these points in relation to their significance in terms of the trading and money cycles.

Explain financial transactions and complete supporting documents

PERFORMANCE CRITERIA

A student must:

1 explain the **purposes** of financial transactions and documentation

2 explain the use of **purchase documents** and complete them clearly and accurately

3 explain the use of **sales documents** and complete them clearly and accurately

4 explain the use of **payments documents** and complete an example clearly and accurately

5 explain the use of **receipts documents** and complete an example clearly and accurately

6 explain why it is important to complete documents correctly and give possible **consequences of incorrect completion**

7 identify and explain **security checks for business documents**

RANGE

Purposes: *monitoring performance, recording purchases and sales, generating accounts, meeting legal requirements, confirming mutual understanding between buyer and seller*

Purchase documents: *orders placed, purchase invoice, credit note, goods received note*

Sales documents: *orders received, sales invoice, delivery note, sales credit note, statement of account, remittance advice*

Payments documents: *cheque (cheque, bank giro form, remittance advice and petty cash voucher), Bankers Automated Clearing Services (BACS), Electronic Data Interchange (EDI), debit cards, credit cards*

Receipts documents: *receipt, cheque, paying-in slip, bank statement*

Consequences of incorrect completion: incorrect purchases, incorrect sales, incorrect payments, incorrect receipts; incorrect accounts, incorrect information about business performance

Security checks for business documents: authorisation of orders, invoices against orders and goods received notes, authorised cheque signatories, segregation of duties

6.2.1 *Explain the purposes of financial transactions and documentation*

PURPOSES

MONITORING PERFORMANCE

Financial information is essential to all organisations so that that they can review their own performance. It is necessary to keep information up to date and accessible for the following reasons:

- for the **planning and control** of the organisation's activities
- in order to keep **shareholders** informed of the organisation's performance
- to ensure that **creditors** are aware of the performance of the organisation
- so that the government **legislation** is adhered to
- for **prospective investors** who may wish to become involved with the organisation

The only way an organisation can monitor its business performance is to obtain information and feedback. This information can be placed into two categories:

1 *Quantitative* – this is a precise measurement of what has been achieved. It may be a percentage e.g. the organisation has achieved 45 per cent of the market share in a certain area.
2 *Qualitative* – this is not so precise. It takes the form of opinions stated when an organisation receives feedback from customers or clients when carrying out market research.

We have mentioned organisations' goals and objectives earlier in the book. Organisations use this quantitative and qualitative information to indicate whether they have achieved their aims, or whether they have to change their plan of action in order to achieve them.

Obviously, the information an organisation requires would not be restricted to one particular area. The information would be needed from as many areas as

student activity

(PC 6.2.1, COM 3.2)
Using the information given above, write a list of the reasons an organisation would need to monitor its business performance.

possible. It would also be vital that this information is accurate – false or misleading information could lead to a series of wrong decisions, which, in turn, would lead the organisation to achieve poor performance.

Different managers within the organisation would deal with different information in order to monitor the business performance of their particular area of work. For example, we may consider the areas of **strategy** and **tactics**, which we have mentioned before:

- managers dealing with strategy would make policy decisions regarding the future of the organisation. They would need precise information from all areas of the organisation. They would also need information from competitors and customers of the organisation in order to compare their performance with that of others
- managers dealing with tactics would need information from the strategy managers. They would deal mainly with information from inside the organisation and would try to ensure that deadlines are adhered to and met
- other managers would need information from both strategy and tactics managers. This would enable them to ensure that the day-to-day running of the

organisation is smooth and trouble free. Any problems they deal with would be short-term operational ones

So, in order to monitor business performance effectively, an organisation needs to produce reliable, accurate and informative material which can be used by a series of personnel. How, then do they achieve this? First, they need to record all purchases and sales generated by the organisation.

RECORDING PURCHASES AND SALES

We look in more detail at the actual documents used for these transactions later in this Unit. But what is the purpose of such documentation?

All organisations will have a **budget**. Whether the organisation is large or small, it will have an objective which it must try to meet. It would be impossible for managers to monitor the performance of the organisation if documents relating to the amount of money spent and the amount of money coming into the organisation were not readily available and accurate.

Obviously, the larger the organisation, the more documentation it will generate. In addition to this, a larger organisation is more likely to purchase goods on a credit basis. This means that it will order and receive goods when the need arises, and pay for them on a monthly basis. Such an organisation is likely to generate its documents by computer software packages, although it is not unusual for an organisation to still be handling transactions manually.

In the same way, an organisation sells its products to customers or clients on a credit basis, and receives payment for them on a monthly basis.

Because so many transactions are dealt with in this way, mistakes such as the following could easily occur unless the organisation records all transactions:

- goods being sent to the wrong customer
- incorrect goods being despatched to a customer
- delay in payments for goods
- complaints being received from customers
- loss of business because of confusion with customers

The activities of different organisations vary, but all organisations use the business documents they generate to plan and control the way the organisation performs. The documentation may relate to the day-to-day work of a small number of workers, or it may relate to a specific job of the production line. Whatever the activity, the accounts department would need to be fully aware of the financial transactions taking place within the organisation. Because so much credit business is conducted nowadays, the accounting team needs copies of each document received or sent out of the organisation in order to generate the accounts of the business.

GENERATING ACCOUNTS

Staff of the accounts department meticulously record in ledgers all the financial transactions of the organisation. This process of using ledgers to record is known as Double Entry Bookkeeping. Most organisations would use the following:

1 *The sales ledger* – all goods or services sold by the organisation will be listed in the sales ledger. Customers are debtors of the organisation until they pay for the goods or services received.
2 *The purchases ledger* – all goods or services bought by the organisation will be listed in the purchases ledger. The organisation will remain the creditor of its suppliers until it pays for the goods or services received.
3 *The cash book* – receipts and payments of both cash and cheques are recorded in the cash book.
4 *The general ledger* – items such as expenses, assets and liabilities are recorded in the general ledger.

In addition to recording information on purchases and sales, the accounts department would also need to record information on the following:

- bank transactions
- timesheets and clock cards
- wages and salaries
- tax and insurance details of staff
- petty cash transactions

More information about these ledgers and other accounting procedures are given later in this Unit and in Unit 7.

The accounts department records this information not only in order to provide details of the transactions for the benefit of monitoring business performance, but also to meet legal requirements laid down by government legislation.

MEETING LEGAL REQUIREMENTS

An enormous amount of government legislation has been passed to determine the way organisations operate. The controls can vary from those on the way food is handled in a food production organisation, to laws governing the health and safety of office workers.

In order to ensure that they comply with these legal requirements, larger organisations employ specialists to keep up to date on such laws. These specialists make sure that they familiarise themselves with all existing legislation and pass this information on to all members of the organisation.

Whatever the size or type of organisation, laws can influence the way it operates. Laws governing business organisations in this country fall into two main areas:

1 *Common law* – these laws tend to be historic. They could have been in place for many years, although it

may not be clear where they originated. Common law can determine, for example, that land or pathways belong to the public, and therefore they cannot be taken over or be built on by anyone.

2 *Statutory law* – these laws can be very complicated, and come about as a result of Acts of Parliament. An example of a statutory law is the Health and Safety at Work Act of 1974. They can be updated should they become out of date, but a new law needs to be passed in order to do this.

In recent years, the existence of EU law has meant that organisations within the UK have had to comply with additional legislation. This legislation covers all aspects of the business activity of organisations, including the requirements for financial transactions. Details of UK and EU legislation governing the way an organisation operates are given in other units of this book.

CONFIRMING MUTUAL UNDERSTANDING BETWEEN BUYER AND SELLER

Another very important purpose of documentation for the recording of the business activities of an organisation is the need to **confirm**. Obviously, it would be foolish to rely on word of mouth. Whatever the size of an organisation, it is necessary for it to confirm an order for goods, or to confirm the amount of money outstanding on an account. Without this written confirmation the organisation would be inefficient and ineffective.

Additionally, with regard to the maintenance of mutual respect between them, organisations need the confirmation of a written document as opposed to a verbal commitment. When goods are ordered and purchased, both the purchasing organisation and the supplier of the goods will need to understand exactly and accurately what is involved in the transaction. Once a written order has been placed, this is a legally binding document, tying the two organisations together in a firm commitment to:

- supply the goods in the exact form and at the price stated, at the time agreed
- pay for the goods on the terms confirmed at the time detailed

Without this mutually agreed document, neither organisation will have any written evidence that the transaction has taken place.

6.2.2 *Explain the use of purchase documents and complete them clearly and accurately*

PURCHASE DOCUMENTS

All organisations need to buy raw materials and services in order to produce or provide their own goods and services. These materials and services may take several forms, from raw materials needed in the production line to the services of specialists, e.g. cleaners or consultants. In order to obtain these materials or services, the organisation will have to complete a series of purchase documents requesting them. It may help you here to refresh your memory concerning the types of goods or services an organisation may require:

1 *Materials* – these can take several forms. They may be raw materials, which the organisation will need to produce its products. They may, however, be things like headed paper needed to produce letters from the organisation, or cleaning products to assist in the sanitation of the production lines. These types of products are known as **consumables**, and they are all ordered on an *Order Form*.

2 *Components* – examples are furniture, new computer equipment, new buildings, etc. These are dealt with in a different way from materials, and a special purchasing system will be in effect within an organisation to deal with these purchases.

3 *Services* – in order to purchase a service from an individual or another organisation, it is necessary for an organisation to complete a contract. The organisation raising the contract would state clearly the terms of the contract, and this would be signed by a representative of the organisation, plus the person providing the service. This contract would be legally binding on both sides.

In a large organisation, the purchasing department is responsible for buying materials or services. This involves the completion of a series of documents. Before we look at these documents in detail, there are a number of terms it may be useful to mention here:

- *trade discount* – this discount is given to an organisation because it is placing a large order. It may also be given if the organisation buys goods on a regular basis from the same company, or if that company is in the same field as the organisation itself

- *prompt payment discount* – this discount is given to an organisation if it pays its bill on time. The term '5 per cent one month' means that the organisation can deduct 5 per cent from its bill if it pays within one month of receiving the goods ordered
- *cash discount* – this discount is given if the organisation pays its bill immediately. The term '2.5 per cent cash discount' means that the organisation can deduct 2.5 per cent from its bill if it pays by cash or cheque immediately the goods are received

The following are the forms of documents that an organisation commonly uses before purchasing goods or services:

1 *Letter of enquiry* – this will be sent to several companies which sell the goods or services required by the organisation. It will help the purchaser find out information before placing an order. This information will include the following:

- price details
- details about the goods
- delivery dates and times
- discounts available

student activity

(PC 6.2.2, COM 3.2, IT 3.1, 3.2)
Using the format given in the example of a letter of enquiry in Figure 6.2.1 on p.493, write your own letter to a supplier requesting five typists' chairs. Your letter should be word processed.

2 *Quotation*– this will state the price of the goods required, the expected date of delivery and any discounts the company may offer. The organisation will then choose the company with the best price, terms and delivery times.
3 *Estimate* – as with a quotation, the organisation may ask several companies to offer estimates to carry out a piece of work. This is not as accurate as a quotation, but again the organisation would choose the company offering the best deal.
4 *Tender* – an organisation may put a piece of work, or a service, out to tender. This means that any company interested in doing the work will 'offer' to do the job

student activity

(PC 6.2.2, COM 3.1, 3.2)
Look at the example of a quotation given in Figure 6.2.2. Why do you think all the different sections are necessary? What does each of the headings mean? In pairs, compile a list of the sections and state the function and importance of each.

for a price. There will be a closing date for tenders to be received by the organisation, and on that date all tenders will be opened. Again, the organisation will choose the company offering the best deal.

Many companies issue catalogues of the goods, products or services they provide. Purchasing departments keep stocks of these catalogues, and need to update them when new price lists are issued. They refer to these catalogues and price lists when they need to compare prices and overall product descriptions.

Once a purchasing department has decided which company it intends to order the goods from, it will issue an order form to that company.

student activity

(PC 6.2.2, COM 3.2, AON 3.2, 3.3)
Look at the three completed quotation forms given in Figure 6.2.3, 6.2.4 and 6.2.5. If you were responsible for ordering goods and sending out letters of enquiry to different organisations, which of the above quotations would you choose? Why would you choose that particular quotation? What does your chosen quotation offer over the others? Write a short statement about each of the quotations itemising your considerations and reasons.

FIG. 6.2.1 *An example of a letter of enquiry.*

Our Ref JT/DEC/JS

25 January 199-

Office Equipment Centre
114 Middle Road
Tottenham
LONDON
NR31 6AW

Dear Sirs

We are interested in purchasing two office desks in pine finish.
We would prefer a three-drawer model, with the drawers on the
left of the desk. In addition, we are interested in an office
chair in black with arm rests.

Would you kindly let us have your quotation for supplying these
goods and include details of your terms and delivery dates.

Yours faithfully

J Sutherland
Chief Buyer

QUOTATION

REFERENCE NUMBER   DATE

TO

In reply to your enquiry dated _____

We have pleasure in quoting you for the following:

Prices include delivery by:

Delivery:

Trade Discount:

Cash Discount:

VAT: Value Added Tax at   % must be added to the price
        quoted.

FIG. 6.2.2 *An example of a blank quotation form.*

FIG. 6.2.3 *A completed quotation form (1).*

QUOTATION

REFERENCE NUMBER 1124   DATE 30 Jan 19..

TO

Smith and Sons
47 Rosamoss Lane
Wisbech
Cambs.

In reply to your enquiry dated 25 JANUARY 199.

We have pleasure in quoting you for the following:

2 PINE DESKS @ £171.00 EACH   TOTAL £342.00

1 CHAIR
@ £170.00 EACH   TOTAL £170.00

Prices include delivery by: COMPANY VAN

Delivery: 3 weeks

Trade Discount: 1.5%

Cash Discount: 2.5%

VAT: Value Added Tax at 17.5% must be added to the price
      quoted.

QUOTATION

E NUMBER 411   DATE 27 Jan 19..

and Sons
samoss Lane
ch

In reply to your enquiry dated 25 JANUARY 199.

We have pleasure in quoting you for the following:

2 PINE 3-DRAWER LEFT HAND DESKS
@ £175.00 EACH   TOTAL £350.00

1 OFFICE CHAIR WITH ARM-RESTS
@ £173.50 EACH   TOTAL £173.50

Prices include delivery by: COMPANY VAN

Delivery: IMMEDIATE

Trade Discount: 2.5%

Cash Discount: 2.5%

VAT: Value Added Tax at 17.5% must be added to the price
      quoted.

FIG. 6.2.4 *A completed quotation form (2).*

QUOTATION

REFERENCE NUMBER 5731   DATE   2 Feb. 19..

TO

    Smith and Sons
    47 Rosamoss Lane
    Wisbech
    Cambs.

In reply to your enquiry dated __25 JANUARY 199.__

We have pleasure in quoting you for the following:

2 PINE 3-DRAWER LEFT HAND DESKS
@ £173.00 EACH   TOTAL £346.00

1 OFFICE CHAIR WITH ARM-RESTS
@ £170.00 EACH   TOTAL £170.00

Prices include delivery by: COMPANY VAN

Delivery: 6 weeks

Trade Discount: 1.5%

Cash Discount: 1.5%

VAT: Value Added Tax at 17.5% must be added to the price
     quoted.

FIG. 6.2.5 *A completed quotation form (3).*

ORDERS PLACED

Order forms are always numbered and dated. This ensures that they can be traced easily should discrepancies occur during the buying process. The distribution of an order form is as follows:

- the top copy will go to the **supplier** of the goods
- one copy will be kept by the **purchasing department** of the organisation buying the goods for its records
- one copy will be needed by the **warehouse** to check the goods when they are received to ensure the order is complete and accurate
- one copy will be sent to the **accounts department** of the organisation buying the goods so that it can pay for the goods when they are received

student activity

(PC 6.2.2, COM 3.2)
Look at the example of a blank order form given in Figure 6.2.6. Why do you think all the headings are required? To what use would each of the headings be put? Carry out the same tasks that you completed for the quotation form in the last Student Activity.

ORDER FORM

TO			ORDER NUMBER	
			DATE	

| DELIVERY ADDRESS | | SPECIAL INSTRUCTIONS | | |

REF NO	QUANTITY	DESCRIPTION	UNIT PRICE	AMOUNT

ORDER AUTHORISED BY: ....

FIG. 6.2.6 *An example of a blank order form.*

1 *Advice note* – this is sent by the seller to the purchaser before the goods are to be despatched. It informs the purchaser that the goods are on their way and ensures that any delay is noticed immediately.

2 *Delivery note* – this is sent with the goods and lists the items that have been despatched. The purchaser will check this to ensure all goods have arrived.

PURCHASE INVOICE

Once the goods have been despatched to the purchasing organisation, the supplier will send a copy of the **purchase invoice**. This invoice will list the quantity and description of the goods sent, as well as the total price owing. The invoice will also state a time by which the payment should be made, and will list any discounts made available to the purchasing organisation. The organisation buying the goods will check the invoice against the order form and the goods received note (see later) to ensure that they all tally. It will check for the following:

- the order number is correct
- the goods listed match those delivered
- the quantity listed matches that delivered
- the price listed matches that quoted
- the calculations are correct
- the discounts are as agreed
- the 'carriage' – this shows how the transport of the goods should be paid for. 'Carriage paid' means that the supplier is covering the cost of transportation. 'Carriage forward' means it is the purchasing organisation who should pay
- the VAT – if the goods are subject to VAT then this will be added to the total cost of the invoice

All invoices contain the letters E&OE at the bottom. This stands for 'errors and omissions excepted' and helps to ensure that the supplier can sent a further invoice if a mistake is found. Most organisations show their VAT number on the invoices they issue.

INVOICE

TO				NUMBER	
				DATE	
				TERMS	
YOUR ORDER NO				DESPATCH DATE	

QUANTITY	DESCRIPTION	UNIT PRICE	TOTAL PRICE	VAT
		Gross Value		
		LESS Trade Discount		
		Net Value of Goods		
		PLUS VAT @ %		
		INVOICE TOTAL		

E & O E

FIG. 6.2.7 *An example of an invoice.*

If items have been delivered, but have been omitted from the invoice, the supplier will send a **supplementary invoice** to cover the difference. A supplementary invoice will also be sent if the customer has been undercharged for some reason.

CREDIT NOTE

The supplier must issue the purchasing organisation with a credit note if he/she has listed items on the invoice by mistake, for example if goods have not been sent. This would mean that the invoice total is too high. Additionally, when faulty goods have to be returned to the supplier, a credit note will be issued if the goods cannot be replaced. A credit note will decrease the amount outstanding on the invoice to be paid by the purchasing organisation.

FIG. 6.2.8 *An example of a credit note.*

CREDIT NOTE

TO   NUMBER

DATE

ORDER NUMBER   INVOICE NUMBER

QUANTITY	DESCRIPTION	UNIT PRICE	TOTAL PRICE	VAT

Gross Value of Goods

LESS Trade Discount

Net Value of Goods

PLUS VAT @   %

CREDIT NOTE TOTAL

GOODS RECEIVED NOTE

NO	DATE RECEIVED	ORDER NO	DELIVERED BY
QUANTITY	DESCRIPTION	NUMBER OF PACKAGES	STORES REF

RECEIVED FROM	ENTERED INTO STOCK		RECEIVED BY
	DATE	INITIAL	
SUPPLIER			STOREKEEPER

FIG. 6.2.9 *An example of a goods received note.*

student activity

(PC 6.2.2, COM 3.2)
Using the example of a blank credit note given in Figure 6.2.8 state why you think each of the headings is needed and to what use each will be put. Once again, list your considerations and reasons.

GOODS RECEIVED NOTE

This document is used internally within an organisation to inform the department requesting the goods that they have arrived. The distribution for a goods received note is as follows:

- one copy to the **department ordering the goods**
- one copy to the **accounts department**

During the purchasing process, there could be problems with goods, as follows:

student activity

(PC 6.2.2, COM 3.2)
Look at the example of a blank goods received note given Figure 6.2.9. Why would each of the headings be necessary? To what use will each be put and by whom? List your considerations and reasons.

- *missing goods* – when the goods received do not tally with the original order for some reason
- *additional goods* – when goods extra to those ordered are received
- *incorrect goods* – when goods different from those ordered are received
- *damaged or faulty goods* – it is essential that goods received are checked before signing for them

6.2.3 *Explain the use of sales documents and complete them clearly and accurately*

SALES DOCUMENTS

The size of the sales department will depend on the size of the organisation and the type of industry it is involved in. The main objective of any sales department is to generate sales for the organisation and to record the transactions in a reliable and accurate way. As we have mentioned earlier in the book, the sales team may work on a regional or area basis, and the information and documentation generated by them may be used by one central department.

It may be that the organisation has received a letter of enquiry from a prospective customer. The sales department would have replied to this by sending either a quotation or a catalogue and price list to the customer. Alternatively, a sales representative might have called in person on the purchasing organisation. As a result of this initial enquiry, the organisation might receive a firm order from the customer.

ORDERS RECEIVED

The completion of an order form by a customer is a legally binding contract that he/she wishes to purchase the goods from the organisation. It is normal for the order to be on credit terms for the customer. In such cases it would be necessary for the sales department to send a copy of the order to the credit control department of their organisation.

It is essential for any organisation to control the credit allowed to customers or prospective customers. It would greatly endanger the performance of an organisation if bills were not paid promptly, and serious problems could result for the company's cash flow. When a new customer applies for goods or services on credit, the organisation may contact a bank for a reference. Alternatively, it may apply for a trade reference from an existing supplier of goods to the customer. Once the creditworthiness of the customer is verified, the sales department will generate the following documentation.

SALES INVOICE

The sales department would issue an invoice to the purchasing organisation once it has received the goods ordered. The invoice would contain the following information:

- a number
- the original order number
- the VAT registration of the supplier
- the name and address of the customer
- the quantity of goods sent
- a description of the goods sent, including any reference or code numbers used by the organisation for stock reference
- the price of the goods
- the discounts allowed to the customer (if applicable)
- the VAT calculation
- the total amount owed by the customer on that particular invoice

An **advice note** would be issued to the customer either shortly before the goods are despatched, or as they are being sent. This informs the customer of the expected date and time of delivery, as well as the method by which they are being sent.

DELIVERY NOTE

This is sent with the goods and describes the content of the parcels/packages being delivered. A signature by the customer is usually necessary as acknowledgement that the goods have been received.

student activity

(PC 6.2.3, COM 3.2)
Using the example of a delivery note shown in Figure 6.2.10, list why you think each of the sections is necessary. To what use will each section be put? Where would you sign for goods received if you had not had the opportunity to check the items? Why should the two sections be necessary here? Again, make a written list of your answers.

SALES CREDIT NOTE

A credit note will be issued if the customer has been charged too much on an invoice, or if the goods received have been faulty or damaged in transit. By issuing a credit note, the selling organisation will be admitting this error and will allow the customer to use the credit note to reduce the amount owing on the invoice.

Alternatively, if the mistake has resulted in the customer not being charged enough on the invoice, then the selling organisation would issue a debit note.

When the customer pays for the goods received will depend on the credit arrangements made. It is usual, however, for the invoices to be paid within one month of receipt. In order to obtain payment it may be the policy of the organisation to issue a statement of account to each of its customers, once a month.

STATEMENT OF ACCOUNT

Each month, the purchaser will receive a statement of account from the seller. It will list all transactions that have taken place during the month and will have two columns – the debit column and the credit column. The **debit column** shows the purchases that have been made. The *credit column* shows the payments that have been made.

Rather than pay each invoice individually, a customer may prefer to settle his/her account on a monthly basis. A statement of account summarises the transactions between the supplier and the customer and would contain the following information:

- the VAT registration number of the supplier
- the name and address of the customer
- the date and description of all goods sent
- the price of all goods sent
- the date of any payments made
- details of any credit or debit notes issued
- the balance owing by the customer

student activity

(PC 6.2.3, COM 3.2)
Using the blank statement of account shown in Figure 6.2.11 on p.501, write a list of each of the headings and beside each state why you consider that heading to be necessary, to whom the information would be sent within the organisation and why they would need such information.

FIG. 6.2.10 *An example of a delivery note.*

DELIVERY NOTE

TO

NUMBER

YOUR ORDER NUMBER

DATE

THE FOLLOWING ITEMS HAVE BEEN DESPATCHED TODAY TO _____

_____ BY RAIL/COMPANY VAN/POST*

QUANTITY	DESCRIPTION	NUMBER OF PACKAGES

I certify that the goods received have been checked and are in good condition

Signed: .... On behalf of: ....

Date: ....

I certify that the number of packages delivered is according to the number stated above, but that the not been checked

Signed: .... On behalf of: ....

Date: ....

* Please delete as appropriate

STATEMENT

TO

DATE

NUMBER

TERMS

DATE	DETAILS	DEBIT	VAT	CREDIT	VAT	BALANCE

PAYMENTS RECEIVED AFTER THE END OF THE MONTH WILL NOT BE SHOWN ON THIS STATEMENT.

FIG. 6.2.11 *An example of a statement of account.*

REMITTANCE ADVICE

On receipt of the statement of account, the purchasing organisation would check the figures sent by the supplier of the goods against its own records. If these figures tallied and the purchasing organisation felt that all was correct and in order, then payment would be made. Depending upon the credit arrangements already in place, this payment could be made by any of the following methods:

- cheque
- credit card payment
- transfer of money from one bank to another

Whichever method of payment the purchasing organisation uses to settle the statement of account sent by the supplier, the purchaser would need to send a document to the supplier of the goods. This document is called a **remittance advice** and it simply serves to inform the supplier that a certain amount of money has been sent to it (via any of the methods listed above) in order to settle, or make a payment on, the statement sent.

6.2.4 Explain the use of payments documents and complete an example clearly and accurately

PAYMENTS DOCUMENTS

All organisations have commitments to make payments to other organisations or individuals on a regular basis. These payments will take a variety of forms, and the method used will depend on the commitment involved. Nowadays, it would be highly unlikely for a large organisation to use cash to make payments. It is more likely to use cheques or other banking facilities.

One of the highest commitments in terms of financial outlay for an organisation is usually the payment of wages and salaries to its employees. Some employees are still paid in cash on a weekly basis. Others receive a cheque on a weekly or monthly basis. More commonly though, employees will receive their salary by means of

a bank transfer. Whichever method of payment is used, each employee should receive a pay slip or pay advice note at the time of each payment. This document is produced by the organisation from details kept on an individual pay record.

An **individual pay record** is kept by the accounts or wages section of the organisation. It contains the details of income tax codes and contributions, national insurance contributions and pension contributions of each employee within the organisation.

The pay slip or pay advice note will be produced from the individual pay record of the employee, and will be issued at the time of payment of wage or salary. The pay slip or pay advice note will contain the following information:

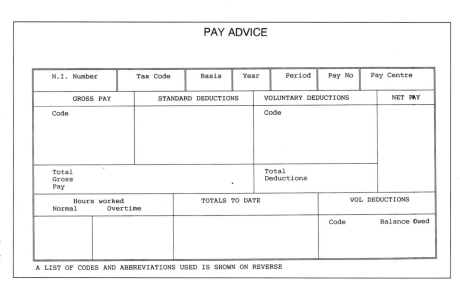

FIG. 6.2.12 *An example of a pay slip issued to employees advising them of their salary details.*

- *gross pay* – the amount earned before any deductions are made
- *statutory deduction* – income tax and national insurance contributions
- *superannuation* – contribution to the organisation's pension scheme
- *voluntary deduction* – these might include trade union membership subscription or social club membership fees
- *net pay* – the amount received once the deductions have been taken from the gross pay

CHEQUE

When a cheque is issued, it is an instruction to the bank to pay the sum of money to the person named. Because of the increased popularity of using cheques as a method of payment (more than eight million each day), it has become a very expensive system for banks. They have used new technology to try to reduce the cost and to increase the efficiency of cheque payments.

Certain conditions limit the use of cheque payments:

- unconditional – means that payment cannot be dependent upon any conditions being met
- the cheque must be written in ink or printed on a computer
- cheques will not be accepted for payment if they are not signed by the drawer (the person paying the money)
- the amount of the cheque must be written in words as well as figures
- the person receiving the money (the payee) must be named
- the life of the cheque is six months – after that it becomes out of date
- any amendments to the cheque must be initialled by the drawer

It is almost impossible nowadays to pay by cheque unless you have a cheque guarantee card to accompany it. This card guarantees that the bank or building society (the drawee) will honour the cheque on behalf

student activity

(PC 6.2.4, COM 3.2)
From the example of the cheque given in Figure 6.2.13, identify the following:

- payee
- drawer
- account number
- bank sort code

of the drawer, even if the cheque book and card are stolen, or if there are insufficient funds in the current account. Once a cheque guarantee card has been used, it is impossible to 'stop' the cheque.

A crossed cheque is one which has two lines drawn or printed down the centre, and the words 'account payee' written between these lines. This means that the person receiving the cheque will have to pay it into his/her bank account and cannot cash it anywhere else. By doing this, the banks and building societies are making it more difficult for people to steal cheques and cash them.

Most organisations tend to pay their bills using a cheque book. In larger organisations, several designated people will be the only ones allowed to sign cheques. We deal with this area of cheque payments later in this Element.

Because banks have found cheque payments so expensive and time consuming, several other banking facilities have been introduced to allow money to be paid or transferred from one bank to another.

❙ *Direct debit system* – regular payments can be made from one account to another using this system. The customer informs the bank of the date and amount

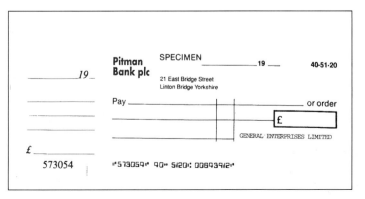

FIG. 6.2.13 *An example of a blank cheque.*

of payment, and the bank transfers the funds accordingly. With a direct debit, the organisation receiving the funds can vary the amount, although it is required to inform the customer prior to taking this action.

2 *Standing order system* – regular payments can be made using this system. A customer can instruct his/her bank to pay by standing order on a certain date for a fixed amount. The recipient cannot change the amount unless the customer informs the bank of the change in advance.

BANK GIRO FORM

Many organisations issue bank giro forms to provide their customers with a quick and effective means of making payments.

A bank giro form states the following:

- the name and address of the customer
- the reference number of the customer
- the account number of the organisation
- the amount due on the account (i.e. the amount the customer must pay on this occasion)
- the date the payment should be made
- the date the payment is made and by whom
- a section which lists the denominations of cash paid into the bank, as well as a section for the amount of a cheque
- the total amount paid by bank giro credit

The customer completes the form and hands it over the counter of any bank to the cashier, together with the cash or cheque payment. The cashier then transfers the payment to the account of the organisation automatically. Obviously, a cash payment is much quicker than cheque payments, as these have to be cleared before the amount can be transferred from the customer's account to the organisation's account.

REMITTANCE ADVICE

As we have already mentioned, an organisation would issue a remittance advice to a supplier of the products or services in order to advise the supplier that the goods have been paid for. Payment may be made by form of cheque, credit card or credit terms, and the organisation receiving the payment would use this remittance advice note for its records to show how much money has been paid. It would also use it to show in its records when the payment was made and by what method.

The purchaser of the products or services would keep a remittance advice note in its records as evidence that the payment was made. Additionally, this note would be used when carrying out a bank reconciliation (reconciling the credit and debit or a bank account).

PETTY CASH VOUCHER

As we have said, most organisations use cash very little for payments. It is likely, however, that an organisation will keep a certain amount of cash for low-value payments. This is known as **petty cash**. The cash would be kept securely and safely by an individual who deals with small purchases on a daily basis. This may be for such items as window cleaning, tea and coffee or for travel for employees. The most commonly used system for recording petty cash transactions is known as the **imprest system**. A certain amount of money is kept for petty cash purposes. This is called the **float**. The process for obtaining petty cash is:

1 The person requesting the money completes a **petty cash voucher**. This contains the number of the voucher, the reason for the payment (i.e. what has been purchased), the amount paid, the VAT charged, the signature of the person claiming the money and the signature of the person authorising the payment.

PETTY CASH VOUCHER	Folio ......

Date ...... 19..

For what required	AMOUNT	
	£	P

Signature ....
Authorised by ....

FIG. 6.2.14 *An example of a petty cash voucher*

2 The person requesting the money takes the petty cash voucher to the person responsible for dealing with these payments (the **petty cashier**).

3 The petty cashier checks that the voucher has been authorised and makes the payment from the float

4 The petty cashier transfers the amount paid on each voucher to the petty cash book. The petty cash book is sectioned into columns:

- money received into the petty cash
- dates of payments from the petty cash (transferred from each voucher issued)
- details of each payment made (also transferred from each voucher issued)
- the number of each voucher
- the total amount of each voucher

- the VAT charged on each voucher
- a series of columns which enable the analysis of petty cash spent on specific items; headings may be:
  - postage
  - travel
  - stationery
  - sundries

5 On a regular basis the petty cashier will request money to bring the float back to its original amount.

6 Usually about once a month the petty cashier will total each of the columns and deduct the total amount issued from petty cash from the original amount of the float. This is known as 'restoring the imprest'.

student activity

(PC 6.2.4, COM 3.2, AON 3.3)
Using the petty cash vouchers given in Figure 6.2.14, complete for the following:

- 2 jars of coffee @ £2.95 each
- 4 boxes of paper clips @ £1.25 each
- window cleaner, payment for 2 weeks @ £2.50 each week

BANKERS AUTOMATED CLEARING SERVICES (BACS)

The Bankers Automated Clearing Service is used for both direct debit and standing order payments. It is also used quite extensively by larger organisations for the payment of salaries to monthly staff. This system reduces the amount of paperwork involved in each transaction it handles.

The information regarding the amount of money to be transferred from one bank account to another is supplied to the bank by means of magnetic tape or disk. This information is processed via the BACS computer centre. Once this detailed information has been processed at the computer centre, the payment(s) are made automatically. In other words, the information regarding the payment is sent to the computer centre. This information is processed and the account of the recipient is located. The money is then transferred from the account of the paying organisation to the account of the recipient.

ELECTRONIC DATA INTERCHANGE (EDI)

In a similar way to that in which the BACS system works, by transferring money from one account to another, the EDI system can transfer information from one organisation to another. This information may take the form of repeat orders or the automatic updating of stock levels. EDI is also a useful tool in accessing information stored in computer libraries or other data bases. Many of the more technologically aware colleges will have links with a variety of American-based computer libraries or data bases, accessed via modem link.

PETTY CASH BOOK															Folio	
DR				(Imprest System)											CR	
RECEIPTS AND PAYMENTS							ANALYSIS OF PAYMENTS									
Imprest		Date	Details	Voucher Number	Payment		VAT									
£	p				£	p	£	p	£	p	£	p	£	p	£	p

FIG. 6.2.15 *An example of a petty cash book.*

Virtually instantaneous electronic data interchange can be achieved through a series of menus and sub-menus. It is rather like browsing in a library, but on screen. Not only can the data be instantaneously transferred to the enquirer's terminal, no matter where that terminal may be, but they can also be printed with the same speed.

Focus study

ELECTRONIC DATA INTERCHANGE

The market researchers Internet Info calculated that in mid-1994 some 38 per cent of the top 2,000 US companies had some kind of linkage with Internet. Indeed, the Internet Society also calculated that 24 per cent of all the Internet hosts (these are separate directories which can be accessed via the Internet) were US organisations, while the UK at this time accounted for some 5 per cent.

On a commercial basis, the Internet can provide information on demand at a cost. You can also buy products via Internet. Organisations have appreciated that making EDI available by the Internet allows them to provide useful direct connection with existing customers in the provision of back up information for their products or services.

DEBIT CARDS

More recently, the need to carry around a cheque book and a cheque guarantee card has become virtually obsolete. Increasingly, banks and building societies are issuing a debit card. This debit card looks very much like a credit card and does operate in much the same way. It simply and immediately debits the current (or cheque book) account of the individual for the amount of the goods purchased. An additional useful safeguard, for the retailer certainly, is that full and prompt payment is guaranteed, as the debit card payment is cleared within three working days. With the swipe card machines now available it is possible to identify any problems with a card holder immediately, as the machine will not accept any cards which have a credit problem (maybe the individual has exceeded an overdraft limit, or perhaps is simply overdrawn).

Some cards which bear the VISA and DELTA logos are used in much the same way as credit cards, although they do not hold credit limits in themselves. Instead they debit the card holder's current account, provided the funds are available, in the same way that a cheque does, but more quickly.

CREDIT CARDS

Not so long ago, it was unusual to see someone paying for goods with a credit card. Nowadays, they are in common use and people feel much more confident about buying goods on credit and using them before they have paid for them. Credit card payments are useful for both individuals and organisations, provided they are used sensibly and by responsible individuals.

All individuals, or organisations, issued with a credit card are given a **credit limit**. This credit limit is the amount they are allowed to spend using the credit facility. Each month a statement will be received from the credit card company, notifying the card holder of any transactions made using the card. It will also state the balance owed and the minimum amount required to be paid that month. If the holder of the card pays the full amount owed, then no interest is charged to the account. If, however, the holder can only pay a small amount (and the credit card company will state the minimum amount to be paid), then the interest charged is high.

It is easy for customers to see which businesses, both in this country and abroad, will accept credit card payments, as they display the credit card symbols in their window or near the counter of their premises.

Offering a credit card in payment for goods or services does not necessarily guarantee that the business will accept it. Organisations have policies regarding the limits on the amount of credit they will accept from a customer. This is called the floor limit and anything above this has to be authorised directly by the credit card company. The business will telephone the credit card company in order to receive an authorisation code. This code is then entered onto the sale voucher. If the credit company will not issue this authorisation code, then the business will not accept payment by credit card and the purchaser will have to pay by a different method. The credit card company may not issue the code if the card holder has already reached his/her credit limit or if he/she has missed a payment (or series of payments) on the account.

Increasingly, it is possible to obtain authorisation from credit card companies automatically, using a special terminal linked directly to the companies. This makes the authorisation easy and quick for both the retailer and the person making the purchase. Sometimes the terminal also prints the sales voucher for the retailer, although this is not, by any means, common practice. It is more usual for the sales assistant to complete the sales voucher by hand. There are four copies of the sales voucher and these are distributed thus:

- top copy to the customer
- second copy sent to the credit card company

- third and fourth copies kept by the retailer for their records

The sales assistant making the sale will complete the sales voucher using an imprinting machine. The details from the credit card are printed onto the voucher, which the customer then signs. The sales assistant should check the following details:

- that the details on the credit card have printed clearly
- that the expiry date on the credit card has not passed

- that the signature on the credit card matches that on the sales voucher

If the organisation is not working under the computer-linked terminal system, the retailer then has to complete a **Retailer Banking Summary** for depositing sales vouchers into the bank. If the terminal system is used, this step is not necessary as the account of the retailer will be automatically credited.

student activity

(PC 6.2.4, COM 3.1, 3.2, AON 3.1, 3.2, 3.3, IT 3.1, 3.2) In the role of a sales assistant, what action would you take if presented with the following problem:

- you suspected that a credit card which had been presented to you was stolen

Discuss this problem in groups.

If an organisation does find a credit card which has been stolen, then the credit card company pays a reward. Find out how much this is.

Credit card companies charge commission. In pairs, find out how much this percentage is and discuss the implications of this to an organisation. You should present your findings in the form of a word processed document.

6.2.5 *Explain the use of receipts documents and complete an example clearly and accurately*

RECEIPTS DOCUMENTS

Just as we expect a receipt for goods we have purchased from a shop, so an organisation expects a receipt for goods or services it has bought.

In order to provide evidence that the purchase has taken place a **sales receipt** is issued. This receipt will include the following information:

- the name and address of the organisation selling the goods
- the VAT registration number of the organisation selling the goods
- the date the transaction took place
- a description of each of the goods purchased
- the cost of each of the goods purchased
- the total cost of the goods purchased
- the payment method

RECEIPTS, CHEQUE AND PAYING-IN SLIP COUNTERFOILS

Receipts must be kept, to prove that the purchase has taken place. They need to be produced if the goods have to be returned for any reason, perhaps because they are faulty, or because they are unsuitable. Normally goods will not be exchanged nor will a refund for goods be given unless a receipt can be produced.

Other documents that prove that a transaction has taken place are the paying-in slip or bank giro credit form produced by banks or a cheque counterfoil kept by the person paying money in. This would contain the amount of the payment, as well as the date and details of to whom the payment was made (the payee). Paying-in slips show the following information:

- the date the transaction took place

```
┌─────────────────────────────────────────────────────────────┐
│                    CASH RECEIPT                              │
│                                                             │
│  Number ........    NUMBER .................. DATE ........  │
│                                                             │
│  Date .........     RECEIVED FROM .........................  │
│                                                             │
│  From .........     .......................................  │
│                                                             │
│  .............      .......................................  │
│                                                             │
│  .............      THE SUM OF ............................  │
│                                                             │
│  .............      .......................................  │
│           £    p                              £    p        │
└─────────────────────────────────────────────────────────────┘
```

FIG. 6.2.16 *An example of a receipt.*

- the branch of the bank where the transaction took place (plus its code number)
- the account name
- the account number
- the amount of the transaction
- the name and signature of the person paying in the money

A paying-in slip is normally used to pay money into one's own account.

A bank giro credit slip can be completed to allow a transaction to take place from one account to another, and can be used for paying bills and for the payment of salaries.

An organisation would use these documents as receipts to be included in the cash book produced by the accounts department.

The organisation would keep a cash book to record receipts and payments made by both cash and cheque. Normally a cash book is two-columned. This means that the page has two columns on the left-hand side of a page for receipts, and two on the right-hand side to record payments.

- the first left-hand column is to record the receipt of cash
- the second left-hand column is to record the receipt of cheques
- the first right-hand column is to record the payment of cash
- the second right-hand column is to record the payment of cheques

The cheque columns are usually headed with the word 'bank' and termed 'money in bank' as opposed to 'cash in hand'.

Usually it is necessary to make transferrals between the columns of the cash book, for instance, when putting cash into the bank. This means that cash is no longer regarded as 'cash in hand' but 'money in the bank'. This is known as a 'contra transaction' and is shown in the cash book by the letter 'c'.

At the end of each month the accounts department would total the columns in the cash book. The column with the smallest amount would be deducted from the column with the largest amount. This figure would be brought down as the balance for the beginning of the next month.

It is important that cash book calculations are checked for accuracy. The amount of 'cash in hand' should be physically counted to ensure that it tallies with the entry in the cash book. There are several reasons why a discrepancy might be found:

- an error when entering the amounts in the cash book
- an error when totalling the columns in the cash book
- incorrect entry because all receipts were not entered
- theft of some of the money

BANK STATEMENT

Just as the 'cash in hand' amounts have to be checked, so do the 'money in the bank' columns. This, however, is not quite so straightforward. In order to check these transactions, a bank statement must be obtained. These are normally issued by banks on a regular basis, although they can be requested by an organisation or individual on a more frequent basis.

In order to check the figures in the cash book with those appearing on a bank statement, a bank reconciliation has to be undertaken. It must be taken into account that the cash book and the bank statement may not tally. This could be due to **time differences**:

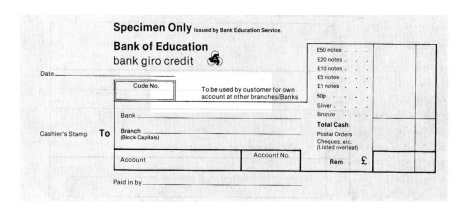

FIG. 6.2.17 *An example of a bank paying-in slip.*

- items may have appeared in the cash book but not yet appeared on the bank statement
- cheques which have been recorded in the cash book may not yet have been cleared by the bank
- standing orders and direct debits may appear on the bank statement but may not have been entered in the cash book
- bank charges may have been incurred – these will appear on the bank statement but may not appear in the cash book
- bank interest may have been paid – this will appear on the bank statement but may not appear in the cash book

In order to carry out a bank reconciliation with the aim of producing a bank reconciliation statement, the following steps should be undertaken:

1 Identify those items that appear both in the cash book and in the bank statement.
2 If items appear in the bank statement but do not appear in the cash book, then the bank columns in the cash book should be updated.
3 Then balance the updated bank column

Once the timing differences have been identified, a bank reconciliation statement should be produced.

6.2.6 *Explain why it is important to complete documents correctly and give possible consequences of incorrect completion*

CONSEQUENCES OF INCORRECT COMPLETION

An organisation will be liable to prosecution under a number of Companies Acts if it has committed an offence in its accounting procedures. In order to ensure the financial integrity of the organisation, it is essential that the accounting systems address the following:

1 Use a **double entry bookkeeping system**, which produces trial balances and reconciliations. This ensures that errors or misappropriations are identified.
2 Systematically **check** all bookkeeping and accounting **systems** and, indeed, check the movement of cash within the organisation.
3 Whether the organisation uses computerised or paper-based accounts systems, the system should be geared up to provide **audit trails**.
4 In addition to having nominated individuals for the purposes of authorisation and signing of cheques, **security measures** should be in place to protect cash.
5 Use efficient **recording mechanisms**, including purchase orders, stock requisition orders, invoices and despatch notes.
6 **Centralise** the accounting systems as much as possible so that the accounting functions can be easily managed and the number of individuals involved in the accounting systems is kept to a minimum.
7 The number of people who handle incoming mail and record payments.
8 Employ independent Chartered Accountants to **audit** the organisation's accounts.
9 Limited companies, in particular, must always have their accounts available for the scrutiny of the **shareholders**.

We can identify the net effect of incorrect completion of documentation in two distinct ways:

- the impact on the **organisation** itself
- the impact on a **third party**, such as a customer or supplier

As we have also mentioned, there are also consequences to a third group of individuals and it is at this point that the organisation does begin to run into serious difficulties. Incorrect accounting systems, once identified, will be the cause of considerable concern for tax, national insurance, customs and excise or other regulators. The organisation may face the prospect of not only having to sort the problem out, but also the payment of fines and other punitive action.

INCORRECT PURCHASES

If an individual incorrectly orders or purchases products from the supplier, then this may have the following implications:

1 If too much has been ordered then the buying organisation is faced with a higher than expected bill, and has to cope with the storage of the over-ordered

products and the trouble of negotiating the return of the excess to the supplier. This is time consuming and may also make the organisation appear foolish.

2 Alternatively, if the product is under-ordered, then this may only come to light when the organisation realises that it is out of stock of a particular item. The consequent expense and trouble caused, which may mean a loss in production or efficiency, is another unnecessary consequence of incorrect purchasing. Normally an organisation will probably purchase slightly more than it actually needs in order to ensure that it receives the maximum discount level available from the supplier. In other words, a single or series of under-orders will add additional costs because the cost per unit will be higher.

For organisations purchasing perishable goods, there is another level of inconvenience and expense. If a retail outlet purchases more fresh fruit and vegetables than it can sell, it may have to dispose of rotten or out-of-date produce. Equally, an under-order can cause an out-of-stock situation especially if the supplier cannot respond quickly enough to remedy the under-stock situation.

INCORRECT SALES

Again, this sort of incorrect completion of documentation can result in two distinct problems. These are:

1 if the number of products ordered by a customer is incorrectly entered onto an order form then they will either suffer an over-supply or an under-supply of the product. It would normally be the responsibility of the supplier to sort this situation out and pay for the collection of over-supplied products, or arrange for the delivery of the balance of an under-stocked order.

2 Alternatively, the individual filling in the order may enter the wrong price per unit or the total cost of the order. Whilst this may be a simple ommission of a figure or the incorrect placement of a decimal point, it could also involve the incorrect calculation of agreed discount levels or VAT payment. Again, the supplying organisation would be required to remedy the situation by:

- the issuing of a credit note for overcharged orders
- the re-invoicing of the order with the necessary amendments

In both situations, the supplying organisation faces an embarrassing situation. It has the responsibility of remedying the situation, but should not take action to fulfil an under-supplied order, collect an over-supplied order or re-invoice without the knowledge of and consultation with the customer. Regrettably, some organisations, if they are over-supplied or under-charged, do not immediately bring this to the attention of the supplying organisation, whereas, if they are under-supplied or over-

charged, then they notify the supplier by telephone at once. It is, therefore, essential, that the supplying organisation has a system of checks and balances which monitor the whole of the invoicing and fulfilment function.

INCORRECT PAYMENTS

Over-payments or under-payments of invoices can obviously result from the incorrect completion of an invoice. However, errors may also occur if an invoice is raised and then paid for as a separate transaction. Again, we can look at this from two different perspectives:

1 If the supplying organisation incorrectly invoices the customer for the wrong amount, then as we mentioned earlier, it is likely to get a different response, depending on the nature of the error. Given that it would be rare for a customer to highlight the fact that it had been under-charged, the supplier needs to have a checking system which systematically compares the invoice components and total against the recommended selling price. This is further complicated by the fact that some deals will have been struck by salespersons, guaranteeing particular pricing levels. If this information has not been passed onto the accounts department, then the customer may well be invoiced for the wrong amount.

2 The supplying organisation needs to have a system enabling it to reconcile payments received against invoices issued. This can be a particularly complex task if a customer does not pay the amount on a specific invoice. Some customers have an agreed credit level with the supplying organisation and simply provide a cheque each month to ensure that they stay within their credit limit. In such cases, there will be no direct reference to a particular invoice issued by the supplier. Consequently, it is nearly impossible to reconcile the payment against the invoices issued and errors and omissions are usually only identified if customers believe that they are under their credit limit, but the supplier informs them that they are not. This situation can come to light if the supplier has over-charged, but it is considerably more difficult to pinpoint the error if they have been under-charged. The only way that this may be highlighted, unless the customers bring it to the attention of the supplier, is if the customers move into credit.

INCORRECT RECEIPTS

Providing a customer with an incorrect receipt may have a number of consequences both to the supplier and the customer. For the supplier, an incorrect receipt can mean that it is impossible to reconcile that receipt against an expected payment. Equally, an incorrect receipt can lead to considerable confusion should the customer have to return the product to the supplier.

The customer will have a receipt for an incorrect amount in relation to the product he/she is returning. Whilst this is still proof of purchase, it may cast doubt upon the validity of the receipt. The customer will, of course, maintain that he/she purchased the product for the amount shown on the receipt. The supplier will have to honour and act in good faith towards the customer and take remedial action as required. The organisation will have to forfeit the amount if the receipt total is in excess of the actual price of the product and will have to make a decision what to do if the receipt total is less than the real value of the product concerned.

student activity

(PC 6.2.6, COM 3.1, IT 3.4)
If an organisation has been operating an unreliable paper-based invoicing and sales system and decides to install a computer-based system, how would you assess the impact of the computerised system in terms of its elimination of errors and ommissions? Would a computerised system be sufficiently reliable and efficient in picking up incorrect completion of sales and invoicing functions?

INCORRECT ACCOUNTS AND INCORRECT INFORMATION ABOUT BUSINESS PERFORMANCE

The main way in which an organisation can assess its performance is by analysing its accounts. If the accounts are riddled with errors and ommissions, then the true business performance will be hidden. An organisation which, as a result of a series of paper errors in its favour, believes it has performed better than it actually has done may face cash-flow difficulties. According to the accounts system, the cash should be there, but of course it is not, because the paperwork was completed incorrectly. In the short term this problem will be compounded by the fact that the organisation will have to institute an investigation into where the phantom money is. It will assume that something fraudulent has occurred. It is only when it has systematically investigated the situation that it will discover that the money never existed.

Whilst it may appear that finding money you did not believe to exist would be positive and useful, an organisation which makes such a discovery may find itself having to make statements to various regulatory bodies or tax collectors and may now realise that it has underpaid them. It is a matter of the honesty and integrity of the organisation whether it admits to the errors that have been made. If the organisation fails to make this admission, there is an ever-present danger that an independent audit will throw up these errors. A consequence of this may be that tax collection agencies will take punitive action against the organisation.

An equally fundamental result of incorrect accounts or information about business performance is the fact that forecasts and decisions on strategies and tactics will be based on incorrect data. If, subsequently, the organisation discovers that its accounting systems have been inadequate in some way, then valuable time and resources will have been wasted in pursuing objectives that can now be seen to be at best doubtful, at worst incorrect.

student activity

(PC 6.2.6, COM 3.1)
If an organisation identifies that its present accounting systems and its employees are incapable of ensuring that the procedures they use guarantee reasonably correct accounting data, what action could the organisation take against both the system and the employees? Would continued error be an acceptable reason for dismissal? Discuss this as a group.

6.2.7 *Identify and explain security checks for business documents*

SECURITY

It is very important that an organisation has security high on its list of priorities. There are different reasons for an organisation to take steps to ensure security measures are complied with.

1 *Security of cash* – not everyone is honest, and money kept in an insecure way may tempt such people.
2 *Security of documentation* – we have already mentioned the importance of keeping and storing documents and various data securely. This is particularly the case with any financial transactions an organisation might make, and is the main reason why the checking of such documents for accuracy and neatness is so important.

student activity

(PC 6.2.7, COM 3.1,3.2)
In the role of the accountant responsible for security, list the actions you would take to ensure that financial information is safely stored but accessible both within the organisation and from outside. Once you have completed your list, compare it to those of the remainder of your group.

3 *Correct procedure* – the security of such documents going out of the organisation is not the only consideration, however. Safeguards have to be taken to ensure that employees follow the set procedures for the completion of documents. This is another form of security.

The three main aspects of security of financial transactions relate to the authorisation of orders, the reconciliation of invoices against orders and goods received notes, and the authorisation of cheques. Let us look at these three main points in more detail:

AUTHORISATION OF ORDERS

It would be very disadvantageous to an organisation if there were not an individual, or a group of individuals, who had the overall say as to what could be ordered.

Obviously, this has to be someone with the right amount of authority within the organisation, who knows its financial commitments. This person or persons have to know what goods are needed and the urgency of this need. It makes sense then, that each department within the organisation should have a person who can authorise requests for goods or services. These people will have a budget to work to and will only be allowed to spend a certain amount of money each month or year. You will already know that these budgets will have been set by the organisation as a whole.

The goods ordered obviously have to be products or services that are required to carry out the work involved, or to improve the way in which the work is carried out. This authorisation is normally the responsibility of the departmental head, and could be carried out with the assistant to that departmental head.

INVOICES AGAINST ORDERS AND GOODS RECEIVED NOTES

As we already know, invoices will be checked thoroughly before being sent out. Some organisations may be more thorough than others. It may be that each person checking the invoice has to sign a verification to that effect before passing it on to the next person.

As we have learnt earlier in this section, reconciliation means the checking of details invoiced against what has been sent. This will be done when an organisation receives an invoice. The person responsible for receiving the invoice will check it against the order sent and the goods received note to ensure that all the details on the invoice are correct. If the invoice is correct, then it will be sent to the accounts department for repayment, either immediately to claim the discount offered, or when the statement of account arrives.

But what if there are discrepancies? If an error on the invoice is discovered when it is compared with the order and the goods received note, then the following steps would need to be taken:

1 If it is only a small error and the organisation has a good relationship with the supplier, then a telephone call is probably all that is needed. In this case the supplier would most likely send the organisation a replacement invoice.
2 However, if the error is a large one, it would be in the interests of the organisation to put this in writing to the supplier.

Obviously, if a series of errors or discrepancies appeared on the invoice of the same supplier, the organisation might well consider changing its supplier for that particular product or service.

student activity

(PC 6.2.4, COM 3.2)
Check the invoice in Figure 6.2.18 and the goods received note in Figure 6.2.19 for accuracy. Can you find discrepancies? List those you can find.

AUTHORISED CHEQUE SIGNATORIES

You may already know that when you open a bank account yourself, the bank will ask you to sign a form so that it has an example of your signature. The same thing applies to an organisation.

For reasons of security, it is not possible to allow just anybody to sign a cheque on behalf of the organisation. To ensure that all cheques that leave the company are authorised to do so, it is normal for an organisation to nominate people with authority to be cheque signatories. This means that their signatures will be held by the bank, and only cheques signed by them will be authorised for payment.

The usual procedure is for the accounts department to complete all the details on the cheques to be sent and then to pass them to the authorised cheque signatory, who signs all the cheques in a batch. However, if the number of cheques leaving an organisation is very large, the organisation would have a rubber stamp made of the signature to cut down on the time spent signing cheques.

The number of cheque signatories depends on the size of the organisation. In a small organisation it may be that only one person can be authorised as a cheque signatory. In much larger organisations, two, three, four or five people may have the authority. It is a form of security to have more cheque signatories when cheques for very large amounts of money are regularly signed. The people signing them are protected from any allegations regarding their 'right to sign', as they have witnesses, and their colleagues have signed as well. Also, if there are several people authorised as signatories, cheques can still be signed if one of the signatories is absent.

The above methods of ensuring the security of documents leaving the organisation protect it to some degree from fraud, theft or misuse of company funds.

SEGREGATION OF DUTIES

In addition to the security of documents both within and outside the organisation, there is the question of information and the way it is dealt with.

Although it is of prime importance that information should be accessible and as comprehensive and useful as possible, it is also a severe security risk for the organisation if that information is allowed to 'leak'. Certainly, if details of customers or clients were allowed to get into the hands of competitors, there would be enormous problems for an organisation and for some of its customers themselves.

In order to ensure that information, both in the form of documented evidence and confidential data which may be accessible to certain individuals, is kept secure, some organisations segregate the duties of their key personnel.

An organisation using this segregation of duties would consider the following points:

- which personnel have access to key information?
- how many other personnel need to know this information?
- how is this information currently stored and accessed?

If the information is very confidential, then the organisation would allow only one or two individuals access to that information. The restriction on access to this information would then segregate the other people in the organisation, making it less likely that the information could actually be leaked.

By segregating the duties of certain individuals the organisation would ensure that information is available only to a few reliable members of staff. These members of staff would have to undergo certain screening tests and would not be allowed to share their duties with anyone else. It would, therefore, become their sole responsibility to deal with certain aspects of the organisation's business activities.

The segregation procedure also provides valuable cross-checking and monitoring system which ensures that individuals do not take unauthorised actions without reference to other members of the organisation. By not allowing a single individual to be involved in all of the processes involved in sales, fulfilment and payment it also ensures that possibly fraudulent action can be picked up.

INVOICE

TO	Smith and Sons 47 Rosamoss Lane Wisbech Cambs.		NUMBER	457663
			DATE	31 January 199.
			TERMS	2.5%
YOUR ORDER NO 156387			DESPATCH DATE	30/1/9.

QUANTITY	DESCRIPTION	UNIT PRICE	TOTAL PRICE	VAT
2	OFFICE DESKS (THREE LEFT HAND SIDE DRAWERS)	£175	£350	£95.00
1	BLACK OFFICE CHAIR WITH ARMS-RESTS	£173.50	£173.50	£33.30
	Gross Value		£523.50	
	LESS Trade Discount		12.50	
	Net Value of Goods		£511.00	
	PLUS VAT @ 17.5%		£128.30	
	INVOICE TOTAL		£382.70	

E & O E

FIG. 6.2.18 *A completed invoice.*

GOODS RECEIVED NOTE

NO 101356	DATE RECEIVED 30 JANUARY 199.	ORDER NO 156387	DELIVERED BY COMPANY VAN
QUANTITY	DESCRIPTION	NUMBER OF PACKAGES	STORES REF
2	OFFICE DESKS	3	BAY 47
2	BROWN OFFICE CHAIRS	1	BAY 48

RECEIVED FROM	ENTERED INTO STOCK		RECEIVED BY
	DATE	INITIAL	
SUPPLIER			STOREKEEPER

FIG. 6.2.19 *A completed goods received note.*

Focus study

SEGREGATION OF DUTIES

Brian Hemmingway Associates is an advertising agency consisting of four partners. Each partner has separate responsibilities, which are:

- Brian Hemmingway, senior partner, responsible for customer liaison and acquiring new orders
- Robert Entwistle, Brian's original partner, and responsible for the day-to-day running of the office
- Stanley Kane, a designer, who works largely from home
- Susan Yallop, a creative consultant, who is the first point of contact for the customers after they have discussed requirements with Brian

The partnership employs six other members of staff who are secretarial, administration or junior design workers. Only the two senior partners are authorised to approve orders or purchases, and normally it is only Robert who handles payments. The partnership recently engaged the services of an auditor to overhaul and check their accounting systems. She discovered that there was a shortfall of some £25,000 in invoices raised against cash received.

0:20

student activity

(PC 6.2.7 COM 3.1)
In pairs, and referring to the above Focus Study, identify whose prime responsibility it is that there is a £25,000 shortfall. In the role of a financial consultant, how would you advise Brian Hemmingway Associates to avoid a repetition of this situation? Should any remedial action be taken against any individual in the organisation?

ELEMENT 6.2

assignment

(PC 6.2.1–7, COM 3.2, 3.3, 3.4, AON 3.1, 3.2, 3.3, IT 3.1, 3.2, 3.3, 3.4*)
This Element, particularly in terms of the Assignment, is essentially a practical one. You will be required to systematically process supporting documentation needed for financial transactions. You may be given the opportunity to use computer-generated documentation or more conventional paper-based systems. The thing to remember is that for every routine action there is a corresponding piece of paper or document. This essential record keeping forms the basis of an organisation's accounts and must, therefore, be both complete and accurate. You should also be aware of the fact that this accounts information forms the basis of an organisation's ability to assess its own performance. Finally, you should also be aware of the fact that, particularly in relation to internal movement of financial data, this is no longer undertaken on paper. The EDI system allows transactions to be undertaken without committing them to paper.

Your tutor will provide you with the following:

- a set of purchase documents
- a set of sales documents
- a set of payment documents

- a set of receipts documents

You will be required to clearly and accurately complete all of these documents, based on information given to you.

TASK 1

(PC 6.2.2)

Clearly and accurately complete the following set of purchase documents from a given set of data:

- purchase order
- goods received note
- purchase invoice

TASK 2

(PC 6.2.3)

Clearly and accurately complete the following sales documents from a given set of data:

- sales order received note
- delivery note
- invoice
- credit note
- statement of account

TASK 3

(PC 6.2.4)

Clearly and accurately complete the following payments documents from a given set of data:

- cheque
- bank giro form
- remittance advice
- petty cash voucher

TASK 4

(PC 6.2.5)

Clearly and accurately complete the following receipts documents from a given set of data:

- receipt
- bank paying-in slip
- cheque
- bank statement

TASK 5

(PC 6.2.1, 6.2.6, 6.2.7)

You should support your set of documents with the following:

- a word processed explanation of the purposes and functions of these documents
- a word processed identification of the need for clarity and accuracy in their completion
- a word processed identification of the importance of security checks

*Applicable only if computer-generated documentation is employed in the completion of these tasks.

Calculate the cost of goods or services

PERFORMANCE CRITERIA

A student must:

*1 explain **direct costs** and **indirect costs** of businesses*

2 identify correctly a unit of production or a unit of service from given data

*3 calculate the **direct costs** of the production or service for a **time period***

*4 calculate **indirect costs** of the production or service for a **time period***

5 calculate the total (absorption) cost of a unit of the production of service

*6 explain **variable and fixed costs** in terms of their relationship with production*

*7 calculate the **variable costs** of a unit of the production or service from given data*

8 calculate the marginal cost of a unit of the production or service

RANGE

***Direct costs:** production materials, machine or assembly wages*

***Indirect costs:** other wages, depreciation, power, management, administration, marketing, other running expenses (rent, rates, telephone)*

***Time period:** monthly, quarterly, annually*

***Variable costs:** raw materials, power*

***Fixed costs:** rent, rates, management, administration*

6.3.1 *Explain direct costs and indirect costs of businesses*

DIRECT COSTS

An organisation can apportion the costs incurred in the production of products or services in either a **direct** or an **indirect** manner. We shall be looking at the indirect costs in the next section. You may also wish to consult other sections of the book and the glossary for a fuller description of fixed, variable, semi-variable, average and marginal costs. In addition, we have considered the break-even point analysis and an organisation's long-term costs.

The **direct costs** can be defined as being the amount **materials** actually cost plus any other directly linked costs, such as **labour**. We shall look at the nature of each of these direct costs in more detail below.

PRODUCTION MATERIALS, MACHINE OR ASSEMBLY WAGES

1 *Labour and wages* – the cost of obtaining, training and retaining labour is a significantly high cost which must be allocated to each unit of production. As we have seen in many of the previous Units, there are many legal obligations as well as social and welfare considerations, which add to this high costs total.

In order to work out the exact labour and wages costs to be attributed to each unit of production, an organisation must make a careful study of the production process and allocate the appropriate expenses. If, for example, an individual earns £10 per hour and processes 10 units during that hour, then £1 of direct costs may simply be added to each unit. Unfortunately, things are not that simple.

student activity

(PC 6.3.1, AON 3.1, 3.2, 3.3)
Using Figure 6.3.1 make the following calculations:

- the percentage increase or decrease in the figures over the two years
- the comparative levels of employment in the three categories identified (show your information in the form of a pie-chart)
- the average wage of the employees, using the 'equivalent number of employees working full time' figure

There are many other additional costs which an organisation must bear in the employment of individuals. These may include employer's national insurance contributions, pension payments and insurance policy payments. In most organisations, labour and wage costs account for the majority of direct costs.

2 *Materials* – the costs of materials differ according to the sector in which an organisation operates. An organisation that operates in the primary sector has comparatively low material costs. At the other end of the scale, in the tertiary sector, the costs of finished goods to a retailer for example, will be extremely

7 Employees		
£ millions	1992	1991
Staff costs:		
Wages and salaries	403.5	372.5
Social security costs	27.4	25.2
Other pension costs	2.1	1.2
	433.0	398.9
Number		
Average number of persons employed:		
Stores	57,087	56,759
Distribution	1,617	1,493
Administration	3,237	3,245
	61,941	61,497
The equivalent number of employees working full time would have been	37,462	37,578

FIG. 6.3.1 *This shows the total wage bill and average number of employees for Kingfisher plc. It compares the figures for the years 1991 and 1992. Note that the 'Stores' category refers to the number of retail outlet employees and not warehousing staff.*

high. The principal elements that affect the costs of materials should be included in the organisation's overall budgetary controls. In addition, an organisation must also consider the cost of materials in relation to market demands, as these will inevitably cause periodic fluctuations in material costs.

Only those materials that are actually used in the production of a product or service should be considered part of the cost of that product or service. Other consumables used by the organisation are classed as indirect costs and are considered under separate budgets.

student activity

(PC 6.3.1, AON 3.1, 3.2, 3.3)
Using Figure 6.3.2 what would be your explanation of the following?

- the drop in the amount (in value) of the finished goods totals from 1991 to 1992
- the nature of the stock under the title 'miscellaneous'
- the importance you would attach to the nearly £3m. drop in the value of stock over the two years

INDIRECT COSTS

Indirect costs are costs incurred in the running of an organisation that cannot be easily apportioned to the production process. In effect, they cover all of the support and management services of the organisation. These indirect costs may be apportioned in percentage terms to each unit produced. However, the optimum balance between direct and indirect costs can be somewhat difficult to ascertain. If an organisation allows its indirect costs to rise in a disproportionate manner to its direct costs and production levels, then we can consider the organisation to be rather 'top heavy'. It will suffer loss of both profit and working capital.

The main forms of indirect cost are:

- other wages
- depreciation
- management
- administration
- marketing
- general running expenses

OTHER WAGES

Obviously, not all employees within a company are directly involved with production. There are many others, from a person in the canteen staff or a security officer, up to the director of the company. These people generally tend to receive salaries rather than wages. Payments to these people, that is, all employees within the business except those directly involved in production itself, are referred to as 'other wages'. The payments to those directly involved in production are known as production and assembly wages).

In some cases, the level of other wages within a company can seem to be very high compared to that of production wages. However, it is of the utmost importance that non-productive wages are kept as low as possible. Essentially, personnel involved in office or clerical and management roles tend to earn higher wages than production staff.

DEPRECIATION

Organisations must always consider the **depreciation** factor when attempting to work out a total for direct costs. Depreciation, as we have already mentioned, refers to the relative reduction in the value of **assets** held by the organisation. The loss of value of machinery used (perhaps the more it is used the less it is worth), or the simple obsolescence of equipment due to technological advances, must be taken into consideration. Depreciation rates are classed as direct costs and, as such, are included in the calculation of costs for each unit.

We must only charge depreciation of machinery actually used in production to direct costs. Machinery used elsewhere, such as a franking machine in administration, has no effect on direct costs or production and must not be included here.

For the purposes of this Unit we will assume all depreciation is calculated on a straight-line basis, for example:

$$\text{Depreciation charge per annum} = \frac{\text{cost of asset}}{\text{useful life}}$$

In other words, a lathe purchased for £80,000 with a useful life of seven years will be depreciated at a rate of:

$$\frac{£80,000}{7} = £11,428 \text{ per annum}$$

Depreciation for indirect costs is worked out in exactly the same way as for direct costs, i.e. on a straight-line basis. But again, we are now concerned with depreciation on non-productive assets such as computers, fixtures and fittings (furniture), and vehicles. A good example is the sales director's car which is not an asset directly used in the production of the good or service itself.

student activity

0:35

(PC 6.3.1, COM 3.1)
With reference to Figure 6.3.3 what do you understand by the following terms:

- acquisitions
- revaluation adjustment
- disposals
- net book amounts

Discuss this in pairs initially, and then feedback to the remainder of your group.

POWER

The **power** used to produce each unit must be considered as a direct cost. This means that the cost of any electricity, gas, fossil fuel or other means of power must be added to the overall cost of each unit. Obviously, certain production processes require disproportionate amounts of power and are thus more expensive in this respect. In addition, we should consider the cost of power needed to light and ventilate the premises in which the production takes place. A certain percentage of these costs will be apportioned to the indirect cost factors also, as administration and warehousing, for example, will similarly benefit from the light, ventilation and warmth provided.

MANAGEMENT

Managers, in particular general managers, need to be 'carried' by the organisation as a whole. These managers, who may have specific administration job roles, may not be involved in the production process at all, but their function is essential to ensure smooth running of the organisation. In this respect, they are vital members

FIG. 6.3.2 *This is a detail from Geest plc's Notes to their 1992 Accounts. You can see that there are four main categories of stock, in their case mostly fresh produce.*

⑪ Stocks

	GROUP		COMPANY	
	1992 £000	1991 £000	1992 £000	1991 £000
Produce and raw materials	9,177	11,629	-	-
Work in progress	109	122	-	-
Finished goods	226	1,878	-	-
Miscellaneous	2,224	1,626	97	92
	11,736	15,255	97	92

Depreciation

At 1st October 1991	–	71	765	40,862	4,989	46,687
Acquisitions	1,334	–	270	14,513	2,289	18,406
Charge for the period	23	212	123	3,839	971	5,168
Revaluation adjustment	–	–	–	1,463	–	1,463
	1,357	283	1,158	60,677	8,249	71,724
Disposals	–	–	–	(388)	(88)	(476)
At 30th September 1992	1,357	283	1,158	60,289	8,161	71,248
Net book amounts						
At 30th September 1992	2,001	10,442	740	9,074	2,938	25,195
At 30th September 1991	–	8,860	429	6,817	1,689	17,795

Plant and equipment includes assets acquired under finance leases in respect of which, at 30th September 1992, the net book amount was £3,341,000 (1991: £180,000) after charging £802,000 (1991: £201,000) depreciation for the year.

Technical plant and equipment has been revalued at 30th September 1992 using price index tables published by the Central Statistical Office. The net book amount calculated on a historical cost basis for these revalued assets would have been £8,429,000 (1991: £6,052,000). All other fixed assets are included on a historical cost basis.

A valuation of the long leasehold property carried out by Sallmans (UK) Limited, and dated 18th April 1991 assessed the depreciated replacement cost of the Television Centre, Leeds and 104 Kirkstall Road, Leeds as £23,073,000. This valuation has not been incorporated into the accounts.

FIG. 6.3.3 *This is a detail from Yorkshire-Tyne Tees Television Holdings plc's Accounts. It covers the depreciation and disposal of assets.*

of staff and their positions require funding. The normal procedure is to apportion in percentage terms the costs of these managers to each unit of production – as part of the general calculation of indirect costs.

Organisations try to ensure that the number of 'non-productive' managers is kept to an absolute minimum as the costs of such people will inevitably affect both profitability and the working capital available.

Managers, by virtue of their position, are more expensive than normal employees and must provide a positive benefit to the organisation.

The more senior a manager is in the hierarchy, the more divorced he or she is from the production process. It is therefore difficult to establish any clear criteria that may be used to apportion managers' costs. This allocation of costs is often the subject of much friction within an organisation, as different departments may wish to see a certain percentage of their managerial costs apportioned elsewhere.

ADMINISTRATION

The **administration** function, as we have seen in Unit 4, plays an important role in the smooth running of a business's activities. Regardless of their position in the overall organisational structure, or, indeed, their responsibilities or competencies, administrative staff do not play an active or direct role in the production process. As with managers, a certain percentage of administration costs will be attributed to each unit of production and spread across all products manufactured or all services provided.

student activity

(PC 6.3.1, COM 3.2, IT 3.1,3.2)
Using the quality press as your sources of information, try to find out the average wage for the following types of director and manager:

- managing director of a plc
- marketing director of a plc
- retail manager (one who manages a whole shop)
- a manager responsible for a specific activity within a business

Present your findings in the form of a word processed table.

Administration units operate as separate cost centres in order to ascertain the full costs of running the administration facilities. These cost centres have to be funded from some other part of the organisation. Organisations attempt to reduce their administration costs while attempting to ensure that their administration is as cost effective and efficient as possible.

Notes on the Accounts

5 Directors' emoluments and other statutory information

The aggregate emoluments of the Directors of British Nuclear Fuels plc for the year were £1,001,451 (1991 £845,104) including fees of £21,737 (1991 £28,057) and payments of £118,805 (1991 £29,800) on retirement.

The emoluments of the Chairman, the highest paid Director, amounted to £191,675 (1991 £162,208).

The emoluments, excluding pension provision by the Company, of the other Directors in the various ranges are as follows:

Range	1992 Number	1991 Number
Nil to £5,000	—	2
£5,001 to £10,000	3	3
£10,001 to £15,000	2	—
£40,001 to £45,000	—	1
£50,001 to £55,000	—	1
£75,001 to £80,000	—	1
£80,001 to £85,000	—	1
£85,001 to £90,000	1	—
£90,001 to £95,000	—	1
£110,001 to £115,000	1	—
£155,001 to £160,000	—	1
£170,001 to £175,000	—	—
£180,001 to £185,000	1	—

Pensions paid to former Directors amounted to £58,910 (1991 £44,101). Included in debtors are interest free loans of £2,042 repaid in April 1992 (1991 £2,917) and £9,000 to Dr W L Wilkinson and Mr K G Jackson respectively. These loans were made prior to joining the Board in accordance with the Company's policy of providing housing assistance to staff who have been relocated.

FIG. 6.3.4 *Part of the costs of British Nuclear Fuels plc are payments to directors. Sir Christopher Harding, the Chairman, is the highest salary earner, with an income in 1992 of £191,675.*

(PC 6.3.1, COM 3.1)
Considering a manufacturing organisation, try to identify the various cost centres. Discuss your opinions in groups of three and then compare your views with those of the remainder of your group.

MARKETING

The **marketing** function can be an extremely expensive aspect of an organisation's costs. The marketing function includes the following:

● market research
● advertising
● sales promotions
● corporate image development

Again, all of these expenses have to be absorbed by other areas of the organisation's activities. Typically, a proportion of the initial set-up costs to launch a new product include most of these marketing functions. Continual marketing support for all products and services is essential, as we have seen, to ensure that the organisation retains and expands its market share.

(PC 6.3.1, COM 3.1,3.2)
With reference to Unit 3, identify, in ranking order, the above marketing activities in terms of their cost to the organisation.
Write down your list and then compare it to those of the remainder of the group.

OTHER RUNNING EXPENSES (RENT, RATES, TELEPHONE)

The general running expenses of the organisation include:

● rent
● leases
● loans
● mortgages
● salaries
● maintenance
● payment to utilities
● warehousing
● transport
● distribution
● insurance
● business rates
● water rates
● communications

(PC 6.3.1, COM 3.2, IT 3.1, 3.2)
Investigate the business rate in your local area. How is it set? What criteria are used to calculate it? How important a consideration is the business rate when an organisation is thinking about locating in an area? Identify at least three areas of the country where business rates are very low as a result of central government funding and assistance. Present your findings in the form of a word processed document.

Obviously, these expenses will depend upon the exact nature of the organisation's business activities.

The most common method for costing products or services is known as **absorption costing**. This means that all direct costs are allocated to the product or service on a standard basis.

The fairest way or apportioning costs may be related to the time (in the case of wages) that the individual spends related to the production process. A full appraisal of absorption costing requires considerable knowledge of an organisation's overheads and relies upon the organisation reaching full capacity.

6.3.2 *Identify correctly a unit of production or a unit of service from given data*

UNIT OF PRODUCTION

A **unit of production** is considered to be one whole finished article of production. For example, one car, one pair of trousers, etc.

If we consider the above example of one car, we do not think of one unit of production as:

- one seat
- one steering wheel
- one engine

and so on. It is only when all these have been assembled and the finished product is ready that we have one unit of production.

Similarly, a toy doll would not be considered to be a unit of production until all the different parts of the doll itself were assembled to make the finished article.

UNIT OF SERVICE

A **unit of service** is much more difficult to identify as there is no tangible finished product. For example, you take your car in to be repaired and (hopefully) when you get your car back it is in fit and running order again. However, it is still the same car, there is no new product. The actual service that has been provided is the labour of the mechanic involved, but how do we identify one unit of service? The effort put in by the mechanic may have been high if it was a difficult job, or may have been quite low for something relatively simple. A relatively easy way to determine how much effort was needed is to see how long it took to complete the repair, as difficult activities take longer than easy ones. Thus we can break down a unit of service, in this case, into time, e.g. 1 hour of labour = 1 unit of service.

Of course, it does not follow that all services can or should be broken down in this manner. For example, it doesn't make sense to break down the service provided by bus and coach companies in terms of how long the driver has been working. Similarly it doesn't matter if he/she has been working 2 or 5 hours, it doesn't change how far you want to travel as a customer of his/her service. In this case the determining factor is distance, for example 1 unit of service = 1 mile. Thus the further you travel the more service units you use and the more it costs.

FIG. 6.3.5 *A British Gas bill.*

student activity

(PC 6.3.2, AON 3.1, 3.2)
Figure 6.3.5 shows a British Gas bill. From the information shown on it determine:

- the total units of gas used
- the cost of one unit
- what does KWH stand for and what does it mean in terms of amount of gas used?

6.3.3 Calculate the direct costs of the production or service for a time period

As previously discussed, direct costs are those costs which are incurred as a direct result of production and include such areas as:

- assembly wages
- production materials
- machine costs
- depreciation
- direct labour
- direct materials

Consider the following example.

TK Harrison Ltd. make a product known as a 'Boxit'. The direct costs of production are:

- Raw materials = £0.50 per Boxit
- Labour = £1.00 per Boxit
- Machine costs = £0.20 per Boxit

Question: If TK Harrison Ltd. make 1,000 Boxits in 1 month, what are the total direct costs of production for this period?

Solution: This is illustrated in Table 6.3.1:

TABLE 6.3.1 *Direct costs for one month*

Direct cost	Cost per Boxit produced	No. of Boxits produced in time period	Total direct cost
Raw materials	0.50	1,000	£500
Labour	£1.00	1,000	£1,000
Machine costs	£0.20	1,000	£200
Total			£1,700

This cost can also be calculated by finding the total direct cost of production per unit (found by adding all the individual direct costs, and multiplying this by the amount produced), i.e.:

- Raw materials = £0.50
- Labour = £1.00
- Machine cost = £0.20
- Total direct cost per unit = £1.70

Therefore

Direct production cost for one month	= total direct cost per unit × quantity produced
£1.70 × 1,000	= £1,700

student activity

(PC 6.3.3, AON 3.1, 3.2, 3.3)
Calculate TK Harrison's direct cost of production for 3 months if:

- direct materials = £0.65 per unit
- direct labour = £0.90 per unit
- machine cost = £0.25 per unit
- and production is constant at 1,000 units per month.

using each of the methods outlined above.

6.3.4 Calculate indirect costs of the production or service for a time period

We know that indirect costs are those costs incurred by the business that are not directly concerned with the manufacture of the good or providing the service in question. Such costs are termed **overheads**, some examples of which are:

- management

- administration
- marketing

and include such expenses as:

- rent
- insurance

- salaries (those not connected to direct production)
- rates
- depreciation (of non-productive assets, furniture, computers etc)

Again consider the following information regarding TK Harrison Ltd.

- Rent on premises per annum = £20,000
- Insurance per month = £250
- Salaries per annum (administration, management, marketing staff) = £75,000
- Rates (business and water) per quarter = £2,000
- Depreciation per annum (on fixtures and fittings, vehicles and machinery not used in production) = £14,000

Question: What are TK Harrison's indirect costs of production for:

- a year
- 6 months
- 1 month

Solution: This is illustrated in Tables 6.3.2 and 6.3.3. Remember it is not necessary to take into account how many units are being produced as indirect costs stay the same whether the company makes 1,000 or 1 million units.

Alternatively the total cost could be found by dividing the total indirect cost of production for one year by two. That is:

- total indirect cost of production per annum = £120,000
- total indirect cost of production for six months $= \frac{£120,000}{2} = £60,000$

To calculate the indirect cost of production for one month:

- total indirect cost of production per annum = £120,000
- total indirect cost of production for one month $= \frac{£120,000}{12} = £10,000$

TABLE 6.3.2 *Indirect costs of production for one year*

Indirect cost	Time period incurred	Adjustment required for 1 year	Total indirect cost of production (£)
Rent @ £20,000	12 months		20,000
Insurance @ £250	per month	× 12	3,000
Salaries @ £75,000	per annum		75,000
Rates @ £2,000	per quarter (3 months)	× 4	8,000
Depreciation @ £14,000	per annum		14,000
Total			£120,000

TABLE 6.3.3 *Indirect costs of production for six months*

Indirect cost	Time period incurred	Adjustment required for 6 months	Total indirect cost of production (£)
Rent @ £20,000	12 months	÷ 2	10,000
Insurance @ £250	per month	× 6	1,500
Salaries @ £75,000	per annum	÷ 2	37,500
Rates @ £2,000	per quarter (3 months)	× 2	4,000
Depreciation @ £14,000	per annum	÷ 2	7,000
Total			£60,000

student activity

(PC 6.3.4, AON 3.1, 3.2, 3.3)
Calculate TK Harrison's indirect cost of production for:

- 1 year
- 7 months
- 3 months

When:

- Rent on premises per month = £1,700
- Insurance per quarter = £1,100
- Salaries: administration per annum = £20,000
  management per annum = £45,000
  marketing staff per annum = £12,000
- Rates per 4 months = £1,500
- Depreciation per annum = £10,000

6.3.5 *Calculate the total (absorption) cost of a unit of the production or service*

We mentioned previously in this Element that absorption costing is the most common method used for finding the total cost of each individual unit. In absorption costing direct costs are allocated to an individual unit reasonably easily, for example:

- Brian can make 4 wooden ducks in 1 hour and is paid £10.00 per hour
- direct labour per duck = $\dfrac{£10.00}{4} = £2.25$
- direct labour per unit = £2.25

Indirect costs which cannot be directly linked into production are apportioned to each unit of production or service on a standard basis. Therefore, each unit receives an equal proportion of the overheads (indirect costs).

Consider our example of TK Harrison again.

- Production of Boxits = 1,000 units per month
- Total direct cost per unit = £1.70 (direct materials £0.50 + labour £1.00 + machine costs £0.20
- Total indirect costs per annum = £120,000 (rent £20,000 + insurance £3,000 + salaries £75,000 + rates £8,000 + depreciation £14,000)

It follows that in one year TK Harrison will make 12,000 Boxits, (1,000 units a month × 12 months) and incur £120,000 of overheads in the process. Therefore each Boxit needs to receive its portion of these overheads. This is given by:

$$\frac{\text{Total indirect costs}}{\text{Quantity produced}} = \text{Indirect cost per unit}$$

So we get:

$$\frac{£120,000}{12,000} = £10 \text{ per unit}$$

Each Boxit produced receives £10 of indirect costs.

The total cost of each unit is calculated by simply adding the direct and indirect cost per unit together.

i.e. indirect cost per unit
$$+ \text{ direct cost per unit} = \text{total cost per unit}$$

$$£10.00 + £1.70 = £11.70 \text{ per unit}$$

Alternatively:

- Direct cost per unit   = £1.70
- Quantity produced in 1 month = 1,000
- Direct cost per month   = 1,000 × £1.70 = £1,700
- Direct costs per annum = £1,700 × 12 = £20,400
- Indirect cost per annum = £120,000
- Total cost of production per annum (total indirect costs per annum + total direct costs per annum)
$$= 20,400 + 120,000 = £140,400$$
- Total production (production per month × 12)
$$= 1,000 × 12 - 12,000$$
- Total cost per unit = $\dfrac{£140,400}{12,000} = £11.70$

student activity

6.3.6 *Explain variable and fixed costs in terms of their relationship with production*

VARIABLE COSTS

Certain production costs come into operation only when they are required. **Variable costs** are costs which are increased or decreased in line with production. In this way, as output increases so will the variable cost incurred, as more of these factors need to be inputted to increase output. For example, if you produce more of a product, you need more raw materials, more production and assembly line workers, more power etc.

From this you can see that direct costs of production are also variable costs.

Let us again look at TK Harrison Ltd. You will remember our direct costs were:

Per unit

Raw materials	£0.50
Labour	£1.00
Machine costs	£0.20
Total	£1.70 per unit

If, as in our original example, we produce 1,000 units:

- Variable cost = 1,000 × £1.70 = £1,700

Using different levels of output we can construct a variable cost schedule:

Output	Variable (direct) cost per unit (£)	Variable cost (£)
1,000	1.70	1,700
2,000	1.70	3,400
3,000	1.70	5,100
4,000	1.70	6,800
5,000	1.70	8,500

This enables us to draw up a variable cost line (curve).

Thus we can see from Figure 6.3.6 that variable costs increase proportionately with output and will always do so.

FIXED COSTS

Fixed costs are costs which do not vary with the level of output. These costs will be incurred whether the organisation is producing anything or not. Fixed costs are therefore not dependent on the level of output of the company and will not change, across a certain range of output even if the level of output changes.

For example, if a business has the capacity to do so, it may increase its output from 15,000 to 20,000 units. But its fixed costs such as rent, rates and administration overheads will still be the same. Remember that these are the same as our indirect costs at 20,000 units of output as they were at 15,000 units of output. This can be shown diagrammatically as in Figure 6.3.7. From this diagram we can see that a fixed costs line is therefore a horizontal line parallel to the X axis at all levels of production.

At this point, however, we need to make a distinction between **short term** and **long term**. In the short term, costs will tend to be fairly fixed as it is often difficult to change the level of expenditure. Over a longer period of time, however, the further we look into a company's future the more variable an organisation's costs may be. So although we say fixed costs, what we are referring to are those costs which do not change within the given period, (one month, one quarter, one year, etc.).

Consider the following situation. If a company wished to increase its level of output and did not possess any spare capacity with which to do so, it would have to buy new machines, build a new factory, or extend its existing one. A company cannot achieve

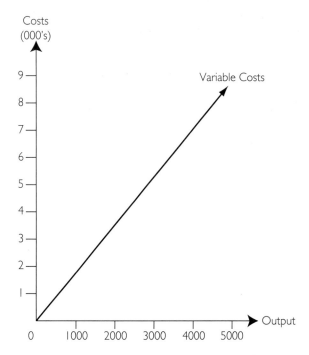

FIG. 6.3.6 *A variable costs curve.*

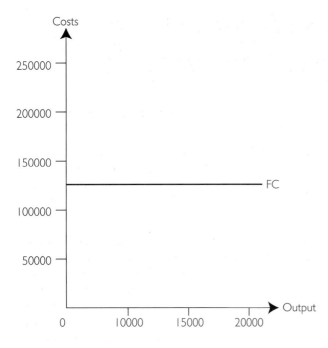

FIG. 6.3.7 *A fixed costs curve.*

Average fixed costs represent the amount of fixed costs incurred by each unit of production. You can assume that indirect costs are also fixed costs. Average fixed cost is given by:

$$\text{Average fixed cost} = \frac{\text{Fixed cost}}{\text{Output}}$$

As output rises the level of average fixed cost incurred by each unit will fall. A good example of this is shown in Table 6.3.4.

TABLE 6.3.4 *Average fixed cost*

	£	£
Fixed costs	100,000	100,000
divided by Output	10,000	40,000
Average fixed cost	£10	£2.50
(or cost incurred by each unit)		

these things quickly. In the long term, however, such adjustments can be made. In this way the company moves to a new and higher level of fixed costs as the new fixed costs are taken on. This is represented in Figure 6.3.8.

This calculation is represented in Figure 6.3.9.

This is an important relationship, for, as we can see, increased production reduces the average fixed cost per unit, and so will also reduce the level of total cost per unit.

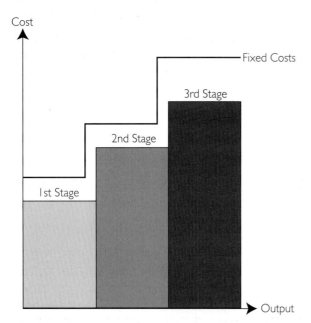

FIG. 6.3.8 *Fixed costs increase as output increases in the long term.*

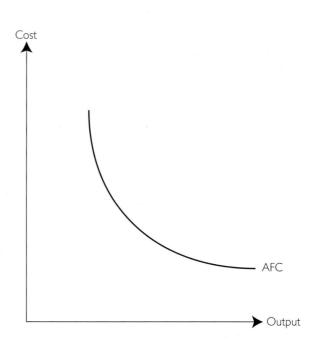

FIG. 6.3.9 *An average fixed costs curve.*

6.3.7 *Calculate the variable costs of a unit of the production or service from given data*

As previously discussed, variable costs are those costs which are incurred in line with production. Consider the following example:

> TK Harrison Ltd. need to buy 850 kg. of raw materials in order to make 1,000 Boxits and these cost £29.41 per 50 kg. It then takes one semi-skilled machine operator 5 minutes to turn the raw materials into a Splodgett and the operator is paid £12.00 per hour. In addition to this, the machine used by the operator takes £0.20 watts of electricity to make each Boxit.

Solution:

1 *Raw materials*
- Raw materials = 850 kg. @ £29.41 per 50 kg.
- Total cost of raw materials $\frac{850}{50} \times 29.41 = 499.97$

That is, 850 kg. of raw materials cost £499.97. From this quantity 1,000 Boxits can be made.

Therefore the cost of raw materials per unit =

$\frac{£499.97}{1,000}$ = 499.997 pence to 3 decimal places

Rounded up this makes £0.50 pence of raw materials per product.

2 *Labour*
The labour cost is £12.00 per hour and each Splodgett takes 5 minutes to make. It is therefore possible to make 12 Splodgetts in one hour. This gives:

- Number of Boxits produced in 1 hour = 12
- Cost of labour for one hour = £12.00
- Cost of labour per Boxit $= \frac{£12.00}{12} = £1.00$

3 *Machine costs*
The machine cost is £0.20 per Boxit. This information was given to us in the question. However, normally you would work this out in the same way as you work out the cost of labour per unit, i.e. how much time does it take to make one Boxit, (or amount of raw materials), and how many is the machine capable of producing, and at what cost?

Solution: The variable cost per unit is simply the sum of all our costs, which vary in a direct relation to output, i.e.:

Per unit	£
Raw materials	0.50
Labour	1.00
Machine cost (power)	0.20
	1.70 = variable cost per unit

You will notice that this figure is the same as the total direct cost per unit from Figure 6.3.3, as those costs which vary with production levels tend to be those directly inputted to the product or service itself.

6.3.8 *Calculate the marginal cost of a unit of the production or service*

The decision as to which costs are fixed and which are variable is not always as clear cut as it may seem. Indeed, neither is the question of which costs are direct or indirect. So far we have assumed, for example, that indirect = fixed and direct = variable. It must be noted that this is not always necessarily the case. Another assumption that we have made is that indirect costs and variable costs are 100 per cent variable. In other words, if output rises by 25 per cent then variable costs also rise by 25 per cent. For example,

production may rise by 25 per cent but the cost of raw materials may only rise by 20 per cent although 25 per cent more raw materials are needed. The reason for this is that as production increases and the amount of raw materials needed also increases, then the producing organisation may be able to benefit from trade discounts or lower prices from bulk buying. Where costing exercises take into account the variable cost of the product rather than the total cost, this is called **marginal costing**.

Marginal costing refers to the extra cost which the business incurs through the production of one more unit.

$$\text{Marginal cost} = \frac{\text{Extra cost}}{\text{Extra output}}$$

In our examples so far, we have assumed that our indirect and variable costs are 100 per cent variable. Therefore, our marginal cost, or the cost of producing one extra unit, is exactly the same as our total direct costs per unit or variable cost per unit, i.e. £1.70.

ELEMENT 6.3

a s s i g n m e n t

(PC 6.3.1–8, COM 3.2, 3.3, 3.4, AON 3.1, 3.2, 3.3, IT 3.1, 3.2, 3.3)

QUIRK AND SONS

Quirk and Sons is a small family-run business producing bedside lamps. It is mainly run by Andrew Quirk and his son Robert. Robert has become concerned lately, because the cost of raw materials has risen from £42.40 per 100 kg. to £44.32 and it takes 8 kg. to make each lamp. In addition to this, their rent and rates have been increased to £800 per quarter. Robert is worried that their selling price may be too low. He also thinks that his father and he should receive more money for their labours. Not only do they do all the finance and administration for the company, they also help run the machinery when necessary, in order to cut down on overtime costs. Robert currently earns £10,000, while his father earns £14,000. Sales and marketing costs are very low at £2,500 per year. They are not worried about sales as they have a contract to a major chain of department stores which will buy all the lamps they make. To this end they have just bought a new machine which allows their machine operator to make 8 lamps an hour instead of 6. Although his pay rise to £20.00 per hour has slightly affected this benefit, they calculated (before buying this machine) that its use of electricity was costing £3.50 per 100 finished lamps, and that the depreciation charge would work out at only 2 pence per lamp. Their current production level is 2,600 lamps per year and

Robert has estimated that insurance costs them £500 per month and depreciation should be worked out on non-productive assets. In total these amount to £20,000. Both Robert and his father agree that these should last the company for nine years.

Produce a report for Andrew and Robert Quirk outlining the total cost of each unit and the marginal cost of each unit. Robert has requested that you explain all your workings clearly in a language that he understands, as the last time they hired somebody to do this this person kept using terms like direct and indirect costs and he did not understand. As part of your report Robert asks if you can explain the terminology that you use.

TASK 1

(PC 6.3.1–5, 6.3.7–8)
Using the above data, show the breakdown of the total costs and marginal costs for each unit of production. You may use a computer generated spreadsheet and your calculations should be supported by an explanation of your thinking behind the numbers.

TASK 2

(PC 6.3.6)
Give a summary of a business's direct and indirect costs, particularly in relation to definitions.
Your work should be produced by the use of a word processing package.

Explain basic pricing decisions and break-even point

PERFORMANCE CRITERIA

A student must:

1 identify **basic factors** which determine price and describe **related pricing strategies**

2 explain **break-even point**

3 draw and **label** a break-even chart from given data

4 **analyse** the break-even chart

5 explain **reasons** for using a break-even chart

RANGE

Basic factors: *need to make a profit, prices of competing products, under-used capacity*

Related pricing strategies: *cost-plus pricing, market-led pricing, marginal cost/contribution pricing*

Break-even point: *the profit or loss of a business, the relationship between total cost and sales over a range of output levels, the relationship between fixed costs and variable costs*

Label: *with sales and costs, units of production, fixed costs, variable costs, total costs, sales, break-even point, profit, loss, selected operating point, margin of safety*

Analyse: *units of production, value of sales, the profit or loss at given levels of production and sales, margin of safety*

Reasons: *starting a business, measuring profits or losses, examining 'what if' scenarios*

6.4.1 Identify basic factors which determine price and describe related pricing strategies

BASIC FACTORS

In Unit 1 we discussed how the interaction of **supply** and **demand** determines the **market price** for a **product**. We also saw that businesses can influence the price at which their particular product or service is sold, depending on the **market conditions** and other influences which prevent the **market forces** from operating smoothly. Consider the following situation:

Milk from a supermarket is considerably cheaper than buying milk from a garage shop or from your milkman.

The first obvious point to highlight is that milkmen deliver their product to your house. Therefore they can justify charging more for their product as it saves you, the consumer, the inconvenience of travelling to acquire it. In addition the daily delivery ensures that the product is fresh. On the other hand, milk sold in supermarkets is usually on sale for a lower price than the organisation paid for it. It should be mentioned, however, that milk sold in a supermarket should also always be fresh. Why is it, then, that the supermarket can charge less than the delivery person for the same product? The theory behind supermarkets making a loss on milk is that the product is needed by people regularly. When they go to the supermarket to buy it, possibly because it is the cheapest place, customers will buy other products as well. The supermarket will make its profit on any additional products which the consumer decides to purchase. In this way the supermarket will make greater profits in the long run. When a supermarket provides such items as milk at a cheaper retail price than the purchase price, these are known as **loss leaders**. We discuss this aspect of **marketing and profit** in Unit 3 of the book.

We have also, in Unit 1, considered various **pricing strategies** used by businesses for a variety of reasons. We need at this point, however, to consider in more depth how and why companies price their products at the level they do.

NEED TO MAKE A PROFIT

Although private businesses have many different objectives, in the long run one of their main aims must be to **make a profit**. In the short term, businesses can sometimes afford to make a loss on a product without necessarily being forced into liquidation. In fact, several organisations do so quite deliberately at times, possibly when launching a new product. However, in the long run the revenue gained from sales must be higher than the costs incurred by the company, otherwise liquidation or bankruptcy (for sole traders) will occur. Therefore the unit price of the product must be higher than its cost. This is termed **cost-plus pricing**.

PRICES OF COMPETING PRODUCTS

In many cases businesses base the price of their product on the price charged by their competitors. This type of pricing is generally used by vulnerable and susceptible companies. Businesses will often keep watch on the prices of competitors, and it is becoming increasingly common for retailers to guarantee that theirs is the lowest price, or they will refund the difference. In order to do this it is vital that the organisation knows exactly what its competitors are doing. This type of pricing strategy is called *market-led* pricing.

There will always be a range of prices open to the organisation to choose from. Obviously, it is a good idea to try to identify the price which will give the organisation the highest level of profit. This can be considered a long-term strategy but there may be also some short-term considerations which have to be addressed. Although we have covered the various different types of **pricing policy** in Unit 1, we can identify some of the major pricing choices open to the organisation again here:

1 *Price skimming or prestige pricing* – when the organisation prices its products to appeal to the customers with the highest income. In other words, the product is highly priced. What these pricing policies mean is that the organisation accepts that it would make bigger profits if it reduced its price because more people would then buy their products. In order to sell more, however, the organisation might have to devote more of its resources to the product. High prices attract competitors, who will seek to take some of the market share by offering similar products at lower prices. Ideally, price skimming or prestige pricing should be applied when the product is new or innovative. Things being as they are, the organisation's product will not remain innovative for long. It is at this point that the competitors step in and the innovative organisation needs to reconsider its pricing strategy.

2 *Low pricing* – as long as the price covers the direct costs and contributes something to the overheads of the organisation, a low price can be acceptable. This

state of affairs should not be maintained for long. The organisation will have other costs or indirect costs which may need a similar contribution. An organisation's main justification for selling products at low prices is that it has spare capacity. In addition it may face the prospect that if it utilises this spare capacity to produce more products, it may not be able to sell these products for higher prices.

Low prices, or, indeed, a **price-cutting war** do not offer advantages to any of the participants. Small businesses, in particular, do not want to engage in such practices. Customers, grateful for low prices, will come to expect those lower prices to continue. If low prices are maintained for a long time, the customers will suffer as a result of some of the suppliers being forced out of business.

An organisation has to consider carefully how to react to a price cut by its competitors. It is probably better to try and focus the attention of the customer on the advantages of the organisation's product rather than to join in the price cutting war. In markets where there is a high level of price sensitivity, however, there may be little choice but to join in the price cutting. In this instance, the only way to survive in the long run is to cut the organisation's costs.

UNDER-USED CAPACITY

Businesses which have high fixed costs often find that it is in their best interests to make use of any spare capacity that they may possess. This would help to spread their fixed costs of production over a wider area of products. In Element 6.3 we discussed how the higher levels of output affect fixed costs, in other words, average fixed costs. Businesses often sell below their standard price in order to receive some return. A good example of this would be airlines who sell as many seats on a plane for the standard price as possible. If there is spare capacity on the plane before the flight departs, it makes sense for the operator to offer these seats for sale at a discounted rate and receive some revenue rather than fly with empty seats and receive no revenue. The cost of the flight would be exactly the same whether there were 20 or 200 passengers on board. This policy of selling seats off cheaply at the last minute is termed marginal or contribution pricing.

RELATED PRICING STRATEGIES

As we discussed in Element 6.3, there are innumerable pricing strategies available to organisations. Specifically relating them to the **basic factors** which determine **price**, we can see that overriding objectives such as the

student activity

desire to make profit, the need to compete on a pricing basis with competitors and the availability of underused capacity may have strong influences on the pricing strategy of the organisation. We will investigate some of the key pricing strategies again in this section of the Element, but for a fuller explanation of the variety of pricing strategies available, you should refer back to Unit 1.

COST-PLUS PRICING

Cost-plus pricing is also sometimes referred to as full-cost pricing. What this means is that companies determine the full cost of a product or service and add an extra mark-up percentage to it. When businesses carry out this strategy it is known that the selling price is always higher than the full cost, or the total production cost per unit. We have already mentioned the subject of total production cost per unit in Element 6.3 of this book. When a business carries out this strategy it ensures that a **profit is made**.

Cost-plus pricing is popular as it is easy to implement and organisations find that they can be reasonably assured of making a profit without too many difficulties. In very simple terms, the system of cost-plus pricing requires the organisation to work out the costs of direct inputs per unit and the total fixed overheads or indirect costs. By using absorption costing, the organisation can apportion each unit its fair share of costs and then add a reasonable and satisfying level of profit.

Let us consider the example of Walker Brothers Ltd.

	£
● Cost of direct materials per unit	4.00
● Cost of direct labour per unit	7.00
● Cost of direct overheads (e.g. power)	1.20
● Total direct cost per unit	12.20
● Total fixed costs= £54,400	
● Output = 16,000 units	

- Add percentage of fixed costs =

$$\frac{54,400}{16,000} \qquad 3.40$$

- Total full cost   15.60

- Add required percentage for profit,
  e.g. 30 per cent =

$$\frac{15.60 \times 30}{100} = \qquad 4.68$$

- Selling price   <u>20.28</u>

Full-cost pricing will not always give the same answer as the method used to determine the amount of fixed costs each unit receives. When absorption costing is used, the amount each unit will receive varies. In other words, the organisation will consider whether the work carried out is done by machines, the amount of time taken, labour hours used or the amount of raw materials each product requires. It should be remembered, however, that this is only a concern when a business makes more than one product.

MARKET-LED PRICING

Market-led pricing differs from cost-plus pricing in that the organisation will do more than research the price that its competitors are charging. In addition, the organisation will also determine whether it can produce the product or service at a level of cost per unit which is below the market price. If this is a viable proposition for the organisation, then it could make a profit at this price.

In reality companies calculate their costs for producing a product or service by looking at the price at which similar products are sold. They would then base their price on those of their competitors. However, as we mentioned at the beginning of this Element, when we considered the question of comparison with regard to the price of milk, we saw that customers will tend to purchase from the cheapest source. In other words, competition pricing or market-led pricing can be very dangerous for organisations as it can lead to price wars. As one competitor tries to undercut another, the price war escalates and can become out of control.

In the modern world, with business becoming more and more competitive, it is becoming increasingly important for organisations to charge a price which is similar to those of their competitors. This is particularly important in view of the fact that more customers have the use of transport and can travel from shop to shop in order to compare prices. In addition, consumers have become more informed about products or services available by means of television and radio advertising.

student activity

(PC 6.4.1, COM 3.1)
Research the price of five different brands of the same product, e.g. cereals, baked beans, canned drinks, etc. Are there any major differences in price between them? Can you account for the reasons behind any price differences you might come across? Discuss your findings in groups of two or three.

We have discussed these issues in some detail in Unit 1.2 and Unit 3.1. You may find it useful to refresh your memory at this stage.

MARGINAL COST/CONTRIBUTION PRICING

In Element 6.3 we discussed the fact that **marginal cost** is the extra cost incurred from producing **one extra or additional unit** of production. This type of cost system shows that when an organisation has spare capacity, it can be more profitable for it to sell any additional units at a price above the product's marginal cost, even if the price the organisation receives for the product is less than the total unit cost of production. Why is this so? It would be useful here to consider again our example of Walker Brothers, which we dealt with earlier in this section:

- Output = 16,000 units
- Fixed cost (overheads) = £54,400

	£
- Cost of direct materials	4.00
- Cost of direct labour	7.00
- Cost of direct overheads	1.20
- Fixed overhead	3.40
- Total full cost per unit	15.60

This is the cost per unit using full absorption cost methods. We determined our selling price as being £20.28. However, if we were to produce one extra unit of production this unit would not incur the full absorption cost. We have already taken into account our fixed costs when we determined our full cost per unit. It is not necessary to do this again. The factory rent, rates and salaries of administration and other staff are not going to change simply because one more unit is produced. The only costs that will be incurred are those directly associated with the production of the product.

The example below may help you to understand this concept:

	£
• Cost of direct materials	4.00
• Cost of direct labour	7.00
• Cost of direct overheads	1.20
• Marginal cost of one extra unit	12.20

Note: Marginal cost = variable cost per unit

If a customer were to order an extra unit of production and offer a price of £15.00, the organisation would be aware that it should accept this offer as the product would still be making a contribution to profit, even though the price is below the total cost per unit of £15.60. It should be noted, however, that this is only the case if the previous level of production and sales was sufficient to cover the fixed costs of the organisation. An additional consideration at this stage would be whether the organisation had spare productive capacity, in other words, if no new machinery had to be bought or hired to make the extra unit. If additional machinery had been purchased or hired, this would have raised the fixed costs.

Another way of looking at this is to consider our fixed costs separately from our variable costs and selling price. Using our previous example once again, we can see that:

- Variable costs of each unit = £12.20
- Selling price of each unit = £20.28
- Difference (20.28 – 12.20) = £8.08

This difference between selling price and variable cost is termed contribution, therefore:

- Contribution per unit = £8.08

Contribution = selling price – marginal (variable) cost. This literally means that each product sold contributes £8.08 towards profit before fixed costs are deducted.
Let us see if our analysis holds true:

- Output and sales = 16,000 units
- Contribution per unit = £8.08
- Total contribution = 16,000 × 8.08 £129,280
  (Less) fixed costs £54,400
- Profit £74,880

Alternatively, to prove the above:

- Total cost per unit = £15.60
- Output = 16,000
- Total cost= 16,000 × 15.60 = £249,600
- Selling price per unit = £20.28
- Units sold = 16,000
- Total sales revenue = 16,000 × 20.28 =£324,480
- Profit = Total sales revenue – Total costs
  = 324,480 – 249,600 = £74,880

With one extra unit of production:

- Profit on 16,000 units = £74,880
- Contribution of the extra unit when sold at £15.00 (less than the full absorption cost per unit) = £2.80
- Profit on 16,001 units = 74,880 + 2.80
  = £74,882.80

Although £2.80 extra profit may seem like a completely irrelevant amount, consider the implications if the extra order had been for 2,000 units at £15.00 and not just one unit.

student activity

(PC 6.4.1, AON 3.1, 3.2, 3.3)
Calculate Walker Brothers' new selling price using cost-plus pricing and level of profit (assuming all output is sold), if their direct costs increase to:

	£
• Direct materials per unit	4.30
• Direct labour per unit	7.20
• Direct overheads per unit	1.24

and output and fixed costs remain the same.
Walker Brothers receive an offer for 1,300 extra units at a price of £13.20.
Should they accept the offer?
Calculate Walker Brothers' profit if they accept this offer.
Outline any limitations they may have on whether or not to accept.

6.4.2 Explain break-even point
6.4.3 Draw and label a break-even chart from given data

Whereas elsewhere in this book we deal with each performance criterion independently, the nature of the break-even point requires us to consider the relationships between the various costs and sales in an integrated manner. By following the line of thought in this performance criterion you will better understand the nature of the break-even point and its significance.

BREAK-EVEN POINT

The break-even point is defined as being the point at which the level of sales is not great enough for the business to make a profit and yet not low enough for the business to make a loss. In other words, earnings from sales are just sufficient for the business to cover its total costs. This occurs when total revenue from sales exactly equals the total cost of production.

Break-even point occurs when total cost = total revenue

From this it can be assumed that if total revenue from sales is greater than total costs, then the organisation concerned makes a profit. Conversely, if the opposite is true, and the total revenue is less than total costs, then the organisation can make a loss. It is essential that organisations take this very important factor into account. The organisation will find that it is essential to determine how many units of output it must produce and sell before it can reach its break-even point. As we have seen, in our earlier analysis in this Unit, the total cost of a unit of production is made up of two factors, the fixed and variable costs, where:

Total cost = fixed costs + variable costs

and the total revenue is given by the number of products sold multiplied by the selling price:

Total revenue = price × quantity

If you sell five chocolate bars at 25p each, your total revenue is £1.25 (5 × 25p).

DETERMINING THE BREAK-EVEN POINT

How do we determine our break even point? The easiest way to do this is by the use of **diagrams**. In Element 6.3 we examined the relationship between costs and output

and we determined that within a certain range of output, provided the capacity was already in existence, **specific costs** remained **fixed**, regardless of the quantity of units produced. This resulted in a horizontal fixed costs (FC) curve line, parallel to the X axis. This is shown in Figure 6.4.1. It can be seen that other **variable costs** changed in direct relation to the level of output. In other words, the higher the output, the higher the variable costs. This gave us an upward left to right sloping variable cost (VC) curve, as shown in Figure 6.4.2.

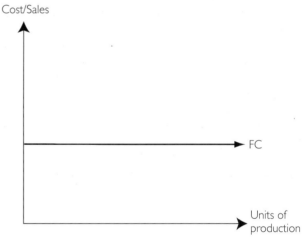

FIG. 6.4.1 *A fixed costs curve.*

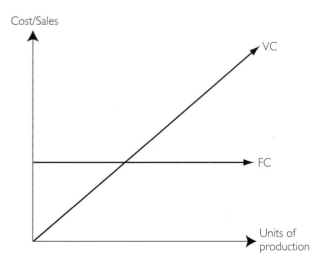

FIG. 6.4.2 *The relationship between output and fixed and variable costs.*

If we add these two lines together we get our **total cost** (TC) curve. This is represented in Figure 6.4.3 and is achieved by simply shifting the variable cost curve upwards at all points by the value of the fixed costs. In other words, instead of starting at the point of origin, we start where the fixed cost line hits the Y axis and then draw a line parallel to the variable cost line. This gives us the total cost, in other words, the fixed costs plus the variable costs.

The next step is to add our **total revenue** (TR) line on to the diagram. Our total revenue line will also be left to right upward sloping, as it follows that the more we sell, the greater the amount of revenue we receive. For example, if we sell five chocolate bars at 25p we receive total revenue equal to £1.25, whereas if we sell 10 chocolate bars we receive total revenue of £2.50. The total revenue line starts from the origin, and we should remember that if we made and sold no chocolate bars, we would receive nothing in terms of revenue. Figure 6.4.4 illustrates the addition of the total revenue line.

From our earlier analysis we determined that the **break-even point** was where the total revenue equalled the total cost. From Figure 6.4.4 this can quite clearly be seen as the point at which the TR curve cuts the TC curve.

Figure 6.4.5 considers this position in more detail. From this figure we can see that the break-even point occurs at BE where TR = TC. At areas to the left of this point the total costs are higher than the total revenue which means that the organisation will make a loss. This occurs because the company must incur all its

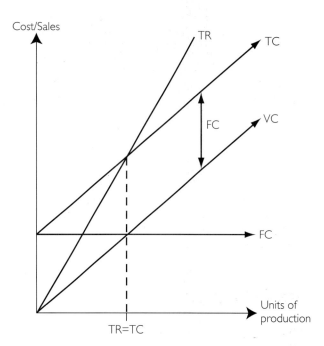

FIG. 6.4.4 *The addition of total revenue – determining the break-even point.*

fixed costs, such as the cost of machines and premises, before it can start to produce anything. In this case, the amount the organisation produces and sells has to catch up with the fixed costs. However, the company does not break-even at this point as every unit produced and sold incurs variable costs as well as earning revenue. Consequently, it does not break-even until sales revenue catches up with fixed costs and variable costs, in other words, where it cuts the total cost line. Essentially, the organisation would not survive if in the long term the selling price were less than the unit cost. Once the position BE has been reached, any unit subsequently sold earns the business some profit, as the difference between the unit selling price and the unit cost remains. This difference increases at higher levels of output, and the distance between TR and TC increases as the output also increases after the break-even point. This is because the percentage of the fixed cost apportioned to each of the units reduces as the output increases. We have dealt with this aspect in the section of this Unit headed **average fixed costs**.

Figure 6.4.5 also shows the organisation's selected operating point and margin of safety. The **selected operating point** shows the number of units of production which the organisation plans to produce and sell. It should be remembered that the selected operating point must always be to the right of the break-even point, as it makes no logical sense for an organisation to plan production and sales to be at a level where it is only able to make a loss. To take this factor into consideration, organisations should build in a margin of

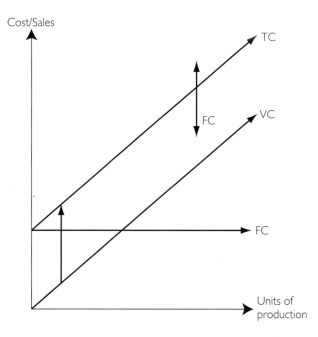

FIG. 6.4.3 *A total costs curve, in which total costs = FC + VC.*

safety to protect them from small fluctuations in price and costs. It should be noted, however, that a small margin probably would not be sufficient to compensate for large surges one way or the other.

When drawing a break-even chart, as with any other type of chart, it is important that it is labelled clearly and correctly. We provide below a quick and convenient checklist to help you ensure that you have considered all aspects when you produce a chart. The following considerations should be taken into account:

1 title
2 axes labelled

- X units of production
- Y costs and sales in £s

3 fixed cost line (FC)
4 variable cost line (VC)
5 total cost line (TC)
6 total revenue line (TR)
7 break-even point (BE)
8 selected operating point
9 margin of safety
10 clear indication of areas of profit and loss

LABELLING A BREAK-EVEN CHART

The break-even chart requires a considerable amount of labelling in order to be able to identify exactly what

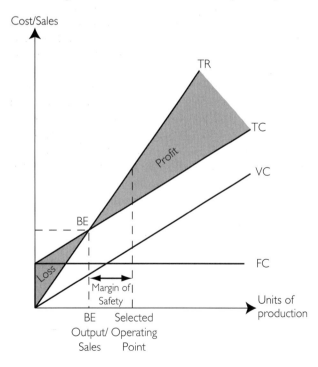

FIG. 6.4.5 *A break-even chart.*

student activity

(PC 6.4.2, AON 3.1, 3.2, 3.3)
Using the following figures, construct a break-even chart.

- selling price = £30
- variable costs per unit = £12
- fixed costs = £18,000
- full production capacity = 2,000 units

From your graph estimate the break-even points for units of production.

Also estimate the level of profit/loss at a selected operating point of 1,500 units.

the chart is telling us about the break-even point. Below we have attempted to define in the simplest possible terms the meanings of the various labels employed.

UNITS OF PRODUCTION

A **unit of production** is considered to be the completed product and not, importantly, the components which make up that product.

FIXED COSTS

Fixed costs are the costs that do not alter in relation to changes in demand or output. They have to be paid regardless of the business's trading level.

VARIABLE COSTS

Variable costs are costs which change in direct proportion to changes in output, such as raw materials, components, labour and energy. Break-even charts require the assumption that some costs vary in direct proportion to changes in output. In fact, it is unlikely that any costs are totally variable as raw materials, for example, are likely to cost less per unit if the organisation buys in bulk. In this instance, you cannot assume that the cost of raw materials will double if output doubles.

TOTAL COSTS

Total costs are simply the sum of all fixed and variable costs.

SALES AND COSTS

Sales are the income generated from the selling of units of production to customers.

Costs, on the other hand, are expenses incurred by the organisation in the purchase of raw materials, other fixed costs and variable costs.

BREAK-EVEN POINT

This is the point at which sales levels are high enough for the organisation not to make a loss but not high enough for it to make a profit. In other words, this is the point where **total sales equal total costs**.

PROFIT

Profit in terms of the break-even chart and the break-even point is achieved when sales exceed total costs.

LOSS

Loss in terms of the break-even chart and the break-even point occurs when revenue from sales has not met the total costs.

SELECTED OPERATING POINT

This is the **planned production and sales level** which is assumed to be the same as that in given data.

MARGIN OF SAFETY

This is the amount by which the selected operating point exceeds the break-even point. This indicates the amount by which sales could fall from the planned level before the organisation ceases to make a profit.

6.4.4 Analyse the break-even chart

In the Element Assignment you will be required to construct a break-even chart and label it fully. You will also be required to analyse the chart and state why a break-even chart would be useful. In order to focus your analysis, it may be valuable to look at the following:

- the units of production
- the value of sales
- the profit or loss at given levels of production and sales
- the margin of safety

It is also useful to consider the **limitations** of the **break-even chart**, and to this end, we have devoted this performance criterion to an analysis of the limitations.

Although break-even analysis can be useful in a variety of different ways, it is a very simplistic way of modelling business costs and revenues. As we have already seen, the fixed costs are likely to change in the long run and a **stepped** fixed cost line would be a more accurate representation. Alongside this, variable costs and sales revenue are unlikely to be linear. Such considerations as trade discounts, special contracts, overtime payments and fluctuations in the cost of raw materials may mean that variable costs, and as a consequence, total cost, and sales should really be curved.

Break-even analysis also makes the highly unrealistic assumption that organisations are able to sell all their output at any given level, whereas, in reality, this is rarely the case.

The final consideration, as with any statistical or diagrammatical analysis of relationships, is that the information gained from the exercise is only as accurate as the information collected. Collecting accurate information for the purpose of producing a break-even analysis is expensive. In many cases, the cost can amount to more than the benefit gained.

6.4.5 *Explain reasons for using a break-even chart*

REASONS

Break-even charts are extremely useful for an organisation, regardless of its age or nature of business. In the case of new businesses, as we will see, the calculation and construction of a break even chart will identify many of the **key considerations** that need to be taken into account in **decision making** right from the beginning. For existing organisations, the break-even chart is an ideal way of **measuring profits or losses** and perhaps looking at the level of business activity required to break even. Since breaking even can mean the difference between the success or failure of the business, the organisation will be able to adapt or change its modes of production, as well as its costing structures to move towards a break-even position. Break-even charts are also useful in examining what is known as a **'what if?'** scenario. These scenarios entail the examination of either external influences on the business and its profitability, or actions taken by the organisation in order to improve or rationalise processes.

STARTING A BUSINESS

Break-even analysis is a very useful tool for people who are considering starting a business. We enlarge on this aspect when we discuss a business plan in Unit 8 of this book.

The break-even analysis is useful in that it is a quick and easy exercise to complete or compile. In addition, it is the main document which managers will have readily to hand when discussing the financial position of an organisation to, say, the providers of finance. This would be a vital piece of information, particularly if the managers concerned do not have a full understanding of the financial requirements of the providers of such finance.

By performing a simple break-even exercise a new business can estimate the level of **output** and the level of **sales** required before it starts to make a **profit**. This can then be compared with any marketing research the organisation may have previously undertaken, in order to estimate whether such a level of output and sales is a realistic proposition. Provided the estimated levels of output and sales in the break-even analysis are positive, then the business should be viable. As we have already mentioned, the break-even analysis should be included in any business plan. It assists with the raising of capital and is a relatively simple way of showing the expected profitability of the business at the planned level of output and sales. In addition, it helps to show prospective providers of finance, or investors, that the business proposition has been researched and considered fully.

MEASURING PROFIT AND LOSSES

One of the main advantages of break-even charts and analyses is the fact that they allow organisations to determine, at a glance, the estimated level of **profit** or **loss**. In addition, it would be easy to determine the different **levels of production and sales**, within a given **production range**. It also allows the organisations to determine a reasonably safe operating level. Organisations do this by building in a margin of safety which would absorb small fluctuations in sales and costs. Alongside this, organisations are also made aware of the minimum number of sales required in order to break-even and avoid making a loss.

EXAMINING 'WHAT IF?' SCENARIOS

As we have already mentioned, a break-even analysis is a relatively quick and easy exercise to perform. In this context it is also relatively cheap. A break-even analysis enables an organisation to examine 'what if?' scenarios on a relatively cost-effective basis.

Should the occasion arise, it is relatively easy for an organisation to re-draw its break-even analysis in order to monitor the effect on its break-even point of any unforeseen circumstances. For example, organisations might consider a change to their position if they had to reduce their selling price and raise output and sales. Additionally they would examine whether or not they should invest in any new machinery which could lower their variable costs through more efficient production, but which would raise their fixed costs. In such cases, a re-drawn break even chart could be used as an aid in making investment decisions.

Focus study

BASIC PRICING DECISIONS AND BREAKING EVEN

The following information has been extracted from the accounts of Birkin and Jones Ltd. for the year 6 June 199x to 5 June 199y.

Production and sales for the year = 200,000 units
Average unit selling price   = £50.00

1 Raw material costs

- Raw material type A = £4.25 per unit
- Raw material type B = £5.70 per unit

2 *Labour costs*

- Unskilled labour = £6.00 per unit
- Skilled labour = £8.00 per unit
- Management salaries = £240,000 per annum
- Administration salaries = £205,000 per annum
- Other salaries = £180,000 per annum

3 *Overheads*

- Management O/H = £64,000
- Administration O/H = £112,500
- Other O/H = £118,500

- Depreciation
  - on productive assets = £0.40 per unit
  - on non-productive assets = £40,000
  - Power = £0.05 per unit

Birkin and Jones have conducted some fairly in-depth research and have estimated that in the following year, due to an increase in popularity of their product (a small pocket-sized walkman), demand and sales will increase by 12 per cent. However due to the shortage of skilled labour in the UK in the electronics industry they have just negotiated a wage increase: their unskilled workers have received a 20 per cent pay rise, skilled workers a 30 per cent pay rise, and a 3 per cent rise in all other salaries. They also expect a 15 per cent rise in the price of raw material A and a 17 per cent rise in the price of raw material B. Birkin and Jones are very much concerned as their three major rivals, who each control approximately 10–12 per cent of market share, have all dropped their selling price by 8 per cent and they think they must do the same in order to achieve the 12 per cent increase in sales. At this point they are not sure what to do.

student activity

(PC 6.4.1–5, COM 3.4, AON 3.1, 3.2, 3.3)
Produce a report detailing their position in relation to their break-even point in 199x and 199y if all changes happen as forecast. How has their position changes? Use break-even charts to help explain your reasoning. Alongside this explain to Birkin and Jones the importance of the break-even position and why you have used this analysis to help them in their decision. Explain any limitations of your analysis you think are relevant.

Do you think Birkin and Jones should lower their price relative to those of their competitors? What type of pricing strategy is this and do you think it is the correct one for them to follow? How does Birkin and Jones' selling price relate to the full cost of one unit of production?

ELEMENT 6.4

a s s i g n m e n t

(PC 6.4.1–5, COM 3.1, 3.2, 3.3, 3.4, IT 3.1, 3.2, 3.3, AON 3.1, 3.2, 3.3, 3.4)

In order to complete the requirements of this Element, you will need to produce a short word processed report addressing the issues relating to the subject of pricing decisions and breaking even.

TASK 1

(PC 6.4.1)

Explain the basic factors which influence the pricing of goods or services.

TASK 2

(PC 6.4.1)

Using the Focus Study above, if you wish, or, using your own data, describe a related pricing strategy for one product or service.

TASK 3

(PC 6.4.2)

Explain the significance of break-even point for a business.

TASK 4

(PC 6.4.3)

Again using the Focus Study above if required, create a break-even chart which is fully labelled. Base this chart on given business information.

TASK 5

(PC 6.4.4)

With reference to the break-even chart which you have just created, provide notes which analyse the chart. You should address the main issues outlined in performance criterion 6.4.4.

TASK 6

(PC 6.4.5)

Having analysed the break-even chart, you must now give at least one reason why it might be useful in the context of the given business information.

NOTES

As this Element is linked to Unit 1 and Unit 3 which look at pricing strategies, you may be able to carry out a single in-depth study by combining the work you have done there with this Element. It is important to remember that the marketing arm of an organisation will make the strategic pricing decisions, but the finance arm will be able to interpret and advise on the financial consequences of various pricing strategies.

UNIT 6

test questions

Focus 1
TRADING CYCLE

1 What is JIT?

(a) a production system which does not require high levels of stock
(b) a method of measuring the speed of the trading cycle
(c) a measurement of the impact of the money cycle on the trading cycle
(d) an evaluation of the supplier's order book

2 The following statements have been made:

(i) an organisation's cost curves will show the most efficient way of producing each product
(ii) if a supplier's order book is full then it will be looking for additional added value

Which of the following best describes the above statements?

(a) True/True
(b) True/False
(c) False/True
(d) False/False

3 Which of the following equations is the correct one for return on capital employed?

(a) $\dfrac{\text{capital employed}}{\text{operating profit}} \times 100$

(b) $\dfrac{\text{operating profit}}{\text{capital employed}}$

(c) $\dfrac{\text{capital employed}}{\text{operating profit}}$

(d) $\dfrac{\text{operating profit}}{\text{capital employed}} \times 100$

Focus 2
ADDED VALUE

4 How many of the following statements are true?

(i) added value is most commonly defined as profit
(ii) added value needs to at least cover direct and overhead costs
(iii) if an organisation has covered its variable costs then it will probably break even
(iv) if added value reaches the break-even point then the organisation is in profit

(a) 1
(b) 2
(c) 3
(d) 4

5 The following statements have been made:

(i) in a price-sensitive market an organisation needs to cut its costs back as much as it can
(ii) the added value concept ceases when the product is passed from the manufacturer to the wholesaler

Which of the following best describes the above statements?

(a) True/True
(b) True/False
(c) False/True
(d) False/False

Focus 3
MONEY CYCLE

6 What do you understand by the term vendor rating?

(a) the way in which a supplier rates a customer in terms of his/her buying potential
(b) the way in which an organisation classifies its suppliers
(c) the way in which an organisation measures the effectiveness of its sales force
(d) the way in which a supplier determines which customer should be supplied as a matter of priority

7 What do you understand by the term residual cash?

(a) the profit made on a product
(b) loans outstanding
(c) cash put aside after all financial commitments have been taken into consideration
(d) cash left over when an organisation has obtained a loan that is larger than is required

8–10 The following are factors to consider when buying and selling:

(a) the taking up of trade references
(b) a record of sales and payments made
(c) the issuing of a writ
(d) the assurance that certain promises will be kept

Which of the above are included in the following:

8 Credit control

9 Chasing bad debts

10 The checking of creditworthiness

Focus 4

FINANCIAL TRANSACTIONS

11 Which of the following can be considered a liability of a business?

(a) petty cash
(b) stock
(c) company cars
(d) bank loans

12 Petty cash can be recorded using which of the following systems?

(a) the impost system
(b) the impest system
(c) the imprest system
(d) the improst system

13 A statement of account will contain two of the following:

(i) the VAT registration number of the supplier
(ii) superannuation
(iii) a space for signature to say that goods have been accepted but not inspected
(iv) details of any debit or credit notes issued

(a) (i) and (ii)
(b) (ii) and (iii)
(c) (i) and (iv)
(d) (ii) and (iv)

14 Which of the following would you not expect to find on a pay slip?

(a) cheque number
(b) gross salary
(c) net salary
(d) national insurance deductions

15 Which of the following headings would not appear on an order form?

(a) quantity ordered
(b) catalogue number
(c) VAT
(d) total amount ordered

Focus 5

COSTS OF GOODS AND SERVICES

16 Which of the following is not a direct cost?

(a) depreciation
(b) raw materials
(c) marketing
(d) assembly wages

17 Decide whether each of the following statements is true or false

(i) direct costs are those costs associated with production
(ii) as the total output of a company rises, so do direct costs

18–20 Listed below are several different types of costs:

(a) fixed costs
(b) variable costs
(c) marginal costs
(d) absorption costs

Which type of cost is best described by the following:

18 the total cost of a unit of production

19 the cost incurred by producing one extra unit

20 a cost which does not change in the time period being considered

21 Which of the following is not a fixed cost?

(a) heating bills
(b) rent
(c) business rates
(d) wages

22 Decide whether the following statements are true or false:

(i) a unit of production is identified in terms of the effort needed to make it, i.e. hours worked
(ii) a unit of production is the finished good at the end of the production process

(a) True/True
(b) True/False
(c) False/True
(d) False/False

23 Decide whether each of the following statements is true or false:

(i) a unit of production or service sold at any price above its marginal cost makes a contribution to fixed costs
(ii) by using marginal costing businesses will always be able to make a profit

(a) True/True
(b) True/False
(c) False/True
(d) False/False

Focus 6

PRICING STRATEGIES AND BREAKING EVEN

24–26 The following statements all relate to pricing strategies:

(a) a system whereby selling price less the total cost of one product equals profit
(b) a system where producers charge less than the existing market price
(c) a system used when suppliers price their products in line with competition
(d) a system when businesses will accept any order so long as it makes some contribution

Which of the following relate to the above descriptions:

24 market-led pricing

25 marginal costing

26 cost-plus pricing

27 The selected operating point of a business is:

(a) the point at which the fixed costs equal total revenue
(b) the company's planned production and sales level
(c) the point at which sales exceed costs to achieve a level of profit
(d) the type of retail outlet used by the business

28 Decide whether each of the following statements is true or false:

(i) the break-even point of a company occurs when its sales revenue is equal to its fixed costs plus its variable costs
(ii) at the break-even point enough units have been sold so that contribution exactly equals fixed costs

(a) True/True
(b) True/False
(c) False/True
(d) False/False

29 Which of the following statements is true?

(a) $TR = TC = profit$
(b) $TC < TR = loss$
(c) $TC > TR = loss$
(d) $TR > TC = profit$

30 Decide whether each of the following statements is true or false

(i) if the selling price of the product is greater than its marginal cost, a business will always break even if it is operating within its existing capacity
(ii) if the business wished to increase its productive capacity it would incur a higher level of fixed costs

(a) True/True
(b) True/False
(c) False/True
(d) False/False

Explain sources of finance and financial requirements of business organisations

PERFORMANCE CRITERIA

A student must:

1 *explain the* **financing requirements** *of a business*

2 *explain* **assets** *and* **working capital**

3 *explain* **common methods of finance** *appropriate to the financing requirements*

4 *explain* **usual sources of finance** *appropriate for different methods of finance*

5 *explain* **characteristics** *of common methods of finance*

6 *explain* **usual sources of finance** *for different* **types of business organisations**

RANGE

Financing requirements: *asset finance, working capital finance*

Assets: *land, buildings, production machinery, transport, office machines, fixtures and fittings*

Working capital: *current assets (stocks of raw materials, work in progress, stocks of finished goods, debtors, cash), current liabilities (creditors)*

Common methods of finance: *trade credit, overdraft, factoring, leasing, hire purchase, loan, mortgage, profit retention, venture capital, equity, grants, gifts*

Usual sources of finance: *sellers, banks, factors, leasing companies, hire purchase companies, building societies, the business, venture capital investors, owner's savings, partner's savings, share issues, government grants, membership fees, charities*

Characteristics: *short-term, long-term, unsecured, secured*

Types of business organisations: *profit making (sole trader, partnership, public limited companies (plc), private limited company (Ltd); non-profit making*

7.1.1 Explain the financing requirements of a business

FINANCING REQUIREMENTS

Before any organisation can begin to do business it needs start-up finance in order to pay for essential items. As we will see in this Element, the organisation will need a variety of different pieces of equipment or assets such as vehicles, premises, shop fittings, machinery, land and, indeed, working capital. We will begin by subdividing the financial requirements into **assets** and **working capital** and identify the financing requirements of the organisation in general.

ASSET FINANCE AND WORKING CAPITAL FINANCE

Broadly speaking, the organisation will need finance to cover the costs of the **essential assets** required for the business. In other words, when we consider assets we are really talking about the actual items that are needed to enable the organisation to operate, such as premises, shop fittings, equipment and transport. All of these are key items or prerequisites, which the organisation must have obtained before it can start business activity.

Working capital is needed to finance the day-to-day running of the business. Working capital is, of course, used to pay for the running costs and raw materials and also to fund credit offered to customers. As we will see in this Element, having sufficient working capital is the key to maintaining liquidity. Organisations which have too much money tied up in assets either fixed or current, against high levels of liability face considerable difficulties.

7.1.2 Explain assets and working capital

ASSETS

Assets are all **items of value** owned by the organisation. They may include any money owed to the organisation by debtors on orders fulfilled but not yet paid. Assets are either **fixed** or **current** and in the first instance, we will be considering the fixed assets of an organisation. These include:

    land
    buildings
    production machinery
    office machines

We will look at these individually in more detail:

LAND

Land can be a valuable asset to the organisation, because of its comparative worth on the open market and the possible uses to which this land can be put by the organisation. Broadly speaking, land may be held either as leasehold or freehold. Land provides the organisation with perhaps its most valuable collateral against which it may borrow.

BUILDINGS

Depending upon the suitability of the building, the organisation probably considers its **premises** to be as important as any land it owns. The building would normally be designed in such a way as to maximise its usage by the organisation. Organisations may own additional premises that are not necessary for their day-to-day business activities, and these may be sub-let or leased to other organisations. This is particularly common in the case of High Street shops, which may own the freehold to the whole building, but lease or rent rooms or whole floors above the retail outlet to other businesses. The value of the buildings will, of course, relate to current market values and, in certain cases, buildings may be very difficult to dispose of in the short term. However, buildings provide a very substantial asset upon which to base applications for loans and financial assistance.

PRODUCTION MACHINERY

Production machinery includes all of the necessary equipment required to carry out production processes. In this category we also include all necessary spares

student activity

(PC 7.1.2, COM 3.1)

Carry out an audit in your local area, looking at the various types of buildings used by organisations. Although you can probably think of some other categories of buildings, here is a brief list of different types:

- light manufacturing unit
- purpose-built industrial unit
- purpose-built office block
- converted office accommodation
- office above retail unit
- purpose-built retail unit
- 'traditional' retail unit

Can you identify the types of organisation which use these premises? How suitable do you think these premises are for their intended purpose? Discuss this in pairs.

and certain consumable machinery items. Production machinery suffers from depreciation (this means that the current value of the asset is lower than its original cost). Because of depreciation, over a period of years, assets in this category will gradually become less and less valuable in real terms to the organisation. A constant updating and replacement of production machinery is necessary, not only to ensure that the organisation makes full use of new technological developments, but also to maintain the relative value of production machinery assets. Typically, production machinery includes all automated, semi-automated and manual machinery of various sizes and complexities.

TRANSPORT

Organisations which distribute products from their premises, or, indeed are required to maintain a fleet of vehicles for their sales representatives would have to consider **transport** as an asset. One of the major problems with transport is that it depreciates very quickly. As we all know, when an individual purchases a vehicle from a car showroom, the moment it is driven off the forecourt it is worth considerably less than the purchase price. This is very much the case with any transport bought by an organisation. The true value of this transport is in the benefits accrued as a result of its use. Organisations frequently do not handle distribution themselves but engage the services of a sub-contractor to carry out distribution activities on their behalf. The majority of organisations lease the transport they require, or obtain it by some form of hire purchase.

OFFICE MACHINES

Within the category of office machinery, we include, of course, typewriters, computers, switchboards, telephones and photocopying machines, for example. In addition, we should also consider office equipment such as desks, chairs, filing cabinets and so on (including small items of office equipment like filing trays, staplers, hole punches, etc.). Again, these suffer, perhaps even more so than production machinery, from depreciation. The value of these assets is related to the current state of the second-hand market, and this, particularly in times of recession, can be very depressed. Office machines tend to have very low values as they are so quickly made obsolete by technological developments. An organisation which has large numbers of typewriters that it wishes to dispose of and replace with computer terminals will find that they have relatively little realisable value.

FIG. 7.1.1 *Ladbroke Property is a division of Ladbroke Group PLC, and is involved in the rented office space sector of business. 'Langham Island', a 1.6-acre development in the heart of London, consists of some 270,000 square feet of office space and adjoins Farringdon Station.*

FIXTURES AND FITTINGS

Fixtures and fittings refer to the non-office machine equipment and other standing items within the premises of the organisation. This category would, of course, include the following:

- tables
- chairs and sofas
- storage cupboards
- carpets and curtains

Again, the realisable value of these fixtures and fittings will be considerably less than the original purchase price. Numerous second-hand office equipment outlets offer an enormous range of obsolete equipment at very low prices. In many respects, the value of the fixtures and fittings lies more in their contribution to the organisation's desire to project a particular image, than in their inherent value. The modern office is a far less cluttered place than it was in the past. Fixtures and fittings, therefore, are considerably more functional and ergonomically friendly than they were. Despite this, they do not last particularly long.

WORKING CAPITAL

There are many ways of considering the **liquidity** of an organisation. This liquidity basically equates to the amount of **realisable capital** available to an organisation. **Working capital** is used to pay immediate debts. If an organisation cannot pay its immediate debts, then it is considered to be **insolvent**. Creditors, such as landlords or suppliers, may be unwilling to allow the organisation to continue its operation if it does not have sufficient realisable assets that can be turned into capital. The main types of working capital are:

- the value of raw materials in stock
- the value of unfinished goods (known as work in progress)
- the value of the stocks of finished goods
- the debts owed to the organisation by other individuals or organisations

We intend now to look at these in more detail:

CURRENT ASSETS (STOCKS OF RAW MATERIALS, WORK IN PROGRESS, STOCKS OF FINISHED GOODS, DEBTORS, CASH)

1 *Stocks of raw materials*
Organisations, through their stock control system, should endeavour to maintain sufficient **stock** to ensure that they are capable of producing at an agreed level. They should hold a **buffer stock** of **raw materials** which may be necessary should

suppliers fail to deliver goods ordered. This buffer stock is also used to ensure that organisations are in a position to increase production at short notice should demand rise. Systems should be in place, in line with available storage facilities, to ensure that organisations can take advantage of raw materials available at a reduced price if the opportunity arises. Normally, raw materials may be found in three locations:

- *in situ* at an organisation's warehouse
- *en route* to the organisation's warehouse from the supplier
- stock earmarked at the supplier's premises destined for the organisation

The value of these raw materials is the current market price, although it may be difficult to realise these assets, depending upon their general availability or suitability. Organisations count raw materials as part of their working capital, since it is possible to turn these raw materials into finished goods and thereby offer them to potential customers. In themselves these raw materials have a basic value.

student activity

(PC 7.1.2, COM 3.1)
In a typical manufacturing organisation, which of the above three locations of raw materials is likely to be of the greatest financial value? Discuss this in small groups.

2 *Work in progress*
The existence of **partially processed raw materials** at the different stages of the production schedule means that the organisation has varying levels of assets throughout the company. Obviously, the closer these part-finished goods are to the end of their production process, the more value will be attached to them. The work in progress may be difficult to identify precisely, since items are scattered throughout the organisation's premises. Typically, **work in progress** is found in the warehouse and along the production lines. These assets can be somewhat difficult to turn into realisable working capital since they may not have a definite value to a potential buyer.

0:20

student activity

(P 7.1.2, COM 3.1)
In terms of the value of work in progress, how much real value would the following have:

- partially finished garments
- partially assembled household goods
- partially processed food

Discuss this in pairs and then feedback your considerations to the remainder of the group.

3 *Stocks of finished goods*

Most organisations try to ensure that they have at least sufficient **stocks of finished goods** to provide for potential demand. Organisations should have identified a particular stock level in relation to known demand, but will also have buffer stock available for unforeseen circumstances. They may well have over-produced in the past and may have been forced to retain these additional finished goods in the hope that demand might increase in the not too distant future. Organisations which rely substantially upon seasonal trade, such as those who sell the bulk of their finished goods around the Christmas period or the summer, build up stocks of finished goods in preparation for their major trading periods. Some stock may be held on behalf of customers, although full payment may not have yet been received. Finished goods in this category cannot be classed as potential working capital. Most of the finished goods, however, could be turned into realisable cash should the organisation consider it advisable to do so. Finished goods may make a major contribution to the working capital.

4 *Debtors*

At any one time organisations will be owed considerable sums of money by a variety of **debtors**. Some of these may be bad debts which may be the focus of factoring in the future. The majority of these debts, however, may become due after agreed credit periods have lapsed. In this sense, debts can be considered to be realisable working capital, as the organisation can substantially rely on the debtors to make the payment when required. Through its credit controller and accounts department, an organisation will ensure that the status of all debts is constantly monitored. It may take steps to encourage debtors to pay on time and it

0:20

student activity

(PC 7.1.2, COM 3.1)
If an organisation found itself to be in possession of unnecessarily high levels of stock in their finished state, what steps could it take to dispose of the excess? Assuming that there is no immediate call for the goods at their current price, how would the organisation offload the excess stock onto the market? Discuss this in pairs.

may be necessary for it to offer additional incentives (such as early payment discounts) for this purpose.

5 *Cash*

When we refer to **cash** as an example of working capital, we are not necessarily referring to a bundle of bank notes hidden in a petty cash tin. Cash in this sense refers to money which is immediately realisable, either within the premises (housed in the safe or petty cash box) or money which may be accessed from a bank current account. Obviously, some businesses operate on a cash only basis, but this is fairly rare, since the majority of organisations will use an invoicing system and receive cheques by means of payment. Cash in limited quantities should always be available in any organisation in order to cater for immediate expenditure. Typically, this will involve the reimbursement of employees for expenses incurred as a result of activities carried out on behalf of the organisation. Other reasons for holding cash may be the purchase of stamps, tea and coffee and flowers for reception.

0:20

student activity

(PC 7.1.2, COM 3.1)
Referring back to Unit 6, where we discussed the role of the credit controller, try to identify the steps this individual would take in order to recover debts. At what point do debts cease to be realisable capital and become bad debts? Discuss this in groups of three or four.

CURRENT LIABILITIES (CREDITORS)

As we will see when we consider overdrafts, debtors inevitably delay payment until the last possible moment. Similarly, an organisation which owes money to various suppliers will likewise attempt to delay payment. In essence, **money owed to creditors** saves the organisation from having to use up available working capital. Favourable credit periods help to ease pressures upon working capital. By careful consideration of the status of its own debts, an organisation can juggle its various debts to ensure that sufficient working capital is available for an unavoidable debt payment.

Recently, the government has been considering legislation which would require organisations to pay their debts on time. What is planned is that legal action would be taken against debtors who consistently refused or avoided payment of aged debts. If the system is fully implemented. then the use of creditors' 'goodwill' as a means to bolster an organisation's working capital would no longer be available.

student activity

(PC 7.1.2, COM 3.1, 3.2)

Assess the relative importance of these methods of obtaining working capital finance to the following types of organisation:

● a retail outlet
● a leisure centre
● a manufacturer of electrical components

How do these organisations differ, in your opinion, in terms of the importance they place on the three methods? Write a list of your considerations and then compare this with the lists of the remainder of your group.

7.1.3 Explain common methods of finance appropriate to the financing requirements and
7.1.4 Explain usual sources of finance for different methods of finance

We have put these two performance criteria together since performance criterion 7.1.3 identifies the *most common methods* of finance and performance criterion 7.1.4 addresses the *sources* of that finance.

COMMON AND USUAL METHODS OF FINANCE

In order to fund the purchase of the capital assets described elsewhere in the book, the organisation will use a number of methods to **raise capital**, including:

● trade credit
● overdraft
● factoring
● leasing
● hire purchase
● loan
● mortgage
● profit retention
● venture capital
● equity
● grants
● gifts

We will now assess the relative importance of and the ease of access to these sources of finance.

TRADE CREDIT/SELLERS

Trade credit is essentially the payment terms agreed between the supplier and the customer. We have discussed this aspect of maintaining working capital in Element 6.1. Essentially, this is a period of interest-free credit which helps the organisation's cash flow at the cost of the supplier's cash flow. Research has shown that although the average period of credit is around 30 days, it actually takes the supplier something like 80 days to get the money in. An organisation would routinely use this form of credit in order to take pressure off its working capital.

OVERDRAFT/BANKS

The size of an organisation's **overdraft** depends upon its working capital requirements. Generally, the amount is agreed annually with the overdraft provider (often a bank). As the organisation's customers will always tend to delay their payments as long as possible, it is prudent for the organisation to try to ensure that its working capital is at least equal to the average monthly sales multiplied by the number of months it takes to collect the debts. Overdraft requirements may also be affected by the level of stock, in terms of raw materials, work in progress and finished goods, that the organisation chooses to hold. Obviously, the more stock the organisation holds, the less working capital there is available.

FACTORING/BANKS AND FACTORS

Factoring agencies or banks will give an organisation around 80 per cent of the value of invoices as a cash advance. The balance will usually be paid when the money is received, less the cost of factoring. Using this method an organisation can release cash which has been tied up with poor-paying customers.

A variation on the factoring offered by banks, is to sell a debt to a specialist debt collector. Again, once an order has been fulfilled, an invoice is sent to the customer. A copy of this invoice is also sent to the factor or debt collector. The factor then sends a cheque for 80 per cent of the invoice to the supplier. At the end of the payment term period the factor contacts the customer with a request for payment of the invoice. When the customer pays, the factor deducts 5 per cent of the total value of the invoice and sends the balance to the supplier. Many organisations consider that even this 5% is too high a price to pay, despite the fact that factoring has the following advantages:

- the supplier has lower administration costs
- the supplier does not have to waste time chasing debts
- the immediate payment of the invoice by the factor helps to increase working capital
- it is the factor that takes on the responsibility of collecting monies and thus the risk of bad debts

LEASING/LEASING COMPANIES

If an organisation chooses to **lease equipment**, then it is never the legal owner of that equipment. The equipment remains the property of the leasing company. The equipment is leased in return for a regular schedule of payments. The organisation leasing the equipment cannot count the equipment as an asset on its balance sheet and does not benefit from tax allowances related to equipment. The organisation is allowed to count the lease payments as a legitimate business expense and may, in this way, include the equipment on the profit and loss account. There are essentially three forms of leasing agreements:

1. *Short-period or closed-ended leases* – these leasing agreements last for up to five years. A particular benefit to the organisation leasing the equipment is the opportunity to buy the equipment at the end of the lease period at a favourable rate.
2. *Long–term or open-ended leases* – these leasing agreements run for an unspecified time period. They can be ended once the minimum leasing period has been completed.
3. *Reduced-payment or balloon leases* – this type of lease offers the advantage of a reduced level of lease repayment during most of the lease period. At the end of this period the organisation leasing the equipment pays a large final payment in order to terminate the lease. This is particularly useful since the leasing company usually allows the organisation leasing the equipment to find another organisation willing to buy the equipment. In this way the organisation can offset some of this final payment by the cash generated from the sale.

student activity

(PC 7.1.3, COM 3.1)
Using the local estate agent(s) as your primary source for research purposes, investigate the relative availability of the following:

- leasehold commercial properties
- freehold commercial properties
- rented commercial properties

Which is the most common? Why do you think this is the case? Discuss this in pairs.

HIRE PURCHASE/HIRE PURCHASE ORGANISATIONS

Hire purchase is not a simple method of purchasing a product. A finance company buys the equipment from the seller and then 'hires' this equipment to the organisation wishing to obtain it. The organisation then has to agree to make regular payments to the finance company until the full value of the goods, plus the interest accumulated over the period, has been fully repaid. In a hire purchase agreement the equipment remains the property of the finance company until all monies have been repaid.

If a hire purchase agreement is broken by the organisation because it cannot continue to make repayments, then certain laws protect the finance company. These laws give the finance company the right to repossess the goods without having to refer to the courts if less than one-third of the repayments have been repaid. If more than one-third has been repaid, then the finance company has to apply to the courts to obtain permission to repossess the equipment. The court will not always grant this permission, but may agree an order by which the organisation can negotiate lower repayments over a longer period of time.

The organisation entering the hire purchase agreement is not the legal owner of the equipment until all the repayments have been made. The organisation cannot, therefore, resell the goods while the agreement is still in force. Because the organisation is not the legal owner of the equipment, the asset can be shown on the organisation's balance sheet and it can claim tax allowances from the time it takes possession of the equipment. The amount still outstanding to the finance company will be shown as a liability on the organisation's balance sheet.

student activity

(PC 7.1.3, COM 3.1)
In the role of a sole trader with limited working capital, consider the relative attractiveness of a hire purchase agreement as against outright purchase. What criteria would you use in trying to determine whether a hire purchase agreement is more beneficial to the cash flow of the business? List the criteria you feel necessary.

The main advantage to an organisation of using the method of hire purchase to obtain equipment is that it is saved the initial outlay of large sums of money. One of the disadvantages, though, is the fact that the repayments include interest in addition to the capital supplied by the finance company and tax relief is only available on the interest the organisation pays.

LOAN/BANKS AND BUILDING SOCIETIES

Loans are usually negotiated with a finance provider (often a bank or a building society) in order to acquire an agreed sum of money which has been earmarked for the purchase of particular equipment or other assets. The loan is usually paid back over a fixed time period with agreed levels of interest and regular payments. The organisation receiving the loan will be required to pay regularly over a number of years and will be expected to meet each payment on schedule. These loans are particularly useful in raising finance to make large purchases. Organisations will be granted loans on the basis of their credit rating. The finance provider will require evidence of income and expenditure so that it can assure itself that the organisation is able to meet all loan payments. Loans can be more easily obtained if the organisation has realisable assets which could be seized should it be unable to maintain the repayment levels.

MORTGAGE/BANKS AND BUILDING SOCIETIES

Many individuals have their own mortgage in order to finance the purchase of their homes. A mortgage is a legal agreement signed by the borrower which gives the lender (a bank or a building society) certain legal rights over the property. The principal right given to the lender is that of repossessing the property and selling it should the borrower be unable to make the required repayments. There are, essentially, two main types of mortgage:

1 *Repayment mortgage* – this is a mortgage paid monthly. It includes payments to both the capital borrowed and the interest accumulated. At the beginning of the payment schedule, the bulk of the repayments will be interest, but in the latter stages of the payment schedule the larger part of the payment will be towards the capital. It is prudent, and often required, that the borrower take out a mortgage protection insurance policy to ensure that the mortgage is 'paid up' in the event of the death of the borrower.
2 *Endowment mortgage* – the main alternative to repayment mortgage is the endowment mortgage. In this case the borrower pays only interest to the lender. The borrower also makes monthly payments

into an endowment life assurance policy which ensures that there is sufficient capital accumulated at the end of the mortgage period to pay off the capital borrowed.

Increasingly, as people have taken out personal pension schemes, they have found it cost effective to take out mortgages linked to their pensions. In effect, the borrower is able to obtain a mortgage on the basis of the funds which will be available in his/her pension scheme. Organisations, however, primarily use the first method of obtaining a mortgage since the mortgage will be based upon the organisation itself and not an individual.

student activity

(PC 7.1.3, COM 3.2, 3.4, AON 3.1, 3.2, 3.3)
Referring to the table in Figure 7.1.2, write a letter of application to Barclays asking for details and terms and conditions of their available loans. What information do you think you should include in this letter? What information do you think they will subsequently ask you to provide?

student activity

(PC 7.1.3, COM 3.4, AON 3.1, 3.2, 3.3)
Again referring to Figure 7.1.2 which shows Barclays repayment schedule, calculate the APR for both endowment/pension and repayment on the basis of 8.8 per cent and 9.0 per cent respectively on a loan of £120,000. Also calculate the monthly interest payments net, the 300 monthly repayments net and the gross total amount payable.

PROFIT RETENTION/THE BUSINESS

You will find a full description of the nature of **profit retention** in Unit 6. However, an organisation would usually seek to put aside a certain portion of any profits gained from previous business activity. This will form an integral part of the working capital available for immediate expenditure. Obviously this form of working capital will not be available to organisations in the early stages of their existence. It is only when the organisation has had a track record of successful

Fixed rate		8.55%	
Fixed until		30th June 1998	
Mortgage term		25 years	
Amount of loan £		40,000	80,000
APR	Endowment/ pension	**9.0%**	**8.9%**
	Repayment	**9.2%**	**9.1%**
Monthly interest payments (net) £	Endowment/ pension	232.63	517.63
300 monthly repayments (net) £	Repayment	279.89	603.27
Total amount payable (Gross) £	Endowment/ pension	126,361.00	251,931.00
	Repayment	98,877.00	197,065.00

Notes to the table

1. The net (re)payments assume tax relief at 25% on the first £30,000 of the loan.

2. A non-refundable booking fee of £150 and an arrangement fee of £150 is payable. The arrangement fee can be added to your mortgage and can be waived – see later.

3. The calculations make allowances for typical valuation fees of £90 and legal costs of £150 for a mortgage of £40,000, and typical valuation fees of £130 and legal costs of £180 for a mortgage of £80,000.

4. The figures do not include the premiums for endowment, pension or mortgage protection policies. Mortgage Indemnity may be payable if the loan exceeds 80% of the purchase price or the Bank's valuation whichever is lower.

5. The endowment and pension options are repaid in one lump sum at the end of the term.

FIG. 7.1.2 *A detail from Barclays Bank's fixed-rate mortgage leaflet which shows repayment schedules and appropriate APRs.*

business dealings that it will be able to put aside some of the profit retained for working capital purposes.

VENTURE CAPITAL/VENTURE CAPITAL INVESTORS

In the UK at the present time, there are approximately 110 **venture capital funds**. The money is provided by pension funds, banks, investment trust, insurance companies, regional development agencies and by individuals. Venture capital funds tend to provide finance for organisations considering expansion, rather than for new businesses who require funds to start up.

Obviously, the venture capital investors have various criteria which they would want organisations to satisfy before they would be willing to lend to them, including:

- a proven record of good management
- they should be operating in a market which either is very large or is growing fast
- they should have profits of £300,000 or be confident of achieving these within three or four years

Any organisation which considers approaching a venture capital fund should note that they are also looking for things like:

- the number of shares of the organisation
- the number of directors on the board
- evidence of the organisation is dealing diligently

In addition to the above considerations, the organisation should remember that the legal and professional fees incurred in approaching a venture capital fund and 'sealing the deal' could amount to between 5 and 10 per cent of the money raised.

EQUITY/OWNER'S AND PARTNER'S SAVINGS/SHARE ISSUES

Equity refers to the initial investments made by the owners of an organisation. The founders of an organisation provide initial sums of money, known as equity, to allow short-term capital to be available. Organisations whose owners cannot raise sufficient funds seek the assistance of financial institutions, which buy shares and thus make up the shortfall in equity. Normally, organisations are reluctant to consider equity finance since, by accepting it, they will lose some control over the business. They are keener to use internally generated funds or some form of **loan**.

The **shareholders** or owners of the business may be a useful source of finance. The issue of shares to raise finance will not only raise this capital but also spread the ownership of the organisation more widely. Organisations tend to avoid this option too since it also may mean that they will lose some of their control of the business. There are other methods linked to shareholders which can be considered if the sale of shares is

not an acceptable option. Shareholders should receive a proportion of the organisation's profits by means of a dividend. However, the organisation may wish to retain some of these earnings, in which case they are known as undistributed profit. They may be used for the acquisition of specific assets.

The term **capital** itself has a number of different meanings, as we will see later in this Unit. In relation to shares, we can consider the following types of capital:

1 *Authorised capital* – this refers to the value of the shares that an organisation is authorised to issue under its Memorandum of Association.
2 *Issued capital* – this is the value of the organisation's capital which has, up to this point, been issued to the shareholders in the form of shares.
3 *Paid-up capital* – this is the amount of capital which has actually been paid to the organisation on the shares which have been issued. It should be noted that it is possible to issue shares which have not been paid for or have only been partly paid for. This is particularly the case of share issues in the privatisation of public corporations.
4 *Unpaid capital* – if shares have been issued, but are not at present fully paid, then the outstanding monies are called unpaid capital. Shareholders will be expected to pay the unpaid remainder to the organisation either at a specified time or when the organisation calls upon them to do so. The organisation may hold this option in reserve and call upon the shareholders to make the additional payment if it faces financial difficulties.

student activity

(PC 7.1.3)
Try to obtain some company reports and identify which of the above forms of shareholder funding are most commonly used by major organisations.

GRANTS/CENTRAL AND LOCAL GOVERNMENT

Grants may be available from a variety of government, local authority or QUANGO sources. Increasingly, the EU provides funds for suitable projects, particularly those linked to social and regional development. As we will see, organisations like European Investment Bank will provide financial assistance for projects relating to

FIG. 7.1.3 *Storehouse, which includes such well-known High Street names as BHS and Mothercare, produces an Annual Report and Accounts for the perusal of existing and potential investors.*

industrial, infrastructure or energy areas of business activity.

In applying for a grant an organisation must substantiate any claims under the grant framework and the organisation will find itself continually monitored and scrutinised by the grant provider.

There are a number of sources of finance available via government agencies, including:

1 *Grant aid schemes* – within this category there are assisted area grants, regional development grants and many other grants specifically targeted towards the regeneration of depressed areas. Organisations can take advantage of these grants if they are willing to relocate or expand within certain areas.

2 *Department of Trade and Industry* – the DTI is keen to encourage research and development in new technological areas, such as:

- microprocessing
- fibre optics
- computers

Within the grant system, the DTI will not only provide financial assistance towards the purchase and development of equipment, but also offer specialist advice at all levels.

3 *Local authorities* – there is a wide variety of grants available via local authorities. They earmark certain funds for particular development projects relevant to the local job market.

4 *European Union funds* – these are funds and grants that have been set aside to provide finance for specified projects. Specifically, as with grant aid schemes, they focus on social and regional development.

5 *Loan Guarantee Scheme* – organisations which lack the necessary assets as security against loans are able to take advantage of the government's Loan Guarantee Scheme. The government essentially acts as a guarantor for loans up to £100,000, but with the limitation that it will only stand as guarantor for 70 per cent of this total. This is a particularly expensive way of obtaining finance since the organisation is expected to pay a premium interest rate. It is, however, the only option available to new or small businesses wishing to expand.

6 *Business expansion scheme* – this government scheme allows private investors to obtain large tax concessions by putting their money into new and growing organisations. The tax concession is available on the personal income tax of the investor, up to the value of £40,000. The investment has to be held for at least five years in order to obtain the tax relief. This scheme encourages investors to provide finance for small and medium-sized organisations.

GIFTS/MEMBERSHIP FEES/CHARITABLE DONATIONS

The concept of **gifts** in relation to working capital is usually only applicable to charities or other voluntary organisations. It is common practice for such organisations to receive a number of different forms of gift. These include:

1 *Covenants* – whereby an individual undertakes to donate a set amount of money to the organisation on a monthly or annual basis. One of the great advantages of the covenant scheme is that the money is channelled to the organisation tax free. In this way, a donation of £10 is actually worth £12.50. Since the money is taken directly from the wage packet of the donor, the inland revenue waives payment of tax on the donation. This does not directly benefit the donor, as he/she would have lost the £2.50 in tax anyway.

2 *Wills* – no doubt we have all heard stories of people who have no close relatives to whom then can leave the proceeds of their estate. These people often leave their money to a named charity. Charities benefit from such gifts as they do not have to pay taxes, in the form of death duty or inheritance tax.

3 *Cash donations* – many organisations routinely make cash donations to charities and other voluntary organisations. These donations are, of course, tax deductible but this is not the sole motive for the donation.

4 *Collections* – with the proliferation of charities and other voluntary organisations every day seems to be collection day. These gifts take the form of casual donations either as a result of street collections or more organised events.

5 *National Lottery* – Many charities have benefitted in recent months from grants allocated to them by a QUANGO set up to distribute the National Lottery funds. Charities are required to make applications for funds and each case is considered on its relative merit.

7.1.5 Explain characteristics of common methods of finance

CHARACTERISTICS

In the previous two performance criteria we have examined the common **methods of finance** and the usual **sources of finance**. In this performance criterion we will simply be looking at the nature of the forms of finance in terms of their **periods of availability** and whether they require collateral or not.

SHORT-TERM

Short-term finance is usually money available for up to a year, and will include:

- bank overdrafts
- creditors
- factoring or invoice discounting

LONG-TERM

Long-term finance is identified as money available for at least a year and possibly as much as ten or more years. Typically, within this category we will find:

- bank loans

- hire purchase
- leasing
- debentures
- share capital
- venture capital
- grants and other governmental or EU funding

UNSECURED

An **unsecured loan** is money borrowed without the backing of collateral or another form of security. Unsecured loans are comparatively difficult to obtain and often have very high interest charges.

SECURED

A **secured loan** will normally require the borrower to risk the loss of a valuable asset if he/she defaults or breaks the conditions of the loan agreement. The acquisition of this asset or collateral will be the last resort of the lender in trying to achieve some degree of repayment if the lender defaults. Typically, **collateral** or security is related to premises, land, machinery or other personal assets.

7.1.6 Explain usual sources of finance for different types of business organisation

TYPES OF BUSINESS ORGANISATIONS

As we will see later in this Unit, specialist accountants plan for the future of an organisation. They would look at the current situation of the organisation and forecast any likely changes they foresee from analysing the data and putting these forecasts to the best advantage of the organisation in terms of meeting aims and goals.

When an organisation is first set up, or if it needs extra finance for future developments, it will be necessary to draw up a business plan. When the organisation needs extra finance, the business plan should provide the information required by all involved in the process.

The identity of the providers of finance depends not only on who is prepared or in a position to offer finance but also on the way the organisation wishes to obtain its money. It might be useful here to look at the various types of organisation separately:

student activity

In the role of a managing director of an organisation, list the items you would want to see on a business plan. Imagine that you need this plan to obtain additional finance for a project the organisation is undertaking.

PROFIT MAKING (SOLE TRADER, PARTNERSHIP, PUBLIC LIMITED COMPANY (PLC), PRIVATE LIMITED COMPANY (LTD)

Sole traders may find it more difficult than any other type of organisation to raise funds, maybe because this type of organisation carries with it a large amount of risk. Very often a sole trader will expand by taking a partner. Obviously, nobody would consider entering into a partnership agreement unless he/she had available very detailed information about the financial stability of the business.

student activity

In the role of a sole trader, list the possible providers of finance that you can think of. Now discuss your thoughts with the rest of your group.

When a sole trader business becomes a **partnership**, it benefits from the additional capital that can be ploughed into the organisation, as well as the additional expertise. However, because there are several restrictions which limit the activities of a partnership, particularly as to the number of partners that can be involved, the opportunities for partnerships to raise capital are limited. In order to overcome this problem and to raise additional capital for the business, many partnerships form themselves into a **registered company**. By legally becoming a registered company the business can offer shares in the organisation. Naturally, no one would wish to purchase shares

without detailed information on the financial stability and future prospects of the organisation

student activity

List the factors to be taken into consideration before a sole trader would enter into a partnership. What would be the sources of finance?

Private limited companies are subject to restrictions on the rights of members to transfer shares, as well as limits on the owning of the shares by the public. A private limited company might try to raise additional finance so that it could become a public limited company. It is obvious that before any such development could take place, a full and detailed breakdown of the financial stability of the organisation would be required. A private limited company always has the word Limited (or Ltd.) as part of its name.

It is much easier for a **public limited company** (plc) than for a private limited company (Ltd.) to obtain additional finance. Once it has been listed on the Stock Exchange it has the following alternatives available to it:

1 *Issue a prospectus* – a public limited company can inform potential shareholders of the dealings of the organisation by producing a prospectus. This invites people to buy shares. Naturally, this is expensive to produce and market. An organisation would need to be financially viable before undertaking such a course of action or before this sort of venture could be successful.
2 *Make an offer for sale* – if a public limited company wanted to raise additional finance it would issue shares to an 'issuing house'. (This may be a concern such as a merchant bank.) The shares are then offered at a fixed price by the issuing house to prospective buyers. Once again, this is a very expensive venture to undertake.
3 *Make a rights issue* – the public limited company could offer shares to its existing shareholders at a special price, but again the shareholders are not likely to invest any further money unless the organisation can prove its financial viability.

The following are ways organisations may choose to increase their finance:

1 *Profit retention* – an organisation might decide to plough back into the business any profits remaining after the Inland Revenue has taken corporation tax from the business's profits, and the shareholders have received their dividends.

2 *Borrowing money* – an organisation could approach any High Street bank for a loan, although merchant bankers are available to provide a more specialist service for businesses. The Stock Exchange also provides a long-term loan service, as does the government. The Loan Guarantee Scheme set up by the government and the Rural Development Commission's scheme both enable organisations to increase their finance

3 *Leasing equipment* – if an organisation wishes to obtain more up-to-date equipment to enhance its production process, then rather than expend money to purchase this, it is possible for it to lease the equipment. Another company owns the equipment and a contract is drawn up between the lessor (the owner of the equipment) and the lessee (who is hiring the equipment). This contract would state the rent and conditions regarding maintenance and breakdown service.

4 *Government assistance* – this scheme was set up to assist, in particular, small organisations which require assistance. The government provides a range of schemes either centrally or at local level.

Chairman's statement   Barclays PLC

The **18% improvement** in operating profit before provisions arose from higher levels of activity in many of our businesses and from increases both in non-interest income and in efficiency. Our commitment to better cost management is reflected in the improvement in the cost to income ratio. Bad debts are, of course, an expected cost in a banking business, but the levels of 1992 were unacceptable and we know we have made mistakes. As a result, we have reviewed the way in which we manage credit policy and portfolio risk, have strengthened credit risk management and are developing a number of tools to improve risk assessment and control.

The provisions of £2.5 billion have arisen predominantly in the United Kingdom, but we have also seen higher levels in parts of Europe, where the trend is not encouraging. However, there has been a welcome fall in the United States. While we have suffered quite substantially in the property and construction markets, a high percentage of the UK bad debts have arisen in the small and medium-sized businesses, of which thousands went into receivership or liquidation during 1992. Although we have made some poor lending decisions, it would have been difficult for us to escape without substantial provisions when we hold about 25% of the corporate market and our customers have been so badly affected by the downturn in business activity.

It is unfortunate that, in some cases, relations in the UK between banks and their customers became strained as a result of the recession. Because of the important part that banks play in the economy, they are sometimes wrongly perceived as utilities rather than commercial businesses. We have been accused of not passing on interest rate cuts, as well as being unsympathetic to the problems of business. All customers with borrowings linked to base rate, however, had the full benefit of the substantial base rate cuts. On the other hand, there is also no doubt that the risk in our lending has increased. It is an obvious, but sometimes overlooked, fact that the interest margin on a loan should reflect the degree of risk and it is quite clear that over the last few years, lending margins have contracted to a level at which this risk is not properly rewarded.

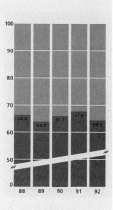

Cost to income ratio
%
Income
Cost

Banks are sometimes wrongly perceived as utilities rather than commercial businesses

FIG. 7.1.4 *Report of the Chairman to shareholders concerning financial transactions and the situation of Barclays PLC, from their Accounts for 1992.*

BARCLAYLOAN REPAYMENT TABLE

New lower rates

All rates and repayment figures in the accompanying Barclayloan booklet (December 1992/January 1993) should be ignored as they have been superseded by those shown in this table. This should be read in conjunction with the accompanying booklet.

The examples in this table are to give you an idea of typical repayments. If the size or period of the loan you have in mind is not shown please ask your branch for a quotation.

The premium for Barclayloan Protection is a once-only payment made when the loan is taken. It is usually added to your loan. However, if you wish you can pay the Barclayloan Protection premium separately in cash.

To apply for a Barclayloan you must be aged 18 or over (20 in Jersey). A written quotation is available on request from your branch or from Barclays Bank PLC, Personal Sector Marketing Department, PO Box 120, Longwood Close, Westwood Business Park, Coventry CV4 8JN.

☐ Loans with Barclayloan Protection

☐ Loans without Barclayloan Protection

	LOANS UNDER £2,500 APR 22.4%			LOANS OF £2,500 TO £4,900 APR 19.9%			LOANS OF £5,000 AND OVER APR 18.9%			
12 MONTHS	£100*	£500	£2,000	£2,500	£100*	£500*	£5,000	£10,000	£100*	£500*
Total to repay £	120.24	601.80	2407.56	2974.32	118.92	594.84	5921.28	11842.68	118.32	592.08
Includes premium £	8.05	40.27	161.07	198.99	7.96	39.80	396.14	792.28	7.92	39.61
Monthly repayment £	10.02	50.15	200.63	247.86	9.91	49.57	493.44	986.89	9.86	49.34
Total to repay £	111.36	557.04	2228.16	2755.08	110.16	551.04	5486.64	10973.40	109.68	548.64
Monthly repayment £	9.28	46.42	185.68	229.59	9.18	45.92	457.22	914.45	9.14	45.72
24 MONTHS										
Total to repay £	136.80	684.72	2739.84	3348.24	133.92	669.60	6637.44	13274.64	132.72	663.60
Includes premium £	11.68	58.42	233.72	285.61	11.43	57.12	566.18	1132.33	11.33	56.61
Monthly repayment £	5.70	28.53	114.16	139.51	5.58	27.90	276.56	553.11	5.52	27.65
Total to repay £	122.64	613.20	2453.28	3005.04	120.24	600.96	5962.32	11924.40	119.28	596.16
Monthly repayment £	5.11	25.55	102.22	125.21	5.01	25.04	248.43	496.85	4.96	24.84
36 MONTHS										
Total to repay £	154.80	775.08	3101.04	3749.40	149.76	749.88	7400.88	14802.48	147.96	739.80
Includes premium £	15.22	76.04	304.22	367.81	14.70	73.57	726.06	1452.16	14.52	72.60
Monthly repayment £	4.30	21.53	86.14	104.15	4.16	20.83	205.58	411.18	4.11	20.55
Total to repay £	134.64	672.84	2691.72	3268.44	130.68	653.76	6462.72	12925.80	129.24	646.20
Monthly repayment £	3.74	18.69	74.77	90.79	3.63	18.16	179.52	359.05	3.59	17.95
48 MONTHS										
Total to repay £	174.72	872.16	3489.60	4175.52	166.56	834.72	8208.48	16417.44	163.68	820.80
Includes premium £	18.59	92.83	371.32	444.32	17.74	88.84	873.38	1746.83	17.46	87.35
Monthly repayment £	3.63	18.17	72.70	86.99	3.47	17.39	171.01	342.03	3.41	17.10
Total to repay £	147.36	735.84	2943.36	3545.76	141.60	708.96	6987.84	13976.16	139.68	698.88
Monthly repayment £	3.06	15.33	61.32	73.87	2.95	14.77	145.58	291.17	2.91	14.56
60 MONTHS										
Total to repay £	196.20	983.40	3933.60	4657.20	186.00	931.80	9117.60	18236.40	181.80	911.40
Includes premium £	22.58	113.13	452.40	535.63	21.45	107.17	1048.55	2097.20	20.95	104.83
Monthly repayment £	3.27	16.39	65.56	77.62	3.09	15.53	151.96	303.94	3.03	15.19
Total to repay £	160.20	802.20	3208.20	3835.80	153.60	767.40	7537.20	15075.00	150.60	753.60
Monthly repayment £	2.67	13.37	53.47	63.93	2.55	12.79	125.62	251.25	2.51	12.56

*Shown for calculation purposes only

BARCLAYS

Published by Barclays Bank PLC, Personal Sector Marketing Department. Reg. No. 1026167. Registered in London, England.
Reg. Office: 54 Lombard Street, London EC3P 3AH. BB620028. Item Ref. 9951235. March 1993. Barclays Bank PLC is a member of the Banking Ombudsman Scheme (UK branches only).

FIG. 7.1.5 *The repayment table for loans provided by Barclays Bank PLC.*

5 *Overdrafts from the bank* – this method of providing finance is the one more commonly used by organisations. If a short-term cash-flow problem has arisen, the organisation can arrange for its business account to have a short-term overdraft facility. Interest is paid while the account is overdrawn, and organisations should always be aware of the fact that an overdraft can be made repayable on demand.

6 *Credit buying* – as we have mentioned before, many organisations purchase their goods on credit. This is a useful way of obtaining goods before actually having to pay for them. It should always be remembered, however, that goods eventually have to be paid for, and it would not be in the interests of the organisation to jeopardise its relationship with suppliers by not paying its accounts on time.

Naturally, any provider of finance to an organisation would want guarantees concerning the current and potential future financial status of the organisation. Sometimes a finance provider will also ask for a personal guarantee from the main shareholder of the organisation that any repayments will be met. They will also demand security or collateral against the amount of the loan. By safeguarding themselves in this way, providers of finance would ensure that they have priority over other lenders or creditors when claiming money should the organisation fail.

student activity

(PC 7.1.6, COM 3.1, 3.2)
In the role of an organisation wishing to obtain additional finance, list the factors you would need to consider. How many different alternatives do you have? Now compare your list to those of the remainder of the group.

NON-PROFIT MAKING

As we mentioned earlier in this Element, the usual sources of finance for a non-profit making organisation are:

- gifts
- donations
- covenants
- membership fees
- inheritances from wills

Since many non-profit making organisations have moved to some degree into the commercial world, there are of course more conventional methods of obtaining finance open to them. As charitable organi-sations, or non-profit-making organisations, produce (or purchase for resale) a range of merchandise sold via mail order catalogues or retail outlets, they should be in a better position to obtain more conventional forms of finance. Many of the more established charities and non-profit-making organisation are considered to be a fairly good credit risk by lenders. This is fortunate for the charities as, due to the recession, many of their more traditional forms of finance (such as donations) have decreased. Some organisations have experienced short-term cash-flow problems which have been financed by loans from banks or extended overdraft facilities.

ELEMENT 7.1

assignment

(PC 7.1.1–6, COM 3.1, 3.2, 3.4, AON 3.1, 3.2, 3.3, IT 3.1, 3.2, 3.3)

In order to achieve the requirements of this Element and the related performance criteria, it would be advantageous to attempt to talk to a building society or bank manager, or, indeed a small business owner, to identify the sources of finance and financial requirements. Bear in mind that work that you undertake throughout this whole Unit will be linked to Unit 8. It would, therefore, be advisable to begin by identifying sources of finance that would be applicable to your own choice of business organ-isation.

TASK 1

(PC 7.1.1–2)

In a word processed report format, explain the dif-ferent financing requirements of business organisations and identify the difference between asset finance and working capital finance.

TASK 2

(PC 7.1.3–6)

In the remainder of your report you should explain the following:

- the different methods of finance
- the sources of these methods of finance
- their appropriateness to different types of asset finance
- their appropriateness for different types of busi-ness organisation

Produce and explain forecasts and a cash flow for a small business

PERFORMANCE CRITERIA

A student must:

1 explain the **purposes** and **components** of **forecasts**

2 produce a capital budget and trading forecast for a 12-month period for a small business

3 explain **capital budget headings** and **trading forecast headings**

4 explain the **purpose of a cash flow** as a component of a forecast to a business seeking finance

5 explain the **significance of timing** in a cash-flow forecast

6 explain **cash in-flow** and **cash out-flow headings**

7 collect data for each heading to support informed forecasts

8 produce feasible forecasts of cash in-flow and cash out-flow for one 12-month period

9 produce monthly and cumulative net balances for a 12-month period

10 explain the **consequences of incorrect forecasting**

RANGE

Purposes of forecasts: to predict what the business thinks will happen; to create opportunities to appraise alternative courses of action, to support business plan, to set targets, to monitor performance

Components of forecasts: capital budget, trading forecast, cash-flow forecast

Capital budget headings: premises, machines, vehicles

Trading forecast headings: sales, raw materials, wages, water rates, telephone, other running costs

> ***Purpose of a cash flow:*** *to highlight the timing consequences of a capital budget and trading forecast, to support an application for finance, lender's confidence, owner's confidence, monitoring of performance*
>
> ***Significance of timing:*** *credit period for: purchases and sales, VAT payments, VAT recoveries, wages*
>
> ***Cash in-flow headings:*** *start-up capital, loan receipts, sales receipts, VAT recoveries*
>
> ***Cash out-flow headings:*** *payments for assets, raw materials, wages, water rates, telephone bills, other running costs, interest payments, loan repayments, VAT payments*
>
> ***Consequences of incorrect forecasting:*** *incorrect working capital, cash-flow problems (liquidity, insolvency)*

7.2.1 *Explain the purposes and components of forecasts*

PURPOSES OF FORECASTS

It is often thought that financial planning is restricted to a single year. Indeed, one-year budgets are very common. Long-term plans are often called corporate plans and short-term investment plans are known as capital budgets. In other words, a business will have two short-term budgets, the **revenue budget** which relates to planned sales and costs over a given period and a **capital budget** which relates to capital investments over that same period.

TO PREDICT WHAT THE BUSINESS THINKS WILL HAPPEN

The importance of establishing a reasonable estimate of an organisation's future sales, costs and cash balances means that the forecasts should be approached in a calm and systematic manner. An organisation would be best advised to obtain all the necessary information required on which to base their forecasts. There needs to be a degree of realism in estimating the figures entered into a forecast. If assumptions have been made, then the organisation needs to be clear about why those assumptions were made and what will be the probable consequences if these assumptions are proved to be wrong. Being able to predict exactly what might happen is not a pure art. Many things can go wrong and equally a vast number of external influences may have an impact on the long-term credibility of the forecast. Indeed, the further the organisation

forecasts into the future, the less likely that forecast is to be accurate.

The best that an organi ion can possibly hope for is to identify probable trends in the short to medium term.

TO CREATE OPPORTUNITIES TO APPRAISE ALTERNATIVE COURSES OF ACTION

Having worked out a forecast based on either current understanding or current sets of figures, the organisation now needs to **analyse the forecast** and attempt to recognise any possible opportunities or alternative courses of action which may result in a more healthy-looking forecast and future. In appraising alternative courses of action, the organisation would normally create an alternative forecast based on the presumed net results of the decisions. In effect, the organisation can begin by either looking at alternative courses of action which will create opportunities or by creating opportunities that require alternative courses of action.

TO SUPPORT BUSINESS PLAN

Any cursory glance at the materials and packs provided by banks and building societies will show that before they consider an organisation as a potential borrower they all recommend and indeed demand a degree of forecasting. When an organisation approaches a bank for finance it is required to provide as much up-to-date information about its business as possibly to enable the bank to complete a thorough credit assessment. This is the only way that the banks can give the organisation the full consideration it deserves. When being assessed as a lending proposition, the organisation will need to make clear what the money may be used for and its net effect on the business. The forecast will show whether the organisation is asking for the right amount of money. The bank will pay particular attention to the amount of money which the owners of the business have invested in it themselves. By looking at the forecasts the bank will be able to ascertain the source of the repayments. It will pay particular attention to items such as the trading profit. Equally, it will also be able to assess whether the purchasing of a fixed asset will generate sufficient income to repay any borrowing needed to purchase it before the end of its useful life.

TO SET TARGETS AND MONITOR PERFORMANCE

When working out a forecast the organisation will have to establish a predicted level of **sales income** over a given period. This is not a particularly easy task since there are so many variables which may influence the performance of the organisation. As we have said earlier, it is always advisable to be pessimistic rather than over-optimistic. Targets and objectives must be set for the the following areas:

- the likely sales income
- the desirable level of direct costs
- the acceptable and manageable level of overhead costs
- the expected profit or mark-up after costs of each product have been taken into consideration
- the expected closing balance at the end of each trading period

The **monitoring of performance** directly relates to the **setting of targets**. An organisation would normally be expected to complete a forecast against which it will be able to insert the real figures as they become available. This may be a basic way of monitoring performance, but the difference between budgeted or forecast figures and actual figures may prove to be very illuminating. Relatively early on, as actual figures become available, the organisation will begin to realise whether its predictions have been correct. In this regard, the organisation may wish to re-examine its forecasts in the light of reality. The real value of monitoring performance lies in the organisation's willingness and ability to do something if the targets that have been set are not being reached.

COMPONENTS OF FORECASTS

There are three main components of forecasting:

- capital budgets
- trading forecasts
- cash-flow forecasts

Throughout the remainder of this Element you will be expected to construct forecasts based on these three components, as well as identifying the meaning and nature of the headings used.

CAPITAL BUDGET

A **capital budget** is a simple statement of intent which specifies the planned acquisition of capital assets. Included in this is the date of the intended purchase and any related costs. Throughout this Element we will be assuming that the cost of the assets is a cash outflow from resources. In reality, many organisations do not actually buy their assets. Strictly speaking, therefore, they are not the organisation's assets. This is particularly true if the organisation has chosen a hire purchase or lease agreement. The organisation has the use of the assets but may not or may never own them.

TRADING FORECAST

Again, a **trading forecast** is a simple statement of intent which specifies planned production schedules, overheads and sales. During this Element we will be working on the assumption that the organisation has no stocks of materials, work in progress or finished goods. Indeed, the assumption goes further to suppose that all production is sold.

CASH-FLOW FORECAST

A **cash-flow forecast** is essentially a prediction by the organisation of how much money it thinks it will receive and how much it will have to spend over a given period of time.

Taken together, these three forecasts or projections provide the organisation with clear and unambiguous sets of figures on which to base their forward planning.

7.2.2 Produce a capital budget and trading forecast for a 12-month period for a small business

In order to fulfil this performance criterion you are directed to the Element Assignment. Working from data given to you by your tutor, you will be expected to produce a capital budget and a trading forecast. Bear in mind that these data and series of calculations may well be more valuable to you if you relate them to your own proposed business plan.

7.2.3 Explain capital budget headings and trading forecast headings

CAPITAL BUDGET HEADINGS

PREMISES

This heading includes any rent, rates or mortgages paid by the organisation for the premises where it conducts its business activities.

MACHINES AND VEHICLES

This heading includes any costs involved in the purchase of new equipment or vehicles for the organisation to use in the carrying out of its business activities.

TRADING FORECAST HEADINGS

SALES

Under this column heading would be the organisation's cash which could be generated by the **sale of their products**. If the organisation is registered for VAT, then the figures expected from the sales, including the VAT, should be entered here.

RAW MATERIALS

Included in this column are the amounts of money the organisation has to pay suppliers for .materials. The longer an organisation can delay paying its suppliers' invoices the better it can be for its cash flow. This positive effect has to be counter-balanced by the ill effects of the organisation's customers being late in their payments. For the purposes of the cash-flow forecast, it would be beneficial to assume that the organisation does not have to pay for its raw materials until one month after it has received them.

WAGES

The amount in this column relates to the **wages** or drawings from the organisation's funds after the deduction of **tax** and **national insurance contributions** under the PAYE system for wages.

The total amount of tax under the PAYE system should be added to the amount of national insurance contributions deducted by the organisation each month from the wages and salaries of their employees. The amount should also include the employer's contribution.

WATER RATES

Water rates can be paid quarterly or monthly, although it is more normal for them to be paid twice-yearly. Again, the amount for the water rate bill would be inserted in this column.

TELEPHONE

The telephone bill will normally be paid quarterly in arrears, although it is possible to delay payment by a further month. The details of the telephone charges would be inserted under this column heading.

OTHER RUNNING COSTS

One of the running costs of an organisation is its heating and lighting bills. These bills will also be paid each quarter in arrears, and once again, payment may be delayed by another month.

7.2.4 *Explain the purpose of a cash flow as a component of a forecast to a business seeking finance*

PURPOSE OF A CASH FLOW

A cash-flow forecast or a projected cash-flow forecast shows the expected income and expenditure for a business over a specified period of time. They are vital components in the preparation of a business plan as well as being useful for more general forecasting purposes. The major benefits of this budgetary control, which is a natural progression from the cash-flow analysis, are:

- it requires the organisation to formulate and define all of its key **objectives**
- individuals within the organisation, or perhaps specialists brought in for the express purpose, will be given responsibilities for aspects of the cash-flow projection. It is possible to measure their **efficiency** in monitoring their part of the projection
- it also ensures that full attention is paid to the **cash requirements** and **when** that finance is actually required
- the various and separate individual budgets of the different parts of the organisation can be co-ordinated
- a clear-cash flow statement enables all employees and other involved in the organisation to be aware of the **cost implications**. In addition they will hopefully attempt to ensure that the most efficient methods are used to carry out their own functions
- it enables the management to concentrate on issues arising out of business activity which do not automatically fall within the cash-flow projection. This particular technique is known as **management by exception** which means that managers are able to concentrate on these exceptions and solve them
- at the same time, the decision makers of the organisation can adopt a **management by objectives approach** to control the activities of the business

In simple terms, the cash-flow forecast will enable the organisation to:

- work out the **income** of the organisation
- work out the **expenditure** of the organisation
- identify short-term **cash-flow problems**
- identify areas where **additional income** may be **generated**
- to know at any point where **money is owed**

student activity

(PC 7.2.4, COM 3.1)
Try to put these functions of the cash-flow forecast in order of importance. Which of the functions would you consider to be the three most important? Discuss your decisions in pairs.

The specific purposes of the cash-flow projection are:

- to highlight the **timing consequences** of a capital budget and trading forecast
- to support an **application for finance**
- to obtain **lender's confidence**
- to ensure the **business owner's confidence**
- to generally **monitor performance**

HIGHLIGHT THE TIMING CONSEQUENCES OF A CAPITAL BUDGET AND TRADING FORECAST

It is readily apparent that an organisation cannot make a long-term commitment to the purchase of an asset if it does not have the wherewithal to meet the repayment schedules, or indeed, to purchase the asset outright. By transposing the capital budget and the trading forecasts the organisation will be in a much better position to predict when and if it can afford to purchase an asset. Also it will be able to understand much more clearly that the purchase of items such as raw materials or components should be linked to the availability of cash as predicted in the trading forecast.

TO SUPPORT AN APPLICATION FOR FINANCE

Any potential **provider of financial resources** will require the organisation to prove that it has a viable business concern. A lender will require the organisation to produce a statement which will include all relevant financial considerations. These considerations will cover all the major income and expenditure of the organisation, together with a reasoned appraisal of the organisation's prospective income and expenditure in the future.

A new business will have to work on reasoned conjecture in order to create a projected cash flow. A lender of finance will expect the organisation to have carried out substantial research into its area of business activity and to have considered all potential opportunities and threats at every stage of the business process. In effect, this means that the organisation is expected to be fully conversant with the requirements of providing products or services for a specified market sector and to be aware of the threats that any competitive organisation may present.

A provider of finance will constantly monitor the performance of the organisation against the projected cash-flow statements and will expect the organisation to do the same. If the organisation's performance is wildly different from the projected performance, then this may give grave cause for concern. The organisation will have to justify any major deviations from the projected cash-flow statement and will be expected to set the problems straight at the earliest possible opportunity.

student activity

(PC 7.2.4, COM 3.1)
Apart from the cash-flow forecast itself, what other information would you need to present in order to support an application for finance? Discuss this as a group.

LENDER'S CONFIDENCE

During the period in which the organisation is being loaned finance, the **lender** will be very interested in the overall performance of the organisation. Regular meetings will be expected when the lender will demand to see current documentation and proof that the organisation is attempting to remain within the projected cash flow. The lender will be keen to see as much information as possible, but will expect to see specific accepted forms of presentation such as cash-flow statements, profit and loss accounts and balance sheets.

student activity

(PC 7.2.4, COM 3.1)
What might be the actions of a lender who lacks confidence in the ability of an organisation to which it has made a loan? Discuss this as a group.

It is in the organisation's best interests to ensure that these documents are as accurate as possible since it may need to rely upon the lender for additional finance at a later date. Equally, it will wish to meet the demands of the lender in order to ensure that a good working relationship is maintained.

OWNER'S CONFIDENCE

Strange though it may seem, the **owners** of the organisation need to be just as confident in the organisation's ability to meet specific targets and continue trading as does a provider of finance. An organisation whose owners do not display confidence in either the product or the organisation may not be taken seriously by a provider of finance. Providers of finance are looking for individuals who feel quietly confident that they can achieve their predicted levels of sale and profit. Equally, if the owners of the organisation approach a lender without having established a degree of confidence based on the forecast, then the chances are that the lender will turn the potential borrower down.

MONITORING OF PERFORMANCE

Just as a lender will wish to see relevant documentation completed accurately, the organisation itself will need to be assured that it is on track to obtain the projected financial objectives. The process of **monitoring performance** is a vital linking process between actual financial success and the processes of the business's activities. By careful consideration of the figures the organisation will be able to match projections with actual performance. It should b able to adjust and amend its activities according to particular circumstances.

7.2.5 *Explain the significance of timing in a cash-flow forecast*

SIGNIFICANCE OF TIMING

Since a new business operates with very little working capital or reserves of cash, the significance of timing both payments and income is vital. Careful control of the budget is essential to ensure that sufficient funds are available when payments must be made. An organisation which does not pay enough attention to the chasing of debts or the recovery of cash from Customs and Excise may suffer serious cash-flow problems. The organisation may have to obtain additional 'unnecessary' loans. Such loans can be extremely dangerous for a new business to have to contemplate as, for reasons already stated, borrowing money can be very expensive.

student activity

(PC 7.2.5)
Investigate the available interest rates for new businesses. How will the amount that they wish to borrow affect the interest rates payable?

CREDIT PERIODS FOR PURCHASES AND SALES

Provided an organisation has supplied acceptable business references, it may be given **credit** by other businesses. The credit period is generally between 30 and 90 days – you will find several references to credit periods in other Units. Just as the organisation will expect credit terms from its suppliers, the organisation's customers will expect credit terms from it. This will be particularly true of an organisation that supplies products or services to the trade. Generally speaking, organisations that make direct sales to the consumer are normally able to rely on immediate payment. Although this may take a variety of different forms and may involve other agencies, such as banks or credit card companies, the money received can still be considered to be 'cash in hand'.

The problem of matching the credit terms acquired by the organisation and the credit terms demanded by customers needs careful consideration. Inadequate monitoring, particularly of late payers, may result in unnecessary cash-flow problems.

student activity

(PC 7.2.5, COM 3.1)
What are the implications for a business that offers 60 days credit to its customers and can only obtain 30 days from its suppliers? Discuss this in small groups.

CREDIT PERIODS FOR VAT PAYMENTS AND RECOVERIES

Organisations whose turnover reaches the current limit of nearly £40,000 per year need to be VAT registered. Registration has considerable advantages and disadvantages, depending on the nature of the business. Let us consider the nature of VAT first, before looking at these advantages and disadvantages.

VAT (Value Added Tax) is essentially a government tax on spending. VAT is added to all items purchased and it is the business's responsibility to collect VAT on behalf of the government. The process of organising this VAT collection includes the following:

- the organisation totals the amount of VAT collected
- the organisation then totals the amount of tax it paid on items bought in
- the balance, if positive (in other words, more VAT was collected than was paid out) is forwarded to Customs and Excise
- if, on the other hand, the balance is negative (in other words the organisation paid out more in VAT than it collected) then the business may claim a refund

Normally organisations are required to present their VAT return quarterly, although in some cases smaller businesses may submit their VAT return annually.

The major **advantage** of collecting VAT on behalf of the government is that the organisation can make use of this money for the three-month period before it is due. However, organisations should take care to ensure that sufficient funds are available to settle VAT bills, as the Customs and Excise Department takes no prisoners! It will demand payment at all costs. If an organisation's business activity is in an area where the products sold are zero rated, that is, not subject to VAT (such as food, books, magazines and children's clothing), then Customs and Excise will provide a very useful 17.5 per cent refund on all purchases made.

student activity

(PC 7.2.5, COM 3.2)
Can you identify at least three types of business that will be able to regularly claim VAT from HM Customs and Excise, rather than pay it to them? List any that you think this may apply to.

CREDIT PERIODS FOR WAGES

Organisations need to ensure that sufficient funds are available to meet any salary or wage bills. When deciding when to pay salaries, organisations will have chosen a particular point in the month when they traditionally have sufficient working capital. With regard to wage earners, an organisation needs to ensure that regular amounts of money are set aside to meet these weekly claims upon the working capital. Organisations tend not to have terribly good relations with their employees if they cannot, for some reason, meet their wages and salaries commitments. You will remember that under employment legislation, particularly that relating to the contract of employment, the employer undertakes to ensure that monies due to employees are made available.

7.2.6 *Explain cash in-flow and cash out-flow headings*

CASH IN-FLOW HEADINGS

We shall now consider cash-flow statements in more detail and look at the meaning of the various headings we shall find on a typical statement. To begin with, we shall consider the cash in-flow headings, which are:

* start-up capital
* loan receipts
* sales receipts
* interest receipts

START-UP CAPITAL

In the case of new businesses, **start-up capital** will include all cash investments made by the owners of the business. These investments will be required to pay any initial expenditures and to provide the basis for the organisation's working capital. This start-up capital may be earmarked for necessary initial purchases, including the acquisition of various assets and raw materials. The organisation will take steps to ensure that it has enough initial start-up capital to cover immediate projected expenditure.

LOAN RECEIPTS

Loan receipts, or rather, the **receipt of a loan**, include any monies given to the organisation as a loan. For the purposes of the cash-flow forecast this will be counted as monies received.

SALES RECEIPTS

Although this heading is not strictly relevant before the business has begun trading, the owners of the business must be able to forecast the probable **income from sales**. This sales revenue will probably form the basis of any major decision made by a provider of finance as to the viability of the business. The sales receipts forecast, in other words, must, as accurately as possible, reflect the true expectations of the business's income from sales.

INTEREST RECEIPTS

Like sales receipts, interest receipts are the receipt of interest from monies invested by the business. Again, providers of finance will want to know the exact nature of any investments made by the business and the probable income derived in the form of interest.

student activity

(PC 7.2.6, AON 3.2, 3.3)
With reference to Figure 7.2.1, calculate the percentage change in the performance from 1992 to 1993. Are there any particular causes for concern that you can identify?

TESCO PLC

GROUP CASH FLOW STATEMENT

52 weeks ended 27th February 1993 (1992 – 53 weeks)	Note	1993 £m	1992 £m
Net cash inflow from operating activities	25	639.4	676.4
Returns on investment and servicing of finance:			
Interest received		89.1	123.3
Interest paid		(117.3)	(136.4)
Interest element of finance lease rental payments		(8.0)	(9.1)
Dividends paid		(121.1)	(103.2)
Net cash outflow from returns on investments and servicing of finance		(157.3)	(125.4)
Taxation:			
Corporation tax paid (including advance corporation tax)		(93.6)	(165.4)
Investing activities:			
Payments to acquire tangible fixed assets		(605.1)	(775.7)
Receipts from sale of tangible fixed assets		81.6	54.4
Increase in investment in associated company		(5.5)	–
Net cash outflow from investing activities		(529.0)	(721.3)
Net cash outflow before financing		(140.5)	(335.7)
Financing:			
Ordinary shares issued for cash		21.2	8.9
Issue of 10¾% bonds		–	200.0
Issue of ¼% deep discount bond		–	50.0
E.C.S.C. loan		–	73.8
New finance leases		26.4	33.6
Increase/(decrease) in other loans		1.8	(40.7)
Capital element of finance leases repaid		(30.3)	(24.7)
Decrease/(increase) in short-term deposits		53.2	(93.2)
Expenses paid in connection with share and bond issues		(0.5)	(1.0)
Net cash inflow from financing	26	71.8	206.7
Decrease in cash and cash equivalents	28	(68.7)	(129.0)

FIG. 7.2.1 *This is Tesco's Group Cash Flow Statement comparing 1992 with 1993. Note all of the variations of investments and financing considerations. Also note that the figures in brackets are negative amounts.*

VAT RECOVERIES

In an earlier section we addressed the significance of VAT payments and VAT recoveries. If you refer back to this you will see that VAT recoveries are, in fact, a **source of finance**. In other words, it is absolutely logical to include this item under the cash in-flow heading.

student activity

(PC 7.2.6, COM 3.1)
In Figure 7.2.1, the sales receipts are noted under the heading 'net cash inflow from operating activities'. In the case of a large retailer like Tesco, what other 'operating activities' could be expected to bring in funds? Discuss in pairs.

student activity

(PC 7.2.6)
Try to identify the ideal types of investment for a business. You should consider the following:

● funds invested to which access may be obtained easily, if required
● funds invested which will be available after a fixed term
● funds which may be invested for a long term, in extremely secure locations

CASH OUT-FLOW HEADINGS

In this section we will be considering the regular expected **expenses** of the organisation. These expenses act as a counter-balance to the cash in-flow (or monies received). Once the cash out-flow totals have been deducted from the cash in-flow totals, the organisation is able to ascertain its closing balance for a particular period. The main cash out-flow headings are:

● payments for assets
● raw materials
● wages
● running costs
● interest payments
● loan repayments

PAYMENTS FOR ASSETS

Payments for assets include the costs of all **capital assets**, such as machinery and office equipment. A new business should be careful to make sure that items such as consumable office materials are not included in this heading. In fact, they belong under the 'running costs' heading. Initially, an organisation may have to earmark considerable amounts of capital to pay for necessary assets. Alternatively, an organisation may be able to arrange for the payments for assets to be made over a number of months, in which case the credit payments will be included under the 'payment for assets' heading each month.

RAW MATERIALS

Raw materials include all consumable items used during the production process. For organisations which require considerable amounts of raw materials, this may be a significant part of their expenses. In the service sector, however, a business is unlikely to need to enter very much under this heading.

WAGES

Under the **wages** heading an organisation totals its entire wages bill. This will include salary payments, weekly wages and any overtime payments. An organisation should be able to predict most of the costs found under this heading quite accurately, with the possible exception of overtime.

student activity

(PC 7.2.6 COM 3.1, 3.2)
Looking at the Kingfisher cash-flow statement in Figure 7.2.2, note the two headings 'payments to acquire tangible assets' and 'receipts from tangible assets'. First, what do you think the word 'tangible' means in this context? Secondly what is the net cost or income from these payments and receipts? Consider this with a partner and compare your written lists with those of the remainder of your group.

WATER RATES AND TELEPHONE BILLS

These two headings are merely examples used to illustrate the fact that some payments may be made in arrears. Typically, an organisation, just like an individual householder, will not necessarily pay its water rates or telephone bill immediately after the production of an invoice by the relevant authority. Many organisations spread the cost by making equal monthly payments based on a prediction of the expected cost of an item. This is a well accepted and tried procedure. In some cases, an organisation may pay in advance for telephone use or for water rates.

OTHER RUNNING COSTS

Running costs include the payment of rent and rates and payments for power and other consumable items such as office stationery. Organisations, particularly in their early stages, have to ensure that these running costs are kept to the absolute minimum.

INTEREST PAYMENTS

If an organisation has purchased assets by taking out a hire purchase agreement or on credit, it will include these payments under the **'interest payment'** heading. Again, the amount of cash involved may depend upon the need of the organisation to gain credit at this early stage of its operations.

LOAN REPAYMENTS

If an organisation has had to obtain a loan in order to purchase assets, then it will include these payments under the **'loan repayment'** heading. Organisations obviously attempt to spread the cost of these repayments over as many months as possible. However, certainly in the case of new businesses, loan repayments

KINGFISHER PLC ANNUAL REPORT & ACCOUNTS 1992

consolidated cash flow statement
Kingfisher plc and subsidiary companies for the financial year ended 1 February 1992

£ millions	Notes	1992	1991
Net cash flow from operating activities	23	239.8	234.2
Returns on investment and servicing of finance			
Interest received		26.5	14.4
Interest paid		(46.2)	(52.5)
Dividends paid		(57.8)	(52.0)
Net cash flow from returns on investment and servicing of finance		(77.5)	(90.1)
Taxation			
Corporation tax paid		(64.9)	(70.3)
Investing activities			
Purchase of subsidiary		–	(35.3)
Payments to acquire tangible fixed assets		(80.3)	(197.6)
Payments for additions to investments		(6.0)	(40.5)
Net purchase of short-term investments		(3.1)	(20.8)
Receipts from the sale of tangible fixed assets		34.7	194.9
Net cash flow from extraordinary items		–	(4.9)
Net cash outflow from investing activities		(54.7)	(104.2)
Net cash inflow/(outflow) before financing		42.7	(30.4)
Financing			
Issue of ordinary share capital		17.7	3.9
Net purchase of short-term investments		(36.8)	(11.9)
(Decrease)/increase in loans		(6.3)	94.0
Expenses paid in connection with issues		–	(0.2)
Net cash (outflow)/inflow from financing		(25.4)	85.8
Increase in cash and cash equivalents	23	17.3	55.4

FIG. 7.2.2 *This is the Consolidated Cash Flow Statement for Kingfisher plc. The group includes Woolworths, Comet, B & Q and Superdrug. 'Consolidated' means the total of all income and expenditure for the whole of the group.*

may be high as providers of finance will insist upon comparatively high rates of interest.

VAT PAYMENTS

A similar logic can be applied to **VAT payments** as to VAT recoveries. We addressed the significance of tim-ing in respect of VAT payments earlier in this Element. Since it is a payment, it is therefore logical that it is included as one of the cash out-flow headings.

7.2.7 Collect data for each heading to support informed forecasts

Your tutor will provide you with, or you will be expected to create yourself, data which will relate to each of the headings which we have identified in Element 7.2.6. Again, you may choose to create data yourself in respect of the business plan which you will be required to complete in Unit 8. This performance criterion forms an integral part of the Element Assignment.

7.2.8 Produce feasible forecasts of cash in-flow and cash out-flow for one 12-month period

Having decided on the source of the data in Element 7.2.7, you must now produce a considered and feasible forecast of cash in-flow and cash out-flow over a 12-month period for your identified business. Once again, this performance criterion forms an integral part of the Element Assignment.

7.2.9 Produce monthly and cumulative net balances for a 12-month period

This simple procedure is derived directly from the information collected and included in your forecast. You are required to produce a running total or cumu-lative net balance for a 12-month period for your cho-sen business. This performance criterion is a feature of the Element Assignment.

7.2.10 *Explain the consequences of incorrect forecasting*

CONSEQUENCES OF INCORRECT FORECASTING

If an organisation incorrectly estimates its levels of expense and income then it may suffer a **lack of working capital** or more serious **cash-flow problems**. Essentially, an organisation must set aside enough working capital to meet immediate running costs and other expenses. Cash-flow problems may be a little more complex, since the problems encountered in one month will have a knock-on effect into the next, and so on, and so on.

INCORRECT WORKING CAPITAL

An organisation that does not have enough working capital has to take drastic measures to ensure that it can

student activity

(PC 7.2.10, COM 3.1)
What short-term solutions can be found for a lack of working capital? Discuss this as a group.

obtain additional funding. This may be in the form of a short-term loan to carry it over the temporary lack of working capital. Since working capital is earmarked to pay for essential purchases and running costs, an organisation unable to meet these costs may have to resort to the disposal of assets in order to raise additional capital.

CASH-FLOW PROBLEMS (LIQUIDITY, INSOLVENCY)

As we mentioned in the previous section, the significance of **timing** in relation to cash flow is all important. An organisation must try to make sure that sufficient funds are entered in the cash in-flow to compensate for expenditure in the cash out-flow. An organisation that does not pay careful attention to this matter risks running out of money. If this happens, it will obviously have a drastic impact upon all areas of the organisation's activities. It will not be able to purchase raw materials, or any assets, cover its running costs, make interest or loan repayments, or meet the wage bill. There is some degree of flexibility here, in the sense that some cash-flow problems may be carried over into the next month. However, this is no real solution, as carrying them over will eat into the available working capital, and this has additional complications, as we have already mentioned. Banks and other providers of finance will be quick to recognise cash-flow problems and will insist that the organisation takes drastic cost-cutting measures to sort out the problems.

ELEMENT 7.2

a s s i g n m e n t

(PC 7.2.1–10, COM 3.2, 3.3, 3.4, AON 3.1, 3.2, 3.3, IT 3.1, 3.2, 3.3)

The purpose of this Element is to introduce forecasts, monitoring and timing consequences of related payments and receipts as expressed in cash-flow forecasts. Your tutor will provide you with data to produce a 12-month capital budget, trading forecast and cash-flow forecast. This Element links quite strongly with both Elements 6.1 and 7.3. Element 6.1 looks at the money cycle, and you may wish to refer back to this to assist you in your understanding of the central role played by accurate cash-flow forecasting in ensuring that an organisation has sufficient cash to continue trading. Element 7.3 helps you to recognise that the capital budget and trading forecast are a part of the profit and loss and balance sheet.

TASK 1

(PC 7.2.2, 7.2.7, 7.2.8, 7.2.9)

Produce a capital budget, trading forecast and cash-flow forecast for a 12-month period for a small business. You should use a spreadsheet package to carry out this task.

TASK 2

(PC 7.2.1, 7.2.3, 7.2.4, 7.2.5, 7.2.6, 7.2.10)

Your capital budget and forecast should be supported by a commentary which explains the thinking behind your budget and forecast figures. You should also comment upon the significance of in-flow and out-flow timing as well as the consequences of a net out-flow of cash. Finally, you should also consider how a cash flow is used to support the seeking of finance.

NOTES

Although you may be provided with data to produce your capital budget, trading forecast and cash-flow forecast, you should also be thinking about being able to construct these three forecasts as preparation for your own intended business which you will be investigating in Unit 8.

You will not be expected to explore the complexity of forecasting in any great detail and you do not need to remember how the timing differences between the capital budget, the trading forecast and the cash-flow forecast produce debtors and creditors on a balance sheet.

Produce and explain profit and loss statements and balance sheets

PERFORMANCE CRITERIA

A student must:

*1 explain a **basic accounting system** suitable for a small business*

*2 identify and explain **accounting periods***

*3 extract a **trial balance** from given accounting records*

*4 identify each account on the trial balance correctly in relation to **profit and loss** or **balance sheet** items*

*5 produce and explain **profit and loss** and **balance sheet** in vertical form from the trial balance figures*

*6 explain the **purposes** of **balances** and **profit and loss** statements*

RANGE

Basic accounting system: *documents, accounting records (ledgers, sales ledger, purchase ledger, cash book, general or nominal ledger), trial balance, financial statements or final accounts*

Accounting periods: *monthly, quarterly, annually*

Trial balance: *owing to creditors, owed by debtors, sales, purchases, money (cash, bank), expenses, drawings, fixed assets (premises, machinery); owners' capital loans*

Profit and loss: *sales, cost of sales, gross profit, overheads; net profit*

Balance sheet: *assets, current assets, current liabilities; owners' capital, profit and loss brought forward, profit and loss for period*

Purposes: *inform owners, inform managers; secure finance, maintain finance; monitor performance; fulfil statutory obligation, assess taxation liability*

7.3.1 *Explain a basic accounting system suitable for a small business*

BASIC ACCOUNTING SYSTEM

An organisation will carry out a series of **financial transactions** when its activities include any of the following:

- the **buying and selling of goods or services**. Because the organisation is buying or selling, then it obviously is making and receiving payments
- the **transfer** of any **mon**ey in or out of its bank accounts
- the **paying** of **wages** or **salaries**

These financial transactions, as we have seen in Element 6.2, are supported by a series of specific documents. Each of these documents is essential to enable the accounting department to carry out its own function. As we will see later, each of these documents has its own purpose in the accounting process.

The organisation needs to record financial transactions for a variety of very important reasons, including:

- the need to **identify** such **figures** as sales, expenses and the profit or loss
- the need to **organise** the **figures** in such a way as to make them a useful tool for monitoring the business performance of the organisation

Essentially, the key purposes of an organisation's accounting system include the following considerations:

1 To meet legal and **statutory requirements**.
2 To ensure that the business activities of the organisation are being **recorded** in an error-free way.
3 To provide continuous **feedback** to the managers of the different sections of the organisation how the business itself is progressing.
4 To ensure that the **financial systems** within the organisation, particularly those which may be concerned with cash or open cheque payments, are **not open to theft** or misappropriation.
5 To form the basis for the production of data which the organisation will use to **monitor** and amend its business **objectives**.

DOCUMENTS

As we have already mentioned, business documents relating to the financial transactions of the organisation are used for several reasons, including:

- to keep **business records**

- to provide information for the **accounting system** of the organisation
- to enable the careful **monitoring** of the business activities to be carried out
- to fulfil legal obligations

The documents we are concerned with here were covered in detail in Element 6.2. They are:

- the invoice
- the order
- the receipt
- the credit note
- the paying-in slip
- the cheque
- the petty cash voucher
- the pay slip

ACCOUNTING RECORDS (LEDGERS, SALES LEDGER, PURCHASE LEDGER, CASH BOOK, GENERAL OR NOMINAL LEDGER)

Most organisations both issue and receive documents such as invoices and credit notes and, in the course of their normal activities, deal with documents related to banking. Obviously, they need to have some method of summarising the information contained on these documents so that the facts and figures relating to the transactions can be transferred to the accounting system. One of the main ways of summarising this information is by transferring it into a series of **ledgers** of books of entry. These ledgers include the following:

1 *A sales day book* – which would list the sales of the organisation (probably completed on a daily basis). The information would be compiled from the invoices issued to customers.
2 *A purchases day book* – which would list the purchases made by the organisation (again, probably on a daily basis) and would be compiled from the invoices received by the organisation from the suppliers.
3 *A sales returns day book* – which would list the goods which have been returned by customers to the organisation and would be compiled from any credit notes issued by the organisation.
4 *A purchases returns day book* – which would list the goods which the organisation has returned to suppliers and would be compiled from any credit notes received by the organisation from suppliers.
5 *A cash book* – which would record the amount of money in the bank account of the organisation and

any money in the form of cash which is held by the organisation. This would be compiled from receipts, paying-in slips and cheques.

6 *A petty cash book* – which would record all small cash transactions which have been made by the organisation and would be compiled from any petty cash vouchers completed.

7 *A journal* – which is a record of any non-regular transactions undertaken by the organisation. This would list any items that have not been recorded anywhere else.

The system which brings together all the information contained in the above documents is called **double entry bookkeeping**. This concerns the keeping of the ledgers. Each ledger is divided into a number of separate accounts which record and categorise the information about each financial transaction. Good examples of this are the 'wages account' or the 'sales account'. So, each account concentrates on only one aspect of the business activities.

Double entry bookkeeping can be quite confusing, but basically, the principle is that two entries are made in the accounts for each transaction that has taken place. For example, if we take the 'wages account', and assuming that the wages were paid by cheque, then one entry would be made in the wages account as a record of the money being paid to the employee and another identical entry would be made in the 'bank account' as a record of the money having been drawn out of the bank account.

Increasingly, organisations are using computer software to enable them to produce their ledgers more quickly and efficiently, although it is likely that some organisations still operate this system manually.

Each of the ledgers listed above is given a specific name and is the prime source for the entries to be made in the double entry system. Because the ledgers involve a large number of accounts, they are normally divided into a number of different sections. Even if the organisation uses computer software to produce its double entry bookkeeping, the same sections are used. The ledger sections are:

1 *Sales ledger* – which includes the personal accounts of the organisation's debtors (customers to whom the business has sold products or services on credit terms).

2 *Purchases ledger* – which includes the personal accounts of the organisation's creditors (suppliers to whom the organisation owes money).

3 *Cash books* – which includes the cash account, the bank account and the petty cash account.

4 *General or nominal ledger* – which includes the remainder of the accounts (e.g. sales, purchases, expenses and real accounts – for items owned by the business).

TRIAL BALANCE

A **trial balance** attempts to make a check on the entries made over a set period of time. A trial balance is carried out in order to ensure that no errors or discrepancies have been made during the completion of the various ledgers. Obviously, if the system is still being carried out manually, errors are quite possible. On the other hand, the fact that two entries have to be made for each transaction means that errors could still be made when using computer programs. The trial balance checks that no errors have been made in the entry of the data into the series of ledgers and calculates the balances of all the double entry accounts. These balances are the amounts left in each of the accounts at the end of a particular period of time or trading period. In addition to being a check on input, a trial balance is also a valuable source of information which can help the organisation in the preparation of its final accounts.

FINANCIAL STATEMENTS OR FINAL ACCOUNTS

The **final accounts** of an organisation are compiled in order to calculate the amount of profit due to the owners of the organisation once a series of expenses have been deducted from the income of the organisation. The information contained in the double entry system would be used (the sales, purchases, expenses of the organisation) in order to provide a statement of profit or loss for a particular trading or accounting period. This trading or accounting period, as we will see later, could be for a month, a quarter, or a year.

The **profit statement** of the organisation incorporates the information contained in the **profit and loss account** which the accounts department has produced. We look in more detail at the information contained in a profit and loss account later in this Element. However, the information contained in the profit statement can be shown thus:

income – expenses = profit

The double entry system also contains information which is included in the compiling of the balance sheet. Again, we look in more detail at the items used to compile the balance sheet later in this Element.

7.3.2 *Identify and explain accounting periods*

ACCOUNTING PERIODS

Depending on the size and nature of the organisation, and on the need of the different managers or the owners of the organisation to monitor its business performance and financial transactions, accounting information may be produced on a monthly, quarterly or yearly basis. Obviously, other considerations here will be the requirements of the providers of any finance the organisation has borrowed and the length of time the organisation has been trading. Another factor to consider is whether the organisation has a good track record of successful business activity, or whether it is experiencing any short-term or long-term cash-flow problems. By producing its accounting information quite frequently, say on a monthly or quarterly basis, the organisation is in a better position to monitor any problems it may be experiencing. Usually trading periods or financial periods are described under the following headings:

MONTHLY

If the organisation is just starting up its business activities and has borrowed money from one source or another, it would be prudent, and possibly essential, to produce a profit and loss account and a balance sheet on a monthly basis. These can be calculated at any time during the month and the trading period runs from the last day of the previous trading period. In other words, if the last set of accounting information was produced on 31 March 19– then the next set would read 'for the trading period 1 April 19– to 30 April 19–.

Additionally, if an organisation has been experiencing a cash-flow problem then it would be in its best interests to produce monthly profit and loss and balance sheet statements so that the management of the organisation can assess whether or not the problem is developing as forecast, or whether more extreme measures will need to be taken. The organisation may be having difficulty meeting its loan commitments and may be under pressure from the providers of finance to prove that these problems are being addressed.

Usually organisations prepare the trial balance which forms part of the accounting information it requires once a month. This trial balance simply lists all of the balances, both debit and credit. Once balanced, it shows the total of the debit balances and the total of the credit balances to be equal.

QUARTERLY

An organisation may choose to produce its accounts on a quarterly basis. Quarterly means, essentially, that the trading period is for three months. Organisations such as British Gas and electricity generating boards issue their statements to customers on a quarterly basis, even though some of their customers choose to pay by budget account on a monthly basis.

The reasons for producing accounts on a quarterly basis could be one or several of the following:

- most of the organisation's customers may be paying for products or services bought from the organisation on a quarterly basis and thus generating accounts for the same trading period is more convenient
- the organisation may have to pay the bulk of its expenses or commitments to other organisations on a quarterly basis and would choose to adopt the same principle for its accounting information
- the organisation may have been experiencing some cash-flow problems, and although these may not necessitate the production of monthly accounts, it is more prudent to assess the financial situation of the organisation on a quarterly basis than an annual one

If an organisation produces quarterly accounts, its documents would state that the trading period is 'from 31 March 19– to 30 June 19–.

ANNUALLY

Most organisations produce their accounts annually. There are several reasons why an organisation would produce annual accounts. These include:

- to fulfil **legal and statutory obligations** – we look at this in the next section of this Element
- to provide the **owners** of the organisation with information
- to provide the **managers** within the organisation with information
- to provide any **providers of finance** with information

The financial year for the purposes of taxation runs from 6 April to 5 April. The Inland Revenue is trying to harmonise the tax years of organisations so that they all begin and commence at the same time. This, obviously, would make the work of the Tax Office easier, but could cause some problems for individual organisations whose tax year currently runs from a different date. Strictly speaking, the first day that an organisation begins trading is the first day of its tax year. For example, if an organisation began trading on 1 September 19– then its tax year would end on 31 August the following year. Each year on this date the organisation would legally be required to produce its final accounts.

7.3.3 *Extract a trial balance from given accounting records*

This performance criterion needs to be addressed in much the same way as the practical parts of Element 7.2. We intend for the fulfilment of this performance criterion to direct you to a set of information which your tutor should provide you with. You will find information about the nature of a trial balance in Element 7.3.1. You now need to extract a trial balance from the information produced by your tutor in order to confirm the accuracy of that accounting data. You should note that you need to be aware that this can be set out in either a single-column form or a double-column form.

student activity

(PC 7.3.3 COM 3.2, 3.4, AON 3.1, 3.2, 3.3, IT 3.1, 3.2, 3.3*)

You should extract a trial balance from the set of accounting information provided by your tutor, ensuring that the following are addressed and the information from each heading is included:

- the amount of money owing to creditors
- the amount of money owed by debtors
- the sales of the organisation
- the purchases by the organisation
- the money belonging to the organisation, either in the form of cash held within the organisation or money in a bank
- any expenses incurred by the organisation
- any drawings from the organisation's funds by the owner(s) of the organisation

- any fixed assets of the organisation (premises, machinery)
- the amount of owners' capital
- any commitments regarding loans that the organisation may have taken out

You should present your trial balance in a suitable format. You should note that there is no need for you to practise any double entry bookkeeping skills. If you have the facilities available, your trial balance could be presented by means of computer software.

This Student Activity will assist you in the completion of the Element Assignment.

* Provided the trial balance has been produced by means of computer software.

7.3.4 *Identify each account on the trial balance correctly in relation to profit and loss or balance sheet items*

PROFIT AND LOSS

When organisations provide a service, they are required to produce a **profit and loss account**. In the service sector, there is no gross profit, so the profit and loss account records the income from clients or customers. Overheads are listed in a similar way to those in a trading account.

SALES

Sales and purchases are items which have been bought by the business, such as machinery and equipment. When they appear on the balance sheet they are classed as **fixed assets**.

COST OF SALES

The **cost of sales**, or cost of goods sold, is the cost to the business of the goods which have been sold in the particular financial year. The calculation used to arrive at this figure is:

Opening stock + purchases − closing stock = cost of sales

GROSS PROFIT

Gross profit is calculated as:

Sales − costs = gross profit

Remember that if costs of sales are greater than net sales then the business has made a loss.

FIVE YEAR RECORD

	1988 £m	1989 £m	1990 £m	1991 £m	1992 £m
Turnover					
Continuing operations	732.2	900.5	1,090.2	1,151.8	**1,211.0**
Discontinued operations	50.7	88.7	96.4	88.1	**73.2**
	782.9	989.2	1,186.6	1,239.9	**1,284.2**
Profits					
Continuing operations	121.9	160.5	218.4	193.5	**117.3**
Discontinued operations	0.2	0.6	7.4	3.9	**0.1**
Trading profit	122.1	161.1	225.8	197.4	**117.4**
Exceptional items	(22.3)	(15.8)	(34.8)	(24.6)	**23.3**
Finance income/(charge)	8.4	2.0	0.9	(10.2)	**(17.1)**
Profit before taxation	108.2	147.3	191.9	162.6	**123.6**
Taxation	(28.5)	(32.1)	(44.6)	(41.4)	**(26.9)**
Minority interests	–	(0.2)	(0.7)	(1.4)	**(1.0)**
Net profit attributable to shareholders	79.7	115.0	146.6	119.8	**95.7**
Dividends	(29.4)	(40.1)	(51.5)	(60.2)	**(60.2)**
Transfer to reserves	50.3	74.9	95.1	59.6	**35.5**
Assets employed					
Long-term assets	266.6	325.6	344.7	380.2	**433.1**
Net current assets	109.5	183.3	149.4	126.8	**169.0**
	376.1	508.9	494.1	507.0	**602.1**
Financed by					
Ordinary shares	147.7	148.8	171.8	172.6	**172.8**
Reserves	181.0	221.8	242.9	273.3	**349.5**
Shareholders' interests	328.7	370.6	414.7	445.9	**522.3**
Minority interests	0.9	1.6	3.4	3.9	**5.7**
Loans	44.6	131.0	70.0	51.1	**68.0**
Taxation accounts	1.9	5.7	6.0	6.1	**6.1**
	376.1	508.9	494.1	507.0	**602.1**
Statistics					
Ratio of activity profit to average operating assets employed	30.3%	31.8%	36.7%	28.8%	**15.2%**
Earnings per share (FRS 3 basis)	14.8p	19.1p	21.5p	17.4p	**13.9p**
Dividend per share (gross including tax credit)	6.67p	8.27p	10.00p	11.6p	**11.6p**
Dividend earnings (times covered)	2.7	2.9	2.8	2.0	**1.6**
Number of shareholders	33,000	30,500	34,000	44,000	**50,000**

FIG. 7.3.1 *This is Fisons' five-year record covering 1988-1992.*

Earnings per share figures have been adjusted for the bonus element of the rights issues of 1 for 6 in 1988 and 1 for 8 in 1990.

OVERHEADS

The general **overheads** included in this classification are such items as:

- administration
- wages
- rent
- telephone
- interest
- travel expenses
- non-production-related power
- insurance
- depreciation

NET PROFIT

The **net profit** is the amount that the organisation has earned during the year. This may not be the amount by which the organisation's bank balance has increased during the year, as some of the transactions will not have had an effect on profit but will have affected the bank balance. Good examples of this would be the purchase of fixed assets and owner's drawings. Net profit

is calculated as:

Gross profit + income from other sources − expenses
= net profit

BALANCE SHEET

The **balance sheet** shows the assets, liabilities and capital of a business at a particular moment in time. It is compiled using information from the double entry system of bookkeeping which we have looked at earlier in this Element. The conventional form in which balance sheets are constructed includes the following headings:

ASSETS

These are essentially **fixed assets**, in other words, the long-term items owned by the business. They have not been purchased with the intention of selling them, but they are classed as assets all the same, since they could be turned into cash. In a full balance sheet each of these fixed assets is listed in terms of its liquidity, in other words, how easy it is to turn into ready cash.

Balance Sheets

As at 31 March	Note	Group 1992 £M	Group 1991 £M	Parent 1992 £M	Parent 1991 £M
Assets employed					
Fixed assets:					
Tangible assets	9	4221	3850	3972	3590
Intangible assets	10	31	33	—	—
Investments	11	58	40	327	300
		4310	3923	4299	3890
Current assets:					
Stocks	12	165	179	152	154
Debtors	13	183	144	184	153
Investments (short-term deposits)		487	568	476	560
Cash at bank and in hand		4	2	1	1
		839	893	813	868
Less creditors: amounts falling due within one year	14	802	707	843	724
Net current assets/(liabilities)		37	186	(30)	144
Total assets less current liabilities		4347	4109	4269	4034
Financed by					
Creditors: amounts falling due after more than one year	15	2612	2564	2597	2552
Provisions for liabilities and charges	16	992	874	967	850
Accruals and deferred income	17	83	99	65	79
Capital and reserves:					
Called up share capital	18	33	33	33	33
Exchange differences		2	2	—	—
Profit and loss account	19	612	521	607	520
Shareholders' interest		647	556	640	553
Minority interests		13	16	—	—
		4347	4109	4269	4034

Sir Christopher Harding
Peter S Phillips } Directors
25 June 1992

FIG. 7.3.2 *This Balance Sheet, for British Nuclear Fuels Ltd., shows how the income and expenditure of the organisation are balanced in each column.*

CURRENT ASSETS

Current assets, conversely, are the short-term assets owned by a business. These are assets which change regularly and include stock, debtors, bank balances and ready cash. In a full balance sheet, each of these current assets is listed in terms of its liquidity, in other words, how easy it is to turn into ready cash.

CURRENT LIABILITIES

Current liabilities are liabilities which are due to be repaid within 12 months of the balance sheet being constructed. Typically current liabilities will include creditors, bank overdrafts and loans.

student activity

(PC 7.3.4, COM 3.1, 3.2)
What other forms of current liabilities might an organisation have to consider? Write a list of your considerations and then discuss with the remainder of your group.

OWNERS' CAPITAL

The **owners' capital**, or the share capital, is included in the balance sheet of a limited company. It is stated in the Memorandum of Association of that organisation and can be divided into two:

● *authorised share capital* – the amount the shareholders have authorised the directors to issue

● *issued share capital* – the amount that has actually been issued to the directors

PROFIT AND LOSS BROUGHT FORWARD AND PROFIT AND LOSS FOR PERIOD

The net total, either negative or positive, from the profit and loss account is entered onto the balance sheet as this accurately reflects the current profit or loss position of the organisation.

The balance sheet is so called because it literally balances in numerical terms the following:

the assets – the liabilities = the capital

Every business transaction which takes place changes the state of the balance sheet and therefore it will change the above equation as well. It is to be noted that, in accounting terms, the balance sheet will **always balance**.

student activity

(PC 7.3.4, COM 3.1)
Having now had the opportunity to consider profit and loss accounts and balance sheets, which do you think is the more valuable document? Consider this value from the point of view of:

● an existing investor
● a potential investor
● the board of directors of the organisation

Discuss these as a group.

7.3.5 *Produce and explain profit and loss and balance sheet in vertical form from the trial balance figures*

As you did in Element 7.3.3, you are now required to carry out another practical exercise. From the information given to you by your tutor, you need now to **construct** a **profit and loss account** and a **balance sheet** in vertical form from the trial balance figures you generated in Element 7.3.3. You also need to show

that you **understand** the function of a trial balance and a profit and loss account and balance sheet. In order to meet the requirements of this performance criterion, you should carry out the following Student Activity.

student activity

(PC 7.3.5, COM 3.1, 3.2, 3.3, 3.4, AON 3.1, 3.2, 3.3, IT 3.1, 3.2, 3.3*)
From the figures generated in the trial balance you compiled in Element 7.3.3 you now need to produce a profit and loss account and a balance sheet for that organisation. You must ensure that you address the following considerations when presenting your **profit and loss account**:

- the **sales** of the organisation
- the **cost of the sales** of the organisation
- the **gross profit** generated by the organisation
- any **overheads** the organisation incurs
- the **net profit** generated by the organisation

  Your **balance sheet** should be sure to address the following considerations:

- the **assets** of the organisation, both **current** and **fixed**

- the **liabilities** of the organisation
- the amount of the **owners' capital**
- any **profit and loss brought forward**
- the **profit and loss generated** for that **trading period**

In addition to producing the above accounting information in the correct format, you need to produce a word processed report which gives you the opportunity to show your **understanding of the function** of the trial balance, profit and loss account and balance sheet. Your accounts documents may be produced by means of computer software if this facility is available to you. Alternatively, you may produce them manually.

  This activity will assist you in the completion of the Element Assignment.

* Provided the accounts are generated by use of computer software.

7.3.6 *Explain the purposes of balance sheets and profit and loss statements*

PURPOSES

As previously mentioned, the compilation of the balance sheet and profit and loss statements is a valuable exercise for an organisation. In addition, the accounting system also provides information both to the owner(s) and to outside organisations that need to be aware of the organisation's performance. We shall break down the type of information required by the different bodies in order to make it easier for you to understand why each different piece of information contained in the accounting system is useful to each different individual or organisation.

INFORM OWNERS

Obviously, the owner(s) of the organisation will need to be fully aware of the financial position of the organisation. The accounting system will give the owners information about the following aspects of business activity at any given time period:

- the amount of money spent on the **purchase of goods for resale** to a given date
- the **turnover** of the organisation, in other words, the sales of the products or services produced by the organisation to date
- the **expenses** incurred to date, including the different types of expenses generated as a result of the production process
- the total amount of **money owed** to the organisation by debtors
- the **names** of the individual **debtors** and the **amount** of money owed to the organisation by each
- the **total** amount of **money owed** by the organisation **to creditors**
- the amount of **money owed** by the organisation to **each** individual **creditor**

- the **total** of the **assets** owned by the organisation
- the **total** of the **liabilities** owed by the organisation
- any **profit or loss** made by the organisation during the specified trading or financial period

INFORM MANAGERS

Managers of different departments or sections of the organisation will also find the information contained in the balance sheet and profit or loss statement of use. They would need to identify from this information any aspects relating to their own section of responsibility which had to be addressed either urgently or not urgently. Specifically, the information contained in the accounting documents would inform managers of the following:

- whether their **key objectives** are being **met** or need to be modified
- whether they are **meeting** their own **cash-flow projections**
- whether they are being **efficient** in **monitoring** their part of the organisation from a financial point of view
- whether they are being successful in **co-ordinating the budget** of their own department/section
- whether a more cost-efficient or **cost-effective method** of carrying out the functions of their section(s) needs to be addressed
- whether, in the case of an organisation making a large profit, they could reasonably suggest **improvements** or **expansion** to their existing section

SECURE AND MAINTAIN FINANCE

As we have already discussed when we considered the different providers of finance and the different finance requirements of the organisation, certain **outside bodies** will also be interested in the balance sheet and profit or loss statement of the organisation. If the organisation has already borrowed money from a bank or another provider of finance, then that organisation will obviously require regular and detailed information about the business activities and the resultant financial position of the organisation on a given date. This monitoring of the financial situation by the providers of finance will take place in a series of meetings, when the owners of the organisation will present the accounts of the organisation.

Should the organisation need to secure a first or additional loan, then the bank manager or building society manager will insist on seeing the detailed accounts information before making any commitment to the organisation.

In addition to this consideration, it should also be noted that the organisation may have invested in the services of a financial **analyst**. This specialist may be giving the organisation advice or may be giving advice to investors in the business. Obviously, this individual or organisation would want detailed and accurate information about the financial position of the organisation in order to carry out their own tasks efficiently and effectively.

MONITOR PERFORMANCE

In much the same way as the provider of finance will need to see detailed and accurate accounting information, so too will the organisation itself. As we have already mentioned above, the organisation will want to constantly monitor its business performance for a variety of reasons. These include:

- to ensure that it is on track to attain any projected financial **objectives**
- to **match projections** with actual **performance**
- to **assess** whether the **level of profit** and sales generated is **sufficient** to be able to make any financial commitments
- to **assess** whether the **level of profit** allows for further purchase of equipment or machinery, or indeed, any **expansion** to the organisation to be considered

FULFIL STATUTORY OBLIGATION AND ASSESS TAXATION LIABILITY

All organisations have a statutory obligation to maintain financial records and to issue correct information and documentation about their performance. These legal requirements include the following:

1. The Companies Acts of 1985 and 1989 require limited companies to maintain **records** which show details of financial transactions. Organisations are required to send every year to Companies House details of their profit and loss account and balance sheet, together with a directors' and auditors' report.
2. The Employment Protection (Consolidation) Act of 1978 states that an employer must provide each of its employees with an itemised **pay slip**. This pay slip must be in writing and must contain all relevant details of deductions and the contribution made by the employer.
3. All businesses, whatever their size or legal form, are required to keep accurate **accounts** so that they can provide information to both the Inland Revenue for tax deduction purposes and HM Customs and Excise for VAT payment purposes. These requirements are strictly enforced and it is less likely than it may have been in the past that organisations will try to evade the payment of tax. The two bodies mentioned above have a legal right to inspect the accounting books of an organisation, and do, indeed, enforce this right.

ELEMENT 7.3

a s s i g n m e n t

(PC 7.3.1–6, COM 3.1, 3.2, 3.3, 3.4, AON 3.1, 3.2, 3.3, IT 3.1, 3.2, 3.3*)

For the purposes of meeting the various performance criteria of this Element, which is very practical in nature, you need to understand the **function** of a **trial balance, profit and loss account** and **balance sheet**.

Your teacher or tutor should provide you with a set of accounting records relating to a single-product business. This accounting information should comprise the following:

- the fixed assets and current assets
- the current liabilities
- the share capital
- the profit and loss brought forward
- the sales and the cost of sales
- the overheads (administration, wages, rent, telephone, interest, travel expenses, etc.)

TASK 1

(PC 7.3.3)

From the information given to you by your tutor, you need to generate a **trial balance**.

TASK 2

(PC 7.3.4–5)

From the information given to you and the generation of your trial balance in Task 1, you should produce a **profit and loss account** and a **balance sheet** for the organisation.

TASK 3

(PC 7.3.1–2, PC 7.3.6)

Produce a word processed document which shows your understanding of the accounting systems used by the organisation for which you have produced your accounts. In addition, you should identify the accounting periods they have used and explain why they have opted for that particular one.

NOTES

If you have the facilities available to you, then your accounts can be generated by the use of computer software. If this is not available, then they should be produced manually.

You do not need to differentiate between trading and manufacturing accounts and between gross and net profit, but you should understand the basic principles involved in summarising and interpreting information from accounting records.

* Provided the accounts are generated by means of computer software.

Identify and explain data to monitor a business

Profitability ratios: return on net assets (per cent) (net profit/net assets); profit margin (per cent) (net profit/sales); gross profit (per cent) (gross profit/sales)

Performance ratios: selling (administration/sales (per cent)): (overheads/sales (per cent)); asset turnover: (sales/net assets); stock turnover (sales/stock); return on capital; gearing; debtors' collection period (debtors/sales/365))

7.4.1 *Identify users of accounting information*

As we have already said, it is important for an organisation to monitor its business performance. We have discussed the type of information such monitoring can produce, i.e. quantitative and qualitative, and the necessity for an organisation to have this information to enable it to achieve its goals or objectives. We have also discussed the strategy and tactics managers use within an organisation. We have realised from this discussion that, however large or small an organisation, or to whatever sector that organisation belongs, each has to deal with financial information of one kind or another. But **who uses** this information and how? We will look at these questions in more detail now.

USERS

The accounts department of an organisation will devise a system of obtaining and recording information which can be used to keep a tight rein on the financial activities of that organisation. The decision-making process of the organisation will be assisted and speeded up when this information is summarised to good effect by the accounts department. Decisions about the performance of the organisation cannot be made without the necessary data, and the accountants within the organisation should be readily able to provide this information. They may do this in several ways:

1 *By the reliable recording of financial transactions* – each time a transaction takes place, it must be recorded. Without this system it would be impossible for an organisation to judge its performance and to forecast future development. The information obtained from transactions should be recorded either manually or through a computerised system. These business activities should be recorded in an orderly and organised way to make information easily and readily accessible.

2 *By breaking down information into different categories* – it would be impossible to analyse information obtained from a variety of sources regarding the organisation as a whole unless this were done. In order to make the information reliable and easy to use, it is necessary to categorise the data.

3 *By summarising the data produced* – the accounts department would be required to summarise the information obtained from its accounting systems, e.g. breaking it down either into departments or specific products the organisation sells.

OWNERS AND MANAGERS

The information produced from such accounting processes would be useless if it were too complicated. The management responsible for decision making and planning for the future of the organisation would probably need to have the financial information interpreted. Other parties who would be likely to need to have this information interpreted would be:

- **shareholders** or prospective investors in the organisation
- **suppliers** of the organisation who might want to check its creditworthiness
- a **bank** from which the organisation has requested a loan
- the Inland Revenue and Customs and Excise departments, which need accurate information in order to assess the organisation for **tax purposes**
- the **employees** of the organisation who would want to know how financially stable their jobs are
- agents representing **investors** who would want to know if the organisation is a viable institution for their clients to invest in

Larger organisations may employ accounting personnel with expertise in different areas, whose skills are deployed in different ways to benefit the organisation. These specialist accountants fall into two main areas:

1 *Financial accountants* – these individuals deal mainly with the way documents and transactions are

recorded and the best way to interpret and present the information gained from them.

2 *Management accountants* – these individuals deal mainly with providing information about the future of the organisation. They provide forecasts and plans which would help the organisation achieve the goals set for the future.

In order for a person to be called 'qualified' in the accounting profession, he/she would usually have passed a series of examinations set by a professional body. Normally, these are examinations in Chartered Accountancy, Certified Accountancy, Management Accountancy or Public Finance Accountancy.

PROVIDERS OF FINANCE

We mentioned earlier some of the people likely to need information about the business performance of an organisation. Among these people are those who are likely to be investing money in one way or another in that organisation. Those people are the **providers of finance**. Obviously, they would need to have a firm statement, from someone who knows what he/she is talking about, concerning the financial position of the organisation.

TAX AUTHORITIES

The business performance of any organisation is also of great interest to the Inland Revenue and Customs and Excise departments. In 1992 the government raised almost £178 billion in taxes. The tax authorities are interested in all organisations, but the reasons for their interest in various organisations may differ. The taxes that business have to pay include the following:

- **corporation tax** – this is tax paid on business profits and all organisations have to pay this on profits over a certain amount
- **business rates** to their local councils
- employers have to pay a contribution to the government of **national insurance** for each employee
- **value added tax** also has to be paid and charged
- **customs and excise duty**

All companies must comply with certain legal requirements:

1 *Auditing* – all registered companies in the UK are required by law to have their final accounts audited by a registered accountant annually. This means the checking of records to testify that the accounts show a 'true and accurate view' of the financial position of the organisation. The auditors will be specialists who are employed by the organisation to carry out this task and they will prepare an audit report when their enquiries have been completed. This audit report will state:

that the financial statements have been audited in accordance with Auditing Standards. In my opinion the financial statements give a true and fair view of the profit and the state of affairs of the company as at 30 April 19– and of the source and application of funds for the year then ended, and have been properly prepared in accordance with the Companies Act 1985.

AUDITORS' REPORT

To the members of Fisons plc

We have audited the financial statements on pages 31 to 51 in accordance with Auditing Standards.

In our opinion these financial statements give a true and fair view of the state of affairs of the Company and of the Group at 31 December 1992 and of the profit and cash flow of the Group for the year then ended, and have been properly prepared in accordance with the Companies Act 1985.

Price Waterhouse

Chartered Accountants
and Registered Auditor

Southwark Towers
32 London Bridge Street
London SE1 9SY
30 March 1993

FIG. 7.4.1 *A copy of the Auditors' Report sent to the members of Fisons PLC after completion of the audits.*

2 *Registrar of companies* – in addition to annual auditing, all organisations must issue a set of accounts to the Registrar of Companies, together with the following:

- a copy of their Directors' Report – this will include a summary of the business activities of the organisation
- a copy of the Audit Report
- a copy of the accounts of each company within the group
- a copy of the accounts and details of any subsidiary companies of the organisation

student activity

(PC 7.4.1, COM 3.2, 3.4)
In the role of an auditor, list the documents that you would expect to have access to during your audit. What information would you gain from these documents and why?

GENERAL PUBLIC

Similarly, the **general public** would also want to be aware of the financial position of an organisation. This might be for a variety of reasons, which may include the following:

- the organisation may have advertised a job vacancy and any potential candidates would want to know that the organisation was viable financially before applying
- an individual may be interested in buying shares in the organisation and would want to know that his/her investment would be a sound one

- an individual may already own shares in the organisation and would be interested to monitor the progress of the investment
- an individual may buy the goods or services of the organisation on a regular basis and would want to ensure that the supply would continue. If the organisation is likely to fail then the individual would want to begin to identify alternative suppliers

EMPLOYEES

The **employees** of the organisation will be personally interested in the progress and development of the organisation itself, as well as its financial stability. The welfare of the individual employees is the responsibility of the organisation, but should an employee suspect that the organisation is likely to cease trading for financial reasons, then he/she would have to seek alternative employment.

An employee would also want to have information available regarding the financial viability of the organisation in the following circumstances:

- the employee may have applied for promotion within the organisation
- the employee may be considering whether to apply for an advertised position for which he/she would be suitable. If the organisation is growing and progressing well, then the individual may not wish to move. However, if there is some likelihood that the employee may become redundant, then the possibility of immediate alternative employment could be in his/her best interests
- the employee will want to know that his/her job is secure for the foreseeable future. The employee is likely to have domestic commitments and will want to take every precaution to protect these
- the employee may have shares in the organisation
- the employee may be thinking of buying shares in the organisation
- the employee may be involved in a profit-sharing enterprise initiated by the organisation

7.4.2 *Explain the reasons for monitoring a business*

REASONS FOR MONITORING

We look at the **reasons for monitoring business performance** in some detail in other sections of this Unit. The main reasons for monitoring a business are as follows:

- to ensure the organisation is **solvent**
- to measure the amount of **profit** the organisation is making
- to ensure the organisation is complying with **legislation** regarding the payment of taxes
- to ensure the organisation is making enough profit

to **maintain payments**

- to compare actual progress with the **objectives** set in the original business plan
- to identify areas where the organisation could **improve** its business performance

If an organisation is to trade successfully, it is important that it is always aware of its current financial situation. In order to monitor its business effectively, an organisation must:

1 *Prepare a budget* – the budget must be realistic and achievable. In addition, it should challenge those involved both in production and in complying with the budget itself.

2 *Monitor* – once the budget has been set, the organisation will need to regularly monitor performance. Monitoring will possibly take place once a month and will be essential if the business is to perform effectively.

The whole process of monitoring can be time consuming. It is, however, essential if the management of the organisation are to remain in control of business activities. Certain key areas will be monitored:

1 *Sales* – variances in the sales price of certain products and those of competitors will need to be noted. In addition, any variances in the volume of sales of particular products and services will also need to be monitored and noted.

2 *Materials* – careful monitoring of the cost of any raw materials will need to be undertaken. Any variances in the cost of materials should be noted, as should any changes in the usage of and demand for such materials.

3 *Labour* – in order to assess the deployment of labour within an organisation, the amount of activity of each area of the workforce must be monitored. Should there be any variances in the amount of work undertaken this should be noted. In addition, any changes in the wages of the workforce must be monitored and noted.

4 *Overheads* – any rise (or fall) in the money the organisation has to allow for overheads (things like heating and lighting) must be monitored carefully, as changes could affect the profit margin of the organisation.

5 *Cash flow* – this is dealt with in more detail later in this Unit, but suffice to say here that careful monitoring of the cash-flow situation of the organisation is essential.

6 *Aged debtors* – this is often one of the most useful reports available when monitoring is being undertaken. It lists the debt for each customer. Increasingly, these reports are prepared by the use of computer systems. The aged debtor report is pre-

pared from the sales ledger of the organisation and states whether customers are paying promptly. Obviously a large number of aged debtors will adversely affect the cash-flow position of the organisation.

7 *Aged creditors* – the reverse of aged debtors, aged creditors are people to whom the organisation owes money. Payment outside the terms of credit can lead to bad feeling with suppliers, which, in turn, could result in their refusing to supply the organisation. Once again, an aged creditors report is compiled when monitoring is being undertaken. This lists the accounts payable and states whether they are being paid within a reasonable amount of time.

8 *Stock* – it should be the aim of an organisation to keep its stock levels to a minimum, but to allow sufficient raw materials to maintain production. In addition, sufficient finished goods should be held in stock to supply the needs of customers. Too high a stock level would mean that too much working capital was being tied up, so it is important that this level is monitored carefully. It is normal to monitor stock levels on an individual product basis.

9 *The balance sheet* – another reason for monitoring all of the above aspects of business activity is to enable the organisation to produce a balance sheet. Some of the items appearing on a balance sheet may fluctuate from one month to another, while others (e.g. the fixed assets) will remain much the same. Increasingly, organisations are preparing their balance sheets by means of computer software, thus enabling this monitoring process to be carried out monthly. If the organisation decides that once a month is too frequent, the process may be carried out quarterly. If a balance sheet is produced only once a quarter, another form of report needs to be produced so that careful monitoring of the cash available, total debtors and total creditors can be undertaken.

In addition to the reasons given above for monitoring business performance, an organisation would also need to look at the following questions:

- are all its **products** making a positive contribution?
- are all the **fixed costs** being covered?
- is production on **target**?
- is the organisation making a **profit**?
- is the list of **aged debtors** becoming too large?
- is the organisation still **liquid**?
- is the organisation still **solvent**?

In an efficient organisation, monitoring will take place continually, thus eliminating the need to monitor all the above all the time. It is essential, however, that the information about these criteria be readily available.

SOLVENCY

Solvency is a measure of the business's ability to survive. It means that the organisation is able to meet its short-term financial commitments and essentially to operate in at least a break-even situation. Organisation which are on the edge of solvency may consider the monitoring of financial transactions to be even more critical than those who are comparatively successful.

PROFITABILITY

The level of **profitability** of a business is measured in relation to its overall productivity and deployment of resources. The levels at which acceptable profit is made differ from organisation to organisation. The profit may relate directly to each unit traded or to the overall turnover of the organisation. In this respect, it is possible for an organisation to be profitable despite the fact that certain elements of the organisation are only breaking even, or are, perhaps, trading at a small loss. It is essential that all financial transactions are monitored in order to ascertain whether projected profit levels have been achieved.

We consider some of the formulae an organisation can use in the monitoring of profitability in Element 7.4.6 of this Unit.

TAXATION

The amount of tax an organisation is liable to pay is a very complicated matter. Many large organisations employ specialists to deal with their taxation affairs.

Most organisations strive to limit the amount of tax they are likely to pay and keep it to a minimum. This is known as **tax avoidance** and it is not illegal to practise this. **Tax evasion**, on the other hand, means that no tax is paid, and this is illegal.

Legally all organisations making a profit are subject to paying corporation tax. This tax is paid nine months after the end of the organisation's own financial year. The organisation has to present its profit and loss account in order that its level of taxation can be calculated. Only those expenses presented in the profit and loss account that can be deemed to be 'wholly and exclusively' incurred in the running of the business can be regarded in the calculation of profits.

Consideration also has to be given to the payment of dividends to shareholders. Advance corporation tax has to be paid when an organisation pays a dividend to its shareholders. Although this payment is compulsory, it is considered to be an advance payment on the corporation tax the organisation is liable for and can be deducted from the final payment of this corporation tax.

Naturally, during the monitoring process, the organisation will need to ensure that it is making enough money to cover the taxation requirements of the Inland Revenue and Customs and Excise departments.

MAINTAINING FINANCE

Another important reason for regularly monitoring progress is to ensure that the organisation can maintain the finance provided either at the commencement of business or to fund a new venture.

The organisation will have used one of the providers of finance that we mentioned earlier to obtain additional funding for this new venture. These providers of finance will obviously have looked very closely at the projected profit margins of the organisation. If these were too optimistic and the organisation is not making the level of profit initially anticipated, then the providers of finance would want some explanation and further guarantees.

Naturally, if the organisation is not making enough money to maintain the repayments on the loan it obtained at the outset, then the provider of that finance will want explanations. It will want assurance that the money will be repaid. Constant monitoring of this aspect of business activity is essential.

COMPARISON WITH TARGETS AND IMPROVING PERFORMANCE

As a matter of course, organisations make forecasts and set targets. However, what is of particular interest to an organisation is projected targets and actual performance. The consistent monitoring of all financial transactions is essential to ensure that the organisation is 'on line' to achieve specific targets.

It is also important for organisations to make constant comparisons (they will not necessarily wait until the end of the year to do this) with projected targets and actual performance so that they can readjust levels of business activity and production as necessary. These comparisons should also identify key problem areas which may require additional financial or advisory input. Areas with particular problems may need a total overhaul of either staff or process. By monitoring financial transactions in relation to targets proposed, an organisation should be able to identify these problem areas before too much damage has been done to productivity, profit or growth.

7.4.3 *Explain the use of comparisons and variance in monitoring a business*

Throughout the course of its business activity an organisation will constantly need to make comparisons between the forecasts it has made in various directions and the actual performance it has achieved. Forecasts and their comparisons tend to be carried out in the following areas:

- the **cash-flow requirements** of the organisation
- the projected **sales figures** of the organisation
- the projected **purchase figures** of the organisation
- the projected **budgets** of each section of the organisation

Although an organisation will have put a great deal of time and effort into the production of such forecasts, this is not the end of the story. Monitoring the actual performance of the business is just as important and can be equally as time consuming. The information compiled needs to be used effectively in order to compare the projected performance with the actual performance of the organisation.

ACTUAL WITH FORECAST FOR THE BUSINESS

The forecasts and comparison with actual performance could be carried out on a weekly, monthly, quarterly or annual basis. On the other hand, an external factor which is beyond the control of the organisation may force it to make comparisons in order to change plans or targets. Such comparisons may be brought about for some or all of the following reasons:

- **cash** generated from **sales** is not as high as forecast – the reason for this could be that the materials used in the production process have cost more than expected, or, indeed, more than expected have been needed. The result of this is a reduction in the gross profit margin of the organisation. In order to remedy this particular problem, the organisation may try to negotiate the price charged by a supplier or to look for ways of reducing wastage. Alternatively, it may seek an alternative supplier
- there could be a **build-up of stock** because the forecasts for projected production and projected sales are not in line. In order to remedy this situation an organisation would need to try to ensure that existing stock is put to immediate use. If this is not possible, then the organisation could have to pay high interest on any loans from a bank related to the stock it holds

- if the price of **raw materials** is increased by the supplier, then the organisation would find that there are problems with the forecasts. In such cases the organisation would again try to negotiate with the supplier. After all, in an organisation where credit is used to purchase raw materials, an increase in the costs could have a knock-on affect in other areas of the business.

Obviously, many more considerations could be mentioned here, but the organisation will have to learn the same lessons whatever the situation. It is imperative that the organisation makes accurate and reliable forecasts. If, for some reason beyond the control of the organisation, actual performance does not meet these forecasts, then at least the potential problems have been highlighted early and some solution can be considered. By concentrating on a monthly profit and loss account and a monthly balance sheet, an organisation will be able to monitor its adherence to its business plan. This control mechanism should enable it to identify any causes for concern and allow the organisation to react in time. The normal procedure is for an organisation to create a cash-flow forecast which includes the budgeted figures for various items. Then, as the actual figures become available, it can compare these with the budgeted figures. Similarly, it will be possible to compare actual output with production targets and actual sales with projected sales.

ACTUAL WITH PREVIOUS YEARS FOR THE BUSINESS

Now we have considered how an organisation can compare its actual performance with that projected in its forecasts, we can consider how it compares its achievements from one year to another.

Obviously, this range statement is very closely linked to the work you carried out in producing accounting information in previous performance criteria.

An organisation would use its accounting information in order to assess the level of increase in profit, or, indeed in loss, from one year to another. We have already identified the importance of such accounting information for monitoring purposes in other sections of this book.

The organisation would also use this accounting information in order to assess increase or decrease of income or expenditure on any given aspect of the business activity.

CASHFLOW FORECAST FOR:		MONTH		TO		MONTH																TOTALS	
		MONTH		MONTH		MONTH		MONTH		MONTH		MONTH											
RECEIPTS		BUDGET	ACTUAL	BUDGET	ACTUAL	BUDGET	ACTUAL	BUDGET	ACTUAL	BUDGET	ACTUAL	BUDGET	ACTUAL									BUDGET	ACTUAL
Cash Sales																							
Cash from Debtors																							
Capital Introduced																							
TOTAL RECEIPTS	(a)																						
PAYMENTS																							
Payments to Creditors																							
Salaries/Wages																							
Rent/Rates/Water																							
Insurance																							
Repairs/Renewals																							
Heat/Light/Power																							
Postages																							
Printing/Stationery																							
Transport																							
Telephone																							
Professional Fees																							
Capital Payments																							
Interest Charges																							
Other																							
V.A.T. payable (refund)																							
TOTAL PAYMENTS	(b)																						
NET CASHFLOW	(a-b)																						
OPENING BANK BALANCE																							
CLOSING BANK BALANCE																							

BARCLAYS

N.B. All figures include VAT. Published by Barclays Bank PLC. Corporate Marketing Department. Reg. No. 1026167. Reg. Office: 54 Lombard Street, London EC3P 3AH. Ultimate Holding Company: Barclays PLC. BB16164l. October 1988. BE. 9971615C. A Member of IMRO.

FIG. 7.4.2 *Barclays Bank's Monthly Cash Flow Forecast pro-forma.*

APPENDIX II

CASHFLOW

MONTHLY/QUARTERLY REPORT

Name of Business:

Month/Quarter ended:

	BUDGET £	ACTUAL £	DIFFERENCE £	REASON	ACTION TAKEN
Cash Sales					
Cash from Debtors					
Capital Introduced					
TOTAL RECEIPTS (a)					
PAYMENTS:					
Payments to Creditors					
Salaries/Wages					
Rent/Rates/Water					
Insurance					
Repairs/Renewals					
Heat/Light/Power					
Postages					
Printing/Stationery					
Transport					
Telephone					
Professional Fees					
Capital Payments					
Interest Charges					
Other					
VAT payable (refund)					
TOTAL PAYMENTS (b)					
NET CASHFLOW (a-b)					
OPENING BANK BALANCE					
CLOSING BANK BALANCE					

NB. All figures include VAT

19

FIG. 7.4.3 *Barclays Bank's Monthly/Quarterly Cash Flow Report pro-forma.*

APPENDIX I

PROFIT AND LOSS BUDGET   MONTHLY/QUARTERLY REPORT

Name of Business:

Month/Quarter ended:

		BUDGET		ACTUAL		DIFFERENCE	REASON	ACTION TAKEN
		£	100%	£	100%	£		
SALES	(a)							
LESS: DIRECT COSTS:								
Cost of Materials								
Wages								
GROSS PROFIT	(b)							
OVERHEADS (FIXED COSTS):								
Salaries								
Rent/Rates/Water								
Insurance								
Repairs/Renewals								
Heat/Light/Power								
Postages								
Printing/Stationery								
Transport								
Telephone								
Professional Fees								
Interest Charges								
Other								
TRADING PROFIT								
Less: Depreciation								
TOTAL OVERHEADS	(c)							
Net Profit before Tax	(b-c)							
Plus: Previous Mths/Qtrs 1.								
2.								
3.								
TOTAL YEAR TO DATE								

NB. All figures exclude VAT

FIG. 7.4.4 *Barclays Bank's Monthly/Quarterly Profit and Loss Budget Reports pro-forma.*

student activity

(PC 7.4.3, COM 3.2, 3.3, IT 3.1, 3.3)
Specifically, how do you consider that an organisation would use the accounts generated from one year to assess the performance during the following year? How would profit and loss accounts and balance sheets help the organisation to compare its achievements in the monitoring of business performance with that of the previous year?

This student activity is essential for you to demonstrate evidence of your understanding of this performance criteriaon. You should present your considerations in the form of a word processed report which fully proves your understanding. This will also assist you in the Element Assignment.

INTER-FIRM COMPARISON

Organisations also make comparisons to assess their own performance in relation to that of their competitors. Organisations need to make the following comparisons:

- increase or decrease in market share
- increase or decrease in turnover
- increase or decrease in prices being charged
- increase or decrease in profits made, and as a result any potential expansion or diversification likely from competitors.

student activity

(PC 7.4.3, COM 3.2)
How would an organisation know the accounting information about its competitors? How would it find out whether its competitors are increasing their market share or making improved profits? Discuss this as a group.

7.4.4 Identify and explain key components of information required to monitor a business

As we have already mentioned, the key components of the monitoring process of making comparisons either with forecasts made or with the performance of previous years include the following:

1 *forecasts* (balance sheet, profit and loss account, cash flow)
2 *actual* (balance sheet, profit and loss account, aged debtors, aged creditors)
3 *previous year's* (balance sheet, profit and loss account, aged debtors, aged creditors)

student activity

(PC 7.4.4, COM 3.2, 3.3, IT 3.1, 3.2, 3.3)
In order to meet this performance criterion, it is advisable for you to have evidence that you understand the components an organisation would use to monitor its business performance.
Notes
You should produce a word processed report which gives details of each of the above headings (and sub-headings) and give detailed information regarding the use of such information both within an organisation and in an inter-firm context.

7.4.5 *Explain the implications for the performance of a business from a given set of accounting information*

Like performance criteria 7.3.3 and 7.3.5, this is a very practical performance criterion. Again, your tutor will give you information about the performance of a business. This data will contain details of accounting information and from this you should explain in your own words what you think the implications are for the performance of the organisation.

Having received the accounting information for the organisation, you should consider the implications for the performance of that business using the following headings:

1 the organisation's **solvency**
2 the organisation's **profitability**
3 the organisation's **ability** to **achieve targets**
4 whether the **achievements** made are **better** or **worse** than targets
5 whether the organisation will be able to establish its **tax liability**
6 if there is any way that the organisation can **minimise its tax liability**
7 whether the organisation will be able to **maintain funding**

8 how the organisation is achieving in **comparison** with others

In order to meet the performance criterion here you should carry out the following Student Activity.

student activity

(PC 7.4.5, COM 3.2, 3.3, IT 3.1, 3.2)
Using the above information and headings, you should produce a word processed report which identifies your thoughts about the implications for the performance of your given business. This Activity will assist you in the completion of the Element Assignment.

7.4.6 *Explain the use of solvency ratios, profitability ratios and performance ratios in interpretating accounting information*

Organisations use a number of the following formulae to ascertain whether they are working at full capacity and obtaining the highest possible level of profitability. There are so many variations of these formulae in use that it would be impossible to ensure that we have covered all of them in this section. You do need to be aware, however, that a substantial section of the Element Assignment requires you to be able to work out the ratios and to explain the significance of the ratios in a business.

SOLVENCY RATIOS

CURRENT (CURRENT ASSETS, CURRENT LIABILITIES)

In terms of the use of its assets, a business will try to see how its performance can be improved by making better use of these assets. This is usually considered from two viewpoints, that of actual asset utilisation and that of stock turnover.

The **asset utilisation** formula shows how fixed assets are being used to generate sales revenue. This is, in effect, a method of showing how efficient the organisation is.

$$\text{asset utilisation} = \frac{\text{sales}}{\text{fixed assets}}$$

This formula can be misleading in some respects since organisations require different levels of fixed assets in order to operate.

ACID TEST (LIQUID ASSETS – CURRENT ASSETS LESS STOCK EQUALS CURRENT LIABILITIES)

Working out the **liquidity** of an organisation (the ability of that organisation to turn assets into cash) is important, particularly when we look at the organisation's ability to pay short-term debts. The easiest way to work out the liquidity ratio of the organisation is to employ the **'acid test'**. The acid test looks at how much money will be available when the creditors require payment. This is best expressed in one of two ways:

$$\text{current assets} - \text{stock} = \text{current liabilities}$$

or alternatively,

$$\text{debtors} + \text{cash balances} = \text{current liabilities}$$

This acid test ratio will be quite accurate since it only includes assets capable of being turned into ready cash in the short term.

PROFITABILITY RATIOS: RETURN ON NET ASSETS (PER CENT) (NET PROFIT/NET ASSETS) AND PROFIT MARGIN (PER CENT) (NET PROFIT/SALES)

Net profit percentage is usually calculated year-on-year and is used to make comparisons with other organisations operating in the same market. As it considers net profit rather than gross profit, it takes into account all of the business's expenses. As a result, the business can identify any increases in the overheads and make adjustments to suit.

$$\text{net profit percentage} = \frac{\text{net profit}}{\text{sales revenue}} \times 100$$

GROSS PROFIT (PER CENT) (GROSS PROFIT/SALES)

Gross profit percentage refers to the ratio of gross profit to sales revenue and will rise or fall in certain circumstances. If the percentage falls, then the organisation is comparatively less profitable. If the percentage rises, then a greater level of profitability has been achieved.

$$\text{gross profit percentage} = \frac{\text{gross profit}}{\text{sales revenue}} \times 100$$

This gross profit percentage is normally calculated at regular intervals throughout the year.

PERFORMANCE RATIOS

SELLING (ADMINISTRATION/SALES (PER CENT))

This ratio is a way of measuring the cost of the administrative support systems and what percentage of the sales revenue which is eaten up by administration costs. This selling performance ratio is:

$$\frac{\text{administration costs}}{\text{sales}} \times 100$$

OVERHEADS/SALES (PER CENT)

Again, this selling performance ratio calculates how much of the total sales revenue is eaten up by overheads. This selling performance ratio is:

$$\frac{\text{overheads}}{\text{sales}} \times 100$$

ASSET TURNOVER (SALES/NET ASSETS)

This ratio measures how effectively the organisation uses its assets to generate sales. The formula is:

$$\text{total asset turnover ratio} = \frac{\text{sales}}{\text{total assets}}$$

STOCK TURNOVER (SALES/STOCK)

The **stock turnover** formula shows the average number of days an item is held before it is used or sold. This will vary from organisation to organisation, depending upon the type of business activity in which it is engaged, e.g. a baker could not hold his stock for the same length of time as a jeweller. The stock turnover formula is calculated by adding together the values of the opening stock and those of the closing stock, and multiplying the two. The stock turnover formula is:

$$\text{stock turnover} = \frac{\text{cost of sales}}{\text{average stock held}}$$

RETURN ON CAPITAL EMPLOYED

This formula is one of the more useful ways of measuring profitability. **Percentage return on capital employed** (ROCE) shows the relationship between the amount of capital used in the operation of the business and profits generated. **Capital employed** is the amount of available finance and is usually generated from profits made in the previous year. The capital employed is all of the net assets before any long-term deductions (such as debts).

$$\text{percentage ROCE} = \frac{\text{net profit for year}}{\text{capital employed}} \times 100$$

GEARING

We should also consider the capital structure of the organisation in terms of its utilisation of share capital, loans and other funds. The **gearing** formula makes a comparison between the capital within the business (provided by shareholders) and any long-term loans or other sources of finance. The gearing formula is:

$$\text{gearing} = \frac{\text{interest-bearing capital}}{\text{risk capital}} \times 100$$

A high gearing percentage means that an organisation must spend a higher percentage of its revenue on interest payments. Inevitably, this means that the organisation's fixed costs are higher and consequently the organisation is at a disadvantage in comparison to other competitors. In recessions, highly geared organisations have tended to fail as interest rates have increased.

DEBTORS' COLLECTION PERIOD (DEBTORS/SALES/365)

There are two other related formulae which we may consider, the **debtors' collection period** and the credit periods available to the organisation. The first formula is used when an organisation is trying to improve its liquidity by cutting down the amount of time it gives debtors to pay outstanding bills. Customers who pay late are, in effect, receiving free credit at the expense of the organisation. The ratio shows the average number of days of credit that customers receive at present. Normally, customers receive somewhere between 30 and 90 days credit as a matter of course. The formula is:

$$\text{debtors' collection period} = \frac{\text{debtors}}{\text{average daily sales}}$$

The other side of the coin is the **credit period available** to the **organisation**. This shows the average credit period suppliers are prepared to offer the organ-

isation. By extending the average credit period, an organisation can increase its liquidity. The formula is:

$$\text{credit period} = \frac{\text{creditors}}{\text{average daily purchases}}$$

As we have already mentioned, the use of these formulae and ratios is strictly limited to the context in which the operation operates. They may not be used for making comparisons between organisations because they do not measure size, structure or type of business activity. These formulae and ratios can only show some of an organisation's aspects, but they are useful in identifying the early stages of potential problems.

student activity

(PC 7.4.6, COM 3.1, 3.2)
As we have already mentioned, there are several other ratios in common use within industry, but for the purposes of this performance criterion range statement, you need only be concerned with the ones we have listed. You do not need to learn these by heart, but if you are given financial information (as you will be in the Element Assignment), then you need to show an understanding of how these are worked out and their significance to businesses.

You should now produce a word processed report which identifies the various ways in which these ratios and formulae are used in industry on a regular basis. What information would an organisation be able to conclude from these data? How often would they be used and in what circumstances?

ELEMENT 7.4

a s s i g n m e n t

(PC 7.4.1–6, COM 3.1, 3.2, 3.3, 3.4, AON 3.1, 3.2, 3.3, IT 3.2, 3.2, 3.3)

To satisfy the requirements of this Element you are again required to produce calculations and information from a given set of data which you tutor should provide you with.

In this case you need to have information on two given sets of accounting information for two comparable businesses. Your work may be produced using the software you have available, or it can be produced manually. Whatever form you use in your presentation, it is important that you provide appropriate graphical representation which you should use to help illustrate your points.

TASK 1

(PC 7.4.1–5)

You should produce a word processed report which details the key components of information used to monitor a business. You must explain the following:

1 who would want the information
2 why they would want to use such information
3 why they would need to make comparisons and variances
4 how comparisons and variances can be useful

TASK 2

(PC 7.4.6)

Now you should produce a summary of the two given sets of accounting information provided by your tutor. You should explain, by the use of illustrations, the following:

- the profitability, both gross and net, of the organisations
- the solvency of the organisations
- the performance of the organisations

You should explain, again in detail, the ratios you think the organisations have chosen to use and why.

UNIT 7

test questions

Focus 1

ASSETS AND WORKING CAPITAL

I Which of the following is a fixed asset?

(a) stock
(b) debtors
(c) mortgage
(d) fixtures and fittings

2 There are two major dangers in not having enough working capital. Which two of the following are correct?

(i) the organisation's inability to be able to buy in bulk
(ii) the organisation's difficulty in being able to offer any credit to its customers
(iii) the fact that investments are held by the creditors
(iv) the net profit of the organisation would be increased

(a) (i) and (ii)
(b) (i) and (iii)
(c) (i) and (iv)
(d) (ii) and (iii)

3 If an organisation pays £500 from its bank account to one of its creditors, the working capital of that organisation will:

(a) be increased
(b) be decreased
(c) remain the same
(d) not be affected

Focus 2

METHODS AND SOURCES OF FINANCE

4–6 The following are all sources of finance

(a) leasing
(b) overdraft
(c) bank loan
(d) profit retention

Which of the above would be the most appropriate for an organisation that has:

4 a desire to use an asset, but does not have the financial resources to pay for it outright

5 a short-term cash-flow problem

6 a wish to improve its financial strength so that it can make expansion plans

Focus 3

FORECASTS AND CASH FLOW

7 In drawing up a cash-flow forecast it is vital to know:

(a) the number and nature of the debtors
(b) the approximate expected dates of the receipts and payments
(c) the amount of working capital available
(d) the profit margins of the products and services sold

8 The following statements have been made:

(i) if an organisation does not forecast its cash flow then it could find itself overtrading
(ii) an organisation that is overtrading could find itself in a position of not having enough cash to pay immediate invoices

How are these statements best described?

(a) True/True
(b) True/False
(c) False/True
(d) False/False

9 If stock is worth £800 and is sold on credit for £1000, then working capital will:

(a) increase by £200
(b) decrease by £200
(c) remain the same
(d) this has nothing to do with working capital

10 At the end of a cash-flow summary will appear the

(a) opening bank balance
(b) total payments
(c) closing bank balance
(d) profit forecast

11–13 The following are four different kinds of costs

(a) direct wages
(b) direct materials
(c) selling overheads
(d) distribution overheads

In which category would you find the following?

11 advertising costs

12 payments to machine operators

13 packing costs

Focus 4

BASIC ACCOUNTING SYSTEMS AND TRIAL BALANCE

14 If an organisation sells products at £500 per unit, variable costs are £100 per unit and total fixed costs are £20,000, what will be the break-even point in the number of units?

(a) 250
(b) 330
(c) 400
(d) 500

15 The total cost divided by the number of units is more commonly known as:

(a) the fixed cost
(b) the marginal cost
(c) the absorption cost
(d) the unit marginal cost

16 The following statements have been made:

(i) a cash-flow forecast which is not reviewed from time to time will probably be more successive as the organisation will not have to continually make changes.
(ii) a cash flow forecast is ideal for helping the organisation to decide on alternative courses of action.

How are these statements best described?

(a) True/True
(b) True/False
(c) False/True
(d) False/False

Focus 5

PROFIT AND LOSS AND BALANCE SHEETS

17–20 The following all appear on a trading profit and loss account

(a) gross profit
(b) sales
(c) net profit
(d) expenses
Which of the above:

17 is sometimes called turnover

18 is calculated by deducting the cost of sales from the sales

19 is also on the balance sheet of a sole trader

20 is deducted from gross profit in order to calculate net profit

Focus 6

MONITORING, COMPARISONS AND PERFORMANCE

21 Absorption costs include

(a) overheads as a part of the total costs
(b) the ability to work out marginal costs
(c) the notion that they are also fixed costs
(d) the exclusion of overheads as part of the total costs

22–25 With reference to the following ratios:

(a) gross profit as a percentage of sales increases in year one from 10% to 12% in year two
(b) ROCE decreases from 12% in year one to 10% in year two
(c) net profit as a percentage of sales decreases from 11% in year one to 10% in year two
(d) the current ratio in year one is 2:1 and in year two is 1.5:1

Which of the above ratios shows:

22 that rising expenses are greater than sales

23 that profitability is increasing against sales

24 that there has been a reduction in liquidity

25 that profitability is better than other investments

26 The rate of stock turnover is:

(a) the level of average stock
(b) the cost of sales times the sales
(c) the value of average stock divided by 2
(d) the number of times that the average stock has been-sold

27 In order to work out whether stock has been damaged or stolen, an organisation would have to:

(a) work out the stock turnover
(b) work out the net profit percentage
(c) work out the current ratio
(d) work out the gross profit percentage

Focus 7

SOLVENCY, PROFITABILITY AND PERFORMANCE RATIOS

28 The financial position at one moment in time of an organisation would be found in:

(a) the trading account
(b) the cash book
(c) the profit and loss account
(d) the balance sheet

29 If output falls by half, the fixed costs will:

(a) double
(b) halve
(c) quarter
(d) be the same

30 The following two statements have been made:

(i)   current assets cannot be easily turned into cash
(ii) current assets change on a day-to-day basis

How are these statements best described?

(a) True/True
(b) True/False
(c) False/True
(d) False/False

ELEMENT 8.1

Prepare work and collect data for a business plan

PERFORMANCE CRITERIA

A student must:

1 explain the **purposes of a business plan**

2 identify the **business objectives** and collect **supporting information** for the business activity for which a plan is to be prepared

3 identify the **legal and insurance implications** of the business objectives

4 discuss the feasibility of proposals with others

5 estimate **resource requirements** to design, produce, promote and sell the goods or services

6 produce a flowchart illustrating estimated **time-scales**

7 identify **potential support** for the plan

8 prepare an action plan identifying actions to be taken to finalise the business plan for presentation

RANGE

Purposes of a business plan: *to seek sources of finance, to gain finance, to monitor progress*

Business objectives: *to make a profit, to break even, to be subsidised; to make goods, to provide services*

Supporting information: *competing products, demand for the product, estimated number of customers, likelihood of repeat business, likely volume of sales, possible value of turnover, possible profit*

Legal implications: *employment law, health and safety regulations, environmental regulations, Trades Descriptions Act; age limits*

Insurance implications: *asset insurance, public liability, product liability*

> ***Resource requirements:*** *human (own skills, others' skills), physical (materials, equipment), financial (capital requirements)*
>
> ***Time-scales*** *for: planning, production, marketing, selling, distribution; lead time to break-even*
>
> ***Potential support:*** *own organisation, other organisations; specialists (financial, legal, marketing, production)*

8.1.1 Explain the purposes of a business plan

When individuals or groups of individuals consider starting to run a business, they have a series of basic choices before them. Essentially, these relate to the **nature of the business** and whether to start a **new business** or buy an **existing** one. We shall look at the basic choices in turn, taking first the question of the nature of the business. The nature of the business depends on which business sector it falls into. These business sectors are, of course, the following:

1 *The primary sector* – which covers all industries involved in the extraction and basic production of raw materials. It should be remembered that this also includes most forms of agriculture and fishing.
2 *The secondary sector* – which covers all industries involved in the processing of raw materials in some way. In other words, these businesses turn raw materials into finished goods or components.
3 *The tertiary sector* – which relates mainly to the service industries. They do not actually involve themselves directly in the processing of materials. This sector includes, therefore, tourism, transportation and financial services.

The choice of a business will largely depend on two main criteria. These are:

● your own or your partner's **knowledge** and expertise of the business activity
● the potential **demand** for the products or services you wish to offer

Whether one wishes to establish a new business or to buy an existing one, there are a number of risks and costs involved. We shall begin by looking at starting a **new business** from scratch.

Inherent in the decisions and circumstances relating to the establishment of a new business are the following risks and costs:

● there are potentially **high financial risks** involved
● **market research** should be extensive
● as you are unknown in the market-place, you will need **time** to establish yourself
● any **mistakes** made in the first few months may prove disastrous
● careful consideration should be given to the **location** of the business
● you must ensure that your new business makes an **impact** very quickly so that your cash-flow is not adversely affected by poor performance in the first few weeks or months

student activity

(PC 8.1.1, COM 3.1)
In the rest of this Unit we will be considering the purposes and nature of a **business plan**. However, when a person is thinking about establishing a new business there is often very little information immediately available which can be used. In the role of an individual considering starting a new business from scratch, what would be your first move in establishing the viability of the business? Who would you need to consult in order to make these initial decisions? Discuss this in groups of four.

If, on the other hand, one is thinking about **purchasing an existing business** which has a track record, perhaps the first consideration is whether it is currently doing well or badly. There are several other considerations to be taken into account. These are:

- although the business may be established and there are all the benefits of the infrastructure being in place, this may mean that, comparatively speaking, it will be more **expensive**
- you may be expected to pay extra for '**goodwill**', that is, the value placed upon the trading name and existing trading relations with customers
- although the business is up and running, this may not necessarily mean that **you** know what to do with it
- you will have to make a careful investigation into the **assets and liabilities** of the business. You may be simply buying someone else's problem
- constant **monitoring** is essential since you cannot really rely on what the previous owner claimed about the strengths and weaknesses of the business

Somewhat different from purchasing an existing business is buying into an organisation which needs to expand or diversify. Although strictly speaking this is not setting up a new business, this could be a way of gaining the advantages of an existing business, while at the same time having the advantages of setting up your own one. If an existing business person is interested in taking a new partner on, or a small limited company is looking to take another shareholder on, then in both cases the injection of new cash may be exactly what both sides are seeking.

student activity

(PC 8.1.1, COM 3.1)
Imagine yourself in the role of an individual considering purchasing an existing business. What financial and other information would you need to see in order to make a considered decision as to whether or not to proceed? Also consider whether you would need to use the services of the following professionals and say what specialist knowledge you could gain from them:

- bank manager
- accountant
- solicitor
- surveyor
- management consultant

At what stage would you bring these specialists in? Discuss this in pairs.

Expanding an existing business, as we have already pointed out, has some risks attached to it. These are:

- you may not be as independent as you would like to be
- you should consider why, if the existing business structure was sound, profits acceptable and management in control of the situation, the organisation needs a new investor
- you should also ask yourself why the business has waited until this point to expand or diversify
- although diversification is a good idea, since it spreads risk across different business enterprises, it does stretch available resources too. Is this a good idea?

student activity

(PC 8.1.1, COM 3.1)
In the role of a financial provider who has been asked to consider further investment and support to an existing organisation, what information would you need? Consider your response to the following two situations:

1 The organisation is making a considered and logical expansion to its business activities. The organisation appears to be reasonably financially sound.
2 The organisation largely requires additional finance to support existing business activities. It proposes to make minor investments to develop new markets. The organisation seems to have a variety of problems associated with both its operations and its management.

What would you insist upon before giving additional funding, particularly in the latter case? Discuss this in groups.

The last business opportunity to consider (we will return to this topic in Element 8.3) is the purchase of a franchise. A successful business may offer its name, operational procedures, products or services to interested parties under a franchising agreement. Inevitably, there are some risks. These are:

- while it is easier to obtain a loan to buy a franchise than some other businesses, the franchisor may require quite high 'set-up' fees

- franchises are considered to be a comparatively low risk but they may only offer fairly low returns. The franchisor will also require a percentage of all of the profits you make
- franchises are usually restricted to a very tight geographical area, so you must remember that you will not be allowed to operate outside of your specified territory

PURPOSES OF A BUSINESS PLAN

TO SEEK SOURCES OF FINANCE

The business plan will seek to identify the organisation's financial situation. The specific financial items that will be covered are:

- the financial resources that are currently **available**
- the financial resources **needed**
- the **cost** of production
- the **prices** of products and services
- the organisation's ability to **repay loans**

Having covered these, the organisation should then be able to identify what finances will be required to ensure that it runs in an efficient and productive manner.

In seeking to obtain additional finance, perhaps to expand or diversify into a new area of activity, the organisation would have to operate from existing sets of information, particularly forecasts and financial statements, as opposed to the projected profit and loss accounts and balance sheets which would be used in the case of a new business.

A bank manager or another individual who may be asked to provide the business with finance will obviously want to know the true state of your proposed business. Some businesses adopt the strategy of creating two plans. These, in essence, are:

1 *An outsider's plan* – which is fairly conservative with regard to projected sales and costs. It will stress the unlikelihood of the business failing and will be used primarily to raise finance. The figures included in this form of plan should be more realistic than optimistic since any experienced financial provider will be able to interpret the figures easily. The figures must be achievable and not misleading. After all, if you mislead the lenders you will end up misleading yourself.

2 *The internal plan* – this plan is for the personal use of the owner(s) of the business. In this plan higher targets will be set, but they must still be within the realms of probability. The figures should not be too low as they will fail to encourage you to strive for higher levels of achievement.

TO GAIN FINANCE

Once the business plan has been completed and any necessary cash-flow and profit forecasts have been made, the next step is to actually acquire the finance. It should be remembered that banks are not necessarily the first port of call. You should think about the amount of finance required before making any moves.

Even if you have projected your financial requirements as carefully as you can, things may not go as well as you have planned. If you need to go back to a lender after a short period of time and ask for additional financial assistance, then this may not instill confidence in you as a business person.

On the other side of the coin, you should not ask for finance greatly in excess of what you feel you actually need. To take on the burden of additional loan repayments when the initial loan is sitting in the bank idle, is to cause unnecessary pressure on the business in the crucial early period.

It is advisable to be pessimistic, but at the same time to be positive and sensible in your financial requirements. Surprisingly, it is easier to find larger sums of money than smaller amounts. Lenders are not particularly interested in advancing many small sums when they could more easily monitor larger sums loaned to fewer borrowers. Equally, there are more investors willing to risk their money on businesses which have some form of track record than investors prepared to back new businesses which have yet to prove themselves. One of the preconditions for obtaining a loan, regardless of the age of the business, is that the management is sound and that the market is buoyant.

If you are starting up a new business you will need money for the following:

- the once-in-a-lifetime expenses – which include spending on the premises, equipment, furniture, professional and legal advice and marketing
- the working capital – which is necessary to bridge the gap between the payment for raw materials or stock and the point at which your customers pay you

As we will see later in this Element and in Element 8.3, there are a wide variety of different sources of finance which, not surprisingly, set a range of different criteria and conditions that the business must meet before they will agree to give financial support.

TO MONITOR PROGRESS

Normally, a business plan is reviewed at regular intervals so that the decision makers within the organisation can assess the relative success and progress of the business. It is better to identify a problem at an earlier stage than have to try to react to it once it has developed. Typically, an organisation will use SWOT analysis

(Strengths, Weaknesses, Opportunities, Threats), to ascertain the current position, both internally and externally. Identifying the **strengths** and **weaknesses** enables the business to assess the internal situation, such as the structure, size, processes, procedures and employees. The **opportunities** and **threats** refer to the external implications for the organisation. In looking at these the organisation attempts to make direct comparisons between competitors whilst looking at the current state of the market.

student activity

(PC 8.1.1, COM 3.1)
It is a good idea to clearly identify your market and consider the most direct competitors and their comparative advantages and disadvantages. In pairs, try to identify how you would do this.

8.1.2 *Identify the business objectives and collect supporting information for the business activity for which a plan is to be prepared*

BUSINESS OBJECTIVES

We can best look at the various objectives of businesses by first remembering that not all organisations have the same objectives. Indeed, they may consider some of the objectives which we will look at below to be of no importance at all. Others may have identified versions of the main objectives, but, in any case, organisations will inevitably put their objectives in different orders. Some objectives may be vital, whilst others are important or desirable. In the business world it is often difficult to make sure that you obtain all of the benefits and successes that you originally intended.

student activity

(PC 8.1.2, COM 3.1)
Look at Figure 8.1.1. How would you identify short-term, medium-term and long-term objectives? Do you think that personal objectives may differ from those of the business? If so, why? Discuss this in pairs.

TO MAKE A PROFIT

Making a profit is, perhaps, the most obvious of all the objectives, and yet, not all organisations will consider this to be the most important consideration. Perhaps, as we shall see from some of the other objectives, simply surviving in a highly competitive world is just as important.

Making a profit has obvious benefits for the owners of the business; the more apparent ones are being successful in their chosen career and obtaining wealth. The employees of the business will benefit too, as they will probably receive better pay and conditions of employment. If the need to make a profit is too powerful and things get out of control, this can have detrimental effects on the business and how it is run. The business may cut corners and risk breaching legislative guidelines, particularly those relating to employees or the environment.

Being profitable, as you will now no doubt be aware, brings additional benefits for the running of the business. These include:

- economies of scale – being able to buy materials more cheaply and producing units at a lower unit cost
- being able to buy environmentally friendly materials
- being able to use environmentally friendly production processes
- being able to obtain the best staff for the job

OBJECTIVES

What are your personal objectives in running the business?

Short-term

_____
_____
_____
_____

Medium-term

_____
_____
_____
_____

How do you intend to achieve them?

_____
_____

What objectives do you have for the business itself?

Short-term

_____
_____
_____
_____

Medium-term

_____
_____
_____
_____
_____

How do you intend to achieve them?

_____
_____

What are your long-term objectives (if any)?

1. _____
_____

2. _____
_____

3. _____
_____

4. _____
_____

5. _____
_____

How do you intend to achieve them?

_____
_____
_____
_____
_____

TO BREAK EVEN

Breaking even, as we know, means covering costs. For most businesses this is the key factor which will signal their survival or failure. Any organisation considering making a loan to a business will at least insist that in the medium term it must break even. Profits may, of course, take a little longer to happen.

The target to aim for is ensuring that the business stays afloat. This is known as the **break-even point**,

FIG. 8.1.1 *Part of Barclays Bank's 'Setting up and running your own business' information pack, which illustrates the need, even before the business has come into existence, of setting out objectives in the short, medium and long term.*

where sales are large enough to cover the overheads of the business. Breaking even may seem fairly straightforward, but, as a business attempts to reach the level of sales required to reach the break-even point, it will have, hopefully, overcome many of the financial pitfalls.

(PC 8.1.2, COM 3.1)

How realistic is it to expect a new business to make a profit in the first year? If a new business must manage its finances in a careful and professional manner in the first year, surely survival must be the major goal? Do you agree with this statement? Discuss this as a group.

Using a break-even chart often gives a false impression in relation to the setting of a particular sales target. The break-even point has the unfortunate habit of moving without telling you. As sales increase, unforeseen expenses may be incurred. However, the longer the business remains afloat, the more chance it has to exceed the break-even point and move into profit.

We have mentioned the problems, but what about the solution to achieving the break-even point? The first thing to realise is that a business cannot hope to break even at all times. It may be necessary, at least temporarily, to obtain additional finance to see the business over a sticky patch. If the business is unable to obtain more funds, then certain steps may have to be taken to control expenditure:

- controlling debtors
- negotiating with creditors
- reducing stock levels

TO BE SUBSIDISED

This objective is quite different from the basic requirements of having to make a profit or breaking even. There are certain circumstances in which organisations may operate at a loss. They receive funds from other sources to ensure their survival. The government, for example, subsidises organisations which operate in designated redevelopment or assistance areas. The government also offers assistance to organisations developing new technological equipment.

A business which is part of a larger organisation, such as a conglomerate or multinational, may receive subsidies while developing a particular market or product. The parent company, in effect, subsidises the running of the business during the expensive start-up period.

Returning to the role of the **government**, we can identify many hundreds of organisations which do not operate on a profitable or break-even basis. Operating from a fixed budget, they are expected to provide a service on behalf of the government. Typically, QUANGOs, other government bodies and, to some extent, local authorities operate on a subsidy basis. Local authorities, in particular, have their own means of raising income in the form of rents, rates and other charges. However, a large proportion of their financial commitments are provided by the government in the form of a grant or subsidy.

The EU also subsidises many different forms of organisations. The Common Agricultural Policy (CAP) provides subsidies designed to support farmers and agricultural businesses, particularly in parts of the EU where traditional forms of production are unable to compete with the more technologically advanced equipment and machinery used by the wealthier members of the EU.

(PC 8.1.2, COM 3.1, IT 3.1)

There are around 300 different types of grants available which are designed to cover the following:

- starting a new project
- acquisition of new machinery
- creating new job opportunities
- expansion of existing business

Try to identify at least one grant which relates to each of the above. Word process your findings and present it orally to the remainder of your group.

TO MAKE GOODS OR TO PROVIDE SERVICES

The foundation of any business is firmly rooted in the nature of the goods or services which it offers. Coming up with the right idea can often be very difficult. When an individual first considers starting a new business, he/she will have to determine what products to sell or what service to offer. A good way of approaching these questions is to consider the following:

- is the business related to assembling things? Examples could include the production of toys, clothes, jewellery or lampshades
- is the business related to arts and crafts? Examples could include drawing, photography, picture framing, pottery, design work or candle making

- is the business related to fashion and beauty? – Examples could include hairdressing, knitting, beauty therapy, aromatherapy, massage or dress making
- is the business related to home-based activities – Examples could include catering, child minding, growing produce, taking in lodgers or curtain making
- is the business related to office services – Examples could include bookkeeping, word processing, desk-top publishing, printing or typewriting
- is the business related to writing – Examples could include translating, copy editing, indexing or proof reading

Perhaps your proposed business does not fall into any of the above categories. After all, there are many other forms of occupation. You could consider some of the following:

- acting as an agent for a mail order, party plan or tele-sales organisation
- teaching or tutoring
- repairing things such as clocks or bicycles
- building work, including decorating and gardening
- removals and doing odd jobs

In relation to the supply of products or services, the business may also have to look into the distribution aspects and see whether it can identify cost-effective methods of bringing products and services to potential customers.

SUPPORTING INFORMATION

A great deal of basic information can be found by referring to statistical information provided by the government or agencies working on behalf of the government. Equally, much information may be gleaned by careful analysis of the competitors. Also, trends in customer spending can provide useful data upon which to base the criteria needed to establish objectives related to the supply of products or services.

COMPETING PRODUCTS

In order to accurately assess your own sales, it is necessary to try to make some kind of judgement about your share of the market. In other words, you will need to have information about your **competitors' business** and their products. This will enable you to position your product and set pricing levels. Many small businesses operate in a market where there are lots of suppliers and no one individual organisation has more than about 5 per cent share.

Being able to measure your market share is relatively easy. However, attempting to wrest market share from competitors may be more difficult. Provided your rep-

utation is good and you have consistent quality throughout all of your activities and operations, then you can move some way towards obtaining a higher market share.

In order to assess your competitors it is essential that you consider the following:

- what are the **competitive products**?
- **how many** do they sell?
- how have they **performed** in the past few years?
- what is the organisational **structure** of the competitor?
- what are their **sales techniques**?
- do they **manufacture** the products?
- **how** do they manufacture the products?
- who are their main **customers**?
- what is their **pricing policy**?
- what is their **delivery service** like?
- how good is their **after-sales service**?

To be in a **dominant** position in any market it is necessary to have a 25 per cent market share. An organisation who is in this position is said to have a **monopoly**. These monopolies are unusual, and it is far more likely that you will find several businesses sharing or dominating a market. This is known as an **oligopoly**.

DEMAND FOR THE PRODUCT

The **market size** is the key factor here. You can measure the potential demand for the product in strictly monetary terms or by the number of units that can be sold. It is important to try to estimate the market **potential** which is, of course, somewhat different from the market size. This refers to the probable growth or contraction of the market. If you have already obtained an overall figure for the market itself, then you need to concentrate on a particular market segment that it is feasible for your organisation to supply. What is the size of this segment and is your organisation capable of providing sufficient products or services to cater for its needs?

ESTIMATED NUMBER OF CUSTOMERS

When trying to acquire new customers it is probably a good idea to begin by carrying out some **market research**. Typically, a business will use the following methods in order to establish the size of the potential customer base:

- using a 'raw' list of names to act as a **blanket mailing list**. This method has its disadvantages since the mailing list is probably too long to allow follow-up and direct sales techniques
- following **leads** from a list of individuals who have approached the business either as a result of mailings or advertisements. These individuals may have asked

for additional information or sales literature

- making use of **referrals** by existing customers. This is particularly valuable as satisfied customers are probably your best advertising and public relations asset
- establishing the name of the decision maker within an organisation that is a potential customer and ensuring that this person receives information about your business. You should also make every effort to find out as much about this organisation as is possible

Whatever method is used, it is vital that the organisation addresses the following points:

- records information about all potential customers
- devises a follow-up strategy
- ensures that potential customers always receive regular updates and information

Trying to establish the exact size and nature of the potential customers base is incredibly difficult. Without having established this, it is almost impossible to make any kind of meaningful financial forecast.

Knowing which **market** your product or service is aimed at will assist you in obtaining statistics and other numerical data. The first step in trying to collate these statistics is to identify the target group itself. You can do this by following the steps given below:

1 Is your target market a consumer one or an industrial or professional market?
2 Does age, sex, family size or marital status form the basis of your target group?
3 Does your product or service rely on the local area alone?
4 Is social class important?
5 Is frequency of purchasing behaviour an important factor?
6 Is your target market characterised by such factors as the wish to appear fashionable or to set trends?
7 Is your target market influenced by the price of the product or service?
8 Where does your target market purchase these products or services currently?
9 If you are selling to an industrial or professional market, how big are these businesses?
10 Does your target market require fast and frequent deliveries?
11 Does your target market require a high level of after-sales service?

To help you understand your customer base and to attempt to put some numerical value, in terms of either numbers or income from that group, you must acquire the above data. You could use your suppliers, asking them to provide you with some analysis of potential customers and to investigate the nature of the products and services they desire.

LIKELIHOOD OF REPEAT BUSINESS

Even when a customer places an order with your organisation, this should not be seen as the end of the transaction. Any business worthy of the name should aim to build up a long-term relationship with its customers. Just hoping that repeat business will happen does not mean that real orders or profits will result. A customer will not return to your business if you do not ensure that he/she is kept happy throughout the entire sales process and beyond. Simple steps can be taken to ensure that a customer remains loyal to you. These include:

- remaining in constant **contact** with the customer
- informing the customer about **special offers** or deals
- making sure that **deliveries** are made on time
- **informing** the customer if the products are likely to arrive late
- giving prompt **attention to complaints** and other criticisms

Many organisations rely on a handful of large customers, a situation in which, perhaps, there is a tendency for the organisation to have its eggs in too few baskets. It is, therefore, essential not only that these important customers remain loyal, but that steps are taken to ensure that there is an ongoing process for acquiring new custom.

Having a good working relationship with your existing customers can also mean that they will recommend you to new customers. They may also be willing to give you vital early sales leads if one of their colleagues or associates is considering purchasing a particular product or service. In other words, they act as a referee for you. It is, therefore, vital that good records are maintained about existing customers so that you can give them the impression at all times that they are valued and important.

LIKELY VOLUME OF SALES

Turnover may be a specific objective of the business. You need to set a particular level of sales in terms of units sold that will enable you to establish a basic level of business activity. The ideal situation is to have in operation a production process that requires equipment or machinery to be running at full capacity. Perhaps the organisation can achieve the volume of sales required by supplying other businesses with part-finished products. In this way, the supporting organisation helps to ensure that volume of sales and production levels are maintained at all times.

Setting the likely **volume of sales** is a procedure that needs to be addressed with considerable caution.

When you state initial sales volumes levels in a business plan, the potential provider of finance is likely to expect you to give assurances that such levels are possible. Again, as with many other things, caution may be the best approach. In this respect, it is probably better to set your volume of sales at a slightly lower level than you actually expect. This will have a twofold impact. First, it will appear to the provider of finance that the business is actually doing better than was anticipated. Equally, the difference between the projected and actual volume of sales may serve as a motivating factor both for you and for any employees.

POSSIBLE VALUE OF TURNOVER

As an alternative to achieving sales volume, we can consider **sales value**. This means that the organisation is concerned with the total **revenue** accrued from its sales. This objective is relevant to both low unit value and high unit value products. Such value will be particularly important to organisations which have high capital expenditure and, as a result, require high revenue in order to service existing loans. The maintenance of high sales value, or turnover, is essential to ensure that the business maintains its competitive edge, as any reduction in turnover may result in a loss of working capital. In extreme circumstances this may mean that the organisation will lose its liquidity and will have to reduce costs elsewhere, such as reducing its workforce.

Another way of achieving high sales value is to increase the profit margin per unit. This is a tricky technique since it may mean that the business's products or services may lose their competitive edge in terms of price.

Again, setting a likely turnover should be approached with considerable caution as it may be a deciding factor in whether potential investors agree to continue their relationship with you at the end of the loan period.

POSSIBLE PROFIT

The **profit forecast** should show the level of profit that you confidently expect your business to produce over a set period of time. There are three basic ways of increasing profits, or at least, maintaining them at an acceptable level, these are:

- cutting costs
- increasing prices
- selling more

Although making a profit seems to be the most obvious objective of any business, this need not necessarily be so. Some organisations do not consider that the maximisation of profits is anessential measure of success. The importance of the profit motive is very much dependent upon the stage of the business has reached. In the early stages of a business's life it is unreasonable to assume that profit maximisation is a key consideration.

With this in mind, it is, therefore, advisable to state on your business plan that profits will be modest, particularly in the first few years. If you claim that profits will be exceptionally high, this will inevitably lead providers of finance to question not only your judgement, but also your figure work.

student activity

(PC 8.1.2, COM 3.1)
Having now considered the principal pieces of supporting information, how detailed and accurate can you confidently expect them to be? Discuss this as a group.

8.1.3 Identify the legal and insurance implications of the business objectives

LEGAL IMPLICATIONS

Businesses are required to ensure that they have complied with various legal guidelines. Further details may be obtained from Units 2 and 4.

The following is a check-list of the legal aspects that a business should consider as an essential part of its business plan:

1 What are the current planning consents or authorised uses of the business premises to be used by the organisation?

2 Do the premises meet HASAW regulations?

3 Do the premises meet fire regulations and do they have a current fire safety certificate?

4 Do the products conform to the Weights and Measures Act?

5 Do the products conform to the requirements of the Trading Standards Office?

6 Do the products conform to the Environmental Health Office requirements?

7 Is there a possibility that the business may breach any environmental protection laws?

8 Do any aspects of the marketing or advertising effort breach the Trades Descriptions Act?

9 Do any aspects of the marketing or advertising effort breach the Consumer Credit Act?

EMPLOYMENT LAW

Particular attention should be paid to providing a contract of employment for all those who work for 16 hours per week or more and adhering to the laws relating to discrimination. For a full list of the relevant employment laws see Units 2 and 4.

HEALTH AND SAFETY REGULATIONS

Employer's liability insurance, as we will see shortly, covers a business against claims that may be made by employees who have suffered injury in the course of their work. The term employee is a broad one in this respect and covers all of those individuals who are under contract in some way to the business.

Health and safety at work has become an increasingly complex area for businesses to consider. In effect, a business should ensure that it complies with the Health and Safety at Work Act 1974 in the following respects:

- providing safe machinery and equipment
- ensuring that regular maintenance is undertaken
- ensuring that all operating procedures for machinery and equipment are carefully monitored
- ensuring that safe methods of handling potentially dangerous or hazardous materials are adhered to
- ensuring that employees receive sufficient training in safety matters
- ensuring that employees are well supervised at all times
- providing healthy and safe working conditions
- ensuring that the access to and exit from the premises are safe, unblocked and clearly marked
- ensuring that any visitors to the premises encounter a safe environment

ENVIRONMENTAL REGULATIONS

Customers are becoming increasingly aware of environmental issues and consequently certain businesses will cite **environmental considerations** as being key

objectives. Specific environmental policies which may be adopted include:

- the use of environmentally friendly products and processes
- the careful disposal of all waste
- the use of energy-efficient heating systems
- the use of bio-degradable packaging materials

student activity

(PC 8.1.3, COM 3.1)

From Figure 8.1.2, you will see that BAA have identified a number of key considerations which relate to their specific business activities. They have funded a number of projects designed to ensure that they minimise the impact of their activities on the local environment. These include:

- the creation of nature reserves
- working closely with local authorities on conservation activities

As a group, investigate similar projects which have been undertaken by businesses in your local area.

The Environmental Protection Act 1990 and its implications for UK businesses have been further supported by a number of EU Directives. These attempt to ensure that businesses take full account of their social and environmental responsibilities at all times. These laws, coupled with considerable consumer pressure, have caused businesses to re-evaluate many of their costs of production. There is no doubt that certain products or services have become more expensive as a result of more stringent environmental protection. However, these costs are far outweighed by the positive impacts which both businesses and the country as a whole enjoy.

When considering environmental concerns, a business will attempt to examine the following aspects of its activities:

- do any of our **activities** involve any environmental risk?
- do any of our **processes** involve any environmental risk?
- do we use any **materials** which are environmentally suspect?

Richard Everitt is a member of the Company's main board, and is responsible for the effective implementation of BAA's environmental policies.

BAA plc owns and operates seven airports in the UK. These account for 73 per cent of the UK's passenger air traffic and 84 per cent of air cargo. In 1992, over 77 million passengers travelled through our airports – an increase of 75 per cent over the last decade. The demand for air travel is likely to double within the next 12 years or so and people's freedom to travel as they need depends on continued airport development.

Airports have impacts on the environment – that's inevitable. And our priority is to continue striving to reduce those impacts where practicable.

While BAA has a long history of successful environmental initiatives, we have never before published an environmental policy. This report sets out our policy and introduces some of the projects we have already undertaken and aim to build upon. We will continue setting new environmental goals and will report each year on our progress.

Richard Everitt

FIG. 8.1.2 *This is the opening page from the British Airports Authority's 1993 Environmental Report. Richard Everitt is a member of the company's main board and has specific responsibility for the implementation of BAA's environmental policies.*

- do our products have a **detrimental impact** on the environment?
- what **type** of **waste** do we produce?
- what **level** of **waste** do we produce?
- can we implement cost-effective ways of **eliminating pollution**?
- if we establish environmental policies will it make us more **efficient**?
- is there a real public or consumer **demand** for environmentally sound products?
- what environmental protection **legislation** is in the pipeline?
- do we have **systems and procedures** in place to ensure that we adhere to existing and expected legislation?
- can we improve our **corporate image** by implementing environmental policies?
- what are the **implications** to our owners, shareholders, investors and providers of finance of our implementation of environmental policies?

student activity

(PC 8.1.3, COM 3.1)
You can see from Figure 8.1.3 that BAA spent £15m. a year on cleaning bills. Can you suggest any ways in which this expenditure could be reduced without environmental implications? Discuss this as a group.

If an organisation decides to implement a comprehensive environmental policy, then this should form an essential part of the business plan. Commonly, an environmental policy will take the form of a statement which will include the following:

BAA aims to reduce its consumption of resources such as energy and water and to reduce waste where possible. We also promote recycling and the use of recycled materials whenever this is cost effective.

Conserving resources

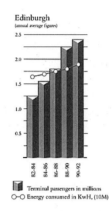

Edinburgh
(annual average figures)

Terminal passengers in millions
O—O Energy consumed in KwH, (10M)

The success of BAA's energy conservation programme can be judged by looking at energy consumption as more and more passengers travel through the Company's airports. For example at Edinburgh, energy consumption went up by only 15 per cent despite a 90 per cent increase in passenger numbers over a 10 year period.

BAA has long recognised the importance of preserving valuable resources, and has introduced various conservation measures as well as commissioning a detailed investigation into the extent to which waste from airports can be recycled. This study will form the basis for a number of new recycling initiatives in the course of this year.

Energy use

In May 1992, BAA signed the Government's "Commitment to Energy Efficiency." The Company's own energy use during 1991/92 was 540 million kWh/year and our airport tenants used a further 660m kWh/year. To ensure that we're using this energy wisely, and thereby helping to reduce air pollution, we've set up energy monitoring throughout our operations. In this way, we can supply managers with the information they need to control energy use more effectively, and set targets for the future. The results can be seen quite clearly at Glasgow, where over the last six years passenger numbers have increased by 50 per cent and terminal facilities have expanded by 60 per cent, but consumption of energy has only increased by 6.2 per cent.

Water consumption

Just as we've done with energy, BAA has also developed ways to save water. A survey of water use at Gatwick led to a £40,000 programme to stop leaks from the mains, saving 140 million litres of water and cutting our water bill by £120,000 a year. Elsewhere, trials with automatic controls on flushing systems in toilets at Gatwick and Heathrow airports have shown that water consumption can be reduced by as much as 90 per cent. At Heathrow alone this could save almost 50 million litres a year.

Waste management

Aircraft arrive at airports with large amounts of waste that has to be disposed of. Each year, Heathrow Airport Ltd has to dispose of around 20,000 tonnes of waste, whilst Gatwick Airport Ltd disposes of around 8,000 tonnes. We have initiated a detailed study of waste management and the type of waste at all our airports to determine possibilities for recycling. BAA also has responsibility for litter control at its airports. With cleaning bills adding up to more than £15 million a year, we are obviously keen to encourage people to dispose of litter in a responsible way. At our airports, we have been actively promoting awareness campaigns such as Tidy Travel Week.

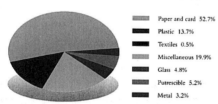

Paper and card 52.7%
Plastic 13.7%
Textiles 0.5%
Miscellaneous 19.9%
Glass 4.8%
Putrescible 5.2%
Metal 3.2%

This chart shows a breakdown of the types of waste handled by contractors for Gatwick Airport. Further research is looking at opportunities for recycling a proportion of this waste.

FIG. 8.1.3 *This is another page from BAA's Environmental Report for 1993, which states its policy of reducing the consumption of resources and, wherever possible, recycling materials.*

1 The business's commitment to make environmental concerns a central part of all planning activities.
2 An undertaking that a series of processes will be put in place to identify possible environmental threats.
3 An assurance that the policy is fully endorsed by both senior management and the board of directors.
4 A commitment that these policies will be communicated to all employees.
5 A commitment to seek assistance and guidance from external agencies as a matter of priority when required.

One of the problems relating to environmental protection is the constant development of new production processes which are not covered under existing environmental protection legislation. Initially, governments and authorities rely on the social responsibility of organisations to carry out their activities in the spirit of environmental protection and existing legislation. It is inevitable that the development of legislation lags behind the development of industrial processes.

TRADES DESCRIPTIONS ACT

There are some key considerations and obligations to be noted here. They relate to the products and services which the business supplies. Essentially, the legislation states the following:

- a product must comply with its description
- a product must be capable of performing to the levels claimed by the manufacturer
- faulty products should be replaced or a refund made to the customer without exception
- products should meet all existing safety standards
- an organisation faces prosecution if it is found to be selling unsafe products

AGE LIMITS

Employees should be 16 years of age in order to be legally in full-time employment. There are some restrictions on the number of working hours for the under-16s in part-time employment. Recently the retirement age has been changed to 65 years. Formerly the retirement age was 60 for women and 65 for men. Individuals, may, of course, work beyond their normal retirement age, but in doing so, there are implications with regard to their pension rights.

INSURANCE IMPLICATIONS

Insurance is, to be frank, an incredibly boring subject. Unfortunately it is not a subject that can be avoided by the business. Sorting out **insurance** should be one of the high priority jobs for anyone starting a new business. If you fail to obtain the correct insurance this could lead to the failure of the business itself. Insurance basically falls into two categories. These are:

1 Insurance **required** by law.
2 Insurance which is **desirable** to cover possible risks or accidents.

Obtaining insurance at the right price and covering the right risks can be tricky. The Association of British Insurers, British Insurance and Investment Brokers Association or the Life Assurance Association can all offer you useful advice in obtaining the right insurance at the right price.

ASSET INSURANCE

Asset insurance attempts to ensure that the business is protected against loss or damage to stock, equipment or processes as a result of various uncontrollable factors. Essentially, there are four different types of asset insurance, these are:

1 *Damage and loss insurance* – which covers the premises and contents of the premises from fire. The term fire used in insurance in actual fact covers floods, lightning, explosions, earthquakes, storms, riots and vandalism.
2 *Theft insurance* – which covers the theft of all removable assets, including computers, machinery, office

student activity

It is wise for organisations to insure various aspects of their business. For an organisation to expose itself to the possibility of theft or fire and their damaging effects is foolhardy.

Barclays, for example, offer the following types of insurance which cover most potential liabilities:

- public liability
- employer's liability
- commercial inclusive policies
- residential building policies
- solo policies for the self-employed
- hotel policies
- nursing and rest home policies
- motor policies
- life insurance policies

In the role of an individual setting up a business for the first time, which of the above would you consider as being essential? Are there any policies available to cover the majority of these risks? In pairs, visit your local banks, insurance brokers and building societies and obtain leaflets. Once you have done this, try to collectively come up with a comprehensive list of insurance needs.

equipment, money and stock. An organisation must ensure that the insurance provides cover for loss both on and off the premises. Additionally, a business must be careful to ensure that the insured value is for the replacement value of items and not the current value. This is known as 'new for old'.

3 *Interruption of business activity insurance* – which may automatically come into operation if the business has suffered damage as a result of a disaster under the fire cover. This insurance also covers the business against loss of business whilst the premises or vital equipment are being replaced or repaired. The cover will also ensure that the business is protected against an interruption in production as a result of the loss of the power supply.

4 *All-risk insurance* – under this type of insurance the business is covered for damage, loss or destruction of items anywhere within the UK. This insurance will compensate the business at full replacement value.

PUBLIC LIABILITY

A business must ensure that it is covered against injury to a member of the **public** as a direct or indirect result of any occurrence or event related to the business. This insurance will also cover loss or damage to the customer's property.

Related to this is the need for the business to obtain employers' liability insurance. It is the responsibility of the employer to compensate an employee who is injured or becomes ill as a result of working for the business. This is particularly true in cases when the business has been judged as being negligent. This cover should amount to at least £2m. The certificate of insurance should also be visible and accessible to all employees.

PRODUCT LIABILITY

In effect, as an extension of public liability insurance, a business needs to insure against claims arising from the use of its products or services. If a customer has suffered injury, loss or damage as a result of faulty products or services, the business will be able to refer this claim to its **product liability** insurance. This insurance also covers the business for any legal costs that may be incurred against claims that are made under consumer protection legislation. Recent damages in the courts have been as high as £1m. It is, therefore, absolutely essential that the organisation protects itself against this potentially crippling burden.

8.1.4 *Discuss the feasibility of proposals with others*

Now that we have looked at the **purposes** of the business plan, the key **objectives**, the **supporting information** and the **legal** and **insurance implications,** we must now begin to put together a **business plan**. In order to do this, we must start with assessing the **feasibility** of your own proposals. To facilitate this the following student activity should be attempted:

 `0:40`

student activity

(PC 8.1.4, COM 3.1)
Using the following list of objectives, you must now present to either your tutor or an external individual the feasibility of your draft plan.

It is hoped that by this stage you have, at least in theoretical form, an idea of the type of business and the nature of the products and services you wish to sell or provide. This initial presentation is aimed at making sure that your plan is realistic. It should be seen as a way of encouraging you to think about your ideas and your ability to discuss them.

Your draft business plan may be delivered in verbal form, but must address all of the following considerations:

1 Likely **demand** for the product.

2 Likely **customers**.
3 Likely **start-up requirements**.
4 Likely year one **expenses** that will need to be financed.
5 The level of sales and profitability needed to ensure survival (in other words your **break-even point**).
6 The **expertise** of individuals required to assist you in setting up the business.
7 The levels of **stock** required.
8 The likely **equipment** needed (including machinery, etc.).
9 The cost and nature of **fixtures and fittings**.

You may find it valuable to write down these considerations and ensure that you have at least given thought to them.

8.1.5 Estimate resource requirements to design, produce, promote and sell the goods or service

RESOURCE REQUIREMENTS

Central issues in the business plan of an organisation are the co-ordination and organisation of the resources that are currently available or those that are required. In this performance criterion we shall attempt to identify the major resource requirements including human, physical and financial.

HUMAN (OWN SKILLS, OTHERS' SKILLS)

Planning the human resources of an organisation basically involves considering not only your own skills but the skills of others. These others may include individuals directly employed by the business, or specialists who are 'bought in' for specific projects or advice. Specifically, we should consider the following:

- the nature and availability of **experienced management**
- the nature and experience of **employees**
- the **employee support systems** that will be required

In order to maximise the effectiveness of a business in the early stage of its development it is essential to deploy human resources. Although we will be considering time-scales a little later on in this Element, it is important to consider the planning needs of human resources in the short and long-term at this point.

The short-term considerations include the skills required in the following areas:

- management
- administration
- marketing
- selling
- accounts
- production
- research and development

It does not necessarily follow that all of these specialists must be supplied by directly employed staff. An organisation may choose to buy in assistance in some of these areas. These will include the following:

- directors who assist only by providing finance
- self-employed individuals contracted to carry out specialist functions
- individuals employed via employment agencies on a temporary basis
- younger or inexperienced employees employed with the intention of training and developing them in specific roles

In terms of its long-term planning an organisation will have to consider the following:

- the maintenance and improvement of **output**
- the maintenance and expansion of **productivity**
- the maximisation of **profit**
- ensuring **job satisfaction**
- maximising the relationship between **labour costs** and productivity

We have looked at the subject of the deployment of human resources in much greater detail in Unit 4. However, relating these human resources needs to the business plan should include the following:

- assessing the precise staff requirements of the organisation
- ensuring the availability and implementation of staff training programmes
- maintaining good industrial relations
- providing staff welfare facilities
- providing competitive wage levels
- establishing mutually acceptable conditions of employment
- adhering to health and safety, employment law and other legal requirements relating to employees

FIG. 8.1.4 *A detail from Barclays Bank's 'Business Plan' form, which considers the cost of employing people or employing their specialised skills.*

PERSONNEL

Estimate the cost of employing any people or buying any services you may need in the first two years

Number of people	Job function	Monthly cost	Annual cost
_____	_____	_____	_____
_____	_____	_____	_____
_____	_____	_____	_____

(Remember to include your own salary and those of any partners you may have in this calculation)

`0:20`

student activity

(PC 8.1.5, COM 3.1)
How many of the above considerations will have to be planned for in the initial stages of the formation of the business? How many of them will be developed as and when the situation arises? Discuss this as a group.

PHYSICAL (MATERIALS, EQUIPMENT)

Planning the **physical resources** will involve consideration of the following requirements:

- premises
- machinery and equipment
- stock
- materials (raw, part-finished and finished)

   `0:45`

student activity

(PC 8.1.5, COM 3.2)
Copy Figure 8.1.5 and attempt to make an initial estimation of the employees required for your intended business. Have you made any decisions which mean that an individual should be an employee when you could really engage his/her services on a less formal basis?

The first major consideration in terms of the physical resources is the **premises**. As we have mentioned earlier, there are a number of legal implications which relate to the nature and use of the premises. Although we will be looking at premises in relation to the production plan in the next Element, perhaps it is a good

Who might you employ?

Name	Role	Age	Total Cost (Salary, NICs etc.)

What experience do they have?

Name	Experience

What specialist skills/qualifications do they have?

Name	Skill / Qualification

FIG. 8.1.5 *A section from Lloyds Bank's 'Business Plan' booklet, which details the role, experience, skills, qualifications and costs of employees.*

idea to look at the fundamentals behind these legal implications now:

1 *Planning* – all premises have a usage designation which is monitored by the local authority. Particular buildings will be considered unsuitable for certain business activities. It should also be remembered that a business operating from the home may render the premises liable for payment of business rates.

2 *Licences* – to trade legally certain businesses may require a licence. The following types of business will require a trading licence which will be monitored by the local authority:

- restaurants, cafes and bars
- food processing and manufacture
- mobile food outlets
- retailers of alcohol
- retailers of tobacco
- nursing homes
- children's nurseries
- scrap metal dealers

3 *Leases, covenants and restrictions* – the lease on a business premises may restrict the business activities allowed. It is also worth considering the length of lease and the possibility of renewing it, before investing considerable sums of money on the improvement of the building. The lease should be available for renewal under agreeable terms and above all, affordable ones. With regard to covenants

FIG. 8.1.6 *This is a section from Barclays Bank's 'Business Plan' form which relates specifically to premises, machinery and vehicles.*

and other restrictions, there may be certain by-laws relating to the building. These may not only restrict the type of business activity allowed, but also relate to any potential development of the site.

4 *Environmental matters* – the location of the premises and the availability of services capable of handling waste and other emissions may make the premises unsuitable. Environmental legislation, for example, does not allow certain business activities to take place in residential areas.

The other major physical consideration relates to the **fixed assets** such as machinery, equipment, materials and vehicles. Specifically, an organisation must consider:

- what machinery, equipment and vehicles should be obtained immediately?
- whether they should be bought or leased
- identifying suppliers who offer the most acceptable terms of purchase

FINANCIAL (CAPITAL REQUIREMENTS)

Planning the **financial resources** involve consideration of the following factors:

- capital available from the **owners** of the business
- **sources** of finance needed

We have covered the main considerations that must be taken into account in the financial planning of resources in Unit 7. Later on in this Unit we will be addressing some of the specific aspects of financial resources planning. At this point, however, we should attempt to identify the following in relation to financial resource planning:

PREMISES/MACHINERY/VEHICLES

Premises:

Where do you intend to locate the business and why? _____

_____

What sort and size of premises will you need? _____

_____

_____

What are the details of any lease, licence, rent, rates and when is the next rent review due? _____

_____

_____

Machinery/Vehicles:

What machinery/vehicles do you require? _____

_____

_____

Are these to be bought or leased and on what terms? _____

_____

_____

_____

How long is their lifespan? _____

- the financial resources required for the purchase and maintenance of **fixed** assets
- the amount of **working capital** required
- how **fixed assets** will be financed
- how **working capital** will be obtained
- **who** will provide the finance

Later in this Unit we will be looking at financial data and forecasting, and, in particular, the following:

- time periods involved
- cash-flow forecasts
- start-up balance sheets
- projected profit and loss accounts
- projected balance sheets

0:30

student activity

(PC 8.1.5, AON 3.1, 3.2, 3.3)
Returning to your own intended business, address the following points:

- the amount of **working capital** needed
- how **fixed assets** would be financed
- **how** working capital will be obtained
- **who** will provide finance

Where would be the best place to start when considering these issues?

8.1.6 *Produce a flowchart illustrating estimated time-scales*

TIME-SCALES

Planning the **time resources** involves undertaking the following tasks:

- accurately **charting** when all other resources will be required
- **co-ordinating** all other resources
- constructing a **time frame** within which all other resources will be needed

Applying a time frame to all of the various resources required to start the business is essential to ensure that the correct resources are available at the right time. The level and complexity of planning needed can be very difficult for new business people and they will require the assistance of qualified specialists to enable them to fully plan the time considerations. Typically, an organisation will use two main techniques for its planning – Critical Path Analysis and Gannt Charts. We shall look at these in some detail:

1 *Critical Path Analysis* – this method relies on the identification of all of the component actions and the minimum time required for each main project. The analysis takes the form of a series of arrows against which are marked the activities and the time required to carry out each activity. Each arrow will come from and go to a node (which is, in effect, an

event). By tracing actions along a series of arrows and events, a business planner is able to identify the maximum time required to carry out particular projects. In addition, activities which take the longest time to complete are identified as critical activities. These will tend to be drawn on the diagram as a thick line. By carefully analysing the completed chart, the planner should be able to identify particular 'bottle-necks' and predict potential future problems.

2 *Gannt Charts* – an alternative method of illustrating the processes and activities in the planning schedule is to create a Gannt Chart. This consists of a number of activities listed against numbered weeks. The activities are cross-referenced against the week in which the activity is intended to begin and end. The process is continued down the list of activities, with the later activities, which rely on the completion of earlier activities, beginning in the week after the previous activity has been completed. Again, it is necessary to identify critical activities which have major implications on the beginning of other activities.

PLANNING

It makes sense to draw up a timetable or control schedule which outlines the tasks, responsibilities and targets which will ensure that the desired progress of the business is maintained. Doing this will also help you to

Critical path analysis

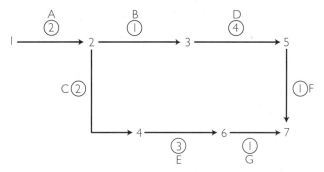

FIG. 8.1.7 *This is a simple critical path analysis network. The numbers on their own refer to the stages. The circled numbers refer to the days that the tasks will take to complete. The letters refer to the tasks themselves.*

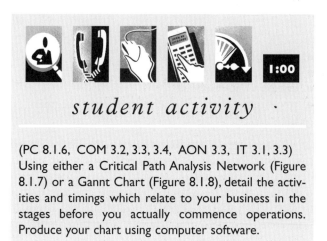

student activity ·

(PC 8.1.6, COM 3.2, 3.3, 3.4, AON 3.3, IT 3.1, 3.3)
Using either a Critical Path Analysis Network (Figure 8.1.7) or a Gannt Chart (Figure 8.1.8), detail the activities and timings which relate to your business in the stages before you actually commence operations. Produce your chart using computer software.

GANTT CHART FOR PLANNING THE CONSTRUCTION OF A HOUSE

Tasks are broken down into the necessary steps

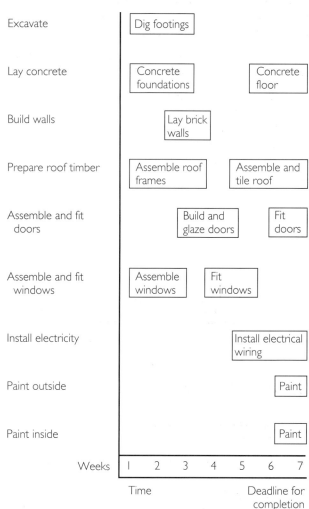

FIG. 8.1.8 *An example of a Gannt Chart.*

identify potential bottle-necks and to decide upon completion dates, which can often be a great source of motivation.

Forecasts, budgets and projections for the business plan can, of course, be set out in any kind of format. During the planning exercise, the plan should be tailored to the needs of the individuals running the business. It is crucial that having settled upon the forecasts and timetable, a systematic method is identified which ensures success. The organisation will already have a set of objectives. These can form the basis of the planning exercise. In this respect, it is logical that the development of the plan, and any calculations which may be needed to create this plan, relate to the fulfilment of the objectives.

Each business will have a different approach to the time-scale of the plan. Some individuals consider a five-year forecast to provide a foundation for continuity. However, looking too far into the future can lead to a series of meaningless calculations that will prove to be unworkable and useless in the future. Practically speak-

ing, a one-year detailed plan, together with indications of the proposed plan for the next two years, will give any new business the necessary clarity of direction and purpose. A forward plan, in essence, only gives an indication of the development of the business and, at best, this should only be an outline and not 'written in blood'.

The overall plan is made up of a number of segments, such as:

- production schedules
- marketing and selling forecasts
- distribution implications
- financial information which refers to the successful reaching of a break-even position

The combination of all of these considerations produces the overall forecast and gives vital information about the resource requirements of the business. It is very important that all of these considerations are discussed, as the plan needs to be developed from a variety of different directions. Likely sales levels, for example, provide us with information on the likely volume of customers as well as figures relating to projected sales and production needs.

PRODUCTION

As we will see shortly, the setting of preliminary sales targets will give us some indication of the production and supply needs. Matching **production** with **sales** can be rather difficult. However, it is essential that a new business attempts to calculate its production needs accurately since being able to fulfil orders on time may mean the difference between success or failure. Equally, if the business builds up too high a stock level at an early stage in its life, then this can be both damaging and expensive.

The main point of this exercise is to try to determine the quantity of products which have to be either produced or assembled in a set period of time. It also gives us information about the quantity of raw materials or components that will have to be bought in order to fulfil these needs. Table 8.1.1 attempts to address these production considerations.

TABLE 8.1.1 *Calculating production costs*

Item to be considered	Basis for calculation
Component costs	Volume
Labour costs and content	Identify production times
Inventory costs	Equipment and stock cover needed
Storage space	Equipment and stock cover needed
Machinery requirements	Volume
Fixed overheads	Space required
Staff costs	Volume
Machinery space required	Utilisation of machinery
Development costs	Development needs/time
Training costs	Manpower level, skills required

MARKETING AND SELLING

For many businesses the **sales forecast** is the most important aspect of their business plan. There are a number of **forecasting models** which may be adopted and which would prove to be of great value in the development of forward plans. The business needs to consider, in addition to its detailed analysis of the first year, the probable sales levels in future years. In other words, the organisation needs to establish what it plans to do in at least the first three years. This is essential as its activities in the first year will determine its activities and success in future years. New businesses, which do not have the benefit of being able to analyse their present

student activity

(PC 8.1.6, COM 3.3, 3.4, IT 3.1, 3.2, 3.3, AON 3.1, 3.2, 3.3)
Using Table 8.1.1 as a guide, design your own table itemising the items you would need to consider for the business of your choice. Can you identify all of them? Are there any other considerations that you feel might be necessary? Produce your table by using a computer software package.

customers, must attempt to make a detailed forecast which links sales to major customers with the following:

- probable **pricing levels**
- **discounts** offered
- **credit** to be provided
- **products** which will sell to each target segment of the market

In our attempt to estimate the benefits and costs of each proposed sales and marketing action, we should begin by considering the resource allocations in both the short and the long-term. We can use a similar model to that which was used for the calculation of production costs and their implications. The considerations are shown in Table 8.1.2.

DISTRIBUTION

As we have already seen, the **distribution policy** of the business is very much related to its production, marketing and selling activities. The choice of distribution method may, of course, depend upon the type of product or service, but, inevitably, there may be a wide variety of different distribution methods available. These need to be assessed in terms of their effectiveness and appropriateness. The business needs to have a clear understanding of what it requires from its distribution network. Perhaps more fundamentally it needs to consider whether its distribution will be carried out as an internal function or provided by an external organisation. Specific requirements may include the following:

- **speed** of distribution
- **efficiency** of distribution
- **safety** of products during distribution

Many organisations rely on specialist distribution companies to ensure that their products reach customers in

TABLE 8.1.2 *Calculating sales and marketing costs and benenfits*

Item to be considered	Basis for calculation
Income from major customers	Volume by customer
Income from other customers	Total volume
Income from possible new customers	Total volume
Income by customer type	Volume by customer type
Possible new customer types	Volume by customer type
Demand by area	Volume by area
Income from individual products	Volume of products sold
Income from new products	Volume of products sold
Price to major customers	Price obtainable
Price to other customers	Price obtainable
Discounts to major customers	Discounts structure
Discounts to other customers	Discounts structure
Credit terms to major customers	Percentage of customers offered 30, 60 or 90 days credit
Credit terms to other customers	Percentage of customers offered 30, 60 or 90 days credit
Advertising expenditure	Advertising costs and returns
Promotional expenditure	Promotional costs and returns
Sales expenditure	Sales costs and returns
Distribution expenditure	Costs of warehouse, employees
Delivery expenditure	Delivery costs, vehicles needed, employees costs
Storage expenditure	Warehouse costs, employee costs, maintenance costs
Sales force expenditure	Employee costs, overheads, training costs
Distributors' expenditure	Training and information costs

student activity

Using Table 8.1.2 as a guide, design your own table, itemising the considerations you would need for the business of your choice. Can you identify all of them? Are there any other considerations that you feel might be necessary?

As you will remember, the break-even point is that point where sufficient goods or services have been sold to cover the costs of sales by the profit generated. The break-even point can most easily be calculated by the use of a graph. The graph in Figure 8.1.9 illustrates the relationship between sales income, fixed costs and variable costs. The point where the volume of sales crosses the line which shows total costs (both fixed and variable) is where sufficient revenue has been generated. Beyond this point the business moves into profit.

It is essential that, regardless of whether a business makes its calculations of the break-even point by means of a table or a graph, the business must show the following:

- a projection of **sales income**
- the **cost of sales**
- **gross profit**
- **net profit**

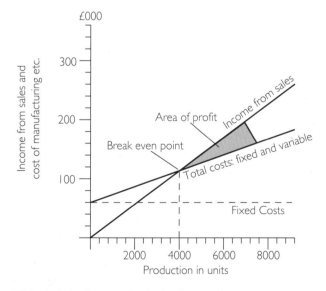

FIG. 8.1.9 *An example of a break-even chart.*

a fast and reliable manner. Some of the benefits which may accrue from using an external organisation far outweigh possible savings which the organisation might enjoy by providing the service itself. These specialist distribution networks offer not only a higher degree of flexibility and responsiveness, but often a more reliable form of security (particularly in terms of insurance, etc.) than any small business could hope to provide.

LEAD TIME TO BREAK-EVEN

One of the principal concerns, not necessarily of the business, but certainly of the providers of finance, is the time period involved before the business reaches a stage at which it covers its costs.

1:00

student activity

(PC 8.1.6, COM 3.2, 3.3, 3.4, AON 3.1, 3.2, 3.3)

To develop the correct pricing plan for your business, you should begin by working out all of your costs. When you know what your costs are, you will be able to work out what your break-even point is. As we have said, this tells you how much you will need to sell before all your costs are covered. You will then be in a position to discover the pricing level required to give you a profit. Unless you identify what your break-even point is, then you may be operating at a loss without realising it.

Your costs can be divided into fixed (overheads) and variable (direct) costs. Fixed costs will include your personal expenses, such as rent, wages and interest charges. These tend to stay the same regardless of your sales level. Variable costs, on the other hand, will change according to your level of sales. The most obvious variable cost change is in the cost of the materials you will need to purchase, but variable costs also include transport, postage and additional labour. Remember that the price you charge will have to cover not only these variable costs, but also your overheads.

In order to facilitate the calculation of your break-even point, you need to make a table that lists the costs of the following:

Personal drawings (wages, etc.)	National insurance
Tax	Stationery
Advertising	Telephone
Rent	Rates
Heating and lighting	Vehicle depreciation
Petrol/diesel	Servicing
Road fund tax	Insurance
Business insurance	Bad debts
Depreciation of equipment	Bank loan
Bank charges	Accountants fees
Total costs	
Price per hour/day/product	
Break-even point	

To help you follow the logic behind all this, we have taken an example from Barclays' leaflet, 'Setting Up and Running Your Business'.

Monty Collyer Hand Car Wash and Valet Services

Item of expenditure	Cost (£)
Personal drawings (wages, etc.)	10,000
National insurance	294
Tax	500
Stationery	100
Advertising	400
Telephone	320
Rent	–
Rates	–
Heating and lighting	–
Vehicle depreciation	1,000
Petrol/diesel	900
Servicing	300
Road fund tax	130
Insurance	320
Business insurance	140
Materials	200
Bad debts	–
Depreciation of equipment	200
Bank loan	200
Bank charges	100
Accountants' fees	300
Total costs	15,404

Monty's essential personal drawings to cover his family's mortgage, food and clothes amount to £10,000. He travels from door to door offering a personal car wash and valet service and expects to work for 46 weeks a year, allowing for holidays, sickness and poor weather. He anticipates that he will work on average 38 hours per week, taking into account the time that he spends travelling from one car to another. He estimates he can wash and valet one average-sized car every 2 hours. His annual work output is, therefore:

46 weeks $\times$ 38 hours $\times$ 0.5 cars per hour = 874

therefore, 15,404 ÷ 874= £17.62 per car

Break-even point   = £17.62 per car

After researching his market, Monty believes that he can charge £20 per car.

Price per hour/day/product = £20 per car

Monty, therefore, makes a profit of £2.38 per car.

Using the formula above, and taking Monty as an example, calculate your own break-even point.

8.1.7 Identify potential support for the plan

POTENTIAL SUPPORT

No business, whatever its size, can realistically expect to be able to form a full business plan by itself. It will inevitably require the assistance of specialists to formulate particular aspects of the plan. In some cases, some of the skills needed may be available within the organisation, but may not yet be identified. In other cases, different organisations will be able to offer support and assistance with procedural or legal matters. Alternatively, an organisation may require the assistance of specifically qualified individuals to undertake monitoring and development tasks on its behalf.

OWN ORGANISATION

Certain individuals or departments within the organisation itself will have been identified as being the source of assistance for particular aspects of the business plan. We considered the responsibilities of individuals and departments when we considered their job roles within the organisational structure in Unit 4. Specifically an organisation would expect the following assistance from each key department:

1 *Accounts* – individuals carrying out accounts functions should be able to identify and construct all necessary profit and loss accounts and balance sheets. They should also be able to give a clear indication of the cost implications of the implementation of particular business plans.

2 *Legal* – the company secretary should be abreast of all current legislation relevant to business activity and should be able to advise the organisation whether new business activities will involve compliance with additional legislation.

3 *Personnel* – the personnel department or personnel manager should be able to identify any additional human resource requirements of any planned new business activities.

4 *Production* – the production manager will be able to advise as to the feasibility of new production requirements. He/she will be able to identify possible suppliers of materials and equipment required to carry out new functions.

5 *Design* – designers in their research and development role will probably have been consulted at an early stage to assess the viability of new products. They will be able to identify any cost implications in consultation with the production manager.

6 *Sales and marketing* – the sales and marketing department or managers will have a clear idea of whether potential new business projects will meet the needs and approval of proposed customers. They will be able to offer advice in the formulation of the marketing plan which we will find to be an integral part of the overall business plan.

7 *Distribution* – there may be distribution considerations, particularly if the organisation is proposing to produce and provide new products or services different from those which it has previously provided. The distribution manager may have to consider alternative distribution and transportation methods in order to ensure prompt and safe delivery of the proposed new products.

8 *Administration* – the administration at various levels of the organisation will be able to provide a key support function to the formulation of the business plan, whether simply in the presentation of the business plan, or whether there are additional considerations that relate directly to the main administration functions.

student activity

(PC 8.1.7, COM 3.2, IT 3.1, 3.2, 3.3)
How would you identify the experience available within your organisation? Devise a skills audit sheet for existing members of staff to detail their specialist knowledge. Present your audit sheet using a computer software package.

OTHER ORGANISATIONS AND SPECIALISTS (FINANCIAL, LEGAL, MARKETING, PRODUCTION)

Sometimes an organisation formulating a business plan may need to call in other organisations or individuals, either because it is very small or because it is deficient in certain areas. These individuals may fulfil many of the functions considered above, but others may be specialists in particular areas of business development. Examples of other organisations or individuals who may be called in to assist the formulation of a business plan include:

- financial advisers
- insurance specialists

- tax consultants
- solicitors
- architects and surveyors
- design specialists
- management consultants
- marketing consultants
- small business advisers
- local authority small business initiatives advisers
- advisers from specific industries
- co-operatives advisers

You will find a much more complete list of potential sources of information in Element 8.3.

These individuals or organisations will be employed only if it is strictly cost effective to do so and if there are positive benefits for the employing organisation. As we have said, these benefits may relate to the specialist knowledge they possess, or the additional advisory skills they can offer.

It is normal for banks and other providers of financial assistance to be able to advise on the employment of particular specialist organisations or individuals. They may well have their own advisers available.

student activity

(PC 8.1.7, COM 3.2, 3.4, AON 3.1, 3.3)
Figure 8.1.10 lists some sources of information, but, as we mentioned in the last section, there are other specialists and consultants who offer advice and support. Using your local Yellow Pages, try to identify any specialists or consultants who may be able to offer advice and support directly related to your own business. You may also try to find out how much it would cost to use their services.

FIG. 8.1.10 *There is a great deal of reliable business information available at low cost, or in some cases free of charge. Much of this information is produced by organisations which are seeking to sell their services and use this free information as a promotional tool. The available information covers all aspects of business activities, including law, finance, taxation, funding and information technology.*

Association of British Chambers of Commerce, 212a Shaftesbury Avenue, London WC2H 8EW (01-240 5831).

British Franchise Association, Franchise Chambers, 75a Bell Street, Henley-on-Thames, Oxon RG9 2BD (0491 579049).

British Overseas Trade Board, 1 Victoria Street, London SW1 (01-215 7877).

Business in the Community (BIC), 227a City Road, London EC1V 1JU (01-253 3716).
(BIC will be able to provide you with the name and address of your nearest local Enterprise Agency).

In Scotland contact Scottish Business in the Community (SCOTBIC), Romano House, 43 Station Road, Corstophine, Edinburgh EH12 7ES (031-334 9876).

Companies Registration Office, Companies House, 55 City Road, London EC1Y 1BB (01-253 9393).

In Scotland contact the Registrar of Companies for Scotland, 102 George Street, Edinburgh EH2 3JD (031-225 5774).

In Northern Ireland contact the Department of Commerce, Chichester House, 43-47 Chichester Court, Belfast BT1 4PJ (0232 234121).

Co-operative Development Agency, Broadmead House, 21 Panton Street, London SW1Y 4DR (01-839 2988).

Highlands and Islands Development Board, Bridge House, Bank Street, Inverness IV1 1QR (0463 34171).

Institute of Export, Export House, Clifton Street, London EC2 4HI (01-247 9812).

London Enterprise Agency, 4 Snow Hill, London EC1A 2BS (01-236 3000).

Mid Wales Development, Ladywell House, Newtown, Powys SY16 1JB (0686 626965).

Rural Development Commission, 141 Castle Street, Salisbury SP1 3TP (0722 336255). The RDC has regional offices throughout the country.

Small Business Bureau, 32 Smith Square, London SW1P 3HH (01-222 9000).

Small Firms Service, dial 100 and ask for Freefone Enterprise. Alternatively here are the regional addresses:

Birmingham – 6th Floor, Ladywood House, Stephenson Street, Birmingham B2 4DT (021-643 3344).

Bristol – 6th Floor, The Pithay, Bristol BS1 2NB (0272 294546).

Cambridge – 24 Brooklands Avenue, Cambridge CB2 2BU (0223 63312).

Cardiff – 16 St. David's House, Wood Street, Cardiff CF1 1ER (0222 396116).

Glasgow – 57 Bothwell Street, Glasgow G2 6TU (041-248 6014).

Leeds – 1 Park Row, City Square, Leeds LS1 5NR (0532 445151).

Liverpool – 1 Old Street, Liverpool L3 9HJ (051-236 5756).

London – Ebury Bridge House, 2-18 Ebury Bridge Road, London SW1W 8QD (01-730 8451).

Manchester – 3rd Floor, 320-325 Royal Exchange Buildings, St. Ann's Square, Manchester M2 7AH (061-832 5282).

Newcastle – 22 Newgate Shopping Centre, Newcastle upon Tyne NE1 1ZP (0632 325353).

Nottingham – Severns House, 20 Middle Pavement, Nottingham NG1 7DW (0602 506181).

Reading – Abbey Hall, Abbey Square, Reading RG1 3BE (0734 591733).

Stevenage – Business and Technology Centre, Bessemer Drive, Stevenage, Herts SG1 2DX (0438 743377).

Wales – The Welsh Development Agency, Treforest Industrial Estate, Pontypridd, Mid Glamorgan CF37 5UT (0443 852666).

Scotland – The Scottish Development Agency, 102 Telford Road, Edinburgh EN4 2NP (031-343 1911).

Northern Ireland – The Local Enterprise Development Unit, Lamont House, Purdys Lane, Newtownbreda, Belfast BT8 4AR (0232 691031).

Rural Development Commission, 141 Castle Street, Salisbury SP1 3TP (0122 336255). The RDC has regional offices throughout the country.

8.1.8 Prepare an action plan identifying actions to be taken to finalise the business plan for its presentation

In writing a **business plan**, you should remember that it includes your long-term objectives, your estimates and your forecasts in a written format. Note that, no matter how detailed the business plan may be, it is not written in stone. Every forecast or estimate that you make may be subject to change, particularly in the light of the experience you will gain once the business is up and running. Your estimates and forecasts should be your best guess based on the information which you currently have. By writing all this down, you are better able to clarify in your own mind the nature of the business and, hopefully, to identify many of the potential weaknesses of your ideas.

The initial plan obviously needs to be well thought through and logical. You need to have devoted sufficient time and resources to organising the business plan. This can best be done by preparing an action plan which identifies the actions that you will have to take in the preparation of the business plan to present to a potential provider of finance or other interested parties.

In the next Element we will be looking at a specific five-part business plan for a small business enterprise. At this point, you need to have assured yourself that you have considered the following points in preparation for that final draft. We will return to the subject of an action plan itself as soon as we have identified what should actually be in the business plan. Essentially, we can identify the main headings for consideration as:

1 A brief **summary** of the business plan which highlights:

- the **nature** of the business
- the potential **market**
- the forecast **profit** figures
- the **finance** required
- the **financial returns** for investors or lenders

2 The **history**, which includes:

- **when** the business was **established**
- a summary of **past performance**
- an indication of **future performance** – this section which is necessary for existing businesses seeking to obtain additional finance, may not be relevant to you in establishing a new business

3 The **management,** which includes:

- your past **employment**
- your **qualifications**
- your **business record**
- your past **achievements**
- details of **employees**
- **weaknesses** identified and **solutions** proposed

4 The **product** or **service**, which includes:

- a non-technical **description** of the products or services offered
- an indication of the **unique nature** of the product or service offered
- a survey of the **competition**
- a description of how products or services will be **developed** in the future
- a statement of patent **trade marks** and registered marks applied for

5 The **marketing** angle, which includes:

- the size of the **market** and its potential for **growth**
- an **analysis** of the **market** by sector
- an identification of the likely **customers**
- an investigation into the **competitors** and their likely responses
- the **promotion** and **advertising** proposed
- a description of your **salespeople** and their sales pitch
- your **pricing policy**

6 **Operational considerations**, which include:

- your location and **premises**
- an identification of potential **suppliers**
- your **manufacturing** requirements
- equipment and machinery required

7 The **financial analysis**, which includes:

- monthly **profit and loss** forecasts
- **profit forecasts** for at least three years
- **cash-flow forecasts** for at least two years
- forecast **balance sheet** for at least two years
- the last three years' **audited accounts** (if applicable)
- **assumptions** you have made in the preparation of your forecasts
- a **risk assessment** which could alter your figures

8 The **future prospects**, which include:

- what are your short, medium and long-term **objectives**?
- **finance** needed, when and why
- **prospects** for investors or lenders

Central to the formulation of a business plan is the need to be sure that the plan is **workable**. We can use this word 'sure' to compare your proposals with a real workable plan. Taking the letters of the word SURE we can make the following comments:

S – is the business soundly based?

U – do you and the business understand what it is actually doing?

R – is the plan realistic and credible?

E – do you have the expertise available?

student activity

(PC 8.1.8, COM 3.2, 3.3, 3.4, AON 3.1, 3.2, 3.3, IT 3.1, 3.2, 3.3)

Design an action plan form which will enable you to ensure that you have covered all aspects of the planning for the preparation of your business plan relating to the business of your choice. Your form should be word processed and must address the following aspects of planning:

1 **Tasks** to be completed.

2 **Individual responsible** for the completion of the tasks.

3 The **sequence** in which tasks will have to be completed.

4 The **time-scale** involved.

5 A section which allows for the **monitoring** of the action plan should it be necessary.

6 **Resource implications** for the completion of the tasks.

7 Potential **sources of advice** and support (when will these sources need to be identified and contacted?).

If you wish, you may visit a bank or building society, who will be able to give you a Starting Your Own Business pack, which includes their own particular version of a business plan, together with advice on completion of the form and possible sources of advice should you require it.

Once you have designed and produced your action plan form, you should attempt to complete it before embarking on the draft version of your actual business plan.

ELEMENT 8.1

assignment

(PC 8.1.1–8, COM 3.1–4, AON 3.1–3, IT 3.1–3)
This Element requires you to initiate a business idea. Essentially, this means:

- converting the idea into a planned activity
- identifying support for that activity
- developing realistic ideas

To begin with, you will need support from your tutor, but specialists such as bank managers or building society managers may be able to help you by providing support and advice. Some students may be involved in Business Education Partnerships or other programmes including Young Enterprise. If you are involved in either of these types of programme, then you will be able to receive valuable advice from them on how to execute your ideas, as well as obtaining financial support.

You should not get 'bogged down' in providing evidence of your design, production, sales and marketing effort, but you must show an understanding of these concerns in your initial business plan draft. The first stage of the draft of your business plan needs to outline the goods or services that will be provided as well as addressing the issue of supporting marketing and financial information.

TASK 1

(PC 8.1.6)
You should identify the planned time-scales involved, in relation to planning, production, market-ing, selling, distribution and lead time to break-even.

TASK 2

(PC 8.1.3)
You should consider the legal and insurance impli-cations.

TASK 3

(PC 8.1.5)
You should provide estimates for resource require-ments.

TASK 4

(PC 8.1.7)
You should identify possible support for the plan from financial, legal, marketing or production spe-cialists.

TASK 5

(PC 8.1.8)
You should identify action points which mark the steps required to complete your business plan.

TASK 6

(PC 8.1.1–8.1.2)
You should support your draft plan by a statement which explains the purposes of producing this busi-ness plan and your business objectives. You should also identify the supporting information from which you have prepared this plan.

Produce and present a business plan

8.2.1 Describe and explain business objectives for a business enterprise

BUSINESS OBJECTIVES

A business plan offers the organisation an opportunity to identify a series of **objectives** with the aim of improving the overall objectives of the organisation. For new businesses this essential objective setting may be not only a basic requirement of any providers of finance but also of fundamental importance to the eventual success or failure of the enterprise. Remember that objectives may change and that they are important for purposes of comparison. They also often depend upon the age and development of the organisation, as well as upon any particular problems or opportunities the organisation may have at any one time.

SUPPLY OF GOODS OR SERVICE

For an existing business the **nature of the business activity** undertaken by the organisation may already be predetermined. However, for an organisation entering the market as a new business, this objective may be the first of many to be considered. An analysis of present market conditions and the comparative successfulness of existing businesses operating in related areas will be of prime importance.

Additionally, to enter a market which provides particular products or services, an organisation will need to ensure that it can source all required resources to maintain production levels.

In relation to the **supply of products or services** the organisation will also have to look at distribution and see whether it can identify cost-effective methods of bringing products and services to potential customers. A great deal of basic information can be provided in statistical form by the government or agencies working on behalf of the government. Equally, a careful analysis of competitors' activities and their published materials, such as company reports, may prove to be valuable. Trends in customer spending can also be useful data on which to base the criteria needed to establish objectives in relation to the supply of products or services.

ACHIEVE SALES VOLUME

One of the objectives of the organisation may be to achieve particular levels of **sales** in terms of units sold or in order to obtain full economies of scale. The nature of the production process may be such that it requires the equipment and machinery to be running at full capacity in order to maintain efficiency. The sales volume generated by this production level may lead to the saturation of the market with the organisation's products. Perhaps the organisation can achieve this volume of sales by supplying other organisations with part-finished products. Food manufacturing organisations achieve high sales volume by supplying 'own-label' products to wholesalers and retailers. The need to achieve high sales volume is particularly common in organisations which produce relatively low-value products.

ACHIEVE SALES VALUE

Sales value is an alternative method of measuring the activity level of the organisation. As we mentioned in Element 8.1, maximising sales value is related to maximising total revenue. This concept is as valid for organisations that produce high-value products as for organisations that produce low-value products. In both cases, organisations may have to achieve high sales value in order to service any loans, ensure maximum use of machinery, or maintain their competitive edge.

Achieving high sales value is particularly important when the organisation has only a small mark-up or profit margin for each unit. Obviously, high sales value will address this problem. Whilst the organisation may not achieve higher profits per unit, it will achieve higher profits , because it will be selling larger quantities of the product. Equally, an organisation which has to reduce its prices and, therefore, its profit margin, may find a higher sales value or total sales value to be crucial in maintaining its level of profit and efficiency.

MAKE PROFIT

Although **making a profit** may seem to be one of the most obvious objectives of any organisation, this need not be so. As we have already mentioned in Element 8.1, certain organisations do not necessarily consider the maximisation of profits to be essential as a measurement of success. Indeed, any, or all, of the objectives identified both in Unit 2 and in Element 8.1 may take precedence over the profit maximisation objective. The importance of profit is also very much dependent upon the stage of development of the organisation. In the early stages of the organisation's life it is unreasonable to assume that profit maximisation is a key consideration. **Survival** may be the main goal.

BREAK EVEN

Breaking even, or even generating enough profit to cover expenditure, may be an objective for an organisation in its early years. By simply breaking even, however, an organisation is not providing additional finance on which to base expansion. It will have to rely on alternative sources of finance if it needs to service any further loan requirements.

Breaking even may be a criterion laid down by a parent company or an organisation providing finance. At a particular stage in the development of a new organisation, the parent company may be satisfied with the level of activity which ensures the continued survival of that operation. This is particularly true of organisations suffering from periods of economic down-turn. Again, as we mentioned in Element 8.1, other organisations may be able to operate at a loss because they are subsidised by a parent organisation, the government or the EU.

MEET TIME-SCALES

Organisations, particularly those that have agreements with providers of finance, may be obliged to meet certain **targets** by a particular date. There may be particular times in the future when the providers of finance will review the organisation's loan situation. It will, therefore, be essential that the organisation has geared itself to maximum efficiency and productivity by these dates.

An alternative way of looking at time-scales is in connection with the fulfilment of orders and deliveries to customers. When a customer requires products to be supplied by a particular date, it is in the organisation's best interests to ensure that these dates are met. Failure to do so may not only result in cancellation of the present order, but will also inevitably mean that the customer will be wary of doing business with this organisation again. Business is a rather small world and unreliable suppliers will be the subject of conversations in both formal and informal situations. It is often the way that good news does not travel very well, but bad news travels extremely quickly.

Another aspect of meeting time-scales may be that the organisation has set itself a series of 'milestones' which it intends to pass by a particular date. These may be related to the development of a product or a market or the achieving of a particular sales total. The organisation must monitor and review these time-scales in relation to any activity at regular intervals.

8.2.2 Outline a marketing plan for a business enterprise

MARKETING PLAN

A marketing plan, or to give it its full name, a **sales and marketing plan** will assist management in controlling a business in a much more efficient manner. Specifically, this part of the plan will cover the following:

- focusing upon the main factors which need to be addressed to remain competitive
- identification and systematic examination of the business's expansion opportunities
- preparation of a series of counter-measures to address potential problems in the future
- setting of identifiable goals and results which it is hoped to achieve from them
- identification of the precise criteria to be met in the achievement of goals and objectives
- setting out of a series of measurement systems to monitor the progress of achieving goals and objectives

- provision of necessary information and supporting data which can be used in negotiations with providers of finance

Drawing up the marketing plan consists of a number of steps which are common regardless of the business's activity or marketing involvement. These are:

1 An assessment of the organisation's **potential performance**.
2 An assessment of the organisation's **historical performance** (if applicable).
3 A detailed analysis of the **competition's performance**.
4 A global investigation of the **market potential** and any possible opportunities or threats.
5 A clear indication of the main **objectives** of the owners of the business.
6 The development and proposed realisation of the business's **strategic plans**.
7 The writing of an **action plan** which details tactics required to fulfil the strategic aims of the business.

student activity

(PC 8.2.2, COM 3.2, 3.4, AON 3.1, 3.2, 3.3)
To assist you in the formulation of a sales and marketing plan it would be advisable to consider the following questions:

- do you understand the **market?**
- what **type of people** buy your product or service?
- do you know **when** they buy?
- do you know **how often** they buy?
- have you **assessed** the product or service they are buying at present?
- what is the **size** of your market?
- is the market **growing**, contracting or is static?
- is it possible to obtain a big enough **market share** in order to be successful?
- does the market have any discernible geographical **boundaries?**
- is the market **local**, national or international?
- what are the likely **costs** in reaching this market?
- do you know how much your customers will be prepared to **pay** for your product or service?
- can you supply a product or service which the market **wants?**
- can you supply the produce or service **when** the market needs it?
- do you have any existing **orders?**
- do you **understand** the product or service you are supplying?
- do you know who you are **competing** against?
- is your product **at least as good**, if not better, than your competitors?
- are there any **legal implications** concerning the sales and marketing of your product or service?
- have you ever sold this product or service **before?**
- can you be assured that you can follow up your existing line of products or services with new **innovations?**

DEMAND FOR PRODUCT OR SERVICE

Researching a market which an organisation believes to contain profitable opportunities is a fundamental task upon which to base a marketing plan, or indeed, a business itself. Some initial criteria to consider are:

- is the market **growing** or is it large already?

- is it supplied by organisations which are either outdated or **inefficient?**
- is the market a **niche** which has not been considered by other organisations so far?
- is the market heavily dependent upon **pricing levels** which determine whether a customer buys one product or another?
- is the market supplied by **branded products** or by products that do not command considerable levels of customer loyalty?
- is the market dominated by a handful of **large suppliers** or is it supplied by numerous smaller competitors?

Perhaps the first place to start is to determine the **market size**. This can be measured either by the **number** of units sold in that market, or the total **value** of that market (in monetary terms).

Estimating the **potential of the market** is a somewhat more difficult task, as it is unlikely that everyone within that market is ever likely to buy your product. Focusing on a particular segment of the market may be the best course of action. Although this may not give you an estimated market potential in terms of sales, the organisation is in a stronger position to take charge of that market segment and become a market leader.

The **market structure** itself is very complex. There are, inevitably, many links in the selling chain before the customer is reached. Even when an organisation sells direct, there may be distributors, agents or dealers through which the product passes before it reaches the retail outlet and then the customer. Knowing how this structure works will enable the organisation to establish, or at least estimate, the potential value of sales. Direct routes can enable you to fix a selling price as well as to estimate the number of products you may be able to sell. If you know this, you will also know the value of sales, so that forecasting potential demand would be easier. When the organisation has to work through a network of distributors then the selling price needs to be low enough to allow each layer of the distribution chain to earn some income, but still allow the product to reach the customer at a reasonable price.

Distribution networks constantly evolve and a comprehensive research study should be undertaken to help the organisation formulate its own sales plan.

Unless the organisation's product is totally new and innovative it is inevitable that it will **share the market** with a number of other businesses. To be able to forecast potential demand, the organisation needs to establish the present market share of the competitors. Knowing this, the organisation will be able to measure how successful its competitors have been. The measurement of market share may be comparatively easy, but **achieving** a **greater market share** is not only a longer-term goal, but also significantly more difficult.

You may have already realised that **market structure**, **market size** and **share of the market** never remain the same. Yesterday, today and tomorrow may be totally different in all respects. Trying to look into the future can be assisted by looking at the past and then projecting the lessons you have learnt into the future. More generally, the economy, legislation and many other external influences may affect the three key considerations. Trying to guess market trends in an environment when there are no external influences would be an easy job. However, this is not reality. Making a realistic forecast of how much the organisation can sell, when it will be able to achieve these sales and how much will have to be spent to achieve these sales, can be a bewildering experience. New businesses, often optimistic of their chances of achieving high sales and market share, are nearly always disappointed.

Time-scales relating to the organisation's objectives should always be doubled. By taking this less optimistic line, the organisation may be able to surprise itself. In any case, ensuring that sufficient cash is available to keep a business going until it reaches the break-even point must be a fundamental consideration. Obviously providers of finance look for a balance between optimism and pessimism with regard to the demand for a product or service. As we have mentioned earlier, looking sufficiently attractive to potential providers of finance is one thing, but achieving your claims is another.

It may be a very good idea to carry out some kind of **test trial** to determine the potential demand for the product or service. If the organisation is intending to set up expensive and complex production facilities or order in large quantities of raw materials, then the last thing it needs to do is to fail in its initial estimation of demand. Before substantial investment in the organisation is undertaken, it is a good idea to satisfy yourself, or, indeed, your lenders, that demand does exist. Test trials will also help define the sales cycle, which is the length of time between the organisation's first contact with a customer and the receipt of an order from him/her.

NAMING

As most businesses offer more than one product or service, the identification of each product or service is essential. This means assigning a **product name** or **brand name** to each of them. This naming process will also help to identify some of the advantages or benefits which may accrue from the use of the product or service. This is often known as the '**unique selling proposition**' (USP), which helps the business to position the product or service in the market-place.

Considerable market research will have already been undertaken to ensure that, at least for the most part, the organisation's perception of the product or service matches that of the customer.

FIG. 8.2.1 *Kwik-Fit's name aptly describes the whole ethos behind the operation.*

As can be seen from Figure 8.2.1, the naming of a business also has considerable implications for success or failure. If you want the name of your business or product to encapsulate emotional or rational feelings about the product, then considerable thought needs to be given to this name. The customer needs to associate your name with good feelings. You should select a name that does not cause annoyance or irritation.

Another aspect to consider is whether your business and major product should share the same name. There is no right or wrong answer to this. However, a new business may not have the resources to create and support two different brand images. In any event, having two different names could prove to be confusing.

When you have carried out market research, you may have considered the necessity of having a **logo** or a logotype. This means that your company or product name is always shown in the same typeface, colour or shape. Your logo should be memorable, slightly unusual and, above all, recognisable. Many small businesses cannot afford the expense of employing a designer to come up with a clever logo. To begin with, any reasonably competent individual who has access to a fairly basic desktop publishing software program can create a bewildering range of different logo designs. A professionally produced logo may cost a great deal of money to create in the first place and also to reproduce.

Some of the key points to consider in choosing a name for your product or business include the following:

- although the name may not create a positive feeling it should not create a negative one
- if you are going to use an existing word or phrase it is best to try it out first
- brain-storming sessions are useful in the production of a list of names for consideration
- you should ensure that the name is not being used by anyone else
- you should avoid the use of initials in your name
- you should be aware that people looking through the Yellow Pages or a similar source of information will inevitably contact those at the beginning of the alphabet first

- you should make sure that your name does not mean something that you did not intend it to mean, particularly in a foreign language
- you should avoid the use of complicated words since customers may have to spell this word, particularly when they are writing you a cheque!
- you should consider using capital letters since these have a tendency to stand out more

PRICING

In setting a **price** or deciding upon a **pricing policy**, you will find that there are a number of factors which will determine where you are in the price range of products generally available. These are:

- your **position** in the market
- the **price sensitivity** of your customers
- the point in its **life cycle** that your product or service has reached
- how your product compares to the **competition**
- what your **price** conveys to the customers

As we have seen in Unit 1, a business may adopt a wide variety of different pricing strategies. Regardless of your choice of pricing strategy, there is one underpinning criterion which you should consider. You must price your product to appeal to the **maximum** number of potential customers. You can make bigger profits if you lower the price, or you can maintain reasonable profits by establishing an average price. If your prices are raised to too high a level, then your profitable business may be the target of competitors who are able to undercut you.

Even if you offer a unique product or service, and can initially charge quite high prices there will be a time when you will have to reduce your prices, as your product or service will not remain unique for very long. There is no point in trying to demand high prices when your product or service does not have a technological or competitive advantage.

On the other hand, if you establish a policy of low prices you are accepting that your product will only just cover its direct costs and make a small contribution to overheads. Low pricing should thus be considered as a last resort if you can actually demand a higher price.

In working out your pricing structure you will, of course have referred to your break-even point. You should remember that direct costs and indirect costs and contribution to overheads are vital if the business is to succeed.

You can justify selling your products or services cheaply if you have spare capacity. In this situation, any sale will contribute to your overheads. This should not be a long-term solution. If you are operating in a market where competition is strong, you may be forced to sell your products and services at low prices. In many markets customers will communicate with one another and aim to force their suppliers to reduce prices. It is very difficult to combat this. Price cutting will trigger off a price war between you and your competitors. A new business will not be able to sustain this price war for very long.

Clearly, if you have excess stock, or poor selling lines of products or services, then price cutting is a possibility. Before reducing prices, however, you should consider using an alternative method and/or market to counteract this down-turn in sales.

Prices should not necessarily be decided on the basis of cost alone. There has to be sufficient **profit margin**. If you have set your prices on the basis of costs, remember that your costs are only forecasts and these can be wrong. You may discover that, having set a price based on forecast costs, you have not covered all of your overheads.

A useful guide in setting your prices is as follows:

1 Look at the position your product or service holds in the market.
2 Has your product achieved a reputation of reliability and has it a good image?
3 Do your customers perceive your product or service as being of good quality?
4 Are you planning to make alterations to your product or services which will affect their position in the market?
5 How do the competitors rate against your products and services?
6 Is there a definable price structure in the market?
7 Where, within the price range of currently available products and services, are you going to pitch your product or service?
8 Decide on some particular prices, then estimate the volume of sales, costs and profit margin, as well as levels of profit for each of these prices.
9 Then choose your price.
10 Finally, test your price out on a test market to allow you to assess the reaction to that price from your customers.

student activity

(PC 8.2.2, AON 3.1, 3.2)
Using the above list, try to establish your pricing policy and the probable reactions and volume of sales.

PACKAGING

Packaging is important, since it offers the business the opportunity not only to give information to the customer, but also to reinforce any image or design qualities. Packaging should be an integral part of the business's **promotional methods**. If you refer back to Unit 3, you will find some specific information regarding the uses and functions of packaging.

Only one hundred years ago packaging was fairly boring. It just involved the printing of the trader's name and product name on a plain bag or carton. In these days of mass production and highly demanding consumer markets, manufacturers have realised that products can sell much better if they have identifiable logos, slogans and names. The packaging reinforces the advertising campaigns and assists point-of-sale merchandising and brand image.

Environmental concerns relating to packaging, particularly in terms of whether the materials used can be recyled, its design and construction, are beginning to oblige manufacturers to produce 'green' packaging. Some retailers in the UK, such as The Body Shop, encourage customers to use old bottles and containers for repeat purchases. Even supermarkets such as Safeway and Sainsbury's offer reusable carrier bags and, indeed, it is not unknown for customers to receive a small discount from their shopping bill if they take away their goods in a box left in one of the box disposal bins near the cash registers.

You may feel that packaging may not be of particular concern to your proposed business. This will be particularly true if you are offering a service rather than selling products. It very much depends upon where you draw the line between packaging and sales literature or promotional materials. Is a folder which contains details of the services you offer packaging or sales literature? You will need to decide this.

PROMOTING

If you refer back to Unit 3, you will find a comprehensive review of all of the viable **promotional activities.**

Many organisations fail to appreciate the value of regularly contacting local newspapers or trade journals with news stories in the form of press releases focusing on their successes. Contrary to opinion, newspapers and magazines are often desperately short of news material and will often print an interesting story, particularly if it is accompanied by a photograph. Exposure in the media can generate interest not only within the industry, but also among the general public – something that can often be very difficult to achieve through conventional advertising.

Many organisations develop a rather fixed attitude towards promotional expenditure. Organisations which manufacture fmcgs (fast moving consumer goods) spend the bulk of their promotional budget on media advertising without really researching the effectiveness of this form of spending.

Research has shown that there is a distinction between **above-the-line expenditure** (this is advertising in the media) and **below-the-line methods** (such as point-of-sale, catalogues, brochures and leaflets). Above-the-line expenditure tends to relate to long-term effects on sales and below-the-line expenditure can drastically affect short-term sales. Regardless of the method used, an organisation can try to measure its effectiveness by looking at the following:

1 Catalogues/leaflets

- number of enquiries/costs
- amount of business/costs

2 Magazines

- number of coupon enquiries/costs
- value of business/costs

3 Samples/merchandising

- volume of orders/costs

4 Exhibitions

- number of enquiries/costs
- value of follow-up business/costs

By identifying each particular type of promotional material the organisation will be able to make an estimate of the most cost-effective method. This cost-effectiveness assessment should always be used in calculating the amount of expenditure that should be used on different promotions.

Customers obtain information about products or services in a variety of different ways, including:

- paid-for promotional activity
- editorial comment in magazines and newspapers
- on-pack information
- personal contacts and word of mouth

In order to ensure that any cash spent on promotional activities is used to the best advantage, an organisation should:

- understand the type of promotional material required
- set a budget or level of investment in that promotional activity
- ensure that the promotional activity fully supports the organisation's objectives and the product's needs
- set a structure for promotional spending
- be able to measure, monitor and improve the effectiveness of the promotional activity

DISTRIBUTING

Organisations should periodically analyse their **distribution policy**. This enables them to discover whether profitability can be improved by changing the distribution method. Any marketing plan should involve this analysis, which addresses the following considerations:

- what is the usual **frequency** of orders?
- what is the usual **size** of orders?
- how many **different products** are usually involved in each order?
- what are the overall **sales per product**?
- what is the nature of the **demand for a produc**t?
- are there any **seasonal factor**s involved?
- is there a significant and identifiable **geographical dimension** to demand?
- what are the **costs** of distribution at present?
- how do these costs compare with those of **alternative distribution** methods?
- what are the **warehouse costs**?
- can these costs be changed by **further investment?**
- how could the **order processing system** be improved?

MERCHANDISING

As we mentioned in Unit 3, there are various methods of **merchandising** a product, all aimed at ensuring that the product is displayed in a prominent and attractive manner in the retail outlet. Sales representatives will visit retail outlets and offer merchandising or point-of-sale materials or equipment in the hope that these two criteria are addressed.

A marketing plan should include any suggestions that could be used by the organisation to enhance its merchandising efforts. Simply supplying a customer or retailer with products may not be enough to ensure that these will be sold. The last thing that suppliers want is for retailers to contact them in two or three months time and tell them that they wish to return the goods as they have not been sold. In order to avoid this, suppliers must provide the retailer or customer with promotional materials in order to make their products more visible to the end-user. It is natural for a customer who enters a shop in search of a particular product to be drawn to attractive point-of-sale material. Dump-bins, posters, sales literature and shelf stickers may greatly enhance the product's attractiveness. Again, as we mentioned in Unit 3, some merchandising equipment is supplied to the retailer under certain terms and conditions. Periodically, the sales representative will check to see whether the equipment supplied is being used under the terms and conditions of the agreement. This checking procedure needs to be tempered with a degree of understanding of the retailer's needs as well as the local market situation.

SELLING (TARGETS, VOLUME)

An organisation's **key customers** will inevitably provide a substantial proportion of the organisation's sales. When these customers are limited in number, the supplying organisation may feel rather vulnerable. There is a simple equation which states that 80 per cent of a supplier's business is provided by 20 per cent of its customers. The loss of a single customer can therefore mean that a large percentage of sales volume will disappear. Obviously, wider sales coverage will reduce this dependency. There are also other benefits of obtaining wider sales coverage. For example, it will give the organisation a greater understanding of the market in general, as well as of the competition. It is known that small businesses export on average only 1 per cent of their turnover. Although sales expansion may require greater short-term investment, spreading into new markets (particularly foreign ones) can reduce the dependency on current customers and the local market.

Assessing the **effectiveness of the sale effort** of the organisation also needs constant review. The points to consider include:

- how good is the organisation at **attracting** and identifying new customers?
- how much **preparation** is made prior to contacting a potential customer?
- how many **sales calls** are made per day?
- how many calls are necessary to **secure an order**?
- **how often** should a customer be visited and how does this relate to the income generated from that customer?
- does the organisation need to employ **more sales staff**?
- would there be an extra positive return if the organisation employed more sales staff?
- do the sales staff spend time handling **repeat orders** when they should be contacting new customers?
- are the **administration systems** streamlined and as efficient as possible?
- how much of the time of the sales force is taken up with dealing with **complaints** and **chasing debtors**?

In the marketing section of the business plan, all of these considerations need to be addressed, perhaps not in detail, but at least they should have been thought about. It would be impossible to create a marketing plan at business start-up level that could possibly address all of these concerns.

TIMING

Timing the various **phases** of the marketing plan is as important as the timing of the overall business plan itself. Certain activities must be undertaken before other key activities may be attempted. For instance:

- the product needs to be clearly **designed**
- the product needs to be clearly **packaged**
- the product needs to be clearly **labelled**
- the **sales force** needs to be fully **briefed**

All this must happen before the product is ready to be launched onto the market.

Another key determining factor in the timing process will be the acquisition and analysis of information gained from **market research**. Sufficient information must be gathered in order to ascertain the nature, size and growth potential of the market, since these factors will determine the direction in which the sales effort will move.

MARKETING COMMUNICATIONS

We have covered the majority of **marketing communications methods** in Unit 3, although it may be a good idea to try to identify some of the key marketing communications methods again here for the purpose of completing the marketing plan. We will identify the main marketing communication methods under two separate headings, these are **consumer marketing communications** and **industrial marketing communications**. We will look at the types of consumer marketing communications first:

1 *Aural and visual* – including television, radio and cinema.
2 *Visual* – including billboards, posters, hoardings and sports equipment.
3 *Read* – including newspapers and magazines.
4 *Oral* – including tele-marketing and direct sales.
5 *Incidental* – including staff uniforms, advertisements on receipts, stickers and point-of-sale material.

Industrial marketing communications include the following:

1 *Written publicity* – including bulletins, technical literature and up-dates.
2 *Display* – including advertising and feature articles.
3 *In-company* – including presentations and demonstrations to employees and potential customers.
4 *Briefings* – including seminars and demonstrations.
5 *Exhibitions* – including trade fairs and consumer fairs.
6 *External visits* – including discussions with customers and wholesalers and distributors.

The identification of the various forms of marketing communication to be used by the organisation must be established at the earliest possible point, since materials and employees need to be prepared. An organisation presenting a business plan with a marketing element would certainly have to identify the viability of the different marketing communications methods and attempt to establish some form of budget or priority for each.

AFTER-SALES SUPPORT

The fundamentals of **customer service** and **after-sales support** are covered extensively in Unit 3. Essentially, the concept of after-sales service recognises the fact that the organisation's relationship with the customer does not end with placing the product in a carrier bag and taking the money. The organisation will have to provide the following:

- friendly and supportive advice
- stocks of spare parts
- an efficient maintenance operation

These features are designed to encourage the customer to make repeat purchases with the organisation.

After-sales service can be undertaken either by the manufacturer or by the retailer. Depending upon the nature of the product or service in question, it may be necessary to have a network of maintenance providers throughout the country who will make home calls or be points of collection for products requiring attention. Whilst many products are covered under guarantee or warranty, the maintenance and repair aspect of the after-sales service is carried out free. The emergence of the concept of extended warranties and guarantees has greatly increased the need for and viability of regional repair centres. Many larger retail chains, such as Dixons, Currys and Comet, will routinely take back items either within or beyond their guarantee or warranty period for despatch either to their own repair centres or to the manufacturer. This vital service provides considerable peace of mind to the customer who is secure in the knowledge that, should the product be faulty, then immediate action will be taken. Inevitably, arguments may arise about the nature of any fault found in the product. The basic rule is that if a product is faulty as a result of inferior parts or poor workmanship, then it is the responsibility of the manufacturer or the retailer to replace the goods. Many people have commented that the emergence of extended warranties merely underlines the fact that products are considerably less reliable than they were in the past. It has to be said that, in trying to convince a customer to take out an extended warranty, retailers and manufacturers are simply attempting to pass potentially expensive repair costs onto the customer. Since many electrical goods, in particular, become technologically obsolete after three or four years, the extended warranty absolves the retailer or manufacturer of any financial responsibility for faulty goods.

Other important aspects of after-sales service include the following:

- in-store advice and information – this service is offered free by the retailer and aims to ensure that the customer is using the product to its best advantage
- care phone lines – these systems have been set up either by retail chains or by manufacturers to provide (usually free) advice and support to customers after purchases have been made. These tend to be either 0800, 0345 or 0891 numbers

After-sales service systems should be included, at least in outline form, within the marketing plan. Depending upon the nature of the product or services involved, the business may have to cope with either a great number of complaints or queries, or simply the occasional one or two. As we mentioned earlier in this Element, it is probably not the best use of valuable staff to require the sales force to field complaints and after-sales service enquiries. If the organisation is large enough, then it may need to set up a customer complaints and after-sales service unit or department. Alternatively, this service could be provided by a sub-contractor working on a fee per complaint or repair handled. In any case, the organisation needs to consider the probable after-sales service implications that may arise from the supply of its chosen products or services.

student activity

(PC 8.2.2, COM 3.1, 3.2, 3.3, AON 3.1, 3.2, 3.3)
You now need to create a draft marketing plan in order to assist you in creating the business plan at the end of this Element. Whilst there is no set format for a marketing plan, you may wish to address the following points as potential headings or sections in your marketing plan:

1 A sound marketing policy should be based on the ability of an organisation to **define** what products or service would be required by the customer. This can best be achieved by some form of **research**.
2 Basic **customer information** is absolutely essential for the development of an organisation. Even very routine enquiries may add to the information base.
3 An evaluation of the **profitability** of each **product** should be a key determining factor in establishing future objectives and how they may be achieved.
4 By investigating the effects of **price rises** within the market, an organisation will be able to gauge how **price sensitive** the market may be. The organisation should also consider possible competitive price changes in the future.
5 By comparing the quality of its own product with both the competition's product(s) and customers' expectations, an organisation will be able to assess the long-term potential of its product.
6 When considering **discounting**, an organisation should establish clear and unambiguous guidelines.

7 The offering of **credit** has important marketing implications and more generally, will affect the availability of working capital.
8 Evaluating the **distribution policy**, whether actual or proposed, should be an integral part of the marketing plan.
9 When considering **exports**, an organisation must take note of two points – that a good distribution network has to be established and that potential export sales may offset any changes in the domestic market.
10 An organisation should continually investigate the **performance** of all of its products to help it in defining objectives.
11 **Product development** should be considered a key feature of business development.
12 The costs and benefits of the **packaging** used by the organisation should be periodically reviewed.
13 The costs and opportunities of **branding** should be continually reviewed.
14 Rather than depend upon a small number of customers, an organisation should consider ways in which to **extend** its **customer base**.
15 When developing the business, and in particular when expanding sales, an organisation needs to consider **development costs**.
16 The promotion of **new products** should be explored and the costs included in any promotional budget.

17 The likely returns from and cost effectiveness of the different methods of **promotion** should be investigated.

18 Employees who have contact with customers will be expected to have a level of expertise. The **training of personnel** is an integral part of the marketing mix.

19 Organisations should review their investment in **various outlets** to ensure that maximum sales are being achieved in relation to the current environment.

20 Organisations should consider whether investment in customer or after-sales service is needed and these costs should be integrated into the marketing plan.

Normally, the key features of the marketing plan, as part of the overall business plan, can be summarised in perhaps four or five pages along with appendices containing market statistics. Using the considerations above, try to formulate a draft marketing plan which at least addresses the following:

1 State the size of the market, its history and its potential for growth.

2 Split the market into definable segments and decide which your business is aiming at.

3 Identify your likely customers and establish how many there are and how they buy.

4 Analyse your competition, determine their size and their position in the market.

5 Analyse your customer service and after-sales service requirements.

6 Identify your sales promotion techniques and advertising methods.

7 Determine how your product will be sold (by self, by retailer, by wholesaler, by distributor).

8 Determine your sales pitch, which includes an identification of the benefits of your products or services.

9 Determine your pricing policy.

At this stage you need not word process your draft marketing plan, but it should be in a legible state so that your tutor can assess whether you have addressed the major considerations required. Bear in mind that any groundwork done at this stage will yield substantial benefits at the end of this Element when you must create your business plan.

8.2.3 Outline a production plan for a business enterprise

PRODUCTION PLAN

Production plans are written to ensure that the resources deployed in the production process will be adequate to meet the potential orders for products and services. It is essential that an organisation makes sure that it has adequate resources in terms of premises, machinery, raw materials and labour in order to produce the products as and when required. If customers are made to wait they may become dissatisfied with the organisation and look for their orders to be fulfilled elsewhere.

DESIGN

New product development and bright ideas that may be associated with such an endeavour must be tempered with the practicalities of production. Whilst many good ideas appear workable on paper, the realities of the situation may mean that the product cannot be produced in a cost-effective and efficient manner.

student activity

(PC 8.2.3, COM 3.2, AON 3.1, 3.2, 3.3)
If relevant to your intended business, try to list the resources that are necessary to ensure that your production process matches your predicted demand for your products or services.

An organisation needs to assess whether it is looking for a new product which its current production processes are capable of producing. It would serve no useful purpose for an organisation to develop an idea for a new product and then discover that the actual production process needs to be carried out by sub-contractors or business partners. After all, one of the key considerations in developing new products, regardless of their design, is that the organisation should make full use of its production facilities.

Designs for new products are often gradually changed as the organisation becomes aware that the design itself presents severe production problems. This process, although depressing for the designer, needs to be put in the context of efficiency and the overall benefits to the organisation.

Whether the design process is undertaken in-house or by consultants, an organisation must ensure that feasibility studies are carried out at the earliest possible stage to ensure that resources are not wasted in developing a new product design when there is no possibility of being able to produce it in a cost-efficient manner. This screening process, as discussed in the last section of this Element, needs to be rigorously enforced to ensure that the organisation does not invest funds in spurious and impractical product designs that will never come to fruition.

PRODUCT DEVELOPMENT

The development of **new products** can be not only time consuming but expensive. The desire to develop new products should be tempered by an awareness that many small businesses fail as a result of over-investing in new product development. However, the success of new products is central to the long-term success and growth of the organisation. It should be noted that only a small percentage of new products are ever successful.

As we saw in Unit 3, it is important for an organisation to plan its new product developments using the following steps:

1 There must be an initial **screening period** in which an investigation is carried out to assess how the product fits in with current products and services.
2 Investigate whether the new product could be produced using **current production methods**.
3 **Test** the production process.
4 Fully **cost** and **price** the production process.
5 Carry out necessary market research.
6 Produce a test batch of new products and test market them.
7 Assuming that all of the above stages are acceptable, introduce the product into the market-place.

PRODUCTION PROCESS AND PRODUCTION LEVELS

Accurate **costing** in relation to production is essential in ensuring that profitability levels remain at a level to allow the organisation to reach its objectives. Some organisations calculate the costs of production, including the contribution to overheads. Many companies, however, do not have a clue how much it costs to produce particular products. Their profits tend to be somewhat erratic and unpredictable.

Control over the production process may be improved by introducing **standard costs**. These may be related to either the amount of time it takes to manufacture the product, or the total costs of that particular finished product. Organisations frequently use an **efficiency ratio** (ER), which is:

$$\text{efficiency ratio} = \frac{\text{standard costing}}{\text{actual costing}}$$

Thus, if an organisation produces a batch of products for £4,000 and its standard costing is calculated as £5,000, then the production line is working more efficiently than the forecast.

A different ratio to control production processes is known as the **capacity ratio** (CR). This relates to the current production level and how it compares with maximum potential production. The ratio looks like this:

$$\text{capacity ratio} = \frac{\text{current throughput}}{\text{maximum throughput}}$$

This ratio is used to identify trends in production and parts of the factory which are not paying for themselves.

By applying these ratios and formulae an organisation is able to assess the efficiency of its production process. As a result it may, perhaps, consider whether certain production functions would be better carried out by sub-contractors.

PREMISES

The **location** of the **premises** is only one of the important questions that need to be considered. In many cases, however, the main factors determining the suitability of premises will be their cost and availability. In choosing an ideal location for a business, it is prudent to consider its accessibility in terms of:

- markets
- raw materials
- employees
- suppliers
- appropriate support services
- main utilities

Another factor, as we have already mentioned, is the availability – in certain areas in the UK – of government development and resettlement grants.

MACHINERY

Depending upon the exact nature of its business, an organisation is more or less reliant upon the guaranteed continuity of production available to it through the use of machinery and other equipment. **Machinery** may be a key physical resource and the organisation must ensure that it has a reliable supplier of such machinery, together with such back-up support services as are essential to maintain production. With regard to the most efficient running of the machinery, it may be necessary to consider a continuous production process, by which the machinery is run on a 24-hour, 365 days a year basis. This will have effects upon the acquisition of other essential resources, such as raw materials, and a well-organised labour force (working in shifts). In relation to its premises, the organisation must ensure that the building not only is fit for the operating of essential machinery, but also has the necessary licensing, insurance and usage clearance by the local authority.

     `2:00`

student activity

(PC 8.2.3, COM 3.1, 3.4, AON 3.1, 3.2, 3.3)
If you have not already identified potential premises from which to run your business, you should now consider how you will identify the correct type and location of building(s). You will find local estate agents to be a valuable source of information in identifying the availability of suitable premises. You will also have to decide, in relation to your available capital, whether you will choose to lease or own your premises.

     `1:30`

student activity

(PC 8.2.3, COM 3.4, AON 3.1, 3.2, 3.3)
Identify all of the types of machinery you will require to run your chosen business successfully. Again, you should consider the following types of ownership:

- outright purchase
- lease
- rental

In the case of retail operations, the need for machinery may be less important, but do not forget that you will need to obtain at least a cash register.

RAW MATERIALS

If an organisation requires large supplies of **raw materials**, not only must the location of the premises be right, but they must also be suitable, to ensure that these large quantities can be handled. Locating the business in an isolated part of the UK can mean unnecessary transportation costs which may affect the viability of the business. Although transport and distribution costs have reduced, comparatively speaking, over recent years, it is still a major goal of most organisations to reduce these costs as far as possible. For this reason organisations operating in the same area of business activity, or in a support function to a number of similar organisations, tend to congregate fairly close to one another. This concentration of organisations is known as the **external economies of scale**. Collectively they achieve these economies of scale by jointly reducing unnecessary costs. In addition, this congregation also ensures that training facilities for staff are available locally. The other major bonus is that smaller support systems, such as servicing contractors and component suppliers, are nearby.

    `2:00`

student activity

(PC 8.2.3, COM 3.1, 3.4, AON 3.1, 3.2, 3.3)
If raw materials are relevant to your business, you should now have some idea of the sources of these raw materials. Have you been able to assess the reliability of supply? The predictability of price? Try to list at least three potential sources of raw materials. If possible try to find out their credit terms.

LABOUR

Labour costs differ widely from area to area and region to region. Employees in the South East of England earn some 50 per cent more than those in Northern Ireland and between 15 and 25 per cent more than those in the rest of the UK. If an organisation wishes to ensure that it has an adequate supply of skilled labour, then it may be forced to locate in an area where wage levels are comparatively higher. The mobility of labour has become greater in recent years, but labour is still not as mobile as some employers would wish. Another major reason for locating in a particular area may be to avoid traditional industrial relations problems which are associated with an alternative

student activity

(PC 8.2.3, COM 3.2)
Does your business require the specialist skills of any individuals? If so, how will you be able to attract them to your business? Even if you do not require specialists, how do you intend to advertise the availability of employment? In earlier Units we looked at the nature and types of employment and identified organisations which assist in the recruitment of staff. You may wish to refer to these sections in the process of deciding how and where to advertise.

region. In areas where there have been considerable job losses, employers can, and often do, exploit the situation by calling on the excess labour pool and employing them at comparatively low wage rates. In terms of an organisation's production plan as a whole, the availability of skilled labour in sufficient numbers is imperative. This ensures that the production process is fully operational at all times and at all levels.

QUALITY ASSURANCE

Although the improvement of **quality** is a gradual process by which the organisation attempts to make small but constant steps towards perfection, investment is necessary.

The concept of **total quality management** (TQM) has begun to be generally accepted as the basis of appropriate practice. Manufacturing processes and all aspects of after-sales service come under the concept of TQM. This approach, Japanese in origin, seeks full quality assurance throughout the organisation. It will hopefully ensure that the organisation addresses the following:

student activity

(PC 8.2.3, COM 3.2, 3.4, AON 3.1, 3.2, 3.3)
In preparation for drawing up your five-part business plan you will need to produce a draft production plan which includes your production intentions and schedules. Some useful considerations are the following:

1 Make a **costing estimate** relating to the products you intend to produce. This should include:

- raw materials
- bought-in components
- machine time required
- packaging
- final processing

2 Appreciate the implications of **long production runs** and effects on stock levels and product range. You will need to calculate the volume necessary to break even.
3 Identify how you can maximise **machine utilisation**.
4 Consider how you will control the level of **raw materials** in stock.
5 Have in place periodic **reviews** of current product range and establish whether the range is too large for maximising production efficiency.
6 Assess how you will deal with **excess stock**.

7 Consider how you will implement **quality control systems**.
8 Consider the advantages and disadvantages of using **sub-contractors**.
9 Consider the implications of **product re-design** and how this will affect efficiency, wastage and profitability.
10 How will you set your **productivity levels**?
11 Consider how you will periodically replace your **machinery** and the effects on production efficiency of doing so.
12 Consider the re-design and layout of your existing **premises** and any costs and benefits that may be associated with moving to new premises.

Addressing these considerations will give you the basis of a strong and credible production plan. Although not all of these considerations may be necessarily relevant to your business, you should try to address ones that are. At this stage you need not word process your draft production plan, but obviously any work done at this stage will save you time at the end of this Element.

- that it is **efficient** at every stage of its activities
- that it makes the best use of all **available resources**
- that it provides **consistency** in its production of products and services
- that it has in place a series of **quality assurance measures** to feedback information on potential quality problems
- that it pays particular attention to the concept of **customer satisfaction**

TIMING

If a production run is long, then the start-up costs of that production are lower per unit produced. Longer production runs produce large quantities of stock and consequently affect cash flow. Organisations which have a wide product range may not have the time to maintain single product manufacture. Obviously, if an organisation were to reduce the number of products it produced then it would be able to improve its production efficiency. However, since longer production runs are most cost-effective, the organisation has to be aware of the **timing** considerations involved in ensuring

that sufficient stock levels are available for immediate purchase.

Many of these timing considerations may boil down to the use of machinery. An analysis of timing will need to include an analysis of machinery utilisation. In order to make a return on capital employed (in the form of its investment in the machinery), an organisation may have to consider round-the-clock production on a seven days a week basis to maximise returns.

Many organisations have been strongly influenced by Japanese manufacturing techniques. They have adopted what is known as a 'just in time' (JIT) strategy. With this philosophy, raw materials arrive at the factory when and where they are required. The timing of these deliveries accords with the needs of the production process. Although just in time strategies may not be necessarily practical or applicable to a small business, an organisation has to ask itself whether there are any ways that it can ensure that the production process is fed efficiently and at the correct time without having to maintain vast quantities of raw materials for components.

8.2.4 *Outline the resource requirements for marketing and production*

RESOURCE REQUIREMENTS

As mentioned in Element 8.1, the **resource requirements** of a business plan are human, physical and financial. One of the main functions of the individuals producing a business plan may be the precise identification of the resources needed to ensure that not only production but general business activity is maintained.

HUMAN, PHYSICAL AND FINANCIAL RESOURCE REQUIREMENTS AND TIMING

As we have already mentioned in previous Units, organisations are concerned with ensuring that they gain economies of scale at the earliest possible opportunity. For example, a production plan which makes up part of the overall business plan will be concerned with the batching of orders so that production runs may be longer so as to ensure economies of scale. This particular technique can have its own drawbacks since it may cause delays in the fulfilment of customer orders. If this is likely to happen, then customers should be kept informed as to the status of their orders at all times.

The resources of an organisation can be deployed to ensure that quality is maintained at all levels of the

production process and the service supplied. It is not sufficient these days for an organisation just to supply products or services required by its customers. They demand much more. An organisation will begin by considering its human and physical resources in the following ways:

1 *Physical resources* – suppliers will be expected to deliver raw and part-finished materials of an acceptable **quality**.
2 *Human resources* – the workforce will be instilled with the notion of **quality**. Special training in quality and **customer service** may also be required. It may be dangerous for an organisation to ignore these features as it is certain that its competitors will be paying close attention to them.
3 *Financial resources* – it is essential that frank and honest contact is maintained with the **providers of finance**. All potential problems regarding cash flow or profitability must be discussed at every stage. If there are shareholders they will demand to know the true state of affairs within the organisation. It may be necessary for them to make additional share capital available to finance short-term cash-flow problems or indeed long-term investments

At this stage in assessing the resource requirements of the organisation, the sales, production and administrative conclusions need to be passed on to a financial expert for further analysis. This expert will attempt to make some projections relating to the following:

- cash-flow forecasts (usually on a month-by-month basis)
- profit and loss assessments (on a month-by-month basis)
- balance sheet calculations (on an annual basis)

All of these **forecasts**, as we will see in the last part of this Element, are strongly interrelated. In planning terms, it is important that the organisation compares forecasts with what has happened in the past.

The **financial projections** will be able to provide an indication of the following:

- the underlying **profitability** as suggested in the forecasts
- the probable **future finance requirements** of the organisation

This analysis will inevitably throw up a number of issues that may require reassessment. Typically, these would include some of the following:

- are there some products which are not performing particularly well that should be dropped and resources channelled into new products?
- are wage levels too high?
- are sales per employee indicating that the organisation is over-staffed?
- how does the discount and credit level structure of the organisation assist or impair profitability?

8.2.5 Produce financial data and forecasts to support a business plan

FINANCIAL DATA AND FORECASTS

Financial data and **forecasts** form the basis of an organisation's ability to raise finance, negotiate the purchase or acquisition of premises and the ordering of raw materials. If an organisation is foolish enough to make an inaccurate forecast then the inevitable outcome may be that insufficient funds are available. Also, if an organisation fails to meet its projected forecasts, then it may be difficult or impossible to acquire further funding. A provider of finance would not look kindly upon an organisation which returns to ask for more money because its forecasting has proved to be inaccurate.

An organisation must attempt to make an estimate of the following:

- sales
- costs
- cash balances

As we have mentioned earlier, over-optimistic sales figures, coupled with low cost figures, will throw a forecast into disarray. An organisation starting out for the first time does not want to have to cope with financial problems created as a result of poor or ill-conceived financial forecasts.

TIME PERIOD

An organisation may choose to detail its financial data and forecasts using different time periods: weekly, monthly or yearly. Certainly, for **cash-flow forecasts**, it is the monthly time period that is the most important concern. Totals will have to be calculated for cash received and cash outgoing for each month. It is probable that certain assumptions will have to be made, particularly in the case of forecasts relating to months in the far future.

Again, a **profit and loss account** is usually formulated on a month-by-month basis. An organisation needs to calculate the total income derived from invoices received during that month and the costs of any outgoings during the same period. This will give a balance per month which indicates the profit or loss in that month.

Balance sheets, on the other hand, tend to be drawn up on a yearly basis, working from information derived from actual cash flow and profit and loss. Remember that a balance sheet only shows what an organisation owes and what it owns at a **particular time on a particular day**. A projected balance sheet will similarly show an estimate of what the organisation will owe and own on a **particular day in the future**.

CASH-FLOW FORECAST

A **cash-flow forecast** in its simplest terms is a record of cash received by the organisation and an indication as to when cash will be needed to be paid out. Within a business plan it is common to make a cash-flow forecast that extends for two to three years. Providers of finance may require an organisation to extend that forecast for up to five years.

You will find a full description of all of the cash-flow headings in Unit 7, but it is worth remembering here that you need to make realistic assumptions about cash received and cash paid out. Remember that the main purpose of the cash-flow forecast is to show an organisation when it needs cash so that the provider of finance knows its funding requirements.

START-UP BALANCE SHEET

A **start-up balance sheet**, in essence, can only contain items of income and expenditure of which an organisation is already aware. It is advisable for a new business to use the services of an accountant to help produce a balance sheet at this stage. A new business is likely to be on a fairly small scale to begin with. If an organisation does not require a great deal of finance its provider of finance may not ask it to supply a start-up balance sheet. You will find a full description of the balance sheet headings in Unit 7. However, it is important to note that the key headings that need to be considered are the following:

1 *Fixed assets* – which include all equipment received, even if these have not yet been paid for.
2 *Current assets* – which include cash in hand, debtors and stock.
3 *Capital* – which the owners have put into the organisation to start the business.
4 *Liabilities* – which include overdraft, any tax or VAT payable and creditors.

PROJECTED PROFIT AND LOSS AND BALANCE SHEET

A **profit forecast** should be made in order to establish the level of profit which the organisation hopes to produce at the end of a specified period.

Taken together, the **projected profit and loss** and **balance sheet** should indicate whether the business will be in a position to either break even or show a small profit. From these two information sources it will be possible to calculate the expected return on capital employed. Again, you should refer back to Unit 7 in the preparation of your projected profit and loss and balance sheets.

student activity

(PC 8.2.5, COM 3.4, AON 3.1, 3.2, 3.3)
You may already have made an attempt to fill in the required financial data pro-formas in Unit 7. It is a good idea to have a look at these again. In the light of what you have just discovered with regard to the business plan, financial requirements and some of the over-arching monitoring procedures, you may wish to make amendments. You should now attempt to complete the following:

● a cash-flow forecast
● a start-up balance sheet
● a projected profit and loss and balance sheet

These will be an integral part of your five-part business plan.

Profit Forecast

Business name _____ **Period covered** _____ 19___ to _____ 19___

Period (eg 4 weeks/Month)		BUDGET	ACTUAL	BUDGET	ACTUAL	BUDGET	ACTUAL	BUDGET	ACTUAL	BUDGET	ACTUAL	BUDGET	ACTUAL	BUDGET	ACTUAL	B

SALES INCOME: (Enter in the month/period when the sale is actually made, not when the money is received.)

Cash sales																
Credit sales																
TOTAL SALES INCOME	A															

DIRECT COSTS: (Include all costs directly related to your service or product.)

Materials and services																
Other expenditure directly related to customers (eg delivery costs)																
Commissions & discounts																
Other																
TOTAL DIRECT COSTS	B															

GROSS PROFIT (Total sales income less total direct costs A-B)	C															
OVERHEADS: Wages, salaries, PAYE and NICs																
Rent, rates																
Heat, light and power																
Repairs and maintenance																
Bank charges and interest																
Insurance																
Legal and professional fees																
Stationery, postage and telephone																
Advertising and promotion																
Bad debts																
Depreciation																
TOTAL OVERHEADS	D															

NET PROFIT (Gross profit less total overheads C-D)	*															
TAX ON PROFIT	*															
DRAWINGS	*															
PROFIT/LOSS (Carried forward)	*															
TOTAL TO BRING FORWARD TO NEXT MONTH/PERIOD	*															

*If a deficit – please enclose in brackets

___ 19___ to _____ 19___

ACTUAL	BUDGET	ACTUAL	BUDGET	ACTUAL	BUDGET	ACTUAL	BUDGET	ACTUAL	BUDGET	ACTUAL	BUDGET	ACTUAL	BUDGET	ACTUAL	BUDGET	ACTUAL	TOTAL BUDGET	ACTUAL

FIG. 8.2.2 *Lloyds Bank's Profit Forecast form.*

8.2.6 *Identify monthly profit and loss and balance sheet monitoring and review procedures for the business plan*

MONITORING AND REVIEW PROCEDURES

By constructing a **monthly profit and loss account** and a **monthly balance sheet**, an organisation will be able to monitor its adherence to its **business plan**. This control mechanism should be able to identify any causes for concern and allow the organisation to react in time. The normal procedure is for an organisation to create a **cash-flow forecast** which includes budgeted figures for various items. Then, as the figures become available, the organisation can compare these with the budgeted figures. Similarly, the organisation will be able to compare actual output with production targets and actual sales with projected sales.

Your business plan will need to explain how financial data and forecasts will be **reviewed**. Simply put, the business has to establish the following:

- **who** will carry out the review
- **how often** reviews will take place
- what **authority** the reviewer will have to institute changes

- what **records** will be kept
- what the **distribution procedure** for information will be and what restrictions there are on that distribution

student activity

(PC 8.2.6, COM 3.2, AON 3.2)
Again, referring back to the pro-formas which you should have filled in, you must now establish exactly how you intend to monitor and review the progress of your business. You need only address this question in outline form, but you should lay down the criteria, timing and remedial procedures that will be undertaken.

8.2.7 *Present and explain a business plan to an audience*

The final part of this Element is to present and explain your business plan to an audience. You will find specific guidance about this task in the Element Assignment. Remember that you need to be prepared and confident that your analysis, projections, forecasts and assumptions are logical and clear.

By this stage you should have established the exact nature of the business that you intend to set up. Alternatively, you will have identified business opportunities which exist in current businesses. You may have decided to make an investment in an existing business or, perhaps, have purchased a franchise operation. In any respect, the ground-work must now be completed.

ELEMENT 8.2

assignment

(PC 8.2.1–7, COM 3.1–4, AON 3.1–3, IT 3.1–3)

The purpose of this Element and its related performance criteria revolve around the presentation of a business plan. By the end of this Element, you should understand the details of the planning process, especially those relating to finance which prospective lenders demand from a business plan.

You will present the business plan, supporting it with visual aids, to an individual or a group who represent a potential source of finance. Your presentation should clearly cover the five-part plan as detailed in the tasks below. You should also be prepared for a question and answer session after the presentation to demonstrate your understanding of the marketing, production and financial implications of your plan.

Whilst the majority of you may wish to present your plan on paper in the appropriate presentational style and format, you may be asked to present your plan on disk.

TASK I

(PC 8.2.1)

In the first part of your business plan for a small business enterprise, you should **introduce** your business and set out the key objectives, as contained in the plan.

TASK 2

(PC 8.2.2/8.2.4)

In this second part of your business plan you must address the **marketing** of your business enterprise. You should state how, where and to whom the business's products or services will be marketed and sold in order to achieve your planned objectives. You will only be expected to outline the marketing plan; you do not have to give specific evidence of having undertaken marketing work. You should, however, identify the resource requirements for marketing and production as these will be required in Part 4 of your business plan.

TASK 3

(PC 8.2.3/8.2.4)

In Part 3 of your business plan, you should deal with the **production intentions** and **schedules** of your business. You should say how the business intends to create the goods or services to satisfy the expected demand for those goods and services.

You should also include here how the goods and services will be acquired or financed, designed or processed and your plans for quality assurance. An outline of these considerations is sufficient, but you should identify the resource requirements, which are needed in Part 4 of your business plan.

TASK 4

(PC 8.2.4)

As we intimated in Tasks 2 and 3, you must now detail the financial requirements, stating those required for marketing and production. This forms Part 4 of your business plan.

TASK 5

(PC 8.2.5/8.2.6)

In Part 5 of your business plan you are required to include relevant financial data and forecasts. These include the following:

- a cash-flow forecast for a given time period
- start-up balance sheet
- projected profit and loss account
- projected balance sheet
- monthly profit and loss statements
- monthly balance sheet

You should indicate how your business plan will be financed in part and in total and where the finance will come from. This part of the plan should also explain how the financial data and forecasts will be reviewed, specifically:

- who will carry out the review
- frequency of review
- what authority the reviewer will have to make changes

- what records will be kept
- to whom and how often the financial information will be distributed

TASK 6

(PC 8.2.7)

Having prepared your business plan you must now explain it to an audience. The exact nature of this audience will largely depend upon the arrangements made by your college. You should be aware, as an integral part of not only the business plan but also the presentation, that other parties such as co-directors, partners, shareholders, investors or employees have a range of needs and expectations of the plan.

TASK 7

(PC 8.2.7)

As we mentioned earlier, you will need to prepare yourself for a question and answer session to demonstrate your understanding of the various aspects of your business plan. This will require you to be able to respond to a variety of questions in somewhat greater depth than the level at which explanations have been made in your business plan. You should attempt to anticipate probable lines of questioning and you should try to ensure that you can support any statements you make in response to questions in a meaningful and logical manner.

Plan for employment or self-employment

PERFORMANCE CRITERIA

A student must:

1 identify and give examples of **types** of employment or self-employment

2 identify **statutory requirements** for employment or self-employment

3 identify **sources of information** and collect information for employment and self-employment

4 identify opportunities for employment or self-employment

5 analyse and discuss **skills** to support employment and self-employment

6 propose a **personal plan** for employment or self-employment

RANGE

Types: *paid (private sector, public-sector), voluntary; own business (family business, business start-up, government enterprise scheme), partnership, franchise*

Statutory requirements: *income tax (individuals, small business), value added tax (VAT), national insurance, pension arrangements, company registration, benefits (for low paid, to people starting a business)*

Sources of information: *Jobcentres, employment/recruitment agencies, media (newspapers, TV, radio), Federation of Self-Employed, Chambers of Commerce, banks, Training and Enterprise Councils (TEC), Department of Trade and Industry (DTI), charitable organisations, other bodies*

Skills: *evaluating own strengths and weaknesses, working with others, working independently, planning, time management, setting targets, reviewing progress, decision making, problem solving, information seeking and handling, communicating, applying number, using information technology, occupational skills*

Personal plan: *time-scales (short-term, long-term), statutory considerations, sources of help and support, information needed, actions to be taken*

8.3.1 *Identify and give examples of types of employment or self-employment*

TYPES

Whilst many people may consider starting up their own business, it is not always practical or possible for them to do so. Equally, many organisations do not necessarily employ people on a full-time basis. There are, therefore, a number of choices and, indeed, restrictions which you must consider before embarking on the writing of a plan for employment or self-employment.

We will begin our investigation of the potentials in employment and self-employment with a brief look at the different types of employment. You will also find details on many of the types of employment and specific job roles in Units 2 and 4. You may wish to refer back to these Units in establishing, particularly in relation to full-time employment, your preferred job role.

PAID (PRIVATE SECTOR, PUBLIC SECTOR)

Paid employment is perhaps the most common form of employment in the UK. Considerable numbers of people, who form the majority of the workforce, work for either the private or the public sector. It is no longer correct to state that the major differences between these types of employment concern the profit motive. Indeed, many public-sector organisations are concerned with profits, or at least, with breaking even.

Paid employment, as the term infers, involves being actually paid for the hours you work or the duties you carry out for or on behalf of an organisation. There are innumerable versions of this type of employment. Essentially, we can identify the following sub-categories of paid employment:

1 *Full-time employment* – this category embraces individuals who work for 35 or more hours per week in return for a wage or salary.
2 *Part-time employment* – this category covers individuals who undertake work for part of a week. Whilst the line between part-time and full-time work has become somewhat blurred, we can normally suggest that part-time workers are those who work for less than 25 hours per week.
3 *Permanent* – this is a sub-category of both full-time and part-time work. It infers that, regardless of the hours worked by the individual, the post is of a permanent nature.
4 *Temporary* – again, this is a sub-category which could include both full-time and part-time employees. Normally a temporary worker would work on a fixed-term contract basis in the knowledge that his/her employment is secure during that period.
5 *Seasonal* – again, this is a variation which could include both full-time and part-time employment. Seasonal workers would be employed during periods of high activity and are normally associated with holiday periods when permanent employees are on vacation, yet the organisation still requires output to be maintained. Equally, additional staff may be required during periods such as the run-up to Christmas when the organisation needs to have as many individuals working for it as possible due to increased demand.
6 *Casual* – this type of employment, which often takes the form of a limited number of hours worked on an as-and-when-needed basis, is usually paid by the hour or by the day. Again this is a method of employing people that does not require the organisation to make a long-term commitment to them. Casual workers may be employed to undertake specific projects or tasks or may also be employed during high demand periods. Casual workers are usually paid relatively low rates and undertake jobs which the permanent employees do not want to carry out.

VOLUNTARY

Non-profit-making organisations, which include charities in the voluntary sector, such as Greenpeace, Friends of the Earth, the Terence Higgins Trust and Oxfam, work on the basis that income generated after running costs and administration have been covered, should be passed onto the relevant charitable cause. For this reason, there are always opportunities for both unpaid and paid employment. With regard to unpaid work, a number of these charities have local retail outlets where they sell a range of second-hand, recycled or 'fair trade' goods. Although the managers of these shops may be paid, the shop assistants tend to be voluntary workers, although in some cases they may receive expenses. The voluntary sector has recently realised that, in order to prosper and support the charitable activities which it finances, it had to become significantly more professional in outlook. As a result charities now employ paid professionals to assist in the efficient running of their organisations. Whilst, in general terms, the pay scales and opportunities offered by voluntary organisations may be more limited than those of consumer-based organisations, many managers, administrators and marketing specialists 'cut their teeth' in voluntary organisations. We will be looking at some specific examples of voluntary sector employment in Element 8.3.3 of this Unit.

OWN BUSINESS (FAMILY BUSINESS, BUSINESS START-UP, GOVERNMENT ENTERPRISE SCHEME)

A great many people who run small to medium-sized businesses began their business life as part of a family business, or else they started a new business, perhaps with assistance from a government enterprise scheme.

Working for a family business has both positive and negative sides. In working in such an environment, a person can be somewhat cushioned from the major business pressures which a self-employed individual would have to face. At the same time, that person may be required to work substantially longer hours and for significantly less pay than in other forms of work. It is a time-honoured tradition for parents to pass their businesses on to their sons or daughters. The gradual repositioning of power and responsibility from parent to offspring can be a difficult and awkward process. As the parent gradually takes a 'back seat' in terms of the decision making and the day-to-day running of the business, the son or daughter will have to have been prepared to cope on their own.

Despite the fact that parents may be prepared to pass their business on to their sons or daughters, there is always the issue of continued 'interference'. This can cause considerable friction between the generations. Equally, the parents will require their offspring to provide for them financially and materially for the rest of their lives. This financial commitment will obviously place a burden of responsibility on the son or daughter. They may find themselves in a position where the business not only has to sustain their own requirements, but also those of the rest of their family. This is not to say that inheriting a family business is a bad thing. After all, much of the hard work in establishing a business has already been done. Developing the business and choosing a new direction or setting new objectives for the business offers the son or daughter ample opportunity to prove themselves.

With regard to the establishment of a new business, the individual is faced with an altogether different set of potential problems and opportunities. As you will have appreciated in the first two Elements of this Unit, there is a need for considerable forward planning and forecasting before embarking on such an enterprise. There is no limit to the possibilities of starting your own business, it is only limited by your own ability to convince potential providers of finance that your business plan will work, and that your business has a reasonable future. As we will see later in this Element, an individual considering starting up a new business will be able to count on the assistance of a number of different organisations. Good relations, particularly with the bank, or other providers of finance, is, of course, essential. Again, the success or failure of the business will be largely dependent upon the individual's ability to use his or her skills to the benefit of the business. Starting up a new business is very much a question of 'learning as you go'. No amount of training, development or advice can ensure that the individual is ready to tackle unforeseen problems. As we will see towards the end of this Element, it is advisable to evaluate your own strengths or weaknesses in a variety of different skills in order to establish, at least in your own mind, that you are capable of running your own business.

Banks, in particular, are very keen on supporting new businesses, provided they can show that the business is viable. It is obviously in the bank's interest to establish a good relationship with the business at the beginning of its life in the hope that the owner of the business will remain with that bank as a client for a considerable period of time.

Assistance from government enterprise schemes can usually be obtained via the local Training and Enterprise Council. Again, we will be identifying specific types of government enterprise schemes in Element 8.3.3. Essentially, these allowances or grants aim to underwrite for a particular period the financial requirements of a person starting up a business, so saving that person from having to take money out of the business in its very early stages. The different forms of support can be tailor-made to suit the circumstances of the individual. Great emphasis is placed on the individual's ability to formulate a credible business plan which can convince the TEC that the business is viable. These government enterprise schemes have different names in different areas of the country and, indeed, in some areas, particularly those which are assisted or urban programme areas, there may be an even greater variety of grants. Local authorities, in their role as local government, also offer advice about grants, premises and loans. The loans tend to be cheap and available in particular to younger individuals.

PARTNERSHIP

Entering into a partnership may be a viable alternative to risking beginning your own business. It is essential that an individual contemplating this course of action should look at the track record, assets and business prospects of the partnership. Remember that as a partner you are jointly and severally liable to the debts of that partnership. In practice, this means that you are responsible for ensuring that bills are paid and you may have to cover other partners' shares if they fail to pay. It is also wise to establish whether the other partners have sufficient assets that can be realised to cover their share of any debts. If a partnership has a history of unpaid bills, or indeed, lacks assets, then the partnership should not be considered.

It is also advisable to establish whether you can get on with the other members of the partnership. Since you will be making decisions which will affect the prosperity of all other partners, a good working relationship must be of prime importance.

It is normal practice for a solicitor to draw up a partnership agreement, or to have a look at a partnership agreement prepared by the existing partners.

FRANCHISE

Franchises offer the opportunity of starting your own business with a greater chance of survival than in other circumstances. The first three years of a new business's life are the most dangerous. Franchises have a much better record of surviving these crucial three years than any other form of new business.

It really goes without saying that an individual who buys a franchise will not acquire this relative peace of mind at no cost. You may have to pay a lump sum as well as paying an amount per year to the person who provided the franchise. The franchisee may also be tied in, contractually, to purchase products or services from the franchisor, and will not be able to benefit from shopping around for better prices.

The franchisor charges a percentage of sales per year, leaving the remainder of the profit (if any) to the franchisee.

In deciding whether or not to buy a franchise, you should follow these careful and precise steps:

1 Never use the franchisor's advisors in helping you to decide whether to pursue the purchase. Their advice may not be objective.
2 Employ an accountant to have a look at the forecasts provided to you by the franchisor.
3 Make sure that you employ a solicitor to look through the franchise contract.
4 Ask the franchisor, or investigate yourself, how many franchises have been sold and how they are doing.
5 Make sure that the franchisor is a member of the British Franchise Association.
6 Visit and talk to existing franchisees.

7 If the set-up charge is high and the ongoing percentage payments are low then this may mean that the franchisor will lose interest in your business. Make sure that you are not bound too much in terms of having to purchase products and equipment from the franchisor.
8 Investigate the franchisor by obtaining references and credit ratings.
9 Check that the franchise territory is clearly marked.
10 Find out whether any market research has been done in that territory.
11 Find out what happens to your franchise should you die.
12 What sort of product or service is involved? Does it have long-term appeal?
13 Check that any products or services have been patented or trademarked.
14 Establish the level of advertising that would be required.
15 Ascertain whether the franchisor's advisers, particularly for ongoing matters, are competent and efficient.

student activity

(PC 8.3.1, COM 3.2, 3.4, AON 3.1, 3.3, IT 3.1, 3.2)
Investigate the number of franchises in your local area. Are there any franchisors actively seeking franchisees in your area? If so, try to discover the following:

● what is the initial cost?
● what is the service fee?
● what is the advertising levy?
● what are the mark-ups demanded by the franchisor?
● are there any hidden costs of financing?
● how appropriate is the territory available to the franchise itself?

When you have carried out your research, present your findings in the form of a word processed report.

8.3.2 *Identify statutory requirements for employment or self-employment*

STATUTORY REQUIREMENTS

Regardless of the size or nature of the organisation, there are a number of **statutory requirements** which it is essential to address. These will relate to either your own personal circumstances or that of your employees or partners. It is imperative that these statutory requirements are addressed, as any breach of them will not only have serious implications in legal terms, but may also undermine the business's financial prosperity.

INCOME TAX (INDIVIDUALS, SMALL BUSINESS)

Self-employed individuals will normally pay their income tax at the beginning of January and at the beginning of July. This arrangement is somewhat different to that of employees who pay their tax on a weekly or monthly basis. The tax is assessed and paid on the previous year's activities. Working out a tax bill can be a complex issue.

It is in the best interests of the individual or small business to have some understanding of how the tax bill is worked out. It is essential to know how the tax system works and what allowances you can set against your income. Accounting records need to be kept so that tax calculations can be made. It is often a good idea to use a professional tax adviser to help you present your accounts properly.

Turning our attention to **partnerships**, the taxable income is worked out in a very similar way to that of a sole trader. You will still be able to deduct business expenses, you can still get tax relief on capital expenditure, on national insurance contributions and on losses. The tax burden placed on each partner is in proportion to the profit share of each individual partner.

The **limited company**, on the other hand, pays corporation tax and the taxation is not assessed against a particular individual. The limited company will pay capital gains tax and corporation tax.

VALUE ADDED TAX (VAT)

If you thought that tax was a difficult subject, then VAT is even worse! The VAT system is a method of using businesses to act as tax collectors for the government. It is an indirect tax in that it is only paid when a customer buys an article. A business person pays VAT on purchases and also charges VAT on goods sold. In basic terms, if a business has charged more VAT on goods sold

than it has paid in VAT on goods purchased, then it owes the Customs and Excise department the difference. If it has paid out more VAT than it has collected, then the Customs and Excise department owes it the balance.

VAT is, at present, 17.5 per cent on most products. There are some exemptions and there are also some items on which the level of VAT is not yet 17.5 per cent though it will rise to this level in the future.

It is the individual and not the business that is registered to pay VAT. For VAT purposes an organisation is an individual. There is, of course, a threshhold below which a business person does not charge VAT, but of course, he/she still pay it. If a business is not registered then it may not claim back VAT.

It is a good idea to contact the local Customs and Excise office to establish whether your business will be liable for VAT registration and the rules and regulations which involve VAT exemptions and payments.

NATIONAL INSURANCE

As a sole trader, or, indeed, as a partner you will have to pay **national insurance** in two ways. You will have to pay class 2 contributions which are a flat rate and class 4 contributions which are worked out as a percentage of your taxable profits.

VAT Notice 700/15/95 *The Ins and Outs of VAT*

The information in this notice was up to date at the month shown on the front cover (March 1995). The notice replaces VAT Leaflet 700/15/91, the Erratum slip dated 1 August 1991 and the Amendment dated 1 June 1992, which have been cancelled.

The changes in this edition of the publication are the result of generally updating and clarifying the guidance.

Other publications to which this notice refers are

> Notice 700 *The VAT guide*
> Notice 706 *Partial exemption*
> Notice 725 *The Single Market*
> Notice 723 *Refunds of VAT in the European Community and other countries*
> Notice 727 *Retail schemes*
> Notice 741 *Place of supply of services*
> Notice 700/1 *Should I be registered for VAT?*
> VAT Leaflet 700/12 *Filling in your VAT return*
> VAT Leaflet 700/51 *VAT Enquiries Guide*

FIG. 8.3.1 *The introductory page from HM Customs and Excise Department's booklet 'The Ins and Outs of VAT', which identifies other useful publications about VAT.*

Again, by law, in the case of employees the business acts as a tax collector. National insurance contributions must be deducted from your employees' pay and contributions must be sent to the Department of Social Security. Contributions entitle the individual to a range of benefits and pensions. By contacting your local Department of Social Security you will be able to obtain useful leaflets and guidelines on your national insurance contributions and collection arrangements and entitlements. National insurance is dealt with in more detail in Unit 7 of this book.

PENSION ARRANGEMENTS

If you are self-employed you pay class 2 national insurance contributions. If you are an employee, you pay class 1 contributions. These contributions entitle you to the basic state pension provided you have paid sufficient contributions during your working life. As an employee you can also make additional payments to the State Earnings Related Pension Scheme (SERPS).

Personal pension plans are a viable alternative in ensuring that you receive sufficient income once you have retired. Personal pension schemes are fairly flexible and include the following features:

- you can make regular contributions
- you can invest a lump sum
- you can alter the level of contributions
- you can factor inflation into your payments and final pension
- you can take a lower amount of pension and receive a tax-free lump sum at the end of the period
- you can use your pension to back up your mortgage
- you can use your pension fund in order to obtain a loan

In choosing your personal pension plan you may wish to investigate the different forms available, which include:

- non-profit
- with profit
- unit linked
- deposit/administration scheme

student activity

(PC 8.3.2, COM 3.2, 3.4, AON 3.1, 3.3)
Investigate the nature and availability of the above forms of personal pension plan. Can you identify which of the above versions would best suit your own purpose?

In the form of a chart, detail the advantages and disadvantages of each form of personal plan.

COMPANY REGISTRATION

It is a relatively simple task to form a company. You can quite easily buy a 'ready-made' company for around £250. Although this company may have a name already, you can change this for a further £50. You will then have to register your new company with the Companies Registration Office. This involves some form filling and will cost you a further £50. It is always advisable to use the services of a solicitor in the formation of a limited company. Automatically you will be required to provide the following:

- an annual return
- notification of changes in the company's directors
- notification of a change of company secretary

Individuals wishing to pursue this course of action would be best advised to obtain the leaflet *Disclosure Requirements* from Companies House. Companies House holds the public records of more than a million companies. We will return to the services provided by this organisation and its role in monitoring companies in the next section of this Element.

BENEFITS (FOR LOW PAID, TO PEOPLE STARTING A BUSINESS)

The Benefits Agency, which is an executive agency of the Department of Social Security, provides a range of benefits for both the low paid and those starting a new business.

Those who are on low incomes can apply for the following benefits:

1 *Income support* – this is a social security benefit for those aged 18 or over and whose income is below a certain level. A claimant may work, but for no more than 16 hours a week. The amount available very much depends on the following circumstances:

- your age
- whether you are with a partner
- the number and age of dependants
- whether you or your family have any disabilities
- how much money you and your partner are earning each week
- how much you and your partner have in savings

The income support payment is usually made up of three parts, which are:

- personal allowance
- a premium for those with special needs
- housing costs, which include mortgage interest payments

2 *Family credit* – this is a tax-free benefit for working families with children. In order to receive family credit you must be responsible for one child under 16 or one under 19 in full-time education. Many of the other restrictions and rules are similar to those which apply to income support.

3 *Housing benefit* – this is paid by local councils to individuals who need assistance in paying their rent. Individuals who are receiving income support and paying rent will usually be able to get maximum housing benefit. There are some restrictions and conditions placed upon the payment of housing benefit, and as with income support, the benefit is made up of three elements, which are:

- personal allowance
- dependants' allowance
- premiums for special needs

4 *Council tax benefit* – the rules which apply to housing benefit also largely apply to this benefit. Again there are certain restrictions, particularly in relation to income, personal circumstances and savings. This benefit takes the form of rebates against council tax bills.

5 *Social fund* – this helps individuals who are faced with expenses that are difficult to pay out of regular income. The social fund provides benefits under the following headings:

- maternity payments
- funeral payments
- cold weather payments
- community care grants

- budgeting loans
- crisis loans

6 *Free and reduced-price milk* – families in receipt of income support, pregnant women and children under 5 receive free milk and vitamins. If you have an infant you will also be entitled to reduced price dried baby milk.

7 *Help with NHS costs* – people on a low income may be able to obtain help to reduce NHS costs. Typically, these will include the following:

- prescription charges
- dental treatment
- sight tests and glasses
- travelling to hospital

There are several other benefits available to those who are self-employed, which are similar to those applicable to those on low income. There are two distinct groups of benefits. The first group consists of benefits which may be claimed provided the individual has paid sufficient national insurance contributions. These are:

- sickness benefit
- invalidity benefit
- maternity allowance
- retirement pension
- widows benefit
- unemployment benefit

The second group, which is not based on national insurance contributions, contains many of the benefits also applicable to the low paid, and, indeed, all employees. These are:

- income support
- housing benefit
- council tax benefit
- family credit
- social fund
- statutory sick pay
- statutory maternity pay
- severe disablement allowance
- attendance allowance
- disability living allowance
- disability working allowance
- invalid care allowance
- industrial injuries disablement benefit
- child benefit
- one parent benefit
- guardian's allowance

The Benefits Agency has produced some reasonably accessible booklets which include:

- Unemployment Benefit (leaflet NI12)
- Young People's Guide to Social Security (leaflet FB23)

- Which Benefit? (leaflet FB2)
- Self-Employed? (leaflet FB30)

All of these booklets contain specific information about many of the benefits listed on the previous page, as well as reference numbers of claim forms.

8.3.3 Identify sources of information and collect information for employment and self-employment

SOURCES OF INFORMATION

JOBCENTRES

Jobcentres are the UK's largest employment organisation. Not only do they guarantee that certain standards of service are maintained, but they are also committed to equal opportunities. Through a Jobcentre you may gain access to a wide variety of services. It should be borne in mind that at the time of writing, many of these services are under review and, indeed, it is widely believed that imminent legislation will lay down a new series of services, conditions and opportunities.

Jobcentres are an ideal place to begin looking for a job. The available job vacancies are clearly displayed on cards and all you are required to do is to note down the vacancies which interest you and take them to the reception desk.

If you are unemployed, a Jobcentre will be able to help you in your job search and will match you with a client advisor. The client advisor will issue you with a **Back To Work Plan**.

The advisor is a good source of information about benefits which you may be able to claim as well as employment and training opportunities available locally.

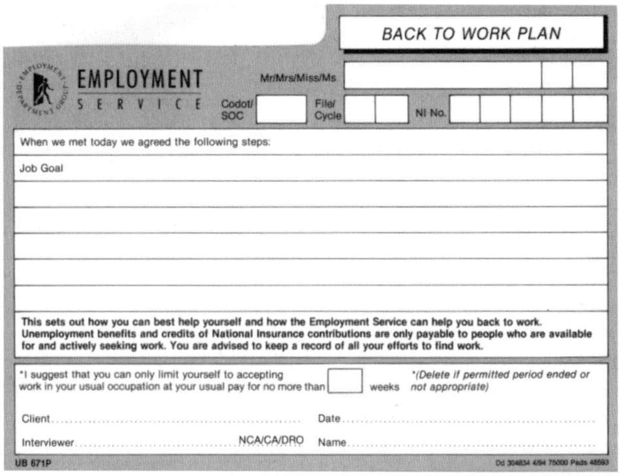
BACK TO WORK PLAN
EMPLOYMENT SERVICE
Mr/Mrs/Miss/Ms
Codot/SOC File/Cycle NI No.
When we met today we agreed the following steps:
Job Goal
This sets out how you can best help yourself and how the Employment Service can help you back to work. Unemployment benefits and credits of National Insurance contributions are only payable to people who are available for and actively seeking work. You are advised to keep a record of all your efforts to find work.
*I suggest that you can only limit yourself to accepting work in your usual occupation at your usual pay for no more than ☐ weeks *(Delete if permitted period ended or not appropriate)
Client.................. Date..................
Interviewer.................. NCA/CA/DRO Name..................
UB 671P
Dd 304834 4/94 75000 Pads 48593

FIG. 8.3.2 *The 'Back to Work Plan' produced by the Employment Service.*

As we will discuss in the next section of this Element, ITV and Channel 4 cover a number of job vacancies. ES Jobfinder provides a 24-hour a day Teletext service showing a selection of vacancies available, both within the UK and abroad. In addition to advertising job vacancies, ES also provides general help and services, and lists events in particular areas. All of the information contained within these services is regularly updated.

Provided you have been looking for a full-time permanent job for at least four weeks, you will be able to claim financial help from the Travel to Interview Scheme. After three months you will be asked to come back to see your advisor who will review and update your Back to Work Plan with you.

There are a number of specific schemes and initiatives available through the Jobcentres, as part of the Employment Department Group. These include:

1. *Job search seminars* – which look at job interviews, letter writing, CVs, making phone calls, typing and other skills. These last for four days spread over five weeks.
2. *Job review workshops* – lasting two days and using a computer programme to help you match your skills and preferences to new areas of work. This is especially useful for those with a professional, administrative or executive background.
3. *Restart interviews* – which are designed to give the individual a fresh start and access to a number of specific services, which include lists of jobs to apply for, a job interview (through job interview guarantee – see below), a place on a training programme, the opportunity for temporary work and help to start your own business.
4. *Job club* – this gives you direct help on telephone and interview techniques, access to telephones, newspapers and stationery all free of charge. These are organised by a job club leader who will also help you prepare job applications.
5. *Job interview guarantee* – which is a scheme which matches skills and qualifications against employers' vacancies and guarantees you an interview for the job.

6 *Job preparation course* – which will help you improve your interview technique and reassess your strengths and weaknesses.

7 *Employment on trial* – which gives you the opportunity to enter employment on a trial basis, provided you have worked there for six weeks.

8 *Work trial* – these last for up to three weeks and are useful for finding out whether you like a particular job. The employer has a real vacancy and this short trial period operates as an opportunity for you to assess the job and for the employer to see whether he/she likes you. You will receive your benefit during the work trial period, as well as receiving up to £5 per day for travel and £1.50 per day for meals.

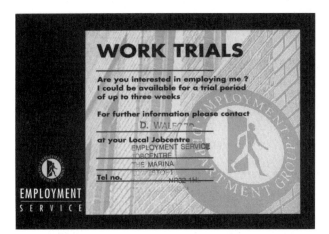

FIG. 8.3.3 *The Employment Service's Work Trials card.*

9 *Job plan* – these are workshops designed to identify your strengths and skills, to encourage you to look at new options and to use a computer program to match your preferences with possible jobs. These last for five days.

10 *Community action* – with an additional allowance over and above any other benefit you may be entitled to, this scheme aims to get individuals involved in environmental and conservation issues as well as administration, caring and research projects.

11 *Restart course* – this part-time two-week course aims to develop techniques to get you back to work, increase awareness of employment and training opportunities, understand the recruitment process and develop a plan of action.

12 *Disability employment advisor* – who helps those with a disability or health problem to find a job which will suit them.

13 *Job introduction scheme* – which allows you to try a job for an introductory period of six weeks. You will be paid the normal rate of pay by the employer during the trial period.

14 *Access to work* – particularly if you are disabled or have a health problem, access to work can offer up

to £21,000 over a five-year period to help you find a job, keep a job, or improve your career prospects. Typical examples of funding entitlements are adaptations to your car, payment of taxi fares, alterations to premises, alterations to equipment and the services of a communicator if you are deaf.

15 *Supported employment* – this scheme offers individuals who have severe disability supported placements, access to the re-employ Interwork and workshops.

It should be noted that a number of the schemes listed above are only available if you have been out of work for six months or more (in some cases three months). However, if you are an ex-offender or ex-services person, or have a disability, you will be entitled to be included on one of these schemes immediately. If you are returning to the job market after being away for more than two years, you will also be able to gain instant access to the schemes.

The Employment Department group's publication 'Just the Job', which is revised annually to take note of changes in the various schemes and initiatives, is a very valuable source of information for those seeking employment or self-employment. Jobcentres boast that they have succeeded in obtaining jobs for around 400,000 people per year.

Another important service which is provided by the Employment Department group is the **career development loan** (CDL) scheme. This enables you to borrow money from various banks – Barclays, Cooperative, Clydesdale or Royal Bank of Scotland. The CDL enables you to borrow between £200 and £8,000 for up to 80 per cent of any course fees. In addition you can claim the full costs of any books, materials or other related expenses. Those who have been out of work for three months or longer will be able to apply for up to 100 per cent of the course fees, as well as living expenses if the course is full-time.

One other service which is provided via Jobcentres is the **Be Your Own Boss** advice service and associated leaflets. These contain a great deal of practical information about self-employment, entering into partnerships or co-operatives, purchasing of a franchise, undertaking commission-only jobs and relevant training and professional advice. This service is run in

FIG. 8.3.4 *This is the 'Positive about Disabled People' symbol.*

conjunction with the local TECs or LECs. In essence, it is very similar to the Enterprise Allowance Scheme which is being phased out and being replaced by Enterprise 2000.

Euro Action is an annual event and promotion supported by BBC Radio 1 and the Employment Department group. It focuses on the following:

- education and training
- student grants, loans, sponsorships and scholarships
- job searches
- setting up businesses
- money management
- identifying opportunities in Europe
- education and training in Europe
- enterprise in Europe

If you are considering a career on continental Europe, then this is an ideal start. The Employment Department group, in association with the Overseas Placing Unit and European Employment Services, produces a range of booklets entitled 'Working in …'. Each of these booklets focuses on job opportunities and sources of information for all the major European countries.

Focus study

JOBCENTRES

As we have mentioned, the Jobcentres also produce very useful information packs on working in various countries. Typically, the pack will include information on the following:

- finding work
- immigration and registration documents
- health
- social security
- taxation
- employment issues
- accommodation
- education
- comparability of qualifications
- culture
- legal matters
- useful addresses
- reading
- checklist

Whilst it is probably inappropriate to focus on any one particular country, we have chosen to focus upon the checklist as a potential pro-forma device for ensuring that you have considered all of the main factors that may be involved in pursuing employment abroad.

student activity

(PC 8.3.3, COM 3.1, 3.4)

If you are interested in employment abroad, the following checklist provides a useful guide to matters that need to be addressed:

1 Find out whether you need a full UK passport or a visitors passport.
2 Find out the method and frequency of payment of any salary.
3 Find out what travel arrangements need to be made.
4 Find out whether the employer is prepared to pay these travel expenses, or indeed, make the arrangements.
5 Find out about the availability of accommodation.
6 Ensure that you have completed an E111 medical expenses cover form or have private health insurance.
7 Ensure that you have sufficient funds to last until you are paid.
8 Ensure that you have put aside sufficient money to pay for a return journey in the event of an emergency.

Some of these points are reasonably obvious, but you should identify who has responsibility for them. Of course, it will ultimately be you, but some other individuals or organisations will have a part in this. Also consider whether you would be prepared to accept employment abroad without knowing some of the above information. Discuss this point as a group.

EMPLOYMENT/RECRUITMENT AGENCIES

Employment and recruitment agencies offer a wide range of advice to a potential candidate in search of full-time employment. Agencies also offer seasonal or part-time job opportunities. Although these two types of agencies cater for slightly different markets, their common aims are to match potential candidates or applicants with the requirements of the employer. In other words, these agencies act as a 'clearing house' or initial selection filtering system for the employer. Normally the agency would receive a percentage of the successful candidates first year's salary in return for successfully placing the individual.

A person who works in a temporary capacity is not paid directly by the organisation for which he/she

FIG. 8.3.5 *Brook Street Permanent Recruitment Service produces this booklet which describes the services it offers to businesses.*

Focus study

RECRUITMENT AGENCIES

The Berkeley Scott Group was founded in 1984 and is market leader in hospitality management recruitment in Europe. This claim is established by the fact that they are the largest in terms of turnover, profitability and successfully placed applicants. They have three operating divisions, which are:

1 Berkeley Scott Selection, which provides a data base selection service for junior, middle and senior line managers.
2 International Service Industry Search (ISIS), which provides an executive search service to companies in order to satisfy their senior executive and non-executive appointments.
3 BSA Advertising and Marketing, which provides recruitment advertising services as well as design and printing facilities.

Working under an ethical code of conduct laid down by the trade association, they guarantee clients and candidates complete protection and confidentiality.

student activity

(PC 8.3.3, COM 3.1)
In relation to your own career intentions, try to identify any local or national employment or recruitment agencies that would be able to assist you in some way. Also consider at what point it would be appropriate to contact them. Should you wait until you need their help or should you establish an initial contact with them at this stage? Discuss this as a group.

works. The employer pays the agency an hourly rate for the employee's services and the employee receives a rather lower hourly rate from the agency. Many agencies, particularly if an applicant has useful and above all 'placeable' skills, will advise him/her on improvements to the CV and on interpersonal skills (particularly in interview situations).

Agencies are usually part of a network. Certainly, High Street employment agencies tend to be part of a chain. The advantage of this is that they are able to investigate employment opportunities in areas other than the immediate locality.

Recruitment agencies, on the other hand, tend to have city-centre locations and may have associations with other recruitment agencies, but tend to canvas for applicants in a slightly different manner.

Whilst employment agencies may advertise in the local press, or more typically, their own shop window, recruitment agencies tend to advertise exclusively in specialist publications to attract potential candidates.

CAREERS SERVICES

Careers services provide a major role both to employers and to potential employees. Essentially, they establish a link between schools and colleges and employers. It is advisable to ask for careers service advice as the advisor may be able to give you useful addresses, telephone numbers and contacts which may save a great deal of research.

MEDIA (NEWSPAPERS, TV, RADIO)

The various sections of the media offer variable levels of assistance in obtaining information about employment. There are very few jobs advertised on TV or on the radio. However, many independent television stations do not broadcast programmes in the early hours of the morning. Instead, using a teletext type service, they show printed details on the screen of employment prospects and specific vacancies in the TV region. Many of these job vacancies and opportunities are provided by the Jobcentres in the local area, or the jobs may be available through agencies. It should also be remembered that there are a number of TV and radio programmes which relate either directly or indirectly to certain employment areas. BBC2 and Channel 4, in particular, broadcast a number of programmes which specifically relate to certain occupations.

Without doubt, newspapers and magazines provide the majority of advertised vacancies and job opportunities. The national press often have specific days which they allocate to occupations in particular fields. Specialist magazines may be a useful source of information on occupations in their field. Employment and recruitment agencies advertise their current range of vacancies in the free newspapers and magazines distributed at tube or train stations. Indeed, the local press, either free sheets delivered to your home or newspapers which may be purchased in retail outlets, contain local job opportunities and vacancy details.

FIG. 8.3.6 *Norwich and Norfolk Great Yarmouth Chamber of Commerce and Industry provides a range of services to businesses in its area.*

Most printed material, such as newspapers and magazines, may be accessed at any local library or at Jobcentres.

FEDERATION OF SELF-EMPLOYED

The Federation of Self-Employed provides a network of regional and local groups to assist and support those engaged in self-employment. The organisation itself and, indeed, its members, provide a wealth of information and advice which is the accumulation of many years of experience.

FEDERATION OF SMALL BUSINESSES

The FSB aims to assist the 400,000 new enterprises which are established each year. With the financial support of Mercury Communications, the FSB is a leading campaign and pressure group. With nearly 60,000 members, it is concerned with bringing about favourable changes in legislation, particularly in relation to the protection and promotion of small businesses. One of the key services it offers is a 24-hour legal advice scheme. In its booklet 'Getting Started in Business' the FSB offers valuable advice on a number of issues, including finance, tax, premises, marketing, customer care and problem solving.

CHAMBERS OF COMMERCE

The network of Chambers of Commerce and Industry offer substantial support, services and facilities to businesses. These include:

● export advice
● adult and youth training
● advice on British Standards, company legislation, import and export documentation
● access to directories and mailing lists
● representation to local and central government
● subscription to magazines and newsletters
● office support services
● European information
● formal and informal social events

BANKS

As you will have already appreciated from the first two Elements of this Unit, banks perform a vital role in the following areas:

● financial facilities, including current accounts, overdrafts, loans, leasing, factoring and import and export assistance
● specialist services – primarily for small businesses through small business centres
● free banking in the first year for new businesses
● frank and objective advice and judgements regarding business problems
● advice on such business matters as insurance

Obviously the relationship you are able to strike up with your bank and bank manager will have a bearing on your willingness to involve them in your business affairs. It should be noted that it is advisable to always separate your business and personal financial affairs so that one does not influence the other.

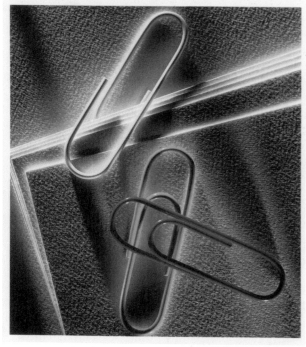

FIG. 8.3.7 *Lloyds Bank's booklet, 'Starting your own Business' is a very useful little guide.*

SOLICITORS

Solicitors offer invaluable advice on the following matters:

- business advice
  - legal forms of business
  - personal guarantees
  - employment law
  - debt collection
- contracts
  - terms and conditions
  - leases
  - franchise agreements
- product protection
  - patents
  - registered trademarks

Choosing a solicitor can be as important as choosing a bank. Solicitors tend to specialise in different areas of the law but if you choose a partnership you will inevitably benefit from the combined skills of the partners. As with accountants, it is also advisable to choose a larger firm as you will be able to benefit from their credibility. It is always advisable to request an estimate of costs before engaging the services of a solicitor.

ACCOUNTANTS

In choosing an accountant, particularly at the beginning of your business venture, you have to weigh up whether you wish to engage the services of a large or small concern. Whilst larger firms of accountants may be unwilling to provide basic bookkeeping services, a small accountancy firm may not be able to assist you in raising finance. It is, therefore, a balancing act which must be based on your own particular requirements. Generally speaking accountants offer the following advice:

- accounts
  - bookkeeping
  - setting up an accounting system
  - advice on computerised accounting packages
  - auditing
- finance
  - managing cash
  - raising and negotiating finance
  - raising venture capital
- tax
  - PAYE
  - national insurance
  - business tax
- general business advice
  - business plans
  - budgets
  - forecasts
  - form of business

It is advisable to ensure that your accountant has some formal accountancy qualifications. This is indicated by certain letters after his or her name, such as ACA or FCA, which means he or she is a member of the Institute of Chartered Accountants (or CA if in Scotland), or ACCA or FCCA, signifying that he/she is a member of the Chartered Association of Certified Accountants. Trying to establish accountancy costs may be difficult as they are usually based on the number of hours the accountant has to spend working on your books.

SURVEYORS/ESTATE AGENTS

You may require the services of a surveyor or estate agent in the course of your search for suitable premises. They will be able to provide you with structural surveys, they will negotiate with landlords or vendors and will give advice on planning permission. It is advisable to ensure that any surveyor you use is a member of the Royal Institution of Chartered Surveyors. Again, it is advisable to make sure that these professionals give you a quote before they carry out any work for you.

DESIGN CONSULTANTS

These individuals can provide a crucial service to the business. Whilst they may not be as central to the success of your business as an accountant or a solicitor, they may be able to advise you on the following:

- the image of your business
- shop fitting
- designing the look of your product
- employee uniforms
- choosing van livery
- production of logos, brochures and leaflets
- design of packaging

TRAINING AND ENTERPRISE COUNCILS (TECS) AND LOCAL ENTERPRISE COMPANIES

There are 82 Training and Enterprise Councils (TECs) throughout England and Wales. Scotland has 22 Local Enterprise Companies (LECs). Both of these organisations offer training and support for small businesses in the interests of addressing the needs of the local community.

Each TEC and LEC has its own particular programme. Generally speaking, the training opportunities include:

- **enterprise awareness events** – which aim to alert potential new businesses to the demands and problems associated with setting up a new business
- specific **business training** aimed at assisting the setting up or development of businesses
- **open learning skills programmes** – business skill seminars on such topics as management and marketing
- information and advice on the **investors in people** IiP) programme
- **training** programmes for **employees**
- co-ordination and planning for **small firms training loans**

TECs and LECs are also involved in the following **business services**:

I *Training access points* (TAPS) – which provide information about local and national training opportunities. These TAPs can usually be found in libraries and High Street locations, as well as in TECs and LECs.

FIG. 8.3.8 *This booklet, 'Run your own business', is issued by Norfolk and Waveney Training & Enterprise Council.*

2 *Counselling and advice* – TECs, LECs and Local Enterprise Agencies also offer advice to both new businesses and existing businesses. Through the services of a personal business advisor, who will be found in **Business Link** (see p. 667), a wide range of problem solving advice is provided.

3 *Consultancy* – the Enterprise Initiative Consultancy Scheme enables small businesses to employ consultants in specific areas. This service is also available through **Business Link**.

4 *Investors in people* – based on the premise that training and development of employees is crucial in the successful development of a business, IiP is an initiative which helps businesses address this consideration. Operating with national standards the TECs and LECs offer guidance in this matter.

TECs or LECs handle a number of other services and initiatives, which include the following:

I *Business Development Centres* – which provide informal advice, information and guidance, as well as other business services. These may be contacted via a freephone number.

2 *Enterprise 2000* – which is designed to give specific help and support in starting your own business. It offers impartial advice from experienced business counsellors as well as seminars on marketing, finance, business administration and preparing a business plan.

3 *Target training* – this offers specialist advice to match your specific ambitions and education. The scheme provides an allowance of £29.50 per week if you are 16 and £35 a week if you are over 17 during the training programme. You will be engaged in on-the-job training which is provided by an employer and a college (or training agency). The studies may take up to two years and there is every chance that you may be offered full-time employment by your employer.

4 *Business Development Fund* – this service provides information on everything you need to know about financial support for your business. It has been primarily set up to help small to medium-sized businesses (i.e. those with up to 100 employees).

DEPARTMENT OF TRADE AND INDUSTRY (DTI)

The DTI itself offers a bewildering selection of advice and networking facilities to new businesses.

Business Link is a business support network for new businesses which calls on the considerable resources of the DTI. It aims to provide a flexible business advice service on a single site where new business can obtain information about all the DTI services available from that location. An integral part of the Business Link is a personal business advisor (PBA) who is there to help small firms in the following ways:

* problem solving
* production of action plans
* access to business support services

There are also a number of regional assistance programmes that are related to the four main government departments involved in business-related matters. These government departments are:

* Employment
* Trade and Industry
* Environment
* Transport

Recently the four departments have been integrated into offices known as Government Offices (GOs) for the regions.

COUNCILS

County councils, in particular, and, indeed, all borough councils offer access to information and advice for small businesses and those considering self-employment.

FIG. 8.3.9 *The Department of Trade and Industry's booklet, 'A guide to help for small firms', includes a comprehensive list of schemes, initiatives, addresses and contacts.*

They produce a number of useful booklets which can be used as a checklist for accessing the names and addresses of relevant organisations. Nearly all councils will have their own business advisors or, at the very least, they will have a business library, which is usually located in a central library.

INDUSTRIAL COMMON OWNERSHIP MOVEMENT

This organisation has assisted 2,500 enterprises since 1971. It is primarily concerned with worker co-operatives where the business is owned and democratically controlled by those who work in it. The assets and reserves of the business are held in common and jointly owned by the members. ICOM acts as an access organisation to other specific specialists and initiatives such as the European Social Fund, the UK Co-operative Council and the European Federation of Worker Co-operatives. Worker co-operatives are a viable alternative to some of the more traditional forms of business enterprise.

CHARITABLE ORGANISATIONS

Charitable organisations, perhaps rather surprisingly, offer the opportunity of both voluntary and paid work. As you may remember when we discussed the marketing of non-profit-making organisations back in Unit 3, we saw that these organisations require specialist skills from their employees in order to survive in an increasingly competitive market. The process of acquiring a full-time paid job for a charitable or voluntary organisation is similar to that you would follow in applying to a profit-motivated organisation. However, there are some significant differences. For example the individual may have to attest that he/she embraces the philosophy and purposes of the organisation.

Alternatively, charitable and voluntary organisations offer an individual the opportunity to engage in meaningful work (without pay) which could not only broaden his or her horizons, but also provide vital job skills and experience. It is quite common for individuals, on leaving full-time education, to offer their services to a voluntary organisation. This meaningful use of their time and skills can be undertaken whilst they seek employment or pursue an interest in self-employment. You will find a variety of voluntary organisations in both your Yellow Pages and via your local library. Many areas have a voluntary services bureau which acts rather like an agency, placing temporary workers, although, of course, no money changes hands.

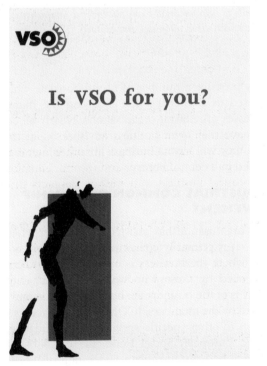

FIG. 8.3.10 *Voluntary Service Overseas produces this booklet, 'Is VSO for you?', which gives you all the information you need in order to decide about working as a volunteer overseas.*

Focus study

VOLUNTARY SERVICE OVERSEAS

Voluntary Service Overseas (VSO) was founded in 1958 and sends volunteers to over 55 countries throughout the world. These individuals are sent abroad as a result of requests from governments or other relief and development agencies and other non-governmental organisations. VSO is open to anyone over 20 who is prepared to spend at least two years overseas. There are some stipulations and restrictions which include:

- no dependent children
- willingness to work for a small allowance
- a full UK passport must be held
- the individual should be qualified
- the individual should have at least 18 months experience.

VSO primarily acts as a recruitment agency for overseas employers. As a volunteer, you are employed by an organisation in the country where you are working.

The UK headquarters of VSO is in London and has a 24-hour answerphone service.

student activity

(PC 8.3.3, COM 3.2, 3.4, IT 3.1)
If you are remotely interested in offering your services on a voluntary basis, contact VSO and establish what qualifications and work experience you would need to have to be a volunteer. Your letter to VSO should be word processed.

COMPANIES HOUSE

As we mentioned in the previous section, Companies House holds the public records of more than a million companies. Companies House itself has four major statutory functions, these are:

1 To incorporate and dissolve companies.
2 To examine and hold documents presented under the Companies Act and other legislation.
3 To make this information available to the public.

4 To exercise certain powers in relation to companies on behalf of the Secretary of State for Trade and Industry.

Every company is legally obliged to provide Companies House with certain information. This includes the following:

- an annual return
- its registered office address
- details of its directors and shareholders
- annual accounts

Companies House attempts to ensure that this information is available to any individual who wishes to gain access to it. In doing this the organisation helps to provide necessary peace of mind for consumers, creditors and shareholders.

As companies are required to meet their filing obligations, this means that Companies House can provide up-to-date and accurate information. If an organisation fails to lodge its details with Companies House then the directors of the company can be liable for fines and the company can be fined up to £5,000. There are a number of offices around the country, including Cardiff (Head Office), London, Manchester, Birmingham, Leeds, Edinburgh and Glasgow.

Companies House provides a twofold service to individuals seeking employment or self-employment. If an individual wishes to check on the status of an organisation for which he/she is considering working, Companies House will provide a great deal of background material. For an individual who wishes to create a new business, the involvement of Companies House is, as we have said, imperative.

PROFESSIONAL ASSOCIATIONS

There are a number of professional associations or organisations which represent the different professions. As you would imagine, these cover the traditional professions, such as accountancy, law, and marketing.

Other professional organisations include the Law Society. There are around 60,000 solicitors practising in England and Wales and the Law Society aims to provide advice on training, qualifications and other opportunities to potential solicitors. It also assists individuals in grappling with the complexities of European law.

LOCAL ENTERPRISE AGENCIES (LEAS)

There are over 400 LEAs throughout the UK which offer business advice and counselling to new or expanding businesses. They also offer extensive assistance in the formation of business plans. The LEAs have very good links with various businesses and organisations in the local area. They will be able to offer you either direct assistance or referral to an organisation which can provide that help. You can obtain the address and telephone number of your local LEA from the TECs, LECs or Jobcentres.

student activity

(PC 8.3.3)
Try to identify a professional association or organisation that it would be advisable to join in your chosen career or profession. What benefits does this organisation offer you and what would be the costs and implications of membership?

EUROPEAN INFORMATION CENTRES

European Information Centres (EICs) aim to provide information about trading with other member states, EU regulations, directives and recommendations. They also assist businesses in making contacts throughout Europe.

RURAL DEVELOPMENT COMMISSION

This government agency plays a key role in helping people in rural areas to expand their businesses. It is primarily interested and concerned with rural areas that are suffering from job losses in agriculture and related industries.

AGRICULTURAL DEVELOPMENT AND ADVISORY SERVICE

ADAS is now known as the Food, Farming, Land and Leisure Consultancy and provides advice to farmers throughout England and Wales.

SPECIFIC REGIONAL ORGANISATIONS

In **Northern Ireland** the Local Enterprise Development Unit exists to offer a range of measures aimed at developing and assisting small businesses.

In **Wales** businesses can seek assistance from the Welsh Development Agency or the Development Board for Rural Wales, as well as from the TECs. These organisations' services include:

- information about the purchase or rental of premises
- inward investment and financial help

In **Scotland**, Scottish Enterprise and Highlands and Island Enterprise are responsible for advising and assisting businesses. In practice their services are contracted out to the Local Enterprise companies.

THE PRINCES YOUTH BUSINESS TRUST/PRINCES SCOTTISH YOUTH BUSINESS TRUST

These organisations offer grants or low interest loans to individuals between the ages of 18 and 29. Specifically they will provide assistance to those who are encountering difficulties in raising finance from other sources. They also provide advice, training and marketing opportunities to businesses.

LIVE WIRE

This initiative, sponsored by Shell (UK) Ltd, offers advice and assistance to young business people. An integral part of this initiative is a competition held annually to reward excellence and achievement by young people.

LOCAL INVESTMENT NETWORKING COMPANY

This nationwide introduction service between investors and small businesses has been set up jointly by the Local Enterprise Agencies. It aims to assist the acquisition of start-up growth capital for the business. This service may be obtained via the TEC, LEC or Business in the Community organisation.

REGIONAL HELP

There are a number of regional enterprise grants available to small businesses. These include the following:

- Regional Selective Assistance Discretionary Grants (RSA), aimed at creating new jobs or safeguarding existing ones
- Regional Enterprise Grants for Investment Projects – available in development areas and some coal closure areas, offering up to £15,000
- Regional Enterprise Grants for Innovation Projects, offering grants of up to £25,000 for new projects
- Regeneration Grants Traditional Coal Mining Areas, offering funding of up to £1m. to most manufacturing and service organisations in the form of loans and equity
- Steel Areas, offering fixed-interest loans for start-up and expansion in steel closure areas
- Inner City Task Forces, offering advice and information regarding finance, particularly useful for new or small businesses with no track record or collateral
- Rural Development Commission (RDC), which provides the following:
  - conversion costs for redundant buildings
  - business advisory services
  - advice on raising finance
  - grants for plant and equipment
  - grants for marketing projects
- small firms training loans – aimed at organisations employing up to 50 people to pay for vocational educational training, available through the Employment Department. Organisations can borrow up to £125,000. The repayment schedule and interest rates are highly competitive.

EUROPEAN UNION

There are a number of initiatives established by the European Union which include the business and innovation centres. The BICs offer a wide range of support services as part of the European Business and Innovation Centre network.

Another EU-related initiative is the EU Value Relay Centres which aim to provide EU research and development programmes. They have access to contacts, experts and other useful resources via UK and EU data bases.

INNOVATION AND TECHNOLOGY

Although these are not strictly within the normal trading opportunities for business studies students, there are a number of specific organisations which relate to technology. These include the following:

- the Engineering and Physical Sciences Research Council (EPSRC)
- Environmental Technology Best Practice Programme
- EUREKA
- Innovation and technology counsellors
- LINK
- The Prince of Wales Award for Innovation
- Regional Technology Centres (RTCs)
- The Senior Academics in Industry Scheme (SAIS)
- The Shell Technology Enterprise Programme (STEP)
- The Small Firms Merit Award for Research and Technology (SMART)

- Support for Products under Research (SPUR)
- The Teaching Company Scheme (TCS)
- UK Science Parks Association

THE BRITISH FRANCHISE ASSOCIATION

The BFA helps to ensure that UK franchising develops in an ethical and responsible manner. The association has 120 franchisor members, accounting for some 10,000 franchised outlets. It has also established links with over 50 professional advisors who are experienced in giving advice to franchisees. The BFA sponsors two national franchise exhibitions held in London in March and at Birmingham's NEC in October. If you were considering purchasing or entering into a franchise agreement then you would be advised to contact the BFA or at least attempt to attend one of its exhibitions.

SMALL BUSINESS BUREAU

Established in 1976, the Small Business Bureau is a lobbying association for small to medium-sized businesses. In its short history it has achieved the following:

- established an influential business newspaper called *Small Business News*
- successfully eased legislative, financial and bureaucratic burdens on small businesses
- published regular information bulletins and discussion documents
- established a policy unit
- launched the Women into Business initiative in 1986

The Small Business Bureau enables new businesses to keep in touch with trends and opportunities across a wide range of business ventures. In addition it offers the opportunity for small businesses to network successfully with other members in their area.

8.3.4 *Identify opportunities for employment or self-employment*

If you have looked at the end of this Element to see what you will be required to do in the Assignment, you will have discovered that you need to identify opportunities for employment or self-employment. In this performance criterion you must begin this process by focusing on specific opportunities in your local area or perhaps nationally, or even in Europe. Any work that you undertake at this point will be of great value when you are required to present your plan for employment or self-employment.

student activity

(PC 8.3.4, COM 3.1, 3.2, 3.4)

One of the first things that you will need to do in order to fulfil the requirements of this performance criterion, and, indeed, the Element as a whole, is to find out the location of possible sources of information. We identified in the previous performance criterion of this Element the principal sources of information, but, since each part of the country is different from others, there is no guarantee that all of these sources of information will be available in your area. You may be fortunate enough to have a local council or local library which serves as an information point for much of this material.

There is one other thing that you should perhaps consider before embarking upon a particular line of investigation. If you can, you should seek an interview with your **Careers Officer**. If you do not have one, then you should attempt to make contact with the Careers Service provided by your Local Authority. At this point, and on the basis of the information gathered from the careers interview, you should have identified the direction in which your investigation should move. Principally, you will be heading in one of three directions:

- full-time employment
- self-employment
- further or higher education

You may have decided to incorporate two or even three of these choices. You may have considered self-employment coupled with part-time education. You may have even considered full-time education and part-time employment. Whatever your choice, you must now address the specific job opportunities available to you.

In the form of an **action plan**, identify at least five separate opportunities. You may find it useful to use the following headings as a guide:

Opportunity	Contact(s)	Finances required	Duration	Leading to

Using this pro-forma, prepare a draft of your plan and present this, along with evidence of research, such as leaflets, brochures and booklets, to your tutor. This will enable your tutor to make an initial assessment of the viability of your plan for employment or self-employment.

8.3.5 *Analyse and discuss skills to support employment or self-employment*

SKILLS

This performance criterion aims to analyse and discuss your own **skills** in relation to your proposed employment or self-employment plans. The format of this performance criterion is somewhat different from the rest of the book. In essence, we have presented this criterion as a series of checklists and activities to help you identify, analyse and make you think about your skills.

EVALUATING OWN STRENGTHS AND WEAKNESSES

Perhaps the best place to start is an analysis of your own general strengths and weaknesses. By doing this you may be able to begin to realise your own potential and limitations.

WORKING WITH OTHERS AND WORKING INDEPENDENTLY

Participation in decision making, problem solving and information seeking may be a day-to-day requirement, regardless of the nature of the job. Individuals who undertake tasks within the environment of a small business may be required to be the sole contributor. In many other cases, even when a business is particularly small, two or more individuals may have to combine their talents and abilities to cope with certain projects or tasks.

The student activity opposite aims to assess whether you are more of a team worker than an independent worker.

PLANNING AND TIME MANAGEMENT

Planning plays an important role in ensuring not only that tasks are carried out at the correct time, but also that they are given sufficient allocation of time and resources. Different people use a variety of planning techniques which aim to establish a forward thinking structure to their proposed activities in the future. As you will be aware, **action planning** is a valuable technique in establishing and monitoring the time and resource implications of tasks to be carried out in the future.

As we have seen in previous Units, **time management** involves not only other people, but also physical, paper, space and other priorities. It involves the constant reappraisal of priorities, but must be tempered with the possible impact on your relationships with others. The second Student Activity on page 674 attempts to analyse your time management potential.

SETTING TARGETS AND REVIEWING PROGRESS

As we have seen in previous Units, it is important not only to set reachable targets but also to have a process of continual review. In doing this the individual will, of course, need to have planned ahead and be able to manage his/her own time. It is worth remembering at this stage that many of the skills that are required for either employment or self-employment overlap one another significantly. It is often difficult, if not impossible, to achieve certain objectives or display particular skills without having laid some foundation via the use of another skill.

`0:40`

student activity

(PC 8.3.5, COM 3.4)

Answer the following questions, using the following responses:

- always
- sometimes
- occasionally
- never

1 Are you able to work long hours?
2 Do you find problems a challenge?
3 Can you come up with good ideas to get out of problems?
4 If you started a new business and it was struggling would you be prepared to keep it going?
5 Are you able to keep going at something until it is completed?
6 Would you always put your own business before any other consideration, including your leisure activities and your family?
7 Do you always show persistence and stamina?
8 Would you always consider success to be measured in terms of financial achievement?
9 Would you be able to live under a constant threat of insecurity in terms of your job and your income?
10 Do you consider yourself to be self-confident?
11 Are you able to take criticism?
12 Do you tend to ask for comments on your performance in the hope that you can do something better next time?
13 Do you tend to believe that your success is dependent upon external factors?
14 Do you tend to take on a leadership role in situations?
15 Are you good at finding the right person or source of information to help you achieve what you want?
16 Do you have the ability to realise that in certain circumstances you may need help?
17 Do you have a tendency to set particularly high standards for yourself?
18 Do you tend to take risks rather than follow a cautious line?
19 Are you invariably healthy?
20 Do you have the ability to delegate?
21 Are you able to distinguish important decisions from unimportant ones?
22 Do others consider you to be a real survivor?
23 Do you find coping with problems a real difficulty?
24 Do you consider yourself to be able to respect others' views and opinions?
25 When others express an opinion or offer advice and information, are you able to accept what they say?

If you have answered these questions with predominantly **always** or **sometimes** responses, then you are probably more suited to self-employment than others. If you have not answered these questions in the way mentioned above, then what do you think you could do to adapt to the demands that you will inevitably face as a business owner?

We will now try to assess your own ability in setting targets and reviewing their progress:

DECISION MAKING AND PROBLEM SOLVING

Decision making is a fundamental skill that any individual within a business context must address. We all make innumerable decisions on a day-to-day basis, but we may not recognise them as such. There is no reason to believe that decisions in a business environment are any different from the choices and the processes that you go through in making decisions in your private life. Often the options available to you will be more extensive than you are used to or they may appear to be more extensive but on closer examination it turns out that they are not. Again, we must refer back to our theme throughout this section of the Element, that all of these skills are **interrelated**. Without having first established **how** you will make the decision, **when** you will make the decision and **why** you will make the decision, you cannot expect to find yourself in a position to **make** that decision.

Problem solving is, to some extent, a variation of decision making itself, but often it concerns a situation that requires an immediate response. In this it differs from decision making, which often deals with longer-term problems. Again, a great many problems will arise without a great deal of notice. As we discussed in Unit 2,

student activity

(PC 8.3.5, COM 3.4)
Respond to the following questions by giving one of the following answers:

- **I agree**
- **I neither agree nor disagree**
- **I disagree**

1 I have a tendency to want to control the tasks and environment around me.
2 I have the desire to be involved in everything.
3 I find it impossible to delegate.
4 I hate being uncertain about things.
5 I generally do not trust other people's ability to do a job.
6 I hate asking other people for favours.
7 I like to be alone when I have things to do.

8 I invariably check and amend other people's work.
9 I would rather stop doing what I am doing than let someone else do what I think I should be doing.
10 I lose interest in a task if someone else interferes in what I am doing.

If you have predominantly **agreed** with the above statements, then you are much more of a solitary creature than a team player. If you have **neither agreed nor disagreed** with the statements, then either you may be unsure of what you may do in certain situations, or it may not actually worry you whether you are working alone or as a member of a team. Those who have **disagreed** with the majority of the statements should be fairly reasonable group workers.

student activity

(PC 8.3.5, COM 3.4)
Try to answer the following statements with either **true** or **false**:

1 I have identified my strengths in relation to time management.
2 I have identified my weaknesses in relation to time management.
3 I can accurately map where I waste my time.
4 I know why I allow my time to be managed badly.
5 I am able to prioritise my tasks in an efficient manner.
6 I can process and evaluate information rapidly.

7 I appreciate the reasons behind my time wasting behaviour.
8 I can employ a variety of different techniques to manage my time.
9 I can cope with other individuals who may divert me from my tasks in hand.
10 I am able to control my time.

If you have responded **'true'** to the majority of these questions, then you have already begun to manage your time effectively. If you have a number of **'false'** responses to these statements, then you may have to consider employing new or more strict conditions upon yourself and rules applying to others.

student activity

(PC 8.3.5, COM 3.4)
Answer the following questions **yes** or **no**:

1 Before setting a target I need to be totally aware of what is required.
2 In setting a target I am aware of the limitations of skills, resources and time.
3 I only set achievable targets.
4 Once a target has been set I will do everything within my power to ensure that it is achieved.
5 In certain cases, it is appropriate to amend the target if circumstances have changed.
6 The review procedures should be an integral part of the planning of the target setting.
7 Reviewing progress should be an ongoing procedure with regular and systematic checks.
8 It is a good idea to use the skills of another individual to assist in the review of progress.
9 Reviewing progress can often throw light upon the reasons that targets are not met.
10 In certain cases, the review procedure may require the target to be changed.

If you have agreed with the majority of these statements, then you have begun to appreciate the importance of setting targets and the integral nature of a review procedure. If you are unsure about some of these statements, then you will need to consider being a little more practical in the setting of your targets and rather more rigorous in their review than you may be at present.

The following Student Activity aims to establish whether you are able to make effective decisions and solve problems:

student activity

(PC 8.3.5, COM 3.4)
Answer the following questions with either a **yes** or **no**:

1 I can identify the potential nature and sources of problems before they happen.
2 I have already established the possible solutions before I make a decision.
3 I have clear criteria relating to acceptable solutions.
4 I am able to compare possible solutions and choose the right one.
5 I can implement and monitor the results of my decisions.
6 I am able to formulate a problem before it really becomes a problem.
7 I never make a snap decision.
8 I would rather consider the problem at length than risk making the wrong decision.
9 I do not find decision making stressful but it is challenging.
10 If I manage information correctly and am aware of its implications, then decision making is relatively easy.

If you have answered yes to the majority of the questions, then you have some grasp of the decision-making process and are reasonably able to solve problems. Alternatively, you may be somewhat over-confident and you should be aware of the potential dangers of over-confidence in the sense that you may not be fully able to predict, process and make logical decisions. If you said no to the majority of or some of these statements, then you are perhaps being a little more honest with yourself. Whilst it is desirable to be able to claim that you can make effective decisions and solve problems, you have obviously appreciated that these skills come with time and experience. There are only a handful of even highly experienced managers who could claim with their hand on their heart that they always make the right decision and they are invariably able to solve problems effectively.

when we looked at the various management and leadership styles, there are very many ways of handling such situations. Despite what we may have said in that earlier Unit, one of the most common forms of problem solving is still **crisis management**. An individual who is forced to follow this panic route will find him/herself unable to plan or manage time effectively since he/she is constantly having to respond to problems of a petty or unimportant nature. If these problems are ignored, however, they may become much bigger than they actually are and consequently may require a decision to be made. The transformation from a problem to a situation that requires a decision can often be a subtle one.

INFORMATION SEEKING AND HANDLING

Following on from the processes involved in decision making and problem solving, the **acquisition of information** and the subsequent **handling** of it are other key skills to obtain. Naturally, the information that you are able to obtain, handle and process will be vital in establishing your ability to communicate to a third party.

The following Student Activity seeks to investigate your information seeking and handling skills:

student activity

(PC 8.3.5, COM 3.4)
Answer these questions with either **yes** or **no**:

1 I invariably know what information I need.
2 I invariably know from whom or where I can obtain the information.
3 I do, of course, know why I want it.
4 I have a good idea of the time-scale involved.
5 I have some requirements about the format in which the information should be delivered.
6 Once I have the information I know what I have to do with it.
7 I can look at the information and know what is valuable and what is useless.
8 I can process the information and present it in a more clear and logical manner.
9 Once I have reformatted the information I can draw clear conclusions from it.
10 I also know the use of the information and to whom it should be relayed.

If you have answered these questions with a predominantly **affirmative** response, then you have a fairly clear understanding of the research, investigation and handling skills that relate to information. You should be aware, however, that in this slightly over-confident stance you may run the risk of overlooking some vital piece of information and may have discarded potentially valuable data by only giving them a cursory glance. Alternatively, if you have a mixture of **yes** and **no** responses, or predominantly **no** responses, you should not consider yourself a failure in this respect. A cautious user of information and, indeed, a careful handler of information may see things that the more confident handler may miss.

COMMUNICATING

The use and development of communication skills is an important consideration when attempting to establish relationships with others. You will encounter a number of different sets of circumstances which may require you to assume certain standards of communication. At other times you will need to display power and authority through your communication ability. The following Student Activity may enable you to identify some of your communication skills:

student activity

(PC 8.3.5, COM 3.4)
Answer these questions with either a **true** or **false**:

1 I can use a variety of communication methods including body language.
2 I can listen effectively and display correct responses.
3 I am able to manage myself in the communication process.
4 I am able to manipulate relationships through my communication.
5 I am able to cope with both formal and informal communications situations.
6 I am able to use a variety of different questioning techniques when seeking information.
7 I am able to read the body language of other people.
8 I appreciate that communication is a two-way process.
9 I am able to communicate well in written form.
10 I am able to present information in a variety of different visual formats.

It will only be the most accomplished communicator that will be able to claim that he/she can display all of the above characteristics. If you have responded **'false'** to a number of the statements above, then you should consider how these communication aspects may be improved.

APPLYING NUMBER

Regardless of your role, either in a business organisation (as an employee) or as a self-employed individual, you will inevitably face a mountain of paperwork. Within this treasure-trove of information you will encounter numerous pieces of data which will require some form of numerical processing. The successful manipulation of numbers or figures in whatever format is another skill that closely relates to other personal abilities.

The Student Activity below aims to assess not only your understanding of numerical manipulation but also your understanding of the importance of getting the answer correct.

USING INFORMATION TECHNOLOGY

Increasingly, the use of information technology has permeated all levels of business activity. It is rare to find an organisation which does not employ information technology to assist in the streamlining and general efficiency of its operations. Whilst it is rare for a person who is not an information technology specialist to be capable of understanding the complexities of information technology, you should by now have a general ability to handle such equipment and systems.

The first Student Activity on page 678 attempts to address the specific information technology requirements of a standard business organisation.

OCCUPATIONAL SKILLS

Obviously, occupational skills refer to specific skills in relation to your chosen profession, career or vocation. You will need to understand that in employment or self-employment, individuals have specific occupational skills which may vary. In general terms, some of the broader skills and knowledge are addressed in the second Student Activity on page 678.

    `0:20`

student activity

(PC 8.3.5, COM 3.4)
You will need to answer the following questions with one of these responses:

- **fully experienced**
- **somewhat experienced**
- **a little knowledge**
- **no knowledge**

In relation to these responses we will not, of course, expect you to have actually carried out these tasks or displayed these skills in a 'real environment'. However, if you feel that you know the implications and procedures involved, you may give the answer that you are experienced.

1 Do you feel that you could keep accurate accounting books such as sales and purchases ledgers and cash books?
2 Do you think that you are able to chase bad debts?
3 Do you feel that you have an understanding of controlling cash flow?
4 Do you feel that you understand the techniques behind break-even analysis?
5 Do you feel that you understand the correct use of an overdraft?

6 Do you feel that you have the ability to present a request for finance?
7 Do you feel that you could understand the complexities of leasing?
8 Do you feel that you could understand the complexities of factoring?
9 Do you feel that you could cope with the estimation of long-term financial needs and raising the necessary finance?
10 Do you feel that you could identify and analyse sources of long-term finance?

If you have claimed competence in the criteria above, then we must assume that you have had considerable work experience in the past. Alternatively, you may consider that the exercises and activities undertaken as a part of this course have been sufficient to prepare you for the real situations. Beware of this over-confidence. If you have, perhaps more commonly, felt that you cannot claim experience in all of these competences, then you should try to undertake some more exercises which address these numerical concerns.

0:20

student activity

(PC 8.3.5, COM 3.4)
Respond to these statements with either **true** or **false**:

1 Most business organisations would achieve significant efficiency improvements if they employed information technology.
2 The use of fax machines, modems and e-mail significantly improves both internal and external communications.
3 An organisation which has a number of computer terminals would be best advised to link them together via a network system.
4 Multi-task programs or software are those which incorporate word processing, data bases and spreadsheet.
5 An organisation would be able to more effectively cater for its customers' needs if it held customer information on a data base.
6 An organisation would benefit from an accounts software package which would enable it to produce an instant picture of the company's financial position.
7 All managers' decision-making and problem-solving tasks would be greatly eased if they had access to a management information system.
8 An organisation which holds considerable quantities of many different components or products would be able to improve the monitoring of its stock control levels by using a stock-control software package.
9 The efficiency of a salesperson or sales representative who is employed to work outside the office would be improved if he/she were issued with a mobile phone or pager.
10 An organisation which has a number of different sites throughout the world would be able to call together its senior managers at very short notice by use of video-conferencing.

These statements have addressed your appreciation of the various uses of information technology, but they have not sought to measure your ability to use them. Practically speaking, you may not have been in a position to have tried video-conferencing, e-mail or mobile phones. Despite this, it is hoped that you have answered **true** to all of the above statements. If you have answered **false** to any of them perhaps you do not yet appreciate the full value of the various information technology systems. Whilst a number of them are not relevant, nor for that matter, accessible to many organisations, as we have said earlier, there are few organisations that do not employ at least two or three of these systems.

0:20

student activity

(PC 8.3.5, COM 3.4)
Answer the following questions with one of these responses:

● **fully experienced**
● **somewhat experienced**
● **a little knowledge**
● **no knowledge**

We will not, of course, expect you to have actually carried out these tasks or displayed these skills in a 'real environment'. However, if you feel that you know the implications and procedures involved, you may answer that you are experienced.

1 Would you feel confident in attempting to sell a product or service to a customer?
2 Do you feel that you could set your own goals and objectives?

3 Do you feel confident that you could select a suitable candidate for a particular job?

4 Do you feel conversant with legislation which relates to your chosen career?

5 Would you feel confident in handling the to day-to-day decision making of a small business?

6 Do you feel confident that you could process customer enquiries and respond in an effective way?

7 Do you feel that you understand the effect that control of costs can have on profits?

8 Do you feel that you understand the requirements of the manufacturing process?

9 Would you feel able to introduce an effective stock control system?

10 If you identified a shortcoming in the administrative systems of your business, would you feel confident of being able to suggest an effective alternative?

We have left these occupational skills rather vague since we cannot predict your chosen career intentions. These 10 questions relate to the overall management and administration of a business and highlight the wide-ranging skills that may be required.

8.3.6 *Propose a personal plan for employment or self-employment*

PERSONAL PLAN

We are now approaching the final stage of the qualification. The requirements of Element 8.3 are to create a personal plan for employment or self-employment. Throughout this Element we have identified the types of employment available, the statutory requirements involved, the nature and use of various sources of information and the personal skills that you will need to analyse to support your job search.

There are some final points which need to be addressed or indeed clarified. Essentially, the format of this last performance criterion entails the actual **planning** of your personal plan. It also attempts to formulate a structure and time-scale.

TIME-SCALES (SHORT-TERM, LONG-TERM)

As defined by the specification for this Element, short-term is considered to be 1–12 months, whereas long-term is 1–5 years. By this stage you should have a reasonably clear idea of your career intentions. You should at least be able to state your intentions with regard to the next year. What must now be done is to develop this further and create a logical **format** in which to state your **objectives**.

STATUTORY CONSIDERATIONS

We have identified all of the major requirements and considerations earlier in this Element. Again, it is your responsibility to identify those which are applicable to your intended career path. Obviously, you should bear in mind that many of the statutory requirements are handled by your employer if you are in full-time or part-time employment. However, even in this case, you should be aware of the obligations, regardless of the fact that you are not personally responsible for implementing them. Conversely, if you are self-employed or

   1:00

student activity

(PC 8.3.6, COM 3.2)
This task is in two parts:

1 First, use the pro-forma headings below to identify your intended actions over the next five years. Just how much you break these proposals down is entirely up to you, and may depend upon the nature of your career intentions. You may find it necessary to take the various stages in smaller portions than yearly ones.

2 Secondly, duplicate the process and suggest a viable contingency plan should your first plan of action prove inappropriate or unsuccessful.

We suggest you use the following headings:

Date	Activity	Outcome	Completion date	Leading to	Notes/ Contacts

considering starting your own business, then you will discover that you must not only be aware of the statutory requirements, but actually implement them yourself.

The following Student Activity attempts to give some form to the **identification** and the **procedures** that must be undertaken:

student activity

(PC 8.3.6, COM 3.2, 3.4)
Complete the following pro-forma. Even if you are in full-time employment, doing this will give you at least some kind of indication of the various statutory requirements and considerations involved.

Statutory requirement	Information source	Advice source	Implemented by	Action needed

SOURCES OF HELP AND SUPPORT

Again, the actual sources of potential help and support will depend upon your intended career plan. Obviously some of the sources that we have already mentioned will be more or less appropriate in different situations. Whatever your intended career plan is, it is always a good start to contact the following:

1 *Your local Jobcentre* – the staff there will be able to give you help and support whether you are intending to be self-employed or employed.
2 *Your local Careers Service* – they should be able to assist you in obtaining help and support from other agencies.
3 *TEC or LEC* – they will be able to advise you about the availability of enterprise schemes and training within your local area.

We have, until this point, left out an individual who can play a vital role in the development of your future. This individual is your tutor. He/she will, at the very least, have a knowledge of the kind of help and support that you will need. Most tutors will have some knowledge of the local job market (which is particularly useful for obtaining contacts in relation to full-time employment) and may know individuals or agencies which can help you set up your own business. Remember, in addition to all of the more conventional forms of help and support, there exists an informal network of contacts. Your tutor may be part of one of these. She/he will know, or know how to find out, a great deal of information

which you will be able to use as a filtering process, hopefully saving you from wasting time and energy pursuing unsuitable or inappropriate channels for information seeking.

student activity

(PC 8.3.6, COM 3.2, 3.4)
As with the other pro-formas in this performance criterion, we have provided some outline headings for you to consider when addressing your help and support needs.

Help needed	Why needed	When needed	Contact	Outcome	Referral

The referral column is there so that you can note suggestions made by the initial contact if this person is not able to provide you with the necessary help and support. At the very least this person should be able to pass you on to another source of help and support.

INFORMATION NEEDED

This category is in many respects very similar to your sources of help and support, but may also include straightforward information on products, equipment and premises. If you are considering employment rather than self-employment, you may wish to obtain information about a particular organisation prior to the recruitment and selection process.

student activity

(PC 8.3.6, COM 3.2, 3.4)
Using the pro-forma below try to make sure that you have covered all of your information needs.

Information required	Request made	Information received	Further information needed	Follow up action
			Yes/No	

ACTIONS TO BE TAKEN

What you have been doing, in essence, is creating an action plan prior to the formation of your **personal plan**. It may a valuable exercise to amalgamate all of the aspects of your personal plan in a single form to enable you to monitor it more effectively. The structure of this action plan should really be considered on an individual basis. However, we can suggest some useful headings and cross-referencing techniques.

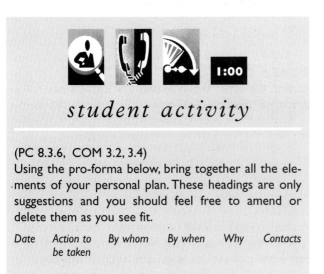

student activity

(PC 8.3.6, COM 3.2, 3.4)
Using the pro-forma below, bring together all the ele-ments of your personal plan. These headings are only suggestions and you should feel free to amend or delete them as you see fit.

Date	Action to be taken	By whom	By when	Why	Contacts

BEING SAFE WHEN JOB SEEKING

Much to their credit, the Employment Department Group have produced a leaflet which addresses the dangers that you may face when you are actively seek-ing work. You can obtain this leaflet from any Jobcentre, but these are the main points the leaflet mentions:

- always tell someone else where you are going and what time you should be expected back
- if your interview is outside normal working hours make sure there is someone around to collect you
- always do some research on the company before-hand – find out as much as you can
- always make sure that the interview takes place at the employer's premises or some other public place

FIG. 8.3.11 *The Employment Service has produced this book-let, 'Be Alert — be safe when jobseeking', which is available from Jobcentres.*

- never apply for a job that appears to offer you too much money for very little work
- be cautious about agreeing to continue the interview over a drink or a meal
- try to avoid allowing the interviewer to stray into personal lines of questioning when they have no rel-evance to the job itself
- never accept a lift from the interviewer

You should also remember that this advice is as applic-able to males as it is to females.

ELEMENT 8.3

a s s i g n m e n t

(PC 8.3.1–6, COM 3.1, 3.2, 3.3, 3.4 IT 3.1, 3.2, 3.3, 3.4)

This is a very broad and complex Element to tackle. There are various **evidence indicators** which you will have to show in order to claim competence and completion of this element. Essentially, this Assignment is in three parts. It covers:

- types of employment
- analysis of personal strengths and weaknesses
- the preparation of a four-part personal plan

TASK I

(PC 8.3.1–4)

In report format, summarise at least three different types of employment or self-employment in which you have a particular interest. Having done this, select one type of employment or self-employment and list the opportunities, along with the relevant sources of information and any statutory requirements.

TASK 2

(PC 8.3.5)

Using the pro-forma lists in the Student Activities of this Element, which you will have already tackled in draft form, analyse your personal strengths and weaknesses in relation to the skills required for your preferred employment or self-employment choices.

TASK 3

(PC 8.3.2, 8.3.3, 8.3.4, 8.3.6)

This task requires you to create a **personal plan** divided into four discrete sections. These are:

I   An identification of the time you will require to realise your employment or self-emloyment opportunities.

2   The information you will need and the sources to assist you in achieving employment or self-employment.

3   Any actions you will need to take in order to become employed or self-employed.

4   An identification of any statutory requirements for your chosen employment or self-employment.

NOTES

You will be expected to understand that all types of employment have certain statutory requirements. If you have chosen to investigate employment opportunities in a country outside the European Union, then you should also identify any restrictions or requirements of that country.

Although you need to gain a clear understanding of any aspects of employment or company law which may relate to the setting up of a business or becoming self-employed, you should concentrate on practical issues and not get bogged down in the mass of regulations, legislation, directives and statutes.

When analysing your own skills, you will need to be able to evaluate and assess your own suitability for employment or self-employment. It should be understood that this discussion is a positive activity and not meant to be a means of criticism.

The various sources of information you will need are offered by local, national, professional and charitable organisations. Gaining access to this information may be difficult and it is strongly suggested that you begin with local sources of information.

Glossary of business terms

Above the line This is a marketing term used to indicate **promotion** by advertising a product or service through consumer media such as television, magazines, newspapers and radio. *Contrast with* **below the line**.

Absorption costing This is a technique which assigns the costing of **materials** and labour and other **overheads** to each unit of production.

Acid test This is an accounting measure which aims to ascertain a business's ability to pay its short-term **current liabilities** with its current assets.

After-sales service This is a form of customer service provided by an organisation to its customers; it includes maintenance, repair and advice.

Aggregate demand This is the total level of **demand** in the economy.

Amalgamation The merging of two or more divisions of a business. *See also* **merger**.

Annual report and accounts This is a yearly report to a company's **shareholders** which includes a **balance sheet**, a **profit and loss account** and other information that is required by law.

Apportioned costs These are **overheads** that have been allocated in an arbitrary way to **cost** or **profit centres**.

Appraisal *See* **performance appraisal**.

Arbitration This is a method of settling an industrial dispute through a third party.

Articles of association These are the rules concerning the relations between individuals within an organisation.

Assembly line This is a method of organising the machinery and labour in an organisation in which the product is assembled in a series of operations along the line.

Asset This is an item which is owned by a business or an individual and to which a monetary value can be attached.

Assets employed The book value of all of a firm's **assets** minus its **current liabilities**.

Assisted areas Defined parts of the UK in which government grants may be given to persuade firms to locate there.

Authorised share capital This is the maximum amount of **share capital** that an organisation can issue at any time.

Average cost This is the total **cost** divided by the number of units produced.

Average fixed costs These are the total **fixed costs** divided by units of **output**.

Average rate of return This is the total **profit** over the life of a product divided by the number of years, divided by **capital** outlay on the product, times 100.

Bad debt This is an accounting term which refers to money owed by customers to borrowers which is unlikely to be paid.

Balance of payments This is the term used to describe the sum of the nation's income and expenditure on foreign trade.

Balance of trade This is the term used to describe that part of the **balance of payments** account that registers exports and imports of **visible goods**.

Balance sheet This is an accounting term which refers to a statement of a business's **assets** and **liabilities** on the last day of a **trading period**.

Bank rate This is the level of **interest** charged by a country's central bank. It forms the basis of the lending rate for all other loans.

Bankruptcy This refers to the position of a business which is unable to pay its **debts** when they fall due.

Batch production This is the manufacture of a limited number of identical products, usually to meet a specific order.

Below the line This is a marketing term used to indicate **promotional** activity other than main media advertising (*see also* **above the line**).

Board of directors This is a group of individuals who are responsible to the **shareholders** for the running of a business.

Bonus issue This is a free issue of shares to **shareholders** on a proportional basis.

Brand This is the name, design, symbol or term which is used to identify an organisation's product or service.

Brand leader This is the term used for the **brand** with the highest percentage share of a specific **market** or market segment.

Brand loyalty This exists when consumers make **repeat purchases** of a product on a regular basis.

Break-even To reach the point when **output** matches **fixed** and **variable costs**.

Break-even point This is when the break-even output equals **fixed costs** divided by **contribution per unit** (**Selling price** minus **variable cost**).

Budget This is an organisation's allocation of money and **resources** for particular projects. It includes a **cash-flow forecast**.

Budgetary control This is an accounting system for controlling **costs** and **revenue** by comparing actual results with estimates.

Bureaucratic This is a term used to describe a system of management that is rooted in paper-based checks and counter-checks on decisions or actions.

Business plan A report detailing the marketing strategy, production costings and financial implications of a business start-up.

Capital This can be defined either as the funds invested by a business to acquire **assets** or as physical **assets** such as machinery or equipment.

Capital employed This refers to the total funds which have been invested in a business, or long-term finance.

Capital expenditure This is the **expenditure** on the acquisition of **fixed assets**.

Capital goods These are goods bought by a business for use in the production of other products or services. Also known as **fixed assets**.

Cartel This is the name given to a group of producers who make an agreement to limit **output** in order to keep prices high.

Cash account This is an account which records all of a company's **incomings** and **outgoings**.

Cash flow This is a system by which an organisation monitors **revenue** and **expenditure** on a monthly basis.

Cash-flow forecast A detailed estimate of a firm's future cash inflows and outflows per month.

Closed shop A workplace where employees must belong to a trade union.

Cluster sample This is a marketing term used to refer to respondents drawn from a relatively small area who are selected to represent a particular aspect of a product's target **market**.

Code of practice A form of self-regulation devised and run by an employers' organisation that lays down appropriate standards for firms operating within the industry.

Collateral This is an **asset** which a borrower is required to deposit or pledge against a loan which will be sold by the lender if the loan is not repaid.

Collective bargaining This is the negotiation process that takes place between employers and representatives of the workforce.

Command economy *See* **Planned economy**.

Comparative advantage This is the idea that countries can benefit from specialising in the production of goods which they are relatively more efficient in producing.

Competition This term refers to the other organisations with which an organisation must contest in order to gain and maintain **market share**.

Consolidated accounts This is the aggregate or total of all accounts from a group of companies.

Consumer durables These are goods which are owned by households but which are not immediately consumed by them.

Consumer panel A group of consumers within a firm's target market used on a regular basis for **market research** exercises.

Contract of employment This is an agreement between an employer and an employee in which the employer lays down the conditions of service and the rewards for work undertaken.

Contribution This is the difference between **sales revenue** and **variable costs**.

Contribution per unit This is the amount each unit sold contributes towards covering the fixed **overheads** of the business.

Corporate identity The design package that aims to create the **corporate image** desired by a firm.

Corporate image This is the view of a company held by its customers, employees and the public at large.

Corporate objectives These are the goals of the whole enterprise.

Corporation This is a publicly registered company which has a separate legal identity from that of its owners.

Corporation tax This is a tax levied by the government on **profits** made by a business.

Cost This is the **expenditure** on **resources** incurred by a business.

Cost-benefit analysis This means weighing up the financial and **social costs** of an action or decision against the financial and social benefits.

Cost centre This is a technique used by some organisations to manage **costs** by attributing them to certain areas of the business's activity.

Cost of living This is the level of prices of products and services usually measured in order to monitor **inflation** via the **retail price index**.

Cost of sales This is **expenditure** incurred in the process of obtaining sales.

Cost price This is the **cost** of a product which a business incurs in the course of its production.

Creditors These are individuals or organisations to which a business owes money.

Current assets These are **assets** owned by a business. They include **stock**, money owed by **debtors** and cash.

Current liabilities These are all the obligations a business has to pay money out for in the near future.

Current ratio *See* **acid test.**

Debentures This is a means of financing a business through fixed-interest loans secured against **assets**.

Debt This is the amount of money owed by one person or organisation to another.

Debtors These are the people or organisations which owe money to a business.

Deindustrialisation This refers to the long-term decline in a country's relative position as a world manufacturer.

Demand This is the amount or quantity of a particular product or service required by organisations and their customers.

Demand curve This is a graphical presentation of the likely level of **demand** for a product at a range of different prices.

Depreciation This term can be used to describe the fall in value of either an **asset** or a currency.

Deregulation This refers to the removal of government rules, regulations and laws from the working of a business.

Deskilling This occurs when a new machine or process changes a job that was once a source of craft pride into a repetitive or mundane task such as feeding or minding a machine.

Direct costs This is the total of **materials** and **labour costs** that can be related to the production of a product.

Direct labour This is a recognisable portion of the workforce which is involved in any aspect of producing a product.

Direct mail This is a form of advertising or promotional material that is posted to specific addresses selected from a mailing list.

Direct marketing This is marketing activity that is aimed directly at the customer.

Director This is an official of a business who is elected by shareholders and given the power and responsibility to run the organisation on their behalf.

Discount This is a deduction from the list price of a product.

Disposable income This is the amount of money which an individual has left after paying compulsory deductions.

Distribution This is the process of storing and transporting products to consumers via various channels.

Diversification This is the process which occurs when a business expands its business activities into new **markets**.

Dividend This is a payment made by a business to its **shareholders** in return for providing **share capital**.

Dividend per share This is the total **dividends** divided by the shares issued.

Division of labour This means breaking a job down into small, repetitive tasks, each of which can be done at speed by workers with little formal training.

Earnings per share This is the **profit** after tax divided by the number of shares.

Economies of scale This is a beneficial reduction in the **average costs** of producing a unit which is obtained by an increase in the size of the business.

Elastic demand This refers to the **demand** for a product which changes as a result of price change.

Elastic supply This refers to the **supply** of a product or service which changes in response to price changes.

Equilibrium This is the term that describes the state of a **market** where **demand** and supply are equal to each other.

Equity This is **ordinary shareholders'** funds.

Excess demand This describes the situation where **demand** exceeds supply.

Expenditure These are the **outgoings** or expenses incurred by a business.

Factoring This is a banking service which provides up to 80 per cent of the value of invoiced sales as a cash advance, and then organises the collection of the **debt**.

Financial management This is advice, usually obtained from an outside source, which allows a business to analyse the flow of money through the organisation.

Financial year This is taken to mean the period from 1 April to 31 March the following year.

Finished goods These are the **stocks** of completed products being stored by an organisation.

Fiscal policy This is the economic term for how the government controls the level of spending in the economy by changing the level of its **expenditure** and of taxation on individuals and businesses.

Fixed assets These are **assets** such as machinery and buildings bought by a business for long-term use.

Fixed costs These are **costs** incurred by an organisation which do not vary even when in the level of **changes**.

Flow production This is the manufacture of an item in a continually moving process.

Franchise This is a business arrangement by which one organisation (the **franchiser**) grants another (the **franchisee**) the right to trade under its name and supply its products or services.

Franchisee This is a person who has bought the local rights to use the name of another company.

Franchiser This is the holder of the **franchise** who sells local rights to suitable **franchisees**.

Genetic brands These are **brands** that are universally and inextricably associated with a particular product that customers treat the brand name as if it were a product category (e.g. Thermos, Hoover).

Goodwill This is the reputation, expertise and contacts of a business, for which a prospective buyer must pay a premium above the **asset** value of the business.

Gross domestic product This is the total value of all products and services produced in the economy in a year. Also referred to as GDP.

Gross margin This is the percentage of **sales revenue** which is **gross profit**.

Gross national product This is the total value of all products and services produced in the economy plus any income from investments abroad. Also referred to as GNP.

Gross profit This is the difference between **sales revenue** and **cost of sales** before selling, distribution and administration are taken into account.

Holding company This is a company which controls another company.

Homeworking This is earning an **income** from work undertaken at home.

Income This is the money received by an individual or organisation.

Income elasticity This is the percentage change in **demand** divided by the percentage change in real **incomes**.

Incomings *See* **revenue**.

Indirect cost This is a **cost** that is not directly attributable to a product or a **cost centre**.

Industrial tribunal This is an informal court room where legal disputes over unfair dismissal or discrimination can be settled.

Inelastic demand This refers to the **supply** of a product or service which does not change even if the price changes.

Inelastic supply This refers to the **supply** of a product or service which does not change even if the price changes.

Inflation This is a general increase in prices which is usually measured in terms of its effect on the whole economy.

Input These are all of the resources used by a business to produce its products and services.

Insolvent This refers to a business which has suffered bankruptcy and cannot pay its debts.

Intangible assets Assets are tangible when they do not have a physical existence. For instance, goodwill, patents, trademarks and copyrights.

Interest This is a charge made for borrowing money.

Internal rate of return This is the **discount** rate which, when applied to a set of **cash flows**, makes their net present value equal to zero.

Inventory This is a comprehensive list of all **finished goods**, **work in progress** and **raw materials**.

Invisible exports Items, often services, which are exported, and for which the country receives payment, but which are not tangible goods. Imports may also be invisible. *See also* **visible goods**.

Issued share capital This is the amount of **authorised share capital** which a business can issue to **shareholders** in order to raise **capital**.

Japanisation This is the process by which Western firms are attempting to follow the Japanese way.

Job analysis This is the identification of the tasks which make up a particular job role.

Job description This is a statement of the tasks and responsibilities which make up a job.

Job enlargement This refers to the process that occurs when the number of tasks and possibly the number of responsibilities involved in a job are increased.

Job enrichment This refers to the situation that occurs when workers are given greater freedom in performing their tasks.

Job evaluation This is a system by which the relative worth of a job is linked to grading and pay.

Job rotation This is the widening of a worker's activities by moving him or her around in a structured programme to carry out a number of different work tasks.

Job satisfaction This is the term that refers to the degree to which an employee feels positively towards his or her present job function.

Job security This is the term that refers to the extent to which a job is, or seems to be, guaranteed for the foreseeable future.

Job sharing This refers to the situation when employees agree to divide the working week or a job in two, so that they each do half of the one job.

Job specification This is a statement or listing of the characteristics required of a person to enable him/her to do a job successfully.

Joint venture This is a business owned by two other independent organisations which have pooled their expertise and **resources**.

Labour costs This is the total of all **expenditure** that can be attributed to the workforce.

Labour turnover This refers to the number of people entering and leaving employment. It is calculated as the number of leavers per year divided by the average number of staff times 100.

Leaseback This is an arrangement which involves the selling of **assets** to a third party and then **renting** them back at an agreed rental.

Ledger This is an accounting record which keeps a running total of the business's financial transactions.

Legislation Rules, regulations and directives imposed by the government or the European Union.

Liability This is a form of **debt** or claim on the **resources** of a business in relation to money owed.

Limited liability This is a type of **liability** in which a **shareholder** is only liable for the amount of money that he or she actually invested in the business.

Liquidation This means turning **assets** into cash.

Liquidity This is the relationship between a business's **current assets** and its **current liabilities**, in other words, the organisation's ability to pay its **creditors**.

Loss leader This is a product sold at a reduced price in order to attract customers to purchase additional products.

Managing Director This is the **director** of an organisation who is responsible for the day-to-day management.

Margin This is the difference between the **cost price** and the **selling price** of a product.

Marginal cost These are extra **costs** incurred by a business when it increases **output**.

Market This is the situation when the buyer and seller of a product or service come together.

Market economy This is an economy which allows **markets** to determine the allocation of **resources**.

Market leader This is a product or service which has the largest **market share**.

Market orientation This is the extent to which a firm's strategic thinking stems from looking outwards to consumer tastes and competitive pressures.

Market penetration This is a pricing strategy for a new product based on a desire to achieve high sales volume and high **market share**.

Market positioning This is where a manufacturer positions a brand within a market-place.

Market research This is the collection and analysis of data regarding a particular **market.**

Market segmentation This is a method of dividing the **market** into segments to target them more accurately.

Market share This is the percentage of the total value of the **market** which is held by an individual organisation.

Market size This is the total sales of all the producers within a market-place, measured either by volume (units sold) or by value (the revenue generated).

Marketing This is a process by which an organisation attempts to identify customer needs and satisfy them.

Marketing mix These are the measures which an organisation employs to attract buyers to purchase its products or services. This is also known as the 4 Ps.

Marketing plan This is a report detailing a firm's marketing objectives and strategy.

Materials These are the items required in order to produce a product. They may take the form of **raw materials** or components.

Memorandum of Association This is a legal document which governs the relationship between the business and all external individuals and organisation.

Merchandising This is a term that refers to the tasks undertaken, including visiting outlets to ensure that a company's products are displayed in as attractive and prominent a way as possible.

Merger This is the mutually agreed combining of businesses into a single business.

Mixed economy This is an economy in which products and services are provided by both private and public enterprises.

Modem This is an accessory that enables one computer to be linked to others.

Monetary policy This is the economic term for how the government controls the level of spending in an economy by regulating the supply of money through the control of **interest** rates.

Monopoly Officially this term refers to the situation where an organisation has a 25 per cent **market share**. *See also* **oligopoly**.

Motivation This is the willingness and enthusiasm of a worker to carry out tasks or a consumer to purchase a product.

Multinational This is a firm which has its headquarters in one country, and has bases, manufacturing or assembly plants in others.

Multiple A store chain that has a number of shops in different places.

Multiplier This is the concept that because income flows in a circular fashion through the economy, small injections of income will be multiplied as the process occurs, and income generally will be raised, although by small increments.

Multi-skilling This means training a workforce to be able to work effectively across a wide range of tasks.

Net assets This is **fixed assets** plus net **current assets** or **fixed assets** plus net **current assets** minus long-term **liabilities**.

Net present value This is the value today of the estimated **cash flows** resulting from an investment.

Net profit This is the difference between a business's **sales revenue** and total **costs**.

Niche marketing This is a corporate strategy based on identifying and satisfying the demands of relatively small **market segments**.

Off-the-job training This includes all forms of training apart from that at the immediate workplace.

Oligopoly This refers to a situation where several relatively large firms dominate the market. *See also* **monopoly**.

On-the-job training This is instruction at the place of work on how the job should be carried out.

Opportunity cost This refers to the next best alternative foregone. In other words, when decisions are made, the opportunity cost is all the benefits that would have been gained by making an alternative decision.

Ordinary shares Also known as **equity**, these are essentially certificates issued to providers of long-term finance. In exchange for their long-term finance, ordinary **shareholders** are entitled to receive **dividends**.

Outgoings See **expenditure**.

Output This is the term that refers to the products or services produced by an organisation.

Overheads These are the **costs** of an organisation which cannot be directly attributed to a product.

Overtrading This occurs when a firm expands within securing the necessary long-term finance, thereby placing too great a strain on its **working capital**.

Own-label (**Own-brand**) These are products that are branded with the retailer's own name, or with a name invented by the retailer, rather than with the name of (or invented by) the manufacturer.

Partnership This is an organisation owned and controlled by two or more individuals.

Performance appraisal This is the process of evaluating the performance of an employee, the purpose of which is to improve performance.

Planned economy This is an economy in which the majority of production is owned and controlled by the State.

Point-of-sale This refers to the materials used to display and promote products at a retail outlet.

Price elasticity This is the percentage change in quantity demanded given by the percentage change in price.

Price-inelastic This refers to the situation where a change in a product's price leads to a proportionately smaller change in the quantity sold.

Price-sensitive This refers to a good the demand for which will react very strongly to a change in its price.

Primary data First-hand information that is related directly to a firm's needs.

Privatisation This refers to the change of ownership of an organisation, from public ownership to private ownership by the sale of **shares**.

Product differentiation This is the extent to which consumers perceive one product as being different from its rivals.

Product life cycle This is the sales pattern of a product over its period of existence.

Product orientation This is a term used by many to indicate an old-fashioned business that ignores customer tastes and needs.

Product range This is the full listing of the products offered by a firm.

Productivity This is a measurement of the efficiency with which a firm turns production **inputs** into **output**.

Profit This accrues when an organisation's **sales revenue** is greater than its total **costs**.

Profit and loss account This is an accounting statement which shows an organisation's **sales revenue** and the **costs** that relate to that revenue during a specific **trading period**.

Profit centre Just as **cost centres** are used to attribute **costs** to various parts of the organisation, profit centres are those which make money for the organisation.

Profit margin This is the difference between the **selling price** of a product and the **cost** of producing it.

Profit share This is a bonus paid on top of employees' salaries to ensure that a proportion of the firm's **profit** is shared out among staff.

Promotion In marketing, this is a method of attracting the attention of consumers.

Public relations These are the methods employed by an organisation to enhance its public image.

Public sector borrowing requirement This term refers to the gap between government income from taxes and other sources, and its expenditure on such areas as defence, education and social security payments.

Pyramid selling This is a system of selling goods in which agency rights are sold to an increasing number of distributors at lower levels (hence 'pyramid'). In effect it is a way of encouraging inexperienced people to part with their cash in exchange for the right to sell a questionable product to others at high prices.

Qualitative research This is in-depth research into the **motivations** behind consumer behaviour or attitudes.

Quality assurance This is the attempt to ensure that quality standards are agreed and met throughout an organisation, to ensure customer satisfaction.

Quality circle This is a discussion group that meets regularly to identify quality problems, consider alternative solutions, and recommend a suitable outcome to management.

Quantitative research This means research using pre-set questions among a large enough sample of people to provide statistically valid data.

Raw materials These are basic items, usually produced in the primary sector of the economy, which are destined to be converted into finished products.

Registered share capital. *See* **authorised share capital**.

Renting This is a method of acquiring an **asset** which is owned by a third party and which may be used by the organisation in return for regular payments.

Repeat purchase This occurs when a first-time buyer purchases the same brand again.

Resources These are human, physical, natural, and time items which can be identified as being 'owned' by an organisation.

Retail price index This is a measure used to determine the rate of **inflation**.

Return on capital This is the percentage return the firm is able to generate on the long-term **capital** employed in the business. In other words, it is the operating **profit** divided by the capital **employed** multiplied by 100.

Revenue This is the income of an organisation derived from sales, **interest** from loans and other investments.

Sales forecast This is a method of predicting future **demand**.

Sales promotion This term refers to the methods used by businesses, other than advertising, to increase their sales.

Sales revenue This is a key item of **revenue** derived from the monies paid by purchasers of a business's products or services.

Secondary data Information collected from second-hand sources such as reference books, government statistics or market intelligence reports.

Selling price This is the price charged by an organisation for its products or services after taking into account the **costs** incurred in producing it and having added a **margin**.

Semi-variable costs These are costs that vary with output, but not in direct proportion.

Share capital This is the money which has been obtained from **shareholders** investing money in the organisation.

Shareholders These are essentially part-owners of an organisation, who have made long-term investments in it.

Shareholders' funds These are that part of a firm's long-term finance owed by the company to its shareholders.

Social cost This measures the cost to the whole of society of a production process or business decision. This cost includes both internal costs and external costs.

Social responsibilities These are the duties towards employees, customers, society and the environment that a firm may accept willingly, or may treat as a nuisance.

Sole trader This is a business owned and controlled by a single individual.

Stock These are the organisation's **assets** in the form of **raw materials**, **work in progress** and **finished goods**.

Stock control This is the process of controlling all **stock** of **raw materials**, **work in progress** and **finished goods**, in order to make best use of warehousing facilities and stock-holding costs.

Stock turnover This is a measurement of the speed with which a firm sells out its **stock**. The **turnover** is worked out by dividing the sales turnover by the **stock**.

Supply This is the amount or quantity of products or services that an organisation are willing to offer the **market**.

SWOT A system by which an organisation can identify its internal Strengths and Weakness and the external Opportunities and Threats.

Tele-working This means working at home, though linked to the office by instant communications such as telephone, fax and computer modem.

Test market The launch of a new or improved product within a tightly defined area, in order to measure actual sales or potential sales.

Trading period This is a specified period of time, a month, a quarter or a year, which is used to monitor business performance.

Turnover This is the amount of money taken in a business. It can also refer to the number of people entering and leaving employment.

Unique selling point This is the feature of a product that can be focused on in order to differentiate it from all competition.

Unit cost *See* **average cost**.

Unlimited liability This is a type of **liability** in which the owners of a business are responsible for all losses.

Value added This is either the difference between the **cost** of producing a product and the price obtained for it (the selling price), or an additional benefit offered to a purchaser in order to convince him or her to buy.

Variable costs These are **costs** which may change in direct proportion to the organisation's level of business activity.

Variable overheads These are **costs** that vary in proportion to changes in **demand** or **output**, but are not related directly to the production process.

Venture capital This is risk capital, usually in the form of a package of loan and **share capital**, to provide a significant investment in a small or medium-sized business.

Visible goods Usually these refer to exports (or imports) of actual goods or commodities. *See also* **invisible exports**.

Wage differential This is the difference between the wage rates for different groups of workers.

Working capital This is an accounting term which identifies the organisation's short-term **current assets**.

Work in progress These are products which are in the process of being turned into **finished goods**.

Index

Absorption costing   522, 526
Acid test   598
Accountants   665
Accounting periods   578
Accounting records   576–7
Accounting systems   576–7
Accounts   351–2, 490
Accounts, final   577
Added value   412–18, 474–86
Administration   350–1, 521
Administration systems   126–53
Advertising   6, 242–51
Advertising Standards Authority   49, 276–81
Advertorials   276
Advisory, Conciliation and Arbitration Services   332, 333–4
After sales service   84, 640–1
Age   263, 617
Agendas   160
Agents   293
Agricultural Development & Advisory Service   669
Articles of Association   100
Asset finance   547
Asset turnover   598
Assets   90, 547–9, 549–51, 617–18, 621–2, 643–5
Assets, current   549–50, 582, 597–8, 621–2, 643–7
Assets, fixed   547–9, 621–2, 643–7
Assistants   347–8
Auditing   588–9
Authorisation   512, 513
Automation   419–20
Average fixed costs   528

Bad debt   484–5
Balance sheet   576–99, 648, 650
Bank Giro Form   504
Bank statement   508–9
Bankers Automated Clearing Services (BACS)   505
Banks   664–5
Belgium   451
Benefits   658–60
Brand loyalty   267–8
Branding   209–11
Break-even   12, 21–3, 477, 478, 532–41, 609–10, 625, 634
British Franchise Association   671

Budgets   564, 565, 566
Business, international   87
Business letters   163
Business, local   86
Business, national   86–7
Business objectives   80–5, 107, 321, 329–30, 360, 489–90, 608–11, 633, 639
Business organisations   80–192
Business plans   80, 563–4, 605–50
Business strategy and tactics (see Business objectives)

Careers Service   663
Cartels   44–8
Cash In-flow   569–70
Cash Out-flow   570–2
Cashflow   563–73, 648
Catalogues   288
Chambers of Commerce   664
Change, management of   322–3
Charities   83, 86, 556–7, 561, 654–5, 668
Chartermark   96
Cheque   503–4, 507–8
Cinema   250–1
Circulars   164–5
Citizens Charter   96
Civil law   95
Code of Advertising Practice   278–81
Communication   156–79
Communication, changes to   176–8
Communication channels   165–6
Communication, effectiveness   173–6, 304
Communication, electronic   166–9
Communication, external   161– 5
Communication, internal   156–61
Communication, objectives   170–3
Communication, special needs   169–70
Community relations   257–8
Companies House   100, 589, 658, 668–9
Company-wide quality control   414–16
Competition   27–36, 43–7, 56–8, 74, 108, 417, 421–2, 447–68, 532–3, 596
Competition Act   44
Competition, imperfect   28, 30, 31, 32, 33
Competition, perfect   27–8, 30, 31, 32, 33
Competitions   259–60
Competitive franchising   56

Complaints   295–6
Computer aided design (CAD)   420
Computer aided manufacture (CAM)   420
Conglomerate   87
Consumer Credit Act   48
Consumer Protection Act   48, 97
Consumer Protection Advisory Committee   47, 48–9
Contract of employment   95, 314, 320, 329, 373–8, 404
Contract of sale   96
Contracting out   420
Contribution   534–5
Control of organisation   90–1, 92, 126
Co-operatives   101–3, 115–16
Corporation tax   67, 69–70, 97
Cost plus   532–4
Costing   474–540
Coupons   260
Credit   482, 483–5, 551–2, 560, 568–9, 599, 625
Credit cards   506–7
Credit clearance and control   305–6, 484, 506–7, 599
Credit note   497, 498, 500
Criminal law   95
Critical Path Analysis   622–3
Curricula vitae   396–8
Customer accounts   306
Customer care   302
Customer loyalty   268–9
Customer relations   358–9, 424–5
Customer requirements   417–18, 476
Customer satisfaction   297–8
Customer service   84, 141–2, 212–13, 307–8, 330, 611–12

Data Protection Act   188–92
Debentures   90
Debit cards   506
Debtors collection period   599
Delivery date   486
Delivery note   500, 501
Demand   1–24, 52–3, 66–7, 611, 635–6
Demand curves   3–4, 17–20, 33
Demographics   109
Denmark   451
Department of Trade & Industry (DTI)   51, 667
Depreciation   519
Deregulation   57, 459
Design Consultants   666
Direct costs   518–19, 524
Direct mail   164–5, 273–4
Direct marketing   273–5
Direct sales methods   285–8
Directors   344–5
Disabled Persons Employment Act   92
Disciplinary procedures   325–6, 331–9, 365–9
Discounts   491–2, 625
Discrimination   315, 318–20, 326–8, 329
Dismissal   365–9
Distribution   139–40, 289–92, 293, 306, 357, 624–5, 639
Door-to-door sales   286–7

EC Directives   92–3, 94
Economies of scale   20–1
Effective demand   3
Eire   452
Elasticity   4–6, 12–14
Elasticity, cross   5
Elasticity, demand   4
Elasticity, price and income   4–5, 13
Elasticity, unitary   5, 14
Electronic Data Interchange (EDI)   505–6
Employee co-operation   340–1
Employee share ownership   341
Employment and employees   38, 39, 53–4, 65–6, 412–68, 480, 589, 614, 654–81, 662–3
Employment Agencies   662–3
Employment Acts   93–4, 614
Employment Protection (Consolidation) Act   93
Employment trends   435–45
Environment   37–8, 49, 426, 614–16
Environmental Protection Act   50
Equal Opportunities   315, 318, 403–4
Equal Pay Act   92, 319
Equilibrium   21–3
Equilibrium market   16, 21–3
Equilibrium point   16, 18–19, 21–3
Equilibrium price   16, 18–19, 21–3
Equilibrium quantity   18–19, 21–3
Estate Agents   665–6
Estimate   492
European Commission   50
European Currency Unit (ECU)   74
European Information Centres   669
European Union   73–4, 461–2, 610
Exchange Rate   447, 458
Exchange Rate Mechanism (ERM)   74
Exchanges   295
Exogenous factors   15

Factories Act   92
Factoring   90, 552
Factory shops   285–6
Fair Trading Act   44, 59
Federation of Self-Employed   664
Federation of Small Businesses   664
Field trials   224–5
FIFO   419
Finance   135–7, 457, 547–99, 642–7
Financial transactions   474–540
Fiscal policy   59–61, 67
Fixed costs   11–12, 527–8, 536–41
Focus groups   224
Foods and Drink Acts   48
Food Safety Act   48
Forecasting   563–73
Forms   161–3
France   450
Franchise   101, 102, 656
Free mail-ins   262
Free market   8–9, 10, 42–3

Gantt Charts   622–3
GATT (see World Trade Organisation)
Gearing   599
Gender   264
Germany   449
Gifts   556–7
Goods Received Note   498, 499, 512–13, 514
Government   42–74, 555–6, 559, 610, 655
Government intervention   42–55, 456–68, 559, 610
Government statistics   234–5
Grants   555–6, 655
Greece   452
Grievance procedures   326, 331–9, 365–9
Guarantees   96–7

Hardware   129–31, 146–7, 182
Health   38
Health and Safety   92–3, 94–5, 145, 174–5, 315, 328, 329, 614
Hire purchase   553
Human resourcing   138–9, 314–405, 424, 456, 619

Income   3, 6
Income tax   69–70, 97, 657
Indirect costs   519–22, 524–5
Indirect sales methods   288–93
Individual performance   361–3
Individual targets   361
Induction programmes   389–90
Industrial Common Ownership Movement   667
Industrial action   334–5
Industrial tribunals   332, 334
Inelastic   4–6, 12–14
Inflation   54–5, 447, 458
Information processing   182–92
Information technology   142, 146–50, 151, 166–7, 354–5
Insurance   617–18
Interest rates   68–9, 480
Interviewee techniques   400–3
Interviewer techniques   398–400
Interviews   220
Investment   39, 72, 477
Invitations   163
Invoices   496–7, 500, 512–13
Italy   450

Japan   453–5
Japanese manufacturing techniques   427–8
Job Centres   660–2
Job descriptions   390
Job enlargement   364
Job enrichment   364
Job functions   348–9
Job responsibilities   359–69, 513, 515
Job roles   344–82
Job rotation   364
Job security   341
Job sharing   378
Just-in-time (JIT) production   416, 427, 475, 486

Labour flexibility   420
Labour mobility   369–70
Leasing   552, 559
Letters of application   393–6
Letters of complaint   164
Letters of enquiry   492
Liability   87–8
Liabilities, current   551, 582
Licensing   56–7
Lifestyle   263–4
LIFO   419
Limited companies   90, 99–101, 558–60
Livewire   670
Loans   553, 557, 559
Lobbying   257, 258
Local authority (see Public sector)
Local Enterprise Agencies   669
Local Enterprise Councils   666–7
Local Investment Networking Company   670
Location   106–7
Loyalty incentives   262
Luxembourg   452

Maastricht Treaty   73–4
Magazines   245–6
Maintenance   140–1
Management Information Systems   419
Management styles   116–20
Managers   345–6, 520–1, 584, 587–8
Manufacturing   81
Marginal costs   529–30
Marginal costing   534–5
Market data, primary   235–6
Market data, secondary   236
Market leader   83
Market orientated   15, 211–13
Market share   30–1, 83–4, 217–18, 297, 462–4
Marketing   135, 198–308, 354, 456–7, 522, 611–12, 624, 634–42
Marketing guidelines and controls   275–81
Marketing matrix   215–16
Marketing mix   208–9, 236–8, 634–42
Marketing plan   634–42
Marketing, principles and functions of   198–218
Marketing research   213–16, 220–39, 611–12
Membership fees   556–7
Memoranda   158
Media planners dilemma   244
Memorandum of Association   100
Merchandising   639
Mergers   45
Minutes of meeting   160–1
Mission statement   80
Mixed economy   9–10, 42–3
Monetary policy   58–9, 61, 68
Money cycle   474, 481–3
Monitoring business performance   128–9, 489–90, 511, 563–99, 607–8
Monopolies   28–9, 30, 31, 32, 58, 59
Monopolies and Mergers Act   44

Monopolies and Mergers Commission   44, 45, 46, 59
Mortgage   553–4
Multinational   113
Multi-skilling   377–8

Naming   636–7
National Insurance   657–8
Needs and wants   2, 294–8
Negotiation   324–5, 331–2, 333–4, 335–9
Netherlands   451
Networks   149
Newsletters   160
Newspapers   244–5
Notes   160
Noticeboards   160

Observation   220–1
Offices, Shops and Railways Premises Act   92
Office of Fair Trading   44, 45, 46, 47, 48, 49, 57, 276, 277, 278
Oligopoly   28–30, 31, 32
Operatives   347
Opportunity cost   8
Order processing   305, 474–5, 495–6, 499
Organisation and methods analysis   126
Organisational structure   106–16, 456
Overdraft   552, 560

Packaging   638
Panel discussions   222–3
Papers and briefs   160
Partnership   90, 99, 555, 558, 655–6
Paying-in slip   507–8
Payment   475–6, 484, 518–30
Payments documents   502–7
Pensions   97–8, 658
Performance ratios   598–9
Person specifications   391–3
Personal skills   671–81
Personnel (see Human Resourcing)
Petty cash   504–5
Piloting   225
Planned economy   9, 10, 42–3
Planning   622–4
Point of sale   254, 302–3
Portugal   452
Posters   248–9, 250
Preference shares   90
Premises   620–1
Press releases   256
Price   3, 7, 10–12, 475–7, 486, 532–5, 637
Price capping   56, 57
Pricing   474–540
Pricing policies   33–6, 418–19, 532–5, 637
Princes Scottish Youth Business Trust   670
Princes Youth Business Trust   670
Private limited company (see Limited companies)
Private sector   85, 654
Privatisation   52, 63–4, 458–9
Product awareness   272–3

Product development   216–17, 238–9, 642–7
Product liability insurance   618
Product lifecycles   269–72
Product mix   217
Product orientated   15, 211–13
Product performance   264–73
Production   137–8, 356–7, 412–68, 482, 518–30, 624, 642–7
Production orientated   15
Productivity   370–1, 414–16, 417, 448, 464, 643
Products   8, 303, 610–11, 618, 642–7
Profit   82–3, 88–9, 296–7, 418, 477–8, 481, 554–5, 559, 580–2, 591, 608, 613, 633
Profit and loss statements   575–99, 648, 650
Profit, gross   580, 598
Profit motive   7
Profit, net   580
Projects   159–60
Prospecting   307
Public liability insurance   618
Public limited company (see Limited companies)
Public ownership (see Public sector)
Public relations   255–6, 358–9
Public sector   52, 62–3, 71–2, 84–5, 86, 103–5, 654, 667
Public service motive   7–8
Public services (see Public sector)
Purchase documents   491–9
Pyramid selling   287–8

Qualitative and quantitative research methods   225
Quality assurance   414–15, 425–6, 427, 645–6
Quality circles   341, 427
Quality standards   328–9, 422, 427–8, 465
QUANGO   105
Quantity sold   18–19
Quantity supplied   10–12, 486
Questionnaires   221
Quotation   492, 493, 494, 495

Race Relations Act   92, 319–20
Radio   249–50, 251, 285
Receipts documents   507–9
Recruitment   322–3, 384–405
References   165, 387
Refunds   295
Regional assistance (see Regional policy)
Regional policy   72–3, 441–4, 670
Registrar of Companies (see Companies House)
Regulation   56–7
Rehabilitation of Offenders Act   92
Remittance Advice   502, 504
Repeat sales   266–7, 612
Resale Prices Act   44
Research and development   134, 355, 423–4, 426, 448
Restrictive Trade Practices Act   44
Retail Price Index   59
Retailers   292–3
Return on Capital Employed (ROCE)   477
Robotics   419–20

Running expenses 522
Rural Development Commission 669

Sale of Goods Act 304
Sales 352–3, 464, 483–5, 580, 612–13, 624, 633, 639
Sales administration 304, 305–7
Sales campaigns 298–300
Sales conferences 299–300
Sales documents 499–502
Sales letters 298–9
Sales literature 252–3
Sales meetings 300
Sales memos 299
Sales persons 300–4
Sales promotion methods 259–64, 638
Security 144–5, 175–6, 178, 187–9, 512–15
Selling off-page 275
Selling off-screen 275
Services 81–2, 610–11
Sex Discrimination Acts 93
Shareholders 82, 88–9, 481, 555, 558, 582, 587–8
Signage 253
Single market (see European Union)
Single sourcing 420
Small Business Bureau 671
Social benefits 39
Social costs 37–8
Socio economic groups 262–3
Software 131–4, 147–8
Sole trader 90, 98, 558
Solicitors 665
Solvency ratios 597–8
Sources of finance 89–90, 547–61, 607, 647–50
Spain 450–1
Special needs 296
Special offers 261–2
Specification 486
Spending 3
Sponsorship 256–7
Staff Associations 331, 335–9
Standard letters 164–5
Statement of Account 500, 501
Stationery 254
Subsidies 610
Summaries 159
Sunday trading 61
Supervisors 347
Suppliers 474–86
Supply 1–24, 633

Supply curves 14–15, 17–20
Supply of Goods and Services Act 97
Surveyors 665–6
Surveys 222, 223–4

Target audience 262–4
Tastes 6
Taxation 584, 587, 588, 591
Team working 340–1
Technology 109–10,. 204–5, 371–2, 419–20, 426, 448, 457, 460
Telecommunications 167–9, 223
Tele-marketing 274
Tele-sales 286
Television 246–8, 285
Tenders 492
Testimonials 165
Threshold concept 244
Total costs 11–12
Total quality control 414–15
Trade Descriptions Act 48, 304, 616–17
Trade Union Act 94
Trade Union Reform and Employment Rights Act 94
Trades Unions 331–9
Trading cycle 474–86
Training 39, 321–2, 364, 426, 460
Training & Enterprise Councils 666–7
Trial balance 577, 582

Underground economy 440–1
Unemployment 53–4
United States of America 453, 455

Vacancies, advertising 384–7
Value Added Tax (VAT) 70–1, 97, 480, 568–9, 570, 572, 657
Value analysis 413–14
Value engineering 413–14
Variable costs 11–12, 527–8, 536–41
Vehicle livery 253–4
Venture capital 555
Voluntary work 654–5

Weights and Measures Act 48
Wholesalers 293
Working capital 90, 549–51
Working conditions 107–8, 316–17, 324–5, 344–82, 426–7, 430–3
World Trade Organisation 462